EXPLOSIVE THIRD EDITION

# DEFRAUDING AMERICA

## Encyclopedia of Secret Operations by the CIA, DEA, and Other Covert Agencies

Written by

*Rodney Stich*

Former Government Investigator

ssisted By CIA & other Spook Whistleblowers

Library of Congress Catalog Card Number 97-65781

Stich, Rodney—Author

**Defrauding America**

EXPANDED THIRD EDITION

1. Drugs–United States; 2. Drugs–CIA; 3. Central Intelligence Agency (CIA); 4. Department of Justice; 5. Airline crashes; 6. Judges–corrupt; 7. Bankruptcy court–corruption; 8. Congress–corruption; 9. Covert agencies–United States; 10. Intelligence agency–Mossad; 11. Savings and loan association–fraud; 12. October Surprise; 13. Inslaw; 14. Bank of Credit and Commerce International; 15. HUD–fraud; 16. Bishop, Baldwin, Rewald, Dillingham, & Wong; 17. Nugan Hand Bank; 18. Whistleblowers.

Hard Cover ISBN: 0-932438-09-1

Published and printed in the United States of America by Diablo Western Press, PO Box 5, Alamo, CA 94507, and PO Box 10587, Reno, NV 89510.

Other related titles:

*Unfriendly Skies—History of corruption and air disasters*. (Third edition, Volume One) ISBN 0-932438-05-9

*Disavow—A CIA Saga of Betrayal.* ISBN 0-9648005-0-0

Mail orders to:
Diablo Western Press, Inc.
P.O. Box 5, Alamo, California 94507
Credit card orders (telephone): 1-800-247-7389, or FAX 510-295-1203.
Checks to DWP, POB 5, Alamo, CA 94507

10 9 8 7 6 5 4 3

CONTENTS

## ABOUT THE AUTHOR

The author spent much of his adult life in aviation as a pilot, commencing as a U.S. Navy pilot and flight instructor in World War Two, followed by years of flying as an airline captain in domestic and overseas operations. He was one of the first pilots licensed by Japan, holding pilot license number 170. During his international flying activities he had many interesting and exciting experiences, including being caught in Iran during a revolution in 1953 as he was flying Moslem pilgrims to Mecca. He experienced all types of aircraft emergencies, including engine fires, engine failures, and serious fuel shortages brought about by adverse winds. These flying experiences brought him into contact with many pilots flying for the CIA, making him privy to clandestine CIA activities as early as 1951.

In the early 1960s he left airline flying and became a federal air safety investigator for the Federal Aviation Administration, being responsible for air safety at several major airlines during the time that a major air disaster occurred in his area of responsibilities on an average of every six months.

The combination of repeated horror in these airline crashes combined with deep-seated fraud in the FAA, NTSB, and at United Airlines, caused the author to become a crusader against corrupt government.

Thirty years of aggressively seeking to expose government duplicity brought him into contact with whistleblowers from the FBI, CIA, DIA, DEA, and other covert agencies.

During the past thirty years he witnessed the explosion of government corruption to a degree that is almost beyond comprehension. His aggressive and imaginative use of legal and other remedies revealed other areas of government corruption, taking him far beyond what he initially discovered as a federal investigator.

In seeking to make the public aware of this corruption and how it is has inflicted brutal harm upon them, he has suffered many years of physical, personal, and financial retaliation. These actions converted him from a multi-millionaire to a state where everything he owned was taken, his civil and constitutional rights nullified, and even imprisoned in retaliation for seeking to expose the criminal and subversive activities involving powerful government officials.

The author is a member of the Association of Former Intelligence Agents, International Society of Air Safety Investigators, Lawyer-Pilots Bar Association, among other professional groups. He has appeared as guest and expert on over 2500 radio and television shows in the United States, Canada, Mexico, Germany, and Holland since 1978.

He has written several widely acclaimed books on aviation and government corruption, including three editions of *Unfriendly Skies* and this third edition of *Defrauding America*. Others are being written.

## AUTHOR'S COMMENTS

The intent of this book is to inform the reader about the bizarre web of intrigue in the three branches of the federal government that I and my large number of sources discovered during the last 30 years. I initially started discovering the misconduct and its brutal consequences after I became a federal inspector and investigator for the Federal Aviation Administration, while I was responsible for air safety at several major airlines.

My attempts to expose and halt the misconduct eventually brought me into contact with people involved in covert activities, causing me to discover corruption far beyond the aviation area. If someone had told me years earlier about these illegal operations I would have thought that person to be paranoid. The world of covert activities is often beyond the comprehension of the average person who has been shielded from the realities of what actually occurs behind the scenes in these United States.

This book reveals criminal and subversive activities implicating high-level personnel in the three branches of the federal government. It reveals why most of the public is dangerously uninformed about the criminal acts perpetrated against the United States and its people by the very people entrusted to prevent such happenings.

Many criminal activities, such as CIA drugging of America, will be difficult to believe by most Americans who have been shielded from the truth by a duplicitous Congress and much of the media. For those of us who have seen these events as insiders, including those who actually participated in them, questioning whether the CIA would engage in drug trafficking is like asking pilots, "Will planes really fly?" Yes, planes actually fly, and yes, the CIA has been smuggling drugs into the United States for the past 50 years. But the crimes related to drug trafficking are only a small part of the overall corruption described within these pages.

For those people who can't believe that these crimes are being inflicted upon the American people by their own government officials, or who feel guilty about not exercising some form of outrage, I suggest that they consider this book a novel.

Although this book is heavily detailed and documented, it is possible that some relatively minor error may occasionally exist, or one of my otherwise reliable informants may have exaggerated some particular matter. However, my extensive cross-checking with other sources reduces this possibility. Any such isolated errors do not cancel the massive amount of various forms of evidence that is prima facie evidence of the criminal activities.

The primary motive that I have had in writing this and other books has been to inform and motivate that small percentage of Americans capable of responding to these serious threats to the nation and its people.

## DEDICATION

This book is dedicated to the memory of those who have suffered so grievously at the hands of corrupt government in the United States. They include:

* Those who perished in fraud-related airline crashes, which the author details and documents in his classic book, *Unfriendly Skies*.

* Those who were fraudulently imprisoned to silence or discredit their disclosure of high-level government corruption.

* Those who were stripped of their life's assets as they were targeted through the misuse of government offices and power, especially through the federal bankruptcy courts.

* Those who died in wars generated by the CIA and other government entities on sham pretenses, such as Korea and Vietnam.

* Those who died in government raids such as at Waco, Ruby Ridge, and the many other incidents that the national media chose to ignore.

* Those who have yet to suffer from financial, personal, and physical harm, even death, as a result of the corruption described within these pages.

* Those people in other countries who were the victims of U.S. invasions and undermining of their governments, economic sanctions, the training, arming and funding of guerilla forces that inflicted torture and death upon them.

* To those brave people who sought to expose different aspects of this corruption and who paid and are paying the consequences for their "foolish" acts. It is unfortunate that the government and most of the non-government checks and balances have become involved through complicity of coverup and disinformation, and that most of the public lacks the courage and integrity to meet their responsibilities in defending against these national outrages.

It is hoped that this book will motivate others to learn about what is being done to America and its people by those in control of the invisible or secret government.

## APPLICABLE EUROPEAN QUOTATION

In Germany they came first for the Communists, and I didn't speak up, because I wasn't a Communist. They then came for the Jews, and I didn't speak up, because I wasn't a Jew. Then they came for the trade unionists, and I didn't speak up, because I wasn't a trade unionist. Then they came for the Catholics, and I didn't speak up, because I was a Protestant. Then they came for me, and by that time no one was left to speak out.

Attributed to Martin Niemoeller

## AN APPROPRIATE U.S. QUOTATION

I didn't speak out when the leaders acting in my behalf destabilized governments throughout the world, invaded foreign countries, and trained terrorists, making possible the deaths of millions of innocent people.

I didn't listen, or care, as Americans went off to wars engineered by people in control of the CIA and other government entities, and remained mute as tens of thousands of America became cannon fodder.

I didn't listen as people told me about the years of CIA drugging of Americans. I didn't listen when I was told about the corruption associated with specific airline crashes. I didn't listen as brave people spoke out and who were subsequently falsely charged and imprisoned. I didn't listen, or care, as fellow citizens were being physically and financially abused by arrogant government agents breaking into their homes and subjecting them to indignities unknown in civilized countries. I didn't listen as voices spoke out about the looting of savings and loans.

I chose to remain ignorant about the depth of corruption by government officials and judges. I ignored the pattern of coverup and criminal activities by members of Congress and much of our media. I ignored the patterns of corruption as if they didn't affect me. I ignored my responsibilities as a citizen, and was indifferent to the tragic plight of those who were directly affected by the massive corruption in government. I shirked my responsibilities by eagerly believing the disinformation and denials given by the mainstream print and broadcast media and federal officials.

The noose is tightening, and more and more of us are being incarcerated, deprived of civil and constitutional protections, and even our freedom. Eventually it will be too late. Many share the blame for these human right outrages. Very few of the victims would have suffered if enough Americans had exercised courage and responsibilities to fight this cancerous growth.

## SAMPLE OF READER COMMENTS SENT TO RODNEY STICH

"In my opinion you deserve the highest commendation this country can bestow on a man. Instead, our subversive and corrupt government has tried to crucify you."

"God bless you sir for the wonderful work that you are doing. I think that you are a modern day American hero."

"First of all, I would like to congratulate you and thank you for your heroic efforts and patriotic morals to the people of this nation in your heart-felt work."

"Just a short note to send my highest regards to you. Your truthfulness is so very refreshing."

"I am writing to thank you for your perseverance and dedication...I don't happen across too many true African patriots anymore...It was hard not to cry through certain parts of the book."

"Ever since the publishing of your book, The Unfriendly Skies, in 1978, I have been a follower and admirer of you–your activities, courage and intelligence."

"I am inspired by men such as yourself who have the courage and conviction to stand against overwhelming odds and aggression all in the name of truth. May God bless you, Rodney, bless you and protect you. I have a strong stirring in my heart that men such as yourself will not be much longer tolerated by the powers to be."

"You sir are a Patriot by the very definition of the truth you shine. May you live long and prosper in the Kingdom of righteous men."

"When I manage to meet a man such as yourself, Rodney, I am reminded of the greatness the nation once had."

"If only there were more people with the courage of Rodney Stich...."

"Dear Mr. Stich, brave, honest, noble, bright. That's Rodney Stich!!"

# AIR DISASTERS AND GOVERNMENT CORRUPTION

These pages detail and document corruption that I, as a former government investigator and then private investigator, and a large number of former CIA and other deep-cover operatives, have experienced or discovered during the past 30 years. This corruption, adversely affecting the national security and the lives of many Americans has been kept from the American people by virtually every government and non-government check and balance. The intent of this and other books that I have written[1] has been to inform the public of the misconduct and harm inflicted upon Americans by people in control of their government and to motivate them into meaningful action and exercise of their responsibilities.

I first discovered criminal misconduct associated with a series of brutal airline disasters that were occurring on programs for which I held federal air safety responsibilities as a federal air safety inspector-investigator for the Federal Aviation Administration (FAA). A major air disaster was occurring on programs for which I had safety responsibilities on an average of every six months, and continued for many years. To this date, not a single one of the guilty parties ever suffered for their crimes, and actually profited.

Because of these tragedies and the arrogance of those who held a key role in making them possible, I started exercising government and non-government remedies. The more that I tried, the greater was the amount of corruption that I encountered. It turned into a David versus Goliath battle against powerful elements in government.

Without that government experience as an insider, I would probably be as uninformed and indifferent to the corruption and the harm as most Americans are today.

## EXTENSIVE AVIATION BACKGROUND

My ability to recognize the relationship between airline crashes and the behind-the-scene problems that caused or made them possible arose from a combination of unusual aviation experiences. The basic aviation knowledge arose from my many years in military and commercial aviation. I joined the navy at the young age of 17 and after training, and before the Japanese attack upon Pearl Harbor,

1 Three editions of *Unfriendly Skies*, Volume One; two editions of *Defrauding America*; and the first edition of *Disavow*.

I became a radioman on a PBY Catalina seaplane. In 1943 I received my wings as a naval aviator and then became a PBY flight instructor, followed by command pilot on four-engine Navy Liberators and Privateers throughout the Pacific.

After World War II I became an airline pilot and captain flying in virtually every type of plane flown by U.S. airlines, including the double-deck Boeing Stratocruiser and Lockheed Super Constellation. My flying included passenger operations throughout most of the world. While flying captain for Japan Airlines I had Japanese copilots, a few of whom ironically were in the same small group of pilots flying out of Wake Island during the war who used to shoot at me when I was flying patrol flights out of Midway Island. In these types of flight operations there were many interesting experiences, including for instance the time that I found myself in the middle of an Iranian revolution in 1953. I had my share of engine failures, engine fires, sudden closing of virtually all airports at my destination, serious icing problems on the North Atlantic, sudden shortage of fuel when the head winds over long over-water flights became more adverse than forecast.

**DISCOVERING THE POLITICS OF AIR SAFETY**

Where I really learned about highly technical air safety matters and the politics of air safety was after I became an air carrier operations inspector for the Federal Aviation Administration. My first assignment was to the FAA Los Angeles District Office. I joined the FAA shortly after the FAA was legislated into being following a spectacular midair collision over the Grand Canyon when a United Airlines DC-7 crashed into a TWA Constellation, causing the deaths of everyone on board. At this time I have many FAA-issued licenses, and had extensive aviation experience.

Among my many safety related responsibilities were conducting flight checks of airline pilots and issuing ratings enabling them to fly that particular aircraft in airline operations. There were problems in the Los Angeles office due to the internal culture within the FAA that continues to this day, but there were more serious problems at another location with one politically-connected airline experiencing more airline crashes than all the other airlines combined.

After an initial assignment to the Los Angeles district office I was asked to volunteer for a crash-plagued program that experienced more air disasters than all the other airlines combined. The corruption that I discovered from that assignment, and concern about the many people who were killed as a result of the deliberate misconduct, started me on years of attempting to expose and bring to justice extremely serious corruption involving federal officials. I constantly discovered other areas of corruption that if someone had told me earlier about it I would have thought them to be paranoid.

The problems that I discovered had already been discovered by other FAA inspectors. Some had transferred to other assignments when their lawful duties were blocked and they were subject to threats by airline and FAA management. My predecessor, who was persistent in seeking to correct the serious safety problems, was ordered transferred to a meaningless assignment in Puerto Rico.

People who also suffered from the politics of air safety were the flight crew members, some of whom were denied the legally required and industry accepted training, and subjected to aircraft that had inadequate safeguards. By denying training to pilots and lowering competency requirements, that particular department saved considerable money. The people responsible for this situation received the benefits that went along with that conduct.

There were other aspects to this misconduct. Government required records were falsified to fraudulently indicate that training was given when the training and competency checks were not accomplished. These were criminal acts, and in light of the repeated crashes associated with the air safety fraud the implications were extremely serious. Almost every crash experienced by that airline was due to pilot competency problems that originated from the violation of training regulations.

Compounding these problems, FAA management in the local district office, in the Los Angeles regional office, and in Washington, knew of the violations and their relationship to the continuing crashes that covered a period from 1960 to 1978. I experienced, as did other inspectors, harassment, intimidation, threats, and adverse personnel actions. It was a nasty situation.

FAA management repeatedly removed and destroyed inspector reports of these safety and criminal violations. Whenever I discovered this occurrence I filed copies of the originals, which simply enraged management.

When weak captains were scheduled for flight checks to be performed by FAA-approved company check airmen, and I made it known that I would be observing the check, as FAA inspectors were required to do, I would be ordered by FAA management not to show up.

I arrived on this tragedy-plagued program shortly after it experienced the world's worst air disaster in which a DC-8 crashed into the heart of New York City. That senseless tragedy was followed within a few months by another senseless crash at Denver.

At that time, FAA inspectors like myself were outraged at the massive safety problems at the airline and FAA actions blocking federal inspectors from performing their duties. One outspoken and concerned inspector, Frank Harrell, took the extraordinary step of circumventing the Denver district office and Los Angeles regional office and went to Washington, complaining to both high-level FAA and National Transportation Safety Board personnel. (The NTSB at that time was known as the Civil Aeronautics Board Bureau of Air Safety.)

Typical of the culture in the FAA, nothing was done in response to these reports. Years later, after many other crashes occurred in that same program due to the same combination of corrupt acts, I also went to the same high-level officials, unknown that my complaints were preceded by other inspectors.

Since we inspectors had the technical ability and authority under federal law to establish the existence of these safety problems and safety violations on the part of the government, the actions taken against us, including the threats and adverse job actions, were extremely serious. Especially so in light of the many people who died in related air disasters.

In response to these serious problems, some inspectors transferred to other assignments where the airlines were more cooperative and in compliance with the law. A very few, like myself, sought to do something about the problems and fought the system, paying a heavy price for trying to comply with our federal responsibilities.

The really "smart" inspectors, and there were plenty of those, simply looked the other way, did not report the problems, and even covered up for them. They gained promotions and higher pay, including outstanding performance awards with their financial bonuses. Of course, people paid the consequences, as many were cremated alive, dismembered alive, and experiencing the horror that accompanies air disasters.

Among the problems that I encountered and reported included:

* Violation of federal air safety training requirements, denying to flight-deck crew members the legally required training and competency checks, and then falsifying records to indicate that these requirements were accomplished.

* FAA-approved company check airmen with an anything-goes safety standard, allowing the airline to eliminate the need for corrective training of pilots and flight engineers who needed additional training. When FAA inspectors, who monitored such checks, reported the problems as they were required to do, FAA and airline management threatened and harassed them.

* Removing FAA inspectors from company-conducted flight checks of known weak pilots.

* Refusing to take corrective action when inspectors reported that the airline was falsifying records, was not conducting important safety training and competency checks of flight crewmembers.

* Refusing to take action on the flight engineer training program and chaotic competency standards of many of the flight engineers.

* Refusing to take action on my reports that the important emergency evacuation training, which was required by law to be accomplished every 12 months, was being accomplished only every three years, and the records falsified to indicate compliance.

* Refusing to correct serious flight instrument deficiencies, which resulted in a foreseeable crash and over 100 deaths during a Los Angeles Airport departure.

* Refusing to provide required corrective training to specific pilots who I reported as having dangerous piloting habits. In one instance, due to the same piloting deficiency that I had reported of a specific pilot, 32 people were cremated alive at Salt Lake City several months after I made the report. That same pilot had been denied the corrective training that was required by federal law. FAA management and the airline had a relationship that played a causative and permissive role in many air disasters over a 20-year period.

**SILENCING FEDERAL INSPECTORS**

When I arrived in the Denver office to take over the new assignment, one of the inspectors who knew of the problems and who was disturbed by them, but who lacked the courage to fight FAA management, clued me in on the many problems. I was surprised when he would motion for me to talk in some remote location of the FAA building, or we would go outside the building, to discuss the serious problems at the airline and within the FAA.

Listing a few of the many crashes caused or made possible by this combination of fraud and criminal misconduct at United Airlines, the following shows how everyone on these flights was subjected to the dangers, and that periodically some of them paid with their lives. For example:

* UAL Douglas DC-7 ramming a TWA Constellation over the Grand Canyon, June 30, 1956. This crash caused the formation of the FAA in 1958.

* UAL DC-8 crash into New York City (December 16, 1960), for many years the world's worst. The crash was precipitated by extremely poor and dangerous piloting technique. And this problem was caused by the airline denying to the crew the legally required training, which was covered up by FAA management.

* UAL Douglas DC-8 crash at Denver (poor knowledge by the entire crew, July 11, 1961).This and other UAL crashes were an extension of earlier company and FAA misconduct.

* UAL Boeing 727 crash Salt Lake City (November 11, 1965). This was caused by poor knowledge and dangerous piloting technique by the entire crew. This consisted of a dangerous approach technique that I had observed on an earlier flight check of that same captain. I also reported that certain check pilots at United Airlines had a similar problem. I had repeatedly reported that the flight engineer training program was the worst that I had ever seen and that the competency checks of the engineers was a sham. In that tragedy the flight engineer failed to shut off the fuel valves and fuel booster pumps, allowing fuel to be pumped out of the aircraft through broken fuel lines. (This same problem exists today as many aircraft, including the huge Boeing 747-400, do not have flight engineers.) The final nail-in-the-coffin for the cremated passengers was the deliberate refusal of airline management to provide the mandatory emergency evacuation training, resulting in the crew poorly performing evacuation of the passengers. United Airlines falsified important records to cover up for these safety violations. This was a criminal act that resulted in many deaths.

* UAL Boeing 737 crash into Chicago due to poor piloting performance, continuing to show the consequences of UAL and FAA management misconduct existing behind 20 years of fatal crashes.

* UAL Douglas DC-8 crash near Salt Lake City due to poor piloting performance, compounded by the alcohol-impaired flight engineer.

* UAL Boeing 727 crash into the Pacific near Santa Monica, caused by several factors: known poor engineer training and competency; illegal dispatch of the aircraft with one generator inoperative and a second generator malfunctioning; absence of backup-powered flight instruments, a known dangerous condition which I had earlier reported.

* UAL Douglas DC-8 crash into Portland as all four engines ran out of fuel due to poor knowledge by the flight crew of the aircraft systems.

* UAL Douglas DC-8 crash out of Detroit due to poor piloting technique.

* UAL Boeing 737 crash into Chicago due to poor piloting technique.

* UAL Boeing 727 crash into Lake Michigan due to known altitude awareness problem that I had repeatedly identified, tried to correct. I was ordered by FAA management to disregard this problem that had already resulted in several major air disasters and near-crashes.

* Many other crashes and incidents.

Typical of the toll in human misery arising from FAA misconduct was the refusal to correct the cargo door problem on the DC-10 that caused the loss of nearly 400 persons, and other crashes with similar misconduct. what was revealed in 20 years of fatal crashes

**SENDING A HATCHET MAN TO SILENCE ME**

FAA management used various tactics to stop my reporting and attempted corrective actions that were required by federal law. But instead of halting my reports, the retaliation caused me to increase my inspection and reporting of the tragedy-riddled misconduct. I had tried to work within the system, making office reports, and filing reports with the regional office, making high-level regional management aware of the serious problems, to no avail.

Showing that this was not a local FAA culture problem, Washington sent a replacement manager to take over the Denver district office, and he spent a major part of his work function seeking to halt my reporting and corrective activities by a pattern of harassment, threats, and job actions.

**AN FAA INDEPENDENT PROSECUTOR**

As the crashes continued to occur from the same basic problems, and pressure increased to silence me, I exercised an internal procedure to force a hearing upon the FAA during which I acted as a form of special prosecutor producing testimony and evidence supporting my charges of FAA corruption related to a series of specific air disasters, including of course the air safety and criminal violations of the airline in question.

FAA management engaged in perjury, subornation of perjury, fraud, using legal arguments to deny the existence of the safety and criminal violations that were already established in the FAA records. Many more people would experience the horror preceding their deaths in subsequent crashes caused by or allowed to occur by these corrupt practices.

This hearing lasted over four months, and produced over 4000 pages of hearing transcript and documents. During the hearing I was opposed by the FAA legal staff, high level management, and an attorney who was on the FAA administrator's staff. During this hearing I discovered still other documents, including an inspection report that I did not even know existed that provided more evidence of misconduct relating to the New York City and other crashes.

**MORE CRASHES AND MORE DEATHS DURING THE HEARING**

During the hearing several other air disasters occurred in my area of responsibility, making it even more obvious how the public pays for the corruption at the airline and within the FAA that I was exposing.

Long before the hearing had started, I had talked by telephone and sent letters to high-level officials in the National Transportation Safety Board (called the CAB Bureau of Aviation Safety at that time), detailing the air safety and criminal violations, associating them with prior air disasters, and warned of still more crashes that could be expected.

Under law, the NTSB is required to investigate any air safety problems brought to their attention. But here we had much more than air safety oversight; we had criminal misconduct that could be directly linked to specific air disasters, and to expose this would expose what would probably be the world's worst aviation scandal.

**NTSB COMPLICITY**

I reminded the NTSB of the obvious, that if they did not immediately conduct an investigation, that the problems would undoubtedly bring about more of the same air disasters. They did nothing. Then, as the FAA engaged in a concentrated effort to cover up for the serious problems during the hearing, engaging in obvious perjury, subornation of perjury, fraud, legal chicanery, I again contacted high-level NTSB officials in Washington, advising them of what was being done, and of the probable consequences in continuing crashes.

**DEJA VU AGAIN AND AGAIN**

During the four-month hearing and hearing coverup several more crashes occurred, due to the same basic problems that I had reported, and which were associated with prior air disasters. The NTSB had to then rush to the accident scenes to investigate the crashes caused by the serious safety problems and criminal violations that I had brought to their attention earlier, and as other inspectors had done.

To protect their own contributing role in these crashes the final NTSB accident report prepared by the politically-appointed Board members had to omit the serious misconduct that I had brought to their attention. Under federal law, this constitutes a false report, and fraudulently misrepresents the report's conclusion. The NTSB had to report the direct causes of the crashes, but omitted the misconduct that made the direct causes possible, or caused the direct causes to occur.

**COVERUPS BY EVERY CHECK AND BALANCE**

As the misconduct, coverups, and crashes continued, I sought imaginative ways to circumvent the high level government blocks. I had gone to various divisions of the U.S. Department of Justice with my complaints, including the FBI, various U.S. attorneys, and the Department of Justice in Washington. I encountered a block, a coverup, obstruction of justice, wherever I went. I sought to circumvent the Justice Department coverup by appearing before a federal grand jury in Denver, where I quickly discovered the power of the U.S. attorney. As the Wall Street Journal frequently writes, the grand jury would indict a ham sandwich if requested by the U.S. attorney. Likewise, most grand juries would not act on their own to render an indictment if the U.S. attorney did not want an indictment to be handed down.

Whenever it was appropriate I would notify the print and broadcast media of my charges when a major air disaster was front page news. Even though the crash occurred in my area of federal responsibilities, and I had federal authority to make these determinations, not a single media source would receive my statements and evidence. Over the years I found this coverup by the media to be standard operating procedure.

**EXHAUSTING JUDICIAL REMEDIES**

Under a federal criminal statute[2] a federal judge is required by federal law to receive evidence of a federal crime from any person. It is also a felony if any person who knows of a federal crime does not promptly report it to a federal judge or other federal tribunal. Since people in control of the U.S. Department of Justice refused to receive my evidence and were themselves implicated through coverups and obstruction of justice, I exercised this right, and this responsibility,

2 **Title 18 U.S.C. § 4 (misprision of felony).** "Whoever, having knowledge of the actual commission of a felony cognizable by a court of the United States, conceals and does not as soon as possible make known the same to some judge or other person in civil or military authority under the United States, shall be fined not more than $500 or imprisoned not more than three years, or both."

under Title 18 USC Section 4.

I filed the first action[3] in the U.S. District Court at San Francisco, seeking to report the corruption within the Federal Aviation Administration. The federal district judge sympathized with my position, but in accordance with the opposing brief filed by the Department of Justice, dismissed my action. I then appealed it, and in argument before the Ninth Circuit court of appeals in San Francisco, the three-judge panel argued that this is a matter for Congress and not the courts. I argued otherwise, saying that it was a responsibility of the courts to receive my evidence, under the federal criminal statute, and also that a federal judge had the responsibility[4] to order a federal agency to halt unlawful actions. Again the action was dismissed, and again, the dismissals caused the deeply entrenched problems to continue, as well as the crashes and the deaths.

I filed similar actions following the PSA San Diego crash, which was at that time the world's worst air disaster, taking the title away from the New York City crash that occurred on the program for which I had air safety responsibilities. In that crash the NTSB had covered up for the all-night partying and drinking of the airline crew whose actions early the next morning resulted in a horrible tragedy into a residential area of San Diego. Following a pattern, the NTSB covered up for the underlying cause of the crash and I petitioned the NTSB to receive my evidence relating to that tragedy. They refused to receive the evidence. I then filed an action with the district court at San Francisco* seeking to have the court order the NTSB to receive my evidence and that of a witness who could testify to the partying.

Shortly after I filed the action an assistant U.S. attorney called and stated to me over the phone that he was supporting my position and was recommending to his superiors in Washington that this be done. That relatively new AUSA with the Justice Department was unaware of the prior Justice Department involvement and coverups, not realizing that supporting my position could expose the air safety and Justice Department scandal that already existed. That AUSA then filed a motion to have my action dismissed, which the judge (and former Justice Department attorney) did.

I also filed a friend-of-the-court brief associated with litigation against Douglas for a scandalous DC-10 crash, which required that I obtain the approval of the various lead attorneys involved in the litigation. I received this approval, but again the district judge dismissed my attempt to provide evidence.

## GOING DIRECT TO THE PEOPLE

Still harboring the fantasy that the public wanted to hear about the corruption that was threatening them when they flew, I decided to circumvent the government and media blocks that I encountered by publishing the first edition of *Unfriendly Skies*, which went to print in 1978, immediately after the PSA San Diego crash. Publishing the book, and appearing as guest and air safety expert on radio and

---

3 *Stich v. United States, et al.*, 554 F.2d 1070 (9th Cir.) (table), *cert. denied*, 434 U.S. 920 (1977)(addressed hard-core air safety misconduct, violations of federal air safety laws, threats against government inspectors not to report safety violations and misconduct);

4 **Title 28 U.S.C. § 1361. Action to compel an officer of the United States to perform his duty.** The district courts shall have original jurisdiction of any action in the nature of mandamus to compel an officer or employee of the United States or any agency thereof to perform a duty owed to the plaintiff.

television shows, the truth would come out.

There is much more to this period of corruption, and I strongly recommend that anyone really interested in how government operates, how government corruption continues year after year, and how this corruption results in tragedies, read the latest edition of *Unfriendly Skies*.[5] Between *Unfriendly Skies* and *Defrauding America*, the reader will learn more about government corruption, as seen by an insider, than found virtually anywhere else.

Were it not for the people responsible for the pattern of air safety and criminal acts and related air disasters I would never have been motivated to become a crusader or activist against corrupt government, and I would never have discovered the endemic corruption detailed and documented within these pages. In a perverse way, these producers of tragedies can be "thanked" for making possible the discovery of even worse corruption and the tragic consequences suffered by many Americans.

The examples given in this book are highlights of events, and only a small part of what I and other federal investigators, and other insiders, discovered. The criminal activities and the harm suffered by Americans and America, have and are occurring in part because of the breakdown in checks and balances, the refusal of Americans to become informed, and massive indifference that became so very clear to me during the past 30 years. These first few pages will detail and document the corruption within the government of the United States that led to the deaths of many people, and still affects to a lesser extent safety in air travel..

FEDERAL AVIATION AGENCY · UNITED STATES OF AMERICA

RODNEY F. STICH
AIR CARRIER OPERATIONS INSPECTOR

DEXTER 3-5475
DEXTER 3-5476

AIR CARRIER DISTRICT OFFICE
STAPLETON AIRFIELD
DENVER 7, COLORADO

---

5 Be sure to get the one authored by me. Doubleday quickly published a title duplicating my long-used title when they knew I was coming out with a very sensitive third edition.

United Airlines crash into New York City, one of many similar crashes resulting from a pattern of corruption at the airline and within the FAA and NTSB.

Showing the horror associated with fraud-related airline crashes: Removing bodies from the UAL crash into New York City.

Another in a long series of airline disasters occurring in the author's area of safety responsibilities: United Airlines crash at Salt Lake City.

# ATTACKING THE WHISTLEBLOWER

My escalating exposure actions threatened many powerful people. I had published the 1978 and 1980 printings of *Unfriendly Skies*. I appeared as guest on hundreds of radio and television shows and had also filed federal lawsuits against the FAA and NTSB, all of which were focusing attention on serious corruption in government. The people and groups threatened by my exposure activities included officials within the Federal Aviation Administration; the National Transportation Safety Board; U.S. Department of Transportation; members of Congress; federal judges, including the Justices of the U.S. Supreme Court, and management at United Airlines. Those who could do the greatest harm to me, however, were Justice Department officials and federal judges, and their influence with state law firms and judges. I had yet to recognize other areas of government corruption far worse than I had already discovered.

The importance of describing what was done to me is that it shows the control over state agencies by federal officials and the type of actions taken, misusing government offices, to obstruct justice, all of which makes possible the infliction of great harm upon the American people.

## INADVERTENTLY GIVING THE CLUE

I inadvertently gave my adversaries the clue as to how to stop my exposure activities. During several radio and television appearances the hosts asked me, "Aren't you afraid of what they might do to you?" The question implied physical harm, but I sidestepped it, saying, "As long as they can't get to my money, I'm OK." I felt there was *no way* that my adversaries could get the assets which funded my exposure activities.

At the beginning of the 1980s, the market value of my real estate properties was close to ten million dollars, and my net worth was over six million dollars. Foolishly, instead of just enjoying life and these assets, I continued my air safety activist activities trying to expose the government corruption that continued to play a role in air tragedies. I was the only person with the evidence and the willingness to fight the powerful thugs involved in this scandal, and perhaps foolishly, felt I had an obligation as a citizen.

## START OF A BIZARRE JUDICIAL PROCEEDING

It took money to continue the activist activities, and I had already inadvertently given the clue to my adversaries that my exposure activities were funded by my assets. A bizarre scheme commenced in late 1982 via a sham lawsuit that had been structured to immediately separate me from my assets, and eventually to take them away from me. Those who carried out the scheme had to have assurances, either specifically or from knowledge of widespread corruption in the judicial branch, that every check and balance in the California and federal courts would protect the scheme and the perpetrators. However, though it was costly for me, it provided me the opportunity to discover a pattern of corruption against America far beyond what I could have imagined at that time. Even though I already knew of very serious corruption in the three branches of government, I felt there was a limit.

To commence and continue the sham lawsuit required repeated violations of blocks of California and federal statutory and case law, as well as constitutional protections. The sham action and the voiding of all state and federal remedies and protections caused loss of the assets that funded my exposure activities.

There are two basic ways to judicially strip a person of his or her assets almost immediately. One is through probate proceedings, but this requires that the person be dead. The other way is through divorce proceedings, seizing the assets on the basis that they are community property. I had been divorced since 1966, and five divorce judgments established that fact.[6] In California where I resided, the 1966 judgment had been entered as a local judgment in the Superior Court, Contra Costa County. Under California and federal law, the judgments were final and conclusive of our divorced status and property rights. The California and 1966 judgments were entered as local judgments in the courts of Nevada, Oklahoma, and Texas. In addition, my former wife, residing in Texas, had been declaring herself divorced for the past two decades, buying and selling real estate as a divorced woman. She applied for higher Social Security payments on the basis of the 1966 divorce judgment, which the federal government recognized when they raised her Social Security benefits. It was safe to say that I was legally divorced.

## THE BIZARRE JUDICIAL SCHEME

In December 1982, several months after the Supreme Court Justices dismissed my action against the NTSB, I was served with a dissolution of marriage action,[7] even though I had been legally divorced for the past two decades. The San Francisco law firm of Friedman, Sloan and Ross[8] filed the action in Superior Court, Solano County, Fairfield, California. The lawsuit alleged that I was married to Friedman's Texas client and that she wanted a termination of that marriage (which in Texas she had declared was terminated in 1966). Using the

---

6 It is common practice, and provided by law (Uniform Divorce Judgment Recognition Act), for original divorce judgments to be entered as local judgments in subsequent states of residence to establish personal and property rights when exercising the constitutional right to change residence and have previously adjudicated rights recognized by the new state of residence.

7 Number 83472.

8 I later learned they carried out covert activities for the Justice Department and Central Intelligence Agency, and were members of the ADL and the ACLU.

pretense of the marital relationship, the Friedman law firm claimed that my assets were community property. On that sham basis, the law firm filed dozens of lis pendens upon them, which halted important segments of my real estate activities, inflicting serious financial harm upon me.

The Friedman law firm claimed that all of my properties were community property, even though they had been acquired years after the 1964 Colorado separation and after the 1966 divorce, which adjudicated all property rights. Under law, these properties were not community. Even if there had been a marriage California judges lacked jurisdiction over separate property in a marriage dissolution action under clearly stated statutes. Building upon the sham divorce proceeding, the Friedman law firm filed lis pendens on all of my properties, preventing necessary such necessary activities as refinancing loans coming due on various properties.

**MASSIVE AND UNPRECEDENTED VIOLATIONS OF LAW**

The lawsuit was filed under the California Family Law Act, which grant state judges limited jurisdiction. It clearly prohibits attacks upon prior divorce judgments.[9] Orders rendered by a judge who lacks personal or subject matter jurisdiction are void, and also subject the judge to lawsuits under the Civil Rights Act.[10] For the next eight years, commencing in 1982, California judges rendered orders lacking jurisdiction for the cause of action filed against me, on the basis of California law. Absence of jurisdiction also arose from other sources.

**CALIFORNIA LAW PROHIBITED THE LAWSUIT**

Technically, jurisdiction could have been obtained to file a lawsuit under declaratory judgment statutes to determine whether the parties were married or not.[11] But to have done that would have prevented immediate seizure of my assets which can be done in a real divorce action on the basis of community property.

In addition, California statutory law prohibits collateral attacks upon *any* prior divorce judgment in any cause of action. The statutes and related case law[12] require mandatory recognition of each of the prior divorce judgments.

---

9 Rules of Court 1201(c) (limits jurisdiction to three causes of action—dissolution of existing marriage, legal separation from existing marriage, nullity of marriage); Rule 1211 (limited to parties that are married to each other); Rule 1212 (prohibiting stating cause of action or claim for relief other than that provided by Rules of Court, including causes especially stated in Rule 1281 petition for dissolution of marriage form); Rule 1215 (limiting Pleadings to those stated in Rule 1281, which does not state attacks upon prior judgments or previously litigated personal and property rights); Rule 1222 (jurisdiction limited to altering existing marital status); Rule 1229 (jurisdiction limited to the causes of action in Rule 1281 petition form and Rule 1282 answer form, which does not list the causes of action attacking prior divorce judgments or relitigating the exercise of jurisdiction basis); Rule 1230(a)(2) (addresses, with C.C.P. § 418.10(a)(1) the court's absence of personal jurisdiction under the Family law Act when there is a prior divorce judgment).

10 **Title 42 U.S.C. §§ 1983-1986**; *Dennis v. Sparks* (1980) 449 U.S. 24.

11 **Code of Civil Procedure § 1060.** To Ascertain Status or Construe Writing. Any person...who desires a declaration of his rights or duties with respect to another, or in respect to, in, over or upon property....may, in case of actual controversy relating to the legal rights and duties of the respective parties, bring an original action in the superior court for a declaration of his rights...

12 Mandatory divorce judgment recognition statutes (Civil Code §§ 4554, 5004, 5164; Code of Civil Procedure §§ 1699(b), 1713.3, 1908, 1913, 1915 (effective when the 1966 judgment was rendered and for nine years thereafter); Evidence Code §§ 666, 665, 622; (statute of limitations, Civil Code §§ 880.020, 880.250; Code of Civil Procedure §§ 318, 338, 343; Statute of limitations: Code of Civil Procedure 318, 338, 343; Civil Code §§ 880.020, 880.250; mandatory requirement to recognize that the prior court acted

California Supreme Court decisions prohibited attacks upon prior divorce judgments.[13]

Attorneys[14] for the Friedman law firm argued that all five divorce judgments were void on the basis that I did not intend to reside forever in the jurisdiction that rendered the 1966 divorce judgment. But that argument had been declared unconstitutional by the U.S. Supreme Court in the 1940s. The Friedman attorneys spent months arguing what my mental thoughts must have been about permanently residing in the 1966 court's jurisdiction. A person getting a divorce does not have to pledge that he or she will reside forever in that jurisdiction. This is the lie that I had to fight during six years of litigation in California courts. Further, the statute of limitations prohibited an attack upon prior judgments three years after they are rendered. Any one of these dozens of state protections barred the action, in addition to the absence of jurisdiction under California law.

## VIOLATING FEDERAL AND CALIFORNIA LAW

In addition to California law barring the sham action, overriding federal law barred the action. Federal statutory and case law, and constitutional safeguards, protect people who change their state of residence from having their prior divorce judgments and personal and property rights voided by a judge in some other state court. The constitution provides that a person cannot suffer loss of previously adjudicated or acquired personal and property rights when the person changes residence to another state. Federally protected rights barred the refusal to recognize residence as a basis for exercising personal jurisdiction in a divorce action. This was settled almost fifty years ago by the U.S. Supreme Court when California judges refused to recognize Nevada divorce judgments obtained after six weeks residence.[15]

Federal law, especially the constitutional and statutory Full Faith and Credit doctrine, requires state judges to recognize the judicial acts of another state.

---

in the lawful exercise of its jurisdiction when the judgment is under attack two decades after its exercise of jurisdiction, and the acceptance of the benefits by both parties: Evidence Code §§ 666, 665, 622.

13 Prohibiting attacks upon prior divorce judgments on refusal to recognize residence, or for any other basis: *Rediker v. Rediker* (1950) 35 Cal.2d 796 ("it must be presumed that the foreign court had jurisdiction and that its recital thereof is true...is not subject to collateral attack on a showing of error in the exercise of that jurisdiction...The validity of a divorce decree cannot be contested by a party who ... aided another to procure the decree."; *Scott v. Scott* (1958) 51 C.2d 249 ("There should be no implication ... that would preclude contacts with the foreign country other than domicile as a basis of jurisdiction." Section 1915 of the Code of Civil Procedure provides: "A final judgment of any other tribunal of a foreign country have jurisdiction, according to the laws of such country, to pronounce the judgment, shall have the same effect as in the country where rendered, and also the same effect as final judgments rendered in this state [which are final and conclusive of the rights and obligations of the parties--C.C. § 4554]"; *Spellens v. Spellens* (1957) 498 C.2d 210 ("The principle of estoppel is applicable [when] the divorce decree was alleged to be invalid for lack of jurisdiction ... The validity of a divorce decree cannot be contested by a party ... who aided another to procure the decree ..."); *Whealton v. Whealton* (1967) 67 C.2d 656 ("When both parties to a divorce action are before the court ... it is questionable whether domicile is an indispensable prerequisite for jurisdiction. ... the prerequisite of domicile may be easily avoided at the trial by parties wishing to invoke the jurisdiction of a court, with little fear in most instances that the judgment will be less effective than if a valid domicile in fact existed.").

14 Jeffrey S. Ross; Lawrence A. Gibbs; Neil Popovic; Carolyn E. Moore; Christopher A. Goelz.

15 *Vanderbilt v. Vanderbilt* (1957) 354 U.S. 416 (requiring the recognition of *ex parte* divorce judgments; *Estin v. Estin* 334 U.S. 541 (1948)(requiring the recognition of prior divorce judgments); *Sherrer v. Sherrer* (1948) 334 U.S. 343; *Coe v. Coe* (1948) 334 U.S. 378 (requiring the recognition of prior divorce judgments); *Perrin v. Perrin*, 408 F.2d 107 (3rd Cir. 1969) (prohibiting denying recognition to prior judgments when exercised on residence, including one day's residence).

This requirement applied to the prior divorce judgments and the property settlement.[16] California statutes also have a full faith and credit mandatory recognition requirement.[17] These protections required that the California judges recognize the California, Nevada, Oklahoma, and Texas divorce judgments. The sham lawsuit also violated fundamental constitutional rights and protections.[18]

**"REMARRYING" LONG-DIVORCED PERSONS**

The California judges held that they had the right to remarry people who had been divorced for decades; to invalidate subsequent marriages; to void prior property settlements adjudicated in other states and jurisdictions, and to order property acquired years after a prior divorce to be community property with the prior spouse. Three judges[19] in the California Court of Appeal upheld these decisions, as did the judges in the California Supreme Court. Their published decision established the right of California judges to void divorce judgments and property rights adjudicated decades earlier, contrary to federal and state statutory and constitutional protections. The person initiating these attacks need not even reside in California, as long as a former spouse resides in the state. Using the published decision as precedence, California judges can order the former spouse to pay your attorney fees for a new "divorce," and pay support at the same time. At the present time, until that published decision is overturned, the same scenario that happened to me can happen to anyone who has been previously divorced.

**SUSPENDING APPELLATE REMEDIES**

The appellate court remedy for a judge's refusal to dismiss an action following a motion to quash is to file a petition for writ of mandamus with the California Court of Appeal. Then, if denied, file a petition for hearing with the California Supreme Court.[20] If the lower court lacks jurisdiction, the upper court *must* grant the petition.[21] Even though the lower court judges clearly lacked jurisdiction, the California court of appeal judges denied the petition for relief. The California Supreme Court justices also upheld the violations of state and federal laws and constitutional protections.

The remedy under California law to vacate an order to pay money is by appeal, and I appealed. The appeal was heard by Court of Appeal judges, Donald King, Harry Low, and Zerne Haning, all appointed by former California governor Jerry Brown. Media articles reported the judges paid bribe money for the judicial appointment. These judges rendered a published decision[22] upholding the violations of state and federal law. That decision was published and is case law in the State of California today. I appealed that decision to the California Supreme Court and, when the violations were approved by California's highest court,

---

16 Article IV, Section 1, and title 28 U.S.C. § 1738.

17 Civil Code Section 5004.

18 Right to unabridged interstate travel, arising in the Privileges and Immunities Clause, Article IV, Section 2, and in the Fourteenth Amendment (right to change residence without losing rights adjudicated and acquired in prior jurisdictions); Fourteenth Amendment, relating to due process and equal protection, giving all persons the right to obtain a divorce, and adjudication of personal and property rights; laws respecting property rights.

19 Judges Harry W. Low; Donald B. King; Zerne P. Haning.

20 California Code of Civil Procedure § 418.10(b).

21 Code of Civil Procedure Section 1086.

22 *In re Marriage of Stich*, 164 Cal. App. 64 (1985).

I appealed to the U.S. Supreme Court. The issues were of utmost importance to thousands of people who were subjected to the same constitutional outrages inflicted upon me. None provided any relief.

This was a major constitutional set-back, something like returning to the fifties when blacks were required to sit in the back of buses in the South. But it was upheld by the California Court of Appeal and the California Supreme Court. The decision was unconstitutional. As long as that decision stands, others risk the same fate I suffered. This little-noticed decision affects everyone who exercises a constitutionally protected right to change residence to California, making them fair game for losing their personal and property rights; making their wives adulteresses; making their children bastards.

**RETALIATION[23] FOR EXERCISING LEGAL DEFENSES**

The Court of Appeal judges held in their published decision that it was frivolous for me to exercise my remedies under California law (motion to quash, petition for writ, and appeal). The decision held that I should have willingly submitted to the jurisdiction of the California judges (who under law had no jurisdiction under the Family Law Act to attack prior divorce judgments); that I should have agreed to be remarried; that I should have agreed to undergo another divorce proceeding, and have the properties and assets I acquired during two decades of divorced status divided with Friedman's Texas client and the Friedman law firm (on the basis of the contingency agreement between Friedman and their client).

Based upon this published decision and the holding that it was frivolous for me to object, the three appellate judges ordered me to pay $50,000 attorney fees and financial sanctions. This order was shortly followed by another order that I pay $170,000 attorney fees to the Friedman law firm.

**"They can't do that!"**

Many attorneys stated to me that the California judges couldn't do what they were doing. I agreed, but they were doing it anyhow. I had not yet recognized that the California lawsuit was a scheme involving federal and state personnel to strip me of the assets I relied upon to fund my exposure activities.

**DOZENS OF ILLEGAL LIS PENDENS**

The illegally filed lis pendens halted my real estate activities. Valuable property was lost, including my mountain-top home that had over a quarter-million-dollar equity in it. Everything I worked for was being lost. Even on the eve of losing valuable properties due to mortgage foreclosures caused by the lis pendens, the Friedman firm and their attorneys refused to allow the existing loans to be refinanced.

Initially, I had legal counsel,[24] but they were as incompetent as the attorney I hired for the Denver FAA safety grievance hearing. I had to terminate them and proceed in pro se status, representing myself. None of my legal counsel

---

23 **Title 18 U.S.C. § 241. Conspiracy against rights of citizens**
If two or more persons conspire to injure, oppress, threaten, or intimidate any citizen in the free exercise or enjoyment of any right or privilege secured to him by the Constitution or laws of the United States, or because of his having so exercised the same; ... They shall be fined ... or imprisoned ... or both.

24 Douglas Page; Maurice Moyal.

argued current California law. They argued fifty-year-old case law from the days of segregated bussing, toilets, and eating establishments, that had been superseded for decades. None of them knew federal law, which under the Federal Supremacy Clause of the United States Constitution takes precedence over state law. To get the law argued, I had to file my own briefs. But in pro per status, due process almost always goes out the window as state and federal judges side with their attorney cohorts.

While under constant judicial attack and suffering severe personal and financial losses due to the sham action, my doctor advised that I must immediately undergo open-heart surgery, which I did, receiving six coronary bypasses (April 1985). Before I left for surgery, I notified the California Court of Appeal judges, King, Low, and Haning, of the hospitalization, and requested they delay their decision on the appeal of the May 10, 1983, order until after I got out of intensive care. Otherwise, I would not have time to request a rehearing from the California Supreme Court judges for the expected unfavorable decision.

I was barely out of intensive care and had just arrived home, when the Court of Appeal judges rendered their decision. Several attorney friends described the decision as the closest thing to a poison-pen letter that they had ever seen. I rushed to prepare a petition for hearing to the California Supreme Court. But the Supreme Court judges had protected the judicial civil right violations since 1983. There wasn't much hope, as the judicial Ponzi scheme protected the renegade judges.

The published decision fabricated facts out of whole cloth. It refused to address any of the California or federal laws that I raised in defense. Contrary to California and federal statutes and constitutional protections, the decision held that California judges could void prior divorce judgments of any party moving to California; could remarry the parties who had been long ago divorced; could order a person (who may have subsequently remarried) to financially pay attorneys on both sides during the "divorce" action; could seize properties and businesses that had been acquired years after the prior divorce, and to convey half of it to a former spouse (even if remarried). They held they had the power to destroy, in this bizarre fashion, the personal lives and possessions of innocent people.

The published decision eulogized the Friedman law firm who filed the action that was prohibited by law. The decision eulogized my ex-wife who openly committed fraud and perjury by simultaneously declaring herself married to me in the California action while declaring herself divorced from me in her resident state of Texas. The published decision approved the rendering of orders inflicting great harm upon people without having jurisdiction under California law to even conduct hearings once the prior divorce judgments were presented to them.

Despite the absence of jurisdiction, the absence of any marriage, the absence of any contact between the former spouses for many years, despite the blocks of state and federal law barring the action, California judges continued to render orders inflicting great financial and personal harm upon me.

California appellate judges (Low, King, Haning) used all types of schemes to block my appeal remedies. They refused to receive my appeal briefs; they misstated the facts and the law; they ordered me to pay huge fines for filing appeals and oppositions; they threatened to impose additional fines if I exercised any of the judicial remedies available under law. In one instance they ordered me to pay over $250,000 in fines to the Friedman law firm for having filed appeals and oppositions, which were rights guaranteed by the statutes and constitution of the state of California.

**BENCH WARRANT FOR MY ARREST**

The judicial outrages didn't stop. When I lacked access to my funds to pay the $170,000 to the Friedman law firm that was ordered by Judge William Jensen, Peterson sentenced me to jail. (California governor George Deukmejian later promoted Peterson to the appellate courts.)

Despite the unconstitutionality of the cause of action, its prohibition under California statutory law, despite the absence of jurisdiction under the Family Law Act, California judges[25] repeatedly protected and rewarded the Friedman law firm. The California judges blocked every attempt to defend against the bizarre action. Something was radically wrong. To support the violations of blocks of law, the California judges blocked every procedural defense.

**RETALIATION FOR EXERCISING FEDERAL REMEDIES**

Another scheme was concocted to put me in jail. Jensen ordered me to appear in court on May 9, 1986, a date that he knew I was calendared to be in federal court at Sacramento. That action was a Civil Rights action I filed against Jensen on the basis of violating my rights under state and federal laws and causing me harm. Jensen retaliated against me for having exercised these rights by ordering me to appear in court to show why I should not be held in contempt for failure to pay the judgments, which he knew I couldn't pay.

I filed papers in the Solano County court notifying Jensen that I physically could not appear on that date (which he already knew). I also stated my inability to pay the money orders since the Friedman law firm, with his help, had tied up all my funds with the lis pendens upon my properties and assets. I again reminded him of the absence of jurisdiction and the wholesale numbers of California and federal laws that barred the attack upon the five prior judgments. I also advised Jensen that an attorney would appear for me at that hearing (which met the requirements of California law).

Despite all this, Jensen held me in contempt of court for not being present, and issued a bench warrant for my arrest. Since I resided in Nevada, this bench warrant kept me from appearing in California for the next year and a half. Seeking relief from the bench warrant, I submitted petitions for relief to the California Court of Appeal and the California Supreme Court. The Ponzi-like scheme of judge-protecting-judge continued, and relief was denied.

**SHAM DIVORCE JUDGMENT**

Without my knowledge, the Friedman law firm and California Judge Dennis Bunting conducted a hearing on July 28, 1988, to terminate the non-existing marriage and order the taking of my properties. During the hearing Judge Bunting rendered a judgment that described the cause of action as a dissolution of marriage action (even though there hadn't been a marriage for over twenty years, depriving

---

25 Judges Dwight Ely, Michael McInnis, William Jensen, John DeRonde, Richard Harris, William Peterson.

the judge of jurisdiction under the Family Law Act proceeding). Having "established" that Friedman's Texas client was married to me, Bunting then rendered an order holding that all my assets were community properties. All of my properties met the legal definition of separate properties since they were acquired years after the 1964 separation and 1966 divorce.

The same order required me to pay $2500 monthly spousal support for the remainder of my life (contradicting the five existing divorce judgments showing there were no spousal support obligations).

There were now six divorce judgments. Five showed me divorced since 1966; showed all properties were separate; and held that neither party had any spousal support rights or obligations. Then we had the sixth judgment rendered twenty-two years later by California judges lacking jurisdiction under California law; lacking jurisdiction under federal law; lacking jurisdiction over properties legally classified as separate; violating dozens of California and federal statutes, constitutional protections, and other laws; in a cause of action barred by forty-five years of U.S. Supreme Court decisions.

Federal statutes provide that a person can obtain a declaratory judgment from a federal judge, declaring his personal and property rights and the validity of the five prior divorce judgments, when these rights are under attack. There is no other place to go but into federal court when judgments from another state are attacked by a state judge. But to render a decision would unravel the scheme concocted against me, expose the civil and constitutional violations, and the criminal conspiracy under which they were perpetrated. To this day, my constitutional and statutory rights to have a ruling holding these judgments and the related personal and property rights declared valid have been unlawfully and unconstitutionally refused to me by at least a dozen federal judges.

I filed a notice of appeal with the California Court of Appeal in San Francisco, which was heard by the same justices that had aided and abetted these violations of law for the past seven years: Justices Donald King, Harry Low, and Zerne Haning. This three-judge panel rendered a decision (July 22, 1990) approving the judgment. They approved the judgment that under law was a void judgment and which violated numerous federal protections, such as the Civil Rights Act. Worse, they placed a frivolous label on my appeal, ordered me to pay $65,000 sanctions to the Friedman law firm for filing the appeal, and ordered me to pay $20,000 sanctions to the State of California! I then filed an appeal with the California Supreme Court, which also had protected the massive judicial violations since 1983. The entire court approved these judicial violations.

It was several years before I recognized what was behind the sham California action. Once the judicial scheme started rendering the unlawful orders, it became necessary for each succeeding judge to enlarge on the violations so as to protect the prior acts and protect those involved in the scheme. This daisy-chain scenario then occurred, time and time again.

Another "routine" air disaster in an area riddled with corruption. United Airlines crash at Denver in the area of the author's air safety responsibilities.

# COMPLICITY OF FEDERAL JUDGES

Any one of the many violations of California and federal law inflicted upon me in the sham California action invoked mandatory federal court jurisdiction. For six years California judges and the Friedman law firm had been violating important civil and constitutional rights, which were escalating. Federal statutory and case law and the Constitution guaranteed declaratory judgment and injunctive relief, and financial damages, for any citizen undergoing these violations.

In their positions of trust, federal judges are paid and have the mandatory duty to provide federal court access and relief.[26] In addition to the statutory right to federal court access and relief the First Amendment to the Constitution[27] provides additional safeguards so that no one suffers as I suffered.

When a divorced person exercises his or her constitutional right to change residence, his or her previously adjudicated personal and property rights in a divorce must be recognized by judges in another state. That person cannot be subjected to another divorce proceeding twenty or thirty years later, invalidating subsequent marriages, as was done to me in the sham California action. In the bizarre action taken against me, one of the remedies arose under the Declaratory Judgment Act and statutes. These remedies required[28] a federal judge to declare the validity of each of the five prior divorce judgments and the validity of my divorced status and property rights.

The refusal by California judges to recognize any of the prior judgments entered in five different states (including California) and refusal to recognize

26 Title 28 U.S.C. § 1331. Federal question. The federal courts shall have original jurisdiction of all civil actions arising under the Constitution, laws, or treaties of the United States.

27 The First Amendment to the Constitution provides that "Congress shall make no law...abridging the [right] to petition the Government for a redress of grievances."

28 Title 28 U.S.C. Section 2201 to declare federally protected rights.

property rights established in those divorce judgments and acquired as a separated and divorced person, invokes federal remedies. In my case, to declare these rights, the U.S. District Judge must first apply federal law that requires recognition of the judgments and then secondarily apply state law if it conforms to federal law. In my case, any one of over a dozen state and federal doctrines of law, constitutional rights, and statutes required the California judges to recognize the rights established in the five judgments. They refused to do so, and even imposed financial sanctions upon me for exercising procedural defense remedies against the grotesque violations of long-established protections.

Because California judges inflicted great financial and personal harm upon me through their violations of my civil and constitutional rights, there were additional federal statutes insuring that I have access to federal court. These remedies also provided jurisdiction to obtain financial damages against the state judges and the Friedman law firm. This relief arises under the Civil Rights Act, among other statutes, which is embodied in Title 42 Section 1983.[29]

When two or more people act to do a certain thing, it is called a conspiracy. It was obvious that the various attorneys in the Friedman, Sloan and Ross law firm and the California judges were acting together to inflict great harm upon me through repeated violations of state and federal law. This conspiracy violated another section of the Civil Rights Act, Title 42 U.S.C. § 1985.[30]

If any person knows that your civil rights are being violated and they have the power to prevent or aid in the prevention of these violations, and they don't do so, other federal statutes provide federal court jurisdiction and relief. This cause of action arises under Title 42 U.S.C. Section 1986[31] and Title 28 U.S.C.

---

29 Title 42 U.S.C. Section 1983: Every person who, under color or any statute, ordinance, regulation, custom or usage, of any State or Territory, subjects...any citizen of the United States ... to the deprivation of any rights, privileges or immunities secured by the Constitution and laws, shall be liable to the party injured in an action at law, suit in equity, or other proper proceeding for redress.

30 Title 42 U.S.C. Section 1985 Conspiracy to interfere with civil rights–Preventing officer from performing duties. (1) If two or more persons...conspire to prevent...any person from accepting or holding any office, trust, or place of confidence under the United States, or from discharging any duties thereof; or to injure him in his person or property on account of his lawful discharge of the duties of his office, or while engaged in the lawful discharge thereof, or to injure his property so as to molest, interrupt, hinder, or impede him in the discharge of his official duties. (2) If two or more persons conspire...for the purpose of depriving, either directly or indirectly, any person...of the equal protection of the laws, or of equal privileges and immunities under the laws...in any case of conspiracy set forth in this section, if one or more persons engaged therein do, or cause to be done, any act in furtherance of the object of such conspiracy, whereby another is injured in his person or property, or deprived of having and exercising any right or privilege of a citizen of the United States, the party so injured or deprived may have an action for the recovery of damages occasioned by such injury or deprivation, against any one or more of the conspirators.

31 **Title 42 U.S.C. Section 1986. Action for neglect to prevent conspiracy**. Every person who, having knowledge that any of the wrongs conspired to be done, and mentioned in the preceding section [42 USCS § 1985], are about to be committed, and having power to prevent or aid in preventing the commission of the same, neglects or refuses to do so, if such wrongful act be committed, shall be liable to the party injured, or his legal representatives, for all damages caused by such wrongful act, which such person by reasonable diligence could have prevented; and such damages may be recovered in an action on the case; and any number of persons guilty of such wrongful neglect or refusal may be joined as defendants in the action, and if the death of any party be caused by any such wrongful act and neglect, the legal representatives of the deceased shall have such action therefor, and may recover not exceeding five thousand dollars damages therein, for the benefit of the widow of the deceased, if there be one, and if there be no widow, then for the benefit of the next of kin of the deceased. But no action under the provisions of this section shall be sustained which is not commenced within one year after the cause of action has accrued.

Section 1343.[32]

Under certain conditions this conspiracy creates still another federal cause of action under the RICO statutes (Racketeer Influenced and Corruption Organization Act)[33].

When federal officials violate a person's civil rights, they are said to be acting under color of federal law. They can be sued. These federal personnel include federal judges, federal trustees, or other federal employees. The authority is the *Bivens* doctrine,[34] which is federal case law applying the Civil Rights Act to violations by federal personnel.

**MANDATORY DUTY TO PROVIDE RELIEF**

I filed the first federal action (January 10, 1984) in the United States District Court in the Eastern District of California at Sacramento.[35] Although I had years of legal experience working with attorneys and in filing federal actions against the FAA and NTSB, and could have filed this lawsuit in pro se, I hired Sacramento attorney James Reed to file the action. He had experience with civil rights as a law school teacher at McGeorge School of Law in Sacramento.

The lawsuit sought (a) a declaratory judgment to declare my divorced status and property rights, as established in the five divorce judgments and under federal and state law; (b) injunctive relief to halt the orders rendered by the California judges who were acting without jurisdiction under California law and violating blocks of state and federal law, and (c) financial damages.

The federal lawsuit raised issues that had been settled in the 1940s by the U.S. Supreme Court. It sought to declare my constitutional right[36] to change residence without being remarried to a person from whom I was divorced decades earlier. It sought to protect the considerable real estate that I had acquired since the 1966 divorce and which was the primary target of the sham action. The lawsuit

---

32 **Title 28 U.S.C. Section 1343**

(a) The district court shall have original jurisdiction of any civil action authorized by law to be commenced by any person:

(1) To recover damages for injury to his person or property, or because of the deprivation of any right or privilege of a citizen of the United States, by any act done in furtherance of any conspiracy mentioned in section 1985 of Title 42;

(2) To recover damages from any person who fails to prevent or to aid in preventing any wrongs mentioned in section 1985 of Title 42 which he had knowledge were about to occur and power to prevent;

(3) To redress the deprivation, under color of any State law, statute, ordinance, regulation, custom or usage, of any right, privilege or immunity secured by the Constitution of the United States or by any Act of Congress providing for equal rights of citizens or of all persons within the jurisdiction of the United States;

(4) To recover damages or to secure equitable or other relief under any Act of Congress providing for the protection of civil rights, including the right to vote.

33 Title 18 United States Code Sections 1961 and 1962.

34 *Bivens v. Six Unknown Agents*, 403 U.S. 388 (1971).

35 January 10, 1984. *Stich v. California Superior Court; Dwight Ely, Judge; Friedman, Sloan and Ross*, C-84-0048 RAR.

36 Under Title 28 U.S.C. §§ 2201, 2202. Among the constitutional rights violated were the rights and protections in the Fourteenth Amendment due process, equal protection, property, liberty, freedom rights; Privileges and Immunity Clause rights under Article IV, § 1, and under the 14th Amendment (depriving right to obtain divorce on universally recognized residence basis, and right to change residence); right to unabridged interstate travel, without losing rights and privileges acquired in prior jurisdictions of residence; Article IV, § 1 (Full Faith and Credit Clause, and Title 28 U.S.C. § 1738, requiring recognition of the personal and property rights in the California divorce judgment, its entry for recognition as local judgments in the courts of Nevada, Oklahoma, and Texas.

sought financial damages against the California judges and the Friedman law firm. In the same year, the U.S. Supreme Court clarified the right to sue state judges who violate state or federal law or who act without jurisdiction.[37] The court clerk assigned the lawsuit to Judge Raul Ramirez.

**THE START OF THE FEDERAL DUE PROCESS GRIDLOCK**

The Friedman law firm and California Judge Dwight Ely filed a motion to dismiss the federal declaratory judgment and civil rights action on the grounds that the California action was a divorce action and, therefore, the federal courts must abstain. The mere fact that I was subject to a divorce action when federal law established that I had been divorced for almost two decades constituted violations of federally-protected rights. These violations invoked mandatory federal court jurisdiction. Many federal laws, and over two dozen California statutes and Rules of Court had been violated, constituting major federal causes of action. Further, even if I had been legally married, federal court jurisdiction over civil rights violations does not cease when federally protected rights are violated.

**REPETITION OF THE FRIVOLOUS TACTIC**

The standard tactic used by the California judges when I exercised my legal procedural remedies was to place a frivolous label on it and call me a vexatious litigant. The frivolous labels were then used to order me to pay huge financial sanctions to the Friedman law firm, who initiated the civil right violations.

U.S. District Judge Raul Ramirez unlawfully dismissed my action, refusing to render a declaratory judgment addressing the validity of the five divorce judgments, or my personal and property rights. Ramirez sought to support his order of dismissal on the argument that the California action was a domestic relations action for which federal courts should abstain. That was a misstatement of the law and facts. First, the Civil Rights Act protections apply to all actions regardless of the label placed upon the suit. Second, I was exercising my rights under the Declaratory Judgment Act to have a federal court declare as valid the prior divorce judgments and the personal and property rights stated in them. Federal law, in addition to state law, required that these judgments and these rights be recognized. Third, the divorce label was a farce as I had been legally divorced for the past two decades. It would not have been much more bizarre to have placed a probate label on the action, ignoring the fact that I was still alive.

Ramirez compounded his refusal to act by ordering me to pay the Friedman law firm $10,000 for having sought declaratory and injunctive relief remedies. If an attorney files a frivolous action, it is the attorney who is ordered to pay, and not the client. But it was I who was the target of the judicial attacks, and this became obvious over the years. Ramirez violated still another federal statute. It is a federal crime to inflict harm upon anyone for having exercised rights

37 *Pulliam v. Allen*, 104 S.Ct 1970 (1984). Followed by other federal decisions: *Harlow v. Fitzgerald*, 457 U.S. 800 (1982); *Dykes v. Hoseman*, 743 F.2d 1488 (11th Cir. 1984). In *Dykes v. Hoseman*, 743 F.2d 1488 (11th Cir. 1984), the Eleventh Circuit federal district court held that a state judge could be sued for money damages when he renders orders without either personal or subject matter jurisdiction.

and protections under the laws and Constitution of the United States.[38]

**DEFINITION OF A FRIVOLOUS ACTION**

The United States Supreme Court and other federal decisions defined the term frivolous as any complaint, appeal, or any other motion from which there is not an arguable point. The U.S. Supreme Court held that they are not frivolous if "any of the legal points [are] arguable on their merits..." *Haines v. Kerner* 404 U.S. 519, 521-522 (1972). Obviously, my federal complaint exercising the right to have my personal and property status declared under federal and state law was not frivolous, and the validity of five divorce judgments, was not frivolous. Nor was it frivolous to seek injunctive relief against the repeated violations of state and federal law by California judges acting without jurisdiction under California law. This judicial charade was repeated time and time again, as the pack of renegade federal judges engaged in a Ponzi-like scheme protecting the scheme and the perpetrators.

**PROTECTION AGAINST WRONGFUL DISMISSAL**

Federal law prohibits dismissing an action if the complaint states a single federal cause of action. The law requires that the allegations stated in the complaint be recognized as true for the purpose of determining whether a federal cause of action is stated.[39] If any *single* federal cause of action is *alleged*, the case cannot be dismissed and the District Judge must exercise his duty to provide a federal court forum.

These and many other protections to which all Americans are entitled were repeatedly violated during a ten-year-period by a daisy chain of federal judges, including Justices of the U.S. Supreme Court.

**SUSPENSION OF APPEAL REMEDIES**

In response to Ramirez's dismissal, I filed a timely notice of appeal with the U.S. Court of Appeals at San Francisco, the same appellate court that had wrongfully dismissed my lawsuits against the FAA and NTSB in 1974 and 1980. These unlawful dismissals continued the practices that played key roles in subsequent air disasters. In those earlier actions I exercised the mandatory responsibilities under federal criminal statutes to report safety and criminal violations to a federal court. By their refusal to receive my testimony and evidence these same federal judges blocked the reporting of serious crimes and became co-conspirators in the criminal acts I sought to expose.

Federal appellate law requires the Court of Appeals to vacate the order of dismissal and the frivolous holding, if the complaint alleges at least one federal cause of action for which federal courts can grant relief. And the allegations stated in the complaint far exceeded that test. For the purpose of this test, all

---

38 **Title 18 U.S.C. § 241. Conspiracy against rights of citizens.** If two or more persons conspire to injure, oppress, threaten, or intimidate any citizen in the free exercise or enjoyment of any right or privilege secured to him by the Constitution or laws of the United States, or because of his having so exercised the same;...They shall be fined...or imprisoned...or both.

39 *Dennis v. Sparks* 449 U.S. 24 (1980)(a section 1983 complaint should not be dismissed unless it appears that the plaintiff can prove no set of facts which would entitle him to relief...For the purposes of testing sufficiency of the complaint, the allegations of the complaint must be accepted as true.); *Gardener v. Toilet Goods Assn.*, 387 U.S. 167, 172 (1967). (An action, "especially under the Civil Rights Act, should not be dismissed at the pleadings stage unless it appears to a certainty that plaintiffs are entitled to no relief under any state of the facts, which could be proved in support of their claims."

allegations must be accepted as true.[40]

The Court of Appeals judges denied my appeal, upholding the violations by the U.S. District Court Judge and upholding the pattern of civil and constitutional violations in the state court. They also upheld the $10,000 financial sanctions ordered by Judge Ramirez[41] in retaliation for exercising defenses guaranteed under the Constitution and laws of the United States. I then sought relief by filing petitions for writ of certiorari with the Justices of the United States Supreme Court. Even they had been implicated in the judicial coverup associated with the air safety corruption. They also protected the scheme.

The Ninth Circuit Court of Appeals and the U.S. Supreme Court dismissed my federal actions seeking relief. Their acts approved the unlawful denial of a federal court forum, the violations of federal law, the unlawful dismissal of the action, and the obvious conspiracy to commit these acts. These higher federal courts gave the California judges and the Friedman law firm carte blanche approval to escalate their attacks upon me, which then occurred. The lis pendens that were placed upon all of my properties prevented the normal replacement of mortgages as they came due, and I lost valuable properties. My personal life and my business were in shambles.

California Judge J. Clinton Peterson[42] sentenced me to jail for five days in 1987, charging me with contempt of court when I failed to pay a money judgment to the Friedman law firm. That same judge had tied up all my assets, leaving me without funds to pay any judgment, valid or not.

**REPEATEDLY SEEKING RELIEF**

As the California judges rendered additional orders, inflicting greater harm upon me, which were new federal causes of action, I filed additional federal lawsuits seeking to halt the escalating harm arising from the unlawful and unconstitutional acts. In every instance, federal judges protected the hard-core civil and constitutional violations occurring in the sham California action, while simultaneously protecting those committing the offenses.[43] I filed numerous petitions with the Justices of the U.S. Supreme Court, making the Justices aware of the pattern of judicially inflicted civil and constitutional violations.

**SHAM OATHS**

All federal judges, including the justices of the U.S. Supreme Court, take an oath to uphold the laws and Constitution of the United States. The oath is as follows:

*I, [name of judge], do solemnly swear (or affirm) that I will support and defend the Constitution of the United States against all enemies, foreign and domestic, that I will bear true faith and allegiance to the same, that I take this obligation freely, without any mental reservations or purpose*

---

40 "In our view, a decision to give less than full independent de novo review to the state law determinations of the district courts would be an abdication of our appellate responsibility. Every party is entitled to a full, considered, and impartial review of the decision of the trial court." *Matter of McLinn*, 739 F.2d 1395 (9th Cir 1983).

41 Ramirez left the federal bench in 1992 and went with the Sacramento law firm of Orrick, Herrington & Sutcliffe. In 1996 he left to become a private judge in mediation services, calling himself Ramirez Arbitration & Mediation Services.

42 Superior Court located at Fairfield, California. He was later promoted to a Court of Appeal judge.

43 Federal Judges Marilyn Petal, Samuel Conti, Charles Legge.

*of evasion, and that I will well and faithfully discharge the duties of the office on which I am about to enter. So help me God.*

Many judges would be impeached if the law was applied as written.

**RECOGNIZING THE JUDICIAL CONSPIRACY**

I had been too close to the trees to see the forest. I recognized the pattern of judicial misconduct but had not associated it with a scheme to silence my reporting of the government corruption. Gradually, it became clear. The California lawsuit was engineered by powerful interests in the federal branches of government, using the Friedman law firm as a front and obtaining the cooperation of California judges in the conspiracy. It was apparently never anticipated, when the scheme was hatched, that I would exercise federal remedies. And when I did, federal judges had to protect the scheme and the attorneys and judges carrying it out. (At a later date, I discovered that the Friedman law firm was either a CIA proprietary or a CIA cutout.)

Once I recognized this relationship, I identified it in my federal briefs and simultaneously identified the criminal activities I first discovered as a federal investigator. I filed a federal action combining the causes of action relating to the ongoing California action, and simultaneously demanded that I be allowed to present testimony and evidence relating to the criminal activities. This action, filed in the U.S. District Court at Sacramento,[44] was assigned to Judge Milton Schwartz.

**"Mr. Stich, these allegations are very serious."**

During the first hearing before Judge Milton Schwartz on May 9, 1986, the judge admitted the gravity of the allegations. "Mr. Stich," he stated, "these allegations are very serious. If you wish, I will continue the hearing and give you time to hire legal counsel." But no legal counsel would touch the case; it was too sensitive. Besides, the cost to pursue the case against powerful federal personnel, who have the unlimited federal funds of the U.S. Treasury behind them, would run into the hundreds of thousands of dollars. And my adversaries would be the judges and Justice Department attorneys who control access to justice. Also, as I would later learn, virtually no attorney would sacrifice his legal career by exposing the misconduct in the courts and the Justice Department.

**RAPID CHANGES IN POSITION**

Within a month after Judge Schwartz admitted the gravity of the allegations stated in the complaint, the Friedman law firm and the California judges filed a motion to dismiss the complaint. Despite the multiple federal causes of actions alleged in the complaint, despite the gravity of the criminal acts which Schwartz admitted during the previous hearing, Schwartz ordered my lawsuit dismissed and ordered me to pay financial sanctions for having exercised these federal remedies.

The dismissal openly violated federal law which bars dismissing lawsuits which state a federal cause of action. Mine stated many causes of actions. Further, I was reporting federal crimes to a federal court for which federal criminal statutes required Schwartz to receive details and evidence.

---

44 E.D. Cal. Nr. C 86-0210 MLS.

Judge Schwartz continued the judicial tactics of the California and federal judges, ordering me to pay financial sanctions to the Friedman law firm for having exercised procedural remedies necessary to halt the harm I was suffering and the violations of statutory and constitutional protections.

The total financial sanctions that federal judges ordered me to pay the Friedman law firm now exceeded $150,000. It is a federal violation to inflict harm upon anyone in retaliation for having exercised rights and protections under the laws and Constitution of the United States. (Title 18 USC Section 241.)

Schwartz compounded these unlawful actions by rendering an unlawful and unconstitutional order forever barring me access to the federal court and forever voiding for me the protections in federal statutes.[45] Neither he, nor any other judge, had authority to suspend the protections under our form of government.

**THE LEGAL BASIS FOR AN INJUNCTIVE ORDER**

The basis for rendering injunctive orders is to protect a party during litigation who is suffering great and irreparable harm. But the injunctive order rendered by Judge Schwartz protected the parties *committing* the harm and deprived me, the victim, of protection intended by federal statutes.

I filed a timely notice of appeal of the dismissal and the injunctive order with the Ninth Circuit Court of Appeals at San Francisco. Instead of vacating the dismissal and injunctive order, the judges in the Court of Appeals upheld the right of a federal judge to block the reporting of federal crimes, upheld the suspension of constitutional and statutory protections, and upheld the civil rights violations inflicted upon me. Again, I sought relief from the Justices of the Supreme Court via an emergency petition and petition for writ of certiorari. And again they upheld the unconstitutional acts by the judges over whom they had supervisory responsibilities.

In response to these new attacks, I filed federal actions against the judges of the California Supreme Court and the California Court of Appeal. The basis for this filing was that they aided and abetted the civil rights violations committed against me. Concurrently, I again sought to have my rights declared in the five judgments which were being violated, as well as demanding that my testimony be received concerning the criminal activities I discovered. The action was assigned to U.S. District Judge Marilyn Patel,[46] who promptly dismissed it *sua sponte*, without any hearing (March 5, 1987), violating still other federal laws.

She ordered me to pay financial sanctions and then rendered an order barring me for life from federal court access. Therefore, for all practical purposes, the judges were voiding, for me, the rights and protections under our form of government, and making possible the continued judicial attacks upon my freedoms and possessions. This obviously unlawful and unconstitutional judicial order was necessary to protect the state and federal judges who were cooperating in the scheme to block my reporting of government corruption that included federal judges and Justice Department attorneys. Patel ordered the court clerk to refuse any filing that I submitted, which violated additional protections in federal statutes

45 The May 30, 1986 injunctive order stated in part: IT IS HEREBY ORDERED that plaintiff, Rodney F. Stich, is *barred from filing any action or actions in any United States District Court, or in any state court,...*

46 N.D. Cal. Nr. C-86-6046 MHP.

and constitutional law.

After every dismissal by a federal judge (and the Supreme Court justices) the Friedman law firm and the California judges increased the frequency and severity of their violations against me, inflicting immense personal and property harm. I had to do something, and under our form of government I had rights that these renegade judges could not legally void.

**PRIMA FACIE EVIDENCE BREAKDOWN OF RIGHTS**

These acts were prima facie evidence of the destruction of constitutional rights and the criminalizing of the federal courts by renegade judges. The involvement of many federal judges, including the entire Ninth Circuit Court of Appeals and the Justices of the U.S. Supreme Court, revealed the enormity of the judicial corruption and its deep entrenchment in the United States.

If any single person can suffer these outrages, or lose their constitutional rights and protections, all U.S. Citizens can suffer the same. If any federal judge can inflict such great harm upon one individual, in clear violation of law, they are capable of inflicting the harm upon anyone else targeted by either that judge or the system of which he is a member.

These corrupt judicial acts are only part of what they did to me, and reflect what can happen to anyone else, regardless of the protections under the laws and Constitution of the United States.

The judicial and Justice Department coverups and retaliation made possible the continuation of the corruption that I sought to expose. This coverup played a role in decades of air disasters made possible by continuation of air safety problems, including the corrupt culture inside the FAA and NTSB. The coverups, obstruction of justice, and retaliation also made possible crimes against the American people that have yet to be revealed in these pages.

Portland. Again and again, people died in airline crashes which were due to fraud by FAA, NTSB and United Airlines management reported by author.

# CHAPTER 11 RETALIATION

This chapter focuses upon still another form of criminal activities which inflicts every year enormous harm upon the American people. The sham California lawsuit and the refusal by California and federal judges to provide relief from the judicial civil right violations were inflicting serious financial harm upon my real estate business. Mortgage loans that periodically came due could not be refinanced because of the lis pendens the Friedman law firm had placed on my properties. Valuable properties with hundreds of thousands of dollars in equities were lost. Other loans were coming due and I had to do something to circumvent the judicial scheme misusing the courts to destroy me financially. The Friedman law firm refused to allow the existing loans to be replaced with comparable loans, even though the properties they claimed their Texas client owned with me as community property would be lost. Their intent was to destroy me financially.

## EXERCISING CHAPTER 11 REMEDIES FOR CIVIL RIGHT VIOLATIONS

Chapter 11 is intended to provide time for people with net worth to pay a particular financial obligation and to remain in control of their business and other assets. I had no financial problems. My problems consisted of the deluge of civil right violations judicially inflicted and the concurrent voiding, for me, the state and federal protections that would have halted the attacks in their track. Taking the plain language of Chapter 11 at its word, I exercised Chapter 11 protections for these violations, which was probably the only time in history this was done. This approach was unorthodox, exercising Chapter 11 courts to force federal judges to provide declaratory and injunctive relief to which I was entitled and long overdue. I filed two cases in May of 1987. One was a *personal* Chapter 11 filing and the other was for my *corporation*, Western Diablo Enterprises.

My plan was to bring the block of civil right violations to the attention of the Chapter 11 judges and have the lis pendens associated with the sham California action dismissed. The idea had merit, but unknown to me at that time, the judicial corruption didn't stop at the state level, or at the federal district and appellate levels. It was even worse in the Chapter 11 courts. I discovered an entirely new area of corruption that had a devastating influence upon thousands of American citizens who fell victim to tentacles of the same corruption.

Because of the media coverup of the bankruptcy court corruption, I had no warning of the endemic corruption in the Chapter 11 courts. I hired a San Francisco area attorney to file a personal and a corporate Chapter 11 case for me, and he in turn hired Las Vegas attorney, Joshua Landish.[47] The cases were filed in Las Vegas where I owned a condominium.

The intent of filing the two Chapter 11 cases was to have federal judges declare my personal and property rights legally established in the five divorce judgments by applying federal law; and to have the related lis pendens removed. The cases were assigned to federal Judge Robert Jones. Instead of providing relief, Judge Jones protected the Friedman law firm and the California judges who committed the civil right violations that Jones was duty-bound to correct. Jones duplicated the tactics of the U.S. District Judges, and refused to address the violations of my federally-protected rights.

However, Judge Jones did provide some relief initially. During a September 11, 1987, hearing, he rendered an order refusing to accept jurisdiction over the two cases, ordered the removal of the lis pendens, and stated he was dismissing the two Chapter 11 filings. He delayed executing the order dismissing the cases for sixty days, permitting me time to refinance the buildings on which mortgages had come due.

On the basis of the verbal order lifting the lis pendens, I obtained a firm refinancing commitment to pay off the $550,000 in mortgages that had come due[48] and felt a sigh of relief that part of my problems were now addressed. But my relief was short-lived. Someone apparently got to Judge Jones after his September 11 decision.

**SABOTAGE BY MY OWN ATTORNEYS**

Las Vegas attorney Joshua Landish, hired to protect my assets, proceeded to sabotage me. He did not notify me that there was a court hearing on September 28, 1987, for the personal bankruptcy case. This hearing was on a motion by attorney Estelle Mannis (Oakland, CA) for mortgage holder Robil, Inc., and Superior Home Loans, both of Hayward, California, to obtain relief from the automatic stay so they could foreclose on several of my properties.[49] They filed this motion immediately after Judge Jones rendered a decision refusing to accept jurisdiction and ordering removal of the lis pendens, permitting me to refinance the mortgage and pay it off.

Disregarding the absence of jurisdiction to hear the motion because of the refusal to accept jurisdiction, that hearing to remove the automatic stay had to be limited to *that issue* and to the *personal* Chapter 11 case, which contained only a small part of the $10 million in assets. Nothing could be addressed concerning the *corporate* filing that contained most of the $10 million in assets.

---

47 Joshua Landish of Las Vegas, Nevada. I also hired Las Vegas attorney Earl Hawley for another corporation, and his conduct was almost as bad as that of Landish.

48 Superior Home Loans-Robil, Inc., Hayward, California.

49 Held by Superior Home Loans and Robil, Inc. of Hayward, California.

Judge Jones' decision refusing to accept jurisdiction had not been vacated (even to this date). There was no jurisdiction to render any further order, except to carry out the dismissal. Robil knew that I would be able to refinance and pay off the mortgage loan due to them. They apparently wanted to foreclose and gain the benefit of the large equities behind the mortgage loans that they had on the properties.

Unknown to me, the attorney I hired to protect my interests, Joshua Landish, met secretly with my adversaries and planned to request Judge Jones to order seizure of my assets and conduct a fire-sale liquidation. In this way, Landish's legal fees would be much higher than if he simply acted to protect my interests.

The official video tapes and transcript of the court proceedings indicated that upon the start of the September 28, 1987, hearing Landish requested Judge Jones to vacate his earlier order providing me relief. Landish requested that Judge Jones order the seizure of my business, my home, my assets, in both the personal and the corporate cases. This attorney sabotage was gross misconduct by the attorney hired to prevent that seizure, and violated my constitutional and statutory rights to a hearing to defend against the seizure of my life's assets.

**UNLAWFULLY SEIZING MY ASSETS**

Federal statutory law[50] requires certain safeguards before judges can strip a person of his or her assets. There must be a noticed hearing to permit the party to defend against the taking of his or her property. There must be a legally recognized reason for taking and destroying the assets. Due process rights must be protected. Each of these requirements was openly violated, and was approved by every appellate court up to and including the U.S. Supreme Court, despite the obvious unlawful and unconstitutional violations.

Chapter 11 law provides that the only authority for seizing a person's properties through appointment of a trustee are (a) gross mismanagement; or (b) major dishonesty, and (c) that creditors must be at risk. There are other protections against seizure, but these are the main ones. Creditors must be at risk. But in my case all creditors were secured by mortgages on the properties that were worth far more than the loan balances. The request for appointment of a trustee must be made by a creditor. My attorney was not a creditor.

I couldn't be accused of mismanagement. It was my hard work and efforts that caused the assets to grow from starting capital of five hundred dollars twenty years earlier to ten million dollars at the time of filing for Chapter 11 relief. There was no dishonesty, and none was alleged. None of the creditors requested the appointment of a trustee; it was my own attorney.

**"Stich is going to be very unhappy when he hears about this."**

Disregarding the numerous protections under the Constitution and federal law, Judge Jones rendered two orders seizing my life's assets. One order seized the Chapter 11 assets in the personal Chapter 11 case (which was on the calendar solely on a motion to remove the automatic stay on several mortgages). The second order seized the assets in the corporate Chapter 11 case, which wasn't on the court calendar and for which there was no notice given. They were both rendered after a prior order refusing to accept jurisdiction was announced. Under

50 Title 11 U.S.C. Section 1104.

federal law these were void or voidable orders. The manner in which it was done met federal case law definition of a conspiracy between Judge Jones, the attorneys, and the trustee. The official court audio tape and reporter's transcript show Judge Robert Jones remarking after ordering the seizure of my assets: "Mr. Stich is going to be very unhappy when he hears about this." Having just lost my life's assets, this would be somewhat of an understatement!

Immediately after rendering the order seizing my assets, Judge Jones was confronted with another problem. The five attorneys who were my adversaries at that hearing (including Landish) presented him with the written order of abstention that Jones rendered at the previous September 11th hearing. He now had to sign an order refusing to accept jurisdiction *after* he had just verbally rendered an order seizing the assets.

Judge Jones got around this problem by signing the abstention order and then signing the orders seizing my assets on October 8, 1987, stating on the orders that there was a hearing on that date. But there was no hearing on that date. The clerk's docket sheet, the reporter's transcript, and other court records proved that there was no hearing on that date. Judge Jones was lying to protect the corrupt seizure of my assets.

Attorney Landish withheld from me knowledge that Judge Jones ordered the seizure of my assets, including my business, my home, my many properties in California and Nevada, and my bank accounts. Unless notices of appeal were filed within ten days, I would lose the right to have those orders vacated. When I accidentally discovered that Judge Jones had rendered the order, but unaware that it was Landish who requested the seizure, I instructed the attorney to file a notice of appeal. Landish agreed to do so, but never did it. Finally, I filed my own notice, and discharged Landish on November 10, 1987, for sabotaging my case.

Even though Friedman had no claim to my assets, in response to a motion by the Friedman group, Judge Jones transferred the Chapter 11 cases from Las Vegas to Oakland, California.

**TURNING ASSETS OVER TO A KNOWN EMBEZZLER**

Before Judge Jones transferred the cases to Oakland, he appointed trustee Charles Duck to seize my assets. Duck had been repeatedly charged by other victims of Chapter 11 courts as having looted their assets after federal judges appointed him trustee. Duck ordered me off my business properties, which I had founded and developed over the past twenty years. He stopped making mortgage payments on most of the ten million dollars in properties and canceled my refinancing commitments, which would have corrected the problem for which I had sought Chapter 11 relief. Duck diverted the $60,000 per month income to his own use, canceled 30-year mortgages and replaced them with 3-year mortgages, incurring huge fees for churning the loans. Over one million dollars disappeared almost immediately, with no trace of the missing money.

United States Trustee Anthony Sousa and United States Attorney Joseph Russoniello, both of whom headed divisions of the Justice Department, with offices at San Francisco, refused to investigate Duck's embezzlement and looting of my assets. Duck's refusal to make mortgage payments caused dozens of mortgages to foreclose, losing valuable properties I had acquired over the years.

Congress knew that the rampant Chapter 11 judicial corruption was known to the Department of Justice; that the Justice Department attorneys protected those committing the multi-billion-dollar-a-year racketeering enterprise. Congress knew that Justice Department officials misused Chapter 11 proceedings through their control over the U.S. Trustees. The Chapter 11 judicial racketeering activities continued as before. The media kept the lid on the scandal, insuring its continuation, and insuring that their readers pay the price.

By law, the U.S. Trustee had the responsibility to *prevent* corruption, as well as the Civil Rights Division of the Justice Department. For two years I made U.S. Trustee Anthony Sousa aware of the corruption that continued without letup. If anything changed, it was for the worse. After Duck was imprisoned in November 1989, Sousa refused to provide relief from what Duck had done to my assets, and appointed another attorney as trustee, who then continued looting my assets as Duck had done.

The new trustee, Jerome Robertson, immediately accelerated the harm done to my estates that Duck had started. Within a few months, Robertson and his retained law firm of Murray and Murray had requested and obtained court approval to take over $250,000 from my assets for legal fees to do things that I routinely did when I controlled my business.

When the U.S. Trustee refused to prevent these corrupt acts, I filed a lawsuit against him—and his boss, the Department of Justice, in the U.S. District Court, District of Columbia.[58] Again, federal judges protected the system of which they were a part. District of Columbia judge Stanley Sporkin dismissed the action on January 17, 1990, without a hearing, and despite the law barring dismissal when the complaint stated federal cause of actions.

**EXAMPLES OF OTHER VICTIMS**

In one case, the Department of Justice forced a publishing company into bankruptcy. The company was set up for the purpose of spreading political ideas, and the Justice Department attorneys did not like the exposures. Presidential candidate Lyndon LaRouche informed the public of corruption by federal officials via the publications *Campaigner Publications*, *Caucus Distributors*, and *Fushion Energy Foundation*.

Without a hearing, the Justice Department obtained an ex parte order forcing the company into bankruptcy. The company argued that the law required three parties to force a person or company into bankruptcy, and sought to have the seizure overturned, without success. The Justice Department used its United States Trustee Division and its control over private trustees and federal judges to force the company into a Chapter 7 liquidation.

Then Justice Department officials secured indictments against LaRouche and six associates for mail fraud on the basis that the companies did not repay earlier loans. LaRouche argued that the loans could not be paid back because Justice Department officials forced the company into bankruptcy. The Justice Department attorneys obtained a fifteen-year prison term for the 67-year-old LaRouche.

---

58 *Stich v. Stanton; U.S. Trustee Anthony Sousa; Richard Thornburgh; United States of America.*

Fortunately, LaRouche had friends outside of prison willing to fight for him. While LaRouche and his associates were in prison, District Judge Martin Bostetter ruled in a 106-page decision on October 25, 1989, that the Justice Department's seizure of the assets and the involuntary bankruptcy action were illegal and a fraud upon the court.

In another case, the husband-and-wife publishing house of *Stein & Day* was induced by attorneys to seek relief in Chapter 11 when a major customer refused to pay a large bill owed to them. Their 26-year-old business had run a small but respectable operation that published about 100 books a year. Their business was good and they were otherwise financially strong. Seeking a time delay in paying pending bills, the primary reason for Chapter 11, owner Sol Stein filed Chapter 11 on the advice of his attorney.

Following the standard script, instead of providing time to pay bills, the Chapter 11 judge seized and then looted the assets of this once profitable company. The husband-and-wife team experienced corruption by the bankruptcy courts that if committed by an ordinary citizen would result in criminal prosecution and imprisonment. Stein lost everything he accumulated for the past three decades. Incensed, he wrote about the judicial Chapter 11 corruption in the book *A Feast for Lawyers*, subtitled *Inside Chapter 11: An Exposé*. Even though Stein recognized only a small part of the criminality in Chapter 11 and 13 courts, he described these courts as inhabited by hacks, vultures and scoundrels, who feed on productive companies and people.

In another of thousands of examples, Chapter 11 judges and officers of the court (trustees) stripped San Diego resident Samuel Shen of millions of dollars of assets he acquired from hard work after immigrating from Hong Kong in 1959. Shen was so badly affected by the trauma inflicted upon him that he was committed to a mental institution for thirty days. As other victims had done, with many succeeding, Shen tried to commit suicide several times. He lost his family, who didn't have the character to support him during these troubling times.[59]

Shen's 1982 Chapter 11 filing showed assets of ten million dollars with liabilities of two and a half million. Everything was almost free and clear. The Chapters 11 and 13 racketeering activities, protected by every level of the federal judiciary, including the U.S. Supreme Court justices, financially destroyed him. Over seven million dollars in assets were looted by the judge-appointed trustee, the trustee's law firm, and whatever hidden interests that Judge Herbert Katz may have had in dummy corporations. There were some who claimed Katz was part of a Jewish Mafia that had stolen hundreds of millions of dollars of assets from people who naively sought relief in Chapter 11.

Real estate investor Jay Sobrinia of San Diego was another typical case. He encountered a sudden cancellation of a verbal permanent loan commitment from his bank. When the bank construction loan came due, the same bank that had promised permanent financing commenced foreclosure on the expensive house. If the bank had been successful, it would have made a windfall profit. This was a common tactic with Bank of America during the depression years and in recent

59 *San Diego Tribune*, July 10, 1989.

times.

Sobrinia's attorney, who had close ties to the Chapter 11 courts, advised him to file Chapter 11 and get a stay of the foreclosure to permit him time to obtain permanent financing. On the lawyer's assurance, Sobrinia then put his entire one million equity estate into Chapter 11. Despite federal statutory law barring seizure of the assets (except when dishonesty or gross mismanagement exists), the Chapter 11 judge ordered Sobrinia's assets seized and turned over to a trustee. The routine destruction of the assets then began, enriching the attorneys, law firms, and corporations that are part of this racketeering enterprise. Sobrinia's million-dollar-equity estate was stolen.

These sad tales are repeated thousands of times, reflecting the theft of billions of dollars a year by pious-appearing federal judges that have stolen more money than many organized criminal enterprises.

The legal and judicial fraternities at every level are a part of the Chapters 11 and 13 racketeering activities. They include federal judges, Justices of the U.S. Supreme Court, attorneys and officials in the Justice Department, trustees, and law firms. In addition, those who aid and abet these crimes by their duplicity of silence include members of Congress and the establishment media. Their victims include many older people who are left destitute, and who are no match for this gang of thugs.

## ONE OF MANY TEXAS VICTIMS

Another victim who told me of the experiences he had with crooked federal judges, trustees and law firms was John Hamilton of Cuero, Texas. He owned a 1,800 acre ranch until he was targeted by the bankruptcy club, and then financially destroyed. Earlier, he had been invited to White House functions as a result of his charitable work.

Hamilton and his wife had obtained a loan of $475,000 on their ranch which was worth almost $4 million, the proceeds of which had been used to build a commercial building. For the next ten years the Hamiltons made payments on the loan, which had a ten-year due date. They expected the bank to renew the loan when its term was up, as is standard practice. Over $300,000 had been paid on the $475,000 loan during the ten years, leaving a balance due of $184,000. Instead of renewing the note, the bank[60] called the loan. Under advice of legal counsel, the Hamiltons filed Chapter 12[61] to gain time to refinance the loan that was only about one twentieth of the property value.

These are the types of filings that are targeted by the "bankruptcy club" members consisting of judges, trustees and law firms. By law, the Hamiltons should have kept control of their assets. But if the law was followed, the assets could not be seized and looted. As is widespread throughout the country, the practice then was for an unlawful seizure of the assets and subsequent liquidation, enriching the criminal enterprise.

U.S. Bankruptcy Judge Richard Schmidt ordered the seizure of the Hamilton's ranch and placed Trustee Gary Knostman in control of the assets, a kiss of death for their life's assets. The trustee hired a closely aligned law firm, and between

60 Bank of Victoria.

61 Chapter 12 Farmers and Ranchers Bankruptcy.

them and their coterie managed to financially destroy the Hamiltons, showing the consequences of trusting the statutory protections to the crooked federal judges and their bank of thieves.

With the seizure of the Hamilton's assets, there was no money to pay for legal counsel, and they had to appear without an attorney, insuring the rapid loss of their life's assets. Eventually the Hamiltons did obtain attorneys, all of whom assisted in the loss of the assets. Today the Hamiltons are destitute, their life's assets stolen from them.

These are only a few of the thousands of cases every year in which honest Americans are stripped of their assets after exercising in good faith the protections of Chapter 11 or 12. They trusted their government, unaware that epidemic corruption of the highest level has taken over many of the federal offices, including the federal courts. Their plight, and the thriving criminality in bankruptcy courts, are well known to members of Congress who have oversight responsibilities; to the media, with its obligation to report criminality in government, that financially destroys many of their own readers; to the checks and balances, every one of which aids and abets the ongoing racketeering enterprise.

Congressman Jack Brooks (D-TX), chairman of the House Economic and Commercial Law Subcommittee, knew about the rampant criminality as a result of having received reports from hundreds of victims in Congressional hearings, and from my reports. Brooks stated:[62]

> *I would tell members, if you've gone broke, go into bankruptcy. But if you've got any money at all, don't take bankruptcy, fight it out. They'll take it all.*

But the statutes provide that Americans can file under Chapter 11, 12, or 13, to get a time delay in paying their debts, and that they will remain in control of their assets. Brooks admitted that the assets were taken, and he certainly knew the rampant criminality by federal judges, trustees, and law firms. He protected the system of crooks that prey upon the American public.

A bankruptcy attorney, Lawrence A. Beck of San Antonio, reported[63] what many attorneys have admitted or known:

> *Unfortunately, most individual debtors who enter bankruptcy with significant assets eventually conclude that they have become trapped in a crooked, dishonest system which is run for the benefit of the panel trustee and his hand-picked attorney, and which is supervised by [crooked] bureaucrats.*

This is the type of criminality that creates the epidemic criminal mindset in the United States. The trustee program was established by Congress in 1986, and is run by the U.S. Department of Justice, to insure honesty in the trustee program and the courts. Before the last page is reached in this book, the criminality by Justice Department attorneys in almost any Justice Department activity should be obvious.

---

62 *Houston Chronicle*, Nov. 7, 1991.
63 ibid.

**STANDARD SILENCING TACTIC PROTECTING CORRUPT FEDERAL JUDGES AND SYSTEM**

Hamilton described the killing of two attorneys who had knowledge of the criminal activities in Texas Chapter 11 courts. He described the death of a bankruptcy trustee, Jane Ford, in June 1993, by a shotgun blast to her head. Her death left behind a twelve-year-old son. Ford reportedly played a key role in the bankruptcy corruption, but eventually the massive theft from bankruptcy estates, carried out with judicial approval and complicity, and the outrage of victimized citizens, caused indictments to be handed down against her. Seeking to reduce her prison sentence, she announced her intention to expose the criminal enterprise in the Texas bankruptcy courts. This was similar to others who announced their intentions to expose federal officials and judges. She ended in the same condition that other many other whistleblowers did, including those who blow the whistle on judicial corruption in the bankruptcy courts: dead. And in a scenario similar to others, the local police and coroner ruled her death a suicide.

Hamilton described another bankruptcy-related killing, in which attorney John Scott was murdered as his charges of bankruptcy corruption started to expose the looting of assets involving federal judges, trustees and law firms. Scott was killed near Austin, Texas.

**GIVING THEMSELVES IMMUNITY FROM THEIR CRIMES**

Federal judges of the Ninth Circuit[64] held that the private trustees, including embezzler Charles Duck who committed the worst reported trustee fraud, were officers of the court, and were therefore immune from liability! Federal judges, therefore, held that a citizen has no claim against an officer of the court (i.e., trustee, attorney, judge, or one of their employees) arising from the criminal acts of that federal official, even though the acts are criminal and inflict enormous harm upon an innocent person. They held in effect that officers of the court could inflict any type of outrage upon the public, and the public has no remedy!

One of the many people victimized by the judicial corruption was Thomas Read of Connecticut. Read obtained a Connecticut judgment against Duck, but bankruptcy Judge Alan Jaroslovsky of Santa Rosa, who had protected Duck's criminal activities, issued an injunction forever barring Read from enforcing the judgment. Read argued that the injunctive order exceeded the judge's authority and filed an appeal with the Ninth Circuit Bankruptcy Appellate Panel (composed of Chapter 11 judges!). The appellate panel rendered a published decision holding that:[65]

> *[J]udicial immunity not only protects judges against suit from acts done within their jurisdiction, but also spreads outward to shield related public servants, including trustees in bankruptcy."*
>
> *This circuit has adopted a...rationale stating that a trustee or an official acting under the authority of the bankruptcy judge is entitled to derived judicial immunity because he is performing an integral part of the judicial process....a trustee, who obtains court approval for actions under the supervision of the*

64 Ninth Circuit Bankruptcy Appellate Panel.

65 September 27, 1989.

*bankruptcy judge, is entitled to derived immunity.*

*It is well settled that the trustee in bankruptcy is an officer of the appointing court. Courts other than the appointing court have no jurisdiction to entertain suits against the trustee, without leave from the appointing court, for acts done in an official capacity and within his authority as an officer of the court....It is...axiomatic that the Trustee, "as a trustee in bankruptcy [and] as an official acting under the authority of the bankruptcy judge, is entitled to derived judicial immunity because he is performing an integral part of the judicial process."*

*Sound policy also mandates immunizing the trustee. The possibility that we would hold trustees personally liable for judgments rendered against them in their representative capacity would invariably lessen the vigor with which trustees pursue their obligations. Immunity is essential because, as Judge Learned Hand noted, "to submit all officials, the innocent as well as the guilty, to the burden of a trial and to the inevitable danger of its outcome, would dampen the ardor of all but the most resolute, or the most irresponsible, in the unflinching discharge of their duties....Accordingly, we hold that the trustee [Charles Duck], acting under the authority of the court, is entitled to derived judicial immunity.*

Fraud, violation of statutory and constitutional protections, are not within the authorized duties of a judge. But this has been conveniently ignored by federal judges protecting themselves against the many forms of judicial misconduct in which they are involved.

As the judicial involvement in the Chapter 11 corruption surfaced, the Ninth Circuit Court of Appeals rendered a judgment[66] protecting judges against responsibility for their criminal acts. The Ninth Circuit rendered the decision holding that regardless of any criminal conduct committed against the public or an individual by a judge or person acting on his behalf, such as a trustee, the public had no remedy against the judges or anyone acting with the judges. The need for these self-protective and unconstitutional decisions is rapidly increasing as federal judges are heavily implicated in some of the worst criminal activities ever exposed in the history of the United States.

Justices of the U.S. Supreme Court enlarged upon the protection against their own criminal acts. The Supreme Court Justices held in *Stump v. Sparkman*[67] that a judge could deliberately commit unlawful, unconstitutional, and corrupt acts upon a citizen, destroy personal and property rights, and be immune from financial liability. This decision was repeatedly stated by U.S. District Judge Marilyn Patel, San Francisco (as I sought relief against California and federal judges).

The Constitution and statutes disagree with judge-made law. Federal civil rights statutes and constitutional rights to seek relief clearly do not provide immunity to federal judges when they violate clear and settled civil and constitutional rights, or against corrupt or criminal acts and who inflict harm upon any member of the American public.

---

66 *Ashelman v. Pope*, 793 F.2d 1072 (9th Cir. 1986).
67 435 U.S. at 362.

In *Stump v. Sparkman* the judge entered into a conspiracy, ordering a young girl permanently sterilized. The Supreme Court held that the girl had no remedy against the judge, as the public's welfare requires that a judge be free to exercise his duties without fear of the consequences.

**THE CORRUPT SYSTEM PROTECTS ITS OWN**

I filed an administrative claim with the Administrative Office of the United States Courts, addressing the judicial misconduct (necessary before filing a lawsuit against the United States government under the federal Tort Claims Act). The claim was based upon the looting of my assets by trustee Charles Duck. The Justice Department denied my claim on October 17, 1989, stating the "claim may not be settled under authority of the Federal Tort Claims Act because that act specifically excludes claims arising from the performance of a discretionary function." In the mindset of Justice Department attorneys and federal judges, Duck's criminal activities were a "discretionary function!"

**SECRET JUSTICE DEPARTMENT MEMORANDUM**

An assistant U.S. Attorney in the San Francisco office, Michael Howard, wrote a July 11, 1990 report describing the rampant criminal corruption by federal officials in Chapter 11 courts in the Northern District of California, stating in part:

*Subject: Alan Jaroslovsky, bankruptcy judge; Charles Duck, former trustee in bankruptcy, convicted; Philip Arnot, Harvey Hoffman, Timothy J. Walsh, Malcolm Biserka, Ruth Harrell, attorneys for numerous trustees in bankruptcy; Susan Euker, Jeff Walk, trustees in bankruptcy; Goldberg, Stinnett and McDonald, law firm that specializes in bankruptcies, primarily Carol Stinnett; David McKim, attorney at law; San Francisco attorney Monseur, first name unknown; Robert and Harrison, law firm in many bankruptcy cases, and primarily Mr. Cook, Esquire; William Kelly, Esquire, attorney for Graham and James law firm in San Francisco; Peter Robinson, private attorney, former Assistant U.S. Attorney.*

*Why Referral to Public Integrity Section: U.S. Attorney's manual, Chapter 3,....states in part, most government corruption cases are both sensitive and of intense public interest. It is particularly important that the appearance of fairness and impartiality always be present [by prosecuting such cases].*

*Considering the possible involvement of bankruptcy court judges, a former U.S. Attorney, and the magnitude of the investigation necessary, it is possible that the U.S. Attorney's office does not have the resources available to investigate the widespread corruption and cronyism which presently exist in the bankruptcy courts. To thoroughly investigate the present quagmire, there is the need for a virtual full-time prosecutor to clean up the system.*

*Main justice would probably have the resources to provide the prosecutors and the investigators necessary to fulfill the present need to clean up the system. I don't believe we have any criminal assistants who have the time to take on such a case as this, for such investigation. Offenses indicated so far: Information provided to me to date indicates that one or more of the above-named subjects have engaged in one or more of the following felonies: (A) Perjury. Submitted false, forged, or altered documents to the courts. (B) Obstruction of justice; (C) Churning of Chapter 11 estates for the exclusive financial advantage of the trustees and the trustees' attorneys. (D) Failure to provide accurate financial accounts and reports to the courts. Most of the problems appear to arise in Chapter 11 [where there are assets].*

Justice Department officials sequestered the report, took no action on the judicial corruption (in which they were themselves involved), and reprimanded the Assistant U.S. Attorney who wrote it. The few concerned Justice Department investigators who sought to expose government corruption faced the same problem that I and other FAA inspectors faced.

**MEDIA COVERUP**

The media was fully aware of the gravity of the Chapter 11 corruption, its nationwide extent, and the pattern of criminality that made many of their own readers victims. The media either didn't report any of the findings by its investigative reporters or, as in most cases, reported the peripheral and minor aspects of the corruption, portraying the acts in a more innocent manner. The *San Francisco Daily Journal* wrote in an October 4, 1990, article that Haley's "pattern of alleged wrongdoing is strikingly similar to that uncovered against her friend and mentor, Charles Duck, who has admitted embezzling $2.5 million from bankruptcy estates under his control."

Occasionally, the media hinted at the problem, but never identified it in a way that the public would react in outrage. The *Journal* had months of articles describing the Chapter 11 corruption, using such headlines as *Bankruptcy Courts, A System in Crisis; The Bankruptcy Club; A System in Crisis; The Road to Ruin.* It avoided the heart of the matter: the epidemic pattern of crooked federal judges, trustees, and powerful law firms, and the coverup by Justice Department officials.

The few newspapers that addressed Chapter 11 corruption reported Duck's embezzlement as the worst by a trustee in the nation's history. And this assessment was given without considering the total amount of what he actually embezzled. Obviously, Duck did not operate in a vacuum, especially with the vocal complaints of his victims, and he needed the protection of federal judges to continue his criminal activities. I notified over a dozen magazines and newspapers[68] of the misconduct from 1988 through 1990, a year and a half before signs of Chapter 11 corruption was exposed.

**DAMAGE CONTROL FOR DUCK**

The Justice Department's prison authorities, where Duck was confined, provided him with unusually lenient conditions. His prison duties were made pleasant, and he was allowed to use prison automobiles for unescorted travel into town where his family was staying. After being released from prison, a large San Francisco law firm hired him as a full time consultant, despite the crimes that he had committed. A law firm is not going to risk unnecessarily alienating federal judges and the Justice Department by hiring a major criminal unless it is with the tacit approval of these government entities.

---

68 Wall Street Journal; San Francisco Examiner; San Francisco Chronicle; Business Week; Newsweek;

Reporter Linda Martin of the *San Francisco Examiner* spent over two months investigating the corruption, interviewing many of those victimized by the "bankruptcy club." During the end of January 1990, Martin revealed to Mrs. McCullough, a California resident and activist against corrupt government, that the *Examiner* refused to print the main part of the judicial corruption, causing her to quit the *Examiner*.

While several San Francisco Bay Area newspapers publicized the Chapter 11 corruption, the mass-media papers kept the lid on the scandal. Reporter Bill Wallace for the *San Francisco Chronicle* explained to one inquirer, Virginia McCullough (September 4, 1990), that the reason they had not contacted me on the Chapter 11 corruption was that I incorporated other areas of government corruption into the discussion. A corollary to that would be a reporter ignoring an informant's description of a murder that took place because the informant also reported another murder. Another reporter for the *Chronicle* gave a different excuse to another inquirer months earlier in answer to a question why the *Chronicle* did not print anything about the air safety corruption that I had earlier reported. His reply: "Stich wouldn't give us any facts."

Reporters Bill Wallace and Jeff Paline came to my home, looked at the volumes of material I had, and went to the federal district courts at Sacramento and San Francisco, examining the papers that I filed describing the corruption in detail. I gave them copies of my earlier book, which explained the serious corruption in detail. All questions presented to me were answered. Nothing was withheld. It was my belief they were under instructions to sequester any mention of the matter in their news stories.

It took a determined effort to keep the scandal hidden, not only in the San Francisco area, but throughout the United States. The number of people financially destroyed by blatant corruption, outright violations of federal statutory and case law, the number of complaints to the Justice Department, to higher federal courts, to members of Congress, reached epidemic proportions.

Most of the mass media knew of the corruption and refused to report it. A scandal affecting thousands of people a year could not have escaped the media's attention. By their coverup the media deceived their readers, some of whom lost their life's assets by being unaware of the judicial racketeering activities. Members of the U.S. Senate and House knew of the corruption, as their constituents pleaded with them to investigate and provide help. The legal fraternity in Congress protected the legal fraternity in the Chapter 11 corruption and made possible the financial destruction of their own constituents.

There were a few exceptions. The *Indianapolis Star* published numerous reports on the Chapter 11 racketeering enterprises, commencing in 1987. The articles described the judicial corruption that most newspapers kept quiet. In an April 19, 1987, article the system was described as follows:

> *The [Chapter 11] court system is burdened with cronyism, political favors and conflicts of interest while a "club" of bankruptcy attorneys reaps the largest fees.... Critics—including other lawyers—use the harshest terms. One described the system as incestuous....subverts the judicial system....Direct and indirect financial relationships between three judges and lawyers or others to whom they award fees....Forged, fraudulent*

*or misleading documents...fraud...At stake is the fate of thousands of economically distressed companies and people, as well as the financial interests of hundreds of thousands of companies and individuals.*

**CONGRESS BELATEDLY FEIGNS AN INTEREST**

As a result of the exposures, one Chapter 11 judge in Indianapolis was sentenced to prison, very possibly to diffuse further investigation. However, the system continued and flourished, and the maverick U.S. Trustee whose effort put the judge into prison was terminated by the Justice Department. Two small-town papers near San Francisco, the *Napa Sentinel* and the *Santa Rosa Press Democrat*, ran articles on the Chapter 11 corruption. But the major newspapers, including the *San Francisco Chronicle*, the *Wall Street Journal*, and others, kept the scheme going by not reporting it to their readers.

The articles by the *Napa Sentinel* and the *Santa Rosa Press Democrat* linked the Chapter 11 corruption with numerous drug enterprises, to federal judges, judge-appointed trustees, the Department of Justice, and to the CIA. This book doesn't go into those areas, but makes reference to these tantalizing issues, especially in light of the revelations of government-protected drug activities by the CIA.

For years, constituents of California Congressman Don Edwards had pleaded with him for help, as they were victimized and financially destroyed by the Chapter 11 racketeering activities. Edwards was known as the "father of the Bankruptcy Code." Attorneys in the Chapter 11 club praised Edwards for the law that so enriched their lives. Edwards had Congressional oversight jurisdiction over the scandal-plagued system, and he also chaired the House Judiciary Committee's subcommittee on (would you believe?) Civil and Constitutional rights. The Chapter 11 corruption obviously violated these civil and constitutional rights.

I had repeatedly reported to Congressman Edwards since 1965 the federal air safety and criminal violations related to a series of airline crashes and the corruption by federal officials, including the Justice Department. From 1988 through 1990, I repeatedly made Edwards aware of the rampant corruption and the specific criminal acts, by Chapter 11 judges and their closely-knit trustees, law firms, and corporations. I reported the shocking pattern of civil and constitutional violations committed for over five years by federal judges and Justice Department attorneys and asked him to help. Instead, he aided and abetted the acts by covering up. Not even once did he respond.

In recent years, Congressional jurisdiction over Chapter 11 was transferred from Edward's subcommittee to Representative Jack Brooks of Texas. The same coverup tactics followed. I had repeatedly notified both of them of the hard-core criminal activities that I had discovered, starting in the mid-1960s.

Brooks did criticize President Bush and the Justice Department[69] for not appointing an executive director to head the U.S. trustee system, which had been vacant for a year at that time. My subsequent 18-page petition to every United States senator by certified mail on April 1, 1991, detailed and documented the ongoing criminal acts, which were crimes against the United States and the

---

69 San Francisco *Daily Journal*, November 2, 1990.

American people. Not a single senator made a meaningful response. Several years later, Congressman Brooks was still "investigating" Chapter 11 corruption, while thousands of American citizens were defrauded of their life's assets.

**ONE OF MANY MURDERS**

Throughout these pages appear the names of some who threatened to expose the criminal activities implicating federal officials, and who conveniently ended up dead. One of those victims was San Francisco attorney Dexter Jacobson. Jacobson was preparing to file several lawsuits against key law firms implicated in the Chapter 11 corruption in the San Francisco area. The San Francisco legal paper, *Daily Journal*, had publicized Jacobson's impending filings, along with the evidence he intended to present to the San Francisco office of the Federal Bureau of Investigation on Monday and Tuesday, August 20 and 21, 1990. His evidence implicated Chapter 11 judges, trustees, powerful law firms and powerful corporations, including Bank of America.

Jacobson and I had exchanged information on the corruption in the Chapter 11 courts several months earlier. He didn't know about the Justice Department involvement in the Chapter 11 corruption, and I did not have time to bring this to his attention.

Two days prior to Jacobson's meeting scheduled with the FBI, his body was found in nearby Sausalito with a bullet hole in his head. Jacobson's death acted to protect Justice Department officials, federal judges, powerful law firms made rich by the Chapter 11 looting, and other members of the "bankruptcy club."

Several Northern California newspapers[70] linked Jacobson's death to the corruption in Chapter 11 courts. Jacobson was the only attorney willing to speak out, as the others either took advantage of the system or kept the lid on it, protecting the legal fraternity from public scrutiny. Many of the attorneys feared retaliation from the judges and trustees who can withhold hefty legal fees. Trustees appoint attorneys to "represent" the estates, and favored attorneys who play the game can be handsomely rewarded.

Jacobson did not practice in the Chapter 11 courts and therefore did not risk the judicial and financial retaliation faced by attorneys who specialize in those courts. He specialized in real estate and business law, mostly in California and federal district courts. Jacobson's murder ended the threat of exposure faced by Justice Department attorneys, judges, law firms, and private attorneys.

**SOME PAPERS REPORTED THE PROBLEMS**

Typical of the media stories after Jacobson's killing included that of the McClatchy News Service (November 24, 1990):

> *"Everybody around here is 100 percent convinced that it was a hit," [quoting Santa Rosa bankruptcy attorney David Chandler]. Jacobson was about to drop a bombshell lawsuit into the burgeoning Northern California bankruptcy court scandal, naming trustees and high-powered lawyers, and was about to take his evidence to the FBI and the Justice Department.... "We both talked about the safety of the documents and we both talked about the safety of each other," recalls Sosnowsksi [referring to his meeting with attorney Dexter Jacobson who was representing the*

70 San Francisco's legal newspaper, *Daily Journal*, *Napa Sentinel*, *Santa Rosa Press Democrat*.

> *formerly defrauded Chapter 11 party]. "We are dealing with some very tough people. They're making big money."...The killing sent a shudder of apprehension through the legal profession....When an examiner concluded in 1988 that Duck had engaged in serious misconduct in the Sosnowski case, and suggested further investigation, Santa Rosa Bankruptcy Judge Alan Jaroslovsky ordered the 49-page report sealed.*

The January 1991 issue of *California Lawyer* magazine ran a nine-page article entitled, "Who Killed Dexter Jacobson?" Reference was made to key parts of the Chapter 11 corruption that had appeared in other publications, including:

> *Jacobson planned to file a civil complaint...that would charge some of San Francisco's top attorneys with involvement in the nation's most costly bankruptcy trustee fraud and embezzlement scandal....Jacobson's secretary, Ginny Morrison, recalls her boss saying shortly before his death that filing the suit was a "dangerous" move.... "He said he was going up against some powerful people, and that this would be on the front page of every newspaper in the country."...attorneys in...tightly knit bankruptcy community were aware of Duck's schemes, and probably had participated in them. Dexter Jacobson was one of the first people willing to investigate that possibility....The final drafts of [Jacobson's] lawsuits have disappeared from Jacobson's house, his office, his car, and from the hard drive of his computer....On the day of his death, Jacobson had planned to meet with FBI Agent Eddie Freyer,...Jacobson was overwhelming his opponents with his meticulous research and questioning. "There is not much doubt in my mind it's tied in with this bankruptcy stuff," one federal source says.*

**COVERUP BY LOCAL POLICE**

The Sausalito police department and the FBI refused to contact me when I advised them in 1990 that Jacobson and I had exchanged information on the Chapter 11 corruption shortly before he was killed. My information may or may not have been helpful, but an investigation into Jacobson's murder demanded that I be contacted to determine what was discussed between Jacobson and myself. But to bring me into the investigation risked exposing a still bigger scandal.

Another attorney was murdered as he was trying to expose the Chapter 11 corruption. Attorney Gary Ray Pinnell, who had been vocal in fighting the corruption within the Chapter 11 system in Texas, was slain in San Antonio, Texas on February 11, 1991. The San Antonio *Texas Express* (March 14, 1991) reported that Pinnell was preparing to turn evidence over to the FBI but was killed before he was able to do so. In both cases Justice Department officials, including the FBI, would have been exposed if these attorneys had succeeded in attracting public attention.

A man was killed in Las Vegas as he was about to testify about an alleged scheme taking the properties of Karin Huffer and her husband, implicating Valley Bank of Nevada (now Bank of America) and the same Chapter 11 judge who corruptly seized my assets, Judge Robert Jones. None of these who died, who were about to present evidence of Chapter 11 judicial corruption to the FBI, realized their evidence threatened Justice Department officials and federal judges, up to and including the Justices of the U.S. Supreme Court.

While these deaths were occurring, the same Justice Department officials and federal judges, who would be implicated by an exposure, were seeking to silence me by repeatedly charging me with criminal contempt of court[71] for seeking to report the criminal activities through federal filings. More about this later.

**CRIMINAL CONTEMPT FOR REPORTING CRIMES**

I had been vocal in exposing the criminality in Chapter 11 courts, and especially that of trustee Charles Duck. In an attempt to silence me, federal Judge Edward Jellen of Oakland charged me with criminal contempt for filing appeals and oppositions to the seizure and looting of my assets. Jellen denied me the right to testify in my defense, denied me a jury trial, denied me legal counsel, and then sentenced me to prison for objecting to the seizure of my assets. U.S. District Judge Samuel Conti approved the prison sentence, and it was sent to U.S. Attorney Russoniello for prosecution.

Several months after federal judges seized my assets and started liquidating them, other federal judges sentenced me to prison for having filed notices of appeal and oppositions to the seizure and looting of my life's assets. Those acts were criminal in nature, violating specific criminal statutes.[72] While I was in prison, federal Judge Edward Jellen (Oakland, California) ordered fire-sale liquidation of my assets. While I was in prison, trustee Charles Duck unlawfully ordered my mail diverted to his office and opened.[73] Postmaster Dennis Hughes in Alamo, California, where I resided, stated to me (after I was released from prison on the first contempt of court charge) that many federal officials came to the post office checking on my mail, and that he expected to be subpoenaed because of the serious irregularities.

The reason for rendering these unlawful orders barring me access to the federal courts was that I had numerous claims against federal officials and judges (and the California judges who cooperated in the scheme to silence me). If federal relief remedies were not denied to me, the escalating corruption and the judicial and legal participants in the scheme would be exposed.

When the initial scheme involving the sham California action backfired, and federal judges involved themselves in the complicity when I exercised federal protections, the number of judicial and legal personnel implicated in the attacks upon me greatly escalated. With each escalation there were new federal causes of action permitting me to sue for damages. The only way to stop that was to render orders, unlawful of course, voiding my protections in the statutes and Constitution of the United States, denying to me the right to court access and relief. More about this in later pages.

In later pages, a more complex web of intrigue is presented, showing other reasons why Justice Department attorneys and federal judges blocked all defenses exercised by the victims, and showing how the CIA has infiltrated all segments of U.S. society, misusing government offices, defrauding American citizens and the United States as a whole. Numerous trustees and judges have been

71 Charges were filed on December 10, 1990 in the U.S. District Court, San Francisco, number CR 90-0636 VRW.

72 Including Title 18 U.S.C. § 241 and §§ 1512, 1513.

73 Title 18 U.S.C. §§ 1702, 1703.

identified to me by deep cover CIA operatives as being deeply involved in corrupt CIA activities, especially Charles Duck and Judge Robert Jones, both of whom brought about the destruction of my life's assets.

## DISCOVERY OF ADDITIONAL CRIMINAL ACTIVITIES THROUGHOUT CHAPTER 11 COURTS

From 1987 to the present I discovered, both in my own case and from reports I received from CIA sources and other victims, that the criminal seizure and looting of assets in bankruptcy courts was epidemic. The criminal acts involved the federal judiciary, including federal judges, trustees, attorneys, law firms, Justice Department attorneys, and CIA personnel.

## DEMANDING BRIBES TO GET OUT OF CHAPTER 7

As my knowledge of this corruption broadened, I discovered other versions of enriching the participants. In Chapter 11 proceedings, for instance, as was earlier described, the incentive was to steal the assets that exceeded the liabilities. But I later discovered from victims that, even when there is no equity in a person's Chapter 7 filing, money is extracted to discharge the case and allow the person to resume a normal life.

Pat Class of Denver and attorney Andrew Quiat described to me another form of extortion. The law provides that a person with liabilities exceeding their assets may file Chapter 7 to completely wipe out their indebtedness, allowing them to basically start all over again. The pattern of court duplicity touches upon every possible source of money, and in Chapter 7 proceedings, where the debtor has the potential of making sizeable income in post-Chapter 7 proceedings, the trustees and judges often demand hidden money to be discharged, even though all issues have been adjudicated.

Pat Class, for instance, described how she was forced into Chapter 7 in the Denver-area HUD and savings and loan related corruption, and then a discharge refused unless she paid the trustee money under the table. Pat and attorney Quiat told me of a case in the Denver courts where the trustee demanded, and received, $1.5 million under the table before a Chapter 7 discharge was granted by the judge.

A CIA contact who had extensive dealings with federal judges in several circuits throughout the United States gave me specific data on the corruption in the San Francisco and Chicago-area bankruptcy courts. More is said about this in later pages. It became clear that the bankruptcy courts serve as one of America's biggest financial frauds inflicted upon the American public, made possible by media coverup.

## EXAMPLE OF FRAUD-RELATED GRIEF

Over the years many people have contacted me who had suffered enormous, often life-long harm as a result of crooked judges and attorneys operating with impunity in Chapter 11, 12, 13 proceedings. Many of the victims have committed suicide. In September 1994, the story of one of these victims reached me.

Before committing suicide on July 12, 1994, in Sonoma, California, near San Francisco, 57-year-old Claire Ann Day wrote a twenty-page suicide note, detailing in it the corrupt acts by bankruptcy judge Alan Jaroslovsky and attorneys working with the judge, as it affected her daughter, Mary. I had heard many stories about this judge's involvement in the crooked bankruptcy courts. One of my CIA contacts stated that Jaroslovsky was a former officer in the U.S. Navy and a part of naval intelligence, and that he was a CIA asset. The CIA was one of the groups involved in the looting of bankruptcy court assets, and this information about the judge fit in with other information.

The suicide note stated in part:

*To: Whomever reads this plea for justice*

*I pray that someone of conscience reads these pages, comprehends the far-reaching implications of what has happened to my family, and take action to prevent this from ever happening again in Sonoma County or anywhere else in this country dedicated to "liberty and justice for all." I do not have the time or propensity to adequately chronicle this good v. evil, David v. Goliath battle, before I die. For every word contained herein are 100,000 missing words.*

A puff of black smoke mushroomed from her body as she ignited the flammable fluid. A neighbor, Bill Anderson, rushed to her, putting his jacket around her to put out the flames. A helicopter rushed Day to the hospital, but she died the next day.

**MEDIA COVERUP**

This woman's painful and horrible sacrifice sought to focus attention on the corrupt judges and legal fraternity. It was in vain. The San Francisco-area newspapers omitted any reference to her immolation. Years ago the immolation of a Vietnamese was pictured throughout the United States. But a similar immolation in the United States would have exposed the corruption in U.S. courts and very possibly the role played by many in the legal fraternity and the CIA in this massive judicially-centered racketeering enterprise. And San Francisco is one of the hubs of corruption described within these pages.

Sonoma County Fire Department Assistant Chief Allyn Lee said, "None of us had ever seen a more severely burned person who had survived."

Anderson said, "It's so sad when things like this happen. I keep thinking how ironic it is. I just fought for my life in the hospital for four months, and then someone just gives up their life." Anderson had fought a life-threatening illness.

The horror of the woman's death caused the county to provide crisis counseling for the people who saw the tragedy.

**THE SYSTEM PROTECTS ITS OWN**

As stated earlier, Charlie Duck still had powerful connections to the system, and was part of it, causing a San Francisco law firm to put him on their payroll in 1995. This would be highly unlikely of a convicted felon accused of the nation's worse bankruptcy fraud, unless the plea bargain was for damage control to prevent further investigations, and that Duck still had his former judicial and CIA connections. If so, it is understandable why the San Francisco law firm coveted his membership.

Author's home (above) and his plane (below), some of many assets taken from him by the combination of Justice Department trustees, federal and California judges, as part of the bizarre scheme to block his reporting of the criminal activities detailed and documented within these pages, and in retaliation for exposing these crimes.

# REPORT CRIMES OF FEDERAL OFFICIALS–GO TO PRISON

The most important tool in the hands of the American public to combat corruption involving federal officials, that circumvents the coverups and obstruction of justice by Justice Department or other government officials, is federal criminal statute Title 18 USC Section 4. The clear wording says:

> Whoever, having knowledge of the actual commission of a felony cognizable by a court of the United States, conceals and does not as soon as possible make known the same to some judge (or other person in civil or military authority under the United States), shall be fined...or imprisoned not more than three years, or both.

Implicit in that statute is that federal judges must receive evidence of a federal crime that is offered to them by anyone having knowledge of the federal offense. As the reader learns about the various criminal activities detailed and documented in these pages, the question may arise as to why I haven't used that statute to produce evidence of the crimes.

I had first used that statute in 1976 seeking to produce evidence to a U.S. District Court judge[74] in San Francisco of the criminal activities within the Federal Aviation Administration (and at United Airlines), associated with several major air disasters.

Later pages show that I exercised the responsibility of that major crime-reporting statute seeking to produce evidence that I had obtained relating to criminal acts by government officials and judges in the bankruptcy courts, in

74 *Stich v. United States, et al.*, 554 F.2d 1070 (9th Cir.) (table), *cert. denied*, 434 U.S. 920 (1977); *Stich v. National Transportation Safety Board*, 685 F.2d 446 (9th Cir.)(table), *cert. denied*, 459 U.S. 861 (1982); *Flanagan v. McDonnell Douglas Corporation and United States of America*, Civil Action 74-808-PH, MDL 172, Central District California.

the CIA drug trafficking, and other major offenses against the United States and the American people.

In every single instance, federal judges blocked me from producing my evidence, something that they had no authority to block. Even worse, they eventually retaliated against me for seeking to comply with that law. If they had not blocked my reporting of these criminal activities, life in the United States would be quite different. Hundreds, if not thousands, of people who know about these criminal activities, including the many CIA operatives who would expose the crimes of the agency if they could, would be exercising that protection.

Early in 1987, in an attempt to thwart my exposure activities, federal judges and Justice Department attorneys commenced charging me with criminal contempt of court in retaliation for seeking to report the criminal acts I had discovered, and for exercising federal remedies seeking to halt the harm inflicted through the sham California lawsuit. They actually sought to put me in prison for exercising federal crime-reporting responsibilities under Title 18 USC Section 4, and for exercising federal defenses against the acts taken to silence me.

The sham California lawsuit had not gone as planned. My exercise of federal remedies was unanticipated, and federal judges had to openly protect the scheme and the participants by unlawfully dismissing the actions. These judicial acts raised additional federal causes of actions, for which additional federal remedies existed. It was a literal perpetual motion scenario as federal judges violated federal law, blocking my exercise of federal remedies, thereby raising additional federal causes of action. The more that was done to me, the greater the number of court remedies that arose.

The method used by this daisy-chain of judicial obstruction of justice was to render a pattern of unlawful and unconstitutional orders barring me from federal court access and voiding all relevant constitutional and statutory protections.

Several months earlier, in late 1987, this same group seized my life's assets, including my real estate investments (motels, apartments, land, rental houses, and my home). The first of a series of orders was rendered, making me a man without a country insofar as the protections of law and Constitution were concerned. Judge Milton Schwartz rendered the first of many orders blocking my access to federal court. This order barred me from reporting federal crimes to a federal court, as required to be reported by federal crime-reporting statutes such as Title 18 U.S.C. Section 4. If I did not report the criminal activities to a federal court or other federal tribunal, I would be guilty of a federal crime. Since I obviously couldn't report the crimes to the same Justice Department officials who had been deeply involved in the criminality, the only avenue open was to report the crimes to a federal court. As a citizen concerned about criminality in government, I also had the *right*, in addition to the responsibility, to submit the reports to a federal court.

From 1974 to this day, I haven't had my day in court on any of the issues raised in any of the federal filings. Every federal judge who received my federal filings blocked my right to have a federal court declare the validity of the five judgments and the important personal and property rights established by those judgments. I was suffering serious personal and financial harm by their refusal to perform a mandatory duty.

In 1986, U.S. District Judge Milton Schwartz at Sacramento rendered an order dismissing my attempts to obtain federal relief from the violations of federally-protected rights inflicted against me in the California courts. In that order, he barred me from ever filing any federal action seeking relief or reporting the federal crimes, which was then followed by an escalation of previous acts by California judges and the Friedman law firm.

Exercising rights and responsibilities under federal law, I filed two lawsuits in the United States District Court in the District of Columbia,[75] naming as defendants the FAA, NTSB, the Justice Department, and Judge Milton Schwartz. In these lawsuits I sought to give testimony and evidence about the criminal acts I had uncovered; to obtain an order halting the violations of federally protected rights; to declare my rights in the five judgments, and to declare as void the order barring me from federal court access. Each of these issues constituted a major federal cause of action requiring the U.S. District Judge to perform his duty.

U.S. Attorney David Levi and U.S. District Judge Milton Schwartz retaliated against me for having exercised these rights and responsibilities belonging to every citizen in the United States. Schwartz issued a March 1987 Order-To-Show-Cause (OSC) for me to appear in federal court at Sacramento on April 23, 1987, to explain why I should not be held in civil contempt for filing the federal lawsuits. Schwartz argued that I was in contempt of court for filing the federal action when his May 30, 1986, injunctive order permanently barred me from federal court access.

Two days before I was to appear, Judge Schwartz's senior law clerk, Jo Anne Speers, telephoned me at my Nevada residence, devoting at least fifteen minutes convincing me not to personally appear, but to appear by legal counsel. "But the order requires that I personally appear," I stated. Ms. Speers answered, "I talked to Judge Schwartz, and it was decided that you do not have to personally appear." I didn't realize it then, but she was lying, and setting me up.

I told Speers that I didn't have an attorney, and she replied I should get any attorney to appear for me, and that he didn't have to know anything about the case. That last statement didn't make any sense at all.

The reason for avoiding a personal appearance was that California Judge William Jensen had issued a bench warrant for my arrest, which was still in effect. Every time there was an appearance calendared for me, the Friedman group alerted the Solano County sheriff's office and sheriff deputies waited to arrest me.

**"They're setting you up!"**

I stated to a friend in Reno, Laura Link (who formerly practiced law in California), what Judge Schwartz's law clerk had stated. "They're setting you up," Laura stated. "Oh, come on," I responded, "I know they're a bunch of bastards, but they wouldn't do anything that obvious." Like most of the public, I was naive about the dirty tricks of federal judges and Justice Department attorneys.

---

75 No. 86-2523; 86-2214.

I made some quick phone calls and Sacramento attorney Joel Pegg agreed to appear for me. But when Pegg appeared on April 23rd, as Judge Schwartz's law clerk suggested, Judge Schwartz already had a multi-page order prepared, charging me with *criminal* contempt for not personally appearing. Schwartz and his law clerk had set me up. Schwartz then ordered me to appear in federal court on May 7, 1987, on a charge of *criminal* contempt, and warned that if I did not appear, a federal bench warrant would be issued for my arrest.

**ARRAIGNED ON CRIMINAL CONTEMPT OF COURT CHARGES**

I appeared on May 7th with attorney Joel Pegg and was promptly arraigned, based on a criminal information filed by U.S. Attorney David Levi. (It is called an indictment when a grand jury is involved, and a criminal information when the Justice Department prepares an indictment on their own.) The Justice Department charged me with a three-count criminal indictment; one for each of the lawsuits in which I sought to report, via federal filings as provided by Title 18 U.S.C. § 4, the criminal activities I discovered, and for seeking relief from the judicial acts taken to silence me.

Federal marshals marched me to magistrate Esther Hix, where I was officially charged with the purported offense of criminal contempt of court. I hadn't realized that reporting federal crimes was an imprisonable offense. Justice Department attorneys sought to have me imprisoned in the federal penitentiary for 18 months. These acts were federal crimes. They inflicted harm upon me for having exercised rights and protections under the Constitution and laws of the United States and for having sought to report federal crimes committed by federal personnel.

**HIGH FLIGHT RISK?**

Assistant United States attorney Peter Nowinski sought to deny me my freedom pending trial, arguing that my offenses made me a high flight risk, and that I had a record of not appearing in court. Magistrate Esther Hix asked why I was considered "a flight risk."

"He failed to appear before Judge Schwartz on April 23rd, 1987," replied assistant U.S. Attorney Novinski. This was the hearing at which Judge Schwartz's law clerk stressed I should not personally appear and at which I appeared by legal counsel. The assistant U. S. Attorney then argued that I failed to appear before California Judge William Jensen in Fairfield on May 9, 1986. That was the date when I appeared before Judge Schwartz, and could not physically be in two places at the same time. I had an attorney appear for me, as permitted by law.

The United States Attorney continued his lying to the court: "The government also has information that Mr. Stich kidnapped a grandchild from Texas and threatened his wife, with whom he was litigating, that she would never see the child again, if she did not terminate the litigation."

That was a fabrication. One of my three daughters, Linda, moved to California from Texas, taking her two children with her. It was those children that I was supposed to have kidnapped. I had not communicated in any manner with my former wife for years, and certainly made no threats. Nor did I know my daughter was moving from Texas until she arrived. I would discover as years went by that it is normal practice for Justice Department attorneys to fabricate whatever lie is necessary to obtain a conviction and to support whatever order they want rendered.

Magistrate Esther Hix read my rights to me, as if I were a criminal, and warned me of the consequences if I tried to flee. For the prior fifteen years I had tried to appear before federal courts to present evidence, and to now imply I might flee was a preposterous statement.

I was treated like a hard-core criminal in retaliation for reporting the crimes in which federal judges and Justice Department officials were implicated. After arraignment, and after signing a stipulation agreeing to a trial before a U.S. Magistrate, I was released on bail. I had to post a $25,000 bond to insure that I would appear in court. I was then booked and my fingerprints and picture taken, like a common criminal. Unknown to me, there was still more trouble waiting.

## FRIEDMAN ALERTED THE CALIFORNIA AUTHORITIES

Waiting to arrest me and take me to Solano County jail were two sheriff's deputies from Solano County with a bench warrant for my arrest, rendered by California Judge William Jensen. Fortunately I had bail money handy, which I paid to the deputies. The deputies were apparently alerted either by the Friedman law firm, California Judge William Jensen, U.S. District Judge Milton Schwartz, or all of them together. At another time during a 1987 hearing in the California action, the Friedman law firm notified the Solano County sheriff's office that I would appear carrying a gun. This was part of the pattern of dirty tricks pulled throughout the eight years of litigation by the Friedman law firm. I was frisked for concealed weapons when I appeared in court.

Trying to retain some semblance of sanity, I had to joke about all of this occasionally. Because the Friedman law firm was heavily Jewish, as were most of the federal judges and Justice Department prosecutors that I encountered, I asked Laura Link: "Do you suppose if I told these bastards I was not of German descent, but of Austrian descent, they would pull back?" She responded, "That won't do any good. Austria was once part of Germany." This conversation was in a light vein, but as I discovered other patterns of corruption far beyond what I had discovered up to this date, I found an inordinate involvement of Jewish attorneys and the Mossad. As shown in later pages, the Mossad is involved in many of the criminal activities inflicting great harm upon the American people.

## KANGAROO TRIAL

To avoid a Kangaroo Court trial, it was important that I receive a jury trial on the criminal contempt charge. Otherwise, I would be prosecuted by the Justice Department and tried by federal judges, who were the two groups most threatened by my exposure activities. The constitutional right to an unbiased tribunal would obviously be lacking.

During my initial arraignment, attorney Pegg instructed me to sign a waiver to permit a trial before a U.S. Magistrate instead of a district court judge. That was a dumb thing to do, as the part-time federal magistrate was employed and retained only so long as he or she pleased my adversaries in the Justice Department and the federal judges. The saving grace was that the waiver contained a stipulation that I would receive a jury trial.

The Sixth and Seventh Amendments to the U.S. Constitution guarantee the right to a jury trial and also a trial before a fair and impartial jury. However, federal judges have ignored this constitutional protection for years, and the U.S. Supreme Court Justices have held that in federal court the right to a jury does not exist if incarceration does not exceed six months. Federal judges euphemistically call this long incarceration a petty offense. There is nothing petty about six months in prison, especially while a person's business, properties, home, assets, and maybe family, are lost.

U.S. Attorney David Levi sought to have me imprisoned for 18 months; six months for each of the three federal actions that were filed. Before the commencement of the trial, my attorney reminded Magistrate John Moulds that a jury trial had been stipulated earlier. Assistant U.S. Attorney David Flynn responded that I wasn't entitled to a jury trial on the basis that he was lowering his requested prison term to six months from the originally requested 18 months. But that reduction in prison sentence had nothing to do with the written stipulation for a jury trial, which arose when I signed a waiver to proceed before a U.S. Magistrate.

Like every other right to which I was entitled during the past several years, that right was violated. Magistrate Moulds denied me a jury trial, and the trial commenced without a jury. (September 16, 1987.) I had notified several of the news services and numerous radio and television stations in the San Francisco and Sacramento area of the government attempt to railroad me to prison for reporting the criminal activities that I had uncovered. Not a single one showed up.

Attorney Pegg raised arguments that held I couldn't be found guilty, but omitted the hard-core constitutional violations associated with Judge Schwartz's injunctive order; the set-up by Judge Schwartz and his law clerk that converted the civil contempt into criminal contempt; the felonious[76] nature of inflicting harm upon a person for exercising rights and protections under law, and the felonious nature[77] of inflicting harm upon a person for attempting to report federal crimes.

**"I find you guilty"!**

Guilty of what? Trying to report federal crimes of his associates! Magistrate Moulds concluded the trial by declaring I was guilty as charged, setting a November 4, 1987, sentencing date. Attorney Pegg then abandoned me, making no effort to submit briefs for reconsideration as provided by law[78] or for filing

---

76 **Title 18 U.S.C. § 241. Conspiracy against rights of citizens.**

77 **Title 18 U.S.C. § 1512. Tampering with a witness, victim, or an informant** –

(b) Whoever knowingly uses intimidation or physical force, or threatens another person, or attempts to do so, or engages in misleading conduct toward another person, with intent to

(1) influence, delay or prevent the testimony of any person in an official proceeding:

shall be fined ... or imprisoned ... or both. [1988 amended reading]

**Title 18 U.S.C. § 1513. Retaliating against a witness, victim, or an informant.** (a) Whoever knowingly engages in any conduct and thereby causes bodily injury to another person or damages the tangible property of another person, or threatens to do so, with intent to retaliate against any person for–(1) the attendance of a witness or party at an official proceeding, or any testimony given or any record, document, or other object produced by a witness in an official proceeding; or (2) any information relating to the commission or possible commission of a Federal offense ...

78 Motion to alter or amend, Federal Rule of Criminal Procedure 60.

notice of appeals and appeal briefs. I felt that he did not wish to offend federal judges or the Justice Department, people with whom he would deal throughout his legal career.

Several months earlier, I was forced to seek refuge in Chapter 11 to protect my assets against the events taking place in the California courts; this matter has been addressed in a previous chapter. When Magistrate Moulds held me guilty of criminal contempt of court, Judge Robert Jones used this decision as the basis for seizing my assets of $10 million. While in prison, these assets were looted and destroyed. My world was tumbling down upon me, a terrible price to pay for having exerted efforts to expose the escalating corruption within the federal government. I often thought that, if I had never taken the United Airlines assignment, and had not reported the pattern of hard-core air safety and criminal violations, my entire life would have been very different.

**RAMPANT CONSTITUTIONAL VIOLATIONS**

After Pegg abandoned me,[79] I filed post-trial motions in *pro se* status, raising numerous defenses, none of which attorney Pegg had raised, including:

1. The underlying injunctive order, voiding for me access to federal court and the statutory and Constitutional protections, was unlawful and unconstitutional.

2. It constitutes a federal crime to retaliate against a citizen for having exercised the right to federal court access, seeking declaratory and injunctive relief from the pattern of civil right violations judicially inflicted. The prosecution and judgment holding me guilty constituted a criminal act under Title 18 U.S.C. § 241.

3. It constitutes federal crimes under Title 18 U.S.C. §§ 1512 and 1513 to prosecute and hold a person guilty of an imprisonable offense in retaliation for having reported federal crimes or having sought to do so.

4. I would have been guilty of a federal crime under Title 18 U.S.C. § 4 if I had not reported the federal crimes, which I sought to report through the federal filings which were used as the basis for the criminal contempt of court charges.

5. The injunctive order barring me from federal court reversed the federal criteria for rendering such an order, which is intended to protect a person suffering great and irreparable harm and not to deprive the person suffering this harm the relief available under law.

6. The underlying injunctive order fraudulently sought support by placing a "frivolous label" on the underlying lawsuit (86-0210 MLS). The major federal causes of actions stated in that action couldn't possibly meet the legal definition of a "frivolous action."

7. Federal case law provides that a person cannot be charged with criminal contempt for exercising a right that would otherwise be lost and that, if I did not file the action, I would lose my right to relief.

8. A federal judge lacks authority to force a person, who knows of federal crimes, to violate federal crime-reporting statutes by remaining silent.

---

79 While Pegg was abandoning me, my other attorney, Joshua Landish, was sabotaging me in Chapter 11 courts by secretly dealing with my adversaries and then requesting the court to seize my assets and begin a fire sale liquidation.

9. A party cannot be punished for contempt when the injunctive order is on appeal. Judge Schwartz admitted this fact in an order he rendered on November 13, 1987:

*This court lacks jurisdiction to entertain the motion for contempt since the underlying judgment in this case rendered by this Court is currently on appeal. The Ninth Circuit follows the general rule with some exceptions not relevant here, that the filing of a proper and timely notice of appeal divests the district court of jurisdiction over those matters that are not on appeal or subject to the appeal.*

Making reference to the verbal order, Judge Schwartz made a written order on December 9, 1987, making reference to the applicable federal law,[80] stating in part:

*The Court denies the Motion of Defendants, Jensen and Superior Court of Solano County for an Order Adjudging Plaintiff in Contempt,...because it is this Court's conclusion that it lacks jurisdiction to entertain the motion since the underlying judgment in this case rendered by this Court is currently on appeal.*

This holding and the law cited made the contempt proceedings before magistrate Moulds illegal and without jurisdiction. But Moulds continued the contempt proceedings and ordered me incarcerated on November 4, 1987. Under federal law I had a statutory *right* to a stay of imprisonment pending appeal if the appeal raised any arguable issues of fact or law.[81] I obviously had many arguable issues.

But Moulds refused to grant me bail, arguing that he did not think the Court of Appeals would vacate his judgment. Federal case law[82] made it plain that bail cannot be denied on the belief by the judge who rendered the judgment that his decision would be upheld. Otherwise, granting bail would depend upon the judge rendering the judgment believing his judgment would be overturned on appeal.

I filed a motion for stay of prison sentence with District Judge Raul Ramirez, pending appeal of the judgment and sentence. Ironically, it was Judge Ramirez's unlawful dismissal of the first federal action seeking relief in 1984 that made possible the escalation of the judicial civil right violations against me. Ramirez also denied bail, holding that he didn't think the judgment would be overturned.

## SUPREME COURT JUSTICE ANTHONY KENNEDY AS CO-CONSPIRATOR

Shortly before Christmas 1987, the Ninth Circuit Court of Appeals at San Francisco turned down my appeal of the prison sentence. The three judges, James R. Browning, Alex Kozinski, and Pamela Rymer, turned down my appeal without addressing a single one of the many defenses that I raised. Incredibly, they approved each and every judicial violation inflicted upon me by the California and federal judges. They approved the judicial voiding of all federal remedies. They approved the imprisonment that constituted prima facie evidence of felony retaliation for trying to report the federal crimes that I had discovered. They

---

80 *Donovan v. Mazaola*, 761 F.2d 1411, 1414, 1415 (9th Cir. 1985; *Matter of Thorp*, 655 F.2d 997, 999 (9th Cir. 1981).

81 Title 28 United States Code section 3143.

82 *U.S. v. Hurst*, 424 F. Supp. 318 (9th Cir. 1978).

approved the obstruction of justice tactics, and the many other wrongful judicial acts. The implications of this judicial mindset were extremely serious. Without addressing a single issue that I raised in the appeal briefs, which they should have done, the Court of Appeals judges simply stated: "The judgment is affirmed."

I quickly filed a petition for writ of certiorari with the United States Supreme Court. In my written arguments, I raised the pattern of judicial suspension of civil rights and the criminal implications by Ninth Circuit judges, their obstruction of justice, their felony persecution of whistleblowers, and reminded the Supreme Court Justices of their supervisory responsibilities over these judges. Aiding and abetting these acts by judges over whom they had supervisory responsibilities, the Supreme Court Justices upheld this conduct, becoming co-conspirators with the criminal acts that I sought to expose.

I was ordered to turn myself in on January 14, 1988; I had to act fast. Over the Christmas holidays I prepared a petition to Ninth Circuit Court of Appeals Justice Anthony Kennedy (before he became a Justice of the United States Supreme Court). I worked feverishly on Christmas Day to finish the petition for submission to Kennedy the following Monday. Kennedy had testified at great lengths during his televised Senate confirmation hearing for appointment to the Supreme Court, expressing repeated concerns for due process, constitutional safeguards, respect for privacy. Kennedy denied me relief. His conduct represented numerous criminal acts, including obstruction of justice, aiding and abetting, accessory before and after the fact, misprision of felonies, fraud, conspiracy, and other crimes. The same applies to the other judges described within these pages.

Judge Kennedy was already involved in the corruption I sought to expose. He was on the appellate panel that heard my appeal of the district court's dismissal of the 1974 federal action against the Federal Aviation Administration. Kennedy knew the consequences of coverup, as several major air tragedies associated with the air safety corruption followed his decision upholding the district court's dismissal of my action. That action sought to report to a federal court the federal crimes I discovered, as a federal investigator, at United Airlines and within the FAA that were associated with a series of air disasters.

After Justice Anthony Kennedy denied the emergency request, I filed a second motion for stay-pending-appeal with Judge Ramirez. When I appeared before Ramirez on February 16, 1988 on the motion, he delayed rendering a decision, continuing the matter until March 4th, 1988, the date I was to be imprisoned. I asked Ramirez to grant a continuance of the incarceration date to permit me to request a stay of the prison sentence pending appeal from the United States Court of Appeals, if he denied my motion. Ramirez assured me that I could request a stay from him on March 4th, implying that he would stay the sentence.

I was at a serious disadvantage by appearing without legal counsel. The Justice Department and federal judges seized all my assets (as discussed in earlier pages), and I was without funds to hire legal counsel. I was entitled to appointment of legal counsel, which I requested. Judge Ramirez appointed federal public defender Carl Larson to represent me. But instead of representing me, Larson acted as damage control for the corrupt judges and Justice Department. Every action he took was to protect the system of corrupt judges and corrupt Justice Department attorneys and defeat my remedies in law. I discovered over the next five years that this type of legal representation (protection of government corruption) occurs in almost every instance.

Larson made no effort to prepare a defense to the multitude of issues that made the guilty verdict a gross miscarriage of justice. He took the position that I was guilty, advising me to prepare for prison. He refused to request a stay of prison sentence pending appeal, a statutory right in federal law. He refused to file any post-conviction motions or to file an appeal. He protected the corrupt system and became criminally implicated.

When Larson learned that I was to appear as a guest on a talk show on government corruption, he became furious and ordered me not to appear. I, of course, ignored him. I finally dismissed Larson and appeared in pro se status so as to file my own briefs raising the important defense issues. Larson refused to raise any of them, protecting the federal judges and Justice Department attorneys with whom he would be working throughout his legal career.

**"Bailiff, do your job!"**

I appeared before Judge Ramirez at the March 4, 1988, hearing without benefit of legal counsel, expecting to receive a stay of the prison sentence pending appeal. Instead, Ramirez denied my request and ordered, "Bailiff, do your job." Two husky marshals seized me and led me to a dirty prison cell in the basement of the federal building, where I was stripped of all my belongings. Handcuffs and leg irons were put on me.

The U.S. Marshals led me to a van in leg irons and handcuffs and transported me to a county jail at Yuba City, California, in what would be one of several prisons for the next two months. Driving up to Yuba City, I passed the motel that I owned, Tahitian Gardens. Staying at the motel was my friend Edith Armstrong, whom I hadn't been able to visit for the past two years because of California Judge William Jensen's bench warrant for my arrest.

No matter how bad life became, it always seemed to get worse, at least for the first month of my imprisonment. Twenty-four hours a day you sit, eat, sleep on a thin, filthy mattress, if you are lucky to have one, and eat under filthy conditions. Life becomes meaningless. I was shocked that this could be happening in America, but things always got worse.

There was also another possible reason for my incarceration. I was recovering from open-heart surgery in which I received six coronary bypasses, and any stress could constrict them and result in a heart attack and possibly death. My death would seemingly end the threat of exposure to those implicated in the various segments of the criminal activities described within these pages. There was no one else with the evidence and the willingness to continue the fight.

While I was in prison and unable to defend myself, the Friedman law firm and California judges rendered orders laying claim to my multi-million dollar estate. They rendered a sham divorce judgment on July 28, 1988, and transferred title to my property, even though there was no marriage to support the divorce judgment.

**DEBATE WITH ACLU WHILE IN PRISON**

My contact with the outside world while in the Sutter County jail was by mail and a telephone in the crowded cell-block. Each prisoner was limited to a scheduled fifteen-minute call. During a late evening phone call from the prison cell, a friend advised that she arranged an appearance for me on radio station KOH in Reno, hosted by Fred Taft. I was to phone the station collect the following morning, and would be on the air for an hour.

In the meantime, Taft arranged that the executive director of the Nevada ACLU, Shelley Chase, would be on the show. On an earlier show, my friend revealed how the ACLU had refused to help me defend against the onslaught of civil right violations, while soliciting money from the public to uphold these protections. Ironically, the Friedman law firm was a key member of the San Francisco ACLU.

I told my friend that it was highly questionable whether I could be on the talk show since I was confined in prison, in a crowded cell, with 16 other prisoners, and limited to a single 15 minute telephone conversation. I explained the situation to the other prisoners, some of whom were bank robbers and drug dealers, explaining that I had the opportunity to debate with the ACLU. The prisoners encouraged me to get on the show. Everyone waived their scheduled telephone schedule so I could make the one-hour talk show possible. Of course, the prison officials knew nothing about it. If they had, they would have put an immediate stop to it.

There were some unusual sounds during the show. Clanking of cell-block doors, screaming of prisoners, and a fight ensuing a few feet from the telephone. During this talk show, ACLU Executive Director Shelley Chase defended and upheld the outrageous civil right violations perpetrated by Justice Department attorneys and the California and federal judges. This is the same ACLU to whom I brought information for the prior twenty years of the ongoing criminal activities that were implicated in a series of air disasters.

Host Fred Taft expressed outrage over the government conduct on two prior shows, relating the government abuse of his cousin by the IRS and his subsequent imprisonment on a tax charge. But during this show Taft changed his colors. He upheld the ACLU's position, causing me to wonder if the station had been pressured by government officials to support the acts taken against me.

**START OF DIESEL THERAPY**

After spending several weeks in the bleak conditions of the Sutter County jail, I went on the "Diesel therapy" route, being transferred from prison to prison. I was transferred to the infamous old Sacramento County jail, where filth, overcrowding, and inhuman conditions took on a new meaning. I wondered how it compared to the infamous Devil's Island Prison. During the frequent changes in prison, I once found myself in a cell with 12 bunks, occupied by over 30 people, with hardly room to sit down. It resembled a cage with animals packed tightly together.

You spend every minute of the day or night sitting or sleeping on the concrete floor, unless you are lucky enough to have a thin mattress for sleeping. The stench of the dirty mattresses was sometimes unbearable. In the Sacramento jail, the open toilet was positioned along a glass wall with constant passing of male and female guards, without any screening or privacy. Many of the prisoners looked as if they hadn't washed or changed their clothes in weeks. They resembled something out of a horror story. Food came in unsanitary containers that resembled feeding time in a dog kennel.

**SILENCING TECHNIQUES IN PRISON**

Diesel therapy is one of many tricks used by the Justice Department to break a prisoner, keep him from his legal counsel, *if* he had counsel, and keep him from communicating with his family or friends. It is common practice in the federal prison system to move prisoners from prison to prison for weeks at a time, the prisoner being "lost" for all practical purposes. After Judge Ramirez ordered my incarceration, he sought to keep me in the county jails where there was no access to legal facilities, thus keeping me from filing legal papers to obtain my release.

**BRUTALITY OF PRISON**

Prison has its own peculiar sounds. The constant slamming of heavy metal doors, night screams, fights in the cells, living, eating, and existing like caged animals. Many prisoners respond accordingly. There is no privacy. Prisoners sleep in crowded inhumane conditions, often within a few feet of a dirty, seat-less toilet used by dozens of occupants. Modesty doesn't exist.

Anyone who hasn't been in prison doesn't know the degradation and the humiliation that goes with it. The first thing that happens is that you are handcuffed, a chain put around your waist and connected to leg irons.

Prisoners are stripped of all belongings, including their watch, rings, and identification, and then put into holding cells. The filthy toilet conditions indoctrinate you to what is yet to come. Fingerprints and mug shots are repeatedly taken at every new jail or prison, and you are stripped naked and subjected to embarrassing body-cavity examinations. Smelly and over-crowded prison cells become routine. The smell of urine and God knows what else is overpowering. One's appetite is easily lost.

**BROKEN, LONELY, DYING MEN**

Under these conditions, broken, lonely, and dying men are found in the medium and high-security prisons. Torn from their families, some for twenty and thirty years, or forever, their lives literally come to an end. There are no hopes, no plans, nothing. In the cases of those framed by the Justice Department attorneys, it is especially pathetic that this could happen in the so-called land of liberty and justice!

I looked at the scribbling on prison walls made by deranged, dejected, and morbid prisoners. Despite the overcrowding, it is terribly lonely, and all meaning to life appears lost. For many, all hope was gone. Under these conditions, a day or a week seems forever. It gave me an entirely different perspective of people in prison and of those who have corrupted our government. Many of these people in prison were railroaded by corrupt Justice Department prosecutors and prosecuted for offenses far less onerous than committed by those making the charges and sentencing them to prison.

**PERSONAL COST TO ME OF UNITED AND FAA CORRUPTION**

My entire life passed before me. I thought of those I loved, and those few people who helped me. I thought of those who didn't seem to care. I thought of the attorneys I hired to defend me, who then conspired with my judicial and Justice Department adversaries. I sometimes wondered what part United Airlines officials played in these events, thinking of how General Motors secretly went after Ralph Nader when he wrote the book, *Unsafe At Any Speed*.

**"My God, this can't be!"**

Many times I thought to myself: "My God, how can this be happening to me! This can't be!" I couldn't believe that what started out with discovering deadly air safety and criminal violations at United Airlines could have such devastating consequences for me. I thought of people who perished in some of the airline crashes closely connected to the corruption I had first found in the aviation arena, and I wondered who suffered the most. I was still better off and had the chance to fight on while, for air disaster victims, it was all over.

How could I be in prison for refusing to commit the crime of coverup? Where was the media, the so-called protectors against government tyranny? Where was Congress? I sent out hundreds of flyers before leaving for prison, notifying these parties that had a check and balance responsibility. I appealed to the ACLU, the Ralph Nader group, civil rights groups, and other checks and balances. Every single one refused to help, choosing instead to aid and abet the criminal subversion of our government.

It was all so incomprehensible. I had been financially well off. I had a good life. I had a reputation throughout the United States as an air safety activist, and suddenly I found myself in prison and stripped of the assets I worked for the past twenty years to acquire, all because I felt a sense of responsibility. How stupid I was! I kept thinking that this must be a dream and I'll wake up, and it will all be over. But that never happened.

Prison life is especially hard on older persons. Medical care that exists in theory is incredibly bad in practice. Heart attacks receive virtually no priority, and a dying person suffering a heart attack can linger for hours before being taken to medical facilities. Often it is too late. Older persons have various medical problems which prison life aggravates, and they become prey to young bullying inmates.

**ELEMENT THAT FIND PRISON SATISFYING**

There is a certain element in society that finds prison life, especially in federal prison, satisfactory. They need not worry about housing or food and have the company of others either like them, or others that they can prey upon. This is the type of individual that will never cease his criminal ways because of the possibility of imprisonment.

**SUICIDE**

Sometimes I just wanted to die. The strain of all this was getting to me. Flung into prison, things looked bleak. Everything was accumulating. The six years of judicial persecution, the loss of my home, my business, my assets, the humiliation, the character assassination, the loss of privacy, and the hopelessness. There is only so much a person can stand. It caused me to think more than once of ending it all. I had been through World War II as a Navy pilot in the Pacific; I had flown for almost fifty years, experiencing all types of aircraft emergencies; I had been caught in Iranian revolutions. All of these stressful conditions put together did not equal the fear that I now experienced. God bless America, where millions of naive Americans recite "with liberty and justice for all," as if it existed!

I looked at the plastic bags used for laundry and other purposes and thought how peaceful things could suddenly become if one was slipped over one's head and the misery ended. The primary thing preventing me from doing such a thing was the hope that I could expose the corruption in government and somehow motivate the American people to exercise their responsibilities under our form of government. What a dreamer I must have been.

**JUSTICE DEPARTMENT CORRUPTION**

While in prison, I learned about other areas of corruption by Justice Department personnel and the harm inflicted upon the American people. I had already seen this misconduct for years, but I discovered areas beyond my earlier comprehension. I found many people in federal prisons who were either falsely convicted or who suffered longer prison terms because of the lying by Justice Department attorneys. Attorneys in the Justice Department are given bonuses for a high conviction rate, motivating this sordid group to send innocent people to prison. Justice means nothing to them, as they seek a high conviction rate, guilty or not.

There are many persons in prison for non-violent crimes who are there because of a lying U.S. Attorney. I got a taste of it several times, as the U.S. Attorney sought to deny me release pending appeal and to incarcerate me for longer periods of time by making false allegations. I heard many stories from inmates who admitted the crimes they committed, who related the fraudulent planting of evidence by Justice Department attorneys.

**TRAVELING IN CHAINS**

From the old Sacramento County jail, I was transported in chains to several other prisons. For as long as twelve hours at a time, I was chained and shackled, unable to properly feed myself or to use the toilet. I ate in the back of crowded prison wagons, stopping at fast-food places for hamburgers. For toilet facilities, we stopped at service stations and were paraded before the public in chains and leg irons. People probably wondered what type of heinous crime we had committed.

Eventually, I reached Terminal Island Federal Prison at Long Beach. Approaching the prison, I could see the tourist attractions that I had visited during happier times. I used to visit these same areas when I appeared on radio and television shows as an air safety activist. To stop these activities the government-funded corruption had me in the same areas, now in chains. How times had changed.

The federal prison at Terminal Island reminded me of pictures I had seen as a child of Sing Sing and Alcatraz. Standing at the bottom of the four story building in unit "J1," all I could see was cell block after cell block four stories high. It was an eerie feeling.

After a couple of weeks at the harsh Terminal Island prison, I was transferred to the Federal Prison Camp at Lompoc, California, where some of the nation's prominent government officials were confined, including former U. S. Attorney General John Mitchell, Wall Street financier Ivan Boesky, and others. Boesky and I worked together on several prison details while I was at Lompoc. The living conditions there were markedly different but I was still suffering the humiliation, the loss of my liberties, and other protected rights that the public takes for granted.

During these prison stays I met numerous people who were formerly employed by the Central Intelligence Agency as operatives or contract agents who described to me the inner workings of this so-called intelligence-gathering agency. I learned about the CIA's looting of America's financial institutions, about the CIA's drug trafficking within the United States, and other criminal activities. These former CIA people had no ax to grind as they described the work they had been ordered to do and how they were silenced by Justice Department prosecutors and federal judges. Much more about this in later pages.

At the Lompoc Federal Prison Camp legal supplies were available, making it possible for me to file legal briefs and contact members of Congress. None answered. I should have known. I had reported the air disaster related criminal acts to them for the past twenty-five years with no response.

While I was in prison, the court appointed another attorney to represent me, Sacramento attorney Clifford Tedmon. He was as bad as every other one I had. He wouldn't file any papers to obtain my release pending appeal. I filed my own motion for release pending appeal on April 13, 1988, addressed to the Ninth Circuit Court of Appeals at San Francisco.

At the same time, Reno talk show host Fred Taft called in on the nationally syndicated Owen Spann show in San Francisco and reported my predicament. It is very possible that this talk show was heard by the federal judges hearing my motion. The next day (April 16, 1988), the Court of Appeals ordered me released pending a decision on my appeal.

But the Justice Department's Bureau of Prisons refused to release me. I didn't even know of the release order until four days later, when I called Tedmon from inside the prison camp at Lompoc, and he was surprised that I had not been released. I then went to the prison authorities and they stated they couldn't find me. Can you comprehend a prison with checks of the occupants occurring seven times a day, unable to find me?

Immediately after the Court of Appeals rendered the order for my release, Justice Department attorneys submitted a motion seeking to void the order. The Justice Department attorneys again misstated the law, arguing that the Court of Appeals lacked jurisdiction to order my release. They argued that I had not filed a notice of appeal of the March 4, 1988, order by Judge Ramirez denying my motion for release pending appeal and that the court lacked jurisdiction to release me.

But the law clearly stated that only one appeal need be filed, which I had done. With that filing, the Court of Appeals had jurisdiction to render any order associated with the appeal, including an order releasing me. Justice Department attorneys were apparently desperate to keep me in prison. I posed the threat of exposing them if I were appeared as guest on radio and television shows. (By then, radio and television stations and their hosts were already avoiding guests exposing government corruption. This greatly increased after the bombing of a federal building in Oklahoma City in 1995.)

## WARM LETTERS FROM CONCERNED CITIZENS

Waiting for me at home was a letter, similar to many others I had received over the years, that was heart warming. Oddly enough, it was from a former

United Airlines management official. The letter stated in part: "Many times I've thought about Rodney Stich and his identification with John the Baptist crying in the desert, but you do make a difference and without you whistle blowers our world gets completely out of synch, so don't ever give up, because you do make a tremendous difference!"

**CONSTANT BAD NEWS**

The freedom didn't last long. On February 26, 1990, I received a notice from the Ninth Circuit Court of Appeals turning down my appeal, upholding each of the unlawful and unconstitutional acts that I brought to their attention. I quickly filed a petition for rehearing with each and every judge in the U.S. Court of Appeals in the Ninth Circuit, called an *en banc* request, and each and every one of them denied my petition. These judicial decisions had ominous implications of the extreme lawlessness of those in control of the federal judiciary.

**SEEKING RELIEF FROM SUPREME COURT**

I quickly filed a petition for writ of certiorari with the U.S. Supreme Court, seeking to halt my imprisonment. And again these nine Justices approved the pattern of corrupt activities perpetrated by judges over whom they had supervisory responsibilities.

**PUBLIC INDIFFERENCE TO THESE CRIMES**

While waiting to hear about my appeal, I appeared as guest on many radio shows, explaining the corruption that I found and which I sought to report and correct, under the authority of several federal statutes. I brought out the outrageous nature and judicial civil rights violations, and the implications of sending a concerned citizen to prison for having sought to report serious federal crimes. Not a single radio host or listener showed any concern, or offered any help. And these were among the people that I sought to help with my crusader activities!

**BACK TO PRISON ON JULY 22, 1990**

On July 22, 1990, I again appeared before U.S. District Judge Raul Ramirez for a hearing. I attempted to discover the nature of the hearing from Ramirez's law clerk but was told they didn't know, which was a lie. When I appeared before Ramirez, he ordered the U.S. Marshal to seize me. The Marshal put handcuffs and leg irons on me and transported me first to the Sacramento County jail, followed by several weeks of transfer from prison to prison in the western part of the United States.

**THE JACOBSON MURDER**

Immediately prior to this second incarceration, a San Francisco attorney, Dexter Jacobson, with whom I had previously discussed the Chapter 11 corruption, was killed. Jacobson was to present evidence to FBI agents in San Francisco on August 20, 1990, relating to corruption that he had discovered among Chapter 11 judges, trustees, and law firms. This is discussed in more detail in other pages.

**SOLITARY CONFINEMENT**

An activist in the San Francisco Bay Area, Virginia McCullough, notified the California prison authorities that I might meet the same fate as Jacobson. This warning caused me to be placed in solitary confinement for six weeks. It is difficult to convey to someone who has never been imprisoned how difficult it is to be in solitary confinement for weeks at a time.

Solitary confinement is being locked into a small dimly-lit cell, unable to talk to anyone for days at a time, with your meals slipped into a slot in the door. Rarely is there any reading material. A person in these conditions must sit and stare for hours and days at a time. In my case, this was particularly distressing. I had a full life, I was a multi-millionaire, had two airplanes, a luxurious home, a house at Lake Tahoe, for which I worked hard, and now corrupt government employees were taking it all. The same systems in government entrusted to protect these outrages were perpetrating them, and then retaliating against me for exercising lawful defenses. Also, the same group perpetrating the crimes were misusing their office to silence me.

It is difficult to express the horror of such an experience without suffering through it, day after day, for what is now fourteen years, and continuing.

The same group of judges and Justice Department attorneys who fraudulently imprisoned me were concurrently looting my life's assets, converting me from a multi-millionaire to a state of poverty. My business, my home, my assets, were all being distributed among those who helped inflict upon me the pattern of government-financed civil right and criminal violations. This horror and the criminal misconduct that it represented were possible because of the criminal aiding and abetting by the Justices of the Supreme Court, the entire Senate, much of the House, and the establishment media.

During this second period of imprisonment, I was eventually transferred to the Federal Prison Camp at Boron, California, where I met several former CIA contract agents who made me aware of a much larger pattern of criminal activities in areas of government to which I had not been exposed. If my efforts ever succeed in waking up the American public and motivating them to act, then this imprisonment may have a redeeming value. (But this is hardly likely to occur.)

Hundreds of hours of face-to-face conversations with these former CIA people provided information about epidemic corruption within the government of the United States that enlarged upon what I found as a federal investigator. Without the benefit of these CIA contacts, I would never have discovered the links between the various criminal enterprises run by federal officials. These contacts helped explain the corruption that I had discovered in the federal courts and in the Justice Department, as the various criminal activities were all interrelated.

I was to have been released on November 23, 1990, after serving out the six-month prison sentence. But Justice Department prosecutors and federal judges had not finished their dirty work on me. Two weeks before I was to be released, U.S. District Judge Marilyn Patel in San Francisco signed an order keeping me in prison and transporting me to the federal prison at Pleasanton, California. The charge? I had filed a federal action[83] in Chicago seeking relief from the corrupt seizure of my assets by Ninth Circuit judges and trustees, and reporting the criminal activities I discovered in Ninth Circuit Chapter 11 courts.

I had named Chapter 11 embezzler Charles Duck as one of the defendants. Patel held that the exercise of these federally protected rights constituted criminal

83 U.S. District Court, Chicago, CV 90-2548.

contempt of court and had me incarcerated without a hearing. Patel had no jurisdiction over me. She sought jurisdiction on the basis of a civil action that I had filed against California court of appeal judges in 1986, which she unlawfully dismissed in 1987. Once an action is dismissed, the judge has no jurisdiction over the parties. But this didn't bother Patel any more than the other judicial outrages bothered the Ninth Circuit Court of Appeal judges or the numerous District Judges that had become implicated in the criminal activities.

While subjecting me to the harsh prison conditions, Oakland, California federal Judge Edward Jellen ordered my home put up for sale, and this was carried out by trustee Jerome Robertson (Los Altos, California) and his Palo Alto, California law firm of Murray and Murray. They gained access to my home, and over 500 floppy disks on which I had sensitive records were either erased, or erased and valueless files substituted. These files contained information about the corruption described within these pages, legal briefs to be filed, and years of legal research that addressed the judicial and Justice Department corruption that I encountered.

## A FORTUITOUS ENCOUNTER THAT BACKFIRED ON MY ADVERSARIES

Leaving Lompoc in chains, I was again on the prison circuit, going from prison to prison, until I eventually ended up at the Federal Correctional Center at Dublin, California. I arrived at Dublin simultaneously with a high-ranking deep-cover CIA operative, Gunther Russbacher. A relationship started that would make possible exposing to the American people unprecedented government crimes against the United States.

Russbacher held a very high covert position within the Central Intelligence Agency and was a warehouse full of insider information about corruption that is beyond the wildest imagination of the average uninformed American citizen. Russbacher and I hit it off well, possibly because we were both pilots and both of us had received our Navy wings at Pensacola, Florida. More about this in later pages.

On December 10, 1990, I appeared in U.S. District Court at San Francisco and was charged by U.S. Attorney Anthony Russoniello with criminal contempt of court,[84] based upon the charges initiated by Judge Patel, and arising from the action I filed in Chicago. An attorney practicing in Berkeley, California was assigned to defend me. He promptly followed the standard pattern of sabotaging my defenses, refusing to file any papers in my defense and refusing to return phone calls. This is typical of court-appointed (or even hired) attorneys when Justice Department employees and federal judges have a strong interest in finding the defendant guilty. The case was assigned to Judge Vaughn Walker, who proceeded to protect the criminal activities that I had uncovered.

I was released on bail but limited in my travels to a small section of the state of California and to Nevada. Five years later, in 1995, I was still confined to this small area while waiting a non-jury trial on the charge of criminal contempt of court for having filed a federal lawsuit in early 1990 seeking to expose the corruption I discovered in Chapter 11 courts.

---

84 *USA v. Stich*, N.D. Cal. No. 90-0636 VRW.

In May 1991, after discovering a great amount of additional government corruption described in the following pages, I filed a declaration in my action putting the court on notice of these criminal activities. I attached to my declaration partial transcripts of sworn declarations given to me by deep-cover CIA operative Gunther Russbacher, describing the criminal activities related to a scandal known as October Surprise, which has yet to be described. The filing of that declaration put on hold all further activities.

**CALIFORNIA ATTORNEYS TOOK ADVANTAGE OF THE JUDICIAL ATTACKS UPON ME**

California attorneys, aware of the suspension of my legal rights, zeroed in like vultures to strip my assets clean. Two California attorneys, Maurice Moyal and Edward Weiss, and California Judge Edward Flier took advantage of the judicial attacks and the voiding of my legal remedies and access to the courts. Knowing that I was to be incarcerated on July 22, 1990, the attorneys calendared a hearing in the Superior Court, Contra Costa County to have my cross-complaint against them dismissed and to obtain a default judgment against me for $500,000. They knew I could not appear to defend myself.

After I was released, I filed a complaint against the attorneys and the judge for fraud and other causes of action and sought to have the default judgment vacated. The developing judicial scandal was known throughout the California judicial system, and it was important that I never prevail in the courts. Otherwise, it was possible that the lid on this can of worms would be pried open. Further, Moyal and Weiss had played a role in helping to inflict financial and other harms upon me, and any attorney assisting in the underlying attacks upon me were protected by the system composed of state and federal judges and the legal fraternity. Contra Costa County Judge Ellen James at Martinez dismissed my action, continuing the ten-year-pattern of judicial gridlock. I filed an appeal, and it was assigned to the same three judges in the California Court of Appeals who played a key role throughout the corruption in the California courts.

But this wasn't all. Without any hearing, U.S. District Judge Vaughn Walker, playing a key role in the latest attempt to have me imprisoned for exposing the escalating criminal activities, rendered an order[85] in a federal case that he opened on his own initiative. In this order, Walker ordered me to pay financial sanctions to the attorneys who had assisted in the attacks against me, Moyal and Weiss, and then entered an order barring the clerk of the court from filing any federal actions presented by me until such actions met the approval of "a Judge of this court."

Anyone can do anything they want to me, in gross violation of state or federal law, and I am totally stripped of the defenses under our form of government. Anyone who thinks these corrupt judicial acts do not affect them, should awaken to reality. The U.S. Department of Justice has a Civil Rights Division whose responsibilities are to uphold and protect the civil rights as articulated in the Constitution and laws of the United States. Obviously, they have corrupted their role and misused their power to cover up for epidemic corruption within the government of the United States.

---

85 *Rodney F. Stich v. State of California*, C-93-0027- MISC-VRW.

Federal judges have a sworn duty to uphold the laws and Constitution of the United States. Their actions, as described in these pages, are clearly to destroy these protections. If they can do this to me, they can do it to you, and they are doing it to many other people. They get away with it because of the orchestrated coverup and disinformation of the establishment media. There isn't much time left for the American public to wake up and rebel against this judicial and Justice Department tyranny.

## MAN WITHOUT A COUNTRY

In the fictional story written by Edward Everett Hale, *The Man Without A County*, the fictional Philip Nolan was stripped of his constitutional rights and protections. An army colonel, acting as a military court, sentenced him to banishment from the United States, imprisoning him for life on a naval vessel.[86] The suspension of my civil and constitutional rights—in the effort to silence me—was perhaps even worse than that suffered by Nolan.

I lost every relevant right and protection under the laws and Constitution of the United States and of the state of California. I was viciously persecuted by those paid and entrusted to uphold the law. I was stripped of my life's assets, my ability to earn income—and my ability to expose the sordid government-funded misconduct that played a key role in many air tragedies.

After each violation of my protected rights occurred, I exercised the remedies provided by law, seeking relief. Each time I did, federal judges dismissed my actions without a hearing or trial in gross violation of constitutional due process and equal protection, and in gross violation of specific statutory and case law. Every time I sought relief from destruction of my personal and property rights arising from some violation of law, federal judges called me a frivolous and vexatious litigant for objecting to the outrages committed by the litany of attorneys from the Justice Department and federal judges. Thereafter, the previous frivolous and vexatious decisions were used to dismiss subsequent actions.

## ABSOLUTE ABSENCE OF ANY PUBLIC CONCERN

Prior to going to prison for having exercised statutory and constitutional defenses, and attempting to expose government corruption that was inflicting great harm upon the American public, I appeared as guest on many radio shows, describing the government tactics to silence me. I also wrote letters to many members of Congress. Not a single person came to my rescue, despite the gravity of the implications and the responsibility of many to have intervened.

Attorneys, who had the training and the opportunity to protect constitutional safeguards, did nothing. Members of Congress with an oversight responsibility did nothing. It started proving to me what a fool I had been to have shown concern and a sense of responsibility.

---

86 The fictional Philip Nolan, an army officer, was tried with numerous other officers for cooperating with the unauthorized military exploits of military commander Aaron Burr. Before sentencing, each officer was asked to make a statement. Nolan, tired of the military life and dirty politics, stated: "Damn the United States! I wish I may never hear of the United States again." The military officer acting as judge (fictional Colonel Morgan) ordered Nolan placed on a U.S. Navy ship, never to see or set foot on the United States again, or to hear the words, "United States." Constitutional freedoms and protections were ignored during this fictional novel. The officers in charge of him during fifty years knew him as "the man without a country."

# EXERCISING FEDERAL PROTECTIONS

I was judicially gridlocked. But I felt that I had to make a judicial record by filing federal actions against those from whom federal law gave me a cause of action. I also filed the actions on the basis that federal filings were examined by the media, and in this way there was a chance that the media would report these charges. (Instead, the media covered up.)

Federal law provides that any person in the United States can file a federal lawsuit seeking a declaratory judgment to establish his personal and property rights when they are under attack, as mine were in the sham California action. Federal law also provides that a person can file a lawsuit seeking injunctive relief halting judicial actions by state judges who violate federally-protected rights. Federal law also provides for seeking damages against others who violate these federally-protected rights.[87] In addition, federal criminal law requires a person to report federal offenses to a federal court or other federal tribunal to avoid being charged with the crime of misprision of a felony.

Every action I filed contained multiple federal causes of action involving violations of rights protected under the Constitution and laws of the United States. Any one of these violated rights invoked mandatory federal court jurisdiction. But the judicial gridlock was everywhere, aiding and abetting the scheme to block my reporting of the serious government corruption and blocking my defenses against the sham California action.

**IMAGINATIVE USE OF LAW**

Realizing that I might never recover from the persecution, I sought to put on notice those who had responsibilities to prevent the criminal activities, including members of Congress who had a duty to act and who, instead, engaged in various forms of criminal coverup and obstruction of justice.

---

87 Federal statutes Title 28 U.S.C. Sections 1331, 1343, 2201, 2202; Title 18 U.S.C. Sections 1961 and 1962, the RICO Act; directly under the U.S. Constitution, including the First, Fifth and Fourteenth Amendments; as a *Biven's* claim; and Title 42 U.S.C. Sections 1983, 1985, 1986.

A federal statute, Title 28 U.S.C. Section 1343, permits any person who has suffered harm due to violation of his civil rights to sue another person who knew about the violations and who could have prevented or assisted in preventing the violations. Members of Congress, for instance, knew about the violations and the harm being inflicted and, under the clear wording of the statute they were liable.

I filed two lawsuits against certain members of the U.S. Senate and House[88] on the basis of section 1343, seeking not only relief but also to draw attention to the government corruption. The defendants knew of the violations of my civil and constitutional rights. They had a far greater responsibility than that of an ordinary citizen to prevent and report the criminal activities. Under federal law, they incurred liability for themselves, and those who were federal employees incurred liability on the part of the federal government under the Federal Tort Claims Act. Another purpose of the lawsuits was to put into a judicial record their responses to the charges I made against them.

## THEY ADMITTED THEIR COVERUP

In response to the filing of these actions, the Senate legal counsel filed a motion to dismiss my complaint on February 27, 1989. The motion to dismiss *admitted* that the defendant senators and representatives knew of my allegations and knew of the consequences of the criminal acts I brought to their attention. Under federal pleading practice, any allegation in the complaint that is not denied is deemed admitted as true.[89] The defendants admitted the truth of the charges in my complaint concerning government corruption and that they had knowledge of my charges.

These members of Congress based their defense on one issue: that, regardless of any wrong they may have committed, they were immune from the consequences of their acts under the Speech or Debate Clause of the United States Constitution. Put this response in perspective. Visualize an air disaster scene and the corruption that led to a series of airline crashes. These members of Congress knew about the criminal acts making the crashes possible, they had a duty to act, and they refused to do so. They admitted this. Their only defense was that they are immune from the consequences. The same conditions exist with other government corruption that has yet to be described.

## IMPLICATIONS OF CONGRESSIONAL POSITION

The response of the senators and congressmen had serious implications. No longer could these members of the Senate and House argue they did not know of my allegations of the corruption that I brought to their attention and for which I sought to produce testimony and evidence. All they could now argue was

---

88 In U.S. District Court in District of Columbia: No. 89-0170 SS. *Stich v. [Senators] Edward Kennedy, Strom Thurmond, Ernest Hollings, Albert Gore, Pete Wilson, Joseph Biden; [Representatives] Jack Brooks, John Conyers, Peter Rodino, Harley Staggers, and Henry Gonzalez*; In District Court at Reno: *Stich v. U.S. Senator Alan Cranston from California, and U.S. Representatives George Miller, Fortney Stark, Norman Mineta, Don Edwards, and Daniel Lundgren*, No. 89-85. February 10, 1989. U.S. District Court at Reno, Nevada, under the provisions of Title 28 U.S.C. Sections 1331, and 1343, and Title 42 U.S.C. Sections 1983, 1985, 1986.

89 Federal Rule of Civil Procedure 8(d): **Effect of Failure to Deny.** Averments in a pleading to which a responsive pleading is required, other than those as to the amount of damages, are admitted when not denied in the responsive pleading. Averments in a pleading to which no responsive pleading is required or permitted shall be taken as denied or avoided.

that regardless of their inactions—which made possible the consequences of the criminal activities I made known to them—they could not be sued. They filed a motion to dismiss, which I of course opposed.

I opposed the motion to dismiss by stating case law showing that the immunity of the Speech or Debate Clause only applied to actions taken on the floor of the Senate and House relating to passage or non-passage of legislation. I recited case law[90] that held the clause did not protect illegal or unconstitutional conduct. I also argued law prohibiting dismissal of lawsuits that state federal causes of action, and that the allegations in the complaint must be accepted as true for the purpose of determining whether federal causes of action were stated in the complaint.

**UNPRECEDENTED SECRECY**

In addition to seeking dismissal of the action that I filed, the defendant senators and representatives requested that the judge **remove all evidence from the court records that the lawsuit was ever filed.** The intent of this motion was to prevent the American public from learning about the complaint and about their response.

This request was unprecedented, and also barred by law. The court filings were public records, protected by the public's right to know. Their destruction would violate federal law. Further, federal law, including Rule of Civil Procedure 60, permits a party to file a motion, years later, to reinstate an action. This right, however, becomes valueless if the record is destroyed.

Even though I raised federal causes of action which under federal rules of court, case law, statutory law, and constitutional due process prevented dismissal, U.S. District Judge Stanley Sporkin rendered an order on May 8, 1989, granting the motion to dismiss, and to destroy all evidence of the filing:

> *On consideration of the motion of defendants to dismiss plaintiff's amended complaint, the entire record, and this court's opinion in this case, it is ORDERED that the defendants' motion be and hereby is granted and the amended complaint is dismissed with prejudice.*

I immediately filed a Notice of Appeal of that order. (Appeal No. 89-00170.) The senators and representatives then filed a motion with the Court of Appeals requesting that my appeal be dismissed without allowing me to present appeal briefs. The Court of Appeals judges promptly came to their rescue and granted the request. The decision stated in part:

---

90 *Miller v. Transamerican Press*, 709 F.2d 524 (9th Cir. 1983); *Kilbourn v. Thompson*, 103 U.S. 168, 204 (1881); *Eastland v. United States Servicemen's Fund* 421 U.S. 491, 502. (1975).

*United States Court of Appeals*
*For the District of Columbia*

---

*No. 89-5163*

---

*Rodney F. Stich*
*Appellant*
*v.*
*Edward Kennedy, et al.,*
*Appellees*

---

*On Appeal From the United States District Court*
*For the District of Columbia*

---

*Motion of Senate Appellees For Summary Affirmance*

*The six senators named as defendants in this action, Edward M. Kennedy, Strom Thurmond, Ernest F. Hollings, Albert Gore, Jr., Pete Wilson, and Joseph R. Biden, Jr., move for summary affirmance of the district court's order of May 8, 1989 (Tab A), dismissing the amended complaint in this case with prejudice....*

*Plaintiff alleges that the Congressional defendants*[91] *"have responsibilities and the power to prevent and aid in the prevention, of violations of these rights and privileges...." Id., par 6, at 3. He states that he "notified members of the Senate and the House of the constitutional violations, and submitted petitions under the First Amendment and other safeguards for relief." Id., § 27, at 12. He asserts that "defendants misused their positions of trust and power, refusing to provide the relief to prevent the violation of rights and privileges suffered by plaintiff," id., par 34, at 14, and that the defendants "actually joined the conspiracy by remaining silent," id., par 36, at 14.*[92]

*In a Memorandum Opinion filed on March 29, 1989, (Tab B), the district court dismissed plaintiff's complaint with prejudice. The court first held that the suit was barred by the Speech or Debate Clause, Article I, section 6, clause 1, of the Constitution, because "[t]he acts and omissions complained of by the plaintiff clearly fall within the legitimate legislative sphere protected by the Speech or Debate Clause." Memorandum Opinion at 3. The court also held that the action failed to state a claim under the First Amendment upon which relief can be granted under Fed. R. Civ. P. 12(b)(6), because "[w]hile the plaintiff's right to petition Congress is guaranteed by the First Amendment, a member of Congress*

91 In addition to the six Senate defendants, plaintiff named as defendants in this action five present or former Members of the House of Representatives: Jack Brooks, John Conyers, Jr., Peter W. Rodino, Jr., Harley Staggers, Jr., and Henry B. Gonzalez.

92 Plaintiff has also filed a substantially identical action in the District of Nevada against Senator Alan Cranston and several other present or former Members of the House. A motion to dismiss that complaint is currently pending. *Stich v. Cranston, et al.*, CV-N-89-85-ECR.

*is not required to 'listen or respond to individuals' communications on public issues.' Minnesota State Board for Community Colleges v. Knight, 465 U.S. 271, 285 (1984)." Memorandum Opinion at 3.*

************************

Judge Stanley Sporkin, one of the judges on the Court of Appeals who rendered that decision, was formerly general counsel to the Central Intelligence Agency and directly involved in several of the criminal activities described in later pages.

**ADDRESSING THE MEDIA COVERUP**

I used the same federal statutes and case law to address the coverup of the corruption by the media. I reported the pattern of corruption to key segments of the media since 1965, including the *Wall Street Journal*, the *Washington Post*, the *New York Times*, and others. They had the ability, and the responsibility, to make these serious charges known to the public.

That action was filed in the United States District Court at San Jose, California,[93] naming these newspapers as defendants, along with the *San Francisco Chronicle*, which became implicated at a later date. The filing of this lawsuit made a judicial record of the charges. This lawsuit was subsequently assigned to Judge Robert Aguilar.

Shortly thereafter, Justice Department prosecutors charged Aguilar with using his office as a racketeering enterprise to obstruct justice on the basis of minor and far-fetched allegations. The specific acts that Aguilar allegedly committed were mild compared to the criminal acts committed by Justice Department personnel. Aguilar had made the mistake of opposing and rendering decisions unfavorable to Justice Department prosecutors in a number of cases.

Many people felt that the Justice Department prosecutors were retaliating against Aguilar because of his opposition, and that Justice Department prosecutors wanted to send a warning to other judges who might become uncooperative.

My lawsuit that included charges of Justice Department misconduct was then removed from Aguilar and assigned to another judge.

The *Wall Street Journal* and its managing editor, Norman Pearlstein, filed a reply (June 15, 1989), requesting that the federal complaint be dismissed. They responded, as did members of Congress, that they knew of the charges; they did not dispute the relationship between the misconduct and the consequences. Therefore, they argued, they were immune from liability, based upon the First Amendment to the United States Constitution. They argued that they did not have to print what any person requested them to print. But I wasn't requesting the news media to print what I wanted printed. I expected them to exercise their responsibilities under federal law to report, in whatever fashion they wanted, the charges and evidence of government corruption that I brought to their attention. They had a responsibility under federal law[94] to aid in the prevention of the corruption that was brought to their attention. Even though the lawsuit against them was newsworthy and raised issues of national concern, none of

93 Number C 89 20262 WAI.

94 They also have a responsibility under Title 28 U.S.C. § 1343 to aid in the prevention of civil right violations that come to their attention. With their ability and responsibility to report federal offenses, they could have aided in the violations of my civil rights, by publishing information on the offenses.

the media printed a single word about it.

The responsibility of the media under the First Amendment was articulated in a Supreme Court decision relating to the Pentagon Papers and the publication of their contents in the *New York Times*. Supreme Court Justice Hugo Black stated:

> *Only a free and unrestrained press can effectively expose deception in government. And paramount among the responsibilities of a free press is the* ***duty to prevent any part of the government from deceiving the people****... The New York Times, the Washington Post and other newspapers should be commended for serving the purpose that the Founding Fathers saw so clearly. In revealing the workings of government... the newspapers did precisely that which the founders hoped and trusted they would do.*

The district judge dismissed my complaint without a hearing, despite the fact it stated numerous federal causes of action. I didn't appeal the complaint as I accomplished the primary goal of making a judicial record of the media's complicity and their responses.

## CULPABILITY OF SUPREME COURT JUSTICES

The same laws that made members of Congress and the media liable and culpable under federal statutes applied even more so to the Justices of the United States Supreme Court. The Justices had covered up the pattern of criminal behavior by federal judges, the Chapter 11 judges, and private trustees such as embezzler Charles Duck, all of whom were officers of the court over whom the Justices had supervisory responsibilities.[95] Like a police chief protecting rampant criminal behavior of their police officers committed against citizens, the Supreme Court Justices protected the criminal behavior of those over whom they had supervisory responsibilities. Because of their positions of trust, the Justices were more guilty of criminal acts for such crimes as misprision of felonies, coverup, accessory after the fact, conspiracy, obstruction of justice, and others.

Since the Supreme Court justices had the responsibility to prevent the commission of these corrupt acts by judges over whom they had supervisory responsibilities, they were liable. I filed a lawsuit against them[96] in the U.S. District Court in the District of Columbia.[97] They were, of course, employees of the U.S. government, acting under color of federal law, so I also named the government of the United States as a defendant. This was probably the first time in history that Supreme Court Justices were sued for civil, constitutional, and RICO violations. The arguments raised in the complaint were based on solid facts and law. But it was bizarre that a person was forced to resort to suing the Justices of the nation's highest court to report federal crimes and seek relief from judicial violations of federally protected rights.

---

95 Rule 17.1(a) of the U.S. Supreme Court. Responsibility to intervene exists when a lower court "has so far departed from the accepted and usual course of judicial proceedings, or so far sanctioned such a departure by a lower court, as to call for an exercise of this Court's power of supervision."

96 William Rehnquist; Antonin Scalia; Sandra O'Connor; Anthony Kennedy; Thurgood Marshall; William Brennan; John Stevens; Byron White; Henry Blackmun.

97 Filed February 17, 1989, No. 89-0470 SS; amended complaint filed March 14, 1989.

The truthfulness of the serious allegations made in the complaint could be easily verified by the media. Every major news service monitors the filing of complaints in federal courts. But again, the media kept the lid on this unusual filing and the gravity of the charges made in the complaint.

**REFUSING TO RESPOND**

Federal law provides for service by certified mail. If the defendants don't respond by returning the acknowledgment-of-service form, personal service is then required, and the defendants must pay for such personal service. Despite their position as Supreme Court Justices, they refused to return the acknowledgement of service. I then had the Supreme Court justices personally served (June 17, 1989).

I filed a 28-page amended complaint on March 14, 1989, stating in part:

> *This suit addresses the wrongful acts and omissions by the defendants, relating to (a) an ongoing, air safety/air disaster scandal, and related air tragedies; (b) upon which has been superimposed a government and judicial scandal of coverup; (c) government and judicial scheme misusing government powers to destroy plaintiff's freedoms, liberties, property rights, privacy, in an effort to halt his exposure activities.*
>
> *Defendants knew of these wrongdoings, and participated in them. The defendants also had the power to prevent them and refused to do so, aiding and abetting those committing the violations. Defendants knew that plaintiff would suffer great and irreparable harm from massive violations of rights and privileges under the laws and constitution of the United States and of the State of California; and knew that by such refusal to act, the misconduct causing and permitting the prior loss of life in fraud-related air tragedies would continue, with continuing loss of life. The defendants willingly sacrificed the lives that were lost, protecting their own vested interests, their own coverup, and the guilty parties involved in what has become the world's worst air-safety air-disaster scandal, upon which has been superimposed the nation's worst government and judicial scandal.*
>
> *Defendants are liable to plaintiff as a result of their wrongful acts. (Title 28 U.S.C. § 1343 and 42 U.S.C. § 1986.) Self-proclaimed qualified judicial immunity does not deprive a citizen of the United States of the rights and privileges under the laws and Constitution of these United States, including the right to redress of the harms suffered from judicial misconduct. The federal government has incurred a liability from defendants' wrongful acts.*
>
> *It is argued that the many persons who perished, and who suffered in airline tragedies caused and made possible by the misconduct of federal officials, have a cause of action against defendants, and against the federal government.*

The specifics in subsequent pages of the complaint related to knowledge by the Justices of the government corruption; the repeated violations of civil and constitutional rights in the sham California action; the coverup of the civil and constitutional violations by Ninth Circuit judges; the false imprisonment for exercising constitutionally protected rights; the Chapter 11 racketeering activities; the seizure of my multi-million dollar assets without any hearing, without cause, and under corrupt conditions, that reflected the corrupt mentality in Ninth Circuit courts.

Justice Department attorneys filed a motion to dismiss my complaint (August 17, 1989), admitting that the Justices knew of my allegations and that they failed to act. Their response did not deny the truthfulness of the charges or the resulting harm, and under federal law my charges must then be accepted as true. The primary defense raised in the motion was that the Justices of the U.S. Supreme Court "enjoy absolute immunity from plaintiff's claims."

The motion to dismiss was riddled with false statements of facts and law, and with trivial matters. The Justices argued that the complaint should be dismissed because "Rule 8 (a)...requires that a complaint be a short and plain statement." After arguing that the complaint was too long (there is no page limit in federal complaints), the justices then argued that the allegations were not specific enough! The justices argued that the complaint did not "state facts with particularity in his complaint that demonstrate who did what to whom and why." The complaint stated very clearly what the Supreme Court justices had done. A complaint does not have to *prove* the allegations, but make reference to them so the defendants know the nature of the alleged wrongful acts.

The justices argued that the complaint stated "unbelievable allegations." The charges were certainly unusual, but not unusual to anyone who knows of the covert activities of the Justice Department, the CIA, and everyday shenanigans occurring within the legal process. Under federal law, the allegations made in a complaint must be recognized as true for the purpose of preventing dismissal of the action.

Many of the facts stated in the complaint were supported by taking judicial notice of legal proceedings in the California courts, in federal courts, and were further supported by my voluminous evidence.

The justices sought to have the action dismissed by making reference to the California action, referring to it as a matrimonial action. The very fact that I was in the seventh year of a so-called matrimonial action, when five divorce judgments showed me as divorced for the past twenty-four years, raised serious federal causes of action. The California action was riddled with a pattern of civil and constitutional violations that were major federal causes of action, raising federal court jurisdiction. On the pretext of that sham divorce action my life's assets, used to expose government corruption, were seized.

The justices argued that the statute of limitations prevented lawsuits against them, but never stated how the *ongoing* wrongful acts could have imposed a statute of limitations defense.

The justices then argued that the allegations were already adjudicated and dismissed by other federal courts. Not one of the federal actions had ever been heard on the merits, and never once did I have my day in court. Nothing had ever been adjudicated. Further, the justices were never named in any lawsuit, so obviously the matters could not have been adjudicated. The Supreme Court justices argued:

> *The nine justices of the Supreme Court are entitled to absolute judicial immunity from plaintiff's claims. A judge will not be deprived of immunity because the action he took was...done maliciously, or was in excess of*

*his authority.*

The criminal statutes, such as misprision of a felony, and civil rights statutes, do not state a judge is immune when he violates either civil and constitutional rights, or violates criminal statutes. The Supreme Court Justices knew of the pattern of federal offenses committed against me and against the United States, and refused to take any action to halt the criminal acts committed by federal judges and Justice Department attorneys over whom they had supervisory responsibilities.

Under a *Bivens* claim, the rights and protections of the Civil Rights Act relating to wrongful acts taken under color of state law extend to federal officials. The Constitution of the United States provides for redress of wrongdoings by government actors and says nothing about judges being immune. The Justices were contradicting their own decision in *Pulliam v. Allen* 466 U.S. 522 (1984). The Supreme Court held:

> *[T]here is little support in the common law for a rule of judicial immunity that prevents injunctive relief against a judge. There is even less support for a conclusion that Congress intended to limit the injunctive relief available under § 1983 in a way that would prevent federal injunctive relief against a state judge. In Pierson v. Ray, 386 US 547, 18 L Ed 2d 288, 87 S Ct 1213 (1967), the Court found no indication of affirmative Congressional intent to insulate judges from the reach of the remedy Congress provided in § 1983. [N]othing in the legislative history of § 1983 or in this Court's subsequent interpretations of that statute supports a conclusion that Congress intended to insulate judges from prospective collateral injunctive relief.*
>
> *Congress enacted § 1983 and its predecessor, § 2 of the Civil Rights Act of 1866, 14 Stat 27, to provide an independent avenue for protection of federal constitutional rights. The remedy was considered necessary because "state courts were being used to harass and injure individuals, either because the state courts were powerless to stop deprivations or were in league with those who were bent upon abrogation of federally protected rights." Mitchum v Foster, 407 US 225, 240,...every member of Congress who spoke to the issue assumed that judges would be liable under § 1983).*
>
> *Subsequent interpretations of the Civil Rights Acts by this Court acknowledge Congress' intent to reach unconstitutional actions by all state actors, including judges....Judicial immunity is no bar to the award of attorney's fees under 42 U.S.C. § 1988.*

Of primary importance of the lawsuit against the justices of the United States Supreme Court was that it put them firmly on notice of the serious corruption perpetrated by federal officials, including federal judges, federal trustees, and Justice Department attorneys, all of whom look to them for guidance.

District of Columbia Judge Stanley Sporkin came to the Justices' rescue. He rendered a *sua sponte* dismissal (January 17, 1990). Again, he violated federal law barring dismissal of a lawsuit that stated federal causes of action.

## HOLDING THEMSELVES IMMUNE FROM LEGAL LIABILITIES

All of the defendants (members of Congress, news media, Justices of the U.S. Supreme Court) responded in similar fashion. They admitted knowing of my charges, that they did nothing in response to them, claiming they were immune from the consequences. Their position was that they could engage in outright criminal acts of coverup, misprision of felonies, and obstruction of justice, and be immune from the consequences.

While Ronald Reagan was president, I notified the office of the President of the misconduct described in these pages. No response. In 1988, while Vice President George Bush was campaigning for the presidency, he promised to get tough with criminals. I assumed he included those within government. After Bush became president and continued to articulate his concern for government ethics and crime, I made him aware of the corruption committed by federal officials over whom he had responsibilities. I sent him a May 1989 certified letter and attachments describing the criminal acts within government, including the Justice Department and the federal judiciary. The White House responded by advising me that the matter had been turned over to the Department of Justice, even though I charged the Justice Department with committing many of the criminal acts. So much for that.

Bush and I were both Naval aviators during World War II. We both got our Navy wings at the same time. We both flew in the Pacific theater of operations. He flew single-engine TBF aircraft, while I instructed in PBY seaplanes and flew as Patrol Plane Commander in four-engine patrol planes (Privateers and Liberators). Even though his piloting experience was very limited and long outdated, Bush surely recognized the consequences of air safety violations, even though sophisticated air safety matters were not part of single-engine, primarily visual flight rules operations.

When Bush became a junior senator from Texas in the United States Senate, he led a group of junior senators purportedly pushing for ethics in the Congress. The *National Observer* stated of Bush:

> *A little-noted event that took place on the floor of the House of Representatives early last week, two days before the House voted to bar Adam Clayton Powell from his seat in the 90th Congress.... With the House chamber nearly empty, freshman Republicans spent an hour philosophizing about Congressional ethics. The seminar of sorts had been organized by a young congressman from Houston, George Bush, 43,...The discussion was remarkable in that Mr. Bush had quietly convinced his rookie colleagues of an almost revolutionary proposition. Although freshmen are traditionally expected to sit back unobtrusively while learning from their elders on matters of legislation and procedure, he contended, the question of ethics is another matter entirely.*
>
> *"True, we lack experience in the House," he told his young colleagues, "but we bring to this problem a fresh look. We feel totally uninhibited by tradition in this sensitive [Congressional ethics] area, because we think we heard the unmistakable clear voice of the people saying on Nov. 8, 'Go there and do something to restore respect for the House.'" Their*

> *proposal is so starry-eyed in its idealism that it looks as if it could have come out of a political-science class on good government. . . . Mr. Powell's [denial of his House seat and] fate was decided by an Ivy League Texan and a freshman philosophy class.*

Bush seems to have forgotten his professed idealism, or else it was a farce. Later pages will show Bush being involved with the CIA in major scandals of enormous consequences to the United States. If these offenses are true, it is obvious why Bush did not respond to my reports of government corruption.

These bizarre and convoluted scandals took me into uncharted waters. My imaginative use of the law was proper, but it was bizarre that the conditions existed that made the unorthodox lawsuits necessary. The fact that the media kept the lid on each of them is another indication of how the media censor the news to protect some of the worst scandals in the United States.

The following grisley picture is a DC-10 crash near Paris that killed 346 people. The tragedy was made possible by corruption within the FAA and NTSB, and assisted by judicial and Justice Department coverups and retaliation.

# LOOTING HUD

As my activities became known, I started winning the friendship and confidence of present and former employees and assets of the Central Intelligence Agency, the Drug Enforcement Administration, the FBI, and other government entities. During literally thousands of hours of deposition-like questioning they provided me details and documentation on government corruption that expanded on what I had already discovered while a government and private investigator and as a victim. For various reasons these people either volunteered the information to me, or they were willing to answer my questions relating to activities in which they actually participated or that they knew about.

A scheme that defrauded the American public of many billions of dollars had its roots in the Department of Housing and Urban Development (HUD). This scheme involved influence-peddling and self-dealing by government officials, bribes by corporations, over-billing, political payoffs, fraud, favoritism, kickbacks, and work that was never performed. This area of criminality cost the American taxpayer many billions of dollars in the 1970s and 1980s. The *Wall Street Journal* called the corruption a "system of spoils and favoritism." To carry out the looting of government funds, former government regulators were hired for their insider connections to obtain contracts that could otherwise not be obtained. That was the HUD scandal.

The HUD program was legislated to fund the rehabilitation of housing, especially for the elderly. Hundreds of millions of dollars, if not billions, were looted through the HUD program. In the 1980s, during the Reagan-Bush administrations, the fraud in the HUD program was epidemic and is continuing to some extent today. The American taxpayers must pay billions of dollars to support the criminal activities in the HUD program.

A major segment of the HUD fraud was centered in the Denver area and committed by a group of closely related people and companies, who had close ties to the Reagan and Bush administrations. Numerous HUD officials left government to work for the Denver group that defrauded the American people of billions of dollars, much of which is hidden away in either off-shore financial institutions or in secret locations throughout the United States. Philip Winn was one of the kingpins in the Denver group. He was a former HUD Assistant Secretary who joined the MDC group in Denver and became a key player in the HUD and savings and loan scandals.

Numerous HUD officials left government service and received high paying jobs with an interrelated group in Denver. This group included, among others: MDC Holdings; Richmond Homes; Silverado Bank Savings & Loan; Aurora Bank; M & L Business Machines; Leonard Millman; Larry Mizel; David Mandarich (president of MDC Holdings); Ken Good; Bill Walters; Neil Bush; Silverado's President Michael Wise; James Metz, major stockholder in Silverado; and dozens of subsidiaries and related companies, limited partnerships, trusts.

It was learned that Leonard Millman, Larry Mizel, and Philip Winn, all members of the ADL, were partners in these schemes, as was Philip Abrams, former HUD under-secretaries.

Federal regulators involved in the HUD scam included HUD Secretary Samuel Pierce, former Assistant Secretary Thomas Demery; Deborah Gore Dean and Lance Wilson, former executive assistantsto Pierce. All except Pierce have been indicted. A number of former HUD officials pleaded guilty to various federal crimes. Dean, an executive assistant to the Reagan Administration's Housing Secretary, was indicted on 13 criminal charges of fraud, perjury, submitting false statements to Congress, and conspiring to steer valuable housing grants to favored developers and consultants.

The group made huge financial contributions to various politicians, including the Reagan-Bush team and the Bill Clinton group. One of the key participants in the fraud, Philip Winn, used part of the money looted from the HUD and savings and loan programs to bribe politicians, especially in the Reagan-Bush presidencies. In return, Winn was appointed U.S. Ambassador to Switzerland and got the protection of the Justice Department through U.S. Attorney Michael Norton, who had secret participation in several of the Denver area real estate projects.

Justice Department officials, with their thousands of investigators throughout the United States, knew of the corruption and did very little. What little they did was usually to prosecute either innocent people or those who played a minor role in the massive criminality. Attorneys, developers, banks, members of the Senate and House were the recipients of the money defrauded from HUD. Consultants, for instance, with political connections, reaped huge fees of as much as $400,000 for a few phone calls or visits to HUD officials or phone calls to powerful members of Congress.

Rampant political favoritism and influence-peddling were part of the HUD scandal, combined with payment of millions of dollars for improvements that were never made. Former HUD personnel acted in collusion with present HUD officials in the fraudulent activities. One of the schemes was buying HUD properties for no-money-down, placing second loans on them for improvements that were never made, and then defaulting on the loans while receiving the rental income.

In 1982, the HUD inspector general made a report to Congress, reporting that insiders, including former HUD officials, were defrauding HUD of hundreds of millions of dollars, especially in the Section 8, and particularly sections 224D, 223F, and 202 elderly housing. Congress did not act until six years later when media publicity forced Congress to conduct an investigation. In 1988, Arlen Adams was appointed Special Prosecutor for HUD, and during subsequent investigations confirmed that developers with the aid of present and former HUD officials were receiving Section 8 rehabilitation units, grossly overcharging the government, often billing for work that was never accomplished. Simultaneously, the group bilking the government was contributing heavily to the Reagan-Bush team.

In March 1989, HUD hearings were triggered by exposure of huge financial donations by the Winn Group and Richmond Homes in Denver.

**TURNING PROSECUTION OVER TO THE BAD GUYS**

In November 1989, Congress asked U.S. Attorney General Richard Thornburgh to recommend to the Court of Appeals in Washington the appointment of a Special Prosecutor. He stalled until March 1990, when Congressional pressure forced him to act. Thornburgh had already blocked the appointment of a Special Prosecutor into Inslaw, October Surprise, and eventually BCCI and BNL. U.S. Attorney Generals Edwin Meese, Richard Thornburgh, and William Barr knew about each of the criminal activities described within these pages, and either aided and abetted them directly, or indirectly, by blocking investigation and prosecution. A corollary to that would be the Mafia controlling the highest law enforcement agency in this country.

**STATUTE OF LIMITATIONS**

One of the reasons for stalling prosecution was to allow the statute of limitations to expire, protecting the widespread criminality in the Denver area HUD and savings and loan corruption, and in turn protecting the part played by the Justice Department, the CIA, and many federal and White House officials.

In another investigation, a report was issued by the Committee on Government Operations, stating that "The Winn Group did not obtain units from HUD on merit alone, but rather from inside favoritism at HUD."

**POLITICAL PAYOFFS**

Key figures in the Denver-based HUD and savings and loan group, Winn and Mizel, contributed heavily to California Congressman's Tom Lantos' Congressional race in 1982. (I had repeatedly reported the corruption that I found to Congressman Lantos, and in typical fashion, verbally addressed the problem while simultaneously protecting it.)

**PART OF THE TAXPAYER LIABILITIES**

Congressional staff investigators discovered thousands of apartments were obtained by the group for rehabilitation, costing the American taxpayer over $100,000 each, when the cost for comparable privately financed units would be approximately $20,000. Congressional investigators discovered that U.S. Attorney Michael Norton owned five large apartment complexes with the Winn Group being investigated.

It was discovered that former FBI Special Agent in charge, Bob Pence, who retired in 1992, had been receiving bribes, along with U.S. Attorney Michael Norton and the head of the Internal Revenue Service's CID unit. Some of these bribes were laundered through the M&L Business Machine Company in Denver.

**USUAL COVERUPS**

When the scandal exposed California Congressman Tony Coelho and Texas Congressman Jim Wright, they took early retirement to defuse the pending investigations. The media and the public did not address the huge losses inflicted upon the American taxpayer. Instead, after key Congressmen such as Wright of Texas and Coelho of California were forced to retire so as to discontinue further investigation, their constituents showed little concern about the criminality and huge financial losses to be paid by the American taxpayer. Their concern was the loss of a powerful Congressman who produced pork barrel benefits for their constituents. Little was said of the huge multi-billion dollar debt inflicted upon the public. If it had been left to the constituents of Congressmen Jim Wright or Coelho, the enormous financial losses would be ignored as long as the voters received benefits from their corrupt Congressmen.

California Representative Tom Lantos (D-Cal.) led a Congressional investigation into the HUD matter, calling it

> *Influence-peddling of the tawdriest kind. The scandal at HUD is one of the most complex national scandals that we have seen in decades. There is a degree of mismanagement, fraud, abuse, waste, influence-peddling that we have just barely begun to touch.*

Representative Charles Schumer, a subcommittee member, said: "Like picking up a large stone only to discover that bugs and slime have grown in the darkness. This investigation has exposed the corruption which flourished unchecked under Secretary Pierce's HUD."

In addition to causing Wright and Coelho to resign (with liberal retirement benefits), Congress tried to stonewall an investigation into HUD by blocking confirmation of HUD appointees expressing an intent to expose the HUD scandal. After Jack Kemp took over HUD and stated his intent to prosecute those involved, Congress blocked confirmation of Kemp's management team. When the Department of Justice started an investigation into HUD, members of Congress then investigated the Justice Department, threatening to cut back its funding. The Justice Department investigation stopped.

Referring to Congressman Wright's blocking of an investigation into HUD corruption, a *Wall Street Journal* editorial (April 17, 1989) stated:

> *What is most disturbing...is the obvious pattern of so many violations extending over so many years....the brazenness is amazing. Obviously, Mr. Wright felt assured there was no prospect that he ever would be called to account for his actions.... When Congress is so powerful it can intimidate the Justice Department from another Abscam case, who should be surprised at corruption?*

**SHADES OF THE SAVINGS AND LOAN DEBACLE**

Investigations showed that House speaker Jim Wright obstructed investigation of the HUD corruption while accepting $145,000 in unreported gifts. The House Committee investigating Wright's dealings with the HUD scandal quickly dropped the investigation after some House members reminded them that an investigation would implicate many other members of Congress. After pressuring Jim Wright to resign on the relatively minor charge of ethics violations, the media attention to the HUD scandal ended. The guilty parties went free; the missing billions of dollars of looted money was never found; and the stage was set for more looting of the American taxpayer.

**JUSTICE DEPARTMENT STONEWALLING**

In typical fashion, after congressional members asked the politically-appointed U.S. Attorney General to investigate their allegations, Thornburgh accused them of introducing partisan politics into the HUD investigations. Representative Charles Schumer of New York replied at a news conference:

> *There's ample evidence of wrongdoing at HUD, but there's stonewalling at the top. And the only way to get to the bottom of the mess at HUD is through the appointment of an independent counsel. Instead of attacking us, the Attorney General should be focusing on making sure that high-ranking officials at HUD don't get away with breaking the law.*

Representative Schumer characterized the attorney general's objections as a "political response." A more correct characterization would probably be felony coverup, obstruction of justice, misprision of felonies.

Another time-honored way that Congress (and the Justice Department) stonewalls sensitive investigations is to withhold funding needed to conduct the investigation. Congress threatens to withhold funding from the Justice Department to dissuade members of Congress from investigating sensitive matters. It was done by Justice Department officials to stonewall investigation of Chapter 11 judicial corruption. It was also done to halt further FBI investigations of Congressional wrongdoings in Abscam. As the FBI's continuing investigations into the conduct of Congressmen became too threatening, members of Congress responded by dragging Justice Department officials in for grueling oversight hearings. It became clear to Justice Department officials that the budget for the Justice Department was in danger if the probes into Congressional wrongdoings did not cease.

**CONGRESS FINALLY CONDUCTED AN "INVESTIGATION"**

Eventually, Congress was forced to conduct an "investigation." A House committee stated in a report that the Department of Housing and Urban Development was "enveloped by influence-peddling, favoritism, abuse, greed, fraud, embezzlement and theft."

Samuel Pierce, Secretary of HUD from 1981 to 1988, refused to cooperate in the HUD investigation, repeatedly invoking his Fifth Amendment privilege against self-incrimination. The House Committee report stated that Pierce gave misleading testimony and that he probably "lied and committed perjury during his testimony on May 25, 1989."

**APPOINTING AN INDEPENDENT PROSECUTOR**

After Congress covered up the HUD scandal, an independent prosecutor was appointed, who then had to set up an office and hire attorneys to investigate, many of whom had no investigative experience.

The Independent Prosecutor found that HUD officials unlawfully allocated federal funds to developers and consultants with whom they had private financial relations, receiving bribes, and other favors. Silvio J. DeBartolomeis, a former deputy Assistant Secretary of HUD, pled guilty to three criminal charges,[98] including conspiring to mislead Congress and HUD's own regional offices concerning a HUD rent subsidy program; and to receiving an illegal salary supplement consisting of a $20,000 loan arranged by developer Phillip Winn. DeBartolomeis was charged with defrauding HUD's Section 8 rehabilitation program, which enriched the developers based in the Denver area.

**INDICTING THE SMALL FRY**

Media attention forced Justice Department prosecutors to file charges in the HUD corruption, years after the criminal acts were known. But the indictments were selective. The power brokers with whom U.S. Attorney Michael Norton was in partnership escaped prosecution or were charged with minor offenses, and evidence was conveniently lost. Federal judges dismissed some charges before the jury could begin deliberation.

The indictments omitted charging the Denver area developers who donated large sums of money to political figures, who had close ties with the CIA, and who contributed large financial contributions or bribes to White House officials and other politicians.

Among the HUD officials who were directly involved in the looting of HUD was HUD Deputy Assistant Secretary, DuBois Gilliam, who pleaded guilty (May 1989) to receiving over $100,000 in payoffs and gifts to approve HUD grants for various developers.

During the investigation, it was disclosed that HUD Secretary Samuel Pierce received over 1,700 formal requests from Congressmen and senators requesting support for specific projects. These same members of Congress were receiving political contributions from individuals for whom they sought HUD favoritism.

Eventually, Winn pled guilty to preparing a false receipt for another HUD official that was submitted to HUD investigators. But these charges were chicken-feed compared to what Winn and his buddies actually perpetrated. My inside sources stated that over $167 million paid by HUD to the Winn group for rehabilitating HUD housing was never spent for that purpose, and sequestered in secret locations.

A nine-count felony indictment was made against a former assistant to ex-Senator Edward Brooke[99] for allegedly lying to the FBI and a federal grand jury, who were looking into Brooke's role in the HUD influence-peddling scandal. Charges against Deborah Gore Dean included improperly steering funds to clients of former Attorney General John Mitchell after Mitchell was released from his Watergate prison term.

A federal jury in Washington, D.C. on October 26, 1993, convicted former HUD aide Deborah Dean, a central figure in the HUD scandal, of being instrumental in funneling millions of dollars to housing projects that enriched politically-connected Republicans.

**GROUP OF HUD WHISTLEBLOWERS**

I became a confidant to several former CIA operatives, private investigators, and insiders, who were heavily involved in the Denver-area operations, and

---

98 *Oakland Tribune,* October 15, 1992,

99 Brooke was a lawyer and consultant for businessmen seeking help with HUD on federally subsidized housing projects in the 1980s.

through them discovered some of the inner workings of the corrupt operations. One of the investigators and insiders, Stewart Webb, was a former son-in-law of Leonard Millman. During four years of marriage from 1981 to 1985, Webb became privy to many of the procedures used to loot billions of dollars from the HUD and savings and loan programs in the Denver area.

Following the divorce, Webb expanded on what he had learned as an insider. Through aggressive investigations, Webb discovered the paper trail of the looted money, including thousands of documents he obtained in recorders' offices throughout the United States. Webb was able to document major schemes implicating the Denver group in various financial scandals. Webb discovered the trail to offshore bank accounts and trusts, and their secret locations.

Describing some of the key players in the Denver area looting of HUD and the savings and loans, Webb stated that among the top players were nationally known and politically connected powerhouses such as Carl Lindner, Larry Mizel, Philip Winn, Albert Rose, George Riter and many others. He described how many HUD officials left Washington and joined the Denver-based group, and how their prior Washington connections made the looting possible.

Additional data was given to me by other insiders, including high-ranking covert CIA personnel. Gunther Russbacher, for instance, operated numerous CIA proprietaries having secret dealings with the Denver group, including money laundering, looting of the HUD and savings and loan programs, and other activities.

Webb initially contacted me on September 17, 1991, advising me of corrupt dealings in the HUD and savings and loan program by his former father-in-law and many of the people and groups that worked with him, including MDC Holdings and dozens of limited partnerships, trusts, and subsidiaries. Webb also told me about the large numbers of federal officials who were in the schemes.

Webb appeared as guest on numerous radio shows, some with investigative reporter Margie Sloan, naming the corporations, the complex paper trail, and the individuals involved. He discovered that the U.S. Attorney in Denver, Michael Norton, was deeply implicated with the group, sharing secret ownership of valuable properties. Webb discovered that the corrupt Denver group gave large financial contributions to Norton when Norton ran for Congress in the early 1980s. This discovery helped explain one of the reasons why Justice Department officials never prosecuted the key figures in the HUD and savings and loan debacle.

Webb reported that he found that the Winn and MDC group owned over 10,000 units in Colorado, Utah, Nevada, Oklahoma, South Dakota, North Dakota, and another 10,000 units in the area controlled by the Texas regional office of HUD.

Webb and IRS agent Walker in the Denver office frequently exchanged information that they found in the HUD criminality. In June 1991, Walker told Webb that he could no longer talk to him about the matter, and when Webb asked, "Is [President] Bush covering this thing up?" Walker replied, "Yes," and then hung up.

Webb stated that his investigation showed that U.S. Attorney Michael Norton was connected to Mizel, a major player in the Denver-area HUD and savings and loan corruption, and that Mizel was Finance Chairman for Norton's unsuccessful Congressional campaign.

Without success, Webb tried to have a Colorado District Attorney in Denver and the U.S. Attorney in Colorado receive his evidence, but they refused.

**PROTECT THEIR FLANKS**

Despite the large sums donated to Michael Norton's campaign for a senate seat, he lost. But the Reagan-Bush team appointed Norton U.S. Attorney in Denver, thereby protecting White House and other federal officials from investigation and prosecution in the HUD corruption.

**JUSTICE DEPARTMENT RETALIATION**

Webb's appearance on many radio talk shows were apparently causing concern in the Justice Department and in the Denver area. Working with Webb's former father-in-law, U.S. Attorney Michael Norton charged Webb with making harassing and threatening phone calls to his former father-in-law, Leonard Millman. Although the language could have been cleaner, the threats were nothing more than a determination to expose the HUD and savings and loan corruption in which his former father-in-law was involved, which threatened to expose the U.S. Attorney's involvement in the criminal activities.

After Webb heard of the warrant for his arrest he went underground for the next year, surfacing only to appear as a guest on radio shows in Denver and throughout the United States. For some of the shows he called me collect, and I would then relay his call to the radio station. I had no knowledge of Webb's whereabouts, and didn't want to know.

**ARRESTING AN IRRITATING WHISTLEBLOWER**

In September 1992, shortly after Webb had talked to Ross Perot by phone and revealed his location in Houston, the FBI arrested Webb. Justice Department prosecutors demanded that Webb be denied release pending trial, an almost unheard of demand in a case involving harassing phone calls. Justice Department officials were trying to silence Webb and keep him off talk shows, especially before the 1992 presidential elections.

I advised Webb that he had the opportunity to get additional information on the HUD and savings and loan scandal by talking to other inmates at the federal prison who were former CIA operatives and insiders in the HUD and savings and loan scandal. It was and is standard practice of Justice Department officials to cause the imprisonment of these people in order to silence or discredit them. By entering prison a writer or investigator has an inside track to information that he would not otherwise have. Sure enough, Webb did discover numerous inmates who gave him additional information, helping to fill in the gaps. While detained in the Federal Correctional Institution at Littleton, near Denver, Webb made contact with a group of former CIA contract agents who were deeply involved with the Denver area group.

**ANOTHER SOURCE OF INFORMATION**

One of these contacts was a former CIA operative named Trenton Parker, who played key roles in numerous covert CIA operations from 1964 until he fell from grace in the late 1980s. Webb and Trenton shared a prison cell in December 1992, until Parker was released pending trial, which was to start in April 1993. Parker had seen some of the material I had sent to Webb and contacted me after being released. This relationship produced extraordinarily secret and sensitive material and added to the mosaic establishing the complex intrigue and corruption described in these pages.

The confidential status report establishing Trenton's highly secret status in the intelligence community prevented Justice Department and CIA personnel from denying his high rank and status. Additionally, Parker gave me information, including briefs that he filed in the U.S. District Court in Denver, that depicted criminal activities by the CIA.

Another insider who contacted me in February 1993 was one of the fall-guys in the HUD scandal, Don Austin. He gave me insider information on the role played by federal officials and the Denver group in looting the HUD program. Austin headed groups of investors buying HUD properties and operated under the name of Nitusa.

Austin described to me how Justice Department officials protected present and former HUD officials who were self-dealing in violation of federal law and were involved in massive fraud, especially in the Denver area. He described how people associated with the savings and loan industry, who had done no wrong, were being prosecuted to make it appear to the public that the Justice Department was punishing those responsible for the huge HUD fraud.

Austin further states how his assets were seized by Justice Department prosecutors under the forfeiture laws, depriving him of money to hire legal counsel to defend against the charges brought by the Justice Department. He described how his court-appointed attorney was incompetent in the complex area involved in the charges. In desperation, Austin discharged the attorney and appeared in pro se, representing himself, and was then overwhelmed by the top guns of the Justice Department.

Austin was a successful real estate investor who worked with the HUD Administration to rehabilitate and sell hundreds of HUD properties. Justice Department officials, under U.S. Attorney Michael Norton, charged Austin with federal offenses and obtained a twenty-one year prison sentence against him. While Norton was covering up for the multi-billion dollar looting of the HUD and savings and loan people with whom he had been financially involved in Denver, he charged Austin with falsifying HUD applications. The alleged falsification of HUD purchase and loan agreements consisted of minor technicalities, such as showing in the cash-down block the value of notes and deeds of trust. It was standard practice to do this and then, on an accompanying HUD form and title company closing documents, the actual form of the down payment was shown.

On the form there was no other way to show the down payment other than as cash. Actually, cash is almost never given, as the standard practice is to give checks, money orders, other properties, or notes and deeds of trust as down payment.

HUD officials and companies acting on their behalf approved the purchase applications submitted by Austin, knew the form of down payment being made, and approved the form of payment on behalf of HUD. But when it came time to prosecute HUD related corruption, U.S. Attorney Michael Norton protected the king-pins of the racketeering enterprise. He selected scapegoats, and Austin was one of them.

Justice Department attorneys wanted to indict Austin because former and present HUD officials, who had purchased many of the properties through Austin, had defaulted on almost all of the units after bleeding them dry. These HUD officials were involved with others implicated in huge HUD and savings and loan fraud. To indict those guilty of this fraud risked blowing the lid on the multi-billion-dollar racket that implicated people like Neil Bush, George Bush, powerful Denver area and Washington politicians and powerful money figures who routinely bribed the politicians.

Austin learned there was a grant from HUD awarding Justice Department attorneys bonuses for the number of criminal counts filed against defendants, encouraging false charges to be filed.

**ATTORNEY SABOTAGE**

Austin related to me the practice of attorneys demanding huge sums of money up front to defend him. After receiving the money, they sabotaged his case. This scenario had been told to me countless times, and I experienced it myself many times. It appears to be standard practice by the attorneys, preying upon people who are unaware of these corrupt practices. Every CIA whistleblower whom I had contacted, including Gunther Russbacher, Ron Rewald, Michael Riconosciuto, the HUD whistleblower Stewart Webb, and others, encountered the same scenario. Every one of them had strong words describing the sordid conduct of the attorneys that they encountered.

Austin's sophisticated lady friend, Pat Class, described the ugly nature of the attorneys she encountered while trying to help Austin. She told of the many instances she paid ten, twenty, and thirty thousand dollars to attorneys up front, who then never performed.

In telephone conversations and writings, Austin described the mechanics of what he had uncovered in the HUD fraud. Austin operated a company called Nitsua, dealing in purchasing and reselling HUD properties. He also told how he and others purchased and paid for HUD insurance, which was kept by the HUD representatives and not applied to their accounts. He described the self-dealing by HUD personnel, including Grady Maples, Regional Director for HUD, and by Gail Calhoon, head of the Denver HUD office. Maples had a major ownership interest in Falcon Development, which in turn acquired the properties that were subsequently looted.

Austin described how drug forfeiture and other forfeiture money was being distributed to federal judges and Justice Department prosecutors, something like the Chapter 11 operations. Even the U.S. Marshals were implicated as they were involved in the seizure of assets.

Austin related one of many transactions in which the Maples Group purchased an apartment complex and then placed secondary financing on it through Greenwood Industrial Bank, owned by a close associate, Bob Hard, one of Maples partners. Rents were collected but no payments were made on the HUD and Greenwood loans.

Also indicted with Austin was James Grandgeorge, who reportedly had been wrongfully convicted but who had offered to pay U.S. Attorney Michael Norton money under the table to get his conviction or his sentence vacated. This plan went haywire after U.S. Attorney General Janet Reno fired Norton in April 1993.

**PROTECTING THE OPERATION AND THE HIERARCHY**

Following the pattern in other scandals involving federal officials, Justice Department prosecutors fabricated charges against innocent people such as Austin. In this way, Justice Department attorneys shifted the blame from those involved in the corruption, including federal officials, former federal officials, and powerful financial figures who orchestrated devastating financial harms upon the American people. Several examples follow, as the information was given to me by people who came to me for help.

During Austin's trial, the Justice Department prosecutor withheld information about the HUD self-dealing, the failure of HUD officers to apply the mortgage insurance money paid by Austin and others, and many other wrongful acts. If the jury had heard this information it would have helped prove Austin's innocence.

Another person set up by Justice Department prosecutors was Paul Jenkins from Utah. Jenkins was one of the owners of six savings and loans in Texas who experienced problems with loans that went bad when the Texas economy slumped in the late 1980s. He arranged with U.S. Homes to purchase all the notes held by the savings and loans that had been taken over by the government at full face value, which would have kept anyone from losing money. But government personnel refused to allow this for several reasons. One, it would diminish the justification for seizing some of the savings and loans and eliminate the criminal charges filed against some of the lower echelon people being prosecuted in the savings and loan debacle.

During the first trial, Jenkins was cleared of the charges against him. Justice Department prosecutors then filed new charges. Jenkins said that he paid over a half million dollars up front to a Texas attorney, Barefoot Sanders, only to have this attorney abandon him the next day, keeping the money for himself. Jenkins then paid money, up front, to another attorney from Texas, Racehorse Haines, and again Jenkins was abandoned. During the second trial, Haines abandoned his client, causing Jenkins, without funds, to rely upon a federal defender. Federal "defenders" have a history of protecting their cohorts in the Justice Department and on the federal bench.

An irony was that most of the victims of Justice Department and government corruption were nice, honest, sincere people. The biggest crooks were those in control of key government offices, including Justice Department attorneys, federal judges, CIA officials, and members of Congress, especially those who are attorneys.

There were other sources, including CIA operatives, who described to me their role in the HUD, savings and loan, HUD, and other scandals, who acted under orders of their CIA handlers. Their roles are described elsewhere in these pages.

**POLITICAL CONTRIBUTIONS**

The illegal political contributions provided to Norton by the Denver group, when he ran for Congress in 1982, were reportedly funded by extorting money from suppliers and their employees. These funds were reimbursed through fraudulent billings later paid by HUD in the rehabilitation program. When these political contributions were publicized and prosecution commenced, Norton had to recuse himself as federal prosecutor. He covered his rear by appointing a special prosecutor, U.S. Attorney Marvin Collins from Texas, for damage control. Federal judges cooperated in keeping the lid on the scandals and protecting key players from prosecution.

Those who paid the heaviest for political contributions were the contractors and suppliers to the Denver group, including MDC Holdings, Richmond Homes, and other subsidiaries, who were forced to make illegal political contributions to Michael Norton. The higher-ups, who demanded the contributions, were either not charged or, after being charged, the charges were either dropped or favorable plea bargains were made. The kingpins responsible for the illegal contributions, Leonard Millman, Larry Mizel, and others, went unpunished.

Although Norton lost the election, the Denver group, heavy financial contributors to the Reagan-Bush team, got Norton appointed U.S. Attorney in Denver. This insured protection against criminal prosecution for the massive fraud in which they were all involved.

The group involved in the HUD scandal was also involved in the fraud associated with the new Denver airport and much more. These were only a very few of the many scandals, protected by federal office holders, for which the American public will be saddled with debt for decades.

**CIA INVOLVEMENT**

As is described later, the CIA, using code names for various operations, had numerous financial companies that played key roles in looting of the HUD program and savings and loan institutions. Different CIA divisions or directorates ran parallel operations, using code names for the HUD and savings and loan operations. These code names included Operation Cyclops and Operation Gold Bug.

**DENVER AIRPORT**

My CIA contacts operating covert CIA corporations in the United States described the massive fraud involving the new Denver International Airport. They elaborated upon the tactics involved in the promotion and development of the airport, including influence-peddling, pay-offs, phony billings, phony land-swaps, sham loans, and other forms of fraud. Denver Mayor Federico Pena reportedly received a large bribe for promoting the airport. He was reported by my CIA contacts as conspiring with the key players in the Denver-area HUD and savings and loan corruption, including James Metz (Silverado's Chairman); Michael Wise (Silverado's President); Charles Keating (who cooperated in phony land-swaps and sham loans); Bill Walters and Ken Good (who defaulted on tens of millions of dollars in loans obtained through the help of Neil Bush); Phil Winn (indicted for bribing HUD officials); Larry Mizel; Norman Brownstein (attorney for Mizel and the MDC crowd and Pena's law partner).

Brownstein allegedly helped hide hundreds of millions of dollars of money looted from various fraudulent schemes of this group, some of the money hidden in trusts filed in remote locations, as described in later pages. Brownstein was portrayed by Senator Ted Kennedy (D-MA) as "the Senate's 101st member."

Brownstein sat on the board of MDC Holdings and represented companies run by some of the biggest crooks in the HUD and savings and loan areas.

**PAYMENT OF BRIBE MONEY?**

Former CIA operative Trenton Parker told me what other CIA sources had also reported, that former Denver Mayor Federico Pena was paid $1.5 million by Leonard Millman to get voter approval for the new Denver Airport. Parker stated that Mayor Pena's office was bugged by the CIA Pegasus group, and that the audio tape shows Millman walking into Pena's office, stating: "OK, here's the million and a half god-damn dollars; now we want the f.... airport to go through. Now, get off your butts and get this thing going."

As in every other known pattern of criminality involving federal officials, hard-core criminality related to the HUD scandals was ignored. For instance, Stewart Webb learned that thousands of remodeled units and homes owned by the government were secretly removed from government records by the group consisting of former HUD officials and then sold, making it very profitable for those involved.

While HUD's internal checks and balances, and Justice Department prosecutors, refused to prosecute HUD corruption perpetrated by HUD officials, they did prosecute members of the public. For instance, in 1994, these same "checks and balances" sought to imprison people who objected to the placement of undesirable housing in their midst. In Berkeley, California, for instance, HUD used federal resources to investigate, intimidate, and threaten with federal prison those people who objected to the placement of housing for drug abusers and the mentally disturbed in their neighborhood.

HUD attorneys investigated for seven months and threatened to charge people with violating federal housing discrimination laws. Nearby neighbors, Richard Graham, Alexandra White, and Joseph Deringer, were threatened with $50,000 in fines and a prison sentence for objecting to the HUD housing plans. HUD charged that the neighbors engaged in "coercion, intimidation and interference" against the potential tenants of the planned housing.

# LOOTING THE SAVINGS AND LOANS

Congress and the Reagan Administration deregulated the savings and loan industry through the Garn-St Germain Act of 1982, which was signed into law by President Ronald Reagan on October 15, 1982. As he signed the far-reaching bill, Reagan announced that it was "the most important legislation for financial institutions in 50 years." He added: "I think we've hit the jackpot." If he meant the jackpot reference for the Mafia, the CIA, and a host of crooks, he was absolutely right. Even the famous bank robber, Willie Sutton, never envisioned such riches.

I had considerable real estate at that time, including motels, hotels, truck stops, golf courses, apartments, and land, and knew the financial frauds that would follow deregulation. It didn't take any great expertise to predict the consequences, and surely members of Congress and the industry recognized that fact even sooner than I.

Developers, Mafia figures and crooks, started buying small savings and loans in out-of-the-way-places. In that manner they gained access to the Treasury of the United States, permitting them to engage in self-dealings, sham transactions, and massive fraud against the American taxpayer. Deregulation and the concurrent fraud were financially fabulous for many people, fueling massive growth in the real estate industry during the 1980s. The price tab was picked up by the public in the 1990s, and they would pay for decades, well into the next century. The losses, much of which were outright theft, exceeded the cost of World War II. Never in the history of the United States had such a massive financial debacle occurred, making the American taxpayer the victim of the biggest scam in the nation's history.

The crooks who held the controlling interests in savings and loan associations paid themselves extravagant salaries, with virtually unlimited expense accounts that bled their companies dry. They made loans to themselves or corporations they owned or controlled and had a fabulous lifestyle that couldn't possibly be supported by the income of the savings and loans they acquired.

Many sordid details of the savings and loan debacle have never been revealed by the mass media. Crooks, with the help of politicians, Justice Department officials and CIA renegades, stripped the American people of hundreds of billions of dollars. The American economy has been badly crippled by this theft, adversely affecting the same American people whose failure to speak out helped bring about their own financial problems.

**WARNING FLAGS PRESAGING DEREGULATION**

It was no secret to members of Congress what would happen if the savings and loans were deregulated. The consequences of relaxing safeguards were seen elsewhere. For instance, the danger of brokered deposits was evident when serious problems arose in California during the 1960s when these deposits were allowed to reach a high percentage of a financial institution's deposits, threatening its solvency. Sudden withdrawal of such large sums of money deposited as a block could easily make the institution insolvent. To correct this problem, regulators ordered a cap of five percent of an institution's total brokered deposits. This restriction remained from 1963 until the limit on brokered deposits was removed in 1982 by the Depository Institutions Deregulation Committee, chaired by Treasury Secretary Donald Regan. This change was enormously profitable to financial institutions dealing in such deposits, including Regan's prior employer before he joined the Reagan administration.

Brokered deposits consisted of blocks of $100,000 deposits from individual depositors, which was the limit for federal insurance guarantees.[100] By dealing in brokered deposits the bank was able to build its capital and engage in huge fraudulent schemes. The danger arose from the high interest rates and fees needed to acquire them, and these costs were greater than what could be earned by lending the money to safe real estate investments.

Just prior to voting for deregulating the savings and loans, the nation's worst bank failure occurred, which was caused by eliminating safeguards and permitting brokered deposits. The Oklahoma City financial institution, Penn Square Bank, failed in 1982 and brought giant Continental Illinois National Bank and Trust Company in Chicago to the brink of failure, as well as other lending institutions that had placed large sums of money into Penn Square Bank.

The American taxpayers had to bail out Continental Illinois to the tune of $4.5 billion (plus the interest that is still being paid on the payout). This amount was in addition to the payments made to the insured depositors at Penn Square. It was the largest federal bailout in the nation's history, and showed the dangers of deregulation and brokered deposits and what could be expected with the subsequent signing of the deregulation act.

Penn Square offered the deposit brokers higher interest rates and substantial brokerage commissions for funds placed with the financial institution, causing brokers to place millions of dollars into the bank on any given day. But the rates and the fees that Penn Square had to pay for these deposits required making loans on high-risk investments and in a Ponzi-scheme. Further, the continual losses due to high costs of the funds and the inadequacy of returns on these funds

---

100 Over strong protests from people who knew what would happen, the federal deposit guarantee was raised from the previous $5,000.

required a continuing infusion of money to continue the scheme.

Common sense and the history of failures made obvious what would happen when Congress voted for deregulation. But many of those who voted for deregulating the savings and loans were recipients of large financial contributions (i.e., bribes).

With brokered deposits there was no money available to make normal home loans; the spread was too much between the rate that homeowners could pay and the rate the savings and loans had to pay for brokered deposits.

The primary problem of deregulation came when the lending institution engaged in self-dealing, land-flips, sham loans, and many other devices used to carry out the massive fraud. All this was obvious to anyone close to the industry, as were members of Congress. But the immediate financial benefits to those voting for deregulation, the law firms and public relations firms, easily took precedence over the harm inflicted upon the United States and the American people, and this attitude prevails throughout these pages.

**EVERY COMMON-SENSE WARNING SIGN IGNORED**

Some of the practices that could be expected to occur, and which did occur after deregulation, included:

1. Inflating the value of properties through land flips, whereby a parcel of land was "resold" numerous times, sometimes on the same day. Each time the new "buyer" paid a higher price. In that way, a borrower could indicate the land was worth far more than it actually was and obtain a larger loan than the property was worth. Oftentimes no payments would be made on the loan after receiving the loan proceeds, and the property allowed to go into foreclosure. The borrower then walked away with the difference between the purchase price of the property and the loan proceeds. In many cases this constituted millions of dollars.

2. Making a loan to a controlled or a dummy corporation far beyond the value of the property, then let the loan go into default and the property taken back.

3. Making a loan that was not intended to be repaid to a controlled corporation. Then when the loan and interest payments are due, making a larger loan on the property to "pay off" the prior loan and accumulated interest, thus showing a sham profit. The loan would be shown as a performing loan on the books rather than a loan in default.

4. Swapping bad loans between cooperating financial institutions and showing the loans as performing loans on the books.

5. Spending lavishly on aircraft, vacation homes, trips, and other expensive life styles and charging it to business expenses. An honestly operated business would not incur such charges when the business was operating in the red.

6. Paying inordinately high salaries to themselves and providing themselves with bonuses when bad non-performing loans are renewed or traded for other bad loans with cooperating institutions.

7. Making sham loans on greatly overvalued real estate owned or controlled by the lending institution, with borrowers never intending to repay the loans.

8. Hiring former federal regulators at exorbitant salaries for their influence-peddling abilities and knowledge, to assist in circumventing regulatory protections.

9. Paying many millions of dollars in bribes to members of Congress to block actions by federal regulators, and blocking corrective legislation.

**TYPICAL LAND FLIP**

A typical example of the fraud associated with land flips was a tract of property northeast of Denver where the new Denver airport was supposed to be located. The original parcel of land, called the Little Buckeroo Ranch, was purchased for $1 million and then flipped over several times in dummy land sales, fraudulently showing its value as $5 million. The Denver group involved in this scam obtained a $5 million non-recourse loan on the property and then defaulted when it was discovered the airport would be built elsewhere. They made a $4 million profit on the deal. People involved in that one example were heavily involved in the HUD and savings and loan fraud in the Denver area and had close ties to the Central Intelligence Agency.

**FINANCING THE LOOTING**

To generate the hundreds of millions of dollars to fund these scams, the parties operating savings and loans needed a steady supply of money, far more than could be expected from local depositors. The answer was in brokered deposits. Money brokers pooled $100,000 deposits from different sources and deposited the funds into whatever savings and loan offered the highest interest and paid the highest brokerage fee.

The deposited funds would either be used for high-risk loans or, as was often the case, to fund sham transactions in which there was no intention to repay the loans. The loss of several hundred **billion** dollars that will be paid by the American taxpayer required more than simply poor judgment. There was no risk to the con-artists, as the American taxpayers were insuring the money.

Brokers would often offer deposits to a savings and loan on condition that the institution make one or more loans on a given piece of real estate. The loan amount would often be made in excess of the value of the property used for security, or made without any security. The institution making the loan may or may not realize that the loan would never be repaid.

There were many variations of these scams. All could be foreseen, and all had occurred in isolated cases the decade before deregulation.

**THE EXPECTED COMMENCED IMMEDIATELY**

The expected started happening immediately. Among the first was Vernon Savings and Loan in Texas, which failed in 1984, involving brokered deposits, land flips, inflated mortgages, and huge personal expenses billed to the financial institutions. Loans that would never have been made with the former safeguards were made to insiders and friends who scratched each other's backs as they made themselves rich.

Ed Gray was sworn in on May 1, 1983, to head the Federal Home Loan Bank Board (FHLBB), and promptly discovered the seriousness of the massive fraud. He tried correcting the problem by returning the restriction on brokered deposits to the previous five percent, thereby halting the primary problem. But those who used the brokered deposits descended upon Congress, handing out money insured by the American taxpayer and succeeding in blocking this change. Treasury Secretary Regan, whose former employer profited by the brokered deposits, and many others sought to discredit Gray as some sort of wacko.

Finally, the discrediting campaign succeeded, and Gray was replaced by Danny Wall, an aide to Senator Jake Garn, Chairman of the Senate Banking Committee. Wall then obstructed corrective action to keep the massive fraud scheme in operation, while simultaneously keeping the money flowing to members of Congress that kept federal investigators at bay. Wall protected Lincoln Savings and Loan from the San Francisco regulatory board which had planned to shut down the corruption-plagued institution, removing Lincoln from the jurisdiction of the regulators who had uncovered the corruption.

In an unprecedented action, Wall transferred regulatory jurisdiction of Lincoln to Washington, and Lincoln continued its corrupt practices of looting assets of U.S. taxpayers and individual investors. One act was to offer bonds of bankrupted American Continental Corporation, Lincoln's parent corporation, to its depositors, falsely claiming they were government-protected. Thousands of elderly people with no other source of income lost their life's savings through this scheme, made possible by Washington and California politicians. These tactics also increased the immediate cost to the American taxpayer to approximately $2 billion plus the triple or so amount that will be paid in interest before the debt is paid off, if it ever is.

Virtually everyone who played the game, who looked the other way, or who blocked corrective action, profited. Members of Congress, including the Keating-Five, received bribes for blocking corrective action by federal inspectors. The media received advertising dollars from large numbers of real estate developments built under a cloud of fraud. The crooks in the savings and loans and others acting with them profited. Everyone knew the American taxpayer would foot the bills. Another group of losers, given very little attention, were the stockholders. Many of them invested their life's savings in the savings and loans, and these savings were usually lost.

Simultaneously,[101] Lincoln's President, Charles Keating, paid $839,000 of taxpayer's money to various election committees to reelect Cranston,[102] and hundreds of thousands more to the senators known as the "Keating Five:" Senators Alan Cranston (D-CA), senior member on the House Banking Committee; Dennis DeConcini (R-AZ); John McCain (R-AZ); John Glenn (D-OH); and Donald Riegle (D-MI). I had notified each of them of the criminal activities I had uncovered, and demanded they receive testimony and evidence that my CIA and DEA whistleblowers and I were ready to present. They all refused.

Members of Congress sought to continue the coverup to the end. In June 1989 Congress quietly rejected a request for $36.8 million to hire investigators to accelerate the investigation and prosecution of corrupt savings and loan officials.

In 1986 the Keating-Five senators applied pressure upon Washington regulators to prevent government investigators from taking actions against Keating's Lincoln Savings and Loan (after the group received huge financial donations from

101 Charlie Keating was chairman of American Continental Corporation, a major land developer in Arizona. American Continental acquired Lincoln Savings & Loan Association of Irvine, California. Keating became its chief executive officer. Lincoln was then used as a private bank for Keating's own investments, many of them highly questionable.

102 *San Francisco Examiner*, October 8, 1989.

Keating). This Congressional obstruction of the regulatory function of the U.S. government increased the costs to taxpayers far in excess of *two hundred billion* dollars for the entire industry. The taxpayers also must pay for the bribes paid to politicians on the California and federal levels and to the former government officials who became high salaried employees of Lincoln.

California's Senator Alan Cranston obstructed the actions of the regulators who sought to prevent others from losing money, including elderly and retired people who invested in the uninsured bonds issued by Keating's enterprises. This obstructive action interrupted the regulatory process, delaying the government takeover of Lincoln Savings and Loan, as it continued selling worthless, uninsured securities to the public.

Even Alan Greenspan, then a private consultant and later chairman of the Federal Reserve Board, sent a letter seeking to block corrective actions, falsely claiming Lincoln was in good financial shape and had good lending practices. This was preposterous. Lincoln's primary assets were grossly inflated desert land. Lincoln had a practice of lending money to closely related investors or their own real estate enterprises, often without any credit check and without collateral.

Eventually the losses were too great to ignore. A new agency was formed to clean up the mess and the same parties who blocked prior corrective action wanted Wall installed as its head, fighting to retain the head of the regulatory agency who helped continue the escalating corruption. Senator Cranston and Representative Donald Riegle fought hard to have Danny Wall confirmed as head of the new agency without a confirmation hearing, avoiding senate questioning of the debacle that unfolded while he held responsibility to prevent such fraud.

Congress' response to the nation's greatest financial debacle consisted of carefully avoiding charging any of their members, including the Keating-Five, with any crimes. They wrung their hands trying to decide whether any of the senators who received huge amounts of money from the crooks, and who blocked corrective attempts by federal regulators, violated ethics. Using this standard on many people sent to federal prison for far less federal offenses would greatly reduce the prison population.

## YOU RAT ON ME AND I'LL RAT ON YOU

Cranston had earlier warned the entire United States Senate that, if the Ethics Committee moved to censure him for his role in the savings and loan scandal, he would blow the whistle on the role played by other senators in the savings and loan matter. As the "investigating" committee considered whether to censor Cranston for ethics violations, Senator Jeff Bingaman disqualified himself, requiring appointment of another senator, which in turn required weeks for the replacement to review the evidence. Bingaman had disqualified himself after "suddenly" discovering, after three years, that a conflict of interest existed: his wife worked for a law firm that once represented two of Cranston's staff members whose legal bill had not been paid. That move took the heat off the ethics committee until media attention focused elsewhere.

Congress repeatedly refused to provide money to shut down the hemorrhaging savings and loans, which then permitted the looting to go on, as well as continuing the political contributions from the insolvent institutions. Congressman Gonzalez stated[103] that the White House and federal officials could simply have placed the looted and failed "institutions under government conservatorship." But Congressman Gonzalez complained to federal regulators in late 1992 that "Regulators can put failing institutions under government conservatorship now, with or without any new funding. This should save the taxpayers the costs of further depletion of the institutions' assets." The refusal to shut down the fraud-racked savings and loans escalated the losses.

**USUAL COVERUPS**

Investigators, trying to blow the whistle on rampant corruption, testified to the House Banking Committee in October 1989 that Washington officials repeatedly overruled or restricted their investigation of corruption-riddled Lincoln Savings and Loan (as they had done after I started exposing hard-core government corruption in the aviation field starting in the mid-1960s).

**ADMITTING TO PAYING FOR INFLUENCE**

Keating admitted giving over five million dollars in political contributions to influence members of the U.S. House and the Senate and state politicians in California and Arizona. Cranston and the four other senators pressured regulators to back off from shutting down Lincoln Savings and Loan, inflicting even greater losses upon the American taxpayer.

Keating wasn't hesitant about stating the effects he expected when he paid bribes to members of Congress, stating several times to the press:

> *One question, among many raised in recent weeks, had to do with whether my financial support in any way influenced several political figures to take up my cause. I want to say in the most forceful way I can; I certainly hope so.*[104]

Despite the huge losses incurred by these practices, Keating paid himself and his family over $34 million in the three years before its demise, even though losses during this time were destroying the corporation.

Representative Henry Gonzalez of Texas initially protected the system by using his post as chairman of the House Banking Committee to obstruct an investigation into questionable banking practices in his home district. Gonzalez pushed an amendment to protect First National Bank of San Antonio and other financial subsidiaries from the regulatory actions of the Federal Deposit Insurance Corporation. But as the savings and loan scandal shot out from under the media blackout Gonzalez, head of the House committee[105] with oversight responsibilities for the savings and loan industry under the Office of Thrift Supervision (OTS),[106] focused attention on the savings and loan problems.

**"Honesty doesn't pay."**

The *Dallas Morning News* reported a conversation by an anonymous Texas state legislator, who said he had to take bribes from the HUD and savings and

---

103 *Wall Street Journal*, October 26, 1992, letter to the editor by Congressman Gonzalez.

104 *New York Times* November 9, 1989.

105 Gonzalez moved up to the chairmanship of the House Banking Committee in 1989 after his predecessor, Fernand St. Germain (Rhode Island) lost his re-election bid because of investigations into his cozy deals with Savings and Loan lobbyists.

106 Successor agency to the Federal Home Loan Bank Board (FHLBB).

loan crowd because he needed the money to maintain his life style on a legislator's salary. He reportedly stated: "It's hard to be pious because in all honesty I could use the money. Honesty doesn't pay."

My CIA contacts described a well-publicized area of the savings and loan corruption in Dallas apartment units along Interstate 30, running east to Lake Ray Hubbard. Hundreds of apartments were built for which there was no demand, no rentals, and no sales. Money was made through land flips and shoddy construction. Some apartment buildings were shown as completed even though the plumbing and other necessities had not been installed. Covert CIA proprietary operations were involved in this scheme that defrauded the American public.

**CALIFORNIA INVOLVEMENT IN THE GREATEST FINANCIAL DEBACLE EVER PERPETRATED**

Corrupt California politics made the Lincoln debacle possible. The California General Services Department (and the California Department of Savings and Loans) obstructed the investigation of Lincoln's corrupt practices, rendering administrative decisions resulting in the loss of almost a quarter billion dollars in savings of the elderly.

In California, Chapter 11[107] judicial corruption was especially acute. California was the state producing numerous attorneys and prosecutors that played a key role in some of the scandals described within these pages. The Justice Department's scheme to silence me used California attorneys, law firms, and state judges, augmented by California-based U.S. district court judges and justices. In this way they joined the conspiracy of criminality I sought to expose.

Many on the Reagan-Bush team were from California, including Earl Brian (of Inslaw fame), Edwin Meese (the U.S. Attorney involved in many of the scandals described within these pages), J. Lowell Jensen (part of the Inslaw scandal yet to be described), and Senator Alan Cranston.

Numerous California officials and friends of California Governor George Deukmejian, mostly attorneys, were heavily involved in these scandals. A Keating enterprise, TCS, made political contributions totaling $48,000 to Deukmejian's campaigns. Keating paid over $189,000 to Deukmejian, in addition to the nearly one million given to California Senator Cranston's interests. Over 23,000 California investors were seriously harmed, as they purchased $250 million in uninsured bonds (most investors thought they were government insured) after California regulators approved their sales, knowing the corporation was insolvent. Many of these elderly people lost their life savings and their sole means of financial support.

In November 1984 Lawrence Taggart, while a California Savings and Loan Commissioner, rendered official decisions allowing Lincoln to continue their fraudulent schemes, causing thousands of investors to lose their life savings. On December 7, 1984, three days before a crucial deadline that nobody was supposed to know about except highest-level federal regulators, Taggart gave Lincoln approval to move almost a billion dollars to its subsidiaries. Taggart then left to became a director of TCS. But records showed Taggart was already

107 Reference to Chapter 11 should be considered reference to other bankruptcy chapters, especially Chapter 13.

hired by TCS at that time. On January 1, 1985, Taggart left his California position, responsible for regulating savings and loans, to work full-time as TCS's highest salaried executive. Additionally, he was to receive half of the after-tax profits earned by the consulting department he headed, and other perks. Three weeks later, Lincoln bought $2.89 million worth of TCS common stock.[108]

Barbara Thomas, a former SEC commissioner, reportedly called the SEC to act as a character witness for Keating during its investigation. Gonzalez said his staff's investigation revealed that Ms. Thomas had received a $250,000 loan from Mr. Keating with unusual payback provisions, suggesting a *quid pro quo* arrangement.

Jack Atchison of the auditing firm of Arthur Young & Company was primarily responsible for auditing Lincoln Savings and Loan, and submitting the reports to the government. Atchison sent several letters to three senators saying that Lincoln was a sound institution and that federal regulators were harassing Lincoln executives. Atchison then left his employment with the accounting firm and went to work for Lincoln at a salary exceeding $900,000 a year. The salary far exceeded what the position justified. It was surely another of hundreds of *quid pro quo* agreements in exchange for the sham report showing Lincoln as being solvent and in good financial condition, when actually it was not.

A California Department of Corporations lawyer-regulator issued a strong warning about uninsured bonds sold in Lincoln's offices. But California officials kept the warning quiet, making possible the sale of worthless bonds to thousands of California investors.

California Assemblyman Patrick Nolan received large financial contributions from Keating after Nolan sponsored legislation removing investment restrictions on state-chartered institutions. More dirty California politics followed. In 1983 I notified Governor Deukmejian, California Attorney General Van De Camp, and numerous state legislators, of the involvement of state judges in seeking to silence my exposure of criminal activities. Instead of investigating the charges and taking corrective action, they protected the judges after I filed civil rights actions in federal court.

California officials denied state examiners and legislative investigators access to records, stating there was high danger of asbestos contamination where the records were stored. Possibly twenty years residence in the building might constitute a danger, but certainly not ten minutes to pick up the files! The building owner denied there was any danger:[109] "They [the records] could have been picked up any time in the last 200 days. They knew there was no problem [of asbestos]."

Assemblywoman Delaine Eastin of the California House Banking Committee stated that subpoenas would be necessary in the Lincoln case to obtain the records from the California Department of Corporations and the California Department of Savings and Loans. Officials under Governor Deukmejian refused to turn over the records, knowing that they contained evidence of California politicians' involvement in the savings and loan scandal. California and Arizona committees

---

108 TCS was losing $70,000 a month and was basically insolvent, paying $2.89 million for a 24 percent ownership of a company with less than $100,000 of solvency.

109 *San Francisco Chronicle* November 1, 1989.

conducted interim hearings dealing mostly in trivia, in that way protecting California officials implicated in the savings and loan scandal.

Both U.S. senators from California, Alan Cranston and Pete Wilson, received money from Keating to block the actions by federal regulators. Wilson received over $75,000 from Keating and received large financial contributions within two months of his election to the U.S. Senate, holding the record for the amount of political contributions in 1990, according to the *San Francisco Chronicle* and *San Francisco Examiner*.

Part of the money, often the life's savings and means of economic survival, lost by investors, went to bribe U.S. senators and representatives who were protecting the crooks in the savings and loans. Widows, retired persons, many of them elderly, testified before a House Banking Committee on November 14, 1989, that they lost their entire life's savings, blaming California Senator Alan Cranston and other members of Congress for their losses. Many, unaware they were uninsured, invested their life's savings in the over $300 million in junk bonds after Cranston and other members of Congress blocked the actions of government inspectors and regulators.

What should have been golden years for thousands of retirees, especially in California, turned into abject poverty, compliments of California regulators and members of Congress, who took bribes to prevent exposure and closure of the corrupt practices of Lincoln Savings and Loan, Keating, and others.

**A FEW EXCEPTIONS**

There were a few members of Congress who spoke out on the rampant criminality in the deregulated savings and loan scandal. Representative Jim Leach told a panel of journalists (May 1989), "You have the opportunity to hold your Legislative Branch accountable, and perhaps bring it down." Referring to the coverup by the government regulatory agency that permitted the corruption to continue, Leach stated: "This Bank Board did the opposite of making timely warnings. It tried to put people to sleep while a fire was raging."

Attorney Joseph Cotchett of Burlingame, California, representing many of the elderly who were swindled in the Lincoln bonds, described the obstructionist tactics by California officials: "And now we have reached the 1,000th coincidence in this case."

**CAN THE MONEY BE RECOVERED?**

Federal Deposit Insurance Corporation's Chairman, L. William Seidman, told of the hopelessness of recovering the huge losses. He warned that the amount of money recovered from anyone found guilty of self-dealing and other insider abuses would be small. "The money is long gone, spent," Mr. Seidman said. "We cannot expect any substantial recovery from criminal abuse."

But it could be traced if they wanted to, as I found through CIA and other sources where many of the trusts were located. Whatever the actual immediate figure is, $250 to $500 billion, these figures exceed many times the total amount looted from publicized savings and loans.

My CIA and other contacts, who had key roles in the HUD and savings and loan scandals and some yet to be exposed, helped move the money to secret offshore and domestic banks, trusts, limited partnerships and other financial vehicles. They told me where some of the funds could be located. In later pages, some of these locations are identified.

**HEAVY CIA INVOLVEMENT**

Several well-documented books[110] have been written of the savings and loan debacle. One thing that most of them missed, which I would not have known except for becoming a confidant to several CIA operatives, was the major role played by the CIA in the looting of America's financial institutions. Among the CIA-related savings and loans listed in these books as being part of the looting but not identified as CIA proprietaries were Silverado Bank Savings & Loan (Denver); Aurora Bank (Denver); Indian Springs State Bank (Kansas City, Mo); Red Hill Savings and Loan; and Hill Financial in Red Hill, Pennsylvania. These authors also failed to discover that many of the other savings and loans were often cutouts for the CIA. More about this in later pages.

**SILVERADO BANK SAVINGS & LOAN**

Much has been written about Denver's Silverado Bank Savings & Loan and its most prominent director, Neil Bush, the son of George Bush. But much has remained secret about Silverado. One of the best-kept secrets was that Silverado was a covert CIA operation; that it funded many covert CIA assets; and that many of the huge financial losses were the direct result of CIA activities. It is ironical that Silverado, a CIA proprietary, had as one of its directors the son of former director of the CIA, George Bush. Because of heavy CIA involvement in Silverado, and for other reasons to be covered, Justice Department prosecutors protected the Silverado gang against meaningful prosecution.

Neil Bush played a key role in looting Silverado, receiving only a token reaction from government agencies that kept a lid on Silverado's criminal activities. Interest payments on money borrowed by the United States to pay off the original $2 billion looted from Silverado may cause the cost to the taxpayer to exceed $6 billion, assuming these debts are ever paid off. It required over two hundred sham loans of one million dollars each, not repaid, for these losses to occur. Neil Bush, like Oliver North in the Contra affair, displayed a look of innocence when questioned about his role in this horrendous fraud.

Neil Bush, while in a position of trust on the board of directors, borrowed over $2 million from Silverado, part of which went into a dry hole drilling for oil in an unlikely location. Most of the money went for his salary and personal expenses. He was not so stupid as not to realize the money would never be repaid if that hole did not produce oil. He drilled this hole where it was known there was no oil. But the drilling served as justification for paying himself a large salary and lots of perks, which the ever-benevolent American taxpayers now must pay well into the next century. Bush made no payments on the money he borrowed and no charges were filed by the Justice Department beholden to his father, President George Bush. It paid to have Justice Department personnel in your back pocket.

Two borrowers from Silverado who were partners with Neil Bush, Ken Good and Bill Walters, got away with $130 million in loans from Silverado that were never repaid. Some of this money went to Michael Norton, who later protected them from prosecution when Norton became U.S. Attorney. The Mafia never

---

110 *Inside Job*, Stephen Pizzo, Paul Muolo & Mary Fricker; *Daisy Chain*, James O'Shea.

had it so good.

When the lending institution failed, the taxpayers were stuck with the tab plus associated costs, including interest on the money borrowed to finance this portion of the national debt. The borrowers in the sham transaction, who had good political connections, often purchased the property at pennies on the dollar from the government after the savings and loans were taken over. Before the taxpayer finishes paying, the cost will probably triple. The infamous Silverado Bank Savings & Loan in Denver was one of the key lending institutions involved in these types of scams.

**MEDIA COVERUP**

Investigative reporters for the establishment media in the United States knew for years about the financial debacle, but kept the lid on the scandal. To have removed the lid would have affected them financially, as major advertisers would have been affected financially. In Denver, for example, three newspapers received considerable income from the advertisements of the group heavily involved in the HUD and savings and loan fraud: *Rocky Mountain News*; *Denver Post*, and *Westword*.

**TAXPAYERS'S BILL: OVER $200,000,000,000**

The greatest financial debacle ever inflicted in the history of civilization is causing American taxpayers to be saddled with a debt that has been estimated as high as 200 *billion* dollars, including interest, an amount far exceeding America's cost of fighting World War II. Probably this large indebtedness will never be paid off. And this is only the savings and loan fraud. Many other corrupt financial scams are pulled on the American public, including HUD, Chapter 11, and others yet to be described. This fraud, and the missing money which no one has sought, requires the American people to pay huge tax increases, and threatens the continuation of basic social programs.

Very little attention has been given to the losses suffered by those people who owned stock in the savings and loans, including the retired people who had their entire savings in worthless stocks, that no longer provided dividend income.

**WHERE WERE THE FBI, JUSTICE DEPARTMENT AND OTHER FEDERAL CHECKS AND BALANCES?**

A good question would be: Where were the hundreds of FBI and Justice Department investigators during this massive fraud inflicted upon the American people? The criminal activities were too extensive for them not to know of their existence. With its many connections within the United States, one could also ask where the CIA was during all this? The fact is, they did know. Later pages will help to explain how these criminal enterprises are linked together, and how people in control of our checks and balances were implicated in them.

A California banking investigator, Richard Newsom, testified that he went to the FBI in July 1988, after he found evidence of serious criminal activities in the savings and loan industry. He testified that he had found that the parent company of Lincoln Savings and Loan funneled over $800,000 to Senator Alan Cranston, and that "the stuff was too hot." The FBI and Department of Justice refused to take any action on the reported corruption. As is shown throughout these pages, the Justice Department's gang of attorneys, including their FBI

Division, are most noted among insiders as being heavily involved in hard-core obstruction of justice when federal officials are implicated.

**JUSTICE DEPARTMENT PROTECTION OF KINGPINS AND WRIST SLAPPING OF THEIR UNDERLINGS**

James Metz, listed as a majority owner of Silverado Savings & Loan, pled guilty (October 16, 1992) to taking $100,000 of savings and loan funds for personal use, and received a six-month sentence in a half-way house. This sentence permitted him to work as president of Richmond Homes and be home during the day, requiring only that he sleep at the location at Colfax and Fillmore Streets in Denver. This token judgment ignored the two billion dollars looted with his help from Silverado. My CIA contacts stated Metz was one of many CIA assets in the Denver area.

David Mandarich was indicted for illegal contributions, of which Michael Norton, U.S. Attorney in Denver, was the major recipient. Since Norton was the primary recipient of the money, he had to stand aside and have Marvin Collins, U.S. Attorney from Texas, act as special prosecutor (directed by Norton) to prosecute the case. Mandarich took the fall for the many other big names but was protected by U.S. Attorney Collins, who deliberately presented a weak case to the jury. U.S. District Judge Richard Matsch then assisted in the coverup by dismissing the charges.

Justice Department prosecutors waited until the statute of limitations had run out for charging Neil Bush and others of the Denver gang before filing nominal charges against Silverado's James Metz and Michael Wise. Corruption and coverup in the Denver area was orchestrated by U.S. Attorney Michael Norton and Assistant U.S. Attorney Gregory Graff in Denver. Investigation of key players would have implicated the CIA and risked exposing White House and other politicians involved in the savings and loan crimes (among others yet to be described).

**COMING DOWN HARD ON SCAPEGOATS**

Many of those charged and prosecuted by Justice Department attorneys in the savings and loan fraud were outside directors of savings and loans, in honorary positions with no knowledge of or control in the institution's activities. By seeking to put these people in prison, Justice Department prosecutors were protecting the kingpins that continued to inflict great financial harm upon the American public. By indicting these people, the prosecutors misled the public into thinking that justice was being done.

**THE FRAUD DIDN'T STOP**

The fraud by the Denver group inflicted billions of dollars in direct losses upon the American people. But it didn't end there. The same Denver group and others, who brought about the collapse of the savings and loan industry by their corrupt activities, used their Washington influence to buy back properties and other assets from Resolution Trust Corporation at ten and twenty cents on the dollar. They made money bringing down the savings and loans and made money buying the assets back, with the help of the same Washington gang. MDC bought from the RTC $750 million in loans that they had obtained from Silverado for $150 million, making a $600 million profit, and defrauding Silverado out of $600 million. This was not mentioned in the investigation of that savings and loan.

**CENTRAL INTELLIGENCE AGENCY INVOLVEMENT**

An article in *Penthouse*[111] detailed the CIA involvement in fleecing financial institutions. Entitled: *The Banks and the CIA, Cash and Carry*, it carried the subtitle, "How Agency rogues fleeced financial institutions to help create one of the greatest scandals in U.S. History." The article, describing the looting of banks and savings and loans by companies fronting for the Central Intelligence Agency, stated in part:

> *Agency rogues fleeced financial institutions to help create one of the greatest scandals in U.S. history...free-lance C.I.A. operatives—in the course of carrying out covert operations, fleeced America's financial institutions....The C.I.A., it was claimed, sanctioned...pulling money out of federally insured financial institutions to fund covert activities, particularly arms deals.*

The article went on to say how Congress had shut off funding needed by the CIA for its covert operations, and how the CIA underground smuggled drugs into the country and looted banks and savings and loans. It further described how the CIA covert operations went underground when President Jimmy Carter ordered disbanding of its covert operations in the late 1970s. The article described how President Reagan's 1981 inauguration reinvigorated the covert CIA operations. Denied funds by Congress, the covert CIA network carried out unlawful and clandestine activities throughout the United States and overseas. These activities violated the CIA charter and were criminal acts.

The *Houston Post* started a series of articles in 1991 revealing connections between the CIA, organized crime, and the savings and loan scandal. Investigative reporter Pete Brewton left the *Houston Post* after pressure was put upon him to withhold key facts. In October 1992 his book was published: *The Mafia, the CIA, and George Bush-The Untold Story of America's Greatest Financial Debacle.*

My investigative activities brought me into contact with deep-cover intelligence agency personnel who revealed to me the part played by the CIA in looting the savings and loans and other financial institutions. In the following pages this relationship is explored.

**SECRET CRIMES BY THE CIA AGAINST AMERICA**

As described in detail in subsequent pages, commencing in 1990 I became a confidant to many former deep-cover CIA and DEA personnel. One of these was Gunther Russbacher, whose father was a former German intelligence officer during World War II. Russbacher held many sensitive positions within the covert segment of the Central Intelligence Agency and was involved in deep cover operations. More is said about Russbacher in later pages, but reference is made to him and some of the CIA activities that he related to me in detail over a four year period.

Russbacher's key covert position within the CIA took him far beyond the limited knowledge many CIA personnel have of CIA operations. The Agency tries to limit knowledge of overall operations by compartmentalizing operations

111 September 1989.

and limiting the knowledge that any one participant has of the overall game plan. But Russbacher's high position within the Agency made him privy to a vast number of secret CIA operations.

Russbacher revealed to me the role played by the CIA in the savings and loan and HUD scandals. He had been with the CIA for over two decades and had been trained by the CIA to operate covert financial operations under various CIA programs, including Operation Cyclops. As he developed knowledge and expertise, the CIA had him organize and operate many CIA proprietary financial institutions.

Russbacher and other deep-cover sources gave me innermost secrets of how the CIA looted America's financial institutions, how the money was laundered, the criminal elements with whom the CIA acted, and where some of the money ended up. These CIA operatives stated how the operations worked and the names of some of the covert CIA financial institutions, fronts, and cutouts. They gave me blank checks, letterheads, copies of corporate filings, and other writings supporting these statements.

For the next few years I conducted hundreds of hours of questioning with Russbacher and other CIA and insider contacts, receiving details of the most secret CIA operations in which he participated during the last three decades. He gave sworn statements during the three years before the first publication of this book. I checked his credibility as a CIA operative with other CIA sources. Most, if not all of what he stated, and what is included in these pages, I believe to be true.

Some banks and savings and loans became fronts for CIA covert operations and often made phony loans, phony appraisals, and phony sales, generating enormous sums of money for clandestine CIA activities.

Russbacher told me that the CIA had given him over forty aliases. During the first two years of his affiliation he was a contract employee of the CIA. Then, in 1965 he entered the United States Navy and was assigned to the Office of Naval Intelligence (ONI). During all but three years of his CIA affiliation, he was in Covert Operations, Consular Operations, and other branches of covert government service. He did two tours of duty in Vietnam and Laos and was an unofficial prisoner during the second tour of duty in Southeast Asia. The U.S. government didn't list its covert personnel.[112]

In a December 6, 1992, sworn declaration, Russbacher described to me part of the CIA operations in which he was involved:

*It is my intent to clarify, once and for all, how the Intelligence Services of the United States of America, have used the savings and loan (Thrift Institutions) to fund their respective covert operations, both within the United States, and abroad. The scheme creating an unlimited money supply was devised after the inside knowledge of how the Federal Reserve operated became known to operatives and case officers.*

*A monetary growth medium had to be found which would enable the Agency (CIA) to have access to an unlimited supply of funds with which*

---

112 His military numbers included 54 329 963; and his various Social Security numbers included 440-40-1417, 471-50-1578, 441-44-1417, and 447-42-0007.

*covert operations might be funded. The key was... "How to utilize/capitalize on the Federal Credit Programs." Careful analysis and study of the Federal Credit Act provided the proper forum.*

*It was decided that small to medium businesses of the Proprietary Operations Unit would be well on line to provide these expert services. Soon, various businesses, owned and operated by either the Agency or utilizing a front directorship, began to deposit funds (legal tender and bogus bearer bonds) into the selected Thrifts. The loading of these institutions was always accomplished with the help of inside information, gained and acquired by and through information garnered by the FSLIC and their respective service members.*

*It was decided that various front organizations would deposit millions of dollars into these selected thrifts, and that such deposits would permit the depositors to make collateral loans for eight-five percent (85%) of the deposit value. The disparity of deposit and secured loan was the carrot for the ailing financial institution. The Agency, through its Proprietary Operations Division, was quick to recognize the Fed. Lending to Deposit Rate for Thrifts, which in turn stated that every dollar taken in on deposit would permit the Thrift to borrow up to seven dollars from the Federal Reserve. It was a lucrative enticement to Agency Operations. The loaned funds were soon gathered from all regional affiliates, and channeled to fund the Charters for our own Thrift institutions. The stage was set. It was merely a question of time until we began re-investing our portfolio.*

*Over a period of approximately 3 years, more than 35 federally insured "Agency Thrifts" were brought on line. Each of the financial institutions was funded in part by Certificates of Deposit (from our own front companies), and various other instruments of financial obligation. Sometimes, bogus (duplicate) Bearer Bonds were used to insure sufficient start-up capital. Slowly, these institutions began making large loans to other Agency front businesses. Many of them flourished regardless of the initial intent to strip them systematically of their assets. Those which failed to provide an unending "money funnel" were soon brought to Court, pursuant to Chapter 11, of the United States Bankruptcy Laws. Prior to permitting entry into such proceedings all visual assets were stripped and/or removed from the insolvent companies.*

*The United States Bankruptcy Courts, as well as the assigned United States Trustees, would permit us to re-channel the obvious assets prior to satisfying the demands of the legal creditors. It must be stated that in the initial stages of such operations there were no legal creditors as the entire operation was an "in-house operation," and subsequently not issues or obligations traded on the open market. Such practices were soon discarded as the volume of the operation was not able to keep out private and corporate investors. Many of the removed assets were sold to other agency operations, which in turn sold said assets to other linked dealers.*

*Brokerage companies of dubious repute were soon spin-offs of the mega industry. In order to provide continuity as well as expert disclosure, I shall reference the history of the funding of Hill Financial, as well as*

*Red Hill Savings and Loan; the establishment of the National Brokerage Companies; the creation of National Financial Services Corporation; National Leasing Corporation; National Realty Corporation; Crystal Shores Development Corporation; Crystal Shores Financial Corporation, and Clayton Financial Planning Corporation. It is imperative that the continuity and creation are uninterrupted.*

*During my time of service within the Proprietary Operations Division of the Central Intelligence Agency, I was approached while using the assigned name of Robert Andrew Walker to initiate contact with a nationally prominent brokerage house. (It must be noted that I had been a part of such brokerage facility under another alias/code name.) I followed the order and began a transfer study, which in turn was to initiate and facilitate the founding of a new savings and loan facility in Red Hill, Pennsylvania. All transfer studies were accurate and the new S&L was soon brought on line. It was funded with corporate paper, other private and corporate bonds/certificates, and other financial obligations.*

*The founding fathers of Hill Financial were Donald Lutz and Robert A. Walker, a/k/a/ Gunther Karl Russbacher. The financial package of the S&L was born from funds derived from SBF Corporation. The new S&L flourished, making numerous loans to the economically depressed local and regional area. These notes were in part non-secured, and no payoff was anticipated from these local trades. We began to diversify, using the Federal Credit Act to gain and secure additional federal funds, by securing other deposits from Agency Operations. Our deposit portfolio was extended on a ratio of 4.3 to 1 and thereby provided considerable additional loan coverage to other more open and more lucrative markets. We began to explore bringing on line additional feeder organizations which could/would add to our real deposit base. The decision for such action was taken after I received orders to charter a brokerage company in the state of Missouri. We, the directors of Red Hill S&L held a closed meeting, wherein it was decided that I would become Chairman of the Board, and elevating Donald Lutz to the presidency. Pledging my continued assistance, I was permitted, nay ordered, to set up shop in St. Louis, Missouri, where I dropped the name Robert A. Walker, and became Emery J. Peden.*

*Within three months I was a registered broker of the Prudential Insurance Company of America. Soon after learning the business, I resigned my position and began a long term relationship with Connecticut Mutual Life Insurance Company. I had an office in Clayton, Missouri, and soon made a significant impact on the financial and insurance industry.*

*<u>END OF SEGMENT ONE (1) of the deposition of Gunther K. Russbacher</u>.*

*I do certify the information contained in this segment of my deposition to be true and correct. Such certification is given under the penalty of perjury. Further, affiant/deponent sayeth not.*

*Gunther Karl Russbacher, deponent in cause.*

*Dated: December 6, 1992.*

Russbacher incorporated and operated a number of covert CIA proprietaries in the United States from the late 1970s to 1986. His main headquarters was in Missouri, but his CIA proprietaries had offices throughout the United States, with heavy involvement in Dallas and Denver, where much of the HUD and savings and loan looting took place.

Russbacher identified as CIA proprietaries or assets numerous savings and loans, including Aurora Bank in the Denver area, Silverado Bank Savings & Loan, Red Hill Savings and Loan, Hill Financial, Indian Springs State Bank, and many others. He described the flow of money from, for instance, Silverado Bank Savings & Loan to start up Hill Financial and Red Hill Savings and Loan. Much of the data that he and other deep-cover CIA operatives gave me still has to be analyzed.

Russbacher made reference to CIA contract agents he encountered, including Heinrich Rupp and Richard Brenneke who worked with the CIA at Aurora Bank in Denver and elsewhere, and Anthony Russo at Indian Springs State Bank in Kansas City.

Russbacher described the links between CIA proprietaries and organized crime and how the CIA worked with the group in Denver, looting the HUD program and savings and loans of billions of dollars. He described the corrupt practices of groups in the Denver area, such as MDC Holdings, Richmond Homes, Mizel Development, and their nearly one hundred subsidiaries, partnerships and other legal entities.

Describing his role in two of the savings and loans, Russbacher stated: "I held the position of Chairman of the Board [Of Red Hill Savings & Loan and Hill Financial]. Let's back up here, and erase that last thing. Robert Andrew Walker[113] held the position of Chairman of the Board." Russbacher used the CIA-provided-alias of Walker for those positions.

Russbacher described the massive corruption associated with the new Denver International Airport that included bribes, land flips, and sham loans.

## TYPICAL CIA PROPRIETARY OPERATION

An example of how the CIA operated secret companies in the United States is seen from the companies that Russbacher operated for the CIA. Russbacher incorporated and operated many CIA proprietaries, hiding the CIA ownership by showing the stock owned by CIA-related personnel. At the top of the group of companies that Russbacher operated for the CIA was National Brokerage Companies, a general partnership located in Missouri. Under National Brokerage Companies were a number of other general partnerships and corporations. The stock in these corporations was held in several names, including Gunther Russbacher and his CIA-provided aliases, Emery Peden and Robert A. Walker.

The various companies and corporations were controlled by covert CIA personnel installed as directors. In 1986 the NBC name was changed to National Brokerage Companies International (NBCI).

Russbacher gave me the names of many financial institutions that he said were CIA proprietaries. He described in great detail his role in Red Hill Savings & Loan and Hill Financial in Red Hill, Pennsylvania. He named other CIA

---

113 One of the aliases provided to Gunther Russbacher by the CIA.

proprietary financial institutions, including National Brokerage Companies; National Fiduciary Trust Company; National Financial Services; Crystal Shores Development; and Clayton Financial Planning, which had several divisions, including Agean Lines and Europa Link. Europa Link allegedly owned W.P.R. Petroleum International, which used leased oil tankers for oil delivery to major refineries.

Also, Badner Bank, which funded Germania Savings and Loan; Commerce Bank of Missouri; Carondolet Savings and Loan in St Louis; Mega Bank Group which owned First State System and operated in about eighteen states; Shalimar Perfumes; Shalimar Armaments; Shalimar Chemical Laboratories; R & B Weapons Systems International, Inc.; Pratislaja Brenneke Munitions Amalgam; KRB Weapons Delivery System; National Realty; and others.

Russbacher said that National Brokerage Companies (NBC, Inc.) was incorporated in Missouri in 1980, and that it was the parent company for many others. He said part of its initial funding came from Silverado Bank Savings & Loan via Red Hill Savings and Loan and Hill Financial. Among its subsidiaries were National Leasing; National Realty (under National Leasing), and Crystal Shores Financial Services.

A division under Clayton Financial Planning was Commercial Federal Savings and Loan, which had connections to National Fiduciary Trust Companies. A division under Clayton Financial Planning was Corondolet Savings and Loan, which also had financial connections to National Fiduciary Trust Companies.

Russbacher stated that under National Fiduciary trust Companies were Badner Bank and International Commerce Bank Holding company. Under Badner Bank were various airlines, including Zantop Airlines; Tower Airlines; Southern Air Transport; Apollo Air; Virgin Air, and RAW World Service.

Under International Commerce Bank Holding Company were Baja Enterprises; property at Cabo San Lucas; Hotel Cabo San Lucas; and Cabo Airport.

Russbacher described the practice of the CIA having their own banks as proprietaries, and named, among others, Commerce Bank of Missouri, and particularly the one in Clayton, naming as a CIA asset the manager, John Bittlecomb. He described the CIA operation known as Valley Bank in Phoenix, which he said played a key role in moving money for the October Surprise operation (and described by former Mossad agent Ari Ben-Menashe in his book, *Profits of War*).

There were several European holdings, including Shalimar Perfumes, Shalimar Arms, and Shalimar Chemical Laboratories. Under Shalimar Armaments was R & B Weapons Systems International, Incorporated. Under R & B were two companies, Pratislaja Brenneke Munitions Amalgam and R.B. Weapons Delivery Systems. It all sounds rather complex, and a further explanation is follows.

**REMOVING HUGE SUMS OF MONEY OVERSEAS**

Russbacher described how the CIA moved large quantities of money from U.S. financial proprietaries during the last few years to off-shore corporations and banks, including those in the Antilles and the Cayman Islands. "The Agency is deadly afraid of exposure within the United States," Russbacher said, "and they have begun to siphon off large and tremendous sums of money to foreign accounts. It must be borne in mind that in the last three years there has been a systematic removal of funds and capital assets from these [CIA] corporations."

Russbacher described how the CIA used the savings and loan institutions to fund their covert operations in the United States and abroad and add to the massive amount of funds secreted in foreign financial institutions. Parallel operations were run by different CIA divisions and directorates, using code names to identify the various operations. Included in the operations affecting financial institutions were Operation Gold Bug, Operation Cyclops, Operation Interlink, Operation Woodsman, Operation Fountain Pen, Operation Thunder, Operation Blue Thunder, and Operation Moth.

**OPERATION WOODSMAN**

Operation Woodsman was a CIA operation that targeted specific companies, forcing the owners out and taking over the assets. Russbacher described several of these operations in which he himself was directly involved. Information used to carry out Operation Woodsman, such as the financial condition of targeted companies, could be obtained by the CIA through a database called the Black Flag file, which is located on a Cray computer in Washington and which is accessed through a government Sentry Terminal (government-secure computer). The Cray computer also contains a list of federal judges, trustees, law firms, and attorneys who covertly work to carry out Justice Department and CIA activities (such as the San Francisco law firm used against me in the sham California action).

**REFERRING TO JUDICIAL INVOLVEMENT**

Russbacher repeated what he had described to me during the past few years about the role of federal judges in the corruption: "More than fifty percent of the judges are compromised through secret bribes or retainers." The bribes take many forms. Sometimes through gambling chips at Atlantic City and Las Vegas casinos, in the form of gratuities, sometimes through second and third parties, inheritances, anything that will whitewash the funds in the property that is given to the judges or trustees. Russbacher stated that these funds are often hidden in offshore financial accounts, adding:

> *Let's say it is property or stock certificates. We'll have phony documentation set up and put in place and show where the stock certificates or the property or the legacy came from. Even if we have to create our own trust with which to do it. It's not like we don't have legally capable counsel available. Now understand this too: these judges received this heavy money regardless of the fact that they have cases pending or not. They get paid whether they do something for us or not.*

Russbacher elaborated on the procedure for gaining access to the Cray computer in Washington, telling how the identification number is first entered and then the security code.

Russbacher stated that he learned about Operation Woodsman when he was assigned to CIA headquarters at Langley, Virginia. "Every damn thing, every crooked thing that the DOJ has done," he said, "involving any and all law firms, is registered under the code name that I have given you."

Russbacher continued:

> *Our intent was to take over the tangible assets of the operating license and licenses, we go through the predetermination hearing with the judge,*

> *trustee and the simple debtors, and then we buy time to reorganize the lines, and transport capabilities. In other words, we use them for ourselves, these little feeder airlines, we try to keep them alive anywhere from six months to a year and a half. Slowly we set our operations and leverage to where the existing financial records are changed to reflect prior debt encumbrance. We falsify the records. We take an existing carrier, their routes, their equipment, push our schedule and freight manifest through their licenses, and then we .. we have no interest in developing a good business or making a go of it, out of the indentured one that we have taken over.*

Russbacher described how the system uses attorney spotters throughout the United States to identify companies that have large equities but have cash problems. CIA proprietaries buy up the company's receivables and indebtedness, and force the company to sign papers making them susceptible to immediate takeover if their financial situation deteriorates. The CIA proprietary then acts to make this happen, after which the owners lose control. Chapter 11 would be included in Operation Woodsman.

The CIA may loot the company and then put it into Chapter 7 or 11 bankruptcy courts, where several options are available to make off with the assets or to have the indebtedness discharged. Russbacher told how the CIA has about seventy percent of the trustees and many of the federal judges in bankruptcy courts on retainer. He also elaborated upon the practice known as "drop-offs" that force companies into Chapter 11, involving companies with valuable assets that have a cash crunch.

Russbacher described some of the company takeovers in which he was directly involved, naming Midway Airlines, Southern Air Transport, and Frontier Airlines. In some cases, the targeted company would be liquidated and, as in the case of Frontier Airlines, the aircraft would go to a CIA proprietary. In Frontier's example, most of the aircraft went to the CIA proprietary, Southwest Airlines. In the case of Southern Air Transport, the targeted corporation was kept as a CIA proprietary.

According to Russbacher, referring to the CIA takeover of Chicago-based Midway Airlines during the last year of its existence, Midway Airlines was first targeted in 1986 because it had a high debt-to-asset ratio, making the airline vulnerable to the takeover scheme of Operation Woodsman. CIA assets began purchasing Midway's debt with the intention of taking over the company and then liquidating the assets in Chapter 7.

Russbacher told how Midway tried to get absorbed by another carrier, Northwest, and that the CIA blocked it, as it wanted Midway's aircraft. The CIA got Justice Department attorneys and the IRS to take actions against the airline through criminal and tax proceedings through mostly bogus criminal and contempt charges, explaining:

> *We put together a bunch of phony allegations, mismanagement of funds, possible fraud. Ninety-five percent of it is totally untrue and unfounded, but the five percent that does remain true and factual are at the forefront, and you push those. Some of the directorships on the Board of Directors were subverted and suborned to CIA tactics.*

The plan by Northwest Airlines to absorb Midway fell through after both Midway and Northwest were pressured by government agencies acting on behalf of the CIA. This scheme caused Midway to go out of business, so the airline's Boeing 737 aircraft went to another covert CIA operation: Southwest Airlines.

Russbacher described similar CIA takeovers which developed into larger companies instead of being liquidated for their assets. These included Southern Air Transport (which started out as Savannah Charter Airlines); Central Airlines of Fort Worth; Allegheny Airlines; and others.

Russbacher explained that some of the directors had their own businesses and that it was easy for the CIA with its control of other government agencies to put pressure on them, adding: "They were not influenced; they were dictated to."

I asked: "How could they be dictated to?" Russbacher replied: "The director, who has other business interests and probably a business of his own, suddenly finds himself in a financial quandary due to various tactics used by the CIA. We put him under our thumb. If he decides not to play ball, we threaten him with criminal charges."

This tactic was used against Charles W. White of Houston, Texas, who was in partnership with CIA-related Jim Bath. When Bath wanted to withdraw $450,000 from an company composed of private investors and use it in a CIA-related operation, and White refused, the power of the courts and covert agencies were misused against White. After many lawsuits, White was financially destroyed.

Russbacher stated that Justice Department attorneys worked hand in hand with the CIA in Operation Woodsman and other schemes, and that the Agency not only has its own private attorneys but "government attorneys on staff as well as the judges. It's a fixed deck all the way across."

Russbacher described another CIA takeover: "We did the same thing with hotels," describing how the CIA took over the Intercontinental Hotels (IH) chain from Pan American Corporation through its CIA front, Global Hotel Management out of Basel, Switzerland.

Among the airlines that were liquidated after acquisition were Central Airlines out of Fort Worth (the agency's first airline acquisition under Operation Woodsman) and Frontier Airlines of Denver. Russbacher described how the CIA created so much friction between Frontier and United Airlines, who had proposed taking over Frontier, that the deal fell through. These problems included union and other problems. The Boeing 737s then went to another CIA proprietary, Southwest Airlines.

Russbacher stated that one reason Southwest Airlines was making money (when all the other airlines were losing money) was that the airline has significant income from CIA-generated business that shows as income on its records, but the source of the income was bogus.

## CONNECTIONS BETWEEN THE CIA AND THOSE LOOTING AMERICA'S FINANCIAL INSTITUTIONS

Russbacher described the relationship between the CIA proprietaries and the Keating group, adding, "The Keating group is a very small group. There is a much larger group that we [CIA] dealt with, of which Keating was only a part." In response to my question as to why the Keating group would work with the CIA, Russbacher stated, "To keep the heat off their backs for one. And number two, some of the companies that were involved were actually proprietary operations."

Russbacher made reference to Anthony Russo, an officer in Indian Springs State Bank, who had financial interest in a CIA proprietary airline, Global International Airways. In 1982 the airline owned by Farhad Azima, an Iranian-born naturalized U.S. citizen, had a fleet of 14 jetliners, making flights to remote airstrips in Central America, carrying military equipment outbound from the United States and often carrying drugs on the return flights. Global flew shipments for CIA operative Edwin Wilson and his company, Egyptian-American Transport and Services Corporation (Eatsco). Well-known national figures involved with Global included Thomas Clines, Theodore Shackley, Richard Secord, Hussein Salem, and others.

**BOGUS BEARER BONDS**

Russbacher described another ongoing CIA operation inflicting hundreds of millions of dollars of losses upon U.S. financial institutions. In this operation, CIA proprietaries obtained loans from various financial institutions on the basis of pledged bearer bonds, all of which were bogus. After obtaining the loans, some CIA proprietaries looted the assets and then filed Chapter 7 or 11 in federal courts where they had control over bankruptcy judges and trustees and were represented by covert Justice Department and/or CIA law firms or fronts.

Russbacher was cautious in divulging the secrets of CIA operations, even though he was trying to blow the whistle on some of its worst and most damaging activities against the United States. As time passed and with my constant probing into different areas of CIA activities, and as Russbacher learned that other CIA operatives gave me information which he had withheld from me, he gradually gave me more data. In early 1993, as I learned the operational names of many of the CIA operations from other sources, including Trenton Parker and Michael Riconosciuto, Russbacher opened up and gave me code names and data. He stated that different divisions or groups within the CIA ran parallel operations and had different names for similar activities. Some of them include the following:

**OPERATION INTERLINK**

Operation Interlink (IL) was the code name for an operation involving financial institutions, whose goal was to raise money for covert CIA activities, and laundering the funds into secret CIA offshore bank accounts.

**OPERATION CYCLOPS**

Operation Cyclops was the name used by the Pegasus unit of the CIA and was an overview over most other Pegasus operations. It included all types of covert financial operations including proprietaries involved in the HUD and the savings and loan programs, and bogus bearer bonds.

**OPERATION MOTH (MH)**

Operation Moth was one of the Agency's names for the operation involved in the savings and loan fraud.

**OPERATION GOLD BUG (GB)**

Operation Gold Bug involved the overall scheme of generating money through various financial activities. Under Operation Gold Bug were a number of other operations. Operation Gold Bug was the development of national and international financial programs to develop sources of income which would be available on a regular basis to support and carry out covert CIA activities domestically and internationally.

Russbacher incorporated and operated over a dozen CIA proprietaries, and outlined the tactics used to loot companies of their assets. When used against savings and loans, Russbacher's section of the CIA gave it the name of Operation Moth. The highly secret Pegasus group within the CIA gave this program the name of Operation Gold Bug. The intent of both groups and operations was to loot the assets of targeted financial or other institutions and wealthy people. The overall operation that targeted other companies was called Operation Gold Finger.

**OPERATION THUNDER (TD)**

Operation Thunder was another name for a CIA covert operation that included the HUD and savings and loan fraud, bogus bearer bonds, and other financial schemes. Russbacher stated that the home base for Operation Thunder was New Orleans and was initially located in a private CIA proprietary. He stated that today the cover for the operation is Telemark Communications, one of the biggest companies in the United States and a CIA proprietary. As with other CIA proprietaries, the top management consisted of Agency people who had liaison with CIA field people who were contract officers or agents, and particularly attorneys and law firms.

Russbacher described the heading sheet on correspondence pertaining to Operation Thunder. On the very top of the sheet would be the words:

Operations Memorandum.

Classification: Top Secret: SOG-SI/6
Copy Number: 4 [or whatever number of copies were authorized]
SOG/ALPHA/-DETACHMENT TS-TS-Q/SOG-D/F: 701
FP399689
Staging Area: New Orleans, Louisiana

**OPERATION BLUE THUNDER (BT)**

Operation Blue Thunder related to the destruction of institutions, including taking them over or forcing them into Chapters 7 and 11. After taking them over, the CIA would take over the corporation's license rights. Basically, it destroyed companies and picked up the assets at fire sale prices.

**OPERATION FOUNTAIN PEN (FP)**

Operation Fountain Pen started with Bank of Zaire, a CIA proprietary, buying banks, corporations and other financial institutions with bogus bearer bonds, treasury bonds, or duplicate issues.

**BOGUS BEARER BONDS**

Several of the covert CIA operations used bogus bearer bonds that had a twenty or twenty-five year due date and were used as collateral for multi-million-dollar loans. After obtaining the loans and laundering the money into other secret proprietaries or offshore financial vehicles, the companies would often file Chapter 7 or Chapter 11. The lender would then think it was covered by the bonds given as collateral, and they would not find them to be bogus until many years later. In some cases the CIA proprietary would make interest payments on the loans secured by the phony bonds. The primary criminal act in those cases would be using forged certificates to obtain a loan.

## AIDING AND ABETTING BY STATE OFFICIALS

Russbacher stated that in 1986 some of the CIA financial institutions he operated were compromised, that connections between the secret proprietaries and members of Congress were in danger of being exposed, and the decision was made to shut them down. He told how Justice Department and CIA personnel conspired with Missouri officials to remove all traces from the state records that the CIA corporations had been incorporated as Missouri Corporations.

Referring to the shutdown of several CIA proprietaries linked to the 1986 downing of a CIA aircraft over Nicaragua, the famous "Hasenfus" flight, Russbacher stated: "All records that were available to the Department of State or to the [state's] Attorney General's office have been seized or closed to where the public cannot get hold of them."

## MONEY-PATH FOR BRIBING FEDERAL JUDGES, TRUSTEES, LAW FIRMS

I was prompted to ask Russbacher about payoffs to federal judges after private investigator Stewart Webb heard of a bribe connection between U.S. District Judge Sherman Finesilver in Denver and a corporation in Ireland. After he passed the information along to me I questioned some of my CIA contacts to determine if they knew anything of it.

In response to my questions, Russbacher explained the path of money for bribing federal judges, trustees, law firms, and attorneys. Russbacher stated that the money for these payoffs came from a company located in Dublin and incorporated in Ireland, called Shamrock Overseas Disbursement Corporation. Its telephone is listed as Shamrock Overseas Courier Service. The function of this company was to place money at regular intervals into numbered bank accounts for the recipients to draw upon. Russbacher chuckled as he stated that the Chief Executive Officer at Shamrock Overseas Disbursement was the same person with whom he had worked at other CIA proprietaries: Donald Lutz.

Russbacher and Lutz were on the management staff of various CIA proprietaries, including Red Hill Savings and Loan and Hill Financial located at Red Hill, Pennsylvania, and at Silverado Bank Savings & Loan in Denver.

Russbacher stated that the routing of the money funded by Shamrock was "From the Netherlands Antilles. And in turn came from Grand Cayman; that in turn came from the Southern Bank in Florida; that in turn came from Southern Savings and Loan in Illinois; which in turn came from National Brokerage Company."

"Where does the money originally come from? Is it from stolen Chapter 11 assets?" I asked. Russbacher replied, "That's part of it. It is a conglomeration of funds. It is what we call an all-purpose account. Arms shipments, the other stuff [drugs, weapons] that we were transporting back and forth. It is what we call the divisible surplus."

I asked if the federal judges he referred to as recipients of these funds were only Bankruptcy Court Judges, to which Russbacher replied, "No, that's not true. You have to include the DJs [U.S. District Judges] too."

"How is it determined the amount that each judge will get, and what judges are paid off?" I asked. Russbacher replied: "It is predetermined. If you will remember from one of my earlier tapes, I told you that the judges receive their funds regardless of whether they have heard a case in six months or not."

"How do they determine which judges are recipients, what qualifies them to be on the payroll?" Russbacher replied, "The fact that they work hand-in-hand with the trustees, and they grant us full power to basically do what we [CIA] want in Chapter 11, 13, and 7 proceedings."

"Are there any other similar corporations in the United States like Shamrock?"

"No, Rodney, they are all funded from Shamrock. In other words, if you pull the plug on Shamrock, you have it all."

Russbacher explained how the recipients pick up the money. "They can get it overseas and pick it up, or they can go to Toronto and pick it up there, at the Royal Bank of Canada." Russbacher stated, "When they go in to make a withdrawal, they request to see the President or Chief Account officer." Russbacher explained that this scheme is part of Operation Woodsman, explained in earlier pages.

Russbacher explained that the recipient's available funds will be found on the bank's terminal screen and that "all they have to have is the account number. No ID is required. Just give them the account number and the four digit identification number." Russbacher stated that Royal Bank of Canada, Manufacturers Hanover Bank in New York, and Valley Bank in Arizona, cooperate in this scheme.

Russbacher repeated what he had told me in the past: that funds would also be disbursed to the recipient judges, trustees, or law firms at gambling casinos, including MGM, Harrah's and Resort in Atlantic City, and Frontier, Stardust, and Horseshoe in Las Vegas. The CIA gave the money to the casino, which in turn gave gambling chips to the recipients when they arrived, after which the chips are cashed in for money. In some cases the casinos report the money as winnings and income tax withheld.

"Would your knowledge of this operation be because you were with NBC (National Brokerage Company)," I asked.

"Yes, because we made deposits and withdrawals through that route," he replied.[114]

**BLACK FLAG FILE**

Russbacher stated that he had seen the list of recipients in this scheme on the computer database while he was at the CIA headquarters at Langley, explaining that the database is called the Black Flag Files (BFF). He stated that the database is on a Cray computer accessed from any government Sentry terminal by typing in an identification entry number. After a flag shows up on the screen, typing in the access code: 3A46915W.

I often asked Russbacher to accompany these statements with a declaration as to their truthfulness, and I did during this questioning. He had also given me declarations attesting to the truthfulness of written information.

---

114 Russbacher was President of NBC, using the alias of Emery J. Peden, and his former wife, Peggy J. Russbacher, was Executive Vice President. There was a National Brokerage, Incorporated, a National Brokerage Company, and numerous other divisions operated by Russbacher.

Russbacher replied: "Sure. All the information that we have discussed on this date, May 17, 1993, from approximately 2020 hours Central Daylight Time, the declaration made to area code 510-944-1930, Rodney Stich, by Gunther Karl Russbacher, 44840417, Captain USN, is true and correct as to the best of my knowledge and belief."

**WHERE IS THE MONEY?**

Losses of approximately half a **trillion** dollars have been the estimated direct cost of just the savings and loan debacle. But where did the money go? It has never been sought or located. The theft of $2 billion by Lincoln or $2 billion by Silverado is a long way from $200 to $500 billion. Neither Congress nor the Justice Department has made any attempt to determine where this money went. Finding it would relieve the American public of a debt load that is affecting the American economy, resulting in a reduction in benefits to individual Americans, thereby causing a staggering tax burden. There is no way that such a huge sum simply evaporated without a trace.

My CIA sources tell me that many of the funds looted by the CIA, organized crime, and such groups as the Denver group have been hidden in offshore financial institutions. Some of the funds that have gone overseas have returned to the United States through foreign shell corporations, buying up vast quantities of U.S. real estate and assets.

**ONE OF THE MANY WAYS IN WHICH CRIME MONEY IS REPORTEDLY HIDDEN**

Investigator Stewart Webb heard from one of his sources that hundreds of trusts are filed with the state of Colorado that contain huge amounts of money looted from the HUD and savings and loan frauds, and also from drug money laundering. He and Russbacher said many of the trusts were filed in the County Recorders office for Baca County in Southeast Colorado. In seeking further information, I asked another CIA source, Gunther Russbacher, "Do you know anything about the Baca trusts?" He replied, "How in the hell did you find out about those?"

Russbacher was especially well informed. He told me that many of the trusts were set up by Denver attorney Norman Brownstein, a key member of the Denver group involved in the HUD and savings and loan scandals. These trusts were reportedly set up for the benefit of such insiders as Larry Mizel, Leonard Millman, MDC Holdings, Richmond Homes, and hundreds of other related legal holdings.

Most of the actual funds associated with these trusts are reportedly located outside the United States. He said that he himself had filed trusts in Baca County for his children. Russbacher said that the location of the money covered by these trusts, which he stated amounted to billions of dollars, were located in offshore financial institutions.

This money includes the billions of dollars stolen from the HUD and savings and loan programs, the billions looted every year from Chapter 11 assets, drug profits, and the other dirty schemes involving the characters listed within these pages. If this information is correct, and if the sources of hidden money divulged to me by my CIA sources were traced, possibly large amounts of the huge losses inflicted upon the American people could be recovered.

**BILLIONS OF HIDDEN TAXPAYERS' MONEY**

Russbacher had several times stated in response to my questions that many billions of dollars of money obtained by CIA proprietaries from the American public were hidden in offshore financial institutions. In Colorado there are located well over a thousand trusts hiding many billions of dollars looted from the American public.

**CONTINUED LOOTING OF AMERICA**

Many of the same crooks who caused billions of dollars in losses were reaping profits through their inner knowledge and political connections, enabling them to manipulate the agency responsible for selling off assets of the seized savings and loans, the Resolution Trust Corporation (RTC).

While waiting for senate confirmation as Clinton's nominee to head the RTC, Stanley G. Tate, announced that upon being confirmed he would be exposing "ubiquitous mismanagement, waste, and fraud at the RTC." Tate told reporters[115] that he planned to release a 36-page statement during the nomination hearings supporting his charges. Tate had discovered the corruption while holding a temporary position on the board overseeing the RTC.

Senator Donald W. Riegle, Jr., (D-Mich.), one of the many senators who ignored my reports of the corruption in federal government, refused to conduct confirmation hearings for the RTC nominee. While Riegle blocked Tate's confirmation, others were making death threats against the nominee. As if these acts were not enough, anonymous attacks were made upon Tate by RTC employees. Media sources wrote articles intended to block his confirmation. The coordinated campaign succeeded; Tate withdrew his acceptance of the nomination on November 30, 1993. Again, public ignorance permitted the same scum to continue looting America.

**RELIEF FOR FELONS**

The conduct of such savings and loan operators as Don R. Dixon and Edwin T. McBirney caused billions of dollars of losses that the American taxpayers will be paying on for many years. They used taxpayer funds for sexual parties, to hire prostitutes, enjoy lavish life styles, none of which came out of profits. There weren't any. In 1993, McBirney was sentenced to fifteen years in prison and Dixon was sentenced to two consecutive five-year terms.

In July 1994, Justice Department attorneys and a federal judge, Robert Maloney, cut ten years from Dixon's sentence, causing his release that same year, after serving a fraction of his prison sentence. McBirney was scheduled for release shortly thereafter. The excuse used was good behavior. But there isn't much else that can occur in federal prison. It is a standard practice where the CIA or some other government agency is implicated and a defendant protects this relationship, that a reduction in prison sentence is promised and then carried out at a later date when media attention no longer exists.

An inordinate amount of the huge savings and loan losses occurred in Texas, where the RTC recovered only about five cents on every dollar of the losses incurred.[116] Despite the many people committing the fraud, the RTC issued

115 *Associated Press*, December 1, 1993.
116 *New York Times*, July 23, 1994.

only about two dozen subpoenas as part of their investigations, which are necessary to follow the money trail to learn where the money went, such as bribes to politicians, kickbacks, money laundering to off-shore bank accounts. The RTC did not issue any subpoenas in its "investigation" of 86 of 137 failed Texas savings and loans. Comparing this with the investigation into Madison Guaranty Savings and Loan as part of the Whitewater investigation, over 160 grand jury subpoenas were issued solely by special counsel Robert B. Fiske Jr.

## FEEBLE "INVESTIGATIONS"

If the RTC had issued the subpoenas required by the nature of the savings and loan crimes of the 1980s, it is probable that the involvement of the CIA and many political figures would have been identified. Also, the way the RTC handled the sales of the seized savings and loan assets made possible even more looting of the American taxpayers as many of the same crooks purchased the seized real estate for pennies on the dollar.

A *New York Times* article (July 23, 1994) headed, "The R.T.C. let crooked thrift owners get away," stated in part:

> *The failures of the RTC to properly pursue the crooked parties, or to obtain maximum money for the seized thrifts, were too purposeful to be simply gross incompetence or negligence. Because of the involvement of people from both the Republican and Democratic parties, none pursued the needed investigations to determine where the enormous amount of money went in the gory looting of U.S. taxpayers.*

Roger Altman, involved in the Whitewater matter, was Deputy Secretary of the Treasury from April 1993 until March 1994, and within a month of taking that position he reversed the RTC's attempt to get Congress to extend the federal statute of limitations for prosecuting savings and loan wrongdoing. Altman said that the RTC no longer needed the extension, when actually this was obviously not correct, since there was virtually no investigation of the big-time wrongdoers.

Altman commissioned a task force that issued a report to Congress defending the RTC investigations and belittled the loss to the American public by the Texas savings and loans. The *New York Times* article of July 23, 1994, stated that "A former chief R.T.C. investigator in Texas told Congress last month that this was a 'whitewash of a national scandal.'"

Former Texas senator Lloyd Bentsen and then Treasury secretary, and Altman, campaigned against extending the federal statute of limitations, insuring that many of the savings and loans thieves would be protected against criminal prosecutions, and that the recipients of the looted money not be discovered.

## FRAUD WAS NO SECRET

It is important to recognize that the looting of the savings and loans were a secret only to the people that would have to pay, and that is the American public. Thousands of government personnel, including investigators in the various divisions of the U.S. Department of Justice, including the FBI, the many CIA personnel throughout the United States, and others, could not have been unaware that this massive fraud was going on. Possibly the CIA involvement in the looting of the savings and loans, the HUD program, and other areas still to be described, was the reason that the criminal activities were covered up.

There is no more powerful government agency, for coverup and obstruction of justice, then the people in control of the United States Department of Justice, the same people who covered up every major scandal and subversive activity described within these pages. I first discovered this practice while an FAA inspector, and in the subsequent years this obstruction of justice became even more obvious.

**ADDING TO SAVINGS AND LOAN LOOTING**

Shortly before this book went to print, I started learning about another scam for which Americans will someday have to pay. This involved HUD mortgage insurance that was paid by the buyers in escrow for the full life of the loans. The money was then siphoned off and the insurance never purchased. Formerly, the buyer of HUD properties paid their insurance premiums on a monthly basis with their mortgage payments. But in 1983, the same Congress that made possible the looting of the savings and loans passed legislation known as "HURRA" (Housing and Urban-Rural Recovery Act) that required up-front payment for years of mortgage insurance premiums. The intended looting of these funds is the most probable explanation for this change. Massive theft of these funds then occurred, with government coverup of the scheme.

Among the companies involved in these activities were the American International Group (AIG), which was the head of hundreds of companies and trusts throughout the world. Among the reinsurance companies controlled by AIG were Transatlantic Holdings and Putnam Reinsurance.

The HUD mortgages for which up-front mortgage insurance premiums were paid were put into "pools" of mortgage loans with Government National Mortgage Association (GNMA), which were then sold off on the secondary market to investors. When large numbers of foreclosures occurred during the 1980s, huge losses were incurred when the mortgage insurance did not exist to pay for the financial losses. CIA asset Gunther Russbacher described to me how he discovered this scam while he headed the CIA's Red Hill Savings and Loan:

> *They were using reinsurance companies with policy premiums that were never paid. Money was paid for the reinsurance but it was never paid [to the reinsurers]. The policy money, the premiums, were never paid in to where the policies were active. American International Groups was one of the big ones [involved in the scam]. Transatlantic Holdings was involved, as well as Transpacific Holdings. Maurice Greenberg, a close associate of Denver's Leonard Millman, headed some of these companies. Dublin International Insurance was part of AI [American International]. We insured Putnam and Company.*

**SECRECY ON THE BASIS OF "NATIONAL SECURITY"**

It is probable that the CIA involvement in this scam is what kept the Justice Department from prosecuting those guilty of the mortgage premium insurance fraud, using the "national security" excuse for withholding this knowledge from the public.

As in other scandals, it pays to have "friends" in the right places to act as damage control. In 1997, according to Standard and Poor, former senator from Texas, Lloyd Bentson, and Carla Hills, were officials in the Department of Housing and Urban Development (HUD), keeping the lid on this scandal.

# OCTOBER SURPRISE

October Surprise is the name given to a scheme that corrupted the 1980 presidential elections. It included payment of bribes to enemies of the United States who held 52 Americans prisoners, seized at the American Embassy in Teheran on November 4, 1979. Shiite Muslim militants attacked and seized the Embassy in Teheran, taking the Americans hostage. The attack upon the American Embassy occurred several months after the Shah of Iran was overthrown and power seized by the Ayatollah Khomeini. The American hostages were subjected to 444 days of brutal conditions, including mock executions. If this scheme had not been carried out, the Americans would have been released months earlier.

**INTENT OF THE SCHEME**

The intent of the scheme was to alter the presidential elections to bring about the defeat of President Jimmy Carter and to elect presidential nominee Ronald Reagan. This was accomplished by blocking the release of the American hostages, causing many Americans to be displeased with President Carter, increasing the chances that Carter would be defeated at the polls.

Months of negotiations to effect the release of these hostages went on between the government of the United States under President Jimmy Carter and the government of Iran. Early in 1980 the U.S. tried a military mission called Operation Desert One to free the hostages, but it failed miserably in the Iranian desert, resulting in the deaths of eight Americans. While the U.S. military was preparing another rescue try, simultaneously negotiating to obtain the hostages' release, the Reagan-Bush team sabotaged the efforts by making public the hostage-rescue plans and warning the American people that Carter was preparing to exchange arms for hostages. One effect of these tactics that were part of October Surprise was the dispersal of the American prisoners throughout Iran, making rescue all but impossible.

**LOSING THE ELECTION IF THE HOSTAGES WERE FREED**

The American public was becoming increasingly disenchanted with Carter, affecting the outcome of the 1980 presidential elections. Analysts in the Reagan-Bush team estimated they would lose the election to President Jimmy Carter if the American hostages were released prior to the November 11, 1980, election.

After the military rescue mission failed, the United States renewed negotiations for release of the 52 American hostages. The Iranians demanded that President Carter release U.S. military equipment that had been ordered and paid for by the Shah of Iran before Iran would release the hostages.

Despite pressures against an arms-for-hostages swap, in mid-1980 President Carter secretly agreed to Iran's terms. Carter agreed to exchange $150 million in previously ordered and prepaid military equipment in exchange for the release of the hostages. Iran desperately needed the military equipment after Iraqi President Saddam Hussein attacked Iran in September 1980.

**SABOTAGING THE UNITED STATES OF AMERICA**

While Reagan and his camp were charging Carter with an arms-for-hostage negotiations, the Reagan team, headed by former OSS officer William Casey, entered into secret negotiations with Iranian factions. Casey and other members of the Reagan-Bush team met secretly with Iranian factions, offering bribes in the form of money and U.S. arms if the Iranians *continued* the imprisonment of the American hostages until after the November 11, 1980, elections.

A series of secret meetings were held between the Reagan-Bush team and the Iranian factions in European cities, with the final meeting occurring on the October 19, 1980, weekend in Paris. The Iranians demanded that either Ronald Reagan or George Bush personally appear in Paris to sign the final agreement. Carrying out this scheme required secrecy and massive coverups by many in the United States and in France.

**VARIOUS INTERESTS WANTED CARTER OUT**

There were special-interest groups wanting President Carter removed from office. Among them was the Central Intelligence Agency, which suffered serious losses to its clandestine operations when Carter ordered the dismissal of large numbers of CIA operatives in 1977. This wholesale firing of Agency employees became known as the "October Massacre."

George Bush, who had CIA connections since the late 1950s, had been Director of the Central Intelligence Agency in 1976 until Carter assumed the presidency and replaced him with Stansfield Turner.

The Reagan-Bush team promised the Iranians billions of dollars of U.S. military equipment and $40 million in bribes to individual Iranians involved in the scheme. The Reagan-Bush team promised to include arms merchants in the lucrative deal and to include Israel as intermediary in the profitable arms sales.

Carter had refused to deal through arms merchants. He limited the shipment of arms to what had already been purchased. Israel was not included in the sales. The secret and treasonous deal offered by the Reagan-Bush team profited everyone, it seemed. The only people who suffered were the 52 American hostages, held captive months longer, and the American people, who felt the fallout in many ways.

Included in Reagan campaign rhetoric was his promise to get tough with the Iranians, saying he would never negotiate with terrorists. Simultaneously, he and his group were bribing the Iranians to continue the imprisonment of the hostages.

The plan worked. The American public believed the disinformation put out by the Reagan-Bush team. Americans, kept ignorant about the truth and dissatisfied with Carter's inability to get the prisoners released, elected a president and vice president who had engaged in a covert scheme involving the CIA.

Within an hour of Reagan's inauguration on January 20, 1981, the Iranians allowed an aircraft to leave Teheran Airport with all but one of the 52 American hostages on board. The flight was prearranged to take off immediately after the Iranians knew that Reagan and Bush had taken their oaths of office.

**"The deal is off."**

When a White House aide told President Reagan that one of the hostages had not been released, Reagan was heard[117] to respond: "Tell the Iranians that the deal is off if that hostage is not freed."

President Ronald Reagan and Vice President George Bush held widely televised homecoming celebrations for the American hostages, saying all the right things about the sufferings the hostages endured. Reagan never divulged that he and his team were responsible for many months of additional imprisonment and suffering. Neither the hostages nor the American people knew about the Reagan-Bush team conspiracy.

It took the cooperation of many people in the United States and Europe to carry out the scheme. Israel's Mossad, acting as a well-paid middle man in the transfer of the arms from U.S. military warehouses to Iran via Israel, played a major role. Without their cooperation, the scheme probably would not have worked.

It also required the cooperation of the French Secret Service and the government of France, which provided security for the secret Paris meetings. It required the cooperation of officials and people in the Central Intelligence Agency; the U.S. Department of Justice, including the FBI, Secret Service, U.S. Attorneys; the Department of State; many members of Congress, among others. It also required the media to cover up.

My CIA sources said that the $40 million bribe money came from the Committee to Reelect the President (CREEP).

**DAMAGE CONTROL**

Many participants in the October Surprise scheme were rewarded with key positions in the U.S. government. Many of these same people engineered or became part of other major scandals that were likewise kept from the American public. The October Surprise plot was the genesis to the Iran-Contra affair, and indirectly to the Inslaw, BNL, and Iraqgate scandals.

To protect the incoming Reagan-Bush team and the many federal officials and others who took part in October Surprise, the Reagan-Bush team placed people, including those implicated in the activities, in control of key federal agencies and the federal courts. Some, like attorneys Stanley Sporkin, Lawrence

---

117 This response was heard by Barbara Honegger, a member of Reagan's White House staff.

Silberman, and Lowell Jensen, were appointed to the federal bench, defusing any litigation arising from October Surprise or its many tentacles. Attorney William Casey was appointed director of the Central Intelligence Agency. Attorney Edwin Meese, Reagan's campaign manager, was appointed to the highest law-enforcement office in the United States, U.S. Attorney General, insuring that there would be no prosecution of the group. Organized crime never had it so good.

**THE FACTS SLOWLY SURFACED**

Although the details of the secret agreement were known throughout Europe, the establishment media in the United States kept the lid on the scandal. But the facts started coming out. A *Miami Herald* article[118] related statements made by CIA operative Alfonso Chardy describing a secret meeting in early October 1980 between Richard Allen, Lawrence Silberman, Robert McFarlane, and Iranian factions. Allen was foreign policy adviser to President Reagan, and Robert McFarlane was an aide to Senator John Tower on the Senate Armed Services Committee.

In 1987, Abol Hassan Bani-Sadr, the President of Iran during the hostage negotiations, wrote a book published in Europe,[119] describing his knowledge of the October Surprise scheme. The information he had received as President disclosed the secret agreement with the Americans, even though he was kept out of the loop by Hashemi Rafsanjani, one of Khomeini's chief lieutenants and later Speaker of the Iranian Parliament.

In 1988, *Playboy* magazine published an in-depth article on the October Surprise scheme. In what would become a pattern of killings that coincidentally protected high U.S. officials, one of the authors, Abbie Hoffman, was killed shortly after bringing the article to *Playboy*. The eight-page article, "An Election Held Hostage," detailed many of the events surrounding the scheme, as did a ten-page *Esquire* article entitled "October Surprise."

A former member of the Reagan-Bush election team, later a member of the White House staff, Barbara Honegger, authored a 1989 book *October Surprise*,[120] based upon knowledge she gained as a White House insider and subsequent investigator. Honegger left the Reagan camp when she became disillusioned with certain practices. Living in Monterey, California, she and a friend, Rayelan Dyer, worked together researching the October Surprise story.

Rayelan was the widow of a former professor and dean of the physics department at the Naval Postgraduate School in Monterey, California. She later married a deep-cover, high ranking officer in the Office of Naval Intelligence, Gunther Russbacher, who was assigned to the Central Intelligence Agency. Unknown to her at the time, her new husband played a key role in the October Surprise operation. Ironically, she initially found out from me about her new husband's role in the matter she and her friend, Honegger, had investigated. More about this in later pages.

In 1991, Bani-Sadr authored another book describing the October Surprise operation, this time published in the United States: *My Turn To Speak*. On April

---

118 April 1987.
119 European publisher *Eagleburger*.
120 *October Surprise*, Tudor Publishing Company.

15, 1991, *Frontline* aired a television show addressing the October Surprise, which was followed the next day by an article in the Op-Ed section of the *New York Times* written by Gary Sick, describing his knowledge of October Surprise. Sick authored a book published in 1991 that copied Barbara Honegger's title, *October Surprise*.[121] Both *October Surprise* books relied upon statements made by dozens of people who were part of the operation or witnesses to it, and who had nothing to gain and much to lose by disclosing what they knew.

Ari Ben-Menashe, a former member of Israel's secret intelligence agency, the Mossad, described in his 1991 book *Profits of War* the role he and the Mossad played in October Surprise, including meetings he attended in Madrid, Barcelona, and Paris.

Ben-Menashe was heavily involved in various secret activities with the Mossad and the CIA, and was one of the first to expose the Iran-Contra activities, for which October Surprise served as the genesis. Ben-Menashe stated that he was a member of the Mossad's advance team working with the French government, which arranged meetings between William Casey, George Bush, and the Iranian factions, including the meetings on the October 19, 1980, weekend in Paris.

Ben-Menashe related that he and others on the Israeli team stayed at the Paris Hilton Hotel, meeting with various members of the Iranian factions, while waiting for George Bush to arrive from the United States. He stated that on Sunday, October 19 at approximately 11 a.m., the Ayatollah Mehdi Karrubi and his body guards appeared in a room on the upper floor of the Hotel Ritz, where Israeli and French intelligence agencies were waiting for Bush to arrive. They were followed several minutes later by George Bush and William Casey. The meeting lasted about ninety minutes and a final agreement was reached, whereby the Iranians were to be given $40 million bribe money and large quantities of arms would be sold to them. In exchange, the Iranians would continue to imprison the 52 Americans until after the November 1980 presidential election and the January 1981 inauguration.

## JUSTICE DEPARTMENT OBSTRUCTION OF JUSTICE

CIA contract agent Richard Brenneke testified in U.S. District Court at Denver in 1988 on behalf of another CIA contract agent, Heinrich Rupp. The purpose of the testimony was to show that Brenneke's friend, Rupp, was a CIA contract agent (as was Brenneke), and that the offenses for which Rupp was being charged were offenses committed under orders of the CIA. Justice Department prosecutors had charged Rupp with money offenses at Aurora Bank in the Denver area.

During Brenneke's testimony, he described other CIA activities, including his role in the October 19, 1980, weekend flights to Paris, in which both Brenneke and Rupp took part. Brenneke testified that he saw George Bush and Donald Gregg in Paris on the October 19, 1980, weekend. Brenneke had nothing to gain by revealing the October Surprise scheme, and much to lose if he was lying. Justice Department officials already knew of the October Surprise activities. U.S. Attorney General Edwin Meese had been on the Reagan-Bush presidential campaign and knew of the criminal activities. Now he held the top law enforcement spot in the United States. Instead of performing his duty, he engaged

121 Random House.

in many criminal acts, including coverup, aiding and abetting, misprision of felonies, obstruction of justice, subornation of perjury, and others. He then compounded these crimes by falsely prosecuting an informant to silence and discredit him, compounding his earlier obstruction of justice.

Instead of prosecuting the guilty people in the October Surprise scheme, Justice Department officials and prosecutors responded to Brenneke's testimony by charging him with perjury for making the statements to the court. This false charge made Justice Department attorneys guilty of felony persecution of an informant under federal criminal statutes,[122] felony coverup, and obstruction of justice.

**JUSTICE DEPARTMENT SUBORNATION OF PERJURY**

The perjury trial was conducted in Portland, Oregon, where Brenneke resided. Justice Department prosecutors brought Donald Gregg, then Ambassador to South Korea, to testify that he was not in Paris on the October 19, 1980, weekend, even though the prosecutors knew Brenneke was telling the truth and that Gregg was lying. They encouraged Gregg to lie under oath, testifying that he was swimming at a beach in Maryland with his family on that weekend. Justice Department prosecutors produced pictures of Gregg and his family in bathing suits on the beach in bright sunshine. They knew the snapshots they were submitting to the court were not taken on that cold October 19th weekend. Encouraging someone to commit perjury is the crime of subornation of perjury.

Brenneke's attorney called a witness from the weather bureau who testified that the sky was overcast during that entire weekend.

Justice Department prosecutors produced two Secret Service agents[123] to testify that Bush never left the Washington area during the October 19, 1980, weekend. But they were vague in their testimony and failed to produce the Secret Service logs showing Bush's activities during a 21-hour period from Saturday afternoon to Sunday evening. The Secret Service agents could not state where Bush was from 9:25 p.m. on Saturday, October 18 until Sunday at 7:57 p.m. My CIA sources told me that several Secret Service agents were on board the BAC 111 aircraft that flew vice presidential nominee George Bush to Paris during the missing twenty-one hours.

Secret Service records, if they are accurate, indicate that Bush gave a speech at 8:40 p.m. on Saturday, October 18, 1980, at Widener University in Delaware County, Pennsylvania, and then did not show where Bush was until Sunday night, October 19, 1980, when Bush gave his speech to the Zionist Organization of America at the Washington Hilton Hotel, arriving an hour late for his 7:30 p.m. scheduled appearance. I obtained sequestered Secret Service documents showing Bush flying into Washington National Airport at 6:37 p.m. Sunday evening.

**PERJURY BY THE SECRET SERVICE?**

In addition to lying about Bush's whereabouts, the Secret Service agents testifying in Brenneke's trial withheld the fact that several Secret Service agents were on the plane that carried Bush to Paris during that October 19, 1980,

122 Including Title 18 U.S.C. §§ 1512 and 1513.

123 Who worked under the control of the U.S. Department of Justice.

weekend.

**BLACKMAIL OF THE UNITED STATES**

As could be expected, when the Reagan-Bush team took office they were then subject to blackmail by Iran, Iraq, Israel, and anyone who had knowledge of October Surprise.

After Reagan and Bush took office, the Iranians received huge quantities of military equipment, many times more than they could have received had they completed the agreement with the United States government under President Carter. In 1982, the Reagan-Bush team took Iraq off the list of terrorist states despite the strong protests of intelligence organizations in the United States and Europe. Israel received huge quantities of military supplies and aid, much of it unknown to the American public, who will be paying the bill for years.

October Surprise also adversely affected the military preparedness of the United States and its European allies. To obtain the arms for Iran promised at Paris, military equipment was stolen from U.S. warehouses in Europe and sent to Iran via Israel.

**CIA CONFIDENTIAL SOURCES**

In later pages, I describe how I met the CIA sources who gave me many of the specific details of the October Surprise scheme. Briefly, they told me in their sworn declarations that October Surprise was primarily a CIA operation, engineered and carried out with CIA personnel and funds. William Casey, a private citizen and covert CIA operative, met several times with Iranians at different European locations in 1980.

One of the key meetings occurred at the Pepsico International Headquarters building in Barcelona, Spain in late July 1980. One of my CIA sources was present with Casey at that meeting, arranging for procurement and shipment of the arms from various European locations to Iran via Israel. The final meeting occurred in Paris on the October 19, 1980, weekend.

Bush flew to Paris from the United States on October 18, 1980, on a BAC 111 owned by a member of the Saudi Arabian family. My CIA contacts have said that the pilots on that flight were Gunther Russbacher, Richard Brenneke, and an Air Force Major.

The BAC 111 reportedly departed Washington National Airport for nearby Andrews Air Force Base on Saturday evening, October 18, 1980. It then departed Andrews at approximately 19:00 pm EST (0000 GMT)[124] for an airport on Long Island in the New York City area, arriving there at 19:45 p.m. (0045). The BAC 111 landed shortly before the arrival of a Gulfstream jet owned by Unocal, from which William Casey deplaned. Casey then joined the passengers on the BAC 111 for the flight to Paris.

The BAC 111 departed Mitchell at 20:00 p.m. (0100 GMT) for Gander, Newfoundland, arriving there at 21:20 p.m. (EST) (22:20 Atlantic Time; 0220 GMT), where it refueled for the flight over the North Atlantic. It departed Gander at 21:40 p.m. EST (22:40 Atlantic Time; 0240 GMT) for Paris, arriving at Le Bourget Airport at 03:40 EST (9:40 a.m., European time; 0840 GMT).

---

124 Greenwich Mean Time.

Unocal's Gulfstream flew non-stop from Mitchell Field to Paris and was waiting at the airport in London when the BAC 111 arrived. Heinrich Rupp was one of the pilots on the Unocal Gulfstream.

In Paris, the plane was met by a fleet of limousines to carry the passengers to their destinations. George Bush and William Casey went straight to the meetings then in progress. At the Paris meetings were numerous Iranians and members of Israel's Mossad, including Ari Ben-Menashe.

A $40 million bank draft on a Luxembourg bank was given to the Iranians as bribe money and a part of the overall agreement which consisted also of the shipment of arms to Iran. CIA-operative Michael Riconosciuto played a key role in arranging for the wire transfer of these funds.

Because it was necessary for Bush to return to the United States quickly in order to attend a late Sunday evening speech at the Washington Hilton Hotel, the CIA provided an SR-71 aircraft. This plane departed from a military field near Paris at approximately 1450 European time (8:50 a.m. EST; 1350 GMT) and took approximately one hour and forty-four minutes to McGuire Air Force Base in New Jersey, arriving there at approximately 10:50 a.m. EST (1550 GMT).

Later that day, Bush boarded the same BAC 111 that had taken him to Paris and then flew into Washington National Airport. The Secret Service reports that I obtained showed Bush arriving at Washington National at 6:37 p.m., in the BAC 111 and then proceeding with Secret Service escort to the Washington Hilton Hotel, where he gave a speech.

**CIA CODE NAME FOR OCTOBER SURPRISE**

As will be explained more fully in later pages, most CIA operations have code names, and the code name for the CIA October Surprise scheme was Operation Eurovan (EV).

**STRONG CIRCUMSTANTIAL EVIDENCE SHOWING OCTOBER SURPRISE EXISTED**

Even discounting testimony from the many people who were involved in one way or another with October Surprise, the circumstantial evidence is far in excess of that used by federal and state prosecutors to convict a person of a crime or to sentence the person to death. The facts exposed by investigative media articles and books were of sufficient magnitude to make President Nixon's Watergate coverup child's play.

The factors indicating that October Surprise did in fact occur include:

1. Statements by former president of Iran, Bani-Sadr, whose 1987 and 1991 books detailed the secret agreement between Iranian factions and the Reagan-Bush team.

2. Statements of numerous people given to Barbara Honegger and quoted in her 1989 *October Surprise*, enlarged upon what she learned as part of the Reagan-Bush team.

3. Statements of numerous people given to Gary Sick and quoted in his 1991 *October Surprise.*

4. Sworn testimony by CIA contract personnel Richard Brenneke and Heinrich Rupp in the U.S. District Court at Denver in 1988.

5. Statements of numerous people given to the authors of various newspaper and magazine articles.

6. Statements made to the press by Ari Ben-Menashe, a former high-ranking Mossad staff officer, who was present at several of the secret October Surprise meetings.

7. Circumstantial evidence in the sequence of events that occurred, including the sudden withdrawal of Iran from further discussions when the United States under President Carter agreed to the terms proposed by Iran, and the release of the American hostages within minutes of President Reagan's inauguration.

8. The implications of guilt by the pattern of coverups.

This is not the end of the October Surprise matter; more follows.

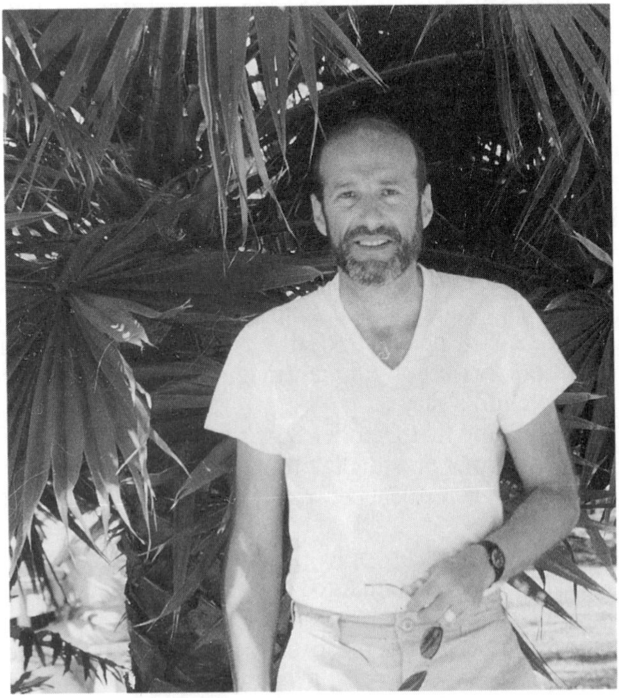

Gunther Russbacher

# CIA WHISTLEBLOWERS

Commencing in 1990, I discovered a number of deep-cover whistleblowers formerly employed by various U.S. intelligence agencies, some of whom had been silenced by Justice Department prosecutors and federal judges. Over a period of six years, and continuing at this time, over a thousand hours of deposition-like questioning of these people occurred, divulging government corruption beyond the wildest imagination of the average American. These people divulged to me the specifics of deep-cover criminal activities that were and are inflicting unprecedented harm upon the United States and the American people.

Despite my personal knowledge of government corruption, commencing while I was a federal investigator, I would probably not have believed what I was told if such a great amount of time had not been expended obtaining specifics and confirmation from other deep-cover sources. Much of what they told me was supported by documentation. Further, highly detailed and documented exposé books and articles helped support the existence of this misconduct.

Ironically, it was the corrupt actions by renegade Justice Department attorneys and federal judges in the Ninth Circuit federal judicial district[231] that brought me into contact with these people.

One of the standard tactics employed to keep the lid on the various scandals and to silence or discredit whistleblowers is to falsely charge the person with a federal crime. This is usually followed by seizing his or her assets, depriving the person of funds for legal defenses. Court appointed attorneys are then furnished, who routinely provide a weak defense so as to protect those in power.

**JUSTICE DEPARTMENT PERSECUTION BACKFIRED**

Justice Department prosecutors and federal judges tried to silence me by the sham judicial action in the California courts and the voiding of all state and federal protections needed to defend against the scheme. When I sought to protect

231 Ninth Circuit comprises the States of California, Oregon, Washington, Nevada, and Hawaii, and is the largest judicial district in the United States.

myself, the coalition of corrupt Justice Department prosecutors and federal judges sentenced me to prison, just as they did when I sought to expose the criminal activities in which they were involved. There is a certain risk in sending a citizen to prison who is determined to blow the lid on these subversive and criminal acts and who is also an author.

Virtually nothing has been written about whistleblowers or concerned citizens who blow the whistle on hard-core criminal acts by federal personnel, especially federal judges and their legal cohorts in the Justice Department. All whistleblowers fare poorly, but none fare as badly as those who expose corruption in the powerful Justice Department and federal judiciary.

It was in prison that many former CIA contract agents educated me about corrupt CIA and Justice Department activities. I met people in prison who, incarcerated for various political reasons, were former CIA operatives or assets operating covert CIA proprietaries, including airlines, banks, and savings and loans. Either their CIA cover was exposed and the CIA and Justice Department chose to make them scapegoats, or the imprisonment was to silence potential whistleblowers or witnesses.

Whatever the reason, CIA and Justice Department officials acted in unison with federal judges, eliminating people who constituted a threat of exposure. The standard tactic is to charge the targeted individual with a federal offense for some act they were ordered to perform by their CIA handlers, deny them adequate legal counsel, deny them the right to have CIA witnesses testify on their behalf, and deny to them the right to present CIA documents. A standard and sham excuse for denying these defenses is that they are not relevant to the immediate charge, when the matter of who gave the person his or her orders is absolutely relevant.

From 200 to 300 former CIA operatives or contract agents had been sentenced to prison by Justice Department prosecutors during the 1980s on charges arising out of the covert activities they were ordered to perform by their CIA bosses. It was their unanimous belief that the prosecution of these CIA operatives was either to silence them or to discredit them if they talked about the operations.

It was in prison that I first met Gunther Russbacher, a CIA deep-cover high-ranking operative. The hundreds of hours of statements given to me by Russbacher, and my book-writing and radio and television appearances, brought me into contact with other former deep-cover personnel and investigators. The thousand and more hours of information gathered during the last few years revealed a convoluted web of intrigue that is bizarre, and irrefutable.

## COMPOUNDING THE JUDICIAL PERSECUTION

If the facts in these pages ever motivate enough people to rebel and throw out the crooks, a tongue-in-check gratitude should be given to the crooked judges and Justice Department attorneys that sent me and others to prison to silence us. And these should especially include U.S. District Judge Marilyn Patel at San Francisco, one of the most corrupt judges I have ever encountered. Her retaliation against me for reporting the criminal activities in Chapter 11 courts made it possible for Russbacher and me to meet.

### GUNTHER KARL RUSSBACHER

Russbacher's parents were members of the Hapsburg group of Austria, and his father was an Austrian in German intelligence during World War II. In 1950, the U.S. government offered many of these intelligence officers the choice of either being prosecuted for war crimes or going to the United States and infiltrating various U.S. intelligence agencies. Russbacher's parents were among those who accepted the move to America. In 1950, the Russbacher family moved to the United States, living in Oklahoma City, Oklahoma and then went to Fallon, Nevada.

When Russbacher reached the age of seventeen, he entered the U.S. Army, later joining the U.S. Navy, and in 1967 received his Navy pilot wings at Pensacola. He then went on to the Naval Air Station at Jacksonville, Florida. (I also received my Navy wings at Pensacola and then went on to Jacksonville, where I became a Navy flight instructor.) Approximately a year later, Russbacher received pilot training in the SR-71 at Beale Air Force Base and flew many SR-71 missions for the CIA. During his CIA activities he was given numerous aliases and service and Social Security numbers.

In 1969, Russbacher was attached to the Office of Naval Intelligence and "sheepdipped"[232] into the Central Intelligence Agency. He had two tours of duty in Vietnam; during his first tour, as a fighter pilot, he was shot down and returned to Fitzsimmons Hospital in Denver for extensive hospitalization. Upon his discharge from the hospital, the CIA sent Russbacher back to Vietnam, where he engaged in various covert activities, including attempting to rescue prisoners of war. During one of these attempts, he was caught and spent about a year in a North Vietnam prison camp until he again escaped. During his imprisonment Russbacher was tortured, including pulling out his finger nails.

The CIA sent Russbacher to Afghanistan in the early 1970s, helping the Afghan fighters against the Russian-backed Kabul government. During this period he helped transfer CIA funds to the newly created Bank of Credit and Commerce International (BCCI). These CIA funds, and those supplied by Bank of America, were a significant source of capital for that bank.

The CIA then put Russbacher into the financial field, starting in Operation Cyclops, a program where CIA operatives are placed into financial institutions to learn the business. He subsequently started up and operated during the late 1970s and 1980s several covert CIA proprietaries in the United States, including savings and loans, mortgage companies and investment companies, dealing in money laundering and other covert CIA activities.

For more than two decades of CIA operations the CIA had given him over thirty aliases for different covert operations. He also had various nicknames including "Gunsel" and "Gunslinger." When undergoing flight training in the SR-71, including at Beale Air Force Base, he used the alias Robert Behler, and the rank of an Air Force Lt. Colonel. When operating covert financial institutions his usual alias was Emery J. Peden with occasional use of Robert Andrew Walker,

---

232 "Sheepdipped" is the term used to describe the transfer of military personnel to the CIA, in which records are falsified showing the person discharged from the respective military organization, and who then works with the CIA in a clandestine position, where the CIA can deny any relationship to the party doing CIA work.

or both. When he wanted to control two positions within a company, he used two different aliases. With Red Hill Savings & Loan and Hill Financial, he used Emery J. Peden for his role as Chairman of the Board and Robert A. Walker as Chief Executive Officer. He also used his real name, Gunther Russbacher.

Russbacher and I spent hundreds of hours dissecting the mechanics of CIA operations during the past four years, some of it sworn declarations when I thought to ask, and I received numerous written declarations from him. Russbacher described some of the CIA affiliated companies or fronts that he operated and their covert business activities. He also mentioned moving money from Silverado Bank Savings & Loan in Denver to start up other covert CIA operations, including Red Hill Savings and Loan and Hill Financial in Red Hill, Pennsylvania.

Several times during the years Russbacher expressed regret to me for having committed some of the things that he was ordered to do by his CIA bosses, including his role in assassinations, both in foreign countries and in the United States. As I became a confidant to other deep-cover high-ranking CIA/ONI operatives I learned that assassination teams were part of their official activities and not simply done by rogue elements.

Russbacher described the various factions operating within the CIA, each with its own agenda and often running similar parallel operations. He fell out of grace with the CIA in the late 1980s for various reasons. Because of Russbacher's role in many CIA activities that implicated high federal officials and his knowledge of criminal activities by the CIA, federal judges, Justice Department officials, and others, Russbacher posed a serious threat to those in control of key segments of the federal government. He was the smoking gun in many national scandals, the exposure of which could create a national emergency.

## SEQUENCE OF SHAM CHARGES

In late 1986 the State of Missouri filed charges against Russbacher for allegedly writing checks to an alias, upon an account that had inadvertently closed; for allegedly defrauding several people out of $20,000, when the money had actually been returned to them, and for allegedly selling unregistered securities (from one CIA proprietary to another). These alleged offenses occurred while he was operating a CIA proprietary known as National Brokerage Company in Clayton, Missouri and Southwest Latex Supply. Russbacher said that no one ever lost any money since people were always compensated for their losses. The charges were not pressed, and Russbacher was not arrested.

In August 1989, Russbacher used a CIA Learjet based at Hayward Airport in California to fly his prospective bride from Seattle to Reno, where they were married, and then back to Seattle. Personal use of government aircraft is not exactly an unknown event, but in this case Justice Department prosecutors, representing Faction One of the Central Intelligence Agency (Russbacher was Faction Two), chose to charge him with misuse of government aircraft and fuel.

Over a period of years I learned of many instances where one government agency seeks to charge an agent of another agency with a federal crime.

Another reason for charging Russbacher with an offense was that he married shortly after signing his latest CIA secrecy agreement in which he agreed not to marry for the next two years. On August 30, 1989, Russbacher married Rayelan

Dyer, the widow of a former professor[233] at the Naval Postgraduate School in Monterey. Among the Naval personnel that Rayelan had met at the school while her husband was alive was Gunther Russbacher, having first met him in 1982. Several weeks before the marriage, Russbacher requested permission to marry from his CIA bosses.

Permission was necessitated by his CIA secrecy agreement barring him from marrying for two years after its latest signing. Russbacher was verbally advised that this approval would probably not be forthcoming because Rayelan was an activist of the 1960s and had sought to expose the October Surprise operation in collaboration with Barbara Honegger, who authored the boo, *October Surprise*.

Rayelan had met Russbacher for the second time in August 1989 while she was traveling in Oregon with her mother, Bess Smith. Several days later, Russbacher called and proposed marriage. After she accepted, Russbacher called the crew of a CIA proprietary aircraft charter operation, Jet Charter International, based at Hayward, California, instructing them to pick him up at Sacramento Municipal Airport and fly him to Boeing Field in Seattle. After the plane was serviced by Flightcraft in Seattle, the Learjet departed for Reno with Russbacher and Rayelan on board. After arriving in Reno they were married, and immediately flew back to Seattle. From Seattle the Learjet pilots, Don LaKava and Jan Pierson, both of whom had served with Russbacher in Central American activities, flew to Modesto, California. The Russbachers then drove to Bess Smith's home in Newman, California.

Within days after the marriage, FBI agents burst into Bess Smith's home (September 1, 1989) in Newman, arresting Russbacher, falsely charging that he kidnapped his wife's niece, Jennifer Smith.[234] The FBI agents told Rayelan and her mother that Russbacher was a con artist, marrying women all over the country and then taking their money. The FBI agents stated that Russbacher was committing all types of fraud throughout the United States. They stated he had no association with the government and was a pathological liar. The FBI agents were so convincing in their lies that they almost had Rayelan convinced.

The kidnapping charges were dropped on December 1, 1989, but the State of Missouri took custody of Russbacher on 1986 charges that he had misappropriated $20,000 through bad checks and sold securities without registering the transaction with the State. Russbacher was denied bail. During trial, the judge declared a mistrial. Waiting for the next trial, which was repeatedly delayed, Russbacher remained in the harsh surroundings of St. Charles county jail in Missouri. His attorney, Timothy Farrell, and the Missouri County Prosecutor, John P. Zimmerman, pressured Russbacher to sign a plea agreement, claiming it would put all of the charges behind him. Russbacher verbally agreed to an Alford agreement, or nolo contendere, wherein Russbacher did not plead guilty but agreed to certain conditions to avoid trial.

---

233 Dean of Science and Engineering.

234 Rayelan's mother received a telephone call from her granddaughter living near Seattle asking that she be allowed to stay in California until the girl's parents recovered from their drug and alcohol problems. Russbacher called the CIA's Learjet to fly him, Rayelan and her mother, to Seattle, where twelve-year-old Jennifer Smith resided. Jennifer's mother agreed to let the daughter go to California.

Russbacher's attorney appeared more interested in appeasing the judge and the prosecutor and failed to provide the defenses expected of even a half-baked attorney.

When Russbacher entered the court room on July 16, 1990, the terms in the written plea agreement, which he had never seen before, were very different from what his attorney and the prosecutor had stated earlier. Russbacher was pressured to sign the agreement, stating he would then be set free. Under the pressure of a year in a county jail and the promise of a return to his CIA status, Russbacher signed the papers. During questioning by Judge Lester Duggan, Jr., Russbacher told the judge that he was not pleading guilty but exercising an Alford plea. But the judge entered into court records that Russbacher pled guilty to the offenses.

**UNAWARE OF THE PITFALLS OF PROBATION**

The wording of the plea agreement was such that he could be incarcerated again whenever it suited Missouri prosecutors, who were working hand in hand with Justice Department and CIA personnel. Russbacher either did not realize it at the time, or he was desperate to get out of jail.

The terms of the plea agreement required Russbacher to remain silent concerning any CIA activities. (This was similar to orders rendered against me by federal judges in the San Francisco area, when they barred me from reporting any criminal activities to a federal court.)

Under the terms of the probation agreement, Russbacher could be returned to prison to serve 21 years, even though there was never a trial on the original charges, if he violated any of the terms of the plea agreement. Almost anything he did for the CIA violated the conditions of the plea agreement, including trips outside of the St. Charles area and failure to report regularly to his probation officer.

**NO SNITCHING**

One paragraph of the plea agreement was obviously meant to keep Russbacher from testifying at any Congressional or other government inquiry. Paragraph number five read:

> *That the defendant enter into no agreements with any governmental or other agency to provide information concerning crimes or bad acts. No snitching for anyone.*

This agreement was signed by the Missouri Assistant Prosecuting Attorney, John P. Zimmerman; by Russbacher's attorney, Timothy Farrell; and St. Charles, Missouri Judge Lester Duggan, Jr. This was another version of the tactic that federal judges and Justice Department prosecutors inflicted upon me, seeking to silence my exposure activities.

The terms of the plea agreement were also spelled out in a July 2, 1990, letter by St. Charles County Assistant Prosecuting Attorney John P. Zimmerman to Russbacher's attorney, repeating the exact words in the plea agreement. There was a determined effort to silence Russbacher, using state officials to carry out the intent of federal officials.

Item number seven provided that Russbacher "not leave the St. Louis area without written permission from his probation officer." But Russbacher's CIA duties required that he immediately leave the area, which he did. The plea agreement also required Russbacher to make weekly reports to the probation officer, which he never did. Nothing was said about it until several years later when Justice Department officials wanted to silence Russbacher.

**ULTRA SECRET OPERATION**

The CIA had an important task for Russbacher to perform upon leaving prison. He was needed for an ultra-secret project associated with the Bush administration's dealings with Iraq's Saddam Hussein. The signature of Russian President Mikhail Gorbachev was needed on a secret agreement prepared and signed by President George Bush. Russbacher stated that the agreement provided that Russia not intervene if the United States attacked Iraq in the near future. Russbacher spoke Russian, had been assigned to the U.S. Embassy in Moscow in the 1970s and mid-1980s, and knew President Gorbachev personally. The signature and agreement had to remain secret.

Russbacher's handlers instructed him to proceed to Offutt Air Force Base for a top-secret briefing. Immediately upon release from prison at St. Charles, Missouri, on July 16, 1990, Russbacher and his wife drove to Offutt Air Force Base. They arrived there on July 18, where CincPac authorization permitted them to occupy living quarters at this high-security Air Force Base. Russbacher was briefed about the mission in which he was to be involved. Among those present at the meeting were Brent Scowcroft, national security advisor, and CIA Director William Webster.

Gunther Russbacher and his wife departed Offutt on July 21, 1990, driving to Reno, where they stayed at the Western Village Inn and Casino in nearby Sparks, awaiting further orders. Late in the afternoon on July 26, 1990, Russbacher boarded a CIA Learjet at Reno, which took him to Crows Landing Naval Air Station, where four CIA SR-71 aircraft were being readied for a non-stop flight to Moscow, carrying out the plans reached at Offutt.

Russbacher described the inflight refueling of the SR-71's on their transpolar flight to Moscow, with the first one occurring northeast of Seattle and the second refueling by Russian tankers as they approached the USSR. Russbacher identified one of the passengers in the SR-71s as national security advisor Brent Scowcroft.

Russbacher was the only person on the four aircraft who spoke Russian, and his previous contacts with Gorbachev was valuable to the success of the mission. Russbacher told me of handing the secret agreement to Gorbachev, obtaining Gorbachev's signature on one of the agreements, and then flying back to the United States, along with two of the other CIA aircraft. One SR-71 was left for the Russians, along with a flight crew to check out Russian pilots. It is believed that one of the flight instructors was a former Air Force Chief Flight Instructor from Beale Air Force Base in Marysville, California, reportedly Abe Kardone. (I owned a 60-unit motel in nearby Yuba City.)

The aircraft refueled twice in the air on the return flight and the three SR-71s landed at Fallon Naval Air Station on July 26, 1990.

On July 25, 1990, the day before Russbacher obtained Gorbachev's signature, U.S. Ambassador April Glaspie assured Iraq's Saddam Hussein that the United States had no interest in its conflict with Kuwait. These assurances were interpreted by Saddam Hussein as clearance to invade Kuwait, which he did several days later. This sequence of events almost suggests that Saddam Hussein was encouraged to attack Kuwait while the United States waited to retaliate.

Upon landing at Fallon Naval Air Station, a Navy helicopter flew him to Reno, at which time he took a cab to the motel where his wife was waiting. While at the motel waiting for further instructions from his CIA bosses, Russbacher received telephone instructions on July 28th from Admiral George Raeder, instructing him to report to Castle Air Force Base for a debriefing on the Moscow flight. Raeder further advised Russbacher that he would be promoted from Captain to Rear Admiral, and that Russbacher should get the proper uniform and a Rear Admiral's cap at nearby Fallon Naval Air Station, which he did.

Bizarre as the Moscow flight sounds to people living a normal life, it must be remembered that the CIA deals in the bizarre. I talked to Rayelan, who saw the CIA Learjet and three CIA SR-71s land. She saw Russbacher enter the Learjet, which immediately departed. I talked to Bess Smith, Rayelan's mother, who lived in Newman, near the Crows Landing Naval Air Station, and who was present at the Navy base during the preparation of the SR-71s. She saw Russbacher get in one of the aircraft. During the debriefing at Castle Air Force Base, she was in one of the adjoining bedrooms and saw the people receiving the debriefing from Russbacher.

The answers Bess Smith gave to my questions showed she wasn't fabricating what she saw. She was a kind, motherly person, who could not fabricate the facts that she witnessed. I also talked to the SR-71 pilot and former instructor at Beale Air Force Base, Abe Kardone of Tacoma, Washington. Kardone, while being circumspect, made statements indicating he was one of the pilots on the flight and that he was the SR-71 instructor who remained behind in Moscow to check out the Russian flight crews.

The Russbachers arrived at Castle Air Force base on July 29, 1990, and CincPac authorization was again waiting from the navy permitting them to be billeted there for several days. (I have copies of the billeting receipts from both military bases.) Russbacher's CIA handlers debriefed him in his apartment-size accommodations while Rayelan and her mother were sleeping in one of the two adjoining bedrooms. After the debriefing, Russbacher waited to receive his promotion to Rear Admiral. Up to this point he had not worn his Navy uniform, which was hanging in the closet in a protective bag. While Russbacher debriefed his CIA people, Bess Smith walked into the kitchen from her bedroom and exchanged greetings with the people there.

On July 31, 1990, the morning after the late-evening debriefing, FBI agents burst into their living quarters, arrested Russbacher for allegedly impersonating a Naval officer. He was then incarcerated at the Fresno County jail while awaiting trial. Justice Department prosecutors soon dropped the charge, but U.S. Attorney David Levi at Sacramento filed new charges. He alleged that Russbacher misused government aircraft, fuel, military facilities and purchase orders associated with the flights to Seattle and Reno when Russbacher married Rayelan.

During the trial, FBI agent Rich Robley testified that Russbacher had worked for the government, and it looked favorable for an acquittal. Before reaching the jury, U.S. District Judge Leonard Pierce declared a mistrial, which was followed by months of delaying tactics by Justice Department prosecutors as they prepared for another trial. Meanwhile, Russbacher languished in jail. When

Russbacher stated he would fight the charges, U.S. Attorney David Levi threatened to charge Russbacher's wife and mother-in-law with unlawfully trespassing on Offutt and Castle Air Force Bases and request six months in prison for each of them.

Despite the constitutional requirement of a jury trial, federal judges have held that six months imprisonment permits eliminating that constitutional protection, allowing federal judges to imprison a citizen without a jury trial. In this way a federal judge, who is often a former Justice Department attorney and usually works in unison with the prosecuting attorney, can sentence a person to six months in prison on fabricated charges. This six months imprisonment often destroys a person financially and inflicts great personal harm upon the individual and family. This unconstitutional imprisonment without a jury trial occurs frequently. It was done to me in retaliation for reporting the federal crimes in which federal judges and Justice Department attorneys were implicated.

The U.S. Attorney promised Russbacher that he would receive only a three-month prison sentence if he pled guilty, and Russbacher agreed. However, U.S. District Judge Pierce refused to honor this agreement and sentenced Russbacher to twenty months in prison. After several months in the county jail, Russbacher was transferred to the federal prison camp at Dublin, California. That is where I met him.

Russbacher and I had a good relationship, possibly due to our prior Navy piloting background. At first, Russbacher was very guarded in what he told me about CIA operations. He described his activities in Central America with the CIA, including Oliver North's involvement, and the disdain that CIA and other people had for North's incompetence and involvement in drug trafficking.

**"My life wouldn't be worth a nickel..."**

At first, there were many CIA operations Russbacher wouldn't disclose to me. When I pressed him for details he stated, "My life wouldn't be worth a nickel if I talked about the hush-hush things." A few weeks after we had met, I was released[235] December 10, 1990[236] and returned to my home in Alamo, California. Russbacher started calling me from prison, and our discussions about CIA and other covert activities continued. Much of the time I asked specific questions about CIA activities and he responded, similar to a deposition. I thought that *I* had discovered major criminal activities while an FAA investigator, but it was child's play compared to what I subsequently learned. Through my contacts with Russbacher, I became acquainted with other deep-cover CIA operatives and contract agents, DEA personnel, and former police and private investigators. This small group had information about virtually every dirty covert activity

235 But the release was only pending still another trial at which the same Justice Department and the same Ninth Circuit judges sought to again send me to federal prison. The FBI and Justice Department again accused me of criminal contempt of court for having filed a federal law suit in the U.S. District Court at Chicago which described additional federal crimes that I had uncovered in Chapter 11 courts, and in which I sought relief from the escalating attacks upon me.

236 San Francisco U.S. District Judge Marilyn Patel had caused me to be incarcerated without charges, without having personal jurisdiction over me, on the basis that I had filed a federal action in the U.S. District Court at Chicago (No. 90-C-2396), reporting a pattern of federal crimes that I had discovered, and for exercising declaratory and injunctive relief remedies to obtain relief from the Judicial persecution inflicted upon me, that initially commenced from the sham law suit filed by the covert Justice Department law firm, Friedman, Sloan and Ross.

of the CIA. The education was priceless and made possible the exposures described within these pages.

Russbacher's health problems necessitated his transfer to the federal prison at Terminal Island near Long Beach, California. But our almost daily telephone conversations continued, going further into CIA activities in which he had been involved.

Russbacher's CIA status and his credibility were proven to me not only by the hundreds of hours of questioning but by the statements given to me by other deep-cover operatives or contract agents, some of whom hadn't seen Russbacher for years.

**OCTOBER SURPRISE**

Rumors about the October Surprise scheme started surfacing in the media in late 1990, causing me to ask Russbacher if he had any knowledge of it. He replied that he was well familiar with the details and that he was part of the operation. But he would only make a few general statements about it. But this suddenly changed.

During an early morning telephone conversation on April 30, 1991, Russbacher said that three Office of Naval Intelligence officers were coming to Terminal Island that afternoon and he would be flying with them to Monterey, California on a special assignment. The flight from Long Beach to Monterey would be in a Learjet, after which a Navy helicopter from the Naval Air Station at Alameda, California would take them to Fort Ord and then on to Santa Cruz, landing at the college. Russbacher's CIA faction occasionally extracted him from prison for short periods of time. But something happened.

Shortly before midnight, my telephone rang. It was Russbacher's wife, Rayelan. She sought my help to determine if her husband was on a helicopter that reportedly crashed several hours earlier at Fort Ord. She had been expecting her husband to arrive at Santa Cruz by Navy helicopter and when she saw on television that a helicopter had crashed at nearby Fort Ord that evening she became worried.

Rayelan had contacted a friend who was CIA Chief of Station at St. Louis, nicknamed "Rabbit," who in turn phoned an FBI contact in California. The CIA station agent then called Rayelan, advising her that a Navy helicopter at Fort Ord had blown apart in the air and that there were no survivors. But he didn't know who had been on board when it crashed. Russbacher's wife asked me to call my FAA contacts to find out if her husband was one of the fatalities.

**"I've been drugged!"**

While Russbacher's wife and I were talking, Russbacher came on the line, calling from federal prison at Terminal Island. He exclaimed, "I've been drugged." Russbacher explained that he had coffee at approximately 2:30 with the Admiral whom he had been expecting. Russbacher said that the Admiral advised that he would return in about an hour and a half to take him to Santa Cruz.

After drinking coffee with the Admiral, Russbacher suddenly felt drowsy and went back to his cell and fell sound asleep. Shortly after 10 p.m., Russbacher woke up when a prisoner shouted that he had an emergency phone call from his wife. He called his wife and the call came through as she and I were talking.

Russbacher described what happened, stating that he felt the Navy Admiral deliberately drugged him to prevent him flying back, and may have done so thinking there was a plot to kill Russbacher, and in that way protect him.

**"Your life may depend on you going public!"**

I warned Russbacher that the information he possessed put his life in danger, which would continue until he disclosed this information to others, and the information made public. "Your life may depend on you going public," I added. Russbacher's knowledge threatened to expose the people involved in October Surprise and many other criminal activities implicating the CIA, members of Congress, federal judges, and others.

It was now about midnight and Russbacher was still groggy. I suggested that he call me the following morning when his mind was clear and give me a sworn declaration of events surrounding the October Surprise operation. I said that I would record his statements and have the recording transcribed, after which I would send portions of the transcript to members of Congress. (What an optimist!)

**REVEALING MAJOR CRIMES**

When Russbacher called the next morning I said, "I need to know the specifics on the flight to Europe, including who was on board the aircraft, who stayed at what hotel; where did the flight start from, and where did it land enroute?" What he stated on that first questioning session was repeated many times during the next few years as other segments of that and other operations were detailed. This was the start of discoveries continuing to this date, of treasonous, subversive, and criminal acts implicating many federal officials. The information and documents I obtained enlarged upon the hard-core criminal misconduct that I had already uncovered.

A partial extract of Russbacher's first declaration reads as follows:

"My name is Gunther Russbacher. I am a captain in the United States Navy; my service number is 440-40-1417. My current location is the Federal Correctional Institution, Terminal Island. I am a federal prisoner, awaiting appeal on a charge of misuse and misappropriation of government properties, misuse of government jets, and misuse of government purchase orders for purchase of fuel. That is my current situation. The date today is May 1, 1991. The time of this interview is 0824. Now that we have the formalities under way, Rodney Stich, we can talk."

"Who were the pilots," I asked.

"On the flight deck were pilots Richard Brenneke, an Air Force pilot, and I was the command pilot."

"Who was in the cabin?"

"In the cabin were George Bush; William Casey (who would be appointed director of the CIA); Robert Gates; Donald Gregg (who at that time was a member of President Carter's National Security Council), and others."

In later sessions, I asked Russbacher to provide a more complete list of the passengers on the BAC 111 flight. He stated that other passengers included several Secret Service agents assigned to vice-presidential candidate George Bush; George Cave (former CIA Iran expert and translator); Richard Allen; Senators John Tower and John Heinz; Congressman Dan Rostenkowski; Jennifer Fitzgerald of the State Department (reportedly a close lady friend of Bush for many years).

"What type of plane were you flying?" I asked.

"The plane was a BAC 111, and we departed from Andrews Air Force Base, to New York, to Gander, and then on to Paris, landing at Le Bourget."

"At what stage of the flight did you see the passengers?"

"I went back into the cabin after taking off from Gander."

"Where did the crew stay while in Paris?"

"We stayed at the Florida Hotel in Paris."

"How long did Bush stay in Paris?"

"Bush only remained a few hours."

"Did you fly the same plane back?" I asked.

"No I didn't. I flew the man [George Bush] back in the SR-71."

"Are you qualified in the 71?"

"Rodney, I flew the 71 for eighteen months."

"Where did the 71 refuel?" recognizing that the SR-71 could not fly from Paris to the United States without refueling.

"The refueling occurred approximately, I would have to say, 1800 to 1900 nautical miles into the Atlantic. We were met by a KC 135."

"Where did you land on the return flight?"

"McGuire," Russbacher replied. [McGuire Air Force Base, New Jersey]

"How long did the flight take?"

"The flight took one hour and forty four minutes."

"What time did you arrive back at McGuire Air Force Base?"

"We arrived at McGuire Air Force Base approximately 10:50 a.m. the following morning."

"Who were some of the people you saw in Paris?"

"Adnan Khashoggi, Hashemi Rafsanjani. Rafsanjani was the Ayatollah's henchman and the second in command. Please look who is in command now; Rafsanjani."

In response to my probing questions, he provided additional data, including rudimentary piloting activities, conversations, airports, and other data that would be hard to fabricate. Russbacher described the route of flight from Washington to New York, to Gander, and then to Paris. He gave specifics that might be meaningless to anyone but a pilot who had been to the airports he described, which provided further confirmation that he was telling me the truth.

After arrival in Paris, Russbacher went to the Hotel Florida and had been asleep only a short time when he received a call from the CIA station chief in Frankfort, advising him that an SR-71 was being flown to Paris for him to fly back to the United States. The SR-71, with vice presidential candidate George Bush as a back-seat passenger and Russbacher at the controls, departed from a military air base near Paris 2:50 p.m. European Time (13:50 GMT, or 8:50 a.m. EST).

The SR-71 was refueled about 1,800 miles from Paris over the North Atlantic by a U.S. Air Force tanker. He landed at McGuire Air Force Base in New Jersey at 10:50 a.m. Eastern Standard Time (6:50 p.m. GMT). After Bush left the aircraft, Russbacher flew the SR-71 to Andrews Air Force Base.

Going back to the October Surprise operation, I asked Russbacher, "What do you know about the first meeting in Madrid between Casey and the Iranians that reportedly occurred in July of 1980?"

"The Madrid meeting was more of a diversionary tactic. The actual meeting occurred in Barcelona. I was in Barcelona at the time of the meetings. I was there at the Pepsico International headquarters building. I gave you the guy's name that was our interface there. V-a-n-T-y-n-e. [Peter Van Tyne]"

"That was approximately what month?" I asked, to make sure we were talking about the same meetings.

"That was in late July of 1980."

"This is the meeting or meetings in which William Casey met with some Iranians?"

"That is correct. That was with Hushang Lavi and Rogovin."[237]

"Referring to all of the reports of Casey having been in Madrid, I believe you stated that Casey was never in Madrid?"

"I said that the meetings, the top-level high-speed meetings, did not take place in Madrid. The suites and conference rooms and everything were rented and cared for. However, the meetings took place, and the people stayed, at the Hotel Princess Sofia, S-O-F-I-A, in Barcelona."

I responded, "And was this at the same time that he was supposedly in Madrid?"

"Right. It was a little subterfuge upon the part of the government [CIA]. But the actual meetings took place in Barcelona. They took place at the Pepsico International Headquarters building."

"And you were there in town with Peggy [Gunther's wife at the time]?"

"That's right. I was there at the meetings."

"So you know what was stated at the meetings?"

"This is where the first discussions were coming up as to what type of arms and munitions that the Iranians wanted."

"And who was there besides William Casey; was that Robert McFarlane?"

"Yes, it was."

"You previously stated that in Barcelona the meetings were held at the hotel, but then you also mentioned in one place about them being held at the Pepsico plant. Can you explain that?"

"Right. The day's meetings were held over at the Pepsico International Headquarters buildings."

"That was the main meetings then? Did you have any at the hotel that you mentioned?"

"Yes."

"What part did Van Tyne play in the meetings? Did he more or less coordinate the meetings?"

"Facilitator. Yes."

Realizing that Pepsico surfaces in numerous CIA activities, including drug processing in the Far East, I asked Russbacher: "Was Pepsico a CIA proprietary corporation?"

---

237 Mitchell Rogovin, lawyer for Lavi.

"No, but they have close connections to each other; they work together."

"A few more questions on the Barcelona meeting,[238] just to get clarified in my mind. Why did they have to use Madrid[239] as a diversionary point when they were trying to cover up for the whole operation?"

"There were also high-level meetings going on in the Spanish cabinet at the same time. It would be easier to hide under the cloak of secrecy as to what transpired in Madrid at that time, without going in and having to create a brand new cover for the meeting in Barcelona."

"Can you give me the details on the hour of the day and how long the meetings lasted?"

"I would estimate, according to my recollection, that the meeting began about ten o'clock in the morning, and lasted probably until one o'clock, at which time they broke for lunch, and the meeting reconvened from about three to six p.m."

"Was it a one-day meeting?"

"No, two days. The first day was full of meetings, and the second day was only about three hours long."

"What was your role at that meeting?"

"The only part that I took part in was to set up a centralized command in Vienna, which would involve being able to draw large containers and to allow freighting weapon containers, and so on."

"From the reforger stores?"[240]

"From the reforger stores, through Austria and down by rail."

"I would presume, referring to some comments you made about Austria being unhappy, were they to be notified when military shipments went through their country?"

"It was a total no-no."[241]

"Even when it is ordered by the United States?"[242]

"The United States cannot order anything. Austria is a sovereign republic. We made weapon shipments from the early contacts with the Iranians through Switzerland. We railed from Zurich to Vienna, and from Vienna on down."

"You said the people at the meeting were Casey and McFarlane; were there any other Americans there?"

"I think Allen was there for a couple of hours."

"And on the other side there was Hushang Lavi, and I think you mentioned Rogovin?"

---

238 The secret late-July 1980 Barcelona meetings, involving private citizen William Casey, preceded the secret October 19, 1980, weekend meetings held in Paris.

239 Investigative reporters and writers charge that William Casey met secretly in Madrid with Iranian factions to prevent the release of the 52 American hostages (last week of July 1980). But this is incorrect. The first meeting in Spain was not at Madrid, but at Barcelona.

240 Reforger stores contain American military weapons and were located in various European locations. To fulfill the Barcelona agreement, US weapons and munitions were fraudulently removed from military warehouses in Austria, Germany, and Italy, commencing in September 1980.

241 Secretly moving the military shipments through Austria violated the laws and sovereignty of Austria.

242 Actually, the duly elected government of the United States neither ordered the shipments of military arms, nor knew about the shipments. The removal was unlawfully done through a criminal conspiracy by private citizen William Casey and Central Intelligence Agency factions, in a literal coup against the United States.

"Yes."

"Rogovin was the attorney for Lavi, wasn't he?"

"Yes."

"Was there anyone else there?"

"There were several other people. But the individual I dealt with primarily was Mr. Peter Van Tyne."

"What was his position?"

"Peter Van Tyne was executive vice-president for Pepsico International. I might add that part of the reason I was there was that I was to set up a large production warehouse and production corporation in Vienna. We are talking about an extremely large warehouse where we could hold container shipments until transshipment took place. We were withdrawing military weapons and munitions from Switzerland, including Swiss military manufacturer Orlikon. We were drawing stores[243] from Germany. We were also drawing stores up from Italy. The shipments from Italy came up through Brenner Pass in overland containers, at which point they ended up in Innsbruck, Austria. In Innsbruck they were replaced by other containers, that were supposedly at that point moving mineral waters from Innsbruck to Third World areas."

"Mineral water?" I asked.

"That was what the code name was. The code name for it was Seltzer Water."

Describing the route of the arms shipments, Russbacher stated he established "transshipment points from Europe, especially Germany, Italy, and Switzerland. In Italy, up through Brenner Pass; from Germany into Austria. We were buying arms from Orlikon, a corporation, a weapons manufacturer in Switzerland. We had a big warehouse, a huge one. Some went through Yugoslavia. It went through Yugoslavia for transshipment through Macedonia, down through Greece, and then to Cyprus, and then across. Hungary was a transshipment point also. At times it went through Hungary. However, most of the times it went through Yugoslavia."

"Because Austria was a neutral country and Hungary was a communist country, we had a choice of transshipment points. Either first from Vienna to Budapest, where they were then transferred onto trains to Yugoslavia, or directly from Austria to Yugoslavia, and Yugoslavia down into Greece, and then to Cyprus. Most of the time it went through Yugoslavia."

This dialogue, and others within these pages, were repeated many times during years of conversations, letters, and affidavits.

In a later written response to interrogatories Russbacher replied in a sworn declaration:

*I was in attendance during the meetings held in Geneva, Switzerland; the meetings in Barcelona, Spain; the meetings held in Madrid, Spain, and the meeting held in Karachi, Pakistan. I was there as agency supply and logistics person, as well as facilitator for the governments involved.*

*The initial meeting was held in Geneva, and was held with Ahmed Heidari and Mohammed Hussein Behishti. Mr. Cyrus Hashemi was the arms specialist present at this meeting. In order to be unknown in this field*

243 Military equipment and supplies.

*we used the following DOS personnel as cutouts: Mr. Sam Carlton and Peter Merrell. This meeting took place six days after my return from Buenos Aires, Argentina, where a meeting of low echelon state staffers and I talked to the Mossad contact man, Ari Ben-Menashe.*

*The meeting with Ari Ben-Menashe was held on or about March fourth to the eighth, 1980. The initial meeting with the DOS persons, Hashemi, Heidari, Behishti and myself, was held in Geneva, shortly after our return from Buenos Aires. We met in Geneva on or about 14 March 1980. The discussion centered around another version of the swap for the hostages.*

*Mr. Adnan Khashoggi permitted us the use of his credit cards for the purpose of purchasing fuel for the aircraft. He indicated that he had specific interest in obtaining a deal for the sale or trade of arms to the government of Iran. We contacted Mr. Behishti and Mr. Heidari (who was the person responsible for coordinating the sale of the arms). Because Mr. Behishti spoke very little English, all conversations were held in either French or German. I was able to function as negotiator and interpreter for several such meetings.*

**LOOTING UNITED STATES MILITARY WAREHOUSES**

During another probing session, Russbacher revealed when the arms and munitions started to flow. The answer was critical and helped explain how the officially elected government of the United States was rendered helpless by the coup d'etat aspects of the October Surprise conspirators.

"After the [July 1980] Barcelona meeting, how soon did these arms start flowing?"

Russbacher hesitated in answering that question. He replied: "My friend, the arms began flowing, I would say, probably in September."[244]

"Were you over there at that time?"

"Yes, I was."

Since Casey, Ronald Reagan, and George Bush, the principal parties in the October Surprise conspiracy, had not held any government office at that time, and the November 1980 presidential elections had not yet occurred, the question arose as to who authorized the shipment of arms, especially since there were laws preventing the shipments, and since the shipments undermined the negotiations by President Jimmy Carter seeking to obtain the release of the 52 American hostages.

"Where did the authority come from to move that military equipment, since Casey and the gang held no government positions?"

Russbacher again hesitated, and then answered: "We [CIA] were already in there. The Agency [CIA] was already out on the limb.[245] And bear in mind

---

244 The gravity of this is that private citizen William Casey (and others) were able to remove military weapons and munitions from United States stockpiles, that were intended for the defense of Europe, and with the obvious cooperation of CIA factions, ship the arms to Iran via Israel, as part of the treasonous and subversive acts to continue the imprisonment of the 52 American hostages. A coup against the United States had occurred.

245 The CIA arranged for Bush and others to fly to the Paris meetings on the weekend of October 19, 1980, at which the secret agreement was finalized (Paying $40 million bribe money and promising billions of dollars in military equipment and munitions, in exchange for continuing the imprisonment of the 52 American hostages).

that Bush was the ex-DCI.[246] Casey had gone back to the days of Wild Bill Donovan. So you are talking about an agency coup that was already in the making at that time."

"What about the military, didn't they have control of those weapons; I mean the US military?"

"Rodney, if I tell you the shenanigans that are pulled, and the shopping that can be done at these reforger stores,[247] you would pull your hair out."

I asked Russbacher who worked with him in procuring the arms and arranging the shipments. "The procurement of them was handled by an associate of mine. The fellow's name was John George Fisher. He is dead."

I asked Russbacher, "What type of paperwork was done to get the U.S. military organizations to release the equipment?"

"It is very simple," Russbacher replied. "All you have to have is a request for transfer; which is commonly referred to as an AF series, duly signed by authorized personnel, or by an authorized officer. And, of course you need a transfer form approved for a transport form. And then you need end-user certificates."

When I asked Russbacher how those in control of the weapon depots allowed the arms to be removed, he referred to the CIA practice of placing CIA people in other government departments: "We [CIA] had already put them in position."[248]

"What about the end-user certificate requirements; you had to show an end-user, and who was that?"

"We [CIA] had end-user certificates available. That's why all shipments went through Cyprus. By the time the weapons came to Cyprus, new end-user certificates, or the real ones, that were going to be used, then showed up. But the end-user certificates that we always provided would have been countries that were friendly to the United States. Some of them were bogus. A lot of them went down to an entity in Spain. We had some sympathetic people."

Continuing, Russbacher stated, "We had embassies in Madrid that provided us end-user certificates. A lot of them were embassies from North African countries, West African countries, including Liberia."

Russbacher referred to the key role played by Israel in the operation, stating, "We worked hand in hand with the Mossad."[249]

During the next few years, I repeatedly questioned Russbacher concerning operations in which he had been directly involved, or of which he had specific details due to the nature of his work. Russbacher repeated details of the various CIA operations that we had previously discussed, oftentimes expanding on the information he had given me earlier.

---

246 Director of Central Intelligence.

247 Term applied to US military warehouses in Europe.

248 It is a standard practice of the CIA to install CIA personnel through the federal government, into state governments, and throughout industry, including the media.

249 Israel played a key role in carrying out the secret activities, including participation/attendance at the Barcelona and Paris meetings, the stealing of the arms from US warehouses, and the secret shipment of arms to Iran. Israel obviously knew that the scheme and activities were treasonous, subversive, and harmful to the United States; and also recognized that they could thereafter blackmail the United States while Reagan and Bush were in the White House.

**ISRAELI PARTICIPATION**

"Were there any Israel people at the Barcelona meeting?"

"I knew there was a discussion that there were some present."

"Was Karrubi there?" [Mehdi Karrubi, presently Iranian Parliamentary Speaker.]" Russbacher replied, "Yes."

In Ari Ben-Menashe's book *Profits of War* and in conversations with Ben-Menashe, he stated that he was present at the Barcelona meeting.

Referring to the $40 million bribe money that was reportedly given to the Iranian factions at the subsequent Paris meetings on the October 19, 1980, weekend, I asked: "Do you know anything about the routing of the reported forty-million-dollar bank draft that was given to the Iranians during the Paris meetings?"

"Michael Riconosciuto would be the best one to answer that."

**THE HELICOPTER CRASH**

I needed details surrounding the helicopter crash that had occurred the night before. "Were the Naval officers that you had coffee with [at Terminal Island Federal Prison], on the helicopter?" I asked.

"Yes," he replied, "I had coffee with one of them."

"What was his name?"

"The first guy's name was Samuel Walters."

"And he was Navy?"

"And that's his true name too."[referring to the alias frequently used; Gunther used the alias of Robert A. Walker.]

"What was his rank?"

"He was a captain."

"Did you meet the other two guys that were on it?"

"Yes, one of them was a Rear Admiral. John D. Burkhardt. He was in defense logistics."

"Office of Naval Intelligence?"

"Yes. And his present job was that he was very strongly implicated in NASA and the SDI initiative." Russbacher continued, "Raye called the Chief of Stations at St. Louis, who is a friend of ours. He made some checks and found out who was on board."

"Were they the ones who were to have gone back with you?"

"Yes. Tricky business, Rodney, I don't know if you want to get into this. If I had been on that helicopter, I would be dead."

Relating what his CIA handlers told him, Russbacher said:

> "The helicopter took off yesterday carrying a rear admiral, two Navy captains, and it should also have carried myself. Everybody here, including the D of J [Department of Justice], was under the impression that I was going to be on that airplane. The aircraft took off from Fort Ord with a flight to Monterey, and from Monterey they were going to discharge one of the crew who was going to stay at the FBO at Monterey. And then the aircraft was going on to Santa Cruz and land back behind the university grounds. The incident occurred about 6:18 p.m. The original incident, as it was described by the radio at Santa Cruz, was that a helicopter exploded about 200 feet above the ground. No pieces. Just general wreckage. What came out about

an hour later was that a helicopter went down with two FBI agents on board. There **were** two FBI agents on board; although they suffered serious injuries, they were O.K. One of them suffered very serious head injuries. Somehow or other they were able to cover up for the initial flight. Rodney, they are after every one that has anything to do with these activities."

Russbacher continued, "Someone saved my butt last night. I don't know how many more times in the future they are going to be able to do it."

"You felt that something was put in the coffee. Did it just make you groggy?"

"I went right to sleep and slept until twenty minutes of ten."

"So after you drank the coffee you were supposed to leave right then and there?"

"Within an hour and a half."

"Then you went back to your cell and went to sleep, expecting them to call you?"

"They never called."

"They never tried to wake you up?"

"As far as I know, no one tried to wake me up. The first inclination I had that it was time to wake up was at twenty minutes of ten; people were screaming at me that I had an emergency call from the [prison] Control Center and that I needed to call home immediately."

"I'm surprised the prison officials gave you that personal service."

"Well, you have to also bear in mind that [my status is] a little different.

"Well, the fact that you can get to a phone that is not monitored indicates that you are in a different category than most prisoners."

"Within four minutes of being awakened, I was on the phone talking to Raye and hearing your voice in the background."

I asked Russbacher how he ended up in prison. He replied, "That could be a book by itself. It dealt with repatriating some of the arms from Central America back to the United States."

Referring to what was done to silence me, Russbacher stated: "Your case is different. It does not address a single issue. Your case addresses multi-issues. If you create sufficient fires, it is extremely difficult to determine where the fires are and how best to put them out. You pose a significant threat. You pose as much of a threat to their little game as I do to the total administration. You pose a significant embarrassment to the federal government. It isn't quite so easy to shut these people down."

## CONFIRMATION OF THE HELICOPTER CRASH AND THE DEATH OF A DEEP-COVER NAVY ADMIRAL

The existence of the Navy helicopter crash was kept secret by the government, as though it never happened. The absence of any report caused me to withhold further mention of it, fearing that reference to a non-reported helicopter crash would discredit the other information Russbacher supplied me. However, during a conversation with *St. Louis Post Dispatch* reporter Phil Linsalata, I described the helicopter crash and qualified the information with the statement that I had no evidence to support its occurrence; that I hadn't told anyone else about it because of lack of evidence. Linsalata said that the *Post Dispatch* had a reliable CIA source and that they would contact him for possibly confirming the crash.

Linsalata contacted me several days later, on May 4, 1991, advising that the CIA contact confirmed the helicopter crash and that a Navy admiral was killed. Linsalata stated that the CIA contact expressed surprise that the *Post Dispatch* knew of the crash and the death of the Navy admiral. During another conversation on May 20, 1991, Linsalata again made reference to the statements made by the CIA source concerning the death of the Navy admiral in the helicopter crash. In response to my questions, Linsalata stated:

*The guy (CIA source) seemed shocked that I had access to this information. His shock seemed sincere. You judge the truth of what a person is saying, such as by the tone of voice. He seemed quite shocked that I had access to this information. He also made a comment that he personally knew who the ranking officer was, the brass, the admiral, and that he knew the guy. He was personally shocked that he [the Admiral] had been killed, and that he was a nice guy. He said the Admiral didn't deserve what happened. The things that he said to me made it impossible to rule out that he was simply offering the information that I gave him. The new information was given to me on his own. I didn't flush it out of him in any way. He just made comments reflecting that he knew what he was talking about. He seemed to be sincere.*

## COVERUP BY ST. LOUIS POST DISPATCH

Harry Martin,[250] publisher of the *Napa Sentinel*,[251] called me (July 8, 1991), stating that he had just received a call from Phil Linsalata of the *St. Louis Post Dispatch* denying that he had ever talked to any CIA contact about any helicopter crash at Fort Ord. Martin said that Linsalata sounded very nervous, as if he was under pressure to make that call. It appeared that the intent of the call was to dissuade Martin from making any reference to the statements Linsalata made to me confirming the existence of the crash and the death of the Admiral.

Martin had been one of the first media sources to respond (May 1, 1991) to the notices that I had a tape and transcript of a CIA operative who had been part of the October Surprise scandal. His subsequent articles were copied by numerous other papers, and members of Congress requested copies of Martin's articles. There was danger of exposing the October Surprise scandal if Martin printed the statements made to me by the *St. Louis Post Dispatch* reporter. Possibly to prevent this from happening, Linsalata's publisher ordered Linsalata to call Martin and deny that he had ever talked to me or to anyone else about the helicopter crash. Martin asked if I had a tape of the conversation and I replied that I did, of both the May 4 and May 20, 1991, telephone conversations. During these telephone conversations, Linsalata went into great detail concerning the information given by his CIA sources.

## WARNINGS TO FORGET THE HELICOPTER CRASH

Several days after the helicopter crash, Gunther and his wife warned me to totally forget about it, warning me that my life would be in danger if I made any reference to it or even made any inquiries. As I started to make reference to the crash during a subsequent conversation Russbacher stopped me: "No

---

250 *Napa Sentinel*, Napa, California.

251 The *Napa Sentinel* had been at the forefront in exposing government scandals, including Inslaw, October Surprise, and other stories.

Rodney, don't bring that up. Don't touch that with a ten-foot pole."

**"Because there is so much coverup in that crash!"**

Russbacher said:

*Rodney, don't even talk about it. I'm telling you. Because there is so much coverup in that crash. Listen to me. Listen closely. And be very guarded. When Raye got a call, she called St. Louis. St. Louis in turn made a phone call and then called her back. There were three people on board and they are all dead. You got that? Stay away from that as far as you can.*

I replied, "It would be important to know the details." Russbacher answered, "This is not the time to know. For your own life. I'm talking about personal safety." At a later date, I discovered additional evidence supporting the existence of that crash and that assassinations were an all-too-common CIA tactic.

**NOTIFYING THE MEDIA**

After I notified various media contacts that I had declarations of a CIA operative concerning the October Surprise operation, journalists from all parts of the United States were calling me for further information. When these journalists contacted Justice Department and White House officials, they were told that Russbacher was a con artist, that he had a long rap sheet and was not believable. This followed the standard line when CIA whistleblowers go public.

Shortly after Russbacher supplied me with his first declaration on May 1, 1991, I mailed partial transcripts to members of Congress,[252] along with a petition demanding that our testimony and evidence be received. I reminded them I was exercising rights[253] and responsibilities[254] under federal law and that they had a responsibility under these same laws and under federal criminal statutes to receive our testimony and evidence. I explained that I was a former federal investigator who held federal authority to make these determinations and that I hadn't lost any of my abilities to do that since leaving government.

I mailed certified letters and transcripts to Independent Prosecutor Lawrence Walsh, who had the duty to investigate all aspects of the Iran-Contra affair, which started with the October Surprise scheme. I reminded Walsh of his responsibilities under federal criminal statutes to receive my testimony and evidence and that of the CIA whistleblowers.

Despite hundreds of certified mailings, each containing over fifty pages of data, no one responded. The non-response was one of the most amazing examples of mass coverup that I had ever witnessed. But it happened time and again. My letters raised very serious charges that, if only a small fraction of them were true, would inflict enormous harm upon the United States. This refusal to perform a duty made possible the continuation of the government corruption that continues to inflict great harm upon America.

As Russbacher provided me with further information and other CIA sources gave me supporting data, I sent additional petitions to members of Congress, demanding that they receive the testimony and evidence from a **group** of

---

252 Every Senator in the United States Senate and to about 250 Representatives.

253 Right to petition government relating to criminal acts by federal officials, including the First Amendment right to petition government and Title 28 U.S.C. § 1361, the right to judicial halting of corrupt acts by federal officials.

254 Federal crime reporting statutes, including Title 18 U.S.C. § 4.

concerned CIA whistleblowers on criminal activities against the United States. I described specific facts that would be revealed. Every senator received at least three certified mailings from me between May 1991 and December 1992, as did the members of the House Judiciary Committee, Foreign Affairs Committee, Oversight and Investigations, government Operations, and Aviation. Not a single reply was received.

As a result of publicity generated by my transcripts and references to Russbacher on my talk show appearances, Russbacher was asked to appear on numerous radio and television talk shows, which he did from prison. Despite all this, the public remained passive, and none of those in government wanted to disturb the status quo.

## ESCALATING MEDIA AND CONGRESSIONAL DISINFORMATION

Shortly after I had first publicized Russbacher's sworn statements, the disinformation to discredit him commenced. Even author Barbara Honegger, who authored the first *October Surprise* book, tried to discredit Russbacher, fabricating facts that I had to address by sending out information identifying the apparent deliberate misstatements. Her tactics tended to discredit the existence of the very scandal that her earlier book sought to expose. It was as if she was being rewarded in some way to discredit the smoking gun in the October Surprise conspiracy.

The charges by Justice Department officials, commencing in 1986, were to discredit Russbacher and minimize the danger to White House and other officials. Russbacher had earlier described the three factions in the CIA as often fighting each other. Faction-One was controlled by the Justice Department and the White House under George Bush. Faction-Two was controlled by the Office of Naval Intelligence, often at odds with Faction-One. And Faction-Three was a small number of former Office of Strategic Services (OSS) personnel.

### "They are deporting Russ!"

Russbacher's appearances on radio and television from his prison environment threatened many people. Justice Department officials addressed this threat by seeking to deport him. Once, upon answering the phone,[255] Russbacher's wife exclaimed, "Gunther isn't in Terminal Island. He is on a flight to Oakdale, Louisiana, a federal prison where prisoners to be deported are sent."

In an attempt to prevent the deportation, I phoned talk-show host Tom Valentine with Radio Free America; senior White House reporter Sarah McClendon; Independent Prosecutor Lawrence Walsh, and appeared on numerous talk shows describing the efforts to sequester evidence relating to October Surprise.

### "I need more information!"

Despite the gravity of criminal activities I listed in the petitions that I sent to Congress, the recipients did nothing. I felt that I needed more information about additional CIA crimes that would force members of Congress to respond. I told Russbacher, "I need more information!" Russbacher went into great detail about other areas of corrupt CIA activities.

---

255 October 13, 1991.

Russbacher detailed the involvement by CIA factions in the looting of savings and loan institutions and insurance companies; the CIA's role in drug trafficking throughout the United States, and much more. He furnished me with blank checks, letterheads, and incorporation papers of some of the covert CIA proprietaries he operated for the CIA, which dealt in unlawful activities.

The information Russbacher gave me in hundreds of conversations was detailed and was presented in a way that I had no reason to question its accuracy. The answers to very specific questions, requiring a very detailed answer, came without hesitation. In those cases when he didn't know, he didn't hesitate to say so, even though he could have fabricated an answer. There were some areas of CIA activity he would not discuss, and information on these areas would often come to me from other sources. Russbacher did back down after refusing to answer questions concerning a certain area when another source described it to me. Then Russbacher would enlarge upon the information in a manner indicating he was well familiar with the operation.

To confirm his answers, I approached the subject from a different angle many months later, and the precise detailed facts would rarely waver. His precise knowledge of people and events in many areas of intrigue was unprecedented and checked out with facts that I obtained from other sources. I was convinced that he was not a con man. He simply could not make up the vast amount of data he gave me in response to questions that covered a broad spectrum. As other CIA whistleblowers came to me I was able to obtain further confirmation of Russbacher's CIA status and of many of the events that he described to me.

Even when I told him information given to me by others, such as former Mossad agent Ari Ben-Menashe, Russbacher often responded with additional information on the person which had never appeared in print. It wasn't Russbacher who sought attention. I was the one that repeatedly told Russbacher to give me information of CIA corruption so that I could force Congress and the media to meet their responsibilities.

Russbacher detailed how the CIA was part of the looting of Chapter 11 assets, and how the CIA used crooked federal judges, trustees, and law firms to accomplish this. He described how the CIA covered up for some of its looted proprietaries by placing the companies into Chapter 7 or 11 where the CIA had control of the judges. He named judges, trustees, law firms and their attorneys, who were present at CIA drug and arms transshipment points in Central and South America, and especially trustee Charles Duck, who looted much of my multi-million in assets. At a later date, Russbacher gave me the name of the overseas corporation that paid the bribe money to the judges, trustees and law firms beholden to the CIA and Justice Department gang.

Russbacher described the interrelationships between the CIA and people looting the savings and loans. He described how Keating-controlled corporations hid over $300 million of depositors' money in Colorado through secret trusts and other financial mechanisms. When I quizzed Russbacher about the CIA's role with Charles Keating, he responded: "It wasn't just Keating. Bear in mind that we are not talking about strictly Keating-controlled corporations. We are talking about a multitude of corporations that were controlled by outside forces. Keating just happened to be one of them."

**REMOVAL OF MONEY FROM THE UNITED STATES**

Elaborating upon the huge outflow of funds generated by CIA proprietaries through various financial scams and drug money laundering, Russbacher stated: "It is a systematic removal of funds from U.S. bank accounts. And these accounts that held large amounts of funds were then channeled to off-shore bank accounts and off-shore investment companies."

I asked, "How are these funds identified; I'm talking about who would be identified as the owner of these funds? Would it be numbered accounts?" Russbacher replied, "It would be numbered or designated accounts, where you have a primary person that is allowed to make transactions. That doesn't necessarily mean that person is the only one."

"I presume that the CIA has numerous operatives who are authorized to place or remove funds from these accounts?"

"There are only ten or twelve people in the whole agency that are permitted to do that. Let's say, no more than two dozen people."

"Are you one of those?"

"Yes, I am. Or I was."

Russbacher's statements as shown in these pages are but a minute fraction of the in-depth discussions between him and myself. These statements were made during late 1990 and up to the date of this book's publication. Much of the details were unknown to the general public and had not been in print. Many people confirmed to me Russbacher's CIA position, and statements made to me by Russbacher were often confirmed by statements made by others, including Ari Ben-Menashe, Michael Riconosciuto, Ronald Rewald, and other CIA related people.

Many hours were spent on what he saw firsthand as a CIA operative in Chapter 11 courts. Russbacher told of the CIA practice of using Chapter 11 courts for two primary purposes. One was to cover up for its looting of CIA proprietaries. The other was to loot the assets of small to medium size companies and individuals who filed Chapter 11 seeking time to pay their debts, and who had large equities.

**PATTERN OF JUDICIAL CORRUPTION IN CHAPTER 11**

Many of the victims didn't understand the blatant illegality of how the racketeering enterprise stripped them of their life's assets. The scheme follows a standard pattern, violating federal statutes and constitutional protections. The Chapter 11 judge, who almost always is a direct participant in the corrupt enterprise, orders the assets seized, usually in clear violation of law, and then appoints a trustee who promptly loots the assets, forcing the Chapter 11 case into a Chapter 7 liquidation.

During liquidation, the trustee, his law firm and attorneys, and others who work together, sell the properties at a fraction of their market value. The person who sought relief in Chapter 11 then becomes the victim of one of the most outrageous racketeering enterprises in the United States. Russbacher gave me details of this racket as seen from his CIA perspective, dovetailing what I had earlier discovered as a victim and an investigator.

I asked Russbacher if, during his CIA activities, he encountered the people who played a major role in seizing and looting my assets. His reply was startling. The federal judge who corruptly seized my assets was Las Vegas Chapter 11

Judge Robert Jones. Russbacher described how the CIA arranged transportation to Atlantic City for this federal judge, where letters of credit would be waiting at different casinos for him to obtain tens of thousands of dollars in gambling chips. Russbacher named other federal judges that he knew who were present at CIA arms and drug or other operations, including Judge Alan Jaroslovsky, a key judge in the Northern District of California, who had repeatedly protected trustee Charles Duck from his accusers. Russbacher later mentioned that he was a CIA-asset and was on a secret financial arrangement.

I asked Russbacher if there could be any legitimate basis for the appearances of federal judges, trustees and law firms at the secret CIA arms and drug trafficking locations in Central America. He confirmed that there was no lawful reason for their appearances at these locations.

Russbacher had flown to Central America CIA sites in CIA aircraft, accompanied by people such as trustee Charles Duck; attorney members of the law firms of Friedman, Sloan and Ross (who filed the sham divorce action against me); Goldberg, Stinnett and McDonald[256] (who seized and looted my assets in conjunction with Duck and Judge Robert Jones); and Murray and Murray (who took over after Duck was sent to prison).

Russbacher had been at CIA meetings in Central America with Duck at John Hull's ranch and at Tegucigalpa,[257] as well as other locations. Referring to Duck, Russbacher described his presence in 1987: "The last time that I had dealings with him, or came close to having dealings with him, he was there in the hotel room with me."

**FUNDING CIA THROUGH SEIZURE OF CHAPTER 11 ASSETS**

Russbacher said that Charles Duck bragged about how he looted the assets of Chapter 11 parties. Referring to Duck and the CIA looting of Chapter 11 assets, Russbacher stated: "Duck has basically siphoned off large sums of money from his assigned cases. He appeared in different areas where we [CIA] were involved. This is the nexus I have been getting across to you, between the bankruptcy issues, and Agency [CIA] operations. It is one of the funding vehicles for the Company [CIA]."

Russbacher stated that the worst Chapter 11 corruption was in federal courts located in the San Francisco, Los Angeles, Chicago, and St. Louis areas. He added, "Let me tell you like this. St. Louis is notorious on Chapter 11. What it amounts to is: one of the bankruptcy judges in each one of the districts gets definite remuneration from the CIA."

**TYPICAL START-UP OF CIA PROPRIETARY**

Describing one of the ways in which the CIA proprietaries generate money, Russbacher stated:

> *Most of them were limited partnerships. The funds would have been from the CIA to start with.*[258] *What they did, they allegedly put a private offering together, and the subscribers for the private offerings were already in*

---

256 Name was changed in 1993 to Goldberg, Stinnett, Meyers & Davis, located at 44 Montgomery Street, San Francisco, California

257 Capital of Honduras.

258 To establish a net worth from which to seek large loans that were never repaid and never intended to be repaid. The funds were diverted to covert CIA domestic and international uses.

*place before the offering was even written up. Each one of these people who subscribed to the offering brought in Agency funds.*

Russbacher stated:

*The corporation or limited partnership would issue corporate paper or whatever, and that's how more funds were created. They used the initial funds for the funding of the LTD partnership strictly as a collateral vehicle for large scale loans.*

He continued:

*If we go in, for instance, with a million or half a million dollars each on a limited partnership, and there are ten of us, let's say we have anywhere from five to ten million dollars in capital assets in the limited partnership, that, along with a good financial statement, and what we planned to do with the limited partnership, can earn us the right to a thirty, forty, fifty million dollar loan. Do you see what I am saying?*

Russbacher described what usually happened after obtaining multi-million-dollar loans. The people default on the non-recourse loans after the money is pulled out, stating, "Generally it was strictly default. We pulled money back out and we would end up with thirty, forty million." Russbacher added, "That particular company would file Chapter 11 in courts where we had control of the judges."

**OTHER CIA SOURCES**

Initially, Russbacher was my best source of information. As I became known in the relatively small intelligence community, other concerned intelligence agency operatives came to me, describing the corrupt activities they had observed or been ordered to participate in.

**MOSSAD-CIA CROSS-CHECK**

Adding to the large amount of information supporting Russbacher's statements was an interesting dialogue between a former Mossad agent, Ari Ben-Menashe, and Russbacher. I arranged for several conference calls between these two former intelligence officers and encouraged them to exchange experiences. In one instance, Russbacher told Ben-Menashe of his friendship with the Mossad's station chief in Vienna, Heinz Toch, a name that would be known to very few people, and then primarily the Mossad. This was one example of Russbacher's intimate knowledge of covert activities. He would not have known this unless he actually was a high-level operative in the CIA.

I talked for many hours to the wives of several operatives who related facts to me as seen from their perspective, corroborating what their husbands told me. I had frequent conversations and written communications with many other former CIA and DEA operatives, including Michael Riconosciuto;[259] Russell Bowen;[260] Trenton Parker;[261] Ronald Rewald;[262] Basil Abbott;[263] Charles Hayes;

---

259 Riconosciuto was a CIA contract agent for many years who was involved in the October Surprise operation, Inslaw, and other activities.

260 Bowen was a member of the OSS during World War II and then continued with a small group of OSS people as moles inside the CIA after OSS was disbanded. He was heavily involved in CIA and Mossad drug trafficking and other intelligence agency operations in Europe, the Middle East, and Central and South America.

261 Long-time deep-cover CIA operative.

262 Rewald was placed by the CIA head of the Agency proprietary, Bishop, Baldwin, Rewald, Dillingham and Wong (BBRDW).

Edwin Wilson;[264] Michael Maholy; Bill Tyree, and others. I was in direct contact with law enforcement people whose investigative functions brought them in contact with CIA activities, especially CIA drug trafficking. These included Jim Rothstein;[265] Ted Gunderson;[266] and others. This vast amount of data, plus what I discovered, developed into a mosaic-like depiction of sordid intrigue, deception, and murder, portraying the worst pattern of criminal activities ever reported against the American people.

My phone was used for hundreds of hours of three-way conference calls between CIA and DEA personnel, their wives, a Mossad agent, and even Ross Perot. Often the conversations were of the nature of one pilot describing to another events that they experienced, each one knowing that any fabrication would be recognized by the other. My position was like a secret mole inside covert CIA activities, adding to the discoveries I made while a federal investigator and while being victimized in one of the many criminal enterprises.

As a former federal investigator holding federal authority to reach conclusions based upon the facts uncovered, based upon the fifteen years of book publishing, and based upon what I had personally observed, the evidence was overwhelming. The American people are being systematically defrauded by a well entrenched group in the federal government.

**CONTINUAL JUSTICE DEPARTMENT ATTEMPTS TO SILENCE RUSSBACHER**

Russbacher was scheduled to be released December 23, 1991. At that time he would pose a greater threat of exposing October Surprise, Inslaw, and numerous other major criminal enterprises implicating White House and federal officials and ongoing criminal operations.

Justice Department prosecutors used another tactic to keep Russbacher in prison. Shortly before Russbacher was scheduled for release, Justice Department attorneys notified Missouri authorities that he had been charged with impersonating a Naval officer at Castle Air Force Base. The attorneys induced them to revoke Russbacher's parole arising from the sham charges for which Russbacher had never had a trial and for which he was induced to enter an Alford plea. (U.S. Attorney David Levi in Sacramento had dropped the impersonating-a-Navy-officer charge shortly after it was made in 1990.)

Russbacher was transported to St. Charles, Missouri for a February 7, 1992, hearing on revocation of his parole on the charge of impersonating a Navy officer. Missouri Judge Donald E. Dalton refused to allow him to call CIA personnel who could attest to his being a covert CIA operative on assignment from the Office of Naval Intelligence. However, he did allow Russbacher to call witnesses from Offutt and Castle Air Force Base, who testified that Russbacher and his wife were billeted there and that the authorization came from Navy CincPac (Commander in Chief, Pacific). The witnesses provided the authorization

---

263 DEA pilot who flew drugs from Central and South America to the United States.

264 Heavily involved in CIA activities in Southeast Asia, Europe, and the Middle East, who worked with key figures in the Iran-Contra affair, and who was made the fall guy and was sent to prison.

265 Rothstein was on the New York City vice-squad for many years. He arrested Frank Sturgis when Sturgis arrived in New York to kill a former girl-friend of Fidel Castro. Rothstein had considerable street knowledge of CIA drug trafficking commencing in the 1950s.

266 Former FBI agent heavily involved in exposing pedophilia.

numbers. This testimony and the Air Force records were strong evidence that Russbacher was on official duty with the United States Navy.

Dalton disregarded the evidence that Russbacher was a covert intelligence officer. He ignored the fact that there had never been a trial on the underlying money offense charge; that there was no evidence presented to show that Russbacher had committed any of the acts charged, or that anyone suffered any financial loss. (Several of the charges arose from Russbacher's transfer of stock from one CIA proprietary to another, without registering with the State of Missouri. Several charges arose from Russbacher writing checks on a CIA proprietary that he owned, to one of his aliases.)

The judge revoked Russbacher's probation and ordered him to start serving the 21-year sentence that had been rendered in 1990 when Russbacher was encouraged to enter an Alford plea (not admitting any guilt but settling for probation).

Russbacher and I continued our almost daily telephone conversations discussing the specifics of CIA operations in which he was involved. As he became more discouraged, he loosened up and gave me more information about CIA/ONI covert (and subversive) activities, most of which were continuing.

Russbacher's health was failing due to an urgent need for coronary bypass surgery. Rayelan, his wife, and I, and other people, worked for his release. I rushed to get the first printing of *Defrauding America* published, with the intent of using the book as the basis for appearing on radio and television shows. In this way publicity would be focused on Russbacher and other CIA scapegoats. The primary intent was to make the American people aware of the well-orchestrated criminality involving government personnel, and to motivate them to take action. That was naive.

The statements made to me by Russbacher that are quoted here are only a small fraction of what he disclosed. Over 200 audio tapes are filled with his answers to my questions given over a four-year period. His precise and sophisticated knowledge of names, dates, and places exceeded anything that I had experienced before or after this time period. In subsequent books, other areas of CIA activities will be described, which Russbacher and other deep-cover operatives described to me.

Russbacher's attorney, Robert Fleming, had filed an appeal of the charges against Russbacher, and in 1994 the appellate court overturned the conviction which had kept Russbacher in prison, causing his release. The prosecutor refiled charges against Russbacher and served Russbacher before he was released from prison, requiring Russbacher to appear for a hearing. Instead of appearing, Russbacher went back to his native Austria. Missouri then filed a warrant for Russbacher's arrest, insuring that Russbacher would be arrested if he returned to the United States.

For reasons not clear to me, Russbacher returned to the United States in 1997 and was promptly arrested. After a few months in county jail in Missouri, a closed-door hearing was held, followed by Russbacher being deported to Austria, accompanied by two INS agents, apparently to be sure he did in fact arrive in Austria.

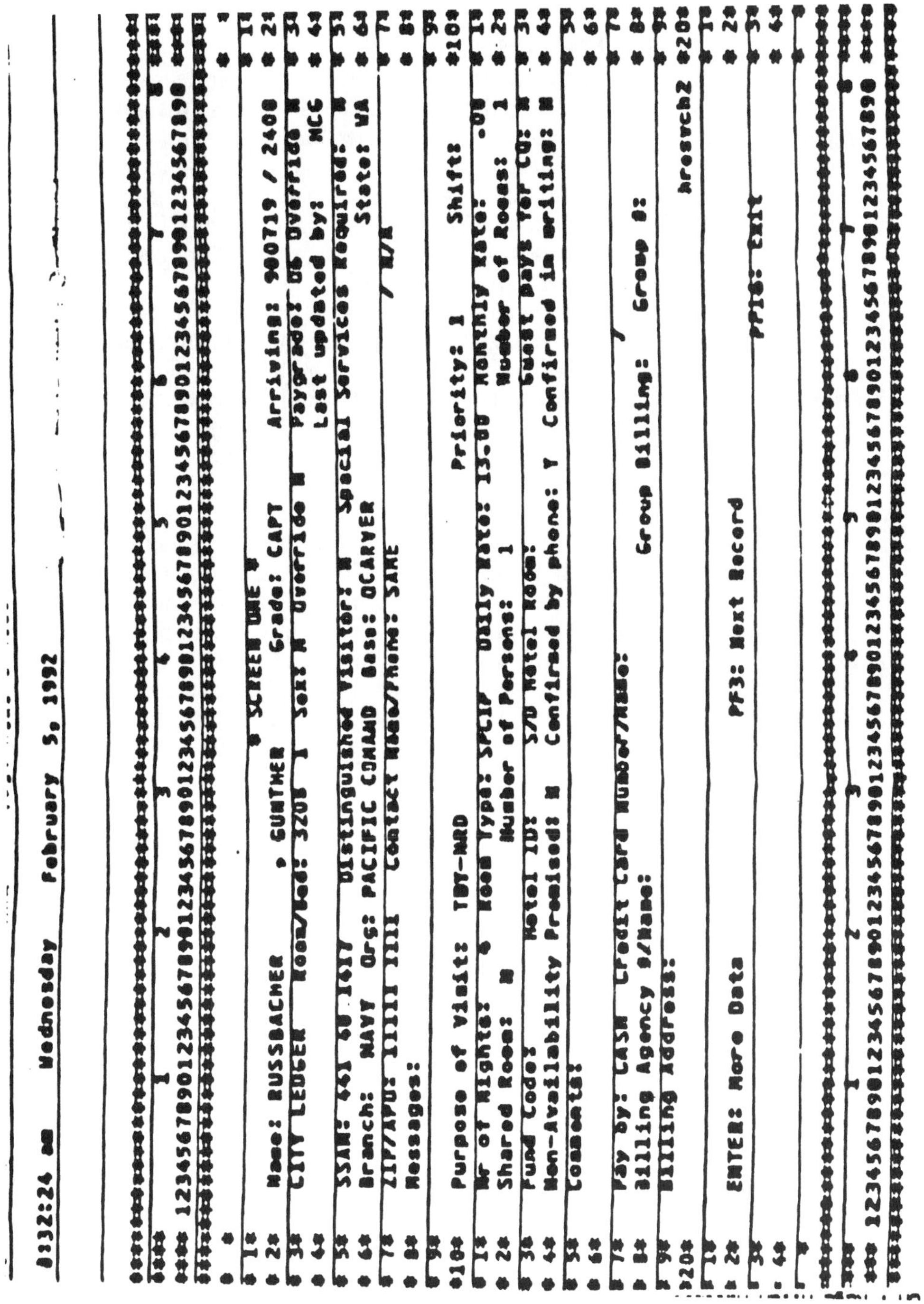

```
8:32:24 am     Wednesday     February 5, 1992

****          1         2         3         4         5         6         7         8 ****
**** 1234567890123456789012345678901234567890123456789012345678901234567890123456789 0 ****
*  *                                                                             *  *
* 1*                             * SCREEN ONE *                                  * 1*
* 2*  Name: RUSSBACHER        , GUNTHER       Grade: CAPT     Arriving: 900719 / 2400 * 2*
* 3*  CITY LEDGER   Room/Bed: 3208  1  Sex: M  Override N     Paygrade: 06 Override N  * 3*
* 4*                                                         Last updated by:   MCG  * 4*
* 5*  SSAN: 461 60 1617    Distinguished Visitor: N   Special Services Required:   N * 5*
* 6*  Branch:  NAVY  Org: PACIFIC COMAND  Base: OCARVER                   State: WA  * 6*
* 7*  ZIP/APO: 11111 1111    Contact Name/Phone: SAME                / N/A          * 7*
* 8*  Messages:                                                                      * 8*
* 9*                                                                                 * 9*
*10*  Purpose of Visit:  TDY-NRD                          Priority: 1      Shift:    *10*
* 1*  Nr of Nights:    6  Room Type: SPCIP   Daily Rate: 13.00  Monthly Rate:    .00 * 1*
* 2*  Shared Room:  N        Number of Persons:   1            Number of Rooms:   1  * 2*
* 3*  Fund Code:         Motel ID:      S/D Motel Room:         Guest Pays for CQ: N * 3*
* 4*  Non-Availability Promised: N   Confirmed by phone: Y  Confirmed in writing: N  * 4*
* 5*  Comments:                                                                      * 5*
* 6*                                                                                 * 6*
* 7*  Pay by: CASH  Credit Card Number/Name:                         /               * 7*
* 8*  Billing Agency #/Name:                          Group Billing:   Group #:      * 8*
* 9*  Billing Address:                                                               * 9*
*20*                                                                     hresvch2   *20*
* 1*                                                                                 * 1*
* 2*  ENTER: More Data                  PF3: Next Record                             * 2*
* 3*                                                            PF15: Exit           * 3*
* 4*                                                                                 * 4*
*  *                                                                                 *  *
****          1         2         3         4         5         6         7         8 ****
**** 1234567890123456789012345678901234567890123456789012345678901234567890123456789 0 ****
```

Copy of official records from Offutt Air Force Base showing Russbacher's status as captain, captain's pay grade as Grade 6, assigned to ONI, with authorization from Commander in Chief, Pacific.

**CIA DISINFORMATION EXPERT**

In 1994, I made contact with Oswald LeWinter, a former deep-cover CIA operative who spent 30 years with the agency and primarily as a disinformation expert. He played a coverup role in the October Surprise operation. He and several associates were responsible for removal of incriminating records from such locations as hotels, cab and limousine companies, and at the airport. LeWinter was with the CIA from 1974 to 1984, assigned to the CIA's achieves at Langley, in Europe, and Israel. He was part of Operation Gladios involving the CIA destabilization of the Italian government.

In 1979, LeWinter was assigned to ITAC, and in 1980 he was asked to get involved in the Reagan-Bush campaign, which led to his involvement in the October Surprise scheme. He said that one of the government officials secretly involved in the October Surprise operation was Donald Gregg, who at that time was head of the National Security Council under President Jimmy Carter. While holding this position, Gregg sabotaged the government of the United States in the operation that helped get Reagan and Bush into office in 1981.

**On the Clean-Up Crew**

LeWinter stated that he started doing advance work for logistics for the October Surprise meetings held in Europe, including Madrid, Barcelona and Paris. When I asked him if he was at the Barcelona meeting at the Pepsico plant he said: "I was there, I made sure that the guys I interfaced with in Spain picked up all the papers. I made sure that the landing and takeoff records from the airport were collected, so there was no evidence that the meeting occurred."

When asked about the Paris meeting, LeWinter said:

"At Paris I coordinated with French intelligence, a man by the name of Picard."

I asked, "At the Paris meeting, did you get to see any of the people, such as Gregg, Bush, or any of the others?" He answered, "Yes, Bush, Gregg, Casey."

"Where did you see them?"

"I saw Casey at the Hilton where he was staying; I got instructions from Casey. I saw Bush in a black Embassy Chevy near the [Hotel] Crillon."

"Did you get involved in any of the arms shipments?"

"No, I knew that they were taken from the reforger stores without telling the European governments, our NATO allies, and shipping them to Iran. They later used me to do some misinformation about that."

# OCTOBER SURPRISE COVERUP

The mainstream media in the United States kept the lid on the October Surprise operation and the other corrupt activities associated with it through a pattern of disinformation and the withholding of evidence. The establishment media sought to discredit the CIA whistleblowers who could prove the existence of the October Surprise operation. They fabricated reasons to discredit a group of former CIA and Mossad intelligence agency personnel who were personally involved in the operation, and who had nothing to gain by giving testimony, and had much to lose, including criminal prosecution. These sources were willing to risk their safety and freedom to expose the corruption against the American people.

The "investigating" committees and the establishment media gave absolute credibility to the statements of those who were part of the treasonous and criminal activities, and who faced impeachment and prison terms if the charges were proven. In this way, as a matter of law, members of Congress and the media became co-conspirators.

The *Village Voice* discredited the testimony of CIA contract agent Richard Brenneke because it found ten-year-old credit card slips for Brenneke that were made in Portland, Oregon on October 18, 1980. These credit card slips were found by Peggy Robahm, who went to Portland where Brenneke resided, from her home state of Connecticut, for the sole purpose of becoming involved with Brenneke. Later, she was hired by the House October Surprise Committee to "investigate" the October Surprise allegations.

My CIA sources state that the signatures on the credit cards were not Brenneke's signature and that it is standard practice for CIA people engaging in covert operations to cause a record to be established showing them to be elsewhere. CIA contract agent, Michael Riconosciuto, a close friend of Brenneke, who also resided in the Portland area, stated to me[267] that "Brenneke's credit card was used by a friend during that weekend."

The same mainstream media discredited CIA operative Gunther Russbacher, the pilot who reportedly flew George Bush and others to Paris on the October 19, 1980, weekend, and then flew Bush back in an SR-71. Former, and probably current CIA asset, Frank Snepp, wrote an article in the *Village Voice* stating that Russbacher didn't even know how to start the engines of an SR-71. This article was then repeated over and over again by the media until the lie was taken as truth.

I had obtained a copy of the formerly secret SR-71 manual, studied its 1000-plus pages, and quizzed Russbacher on the operation of the aircraft, including the starting procedures for the engines. I was qualified to determine his competency in this area since it was my job for many years to conduct pilot competency checks for airline pilots on jet aircraft. Russbacher certainly knew how to start the engines on the SR-71. The start-up procedures are quite different than other jet aircraft, but amazingly simple.

A *Newsweek* article[268] fabricated facts to discredit the October Surprise charges, stating on its cover: "The October Surprise Charge: Treason; Myth." It misstated and omitted facts so as to support the front page cover. The magazine sought to discredit the testimony of former Mossad agent Ari Ben-Menashe, who was present at the Madrid, Barcelona, and Paris meetings.

Authors of several books and many magazine and newspaper articles found Ben-Menashe credible and quoted him in their writings. Gary Sick quoted him numerous times in his 1992 *October Surprise* book, as did Seymour Hersh in *The Samson Option*.[269] Russbacher said to me many times that he saw Ben-Menashe at the Barcelona meetings. The establishment media sought to discredit Ben-Menashe by stating he was only a low-level file clerk who never left Israel.

Denying the existence of the October Surprise operation required undermining the credibility of these whistleblowers and informants who were present. *Newsweek* portrayed Ben-Menashe as being a "shadowy, Israeli exile, a former translator for the Israeli government,...does not seem to check out." Perhaps they expected an espionage agent to live the life of a nun!

*Time* magazine also joined the disinformation tactics. Its October 28, 1991, issue called Ben-Menashe a "veteran spinner of stunning-if-true-but yarns," and a "fabricator." An eleven-page deceptive article in *The New Republic*[270] was entitled "The Conspiracy That Wasn't" with the subtitle, "The hunt for the October Surprise." The deceptive article, written by Steven Emerson and Jesse Furman, stated in part:

> *The conspiracy as currently postulated is a total fabrication....Almost every source cited by Sick or Frontline has been indicted or was the subject of a federal investigation prior to claiming to be a participant in the October Surprise.*

---

267 During a phone call with Riconosciuto and attorney Jim Vassilos on October 27, 1992.

268 November 11, 1991.

269 Described Israel's nuclear program and the part played by Robert Maxwell in various forms of skullduggery.

270 November 18, 1991.

Ben-Menashe authored the 1992 publication of *Profits of War*,[271] subtitled "Inside the Secret U.S.-Israeli Arms Network," which contained copies of Israeli government documents showing Ben-Menashe as a high-level staff officer for Israel's Mossad and military agencies.

**THE CIA'S MEDIA WURLITZER**

The CIA has many media personnel on its payroll to plant stories or discredit charges against it. The Agency secretly pays out large sums of money for articles and books to be written on the CIA's behalf. Its control over the media is like a Wurlitzer, orchestrating and manipulating all segments of the written or broadcast media. The CIA uses taxpayer funds to control reporters and publishers of newspapers, magazines and books.

**SERIOUS IMPLICATIONS**

The evidence supporting the October Surprise charges required impeaching President George Bush and filing criminal charges against key officials in the executive, legislative, and judicial branches of the federal government. Never in the history of the United States was there such a serious criminal conspiracy inflicted upon the United States by people in control of the White House and government. There was no comparison between the relatively minor coverup of Watergate and the hard crimes associated with October Surprise. The media exaggeration of Watergate inflicted immense harms upon the United States. The media *coverup* of October Surprise inflicted far greater harm upon the United States but in a form not recognized by the uninformed American public.

October Surprise was many times more serious, involving people scattered throughout the three branches of the federal government. Failure to deny the existence of October Surprise could cause mass impeachments, criminal prosecution, and awaken the American public to the criminality in government. The fallout would affect both political parties.

Consider the difference between the political turmoil associated with exposing the October Surprise crimes and the seeming tranquillity following its coverup. The surface tranquillity, however, hid the hard-core corruption and harm that continued to be inflicted upon the American people in ways not recognized by the public.

**"We couldn't stand another disgraced presidency."**

The coverup by some of the media was for reasons other than protecting the guilty or vested interests. Several syndicated columnists, including Jim Fain of *Cox News Service*, explained the reason for the October Surprise coverup in an April 23, 1991 column: "A consensus grew that we couldn't stand another disgraced presidency. Democrats in the bungled Congressional hearings said as much."

One of the tactics used to discredit October Surprise and other scandals was to discredit and make a mockery of those who describe the criminal acts and who use the word conspiracy. This tactic plays upon the ignorance of the public as to what constitutes a conspiracy. A conspiracy exists in almost any type of crime and consists of two or people agreeing to do one or more acts. There is obviously no shortage of conspiracies anywhere, even though the standard

---

271 *Profits of War*, Sheridan Square Press.

disinformation tactic is to ridicule anyone who makes reference to a conspiracy.

Another coverup tactic is to discredit statements or charges made by someone accused of a federal offense, calling him or her a felon and a person whose statements cannot be believed. Many CIA operations have been criminal under law, making it easy for Justice Department officials to silence any potential CIA whistleblower by charging them with committing a crime. Using this argument, the only witness who could be considered reliable would be someone like a nun, someone who couldn't possibly have access to information about criminal activities.

However, when the shoe is on the other foot and Justice Department prosecutors are trying to sentence a person to prison, they not only use the testimony of felons but even reward them for their often-fabricated testimony. Paid testimony comes in the form of pardons from earlier convictions, dropping of pending charges, money, including supporting the witness for years in the witness protection program.

If witnesses didn't testify as Justice Department prosecutors wanted, they would face long prison terms or other consequences. In addition, they don't have to worry about prosecution for perjury; the only law enforcement agency holding authority to prosecute them *wanted* them to commit perjury. In the criminal trial against Mafia figures Gotti and Thomas Gambino, long prison sentences were based upon the testimony of other felons, who were rewarded for their testimony through sentence and charge reductions.

**GREAT PRETENSE**

President George Bush, speaking (August 14, 1991) before an audience of nearly 3,000 delegates to the national convention of the Fraternal Order of Police, the nation's major police labor organization, stated:

> *The time has come to show less compassion for the architects of crime and more compassion for its victims. Our citizens want and deserve to feel safe. We must remember that the first obligation of a penal system is to punish those who break our laws. You can't turn bad people into saints.*

So much for hypocrisy. The initial media attention to October Surprise forced the Senate and House to form committees supposedly investigating the charges. But the Republican members of the House and Senate vigorously opposed any investigation, afraid of what would be revealed. When continuing media pressure forced an investigation, safeguards were installed, including bringing people from other government agencies that could be counted upon to insure a coverup. These "investigators" then barred witnesses who would expose what was being investigated. They conducted closed-door hearings of witnesses, preventing the public from making their own decision as to the truthfulness of what was written in the final reports, or what was omitted. By omitting key testimony, the final report would be a farce.

Another tactic is to label key witnesses as unreliable or discredited, as was done with U.S. and Israeli intelligence agency witnesses: Mossad agent Ari Ben-Menashe; CIA contract agent Richard Brenneke, and deep-cover CIA operative Gunther Russbacher. These witnesses had no reason to lie. They were not at risk because of the role they played in the October Surprise scheme. Instead, they risked persecution by Justice Department prosecutors if they testified falsely. In a Catch-22 scenario, they knew that they faced false prosecution from Justice Department attorneys even if they testified truthfully and disclosed government corruption. Brenneke discovered this when he testified during a Denver hearing about George Bush and Donald Gregg's trip to Paris, which Justice Department attorneys sought to cover up.

**TROJAN HORSES**

In 1991, the Senate refused to conduct an investigation into the October Surprise charges, but the Senate Foreign Relations Committee conducted a small-scale investigation with virtually no staff and very little funding. The Senate Committee selected attorney Reid Weingarten[272] to be Special Counsel controlling the investigation. He was formerly employed by the U.S. Department of Justice and could be expected to protect the Justice Department's coverup and involvement in the October Surprise operation. Immediately after Weingarten was named Special Counsel, I sent to him portions of the transcript of Russbacher's sworn declarations which described details of the October Surprise operation. They now had Brenneke's sworn statements in the Denver U.S. District Court and Russbacher's declarations. The committee refused to respond to my petition and refused to receive Russbacher's and Brenneke's testimony.

A key member of the Senate committee was Cecilia Porter, on loan from the GAO's Office of special investigations. Her previous "investigation" into October Surprise discredited key witnesses, including Richard Brenneke (without obtaining his testimony), and then she helped write a report claiming that the October Surprise scheme did not exist.

The chief investigator on the Senate October Surprise Committee was an agent from the Treasury Department's Secret Service, a federal entity that played a major coverup role in the October Surprise operation. The chairman of the Senate October Surprise Committee, Senator Terry Sanford, was formerly the attorney for Earl Brian, one of the principal participants in the October Surprise scheme. Brian was a CIA asset involved in numerous corrupt CIA and Justice Department activities, including the Inslaw affair.

**BLOCKING THE INVESTIGATION**

The senators on the committee placed numerous restrictions on the investigation, which were admitted in their final report:

* Imposed travel restrictions, barring the investigators from traveling to Europe, the travel necessary to obtain the testimony of numerous people identified with the October Surprise operation. The report stated that "Senator Jesse Helms, Ranking Minority Member of the Committee, served notice to Chairman Claiborne Pell that he would not authorize any such foreign travel [barring testimony from key witnesses]." The report stated that "Special Counsel was denied authority to travel abroad, thereby precluding the possibility of interviewing Iranian exiles in Europe, Israeli public officials and intelligence operatives, international arms dealers, and prominent Iranian political figures such as Hashemi Rafsanjani and Mehdi Karrubi, who may have knowledge relating to the allegations at issue."

---

272 Special Counsel Weingarten was appointed on December 16, 1991.

* Denied subpoena power to the investigators that was needed to compel the attendance of witnesses or the production of documents. The investigators had to submit their request for subpoenas to the full committee of senators and obtain majority approval for the Chairman of the Committee to sign the subpoenas. The Republicans on the committee were primarily responsible for this restriction. This awkward restriction was further compounded by the senators refusing to approve many of the subpoenas. Out of 47 witnesses and 15 entities for which subpoenas were requested, the senators refused to issue 44 of them. Without subpoenas, many government agencies, directed by Justice Department officials, refused to provide important testimony or evidence.

* Limited the funds and the time for completing the investigation. The Senate October Surprise Committee spent only $75,429 by the time it issued the November 19, 1992, report. In comparison, Iran-Contra Independent Prosecutor Lawrence Walsh spent over $40 million and six years investigating White House personnel to determine who withheld evidence from Congress. Compare the $40 million spent for the relatively minor offenses of determining who withheld evidence to the $75,000 spent to investigate the treasonous and subversive criminal acts involved in the October Surprise operation.

**MORE EVIDENCE**

In June 1991, the committee took the testimony of Ari Ben-Menashe behind closed doors. Ben-Menashe described his presence at the various October Surprise meetings in Spain and France, including the presence of George Bush at the Paris meetings. His testimony was dynamite, describing in a credible manner the specifics of what he had witnessed in the October Surprise scheme. The American public was deprived of this information. Their massive ignorance and indifference to government misconduct made the sham investigation possible.

The Secret Service refused to allow the committee to question their agents who personally followed Bush during the October 19, 1980, weekend. Instead, they limited the questioning to Secret Service agent Leonard J. Tanis, who had not seen Bush on that October 19, 1980, weekend and had simply read the agents' reports placed before him. If the reports were altered, his testimony would be based upon the altered documents. Tanis' lack of knowledge was revealed during questions about contradictions in his statements.

Tanis testified: "Evidently, I've either mixed up the date or something." If he was deliberately perjuring himself and his testimony shown as false, it would be easy to state he had the dates confused. Secret Service officials were covering up. The refusal to allow the Secret Service agents who were with Bush to testify could only be to hide his actual whereabouts.

**ADDITIONAL CONFIRMATION FROM MOSSAD AGENT**

In his book *Profits of War*, author Ari Ben-Menashe described his role as a Mossad agent in the transfer of bribe money for Iranians as part of the October Surprise conspiracy. He also detailed the partial diversion of these funds to Earl Brian, a friend and business associate of California attorney Edwin Meese. Meese was rewarded for his treachery in October Surprise by being appointed Attorney General of the United States, and was able to block any subsequent investigation, and retaliate against any whistleblower.

Ben-Menashe described receiving $56 million from the Saudi ambassador in Guatemala and leaving $4 million of this in the CIA-related Valley National Bank of Arizona in a bank account belonging to Earl Brian. Ben-Menashe's boss, Director of Israel Defense Forces/Military Intelligence Yehoshua Sagi, explained that it was CIA money and that the Saudis helped arranged the banking and transfer. Ben-Menashe wrote that this money came from Central America drug deals involving some Israelis and the CIA. Ben-Menashe described being met by CIA Deputy Director Robert Gates at Miami, who then went to Phoenix to insure that Earl Brian got his bribe money.

Ben-Menashe described how Brian was involved in other secret deals involving the CIA and other U.S. agencies. Ben-Menashe wrote that bribe money was given by the CIA to the West Australian Labor Party for allowing Australia to be used in the transfer of arms to Iran following the October Surprise agreement. He stated that Richard Babayan, a CIA contract agent, received a $6 million dollar check from Earl Brian, who was acting on behalf of a CIA cut-out. Hadron and Earl Brian figured prominently in a later scandal given the name of Inslaw. The CIA connections help explain how they avoided criminal prosecution and how Attorney General Edwin Meese, deeply involved in these criminal activities, protected all parties involved, and misused the Justice Department to persecute and imprison informants.

**GEORGE BUSH, CIA ASSET**

George Bush was a necessary participant in the October Surprise scheme because the Iranians wanted final approval by either presidential candidate Ronald Reagan or his running mate, George Bush. Bush was far more capable of carrying out this type of covert operation. He had been the director of the CIA in 1976 and 1977, and a CIA operative since at least 1960, prior to the assassination of President John F. Kennedy. A document dated November 29, 1963, from John Edgar Hoover, Director of the FBI, to Director of the Bureau of Intelligence and Research in the U.S. Department of State, identified Bush as a CIA asset. Referring to information given to the CIA, FBI Director Hoover wrote of the person providing the information:

> *The substance of the foregoing information was orally furnished to Mr. George Bush of the Central Intelligence Agency and Captain William Edwards of the Defense Intelligence Agency on November 23, 1963, by Mr. W.T. Forsyth of this Bureau.*

Attached to the letter was a self-explanatory FBI report:

1
DL 89-43
HJO:mvs
Re: <u>James Milton Parrott</u>

*Houston on November 22, 1963, advised that George H.W. BUSH, a reputable businessman, furnished information to the effect that JAMES PARROTT has been talking of killing the President when he comes to Houston. A check with Secret Service at Houston, Texas revealed that agency had a report that PARROTT stated in 1961 he would kill President KENNEDY if he got near him.*

**THE SENATE OCTOBER SURPRISE REPORT**

The Senate October Surprise Committee issued its report[273] on November 19, 1992. It is a standard tactic for a good liar or an attorney to admit certain things to establish a facade of honesty and then follow with lies to complete the cover-up. The report properly identified the severity of the charges, a standard practice to give the impression of credibility by admitting one or more facts. The report then proceeded to discredit the witnesses whose testimony proved the existence of the October Surprise scheme. The witnesses being discredited had nothing to gain by giving false testimony, and much to lose, but this basic reasoning was ignored. The report gave absolute credibility to federal officials who would have been impeached and prosecuted if the charges were proven true. This report was prepared by former Justice Department attorney Reid Weingarten.

**THE REPORT MET THE DEFINITION OF COVERUP**

The committee refused to receive the testimony of Gunther Russbacher. They called him an imposter (without questioning him) and refused to address the transcript of his sworn declarations that I sent to them. The report discredited Russbacher by making reference to an attorney friend, Paul Wilcher, who reportedly failed to produce a copy of a video[274] that allegedly existed of an SR-71 flight from Paris to Andrews Air Force Base on the October 19, 1980, weekend. The failure of someone else to produce a copy of a video tape had nothing to do with the importance and credibility of Russbacher's testimony.

Richard Brenneke gave sworn statements to a U.S. District Court in Denver in 1988, describing his role in the Paris October Surprise meetings. His testimony coincided with statements and testimony of other people. Without requiring Brenneke to testify, the committee's report discredited the former CIA contract agent on the basis of newspaper articles, primarily those written by former or current CIA operative Frank Snepp. The report said:

*On the basis of these published [media] reports, and on the GAO's inquiry (in which Brenneke declined to cooperate), this investigation determined that it would not be fruitful to devote further resources to pursue evidence originating from Brenneke.*

On a matter of such urgency, investigators don't ask a key witness to testify; he is ordered to do so. Brenneke had been threatened, just as CIA contract agent Riconosciuto had been threatened, by Justice Department attorneys not to testify. Under these conditions, Brenneke had no alternative but to decline a voluntary request for testimony.

---

273 The Senate October Surprise Committee commenced operation after Senate Majority Leader George J. Mitchell requested that the committee, through the subcommittee, investigate the October Surprise charges. The committee was headed by Senator Terry Sanford, Chairman, and Senator James Jeffords, ranking member, and was a subcommittee on Near Eastern and South Asian Affairs of the Committee on Foreign Relations.

274 CIA SR-71 aircraft made a continuous video recording of the two seats in the SR-71 aircraft, making a permanent tape recording and simultaneously sending transmissions to a satellite which beams the signals to an earth station. The tape recordings are kept at the National Archives in Camp Mead, Maryland.

The Congressional Committee report also sought to discredit Brenneke on the basis of ten-year-old credit card slips showing that someone made charges on his credit card in Portland, Oregon on October 18, 1980. Obtaining Brenneke's testimony would have clarified the matter of the credit cards.

Barbara Honegger, author of the first book bearing the title *October Surprise*, reportedly had the signatures on these controversial credit cards examined by a handwriting expert, who stated they did not compare with Brenneke's signature. She reportedly stated this fact to Lawrence Barcella, head counsel of the October Surprise Committee, in December 1992. Several years earlier, Honegger had questioned people present at the places covered by the credit card receipts, who knew Brenneke. They stated that Brenneke was not at the places shown by the credit cards, and had not signed the credit card slips.

The General Accounting Office (GAO) had earlier discounted Brenneke because he refused to participate in any hearings, conveniently ignoring the fact that Justice Department employees had threatened Brenneke, warning him that he would suffer the consequences if he testified.

Brenneke had been a CIA contract agent carrying out CIA covert activities, which included drug trafficking. Any one of these CIA-ordered activities could be used for subsequent prosecution by Justice Department attorneys. He saw what happened to CIA contract agent Michael Riconosciuto and to many other CIA assets who were sent to prison on trumped-up charges solely to silence them. Brenneke saw the discrediting and coverup tactics by the mainstream media and the coverup by the entire Senate and House. He was certainly smart enough to recognize that the safest approach was to say nothing.

The Senate report discredited the testimony of Jamshid Hashemi, an arms merchant present at meetings between William Casey and Iranian representatives in Madrid in July 1980. I had obtained secret CIA and State Department documents showing Hashemi's involvement in the arms-for-hostages operation, in which government officials expressed confidence in his credibility. Copies of these reports, sent to the Senate and the House October Surprise Committees, were ignored.

The report stated of Mossad agent Ari Ben-Menashe and other witnesses, none of whom had reason to lie, that they "have proven wholly unreliable." This decision was based upon their testimony having contradicted the testimony of those who were part of the October Surprise conspiracy.

I sent the Senate committee copies of Secret Service reports showing Bush flying into Washington National Airport on Sunday evening, October 19, 1980. These reports disputed Secret Service reports furnished to the committee. I had obtained the reports from Russbacher, who had received them while he was assigned to the CIA at Langley in 1981. They had been sent by the Secret Service to the CIA shortly after the events occurred and before the Secret Service found a need to alter the reports years later.

After discrediting the sworn testimony of people who were innocent participants in the October Surprise operation, after placing irresponsible restrictions on the investigation, and after encountering great numbers of people who refused to testify, the Senate committee held there was no such scheme:

*The vast weight of all available evidence—including sworn testimony from Secret Service agents assigned to protect Bush, extensive Secret Service records and logs, as well as statements by campaign staff—indicates that Bush did not travel to Paris in October 1980 or, for that matter, at any time during the 1980 presidential campaign.*

The committee report referred to former President Reagan's refusal to cooperate, stating that the investigators were "disappointed by President Reagan's declination of the request for an interview. President Reagan's written reply was wholly inadequate to explain his off-hand but apparently relevant comment to a reporter that he had acted in some fashion as a candidate in connection with the hostage crisis." The report identified the refusal of the FBI to cooperate:

*The history of the FBI's handling of evidence in this case—from the disappearance and discovery of the "Pottinger Tapes," to the disappearance and discovery of the entire Hashemi electronic surveillance, to the discovery of an eight-day period in which the Hashemi New York wiretaps were apparently discontinued—is a curious one. It is not typical for the FBI to simply "lose" evidence.*

Basically, the committee sought to support its coverup decision that there was no October Surprise operation and that George Bush had not gone to Paris, based upon the following:

* Secret Service reports purporting to show that Bush never left Washington during the October 19, 1980, weekend. But the Secret Service agents were barred from testifying, and Secret Service agents were reportedly on the BAC 111 to Paris and would be implicated in a coup against the United States. October Surprise was a coup. Secret documents that I later obtained indicate these were altered. From my experience as a federal and private investigator I have found that it is a common practice for Justice Department attorneys and the CIA to falsify documents.

* A Government Accounting Office (GAO) investigation that concluded there was no evidence of the reported October Surprise operation. I had repeatedly contacted GAO for the prior two decades with hard evidence of criminal activities I uncovered first as a federal investigator and later as a victim in Chapter 11 proceedings, and they refused to investigate. The GAO refused to question any CIA operatives and contract agents who were part of the October Surprise operation.

* The testimony of White House personnel implicated in the criminal activities, who faced long prison terms if convicted of the crimes in which they participated. The committee wrote:

*No credible evidence has been found to indicate that high-ranking Republican campaign figures or other prominent American political officials—including Bush, Casey, Robert McFarlane, Robert Gates and Richard Allen—attended any October 1980 Paris meetings. Moreover, the Special Counsel has concluded, after a review of Secret Service records and testimony from Secret Service agents, that candidate Bush was in the United States through October 1980.*

**COVER-YOUR-REAR TACTICS**

Should the coverup backfire, the Senate October Surprise Committee sought to cover their rear ends. The report stated that certain obstacles existed to determining the truth of the October Surprise charges: "The investigation was handicapped by several factors which made reaching final conclusions an almost impossible task." There were certainly obstacles, and many of them deliberately put in place by the "investigating" committee. The "CYR" tactics included the following:

* The investigation was hindered by the unavailability of certain key witnesses.
* Key witnesses who would have implicated themselves refused to cooperate, including Ambassador to South Korea Donald Gregg (who was on the BAC 111 flight to Paris). The report stated that Gregg declined to be interviewed by the investigators. The great harm inflicted upon the United States (if the charges were true) demanded ordering him and every other relevant witness to testify.
* The senators refused to issue a subpoena for the testimony of former President Ronald Reagan. They satisfied themselves with a letter from Reagan's attorney, John A. Mintz, who wrote "that he has no recollection or other information relevant to the issues raised in any of your questions."
* Refusal by the Reagan Presidential Library to produce requested records until after the investigators had already been reassigned and the investigation completed.
* The report admitted that lack of funds and personnel greatly hindered the investigations, forcing investigators to rely upon other federal agencies to conduct an investigation, even though those agencies were implicated and engaged in a coverup.
* The Treasury Department refused to allow the investigators to question the Secret Service agents who had actually been with Bush during the time in question. There would be no reason for refusing to allow these low-level federal employees to be questioned, other than to cover up.
* The family of former CIA Director William Casey (who died in 1987) impeded the investigation by delaying and refusing to provide his personal and business records, including his diary and passport.
* Failure of Donald Gregg, who was on the flight to Paris on October 19, 1980, to pass a lie-detector test. The Senate October Surprise Committee gave Gregg the test. He failed it. But rather than call the test a failure, the committee report stated that "Gregg's response was lacking in candor." CIA assets Gunther Russbacher and Richard Brenneke, and Mossad's Ari Ben-Menashe, had stated that Gregg was at several October Surprise meetings in Europe.

There was far more evidence showing the October Surprise charges to be true than existed in many criminal cases resulting in sentences of death. The testimony of criminals, paid to give testimony wanted by the prosecutors, is sufficient to result in life-long incarceration or death and accepted by the media, the courts, and the Justice Department. But the testimony of whistleblowers exposing corruption by federal officials, who risk perjury charges and prison if their courageous testimony is proven false, is not accepted by those interested in coverup.

People who testify falsely, in response to pressure from Justice Department attorneys, are assured of freedom against perjury charges. If people refuse to testify as Justice Department prosecutors want, they suffer consequences that can often destroy their lives. Testifying falsely, as requested by Justice Department attorneys, is rewarded. Criminal charges against them may be dropped; if in prison, they may be paroled; they may be put in the witness protection program and supported financially.

On the other hand, patriotic Americans seeking to testify about government corruption face fraudulent perjury charges and prison.

**HOUSE "INVESTIGATIVE" TEAM**

In response to media pressure, the House of Representatives on February 5, 1992, created a task force to report on the October Surprise operation. The House committee repeated the age-old practice of staffing the committee with people who would carry out the coverup. Its chief counsel, Lawrence Barcella, Jr., followed the standard practice of former Justice Department attorneys of protecting Justice Department officials who were implicated. He had a history of protecting federal officials who had committed criminal acts against the United States.

Barcella had covered up for a CIA operation that went sour, in which the CIA was secretly supplying Libya with war supplies. Justice Department prosecutors charged CIA operative Edwin Wilson with illegal arms sales to Libya that the CIA had earlier sanctioned. Barcella was the Justice Department prosecutor who prosecuted Wilson and insured that the CIA involvement did not surface.

Barcella was the attorney for Lynn Nofziger, President Ronald Reagan's chief political adviser during the 1980 presidential campaign. He was also a member of former Senator Paul Laxalt's Nevada law firm when Laxalt was Reagan's Campaign Committee Chairman in 1980. If the October Surprise conspiracy did in fact occur, these men could be expected to know about it and, at the very least, be guilty of felony coverup. The same could be said of Barcella.

Barcella was one of the key public relations or coverup men for the corrupt bank, BCCI, and one of its most forceful apologists. Attorneys Clark Clifford and Robert Altman hired him to deceive the American public through aiding and abetting the criminal acts of that rogue bank. Barcella was one of four attorneys who requested Senator Orrin Hatch (R-Utah) to give a speech on the Senate floor in defense of BCCI, seeking to block a Congressional investigation into the criminal activities of the Bank. Barcella was known to be a friend and protector of the U.S. intelligence community while he was a federal prosecutor. The October Surprise charges that Barcella was entrusted to investigate threatened to expose this CIA operation and the coverup by his former Justice Department bosses.

After the BCCI scandal broke, Barcella was asked about BCCI's compliance with U.S. banking laws, to which he falsely replied: "BCCI's policies and procedures were consistent with industry norms in the countries in which they were operating."[275] This bank inflicted the biggest bank fraud in the world's history. It had long been established that BCCI was engaging in criminal activities: drug-money laundering, financing of terrorists, secret takeover of U.S. banks, and bribing of government officials wherever it operated, including the United States.

Another "investigative" committee member was Richard Pedersen, who was involved in other coverups of government corruption. In early 1992, Pederson threatened Garby Leon (Columbia Pictures) and Rayelan Russbacher during a telephone call, warning them to cease further activity in the October Surprise matter.[276]

Shortly after the House October Surprise Committee was formed, I submitted several petitions to its chairman, Congressman Lee Hamilton (D-IN). I enclosed my declaration and a partial transcript of Russbacher's declarations giving specific details of the October Surprise operation in which Russbacher was involved. Hamilton and the committee repeatedly refused to respond to these petitions.

## CIRCUMVENTING CONGRESSIONAL COVERUPS

I submitted numerous documents to the House Committee showing that the October Surprise operation existed (along with other documents showing that the Iran-Contra arms and drug trafficking existed long before the publicized 1986 starting date). Several of the copies indicated that the Secret Service was lying about the whereabouts of George Bush on the October 19, 1980, weekend.

One Secret Service report dated October 30, 1980, reported that "Bush arrived Washington National aboard a UAE BAC 111 Charter at 8:25 p.m." Another dated February 17, 1981, was titled, "Visit of George Bush to Capitol Hilton Hotel, Washington, D.C. on October 19, 1980." A report directed to Stuart Knight, Director, U.S. Secret Service, Washington, D.C., stated:

> *On October 19, 1980, at 8:00 P.M. nominee Bush arrived via motorcade at the Capitol Hilton Hotel. Nominee Bush attended a dinner in the main ballroom.*

## NO EVIDENCE, NO WITNESSES CALLED

In July 1992, the Hamilton committee released an interim report stating there was no evidence that Bush was in Paris or that there was any support for the October Surprise charges. The Hamilton Committee didn't obtain testimony of any of the parties willing to testify that would prove the existence of the scheme and Bush's presence at the Paris meetings. The only parties the committee questioned (not under oath and in private) were two Secret Service agents who guarded vice presidential candidate Bush when Bush was reportedly in Paris. The agents stated that Bush had not been in Paris during the October 19, 1980, weekend. In later pages it is shown that Secret Service agents were on the flight to Paris and that they lied.

Congressman Hamilton had close ties to President Reagan's aide, Earl Brian (who was deeply involved in the Inslaw scandal described in other chapters). Hamilton had close ties to CIA operative John Hull, who operated an arms and drug transshipment point on his ranch in Costa Rica. Hull is wanted by Costa

---

275 *False Profits*, Peter Truell and Larry Gurwin, Houghton Mifflin Company.
276 Told to the author in conversations with Garby Leon and Rayelan Russbacher.

Rican authorities on drug and murder charges. He also had close ties to Dan Quayle while Quayle was a U.S. senator from Indiana. Hull is being protected in the United States by CIA and Justice Department officials.

**AGAIN PUTTING CONGRESS ON NOTICE**

I wrote to Congressman Hamilton on November 27, 1992, enclosing copies of the Secret Service reports, stating that they "showed vice presidential nominee George Bush arriving in Washington, D.C. on a United Arab Emirates BAC 111 at approximately 8.00 p.m., and his departure for the Washington Hilton Hotel." I emphasized the significance of the documents, writing that they showed Bush and Secret Service agents were lying when they stated Bush had not left the Washington area on the October 19, 1980, weekend.

Arguably, those Secret reports had less significance in establishing Bush's Paris presence than the sworn testimony of CIA operatives Russbacher, Brenneke and Riconosciuto, or former Mossad agent Ari Ben-Menashe.

Treasury Agent Richard Pedersen called me several days later, asking where I obtained the Secret Service reports. He said those reports were forgeries, that the date of October 19, 1980, had been altered from the October 18, 1980, date he had on his copies. He stated that the airline identification had been changed from United Airlines to United Arab Emirates (UAE). I responded that I would check my source and get back to him. If this was correct, the committee had a responsibility to look at my documents and question the person who gave them to me. It is a federal crime to falsify government documents. If Pedersen actually thought that my copies were forged, he had a duty (and surely would have done so) to obtain my testimony to determine where I obtained the documents. They never asked.

I asked Pedersen why the committee didn't call Gunther Russbacher to testify. He said Russbacher was a phony and an impostor; that he was charged in Oklahoma City with being mentally unbalanced; that he had been in prison from 1976 to 1983, and could not have been involved in October Surprise. Further, that Russbacher's attorney friend, Paul Wilcher, had set up conditions they could not meet.

Several times I had told Russbacher that Wilcher's demand for immunity was giving the committee an excuse for not calling him to testify and that there was no reason to ask for it. Russbacher didn't need immunity if the questions were limited to the October Surprise flights. Because of his wide-spread involvement in CIA-directed activities such as money-laundering, drug trafficking and bank fraud, he was subject to prosecution, especially if the CIA pulled the standard disavowal on him. Russbacher could raise the immunity issue if the questioning went into areas other than October Surprise, which was unlikely. However, Wilcher's request for immunity was no excuse for the October Surprise committee not to obtain Russbacher's testimony. The October Surprise offenses were of such great importance that prejudgment of Russbacher's credibility and refusal to obtain his testimony was out of order, but consistent with the coverup pattern.

I asked Pedersen if he had read Ben-Menashe's recently published *Profits of War*, stating that the book contained copies of Mossad documents showing Ari Ben-Menashe to be a high staff officer with Israel's intelligence agency.

Pedersen responded, "Ben-Menashe had been discredited," without providing any support. It was obvious that Pedersen was determined to discredit anything and anyone who supported the October Surprise charges.

I contacted Russbacher for a history of the Secret Service reports he had given me that did not coincide with reports the investigative committee had. He said the Secret Service sent copies of those reports to the CIA at Langley, Virginia shortly after they were filed and they were routed through him while he was at CIA headquarters. Russbacher advised that the initials "RAW" in the upper right hand corner of the documents stood for Robert Andrew Walker, one of his CIA-provided aliases. I sent the following letter to Congressman Hamilton:

*December 12, 1992*

*Congressman Lee Hamilton*
*October Surprise House Committee*
*RHOB, Room 2187*
*Washington, DC 20515* *Certified Mail: P 888 324 843*

*Dear Congressman Hamilton:*

*This letter makes reference to a telephone call that I received from Agent Richard Pedersen who is a member of the House October Surprise "investigation," and who was borrowed from the Treasury Department's Secret Service, and puts you on notice of the following facts:*

*These comments are in response to Mr. Pedersen's recent phone call to me:*

*1. Agent Pedersen telephoned me recently in response to the letter I sent to you and the attached copies of Secret Service agent reports showing Vice-President nominee George Bush arriving at Washington National Airport at 18:35 on October 19, 1980, and a motorcade to the Washington Hilton.*

*The significance of that time and date is that it shows Secret Service Agents and George Bush, among others, lying when they stated that Bush had not left the Washington area on the October 19, 1980 weekend.*

*2. Mr. Pedersen stated that the multi-page Secret Service agent reports which I sent to you had been altered. He stated that his copy shows 10/18/80 (Saturday) as the date that Bush flew into Washington National Airport, while my copies show 10/19/80 (Sunday) as the date.*

*The significance of this is that the Secret Service and George Bush claim Bush never left the Washington area during the October 19, 1980 weekend, and that if the flight into Washington occurred on 10/19/80, it would show both the Secret Service and George Bush were lying and obstructing justice. Further, even if the flight arrived in Washington on the evening of the 18th, for argument, it appears that this conflicts with the schedule reported by Bush and the Secret Service.*

*3. Mr. Pedersen stated that whoever altered the document would be guilty of a federal offense, and he asked me where the documents came from. I had found these Secret Service agent reports several months ago in the inflow of papers that I receive in the mail, by FAX, and sometimes given to me. I don't usually keep track of who has sent or given to me any particular papers. I knew that numerous people have the same copies that I sent to you, and which are the subject of Mr. Pedersen's questions.*

*4. Seeking to establish the history of the documents, I questioned CIA operative Gunther Russbacher about them. He stated that the reports were received by him while he was working as a CIA operative at CIA headquarters in Langley, some time after he had played key roles in the October Surprise operation. He stated to me that he placed the initials of one of his CIA-provided aliases, RAW (Robert Andrew Walker), on the upper right hand corner of several of the Secret Service reports. He acknowledged to me that the dates shown on my reports are the same dates as on the reports that he initialed while in his capacity as a CIA deep-cover operative.*

*5. If your October Surprise Committee was an investigative committee instead of a white-wash committee, the answers could be obtained by having this CIA operative, Gunther Russbacher, testify in open door hearings. That same operative can testify to the details of the October Surprise operation, including where the meetings were held in which he participated; when the shipment of arms commenced; how the arms were stolen from U.S. reforger stores; the part played in the treasonous activities of the CIA and high White House officials, and others. He can also describe other patterns of corrupt activities, including the CIA looting of financial institutions; CIA drug trafficking within the United States; CIA participation in looting of Chapter 11 assets as part of a vicious racketeering enterprise preying upon American citizens and small businesses who exercise Chapter 11 protections; and other racketeering enterprises implicating federal officials. He can also testify to the Secret Service Agents that were part of the October Surprise operation, along with White House officials, people who are now federal judges, members of Congress who participated, including Senators John Tower and John Heinz, among others.*

*6. Sworn declarations given to me by CIA informants indicate that four or five Secret Service Agents accompanied the group of Americans who traveled to Paris for the October 19, 1980 weekend meetings that finalized the October Surprise operation. The involvement of the Secret Service, the CIA, members of President Carter's staff, and others, in the subversive acts against the United States may constitute one of the worst criminal conspiracies ever exposed against the United States, and surely constitutes an unpublicized coup. Having a Treasury Department agent play a major role in the October Surprise investigation, when Treasury Department agents assisted in carrying out the coup or scheme, is typical of Congressional "investigations," but hardly meets the definition of an investigation.*

*7. Mr. Pedersen stated that the Secret Service reports were not confidential or secret but simply not released. However, various news media sources claim they have copies of the reports, and presumably this supports his statement indicating that the reports are not classified. I am requesting copies of the reports that your committee has in its possession, and any other reports commencing from Friday, October 17, 1980 through October 20, 1980, Monday.*

***SIGNS OF COVERUP BY YOUR COMMITTEE***

*8. In response to my comment that Ari Ben-Menashe's credibility has been established by the copies of Mossad documents in his recently published book,*

*Profits of War*, Mr. Pedersen responded that he was totally discredited. Ari Ben-Menashe testified before Congressional committees that he was present at several of the October Surprise meetings, and saw George Bush, William Casey, Robert McFarlane, Donald Gregg, among others, at these meetings. He knew he would be charged with perjury if he lied, and he had nothing to gain. His recent book, *Profits of War*, include Mossad documents showing him to be a high staff officer possessing details of the October Surprise operation that dove-tails with the testimony, the testimony offered, and the investigative findings of numerous journalists and authors.

*9. In response to my question as to why the testimony of CIA contract agent Richard Brenneke was not accepted, Mr. Pedersen responded that he was totally discredited. But Brenneke knew that he would probably be charged with perjury if he lied. He had nothing to gain by his testimony before a U.S. District Court Judge in Denver in 1988. He was simply trying to show that he, and Rupp who was on trial in the Aurora Bank fraud case, were CIA contract agents. Further, his testimony coincided with other CIA operatives, with dozens of people who described their part in the October Surprise operation to various investigative journalists and authors. They, like Brenneke, had nothing to gain by their statements.*

*10. In response to my question about why the committee did not accept testimony from CIA contract agent Michael Riconosciuto, Mr. Pedersen totally discredited him. Again, as with Brenneke, Riconosciuto gave sworn testimony concerning the October Surprise operation, and he knew that he faced perjury charges if he gave false testimony. He had no reason to lie. He testified to assisting in the relay of the $40 million bribe money in the October Surprise operation.*

*11. In response to my question asking why the House October Surprise Committee didn't have CIA operative Gunther Russbacher testify, Mr. Pedersen justified refusing to allow Russbacher to testify on the basis that Russbacher had been continuously in prison from 1977 to 1983, and thereby couldn't have been part of the October Surprise operation. But Russbacher has given me sworn declarations that he had not been in prison continuously during this time, and only was imprisoned for short periods to provide a background for his covert CIA activities with factions in Europe and the U.S. underworld. Further, Russbacher would not risk further imprisonment from perjury charges and could be expected to testify truthfully. I already have hundreds of sworn statements by Russbacher, describing the specifics of the October Surprise operation, which I have personally checked out with Ari Ben-Menashe, and through contacts with various personnel reportedly implicated in the European meetings associated with the October Surprise operation.*

*12. Mr. Pedersen stated awareness of the SR-71 video tape described by Paul Wilcher, on the purported flight from Paris in which Gunther Russbacher was reportedly the pilot and George Bush the passenger. Your committee could have proved or disproved the existence of that video tape by requesting the tape from the archives at Camp Mead, Maryland. You never did that.*

*13. Gunther Russbacher, CIA operative and Captain in the U.S. Navy and Office of Naval Intelligence, has offered to testify under oath to your committee and others, describing his role in the October Surprise operation, knowing that he would be charged with perjury if he lied. Congressman Hamilton and his committee knew he offered to testify and that Russbacher would undoubtedly not risk a prison term to lie, especially when it would not be to his benefit to testify.*

*14. I provided to your committee a partial transcript of sworn declarations by Gunther Russbacher, describing details of the October Surprise scheme, claiming that he was at several of the meetings, and that he arranged for the procurement and shipment of arms following the Barcelona meeting. I am prepared to testify to what Russbacher stated to me during the past two years concerning his role in the October Surprise (and other corrupt) CIA operation. As a former federal investigator I am quite competent to evaluate the sincerity and truthfulness of almost 300 hours of statements. Russbacher has offered to testify to a Congressional committee, including that chaired by Congressman Hamilton, knowing that he would be charged with perjury if he lied.*

*15. Your group has ignored the statements made by former Iranian president Bani-Sadr in his two books describing details of the October Surprise operation. Presumably he too is totally discredited.*

*16. I am a former federal investigator who held federal authority to make certain determinations. I witnessed a pattern of hard-core federal crimes perpetrated by federal officials. I have government documents showing the crimes to exist. I have made judicial records of the criminal activities, and the responses of rogue Justice Department personnel and federal judges constitute additional criminal acts on their word. I have questioned CIA operatives, others, and have uncovered a pattern of criminal activities against the United States that are inter-related with the October Surprise operation. I have seen the criminal obstruction of justice by every government check and balance, including Justice Department personnel and members of Congress, among others. These findings coincide with the crimes charged by Brenneke, Riconosciuto, Russbacher, investigative journalists and authors, and the crimes implied by the felony coverups.*

*17. Even worse, the conduct of your committee includes threats against those seeking to report the October Surprise crimes. Garby Leon of Columbia Pictures and Rayelan Russbacher stated to me that during an early 1992 telephone conversations with Secret Service agent Pedersen, that he threatened them if they continued with their October Surprise exposure activities.*

*18. Threats reportedly made by Agent Pedersen of your committee against attorney Paul Wilcher as Wilcher sought to give data to your committee showing details of the October Surprise conspiracy. Wilcher states that he was physically shoved against the wall by Pedersen and warned to halt his exposure activities.*

*19. Agent Pedersen threatened me for having copies of the Secret Service reports, displaying no interest, obviously, in reaching the truth.*

*20. Aiding and abetting the coverup by this committee are Justice Department prosecutors and federal judges, seeking to cover up for their own involvement in October Surprise and its many related tentacles, by charging me with federal crimes in retaliation for having reported the crimes to a federal court, and in retaliation for seeking to defend against the felony persecution associated with the obstruction of justice.*

*21. These threats against informants to keep them from reporting criminal acts are criminal violations.[2] The refusal to receive evidence, the threats against informants, the staffing of your committee with people that have a vested interest in coverup, violate blocks of federal criminal statutes.[3]*

***COMPOSITION OF HOUSE OCTOBER SURPRISE COMMITTEE***

*The composition of Congressman Hamilton's October Surprise "investigative" Committee parallels many other Congressional investigative committees:*

*A. Chief counsel Larry Barcella is a former (and probably present) CIA asset. Since October Surprise was a CIA operation he could be expected to block any exposure, and his conduct reflects that approach. Further, Barcella was a Justice Department hatchet man and also represented BCCI, defending their corrupt acts and trying to block their prosecution. His partial success in this respect enabled BCCI to continue their looting of assets in what has become the world's worst bank fraud.*

*B. Richard Pedersen is an agent with the Treasury Department. The Treasury Department's Secret Service agents were present during Vice-president nominee George Bush's flight to Paris on October 18, 1980. Pedersen's role, and certainly his conduct, has been to block any exposure of the October Surprise treasonous and subversive acts against the United States.*

*C. Peggy Robahm, one of your "investigators," was reportedly used by the CIA and Justice Department to discredit Richard Brenneke, by tactics that are better described in a fiction book. This same Peggy Robahm was then placed on Congressman Hamilton's October Surprise Committee to discredit the existence of the operation.*

*The impression I received from Mr. Pedersen was that the House October Surprise Committee's "investigative" report would be released shortly, and reveal that no such event occurred. From what I have observed, starting as a federal investigator and then a private investigator for the past thirty years, what else could be expected! For crimes against the United States, the members of the House October Surprise Committee have met past standards.*

*With tongue in cheek, I offer my services to expose the crimes involved in October Surprise and the various other associated tentacles. Obviously I don't expect the offer to be taken. If you wish, I will send you a copy of Defrauding America when it is released, which puts these events in the proper perspective.*

*Sincerely,*

*Rodney F. Stich*

*Enclosures:*

*October 3, 1980 CIA: "Proposal to Exchange Spare Parts With Hostages."*
*October 9, 1980 Department of State: "Approach on Iranian Spares."*
*October 21, 1980 Department of State: "Talk with Mitch Regovin."*
*October 29, 1980: "Two Related Items on Iranian Military supply."*
*October 1980 Secret Service reports: Bush's security detail.*
*June 3, 1983(?) CIA: Release of Hostages.*

*July 5, 1985: "New Developments on Channel to Iran."*
*August 19, 1985: "Status of Hashemi-Elliot Richardson Contact."*

******************************

## *ENDNOTES*

*1. The criminal activities include: (a) pattern of air safety and criminal acts related to a series of fatal airline crashes; (b) CIA scheme known as "October Surprise," in which U.S. military equipment was stolen and given to Iran in exchange for continuing the imprisonment of 52 American hostages held by Iran in 1980; (c) CIA embezzlement and looting of America's financial institutions; (d) criminal misuse of Chapter 11 courts by the CIA/federal judges/federal trustees/law firms to sequester evidence of the looted CIA proprietaries; (e) criminal misuse of Chapter 11 courts by the same group to fund covert and corrupt CIA activities (including corrupt seizure and looting of Petitioner's assets in the Oakland Chapter 11 courts, cases Nrs. 487-05974J/05975J); (e) CIA drug smuggling into the United States, enlarging upon its history of drug trafficking in foreign countries; (f) felony coverup and conspiracy to coverup by persons in the U.S. Department of Justice and by federal judges/justices; (g) felony persecution of informants, whistleblowers, and protesting victims by corrupt federal judges and prosecutors; (h) criminal activities related to the stealing of software belonging to Inslaw, and criminal misuse of the Justice Department and Chapter 11 courts; and other criminal activities.*

*2. **Title 18 U.S.C. § 1512. Tampering with a witness, victim, or an informant—***
*(b) Whoever knowingly uses intimidation or physical force, or threatens another person, or attempts to do so, or engages in misleading conduct toward another person, with intent to—*

*(1) influence, delay or prevent the testimony of any person in an official proceeding:*

*shall be fined...or imprisoned...or both. [1988 amended reading]*

*Title 18 U.S.C. § 1513. Retaliating against a witness, victim, or an informant. (a) Whoever knowingly engages in any conduct and thereby causes bodily injury to another person or damages the tangible property of another person, or threatens to do so, with intent to retaliate against any person for—(1) the attendance of a witness or party at an official proceeding, or any testimony given or any record, document, or other object produced by a witness in an official proceeding; or (2) any information relating to the commission or possible commission of a federal offense...*

*3. Title 18 U.S.C. § 1505 (obstructing proceedings before federal courts, and earlier, before FAA, NTSB, before federal grand jury, to prevent presenting testimony and evidence of federal offenses); § 1512 (tampering with a witness or informant, and specifically, preventing Stich's communication to a federal court of the federal air safety and criminal offenses, using felonious means to block such federal proceedings); § 1513 (retaliating against a witness, victim, or an informant, and specifically against Stich, to prevent his reporting of the federal crimes by federal officials); §§ 1961-1965 (RICO violations, by conspiring to harm an informant, and adversely affecting interstate and international commerce); § 241 (conspiracy against rights of any citizen, including conspiracy that violated wholesale numbers of federally protected rights); § 371 (conspiracy to commit offense against, or to defraud, the United States); § 1951 (interference with interstate and international air commerce, and specifically the FAA, NTSB, wrongful acts, and blocking and retaliating against Stich for seeking to report federal air safety and criminal acts affecting air safety); § 2 (principal); § 3 (accessory after the fact); § 4 (misprision of felony); § 35 (imparting or conveying false information); § 2071 (Concealment, removal, of official reports); § 34 (changing federal offenses to capital offense when death results); § 111 (impeding FAA inspectors or other federal employees); § 1621 (perjury, at FAA hearing); § 1623 (subornation of perjury, at FAA hearing); § 1623 (false declarations before federal grand jury); 28 U.S.C. § 1343 (Failure to prevent the violations of a person's civil and constitutional rights); Title 42 U.S.C. §§ 1983-1986 (Violating civil and constitutional rights of another, conspiracy to do so, failure to prevent the violations when the ability and responsibility to do so exists); Treason, Art 3 § 3 of US Constitution.*

*****************************

I mailed another letter to Congressman Hamilton on December 29, 1992, enclosing copies of secret CIA and State Department documents describing arms-for-hostages meetings from 1980 through 1985. The documents clearly showed that the arms flow to Iran started not in 1986, as reported in the Iran-Contra prosecutions and media reports, but years earlier, commencing in September 1980 as part of the October Surprise operation.

To determine whether the Secret Service report in my possession or the one cited by the House October Surprise Committee was correct, I filed a Freedom of Information (FOI) request with the Secret Service, enclosing a copy of my document showing Bush arriving at Washington National Airport on a UAE BAC 111. I requested their copy of the document. The Secret Service acknowledged finding their copy, but refused to release it to me.

**REPORTS OF THE HOUSE COMMITTEE**

On July 1, 1992, the House committee issued an interim report on October Surprise, stating its investigation had not been completed, that a final report would be released in January 1993, and that they believed there was no truth to the charges. Special counsel Lawrence Barcella, Jr., issued the preliminary report.

The final report, consisting of 968 pages, was issued on January 3, 1993. It followed the standard Congressional pattern of withholding incriminating evidence, discrediting witnesses who supported the original charges, and lending credibility to those government officials who were implicated in the charges. The report withheld knowledge of the Secret Service reports and Russbacher's declarations that I submitted in November 1992.

A number of factors struck me, in the report, including:

* Most of the investigators consisted of current or former Justice Department and Secret Service personnel.

* Withheld knowledge of the Secret Service documents that I submitted to Congressman Hamilton in November 1992, which contradicted the statements made by Secret Service personnel as to George Bush's location on the October

19, 1980, weekend.

* Withheld knowledge of the 40-plus-page sworn declarations given by former CIA operative Gunther Russbacher and other CIA and Mossad assets.

* Refused to receive my testimony and evidence relating to statements made to me by Russbacher over a two-year span that described many specifics involved in the October Surprise operation.

* Refused to allow Russbacher to testify, giving sham excuses for not doing so.

* Fraudulently discredited the testimony of former Mossad operative Ari Ben-Menashe, who was present at several of the European meetings, including the Paris meetings and meetings at which Russbacher was present. The Task Force report stated:

> *The Task Force has determined that Ben-Menashe's account of the October Surprise meetings, like his other October Surprise allegations, is a total fabrication.*

A September 4, 1987, letter written by Colonel Pesah Melowany in the Israel Defense Forces states of Ben-Menashe:

> *Mr. Ari Ben-Menashe has served in the Israel Defense Forces External Relations Department in key positions. As such, Mr. Ben-Menashe was responsible for a variety of complex and sensitive assignments which demanded exceptional analytical and executive capabilities.*

IDF Colonel Yoav Dayagi wrote on September 6, 1987:

> *[Ben-Menashe] served in the IDF External Relations Department in key positions...is a person known to keep to his principles, being always guided by a strong sense of duty, justice and common sense.*

Ben-Menashe's book had copies of other letters from the Israel Defense Forces attesting to his high level position. There are copies of Telex messages from Ben-Menashe to Iranian president Rafsanjani and other Iranian officials quoting prices for war material to be shipped by Israel.

* Falsely discredited Ben-Menashe's testimony by stating he was only a low-level translator, even though he presented letters and documentation during a closed hearing showing otherwise. Several of my CIA contacts described encountering Ben-Menashe in Europe, Central and South America and other locations, engaging in covert activities for Israel.

* Accepting at face value written denials by Israel officials[277] that they were not involved in any of the October Surprise activities. These denials contradicted testimony by former Mossad agent Ben-Menashe and my CIA contacts, including Gunther Russbacher. The disclaimers by Israeli officials were made indirectly to the Task Force, as the Israeli government refused to allow them to be questioned. Obviously they had something to hide! Israel has a strong vested interest to make sure the American people never learn of its complicity in October Surprise.

* Refused to have former CIA operative Richard Brenneke testify, despite his key role in October Surprise and other deep-cover CIA operations.

* Discredited Brenneke on the basis of deceptive credit card charges routinely

277 David Kimche, Shmuel Moriah, Rafi Eitan.

made on behalf of covert CIA operatives for later use as disclaimers.

* Falsely stated that Paul Wilcher, who made numerous attempts to have the Task Force obtain Russbacher's testimony, was an unlicensed lawyer, when in fact he was admitted to practice in the state of Illinois.

* Referred to witnesses who risked Justice Department retaliation by coming forth with the truth as "utter fabricators." This group included Ari Ben-Menashe, Gunther Russbacher, Richard Brenneke, Michael Riconosciuto, Heinrich Rupp, and Jamshid Hashemi. It accepted without question recanted statements made to journalists by Oswald LeWinter, Admiral Ahmed Madani, and Arif Durrani.

* Accepted as true the self-serving statements and denials by those who would be implicated, including Donald Gregg, Robert McFarlane, and Israel officials. The U.S. personnel would be impeached and charged with major crimes if the truth was admitted.

* Refused to contact the National Archives at Camp Mead, Maryland to obtain a copy of the video tape showing George Bush and Gunther Russbacher in an SR-71 aircraft on a flight from Paris to McGuire Air Force Base on Sunday, October 19, 1980. This is the tape that the report stated Wilcher did not deliver.

* Refused to have Riconosciuto testify about the electronic transfer of the $40 million in bribe money given to the Iranians during the October 19, 1980, weekend meetings in Paris.

* Refused to address Donald Gregg's failure to pass a lie detector test given by the Government Accounting Office.

* Refused to make reference to the transcript of sworn declarations that I had obtained from Russbacher, while including hearsay statements that denied the existence of October Surprise.

The Task Force report dismissed the charges of an October Surprise scheme as "bizarre claims." The American people have been victimized by the subversive criminal conspiracy and its many tentacles, including the brutality of the Iran-Contra operation. These criminal acts against the American people were then followed up with the coverup.

Aiding in the coverup was the media. A classic example was a January 16, 1993, article in the *Wall Street Journal* praising the House report and suggesting that Justice department officials charge the witnesses, who had risked so much, with perjury. Since the mid-1960s I had sent evidence to the *Wall Street Journal* of hard-core criminal acts committed by federal officials. Several of my CIA confidants believed that the *Journal's* preoccupation with protecting Israel was the reason behind their efforts to cover up for the October Surprise operation.

**GUILTY AS THE PERPETRATORS BY THEIR SILENCE**

I sent letters to people who were part of the October Surprise operation or who had evidence of its existence, advising them that I was going to publish in this book their involvement unless they gave me contrary information. Members of the French Secret Service present during the October 19, 1980, meetings in Paris would have filed reports on their activities. I mailed a registered letter to French President Francois Mitterrand on April 4, 1992, requesting a copy of the French Secret Service report of the October 19, 1980, October Surprise meetings in Paris. Several of my sources told me that French government agents were present during the meetings and that reports were made. My letter stated in part:

*This letter is a request for information, and copies of official writings, relating to the following:*

** Barcelona meetings that occurred in late July, 1980, at the Pepsico International Headquarters Building, at which William Casey (subsequently Director of the United States Central Intelligence Agency) was present, along with Robert McFarlane, Gunther Russbacher, and Iranian nationals. The intent of this meeting was to provide Iranian factions with bribe money and military equipment and munitions stolen from United States military warehouses, and which started flowing to Iran via Israel in September 1980. These meetings consisted of a criminal conspiracy to defraud the United States.*

** October 19, 1980 weekend meetings in Paris, furthering the treasonous and subversive acts, in which a scheme was finalized to pay large amounts of money, and billions in secret military equipment and ammunition, from the American conspirators, to Iranian factions, to continue the imprisonment of 52 American hostages.*

*These acts were subversive and treasonous, and required the felony coverup by many people. Until these criminal acts are uncovered, the same people who unlawfully and corruptly gained control of the United States government are continuing to inflict great harms upon the United States, with international implications.*

*I know that the French secret police knew of these meetings, were present at these meetings, and made reports of them. I also know that you were made aware of them. I therefore request that you send to me copies of these reports, and related writings, so I can take actions to have these American officials impeached and prosecuted.*

*If you refuse to do so, you should be advised that you, as the head of the government in France, will be aiding and abetting the treasonous, the subversive, the criminal acts, that continue to inflict great harms upon the United States and its people. This letter, and your response, will be included in the nearly completed book describing the criminal cartel that is defrauding the American people.*

When the president of France did not respond to that request, I sent another request for documents by registered mail on July 7, 1992. The French government again refused to answer or deny my charges. I had advised that their refusal to respond would be included in this book as support for the charges being true.

A manager at Columbia Pictures in Los Angeles, Garby Leon, told me in early 1992 that he had spoken to ABC News' Paris bureau chief, Pierre Salinger, who had admitted to him that he had a copy of the French Secret Service report describing the October Surprise meetings in Paris. Salinger said that he would show the report to him if he came to London. I sent a request to Salinger and to ABC's corporate headquarters by registered mail, requesting a copy of that report. My letter stated in part:

*This is a request for information, and a copy of documents in your possession, relating to the activities known as "October Surprise." I have been advised by several sources that you, and American Broadcasting Corporation, have writings supporting the existence of these treasonous and subversive activities which were a CIA operation. I am writing in my book that is nearly completed, and it is being stated...that ABC has these writings in its possession, and...that ABC has become, as a matter of federal law, co-conspirators, and liable criminally as principals.*

**FURTHER OCTOBER SURPRISE SUPPORT**

Neither Salinger nor ABC responded. However, in 1995, Salinger admitted in a book called "P.S.," originally published in France and then in English in the United States, that he knew of the October Surprise meetings in Paris. In an eight-paragraph section of the French publication (omitted in the English translation) he described the secret meeting that Bush attended. Salinger wrote that he determined through his high-level sources in France that the secret meetings did in fact take place .

Salinger wrote in his book that "a man named Jacques Montanes showed up at my ABC office with a big bag full of papers." The papers documented the airlift of military supplies to Iran in October 1980, prior to the U.S. presidential elections, and as Gunther Russbacher, who arranged for much of the military equipment, had described to me. Montanes had been involved with the arms shipments, obtaining documents showing companies contributing to the military equipment shipments from Spain, France, Great Britain, and Israel. Salinger's book continued, "Obviously, I broke this story on ABC News, something that shocked the American government."

Salinger described his long relationship with top officials in French intelligence who confirmed to him that the U.S.-Iranian meeting did take place on October 18 and 19. In his book Salinger write that "Marenches had written a report on it which was in intelligence files. Unfortunately, he told me that file had disappeared."

Salinger described his conversations with respected American journalist, David Andelman, who was the ghost writer of the 1992 memoirs of Alexandre de Marenches, French spy chief. At Salinger's request, Andelman asked Marenches about the alleged Paris meetings involving Casey and Bush. Salinger wrote in his book, "Andelman came back to me and said that Marenches had finally agreed [that] he organized the meeting, under the request of an old friend, William Casey.... Marenches and Casey had known each other well during the days of World War II. Marenches added that while he prepared the meeting, he did not attend it."

Andelman testified to this admission before the House October Surprise task force in December 1992, but as with other creditable witnesses, this testimony was ignored so as to deny the existence of this crime.

Salinger referred to the coverup by such U.S. magazines as *The New Republic* and *Newsweek*, who debunked the charges. In this way major crimes against America went unpunished and continued to flourish.

**U.S. PUBLISHING CENSORSHIP**

The English edition of Salinger's book omitted any reference to these facts or to October Surprise. I continually ran into this media coverup. The book, *Trail of the Octopus*, written by a former Defense Intelligence Agency agent, Lester Coleman, published in England, exposed Justice Department coverup of the CIA-DEA drug smuggling operation that permitted the bomb to be placed on board Pan Am Flight 103 that blew up over Lockerbie. In 1996 American West Distributors in Berkeley, California, was forced to halt its plan to distribute the book due to pressure. The television documentary, *Maltese Doublecross*, produced in England, also describes how this conduct by CIA and DEA personnel led to the bombing of Flight 103, could not get any distributors in the United States. I met with its producer, Allan Francovich, in Berkeley, and he described his inability to get anyone to show the film.

**PEPSICO AS A CIA ASSET**

Pepsico International Headquarters in Barcelona was the site of one of the meetings held in Barcelona in July 1980.[278] I sent a registered letter to Wayne Calloway, CEO and Chairman of the Board of Directors of Pepsico, in Purchase, New York, advising that I was describing in my book the part they played in the October Surprise operation unless I heard otherwise from them. The letter stated in part:

*I am in possession of declarations/transcripts showing that the Pepsico Corporation played key roles in the treasonous and subversive acts known as October Surprise.[279] These declarations and transcripts, by a deep cover CIA officer, who was present at the Barcelona meetings in late July 1980, at the Pepsico International Headquarters Building, describes the part played by Pepsico in helping to sabotage the United States by becoming a part of the conspiracy known as October Surprise. Other declarations show the part played by Pepsico in other CIA schemes. The Pepsico official directly involved in the Barcelona caper was Peter Van Tyne.*

*Pepsico's part in the CIA-related schemes is being described in the nearly completed Defrauding America book, which is a follow-up to my last one, Unfriendly Skies—Saga of Corruption. To fill in areas that are not yet clear, would you kindly provide me with the following information:*

*1. The address of Peter Van Tyne, and what his position was with Pepsico in mid-1980.*

*2. Peter Van Tyne's present address for receiving correspondence.*

*3. Who in the CIA, and any others, arranged with Pepsico for the use of its International Headquarters facilities in the subversive acts associated with October Surprise?*

*4. What is the relationship between Pepsico and the Central Intelligence Agency in the United States and overseas?*

*5. What other covert relationships existed, and exist, between Pepsico and the CIA?*

*6. What are the rewards, financial and otherwise, arising from these relationships?*

*For your information, copies of the transcripts showing Pepsico's involvement with these very serious crimes against the United States have been attached to federal briefs, and have been sent to many members*

278 Stated by Russbacher and Ben-Menashe.

279 The conspiracy involved private citizens, renegade federal officials, Central Intelligence Agency personnel (all sabotaging the elected Government of the United States), and Iranian factions who were holding 52 American citizens in Iranian prisons.

*of Congress (despite its record as the world's most reliable coverup body), and others. Many more will be sent out. Your answer to these questions would be useful in clarifying the covert relationships that helped inflict such great harms upon the United States.*

*If you don't provide this information, the book will show the implications of what Pepsico has done, and what can be implied by your refusal to respond.*

There was no response and no denial.

Russbacher told me that William Casey boarded the BAC 111 at a New York City area airport after deplaning from a Unocal Gulfstream aircraft. I contacted Unocal[280] by certified mail on June 7, 1992, advising them of the serious charges associated with the October Surprise operation in which they were a part and advising that unless I heard otherwise from them I would describe the part they played in the operation. No response and no denial.

The House October Surprise Committee advised me that my Secret Service report showing George Bush flying into Washington National Airport in a UAE BAC 111 should read United Airlines, and the date should be October 18, 1980. I wrote to United Airlines via certified mail asking for their confirmation of the flight and date. They refused to answer.

**OCTOBER SURPRISE CLEANUP CREW**

As stated earlier, I started communicating in December 1994 with a former CIA operative, Oswald J. LeWinter, and we were in frequent contact. He gave me details on various deep-cover CIA activities in which he had been involved, including the October Surprise cleanup operation. He described how this team went to hotels and other suppliers of services in Paris, removing records and other evidence relating to the October Surprise meetings.

LeWinter was involved in many CIA operations throughout the world, and one of the few agents who whose knowledge and experience was compartmentalized. He was a CIA mole in NATO, and had top-level contacts in Vietnam. He said that his primary duty during his 30 years as a CIA operative was disinformation. This included planting false stories, removing evidence to hide CIA activities, and putting different spins on the facts. He was involved in undermining foreign governments and described some of these activities that occurred in South America. He acknowledged knowing of several of my CIA sources, including Bob Hunt and Gunther Russbacher.

Larry Barcella had contacted LeWinter for information about October Surprise. LeWinter asked, "What version do you want; that it existed, or didn't exist?" Barcella replied, "The version that shows it did not exist." LeWinter than denied any knowledge of October Surprise.

At a later date, LeWinter was interviewed by a reporter from the German newspaper *Der Spiegel* at which time LeWinter admitted the existence of October Surprise, giving details, and stating that he lied to Barcella, giving Barcella the version the investigator wanted to hear. LeWinter even gave the reporter an affidavit containing these statements.

---

280 Richard Stegemeier, Chief Executive Officer, Unocal Corporation P.O. Box 7600, Los Angeles, CA 90051; Certified P 790 780 431.

The *Der Spiegel* reporter then contacted Barcella with the statement by LeWinter admitting lying to a congressional investigator. Barcella did nothing, not wishing to risk exposing the October Surprise operation.

In early 1996, LeWinter stated to me that he was preparing a manuscript on his CIA activities, and had a tentative name for it of *For the Honor Of Lying*, a fitting title for his CIA-ordered disinformation.

**EVIDENCE THAT THE SUBVERSIVE OPERATION OCCURRED.**

1. Sworn declarations and testimony of CIA operatives, including Gunther Russbacher, Richard Brenneke, and Michael Riconosciuto, who were part of the operation, and had much to lose if they lied, and even if they came forward.
2. Sworn testimony of Mossad officer Ari Ben-Menashe, who was present at several October Surprise meetings.
3. Secret Service documents disproving the statements of Secret Service agents and George Bush relating to Bush's absence from Washington on the October 19, 1980, weekend.
4. Statements by dozens of people in the United States, Europe and the Middle East, describing their knowledge of the October Surprise operation.
5. Refusal of people to deny the charges that I advised would be made against them if they did not respond to my mailings.
6. Large amount of anecdotal and circumstantial evidence.
7. Many people who were killed or who mysteriously died, who had knowledge of the October Surprise operation, and who were a threat to Iranian and U.S. officials implicated in the scheme.
8. Intense opposition by Republican members of Congress to conduct investigations into the charges.

**ENORMOUS CONSEQUENCES IF THE PUBLIC WAS TOLD THE TRUTH**

The resulting consequences of being caught in a coverup were minor compared to the consequences suffered by Washington officials if the October Surprise was admitted. Among the potential consequences of admitting that October Surprise conspiracy occurred:

1. Impeachment and criminal prosecution of many federal officials.
2. Exposing the role played by the CIA and possibly exposing other criminal activities of this agency.
3. Many Congressmen would be criminally implicated by their coverup, calling for impeachment and criminal prosecution.
4. Federal judges, who gained their positions by having played a role in the October Surprise scheme would be exposed, undermining public respect for the federal judiciary.
5. Past presidents of the United States would be exposed as guilty of treasonous and criminal activities.
6. Powerful law firms, lobbyists, and many other private interests with fortunes tied to those in power would be adversely affected if their benefactors were prosecuted and removed from office.
7. All political parties would suffer as a result of the public's awareness of the level of criminality in government.

## RESPONSIBILITIES AND OBSTRUCTION OF JUSTICE PARTIES

Every member of Congress had a responsibility under federal criminal statutes to receive testimony and evidence of the criminal acts described within these pages. The oath states:

> *I, [name of Congress person], do solemnly swear (or affirm) that I will support and* ***defend*** *the Constitution of the United States against all enemies, foreign and domestic; that I will bear true faith and allegiance to the same; that I take this obligation freely, without any mental reservation or purpose of evasion, and that I will well and faithfully discharge the duties of the office in which I am about to enter. So help me God.*

## FURTHER SUPPORT FOR SR-71 FLIGHT TO MOSCOW

In March 1996 I received a phone call from John Lear, an airline pilot, who was one of the sons of the famed builder of the Learjet airplane. He had just read the second edition of *Defrauding America* and said he found it very accurate. Lear had flown for CIA-related airlines for many years. When he got to the part in which Gunther Russbacher described an SR-71 left in Moscow in 1990, he remembered a conversation that he had with a pilot friend, Ken Polzin. Polzin had flown as captain for Buffalo Airways into Budapest in 1990, and while there, his Hungarian copilot, Gabor Szabo, told him about seeing an SR-71 in a hangar at Moscow several months earlier. I called Polzin for further information, and he related his Hungarian copilot telling him, on a flight to Budapest, Hungary, about seeing the SR-71 in a hangar. Szabo had recently been to Moscow receiving flight training on the Tupolov aircraft while flying for Malev Hungarian Airlines, and had seen the SR-71. There is certainly something strange about giving our supposed adversary one of our most secret aircraft during the Cold War.

Gunther and Rayelan Russbacher in "happier" times:

# IRAN-CONTRA

Without the October Surprise operation there could not have been an Iran-Contra scandal. The Iran and the Contra portions of what is known as Iran-Contra are really separate scandals with some relatively minor connections. The media and Congress have joined them together and have loosely described Iran-Contra as unlawful arms sales to Iran in exchange for American hostages seized in Lebanon and unlawful arms sales to Nicaragua. The Teheran hostage seizure associated with the October Surprise operation showed terrorists the profits to be realized in seizing Americans as hostages.

## THE IRAN CONNECTION

U.S. media and congressional publicity on Iran-Contra focused on the illegal arms sales to Iran in the mid-1980s, but these sales began years earlier, as part of the October Surprise operation. Although the arms sales were allegedly to obtain the release of American hostages seized in Lebanon, there was also a profit motive for many of the participants. Sharing in the profits from these arms sales to Iran were arms brokers, Israel, and a private network composed of CIA and National Security Council players. These arms sales to Iran violated U.S. law, and the criminal acts involved the president and vice president of the United States, members of the National Security Council, the CIA, and others.

## MOTIVES FOR THE ARMS SALES

The sales occurred partly because huge profits could be made by many participants. The arms would be purchased from U.S. or foreign governments, and then resold to Iran. Profits from these unlawful arms sales were stashed away in secret offshore bank accounts.[281] Ironically, about $10 million was placed in the wrong-numbered Swiss bank account that was intended for Air Force Maj. Gen. Richard Secord and his business partner, Albert Hakim.

281 One such account was in the name of Lake Resources, number 386-430-22-1.

Another motive for the illegal arms sales was for the CIA and NSC participants to purchase arms through their front companies. The money generated by the Iranian arms sales were not gifts to the Contras, as implied by the Reagan-Bush White House and the media. The profits from the arms sales to Iran were used to purchase additional arms, which were then traded to the Contras for drugs. These drugs constituted a large portion of the huge cocaine trafficking into the United States from Central and South America. The aircraft flying arms to Nicaragua and other Central and South America locations returned to the United States with drugs. This was a giant operation resembling a corporation structure such as General Motors.

**NAIVETE OF PAYING FOR HOSTAGES**

It can only be guessed if the selling of arms to Iran in exchange for the American hostages seized in Lebanon was the primary intent or simply an excuse for the Iran-Contra operation. It is difficult to believe that intelligence agency renegades thought the hostage situation could be solved by paying for their release, thereby encouraging a continuation of the hostage-taking. It appeared that for every hostage returned upon the payment of money or arms, additional hostages were seized. A "cottage industry" flourished. Its sole purpose was seizing American hostages in Lebanon. American hostages seized in Iran as part of October Surprise showed that profits could be made from hostage-taking, especially if they were Americans.

**UGLY SIDE OF THE CONTRA CONNECTION**

The ugly side of the Contra connection was carefully kept from the American public by the establishment media and Congress. Oliver North and others involved sought to place a humanitarian cloak over their activities with the Contras. They claimed U.S. involvement in Nicaragua was humanitarian by helping an oppressed people fight communism. But the CIA, representing the American people, traded arms for drugs. Aircraft carrying arms from the United States to Central America often returned with the drugs that were used to pay for the arms. The logistics used in the war against the Nicaraguan government and people facilitated the CIA-DEA drug smuggling into the United States. In the CIA's Vietnam War the logistics associated with sending arms to fight the Vietnamese people were used on the return trips into the United States to smuggle drugs. Enormous profits resulted, and many CIA operatives did quite well financially.

It wasn't only the Contras to whom the CIA furnished arms. The CIA, joined by Israel, arms merchants, and others, were selling and delivering arms to the opposition Sandanistas. One CIA operative said to me, "How else could we keep the fighting going!"

Drug trafficking from Central and South America into the United States by the CIA, DEA, and the Mossad was well underway in the 1960s. The CIA's stirring of the pot in Nicaragua greatly aided this by providing a great increase in aircraft availability and an excuse for the trafficking. Various code names were given to these arms and drug flights, as described in later pages.

As in any CIA operation, there were terrible brutalities inflicted upon innocent people. The Contra affair funded the intrusion by the CIA, representing the United States and the American people, into the affairs of a foreign country, using the same tactics and excuses as in Vietnam. The CIA prepared an assassination manual on torturing and killing people in Central America, resulting in the deaths of thousands of villagers, similar to the infamous Phoenix program in Vietnam that assassinated over 40,000 South Vietnamese villagers.

Numerous books have been written depicting these atrocities.[282] An October 19, 1992, *New York Times* article showed pictures revealing the 1981 massacre of almost 800 villagers at El Mozote, El Salvador. Reporters from the *Times* and *Washington Post* were in agreement that the killings were perpetrated by groups financed and supplied by the White House gang and the CIA. Searchers found many bodies, including those of children, under the floor of a parish house.

Most of the media discredited these assassination reports when they first came out, even though the media knew the reports to be true. The CIA infiltration of the media and the government's furnishing of much of what passes as news, along with the money dispensed to the media by the CIA, made this cooperation quite easy.

The arms sales to Nicaragua or any other Central American country violated U.S. law and specifically the 1984 Boland Amendment. Those involved in the sale of arms, including the trading of arms for drugs, deliberately continued violating the law. If the arms trafficking stopped, so would much of the drug trafficking into the United States on the return flights.

**CONGRESS FORCED TO CONDUCT AN "INVESTIGATION"**

Several events caused the American public to become aware of at least peripheral segments of the Iran and Contra operations. One event was the shooting down of a CIA proprietary aircraft[283] over Nicaragua in 1986. This was the highly-publicized shooting down of the C-123 aircraft with three crewmembers on board, and the survival of one of them: Eugene Hasenfus. Despite instructions for all evidence of CIA involvement to be removed from the aircraft and in the crew's possession, there was much evidence that the arms-carrying flight was a CIA operation.

Nicaraguan authorities put Hasenfus on television, during which he admitted that he was working for the CIA. As U.S. media stopped publicity on that event, other events occurring in Europe and the Middle East focused attention on the Iran segment of Iran-Contra.

An Iranian politician, incensed about his opponent's participation in the Iranian arms deals, distributed thousands of leaflets in Iran exposing these dealings, followed by an article in the Lebanese newspaper *Al Shiraa*. Israeli arms dealers who were taken out of the loop by direct arms sales from U.S. officials to Iran sought to eliminate the American competition, and they caused publicity to be generated.

This combination of publicity forced the U.S. media and Congress to focus on at least the outer fringes of the Iran and Contra affairs. Congress conducted

---

282 *Dangerous Liaison*, Andrew and Leslie Cockburn; *The Politics of Heroin*, Alfred McCoy; *Cocaine Politics*, Peter Dale Scott and Jonathan Marshall; *Everybody Had His Own Gringo*, Glenn Garvin.

283 The aircraft was owned by Southern Air Transport, a CIA proprietary. Three crew members were killed after the plane was hit by a ground-to-air missile. The cargo-pusher, Eugene Hasenfus, whose job was to push the military equipment from the aircraft while airborne, had carried a parachute with him, and parachuted from the falling aircraft. He survived, was captured, and testified to Nicaraguan authorities about his CIA connections.

one of their "investigations," and then requested that U.S. Attorney Edwin Meese recommend to the U.S. Court of Appeals in Washington appointment of an Independent Counsel (December 1986) to investigate further.

**AUTHORITY FOR INDEPENDENT PROSECUTOR**

Authority for the appointment of an independent prosecutor to investigate misconduct, criminal and treasonous activities of high officials in the executive branch was granted in 1978, following the Watergate affair. Congress passed the Independent Counsel Act,[284] providing for the appointment of an independent prosecutor to investigate crimes by high federal officials, *but exempted themselves from being investigated.* The mechanics of the legislation provided that the Judiciary Committee of either the House or Senate must request the U.S. Attorney General to submit a request to three judges on the Washington, D.C. Court of Appeals for the appointment of an Independent Counsel.

The Attorney General then decides whether to comply with the request. If the Attorney General does submit a request to the three-judge panel, the panel then decides what law firm or attorney will conduct the investigation. There are several judges on the Washington Court of Appeals who played key roles in October Surprise and the Iran and Contra operations. One of these judges is Lawrence Silberman.

A disadvantage of the Independent Prosecutor is that the attorney selected may be unqualified and without sufficient experience to conduct a criminal investigation. The attorney selected to act as Independent Prosecutor may be biased or have hidden interests, and often has profitable ties to the Justice Department, CIA, or other government entity. The attorney will rarely jeopardize these lucrative ties. The attorney selected may be a former Justice Department employee still loyal to the mindset of that agency.

**LIMITING THE RISKS**

Meese made the request, limiting the investigation to determining which of the people who gave testimony to Congress had either lied or withheld evidence. Meese himself was implicated in the Iran and Contra operations and had a vested interest in insuring coverup of the sordid operation. Court of Appeals judges selected former head of the American Bar Association, Lawrence Walsh, an 80-year-old Oklahoman, to conduct a limited investigation as Independent Counsel. The investigation focused on personnel assigned to the White House, the National Security Council, and the CIA.[285]

Walsh eventually filed charges against many of them. Caspar Weinberger was indicted on June 16, 1992, on charges of obstruction of justice and of Congress, perjury, and false statements to Iran-Contra investigators. Duane

284 Legislation was enacted in 1978.

285 Among those who were investigated were Caspar Weinberger (Secretary of Defense); George Schultz (Secretary of State); George Bush (Vice President of the United States); Edwin Meese (Attorney General); Donald Regan (White House Chief of Staff); John Poindexter (National Security Advisor); William Casey (CIA Director); Alton Keel (Poindexter's deputy); Robert McFarlane (National Security Advisor); Elliott Abrams (Assistant Secretary of State); Duane Clarridge (CIA Chief of European operations); Clair E. George (CIA); Alan G. Fiers, Jr. (Head of CIA Central American Task Force); Richard V. Secord (retired Air Force Major General); Thomas G. Clines (CIA contract agent); Joseph F. Fernandez (CIA station chief in Costa Rica); Oliver L. North (Marine Corps officer and staff member of the National Security Council); among others.

Clarridge was indicted on November 26, 1991, on charges of perjury and making false statements to Congress. Oliver North was found guilty on May 4, 1989, of altering and destroying government documents, aiding and abetting, and obstruction of Congress. This case was dismissed on the technicality that he was immune against prosecution on the basis of testimony given to Congress.

Claire George was indicted and found guilty on December 9, 1992, of making false statements and perjury before Congress. Elliott Abrams was indicted and pled guilty on October 7, 1991, to withholding information from Congress. Alan Fiers, Jr., pleaded guilty on July 9, 1991, to withholding information from Congress. Robert McFarlane was indicted and pled guilty on March 11, 1988, to withholding information from Congress. Thomas Clines was charged and found guilty on September 18, 1990, of tax-related crimes and sent to prison.

Richard Secord was charged and pled guilty on November 8, 1989, to making false statements to Congress. Albert Hakim was charged and pled guilty on November 21, 1989, to supplementing the salary of Oliver North. Carl Channell pled guilty on April 29, 1987, to conspiracy to defraud the United States. Richard Miller pled guilty on May 8, 1987, to conspiracy to defraud the United States. John Poindexter was found guilty on April 7, 1990, of conspiracy, obstruction of justice, and making false statements to Congress. Joseph Fernandez was charged but the case dismissed on November 24, 1989, after the CIA refused to turn over documents relevant to his defense.

Vice President George Bush denied any knowledge of the Iran-Contra affair until it was made public in the American mainstream media in December 1986, just as he denied his involvement in October Surprise. My CIA contacts described Bush's heavy involvement in Central America operations in which drug trafficking constituted a major role. Testimony and numerous books describe Bush's long-time involvement in the Central America operations. Felix Rodriguez, known to be involved with the entire sordid operation, reported regularly to Bush in the White House.[286] Many of North's notes referred to the drug trafficking, relying upon the drug profits to fund other elements of the operation.

The large-scale smuggling of arms out of the United States to Central America and return flights loaded with drugs surely were not unknown to Justice Department officials, to the CIA, to Customs, or the Drug Enforcement Agency in the Justice Department. My CIA contacts who were part of the operation detailed how they continued in their CIA-related drug trafficking unmolested.

Secord and others ran a private company selling arms to Iran, making huge profits, which they put into private bank accounts in Europe. My CIA contacts state that many in this same group managed CIA drug trafficking operations in Central America and in the Golden Triangle area.[287] Poindexter was charged with obstructing and conspiring to obstruct justice, and making false statements to Congress. North was convicted of aiding and abetting obstruction of Congress, destroying security council documents and accepting an illegal gift.

---

286 Statements made to the media by Americans and Israelis involved with the operation; highly documented books, including *Honored and Betrayed*, by former Air Force Maj. General Richard Secord; Felix Rodriguez, a former CIA operative, was in frequent telephone contact with Bush, and described these contacts.

287 Burma, Laos, Thailand.

Aside from the coverup of the sordid aspects of the so-called Iran-Contra affair there are some contradictions to the prosecution of these people, arising out of their withholding of information from Congress and false statements. For example:

* Members of Congress have engaged in criminal coverup, misprision of felonies, obstruction of justice, falsification of hearing records, and other crimes for years, and it is shown throughout these pages.

* Members of Congress have obstructed the reporting of federal crimes against the United States as a standard practice. I repeatedly petitioned Congress to introduce my testimony and evidence and that of our group of CIA and DEA whistleblowers. These were criminal acts.

* Members of Congress routinely cover up for serious crimes discovered during closed-door hearings and then render decisions that are contradicted by the evidence being withheld.

* These acts violated numerous criminal statutes, including:

  * Misprision of felony (refusing to make known criminal acts against the United States).

  * Obstruction of justice

  * Conspiracy to obstruct justice.

* Many members of Congress already knew of the criminal acts involved in Iran-Contra including the CIA and DEA drug trafficking that they continued to sequester.

* Conspiracy to commit these crimes and others and defrauding the United States.

**CRIMINAL COVERUP BY INDEPENDENT PROSECUTOR**

Walsh spent over $40 million focusing on the relatively minor issues of who knew about the arms for hostages and who withheld information from Congress. Walsh focused for six years on these trivial issues, while covering up for the hard-core drug trafficking into the United States as part of the Contra operation. He also covered up for the genesis of Iran-Contra: the October Surprise scandal. Walsh committed acts far more serious than the people he charged with federal crimes. He covered up for treasonous and criminal activities.

In early 1992, I mailed several petitions to Independent Prosecutor Lawrence Walsh including transcripts of sworn declarations by some of the CIA and DEA whistleblowers, requesting that he receive our testimony and evidence, which he was required to receive as a matter of law. He never answered.

The petition and declarations exposed corrupt activities by federal officials including the Iran and Contra operations, October Surprise, CIA and DEA drug smuggling, looting of savings and loans, Chapter 11 corruption, and the criminal activities in the federal courts where he was once a federal judge and federal prosecutor. He ignored it all, covering up for crimes against America.

**PRESIDENTIAL PARDONS**

Caspar Weinberger, former Defense Secretary, was scheduled to stand trial in January 1993 on charges of perjury, making false statements to Congress, and obstructing Congressional investigators. His testimony would implicate President George Bush and other high federal officials. Shortly before the trial was to start, Bush executed a Christmas Eve pardon for Weinberger, forestalling that risk. He also pardoned Duane Clarridge; Clair George; Robert McFarlane; Elliott Abrams; and Alan Fiers, Jr.

**REPERCUSSIONS IF PARDONS NOT ISSUED**

If Bush had not issued these pardons, the danger existed that the sordid parts of the Contra operation would surface, including the drug trafficking into the United States. Further, former President Ronald Reagan's involvement would probably have surfaced.

After Bush issued his pardon, I sent another certified letter and petition to Walsh, again putting him on notice of the criminal activities associated with the Contra operation, attaching copies of secret government documents supporting some of the charges.

I should have saved my time; many state and federal investigators sent boxes of evidence to Walsh showing crimes far worse than those that he identified and prosecuted. He was simply repeated the practice of prior independent prosecutors in addressing only the minor issues and insuring that the hard-core criminal activities involving high-level government figures remain hidden. IRS investigators, and state investigators in Arkansas, sent boxes of evidence to Walsh proving that the Iran-Contra figures were involved in criminal and subversive activities against the United States. More about this in later pages.

The petition that I sent to Walsh is shown, in part, in the following pages:

*December 27, 1992*

*Mr. Lawrence Walsh, Independent Prosecutor*
*Office of Independent Counsel, Suite 701 West*
*555 Thirteenth Street, NW*
*Washington, DC 20004 Certified: P 888 324 857*

*Dear Mr. Walsh:*

*This letter and the enclosures address the Iran-Contra affair that you were hired and paid to investigate. I had several times offered to present evidence to you concerning the hard-core criminal acts associated with Iran-Contra, and you refused to receive the evidence. In your investigation you chose to limit your investigation, similar to limiting the investigation of Murder Incorporated to parking ticket violations.*

*While you deserve credit for objecting to President Bush's pardons, you share blame for cover up of the serious Iran-Contra violations of federal law, the arms and drug trafficking into and out of the United States by the network, and of the treasonous and subversive October Surprise operations which you chose to cover up, and which were the genesis of Iran-Contra.*

*This letter, and the attachments, again puts you on notice and under federal criminal statutes and constitutional right to petition government, demands that you receive the testimony and evidence of myself and the parties who have knowledge of the criminal activities of which Iran-Contra and October Surprise are only a part. (I won't hold my breath waiting for you to meet your duty.)*

*The enclosed documents include Secret Service agent reports as received by the CIA, prior to their alterations to accommodate the coverup. The information that I have is that the Secret Service reports were routed through deep-cover CIA officer Gunther Russbacher, who then placed the initials of one of his CIA-provided aliases on many of them: RAW, standing for Robert Andrew Walker, who also operated a number of cover CIA financial proprietaries.*

*The documents not only support the charges that October Surprise did in fact occur, but also provide information on the Iran-Contra affair.*

***SIGNIFICANCE OF DATES ON THE SECRET SERVICE REPORTS***

*The correct dates and aircraft have great significance:*

*1. If Bush arrived by aircraft at Washington National Airport on Sunday, October 19, 1980, it would indicate Secret Service personnel lied (as well as George Bush) when reporting that Bush never left the Washington area on the December 19, 1980 weekend. (Wouldn't the false statements also be shown by an October 18, 1980, arrival by aircraft in the Washington area?)*

*2. If Bush arrived via a United Arab Emirates BAC 111, and several CIA operatives and contract agents testified (and declared in sworn declarations) that Bush and others departed Washington for Paris in a UAE BAC 111 on October 18, 1980, it appears that Bush returned to Washington on the same aircraft.*

*3. It would indicate that the several dozen people who testified before*

*Congress and in federal court; CIA operative Gunther Russbacher who made sworn declarations that I have in my possession; and those who described to investigative journalists and book authors particulars of the October Surprise operation, were truthful about the October Surprise operation.*

*4. If the hard-core October Surprise conspiracy and its implications were exposed to the public, the consequences would be endless. Other criminal activities arising from the operation would surface. The felony persecution of whistleblowers and informants would be exposed, as well as the perennial coverup and obstruction of justice by members of Congress. Key personnel in all three branches of government would be shown implicated in the October Surprise and related criminal enterprises, culminating in a political disaster of unknown consequences.*

***DETERMINING THE VALIDITY OF THE DISPUTED REPORTS***

*It is very important to the United States to determine the truth in this matter. A coverup will simply escalate the criminal mindset that has escalated in the federal government. Numerous people have copies of the Secret Service reports that I sent to you, showing George Bush arriving at Washington National Airport on the evening of October 19, 1980 in a UAE BAC 111. These reports have the initials, RAW, in the upper right hand corner.*

*My investigation indicates that the initials "RAW" stand for Robert Andrew Walker, an alias provided by the CIA to Gunther Russbacher, reportedly a deep-cover CIA and Office of Naval Intelligence officer. I recently questioned Russbacher about these reports, whether the initials were his, and whether the October 19, 1980 dates and the United Arab Emirates BAC 111 information were the same as when he first initialed the reports. He confirmed that the facts on my reports are the same as when the reports came to him.*

*Russbacher stated that he placed the initials, RAW, in the upper right hand corner of the Secret Service reports when the reports came to him at the Central Intelligence Agency at Langley, Virginia. Apparently the reason the reports came to him was that he was present at several activities related to the October Surprise operation. I have previously sent to Congressman Hamilton partial transcripts of Russbacher's sworn declarations describing the October Surprise activities in which he participated.*

*If Secret Service agents were on board that flight, then it would indicate further that a coup against the United States did take place, and that the Secret Service (and many others) are now trying to deny that fact. The only way to establish which Secret Service reports are correct and which are forgeries is to have Russbacher testify in open hearings before the Senate October Surprise committee. Russbacher has advised me that he is willing to testify how and when he received these Secret Service reports; that the October 19, 1980 date was on these reports when he first saw them at the CIA; and the role that he played in the October Surprise operation.*

*If the hearings are closed to the public, then the usual Congressional coverup will prevail. If you remember, I'm a former federal investigator who is well familiar with the pattern of coverup, obstruction of justice, altering documents and reports. I have reported these crimes for years, with the felony coverups escalating in frequency and severity. Based upon my knowledge over the past thirty years, lying, perjury, obstruction of justice, are routine practices by many in federal government. I describe these acts in my various books and in prior federal court filings.*

***RUSSBACHER'S CREDIBILITY***

*Russbacher's credibility has been established to my satisfaction, and can be established in numerous ways:*

** He has given me many hours of sworn declarations in deposition-like questioning relating to the specific October Surprise operation in which he was ordered to participate by his superiors (in addition to other CIA operations that have inflicted great harms upon the United States). During the past two years I have questioned Gunther Russbacher extensively, during a minimum of 200 hours of deposition-like questioning, uncovering facts supporting the criminal activities against the United States.*

** Russbacher has tried to give testimony to Congress concerning some of his CIA activities, including the October Surprise operation, and is willing to do so at this time. These efforts have and are being made with full recognition that if he commits perjury the present Justice Department staff and the past three U.S. attorney generals (all of whom are implicated in the crimes) would promptly charge him with criminal perjury. The Senate and House October Surprise committees had a* ***duty*** *to obtain his testimony, rather than fabricate excuses for not doing so.*

** The tone, the conditions under which Russbacher gave me the sworn declarations, and the specifics in these declarations, strongly suggest the truthfulness of these sworn statements. The sworn declarations contain data on the October Surprise activities that have never before been exposed. The declarations coincide with facts that came out a year and two years later, including those in Gary Sick's October Surprise and Ari Ben-Menashe's Profits of War.*

** Locations of meetings that have never before been exposed. Ari Ben-Menashe confirmed the meeting site when I told him of the meeting in Barcelona at both a hotel and the Pepsico International Headquarters building. It is my belief that most if not all of Russbacher's statements and sworn declarations made during the past two years are true, and coincide with statements made to me by Ari Ben-Menashe and by numerous investigative journalists and authors.*

***FEDERAL CRIMES AGAINST U.S. REPORTED BY RUSSBACHER***

*In numerous deposition-like sessions, Gunther Russbacher had declared under oath the following activities related to the October Surprise operation (and much more):*

*D. Description of several of the secret October Surprise meetings by a deep-cover CIA officer who was present, including the key Barcelona meetings that have not been publicized before. When I made reference to the Pepsico meeting site it refreshed the memory of Ben-Menashe and he confirmed the meeting site.*

*E. The people who were on board the flight to Paris on the October 19,*

*1980 weekend were identified as including four or five Secret Service agents,[288] George Bush, William Casey, Donald Gregg, Robert McFarlane, and others.[289] If Secret Service agents were on board that flight, as Russbacher's sworn declarations state, it would be understandable that Treasury Department officials are desperately trying to discredit the Secret Service reports allegedly received at the CIA showing that Bush flew into Washington National Airport on Sunday evening, when he and the Secret Service claim he never left the Washington area.*

### *PRIMA FACIE EVIDENCE OF OCTOBER SURPRISE OPERATION*

** Specific statements by dozens of witnesses interviewed by investigative journalists and authors, detailing segments of the October Surprise operation, who have nothing to gain by their statements.*

** Testimony given to the House and Senate October Surprise committees by people who were in a position to know; who had nothing to gain; and who risk prison through criminal perjury charges if the testimony was false.*

** Refusal by certain individuals to deny their role in the October Surprise operation when I questioned them in writing. These people and firms include Pepsico International Corporation; Pepsico official Peter Van Tyne; Pierre Salinger, who has copies of the French Secret Service report of the Paris October 19, 1980 meetings; French President Francois Mitterrand, who refused to provide copies of the French Secret Service reports; refusal of members of Congress to receive testimony and evidence offered by me in petitions, relating to the multiple criminal activities.*

** Outright misstatement of facts by the House and Senate October Surprise committees, and using phony reasons to discredit people testifying to what they saw.*

** Obstructing a thorough investigation by members of Congress, Justice Department officials, U.S. attorney generals, including threatening and prosecuting informants.*

### *PATTERN OF FELONY COVERUP*

** Pattern of felony persecution[290] of informants and whistleblowers by corrupt*

---

288 If Secret Service agents were actually on board that flight, the coup against the United States takes on wider dimensions, explaining the discrepancy between the Secret Service reports showing Bush flying into Washington National Airport on the evening of October 19, 1980, in contradiction to Bush's arrival the night before.

289 The other passengers reportedly on the BAC 111 to Paris included, among others, Senators John Tower (Iran-Contra coverup chairman); John Heinz; Congressman Dan Rostenkowski; Jennifer Fitzgerald.

290 **Title 18 U.S.C. § 1512. Tampering with a witness, victim, or an informant—**

(b) Whoever knowingly uses intimidation or physical force, or threatens another person, or attempts to do so, or engages in misleading conduct toward another person, with intent to–

(1) influence, delay or prevent the testimony of any person in an official proceeding:

shall be fined...or imprisoned...or both. [1988 amended reading].

**Title 18 U.S.C. § 1513. Retaliating against a witness, victim, or an informant.** (a) Whoever knowingly engages in any conduct and thereby causes bodily injury to another person or damages the tangible property of another person, or threatens to do so, with intent to retaliate against any person for—(1) the attendance of a witness or party at an official proceeding, or any testimony given or any record, document, or other object produced by a witness in an official proceeding; or (2) any information relating to the commission or possible commission of a Federal offense....

**Title 18 U.S.C. § 241. Conspiracy against rights of citizens.** If two or more persons conspire to injure, oppress, threaten, or intimidate any citizen in the free exercise or enjoyment of any right or

*Justice Department prosecutors and federal judges, as felony retaliation is inflicted upon people offering testimony. The pattern of felony retaliation by a conspiracy of federal prosecutors and federal judges have been inflicted upon:*

** CIA contract agent Richard Brenneke, charged with perjury when he testified to his role in the October Surprise operation and having seen George Bush and Donald Gregg at the Paris meetings.*

** CIA contract agent Michael Riconosciuto, threatened by Justice Department officials if he testified before Congress concerning the Inslaw corruption and October Surprise. The threats were then carried out against him and his wife, as threatened. Importing a CIA prosecutor specifically for the purpose, Justice Department personnel prosecuted Riconosciuto and caused him imprisonment. As warned by Justice Department official Videnieks, Riconosciuto's wife lost custody of her three children and she was imprisoned for removing them to a safer location.*

** CIA operative Gunther Russbacher, falsely charged with money offenses while operating covert CIA financial proprietaries and given 21 years in prison for a $20,000 offense in which no monetary loss was suffered by anyone, in which he pleaded nolo contender, and in which there was never a trial; 18 months in prison for [misuse of government purchase orders while a CIA operative.] Arrested at Castle Air Force Base for allegedly impersonating a Naval Officer, after debriefing his CIA superiors concerning a secret flight of SR-71s to Moscow on July 26, 1990.*

** Informant and whistleblower Rodney Stich, repeatedly threatened and imprisoned since mid-1987, as corrupt federal judges*[291] *and Justice Department prosecutors retaliated against me for filing federal actions reporting the federal crimes (in which their group and they were implicated).*

** Ari Ben-Menashe, high-ranking officer in the Mossad, possessing information concerning the October Surprise operation and other corrupt acts against the United States in which present federal officials were implicated. He was falsely charged by Justice Department officials in an attempt to silence and discredit him.*

*The criminal mindset of those now in control of the Justice Department, and in control of the federal judiciary, is reflected by these repeated prison sentences inflicted upon informants and whistleblowers, in retaliation for reporting the criminal activities previously brought to your attention, to Congressman Hamilton's attention, and to every senator in the U.S. Senate. Since 1987, and continuing at this very moment,*[292] *corrupt federal judges and Justice Department prosecutors are threatening to put me in federal prison in retaliation for filing a federal action reporting certain segments of the criminal activities that I have repeatedly brought to the attention of your committee and others via petitions.*

---

privilege secured to him by the Constitution or laws of the United States, or because of his having so exercised the same;...They shall be fined...or imprisoned...or both.

291 Including District court judges David Levi; Milton Schwartz; Raul Ramirez; Garcia; Marilyn Patel; Samuel Conti; the entire Ninth Circuit Federal Court of Appeals; Justices of the U.S. Supreme Court who knew and aided and abetted the corrupt and criminal acts of the judges over whom they have supervisory responsibilities and duty to act.

292 U.S. District Court, N.D. Cal. Nr. 90-0636 VRW.

## *MY CREDIBILITY*

*My findings and determinations have considerable credibility:*

** Former federal investigator holding federal authority to make such determinations, possessing evidence supporting many of my charges, including judicial records which establish the felony persecution of informants and victims by Justice Department prosecutors and federal judges.*

** Private investigator for many years expanding my investigations into other and related areas of criminal activities against the United States and its citizens.*

** Author of several books exposing government corruption through specific examples, based upon hard evidence and judicial records, having devoted thousands of hours and many years of investigations to this cause.*

** Victim of the criminal activities seeking to obstruct justice, as rogue Justice Department personnel, federal judges, cooperating law firms and attorneys, targeted me for the past decade, misusing the judicial process, blocking my reporting of the crimes, and retaliating against me for exposing the criminal activities of which they were a part. These crimes were committed while a majority of the U.S. Senate and House withheld their duty to act, and thereby became accomplices.*

** Statements and sworn declarations given to me by deep-cover CIA operatives and contract agents, describing the pattern of criminal activities that I have made reference to in prior petitions to members of Congress and which I have entered into judicial proceedings.*

** Over 1,800 radio and television appearances since 1978, in which my reports of corruption have been given major credibility.*

** Judicial records confirm many of my charges, especially relating to criminal acts related to a series of airline crashes; the pattern of corruption in Chapter 11 courts; the pattern of felony coverup and felony persecution of informants by Justice Department personnel and federal judges.*

## *OBSTRUCTING JUSTICE AND MISSTATING THE FACTS*

*Federal crime reporting statutes make it a federal offense if any person, knowing of a federal crime, does not promptly report it.*[293] *Justice Department personnel and federal judges have perverted this requirement by retaliating against informants, whistleblowers and victims who seek to report aspects of these various criminal activities.*

*It is a federal crime if anyone retaliates against an informant or victim, as Justice Department prosecutors and federal judges have done. It is a federal crime for a federal officer, such as a member of Congress or a Congressional committee, to refuse to receive evidence offered by an informant or victim.*

** It is a federal crime to refuse to provide relief to an informant or victim who is suffering such retaliation, especially when the retaliation is perpetrated by a federal employee and agency over whom members of Congress have oversight responsibilities.*

293 **Title 18 U.S.C. § 4 (misprision of felony).** Whoever, having knowledge of the actual commission of a felony cognizable by a court of the United States, conceals and does not as soon as possible make known the same to some judge or other person in civil or military authority under the United States, shall be fined not more than $500 or imprisoned not more than three years, or both.

** It is a federal crime to misstate the facts in a federal report, and this includes Congressional committees, and that includes the House and Senate October Surprise Committees. As a former federal investigator, it is obvious that these Committees are engaging in a felony coverup, withholding of evidence, misstating the evidence.*

***DETERMINATION OF WHICH SECRET SERVICE REPORT IS CORRECT***

*As part of the long-time effort to expose the escalating pattern of criminal activities against the United States by corrupt federal officials, I have repeatedly discovered federal officials falsifying documents, covering up for documents, misstating the facts, showing that perjury by federal personnel and falsified federal documents are normal coverup tactics. In evaluating whether Congressmen Hamilton's copy of the Secret Service reports, or my CIA related Secret Service reports, are accurate, the following actions should be taken:*

** Obtain the testimony of Gunther Russbacher concerning these reports, in open hearings, and giving the media access to him before and after his testimony.*

** Allow the CIA operatives to testify,*[294] *and compare their testimony, as it relates to October Surprise and peripheral activities.*

** Obtain the sworn testimony of the Secret Service agents who were with Bush from October 18 through October 20, 1980, in open hearings, making it clear that the Justice Department (in the next administration) and an independent prosecutor (if the statute is renewed) will prosecute for criminal perjury if the statements are false.*

** Consider the overwhelming pressures upon Secret Service agents (and others), to lie, concerning their observation of Bush's activities from October 18, 1980 to October 20, 1980, and their knowledge of the October 19, 1980 report date.*

** Obtain CIA records and testimony relating to the routing of the Secret Service report that Russbacher initialed.*

***OBSTRUCTION OF JUSTICE BY THE HOUSE "INVESTIGATIVE" COMMITTEE***

*It is my evaluation that Congressman Hamilton's October Surprise Committee will continue to cover up and obstruct justice in relation to the October Surprise matter:*

** Agent Pedersen, on loan from the Treasury Department, seeks to protect the Secret Service's involvement in the October Surprise operation.*

** Credible witnesses such as former Mossad staff officer Ari Ben-Menashe, CIA contract agents Richard Brenneke and Michael Riconosciuto, who testified under risk of criminal perjury charges, were dismissed by simply calling them not creditable, and giving sham reasons that only a gullible public could swallow.*

** Credible deep-cover CIA whistleblowers, such as Gunther Russbacher, are not given the opportunity to testify, eliminating one of the primary sources of establishing the existence of the October Surprise operation and its many*

---

294 Gunther Russbacher; Michael Riconosciuto; Richard Brenneke.

*tentacles.*

* *Conducting closed hearings to prevent the public discovering the crimes against the United States on the basis of testimony offered, or the refusal to ask questions that would result in the answers establishing the crimes. This is a standard Congressional tactic of many years.*

* *Aiding and abetting the felony persecution of informants by corrupt Justice Department officials and federal judges, as a part of the pattern of felony obstruction of justice by Congressional "investigative" committees.*

* *Refusing to receive testimony and evidence relating to the petition that I submitted, including the declarations of Russbacher and myself, describing the criminal activities that both of us discovered while we were federal employees.*

***OBSTRUCTION OF JUSTICE BY THE SENATE "INVESTIGATIVE" COMMITTEE***

*As a former federal investigator my evaluation of the November 19, 1992 Senate October Surprise report is that it is a blatant and felonious coverup, misstating the facts, omitting key facts, refusing to have key witnesses testify, for the purpose of cover up and of course, obstructing justice.*

*The report discredits the many witnesses who testified to what they witnessed in their participation in the October Surprise operation. They had nothing to gain by their testimony and risked imprisonment on charges of perjury. Many knew the fate of Richard Brenneke and Michael Riconosciuto when they testified, and yet they had the courage to come forward. Deep-cover CIA officer Gunther Russbacher is suffering greatly from his attempts to report the great crimes committed against the United States in the October Surprise and other criminal activities. I have been stripped of my multi-million dollar assets and have been subjected repeatedly, and at this time, to criminal contempt of court in retaliation for seeking to report the crimes that you coverup, and for seeking relief from the great harms inflicted upon me by criminal misuse of the agencies over which you have oversight responsibilities. These criminal acts and outrages reflect the subversive activities rampant in the United States and made possible by your coverup.*

*My book describes the felony coverup by members of Congress, Justice Department personnel, others, including Independent Prosecutor Walsh, and describes the criminal aiding and abetting of activities that are destroying the United States form of government from within.*

***RESPONSIBILITIES OF MEMBERS OF THE COMMITTEE***

* *Obtain Russbacher's testimony in open hearings. He has repeatedly stated, and reconfirmed it today, December 26, 1992, that he is ready to testify concerning:*

* *The CIA origin of the Secret Service reports that I mailed to Congressman Hamilton;*

* *The specific details of the October Surprise operation in which Russbacher was ordered to participate by his CIA superiors, including meetings in Barcelona and Paris; the shipment of arms after the Barcelona meetings; where the arms were obtained; how they were shipped; names of people involved in the shipping of the arms; names of those on the BAC 111 to Paris*

*on the October 19, 1980 weekend.*

** With immunity, he would be willing to testify to other activities in which he was ordered to participate, that have inflicted great harms upon the United States. These activities include looting of financial institutions (many of the participants still escape prosecution because of CIA and Justice Department involvement, and especially in the Denver area, involving the many financial institutions related to Metropolitan Development Corporation); CIA drug trafficking in the United States (and the coverup of these activities at Mena, Arkansas, by president-elect Bill Clinton); the CIA role in the BCCI banking scandal; and others.*

** Obtain my testimony and evidence in open hearings, relating to the direct and indirect knowledge that I have of these criminal activities.*

** Obtain the testimony of other CIA operatives, whose testimony would reinforce that of other informants.*

** Include as part of your "investigation" the contents of my manuscript which shows the intricate relationship between the various criminal activities.*

*This is a request that you include in the final report of your October Surprise "investigation" the comments made in this and earlier letters.*

*Sincerely,*

*Rodney Stich*

*Enclosures:*

*October 3, 1980 CIA: "Proposal to Exchange Spare Parts With Hostages."*
*October 9, 1980 Department of State: "Approach on Iranian Spares."*
*October 21, 1980 Department of State: "Talk with Mitch Regovin."*
*October 29, 1980: "Two Related Items on Iranian Military supply."*
*October 1980 Secret Service reports: Bush's security detail.*
*June 3, 1983(?) CIA: Release of Hostages.*
*July 5, 1985: "New Developments on Channel to Iran."*
*August 19, 1985: "Status of Hashemi-Elliot Richardson Contact."*

Walsh refused to receive my testimony and evidence, and that offered by Gunther Russbacher. He also refused to act, or even make reference to boxes of documents sent to him by Arkansas and congressional investigators proving the existence of massive drug trafficking into the United States as part of the Contra operation.

## SILENCING THE CHRISTIC INSTITUTE

The public-service-oriented Christic Institute based in Washington, D.C., investigated the atrocities associated with CIA activities in Central America and filed a federal lawsuit against White House officials who were implicated. Their complaint stated numerous federal causes of actions invoking mandatory federal court jurisdiction. But the Christic Institute encountered the same judicial obstruction of justice that I had encountered, and similar retaliatory actions.

The U.S. District Judge unlawfully dismissed the case and then ordered the Christic Institute to pay one million dollars damages for having exercised their constitutional and statutory right to file the action and report the criminal activities. The Christic Institute filed an appeal and was ordered to pay additional sanctions for exercising that right. The Justices of the U.S. Supreme Court approved this judicial misconduct by refusing to provide relief, just as the Supreme Court Justices had done to me.

**ELIMINATING THE INDEPENDENT PROSECUTOR**

Toward the end of 1992, as the number of crimes directly involving federal officials escalated to an unprecedented number threatening Justice Department and White House officials, as well as members of Congress, the Independent Prosecutor authority was allowed to expire. Congress refused to renew it. Republicans were under great threat of exposure from a decade-long pattern of corruption and they threatened to filibuster if a vote was taken to renew the legislation. Democrats were also threatened for their role in numerous scandals and didn't press the matter. Further, the legislation carried a provision that members of Congress could also be investigated by an independent prosecutor.

**FINAL REPORT BY INDEPENDENT PROSECUTOR WALSH**

The final report by Independent Prosecutor Walsh was sent on August 5, 1993, to a special tribunal of the federal appeals court in Washington, D.C. Copies of the report were sent to the parties named in the report with an opportunity to object. The special tribunal, headed by Judge David B. Sentelle, gave these parties until December 3, 1993, to raise objections to Walsh's findings.

Walsh's report, avoiding the ugly nature of the ongoing criminality, did identify some of the parties. The report stated that President Reagan, former Attorney General Edwin Meese, and former Defense Secretary Caspar Weinberger engaged in a "broad conspiracy" to conceal the criminal activities.

Walsh avoided revealing to the American people the ugly side of the Iran-Contra affair, including the massive drug trafficking into the United States by U.S. intelligence agencies and the Mossad. The CIA-DEA drug smuggling into the United States has greatly contributed to the worst crime wave America has ever experienced.

**DOCUMENTATION RELATING TO OPERATION MAGG PIE**

The secret, unlawful arms-for-hostages conspiracy carried the code name Operation Magg Pie. One CIA document dated May 20, 1986, signed by CIA Director Bill Casey, related to a flight from Tel Aviv to Teheran which received considerable Congressional attention. This was the flight carrying a cake and dueling pistols for Iranian officials. A key reference was to the two pilots who would fly the plane from Israel's Ben-Gurion Airport to Teheran. These two pilots were John Robert Segal (CIA) and Gunther Karl Russbacher (ONI). The memorandum, written six months before the U.S. press publicized the Iran-Contra activities, showed George Bush as receiving a copy. Bush repeatedly denied knowing anything about the arms-for-hostages until after the November 1986 media publicity.

Another document from the National Security Agency dated May 30, 1986, relating to Operation Magg Pie, written by Oliver North to Admiral John Poindexter, NSA, showed Vice President George Bush being advised of the operation.

Still another document, this one from the Israeli government, identified Gunther Russbacher as one of the pilots on Operation Magg Pie. The Israeli letter listed the names of U.S. personnel who were at Tel Aviv's Ben-Gurion Airport in May, 1986.

There was also the record from Offutt Air Force Base at Omaha, Nebraska describing Russbacher's stay at that high-security base, listing him as captain in the U.S. Navy and showing the authorizing government agency as CincPac, along with his serial number, 441 40 1417.

Almost all these documents, showing Russbacher as a key officer with the Office of Naval Intelligence, were known to members of Congress who stated Russbacher was a phony. They were known to the prosecutors and officials in the U.S. Department of Justice, who continued to prosecute Russbacher. I brought them to the attention of state officials in Missouri who had caused Russbacher's imprisonment on the sham charge that he was impersonating a naval officer. The establishment press knew about the documents and maintained their usual duplicity of silence.

Gunther Russbacher, Bristol, England, August 1997

NATIONAL SECURITY AGENCY
CENTRAL SECURITY SERVICE
FORT GEORGE G. MEADE, MARYLAND 20755-6000

August 22, 1985

Robert C. McFarlane
National Security Advisor
Old Executive Office Bldg. Rm. 306
Washington, D.C. 20506

CONFIDENTIAL

Re: MAGG PIE

Dear Mr. McFarlane:

The first transaction on August 17, 1985 involved the sale of 100 TOW missiles. In return for the release of an undetermined number of United States citizens held hostage in Lebanon. The missiles were to be provided from the weapons stock of the Israeli Defense Forces.

We have agreed to replenish the Israeli weapons stock after the transaction with Iran is completed.

As of August 20, 1985, our DC-8 transport aircraft, piloted by Gunther Russbacher (ONI) and John R. Segal (CIA), along with Robert Hunt (ONI), Oliver North (NSC) and George Cave (CIA), flew from Israel to Iran loaded with 96 TOW missiles. (Rather than the agreed upon 100).

Contrary to the agreement as you know, none of the hostages were releas

Manucher Ghorbanifer contended that the TOWS were mistakenly delivered to the commander of the Iranian Revolutionary Guard rather than to the Iranian faction for whom they were intended.

Please respond to any clarifications.

Yours truly,

John M. Poindexter
Deputy Director
National Security Council

cc: V-P Bush
William Casey

JMP/sv

August 22, 1985, document from National Security Agency's John Poindexter to Robert McFarlane referring to the sale of missiles to Iran. Gunther Russbacher and Robert Hunt, two of my contacts, are named in the document.
A copy was sent to Vice President Bush, who assured the American public while vice president and president that he knew nothing about the arms-for-hostages conspiracy.

NATIONAL SECURITY AGENCY
CENTRAL SECURITY SERVICE
FORT GEORGE G. MEADE, MARYLAND 20755-6000

September 20, 1985

Robert C. McFarlane
National Security Advisor
Old Executive Office Bldg. Rm. 306
Washington, D.C. 20506

CONFIDENTIAL

Re: MAGG PIE

Dear Mr. McFarlane:

Despite the failure of the first arms transaction, the Iran Initiative was continued. Our negotiators agreed, the United States, through Israel, would provide Iran with 400 TOW missiles. In return, the Iranians would arrange for the release of any U.S. hostage, except for Buckley.

The transaction was to take place in the same manner as the first. Israel would provide the missiles and the U.S. would later replenish the Israeli supply.

Lt. Col. Oliver North and Ltjg. Robert Hunt, on staff to the National Security Council, who in their official capacity were to make the necessary arrangements to receive any hostages who might be released.

On September 15, 1985, a DC-8, piloted by Gunther K. Russbacher (ONI) and John R. Segal (CIA) along with Oliver North (NSC) and Robert Hunt (ONI), Howard Teicher (CIA), flew to Tabriz, Iran, loaded with 408 TOWS. ON the same day, American hostage Benjamin Weir was released in Beirut on information and belief this transaction was effected to demonstrate the ability of the negotiators on each side to deliver by providing TOW missiles and releasing a hostage respectively.

On September 17, 1985, Manucher Ghorbanifer paid $290,000 to the Israeli intermediary to cover the costs of transporting the TOWS. The following day, Iran paid $5 million into Ghorbanifer's Swiss bank account at Credit Swiss, No. 913-216-83-7.

Any further clarifications or changes should be acknowledged.

Sincerely,
John Poindexter
John M. Poindexter
Deputy Director
National Security Council

CC: V-P BUSH
WILLIAM CASEY

JMP/sv

September 20, 1985, document describing the arms-for-hostages scheme showing Israeli involvement; identifying as ONI, Gunther Russbacher and Robert Hunt; and informing Vice President Bush of the scheme.

UNITED STATES GOVERNME
memorandum

DATE: 20 May 1986

REPLY TO ATTN OF: Bill Casey HQ. CIA.

SUBJECT: Russbacher Karl Gunther ONI. Segal Robert John CIA.

TO: John Poindexter NSA.
RE. Operation MAGG PIE.

Please be advised these men will meet with agents Robert Hunt ONI. Bud McFarlane NSA. Oliver North NSA. George Cave CIA. and Howard Teicher also CIA. They will give complete briefing at TelAviv Ben Gurion airport. Pilot selection is now finale. If you have any questions please call me soon. We leave Sunday the 25. Im keeping my fingers crossed.

Good Luck.

Bill Casey CIA.

CC.
VP. Bush

May 20, 1986, document from CIA Director Casey to Admiral Poindexter, listing the names of intelligence personnel involved in the arms-for-hostages scheme including Gunther Russbacher and Robert Hunt, and showing copy sent to Vice President George Bush.

UNITED STATES GOVERNMENT

# memorandum

DATE: 22 May, 1986

REPLY TO ATTN OF: John M. Poindexter (NSA)

SUBJECT: MAGG PIE PROFS: 31305B 89

TO: William J. Casey, Hq. CIA

Bill:

This is a note for the funds that Oliver North (NSC) and Robert Hunt (ONI) have worked out on behalf of the Iranians to deposit $15 million into an Enterprise bank account, and an additional deposit of $1.46 million was made to the Enterprise account to cover 508 additional TOWS which were to be provided to Israel as replenishment for the previous Israeli TOW shipments.

Of the approximate $16.5 million, the Enterprise received for this hardware, the agents caused only $6.5 million to be paid to the United States to cover the cost of the HAWK spares parts and the 508 TOWS, leaving a profit for the Enterprise of almost $10 million. If you have any questions, please call me at the executive office building.

Yours truly,

John Poindexter

John Poindexter

cc: V-P Bush
O. North

May 22, 1986, document from Poindexter (NSA) to CIA Director William Casey describing receipt of money from the sale of missiles to Iran, the profits, and the deposit of funds by Oliver North (NSC) and Robert Hunt (ONI) into a private bank account.

UNITED STATES GOVERNME

memorandun

DATE: 27 May, 1986

REPLY TO ATTN OF: Mr. John M. Poindexter, NSA

SUBJECT: MAGG PIE PROFS: 31305B 90

TO: William J. Casey, Hq. CIA

Bill:

Several days after the last of Khashoggi's payment was deposited in Lake Resources account - number 386-430-22-1, Agents Robert Hunt (ONI) and Oliver North (NSC) worked on Albon Valves - a shell company for additional funding. They deposited $26,490 to an account named "Korel." Four days later, Hyde Park Square, another account dispensed $200,000 as capital for the Button Account set up for Robert Hunt, Oliver North, George Cave, Howart Teicher, Gunther Russbacher and John Segal and their families. We considered the personal benefits of these agents. These accounts must be kept confidential for security reasons.

Yours truly,

John Poindexter

John Poindexter

cc: VP Bush
O. North

May 27, 1986 document to Bill Casey from John Poindexter listing the bank account number of a CIA proprietary, and showing money expended for arms. Also listed were some of the author's contacts and their CIA/ONI status, including Gunther Russbacher and Robert Hunt. Further, the documents show Vice President Bush being kept informed of the operation (Bush repeatedly denied, while vice president and president, knowledge of the unlawful scheme, while being an accomplice to the unlawful actions).

UNITED STATES GOVERNMENT
# memorandum

DATE: 30 May, 1986

Y TO N OF: Oliver L. North NSA.

JECT: MAGG PIE. PROFS: 31305B86

TO: John M. Poindexter. NSA.

miral

eir has been a problem in negotiations in Tehran. Manucher Ghorbanifar had sured us that we would be meeting with Hashemi Rafsanjani and president Ali amenei on this trip. Instead we met with Dr. No. and the Australian. During is meeting we were told that our pilots Russbacher Gunther Karl and Segal hn Robert were being brought to our hotel. Agents Hunt Robert and Cave George d spoken to Robert McFarlane and had decided to cancel negotiations due to curity and nature of this trip. Please get back to me on this as soon as ssible. I will call you in the morning.

Semper Fidelis,

Oliver L. North

C:
VP. G. BUSH
CIA. W. Casey

May 30, 1986, document from Oliver North to Admiral Poindexter, showing Gunther Russbacher to be a part of ONI, with copy to George Bush. Significance is that Russbacher is who he said he is and that Bush lied, while vice president and president, when he stated he did not know about the arms-for-hostages scheme.

OFFICE OF THE VICE PRESIDENT

WASHINGTON

June 16, 1986

Mr. John M. Poindexter
National Security Advisor
Old Executive Office Building
Washongton, D.C. 20506

CONFIDENTIAL

Dear Admiral Poindexter:

I would like to take this time to offer my gratitude and appreciation for your hard work and assistance in Operation MAGG PIE.

Your negotiations on our behalf have proven to be quite effective in obtaining the release of United States Citizens held hostage in Lebanon.

I would like you to personally thank Robert McFarlane for his willingness, daring and efforts in meeting with Iranian factions.

I would also like you to thank the Staff of the National Secu ity Council, including Agents, Lt. Col. Oliver North (USMC), and Lt. Robert Hunt (USN) for their dangerous assistance and diligence, without which Operation MAGG PIE would never have been successful.

Finally, you must offer my gratitude to the C.I.A.and their Agents, George Cave, Howard Teicher, John Segal and Gunther Russbache These men are dedicated and blessed with the gift of courage. They to truely believe in the pursuit of freedom for all mankind. May God bless you all.

Respectfully,

George Bush

George Bush

GB/fr
cc: R. Reagan
W. Casey

June 16, 1986, letter from Vice President George Bush to John Poindexter referring to the arms-for-hostages scheme. Both Ronald Reagan and George Bush are shown as being sent a copy of this document describing part of the arms-for-hostages scheme. Reagan and Bush repeatedly stated they knew nothing about the arms-for-hostages scheme until after the November 1986 shoot-down of a CIA aircraft in Nicaragua. This lying was many times worse than Richard Nixon's coverup of the Watergate break-in.

## SIGNIFICANCE OF THE GOVERNMENT DOCUMENTS

Watergate has been cited as one of the biggest scandals in the United States government by the CIA-protective *Washington Post* and members of Congress. But Watergate was a two-bit burglary by CIA and White House personnel, which President Richard Nixon sought to cover up after learning about it. It took months and months of drum-beating by the *Washington Post* and related hyperbole as to its seriousness to bring down a president who was hostile to the CIA. Either the Iran or the Contra portions of the Iran-Contra scandal were many times more serious than the Watergate affair.

Not only did Ronald Reagan and George Bush cover up for these criminal activities but they participated in them as the operations developed (unlike Watergate where Nixon did not learn about the break-in until after the fact). Tens of thousands of people died as a result of the U.S. arming of Iran. The Contra operation included CIA-funded assassination squads intruding into the affairs of a foreign country and massive drug trafficking into the United States. Where were the *Washington Post* and the many other newspapers that exaggerated the Watergate affair? Where were members of Congress who piously condemned President Nixon? They were engaging in felony coverup and obstruction of justice, and the public has paid and is still paying the price for the crimes of their leaders.

## STEALING AIRCRAFT

One of the little-known criminal activities involved with the arms and drug trafficking aspect of Iran-Contra was the theft of single and twin-engine general aviation aircraft. After the aircraft were stolen the registration numbers would be altered and then would be used for hauling arms to Central America and drugs on the return trips.

Gunther Russbacher had first told me about this operation. A former Federal Aviation Administration security investigator, Curt Rodriguez, also described the practice. He had discovered that many of the crashed drug-carrying aircraft had their manufacturer's identification plates removed, and then installed on aircraft stolen.

Rodriguez discovered this problem as he discovered single and twin-engine aircraft involved in drug trafficking. He told me that his FAA supervisors ordered him to stop investigating this matter, and not to make any reports relating to it. Rodriguez stated that when he ran an aircraft search through the FAA registry in Oklahoma City, on certain aircraft, Justice Department personnel would be notified of the check. He would then be ordered to halt his investigation. He felt that these aircraft were used by the CIA and other "intelligence" agencies for drug trafficking.

Oklahoma City investigative reporter and talk show host Jerry Bohen also discovered the practice of stolen aircraft used by the CIA. Former CIA asset Terry Reed, who conducted flight training in Arkansas of Contra pilots, also writes about the practice, and that Oliver North and Attorney General William Barr were either aware of it or were involved in ordering the operation to occur. The CIA used their inside contacts with the FAA to determine what substitute aircraft registration numbers to use.

**PROJECT DONATION**

In some cases the theft of the aircraft occurred with the owner's permission. The scheme worked like this: The CIA would instruct people owning insured airplanes to report them as stolen, after allowing CIA personnel to take the aircraft. The owner would report the "theft" to the insurance company and then collect the insurance proceeds. This plan appealed to aircraft owners who had trouble selling their aircraft and wanted their equity out of it. This was called Project Donation. I remember seeing advertisements in various aircraft newspapers such as *Trade A Plane* seeking people who wanted to donate their aircraft. Reed describes how Oliver North explained the operation to him in 1983 when they met in Oklahoma City.

In some cases the insurance would be carried directly or indirectly by an insurance company that was a front for the CIA. When the donated aircraft disappeared the "theft" would be reported to the insurance company holding the original policy and then charged to the CIA-controlled insurance company which had earlier purchased the theft portion of the original policy. It is a common practice among insurance companies to buy the insurance coverage from an unsuspecting insurance company that issued the original policy.

# CIA REVIEW

The CIA was legislated into existence in 1947 via the National Security Act while Harry Truman was president. The primary purpose of the legislation was to centralize intelligence material gathered by U.S. intelligence agencies. This need was made obvious by the disaster at Pearl Harbor in 1941. The Pearl Harbor debacle resulted in 2,500 deaths, loss of many ships and aircraft, and allowed Japan to escalate the global conflict that resulted in millions of deaths and atrocities. If White House and military officials had used street-smarts in defending against that Pearl Harbor attack, Japanese aggression could have been prevented or halted. (I was a crewmember on a PBY aircraft at the time of the attack and was in Hawaii with replacement aircraft within two weeks.)

Of course, even then, the intelligence was available to people with a duty to react, but as usual, they didn't react. Even when radar showed hundreds of planes approaching Hawaii from the Northwest, nothing was done. The same can be said of the many Japanese messages that were decoded, showing that an attack was imminent. I was a young Navy radioman in a PBY squadron at that time, and saw the ineptitude that is no rarity in American culture, and certainly more so today.

The Central Intelligence Agency is referred to by CIA personnel as "The Company," the Agency, or the CIA, and these terms are used throughout these pages.

**INTENT HAS BEEN REPEATEDLY NEGATED**

The Aldrich Ames spy scandal is only one instance of how the CIA has failed in its legislated duties. This failure could have, and may still bring about, catastrophic harm to the United States if a sufficiently powerful adversary took advantage of the internal CIA problems. As a result of Ames' treasonous acts, and the CIA's failure, or refusal, to halt Ames' activities, the CIA knowingly passed on to high-level planners in the United States information that the CIA knew was not accurate.

In evaluating the competency of the CIA to gather and evaluate intelligence, consider its competency or willingness to halt the incredibly harmful acts of this top agent. The CIA knew it had a spy in its top level ranks, with access to highly sensitive documents and information. It surely knew that national security was being seriously harmed. It knew that:

* Ames had paid $540,000 cash to purchase his home.

* Ames drove a Jaguar whose $60,000 cost equaled his yearly salary.

* Ames frequently charged as much as $30,000 monthly on his charge account.

* Ames had been filmed several times by FBI surveillance cameras entering the Russian Embassy in Washington.

* Other CIA agents had reported for several years suspicious conduct by Ames.

The CIA conduct appeared to be protective of Ames. Not only were these warning signs of substantial income other than from government employment ignored, but lie detector tests omitted any questioning of these tell-tale signs.

Under these conditions, it is obvious that the tell-tale signs warning of the Japanese Pearl Harbor attack would go unheeded.

**PAPER CHECKS AND BALANCES**

The National Security Act provided for checks and balances that have become meaningless. The Act required that the National Security Council authorize any covert action taken by the CIA. The Council is composed of the president of the United States, the vice-president, secretary of state, and secretary of defense. The CIA can lawfully perform only those operations specifically authorized by the National Security Council. In practice, the CIA either does not inform the NSC of its covert operations or notifies it after the operations have commenced or been completed.

**NATIONAL SECURITY ACT**

The National Security Act establishing the CIA authorized and limited the Agency to certain functions. Portions of the Act state:

(d) **Powers and duties.**

For the purpose of coordinating the intelligence activities of the several government departments and agencies in the interest of national security, it shall be the duty of the Agency, under the direction of the National Security Court–

(1) To advise the National Security Council in matters concerning such intelligence activities of the government departments and agencies as relate to national security;

(2) To make recommendations to the National Security Council for the coordination of such intelligence activities of the departments and agencies of the government as relate to the national security;

(3) To correlate and evaluate intelligence relating to the national security, and provide for the appropriate dissemination of such intelligence within the government using, where appropriate, existing agencies and facilities: *Provided,* That the Agency shall have no police, subpoena, law-enforcement powers, or internal-security functions; *Provided further,* that the departments and other agencies of the government shall continue to collect, evaluate, correlate, and disseminate departmental intelligence: *And provided further,* That the Director of Central Intelligence shall be responsible for protecting

intelligence sources and methods from unauthorized disclosure;

(4) To perform, for the benefit of the existing intelligence agencies, such additional services of common concern as the National Security Council determines can be more efficiently accomplished centrally;

(5) To perform such other functions and duties related to intelligence affecting the national security as the National Security Council may from time to time direct.

**UNHEEDED WARNINGS**

The lawful functions and restraints given the CIA by the statutes have been violated almost from its inception and warnings about the CIA problems have gone unheeded. President Harry Truman warned the American people of the CIA danger, stating as quoted in the December 21, 1963, *Washington Post*:

*For some time I have been disturbed by the way the CIA has been diverted from its original assignment. It has become an operational and at times a policy-making arm of the government....I never had any thoughts that when I set up the CIA that it would be injected into peacetime cloak-and-dagger operations. Some of the complication and embarrassment that I think we have experienced are in part attributable to the fact that this quiet intelligence arm of the President has been so removed from its intended role that it is being interpreted as a symbol of sinister and mysterious foreign intrigue and a subject for cold war enemy propaganda.*

Truman's warnings were echoed by President Dwight Eisenhower as he was leaving office, warning the American people of the dangers posed by the military-industrial complex, of which the CIA is a part.

**A SECRET GOVERNMENT**

Instead of the CIA being primarily an intelligence gathering and coordinating agency acting under the National Security Council, the CIA has become so powerful that it can destroy any politician who seriously questions its activities. This is especially true when combined with the criminal misuse of power by Justice Department attorneys and federal judges.

The average American is unaware of the gravity of the CIA's criminal activities, thanks to the orchestrated coverup and disinformation by the establishment media. The corrupt mindset has existed for years. Initiating wars, as in Vietnam, and assassination operations, as in Vietnam and Central America, are routine. Engaging in drug trafficking in foreign countries and the United States, a key reason for world-wide proliferation of drugs, is the type of criminal activities this dangerous agency considers proper. It conspires with underworld figures including the Italian and Jewish Mafia to carry out all sorts of criminal activities.

Although the CIA is not permitted by law to operate within the United States, it has done so. It has engaged and is engaging in many forms of criminal activities against the American people. Through fronts, cutouts, and proprietaries, the CIA has defrauded all types of U.S. financial institutions, including savings and loans, banks, and insurance companies. The CIA is a major player in the looting of Chapter 11 assets, making the exercise of Chapter 11 statutory protections a trap for unwary Americans.

The CIA has corrupted the election process in the United States and in foreign countries. The CIA's October Surprise operation corrupted the 1980 presidential election and placed into office a group that embarked on a barrage of criminal activities. The CIA-related Watergate affair caused removal from office of President Richard Nixon. The JFK assassination, with its strong CIA overtones, removed another president elected by the people.

**U.S. PRESIDENTS WHO INCUR CIA WRATH**

Opposing the CIA has been dangerous, possibly even fatal, for presidents of the United States. President John F. Kennedy, recognizing the dangers of the CIA before his assassination in 1962, threatened to muzzle the CIA after the Bay of Pigs fiasco and stated his intention to pull U.S. personnel out of the CIA's Vietnam operation. There is considerable circumstantial evidence indicating CIA involvement in Kennedy's assassination. When the many ugly acts of the CIA are recognized, assassinating a president of the United States is not far-fetched.

President Richard Nixon, recognizing the dangers of the CIA, stated his intention to rein in the agency. It was the CIA-related Watergate affair, augmented by the panic-generating antics of CIA's friends, including the *Washington Post* and reporter Bob Woodward, that expanded President Nixon's after-the-fact coverup of the relatively minor break-in into a major scandal that brought the U.S. government to a standstill and global disgrace. Compare the after-the-fact coverup by Nixon with the massive coverups committed by CIA-affiliated President George Bush and the silence by the same *Washington Post* and Bob Woodward.

President Jimmy Carter suffered at the hands of the CIA after he fired many of its covert operatives in 1976. Carter was a threat to the CIA, and they retaliated against him several years later by engineering the October Surprise scheme, which helped insure Carter's defeat in the November 1980 presidential election.

**BENEFITING FRIENDS**

Ronald Reagan and George Bush, who benefited from the CIA's October Surprise, were the only presidents of the United States since before President Kennedy who were not adversely affected by CIA tactics. Bush was director of the CIA in 1975 and 1976, and reportedly a CIA agent since 1960. Reagan and Bush, and those who aided and abetted these acts, were beneficiaries of the CIA October Surprise operation and other CIA dirty tricks.

**NAZI INFLUENCE AFFECTING THE UNITED STATES?**

After World War II many former Nazi intelligence officers were brought to the United States and placed into various intelligence agencies, including the Office of Naval Intelligence and the Central Intelligence Agency. Many had been given the choice of being prosecuted for World War II war crimes or joining the U.S. military and intelligence agencies. This practice was called Operation Paperclip. These former Nazi officers gained key covert positions in the CIA and other intelligence agencies, engaging in activities that inflicted great harm upon the United States. This Nazi influence could explain the enormous harm inflicted upon the United States by the CIA. Russbacher arrived in the United States as the young son of a recipient of this program.

In *Blowback*, author Christopher Simpson describes how the U.S. officials secretly brought into the United States under this program people such as Klaus Barbie, not only in spite of their atrocities performed at Nazi extermination camps, but *because* of this experience.

**EXPOSÉ BOOKS BY INSIDERS**

Many books have been written by former CIA insiders describing the agency's covert activities and misuse of power. In *Secret Team,*[295] written by CIA insider Colonel Fletcher Prouty, he describes his discoveries during many years as Chief of Special Operations (clandestine activities) with the U.S. Joint Chiefs of Staff. Prouty writes: "The CIA is the center of a vast mechanism that specializes in covert operations," which is, of course, obvious to anyone with a basic knowledge of CIA activities. Prouty writes: "The CIA is the willing tool of a higher level Secret Team, or High Cabal, that usually includes representatives of the CIA and other instrumentalities of the government, certain cells of the business and professional world and, almost always, foreign participation."

**CIA PLANTS EVERYWHERE**

Referring to news management that enables the CIA to escape unfavorable publicity, Prouty writes about the media's reliance upon CIA "news" handouts and the infiltration of the media by CIA personnel:

> *Leaders of government and of the great pressure centers regularly leak information of all kinds to columnists, television and radio commentators, and to other media masters.... [fabricated data] will be skillfully leaked to the press and to selected businessmen...designed especially for "Periscope" in Newsweek, or perhaps for its old favorite, Joe Alsop....advance top-level information is a most valuable and saleable commodity.*

To defuse any criticism or exposure of the CIA's unlawful activities, the CIA has people widely dispersed throughout the U.S. government and industry. Prouty writes:

> *There are CIA men in the Federal Aviation Administration, in State [Department], all over the DOD, and in most other offices where the CIA has wanted to place them. Few top officials, if any, would ever deny the agency such a service, and as the appointive official departed, and his staffs came and went, the whole device would be lost with only the CIA remembering that they were still there. Many of these people have reached positions of great responsibility.*

**CHURCH COMMITTEE REPORT**

A congressional investigation of the CIA resulted in a 1976 Church Committee report which stated in part in the sections that were not kept from the American public:

> *[The CIA provided] financial support to individual candidates, subsidies to publications including newspapers and magazines, involvement in local and national labor unions, all of these interlocking elements constituted the fundamentals of a typical political action program. Elections, of course, were key operations, and the Agency involved itself in electoral politics*

295 *The Secret Team*, L. Fletcher Prouty, Institute for Historical Review, Costa Mesa, California.

*on a continuing basis.*[296]

*The Agency was also establishing close links with both book publishing houses and media organizations in the U.S. at this time.... Altogether, from 1947 until the end of 1967, the CIA produced, subsidized, or sponsored well over 1,000 books. Approximately 20 percent of them were written in English. Many of them were published by cultural organizations backed by the CIA.*

*The Agency was also conducting extensive operations with newspaper, magazine, and television organizations. It maintained liaison relationships with about 50 American journalists or U.S. media organizations. They are part of a network of several hundred foreign individuals around the world who provide intelligence for the CIA and at times attempt to influence foreign opinion through the use of covert propaganda.*

**A KEY REASON WHY AMERICAN PUBLIC REMAINS ILLITERATE ABOUT CIA AND OTHER GOVERNMENT CORRUPTION**

In an article written by columnist Carl Bernstein, he wrote that "The CIA and the Media" had more than 400 American journalists carrying out assignments for the Agency. My CIA contacts confirmed that the CIA has hundreds of paid journalists and management working in U.S. and world-wide media sources, providing protection against disclosures, disinformation requested by the Agency, and providing national leaders with false information upon which to base national policy.

With this type of support, it is improbable that the American public will ever learn or be convinced of the sinister subversive and criminal activities by people who have taken over control of key government entities.

High-level CIA personnel are able to control other government agencies in carrying out its oftentimes corrupt activities. The CIA infiltrates Customs and other agencies, blocking the checks and balances that could otherwise threaten the various CIA operations.

Criminal activities in which the CIA or other federal officials may be involved can be kept from the American public. These areas include what has already been described and what has yet to be described, including for instance, CIA involvement in October Surprise, the HUD and savings and loan scandals, looting of Chapter 11 assets, Inslaw, BCCI, Iraqgate, defrauding U.S. financial institutions, drug trafficking in the United States, and other criminal activities. Throughout these pages it will be seen that these paid media sources were instrumental in covering up these crimes.

**FAILURE TO REPORT CRIMES AGAINST THE UNITED STATES**

If the CIA had not, itself, been involved in many of the corrupt activities, its vast intelligence network should have discovered the criminal activities against America. Other government agencies whose vast investigative powers probably discovered these crimes include the FBI, its parent the Justice Department, Customs, DEA, and others. How could such vast safeguards not have discovered

296 The Church Committee report. The Select Committee to Study Governmental Operations with Respect to Intelligence Activities, Foreign and Military Intelligence, 94th Congress, 1976.

these crimes? Were they incompetent, were they either part of the criminal activities, or blocked by the top law enforcement officer, the U.S. Attorney General, from doing so? As shown in these pages, the Justice Department has been made into a vast criminal enterprise.

**HUNDREDS OF THOUSANDS OF DEATHS**

Former CIA agent Fletcher Prouty tells how the CIA got the United States embroiled in military conflicts, including the Korean and Vietnam Wars, that resulted in enormous casualties. Prouty tells how independently acting CIA groups initiated the conflict leading to the U.S. involvement in Vietnam. Supporting this position was the Asian scholar, Eugene Windchy, in *The New Republic*: "What steered the nation into Vietnam was a series of tiny but powerful [CIA] cabals."

Prouty wrote, "By the time of the Bay of Pigs operations, the CIA was part of a greater team, which used the Agency and other parts of the government to carry out almost any secret operation it wanted." He continued, "In this unusual business I found rather frequently that the CIA would be well on its way into some operation that would later require military support before the Secretary and the Chiefs had been informed."

Prouty explains that the CIA contains the real power structure in the United States, and how the CIA has infiltrated other government agencies and private enterprises with people loyal to the various CIA hierarchies.

**SECRET DOMESTIC CORPORATIONS**

The CIA has hundreds of dummy corporations in the United States, such as in the form of proprietaries, fronts, and cooperating assets. These include, for instance, law firms; financial companies, such as banks and bond brokerage houses; insurance companies, and airlines. The CIA can control virtually anything that occurs in the United States or any person or group, including members of Congress, state and federal judges, elections, coverups, and murder.

Examples of the many past or present CIA proprietary airlines or assets are the following: Civil Air Transport (CAT); Air America; Southern Air Transport; Global International Airways; St. Lucia Airways; Intermountain Airways; Summit Aviation; Arrow Airlines; Apex Aviation at Spirit of St. Louis Airport; Evergreen International Airlines and its related subsidiaries; Race Aviation; Ransom Aircraft; Resorts International; Flying Tiger Line; Response Air; Seagreen Air; Skyways Aviation; International Air Tours; Capital Airlines; Air Asia; Rich Mountain Aviation; Southwest Airlines.

It becomes very easy for the CIA to deny blame for their acts. They simply deny any knowledge of what the front-company or contract agent are doing, in addition to their standard practice of lying. There is no danger to this practice since Justice Department officials protect their lying, and their corrupt operations, and most of the mainstream media also covers for them, as well as members of Congress.

**CIA PROPRIETARIES**

One of many ways used by the CIA to hide its activities is through the use of proprietaries. This is a corporation secretly owned by an intelligence agency that operates or appears to operate as a private company. It launders money, provides cover for CIA personnel, gathers intelligence, and facilitates covert operations.

**ASSASSINATIONS**

Assassinations have been a routine part of the CIA mindset. In Vietnam, the CIA Phoenix Program assassinated over 40,000 people. Numerous books have identified CIA operatives with the assassination of President John F. Kennedy.[297] Congressional hearings had brought out the CIA's plans to assassinate Cuba's Fidel Castro and other heads of state. Leaders of other nations and people considered a threat to the CIA's interests have been assassinated. Many people throughout the world with knowledge of the CIA October Surprise operation have been killed or have mysteriously died. Francis Nugan, who assisted in operating the covert CIA money operation known as Nugan Hand Bank, was killed in Australia after the CIA's cover was blown, keeping him from testifying about the CIA operation.

In trying to comprehend what these CIA-induced deaths mean and to equate the brutality with the CIA, think of thousands of people disemboweled, decapitated, dismembered, the napalming of children and others, and other types of brutality.[298]

If the American public exercised its responsibilities, especially in the misuse of its tax dollars needed to finance these CIA outrages, many of these tragedies would not have occurred.

Entire continents such as Central and South America have been converted to constant and brutal upheavals with the money and the arms given by the CIA. Death, destruction, and horror follow wherever the CIA goes.

Former Mossad operative Ari Ben-Menashe described in his book the assassinations carried out by the Mossad, many of which required the specific approval of Israel's leaders. He related how Amiram Nir was killed by a CIA asset to keep him from testifying to a Congressional committee investigating the Iran-Contra affair that would have implicated President Reagan, Vice-President Bush, Oliver North, Israel's Mossad, Israeli officials, including Shimon Peres. In later pages assassination tactics of various CIA factions or fiefdoms are described.

The CIA has its own assassination teams, as will be explained in later pages. They carry out their deadly tasks in foreign countries and in the United States. One of my CIA sources, commander of a Navy SEAL Team, described how his group taught methods of assassination to various intelligence agency personnel. Gunther Russbacher did the same.

It has been reported that CIA covert activities in inciting wars, revolutions and social unrest throughout the world, have resulted in over six million deaths, including the 58,000 American GIs who perished in the Vietnam War.

**CIA HIRING MASS KILLER**

Employed by the CIA and the National Security Council, and in frequent contact with Oliver North and George Bush, was Posada Cariles, a Cuban who had placed a bomb on a Cuban airliner that exploded in midair after taking off from Jamaica, killing all 76 people on board. (October 6, 1976.) Cariles had

---

297 *Plausible Denial*, Mark Lane; *JFK, The CIA, Vietnam and The Plot To Assassinate John F. Kennedy*, L. Fletcher Prouty; *Act Of Treason*, Mark North; *Crossfire*, Jim Marrs.

298 National weekly, *Spotlight*.

been convicted of the crime and imprisoned, but escaped. He was placed on the CIA's payroll, managing covert operations in El Salvador.

Felix Rodriguez, a close associate of Vice-President and then President George Bush, said that the CIA arranged for Cariles' escape and then employed him in covert CIA operations. No one showed any concern for the 76 people who suffered and died a brutal death. One of Rodriguez's aliases was Max Gomez. He worked closely with Donald Gregg and George Bush, both of whom were heavily involved in the infamous October Surprise scheme.

**AVOIDING RESPONSIBILITY FOR THEIR ACTS**

The CIA uses various methods to avoid responsibility for its actions. One method is to use cut-outs acting in place of the CIA. In this way the CIA can distance itself from the operation if its cover is blown. The CIA makes a standard practice of sheep-dipping those people carrying out their dirty tricks, including military personnel. The person's records are removed from the military agency and placed in a special intelligence file. Fictitious records are processed showing the military person to have been released from the agency. His or her records are changed and letters sent to civilian agencies, banks, friends, indicating discharge from the service. The CIA helps the sheep-dipped person to change his credit and employment records and the many things that a person does when discharged from service. The sheep-dipped people are often eventually returned to military service, and the time spent with the CIA counts toward retirement and other benefits.

An individual or a company can be used by the CIA to act on the CIA's behalf, giving the CIA plausible denial. While it is usually very profitable for an individual or company to carry out the dirty work of the CIA, it is sometimes costly (even fatal). Irwin Rautenberg suffered financially from this arrangement when the CIA cut him off, leaving him with lots of unpaid bills.

**AIR-SEA FORWARDERS**

An example of how the CIA uses established companies as a front was an air freight forwarding company in Los Angeles operated by Rautenberg, under the name of Air-Sea Forwarders. The CIA asked him for help in 1956 to provide a cover for the CIA, and an agreement was reached with the CIA, allowing the Agency to use his company name. Air-Sea became two companies, the real one being Air-Sea Forwarders, and the false one owned and operated by the CIA, but bearing the Air-Sea name. This permitted the CIA to hide their shipments under the name, Air-Sea Forwarders.

Air Asia operated the largest airplane maintenance facility in Southeast Asia during the Vietnam War. Until 1956, the CIA proprietary worked through a company called Slick Airways (for whom I flew as pilot for a brief period while furloughed from my regular airline, Transocean Airlines).

In 1975, the CIA "sold" Air Asia to another CIA proprietary, E-Systems of Dallas, Texas, which had government contracts exceeding $2 billion a year. In 1981, E-Systems notified Rautenberg that they were terminating their relationship with him, leaving him holding millions of dollars in unpaid bills and taxes that were the responsibility of the CIA.

Rautenberg filed a breach-of-contract suit against E-System and against Air Asia. In November 1984, before his suit came to trial, Rautenberg met with attorneys for the CIA and Justice Department at the office of his lawyer, Mickey Kantor (later a U.S. trade representative). His own attorney and the attorneys for the CIA and Justice Department demanded that he sign a secrecy agreement, refusing him from introducing any evidence of CIA-related activities at the trial, and barred him from even making reference to the agreement. Rautenberg then sought another attorney.

Los Angeles district court judge Richard A. Gadbois, Jr., who presided over the case, also issued a secrecy order preventing Rautenberg from presenting his evidence. Despite this order the jury awarded Rautenberg $6.2 million in damages in 1986. In an unusual act Judge Gadbois secretly met with CIA and Justice Department attorneys and overturned the jury's verdict.

Rautenberg petitioned the U.S. Supreme Court to have the court rule that the judge's order barring submission of evidence was in error. The Supreme Court refused to rule on the request in a May 1993 decision. In the meantime, a federal appeals court ordered a new trial, which was to start after the Supreme Court rendered a decision.

Rautenberg was a survivor of the Nazi death camps. He said that he had always thought that dealing with the U.S. government through the CIA was safe, thinking "that Uncle Sam wouldn't let me down."

The CIA's denial of involvement is willingly accepted by Congress and the establishment media over statements made by brave whistleblowers. This, combined with the absence of responsibility by checks and balances, are key reasons why whistleblowers are little known to the American public. Lying to the media, to Congress, in criminal trials to imprison CIA assets, has long been recognized as standard practice. One of the documents shown in later pages, relating to CIA operative Trenton Parker, clearly shows this practice by the statement: STANDARD DENIAL.

**PLAUSIBLE DENIAL**

It is standard practice for the CIA to use contract employees and mercenaries to carry out CIA activities within the United States and abroad, and in this manner fraudulently deny any involvement. Another standard practice is for the CIA to conspire with Justice Department attorneys to charge covert employees with violating federal law, and seek long prison sentences so as to silence or discredit them. Some die in prison or are too old to cause trouble for the CIA when they are released.

**SILENCING CIA WHISTLEBLOWERS**

Many CIA personnel became disenchanted or outraged by the harm inflicted by the Agency's corrupt activities and would like to blow the whistle, but fear the consequences. The years of CIA drug trafficking, for instance, the CIA's major involvement in looting savings and loans, its role in looting bankruptcy court assets, require that there be some mechanism in place to silence anyone who tries to blow the whistle. The mechanism includes:

* Charging potential CIA whistleblowers with federal offenses for having performed duties ordered by their CIA superiors. This tactic has the cooperation of Justice Department officials.
* With the cooperation of federal judges, stripping the targeted person of his defenses, including refusing to allow him to call CIA witnesses; refusing

to provide CIA documents; stripping him of his assets so he cannot hire attorneys and investigators; assigning a court-appointed attorney whose loyalty is to the system.

* Justifying the refusal to permit CIA witnesses to appear, and documents to be introduced into evidence, on the grounds of national security, a catch-all phrase used to block exposure of government misconduct.[299]

* Assassinations and mysterious deaths affecting those who are exposing or who could expose an illegal operation.[300]

299 This tactic has been repeatedly used to deprive defendants of evidence showing that they were acting under CIA orders and had some form of CIA association when they performed some particular act for which they were then being charged.

300 Throughout these pages will be found examples of this silencing tactic.

# NUGAN HAND BANK

A primary CIA money laundering operation in the Pacific area was Nugan Hand Bank, with headquarters in Sydney, Australia and branch offices throughout the Far East, Europe, and the United States. Nugan Hand Bank was incorporated in 1976 in the Cayman Islands, a popular money-laundering location. It is believed that Nugan Hand Bank was a replacement for Castle Bank & Trust, incorporated in Nassau, Bahamas. After Castle failed, Nugan Hand commenced operation. It had branch offices in Far East countries, laundering drug money from the Golden Triangle drug producing area.

Secondary functions were arms sales and funding covert activities, such as undermining governments and funding assassination squads. Nugan Hand was a covert CIA financial operation comprised primarily of those with ties to the U.S. intelligence community. The primary partners were Francis Nugan, Michael Hand, and Maurice Bernard Houghton.

Vast amounts of money were hidden in assets and financial holdings throughout the world. Either to appear as a legitimate international investment operation, or to defraud people out of millions of dollars, Nugan Hand took deposits from individuals throughout the world, money that would eventually be lost by these investors. When the cover for this CIA-related operation was blown, these funds were quickly moved to other CIA proprietaries, inflicting financial losses upon the investors and depositors. Many of the individuals putting money into the CIA's Nugan Hand Bank were military personnel, who eventually lost everything they deposited.

## EXPOSING NUGAN HAND FRAUD

Nugan Hand's cover was blown on April 11, 1980, by a reporter for *Target*, a Hong Kong financial newsletter. This required the CIA to shut down the operation and destroy evidence of its CIA links. Francis Nugan was one of the most visible players in the Nugan Hand operation. He was an alcoholic with a reputation for talking too much, a trait that threatened to expose the CIA's role in the operation. Assassins killed Nugan,[301] leaving his body in a car alongside a lonely road outside of Sydney, Australia. A bolt-action rifle was found alongside the body, and the scene was made to look like a suicide.

An unspent bullet remained in the firing chamber of the bolt action rifle. For an unspent bullet to be in the chamber after firing the shot that was instantly fatal, someone, other than Nugan, had to manually operate the bolt handle. Nugan obviously did not do this. The bullet had killed Nugan instantly, blowing away much of his skull and scattering it throughout the car. There were no fingerprints on the gun, indicating that whoever fired the fatal bullet wiped the fingerprints from the rifle.

The only identification on Nugan's body was a calling card apparently overlooked by the killers, belonging to William Colby, former Director of the Central Intelligence Agency, with a meeting date written on the back. Colby was legal counsel for Nugan Hand. He also had connections to the Wall Street law firm of Reid & Priest, suggesting that this firm was a front for the CIA or a CIA proprietary.

After Nugan's death, the CIA removed the funds from the various Nugan Hand offices and laundered them into other CIA operations. Misinformation commenced immediately, denying that the CIA had any connection to the rogue bank, despite the many intelligence agency officers in the operation.

Before Australian authorities started an investigation, Michael Hand disappeared, along with most of the Nugan Hand records. Although the media reported that Hand had disappeared, leaving no trace, two of my CIA sources had been in contact with him after he fled Australia. Hand secretly surfaced in Iran, followed by his participation in the CIA Central America drug trafficking.

Hand disappeared as Australian authorities sought to question him about Nugan's death, the Nugan Hand Bank operation, and the disappearance of approximately one billion dollars from the bank. Hand first went to Thailand under CIA cover and then showed up in Florida and the Caribbean area. One of my deep-cover CIA contacts, Trenton Parker, told how he and Hand had worked together in the early 1980s. Parker's CIA faction was interested in discovering Hand's operation, and Parker met Hand in Jamaica on February 2, 1980. They then worked together on Operation Interlink and Operation Anacondor.

Parker said that Hand and Vice President George Bush were in frequent contact after Bush became vice president, and while Australian authorities were searching for Hand. Parker stated that CIA Director William Casey frequently met with Hand in Panama in the early 1980s concerning arms sales and drug trafficking.

Parker stated that he and Hand took over one of the drug trafficking operations for the CIA in Central and South America. He said that Hand's experience in developing the Golden Triangle drug operations for the CIA made him useful in expanding the drug operations from Central and South America into the United States.

Investigation by Australian authorities into Nugan Hand revealed the CIA's meddling in Australian affairs, inciting political unrest, intrusion into Australian

301 January 27, 1980.

elections, deception, invasion of its sovereignty, and other dirty tricks.

Like most CIA-related operations, Nugan Hand Bank relied upon a pattern of fraud and deception. Large amounts of currency were moved in and out of various countries, including Australia and the Golden Triangle areas.

Michael Hand was a Green Beret and a colonel in the U.S. Army, assigned to the CIA. Earlier, Hand was handling the CIA's drug business and laundered the money from the Golden Triangle area of Asia. In the 1960s, the CIA transferred Hand from the Golden Triangle assignment to Teheran, where he set up the secret police for the Shah of Iran. (I was flying as pilot in Iran at that time.)

The Nugan Hand affair received considerable media attention in Australia, but the mainstream media in the United States said virtually nothing about this CIA operation and its implications. Australian authorities conducted numerous investigations, but in their final report they white-washed the Nugan Hand affair. The CIA had an ongoing relationship with Australia's Security Intelligence Organization (ASIO), which probably played a role in the coverup of Nugan Hand.

One of Nugan Hand's CIA assets was John Fredericks. He suffered a fate similar to Francis Nugan. Fredericks and his bodyguard were killed (July 28, 1991) in Australia.

**STAFFED BY THE CIA**

Most of the management personnel of Nugan Hand Bank were intelligence community personnel.[302] When Nugan Hand shut down, most of them moved to other CIA operations, including Bishop, Baldwin, Rewald, Dillingham and Wong in Hawaii. These players, with a long CIA and military intelligence background, included, for instance, Admiral Earl Yates, General Leroy Manor, and General Edwin Black.

Many people holding check-and-balance responsibilities covered up for the Nugan Hand scheme. These checks and balances included the oversight agencies in Australia; the Reserve Bank in Australia that had responsibilities over Nugan Hand; Citicorp, which traded securities with Nugan Hand; taxing authorities in Australia, who were familiar with Nugan Hand's operation; the accounting

---

302 Michael Jon Hand, CIA operative, former Green Beret, vice-chairman and part owner of Nugan Hand Bank; General Edwin F. Black ran Nugan Hand's Hawaii office; Paul Helliwell was a CIA asset heavily involved in drug money laundering; General Earle Cocke, Jr., ran the Nugan Hand Washington office and headed the American Legion; William Colby, retired Director of CIA, was the attorney for Nugan Hand; Dale Holmgren headed flight services for several CIA airlines and ran Nugan Hand's Taiwan office; Robert Jantzen, CIA station chief in Thailand, was Nugan Hand's officer in Thailand; General Leroy Manor, chief of staff for U.S. Pacific Command, ran Nugan Hand's Philippine office; Walter Macdonald, former deputy director of CIA for economic research, was a consultant to Nugan Hand; Theodore G. Shackley, top clandestine officer at the CIA, had numerous dealings with Nugan Hand; Admiral Earl Yates, chief of U.S. strategic planning for Asia and the Pacific, was president of Nugan Hand Bank. Yates had been commander of the aircraft carrier, *John F. Kennedy*. He retired (or was sheep-dipped), from the Navy in 1974 and became president of Nugan Hand Bank in 1977; Gordon (Billy) Young, CIA asset, represented Nugan Hand in the Golden Triangle drug zone of Southeast Asia; George Farris was a military intelligence specialist working in the Hong Kong office of Nugan Hand; Guy Pauker was an advisor to Henry Kissinger; Edwin Wilson, a CIA operative, had frequent dealings with Nugan Hand Bank; Thomas Clines, a CIA operative and deputy to Major General Richard Secord in the Iran-Contra arms network, had frequent dealings with Nugan Hand. After Nugan was killed, and before Australian authorities started investigating the bank, Clines rescued Houghton from Australia.

firm that certified the Nugan Hand records; U.S. Consul General in Australia who knew of the CIA operation; the Premier of Australia, who had offices adjacent to Nugan Hand; Irving Trust Company, the correspondent bank for Nugan Hand in the United States; Corporate Affairs Commission in Australia that stonewalled requests for information; prominent Australian attorneys who worked closely with Nugan Hand; Australian Department of Commerce, who had considerable information about Nugan Hand's activities; Australian intelligence agencies that worked with U.S. intelligence agencies, and who knew about the rogue operations, and others.

After Nugan's body was found, intense activities were initiated to destroy evidence linking Nugan Hand Bank to the CIA. Retired three-star U.S. General Leroy J. Manor (formerly chief of staff for all U.S. forces in Asia and the Pacific), who had been head of Nugan Hand's Philippine office, tried to have the wire services block the reporting of Nugan's death. Recently retired Rear Admiral Earl P. Yates (formerly chief of staff for strategic planning for U.S. forces in the Pacific and Asia) flew to Australia to direct the shredding of documents. Yates was president of Nugan Hand, and lived near CIA headquarters at Langley, Virginia. Michael Hand joined in the shredding. Maurice Houghton and his attorney, Michael Moloney, also arrived. Hand threatened lower-level employees, stating if Maloney's orders to sanitize the files before the law arrived weren't followed, "terrible things would happen; your wives would be cut up and returned to you in bits and pieces." (*Wall Street Journal*, August 24, 1982.)

Two in a series of *Wall Street Journal* articles (August 25 and 26, 1982) described Nugan Hand Bank as a drug and arms-related operation, staffed by CIA and military personnel. The articles stated in part:

> *Nugan Hand bank was deeply involved in moving funds about the world for big international heroin dealers... U.S. servicemen are big losers in failure of Nugan Hand Bank.*

Australia's Royal Commission on Drugs found so much evidence of drug and drug-money trafficking by this CIA operation that it recommended a separate Royal Commission be appointed just for the bank's operations. But Australia's intelligence agency, ASIO, blocked an investigation, reflecting the common practice of intelligence agencies to protect each other rather than their own country. U.S. officials stymied every attempt by Australian authorities to obtain information about Nugan Hand Bank.

During its investigation, the Royal Commission found that drugs were flown into a landing strip by former Air America pilot K.L. "Bud" King and Michael Hand. The strip was on a real estate development promoted by U.S. singer Pat Boone and financed by wealthy shipping magnate D.K. Ludwig. King, who also worked for the Boone-Ludwig project, whose testimony could have been very damaging to Nugan Hand and U.S. officials, died mysteriously in a fall.

Australian authorities connected Nugan Hand not only to drug and arms transactions, but also to contract murders, of which there were several associated with Nugan Hand's demise.

Australian attorney John Aston and his law firm were found to represent Nugan Hand and various drug traffickers, and the law office was used as a drop point for money to be secretly deposited and moved by Nugan Hand.

The Australian investigations left no doubt that Nugan Hand management was heavily involved with drug dealers, including Khun Sa, the Golden Triangle's biggest opium producer.

**PATTERN OF LIES**

One of the most pervasive traits of CIA-related companies is the lying by government officials, including those at the CIA, the State Department, the Defense Department, and elsewhere in government. Throughout these pages, in scandal after scandal, government officials "assure" the public that government officials were not involved. And the public swallows these denials hook, line and sinker. U.S. officials "assured" Australia's prime minister, Malcolm Fraser, that the United States had no connections to Nugan Hand Bank. These "assurances," given routinely to Americans by their government, were, of course, lies. Vice President George Bush, while visiting Australia, also gave his assurances that the CIA wasn't involved with Nugan Hand Bank.

In Australia, the CIA worked secretly with ASIO to topple Australia's Labor government led by Prime Minister Gough Whitlam.

Many of Nugan Hand's records related to troop movements, hardly subjects that a bank would be interested in.

Hand's death and the sudden publicity focused on Nugan Hand Bank caused its liquidation in April 1980. With its demise, the CIA company concentrating on arms and drug sales and money laundering had to be replaced with another company. That company was Bishop, Baldwin, Rewald, Dillingham and Wong, which is described in the following chapter.

# BBRDW

After Nugan Hand's cover was blown and the operation abandoned, the CIA redirected many of the Nugan Hand operations to another Pacific financial institution based in Hawaii: Bishop, Baldwin, Rewald, Dillingham and Wong (BBRDW). This CIA proprietary was started, operated, and funded by the CIA in 1979, using many of the same high-level people that had staffed Nugan Hand Bank. By the end of 1980, BBRDW began setting up offices in Hong Kong, Taiwan, Indonesia, Singapore, and Australia, all former Nugan Hand locations, staffing the offices with over 30 CIA agents, including some of the same high-level people that operated Nugan Hand Bank. (General Edwin Black; General Leroy Manor; Admiral Lloyd Vassey; Admiral Earl Yates; Walter McDonald; Maurice Houghton). As in most CIA-related proprietaries, its key management was comprised of CIA-related personnel.[303]

The CIA used BBRDW as a international investment company cover, with 120 employees staffing offices in sixteen countries, including Hong Kong, India, Indonesia, Taiwan, New Zealand, Singapore, London, Paris, Stockholm, Brazil and Chile. CIA personnel opened and operated these far-flung offices.

For appearances, the CIA placed in charge of its BBRDW proprietary a Honolulu businessman, Ronald Rewald, who had worked for the CIA years earlier while attending Milwaukee Institute of Technology. That CIA college project was called Operation MH Chaos, and consisted of spying on student groups during the mid-1960s. The CIA gave Rewald the alias WINTERDOG. Other CIA divisions had parallel programs called Operation Mother Goose and Operation Back Draft.

Rewald left the CIA after college, married, and had five children, and lived comfortably in a home on Lake Michigan. Business changes caused Rewald

303 Including retired Pan American chief pilot, Captain Ned Avary, reportedly a CIA contract Agent; Sue Wilson, former National Security Agency employee; Jack Kindschi, former CIA Station Chief; Charles Richardson, Chief of Base, Foreign Resources, CIA; John Sager, former Moscow Station Chief; Clarence Gunderson, CIA/Air Force Intelligence Officer; General Hunter Harris, retired four-star Air Force commander; and General Edwin F. Black, former head of Nugan Hand operations based in Hawaii.

to move his family to Hawaii, where he opened an investment consulting company under the name Consolidated Mutual Investment Corporation (CMI). It was here in 1978 that the CIA lured Rewald back into the Agency and used his company as a cover.

The Agency felt that Rewald's athletic activities could snare dignitaries from foreign counties, and encouraged Rewald to become active in polo and other high-profile activities at which these dignitaries were hosted. Rewald became an international polo player, later using BBRDW to purchase the Hawaii Polo Club, which enabled him to cultivate friendships with many influential people throughout the world. These included the Sultan of Brunei, who later transferred seven billion dollars from British banks to U.S. banks. The CIA wanted Rewald to maintain a lavish life style to attract these people, and funded these activities through other covert companies, especially law firms and consulting firms.

Rewald's first CIA station chief and handler was Eugene J. Welch, who was later replaced by Jack Kindschi, followed by Jack W. Rardin, all of whom coached Rewald on CIA operations. Several years later, Rewald would be the fall-guy when the cover was blown on BBRDW.

**COVERT FUNDING FOR CIA PROPRIETARIES**

Funding for these CIA proprietaries came from other CIA-related companies. BBRDW would send fictitious bills to them to explain why the funds were received. These companies were located in California, Virginia, Hong Kong and Paris.

BBRDW was active in numerous covert CIA activities, including:

* Supplying arms to Taiwan, India, and other countries, which was unlawful under federal law, but carried out under CIA orders.

* Setting up banking and trust companies for CIA money laundering.

* Secretly acquiring Japan's secret plans for the Japanese High Speed Surface Transport (HSST) by paying a $27,000 bribe to a Japanese businessman.

* Targeting foreign political, military and business leaders whose funds were placed in accounts alongside money obtained through clandestine CIA operations.

* Funding worldwide CIA operations, including assassinations.

* Soliciting private investors in order to appear like a legitimate international investment concern, commingling their funds with those of the CIA.

* During the Falklands War, Rewald traveled to Chile and Argentina under cover of playing polo, obtaining intelligence information for the CIA.

* Rewald was kept uninformed about the more lurid activities carried over from the Nugan Hand operation.

**INNOCENCE IN AN AREA OF CORRUPT ACTIVITIES**

The CIA started, funded, and staffed BBRDW and its many subsidiaries. Its high-level CIA agents, including Welch, Kindschi and Richardson, directed the sordid and illegal operations, keeping the details from Rewald. Once, when Rewald was approached by CIA agent Richard Armitage to handle drug transactions and launder the drug money, Rewald responded that the company did not have expertise in these areas and he didn't want to get involved in them.

The CIA's foreign resource chief, Richardson, later told Rewald that CIA people in BBRDW and its subsidiaries did have expertise to handle these matters, and made reference to former Pan Am pilot Ned Avary. At a later date, Rewald described this encounter in a memo to his attorney, and added that he knew that Ned Avary, General Hunter Harris, and Richard Armitage were involved in these areas.

**CIA COVER BLOWN BY TV REPORTER**

Honolulu TV reporter Barbara Tanabe drew attention to BBRDW in July 1983 after receiving a tip about BBRDW irregularities. The tip was planted by Chinese intelligence agents who were dissatisfied with BBRDW's campaign seeking to frighten Hong Kong financiers to move their money out of Hong Kong to Hawaii. This attempt to move capital from Hong Kong before China took over the British crown colony disturbed Chinese officials, and they retaliated by seeking to discredit BBRDW, not knowing it was a CIA operation.

This publicity caused Hawaii officials to commence an investigation of BBRDW's financial activities. When a CIA proprietary is investigated by any outside agency, state or federal, the standard practice is for Washington CIA and Justice Department officials to block the investigation.[304] This time, however, the CIA proprietary had received too much media attention for this past practice to work.

Using typical CIA tactics, the Agency pulled funds out of the various bank accounts in Hong Kong, Singapore, London, Switzerland, and the Cayman Islands, transferring the money into other foreign CIA proprietaries and financial institutions. The looted assets consisted not only of CIA money, but also funds invested by private citizens residing in Hawaii and California.

Before the cover was blown on BBRDW, millions of dollars were received from investors in Hawaii and California by the CIA proprietary operation. During a Board of Directors meeting shortly before the cover was blown, Rewald had ordered these investors to be paid off and no further private investment money taken in. This plan was shown by minutes of a board meeting. Rewald's explanation was that these funds were too much trouble, and interfered with Agency operations. But after the cover was blown, and without Rewald's knowledge, the CIA removed these funds, just as it had done after the Nugan Hand Bank cover was blown.

For over 12 months the local media focused considerable attention on the BBRDW affair. It was Hawaii's most famous legal case.

Shortly after the cover was blown, Rewald became depressed by being made the scapegoat, and the lack of support by his CIA handlers. He checked into room 1632 at the Sheraton Waikiki with thoughts of committing suicide. Before checking into the hotel, Rewald visited the office of the CIA station chief in the federal building in downtown Honolulu. Finding Jack Rardin out of the office, Rewald placed a message on Rardin's answering machine:[305]

*Jack, this is the Chairman. I am checking into the Sheraton Waikiki under the name Ronald Imp. Status urgent. Mayday. I'll be waiting for your*

304 Security Exchange Commission, Internal Revenue Service, Banking Commission, and other regulatory agencies.

305 Rardin's number was 531-1023.

*call.*

A bottle of Codeine # 3, which Rewald contemplated taking, and a Bible, sat on the end table alongside the bed. This was not the behavior of a person intentionally engaging in criminal activities, but more the conduct of a person who was distraught at being used, as Rewald's CIA handlers had done to him.

Rewald had kept highly sensitive records of key financial transactions in a green-cover book, which the CIA wanted. The book contained information showing secret bank account numbers and aliases, including bank accounts for high level people in politics and in the intelligence community in such banks as Union Bank of Switzerland, Grand Caymans Bank, and the Hong Kong and Shanghai Bank. If this information was publicized, and understood, it would send shock waves through the government.

In an effort to obtain possession of the valuable book, two CIA agents, Angelo Cancel and Richard Allen entered Rewald's hotel room and attempted to force Rewald to reveal its location. Rewald was groggy from taking a heavy dose of the Codeine tablets and wasn't responding to their requests. They dragged him into the bathroom, placed him against the tub, and plunged a knife deeply into his arms. Bleeding profusely, Rewald lapsed into unconsciousness. Unable to find the book, Allen and Cancel left Rewald to die from loss of blood. Fortuitously, a hotel maid discovered Rewald's bleeding body and he was rushed to Honolulu's Queens Hospital, saving his life.

**THE HIDDEN GREEN BOOK**

While Rewald was recovering in the hospital, he was warned by his CIA handlers to remain quiet, to say nothing, and the CIA would financially support his family. That was never done. The former CIA station chief, Kindschi, visited Rewald in the hospital and asked: "Ron, where is the green book?"

"It's safe," replied Rewald.

In response to a question from Honolulu detective Ed Lingo, the present CIA station chief, Rardin, claimed he didn't know Rewald, that he didn't know anything about BBRDW except what he read in the papers, and that he had no connection to either. He was of course lying. Rardin socialized frequently with the Rewald family and was in almost daily contact with Rewald as his CIA handler.

Agents Allen and Cancel, who had tried to kill Rewald in the hotel, threatened Rewald's secretaries, Sue Wilson[306] and Jackie Vos, ordering them to leave Hawaii immediately and never return. Their departure would prevent them from testifying about the CIA operation.

**DON'T CALL THE FBI**

As the two women later discussed their problem, Sue told Jackie that if she hadn't heard from her in the next thirty days to call the local police. When Jackie asked Sue if the FBI should be called, Sue responded: "They won't help us. They're all in this together. We might be able to trust the local guys. They're not part of the system."

While these events were taking place, another CIA contract agent and close

---

306 Wilson had been a semifinalist in the Miss Teenage America pageant, after which she worked with the National Security Agency in Washington and Honolulu, before joining Bishop Baldwin.

friend, Thomas Wilhite of San Rafael, California, became outraged at what the Agency was doing to Rewald. He said to Rewald:

*There's a big coverup going on. They've completely disavowed any knowledge of you. You are being left out to dry, pure and simple. I'm calling a press conference for tomorrow at the ranch. I'm going to tell the media everything. Tell them this is all a CIA coverup and that you were just following orders.*

Rewald responded:

*Tom, you can't do that. I have an agreement with the Agency. They assured me that as long as I keep quiet, Nancy and the children will be taken care of. They will take care of me as soon as all this cools down, so don't do this. It's not necessary.*

Wilhite replied:

*They're lying to you, Ron. I assure you they are destroying every bit of evidence. They are shutting us all up, transferring others to who knows where. All the bank accounts are being emptied. Believe me, you are being abandoned and set up. You know what plausible deniability is all about.*

Before the press conference the following morning, Wilhite took his red aerobatics Pitt Special bi-plane for a customary morning flight. Taking off from the grass runway on his ranch, the plane climbed steeply to 1,000 feet and then suddenly plunged to the ground. The crash killed him. The aircraft had apparently been sabotaged. Wilhite's death wasn't the only one connected to BBRDW. Two attorneys were killed in Washington as they searched for evidence linking BBRDW's client, President Ferdinand Marcos of the Philippines, to the CIA.

A CIA agent working under Richardson through the BBRDW operation, Richard Craig Smith, had spied on the Russians in Japan and secretly pretended to the Russians to be a double-agent, as directed by Charles Richardson. Now, without CIA support (or maybe he was deliberately turned in), he was arrested by the Justice Department and charged with the serious offense of espionage, allegedly selling secrets to the Russians. Smith's federal case was tried in Virginia. (*U.S. v. Smith*, 592 F. Supp 424 (E.D. Va. 1985); 750 F.2d 1215 (4th Cir. 1984); and 780 F.2d 1102 (4th Cir. 1985).

**KING PIN OF CIA OPERATIONS IN THE PACIFIC**

After BBRDW's collapse, the British Broadcasting Company (BBC) referred to Rewald as "King Pin of CIA Operations in the Pacific."

The judge aided and abetted this coverup by issuing dozens of orders depriving Rewald of the defenses guaranteed under law. He issued gag orders barring Rewald's attorney from repeating what Rewald had told him; refused to allow the introduction of thousands of CIA documents that would show where the money came from (sham CIA front companies), where the money went (for CIA expenditures), and that Rewald was a CIA agent. Case records, normally available to the public, were sealed from public view. Rewald was ordered not to talk about the CIA. These measures would not have been necessary if the CIA had not been deeply involved in BBRDW. The public, especially the investors who lost millions of dollars, had a right to have access to whatever records and testimony applied to the case.

Justice Department officials, seeking to protect the CIA, charged Rewald with 100 counts, including defrauding the many investors who put money into the operation and who lost their investment when the CIA looted the assets. Many of these investors blamed Rewald for their losses, apparently assuming that Justice Department prosecutors were telling the truth and would not lie.

**DENIAL OF DEFENSES BY JUSTICE DEPARTMENT**

Justice Department prosecutors used the standard procedures to keep the public from learning about this covert CIA operation. These included:

* Charging Rewald with the federal offense of defrauding the investors, while simultaneously protecting those who actually perpetrated the crime.
* Seizing all of Rewald's assets, depriving him of the funds necessary to hire legal counsel.
* Transferring a key CIA attorney, John Peyton, to Honolulu to prosecute the case against Rewald. Peyton insured that CIA witnesses and documents were not available to Rewald. Prior to this transfer, Peyton was chief of litigation for the Central Intelligence Agency, taking a demotion to become assistant U.S. Attorney.
* Withholding evidence that would have shown that the CIA looted the BBRDW assets.
* Engaging in various forms of deception.

**DENIAL OF DEFENSES BY FEDERAL JUDGES**

Judge Fong cooperated with the Justice Department prosecutors by:

* Dismissing Rewald's experienced attorneys, Los Angeles attorney A. Brent Carruth and San Francisco attorney Melvin Belli, and appointing inexperienced legal counsel to represent Rewald. He appointed a young attorney just out of law school who had never tried any case, and who had no knowledge of the legislation relating to classified documents, CIPA.[307] This lack of knowledge contributed to Rewald being denied the use of classified documents and CIA witnesses that would show the CIA controlled all of BBRDW's activities. That attorney, Brian Tamamaha, had an application for employment with the Justice Department and was simply waiting for a routine security check.
* Denying Rewald the right to call CIA witnesses and produce any of the thousands of CIA documents showing him as head of a covert CIA proprietary, carrying out orders as shown on hundreds of cable messages and letters. This denial emasculated Rewald's defense and prevented the public from learning about the CIA operation.
* Denying to Rewald's attorney the right to introduce important documents, refusing to allow Rewald to testify to his CIA activities, and refusing to allow testimony as to who funded the CIA operations and where the money was spent.

Justice Department and CIA officials suborned perjury from its witnesses. In one case, when Rewald's attorney subpoenaed CIA agent John H. Mason, who had given Rewald many orders in the past, the person appearing was not the John H. Mason that Rewald knew. This same trick, substituting another person

307 Legislation dealing with classified government documents and information was called the Classified Information Procedure Act (CIPA).

for Mason, was used in the sham espionage trial against another CIA agent, Richard Craig Smith.

During Rewald's trial, Justice Department prosecutors and CIA witnesses denied that Rewald was a CIA employee, and denied that BBRDW was set up by and for the CIA, funded by the CIA, and all activities controlled by the CIA. Rewald had to sign a standard CIA agent security agreement. (Because of the poor print quality of the original security agreement, it is copied word-for-word as follows):

*SECRECY AGREEMENT*

*1. I, Ronald Rewald, hereby agree to accept as a prior condition of my being employed in, or otherwise retained to perform services for, the Central Intelligence Agency, or for staff elements the Office of the Director of Central Intelligence (hereinafter collectively referred to as the Central Intelligence Agency), the obligations contained in this agreement.*

*2. I understand that in the course of my employment or other service with the Central Intelligence Agency I may be given access to information which is classified with the standards set forth in Executive Order 12065 amended or superseded, or other applicable Executive Order, and other information which, if disclosed in an unauthorized manner, would jeopardize foreign intelligence activities of the United States government. I accept that by being granted access to such information I will be placed in a position of special confidence and trust and become obligated to protect this information from unauthorized disclosure.*

*3. In consideration for being employed or otherwise retained to provide services to the Central Intelligence Agency I agree that I will never disclose in any form the following categories of information or materials, to any person not authorized by the Central Intelligence Agency to receive them:*

*a. information which is classified pursuant to Executive Order and which I have obtained during the course of my employment or other service with the Central Intelligence Agency.*

*b. information, or materials which reveal information, classifiable pursuant to Executive Order and obtained by me in the course of my employment or other service with the Central Intelligence Agency but which because of operational circumstance or oversight, is not formally marked as classified in accordance with such Executive Order, and which I know or have reason to know has not been publicly acknowledged by the Agency.*

*c. information obtained by me in the course of my employment or other service with the Central Intelligence Agency that identifies any person or organization that presently has or formerly has had a relationship with a United States foreign intelligence organization, which relationship the United States government has taken affirmative measures to conceal.*

*4. I understand that the burden will be upon me to learn whether information or materials within my control are considered by the Central Intelligence Agency to fit the description set forth in paragraph 3, and whom the Agency has authorized to receive it.*

*5. As a further condition of the special confidence and trust reposed in me by the Central Intelligence Agency, I hereby agree to submit for review by the*

*Central Intelligence Agency all information or material including works of fiction which contain any mention of intelligence data or activities, or contain data which may be based upon information classified pursuant to Executive Order, which I contemplate disclosing publicly or which I have actually prepared for public disclosure, either during my employment or other service with the Central Intelligence Agency or at any time thereafter prior to discussing it with or showing it to anyone who is not authorized to have access to it. I further agree that I will not take any steps toward public disclosure until I have received written permission to do so from the Central Intelligence Agency.*

*6. I understand that the purpose of the review described in paragraph 5 is to give the Central Intelligence Agency the opportunity to determine whether the information or materials which I contemplate disclosing publicly contain any information which I have agreed not to disclose. I further understand that the Agency will act upon the materials I submit and make a response to me within a reasonable time.*

*7. I understand that all information or materials which I may acquire in the course of my employment or other service with the Central Intelligence Agency which fit the descriptions set out in paragraph 3 of this agreement are and will remain the property of the United States government. I agree to surrender all materials reflecting such information which may have come into my possession or for which I am responsible because of my employment or other service with the Central Intelligence Agency, upon demand by an appropriate official of the Central Intelligence Agency, or upon the conclusion of my employment or other service with the Central Intelligence Agency.*

*8. I agree to notify the Central Intelligence Agency immediately in the event that I am called upon by judicial or Congressional authorities to testify about, or provide information which I have agreed herein not to disclose.*

*9. I understand that nothing contained in this agreement prohibits me from reporting intelligence activities which I consider to be unlawful or improper directly to the Intelligence Oversight Board established by the President or to a successor body which the President may establish. I recognize that there are also established procedures for bringing such matters to the attention of the Agency's Inspector General or to the Director of Central Intelligence. I further understand that any information which I may repeat to the Intelligence Oversight Board continues to be subject to this agreement for other purposes and that such reporting does not constitute public disclosure or declassification of that information.*

*10. I understand that any breach of this agreement by me may result in the Central Intelligence Agency taking administrative action against me, which can include temporary loss of pay or termination of my employment or service with the Central Intelligence Agency. I also understand that if I violate the terms of this agreement, the United States government may institute a civil proceeding to seek compensatory damages or other appropriate relief. I understand that the disclosure of information which I have agreed herein not to disclose can, in some circumstances, constitute a criminal offense.*

*11. I understand that the United States government may, prior to any unauthorized disclosure which is threatening me, choose to apply to any appropriate court for an order enforcing this agreement. Nothing in this agreement constitutes a waiver on the part of the United States to institute a civil or criminal proceeding for any breach of this agreement. Nothing in this agreement constitutes a waiver on my part of any possible defenses I may have in connection with civil or criminal proceedings which may be brought against me.*

*12. In addition to any other remedy to which the United States government may become entitled, I hereby assign to the United States government all rights, title, and interest in any and all royalties, remunerations, and emolument that have resulted or will result or may result from any divulgence, publication or revelation of information by me when carried out in breach of paragraph 5 of this agreement or which involves information prohibited from disclosure under terms of this agreement.*

*13. I understand and accept that, unless I am provided a written release from this agreement or any portion of it by the Director of Central Intelligence or the Director's representative, all the conditions and obligations accepted by me in this agreement apply both during my employment or other service with the Central Intelligence Agency, and at all times thereafter.*

*14. I understand that the purpose of this agreement is to implement the responsibilities of the Director of Central Intelligence, particularly the responsibility to protect intelligence sources and methods, as specified in the National Security Act of 1947, as amended.*

*15. In any civil action which may be brought by the United States government for breach of this agreement I understand and agree that the law of the Commonwealth of Virginia shall govern the interpretation of this agreement.*

*16. Each of the numbered paragraphs and lettered subparagraphs of this agreement is severable, if a court should find any of the paragraphs or subparagraphs of this agreement to be unenforceable. I understand that all remaining provisions will continue in full force.*

*17. I make this agreement in good faith, and with no purpose of evasion.*

____________________________

*Signature*

____________________________

*Date*

*The execution of this agreement was witnessed by the undersigned, who accepted it on behalf of the Central Intelligence Agency as a prior condition of the employment or other service of the person whose signature appears above.*

***WITNESS AND ACCEPTANCE:***

__________________________

*Signature*

__________________________

*Printed Name*

*Date*

__________________________

I gained possession of hundreds of CIA documents relating to BBRDW, and they clearly show that BBRDW and its subsidiaries were organized, funded, operated and controlled by the CIA through its over two dozen CIA agents within the companies.

**THE VERDICT AND OUT-OF-PROPORTION PRISON SENTENCE**

The trial started in mid-1985 before a federal jury in Honolulu, and a guilty verdict was reached on most charges on October 21, 1985. Judge Fong, who had repeatedly violated important due process protections, sentenced Rewald to eighty years in prison. (Under the mandatory guidelines for that type of offense, which came into play shortly thereafter, if Rewald had actually committed the offenses, was three and a half years). This 80-year prison sentence insured that Rewald would die in prison and his knowledge of CIA activities would go to the grave with him.

Making matters worse for Rewald during his remaining life in prison, he had suffered an injury in a polo accident that caused him serious health problems, which were made worse by the incredibly bad medical care in prison. Eventually Rewald lost control over his bladder and bowel movements and was confined to a wheel chair.

**SUSPICIOUS REWARD FOR TANABE**

Barbara Tanabe[308] became affiliated with a CIA proprietary or asset after Rewald was sentenced to federal prison. She left station KHON and became president and chief operating officer of the Pacific division of a powerful public relations firm based in Washington, D.C., that was reportedly a CIA proprietary or asset: Hill and Knowlton Communications, Pacific. Hill and Knowlton is famous for its CIA connections and for its propaganda news releases, one of many media assets receiving CIA money.

**AIDING AND ABETTING BY NINTH CIRCUIT COURT OF APPEAL JUDGES**

Rewald filed a notice of appeal with the Ninth Circuit Court of Appeals (No. 85-1353) on December 20, 1985, and his attorney, A. Brent Carruth of Van Nuys, California, filed the two appeal briefs on March 21, 1988. Because of classified documents involved in Rewald's defense, one brief of 108 pages was marked Secret and sealed as required by CIPA rules.

I had learned from 1974 to the present date that the Ninth Circuit Court of Appeals judges routinely engaged in a coverup, as will be well recognized by the time the reader gets to the end of this book. They refused to provide relief to Rewald from the travesty of justice. They aided and abetted the gross injustice. They allowed the 80-year sentence to stand, fabricating facts to support their decision.

**AIDING AND ABETTING BY SUPREME COURT JUSTICES**

Also aiding and abetting this travesty of justice and the coverup of CIA activities were the Justices of the U.S. Supreme Court, another group that I found routinely covering up.

308 Tanabe was reported to be a member of the Honolulu Committee on Foreign Relations (HCFR), associated with the New York-based Council on Foreign Relations (CFR).

Even while Rewald languished in prison, the CIA attempted to have him assassinated. American Broadcasting Company (ABC) presented a two-part report on *World News Tonight* that aired on September 19 and 20, 1984. The program featured a former CIA contract agent, Scott Barnes, describing a plan in which the CIA hired him to infiltrate the prison where Rewald was an inmate and check on Rewald's activities. According to Barnes, two CIA agents, John Stein and Gene Wilson, hired him to investigate whether Rewald was blowing the whistle on the CIA's operations. Barnes said during the ABC show that in November 1984 he met two men whose last names were Stein and Wilson, and two Office of Naval Intelligence agents at the Royal Hawaiian Hotel in Waikiki, and that during the meeting Barnes was told: "Rewald is no longer an asset; he is only a liability." Barnes stated that he was then directed to kill Rewald. Barnes refused.

## CIA THREATENING, AND THEN BUYING, A MAJOR NEWS SOURCE

In November 1984, CIA Director William Casey complained to the Federal Communication Commission about the ABC television network for having aired a show featuring CIA agent Scott Barnes. In the television presentation Barnes said he was asked by two CIA agents in Honolulu to kill Ronald Rewald. This airing had the danger of revealing the CIA role in BBRDW and could expose an endless number of other covert CIA proprietaries and operations. Casey was a founder,[309] major investor, and director in Capital Cities Corporation, which then took over the ABC television network a few months later, in March 1985. As stated in *National Affairs*:

> *The CIA director openly attacks a leading network and threatens its broadcast license, ultimately causing it to issue a retraction of a [highly sensitive] story. Meanwhile, wearing his other hat as an investor, founder and close confidante of the Capital Cities management, Casey also stands to further his private business interests, as well as those of his friends, who were mounting a takeover of ABC.*

The combination of the media being infiltrated by CIA assets, funding of all forms of media activities, threats to revoke its government-granted license, and business interests linked to government officials, are key reasons why the media has engaged in a complicity of silence at a great cost to America.

In April 1993, prison officials at Terminal Island placed a block on Rewald's outgoing phone calls so that any calls to me would be automatically blocked. The following November, after the first printing of *Defrauding America* came out with reference to Rewald, prison authorities seized all of his records, preventing him from disclosing to me evidence of CIA-related corruption.

## CIVIL SUIT AGAINST GOVERNMENT

Rewald filed a lawsuit against the CIA, seeking to have the investors who were defrauded by the CIA join in the action. Justice Department attorneys sought to dismiss Rewald's action on the grounds that Rewald "seeks monies based on his intelligence gathering services on behalf of the United States," citing

309 Along with Lowell Thomas and others.

*Totten v. United States*, 92 U.S. 105 (1875).[310] At his criminal trial, Justice Department prosecutors claimed Rewald had no significant CIA connections. During the civil trial they reversed themselves.

**EXAMINING THOUSANDS OF PAGES OF JUDICIAL PAPERS AND OTHER GOVERNMENT DOCUMENTS**

It became obvious to me after examining thousands of pages of court documents, briefs, appeal court decisions, and other papers, that Rewald had been framed by people in control of the Justice Department and the CIA, and federal judges. The court documents established that Rewald was in fact a CIA agent. The tactic used by federal judges to insure that Rewald is forever silenced and discredited, and would die in prison, would prevent Rewald from introducing evidence showing that BBRDW and its subsidiaries were primarily funded by CIA funding sources; that the movement of money, including the investors funds, were controlled by the CIA, that the many off-shore bank accounts controlled by this CIA proprietary had ample funds in them until the funds were secretly removed shortly after BBRDW's cover was blown.

These and other documents would have shown that Rewald was the titular head of a CIA proprietary, in which much of the money flow and other activities were controlled by the many CIA agents operating inside BBRDW and its subsidiaries. Funding the operation of the many world-wide offices over a six-year period could never have been accomplished through the relatively small amount of investors' funds placed in BBRDW. Without being able to show that BBRDW was organized by, funded and controlled, by the CIA, Rewald was made a scapegoat to cover up for the covert CIA operation.

The Ninth Circuit Court of Appeals judges (Arthur L. Alarcon, Cynthia Hall, Alex Kozinski) covered up for this travesty of justice as I repeatedly discovered since 1975, when I sought to report the criminal activities described within these pages, and sought relief from the actions taken to silence me.

**HAPPY DAY FOR REWALD**

Although Rewald had 70 years to go on his prison sentence, and would not be due for parole for many years, the parole board notified Rewald in 1995 that they were holding a parole hearing concerning him. I and many other people submitted papers on his behalf, referring to the outrageous travesty of justice associated with the judicial and Justice Department attacks upon Rewald.

In my writings to the parole board I submitted a copy of the second edition of *Defrauding America* and a letter to the board, outlining the outrageous nature of Rewald's sentence. I ended the letter with a statement that I would like to show in the next edition that the great injustice inflicted upon Rewald finally ended.

Famed attorney Melvin Belli wrote letters outlining the outrageous attacks by Justice Department and CIA officials, and the federal judge, against Rewald, clearing outlining the misconduct being perpetrated.

---

310 The denial of compensation for intelligence gathering services during the Civil War were denied because, "The service was secret and to be obtained clandestinely, and communicated privately; the employment and service were to be equally concealed. Both employer and agent must have understood that the lips of the other were to be forever sealed. In sum, any person who allegedly enters into an intelligence gathering agreement must recognize that such an agreement must remain forever secret."

Rewald was released in June 1995, and went to live with a daughter in Los Angeles. Several days after Rewald's release, his wife was diagnosed as having cancer, which necessitated months of surgery and chemotherapy.

**FUNDING SECRET BANK ACCOUNTS FOR U.S. OFFICIALS**

In March 1996, I acquired several boxes containing hundreds of CIA documents generated from the CIA's secret operation in Hawaii, and within these boxes I found highly sensitive material, including notes that Rewald had made while the titular head of BBRDW. Certain notes and information provided to me by Rewald divulged CIA drug related activities, including drug money laundering. As I gathered from looking over the material and by talking with Rewald, he was unaware of much of the CIA activities originating out of BBRDW.

**DYNAMITE DISCLOSURES OF CIA-FUNDED BANK ACCOUNTS FOR HIGH-LEVEL OFFICIALS**

Deeply imbedded in these documents was an envelope labeled "Attorney-Client information." The information was dynamite, divulging secret activities, including CIA drug trafficking, and CIA funding of secret overseas bank accounts for high U.S. officials.

The information in this envelope included information from the "Green Book" that the CIA sought to get from Rewald while he was in the hospital recovering from the combination suicide and assassination attempt. The notes in the envelope listed high-level people with secret CIA-funded accounts. The names on the left side of the notes were the aliases Rewald used to identify the people on the right for which there were secret bank accounts opened and funded by the CIA through BBRDW.

| | |
|---|---|
| *Irwin M. Peach* | *George Bush* |
| *Mr. Bramble* | *George Bush* |
| *Commander Quinstar* | *General Hunter Harris* |
| *Mr. Apan* | *Robert W. Jinks* |
| *Mr. Grey* | *Robert Allen* |
| *Farrah Fawn* | *Jackie Vos* |
| *General Shake* | *Arnold Braswell*[311] |
| *Mr. Branch* | *Richard Armitage*[312] |
| *Mr. Denile* | *William Casey*[313] |
| *Slimey Affirm* | *Stanley Sporkin*[314] |
| *Captain Perjury* | *Ned Avary* |
| *Attorney Doright* | *Robert Smith* |

Rewald's notes also indicated that fictitious names were used to hide money for B.K. Kim, Philippines' President Ferdinand, and Imelda Marcos, among others.

311 Arnold Braswell was Commander-in-Chief of U.S. Pacific Air Force (CINCPACAF).

312 Richard Armitage was U.S. Assistant Secretary of Defense and reportedly heavily involved with drug trafficking while in Vietnam.

313 William Casey, Director of Central Intelligence.

314 Stanley Sporkin was legal counsel for the CIA, and then a federal judge in Washington, D.C. In this capacity he unlawfully dismissed one of my federal actions seeking to expose the government corruption in which he was involved.

Former senior editor of Forbes, James Norman, had been reporting[315] that a secret group in the intelligence community, outraged at what was going on, infiltrated bank money transfer systems and discovered large quantities of money sequestered in overseas bank accounts for government figures. One of these people was allegedly Vincent Foster, who made a number of one-day trips to Switzerland to conduct bank activities.

These notes, written by Rewald over ten years earlier, when he was head of BBRDW, provided additional evidence of U.S. officials hiding their money in secret bank accounts overseas. The accounts were in financial institutions in Hong Kong, Switzerland, and the Caymans.

Information on another sheet that I found in Rewald's papers revealed activities engaged in by CIA agents embedded into BBRDW and its various subsidiaries. These are the activities in which Rewald refused to get involved, including CIA drug trafficking.

These notes revealed other activities that I hadn't known about earlier. While Rewald was hospitalized in Honolulu, sources kept him informed of some activities being taken to remove and hide the funds being removed from BBRDW and subsidiary accounts. General Hunter Harris called President George Bush to alert him that the cover on BBRDW had been blown, and wanted instructions as to how to proceed. CIA head, William Casey, then called Robert W. Jinks, and told him to work with Robert Allen. Jinks was then ordered to proceed to Texas to get bank account numbers and then to go to the Cayman Islands where the accounts were located.

Rewald's notes indicated that someone from CIA headquarters at Langley, or an associate of Robert Allen, eventually went to the Cayman Islands and moved BBRDW's funds to another offshore country. Robert Smith, who wasn't directly involved in the money transfer but aware something was going on, learned that a General in Texas was to give Robert Jinks bank account information and that he, Robert Smith, was to go to the Caymans to retrieve the hidden money. General Arnold Braswell was to assist in this removal, but he was too shook up by what was going on and, combined with his drinking problem, was unable to carry out any instructions. Braswell was not used.

Similar efforts were being taken to remove funds from BBRDW and subsidiary accounts in Hong Kong and Switzerland. About this time, funds were being received from secret arms sales and Rewald said that Ned Avary diverted these funds away from BBRDW.

While these events were taking place, Robert Allen sought to force Jackie Vos to disclose the whereabouts of the Green Book that listed these accounts so as to destroy the records.

**SEEKING HELP FROM THE FBI**

Vos sought help from the FBI from the threats made by Allen, but higher Justice Department officials ordered the FBI to stay clear of all activities related to the CIA's BBRDW.

Rewald wrote in his notes that he had met President George Bush twice in Hawaii, and had been invited to meet with the president in Washington for lunch

---

315 *Media Bypass* issues commencing in February 1996.

or dinner, along with someone that Rewald identified as "Brady." All of these people were described in Rewald's notes by their code names, but a separate sheet of paper identified who they were, except for "Brady."

I asked Rewald about these, and he stated that he made the list of names with secret offshore bank account numbers. I asked Rewald, "Referring to the fictitious names for offshore bank accounts, do I correctly understand that you made up the alias names yourself?"

*"You mean, Peach for Bush? That was done well after the collapse [of BBRDW] and was done to disguise my reference to the accounts so that someone picking it up wouldn't know what I was talking about. These people certainly had these accounts."*

**PEROT'S KNOWLEDGE OF THE BANK ACCOUNTS**

Responding to my questions about the secret bank accounts listed in his memorandum, Rewald said:

*The names you are talking about, Perjury, Quinstar, Peach, and so on, that was in response to an inquiry from a politician out of Texas, a little bald-headed guy [Ross Perot], who ran for president about four or five years ago. He had hired an investigator who contacted me and they had a lot of facts and information on some of our operations, and he was trying basically to find out whether someone that they had an argument with was involved in this operation. That's when I put together those names and I passed the information on, and I said that is what this person did and what that person did.*

I asked, "Were these people informed of their balances?"

*"We sent out monthly statements."*

I asked, "Where did the money come from to put in those accounts?" His answer opened open still another can of worms.

*"They came from the Agency funding mechanisms."*

"Were these substantial amounts," I asked?

*"Oh yes, our bank accounts were always full. It was not unusual for us to have hundreds of millions of dollars in various banks in Hong Kong and Shanghai banks, in Cayman banks, Netherland Antilles banks, Swiss bank accounts."*

Referring to the serious implications of what he had just said, I remarked, "For Bush and the others to have secret bank accounts, funded by the CIA, there are serious implications in that fact."

*"Well, there are."*

Seeking to enlarge upon what he had just told me, "You say that the CIA was putting money into his account?"

*The original money was put in by him or for him. The percentage rate that we were paying was set by the Agency. That was twenty percent. But that was the same as Hong Kong was paying on accounts. So it is not unusual. That was just to be competitive with what investment banking operations were giving at that particular time. You must remember this was 1980, 81, 82. At that time, twenty percent was not an unusual amount to pay in Hong Kong and other areas.*

Referring to the notes listing the secret bank accounts, Rewald said: *After I was found in the Sheraton Waikiki Hotel in 1983 (first thought by the CIA to be dead), I was taken to the hospital. The very first thing that was done [by my CIA handlers] was a phone call from Commander Quinstar to Irwin M. Peach to alert him, and get instructions.*

*The DCI had Mr. Apan called back from Australia or the Far East (I am not sure which location he was at that day), and he was told to work with Mr. Grey. They made arrangements for Mr. Apan to travel to Texas, to get account numbers and banking instructions and he was to go to the Caymans where we had hidden bank accounts. I knew of at least two occasions when he was about to leave, but I think either someone from Langley or an associate of Mr. Grey was finally sent. In any event, I was told that the funds were all removed and transferred abroad. Attorney Doright was aware of Apan being asked to make this trip, but little else. He was helping me at the time (however he was lost, because he had only little bits and pieces of the picture and what was really going on). He did know that a General in Texas was to give Mr. Apan bank account information and that he was to travel to the Caymans to give Mr. Apan bank account information, and that he was to travel to the Caymans to retrieve some money. General Shake was supposed to help, but was falling apart through this whole mess.*

*The same effort to clear out all funds from private company accounts was at the same time being done in Hong Kong and Switzerland. Also, after a payment came from an arms transaction, those funds were diverted away from Bishop, Baldwin account by Captain Perjury.*

*Mr. Grey tried to force Farah Fawn to retrieve my green book (this contained a list of all foreign accounts and the cover names used to hold funds for special people). I had already destroyed my copy of the green book while I was in the hospital because I feared it would fall into the wrong hands. Local police were trying to sneak in and talk to me, and they were not under control. Mr. Grey did get the second copy of the green book, but this was after he had approached Farrah Fawn (who was unwitting in this whole affair). She was threatened and forced to help them. She sought help from the FBI, but they were called off.*

*I had met with Mr. Bramble on two occasions in Hawaii and was invited and scheduled to meet with him again in Washington. I was also to travel with him to the Far East to meet with others, including President Marcos.*

*Bramble wanted to meet and get involved with the Sultan of Brunei who came to Hawaii to play polo with me. I was to contact Bramble if it looked as if he would meet with the Sultan. However, it was too early in the relationship with the Sultan for that type of introduction. While the Sultan and Ricky Zobel and I agreed to do some joint business ventures, and the Sultan put several million dollars into a project with the two of us, I felt that I would blow my polo and business cover with an introduction to Bramble. I do know that Bramble traveled to Brunei and met with him some time later. Except for the Sultan of Brunei, Ricky Zobel, and Ferdinand Marcos, all names were aliases.*

Making reference to one of the officers in BBRDW, I asked Rewald if Haughton was an active part of the CIA's operation. Rewald responded:

*He was briefing us on operations that we had taken over that were existing operations for Nugan Hand. He was also representing the Agency. He tried to convince me that drugs were something we had to get involved in. He is the one who said that we had other people in our operation that had the experience. I said we didn't, and he named Avary.*

*Richard Branch [Richard Armitage], now Assistant Secretary for Defense, was a close personal friend of Commander Quinstar [General Hunter Harris] and Mr. Bramble [George Bush]. When I was first approached [by Bernie Haughton, CIA agent with Nugan Hand] to handle drug transactions and launder the money from them through various conduits we were setting up, I turned it down, saying that I would not be involved in drugs in any way. I also said that we had no expertise in these areas. I was [later] told by my FR Base Chief [Charles L. Richardson] that we did have experienced people in our cover at BBRD&W to handle such transactions, and Captain Perjury [Ned Avary] was named. I knew that Perjury, Quinstar, and Branch, were playing around in these areas, and we may have helped move funds around. But I never knowingly handled anything involving drugs.*

*I was never received quite as warmly as before this by any of my superiors. I also know that all of these people, plus General Branch worked together during Nugan Hand, and constantly sought covert operations in Southeast Asia, I think more to handle whatever it was they were doing than to further our missions. I am sure the source of funds in both the Cayman Islands and Swiss accounts were more from these transactions unknown to me, than the arms shipments we were running through the Hong Kong banks. It was during this same time that Irwin Peach [George Bush] met with me to tell me how great I was doing and how they could not afford to lose my help. And after all, there was a considerable investment made in me and my cover. After this, both Quinstar, and more so, Captain Perjury made many trips to Washington, reporting to someone supposedly at the Pentagon on various things we were doing. This normally would have been handled through the Chief of Station or Base Chief as in the past. I had no need to know why these briefings were being handled differently. The contact number we were always left with was at the Pentagon, or routed through it. I believe it was a General named Allen.*

Even through Rewald wasn't involved in the drug-related activities, he was hesitant about disclosing these CIA activities to me. He had visions of the CIA as an honorable agency, despite what had been done to him that showed otherwise. I felt that his refusal to get involved in the drug-related activities isolated him from the hard realities of what was actually going on in the CIA.

## KEEP UNINFORMED WHILE TITULAR HEAD OF A LARGE CIA FINANCIAL OPERATION?

During my several years of telephone, personal, and letter contact with Rewald, I felt he was sincere, and felt he was doing a patriotic duty for the United States and that he was not made aware of the many CIA activities carried on by the many BBRDW global offices, or even many of the CIA activities carried out by CIA agents in the Honolulu home office.

Not only were secret bank accounts a violation of law, but the fact that the CIA was the funding source, part of which probably came from the CIA's drug trafficking, constituted major crimes, especially when the participants hold high office, such as Bush, William Casey, and Stanley Sporkin.

**AIDING THE MISCARRIAGE OF JUSTICE**

Typical of the misinformation put out by the mainstream media was an article in the *Honolulu Advertiser* (July 4, 1995) after Rewald was released from prison after 10 years. The article written by senior staff writer Walter Wright appeared to be another piece paid for by the CIA. The article was headed, "Con Man Rewald Let Out of Prison." The *Honolulu Advertiser* continued its long-term coverup of the CIA operation in Hawaii.

SECRECY AGREEMENT

1. I acknowledge the fact that because of the confidential relationship between myself and the U.S. Government, I will be the recipient of information which, in itself, or by the implications to be drawn therefrom, will be such that its unlawful disclosure or loose handling may adversely affect the interest and the security of the United States. I realize that the methods of collecting and of using this information, as well as the identity of persons involved, are as secret as the substantive information itself and, therefore, must be treated by me with an equal degree of secrecy.

2. I shall always recognize that the U.S. Government has the sole interest in all information which I or my organization may possess, compile or acquire pursuant to this understanding. No advantage or gain will be sought by me as a result of the added significance or value such information may have, due to the Government's interest in it.

3. I solemnly pledge my word that I will never divulge, publish, nor reveal either by word, conduct, or by any other means such information or knowledge, as indicated above, unless specifically authorized to do so, by the U.S. Government.

4. Nothing in this understanding is to be taken as imposing any restriction upon the normal business practices of myself or my organization: i.e., information normally possessed by us or gathered in the regular course of business will continue to be utilized in accordance with our normal practices.

Declassified By 134025
date 8/25/85

| SIGNATURE: | SIGNATURE: |
|---|---|
| Signature of John H. Mason | |
| [redacted] | |
| REPRESENTATIVE OF U.S. GOVERNMENT | Ronald R. Rewald |
| [redacted] | CMI Investment Corporation |
| DATE | ORGANIZATION |
| Handwritten date 25 June 1979 | [redacted] |
| | DATE |

CIA secrecy form for Ronald Rewald, under CIA cover of Consolidated Mutual Investment Corporation.

**SPEED LETTER**

REPLY REQUESTED

DATE 21 September 1979

LETTER NO.

TO : CCS/OFB

ATTN:

FROM: CCS/CCB

1. This will confirm discussions with [redacted] hat Hudley, Johnson and Moore (H-482) will be used as a funding facility to LPBURGER which will backstop [redacted] (P) under his operational alias of Richard P. Canannaugh during his tour in FR/Los Angeles.

2. Please refer any questions you may have on the above to [redacted] or the undersigned on extension [redacted]

WARNING NOTICE
SENSITIVE INTELLIGENCE SOURCES
AND METHODS INVOLVED

[redacted]

SIGNATURE

REPLY

DATE

ALL PORTIONS OF THIS DOCUMENT ARE CLASSIFIED SECRET

[redacted]

DISTRIBUTION
Orig - Addee
1 - CS-3938
1 - 11120
1 - Reading Board
1 - Chrono
1 - [redacted] Chrono
1 - [redacted] Chrono

DERIVATIVE CL BY 025298
CL REVW ON 21 Sep 99
ED FROM DSC 12E

SIGNATURE

RESPONDER'S FILE

SECRET

CIA form approving full funding for LPBURGER (Rewald) and Richard P. Cavanaugh, using the CIA public relations firm of Hudley, Johnson and Moore.

**WARNING OF MISSILE ATTACKS ON U.S. AIRLINERS**

While Rewald was in prison at Terminal Island he met another prisoner, Mohammad Akbar Bey, the son of one of the Afghan rebel leaders who he had previously met while Rewald was the head of the CIA operation in Hawaii. As a result of this meeting, negotiations commenced between Afghan rebels and Justice Department and CIA officials in which the rebels offered 30 to 40 SAM missiles to the United States at virtually no cost. These were missiles being sought by terrorists at the same time. The rebels would give these missiles to the United States in exchange for the release from federal prison of the son of one of the rebel leaders. Bey was in prison for a drug-related offense.

Rewald was a key part of the negotiations because the rebels trusted him, while they did not trust Justice Department and CIA officials. Also involved in these negotiations was Long Beach attorney, John J. Reed, who was believed to be one of the many attorneys fronting for the CIA.

Justice Department and CIA officials knew that terrorists were bidding on these missiles and that if they rejected the missiles, terrorists would acquire some or all of them. At that time, 25 commercial aircraft had already been shot down by SAM missiles in Africa, the Middle East, and the Soviet Union. Terrorism against the United States was increasing and it could be expected that U.S. commercial aircraft would be targeted with any missiles acquired by terrorists.

**QUESTIONABLE AGENDA**

After months of negotiations frustrated by Justice Department and CIA officials, the missiles were rejected. Anyone familiar with the mentality of these two agencies would not have any problem believing that Justice Department and CIA officials **wanted** the missiles to fall into the hands of terrorists. The downing of one or more commercial aircraft would justify their existence and expansion, as well as "justifying" imposing draconian security measures upon the American people.

Concerned about the probable consequences of rejecting the SAM missiles, Rewald provided me with information and documents concerning the missile negotiations. I then sent by certified mail a detailed three-page letter to Senator Arlen Specter and every member of the House and Senate intelligence committees, warning that surface-to-air missiles were about to be turned over to terrorists because of the actions by Justice Department and CIA officials. I stressed that I had considerable documentation and memorandums outlining the negotiations, and that failure to immediately contact me and my CIA source would permit the terrorists to acquire the missiles, and that one or more U.S. aircraft would probably be eventually shot down. Not a single one responded.

**HISTORY OF COMMERCIAL AIRCRAFT DOWNING BY MISSILES**

In the preceding two decades, over two dozen commercial aircraft have been shot down by surface-to-air missiles in Africa, the Middle East, and Russia. It could be assumed that it is only a question of time before missiles are used to down aircraft in the United States. For any responsible person or group, such as the members of Congress who received the warning letters, to ignore the threat of missiles falling into the hands of terrorists is contempt for the lives that would be lost. My three-page letter to member of Congress follows:

**From the desk of Rodney Stich**
**P.O. Box 5, Alamo, CA 94507; phone: 510-944-1930; FAX 510-295-1203**
**Author of *DEFRAUDING AMERICA-A Pattern of Related Scandals* and *UNFRIENDLY SKIES-History of Corruption and Air Tragedies***

October 20, 1995

Senator Arlen Specter
United States Senate
Washington, DC 20510 Certified: P 427 892 268

Ref: Refusal by CIA and Justice Department officials to accept the "gift" of 30-40 Stinger missiles, suggesting a hidden agenda, with possible catastrophic consequences in shooting down commercial airliners.

Dear Senator Specter:

My sources in the intelligence community have recently given me details of efforts by Afghani rebels to turn over to the United States, without charge, 30 to 40 Stinger missiles (SAM), with a possibility of an additional 100 missiles thereafter. Incredibly, this offer was *rejected* by Justice Department and Central Intelligence Agency officials. There is a strong probability that one or more of these rejected missiles will be used to shoot down commercial airliners. If this occurs, not only will the carnage be horrendous, but it will inflict severe financial havoc upon the aviation industry and upon air travel. The following is a brief description of what has transpired:

**Synopsis of CIA and Justice Department Tactics Insuring That the SAM Missiles Will Be Available to Terrorists**

Recent information provided to me by one or more of my many contacts in the CIA community describes the dates, places, and people involved in offering the missiles to the United States, and the rejection of this offer. These sources provided me with precise details of the negotiations to give the missiles to the United States, the agreement by Afghan rebel leader, General Rashid Dostom, and a CIA attorney.

CIA headquarters was initially made aware of the offer through a letter sent by a former CIA agent whom I have known for about five years, and who I consider very honorable and reliable. That letter went unanswered. The agent, concerned about the consequences of commercial airliners being shot down with these missiles, then contacted another CIA employee at CIA headquarters, who then tried to force a response from high CIA officials. This latest action forced CIA officials to finally respond.

Negotiations then commenced, which involved, among others, the former CIA agent who headed a major CIA proprietary in Hawaii; a CIA attorney in the Los Angeles area; an Afghani located in California; and an Afghani rebel general in Afghanistan (who had previously turned over 20 Stinger missiles to the United States).

The general agreed to turn over the missiles without cost to the United States, and simply requested the release of an Afghani being held in federal prison on a drug charge arising from a possible KGB setup. At the same time that the Afghan general was offering to give these missiles to the United States, these same missiles were being sought by terrorist groups who bid large amounts of money for them. One obvious possible use for these missiles in terrorist hands would be to shoot down commercial airlines.

Incredibly, CIA and Justice Department officials rejected the offer, insuring that the missiles would fall into the hands of terrorists, where some of them may be at this very moment.

The Afghani initially offered to give to the CIA 30 to 40 Stinger (following an earlier return of 20 Stinger missiles), with a possibility that 100 more would be delivered thereafter. The CIA and Justice Department requested serial numbers for several of the missiles to determine that the missiles were actually available. These serial numbers[1] were then provided, and the numbers were confirmed by U.S. authorities as authentic.

After telephone contact was made with this Afghan general (General Dostom), a written agreement was signed by a Los Angeles area CIA attorney, the Afghani in California, and the former CIA agent who the Afghans were using to insure that the CIA and Justice Department kept their word.

**Knowledge of corrupt CIA and Justice Department activities**

My prior experience as a federal and then a private investigator, and a confidant to many former CIA and other deep-cover people seeking to expose government corruption, has enabled me to recognize the corrupt conduct of these two government agencies. I strongly feel that this rejection indicates a secret agenda that could inflict additional great harm upon America. This conduct would be compatible with the corrupt activities and harm that I have detailed and documented during the past 30 years of attempts to expose the activities of corrupt government officials and employees.

**POSSIBLE REASONS FOR REFUSING THE MISSILES**

There are several possible reasons for the CIA and Justice Department refusing to accept the missiles, and each of them is in character for these two groups. Two of these reasons are listed here:

* **Attempt to prevent exposure of an earlier CIA and Justice Department scandal.** The offer to provide the missiles at no charge went through a former CIA agent who was made the titular head of a large and covert CIA proprietary in Hawaii: Bishop, Baldwin, Rewald, Dillingham and Wong (BBRD&W). This covert operation that was based within the United States (Honolulu) had offices in 17 countries, and replaced another CIA operation and scandal known as Nugan Hand Bank with headquarters in Australia. After a Honolulu television station blew the cover on BBRD&W, officials in control of the CIA and Justice Department sought to cover for the CIA operation by fraudulently charging with criminal conduct the head of that CIA proprietary.

If the missiles had been accepted, it is possible that this sacrificed agent would be identified and the massive fraud involving the Hawaiian and Nugan Hand operations would then surface. (Exposure of this type of misconduct would reveal that the Justice Department's conduct at Ruby Ridge and Waco are only the tip of the iceberg.)

* **CIA need for continuing crises.** Another possibility for CIA and Justice Department rejection of the Stinger missiles is that the CIA *wants* the missiles to fall into terrorists' hands, and actually wants an airliner to be shot down. The shoot-down of a commercial airliner could then be used to justify the continuation of CIA activities. This scenario is not as bizarre as it sounds when a person understands the history of corrupt CIA and Justice Department activities and the great harm inflicted upon the United States through criminal activities. I describe these activities in books that I have written, *Defrauding America* and to a lesser extent, *Unfriendly Skies*.

**A Prior Air Tragedy Involved With CIA-DEA-Justice Department Misconduct**

**Pam Am 103.** Despite the coverup by the CIA and Justice Department (and by Congress and much of the mainstream media), substantial evidence indicates that the Pan Am 103 tragedy was made possible by CIA-DEA misconduct associated with a pattern of illicit drug smuggling into the United States. My deep-cover contacts, along with information obtained from other sources, indicates that the CIA and DEA had an established drug pipeline from Nicosia and Beirut into the United States using Pan Am aircraft. Pan Am's involvement started at Frankfort, Germany. Ironically, one of the same DEA agents involved in that drug pipeline, Michael T. Hurley, was used to retaliate against a witness who testified to Congress concerning the Justice Department's involvement in the Inslaw scandal. Justice Department officials retaliated against Michael Riconosciuto for testifying before Congress about the Justice Department's involvement in the Inslaw scandal. This is a routine criminal misuse of Justice Department offices and power. Officials prosecuted Lester Coleman, a former intelligence agency asset who blew the whistle on the CIA-DEA involvement in the Pan Am tragedy. Justice Department officials prosecuted Juval Aviv in retaliation for uncovering evidence showing CIA-DEA involvement in that tragedy. (I have a long list of others who were fraudulently prosecuted to silence them, including the long persecution of me in retaliation for exposing these crimes against America.)

[1] The Stinger missiles serial numbers provided by the Afghans included the following: Lot Nos. GDP 84D 001-320 362956; GDP 84J 001-320 363602; GDP 86G 001-387 369587; GDP 84G 001-320 363387.

**Pattern Of Congressional and Media Coverup**

None of the corrupt government activities that I identify could continue without the criminal coverup by members of Congress and by most of the U.S. mainstream media. I repeatedly offered to provide evidence to you and other members of Congress (and the media) of hard-core criminal activities involving federal officials, and the only response was silence (i.e., misprision of felonies, coverup, obstruction of justice). This same misprision of felonies has put many citizens in prison (Title 18 USC § 4), even though they were less guilty than government officials, members of Congress, and the media, who have a greater responsibility to report these crimes.

On the surface, although very serious, this missile matter does not appear to have the subversive and criminal nature of other criminal conduct that I exposed. However, it demands a full, open, congressional investigation.

Fortunately for everyone involved in these criminal activities, the mainstream media has kept the lid on the scandals, and most Americans are too preoccupied with trivia, and totally unwilling to meet their responsibilities under our form of government.

**Vested Interest In Continuing the Coverup**

Based upon 30 years of experience in attempting to expose hard-core government corruption, starting while I was a federal investigator, it would be my expectation that you will cover up this matter. For many years, and especially during the past five years, I have made you aware of criminal activities[3] involving government employees and officials, including corrupt officials within the Central Intelligence Agency, the Justice Department, and crooked judges. Each of you therefore have a vested interest in preventing the American people from learning about these criminal activities and what has been done to the American people.

But there is the possibility that despite the media coverup, and the public's incredible illiteracy about government misconduct, that a small percentage of the American people will learn about it and demand justice. If one or more commercial aircraft are blown out of the sky, your prior knowledge will be publicized. So you have a dilemma as to what to do with this information. You certainly can't meet your responsibilities by turning this information over to the same Justice Department that is corruptly involved with the various criminal activities that I brought to your attention.

Sincerely,

Rodney Stich

cc: Broadcast and print media.
Every member of the Senate and House intelligence Committees via identical letter.

[3] The criminal activities that Stich initially discovered while a federal investigator included: (a) widespread and deeply entrenched pattern of CIA and DEA drug smuggling into the United States, aided and abetted by persons in employed by Customs, Justice Department, and other government agencies and branches; (b) converting federal bankruptcy courts into criminal enterprises through looting of assets by a conspiracy consisting of federal judges, trustees, covert Justice Department and CIA law firms; (c) CIA involvement in looting U.S. financial institutions, including the savings and loans; (d) CIA scheme known as "October Surprise," and its coverup; (e) Inslaw corruption involving Justice Department personnel and federal judges; (f) Operation Mount Rushmore, a CIA/Mossad scheme to assassinate presidential candidate Bill Clinton in San Francisco; (g) criminal coverup and obstruction of justice by Justice Department personnel, federal judges, and others, of each of these and other crimes; (h) felony persecution of informants, whistleblowers, and protesting victims by federal judges and prosecutors; (i) involvement of California judges in helping to carry out several of these schemes, including a ten-year pattern of judicial acts against Rodney Stich while violating blocks of California and federal statutes and constitutional protections, making them co-conspirators.

Law Office of
John J. Reed

John J. Reed
Attorney at Law

Douglas P. Linn
Legal Administrator

Mr. Mohammed Akbar
(27666-053)
FCI, Terminal Island, CA.

September 22, 1994

Re: Agreement with U.S. Government

Dear Mohammed Bey:

This is a letter to memorialize the Agreement I have made, in your name and on your behalf, with officials of the Government of the United States.

The Agreement is as follows:

> MOHAMMED AKBAR will arrange to have two (2) complete and functional STINGER MISSILES delivered to an agent of the United States Government, in his name and on his behalf.
>
> Immediately upon the delivery of the two (2) STINGER MISSILES to an agent of the United States Government, that agent will notify the appropriate officials in Washington, D.C. who will order the immediate release of Mohammed Akbar for immediate return to his homeland.
>
> After his arrival in his homeland, MOHAMMED AKBAR agrees, and pledges his word, to [make every effort] effect the delivery to an agent of the United States Government an additional eighteen (18) complete and functional STINGER MISSILES.

Akbar

I, JOHN J. REED, Attorney for MOHAMMED AKBAR, declare and affirm that I have made the Agreement set forth above on behalf of MOHAMMED AKBAR and that I have been assured by officials of the United States Government that they will abide by the Agreement set forth above.

Signed and Accepted: Akbar
MOHAMMED AKBAR

Witnessed by:
RON REWALD

Signed,
John J. Reed
JOHN J. REED

One World Trade Center Suite 1850 • Long Beach, California 90831-1850 • (310) 432-4490 Fax (310) 432-5409
Marina Office — (310) 436-9847 Fax (310) 436-9847

**TWA FLIGHT 800, *DEJA VU***

Before a year passed, a surface-to-air missile shot down a huge Boeing 747, TWA Flight 800, off the coast of Long Island, shortly after it had taken off from New York's JFK Airport. Evidence of the missile came from the reports of over 150 people who saw the missile trail, many of them professionals, including two pilots on an Air National Guard helicopter as they were taking off from Francis S. Gabreski Airport on Long Island. As the helicopter lifted off from runway 24, heading southwest, and started a left turn to the south, they noticed through their windshield the fast-moving missile streak and then a violent explosion.

To understand what these professional pilots saw, picture the scene out of their windshield at night, a totally black environment, suddenly pierced by the streak of a missile going from the surface toward TWA Flight 800. This evidence alone far exceeds evidence that the NTSB has used in the past to determine the most probable cause of an airline crash.

Elsewhere on Long Island, over 150 people, many of them professionals, saw the missile-streak in the sky. The statement of those witnesses far exceeds the evidence available to the National Transportation Safety Board (NTSB) in the past when it made a determination of the most probable cause of an airline crash. Linda Kabot was taking pictures at a fund-raiser dinner for Mayor Vince Cannuscio at East Quogue Beach on Long Island. During the picture taking, a blast was heard nearby, but nothing was thought of it. Unknown to Kabot at that time, her camera recorded an object streaking through the sky toward where TWA was flying.

Investigators examining the wreckage immediately after it was removed from the ocean found and reported traces of explosive residue. But when these parts were examined by the FBI crime laboratory in Washington, the FBI report said there were no explosive traces. At about this same time, the media reported the complaints by FBI lab technicians that the FBI lab often falsified evidence to support Justice Department prosecutors. Covering up for evidence would fit into that pattern.

**DANGER IF A MISSILE IS OFFICIALLY RECOGNIZED AS THE CAUSE OF DOWNING OF TWA FLIGHT 800**

The conduct of Justice Department and CIA officials described in my letters to Congress threatened to expose their conduct in making it possible for terrorists to obtain the SAM missiles. Questions could be asked as to why they acted to make missiles available to terrorists, and members of Congress could suffer from disclosing their cavalier attitude in response to my urgent letters. In addition, the question arose as to where and when would a U.S. airliner be shot down by the rejected missiles.

**UNPRECEDENTED MISINFORMATION AND COVERUP**

Never in the history of aviation had there been as much government misinformation about an air disaster as with TWA Flight 800. Justice Department and NTSB officials were fabricating implausible theories while refusing to give credit to the heavy evidence of a missile strike. In my book, *Unfriendly Skies*, I detailed many instances of NTSB coverups.

An anonymous letter appearing in the October 1996 *California Sun* (Ojai, California) described the experience of a California couple who were vacationing on Long Island at the time of the blast and who saw the missile trail. He made a report to the FBI about the missile trail, and received a reaction many others received. His letter stated in part:

*They questioned us in separate rooms and made us feel like criminals. They said that what we must have seen was a shooting star or some fireworks being shot from a boat. I told them that it was not anything like that at all. I said that it was definitely a flare type rocket heading toward the aircraft, then it exploded. It was then suggested that we did not see anything at all and that we were going along with what other people said they saw. Just for the excitement of it. I told them, "No way, I know what I saw...They scared the hell out of us."*

**MORE INTRIGUE**

I appeared as a guest on the Los Angeles radio show hosted by Peter Ford, the son of Glenn Ford and actress Eleanor Powell (December 4, 1996), along with Jeremy Crocker, a person who allegedly was a former Department of Defense (DOD) employee. Crocker had conducted considerable research into the downing of TWA Flight 800, interviewing people in different parts of the United States. Shortly after the show, Crocker disappeared and at the time of this writing, he had not been found.

**FBI THREATS TO REMAIN QUIET**

Numerous reports surfaced of FBI agents warning people to remain quiet about their knowledge of a missile sighting. I was also warned. A copy of my October 20, 1995 letter to Senator Arlen Specter, warning of a missile attack on U.S. aircraft, was put on the Internet by unknown people, and this became known to the FBI. On July 24, 1996 two FBI agents contacted me and wanted to meet with me, which I did. But they didn't want any information on the rejected missiles. Their only interest was to warn me to remain quiet about what I knew. In a phone call that took place about a hour after we met, Special Agent V. Stewart Daley warned me to remain quiet about the missiles. I told him that I encountered FBI coverup for the past 30 years, starting while I was a federal investigator, and I was not about to remain silent now.

To make a record of the FBI's meeting, their total indifference to any information about the rejected missiles, and their threats warning me to remain quiet, I sent a July 30, 1996 letter to the FBI describing the events as I saw them. A copy of my letter to the FBI follows.

**From the desk of Rodney Stich** ()
**P.O. Box 5, Alamo, CA 94507; phone: 510-944-1930; FAX 510-295-1203**
**Author of *DEFRAUDING AMERICA–Dirty Secrets of the CIA & other Government Operations***
***DISAVOW–A CIA Saga of Betrayal***
***UNFRIENDLY SKIES–History of Corruption and Air Tragedies***
*Member*
*Association Former Intelligence Officers (AFIO)*
*International Society of Air Safety Investigators (ISASI)*
*Former FAA air safety investigator*
*Association of National Security Alumni*
*Lawyers Pilots Bar Association (LPBA)*
*Former airline captain and Navy pilot*

July 30, 1996

V. Stewart Daley, Special Agent
Federal Bureau of Investigation
1850 Gateway Blvd, Suite 1010
Concord, CA 94520

Certified: P427 892054

Ref: TWA Flight 800; SAM missiles offered to US and rejected; and July 24, 1996 meeting with FBI agent.

Dear Sir:

The purpose of this letter is to make a record relating to what transpired during a meeting and subsequent telephone conversation between myself and FBI agent V. Stewart Daley on July 24, 1996:

* The San Francisco FBI office contacted me on July 24, 1996, arranging for a meeting that afternoon between myself and FBI agent V. Stewart Daley, which did occur, outside of the Rossmoor Diner in Walnut Creek, California.

* The purpose of the visit by FBI agent Daley was supposed to discuss the letters that I had sent to members of the House and Senate intelligence committees on October 20, 1995, and a copy of those letters to FBI agent Jim Kallstrom on July 21, 1996. Kallstrom is the lead FBI agent in charge of the criminal investigation involving TWA Flight 800.

* The intent of my October 20, 1995 letter to those members of Congress was to alert them to a very serious matter, requiring their immediate attention, that would otherwise probably culminate in one or more missiles being acquired and used by terrorists to shoot down commercial airliners.

* Prior to my sending that October 20th letter, one of my many CIA sources had expressed concern to me in October 1995 that surface-to-air missiles (SAM) would be made available to terrorists by the inexplicable actions of Justice Department and CIA personnel. My source described his participation in the efforts of Afghan rebels who were offering 40 to 60 missiles to the United States, through the Justice Department and Central Intelligence Agency, at no cost to the United States. They also advised that an additional 100 missiles may also be made available. The only consideration attached to this gift of SAM missiles was that a young son of one of the rebel leaders be released from federal prison at Terminal Island. He had been convicted of a drug-related offense.

* It was known to these Justice Department and CIA employees that terrorists were offering $100,000 each for several of these missiles. Knowing this, and knowing that the missiles would probably be used to shoot down commercial airlines, Justice Department and CIA officials refused to accept them. This CIA source recognized this probable consequence of the rejection, and conveyed his concern to me. He then provided me with sufficient documentation to establish the truth of his statements, including copies of letters to and from the Justice Department, serial numbers of some of the missiles, and other

data.

**Informing Congress of Impending Shootdown of Passenger Airliners**

* I then informed each member of the House and Senate intelligence committees through that October 20, 1995 letter, making them aware of the probable shoot-down of a passenger airliner if they did not immediately intervene and seek to halt the sale of these missiles to terrorist groups. I made it clear that I had documents to support these statements and could provide them with other information. I urged them to immediately contact me for further information.

* Despite the horror that would probably follow failure to take immediate actions, not a single member of Congress contacted me.

* My credibility could not have been an issue. Those letters provided information on my background, including years as a former federal investigator in the Federal Aviation Administration, a member of sophisticated intelligence and aviation groups, a writer of highly technical, detailed, and documented books, and long experience in these areas.

**Standard FBI Coverup and Obstruction of Justice**

* During this July 24, 1996 meeting with FBI agent V. Stewart Daley, I described in general terms the nature of the missile problem and the possibility that TWA Flight 800 was shot down by a missile, and that other passenger airliners would probably be shot down by the missiles made available to terrorist groups by the conduct of these Justice Department and CIA officials. I also made it clear that I was using this meeting to make the FBI aware of other criminal activities that I had discovered. These were major criminal activities inflicting death upon many people, and were inflicting great harm upon national security. These criminal activities included, among many others:

* **Pattern of FAA corruption related to a series of airline crashes and deaths.** I detailed and documented these activities in the third edition of *Unfriendly Skies*, the second edition of *Defrauding America*, in thousands of pages of testimony and evidence placed into a FAA hearing that I forced upon the agency. I charged the existence of deeply entrenched FAA corruption (and corruption at a major airline) associated with a series of fatal airline crashes that I and other federal inspectors had uncovered as part of our official duties. These corrupt activities were made known to high level management in the FAA, NTSB, Justice Department, and to members of Congress, some of whom had already been advised of these problems by other FAA inspectors. They all covered up, making possible the continuation of the FAA culture, the air safety misconduct, and the resulting crashes. This mindset continues, making possible many of the airline crashes that continue to occur.

* **Pattern of corruption implicating high-level federal officials relating to long-standing drug trafficking into the United States**, This would include evidence that I have accumulated for the past seven years (and longer) from my many CIA and other deep-cover sources. Heavily involved in this coverup (and prosecution of whistleblowers) are Justice Department employees and federal judges, as described in part in my two detailed and documented books.

* **Massive corruption in the Ninth Circuit bankruptcy courts,** looting the assets of people who exercise the statutory protections of Chapter 11, unaware of the enormous fraud involving judges, US and private trustees, law firms, and attorneys.

* **Justice Department coverup of the CIA-DEA drug pipeline, misusing Pan Am aircraft, making possible the placement of the bomb on Pan Am Flight 103,** and the fraudulent prosecution of people who seek to expose the truth. There is similarity between Justice Department coverup between the two TWA mishaps in the New York City area and the Lockerbie disaster.This coverup of the CIA-DEA drug pipeline has protected the terrorists who actually placed the bomb on board Pan Am 103. It was the illicit activities of CIA and DEA personnel that made possible the placement of the bomb on board the aircraft, making these US employees partly responsible

for the bombing and deaths.

**Coverup of Tragedy-Related Corruption Combined With Threats[1] To Remain Quiet**

* Shortly after I returned home from that meeting, FBI agent Daley contacted me by phone, and warned me not to repeat any of the information that I had provided to him. He had no interest in any of these criminal matters, despite the gravity of the matters and their harmful effects upon national security.

* No interest was shown in any of these areas by FBI agent V. Stewart Daley, including specifics on the missiles.

* I reminded him that he had a duty under Title 18 USC Section 4, and other criminal statutes, to arrange for me and my sources to give evidence to a proper investigative body. He repeated his warning that I keep this information to myself.

**How the American Public Has Paid For These Crimes and the Coverup**

* **TWA Flight 800. If** this flight was actually shot down by a missile, the matter of Justice Department and CIA rejection of the SAM missiles is of grave concern to the United States. What agenda do these officials have that are subjecting the United States to such tragic consequences? And if TWA Flight 800 was **not** shot down by a missile, when will the missiles, in the hands of terrorists, be used to shoot down a passenger airliner?

* Further complicating this matter is the refusal by any of the two dozen members of the Senate and House intelligence committees to obtain from me the confidential data that I have acquired after they received that urgent letter. They also appeared willing to sacrifice the lives that would very probably be lost through missile attacks.

* **Coverup behind the downing of the TWA Flight over Staten Island many years ago, killing everyone on board.** A prior tragedy befalling TWA, within miles of the downing of TWA Flight 800, was associated with criminal misconduct on the part of FAA management (and others), and occurred on a program for which I held federal air safety responsibilities shortly after that tragedy occurred (the world's worst at that time). Evidence of this relationship (and of the criminal misconduct in other airline crashes occurring in my area of federal air safety responsibilities) is found in the records of an unprecedented four-month-long FAA safety hearing (E20GFAA) that I forced upon the FAA while holding federal authority to make such determinations. During that hearing I acted as a prosecutor, producing official documents and testimony to support my charges. FAA legal staff and the top aide to the FAA administrator engaged in coverup during the hearing, in perjury, subornation of perjury, that continued the FAA culture, the serious air safety and criminal violations, which then caused or made possible other crashes in my area of air safety responsibilities.

* This hearing was preceded by several air disasters on programs for which I had federal air safety responsibilities, followed by identical air disasters (plus two air disasters occurring during the hearing).

---

[1] **It is a criminal offense to threaten any person who seeks to report federal crimes.**

Title 18 U.S.C. § 1513. **Retaliating against a witness, victim, or an informant**. (a) Whoever knowingly engages in any conduct and thereby causes bodily injury to another person or damages the tangible property of another person, or threatens to do so, with intent to retaliate against any person for – (1) the attendance of a witness or party at an official proceeding, or any testimony given or any record, document, or other object produced by a witness in an official proceeding; or (2) any information relating to the commission or possible commission of a Federal offense ...

Title 18 U.S.C. § 1512. **Tampering with a witness/informant**. Applies to anyone who (b) uses intimidation or physical force, or threatens another person, or attempts to do so, or engages in misleading conduct toward another person, with intent to (1) influence, delay or prevent that person's testimony in an official proceeding; (2) cause or induce any person to (A) withhold testimony; or withhold a record from an official proceeding; (B) alter, destroy, mutilate, or conceal an object with intent to impart the object's integrity or availability for use in an official proceeding; (3) hinder, delay, or prevent the communication to a ... judge of the United States of information relating to the commission or possible commission of a Federal offense, ...

**§ 1512. Tampering with a witness, victim, or an informant –**

(b) Whoever knowingly uses intimidation or physical force, or threatens another person, or attempts to do so, or engages in misleading conduct toward another person, with intent to –

(1) influence, delay or prevent the testimony of any person in an official proceeding:

shall be fined ... or imprisoned ... or both. [1988 amended reading]

3

These activities were accompanied by coverup involving officials in various divisions of the U.S. Department of Justice, members of Congress, and others. They all played a role in the deaths associated with the specific air disasters.

* **Harm to national security**, to US institutions, and the deaths of many people, and establishing a corrupt culture in government institutions, especially the FAA, Justice Department, and Central Intelligence Agency.

**FBI Reaction To This Pattern of Tragedy Related Criminality**

Despite the gravity of the matters brought to your attention, and to other divisions of the Justice Department by a former federal investigator, no attempt was made to receive my evidence and testimony, and that of my sources.

Your telephone conversation consisted of a warning for me to remain quiet. This coincides with prior actions and inactions of Justice Department officials. It is of interest that a federal criminal statute[2] provides for any citizen to report a federal crime to a federal judge (or other federal tribunal), and if a citizen fails to promptly do this, he has committed a criminal act. It should be of great concern to Americans that every attempt to report these criminal acts to federal judges has been judicially blocked. These judges, with the assistance of Justice Department employees, have prevented me from making such reports. They have rendered orders barring me from federal court access, which blocks me from making the reports that they are required to receive under Title 18 USC Section 4. The two books, *Unfriendly Skies* and *Defrauding America* detail and document these and many other examples of misconduct involving federal employees.

Sincerely,

Rodney Stich

cc: Janet Reno, U.S. Attorney General, Constitution Avenue and 10th Street, NW, Washington, DC 20530. FAX 202-514-4371.
Internet; Senate Intelligence Committee FAX 202-224-1772; House Intelligence Committee FAX 202-225-1991.

[2] **Title 18 U.S.C. § 4 (misprision of felony).** "Whoever, having knowledge of the actual commission of a felony cognizable by a court of the United States, conceals and does not as soon as possible make known the same to some judge or other person in civil or military authority under the United States, shall be fined not more than $500 or imprisoned not more than three years, or both."

After TWA Flight 800 was downed, I made the media aware of the role played by Justice Department and CIA officials that made possible the acquisition of surface-to-air missiles by terrorists by rejecting the "gift" of the missiles. Virtually none of the major mainstream media responded, insuring that this relationship would be kept from the public.

As the first anniversary of the downing of TWA Flight 800 approached, the *EXTRA* television program on the CBS network spent half a day filming me and my letter to members of Congress warning of missile attacks upon commercial aircraft. I had already been cancelled at the last moment on four prior network shows during the past year (including CNN, CBS, CBN) and I thought my appearance would probably be scratched in this case also. I was right.

What may have assisted in this cancellation was turning over one of the documents relating to the Afghan-Justice Department missile negotiations that had the name of the CIA's attorney on it. By contacting this attorney, pressure could be expected to be applied to the *EXTRA* television producers to remove me from the program. And that, of course, was done.

I wrote a letter to producer Jackie Pratt at the Glendale, California studios, reminding them that by covering up for the rejected missile matter that they were keeping the public from learning about missiles that might have been involved in shooting down TWA Flight 800 and were in terrorist hands for possible shooting down of airliners in the future.

Ronald Rewald

**From the desk of Rodney Stich**

**P.O. Box 5, Alamo, CA 94507; phone: 510-944-1930; FAX 510-295-1203**

**Author of *DEFRAUDING AMERICA–Dirty Secrets of the CIA & other Government Operations***
***DISAVOW–A CIA Saga of CIA Betrayal***
***UNFRIENDLY SKIES–History of Corruption and Air Tragedies***

*Member*
*Association Former Intelligence Officers (AFIO)*
*Association of National Security Alumni*
*International Society of Air Safety Investigators (ISASI)*
*Lawyers Pilots Bar Association (LPBA)*
*Former FAA air safety investigator*
*Former airline captain and Navy pilot*
*E-mail: stich@defraudingamerica.com* *Web sites: www.defraudingamerica.com; www.unfriendlyskies.com*
*Internet search engine: "Rodney Stich"*

July 22, 1997

Jackie Pratt, Producer
EXTRA Television Show
1840 Victory Blvd
Glendale, CA 91201

Ref: July 17, 1997 television show on TWA Flight 800

Dear Ms. Pratt:

This letter makes a record of events associated with the downing of TWA Flight 800, and will be especially appropriate when commercial aircraft in the future are destroyed by surface-to-air missiles. The highly sensitive matters that I brought to the attention of the Extra staff will probably play a role in subsequent missile attacks on aircraft. Here are the facts as we both know them:

* A camera crew from the Extra television program arrived at my home for filming on July 8, 1997. The filming crew spent about four hours filming:

  * My comments relating to TWA Flight 800, the pattern of "doctored" reports by the NTSB and FBI which I have documented over the years, starting while I was a federal investigator. My many years in aviation, especially as a professional air safety and accident investigator for the FAA, and knowledge I acquired from a close CIA source, makes my information especially valuable in understanding much of the truth about the TWA tragedy.

  * Documents that I had acquired from one of my former CIA sources who was directly involved in secret negotiations relating to SAM missiles being offered to the United States. These missiles were being simultaneously sought by terrorists, who would acquire some or all of them if the "gift" of missiles was rejected by CIA and Justice Department officials involved in the negotiations. The documents consisted of letters by one of the attorneys involved in the negotiations, and dozens of pages of memorandums describing the negotiations in detail.

  * Urgent letters sent to members of Congress before the downing of TWA Flight 800, relating to missile attacks upon commercial aircraft, associated with the rejected SAM missiles. These letters stated facts, warned of impending missile attacks upon commercial aircraft, and urged the congressional recipients to immediately contact me and my CIA source for further information so as to block the transfer of SAM missiles to terrorists.

  The *significance* of this material is as follows:

* The material shows that CIA and Justice Department officials knowingly acted in such a way that the missiles being offered as a "gift" to the United States would be acquired by terrorists. The history of over two dozen commercial aircraft being shot down by SAM missiles

in the last two decades made it clear that other commercial aircraft would be downed by the rejected missiles, and that hundreds of people could be expected to perish.

* This scenario explains the most probable reason for the unprecedented deliberate NTSB-FBI disinformation about the downing of TWA Flight 800 and the refusal to recognize the validity of the many missile-sighting reports.

* Realizing that the filming of these matters by the Extra producers would help to inform the public of the serious matter relating to the rejected missiles, how the rejected-missile scenario placed missiles into the hands of terrorists, and the threat faced by air travelers from these missiles, I was pleased to have this opportunity to help the Extra film crew. I even rented an aircraft that the film crew then used to give a better understanding to the program viewers of what the two military helicopter pilots saw when they spotted the missile ascending from the surface to where it then exploded upon reaching TWA.

* I realized that pressure would be applied by Justice Department and CIA personnel to stop your airing of this information, and have repeatedly encountered this media reaction. The consequences in the past of such a coverup resulted in continuing the problems that played key roles in subsequent crashes, and I presume this coverup reaction will continue with the subject of missile attacks upon airliners.

* After completing the filming, the film crew advised that the information and material that I provided was very good and that it would be included in the Extra television program appearing at the anniversary of the shooting down of TWA Flight 800.

* Extra had an opportunity to provide a very important public service and which could focus on the problems resulting in aircraft missile attacks. Obviously, this is a life-or-death matter and as time goes on, I'm sure the Extra personnel will see the consequences of keeping this information from the public. I have detailed and documented many and continuing consequences from media coverup in my books, *Unfriendly Skies* and *Defrauding America*.

* When the next missile strikes a commercial aircraft, remember the role that this coverup may have played that made the tragedy possible.

Sincerely,

Rodney Stich

# INSLAW AND CRIMES AT JUSTICE

Another of the many scandals surrounding Justice Department officials was called the Inslaw affair, and provides additional examples of the criminal mindset of Justice Department officials and other government employees. It provides additional evidence of the criminal mindset by those in control of the highest law-enforcement agency of the United States.

Inslaw was a small computer programming company owned by William and Nancy Hamilton that was subjected to criminal activities and a conspiracy by high Justice Department officials (some of whom were later promoted to federal judges). By misusing the power of their office, these officials misappropriated, or aided and abetted, the theft of the PROMIS software from the small company.

## FORCING A SMALL COMPANY INTO BANKRUPTCY

The tactics used by Justice Department officials to steal the software forced the small company to seek protection in Chapter 11. Justice Department officials then misused the office of the U.S. Trustee (division of the Justice Department) to force the company into a Chapter 7 liquidation, at which time they would purchase the PROMIS software at pennies on the dollar.

In 1982, the U.S. Department of Justice signed a $10 million contract with Inslaw to install an enhanced version of software known as PROMIS in 42 U.S. attorney offices. The Inslaw company went heavily into debt, obtaining a loan to complete the contract. After the software was installed in the Justice Department and found to be satisfactory, and its value recognized for an upcoming half-billion-dollar government contract, Justice Department officials refused to pay Inslaw, knowing that it would force them into bankruptcy.

## STANDARD JUSTICE DEPARTMENT PROCEDURE

Once Inslaw filed Chapter 11 in the bankruptcy court, seeking time for paying its bills, Justice Department officials forced the company into a Chapter 7 liquidation through its U.S. Trustee division and control of the bankruptcy process.

As stated elsewhere in these pages, it is a standard practice for people in control of the CIA and other government agencies to target selected companies and force them into bankruptcy, and then have associates take over the assets.

Earl Brian, a close friend of Attorney General Edwin Meese, had a controlling interest in a software company seeking to obtain the government computer contract: Hadron Incorporated. The company was primarily owned by Earl Brian,[316] who served in the White House as chairman of a task force which reported to Attorney General Edwin Meese. Meese and his wife had a financial interest in Hadron.

Key Justice Department and White House people who were part of the scheme included the three U.S. attorney generals (Edwin Meese, William Barr, Richard Thornburgh), Earl Brian, and Deputy Attorney General D. Lowell Jensen, among others. Most were from California, and, except for Brian, were attorneys. Earl Brian and Edwin Meese were from California and in former Governor Ronald Reagan's administration. Brian wanted the Inslaw software, which would subsequently be sold to the Justice Department and other government agencies in a $500 million contract.

Brian expected to obtain the contract through his influence with Meese. The value of that stock, and the company's profits, would soar into the hundreds of millions of dollars upon obtaining the rights to Inslaw's Enhanced PROMIS software and the government contract.

Earlier, the chairman of Hadron, Dominic Laiti, attempted to purchase the PROMIS software from Inslaw, but Inslaw refused to sell. Laiti warned William Hamilton that Hadron was politically connected to Attorney General Meese, and, "We have ways of making you sell."

After this threat was made, Deputy Attorney General Lowell Jensen, another former California attorney, directly responsible for approving payment to Inslaw, refused to pay for the installed software. Unable to pay their employees and the bank loan, the Hamiltons sought refuge in Chapter 11.

In what was probably a *quid pro quo* for his cooperation in the scheme against Inslaw, Meese recommended to President Reagan that Jensen be appointed to a U.S. district judge position in San Francisco. Judge Jensen played key roles in the obstruction of justice when I reported these crimes to federal courts in the San Francisco area. He was one of several October Surprise and Inslaw participants who profited by their role in October Surprise, Inslaw, and other crimes against the United States.

Another federal official involved in the scheme against Inslaw was Edwin Thomas, assistant counsel to President Reagan, and a friend of Meese. Thomas loaned Meese's wife, Ursula, $15,000 in early 1981 to buy stock in Infotech (then operating under the name of Biotech Capital Corporation), and which was a division of Hadron Corporation. Thomas was working directly for Meese as assistant counsel to the President, and Earl Brian loaned him $100,000 in July 1981. Thomas, using his official White House position, made calls to the Small Business Administration to have the SBA approve a loan application to a Biotech subsidiary owned by Thomas which was involved in computer software.

316 Brian owned United Press International.

Biotech hoped to obtain Justice Department contracts worth an estimated half billion dollars, using the stolen Inslaw software. The insiders to this scheme anticipated they would be multi-millionaires. But the scheme required that Hadron obtain the enhanced PROMIS software from Inslaw, which the owners, William and Nancy Hamilton, refused to sell.

Justice Department officials pressured the IRS to force Inslaw into a Chapter 7 liquidation after Inslaw filed Chapter 11, hoping to have Hadron acquire the PROMIS software at pennies on the dollar. This software would then be offered to the government for the estimated half billion dollars in contracts. The same Justice Department officials who engaged in the criminal conspiracy would then recommend that the company, in which they had an interest, be awarded the software contract.

In an unusual refusal to cooperate with Justice Department dirty tricks, Chapter 11 Judge George F. Bason blocked that attempt.

**SELLING THE STOLEN SOFTWARE**

After receiving the leased software from Inslaw, Justice Department officials gave the software to Earl Brian,[317] who then used CIA contract agent Michael Riconosciuto to alter the program at the Wackenhut-operated facilities on the Cabazon Indian Reservation near Indio, California. Prior to selling the software to foreign countries for use by their intelligence and military agencies the software was altered to permit the CIA to secretly tap into it and extract information.

Riconosciuto made modifications to the software in order to meet the requirements of the Canadian Mounties and the Canadian Security and Intelligence Service. He reported that it was Brian who sold Inslaw's software to the Canadians.

Riconosciuto had played a role in the 1980 October Surprise scheme. He and Earl Brian played a part in the wire transfer of $40 million in bribe money given to the Iranians in Paris during the October 19, 1980, Paris meetings.

Another CIA operative knowing of the sale of the PROMIS software was Gunther Russbacher, who carried the software to Australia and provided me with a sworn statement to that effect which I, in turn, provided to the Hamiltons and their attorney, Elliott Richardson.

Ari Ben-Menashe, a former member of Israel's Mossad, told the Hamiltons that he had obtained the enhanced PROMIS software from Earl Brian and Robert McFarlane (who at that time was Reagan's national security adviser). Documents and CIA statements made to me indicated that McFarlane played a role in the 1980 October Surprise scheme and the following Iran-Contra scandal.

Ben-Menashe said that he was at a meeting in Israel when Brian said he owned the PROMIS software and was trying to sell it to Israel. Ben-Menashe stated that Chilean arms dealer Carlos Cardoen told him that "he brokered a deal between Brian and a representative of the Iraqi military intelligence for the use of PROMIS." Iranian arms dealer Richard Babayan stated in a 1987 affidavit that a member of Iraqi intelligence told him Iraq had acquired PROMIS

317 *The Financial Post* August 19, 1991, issue linked Brian to covert operations with the United States and Israeli intelligence communities. He was reportedly involved in the sale of weapons to Iran in the 1980s. He reportedly worked with the CIA. He was reportedly implicated in the many scandals involving Ed Meese.

from Brian on the recommendation of the Libyan government.

**SALE OF STOLEN SOFTWARE TO CANADA**

The Hamiltons, who owned the Inslaw Company, discovered the unlawful sale of their software by Justice Department officials and Earl Brian to Canada when Canadian government personnel inadvertently contacted Inslaw for information on the software which had been sold to them. The Hamiltons visited the Canadian offices that had requested information, learning that numerous Canadian offices were using it. After the Hamiltons reported that they had not sold the software to any Canadian offices, and that they were not authorized to use it, Canadian officials falsely claimed that none of their offices were using the software. Canadian authorities covered up for the theft and protected Justice Department officials. Brian and others who worked with him sold the stolen Inslaw software throughout the world for tens of millions of dollars. Crime does pay.

**CIVIL SUIT AGAINST JUSTICE DEPARTMENT OFFICIALS**

While in Chapter 11 proceedings, the Inslaw Company filed a civil action[318] against the U.S. Department of Justice and the officials who stole the PROMIS software. In court filings, Inslaw and its attorney, former U.S. Attorney General Elliott Richardson, claimed that Inslaw was a victim of a conspiracy by Meese and his friends, who capitalized on their government positions for the purpose of stealing the software and converting it into private use and personal gains.

Justice Department officials sought to block this lawsuit by misusing the power of the Justice Department. The first attorney representing Inslaw against the Justice Department was Leigh Ratiner in the Washington law firm of Dickstein and Shapiro. As Ratiner learned, Justice Department officials put pressure upon his bosses, causing his dismissal from the law firm. However, they paid him the fabulous sum of $120,000 yearly for the next five years on the condition that he not practice law during that time.

In this way the attorney could not represent the Inslaw firm in its lawsuit against Justice Department officials and the Hamiltons, now without funds, would have great difficulty finding a law firm that would take their case. This inability to obtain legal counsel is made worse by attorneys' refusal to take cases against the Justice Department when that powerful agency can retaliate.

Ari Ben-Menashe saw a cable from Israel's Joint Committee[319] to the United States requesting that $600,000 be transferred from the CIA-Israeli slush fund to Hadron. The cable stated that the money would be transferred to the law firm of Dickstein and Shapiro as compensation to remove Inslaw's attorney, Ratiner, from the case. Talk about conspiracies!

**TWO FEDERAL JUDGES RULED AGAINST JUSTICE DEPARTMENT**

At the end of the civil trial against the Justice Department in the Inslaw case, Judge George Bason ruled in favor of Inslaw and awarded Inslaw $6.8 million. Bason lambasted Justice Department officials, charging that they were guilty of deceit, theft and trickery. Justice Department officials appealed the judgment

318 *Inslaw v. Thornburgh*, CIV. 89-3443.

319 Israel's Joint Committee was formed to deal with Iran-Israel relations.

to the U.S. district court,[320] where U.S. District Judge William Bryant upheld the decision, praising Judge Bason's "attention to detail and mastery of evidence."

That decision was then appealed to the U.S. Court of Appeals in Washington, D.C., where several of the October Surprise participants had received federal judgeships from the Reagan-Bush administration. The decision was reversed, claiming that the lower court judges had no jurisdiction to render such a decision.

A practice in federal courts, little understood by the public, is to appoint U.S. attorneys to the federal judiciary who are loyal to the Justice Department's controlling clique. These insiders then act to protect the dirty business in the Justice Department, the CIA, or any other federal agency. Judges who don't cooperate are sometimes charged with criminal offenses by Justice Department prosecutors for some real or fabricated minor offenses and removed from the bench.

**JUSTICE DEPARTMENT RETALIATION**

Bankruptcy court judges must be reappointed every fourteen years, and that reappointment was denied to Judge Bason after the unfavorable ruling against Justice Department officials. Justice Department officials then recommended for appointment to Bason's former position the Justice Department attorney who defended against the Inslaw litigation. Judge Bason later testified to a Congressional committee: "I have come to believe that my non-reappointment as bankruptcy judge was the result of improper influence from within the Justice Department which the current appointment process failed to prevent."

It is normal for over 90 percent of the incumbent bankruptcy judges who seek reappointment to be reappointed. Bason's replacement had no bankruptcy experience but could be counted upon to carry out Justice Department wishes. It is also normal to appoint to key judicial positions attorneys who can be controlled.

**ALTERING TESTIMONY, A CRIME**

In March 1987, Justice Department officials pressured an important witness, a federal judge, to change testimony that he had previously given under oath in the Inslaw matter. A Justice Department attorney also was pressured to recant his previous testimony, given under oath, which was favorable to Inslaw. For them to recant their earlier testimony given under oath, and now testify the opposite, meant that they lied the first time they testified, thereby committing perjury. Justice Department prosecutors should have filed perjury charges. Actually, Justice Department attorneys were suborning the perjured testimony, compounding the crime of the prior or subsequent perjury.

**YEARS OF SELECTED MEDIA EXPOSURE**

Most of the mainstream media kept the lid on this scandal. But articles did appear, and an article in *The American Lawyer* (December 1987) referred to the Inslaw affair:

> *No sooner had the Justice Department awarded Inslaw a $10 million contract than things began to go wrong. Hamilton couldn't understand why. Suddenly Inslaw's finances were in shambles. By February 7, 1985,*

320 The United States Court of Appeals in Washington vacated the judgment against the Justice Department, ruling that the bankruptcy courts lacked jurisdiction over the matter.

*the government had withheld payments on $1.77 million in costs and fees. Inslaw, the market leader, filed for bankruptcy. Hamilton says he was mystified. How could everything he had built fall apart so fast—and with no explanation? [Hamilton said] "I think, in a perverse way, I was...slow to catch on. I feel silly. I wasn't paranoid enough."*

*A story of government conniving and manipulation...and in Elliot Richardson's words, "complemented and allowed to run its course by ill will at the higher level," meaning former Deputy Attorney General Jensen. [Now a federal judge at San Francisco.]*

**SERIES OF KILLINGS PROTECTED FEDERAL OFFICIALS**

Following a pattern, many people who posed a threat to U.S. officials because of what they knew turned up dead. The most publicized killing related to Inslaw was free-lance reporter and author Danny Casolaro, who was investigating criminal activities implicating Justice Department officials and writing a book on the subject. Casolaro was killed at the Sheraton Inn in Martinsburg, West Virginia on August 10, 1991.

A CIA operative had met Casolaro earlier at a restaurant, advising Casolaro that he knew of a person who could give Casolaro additional evidence proving the link between Justice Department officials and the Inslaw scandal.

Shortly before his death, Casolaro met with a former CIA Special Forces operative who had worked for a company involved in the Inslaw case and who was also a good friend of Justice Department official Peter Videnieks. Videnieks was the Justice Department official who later threatened Riconosciuto if he testified before a Congressional committee in the Inslaw investigation or gave affidavits into the Inslaw civil action. The CIA operative set up a meeting between Casolaro and Videnieks, and it is at this meeting that Casolaro was killed.

Casolaro traveled to Martinsburg, Virginia, about 40 miles from Washington, to meet the informant. The following morning, August 11, 1991, Casolaro was found dead in the bathtub of his room in the Sheraton Hotel, his wrists slashed ten times. His briefcase and all his notes were missing.

Casolaro had been talking almost daily with CIA contract agent Michael Riconosciuto, and had stayed with Riconosciuto and his common-law wife, Bobbi, at their residence near Tacoma, Washington obtaining additional evidence. Casolaro's death was one of at least half-a-dozen closely linked to the Inslaw matter. Casolaro's death bred numerous articles linking Justice Department officials with Inslaw.[321]

Despite identification in Casolaro's personal belongings listing his relatives, the police made no effort to contact Casolaro's family before placing a suicide label on the death and ordering an immediate and unprecedented embalming of the body. No permission was sought from Casolaro's family and no check was made for incapacitating drugs that may have been given to him. This unusual response destroyed any evidence that might have linked Casolaro's death to others.

Casolaro had suspected his life may have been in danger and said several

321 A typical article was entitled, "The Dark World of Danny Casolaro," a four-page article in the October 28, 1991 issue of *The Nation*.

times to his brother, a medical doctor, that if anything happened to him that looked like an accident, for him not to believe it.

After Casolaro's murder, Inslaw's attorney Elliott Richardson again demanded that the Justice Department conduct an investigation, citing the fact that Casolaro found evidence proving the existence of misconduct by high Justice Department officials over whom the Attorney General had supervisory responsibility. Richardson was in effect asking the U.S. Attorney General to investigate criminal misconduct implicating Attorney General Edwin Meese and his staff.

**SENATE "INVESTIGATION"**

Probably motivated by media attention to the Inslaw matter, the Senate Permanent Subcommittee on Investigations, chaired by Senator Sam Nunn, conducted a typical Congressional investigation in 1989 into the theft of the PROMIS software and into problems in Chapter 11 courts. Justice Department officials blocked the investigation by refusing to produce documents and refusing to allow Justice Department personnel to be questioned under oath. Attorney General Thornburgh refused to appear before the committee, even though he had a duty to do so. The senate committee also had a duty to force the attorney general and other federal employees to appear. Instead, the committee disbanded the investigation and issued an incomplete report.

**CONFIRMATION BY CIA ASSETS**

Several CIA operatives and contract agents, including Gunther Russbacher and Michael Riconosciuto, offered to testify before the Congressional committees to provide evidence. Only Riconosciuto was allowed to give testimony, showing that the PROMIS software was stolen by Justice Department officials, given to Earl Brian, and sold to numerous foreign countries, including Canada, Libya, Iran, Iraq,[322] and South Korea.

The Inslaw contract with the Justice Department to install the PROMIS software did not constitute a sale. Similar to the purchase of software such as WordPerfect, the buyer of that software only has a license to install and use it, and not to turn around and sell it, as Justice Department officials and their associates subsequently did.

**THREAT OF PRISON IF THE TESTIMONY WAS FALSE**

The Senate reported the stonewalling, stating that its inquiry into Inslaw's charges had been "hampered by the [justice] department's lack of cooperation." The report stated that it had found employees "who desired to speak to the subcommittee, but who chose not to, out of fear for their jobs." The report addressed not only the Justice Department's misconduct in the Inslaw affair but also its misuse of Chapter 11 through its U.S. Trustee Division. The report concluded that the Justice Department politicized the U.S. Trustee program, forcing the Inslaw company with whom it did business into bankruptcy, by refusing to pay for the PROMIS software program.

These were serious charges of misconduct by officials in an agency over whom Congress had oversight responsibilities, requiring Congress to fully investigate the matter and bring it to a satisfactory conclusion. As usual, they

322 The PROMIS software was reportedly sold to Iraq in 1988, while the Bush Administration was supplying Iraq with billions of dollars in grain subsidies that were diverted to arms purchases.

engaged in, at best, misfeasance by allowing the criminal and corrupt activities to go unpunished and to continue.

The report agreed with the findings of Judge Bason, who blasted the Department of Justice in his decision. The judge's decision stated in part:

> *[Justice Department officials] took, converted, stole, [the plaintiff's property] by trickery, fraud and deceit. [made] an institutional decision...at the highest level simply to ignore serious questions of ethical impropriety, made repeatedly by persons of unquestioned probity and integrity, and this failure constitutes bad faith, vexatiousness, wantonness and oppressiveness.... engaged in outrageous, deceitful, fraudulent game of cat and mouse, demonstrating contempt for both the law and any principle of fair dealing.*

The Senate report included articles appearing in *Barron's*[323] and *The American Lawyer*[324] which went into great detail describing the Justice Department and U.S. Trustee misconduct. One article in *Barron's*[325] described the Justice Department's attempts to bankrupt and destroy Inslaw, misusing the U.S. Trustees and the bankruptcy judges to carry out their scheme. The article stated in part:

> *Justice officials proceeded to purposefully drive the small software company into bankruptcy, and then tried to push it into liquidation. Ultimately, the series of "willful, wanton, and deceitful acts" led to a cover up. Bason called statements by top Justice Department officials "ludicrous...incredible...and totally unbelievable."*
>
> *Some of the evidence against the department came from one of its own. During the course of the litigation, Anthony Pasciuto, Deputy Director of the department's Executive Office for United States Trustees, told...how the Justice Department had pressured Trustee officers to liquidate [Inslaw]. Later, a superior confirmed Pasciuto's story. But at the trial, a horrified Pasciuto listened while his superior changed his testimony. Close to tears, he, too, recanted.*
>
> *Judge Bason...ordered Justice to pay Inslaw about $6.8 million in licensing fees and roughly another $1 million in legal fees....In November, Judge Bason rejected a Department of Justice motion to liquidate Inslaw.... one month later, the Harvard Law School graduate and former law professor discovered that he was not being reappointed.*

The report described the normal process of government obfuscation followed by loss of interest by the press, stating:

> *It seemed as if the controversy was winding down....It would follow a natural course in the press, and then fade from view. Inslaw would become another shocking event that slinks off into obscurity: Someone occasionally might dimly remember and idly ask, "What ever did happen to Bill Hamilton and those Inslaw people? A real shame...I heard the judge was back teaching law somewhere..."*

---

323 March 21, and April 4, 1988.

324 December 1987.

325 March 21, 1988.

The *Barron's* article described the efforts of Anthony Pasciuto, a Department of Justice insider, who blew the whistle on the Justice Department's misuse of this powerful federal agency against Inslaw and his small company:

*In an interview with Barron's...Pasciuto explained how the Justice Department blacklisted Inslaw. It was a tale that involved two U.S. trustees, a federal judge who told two versions of the same story, and a Justice Department that routinely refused to pay certain suppliers.*

*Pattern of harassment [by the Justice Department] that helped drive Inslaw into Chapter 11....the Justice Department was trying to starve Inslaw. They didn't just push to bankrupt the software firm,...they wanted to liquidate it, converting it from Chapter 11 to Chapter 7, as soon as possible. Why?*

*Tony Pasciuto [said] that his boss, Thomas Stanton, director of the Justice Department's Executive Office for U.S. Trustees, was pressuring the federal trustee overseeing the Inslaw case, William White, to liquidate Inslaw.*

*Cornelius Blackshear, the U.S. Trustee in New York at the time of Inslaw's Chapter 11 filing, knew all about Stanton's plan. Pasciuto said that Judge Blackshear had repeated this tale of pressure in the presence of United States Court of Appeals Judge Lawrence Pierce in the judge's chambers in Foley Square in New York.*

*Blackshear met with a Justice Department representative, and signed a sworn affidavit, recanting, and said that he had confused Inslaw with another case—United Press International, which had also been involved in bankruptcy proceedings in Judge Bason's court.*

*Cornelius Blackshear left his position as United States Trustee and became a United States bankruptcy judge the following fall.*[326]

**"A Lot Dirtier Than Watergate."**

Ronald LeGrand, Chief Investigator for the Senate Judiciary Committee, told William Hamilton and his attorney that a trusted Justice Department source confided that the Inslaw case was "a lot dirtier for the Department of Justice than Watergate had been, both in its breadth and its depth."

Despite the oversight responsibilities of this Senate group, despite the requirements of federal criminal statutes, the Senate committee refused to take any action against the criminal acts of federal employees in the U.S. Department of Justice, and did nothing to alleviate the harm inflicted upon the innocent owners of the Inslaw company. In this way they aided and abetted the criminal activities, of which Inslaw was only the tip of the iceberg.

**HOUSE "INVESTIGATION"**

The Congressional Subcommittee on Economic and Commercial Law of the Committee on the Judiciary, also held hearings concerning the Inslaw matter and the related death of Danny Casolaro. Congressman Jack Brooks (D-Texas) chaired the committee investigation. U.S. Attorney Meese and the Justice Department group stonewalled the House committee just as they had done with the Senate committee, refusing to turn over requested documents, fraudulently

---

326 For those who cooperate with the Justice Department, federal judgeship positions are the carrot.

stating that the key documents had been accidentally destroyed or could not be found. How convenient! At the start of the hearings Congressman Brooks stated:

*As incredible as this sounds, federal Bankruptcy Judge George Bason, who will be testifying later, has already found much of the first part of the allegation to be true. In his decision on the Inslaw bankruptcy, Judge Bason ruled that the Department "took, converted and stole" Inslaw's proprietary software using "trickery, fraud and deceit." The judge also severely criticized the decisions by high-level Department officials to "ignore the ethical improprieties" on the part of the Justice Department officials involved in the case.*

Over thirty people testified during the committee hearings, revealing how Justice Department officials had stolen the software, schemed to force Inslaw into bankruptcy, and then stole the computer program. Among those who testified before the House committee was former Chapter 11 Judge Bason, who heard the case against the Justice Department. He testified:

*The judicial opinions that I rendered reflected my sense of moral outrage that, as the evidence showed and as I held, the Justice Department stole Inslaw's property and tried to drive Inslaw out of business. Those opinions were upheld on appeal by Judge Bryant in a memorandum that noted my attention to detail and mastery of evidence.*

Revealing Justice Department retaliation for rendering a decision unfavorable to that agency, Judge Bason testified:

*Very soon after I rendered those opinions, my application for reappointment was turned down. One of the Justice Department attorneys who argued the Inslaw case before me was appointed in my stead. Although over 90 percent of the incumbent bankruptcy judges who sought reappointment were in fact reappointed, I was not among them.*

By placing one of their own as a judge on the federal court system (a common practice), the Justice Department officials expanded their pattern of influence.

Congressman Brooks stated in the final committee report: "Despite the dramatic findings by the two courts, the Department has steadfastly denied any wrongdoing by its officials, claiming that its conflict with Inslaw is nothing more than a simple contract dispute. I find this position a little hard to swallow."

The September 10, 1992, report accused high Justice Department officials of criminal misconduct and recommended appointment of a special prosecutor. The 122 page report stated in part:

*There appears to be strong evidence, as indicated by the findings in two federal court proceedings, as well as by the committee investigation, that the Department of Justice "acted willfully and fraudulently,"*[327] *and "took, converted and stole," Inslaw's enhanced PROMIS by "trickery, fraud, and deceit." It appears that these actions against Inslaw were implemented through the project manager from the beginning of the contract and under the direction of high level Justice Department officials.*

*What is strikingly apparent from the testimony and depositions of key*

327 *INSLAW, Inc. v. United States*, opinion of U.S. District Court Judge William Bryant.

*witnesses and many documents is that...[The Department] engaged in an outrageous, deceitful, fraudulent game of cat and mouse, demonstrating contempt for both the law and any principle of fair dealing....high level officials at the Department of Justice conspired to drive Inslaw into insolvency and steal the PROMIS software so it could be used by Dr. Earl Brian, a former associate and friend of then Attorney General Edwin Meese. Dr. Brian is a businessman and entrepreneur who owns or controls several businesses including Hadron, Inc., which has contracts with the Justice Department, CIA, and other agencies....the circumstances involving the theft of the PROMIS software system constitute a possible criminal conspiracy involving Mr. Meese, Judge Jensen, Dr. Brian, and several current and former officials at the Department of Justice....the committee's investigation largely supports the findings of two federal courts that the Department "took, converted, stole" Inslaw's enhanced PROMIS by "trickery, fraud and deceit," and that this misappropriation involved officials at the highest levels of the Department of Justice.*

*One of the principal reasons the committee could not reach any definitive conclusion about Inslaw's allegations of a high criminal conspiracy at Justice was the lack of cooperation from the Department. Throughout the two Inslaw investigations, the Congress met with restrictions, delays, and outright denials to requests for information and to unobstructed access to records and witnesses since 1988. [fraudulent claims] Some of the documents held by the Department's chief attorney in charge of the Inslaw litigation had been misplaced or accidentally destroyed.*

*The ultimate goal of the conspiracy was to position Hadron and the other companies owned or controlled by Dr. Brian to take advantage of the nearly 3 billion dollars' worth of automated data processing upgrade contracts planned to be awarded by the Department of Justice during the 1980's.*

*The enhanced PROMIS software was stolen by high level Justice officials and distributed internationally in order to provide financial gain to Dr. Brian and to further intelligence and foreign policy objectives of the United States.*

*Numerous potential witnesses refused to cooperate, for the stated reason that they were fearful for their jobs and retaliation by the Justice Department, or that attempts had already been made to intimidate them against cooperating.*

*The Department's unwillingness to allow Congressional oversight into its affairs, in spite of an alleged coverup of wrongdoing, greatly hindered the committee's investigation of the Inslaw allegations. The committee also encountered serious problems with obtaining cooperation from U.S. intelligence and law enforcement agencies. The committee also encountered virtually no cooperation in its investigation of the Inslaw matter beyond U.S. borders. The government of Canada refused to make its officials available to committee investigators for interviews without strict limitations on the questioning.*

Referring to an even worse level of corruption, the committee report stated:

*According to LeGrand, a trusted source, described to the Hamiltons as a senior DOJ official with a title, had alleged that the two senior Criminal Division officials were witnesses to much greater malfeasance against Inslaw than that already found by the Bankruptcy Court, malfeasance on a much more serious scale than Watergate. LeGrand told the Hamiltons that D. Lowell Jensen did not merely fail to investigate the malfeasance of Videnieks and Brewer but instead had "engineered" the malfeasance "right from the start" so that Inslaw's software business could be made available to political friends of the Reagan/Bush administration.*

*Can identify about 300 places where the PROMIS software has been installed illegally by the federal government. Dr. Brian sold PROMIS to the Central Intelligence Agency in 1983 for implementation on computers purchased from Floating Point Systems and what the CIA called PROMIS "Datapoint." Dr. Brian has sold about $20 million of PROMIS licenses to the federal government. Department officials hinted to CIA officials that they should deny that they are using PROMIS.*

*[A DEA agent] reassignment in 1990 to a DEA intelligence position in the State of Washington, prior to Michael Riconosciuto's March 1991 arrest there on drug charges, was more than coincidental....the agent was assigned to Riconosciuto's home State to manufacture a case against him. Mr. Coleman stated he believes this was done to prevent Mr. Riconosciuto from becoming a credible witness concerning the U.S. government's covert sale of PROMIS to foreign governments.*

*The committee encountered numerous situations that pointed to a concerted effort by Department officials to manipulate the litigation of the Inslaw bankruptcy, as alleged by the president of Inslaw. During this controversy, one key Department witness was harassed and ultimately,....*

*Unauthorized destruction of government documents...Department employees were involved in the illegal destruction (shredding) of documents related to the Inslaw case.*

*Riconosciuto stated that a tape recording of the telephone threat was confiscated by DEA agents at the time of Riconosciuto's arrest....the timing of the arrest, coupled with Mr. Riconosciuto's allegations that tapes of a telephone conversation he had with Mr. Videnieks were confiscated by DEA agents, raises serious questions concerning whether the Department's prosecution of Mr. Riconosciuto was related to his cooperation with the committee.*

*IX. CONCLUSION*

*Based on the committee's investigation and two separate court rulings, it is clear that high level Department of Justice officials deliberately ignored Inslaw's proprietary rights in the enhanced version of PROMIS and misappropriated this software for use at locations not covered under contract with the company....Instead of conducting an investigation into Inslaw's claims that criminal wrongdoing by high level government officials had occurred, Attorney Generals Meese and Thornburgh blocked or restricted Congressional inquiries into the matter, ignored the findings of two courts and refused to ask for the appointment of an independent counsel. These actions were taken in the face of a growing body of evidence that serious wrongdoing had occurred which reached to the highest levels of the Department. The evidence received by the committee during its investigation clearly raises serious concerns about the possibility that a high level conspiracy against Inslaw did exist and that great efforts have been expended by the Department to block any outside investigation into the matter.*

*Finally, the committee believes that the only way the Inslaw allegations can be adequately and fully investigated is by the appointment of an independent counsel.*

*X. FINDINGS*

*... the Department ignored Inslaw's data rights to its enhanced version of its PROMIS software and misused its prosecutorial and litigative resources to legitimize and coverup its misdeeds.... Several witnesses, including former Attorney General Elliot Richardson, have provided testimony, sworn statements or affidavits linking high level Department officials to a conspiracy to steal Inslaw's PROMIS software and secretly transfer PROMIS to Dr. Brian.... the PROMIS software was subsequently converted for use by domestic and foreign intelligence services. This testimony was provided by individuals who knew that the Justice Department would be inclined to prosecute them for perjury if they lied under oath. No such prosecutions have occurred.*

*The reviews of the Inslaw matter by Congress were hampered by Department tactics designed to conceal many significant documents and otherwise interfere with an independent review. The Department actions appear to have been motivated more by an intense desire to defend itself from Inslaw's charges of misconduct rather than investigating possible violations of the law.... the Department "stole through trickery, fraud and deceit" Inslaw's PROMIS software.*

*13. Further investigation into the circumstances surrounding Daniel Casolaro's death is needed.*

*14. The following criminal statutes may have been violated by certain high level Justice officials and private individuals:*

*18 U.S.C. § 371–Conspiracy to commit an offense.*

*18 U.S.C. § 654–Officer or employee of the United States converting the property of another.*

*18 U.S.C. § 1341–Fraud.*

*18 U.S.C. § 1343–Wire fraud.*

*18 U.S.C. § 1505–Obstruction of proceedings before departments, agencies and committees.*

*18 U.S.C. § 1512—Tampering with a witness.*

*18 U.S.C. § 1513—Retaliation against a witness.*

*18 U.S.C. § 1621—Perjury.*

*18 U.S.C. § 1951—Interference with commerce by threats or violence (RICO).*

*18 U.S.C. § 1961 et seq.—Racketeer Influenced and Corrupt Organizations.*

*18 U.S.C. § 2314—Transportation of stolen goods, securities, moneys.*

*18 U.S.C. § 2315—Receiving stolen goods.*

**AIDING AND ABETTING**

Every Republican Congressman[328] on the committee voted against the report, claiming there was no support for the findings by the two federal judges and the committee investigators. This coverup tactic duplicated the obstruction of justice in the October Surprise scheme (and in every other scandal described within these pages). The Republican block stated in their dissenting report:

*Those entrusted with the enforcement of our laws in the Executive Branch are better qualified than Members of Congress to assess the utility of settling a legal controversy on terms favorable to a private litigant.*

These Republican Congressmen held that the very same Justice Department officials (committing the criminal acts, including the obstruction of justice, the destruction or withholding of documents, the threatening of informants) should be the only persons permitted to investigate their own misconduct. The Republican Congressmen eulogized the very same Justice Department officials who had been found by two federal courts to have engaged in corrupt acts. The dissenting opinion by the Republicans stated "Fairness to DOJ requires..." Fairness? Justice Department employees destroyed documents (a felony), threatened witnesses (a felony), used government agencies to steal the livelihood of innocent citizens (another felony)!

**TRAP DOOR ALTERATIONS**

Assured that the Congressional investigation would go no further, Justice Department officials and their business associates continued their sale of the stolen PROMIS program. Meese's friend and business associate, Earl Brian, sold copies of Inslaw's software to intelligence agencies all over the world, collecting millions of dollars in the process. Who says crime doesn't pay!

Israel's Mossad, which knew the software was stolen, obtained the PROMIS software from Earl Brian in 1982 through a front company called Degem. The Mossad installed their own "trap-door" into the software, permitting the Mossad to secretly enter the database after it was sold to other countries, including Nicaragua, Colombia, Chile, and Brazil. In this way the CIA and the Mossad could spy on the countries that bought the program, including friendly nations.

The trap door alteration of the PROMIS program was accomplished for the Mossad through Ben-Menashe, using a computer software company in Chatsworth, California.

After the CIA and Justice Department, working together, made the trap door changes, Brian sold the first program to Jordan via his company, Hadron. The Mossad then secretly entered the computer program without Jordan's knowledge, revealing the success of the trap-door.

The CIA and Mossad approached Robert Maxwell, a British citizen and secret Mossad agent, through Senator John Tower in 1984, authorizing Maxwell to sell the PROMIS software to East Bloc countries, including Russia. Maxwell's Berlitz language schools, scattered throughout the world, made him an excellent source to carry out the plan. Maxwell also purchased an existing computer company owned by the Mossad, Degem, which had offices in several foreign

328 Congressmen Hamilton Fish, Jr.; Carlos J. Moorhead; Henry J. Hyde; F. James Sensenbrenner, Jr.; Bill McCollum; George W. Gekas; Howard Coble; Lamar S. Smith; Craig T. James; Tom Campbell; Steven Schiff; Jim Ramstad; George Allen.

countries, to install the software.

According to Ari Ben-Menashe, by 1989, sales of the stolen PROMIS software brought in $40 million. Not bad for criminal activities using U.S. Department of Justice facilities, with the activities financed by U.S. taxpayers' dollars.

**SOFTWARE FOR DRUGS**

Guatemala purchased the PROMIS software. The vast network of computers needed to operate the program was furnished by IBM in 1985, using money obtained from shipping drugs to the United States. Even the drug cartels used the PROMIS software.

Unhappy with the U.S.-sanctioned shipment of chemical weapons to Iraq from Cardoen Industries in Chile, Ben-Menashe threatened to expose the sale of PROMIS software and the hidden trap-door, if the U.S. did not discontinue the shipments. Justice Department officials retaliated, seeking to silence him by charging Ben-Menashe with selling aircraft to a foreign country. Justice Department prosecutors and a federal judge caused Ben-Menashe to be imprisoned for a year pending trial, until a New York federal jury acquitted him.

**SELECTIVE MEDIA COVERAGE**

A February 5, 1990, article in the legal newspaper, *The Recorder*, criticized Michael Shaheen, Jr., head of the Justice Department's Office of Professional Responsibility, for "outrageous, deceitful, fraudulent" acts and the coverup of such acts. Professor Bennett Gershman at New York's Pace University School of Law and author of *Prosecutorial Misconduct* was quoted as stating, "It is a joke to say Justice [Department] polices itself."

The heading in a March 15, 1991, *Miami Journal* article read: "Justice Department perverts justice in Inslaw case." The article stated in part:

> *In the matter of the Department of Justice and the Inslaw case, a remarkable thing is happening: The stench gets worse. Until recently, it could be said of this shameful affair that it smelled only to high heaven. It is now beginning to smell to outer space. As Attorney General, he ought to be doing his damnedest to get to the bottom of this disgraceful matter. Instead, he has stalled; he has stonewalled; he has taken refuge in legalisms; he has obstructed efforts of two Congressional committees to dig out the facts. And this isn't even his scandal. He inherited the mess from Ed Meese.*

A *Vancouver Sun* headline on April 5, 1991, stated: "Probe of hot-software charge urged." The article stated in part:

> *Solicitor-General Pierre Cadieux should go before a parliamentary committee to answer charges the RCMP and CSIS are using stolen computer software, opposition Mps said Thursday. The PROMIS software was allegedly pirated by U.S. Justice Department officials and sold by associates of former president Ronald Reagan to government agencies in Canada, Libya, Iraq,*[329] *and Israel, according to affidavits filed in U.S. bankruptcy court last week.*

An article in the *Financial Times* of London on April 5, 1991, referred to the Inslaw matter:

---

329 It is believed that Iraq used the PROMIS software during the Persian Gulf war.

*A BIZARRE series of allegations—including claims of misconduct by Mr. Robert McFarlane, the former National Security Adviser to President Ronald Reagan—have surfaced as a result of a seemingly obscure legal action involving the US Department of Justice and a small Washington computer software company called Inslaw....the charge Israeli intelligence forces are using an Inslaw computer software system illegally provided by Mr. McFarlane....several members of the Washington establishment and US press reports suggest Inslaw may be only the tip of an iceberg that could have implications for US foreign policy in the Middle East.*

An October 25, 1991, *Daily Journal* headline stated: "The Promisgate Plot Thickens," with the subtitle: "Scandal over Justice Department Software Could Run Very Deep." The article revealed that the scheme was to deliver Inslaw's stolen software to a company in which Attorney General Edwin Meese had an interest and then the stolen software would be sold to the Justice Department in a $250 million contract to automate Justice Department litigation divisions.

Syndicated columnist James Kilpatrick headlined his August 29, 1991, article stating, "Odor Of a Situation Needing a Probe." The article stated in part:

*Some months ago, writing about the Inslaw case, I said the affair was beginning to stink to high heaven. With the death of Danny Casolaro, a free-lance investigative reporter, the stench grows worse....There is reason to believe that Danny Casolaro went to Martinsburg to crack the [Inslaw] case. He had told friends that Inslaw was part of an "octopus" of criminal activities in high places, including the BCCI and the savings and loan scandals.*

## ORGANIZED CRIME IN THE JUSTICE DEPARTMENT

An October 27, 1991 article written by former U.S. Attorney General Elliot Richardson, appearing in newspapers throughout the United States, stated:

*Organized crime in the U.S. Justice Department—The Stench at the U.S. Justice Department. The former Attorney General called for appointment of independent counsel to investigate the alleged corruption by Justice Department officials*[330] *in the Chapter 11 misconduct involving Inslaw. Richardson called for an independent counsel to investigate the Justice Department's misconduct on the basis that the nation's highest law enforcement agency was heavily implicated in Chapter 11 corruption.*

Richardson's charges that the Justice Department was a criminal enterprise was more correct than his words suggested. I found out about the criminality of those officials and prosecutors in the Justice Department (including the FBI) for the past thirty years, starting while I was a federal investigator.

Attorney General William Barr, for instance, was legal counsel for the CIA during 1976 and 1977 while George Bush was director of the Agency. In the mid-1980s Barr was reportedly an attorney for the CIA's Southern Air Transport, using the alias of Robert Johnson.[331] He coordinated and directed the unlawful weapons shipments to Central America from Arkansas, drug smuggling on the

330 Earl Brian, California health secretary under Governor Ronald Reagan, and a friend of Attorney General Edwin Meese, linked to a scheme to steal Inslaw's computer software used by the Justice Department.

331 As stated by former CIA asset Terry Reed in his book, *Compromise*.

return flights, and drug-money laundering from the drug operations. After Barr became Attorney General he obstructed justice and covered up for these crimes against the United States.

He, and prior attorney general Edwin Meese knew about the treasonous and criminal October Surprise operation, Inslaw, Iran-Contra, and other crimes against the American people. The list goes on and on, with the heads of the Justice Department guilty of far worse crimes than many prisoners languishing in federal prisons.

**OTHER CRIMINALITY SURFACED**

Another pattern of corruption surfaced as Congressional investigators questioned Michael Riconosciuto. They learned that he helped arrange the transfer of $40 million bribe money from the Reagan-Bush team to the Iranians during the October 19, 1980, weekend meetings in Paris. This revelation provided further evidence that the October Surprise operation did indeed take place, but the Senate and the House kept the lid on this awesome scandal.

Inslaw's attorney, Elliott Richardson, requested an affidavit from Riconosciuto concerning his knowledge of the Justice Department's role in the Inslaw matter. When Justice Department officials learned of these requests, Peter Videnieks of the Justice Department threatened Riconosciuto during a telephone call. Videnieks warned Riconosciuto that if he gave evidence to the Congressional committee (and a pending Inslaw civil suit against the Justice Department), serious things would happen to him and his wife, Bobbi. Riconosciuto taped this telephone conversation.

Despite Justice Department threats, Riconosciuto submitted testimony to Congress and an affidavit to Inslaw's attorney. The March 21, 1991, affidavit stated:

*UNITED STATES BANKRUPTCY COURT*
*FOR THE DISTRICT OF COLUMBIA*

| | | |
|---|---|---|
| *IN RE:* | ) | |
| | ) | *Case No. 85-00070* |
| *INSLAW, INC.,* | ) | *(Chapter 11)* |
| | ) | |
| *Debtor,* | ) | |
| | ) | |
| | ) | |
| *INSLAW, INC.,* | ) | *Adversary Proceeding* |
| | ) | *No. 86-0069* |
| *Plaintiff,* | ) | |
| | ) | |
| *v.* | ) | |
| | ) | |
| *UNITED STATES OF AMERICA,* | ) | |
| *and the UNITED STATES* | ) | |
| *DEPARTMENT OF JUSTICE,* | ) | |
| | ) | |
| *Defendants.* | ) | |
| | ) | |

*AFFIDAVIT OF MICHAEL J. RICONOSCIUTO*

| | | |
|---|---|---|
| *State of Washington* | ) | |
| | ) | *ss:* |
| | ) | |

*I, MICHAEL J. RICONOSCIUTO, being duly sworn, do hereby state as follows:*

*1. During the early 1980's, I served as the Director of Research for a joint venture between the Wackenhut Corporation of Coral Gables, Florida, and the Cabazon Bank of Indians of Indio, California. The joint venture was located on the Cabazon Reservation.*

*2. The Wackenhut-Cabazon joint venture sought to develop and/or manufacture certain materials that are used in military and national security operations, including night vision goggles, machine guns, fuel-air explosives, and biological and chemical warfare weapons.*

*3. The Cabazon Band of Indians are a sovereign nation. The sovereign immunity that is accorded the Cabazons as a consequence of this fact made it feasible to pursue on the reservation the development and/or manufacture of materials whose development or manufacture would be subject to stringent controls off the reservation. As a minority group, the Cabazon Indians also provided the Wackenhut Corporation with an enhanced ability to obtain federal contracts through the 8A Set Aside Program, and in connection with government-owned contractor-operated (GOCO) facilities.*

*4. The Wackenhut-Cabazon joint venture was intended to support the needs of a number of foreign governments and forces, including forces and governments in Central America and the Middle East. The Contras in Nicaragua represented one of the most important priorities for the joint venture.*

*5. The Wackenhut-Cabazon joint venture maintained closed liaison with certain elements of the United States government, including representatives of intelligence, military and law enforcement agencies.*

*6. Among the frequent visitors to the Wackenhut-Cabazon joint venture were Peter Videnieks of the U.S. Department of Justice in Washington, D.C., and a close associate of Videnieks by the name of Earl W. Brian. Brian is a private businessman who lives in Maryland and who has maintained close business ties with the U.S. intelligence community for many years.*

*7. In connection with my work for Wackenhut, I engaged in some software development and modification work in 1983 and 1984 on the proprietary PROMIS computer software product. The copy of PROMIS on which I worked came from the U.S. Department of Justice. Earl W. Brian made it available to me through Wackenhut after acquiring it from Peter Videnieks, who was then a Department of Justice contracting official with responsibility for the PROMIS software. I performed the modifications to PROMIS in Indio, California; Silver Springs, Maryland; and Miami, Florida.*

*8. The purpose of the PROMIS software modifications that I made in 1983 and 1984 was to support a plan for the implementation of PROMIS in law enforcement and intelligence agencies worldwide. Earl W. Brian was spearheading the plan for this worldwide use of the PROMIS computer software.*

*9. Some of the modifications that I made were specifically designed to facilitate the implementation of PROMIS within two agencies of the government of Canada; the Royal Canadian Mounted Police (RCMP) and the Canadian Security and Intelligence Service (CSIS). Earl W. Brian would check with me from time to time to make certain that the work would be completed in time to satisfy the schedule for the RCMP and CSIS implementations of PROMIS.*

*10. The proprietary version of PROMIS, as modified by me, was, in fact, implemented in both the RCMP and the CSIS in Canada. It was my understanding that Earl W. Brian had sold this version of PROMIS to the government of Canada.*

*11. In February 1991, I had a telephone conversation with Peter Videnieks, then still employed by the U.S. Department of Justice. Videnieks attempted during this telephone conversation to persuade me not to cooperate with an independent investigation of the government's piracy of INSLAW's proprietary PROMIS software being conducted by the Committee on the Judiciary of the U.S. House of Representatives.*

*12. Videnieks stated that I would be rewarded for a decision not to cooperate with the House Judiciary Committee investigation. Videnieks forecasted an immediate and favorable resolution of a protracted child custody dispute being prosecuted against my wife by her former husband, if I were to decide not to cooperate with the House Judiciary Committee investigation.*

*13. Videnieks also outlined specific punishments that I could expect to receive from the U.S. Department of Justice if I cooperate with the House Judiciary Committee's investigation.*

*14. One punishment that Videnieks outlined was the future inclusion of me and my father in a criminal prosecution of certain business associates of mine in Orange County, California, in connection with the operation of a savings and loan institution in Orange County. By way of underscoring his power to influence such decisions at the U.S. Department of Justice, Videnieks informed me of the indictment of these business associates prior to the time when that indictment was unsealed and made public.*

*15. Another punishment that Videnieks threatened against me if I cooperated with the House Judiciary Committee is prosecution by the U.S. Department of Justice for perjury. Videnieks warned me that credible witnesses would come forward to contradict any damaging claims that I made in testimony before the House Judiciary Committee, and that I would subsequently be prosecuted for perjury by the U.S. Department of Justice for my testimony before the House Judiciary Committee.*

*FURTHER AFFIANT SAYETH NOT.*

*Michael J. Riconosciuto*

*Signed and sworn to before me this 21 day of March 1991.*

*Notary Public*

**********************************

Richard Babayan submitted an affidavit dated March 22, 1991 into a federal court proceeding[332] in the District of Columbia, describing the sale of Inslaw's software by Earl Brian to Iraq, Korea, Libya, and Chile. The affidavit follows:

332 Case number 85-0070, U.S. Bankruptcy Court, District of Columbia.

*UNITED STATES BANKRUPTCY COURT*
*FOR THE DISTRICT OF COLUMBIA*

| | | |
|---|---|---|
| *IN RE:* | ) | |
| | ) | *Case No. 85-00070* |
| *INSLAW, INC.,* | ) | *(Chapter 11)* |
| | ) | |
| *Debtor,* | ) | |
| ______________ | ) | |
| | ) | |
| *INSLAW, INC.,* | ) | *Adversary Proceeding* |
| | ) | *No. 86-0069* |
| *Plaintiff,* | ) | |
| | ) | |
| *v.* | ) | |
| | ) | |
| *UNITED STATES OF AMERICA, and the UNITED STATES DEPARTMENT OF JUSTICE,* | ) | |
| | ) | |
| *Defendants.* | ) | |
| ______________ | ) | |

*AFFIDAVIT OF RICHARD H. BABAYAN*

| | | |
|---|---|---|
| *State of Florida* | ) | |
| | ) | *ss:* |
| *Palm Beach County* | ) | |

*I, Richard H. Babayan, being duly sworn, do hereby state as follows:*

*1. During the past several years, I have acted as a broker of sales of materials and equipment used by foreign governments in their armed forces, intelligence and security organizations.*

*2. In the capacity described in paragraph # 1, I attended a meeting in Baghdad, Iraq, in October or November, 1987, with Mr. Abu Mohammed of Entezamat, an intelligence and security organ of the government of Iraq. Mr. Abu Mohammed is a senior ranking official of Entezamat and a person with whom I had extensive dealings over the previous three years.*

*3. During the aforementioned meeting with Mr. Abu Mohammed, I was informed that Dr. Earl W. Brian of the United States had recently completed a sale presentation to the government of Iraq regarding the PROMIS computer software. Furthermore, it is my understanding that others present at Dr. Brian's PROMIS sales presentation were General Richard Secord, of the United States, and Mr. Abu Mohammed.*

*4. In early to mid-1988, in the course of subsequent visits to Baghdad, Iraq,*

*I was informed that Dr. Earl W. Brian had, in fact, provided the PROMIS computer software to the government of Iraq through a transaction that took place under the umbrella of Mr. Sarkis Saghanollan, an individual who has had extensive business dealings with the government of Iraq since the late 1970/s in the fields of military hardware and software. I was also informed that the government of Iraq acquired the PROMIS software for use primarily in intelligence services, and secondarily in police and law enforcement agencies.*

*5. During the course of the visits described in paragraph # 4, I also learned from Mr. Abu Mohammed that the government of Libya had acquired the PROMIS computer software prior to its acquisition by the government of Iraq; that the government of Libya had by then made extensive use of PROMIS; and that the government of Libya was highly recommending the PROMIS software to other countries. I was informed that the high quality of the reference for the PROMIS software from the government of Libya was one of the principal reasons for the decision of the government of Iraq to acquire PROMIS.*

*6. In the capacity described in paragraph # 1, I attended a meeting in early 1988 in Singapore with Mr. Y.H. Nam of the Korea Development Corporation.*

*7. The Korea Development Corporation is known to be a cutout for the Korean Central Intelligence Agency (KCIA).*

*8. I learned from Mr. Y.H. Nam during the meeting described in paragraph # 6 that the KCIA had acquired the PROMIS computer software, and that Dr. Earl W. Brian of the United States had been instrumental in the acquisition and implementation of PROMIS by the KCIA.*

*9. In the capacity described in paragraph # 1, I attended a meeting in Santiago, Chile, in December, 1988, with Mr. Carlos Cardoen of Cardoen Industries. During this meeting, I was informed by Mr. Cardoen that Dr. Earl W. Brian of the United States and Mr. Robert Gates, a senior American Intelligence and national security official, had just completed a meeting in Santiago, Chile, with Mr. Carlos Cardoen.*

*10. I hereby certify that the facts set forth in this Affidavit are true and correct to the best of my knowledge.*

*FURTHER AFFIANT SAYETH NOT.*

______________________________

*Richard A. Babayan*

Gates was later appointed director of the Central Intelligence Agency, following the standard practice of placing people in key positions who are already implicated in misconduct.

**AFFIDAVIT OF FORMER MOSSAD AGENT**

Affidavits exposing Justice Department corruption in the Inslaw scandal came from many areas, and from people who had nothing to gain and much to lose. Former Mossad agent Ari Ben-Menashe provided an affidavit to Congress showing that Earl Brian brokered the stolen PROMIS software to Iraq through the office of Carlos Cardoen in Santiago, Chile. Cardoen was a CIA asset selling chemical weapons and arms to Iraq.

Ben-Menashe testified before Congress about the Justice Department's theft of the PROMIS software and submitted an affidavit into the Inslaw litigation. The affidavit also gave details of the October Surprise operation, including: that there were three meetings in Madrid between the Reagan-Bush campaign group and Iranian factions; that there was a fourth meeting in Barcelona; that he saw Bush, William Casey and key Iranian officials in Paris at the October 1980 meeting; that the head of the French intelligence (SDECE) was at the Paris meetings; that Hamid Nagashian, deputy director of the Iranian Revolutionary Guard, aides to high ranking Iranians, were present in Paris. The affidavit stated that Bush showed the Iranians a check for $40 million made out to them, which was then deposited in a Luxembourg bank.

Former U.S. Attorney General Elliott Richardson, the attorney for the Inslaw company, requested the present U.S. Attorney on October 27, 1991, to request appointment of an Independent Prosecutor to continue the investigation and to prosecute the involved Justice Department officials. His statements appeared in media articles under the title: "Organized crime in the U.S. Justice Department–The Stench at the U.S. Justice Department." Richardson cited charges made by thirty people supporting the existence of criminal acts by Justice Department officials in the Inslaw case.

**SHIFTING RESPONSIBILITIES**

The Congressional committees had the power and the responsibilities to commence impeachment proceedings against Justice Department officials, but avoided the fight and the possibility of Justice Department retaliation. Instead of taking meaningful action, it issued a report condemning the Justice Department and let it go at that.

**AT BEST, A GROUP OF COWARDS**

Not a single member of that Congressional committee, or of any other Congressional committee who knew of the threats and the carrying out of the threats, exercised his or her duty to investigate and provide corrective actions against the ongoing criminal activities. They were like crooked police officials who looked the other way.

The House committee recommended to the Justice Department that it request the Court of Appeals in Washington, D.C., to appoint an Independent Prosecutor to investigate and prosecute the criminal acts by several U.S. attorney generals and Justice Department officials.[333] Attorney General William Barr[334] refused to do that. What else could be expected? Attorney General William Barr, who was also implicated, refused to do so, just as the attorney generals have refused to appoint an independent prosecutor in October Surprise, BCCI, Bank of Lavoro, and other scandals.

## SPECIAL COUNSEL "INVESTIGATION"

Media publicity forced Barr to do something. He appointed a former Justice Department crony to conduct an "investigation" of the Inslaw matter and then report back to him. The special counsel would be selected by Barr; would be subservient to him; and would report to him. Barr could then ignore the recommendations in the remote possibility the special counsel did not cooperate in the expected coverup. Barr hand-picked Chicago attorneys Nicholas Bua, a former U.S. District Judge, his law partner, Charles Knight,[335] and five Justice Department prosecutors to investigate the Justice Department's criminal misconduct. Bua then impaneled a federal grand jury to conduct an "investigation" into the Inslaw affair. Bua's law partner, attorney Charles Knight, controlled the witnesses and questioning before the grand jury in a manner almost guaranteed to avoid a grand jury indictment.

## UNLAWFULLY DISMISSING THE GRAND JURY

The first grand jury[336] started listening to the evidence and giving it credibility. Bua quickly dismissed that jury and impaneled another one, which would rubber-stamp the acts of the special counsel. Grand juries that exercise the independence they are expected to have, and which act contrary to the U.S. Attorney, are called "runaway" grand juries.

A rare example of a runaway grand jury happened in Denver in November 1992, as the jury received evidence of massive pollution at the Rocky Flats nuclear weapons plant. U.S. Attorney Michael Norton sought to block the investigation and the jury ignored his attempts. Instead of covering up for large-scale problems at Rocky Flats, the grand jury, under the guidance of a rancher and grand jury foreman, Wes McKinley, prepared a letter for President-elect Bill Clinton to appoint an independent prosecutor to circumvent the Justice Department and investigate whether any federal criminal laws were violated at Rocky Flats. Nothing ever came of this.

## CITIZEN COMMITTEE CHARGING THE INSLAW SPECIAL COUNSEL WITH OBSTRUCTION OF JUSTICE

The coverup by the Inslaw special counsel aroused the ire of the Citizens' Committee to Clean Up the Courts,[337] causing them to file a September 1992 lawsuit in the U.S. District Court[338] at Chicago naming as defendants attorneys

---

333 An independent prosecutor (or counsel) is appointed by a panel of three judges in the U.S. Court of Appeals at Washington, following the recommendation by the U.S. Attorney General.

334 Former legal counsel with the Central Intelligence Agency, who is deeply involved with the stolen PROMIS software.

335 Partners in the Chicago law firm of Burke, Bosselman & Weaver.

336 Chicago, No. 92 GJ 811.

337 A citizen's group in Chicago that investigates and exposes government corruption, especially that which involves corrupt state and federal judges.

338 Number 92-C-6217.

Nicolas J. Bua[339] and Charles Knight. This lawsuit was in response to the coverup and obstruction of justice by Bua and Knight in the Inslaw investigation.

Two of the plaintiffs[340] in the action, Sherman Skolnick[341] and Mark Sato,[342] had been in Bua's law offices, advising that they were going to circumvent the special counsel and give evidence and testimony to the foreman of the grand jury relating to Justice Department misconduct in the Inslaw matter. According to Skolnick and Sato, Bua stated (referring to the Inslaw investigation) "I do not intend to prosecute anyone. I want the matter behind me." Bua told the Citizens' Committee group that he would block the giving of testimony and evidence to the grand jury and would hold them in contempt if they tried to give evidence to them.

**TRYING TO CIRCUMVENT THE COVERUP**

Recognizing the imminent coverup, several members of the Citizens' Committee to Clean Up the Courts[343] advised Bua that they were presenting evidence to the grand jury investigating the Inslaw scandal. Bua angrily responded that he would bring charges against the group and against any grand jury member who acted on the evidence. Bua warned the group that he wanted to get Inslaw behind him and that he had no intention of prosecuting anyone in the Justice Department.

The Chicago federal grand jury subpoenaed Riconosciuto in November 1992 to testify concerning the Inslaw affair.[344] On the first day of testimony, Justice Department officials moved Riconosciuto from his jail cell without advising him that he would be testifying, preventing him from bringing his evidence with him. Justice Department officials then took Riconosciuto before the grand jury in shackles, leg irons, and handcuffs, creating the impression that he was a dangerous criminal rather than a former CIA asset involved with sensitive matters including the Justice Department's theft of the PROMIS software.

Knight sought to discredit Riconosciuto by admonishing him for not having brought any evidence to support his testimony, even though it was the Justice Department that was responsible for that matter. Seeking to influence the jury against Riconosciuto, Knight warned Riconosciuto in a sneering tone that he would be criminally prosecuted if he gave false testimony (i.e., if he told the truth).

Bua kept witnesses from the grand jury investigation who would have revealed the truth of the Justice Department's criminality in the Inslaw matter.

Riconosciuto was already aware of how Justice Department prosecutors charged CIA agent Richard Brenneke with perjury when Brenneke had truthfully testified to being employed by the CIA and having seen George Bush and Donald

339 Bua was a Federal District Court judge in Chicago until 1991. He then joined the Chicago law firm of Burke, Boggelman & Weaver.

340 The third plaintiff was Michael Riconosciuto, charged with reportedly trumped-up amphetamine charges shortly after giving testimony to the House committee investigating the Inslaw matter. A week earlier a high Justice Department official, .... Videnieks, warned Riconosciuto that he would suffer the consequences if he gave testimony to Congress. (These threats constituted federal crimes.)

341 Skolnick is chairman of the Chicago based Citizens Committee to Clean Up the Courts.

342 Sato is a legal researcher and writer.

343 9800 So. Oglesby, Chicago, IL 60617.

344 Riconosciuto was in federal prison at Terminal Island, California, as a result of the charges filed by Justice Department officials after Riconosciuto testified to the Congressional committee.

Gregg in Paris on the infamous October 19, 1980, weekend. Brenneke had nothing to gain by his testimony. Neither did Riconosciuto. They were both disillusioned with the corruption in the CIA and sought to exercise their responsibilities under federal crime-reporting statutes and as citizens. As a result, they had both suffered from Justice Department retaliation.

## ANOTHER JUSTICE DEPARTMENT COVERUP

In June 1993, Nicholas Bua sent his report to his Justice Department employer, exonerating Justice Department officials, stating that there was no truth to any of the charges. The evidence showed otherwise, including the findings of two federal courts, a host of investigators, and the testimony of independent witnesses. Bua's report discredited the testimony of the victims and witnesses who risked Justice Department retaliation by coming forward, and accepted as true the statements made by those implicated in the wrongdoings, and especially those made by Earl Brian. The Bua Report stated facts absolutely contrary to the findings of the U.S. Bankruptcy Court judge, the U.S. District Court judge, and the Congressional investigations.

Former Attorney General Elliott Richardson, the attorney for the Inslaw Company, issued a statement on June 18, 1993:

> *What I have seen of [the report] is remarkable both for its credulity in accepting at face value denials of complicity in wrongdoings against Inslaw and for its failure to pursue leads making those denials implausible.*

Former Attorney General Elliot Richardson and his staff prepared an eighty-page report plus exhibits exposing the errors and falsehoods in the Bua report. Richardson's report referred to the obvious absurdity of Justice Department officials using their own personnel to investigate themselves. The report pointed out the lunacy of the Bua Report taking at face value the statements of those people who were part of the corrupt acts and who had everything to gain by lying, and for discrediting the testimony of those who had no reason to lie and risked perjury charges if they did lie.

The Richardson Report exposed the refusal of the Bua group to obtain the testimony and documentary evidence that would expose the Justice Department misconduct and which would have contradicted the Bua Report findings. The Richardson Report stated in part:

> *The Bua Report denigrates the findings of the Bankruptcy Court without clearly acknowledging that those findings were affirmed and supplemented by two other entities independent of DOJ, the U.S. District Court and the House Judiciary Committee [including the 44-page opinion by District Judge William B. Bryant, Jr.]*
>
> *The Bua Report focuses only on those facts that its authors deemed relevant to the conclusions they intended to reach. The report's remarkable credibility toward professions of innocence by the very individuals heretofore identified as the principal culprits in the theft of the software. To accept the self-serving, long after-the-fact and post hoc rationalizations of these individuals over their testimony at trial, which testimony clearly evidenced their propensity for lying and covering up the truth, as found by two federal courts, is ludicrous. A separate adversarial hearing ensued on this subject, and the bankruptcy court found that DOJ officials had,*

*in fact, secretly attempted in 1985 forcibly to convert INSLAW from a Chapter 11 reorganization into a Chapter 7 liquidation in order to prevent INSLAW from seeking redress in the courts for DOJ's theft of the PROMIS software in April 1983.*

**COVERUP BY ATTORNEY GENERAL JANET RENO AND CLINTON ADMINISTRATION**

Attorney General Janet Reno then accepted the Bua report as the final word, and stated that she would not conduct any further investigation into the matter. That decision covered up for the criminality related to Inslaw and the criminal mindset in the Justice Department. She also acted to cover up for other criminal activities of federal officials, including BCCI, BNL, and others, as described elsewhere in these pages. The Clinton Administration, through its Attorney General, was continuing the pattern of criminal coverup and related crimes that I had discovered in that department for the past thirty years.

**SIMULTANEOUS MURDERS AND RETALIATION**

Riconosciuto sought help from various people to gather supporting documents for this grand jury proceeding. Among those gathering documents were his wife, Bobbi, and CIA contacts, including Ian Spiro, who resided near San Diego with his wife and their three children. Spiro had reportedly worked with Riconosciuto and the CIA.

Spiro never provided Riconosciuto with the Inslaw data. Spiro's wife and three children were found murdered in different rooms of their home near San Diego on November 1, 1992. Each of them had been shot in the head. Several days later, police found Ian Spiro's body in a parked car on the Borego Desert east of San Diego. Even though the murders were a state responsibility, the FBI did damage control by intruding into the investigations, stating that Spiro had killed his family and then committed suicide.

**LARGE NUMBER OF RELATED MURDERS PROTECTING JUSTICE DEPARTMENT AND OTHER OFFICIALS**

Danny Casolaro had evidence that would have assisted Riconosciuto, but he was killed. Earlier legal counsel and others who had worked with Riconosciuto were also killed, including attorneys Alan D. Standorf and Dennis Eisman. Earlier, an investigator hired by Riconosciuto, Larry Guerrin, was killed. The skeletal remains of Riconosciuto's friend, Vali Delahanty, were found on April 12, 1993, in a nearby ravine. Another attorney, John Crawford, who worked with Riconosciuto, died of a reported heart attack in April 1993.

Riconosciuto had relied upon Ian Spiro to obtain evidence needed for his defense, but Spiro and his family were killed. Almost simultaneously, a business and social acquaintance of Spiro was killed. Several months later, attorney Paul Wilcher, who sought to expose the Inslaw and October Surprise scandals, who shared data with me, was found dead in his Washington, D.C. residence. These deaths, and dozens of others, protected key officials in the government of the United States, especially within the U.S. Department of Justice.

**ANOTHER "CYA" OPERATION BY JUSTICE DEPARTMENT OFFICIALS**

A state civil trial that had the potential of exposing criminality on the part of Justice Department officials occurred during 1994 in Los Angeles, involving

Inslaw figure Earl Brian. Justice Department officials sent Assistant U.S. Attorney Stephen Zipperstein to Los Angeles to either block the start of the trial or prevent exposure of information relating to the Inslaw affair. Zipperstein was put in charge of the Justice Department "investigation" into the death of Danny Casolaro, whose death was linked to Inslaw. Zipperstein was also the Justice Department official who intercepted Paul Wilcher when Wilcher sought to deliver his one-hundred-page declaration to Attorney General Janet Reno. Wilcher was found dead shortly after giving his information to Zipperstein.

**COVERUP BY CLINTON'S JUSTICE DEPARTMENT**

For whatever reason, President Clinton's Justice Department conducted an "investigation" into the Inslaw affair in 1994. The investigation was conducted under the control of Webster Hubbell, the *de facto* head of the Justice Department, close associate of President Clinton, and Rose Law Firm partner with Hillary Clinton. As expected, Hubbell cleared the Justice Department of any wrongdoing in the case. Ironically, before the year was out, Hubbell pleaded guilty to several criminal offenses, adding to the list of former Justice Department officials found guilty of criminal acts (and to the much longer list of those who did commit federal crimes but were never prosecuted). Hubbell went to prison.

**FRAMING RICONOSCIUTO**

After Riconosciuto testified to Congress about the Justice Department's theft of the Inslaw software, Justice Department officials carried out their threat. Justice Department prosecutors charged Riconosciuto with a criminal offense, claiming he had *intended* to manufacture amphetamines at his mining operation in Washington.

To insure the success of this prosecution against Riconosciuto, Justice Department officials transferred DEA agent Michael Hurley from his Middle East assignment in Nicosia to Tacoma. According to information received from reliable sources, Hurley was DEA agent-in-charge at the infamous Mena, Arkansas drug center for CIA operations in the early 1980s before being assigned to Iran and then Nicosia.

The jury apparently believed the Justice Department prosecutors and Hurley's testimony, and returned a verdict of guilty, causing Riconosciuto to be sentenced to a long prison term.

Former Defense Intelligence Agency (DIA) agent Lester Coleman, III worked for the DIA in the Middle East, alongside Hurley in the DEA's Nicosia office. Coleman stated that he discovered the DEA had copies of the stolen Inslaw's PROMIS software and that the DEA was involved in selling it. According to a book authored by Coleman called *Trail of the Octopus*, the DEA was involved, or covered up for, a CIA-DEA-Lebanese-Syrian drug operation using Pan Am aircraft out of Frankfurt. This operation made possible the placement of the bomb on Pan Am Flight 103 which exploded over Lockerbie, Scotland. More about this in later pages.

On July 24, 1997, I received a fax from Hurley threatening to sue me, which appeared to be an attempt to block the printing of this book.

# BCCI, BANK OF CROOKS AND CRIMINALS

The world's worst banking scandal, inflicting huge financial losses on thousands of people worldwide, surfaced in the media in 1991. This was the Bank of Credit and Commerce International (BCCI). As could be expected, it had heavy ties with the CIA, terrorist organizations, drug traffickers, and any other crooked financial transaction shunned by most other banks. It financed terrorist activities, financed drug trafficking deals, defrauded depositors.

Following a standard pattern, Justice Department officials and the various divisions including the FBI and other government agencies kept the lid on the worldwide criminal activities of the bank. It wasn't until law enforcement agencies in Europe and a state prosecutor in New York City prepared to file charges that the bank's corrupt operations were shut down in the United States.

BCCI was a private bank operating in over seventy countries, including the United States. At one time BCCI had over 400 branches in 78 countries and assets of over $20 billion. Its holding company was based in Luxembourg and its principal operation in London. The primary bank supervisor for BCCI was Luxembourg Monetary Institute, the central bank of Luxembourg.

The BCCI scandal was related to other criminal activities including BNL, Iraqgate, Iran and the Iran-Contra affair, among others. BCCI and BNL both played a role in the Iraqi armament buildup, during which funds provided by U.S. taxpayers were forwarded by the Atlanta branch of Italy's Banca Nazionale del Lavoro. There were numerous cross-dealings between the banks. BCCI used its international connections to fund loans to BNL, which funded the Iraqi weapon buildups, which then required the U.S. taxpayer to fund much of the Persian Gulf War.

**COVERUP OF THE BANK OF CROOKS AND CRIMINALS**

Millions of people throughout the world lost billions of dollars, made possible by the coverup actions of officials in foreign countries and in the United States. Part of these losses would not have occurred had officials and attorneys in the United States not engaged in criminal activities, including coverup, misprision of felonies, obstruction of justice, aiding and abetting the criminal activities. Congressional committees, Justice Department personnel, the FBI, and the CIA, all knew about the corrupt BCCI operation for years.

### SOURCE OF STARTUP FUNDING

BCCI commenced operations in Pakistan in 1972, with much of its funding provided by Bank of America and the CIA.[345] Bank of America claims that it sold its BCCI interest in the early 1980s, but records indicate that the bank continued to control much of BCCI's operation until shortly before BCCI was shut down. In the early 1970s, CIA operative Gunther Russbacher described to me how he transferred sizable amounts of CIA funds into the bank for the start-up operations.

### MADE TO ORDER FOR CIA ACTIVITIES

The CIA knew about BCCI's activities, finding this mindset suitable to its own operations. If, for argument, the CIA had not been partners in the corrupt BCCI activities, its world-wide network of operatives and assets should have discovered the BCCI activities that brought about the world's worst banking loss. BCCI was custom-made for the covert and corrupt activities of the CIA, the Mossad, drug dealers, and terrorists. My CIA contacts, including Russbacher, told how CIA operatives used the bank to launder money from CIA enterprises. These included drug trafficking proceeds, the looting of savings and loans, funding unlawful arms shipments, financing terrorist operations,[346] undermining foreign governments, and other covert activities.

### MANIPULATING U.S. CHECKS AND BALANCES

Investigative reports indicated that BCCI was able to manipulate the spy agencies of numerous countries, including the U.S., Israel, China, Saudi Arabia, and Pakistan, among others. BCCI was supplying funds for terrorist organizations such as Abu Nidal. BCCI rigged international commodity markets that permitted certain insiders to make hundreds of millions of dollars in profits, offset by the same amount lost by depositors. BCCI was laundering drug money for drug cartels throughout the Americas, Europe, and the Middle East.

### BANK OF AMERICA INVOLVEMENT

Bank of America was heavily involved in BCCI from the date of its inception in 1972. It put up an initial cash investment amounting to 25 percent of the stock, which was later increased to 45 percent. (Some argue that Bank of America had a 60 percent interest.) Bank of America and the CIA had a major ownership in BCCI at that time.

Bank of America loaned money to people to buy stock in BCCI, possibly as fronts, making Bank of America's interest considerably higher. Three out of seven members of BCCI's board of directors were former senior executives

---

345 The author's CIA informants described how they diverted funds from secret CIA bank accounts in Europe to BCCI in 1972. CIA operative Gunther Russbacher informed me that while he was in Afghanistan he placed a large amount of CIA money into BCCI.

346 The Abu Nidal terrorist group and others obtained funds through BCCI, which helped to bring about the Pan Am 103 tragedy and others.

at Bank of America, some of whom were on leave from BofA.

A class action lawsuit[347] filed in San Francisco courts[348] by a class of defrauded BCCI depositors charged that Bank of America officials had considerable control over BCCI and had more knowledge of its illegal operations than previously disclosed. The lawsuit charged that Bank of America had a major ownership interest and control in BCCI, and that Bank of America loaned millions of dollars to BCCI front men so that they could unlawfully purchase financial institutions in the United States. The suit charged that five Bank of America officers were either on BCCI's board of directors or helped manage the bank. One of them, P.C. Twitchin, allegedly approved all BCCI loans over $5 million.

The suit charged that in 1978 Bank of America hired the son of Pakistani General Zia for a position, even though he was completely unqualified, solely to bribe important Pakistani officials. The suit charged that through a correspondent banking relationship with BCCI, Bank of America continued to conspire with and aid and abet BCCI activities until the summer of 1991. The suit charged that the wrongful acts of BCCI could not have been accomplished without the active and knowing assistance of Bank of America.

The president of an Atlanta Bank controlled by BCCI was a Bank of America official, adding to the evidence that BofA had heavy interests in the activities constituting the world's worst banking fraud. Bank of America had a symbiotic relationship with the "Bank of Crooks and Criminals," which continued years after the criminal activities became public. Bank of America made large profits from its relationship with the rogue bank. But fearing that its direct ownership in BCCI could be embarrassing, Bank of America officials started selling (1977) its interest in BCCI, lending money to front men to acquire these interests.

"The mother of all scandals," stated syndicated columnist Jack R. Payton in the *San Francisco Examiner*,[349] as he wrote of the BCCI affair. "Top BofA Alumni Filled Major Posts At BCCI," was another headline in the *San Francisco Chronicle*. The article named top executives of Bank of America who filled high-level positions at BCCI.

Another *San Francisco Chronicle* article was entitled, "BofA, BCCI Dealings Hit $1 Billion-Plus a Day." Bank of America was a crucial repository for large infusions of cash needed by BCCI to keep its worldwide financial empire afloat. The article stated that the transactions continued throughout the 1980s, long after BCCI's corrupt activities were known to thousands of people.

The article also mentioned Congressional sources who found that Bank of America's daily activities with BCCI reached $1.3 billion a day in some years, and that the relationship continued even after the U.S. government indicted two BCCI officers and nine BCCI executives in 1988 on charges of laundering over $32 million in drug money. The article quoted banking sources stating that the level of financial transactions that Bank of America conducted with BCCI was rare for a foreign correspondent bank.

According to a *San Francisco Chronicle* article quoting a Congressional source, Bank of America did not sever ties after BCCI's corrupt activities became

347 Filed by the San Diego law firm of Milberg Weiss Bershad Specthrie & Lerach.
348 *San Francisco Chronicle*, with the column headed, "Lawsuit Links BofA to BCCI."
349 October 9, 1992.

common knowledge. The Congressional source added that as late as March 1990, Bank of America kept two of its accounts open with BCCI's Miami office, two years after the Miami office had been indicted and was widely known for alleged money laundering deals involving drug money for former Panama dictator Manuel Noriega, among many others.

## BANK OF AMERICA KEPT BCCI IN BUSINESS

Without these financial transactions from Bank of America, BCCI would have occasionally run out of funds. Bank of America was instrumental in permitting BCCI to continue stealing depositors' money. Without this help the corrupt activities of BCCI would have been discovered years earlier.

The author of numerous books on financial institutions[350] told how Bank of America's $1 billion daily money transfer was strange and unusual. He estimated that the deposits were a Ponzi game probably involving letters of credit, which banks use to handle foreign trade payments. Mayer wrote that a great deal of BCCI sham activities were in bogus letters of credit.

Bank of America sold some of its stock to a BCCI subsidiary called International Credit and Investment Company, making a $27 million profit on the transaction. That same company, ICIC, has since been identified as the BCCI entity that handled some of BCCI's most notorious deals. These included fraudulent insider loans that were never repaid.

Congressman Frank Riggs (D-Calif) asked the House Committee on Banking, Finance and Urban Affairs to investigate Bank of America's ties to BCCI, stating in a letter to Congressman Henry Gonzalez, chairman of the Committee, that there is "very clear evidence" that Bank of America had links to the scandal ridden BCCI. In his letter to Gonzalez, Riggs wrote, "I believe that the links that have already been found between BCCI and BofA are of such far-reaching implications that a hearing is needed now." Riggs continued, "It troubles me that BofA continued to handle as much as $1.3 billion of BCCI deposits per day even after BCCI was indicted for money laundering in 1988."

Riggs pointed out that there existed a close financial relationship between Bank of America and International Credit and Investment Company (ICIC), a BCCI subsidiary in the Cayman Islands. Riggs added, "We know that Bank of America, a founder of BCCI, also provided a start-up loan to ICIC. We also know that BofA later sold its BCCI holdings to ICIC and provided financing to ICIC for the purchase. BofA made more than a 600 percent profit off this transaction."

## BANK OF AMERICA MONEY LAUNDERING

Bank of America was fined $7 million in 1986 for 17,000 separate acts of money laundering.[351] Bank of America's name surfaces throughout BCCI's sordid history. Despite the widespread knowledge by U.S. banking and intelligence agency personnel of the BCCI criminal activities during its two decades of corrupt operations, Bank of America officials, who controlled much of the BCCI operation, claimed they knew nothing about the corrupt unlawful activities.

350 Mayer.
351 *Time*, October 7, 1991.

## UNLAWFUL ACQUISITION OF U.S. BANKS AND SAVINGS AND LOANS

BCCI, as represented by Clark Clifford and Robert Altman, tried to convince U.S. regulators in the 1970s to allow BCCI to purchase a bank holding company. When U.S. regulators refused to allow this purchase that was barred by U.S. law, BCCI then loaned money to people who bought shares in American banks, including Financial General Bankshares, Inc.

When BCCI secretly sought to acquire in 1978 Financial General Bankshares, Inc., the stockholders of Financial went to court to block a takeover attempt, citing questionable activities by the BCCI front men. The stockholders requested supporting documents from Bank of America. To keep the BCCI activities from the public, from the stockholders, and from the government, Attorneys Clark Clifford and Robert Altman threatened to sue Bank of America if the bank produced the requested documents.

Bank of America officials then refused to produce documents that would otherwise expose these activities.[352] With the help of powerful U.S. law firms willing to subvert U.S. laws and interests, BCCI was able to violate U.S. banking laws, engage in a pattern of criminal activities, and inflict billions of dollars of harm to people throughout the United States and other countries. But U.S. taxpayers came to the rescue, and are now paying the price for these corrupt acts heavily involved with U.S. officials and law firms.

After secretly and unlawfully purchasing Financial General Bankshares, its name was changed to First American Bankshares. Altman was rewarded by being named president of the holding company and given stock that eventually netted him several million dollars profit, in addition to his monthly compensation. Many politicians were also paid off handsomely. When billions are stolen it is possible to pay well for those helping in the scheme. They all played the part of the amiable dunce, claiming they did not know First American Bankshares was controlled by BCCI or that the criminal activities existed.

These covert ownerships that were harming U.S. interests were fraudulently hidden by many law firms and attorneys, including Clifford and Altman. Clifford, chairman of First American Bankshares, said he didn't know of any ties to BCCI, in spite of the fact that his law firm represented BCCI; he was Chairman of BCCI front companies, and was the main U.S. lawyer for BCCI in the late 1970s. Clifford was frequently called the number one fixer in the Democratic party.

First American Bank in New York was part of the BCCI operation. BCCI secretly acquired First American's parent, First American Bankshares of Washington, D.C., in 1983. Federal law restricted the operations of BCCI's offices, prohibiting BCCI from accepting deposits in the United States. This restriction was violated, causing many depositors to lose their deposits. BCCI secretly acquired Independence Bank in Encino, First American, and invested in CenTrust in complex financial deals that were difficult to detect. BCCI acquired various U.S. banks including First American Bank in Washington with its many branches; National Bank of Georgia; Independence Bank in Encino, California.

---

352 *San Francisco Examiner*, September 22, 1991.

**SAUDI ARABIA INVOLVEMENT**

The biggest and most prestigious bank in Saudi Arabia, National Commercial Bank, was implicated in the BCCI scandal. District Attorney Robert Morgenthau, County of New York, brought a fraud indictment against the largest banker in Saudi Arabia, Sheik Khalid bin Mahfouz, charging the Saudi bank with failing to report purchases of stock in Washington's largest bank holding company, First American Bankshares, which was illegally and secretly controlled by BCCI. The purchase of the stock was financed by loans from the Saudi bank to people acting as fronts for BCCI. The Saudi bank loaned money to BCCI in a manner that permitted BCCI's illegal operations to continue.

**CANADIAN INVOLVEMENT**

Canadian politicians were also implicated. When members of Canada's Parliament were forced to investigate BCCI activities, they learned that the former deputy commissioner of the Royal Canadian Mounted Police (RCMP), Henry Jensen, who had supervised the BCCI investigation from 1987 to 1989, had gone to work for BCCI as a paid consultant shortly after his retirement.

Canadian officials refused to cooperate in the Inslaw investigation. Canadian officials have been charged with covering up sensitive facts relating to the Arrow Airlines DC-8 crash at Gander that killed 248 American GIs under suspicious circumstances. Arrow was a CIA front company.

**CONGRESSIONAL HEARINGS**

A BCCI insider, Abdur Sakhia, testified at a Senate Foreign Relations Subcommittee on Terrorism, Narcotics and Internal Operations about events that he had seen as a BCCI officer. He described a July 1988 meeting at the Washington offices of Clifford and Warnke, at which Clifford joked to one of the BCCI officers: "Welcome aboard. We will tell more lies now." Sakhia testified to meetings at which Altman and other senior BCCI executives referred to secret agreements under which BCCI retained control of Independence Bank of Encino. Clifford and Altman have consistently denied knowledge of any relationship to BCCI. Sakhia told how the CIA used BCCI for money transfer in the Iran-Contra affair.

Former federal budget director Bert Lance in the Carter Administration testified before Congress (October 23, 1991) that he was convinced the CIA recruited the founder of the Bank of Commerce and Credit International to use the bank for CIA purposes.

Acting director of the CIA, Richard Kerr, testified to the Senate subcommittee (October 26, 1991) that the CIA knew in 1985 that BCCI had secretly gained unlawful control of Washington's largest bank holding company.

**SAVINGS AND LOANS AND BCCI**

The savings and loan debacle had numerous connections with the BCCI scandal. Savings and loan figure Charles Keating served on the board of a Bahamas-based investment company, Trendinvest Ltd., along with Alfred Hartmann, who was a director of BCCI. Reports given to me by CIA sources state that the Keating group, among others, moved hundreds of millions of dollars into offshore bank accounts and trusts. Attorneys at the law firm of Alvarado, Rus & Worcester, representing over 15,000 investors who were defrauded by the Keating group, stated: "It was clear to us back in 1989 that Mr. Keating had been involved in significant movement of cash offshore."

Two failed savings and loans, CenTrust Savings Bank in Miami and Viking Savings in Santa Monica, California had direct or indirect connections to BCCI. Viking Savings and Loan was secretly acquired through money provided in part by California Democratic State Senator Alan Robbins, who contributed $900,000. Robbins allegedly obtained the money from BCCI Independence Bank of Encino, California. Viking was acquired by Michael Goland, a pro-Israeli candidate. Goland used money to mount a 1984 Senate campaign against Republican Charles Percy, who Goland felt was anti-Israel.

BCCI had a secret and illegal 28 percent ownership in CenTrust Savings Bank. CenTrust's failure will cost the American taxpayer over $2 billion. CenTrust was run by David Paul, a major fund raiser for the Democratic Party and a close friend of Senator Kerry, who investigated the BCCI scandal, and to this day hasn't taken any significant action. Senator Kerry was chairman of a key campaign committee for Senate Democrats in the late 1980s, while Paul was the chairman of the committee's fund-raising arm. Ghaith Pharaon, a Saudi Arabian financier, openly acquired a 28 percent stake in CenTrust, acting as a front man for BCCI.

A BCCI front purchased the Bank of Georgia in 1977, in which former budget director during the Carter administration, Burt Lance, had a substantial financial interest. Lance sold his shares in National Bank of Georgia to Saudi businessman and BCCI front man Ghaith Pharaon, who then sold them to First American Bank Holding company in Washington, D.C., another secretly controlled BCCI operation.

BCCI had tentacles in other criminal activities including Iraqgate and the bank primarily owned by the Italian government: Banca Nazionale del Lavoro (sometimes referred to as Bank Lavoro, or BNL for short). Both of these scandals implicated high U.S. officials.

## BCCI, BUSH, AND CLINTON

One of the men behind the founding of BCCI was Jackson Stephens who headed Stephens, Inc, located in Little Rock, Arkansas. Stephens, Inc. was a large U.S. investment bank with numerous hidden connections, including one with Harken Energy, to obtain the oil drilling rights off Bahrain. George Bush, Jr., was a consultant and member of the board of directors of Harken, before the oil drilling contract was signed. Stephen's firm helped secure a loan from a BCCI affiliated Swiss bank for Harken Energy.

Bill Clinton's involvement in the BCCI affair was shown in a February 1992 article[353] under the headline "Clinton and BCCI." The article reported that the Clinton campaign had a $2 million credit line from a bank with connections to BCCI. The credit line was from Worthen National Bank in Little Rock, Arkansas, controlled by Little Rock billionaire Jackson Stephens and managed by Curt Bradbury. Stephens was involved in the 1970s deals in which BCCI unlawfully acquired Washington's First American Bank.

Stephens' links to BCCI were reported in an *Arkansas Democrat* article

353 The article first appeared in the *New York Times*, and reported in the *Wall Street Journal*, February 10, 1992.

(December 1991) titled "Reports link Stephens to BCCI." The article stated that an employee of Stephens acted as chairman, president, and chief executive officer of Worthen National Bank. In addition, the article stated that in 1977, Stephens, Inc. assisted BCCI to unlawfully take over First American Bankshares. Another *Arkansas Gazette* article (August 1991) entitled "Little Rock on the BCCI route to power," stated in part:

> *Curt Bradbury, then a financial analyst for Stephens, Inc., and now chairman and chief executive officer of Worthen National Bank of Arkansas, provided [a BCCI officer] research about Financial General, including a copy of its latest annual report. Financial General was the parent company of the National Bank of Georgia, the bank run by Bert Lance [longtime crony of former President Jimmy Carter].*

It was the purchase of Financial General and the National Bank of Georgia that evolved into First American Bankshares, operated by attorney Clark Clifford in Washington.

An article in *Spotlight*[354] tied Democratic presidential candidate Clinton to the BCCI scandal and charged that the mainstream press was concentrating on Clinton's extramarital activities and his draft-dodging during the Vietnam war while ignoring Clinton's involvement in the BCCI scandal. The article referred to *New York Post* writer Mike McAlary's reporting of the connections between Clinton and the BCCI mess. Money allegedly came from Arkansas billionaire Jackson Stephens, who reportedly brokered the transaction that enabled BCCI to gain unlawful and covert control of two U.S. banks, First American Bankshares and the National Bank of Georgia.

Houston oil consultant Michael Ameen, who was on the payroll of the U.S. State Department as a consultant, was highly instrumental in working out the Bahrain deal. Ameen had close contacts with a major BCCI shareholder, Kamal Adham, who was also a former chief of Saudi Arabian Intelligence.

**MANY LINKS**

Alfred Hartmann, a Swiss banker, was a BCCI director and chairman of its Swiss unit, Banque de Commerce et Placements S.A., or BCP for short. Hartmann was also chairman of BNL's unit in Zurich, Switzerland, known as Lavoro Bank. Hartmann was vice chairman of a joint-venture institution in Geneva called Bank of New York-Inter Maritime Bank. Hartmann was involved in the BCCI and BNL banks and in the Bank of New York-Inter Maritime Bank. An officer of Bank of New York, Bruce Rappaport, also had close ties to the CIA and the Mossad.

**PROFITS FOR SABOTAGING AMERICA'S INTERESTS**

Many attorneys, public relations firms, members of Congress, and others made handsome profits at the expense of the American taxpayers and the thousands of depositors who lost their life's savings.

Carter, while President of the United States, owed money to a bank with connections to BCCI and was bailed out along with his banker friend, Bert Lance, by Pharaon. Pharaon first loaned $3.5 million to Lance through BCCI and then

354 March 2, 1992.

bought control of Lance's bank for an additional $2.4 million.[355] Several days later President Carter approved the sale of F-15s to Saudi Arabia. BCCI paid for former President Jimmy Carter's trips around the world after he left the White House.

BCCI wrote off a $160,000 loan to an Atlanta consulting firm operated by Andrew Young, former mayor of Atlanta.[356] The loan had been made by National Bank of Georgia, which had been acquired by BCCI front man Ghaith Pharaon. Young had served as U.S. ambassador to the United Nations during the Carter administration. Enlarging on his many trips to Africa, Young promoted BCCI to individuals and governments in Africa and Central America. Mayor Young received a retainer for introducing Third World leaders to BCCI. A former BCCI official provided about $11,000 in travel accommodations to Reverend Jesse Jackson.

White House aide and attorney Ed Rogers went to work for a BCCI front man, Kamal Adham, in October 1991. Adham was a front man in the illegal purchase of Washington's First American Bank. In a press conference, President Bush denied knowing Adham, although the facts indicated otherwise. Adham was head of Saudi Arabia's spy agency while Bush was head of the U.S. Central Intelligence Agency. Despite Rogers' young age, 33 years, and his lack of legal experience, BCCI offered him $600,000 up front for two years work plus expenses to leave his job as White House aide and assistant to chief of staff John Sununu. He obviously wasn't being paid for his legal knowledge, but for his political contacts with the Bush Administration.

Rogers, a young attorney who had never practiced law and had relatively little experience, stated on his application to register as a foreign agent that he had been hired for his legal expertise. The two most probable reasons for Rogers to be hired by a mastermind in the BCCI web were (a) either for his influence in the White House, or (b) with the urging of the White House to facilitate the various covert activities between President George Bush, other White House officials, or the CIA.

Abu Dhabi's role takes on political dimensions because the ruling family of Abu Dhabi contracted with a firm operated by President Bush's deputy campaign manager, James Lake, to handle public relations. That firm has been paid over $1 million over a twelve-month period to have the U.S. media define Abu Dhabi as a victim of the scheme to illegally gain control of banks in the United States. Abu Dhabi was uncooperative in providing documents and refused to allow any of its citizens to testify. Lake was sitting in on White House campaign strategy meetings while also providing information to Sheik Zaved bin Sultan al-Nayhan,[357] who controlled a major portion of BCCI's shares.

**PUBLIC RELATIONS FIRM'S SELLOUT OF U.S. INTERESTS**

BCCI hired a public relations firm led by prominent Republican Robert Gray and Democrat Frank Mankiewicz, which was paid fees of $50,000 a month while it spread false information to Congress and the public protecting BCCI. The accounting firm responsible for inspecting BCCI, Price Waterhouse, received

355 The Jack Anderson syndicated column.

356 *Wall Street Journal* September 3, 1991.

357 Sheik Zaved bin Sultan al-Nayhan was president of the United Arab Emirates.

a $600,000 loan from BCCI.[358] An employee of Price Waterhouse, who audited the financial statements of BCCI and covered up for the irregularities, received over $100,000 from a BCCI affiliate within two years after leaving the accounting firm. The same practice continued as private auditors (hired by those looting the savings and loans, and receiving exorbitant salaries) kept the lid on the corrupt activities.

San Francisco attorney Henry Fields and the law firm of Morrison & Foerster were used by BCCI front man, Ghaith R. Pharaon, to obtain regulatory approval for the purchase of Independence Bank of Encino, California. Fields assured regulators that Pharaon would be the sole owner of Independence. But Pharaon signed an agreement putting 85 percent ownership of the California bank in the hands of a BCCI subsidiary. Immediately after the California bank changed hands, Pharaon hired another Morrison & Foerster attorney to be on the board of directors of Independence Bank.

Many attorneys in the United States and overseas were involved in the complex activities of BCCI, and not a single one spoke out, typical of their role in almost every scandal I have already mentioned.

**CIA CONNECTIONS**

The CIA provided part of the startup funding for BCCI. It moved large amounts of money through BCCI during its entire operation. Former CIA Director Richard Helms tried to arrange for the purchase of First American by BCCI and failed. Clark Clifford then sought to arrange the purchase using BCCI front men, obtaining U.S. regulatory approval based upon Clifford's false representations.

**JEB BUSH**

One of President Bush's sons, Jeb Bush, had numerous dealings with BCCI and was frequently in BCCI's Miami office. Jeb Bush's company invested in real estate with a company controlled by a BCCI customer, who was later sent to prison for defrauding BCCI and other banks.

**BRIBERY WAS EVERYWHERE**

BCCI had a bribery list of U.S. elected public officials. Reference was made to this list during Congressional testimony (September 13, 1991) before the House Banking Committee, which was chaired by Representative Henry Gonzalez. One method reported for conveying bribes to members of Congress was through the Chicago Commodity Exchange, Chicago Board of Trade, Chicago Board Options Exchange, and the Chicago Mercantile Exchange. Money was put into commodity exchange accounts overseas under the name of a particular member of Congress. Periodically the Congressman would be informed that there was money in his account, and he was then advised how he could withdraw it if he wished. Huge amounts of cash were brought into Chicago to orchestrate this scheme.

**BOTH POLITICAL PARTIES IMPLICATED**

As in many of the scandals mentioned in this book, both political parties were implicated, receiving large financial contributions or bribes from the illicitly operated bank. As in the savings and loan scandal, members of Congress were

358 *Wall Street Journal* article by Peter Truell.

handsomely rewarded for either looking the other way or obstructing any investigations. The key to continuing the corruption and harms inflicted throughout the world by BCCI was bribing U.S. and other officials.

Senator Orrin Hatch (R-Utah), the senior Republican on the Judiciary Committee, was one of hundreds of Congressmen who received money from BCCI officials. He was more openly protective of the BCCI corruption. Senator Hatch issued a glowing endorsement of the Justice Department's plea bargain settlement with BCCI's money-laundering operation in Tampa, Florida, which was a slap-on-the-wrist settlement blocking further investigation into high-level BCCI corruption. It also prevented investigation of Hatch's involvement with BCCI.

Although BCCI pled guilty to several dozen felony counts, Senator Hatch said in his Senate floor speech that "There was no systematic money laundering uncovered in the BCCI case." Hatch has extolled "senior management, directors and shareholders of BCCI for the responsible way" they behaved. This probably reflected the mindset of U.S. Congressmen (and Congresswomen).

Senator Hatch's speech had been prepared by the same BCCI cutouts that perpetrated the sham against the American people: Washington attorney Robert Altman and his law office. Immediately after giving the unusual speech defending the crime-infested bank and those who made the crimes possible, Senator Hatch placed a telephone call to BCCI's chief executive officer, Swaleh Naqvi. Hatch requested a loan for his business associate, Munzer Hourani, a Houston businessman.

In another instance, Senator Hatch's office misused his senate office trying to protect BCCI against drug money laundering charges. When the media exposed this attempt, Hatch sought to divert attention from himself by blaming a former member of his staff, Michael Pillsbury. Pillsbury had represented Senator Hatch by seeking a more favorable outcome in the 1989 money laundering indictment in Florida against BCCI officials. Hatch sought to sidestep blame by asking the Senate Ethics Committee to investigate his former aide.

Senator Hatch was involved with a part owner of BCCI, Mohammed Hammoud, a front man for BCCI in First American Bankshare purchases. Hammoud's loose talk about the BCCI operations threatened politicians and crooks worldwide, possibly causing his May 1990 death under mysterious circumstances in Geneva, Switzerland. The insurance company refused to pay death benefits because the corpse was four inches shorter than shown on Hammoud's last physical examination.

Senator Hatch was one of the senators to whom I sent evidence of these various scandals and who refused to receive my evidence. It is understandable that a member of Congress already implicated in one or more scandals or criminal activities would refuse to receive evidence of other criminal activities. The same argument can surely be applied to each of the other senators and representatives who refused to receive the testimony and evidence of our group of whistleblowers.

One of the infamous Keating-Five senators from the savings and loan scandal, Senator Alan Cranston (D-Calif.), intervened on behalf of BCCI.[359] Cranston

359 *Los Angeles Times*, October 7, 1991.

wrote a letter to the Federal Home Loan Bank Board at the request of David Paul, owner of BCCI-related CenTrust Savings Bank[360] of Miami, requesting relief from regulatory actions, while simultaneously receiving political contributions which are usually bald-face bribes. Senator Cranston repeatedly intervened on behalf of the biggest crooks in the savings and loan debacle while refusing to receive my evidence of massive criminal activities. He also intervened on behalf of the crooks in the world's worst banking scandal. That same scenario applied to many other members of the Senate and House.

## CONGRESS FORCED TO "INVESTIGATE"

The media attention over BCCI's activities forced Congress to conduct an "investigation." The Senate Foreign Relations' Subcommittee on Terrorism, Narcotics and International Operations, chaired by Senator John Kerry (D-MA), conducted an investigation. At the same time, Kerry received financial contributions from BCCI's front man David Paul, of Florida's CenTrust (a U.S. financial institution unlawfully affiliated with BCCI). CenTrust failed, costing the American taxpayer over two billion dollars. CenTrust Chairman, David Paul, arranged for BCCI to invest $25 million in CenTrust bonds in 1988, and then repurchased the bonds two months later. The intent was to make CenTrust temporarily look healthier than it really was. This temporary financial support further substantiated the BCCI-CenTrust relationship.

The bribe to Kerry, or whatever one wishes to call it, may be the reason that the Senate Committee did not request the appointment of an Independent Prosecutor despite the serious corruption uncovered by the committee investigators. Many members of Congress were involved in the scandal, which also helped to eliminate any desire for an Independent Prosecutor.

## COVERUP OF VERY SERIOUS CRIMES IGNORED BY THE SENATE COMMITTEE

Senate investigator Jack Blum unsuccessfully sought to have Congress act on the alarming disclosures that he had uncovered. When much of the criminality focused on corrupt members of Congress, other U.S. officials refused to delve into those areas. In desperation, Senate Investigator Jack Blum quit his Senate investigative function and tried to get Justice Department officials to act. After being stonewalled there, Blum sought to interest Manhattan District Attorney Robert Morgenthau in the scandal that had tentacles in New York.

The overwhelming evidence that Blum presented resulted in Morgenthau obtaining a grand jury indictment (July 29, 1991) against BCCI and two cutouts, Clark Clifford and Robert Altman. They were charged with engaging in a multi-billion-dollar scheme to defraud depositors, falsifying bank records, concealing illegal money-laundering, and engaging in larceny. Even after the indictment, Justice Department officials refused to produce requested documents. By July 1991, Morganthau had enough evidence to indict Clifford and Altman. They were charged with bank fraud and with receiving $40 million in bribes from BCCI as part of a conspiracy to give BCCI control of several banks in the United States.

---

360 About one fourth of CenTrust's stock was owned by BCCI before it collapsed.

**THE SENATE REPORT**

The committee issued a nearly 800-page report (October 1, 1992), accusing BCCI of using political insiders to commit fraud upon the United States on a global scale. The report stated that there exists "an elaborate corporate spider-web with BCCI's founder, Agha Hasan Abedi and his assistant, Swaleh Naqvi, in the middle." The report stated that BCCI's *modus operandi* throughout the world, including the United States, was bribery and subversion of government officials.

The report stated that BCCI "systematically bribed political figures around the world." Senator Hank Brown, a member of the Senate committee, stated at a news conference, "We found it was BCCI's overpowering use of the nation's political insiders like [former Defense Secretary] Clark Clifford...that permitted BCCI's secret expansion in the United States."

The report described an international operation that would exceed SPECTRE, the fiendish "Special Executive for Counter-intelligence, Terrorism, Revenge and Extortion," found in James Bond novels and movies. Senator Kerry said that "BCCI constituted international global crime on a level that boggles the mind." The report criticized U.S. bank regulators, the CIA, and the Justice Department, and offered a scathing portrait of political influence, international bribery, and inaction by agencies having the duty to act, becoming the catalyst for one of the biggest financial frauds in the world's history.

The report listed the financial contributions or bribes paid to various members of the U.S. Congress, including former Senator John Culver (D-Iowa) and Senator Orrin G. Hatch (R-Utah). The report severely criticized two attorneys, Clark M. Clifford, a former Cabinet member and adviser to various Presidents of the United States, and his protege, Robert A. Altman, who have been charged with taking bribes from BCCI in exchange for hiding BCCI's ownership of First American Bankshares, a Washington holding company of which Clifford was the chairman.

Senator Hank Brown (R-CO), who was the subcommittee's ranking minority member, substantiated the fact that BCCI's financial contributions were so extensive that "there was not a single committee of this Congress that wanted to conduct a complete, thorough investigation."

The report stated that while Senator Hatch and Mr. Pillsbury, a former State Department official, worked on behalf of BCCI to halt investigations, Senator Hatch was requesting BCCI to lend $10 million to a business associate with whom the Senator was in partnership.

The report stated that BCCI used political insiders such as former Defense Secretary Clark Clifford and members of Congress to commit fraud on a global scale. It told how BCCI paid members of Congress, lobbyists, and attorneys to obstruct the investigation into its terrorists and drug-money-laundering activities. The report implicated Democrats and Republicans, lawyers and lobbyists, public relations firms, Congressional staffers and former senators.

The report treated with kid gloves Senator Hatch's frequent attempts to protect BCCI and to obstruct criminal investigations while receiving BCCI money. The report tried to make Senator Hatch's aide the scapegoat and recommended that the aide be "investigated" by the Senate Ethics Committee. The activities of attorney and former Senator John Culver (D-Iowa), were stated, in part:

*Sen. Culver's role in lobbying Congress to assist BCCI was more significant than had been publicly understood, and...he provided valuable advice to BCCI on how to handle Congressional attempts to investigate the bank.*

Despite the gravity of the crimes depicted in the Senate report, much remained to be learned when the Senate committee discontinued its investigation and issued its report.

CIA officials refused to produce hundreds of documents that it had on the BCCI operations, in which the CIA itself was involved.

**REFUSAL TO REQUEST INDEPENDENT PROSECUTOR**

Despite the many unanswered questions concerning involvement of U.S. officials, the Senate committee refused to request appointment of an *independent* prosecutor. To have done so would have implicated many members of Congress in both major political parties. When questioned by reporters as to whether he would request appointment of an independent counsel, Senator Kerry replied, "There already is an independent counsel, Bob Morgenthau." That answer was a farce.

A county district attorney has a limited budget, and has neither the funds nor the authority, nor the responsibility, to investigate a complex scandal with international implications of the magnitude of the BCCI scandal. The authority of a local county prosecutor is obviously inadequate to investigate the national and international aspects of the BCCI scandal. Morgenthau's yearly budget for prosecuting *all* criminal acts in Manhattan was approximately $50 million. Independent prosecutor Lawrence Walsh, for instance, spent over $40 million just to determine who was lying to Congress in the Iran-Contra affair.

**HUNDREDS OF TIPS FROM INFORMANTS, AND THE USUAL JUSTICE DEPARTMENT OBSTRUCTION OF JUSTICE**

Federal agencies received hundreds of tips for over ten years detailing BCCI criminal activities. Federal agencies, including the FBI, Justice Department, Drug Enforcement Administration, and the Internal Revenue Service, had thousands of investigators, many of whom knew about the corruption for years, and no action was taken. As in every other scandal, Justice Department officials blocked corrective actions.

An initial investigation in 1989 by Justice Department officials into BCCI's secret ownership of First American had been abruptly canceled, protecting the criminal elements within BCCI, powerful Washington law firms, members of Congress, Bank of America, and others.

Former BCCI officers informed the Senate committee that they believed the Justice Department's coverup and failure to properly investigate BCCI was due to BCCI's extensive connections with the CIA and other U.S. intelligence agencies. An investigation would expose the unlawful Iran-Contra arms flow, the drug trafficking into the United States from throughout the world, CIA money laundering from its covert domestic proprietaries, bribing of U.S. officials, especially members of Congress, and God knows what else.

The BCCI scandal would most likely have slowly drifted away and become worse, if it had been left up to those in charge of the U.S. Department of Justice and Congress. It would be one more major scandal kept secret from the American public. But a persistent investigator, Jack Blum, went to a County Prosecutor in New York when Congress and the Justice Department stonewalled the matter, and convinced a 73-year old County Prosecutor, Robert Morgenthau, to prosecute BCCI and the crooks associated with it. Soon after commencing the investigation, Morgenthau encountered the obstruction of justice tactics by Justice Department attorneys, who wanted to keep the lid on the scandal.

**OVER A DECADE OF IGNORING INFORMANTS**

Thirteen years before BCCI was seized in 1991, an American bank examiner, Joseph Vaez,[361] warned in a memo that BCCI was rife with bad loans and that the bank used front men to disguise fraudulent transactions. The memo described the incestuous lending and ownership arrangements with affiliate companies in offshore havens, the practice of almost limitless lending to favored customers, and other serious banking irregularities.

The memo referred to the ICIC Group, a Cayman Islands affiliate that the Federal Reserve called BCCI's alter ego, and estimated that it controlled 70 percent of BCCI, and that BCCI's front men operated through ICIC. Vaez testified before a Senate subcommittee[362] concerning the memo, which mysteriously disappeared from the government files. Vaez then produced his copy of the document. The Senate committee then requested the original from the comptroller's office, which refused to produce it. The committee then subpoenaed the document.

Assistant Secretary of Intelligence at the State Department, Douglas Mulholland, testified about another hidden memo on BCCI. In January 1985, while he was special assistant for national security to the Secretary of the Treasury, he received an unusual report from the CIA relating to BCCI. Mulholland further testified that the CIA forbade him from discussing the memo on the basis of national security.[363]

A CIA telex message from CIA Director Richard Helms was entered into the Senate hearing record showing the CIA knew of the BCCI activities a decade before the scandal surfaced. The telex related to the wording of an agreement to grant power of attorney to a Washington law firm relative to a transaction involving Financial General Bankshares of Washington, D.C., later renamed First American Bankshares.

**HOUSE "INVESTIGATION"**

The House also conducted an "investigation" into the BCCI scandal. Representative Charles Schumer chaired the House committee, and the report was for all practical purposes a coverup. Congressional investigator and coverup artist Lawrence Barcella helped persuade Senator Orrin Hatch to give a speech on the Senate floor praising BCCI.[364] This is the same Barcella who in 1992 engaged in a coverup of the House October Surprise "investigation." Barcella also helped to conceal a covert CIA operation supplying military equipment to Libya's President Moamer al Kadhafi, after its cover was blown, by charging

361 Vaez was an examiner for the Office of the Comptroller of the Currency testifying before a Senate subcommittee.

362 *New York Times*, February 20, 1992.

363 The "national security" label is routinely used to prevent the disclosure of information on internal misconduct by government officials.

364 *Newsweek*, August 26, 1991.

CIA-operative Edwin Wilson with a federal crime for carrying out CIA operations.

CIA Deputy Director Robert Gates had stated in 1988 to the head of Customs, William von Raab, that BCCI stood for the "Bank of Crooks and Criminals International." Yet, the CIA continued to deposit and launder funds in BCCI, covering up the criminal activities that would defraud people all over the world who had put their money into the bank.

In the 1980s, U.S. Customs Commissioner William von Raab unsuccessfully tried to get the Justice Department to act on the serious federal violations committed by BCCI. Raab testified to Senate investigators that in 1988 he told Gates of the drug money laundering at BCCI, and that Gates refused to proceed with the information. Raab did not know, apparently, that the CIA was *itself* laundering drug and other illicit money through BCCI.

BCCI officer Nazir Chinoy tried to provide information to federal prosecutors about covert arms deals involving BCCI and the CIA.[365] Instead, Justice Department officials indicted Chinoy, and in that manner, the CIA drug smuggling was again kept under wraps.

Justice Department officials were put on notice during a 1985 federal heroin investigation that money was being laundered in BCCI's Independence Bank of Encino in California. The Justice Department's DEA and the Treasury Department's Internal Revenue Service learned of the BCCI connection and the drug money laundering, and did nothing about it. To have done so would have exposed the CIA and bribing of federal officials. Tape recordings of a BCCI officer talking to an undercover investigator included the following statement:

> *Now we are trying to extend our operations into the United States, we have offices in New York, Atlanta, Miami, Houston, San Francisco, also we have acquired some local bank which we take over very shortly.*

Kidder, Peabody & Company notified federal regulators from 1978 through 1981 that it was helping BCCI acquire an interest in First American Bankshares, Inc, while First American was telling banking regulators that First American had no connections to BCCI.[366] This information was prepared by Martin Siegel, showing that BCCI was behind the ownership change involving First American, the largest bank holding company in Washington. After the acquisition was approved in 1982, Kidder renewed its registration as an agent for BCCI, working in connection with the acquisition of First American. No reference was made on the application form that Kidder was working with the front men.

Seeking to circumvent the block by Justice Department officials, U.S. Customs officer Robert Mazur wrote to Senator John Kerry (D-Mass.), chairman of the Senate Subcommittee on Terrorism, Narcotics and International Operations, complaining about the coverup within the Justice Department and Customs. Mazur wrote:

> *Tons of documents were not reviewed...and the CIA put a halt to certain investigative leads into a 1988 Florida inquiry that led to the indictment*

---

365 *San Francisco Daily Journal*, November 13, 1991.
366 *Wall Street Journal*, September 10, 1991.

*of BCCI officers in Tampa. We had drug traffickers, money launderers, foreign government involvement, Noriega and allegations of payoffs by BCCI to U.S. government political figures. I will not elaborate on who these U.S. government figures were alleged to be, but I can advise you that you don't have all of the documents. Some were destroyed or misplaced.*

Senator Kerry refused to release the letters written by Mazur, but those who have seen them state they were political dynamite, exposing serious misconduct by many members of Congress. Dozens of members of Congress received political contributions or bribes from BCCI and its unlawful outlets in the United States, including the chairman of the investigating committee, Senator John Kerry, who received the highest reported amount of contributions. Kerry also failed to recommend appointment of an independent prosecutor into the BCCI scandal.

In testifying before the Senate committee,[367] Mazur testified to the following facts: (1) that his group discovered hundreds of leads indicating gross misconduct by BCCI officials; (2) that Justice Department officials refused to send investigators who were needed to follow through on the leads;[368] (3) that the leads indicated large political payoffs in the United States; (4) that BCCI was financing unlawful arms transactions; (5) that BCCI secretly owned U.S. banks, and other federal violations; and (6) that Justice Department officials blocked exposure of these matters in numerous ways, including refusal to provide additional personnel, refusal to grant permission to obtain testimony outside the United States, and by reaching a plea bargain with BCCI before higher-ups were implicated.

Mazur further testified that he resigned from the U.S. Customs Service[369] because of his frustration at the coverup by Justice Department officials and within the Customs Service. He described the discovery of BCCI's money-laundering activities in Tampa, Florida, and the political payoffs, along with the secret ownership of U.S. banks.

### JUSTICE AND CIA CAUGHT RED HANDED

Feisty Congressman Henry Gonzalez's (D-TX) persistent investigations and demands for documents exposed the coverup by Justice Department and CIA officials. Each of them had reported to Congressional committees that every document in their files pertaining to BCCI had been released to the Congressional investigative committees. These statements were proven false after the CIA inadvertently released sensitive documents disproving the statements. Media attention and charges of coverup created a crisis situation, each of the two agencies blaming the other for coverup.

Acting CIA Director Richard Kerr testified to the Senate committee on November 11, 1991, revealing that between 1983 and 1985 the CIA had sent several hundred reports to government agencies, including the Justice Department, chronicling BCCI's illegal activities. Justice Department officials had lied to Congress, stating initially they did not have any other documents. Thereafter, Justice Department officials sought to have CIA officials explain the discrepancy

367 November 21, 1991.
368 *Los Angeles Times*, November 22, 1991.
369 Resigned in April 1990.

by lying, but without success.

**RETALIATING AGAINST FBI DIRECTOR**

Congress and the media demanded that an independent prosecutor be requested to investigate the Justice Department and the CIA. FBI Director William Sessions assured Senator David Boren (D-OK) that the FBI would investigate the conduct of Justice Department officials. This statement was an unprecedented threat to his bosses in the Department of Justice, and who were implicated in several major scandals. Two days after Boren announced Sessions' intention this to the press, U.S. Attorney General William Barr announced an investigation of Sessions for ethic violations.

The basis for the investigation of the FBI head? Sessions used government telephones for private business, allowing his wife to ride with him on government aircraft on a space available basis, and installing a security fence at his home to protect government secrets. Big deal! If applied in the same manner, this charge could be leveled at major segments of the federal and state governments.

Recognizing the phony and retaliatory nature of the charges, Senator Boren was among the Congressmen who charged Justice Department officials with trying to obstruct justice by threatening the Director of the FBI with phony charges.[370]

It was ironical that while Attorney General William Barr was engaging in widespread coverup and obstruction of justice of many of the crimes described within these pages, he sought the removal of the FBI Director on these sham charges.

**PRESIDENT ASSISTED IN COVERUP**

Clinton had already played a key role in obstruction of justice relating to the vast CIA drug trafficking near Mena, Arkansas, while Clinton was governor of that state. After Bill Clinton became president and appointed Janet Reno as U.S. Attorney General, the two of them carried out Barr's previous plan to remove the Director of the FBI who constituted a threat to government corruption. Without allowing Sessions to defend against the obvious sham charges, Reno and Clinton removed the FBI Director.

The lapdog press eulogized this removal and said nothing about its relationship with Sessions' intent to investigate Justice Department corruption.

It is estimated that the BCCI corrupt practices cost innocent depositors from $5 to $15 **billion** in losses. Over a million depositors in 69 countries, including the United States, lost all or most of their savings and deposits. Part of BCCI's losses will be paid by the U.S. taxpayer through the losses of secretly owned savings and loans and the stockholders in the U.S. banks secretly owned by BCCI. The Independence Bank of Encino, California,[371] a BCCI bank, caused losses of $130 to $140 million. These losses are insured by the American public, who will pay the tab.

U.S. investors in the bank-holding company secretly acquired by BCCI lost large sums of money. First American Bankshares paid $225 million to acquire

---

370 Very few government employees have not used government phones for private calls. Many government employees, including myself, used government aircraft for flight experience which concurrently had an element of private use attached.

371 Independence Bank had fourteen branches in the Los Angeles area.

National Bank of Georgia in 1985, receiving only $90 million from its 1992 sale after the BCCI scandal broke. The $135 million difference is a loss to the U.S. investors who owned part of the bank holding company.

Central banks and governments of Third World Nations will lose billions. These losses could have been prevented if the CIA or any of the other U.S. officials had performed their duties instead of engaging in felony coverup. And the same goes for the members of Congress who also covered up. Of course, the same goes for each and every one of the other corrupt activities described within these pages.

**VATICAN BANK SCANDAL**

Similar to the deaths of informants in other scandals such as Inslaw, Chapter 11 corruption, and October Surprise, witnesses and informants to the BCCI scandal were killed or mysteriously died. The 1988 death of a New York City attorney, Cornelius Ahearn, is believed due to the fact that he knew too much about the links between the BCCI scandal and the Vatican Bank scandal[372] of the 1980s.

**WHITE HOUSE INVOLVEMENT**

The White House had numerous tentacles to the BCCI scandal, and through its control over the Justice Department blocked or greatly reduced action against BCCI for years, despite knowledge of the bank's criminal activities. President Bush's deputy campaign manager, James Lake,[373] simultaneously worked in 1992 for the main owner of scandal-riddled BCCI.[374]

Attorney Ed Rogers, the right-hand assistant to President Bush's Chief of Staff, John Sununu, signed a lucrative employment agreement with a BCCI participant, Sheik Kamal Adham, the former chief of Saudi intelligence. Adham was at the heart of the BCCI bank swindle.

At the same time, the U.S. Attorney General and his Justice Department were blocking prosecution of BCCI. It was an interesting connection, to have a top-level campaign adviser for President Bush representing a major owner of the corruption-riddled renegade bank while the Justice Department was blocking prosecution of the multiple crimes involved in the BCCI scandal.

**BRITISH COVERUP**

It was the English government that first acted to shut down BCCI in 1992 when the scandal became public. BCCI was chartered in Luxembourg but actually operated primarily in England under British regulators and investigators. The Bank of England and other British checks and balances knew about BCCI corrupt activities for years, and covered up. England's security agencies, MI5 and MI6, surely knew what was going on, and did nothing.

British media attention forced an "investigation," conducted by Lord Justice Bingham, who issued a report in October 1992. The report did nothing to prevent another BCCI, and did not delve into those responsible for the world's worst banking scandal. The report described BCCI's performance as "a tragedy of

---

372 The Vatican bank scandal surfaced in 1982, following the collapse of Calvi's Milan-based bank. The Vatican settled law suits for $250 million.

373 Lake worked as a senior communications adviser to the Bush campaign, being promoted on February 27, 1992 to deputy campaign manager for surrogates, advance and scheduling.

374 *Associated Press*, February 28, 1992.

errors, misunderstandings and failures of communication." It wasn't a misunderstanding, nor failure of communication, that permitted BCCI to engage in world-wide money laundering, financing terrorists and drug cartels, threats and murders; it was criminal coverup by every check and balance.

The people sabotaging their own country's interest were not only in the United States. The Bank of England reported (September 28, 1992) that it would seek a probe into allegations revealing that several of its employees took bribes from BCCI. It subsequently issued a white-wash report, stating that no evidence was found of bad faith, duplicity, coverup, or conspiracy by British subjects in the BCCI corruption. The Bank of England entered into an arrangement with the bank's principal owner, Abu Dhabi, and under this agreement, important records and witnesses were allowed to leave England. In that way, those in England who aided and abetted the BCCI scheme escaped exposure.

## JUSTICE DEPARTMENT COVERUP

"Something fishy is behind this government's reluctance to prosecute aggressively the well-connected predators of BCCI," stated William Safire in his November 1991 syndicated column.

Until January 1992, high Justice Department officials blocked an investigation into BCCI corruption, according to the testimony of a former U.S. Attorney in Miami, Dexter Lehtinen.[375] He testified that in 1991, when he was building a case against BCCI, Justice Department officials in Washington blocked court orders to obtain documents from foreign countries concerning BCCI corruption. Lehtinen also testified that in late August 1991 he received a phone call from a high Justice Department official who said he was calling on behalf of Acting Attorney General William Barr. The official said that Barr wanted him not to seek an indictment against BCCI. Congress also assisted in this coverup by refusing to approve Lehtinen's temporary U.S. Attorney position to a permanent position, causing him to resign.

Members of Congress demanded in 1992 that Attorney General William Barr request the appointment of an Independent Prosecutor to investigate BCCI. Barr refused to do so. He had earlier refused to appoint a Congressionally-requested independent prosecutor in the Inslaw matter, in the Bank of Lavoro matter, and in the Iraqgate matter.

The prosecution of BCCI on the money-laundering charge was not initiated by the Justice Department but on the initiative of local Customs Service agents. Justice Department officials had sought to block that prosecution, but this proved difficult due to media attention, Justice sought to limit the scope of the investigation by reaching a plea agreement allowing BCCI to ensure that the evidence collected during the investigation wouldn't be used against BCCI in any future federal charges.

## ONE OF MANY REASONS FOR JUSTICE DEPARTMENT COVERUP

Before William Barr came to the Justice Department, he was an attorney with the Washington law firm of Shaw, Pittman, Potts & Trowbridge. This

---

375 Testified on May 14, 1992, before the Senate Subcommittee on Terrorism, Narcotics and International Operations.

law firm represented BCCI for several years. A partner in the law firm, Kenly Webster, was representing a former BCCI chief executive, Swaleh Naqvi, who had been indicted by a Manhattan grand jury on fraud, false accounting, money-laundering and other charges. Naqvi had also been indicted in Tampa, Florida, on similar charges. Barr's former law firm also represented B. Francis Saul II, a director and powerful shareholder in Financial General Bankshares, Inc. Financial later became First American Bankshares, a covert BCCI operation.

Further, Barr had been legal counsel for the CIA, the same agency that was heavily involved with BCCI corrupt activities. He was CIA counsel during the time that George Bush was Director of the CIA. Barr appeared with CIA Director Bush in hearings before Congress.

**ATTORNEY GENERAL OF THE UNITED STATES INVOLVED IN MASSIVE DRUG TRAFFICKING**

Terry Reed wrote in his book, *Compromised*, that William Barr was an attorney for Southern Air Transport, to whom Reed routinely reported for coordinating arms shipments from Arkansas to Central America and drug shipments on the return flights. Reed wrote that he knew Barr during the 1980s as Robert Johnson.

Miami attorney James F. Dougherty II, representing an insurance group that had sued BCCI, appealed directly to Attorney General Richard Thornburgh (December 1990) when evidence surfaced that BCCI was planning to destroy or move records of its corrupt activities. No response was received.[376]

Justice Department officials blocked the testimony of two key witnesses before a Senate hearing on BCCI,[377] who would have exposed not only BCCI's criminality but also the coverup by Justice Department and CIA officials. Robert Mazur, who headed the Customs Service's investigation of BCCI in Tampa, and an assistant U.S. Attorney, Mark Jackowski, had sought to file charges against BCCI, but Washington officials blocked the investigation.

Justice Department officials shut down an investigation into the BCCI ownership of First American Bankshares in October 1989, allegedly so that it could focus on another probe. But when that probe was completed, Justice Department officials never went back to the far more serious matter of illegal ownership of First American Bank Holding Company. It wasn't until the Manhattan prosecutor started exposing the BCCI corruption and the Bank of England seized control of BCCI that Justice Department officials showed signs of life. At that point Justice Department officials had to do something. Some reports state that as many as twenty percent of the members of both houses of Congress received bribes from BCCI.[378]

Although known for years, the corruption surfaced in September 1991. BCCI accomplished its corrupt activities by bribing prominent citizens and high government officials throughout the world, including the United States.

Top law firms and public relation firms in the United States fronted for the rogue bank, secretly enabling it to operate in the United States. Members of Congress, the CIA, Justice Department, and other U.S. government agencies

376 *Daily Journal*, October 21, 1990.
377 *New York Times* October 2, 1991.
378 *Spotlight*, October 21, 1991.

were responsible for the continuation of most if not all of the criminal activities described in these pages. The mentality of BCCI suited to a "t" much of the criminality by U.S. officials.

BCCI secretly and unlawfully owned several American banks in violation of federal law. Included in these banks secretly owned by BCCI were First American Bank of the District of Columbia and its 43 branches in New York City.

U.S. authorities had known of BCCI's corruption and looting of deposits for years. Dozens of informants notified Justice Department officials and members of Congress of the corrupt activities. But, as in every other scandal within the federal government, nothing was done to stop BCCI's corrupt activities until the scandal broke (July 1991) in England, causing the bank to be closed.

**HUNDREDS OF WARNINGS**

Before the bubble burst on this racketeering operation, depositors lost billions of dollars, wiping out the life savings of many people, especially those in undeveloped countries. Insiders, including drug traffickers[379] and the CIA,[380] had advance notice of the pending collapse and took their money out before BCCI collapsed.

Just prior to the Justice Department crackdown on the BCCI secretly-owned bank in Tampa, forewarned drug dealers made a run on the bank, withdrawing over $10 million.

Front men such as former Defense Secretary Clark Clifford and Robert Altman acted as cutouts or front men to cover up for the unlawful BCCI ownership. In 1979, attorneys Clifford and Altman deceptively acted to permit BCCI to unlawfully acquire ownership of First American Bank in Washington, D.C. Clifford was an attorney and veteran power broker in Washington, and he was a pillar of the Washington Beltway establishment.

Other U.S. financial institutions were later acquired through attorneys acting as BCCI front men, or with their connivance. These included Independence Bank in Encino, California, and CenTrust Savings in Miami.

The Atlanta branch of BNL loaned or pledged nearly $5 billion to Iraq between 1985 and the summer of 1989.

Jack Blum, who initially learned of the criminal activities while an investigator for the Senate, believes that both Republicans and Democrats blocked an investigation because members of their own parties were responsible for covering up early warnings of the criminal activities. The same can be stated of the 1980 October Surprise scandal and the many others within these pages.

Prominent Washington figures made the BCCI scandal possible. There were numerous members of Congress; prominent attorneys Clifford and Altman; former Treasury Secretary John Connally, who bought a Texas bank with BCCI front man Ghaith Pharaon; former Atlanta Mayor Andrew Young, who borrowed money from BCCI and never paid it back; Ron Brown, chairman of the Democratic Party, a partner in the Washington law firm of Patton, Boggs and Blow, which received $1.3 million in fees from BCCI, later joined President

379 *New York Times* October 28, 1991.
380 Statements made to me by CIA informants.

Clinton's Washington staff.

In February 1992, a federal grand jury indicted David Paul, the former chairman of CenTrust Savings Bank in Miami, on fraud charges. The charges arose from a $25 million securities deal involving an investor linked to BCCI. Also charged were Ghaith Pharaon, reportedly a front man for BCCI, and William Christopher Berry.

**THE USUAL CONGRESSIONAL BRIBING**

BCCI penetrated the U.S. financial system through American law firms and attorneys who helped inflict upon the United States and other countries great financial harm and aided and abetted the drug-money laundering, financing of terrorists, and other unlawful activities. They turned their legal expertise against the United States for profit.

**CRIMES AIDED BY JURY MEMBERS**

The trial of attorney Robert Altman as part of the largest bank fraud in the nation and the world's history occurred in 1993 in New York City. Altman, with his boyish smile of innocence (similar to Oliver North), was accompanied throughout the trial by his attractive wife and former television star, Lynda Carter. Her lifestyle was enriched by the money her husband made through his role in the BCCI fraud. She was a popular sideshow to the trial.

The jury, composed of many unsophisticated people, some of whom couldn't be expected to balance their personal check books, were confronted with complex matters, compounded by the usual misrepresentation of legal counsel. On August 14, 1993, the jury acquitted Altman of the charges, proving again that crime pays, especially when cloaked in complex legal activities.

The outcome of a jury trial by unsophisticated jury members is similar to playing a slot machine. There are those jury members who believe everything the prosecutor says, assuming that **surely** an innocent person would not be charged if the facts were not true. There are the jurists who are influenced by legal chicanery that tricks the jury. There are those jurists who are influenced by the look of innocence, such as displayed by Oliver North and Robert Altman.

The BCCI corruption was effectively covered up by the New York jury members, followed by the coverup of President Clinton's Justice Department. It remained for foreign countries to prosecute and punish many of those who played key roles in the BCCI debacle.

**INDEPENDENT COUNSEL VERSUS SPECIAL COUNSEL**

There are vast differences between an "independent counsel" (or independent prosecutor as they are sometimes called) and a "special counsel." A special counsel is selected by the U.S. Attorney General, works under Justice Department officials, and submits a report to the Justice Department. If Justice Department officials are implicated, the most obvious expectation is that it will be a coverup. The Attorney General's selection of the special counsel will be almost sure to obtain that result.

An Independent Counsel or Independent Prosecutor, on the other hand, is selected by a panel of three appellate judges in the District of Columbia, following a request by the U.S. Attorney General. The Attorney General considers the request for an independent counsel following the request by a majority of the House or Senate Judiciary Committees. But even an independent counsel has its limitations. The person appointed by the federal appellate judges is often inexperienced, and may have a coverup agenda.

# BANK OF LAVORO AND IRAQGATE

Another of the many scandals involving high-level federal officials surfaced in the late 1980s, referred to as Iraqgate. It evolved around the Banca Nazionale del Lavoro (BNL), owned primarily by the Italian government. Implicated in the scandal with the bank were White House and Justice Department officials. The details of this scandal first surfaced in the alternate media, as is so often the case.

While other members of Congress engaged in the usual coverup of this scandal, Congressman Henry Gonzalez of Texas exposed the BNL corruption in 1991. He had to surmount the coverup by other members of Congress, the CIA, Justice Department personnel, and the White House. BNL first attracted his attention when he learned that the small Atlanta branch of BNL had made over $5 billion in loans to Iraq.

BNL was tied in with the Persian Gulf war and President Bush's arming of the Iraqis through loans which the American taxpayers will be paying for the next few decades. These loans made it possible for Iraq's Saddam Hussein to wage war against Kuwait and caused the U.S. taxpayers to be saddled with over ten billion dollars in debt over the next several decades.

In November 1989, White House officials guaranteed the payment of loans made by banks to Iraq for the purchase of U.S. farm products under a program run by the U.S. Agriculture Department's Commodity Credit Corporation (CCC). The approval provided that United States taxpayers would indemnify the banks lending money to Iraq for the purchase of U.S. food supplies, if Iraq defaulted on the loan payments. Iraq had already made a name for itself by defaulting on earlier loans, and its income left little possibility of repayment.

Instead of using the money to purchase U.S. food supplies, Iraq diverted billions of dollars of these farm loans to purchasing military equipment. In some cases Iraq exchanged food shipments for arms, including poison gas and chemicals.

When farm products were actually purchased in the United States, the ships supposedly hauling the products to Iraq would be diverted in Europe, and the food supplies traded for military equipment and supplies. These loans, which would not be repaid by Iraq under the existing conditions, would unknowingly be paid by the American taxpayers.

It was also obvious to U.S. officials that the war material being secretly purchased by Iraq would require some form of U.S. intervention in the future, in either money or lives, or both. The U.S. taxpayers, through their leaders, made possible the terrible bloodshed that occurred in the Gulf War.

Billions of dollars were spent every year to fund U.S. intelligence services. Intelligence-gathering agents are located throughout the United States and overseas. Obviously high-level government officials knew of the fraudulent use of the loans, and the massive military buildup by Iraq. (The same could be said for all of the scandals described in these pages.) But despite repeated warnings to the White House, President Bush pushed to continue the program. It was as if Bush, a former CIA director, wanted Iraq to escalate its military might and start a Middle East war.

**U.S. KNOWLEDGE OF CHEMICAL WEAPONS**

Of the many insiders feeding me information were two people closely associated with production of chemical weapons in the United States for Iraq, who warned federal agencies of the problem prior to the Persian Gulf War, and who then experienced Justice Department persecution. (This has become so obvious over the years that it is standard Justice Department procedure to silence and discredit whistleblowers against government misconduct.)

One of these contacts was Louis Champon, who owned and operated Champon Flavors, a Florida company making flavoring, including bitter almond oil, a cherry flavoring, made from fruit pits. Champon had developed a technique for extracting a cyanide by-product out of the fruit pits, and this fact became known to Iraq and Libya.

Dr. Ihsan Barbouti and his son, Haidar Barbouti, approached Champon in February 1988, with a proposal to form a joint venture for the purpose of extracting a cyanide by-product. Barbouti stated that the cyanide would be used for industrial purposes by a company in Europe.

Unknown to Champon at the time, the Barboutis had ties to the Central Intelligence Agency, and had reportedly dealt with Iran-Contra figure Secord. They were also procuring agents for military supplies for Iraq and Libya.

Champon entered the partnership with Barbouti, forming a new company called Product Ingredient Technology (PIT). Champon later discovered that his partners were shipping the cyanide to a CIA-affiliated weapon manufacturer in Chile, Cardeon Industries, and that the cyanide was used to manufacture weapon-grade cyanide. The Barbouti side of the partnership brought in the CIA-related Wackenhut Corporation to provide security at the plant.

After Champon became suspicious that weapon-grade cyanide was being produced under Barbouti's direction, Champon reported these facts to a Mr. Cabelly of the State Department on December 20, 1988. Nothing happened.

The following January, Champon saw press reports stating that Dr. Barbouti was the designer and builder of a Libyan chemical warfare plant located near

Rabta, Libya, causing Champon to again call the State Department (February 1989), providing further information. Again, Cabelly stated he would look into the matter and again, nothing happened.

In July 1990, shortly before Iraq invaded Kuwait, Mr. Pucillico of the State Department called Champon, advising him to contact U.S. Customs' agent Earl Miller in Miami, who put Champon in touch with Customs agents Jack Bigler and Martin Schramm in Houston. They advised Champon not to divulge the information to anyone, that the matter was highly political, and that there would be no investigation or prosecution of the matter.

Champon disclosed his information to investigative reporters at the *Dallas Morning News* and NBC. NBC aired the story nationally, which was then followed by the usual retaliation by officials in control of U.S. Customs, Internal Revenue Service, and the U.S. Department of Justice, bringing about the loss of Champon's business, followed by threats of death if Champon did not remain quiet.

A year after Champon provided me with this information, another insider contacted me, Peter Kawaja. He had operated a security company called International Security Group, ISG, and a computer database company that became involved with U.S. intelligence agencies and the plant making the cyanide. His computer company was asked to install a computer-based system for Product Ingredient Technology (PIT), and became prime security for Ihsan Barbouti International (IBI), including providing bodyguards.

Kawaja was also asked to install a hydrogen cyanide detection system at IBI. During these activities, Kawaja made recordings of telephone conversations and data transmissions. The information disclosed, among other things, CCC-BNL documents and letters of credit relating to the weapon-grade cyanide. Kawaja became suspicious, and conveyed his concerns to the CIA, the FBI, and Customs, who then undertook an investigation.

## STANDARD REACTION TO EXPOSING U.S. CORRUPTION

Again, there was no cessation of activities. Instead, his wife, Eileen, suddenly died under mysterious circumstances. Kawaja received death threats over the phone. The local police started harassing him. The IRS harassed him with what Kawaja claims were unfounded liens and levies, followed by CalFed Bank foreclosing on his business. These were standard tactics used by U.S. agencies against whistleblowers.

The plant producing the weapon-grade cyanide was eventually shut down, and a company called Century Arms International occupied the building. Kawaja said as late as 1995 he had seen missiles and bombs in the building, suggesting another covert operation.

## DEFAULTING ON U.S. GUARANTEED LOANS

Iraq's invasion of Kuwait on August 2, 1990, caused it to default on its loans to the BNL bank. The loans guaranteed by the U.S. taxpayers to the participating banks then became due. Making matters worse, Iraq had part ownership interest in some of these banks and stood to gain not only from receipt of the initial $5 billion, but would gain when the United States paid the various banks that loaned the money guaranteed by the U.S. Again, and again, and again, the U.S. taxpayers paid the tab and the interest required to finance it. In effect, they paid for their ignorance or indifference to government misconduct.

Some of the money furnished by the United States was used to purchase poison gas that was used on Iraqi Kurdish villages,[381] much of it purchased through Cardoen Industries in Chile, a CIA asset. Cardoen supplied considerable war materials to Iraq and other countries under the guidance of the CIA.

The Rome-based Bank of Lavoro, through its Atlanta branch, loaned directly and through other participating banks over five billion dollars to Iraq under this program. The young manager of the Atlanta branch of BNL, Christopher P. Drogoul, was ordered by his superiors in Rome to fund the loans and falsify the paper work so that U.S. authorities would not discover the fraudulent diversion of funds from farm to military uses. In carrying out the scheme the Bank of Lavoro borrowed money from other banks and then reloaned the money to Iraq at a slightly higher interest rate, relying upon the United States loan guarantees to protect itself from losses.

The scheme required secret telexes, separate sets of books, phony taxes, and other devices to escape detection by bank examiners. The fraudulent program was known to bank employees as Perugina, the name of an Italian candy factory.

Britain was also involved in the diversion of funds that made it possible for Iraq to invade Kuwait. Matrix Churchill, a machine tool company in England, secretly and unlawfully supplied military equipment to Iraq during this period, even while the company knew that Iraq was using poison gas on the Kurds. As usual, it appeared that the only people in the western hemisphere who didn't know about the scam were the American people, made possible by U.S. media coverup and the public's refusal to devote enough time to reading something other than the bland news in the mainstream media.

Two BNL employees reported the scheme to the local U.S. Attorney in Atlanta, causing the local U.S. attorney to raid BNL's Atlanta office and seize incriminating documents. The U.S. attorney discovered that bank officials in BNL's home office in Italy knew of the scheme, directed it, and ordered the local bank manager in Atlanta to carry it out. But Justice Department officials in Washington did not want Italian officials blamed, which would implicate U.S. officials.

To divert attention elsewhere, Justice Department prosecutors charged the young Atlanta bank manager, Christopher P. Drogoul, with defrauding his bank by disbursing the $5 billion in loan proceeds without home office knowledge and approval. The Justice Department's indictment was based upon charges that the bank manager acted alone, disbursing $5 billion in funds without the knowledge and approval of BNL's home office in Italy, and therefore committed fraud.

If the home office had known and approved of the scheme, the bank manager and employees could not be charged with defrauding the bank. Further, if home office officials were aware of the scheme, it would have serious political implications in Italy. Additionally, if BNL officials in Rome knew of the fraud associated with disbursing the funds guaranteed by the U.S. taxpayers, the liability of U.S. taxpayers to pay the billions of dollars that were fraudulently diverted

381 *San Francisco Examiner* July 26, 1993.

would not exist. For the U.S. taxpayers to be liable, the young manager of this small branch bank had to be solely responsible and knowledgeable of this gigantic fraud.

By covering up for the corruption, Justice Department officials and the White House were causing the U.S. taxpayers to pay $5 billions and several times more in interest charges. Is it any wonder that social programs such as Medicare, Social Security, and others must be cut?

Following a standard pattern, Drogoul's court-appointed attorney, seeking to protect the Justice Department and other federal officials, urged him to plead guilty. Drogoul wanted to go to trial to clear his name. By pleading guilty, he faced twenty years in prison. The court-appointed attorney had falsely assured Drogoul that if he pled guilty he would receive a suspended sentence. A week before trial, on September 2, 1993, Drogoul reluctantly pleaded guilty to something that he had not done. The guilty plea avoided the trial that would have exposed much of the U.S. misconduct and that of Italian bank officials.

In an unusual twist of not going along with Justice Department prosecutors, U.S. District Judge Marvin Shoob demanded that Drogoul explain truthfully at the sentencing hearing what had actually happened.

Fearing a long prison term instead of the suspended sentence promised to him by his attorney and the federal prosecutor, Drogoul obtained other legal counsel for his appearance at the sentencing hearing. The new attorney, Bobby Lee Cook, moved to have Drogoul's guilty plea rescinded on the basis that the BNL bank manager acted in the multi-billion-dollar scheme with the knowledge and approval of his superiors in Italy. Judge Shoob bravely granted the motion and rescinded the guilty plea, over the protests of Justice Department prosecutors, who knew the bank manager was not guilty.

Cook demanded documents from the CIA and Justice Department that would show federal agencies had prior knowledge of the fraudulent BNL activities, and knew that high Italian officials in Rome had approved the activities that were apparently sanctioned by the Bush Administration.

At first, Justice Department officials denied having such reports. Congressman Henry Gonzalez, who had been exposing the BNL corruption for months on C-SPAN, submitted a CIA document to the court showing that Italian officials in Rome had knowledge of the multi-billion-dollar transactions and fraud.

Several days later, CIA officials sent a letter to Justice Department prosecutors omitting the fact that the CIA had evidence that Rome officials were cognizant of the scheme. CIA officials then accused Justice Department officials of trying to get the CIA to provide U.S. prosecutors and the court with misleading information to support the imprisonment of the young BNL bank manager. As Congressman Gonzalez released more documents, it became obvious that the CIA possessed numerous documents showing that BNL officials in Rome knew of the loans and the diversion of the funds from farm products to military supplies. Further, that the CIA deliberately withheld this evidence from the court.

It also turned out that federal officials had altered a list of high technology items that were sent to Congress to obtain approval for the shipment to Iraq. The evidence indicated that high federal officials knew about the fraud being perpetrated by BNL and Iraq against the United States and had not only deliberately covered up for it, but *enlarged* upon it. Evidence indicated that President Bush was determined to arm Iraq for attack upon its neighbors.

Among the documents that surfaced was one written by Secretary of State James Baker, urgently warning the White House that Iraq was secretly using technology provided by the United States to build up its chemical, nuclear, biological and ballistic missile capabilities.

Not only were Justice Department attorneys seeking to imprison an innocent bank manager, but were imposing a huge cost upon the American public.

**JUSTICE VS CIA VS FBI**

Foreign media exposure of the BNL scandal forced Justice Department officials to engage in tactics to protect officials in the United States and Italy, fraudulently charging Drogoul with defrauding the Italian bank.

Robert Gates, Director of the CIA, and other government officials, told the House Banking Committee that the CIA knew nothing about the huge loans to Iraq. Congressman Henry Gonzalez, Chairman of that committee, produced evidence showing they were lying.

Drogoul was pressured to plead guilty, despite the evidence and common sense showing he was not guilty. The federal judge in the Drogoul case refused to support the Justice Department's attempts to settle the case by laying the blame on Drogoul. Unable to control the judge (a rare occasion), Justice Department prosecutors attempted to disqualify him and to go shopping for a judge that it could control.

The scenario leading to the rift between Attorney General William Barr and his Justice Department gang, the CIA, and FBI Director William Sessions, followed this schedule:

* CIA officials submitted a document to an Atlanta district court that contained misleading information, conveying false information covering up the real facts. The document was intended to deceive,[382] to deny that the CIA had knowledge of the BNL fraudulent loans for several years. The CIA would have been highly incompetent if, with all its agents worldwide, it did not know of the fraud that required participation of many people.

* Senator David Boren, suddenly showing an unusual display of duty, substantiated the fact that the document contained false information. In response to this public rebuke, the CIA drafted a memorandum to correct the falsified document. Justice Department attorneys objected to the CIA correcting the original report, as the Department of Justice would then have to explain its own deception.

* The CIA then acquiesced to the Justice Department's demands to continue the coverup. But the next day, the CIA prepared a document for Justice Department officials to sign that would protect the CIA's lying. Justice Department officials refused to sign this document, as it would further show that they lied.

* CIA officials then testified in a closed-door Senate Intelligence Committee hearing, describing what happened. The CIA attorneys placed the blame for

382 Submitting documents knowingly stating wrong facts and wrong conclusions, or withholding facts that would show a different conclusion, is a crime under federal law.

their coverup on pressures from Justice Department officials.

**"Never In the History Of the Republic"**

*New York Times* syndicated columnist William Safire stated (October 12, 1992) that "Never in the history of the Republic...has the nation's chief law enforcement officer been in such flagrant and sustained violation of the law." Safire stated in a mild way what was normal conduct in the Justice Department, which I continuously observed for the past 30 years.

**ANOTHER COVERUP COSTING THE AMERICAN PUBLIC BILLIONS OF DOLLARS**

If the case against the young bank manager of BNL in Atlanta had gone to trial, the involvement of President George Bush and members of his Administration, and of the government of Italy, would have been exposed. U.S. District Judge Marvin Shoob, after hearing evidence, stated:

> *[The five defendant employees of BNL] were pawns or bit players in a far larger and wider-ranging sophisticated conspiracy that involved BNL-Rome and possibly large American and foreign corporations and the governments of the United States, England, Italy and Iraq.*

Justice Department attorneys lied[383] as they told Judge Shoob that the manager of the small BNL branch acted on his own to lend five **billion** dollars to Iraq, without knowledge or approval of BNL's home office. Judge Shoob replied:

> *Based on the information that I have seen and that has been revealed, that kind of conclusion could only come about in never-never land.*

During an August 23, 1993, sentencing hearing for five BNL employees, Judge Shoob stated he would not sentence any of them to prison because the Justice Department's contention that they defrauded the parent bank in Rome was too incredible.

He added that they were merely "pawns and bit players in a far more wide-ranging conspiracy." Judge Schoob said there were too many circumstances that made it implausible that the conspiracy was a small one involving only the Atlanta bankers, adding: "Smoke is coming out of every window. I have to conclude the building is on fire."

Congressman Gonzalez had argued for an independent prosecutor to investigate the BNL affair. As in the Inslaw and BCCI case, the Attorney General appointed one of its own to investigate itself, former U.S. District Judge Frederick B. Lacey, to conduct a Justice Department investigation. Judge Shoob said of the Lacey report: "If Judge Lacey had investigated the Teapot Dome scandal," referring to the 1922 scandal which almost caused removal of President Warren G. Harding, "he would have given out a medal instead of a jail sentence."

Justice Department officials didn't care for this type of honesty and lack of control over the judge, and moved to disqualify him from presiding over the trial for BNL bank manager Drogoul, which was set to start on September 8, 1993. Another judge was then selected to conduct the trial.

Risking exposure of the role played by many people still in office, and especially the Justice Department, former president George Bush was subpoenaed to testify during the trial of bank manager Drogoul. The subpoena was accepted

---

383 *Wall Street Journal*, August 24, 1993.

by the Clinton Justice Department, which is responsible for defending the acts of past presidents while they were in office.

**STANDARD JUDICIAL COVERUP TACTIC**

The new judge, Ernest Tidwell, was more amenable to the Justice Department coverup. Drogoul's attorney, Robert Simels of New York, stated that the judge issued two rulings refusing to allow the bank manager to give evidence showing that President George Bush and White House officials acted to carry out the fraud. He said that the judge blocked him from introducing evidence concerning the role of U.S. intelligence agencies in making the sham loans to Iraq, and the Italian government's efforts and pressures upon the Bush Administration to avoid indicting BNL. Judge Tidwell stated that this evidence was not related to the charges against Drogoul. That was not so.

This judicial strategy is repeatedly used against CIA personnel who for various reasons are charged with criminal offenses for carrying out their orders. The compromised judge renders orders barring the defendant from showing his CIA employment and that he was carrying out orders. They are barred from introducing CIA documents and barred from having CIA personnel appear. It happened to almost every CIA operative named in these pages.

The Drogoul trial was to have been the main stage for exposing the misconduct by the Bush Administration leading up to the Gulf War.

**GASSING OUR OWN SOLDIERS**

Strong evidence exists that Iraq used chemical and biological agents against U.S. and other troops in the Persian Gulf war, and that U.S. intelligence agencies supplied these weapons to Iraq through a layer of intermediaries. Cardoen Industries in Chile was one of the CIA's suppliers.

Under-secretary of Defense for personnel and readiness, Edwin Dorn, stated that the Pentagon had concluded that Iraq did not use chemical or biological weapons during the war. To have said otherwise could have precipitated an investigation that threatened to expose the major role played by U.S. intelligence agencies in the arming of Iraq, including the sale of chemical and biological weapons.

During a limited congressional investigation, Senator Donald Riegle (D-Mich.) said that exposure to chemical and biological agents was widespread during the Persian Gulf war. In response to the denials by government officials, Riegel stated, "I've seen our government lie to us before in other war situations. This is not going to be an issue that gets swept under the rug." But it was swept under the rug, as Riegel surely knew it would be.

The U.S. military-industrial group profited from the military buildup of Iraq, which cost the American taxpayers huge amounts after it became necessary to invade that county in 1990. Further, the Gulf War Syndrome could very possibly be linked to the chemical grade cyanide produced in the United States.

**KISSINGER'S ROLE IN THE GULF WAR**

*Spotlight* wrote (November 9, 1992) that as early as 1984 Kissinger Associates were involved in arranging some of the loans from the Banca Nazionale del Lavoro (BNL) to the Iraqi government to finance its arms acquisitions from a little-known subsidiary of Fiat corporation. Referring to a confidential report prepared for the Economic Planning Group of the European Community by the Centre Des Etudes Transatlantiques (CETRA), *Spotlight* reported that the deal set up by Kissinger Associates involved the secret sale of five million land mines and other war material.

BNL was used for this transaction, funneling over one billion dollars through a small BNL branch in Brescia. At the same time the U.S. taxpayers were saddled with billions of dollars in debt to finance arm sales to both sides in the Iran-Iraqi war. Profiting from these secret deals were U.S. and foreign arms manufacturers, the arms merchants, Israel, and those in the United States who aided and abetted the activities.

Brent Scowcroft and Lawrence Eagleburger were employed by Kissinger Associates. Scowcroft would become President Bush's National Security Adviser and Eagleburger acting Secretary of State.

*Spotlight* stated: "CETRA's data prove the scheme for financing and supplying Iraq's military purchases was set up by Kissinger Associates long before BNL's Atlanta branch became involved." The article continued: "[It is] time we forgot those scapegoats in Atlanta [and] focus on the real culprit: Kissinger Associates."

Referring to Charles Barletta, a former Justice Department investigator, *Spotlight* wrote:

> *Barletta added that federal probers had collected dozens of such incriminating case histories about the Kissinger firm. But Henry Kissinger seems to possess a special kind of immunity. I'm not sure how he does it, but Kissinger wields as much power over the Washington national security bureaucracy now as in the days when he was the Nixon administration's foreign policy czar. He gets the payoff; others get the blame. Kissinger will remain unscathed until Congress finds the courage to convene a full-dress investigation of this Teflon power broker.*

## SOMETHING FISHY OCCURRED

On July 25, 1990, U.S. Ambassador to Iraq, April Glaspie, assured Iraq's Saddam Hussein that the United States was not interested in its dispute with Kuwait. Some reports state that April Glaspie assured Saddam Hussein that if Iraq invaded and seized only the northern part of Kuwait, the United States would not object.

As stated in earlier pages, CIA operative Gunther Russbacher had several times described to me the details of the flight of SR-71 aircraft to Moscow associated with delivering an agreement to President Gorbachev for signing. This agreement provided that the USSR would not intervene if the United States invaded Iraq. Possibly as a sign of good faith, one of the highly secret SR-71 aircraft was left in Moscow. Bizarre as this sounds, and as stated earlier, a well-known and respected pilot admitted to me in 1995 that an SR-71 was seen in a hangar at Moscow's airport.

## CONGRESSIONAL HEARINGS

During Congressional testimony before the House Banking Committee on November 10, 1993, Christopher Drogoul was brought from federal prison to testify about the BNL scandal. He testified that he tried to report the criminal activities involving Iraq, his bank, and U.S. officials, but that the U.S. attorney's office in Atlanta repeatedly barred him from telling the truth. They wanted to protect the U.S. officials, Italian officials, and Iraqi officials, and to blame him for making loans totaling about five-and-a-half billion dollars that were beyond his ability to make.

Drogoul testified, and the facts indicated, that he was merely a pawn in the scheme involving the United States, Iraq, Italy, Britain, and Germany to secretly arm Iraq. Not only did this conspiracy result in thousands of needless deaths, but the American public must pay this amount and the interest that will surely triple the original figure before the money is repaid somewhere in the twentieth-first century.

Regardless of his innocence, a federal judge sentenced Drogoul to federal prison in 1994, on the basis that his superiors did not know his small branch was dispensing five billion dollars, and that the United States government did not know of the scheme.

**CLINTON'S RHETORIC**

While on the campaign trail, Clinton stated he would recommend the appointment of an independent prosecutor to investigate U.S. involvement in the BNL fraud. But upon assuming the presidency, and through Attorney General Janet Reno, who appeared to be more of a figurehead for the Justice Department, the position was changed. The Clinton Administration, including the Attorney General, argued that there was no U.S. involvement in the BNL corruption and that the BNL headquarters in Italy and the Italian government were not involved. Attorney General Janet Reno and President Bill Clinton were lying.

**COVERUP COSTING AMERICANS BILLIONS**

Attorney General Janet Reno refused to appoint a special counsel to investigate the BNL scandal and in February 1995 agreed that U.S. taxpayers had to pay BNL the loan guarantees that made possible the arming of Iraq. She was stating in effect that the manager of a small BNL bank branch in Atlanta approved $5 billion in loans without the knowledge of bank officials in Italy. This was of course ridiculous.

**EXPOSURE OF US CULPABILITY**

A 340-page report by an Italian parliamentary commission[384] said that the illicit loans to Iraq from BNL were part of a U.S. policy to channel military aid to Iraq, under the direction of President George Bush. The report stated in part:

> *That the political direction of the whole operation was always firmly based in Washington is evident....Personalities in the Italian government and of BNL were aware of what was happening, or had received authoritative advice not to look too closely at the Atlanta branch operations....It is now evident...that the affair constituted an American political scandal.*

---

384 *Wall Street Journal* January 27, 1994.

# CIA AND DEA DRUG TRAFFICKING

The CIA's role in drug trafficking into the United States has been the subject of many magazine and newspaper articles, books, Congressional testimony, and television presentations. I first became aware of it in the 1950s while an airline pilot flying into Japan and while flying in the Middle East, out of Teheran, Beirut and other places. During matter-of-fact conversations with other pilots they described the drug loads they were carrying for CIA-related airlines. At that time there was very little attention given to the drug trade and I was as naive and indifferent to the problem as the remainder of the population.

One of the first books linking the CIA to drug trafficking was Alfred McCoy's[385] *The Politics of Heroin in Southeast Asia*[386] published in 1972, and his heavily documented 1991 update *The Politics of Heroin—CIA Complicity in the Global Drug Trade*.[387] McCoy is a professor of Southeast Asian history at the University of Wisconsin in Madison and has made an exhaustive study of the CIA's involvement in drugs while living in various parts of the world.

Professor McCoy started investigating the drug trafficking in the 1950s, questioning people in all phases of the drug culture from the growers to the end users. He spent considerable time in Southeast Asia and throughout the world obtaining first-hand knowledge of the drug trade. His books describe how CIA helicopters, supposedly fighting communists in Vietnam, were hauling drugs from the fields to distribution points, and how this CIA operation included heavy sales to the American GIs. McCoy described the role of the PepsiCo bottling plant in the drug processing.

Adolfo Calero was an executive with the PepsiCo bottling plant in Nicaragua, and as shown in several congressional hearings he was a known major drug trafficker, and working with the National Security Council and the CIA in their

385 Professor, University of Wisconsin.
386 Harper & Row.
387 Lawrence Hill Books.

war activities in Nicaragua. Statements given to me over the years by my various deep-cover sources clearly show that the Pepsico and Coca Cola companies, or their agents in foreign countries, were involved in drug trafficking.

McCoy describes the pressure put upon the media by the CIA to halt his book. He describes the many people who testified in closed-door congressional hearings for the past twenty years, leaving no doubt that the CIA was involved and primarily responsible for the drug scourge in the United States.

Many other highly detailed books have been written about CIA drug trafficking by people who were part of the operation. These include, among others, *Dope, Inc.*;[388]*The Big White Lie*;[389] *Cocaine Politics*;[390] *Out of Control*;[391] *Bluegrass Conspiracy*;[392] *The Cocaine Wars*;[393] *The Crimes of Patriots*.[394] But only a fraction of one percent of the American people have read them, insuring that they remain ignorant about the criminal and subversive activities by those in control of key government entities.

## BIZARRE ASPECTS OF TAXPAYER-FUNDED DRUG TRAFFICKING

There are many bizarre aspects of the epidemic drug trafficking into the United States by the CIA and its co-conspirators. One is the billions of dollars spent each year to "fight" drug trafficking, using the same government agencies to "fight" the battle as are themselves implicated in the drug trafficking. The American public is paying the salaries and government-related costs associated with the drug smuggling, and drug interdiction.

Entire communities have been turned into war zones, with thousands of people killed, thousands of people incarcerated, sometimes for life, and civil liberties taken away on the pretense of fighting the war on drugs.

## CONGRESSIONAL COVERUP

Another bizarre and criminal aspect related to the CIA-related drug problem is the coverup by members of Congress and much of the mainstream broadcast and print media. Dozens of people directly involved in the drug trafficking have testified to members of Congress (usually in closed-door hearings) of the drug trafficking. Hundreds of letters have been sent to members of Congress by informants describing the specifics of the drug trafficking and the involvement of people in control of the federal government.

McCoy describes giving testimony in 1972 to congressional committees, including Senator William Proxmire, about the CIA role in the developing global narcotic trade. He describes how members of Congress enthusiastically accepted the CIA's denial of any role in drug trafficking, despite the overwhelming evidence of its existence. Two decades later, despite many closed-door hearings receiving testimony further supporting the CIA and DEA drug smuggling into the United States, members of Congress still keep this information from the public.

---

388 *Dope Incorporated*, by the Editors of Executive Intelligence Review.
389 *The Big White Lie*, by Michael Levine.
390 *Cocaine Politics* by Peter Dale Scott and Jonathan Marshall.
391 *Out of Control* by Leslie Cockburn.
392 *Blue Grass Conspiracy* by Sally Denton.
393 *The Cocaine Wars* by Paul Eddy, Huygo Sabogal and Sara Walden.
394 *The Crimes of Patriots* by Jonathan Kwitny.

Dozens of highly documented books have been written about the subject by people who either investigated the subject or who were pilots involved in the drug trafficking. I mailed petitions via certified mail to members of Congress since 1991 describing the operation and demanding that they receive the testimony and evidence of our small group of former government investigators or present and former CIA personnel. The only people who don't know about the sinister practice by government personnel, whose criminal conduct they fund as taxpayers, are the majority of the American people.

As part of their jobs, those in the media are aware of this overwhelming amount of evidence, and are aware of the implications and the consequences. Their coverups are criminal acts under federal crime statutes.

**ONE OF MANY DEA WHISTLEBLOWERS**

Michael Levine, a twenty-five-year veteran of the Drug Enforcement Administration (and prior drug agencies), authored the 1993 book *The Big White Lie,* exposing the drug trafficking sanctioned by federal officials. The former DEA agent wrote that the so-called war on drugs is the "biggest, whitest, and deadliest lie ever perpetrated on U.S. citizens by their government." He described how the CIA, the DEA, and other intelligence agencies blocked investigations and prosecution of high-level drug traffickers. Levine described how the CIA was primarily responsible for the drug epidemic as seen from his perspective.

Levine repeatedly uncovered CIA links to the drug trafficking while he was a DEA agent. He discovered that the CIA was primarily responsible for the burgeoning drug activity from Central and South America into the United States, and that the biggest drug dealers were CIA assets. He found that federal judges and Justice Department prosecutors dramatically dropped the amount of bail for high-level drug traffickers who were CIA assets, and who had been accidentally charged.

Levine described how the CIA supported drug traffickers who then seized control of the government of Bolivia. He went into detail describing how the top people involved in drug trafficking, such as the government of Bolivia, are protected against exposure and prosecution, and how these protected individuals are CIA assets. He wrote that U.S. officials are "afraid the world would find out there wouldn't be a cocaine government in Bolivia if it wasn't for the CIA." He described how high DEA and Justice Department officials "intentionally destroy drug cases" and put conscientious DEA agents at risk, even causing their deaths. Levine uncovered how major drug cases involving CIA assets receive little or no media publicity, thereby protecting the vast criminal activities. Levine stated in his book the problem with raiding suspected drug labs, that when the site was raided there was evidence of a prior drug lab but it no longer existed.

**FAILED DRUG RAIDS**

Two of my contacts who worked for the DEA told me why this occurred. William Coller, a former mid-level DEA agent would learn about the planned drug raid and then instruct DEA contract agent (and pilot) Basil Abbott, to warn the people running the labs of the impending raid. Abbott spoke Spanish well, and had become friends with key government contacts throughout South America, including Sonia Atala and her husband, Walter. During several years of frequent contacts with Abbott he described in detail the hauling of arms to Central and

South America for the DEA and return flights loaded with drugs, often unloaded at DEA facilities. Abbott explained that this was why, as Levine stated in his book, *The Big White Lie*, that Levine couldn't figure out how the drug labs in Bolivia were found abandoned when they were raided.

I asked Abbott the names of some of the people he warned, and he named, among others, Sonia Atala and her husband, Walter. Both of these drug traffickers, responsible for huge quantities of drugs coming into the United States, were protected against prosecution by officials in control of the U.S. Department of Justice. Levine described the huge drug trafficking by Sonia and Walter Atala and how the CIA, DEA, and Justice Department protected them.

**JUSTICE DEPARTMENT OBSTRUCTION OF JUSTICE**

Levine wrote about the situation that I encountered over a 30-year period, commencing while I was a federal investigator. When Levine sought to expose drug trafficking by CIA or DEA assets, Justice Department management commenced harassing him, fabricating charges, and even threatening to put him in prison. (As they have been doing to me continuously since 1986.)

Terry Reed, a former CIA asset, and author of *Compromised*, ran into the same retaliation. When he discovered the CIA drug smuggling activities into the United States involving the CIA, DEA, and the National Security Council, Justice Department and Arkansas prosecutors sought to put Reed and his wife in prison through false charges.

**INPUT FROM TALKSHOW LISTENERS**

It frequently happened during my over two thousand talkshow appearances that callers would supply knowledge of government-related drug trafficking that they witnessed, adding to what I had learned. During a July 27, 1993, appearance on the syndicated talkshow *Radio Free America*, hosted by Tom Valentine, a caller from Houston, Texas described his conversations with DEA pilots at a Houston-area airport. The pilots had admitted to him that the crates on board the aircraft contained cocaine from Central America, but that the drugs were being used for sting operations. This excuse was a farce used to cover up for the criminal activities and silence the inquisitive pilots who may question the apparent illegality of the drug shipments.

Another caller on that same program, an Air Force officer, told about the many large Air Force aircraft flying into Homestead Air Force Base with large quantities of drugs on board. One of my sources, a former DIA asset, Frank Nesbitt, described how the drug trafficking into the base was common talk among military personnel.

The involvement of government personnel in drug trafficking, especially the coverup by Justice Department officials, establishes the mindset throughout the United States.

Among the many articles on CIA drug trafficking was the April 1988 story in *The Progressive*. The article described the testimony given by Michael Toliver concerning his flights for the CIA hauling drugs from Central America into the United States, including landing with 25,000 pounds of marijuana at Homestead Air Force Base in Florida. The article stated that Federal Judge Patrick Kelly "found the testimony compelling enough that he called it to the attention of President Ronald Reagan, as well as the CIA, the FBI, special prosecutor

Lawrence Walsh, and Congress." Judge Kelly directed federal marshals to deliver the transcript of Toliver's deposition directly to President Reagan. Toliver's story was broadcast on CBS television's *West 57th Street*. According to the article no one from the Justice Department questioned Toliver about his serious charges.

**DEA AGENTS BLOWING THE WHISTLE**

One of many former DEA officials who sought to expose the involvement of U.S. officials in the drug trafficking was Richard A. Horn, based in Myanmar (formerly Burma). He sued the former top State Department and CIA officials in that Asian nation for subverting his official drug fighting activities.[395] This suit provided still another sign of how top U.S. officials blow any interference in the highly-profitable and destructive drug trade into the United States.

Horn charged in his lawsuit that State Department and CIA officials retaliated against him because his exposure of drug traffickers interfered with the drug-related activities of State Department and CIA officials. Horn's lawsuit charged that Myanmar's government was making substantial progress in reducing the drug trade, much of it produced by Khun Sa, the opium warlord who worked with the CIA, and that the U.S. government was retaliating against the government for these drug-eradication efforts. Other government agencies knew that Myanmar produced over half the heroin on the world market.

Horn charged that the State Department's chief of mission in Myanmar, Franklin Huddle, Jr., worked with the CIA station chief to sabotage Horn's anti-drug efforts, and tried to bring about the death of an informant who had been assisting Horn in his activities.

Clashes between conscientious government agents and corrupt government personnel are common. Yet, every government check and balance supports the officials involved in criminal activities. An October 27, 1994, *Wall Street Journal* report made reference to various DEA agents whose efforts have been blocked by CIA officials [and government officials acting in unison]:

> *Drug-enforcement agents and C.I.A. officers have clashed in Venezuela, Colombia, Haiti and other countries where military and government officials have been accused of complicity in the drug trade.*

Supervising federal agent for the Drug Enforcement Administration, Celerino (Cele) Castillo, had repeatedly reported the large amount of cocaine being smuggled to Florida, Texas, and California, by mercenary pilots used by Oliver North. In an interview with *The Texas Observer*,[396] and as written in his 1994 book on drugs, Castillo stated that he observed large quantities of drugs shipped to the United States through Ilopango Air Force Base in El Salvador. He said that in 1986 he reported these findings to his superiors in the DEA and to the U.S. ambassador to El Salvador, Edwin Corr. Castillo said that he told Bush about the drug trafficking during a cocktail party in Guatemala City in 1986, and that Bush "just smiled and walked away from me."

**SOUTHEAST ASIA DRUG TRAFFICKING**

For decades the British and the French controlled the huge drug operations in Southeast Asia, which were taken over by the United States through the CIA

395 *Wall Street Journal*, October 27, 1994.
396 *Associated Press* June 17, 1994.

in the 1950s. Vietnam was a CIA operation that escalated, either intentionally or unintentionally, providing the logistics for the CIA to greatly expand the drug trafficking into the United States.

Many Americans, brainwashed to believe that the Vietnam war was in the interest of freedom and to fight communism, supported the war that sacrificed the lives of 58,000 Americans. Great numbers were painfully injured and maimed for life.

**EVEN IN DEATH THE GIs WERE MISUSED**

The CIA drug trafficking required large numbers of drug addicts. The drug addiction of many American GIs in Vietnam was highly profitable and made possible by the CIA drug trafficking. Even in death the GIs became unwitting participants in the drug trafficking. Plastic-wrapped drugs were shipped into the United States in the bottom of caskets, in body bags, and in body cavities. Upon arrival at Air Force bases, and especially Travis Air Force Base in California, the drugs would be removed from the caskets and bodies. These were identified by secret codes.

Many articles have been written about this sordid practice in the alternative press, but withheld by the mass media. In one instance, an officer from the army's Criminal Investigation Division uncovered a large-scale heroin smuggling scheme using the bodies of dead GIs who perished in the CIA's Vietnam War. His group filed reports with the Pentagon describing how the bodies were cut open, gutted, and filled with sacks of heroin. Approximately fifty pounds of heroin with multi-million-dollar street value were stuffed into each body.

Crates returning to the United States from Vietnam on military aircraft often contained bags of heroin, and also identified by coded labels. The coverups in the military, in the CIA, in the Justice Department, weren't isolated rogue acts, as the practices were too widespread, and exposure blocked by high-level officials. Any time an investigator reported the problem, he or she was ordered to stop.

These aspects of the CIA's Vietnam War that used Americans as pawns are never brought up at Memorial Day ceremonies. The American public is led to believe that the hundreds of thousands of dead, maimed, or injured Americans suffered for an honorable cause. This is not to discredit those who endured the fighting, but to bring reality into the picture.

In typical fashion revealed throughout these pages, the military hierarchy reacted to the report by disbanding the investigative team. Other reports plus those given to me by my CIA contacts provide further confirmation of this sordid practice. This coverup made possible the continued drug smuggling and constituted criminal coverup.

The CIA's war in Nicaragua had many of the same qualities, except that American GIs were not sacrificed as in Vietnam. The CIA's war in Nicaragua provided the logistics for bringing large quantities of drugs into the United States. Again, the American public was manipulated to believe that Nicaraguans did not have the right to choose their desired form of government. CIA-funded and directed assassination squads killed tens of thousands of people, while the CIA smuggled large quantities of drugs into the United States.

**OPERATION CODE NAMES**

The CIA drug trafficking is handled in an organized manner, like major corporations, such as General Motors. Different geographical areas and different types or levels of operations are given code names. In the Golden Triangle area of Southeast Asia, the code names included Operation Short Flight; Operation Burma Road; Operation Morning Gold, and Operation Triangle.

The CIA transferred some of its operatives who developed the drug trafficking in the Golden Triangle area of Southeast Asia to develop and operate drug trafficking into the United States from Central and South America. They reportedly included Theodore Shackley; Edwin Wilson (who is in federal prison); and Frank Terpil. In Central and South America the code names for CIA drug trafficking included Operation Snow Cone, Operation Toilet Seat, and Operation Watchtower.

**OPERATION TOILET SEAT**

The CIA used Boeing 727 and C-130 type aircraft to haul drugs from Central and South America to offshore locations in the United States, throwing the drugs out the rear ramp into the ocean in water-proof containers. The planes were leased or operated by CIA proprietary airlines and flown either by CIA/DIA/DEA crews or by airline pilots supplementing their regular income by becoming contract agents.

**PILOTS HEAVILY INVOLVED IN DRUG TRANSPORTATION**

One of my confidential sources, Gunther Russbacher, gave me the names of several airline pilots who regularly flew drug operations for the CIA, including two captains from United Airlines and a retired Pan American pilot. One of the United Airline pilots bragged that he made twice as much money flying illegal cargo as he did on his regular airline job.

Many pilots have admitted to me during the past 40 years that they hauled drugs under the direction of the CIA, DEA, and the military. These contacts were my early indication of CIA drug trafficking, commencing in the early 1950s. Numerous aircraft charter operators engaged in hauling drugs.

CIA-fed media releases claimed that the United States had to fund the Contras for freedom purposes and to combat communism. The real reason appeared to be the profitable drug trafficking. My CIA contacts stated the CIA was shipping arms to *both sides*, defending this practice in a tongue-in-cheek comment, "How else can the CIA keep the war going!"

The CIA sought support from Congress for its Contra operation by reporting that the Sandinistas were trafficking in drugs and claimed that the Contras were not doing the same. Actually, U.S. intelligence agencies were selling arms to both the Contras *and* the Sandinistas and taking drugs as part payment. The drugs were then shipped back to the United States in the same aircraft used for shipping the arms.

To stimulate Congressional and public support for continuing to support the Contras, the CIA installed video cameras in an aircraft flown by CIA pilot Barry Seal and secretly video-recorded the placement of drugs on board the aircraft at a Central America arms and drug transshipment point. The White House stated that the drugs were loaded by the Sandinistas, making the tapes available to Congress and the media. The White House sought to inflame public opinion against the Sandinistas so that Congress would vote for funding the Contras. The people represented as Sandinistas loading drugs in that video were actually Contras. The scheme worked: Congress voted money for the Contras and the public generally was oblivious to having been duped.

All types of aircraft were used for flying arms to Central and South America and returning with drugs. Many CIA aircraft were large airline or military types, landing in the United States at military or general aviation airports.[397] DEA aircraft used for drug trafficking operations were usually single and twin-engine general aviation aircraft and usually landed at private airports.[398]

Among the well-known names operating out of Mena Airport was Barry Seal, one of the CIA's drug pilots. He coordinated frequently with Oliver North, who used the drug profits to purchase arms that went to Central America. Seal was becoming a threat to the CIA drug operations. He knew too much, and he talked too much. He thought that the threat of exposing high-level CIA and DEA officials in the drug trafficking to Congress was insurance for him. If he had known that Congress already knew about the drug trafficking and kept the lid on the scandal by coverups, he surely would not have been so confident and cocky.

Seal was killed on February 19, 1986, and on the day he was killed the FBI seized his personal belongings, hiding evidence of his CIA-sanctioned drug operations.

**VAST DISTRIBUTION NETWORK**

After the drugs were unloaded at drug transshipment points, CIA-affiliated trucking companies transported the drugs throughout the United States.[399] Organized crime took much of the drugs upon arrival in the United States. Details of this CIA-organized crime relationship is found in other pages.

**CIA DRUG MONEY LAUNDERING**

The CIA laundered some of the money obtained from drug trafficking in the Far East through covert CIA financial institutions and other banks that knowingly accepted the funds. These included Nugan Hand Bank; Bishop, Baldwin, Rewald, Dillingham and Wong; the Vatican Bank; Bank of Lavoro; and Bank of Credit and Commerce International (BCCI).

**OPERATION BACK BITER**

A code name identifies the situation where a CIA or DEA drug pilot is set up and sacrificed: Operation Back Biter. Targeted CIA or DEA drug pilots are

---

397 Almost all military bases became drug transshipment points, and especially Homestead (Florida); Davis-Monahan (Arizona); Luke (New Mexico); McGuire (New Jersey); McClellan and Travis (California).

398 Frequently mentioned airports include Mena Airport and others in the vicinity (Arkansas); Angel Fire Airport (New Mexico); Marana Airport (Arizona); Spirit of St. Louis Airport (Missouri); McMinnville Airport (Oregon); Coolidge Airport (Phoenix); Midland-Odessa (Texas); Lakeside Airport (Chicago); Addison Airport (Denton, Texas); Shamrock Airport (Houston); Pietra Negro (Black Rock), northeast of El Paso; and Redbird Airport in Dallas, (where I had once taught aviation flight and ground training). The airport at Mena, Arkansas, was a well-known CIA arms and drug transshipment point, and was featured on two television shows, *Frontline* and *Now It Can Be Told*, and in numerous newspaper stories.

399 CIA contacts identify some of the CIA-related drug haulers: MNX Trucking; Jayes' Truck Driver Training School; Jiffey Truck Driver Training School; and Zapata Trucking Company, a division of the Zapata Corporation in Houston.

routinely set up by top echelon people. Customs and DEA officials are told about the arrival of a targeted pilot at a certain airport and he is arrested upon arrival. The pilots are charged and prosecuted, denied the right to have CIA or DEA personnel testify in their behalf, and refused the right to obtain government documents on the basis of national security.

**OPERATION WATCHTOWER**

Operation Watchtower[400] was one of many drug trafficking operations from Central America consisting of the placement and operation of low frequency radio beacons to guide low-flying pilots from Colombia to Panama. It also consisted of making available to the pilots the radio frequencies and schedule of drug interdiction aircraft so as to avoid detection. Because of the extremely low altitude that these drug-laden aircraft flew, often at only five hundred feet, they could not receive the line-of-sight radio signals ordinarily used. Radio signals from an aircraft on a particular frequency actuated a relay at the radio beacon site that started up the gasoline-engine-powered generators and the radio transmitters.

**MILITARY INVOLVEMENT**

The CIA utilized the Army Intelligence Agency in Operation Watchtower, which began in the mid-1970s. U.S. Army Colonel A.J. Baker was ordered to oversee part of Operation Watchtower and turned the operation over to Army Colonel Edward P. Cutolo, who also commanded the 10th Special Forces based at Ft. Devens, Massachusetts. Cutolo had supervised Operation Orwell for the intelligence agencies. This operation spied on political figures for the purpose of blackmail. Many of my deep-cover sources described the military's passive or active role in the drug trafficking into the United States.

Army Colonel Edward P. Cutolo, who had been ordered by the CIA to supervise Operation Watchtower, grew increasingly concerned about its flagrant illegality, and conducted an investigation in an attempt to bring it to a halt. Fearing he might be killed because of his investigation, he prepared a fifteen-page single-spaced affidavit dated March 11, 1980, describing the CIA drug trafficking and other activities. Cutolo gave copies of it to several trusted friends[401] with instructions to release the affidavit to government officials and the media if he was killed or died. He was prophetic. Cutolo was killed, as were several other people working with him to expose the drug trafficking operations. Their deaths, as with dozens of others, protected high U.S. officials and the sordid operations they inflicted upon the United States.

The affidavit described the installation and operation of the radio beacon towers and several of the drug flights in which he participated. The first one occurred in December 1975, headed by Colonel A.J. Baker, under whom Cutolo worked. Cutolo stated in his affidavit that, in the February operation, "30 high-performance aircraft landed safely at Albrook Air Station," and "the mission was 22 days long."

---

400 *The Spotlight*, Oct 14, 1991; *Riders X-Change*, Oct 1991 Edition; *Called To Serve*, 1991 Author Colonel James Gritz; *Freedom*, Nov-Dec 1993; *Freedom*, Jan-Feb 1993; *Freedom*, Jan-Feb 1995, authored by U.S. Army Colonel William Wilson.

401 Colonel A.J. Baker; Hugh B. Pearce; Paul Neri, and eventually to Colonel James Gritz and William Tyree.

The affidavit listed key people meeting the aircraft, including Colonel Manuel Noriega, who was then Panama's Defense Force Officer assigned to Customs; CIA operatives Edwin Wilson and Frank Terpil; and Mossad operative Michael Harari. Harari worked closely with U.S. intelligence agencies in the drug trafficking operation, sharing the profits for Israel and sharing the blame for the U.S. drug epidemic and associated crime wave. Harari had authority from the U.S. Army Southern Command in Panama to operate on military bases. Israel's Mossad participation in drug trafficking made Israel a participant in undermining the welfare and security of the United States, a very grave offense.

**OPERATION ORWELL**

The Cutolo affidavit described another unlawful mission, Operation Orwell,[402] which consisted of spying on politicians, judicial figures, state law enforcement agencies, and religious figures. Compromising information was distributed to certain members of the military-industrial complex. Colonel Cutolo stated in his affidavit that the compromising information was needed to silence these people if information on the criminal activities leaked out:

> *Mr. Edwin Wilson explained that it was considered that Operation Watchtower might be compromised and become known if politicians, judicial figures, police and religious entities were approached or received word that U.S. troops had aided in delivering narcotics from Colombia into Panama. Based on that possibility, intense surveillance was undertaken by my office to ensure that if Watchtower became known, the United States government and the Army would have advance warnings and could prepare a defense.*

This was another way of accomplishing the CIA's "plausible deniability...to downplay and defend against inquiries." The affidavit listed some of the people against whom the surveillance was directed:

> *I instituted surveillance against Ted Kennedy, John Kerry, Edward King, Michael Dukakis, Levin H. Campbell, Andrew A. Caffrey, Fred Johnson, Kenneth A. Chandler, Thomas P. O'Neill, to name a few of the targets. Surveillance at my orders was instituted at the Governors residences in Massachusetts, Maine, New York, and New Hampshire. The Catholic cathedrals of New York and Boston were placed under electronic surveillance also. In the area of Fort Devens, all local police and politicians were under some form of surveillance at various times.*
>
> *I specifically used individuals from the 441st Military Intelligence Detachment and 402 Army Security Agency Detachment assigned to the 10th Special Forces Group to supplement the SATs tasked with carrying out Operation Orwell.*
>
> *I also recruited a number of local state employees who worked within the ranks of local police and, as court personnel, to assist in this Operation. They were veterans and had previous security clearances. They were told at the outset that if they were caught they were on their own.*

---

402 Authority for the Army to become involved in this CIA operation came directly from FORSCOM through CIA operative Edwin Wilson, under Army Regulation (AR) 340-18-5 (file number 503-05).

The Cutolo affidavit described the killing of an Army servicewoman, Elaine Tyree, who had knowledge of Operation Watchtower which she described in her diary. To shift attention from the actual killer and his connection to the ongoing drug operation, the military charged Tyree's husband with the killing.

The Cutolo affidavit continued:

> *It was too risky to allow a military court to review the charges against Pvt. Tyree with Operation Orwell still ongoing and Senator Garn's office requesting a full investigation. Pvt. Tyree therefore had to stand before a civilian court of law on the criminal charges.*

At the first military hearing, the presiding judge found no reason to bind Pvt. Tyree's husband over for trial for the murder of his wife. This decision risked further investigation and possible exposure of the corrupt operation. Army pressure caused the county prosecutor to indict the husband for murdering his wife, even though the army knew the actual killer was someone else. The Cutolo affidavit stated:

> *On 29 February 1980, Pvt. Tyree was convicted of murder and will spend the duration of his life incarcerated. I could not disseminate intelligence gathered under Operation Orwell to notify civilian authorities who actually killed Elaine Tyree.*

To prevent further investigation into the murder, Army officials conspired with Lieutenant J. Dwyer of the Middlesex District Attorney's Office and the County District Attorney. They went to the Massachusetts Supreme Court and obtained a ruling prohibiting any court but the Massachusetts Supreme Court from ordering the arrest of suspects in the Tyree murder. This was without precedent, as any court in Massachusetts could issue arrest warrants for murder suspects. But the ruling protected the real murderer, Michael Peters, who, if charged, would have exposed Operation Watchtower and Operation Orwell.

The Cutolo affidavit continued: "I have seen other men involved in Operation Watchtower meet accidental deaths after they were also threatened." It then identified the people who died in strange fashion and who had posed a danger of exposing the drug trafficking.

Sgt. John Newby received threatening phone calls and then died in a parachuting accident when his chute failed to open. Colonel Robert Bayard was murdered in Atlanta, Georgia in 1977, as he went to meet Mossad agent Michael Harari.[403] Colonel Cutolo died in a one-car accident near Skullthorpe, England, in 1980, while on a military exercise near the Royal Air Force base at Skullthorpe. Cutolo's death was under strange circumstances, and occurred shortly before he was to meet Harari.

Colonel Baker died while trying to determine if Harari had killed Colonel Cutolo. Colonel James Rowe was assassinated on April 21, 1989, in the Philippines within three days after Mossad agent Harari arrived in that country. Rowe had been investigating Harari's links to Cutolo's murder and to CIA operatives Edwin Wilson and Thomas Clines. Pearce was killed in a helicopter accident in June 1989 under mysterious circumstances. Congressman Larkin

---

403 Harari had been the station chief for the Mossad in Mexico. He also headed Mossad assassination teams in Europe. He was responsible for assassinating a waiter in Norway in a case of mistaken identity and was sent by the Mossad to Central America.

Smith died in an airplane accident on August 13, 1989.

The affidavit stated that Mossad agents associated with Operation Watchtower were being protected by CIA Director Stansfield Turner and George Bush and that Washington military authorities had approved the drug trafficking operation:

> *Harari was a known middleman for matters involving the United States in Latin America [and] acted with the support of a network of Mossad personnel throughout Latin America and worked mainly in the import and export of arms and drug trafficking.*
>
> *Edwin Wilson explained that Operation Watchtower had to remain secret...There are similar operations being implemented elsewhere in the world. Wilson named the "Golden Triangle" of Southeast Asia and Pakistan....Wilson named several recognized officials of Pakistan, Afghanistan, Burma, Korea, Thailand and Cambodia as being aware and consenting to these arrangements, similar to the ones in Panama.*

Referring to the huge profits received by the CIA from the drug trafficking, the affidavit continued:

> *Edwin Wilson explained that the profit from the sale of narcotics was laundered through a series of banks. Wilson stated that over 70% of the profits were laundered through the banks in Panama. The remaining percentage was funneled through Swiss banks with a small remainder being handled by banks within the United States. I understood that some of the profits in Panamanian banks arrived through Israeli Couriers. I became aware of that fact from normal conversations with some of the embassy personnel assigned to the Embassy in Panama. Wilson also stated that an associate whom I don't know also aided in overseeing the laundering of funds...Wilson indicated that most of Operation Watchtower was implemented on the authority of Clines.*

Referring to Operation Orwell, which spied upon politicians for subsequent blackmail:

> *I was notified by Edwin Wilson that the information forwarded to Washington, D.C., was disseminated to private corporations who were developing weapons systems for the Dept. of Defense. Those private corporations were encouraged to use the sensitive information gathered from surveillance of U.S. senators and representatives as leverage [blackmail] to manipulate those Congressmen into approving whatever costs the weapon systems incurred.*
>
> *As of the date of this affidavit, 8,400 police departments, 1,370 churches, and approximately 17,900 citizens have been monitored under Operation Orwell. The major churches targeted have been Catholic and Latter Day Saints. I have stored certain information gathered by Operation Orwell on Fort Devens, and pursuant to instructions from Edwin Wilson have forwarded additional information gathered to Washington, D.C.…Certain information was collected on suspected members of the Trilateral Commission and the Bilderberg group. Among those that information was collected on were Gerald Ford and President Jimmy Carter. Edwin Wilson indicated that additional surveillance was implemented against former CIA Director George Bush, whom Wilson named as a member*

*of the Trilateral Commission.*

It is easy to understand why members of Congress can be blackmailed into covering up for criminal activities involving personnel of intelligence agencies or the Justice Department when information on their personal lives is secretly collected by the FBI and U.S. intelligence agencies for blackmail purposes.

The affidavit described some of the weapon manufacturers who received this CIA information:

> *Edwin Wilson named three weapons systems when he spoke of private corporations receiving information from Operation Orwell. (1) An armored vehicle. (2) An aircraft that is invisible to radar. (3) A weapons system that utilizes kinetic energy. Edwin Wilson indicated to me during our conversation, which entailed the dissemination of Operation Orwell information and the identification of the three weapons systems, that Operation Orwell would be implemented nationwide by 4 July 1980.*

The affidavit made reference to classified information and "the activities of the CIA in the United States and in Latin America." Referring to people working with Edwin Wilson, the affidavit continued:

> *Each operation had basically the same characters involved...with Edwin Wilson...Robert Gates and William J. Casey...*

As Colonel Cutolo suspected, Neri was killed, apparently to silence him. Paul Neri[404] was one of the people that Cutolo entrusted with the affidavit and who had been requested to make the affidavit public upon his death. In distributing the affidavit to members of Congress and the media, Neri wrote:

> *Both Col. Rowe and Mr. Pearce agreed to go public, after the meeting with Larkin Smith, to call for a full investigation into the events described in Col. Cutolo's affidavit. But both men died prior to the meeting with Smith.*

Referring to the Mossad, Neri's cover letter stated:

> *With the deaths of Col. Cutolo, Col. Baker, Col. Rowe (and Col. Robert Bayard named in Col. Cutolo's affidavit) it is hard to believe the deaths of these men are not the work of the Israeli Mossad. It is equally easy to attribute the death of Col. Cutolo directly to Operation Watchtower inquiries.*

Meeting the same coverup response that I received for the past thirty years from the establishment media, Neri's letter stated:

> *For your information a copy of the affidavit will be sent to the New York Times, the Washington Post and the Boston Globe....The men who died so far...were good men. They attempted to let the public know what really occurred in Latin America, and in the never ending drug flow.*
>
> *In 1980 Col. Cutolo died in an accident while on a military exercise. Just prior to his death he notified me that he was to meet with Michael Harari, an Israeli Mossad agent. It is my belief, though unsubstantiated, that Harari murdered Col. Cutolo because of the information Col. Cutolo possessed. I believe that Col. Cutolo died in his attempt to [expose] Operation Watchtower...*

---

404 Neri was an employee of the National Security Agency.

*Colonel Baker enlisted the aid of Colonel James N. Rowe, and between Col. Baker, Col. Rowe and myself, we set out to prove that Harari murdered Col. Cutolo, and that Operation Watchtower...netted Edwin Wilson and Frank Terpil of the CIA a large sum of tax free dollars.*

*Prior to getting very far into the investigation, Col. Baker died... We had no doubt as to the guilt of Thomas Clines, whom we suspect was the master mind behind Operation Watchtower.*

Neri went on to describe how Harari and Col. James Rowe[405] were in the Philippines when Rowe was assassinated and that "It is my unsubstantiated belief that Harari murdered Col. Rowe or arranged it." Neri's letter continued: "I believe Harari's motive for murdering Col. Rowe was due to Col. Rowe's inquiries about Harari's movements and relationships to Edwin Wilson, Thomas Clines and Manuel Noriega."

Referring to another death in the small group seeking to expose Operation Watchtower and the associated deaths, Neri wrote:

*In June 1989, Mr. Pearce was killed in a helicopter accident. The accident has a story of its own I am told. Both Col. Rowe and Mr. Pearce agreed to go public, after the meeting with Larkin Smith, to call for a full investigation into the events described in Col. Cutolo's affidavit. But both men died prior to the meeting with Smith.*

Paul Neri continued:

*Since the Israeli Mossad openly trafficks in arms and drugs in Latin America, a theory that Clines, Wilson, Terpil, Harari and Noriega engaged in Operation Watchtower is very easy to believe at this time, especially following the Libyan situation and the Iran-Contra affair. It all fits, this entire scenario carried over from Operation Watchtower directly into the Iran-Contra affair with the same characters.*

Referring to the deaths associated with the attempted exposure of the CIA's Operation Watchtower and the Mossad involvement, Neri wrote, "I'm sorry that I am unable to carry the work any further. This is now your Pandora's Box."

Before he was murdered, Colonel Rowe also tried to get CBS's *60 Minutes* interested in the contents of the Cutolo affidavit, the murders, and the CIA crimes. CBS replied on July 13, 1987, refusing to proceed with the matter. Despite the responsibility of the media to expose government corruption, CBS chose to cover up. This coverup made possible the continuation of the drug trafficking and more murders. Over the years I encountered many deep-cover drug-pilots who offered evidence of the CIA drug trafficking to each of the television and radio networks, and discovered the usual coverup.

Tyree wrote, "It is not uncommon for Israeli Mossad agents to kill Americans who the Israeli's deem a threat to the security of Israel." This belief has been stated to me numerous times by CIA contacts.

**FINALLY THEY GOT NERI**

On April 29, 1990, Paul Neri died. An unknown person wrote a short letter that was sent out with the Cutolo affidavit and Paul Neri's accounting of what had happened, writing:

---

405 Rowe was in the Philippines serving as chief of the Army Advisory Group.

*Mr. Paul Neri, of the National Security Agency, died on April 29, 1990. Before his death, he requested that I mail the enclosed affidavit to you. Paul Neri was concerned that he would be killed or lose his security clearance if he revealed the affidavit before he died. According to him, these facts are true. If you investigate and interview the parties named within the affidavit, you will find the information is true. I am simply carrying out the wishes of a good friend, but do not want to get involved any further; therefore, I shall remain anonymous.*

**HEARING FROM TYREE**

I made initial contact in 1994 with Tyree, who then furnished me with considerable details and documents on Operation Watchtower and Operation Orwell, and other covert operations in which the military was involved. I am convinced that Tyree was framed by military officers and prosecutors in Massachusetts, for the murder of his wife.

Tyree prepared several highly detailed affidavits describing what he himself had observed of the drug-related Watchtower operation. He elaborated on Operation Watchtower as a U.S. Army Special Forces secret operation.

Tyree was crew chief on a "sterile"[406] helicopter used in Operation Watchtower. The Special Forces Teams were used to install and maintain the radio beacons. Tyree described an incident in which a group of Green Berets[407] identified as Special action Team Number 1, were ambushed in Colombia near the village of Turbo, by about four dozen soldiers from a Colombia Army Unit who mistook the SAT members for local bandits. Two of the SAT team members were shot before their radio request for air evacuation was accomplished.

Tyree had the impression that Operation Watchtower was either a part of Task Force 157,[408] or that task force was being used as a shield behind which Edwin Wilson and others were conducting Operation Watchtower.

Colonel Rowe took command of Operation Orwell after Colonel Cutolo's death. Rowe advised Tyree of the continued surveillance activities, including that of Harvard Law School Professor Lawrence H. Tribe. The surveillance activities were initiated by Special Forces personnel because of the people's opposition to Washington policies. Rowe told Tyree that he had substantial evidence showing that Colonel Edward Cutolo, Colonel James Baker, and Colonel Robert Bayard, were all victims of foul play, and that Mossad operative Michael Harari was involved in the deaths.

Tyree wrote that the last message he received from Colonel Rowe was just prior to his departure for Manila, where Rowe was assassinated in April 1989. Rowe told Tyree that if he remembers any more details on what Tyree had earlier told him, to call a certain phone number and leave a message.[409] After Rowe was assassinated, Tyree called the number and reached a Colonel Richard Malvesti,[410] who stated that he was in possession of the material on which Colonel

---

406 Special forces used the term "sterile" to indicate the aircraft was stripped of all identification, the purpose of which was to deny the role of the United States in the operation.

407 The Green Berets were divided into three Special Action Teams, each one consisting of approximately seven men.

408 Task Force 157 was a secret intelligence gathering project of the U.S. Navy.

409 Phone number for Colonel Rowe was 919-396-3832.

410 Malvesti was director for operations of the Joint Special Operations Command.

Rowe was working. From time to time Tyree received news-clippings in the mail relating to personnel involved in Operations Watchtower or Orwell, without the name or address of the sender. Tyree stated that he thought the mailings were from Colonel Malvesti or Paul Neri of the U.S. National Security Agency.

Malvesti's activities on behalf of exposing Operation Watchtower and Orwell probably played a role in his subsequent death[411] on July 26, 1990. During a routine parachute jump in 1990, his parachute failed to open. This failure could easily be brought about by someone tampering with the chute.

General Carl W. Stiner, a four-star general who was commander in chief of the U.S. Special Operations Command, spoke at Malvesti's funeral, stating, "The Ranger experience is not for the weak or the faint-hearted." Excellent rhetoric, but it didn't address the criminal activities associated with Malvesti's death or the many others, or of the subversive and criminal activities against the United States by people allegedly representing and protecting the interests of the United States.

Tyree said that on July 23, 1990, he received the affidavit of Colonel Cutolo that was sent on behalf of Paul Neri, and that the information that pertained to Tyree and his personal observation was correct.

Tyree overheard several of the Panamanian military officers give credit for assisting the success of Operation Watchtower to a Colombian armed forces officer named Eber Villegas.

In 1976, Tyree was honorably discharged from military service, and then re-enlisted in 1977. He was sent to Fort Devens, Massachusetts, where he again served under Colonel Cutolo, and was part of the 2nd Battalion, 10th SFG (A). From this group Tyree was transferred to the 441st MID, which at that time was commanded by Captain Jimmy W. Williams. It was here that Tyree took part in Operation Orwell.

Tyree stated in his affidavit that the intent of the operation, which was referred to as Operation Orwell, was to monitor civilian targets to determine if Operation Watchtower had been discovered, and the probability that an investigation or governmental inquiry would be requested as a result of such discovery.

Tyree stated in his declaration that of the ten surveillance operations that he was part, two of them were of prominent civilian officials in the New England area. One was the Mayor of Lunenburg, Massachusetts, a small town near Fort Devens. The other one was district attorney of Middlesex County, Massachusetts, John Droney.

Sergeant John Newby, who also worked on Operation Orwell, told Tyree that his surveillance targets included U.S. Senators John Kerry and Ted Kennedy, judges (including Levin H. Campbell, Andrew A. Caffrey, Fred Johnson). Another Operation Orwell team member was Major Arnett who reportedly conducted surveillance of U.S. Senator Jesse Helms.

**KILLING OUR OWN PERSONNEL**

Tyree stated in his affidavit that once the rescue helicopters entered Colombian airspace they and the extracted SAT team became liabilities, and orders were given to three U.S. Army "Cobra" attack helicopters to shoot them down upon

411 Malvesti is buried in the Massachusetts National Cemetery in Bourne.

their return to Panama. The orders allegedly were not carried out because of the presence of U.S. troops in the area, and that the troops would witness the shoot-down and associated deaths.

Sacrificing personnel is common in covert U.S. operations This happened with Rewald, Riconosciuto, Russbacher, Brenneke, among others. U.S. servicemen in Vietnam were addicted to CIA-furnished drugs.

Tyree told how members of the Panamanian Defense Forces (PDF) assisted in unloading the cocaine at Albrook Air Station. In one of his affidavits Tyree said:

> *I personally witnessed members of the Panamanian Defense Force (PDF) help unload the bales of cocaine from the aircraft onto the tarmac of Albrook Air Station. Among the PDF officers were Colonel Manuel Noriega, major Roberto Diaz-Herrera, Major Lis del CID, and Major Ramirez. These men were always in the company of an American civilian identified to me by other personnel involved in the operation as Edwin Wilson, of the CIA. Another civilian in the company of Wilson, I have since learned, was Israeli Mossad Agent Michael Harari.*

Tyree described seeing Wilson provide PDF officers with manila folders containing the following addresses: CIA, Office of Naval Intelligence, and Defense Intelligence Agency. The contents appeared to be photographs taken by satellites or SR-71 high-altitude spy aircraft.

Colonel Cutolo, who commanded the second and third Watchtower missions, and Tyree, were transferred to the 10th Special Forces Group at Fort Devens, Massachusetts, along with another participant, Sergeant John Newby. As stated earlier, Newby started receiving threats upon his life, and his life ended in October 1978.

During the 1976 Watchtower operation, Tyree said that the pilots appeared to be mercenaries who spoke several foreign languages and had German, French, and English accents, while the pilots and lead personnel in the first 1975 operations appeared younger and acted as if they were U.S. Army or U.S. Navy personnel. He thought that British Special Air Service (S.A.S.) pilots were on some of the flights.

Tyree said that Ted Shackley, a former high-ranking CIA operative now living in Colombia, was deeply involved in Operation Watchtower and other CIA-related drug operations. He believed that the Navy's Task Force 157 operated in full or in part the drug operation known as Operation Watchtower. He said that "Col. Baker, Col. Rowe and I believed that Thomas Clines, with the aid of Edwin Wilson and Frank Terpil orchestrated Operation Watchtower...with full CIA auspices."

**DEATH OF TYREE'S WIFE**

Tyree's affidavit described how his wife started receiving threatening phone calls and notes left on parked vehicles in October 1978, warning Elaine Tyree to stop writing and reporting the secret activities, including Operation Watchtower and Operation Orwell, among others. Tyree identified the military superiors and members of Congress[412] to whom he reported the threats.

---

412 Including U.S. Senator E.J. Garn (R-Utah).

Tyree and his wife started receiving threats at the same time, and Tyree made these telephone threats known to Colonel Cutolo, First Sergeant Frederick Henry, and Sergeant Kenneth Garcy. Garcy stated in an affidavit dated September 29, 1990, that Elaine Tyree was keeping a record of what she had learned about the drug operation and that she intended to turn the diary-style book over to the Criminal Investigation Division (CID). Garcy wrote in his affidavit that Tyree was concerned about the safety of his wife.

On January 30, 1979, Elaine Tyree was stabbed to death at the Tyree's off-post residence.[413] Subsequently, Erik Y. Aarhus (U.S. Army SP4) and Earl Michael Peters were charged with her murder. Local district attorney John Droney obtained an unusual ruling from the Massachusetts Supreme Judicial Court (SJC), dismissing the murder charges against Peters, even though he was seen leaving the murder scene, and that only that court could order the arrest of anyone involved in Elaine Tyree's murder.

Prior to his wife's death, Tyree had repeatedly contacted members of Congress[414] about his findings of drug trafficking from Central America; of the drugs and arms trafficking at Fort Devens, and the threats to him and his wife.

In the first decision exonerating Tyree dated May 15, 1979,[415] Special Justice James W. Killam, III held that Erik Aarhus and Earl Michael Peters should be tried for the murder of Elaine Tyree. The district attorney refused to accept this decision. Instead, he moved to prosecute Tyree and blocked all prosecution of Peters.

Francis M. Gardner, the manager of the apartments where the Tyrees lived at the time of Elaine Tyree's death, signed a statement before a notary public stating that he observed a person identified as Earl Michael Peters leaving the Tyree's apartment carrying a box (which the Tyrees had stored for him). Police arrived shortly thereafter and Elaine Tyree was found stabbed to death. According to Tyree the police never interviewed Gardner. Gardner stated to investigators that he saw the police remove the diary kept by Elaine Tyree and other papers. The police denied this.

After Tyree was held guilty in the murder of his wife the military at Fort Devens, Massachusetts gave Tyree an honorable discharge. If Tyree had actually murdered his wife, the Army would undoubtedly have given him a dishonorable discharge. Even Elaine Tyree's father felt, and wrote, that he did not believe Tyree to be the murderer.

In his February 10, 1992, affidavit, Tyree described reports of drug experiments on American GIs in Europe during the early 1950s by Doctor James P. Cattell. This information was given to PDF personnel (PF-8) by Edwin Wilson for the purpose of interrogations.

Tyree explained giving Secret and Top Secret U.S. documents to the PDF and Israeli agents, possibly explaining how the drug-laden aircraft obtained the radio frequencies and flight schedules of drug-interdiction aircraft.

---

413 104 1/2 Washington Street, Ayer, Massachusetts.

414 Including Senator J. Garn of Utah.

415 Trial Court, First Northern Middlesex Division, Cases No. 271-272-273 of 1979 308 & 367.

**JUDICIAL OBSTRUCTION OF JUSTICE**

Massachusetts Judge James F. McHugh[416] refused to accept testimony from active duty personnel of the U.S. Army Special Forces who came forward to corroborate the existence of Operation Watchtower. The judge even threatened to charge Tyree with perjury if *he* decided that the statements were false. (This is similar to the obstruction of justice and threats made by federal judges in the Ninth Circuit district and appellate courts at San Francisco.) Army attorneys warned Tyree he would be prosecuted for divulging classified information, the military-CIA drug trafficking being considered "classified information." Judge McHugh refused to accept live testimony from active duty U.S. Army Special Forces personnel, who could expose the truth.

**DESTROYING EVIDENCE**

In a December 5, 1979, letter on official letterhead of the Commonwealth of Massachusetts, District Attorney John J. Droney wrote to Colonel Cutolo:

*I recommend that you destroy the surveillance material collected at the Tyree residence on January 30, 1979, if you have not already done so.*

Droney was using, as the primary witness against Tyree in the murder of Elaine Tyree, the same person seen crawling out the bedroom window of the Tyree residence at the time of the murder.

Prior to Tyree's February 1980 trial, he sent a certified letter to the Pentagon detailing the criminal activities involving U.S. personnel in Operations Watchtower and Orwell. He received no response.

During several years of corresponding with Tyree I found him to be very precise, knowledgeable about deep-cover type of activities, and with many contacts. He was a good source of information and cross-check on what other sources had told me. He sent me considerable written data supporting the existence of Operation Watchtower and Operation Orwell, and of his own innocence. He had many letters from responsible people, including investigators, confirming his innocence.

**CONTINUING DEATHS**

Before leaving on his trip, Cutolo wrote a note to Colonel Rowe, informing him that he had arranged to meet with Michael Harari (in Manila). Why would a U.S. military intelligence officer meet secretly with a Mossad operative if the two intelligence agencies routinely met with each other? Cutolo died on May 26, 1980, his death caused by multiple fractures to the skull, other fractures, and punctured organs. These were out of the ordinary for the type of auto accident in which he was involved.

Deaths of others involved in Operation Orwell included Master Sergeant Mark Larochelle. He was killed during a helicopter training mission at Fort Chaffee, Arkansas in July 1990.

Kenneth Garcy, formerly with the 10th and the 1st Special Forces Group, Airborne (SFGA), prepared an affidavit on September 9, 1990, describing the drug trafficking associated with Operation Watchtower; the threatening phone calls to Elaine Tyree; knowledge of the CID's determination to retaliate against Tyree for attempting to expose Operations Watchtower and Orwell; harassment

416 Middlesex Superior Court, Middlesex County, Massachusetts.

by the CID of anyone talking to Tyree; criminal activities of Earl Peters; considerable illegal activities at Fort Devens, and that Elaine Tyree was making a record of it; CIA drug trafficking out of the Golden Triangle area of Southeast Asia during the Vietnam War; that Earl Peters had a key to Tyree's apartment; that members of the 1st Special Forces Group (Airborne) at Fort Lewis, Washington, stole ammunition and weapons and shipped them to Japan via Thailand, for sale to the Japanese "mafia" known as "The Yukuza."

Colonel William Wilson, a Green Beret, also described the drug trafficking in Operation Watchtower. After retirement he authored two articles appearing in *Freedom* (Nov-Dec 1993 and Jan-Feb 1995) describing his knowledge and role in the operation. Wilson served with the Army's Office of Inspector General, and assisted in uncovering and documenting the massacre of hundreds of Vietnamese civilians by American troops at My Lai on March 16, 1968.

**INVOLVEMENT OF JOINT CHIEF OF STAFF?**

In 1994, President Clinton appointed Army General John Shalikashvili Chairman of the Joint Chiefs of Staff. Shalikashvili was the commander of the army unit that carried out Operation Watchtower shortly after he went to another command. Colonel Cutolo succeeded Shalikashvili as the group commander of the 10th Special Forces Group, Airborne (SFG(A)). Since Colonel Cutolo was disturbed by the drug trafficking in Operation Watchtower, it can be assumed that the operation was originated by higher authority, or prior command.

**JONESTOWN TRAGEDY**

Tyree had been part of a team operating in Surinam and French Guiana, among other countries, and had insider information about Jim Jones and Jonestown in Guayana. Tyree wrote about former personnel from Army special forces groups training some of the enforcers at Jonestown prior to the mass murders and suicides. Tyree wrote that Congressman Leo Ryan who had traveled to Jonestown to investigate allegations of wrongdoings was to have been protected by an Army Special Forces team, but that the team did not appear until after the congressman had been assassinated. Tyree wrote:

> *[The congressman] was hated by many different factions in the United States...the perfect place to assassinate him would be outside the U.S., where the law enforcement authorities are not as apt to control the evidence, crime scene, etc. This fact was known to [the state department], and they acted on it as a precaution....the Special Forces team assigned to guard the U.S. Representative didn't arrive on the ground in Jonestown until minutes after the U.S. Representative was dead. Two facts in dispute are:*
>
> *(A) Did the Special Forces team deliberately delay in reaching Jonestown? If so, why did they delay, and on whose orders did they delay?*
>
> *(B) That the Special Forces team were the people that actually killed the U.S. Representative. This is possible, as the person who told me that version is a person who has always proved to be a creditable source.*
>
> *A number of Special Forces were training the ranchers in and around the Jonestown complex in security measures.*

**MOSSAD'S DRUG TRAFFICKING**

Several of my CIA and DEA sources who were directly involved in the drug trafficking described the Mossad's role in Central and South American drug trafficking. These sources described how the Mossad marked their drug packages, how the Mossad shared space on CIA aircraft flying drugs into the United States, and about the vast network of Mossad operatives throughout Central and South America engaging in drug smuggling.

Mossad operatives connected with the drug operations included Michael "Freddy" Harari and David Kimche. Both worked hand-in-hand with the CIA and the drug traffickers, including the Medellin and Cali Cartels. When U.S. forces invaded Panama to arrest Noriega, Harari was caught in the fighting. Despite the fact that the Mossad's role in drug trafficking was serious and that he was a co-conspirator with Noriega, the U.S. intelligence agencies allowed Harari to escape in an Israeli jet. If Harari had been captured and questioned, Israel's involvement in the drug trafficking could have come out, as well as that of U.S. intelligence agencies.

Former OSS operative Russell Bowen worked with or alongside the Mossad and Harari for many years. He told me that Harari had started his vast Central and South American operations by hauling cigarettes and then branching out into drugs.

**ANOTHER CIA OPERATIVE CAME FORWARD**

Another of the many confidential sources with whom I had contact was Trenton Parker who played a key role in CIA activities in the Caribbean. Ironically, Parker had crossed paths with Russbacher in the early 1980s, which provided further confirmation of Russbacher's status, and Parker provided me with information on CIA activities that Russbacher had withheld. Once Parker gave me preliminary information about the activities Russbacher then enlarged upon it.

Parker provided me with a confidential employee status report showing his CIA status from December 23, 1964, to May 24, 1992, and his last rank was Colonel in the United States Marine Corp. It showed that he had a top secret clearance, and that he was attached to the Marine-Naval intelligence and to the CIA. His serial number was 553-60-1458, with an additional MSID identification number of 2072458. The reports identified Parker as a member of the ultra-secret Pegasus group, with headquarters in the U.S. Department of Labor offices in Fairfax, Virginia. The status report listed his alias, Pegasus 222.

Parker stated that the CIA and Justice Department had sacrificed him in 1982 to protect an ongoing secret scheme called Operation Snow Cone. He had been charged by the Security Exchange Commission (SEC) with a money laundering operation, which was part of a CIA operation under Operation Interlink and Operation Gold Bug. This CIA operation was accidentally exposed by the SEC which was unaware of the CIA's role in the ongoing unlawful operation. Usually Justice Department officials in Washington quickly step in and the charges are dropped. But in this case the SEC charges were filed and publicized by the media. It was therefore too late to pressure the SEC to retract the charges.

There was another possible reason for filing charges against Parker. Parker stated that his handlers had asked him to be part of an expanding drug operation in Nigeria called Operation Indigo Sky, and that he refused. He didn't care to get involved in drug trafficking, and living conditions in Nigeria were deplorable.

Justice Department prosecutors and CIA personnel encouraged Parker to plead guilty, assuring him that he would be released as soon as attention to his case no longer existed. Parker pled guilty in 1982, he refused all newspaper interviews, and was promptly hidden in the federal prison system, including months of diesel therapy which kept him from a law library and telephone.

The opportunity to seek legal relief arose while Parker was in an Arizona prison where he could prepare and file a post-conviction motion. This motion was heard by U.S. District Judge Marquez in Tucson on February 12, 1986, after which the judge ordered the prison warden and the U.S. Attorney to release Parker immediately.

In 1992, U.S. Attorney Michael Norton in Denver charged Parker with money laundering charges that had been part of his CIA operations. At his arraignment in Denver the judge ordered him released pending trial, set for April 1993. Before his release, Parker occupied a cell with Stewart Webb, a private investigator whom I had met earlier, and who was trying to expose the HUD and savings and loan corruption in the Denver area. Webb showed Parker some of my writings, and Parker contacted me upon his release.

Parker said that he had been with the CIA for approximately 30 years and was part of faction "B"[417] in the CIA, and was identified as Pegasus 222.

While waiting for trial, Parker filed papers with the court listing the secret CIA operations that he would reveal at his trial. He also filed a list of documents that he would submit, including the confidential status report showing him to be a Colonel in the U.S. Marines assigned to the Office of Naval Intelligence and to the Central Intelligence Agency.

Once Parker filed the list of documents with the court an assistant U.S. attorney in Denver complained to the judge that Parker should have filed the documents under seal because they revealed secret CIA activities. Because of those revealing documents U.S. Attorney Norton dismissed all charges against Parker, which avoided revealing the Agency's dirty linen. Parker called me on March 23, 1993, stating: "All charges have been dropped. I'm going underground. Don't ask any questions." He then hung up.

As time went on, over the years, I occasionally talked to Parker. He was adamant that he wanted nothing else to do with any of the corruption in government, feeling as I did. He felt that the nation's checks and balances were too corrupt, and the public too illiterate about government misconduct and too indifferent, for anyone to show any meaningful concern.

---

417 The CIA reportedly has three covert factions. Faction One or sometimes referred to as faction A, appears to be under the control of the Justice Department. Faction Two or B, as it is sometimes called, is under the control of the Office of Naval Intelligence. Faction Three is small, including former OSS operatives, and reportedly a loose-knit group of rogues.

ORIGINAL TRANSMISSION DATE: 3/3/93 - RETRANSMISSION DATE 3/10/93

DOCUMENT CLASSIFICATION STATUS: <u>T O P  S E C R E T</u>

TO: MONA B. ALDERSON,
LITIGATION DIVISION, OGC,
CIA/WASHINGTON D.C.
PHO: 703-874-3107
FAX: 703-874-3208

**CONFIDENTIAL**

RE: INQUIRY OF 3/3/93
MR. JOSEPH MACKEY,
ASST. U.S. ATTORNEY,
DENVER, COL.
PHO: 303-844-2081
FAX: 303-874-3208

Defense Exhibit No. G-47-P-222

<u>NOTICE</u>: PURSUANT TO THE NATIONAL SECURITY ACT OF 1947, 50 USC 401 & 402, ET. SQ. - THE FOLLOWING INFORMATION IS CONSIDERED INFORMATION OF A CLASSIFIED NATURE INVOLVING NATIQNAL SECURITY AND SHOULD BE TREATED BY YOU AND YOUR DEPARTMENT/OFFICE ACCORDINGLY.

RE: BACKGROUND INFORMATION AND CURRENT OPPS-STAT ON SUBJECT:
TRENTON H. PARKER AKA PEGASUS-222 - 2/2/45-COL.USMC/GS18
ATTACHED MARINE-NAVEL ITLG-SEC/TAD-CIA-12/23/64 TO 5/24/92.
SECURITY LVL/TOP SECRET/EXP 5/24/92. MSID NO. 2072458.
SS NO. 553-60-1458. NSA/SPL-DDO/SEC-CHIEF-SP/AG PEGASUS UNIT.
CONFIRM/REG/CIA/DENVER,CO. SBS/CUR/RES - DENVER, CO.
ALL OPPS/ASSIGS CLASSIFIED TOP SECRET/UAVAILABLE.
CUR/SEC/STAT: HIGH RISK. FED/CR/IDC/DENVER-1/27/93.

NO ADDITIONAL RECORDS OR BACKGROUND INFORMATION AVAILABLE FOR RELEASE TO YOUR OFFICE AT THIS TIME ON SUBJECT DUE TO MATTERS OF NATIONAL SECURITY AND PRESIDENTIAL DIRECTIVE/G-BUSH 5/24/92.

DO/DA RECOMMENDATION: - <u>STANDARD DENIAL</u>

ANSWER BACK/REF/P-222,
DO/COMM-CTR/3/3/93,
FOR/ITL/SEC - DDO/DDA,
DRC/CIA/LANG/VA.

**CONFIDENTIAL**

Copy of the CIA confidential document showing Parker's ONI and CIA status. Its use of the term Standard Denial, shows the CIA practice of lying.

**SHAM AND PROFITABLE DRUG BUST**

Parker told me that the CIA, with Vice President Bush's approval, set up a sham drug bust in Miami during March 1980 using 4,000 pounds of cocaine, the biggest drug bust at that time. The purpose of the scheme was to generate support in the United States for the newly appointed drug czar, Vice President George Bush, justifying the use of the U.S. military in the so-called war against drugs.

In carrying out the scheme, the CIA reportedly coordinated with Jorge Ochoa, a Colombian drug dealer. Ochoa organized many of Colombia's drug dealers to contribute cocaine for a large shipment into the United States, advising that there was safety in numbers. Most of the dealers didn't know that this was a planned drug bust and that they would lose whatever cocaine they contributed to the shipment. After the drug dealers contributed their cocaine into Ochoa's warehouse, Ochoa switched large quantities of bad cocaine that he had accumulated with good cocaine contributed by other dealers. Later, Ochoa sold the cocaine obtained in the switch for about fifty million dollars.

The 4,000 pounds of cocaine, including the bad cocaine that Ochoa had switched, was then shipped to Miami and seized by U.S. Customs as planned. Bush got good publicity for his role as drug czar and Ochoa and his insiders made over fifty million dollars by replacing good cocaine with bad cocaine.

The sting operation in which Parker participated used an informer to notify DEA agent Phelps in Bogota that the drugs were arriving at Miami International Airport on a particular flight at a given time. Phelps then notified DEA and Customs at Miami, so they could be present at the aircraft's arrival and to seize the drugs.

There were comical elements to this planned drug bust. Parker described what he observed at Miami International Airport when the 4,000 pounds of cocaine arrived on board TAMPA Airlines. Watching the scene from an unobserved distance via binoculars, Parker said that the airplane with the two tons of cocaine arrived at the parking area but there were no Custom agents there to seize the drugs, despite the considerable planning that went into the operation.

Several people working with Parker were at the aircraft, presenting the appearance of being there to unload the cargo. However, they intended to run off as the DEA and Custom agents appeared. But there were no agents. The pilots wanted the drugs unloaded fast and wanted to leave. To avoid losing the drugs intended for the planned seizure, Parker's people unloaded the crates containing the drugs onto the tarmac.

The cocaine was hidden in boxes of Levi jeans, with yellow bands on the boxes containing the real Levi's, and white bands on the boxes containing the cocaine. Parker's people sprayed the boxes containing the cocaine with ether so the Custom agents couldn't possibly overlook the presence of drugs. (Ether is used in the preparation of cocaine.)

The absence of the expected DEA and Custom agents presented Parker with a problem. He advised his men by radio to stand by. An hour later, Parker saw through his binoculars a couple of Custom agents, engaging in frivolity, walking slowly toward the boxes, obviously unaware of the presence of drugs. Parker then radioed his men to stay clear of the area.

Parker watched through his binoculars as the agents poked holes in the boxes to check for possible drugs. The third box that they poked caused white cocaine powder to escape. Parker then radioed his people to immediately leave the area.

Parker boarded a commercial airline for return to Denver. That night the U.S. media described the drug find as the largest discovery in the nation's history. DEA and Customs officials described the drug find as the result of an intensive coordinated effort between the DEA and Customs.

### CIA COMPLICITY IN ESTABLISHING THE MEDELLIN CARTEL

Parker told how the CIA set up the meetings in which various Colombian drug dealers organized into a drug trafficking cartel. Parker mentioned two preliminary meetings in late 1981 arranged by the CIA, in which the individual drug dealers in Colombia planned to organize into a cartel for shipping drugs to the United States. He stated that the first meeting occurred with twenty of the biggest cocaine dealers in Colombia present; that the second and final meeting was held at the Hotel International in Medellin attended by about two hundred drug dealers, pushers, and smugglers. The Medellin Cartel was established in December 1981, and each of the members paid an initial $35,000 fee to fund a security force for the cartel members to protect their drug operation.

Russbacher confirmed the meetings that Parker mentioned, and that there had been a preliminary meeting in September 1981 in Buenaventura, Colombia which established the format for the subsequent meetings. Russbacher attended the September 1981 meeting which was initiated by the CIA to facilitate drug trafficking into the United States, permitting the CIA to deal with a group rather than many independent drug dealers.

At least half a dozen former CIA, OSS, and DEA personnel gave me many hours of statements over a three year period concerning Central and South America drug operations in which U.S. intelligence agencies and the Mossad participated.

### CIA PLANNING AND FUNDING THE KIDNAP OF OCHOA'S SISTER

Prior to organizing the Medellin cartel the CIA created a crisis situation, providing an impetus for the Colombian drug dealers to form the Medellin Cartel. Parker described the CIA operation in early December 1981 that led to the kidnapping of Jorge Ochoa's sister, Leona, from a University outside of Bogota. Parker said that, acting in his CIA capacity, he paid a group known as M-19 to carry out the kidnapping and to also kidnap Carlos Lehder. Lehder escaped after he was captured. The CIA paid the M-19 group three million dollars, of which two million dollars was in guns and one million in cash.

Parker said, "We made arrangements with Colonel Noriega, and this was the point where Noriega became involved with the CIA and the drugs." He continued: "The deal was that the meeting between M-19 and Ochoa and Escobar would be held in a neutral point, namely Panama. During the second week of January 1982, everything was set up."

Another one of my CIA sources, Russell Bowen, played a role in the kidnapping of Ochoa's sister. He piloted the DC-3 aircraft that flew Ochoa's sister, Leona, to a remote location, where she was held until the ransom was paid and she was released.

**CROSSING OF PATHS**

As Parker was elaborating upon one of his money-laundering flights, I learned that his path had crossed that of Gunther Russbacher, adding further confirmation to Russbacher's ONI status. Parker described the purpose of a flight from Dobbins Air Force Base near Marietta, Georgia in January or February of 1982, and included a description of the pilot. He said the pilot was a Navy Lt. Commander with the nickname of "Gunsel." Russbacher had told me that Gunsel and Gunslinger were nicknames he used. Parker stated that the pilot was very articulate, which fit Russbacher's description. Russbacher confirmed that he did fly such a flight, and that the route of flight and the name of one of the passengers coincided with Parker's description.

Parker described the series of short flights with the first landing at Grand Cayman Island, where Parker picked up five million dollars in cash from a CIA source. The plane then went to Nassau, where Parker paid Prime Minister Lynden Pindling[418] one million dollars to get rid of a place called Norman's Cay. Parker explained that Norman's Cay was a main drug transshipment point operated by Colombian drug dealer Carlos Lehder, whom he described as one of the five keys of the Medellin Cartel. Parker stated:

> *Lehder was getting way out of line; he was shooting at people and when he finally shot at Walter Cronkite who happened to be sailing around in the area, Walter broke the news and a lot of people were saying how can this guy be operating out of Norman's Cay just off the shores of the United States?*

Parker stated that Lehder was then forced to leave Norman's Cay and return to Colombia, where he joined the Medellin Cartel. Parker said that before leaving Nassau he was joined by Robert Vesco (wanted in the United States for money fraud), and then the CIA aircraft flew them to Havana, where they were met at the airport by security guards and Fidel Castro. Parker said:

> *I personally delivered two million dollars to Fidel Castro. And for those two million dollars he was to see that a shipment of arms was to go to M-19, which was a right-wing revolutionary force that we wanted to keep active so that we could have pressure on the government to bring about certain things that we wanted to do. And we needed pressure from below and pressure from above. He agreed to do that and he did do that.*

Parker continued: "I took the remaining two million dollars and flew into Panama City, Panama and there I checked into Holiday Inn," where he met with the head of Colombia's M-19. Parker added: "I delivered my one million dollars to him and then I met with Colonel Noriega and delivered one million dollars to him. That one million dollars was to pay Noriega to act as the neutral party to negotiate the release of Ochoa's sister. Sure enough, Ochoa's sister was released." Parker continued:

> *And then he was also supposed to make an offer that he could and would provide protection for the drugs coming into the United States through*

418 Lynden O. Pindling.

*the back door to the midway. And what that was, is that we had already made a move on the cartel to close down some of the small operations. At that time Noriega offered a connection into the Sandinistas, the drug operations. Refinery plants were set up there. And that's what we wanted, as we wanted to show the Sandinistas as being the bad guys and justify U.S. involvement.*

*What we were doing was also financing operations because a certain group in the CIA was going ahead and flying guns down into Nicaragua, dropping them off by parachutes to the Contras. They then went over to the Sandinistas, picked up drugs and flew them into the United States, after which the money would be returned to the Sandinistas. In effect we were taking over some of the flying services for the Medellin Cartel. The money from the drugs produced the money for the guns and that is how the operation worked, and Bush knew the whole god-damn thing.*

Parker explained that after completing that trip, he flew back to Denver where he was to go to trial on charges relating to a CIA operation called Operation Gold Bug. He explained that he was on a one-million-dollar self-recognizance bond, which was rather bizarre since any offense requiring that large a bond would be too serious to permit release on one's own recognizance.

Parker thought that charging him was a mistake unless it was to silence or discredit him. Parker said, "First, my trial was to start on February 2, 1982. Second, when it came up it came up by a pure fluke." He explained how the CIA was to protect him from prosecution. Prior to trial his CIA handlers instructed him to remain silent about the CIA operation as it was ongoing and that any exposure of it would have serious consequences. His handlers stated that he would receive a very light prison sentence or probation and would soon be free.

### MORE FUEL FOR CHARGES THAT CIA WAS INVOLVED IN KENNEDY'S ASSASSINATION

Parker said that after President Kennedy decided to pull U.S. troops out of the CIA Vietnam operation, which would cause the loss of billions of dollars from the CIA drug trafficking, certain CIA factions decided to assassinate Kennedy. Pegasus people learned of the plot and told Kennedy two weeks before he was assassinated.

These statements by a deep-cover CIA operative and Marine Corps officer certainly raise serious questions and add further fuel to the speculation and charges that the CIA was involved in Kennedy's assassination. In light of other CIA criminalities, there should be little doubt that the CIA has the mindset to assassinate a president of the United States.

Parker stated that after Kennedy's death the Pegasus unit was not able to function as intended because of the corrupt activities of U.S. presidents after the Kennedy assassination. He named Johnson, Nixon and Bush, as knowing of the planned assassination, and that the Pegasus group had taped telephone conversations making reference to the operation. He stated that Reagan was not implicated like the others; he was more of a figurehead for powerful factions controlled by former CIA Director Bush.

Parker described the necessity of Pegasus going underground within the CIA because of the inability to report to a president, and that the files on corrupt CIA operations gathered by the Pegasus group were moved to various secret locations. Denver was one of the sites.

Parker said that his Pegasus group secretly gave files on the CIA criminal activities from 1976 to 1982 to a member of the Joint Armed Services Committee, Congressman Larry McDonald. These files revealed corrupt activities by several U.S. presidents, federal officials, the CIA, and other members of government.

Parker said that McDonald let it be known to the press that he was going to reveal startling evidence upon his return from the Far East showing that the CIA and certain high-ranking public officials were part of an operation responsible for drug trafficking since 1963 from Southeast Asia. McDonald boarded KAL Flight 007, which was shot down by the Russians.

**REFERRING TO THE THREE NAVAL OFFICERS KILLED AT FORT ORD**

Parker had seen one of my petitions to Congress reporting, among other matters, the crash of a Navy helicopter at Fort Ord on April 30, 1991, and the death of three naval officers from the Office of Naval Intelligence, one of whom was a woman. He was interested in knowing their names and physical descriptions, as two men and a woman disappeared from his Pegasus group at about that time. He thought the crash might explain their sudden disappearance. He added: "The Pegasus units have been systematically exterminated; people have been knocked off." Since the Pegasus unit was collecting evidence of CIA criminality, the members were frequent targets of assassination by other CIA and intelligence groups.

Parker described many of the CIA operations in which he played a role, and his description coincided with information given to me by Gunther Russbacher and other CIA sources.

**OPERATION MOTHER GOOSE**

Parker told me his various assignments in the CIA from when he first joined the Office of Naval Intelligence. He was involved during 1964 in the CIA scheme called Operation Mother Goose dealing with joint military selection, recruitment, and training of qualified enlisted men with security ratings. These people were educated and trained in basic covert and undercover activities. After training they were released from active military duty to enroll in colleges and universities under the GI Bill. While under CIA supervision, they infiltrated student activities and student movements as they related to the Vietnam War and other political areas. Parker trained at the United States Marine Corps base at Camp Pendleton, California.

**OPERATION BACK DRAFT**

Parker's next CIA assignment was an enlargement upon Operation Mother Goose called Operation Back Draft. This operation provided financial assistance to students while attending college and trained them to infiltrate and disrupt student activities. Parker participated in this program while attending college and university programs in Southern California.

Another CIA contract agent, Ron Rewald, was used in a similar operation and was later recruited by the CIA to operate a proprietary in Hawaii known as Bishop, Baldwin, Rewald, Dillingham and Wong (BBRDW).

To qualify Parker for use in financial operations, the CIA obtained employment for him with New York Stock Exchange brokerage firms from 1971 until 1974 in California and Colorado. While in this position he supplied confidential information to the CIA on customer accounts and transactions. Eventually he opened his own brokerage firm as a front for the CIA through the SEC and NASD.

This is similar to the operation described to me by CIA operative Gunther Russbacher in which Russbacher received training at Mutual Life Insurance Company, and then incorporated and operated a number of CIA financial institutions headquartered in Missouri. These institutions had offices throughout the United States including Denver, Dallas, Houston, Atlanta, and Traverse City, Michigan.

**OPERATION ANACONDA**

Another CIA assignment was participation in Operation Anaconda in the mid-1970s, through which CIA personnel ran for state and federal political office. Another purpose of the operation was to swing key elections to a particular candidate, away from one whose interest may be detrimental to the CIA. This was used against Senator Church and Representative Pike after their committees exposed CIA misconduct.

Parker elaborated upon other CIA operations in which he was involved, including infiltration of U.S. financial institutions, drug operations in Central and South America, and the Nigerian operation known as Indigo Sky.

Parker appeared as guest on several talk shows with Tom Valentine of *Radio Free America*.[419] During one appearance on July 29, 1993, he shared the two-hour program with former CIA employee and author Fletcher Prouty,[420] describing the mechanics of the CIA's Operation Interlink. Prouty stated during the show that Parker's revelations "make this one of the most important shows on the CIA that has ever occurred."

**PRISON RELEASE BROUGHT ABOUT BY *DEFRAUDING AMERICA* BOOK**

After federal charges were dropped against Parker the State of Arizona filed money-laundering charges against him, arising from Parker's earlier CIA activities. Extradition papers were filed with Colorado authorities where Parker was residing, seeking to have him extradited to Arizona. Parker felt that this charge arose from activities of the United States Department of Justice.

Fighting extradition, Parker filed into court records the Expanded Second Edition of *Defrauding America*, referring to the sections explaining Parker's CIA activities and telling how Justice Department officials sought to silence or discredit CIA assets by filing sham charges and incarceration. The judge refused to honor the extradition papers from Arizona, ordering Parker released from custody. Parker felt that the book played a key role in his release.

---

419 A syndicated show of Sun Radio Network, heard throughout the United States, and on short wave five nights a week.

420 Prouty authored *The Secret Team*, and other CIA books.

ORIGINAL TRANSMISSION DATE: 3/3/93 - RETRANSMISSION DATE 3/10/93

DOCUMENT CLASSIFICATION STATUS: T O P S E C R E T

TO: MONA B. ALDERSON,
LITIGATION DIVISION, OGC,
CIA/WASHINGTON D.C.
PHO: 703-874-3107
FAX: 703-874-3208

CONFIDENTIAL

RE: INQUIRY OF 3/3/93
MR. JOSEPH MACKEY,
ASST. U.S. ATTORNEY,
DENVER, COL.
PHO: 303-844-2081
FAX: 303-874-3208

NOTICE: PURSUANT TO THE NATIONAL SECURITY ACT OF 1947, 50 USC 401 & 402, ET. SQ. - THE FOLLOWING INFORMATION IS CONSIDERED INFORMATION OF A CLASSIFIED NATURE INVOLVING NATIONAL SECURITY AND SHOULD BE TREATED BY YOU AND YOUR DEPARTMENT/OFFICE ACCORDINGLY.

RE: BACKGROUND INFORMATION AND CURRENT OPPS-STAT ON SUBJECT:
TRENTON H. PARKER AKA PEGASUS-222 - 2/2/45-COL.USMC/GS18
ATTACHED MARINE-NAVEL ITLG-SEC/TAD-CIA-12/23/64 TO 5/24/92.
SECURITY LVL/TOP SECRET/EXP 5/24/92. MSID NO. 2072458.
SS NO. 553-60-1458. NSA/SPL-DDO/SEC-CHIEF-SP/AG PEGASUS UNIT.
CONFIRM/REG/CIA/DENVER,CO. SBS/CUR/RES - DENVER, CO.
ALL OPPS/ASSIGS CLASSIFIED TOP SECRET/UAVAILABLE.
CUR/SEC/STAT: HIGH RISK. FED/CR/IDC/DENVER-1/27/93.

NO ADDITIONAL RECORDS OR BACKGROUND INFORMATION AVAILABLE FOR RELEASE TO YOUR OFFICE AT THIS TIME ON SUBJECT DUE TO MATTERS OF NATIONAL SECURITY AND PRESIDENTIAL DIRECTIVE/G-BUSH 5/24/92.

DO/DA RECOMMENDATION: - STANDARD DENIAL

ANSWER BACK/REF/P-222,
DO/COMM-CTR/3/3/93,
FOR/ITL/SEC - DDO/DDA,
DRC/CIA/LANG/VA.

CONFIDENTIAL

Copy of the CIA confidential document showing Parker's ONI and CIA status, and showing lying to be the standard practice of the CIA.

A year later, in June 1994, the State of Arizona again sought to extradite Parker from Colorado. Colorado attorney Dennis L. Blewitt said to me that almost twenty law-enforcement personnel surrounded Parker's home and arrested him, based upon the Arizona extradition papers.

Parker then sought to have the papers filed in the previous extradition attempt, in the possession of another judge, sent to the court where the new extradition request was to be heard. Blewitt and several friends went to the clerk of the court where the case was pending, requesting help in getting from the other judge the necessary documents. When the clerk heard the name of the book *Defrauding America* she reached under the counter and pulled out a copy. When she realized that Parker was in the book she told the group not to worry, that she would get the records for Parker.

Reportedly, the clerk and the two judges had a copy of the book with Parker's activities described in detail. Arizona requested that a $500,000 cash bond be required for Parker's release pending a hearing on the extradition request. The judge settled for $3,500. After Parker was released he called me, describing the events, and said that even the Thornton city police, who arrested him, had a copy of *Defrauding America* in the police station, and it was being read by the people on duty. Several times Parker credited the book with bringing about his release. The way he described the events caused me to chuckle.

**DESCRIBING MEETING FOSTER AT MENA**

Parker described[421] a meeting he had at Mena, Arkansas at which there were present CIA asset Terry Reed and Rose Law Firm partner Vincent Foster. Parker said that CIA money laundering was the primary topic of discussion. This meeting provided extra support for the fact that the law firm was involved in the CIA-related activities.

**AN OSS MOLE INSIDE THE CIA**

Russell Bowen was one of many intelligence agency sources who gave me many hours of information concerning his activities for the OSS and CIA. Ironically, Bowen said he was a mole within the CIA representing a group of about seventy-five people from the former Office of Strategic Services (OSS). During World War II Bowen was a Lieutenant Colonel in the military and was one of the youngest P-38 fighter pilots during the war. He received the Distinguished Flying Cross, the Distinguished Service Medal, and other decorations for meritorious service.

During World War II he was brought into the OSS by General William Donovan, who was selected by President Franklin Roosevelt to form this intelligence unit. When President Truman disbanded the OSS in 1947, several dozen OSS members secretly maintained their organization under the cover of the CIA and were known as Faction Three in the Central Intelligence Agency.

After the war, in his OSS/CIA role, Bowen was the pilot for United Nations Secretary General Dag Hammerskjold, the Shah of Iran, and eventually Fulgencio Batista, the former dictator of Cuba. He and I had crossed paths when my piloting duties took me to the Middle East on temporary assignment from my base at Oakland, California.

421 During a telephone call in June 1994.

Bowen was flying DC-3 and C-46 aircraft from Kabul to Beirut via Teheran, and I flew the same type of aircraft in the same general area. Bowen was flying "material" for the CIA, and I was flying Moslem pilgrims to Mecca from throughout the Middle East including Baghdad, Teheran, Beirut, Jerusalem, Jidda, and Abadan.

Bowen surprised me when he said that two employees of the same airline that I worked for, Transocean Airlines, were CIA operatives: Allan A. Barrie, General Manager for Iranian Airways in Teheran, and Henry F. "Hank" Maierhoffer. I had flown for Transocean Airlines and had known them when I flew in the Middle East during the early 1950s but had no idea they were engaged in such activities.

Bowen told how he started up several airlines in South America after the war that served as covers for the CIA. He also mentioned knowing a friend of mine, King Parker, who also started several airlines in South America and who occasionally flew with me in the 1980s in my Beech Twin Bonanza aircraft. Parker has since passed away. Parker had flown PBY aircraft for the Royal Canadian Air Force during World War II while I was a Navy flight instructor in PBY seaplanes at Jacksonville, Florida in 1944.

**CASEY'S UNDERCOVER CIA OPERATIONS**

Bowen said that he reported directly to William Casey in the CIA during the 1960s and 1970s. He indicated that Casey was with the CIA in a covert capacity after World War II and long before becoming its director in 1981. Bowen said that he flew dozens of covert CIA operations in the Middle East and Latin America, under Casey's direction. Bowen also mentioned meeting Casey and other handlers on his trips to Washington at secret places and receiving verbal instructions and suitcases filled with money.

Casey was part of the OSS during World War II until it was disbanded by President Truman in 1947. He then became a covert operative for the CIA with no publicized connection to the Agency until 1981, when President Reagan appointed him Director of the CIA.

**"GARBAGE COLLECTOR"**

Bowen was known in the CIA as a "garbage collector," a term used to extract CIA operatives from foreign countries who had been compromised or were wanted by the local police or military. Bowen told me of the time in 1983 when Theodore Shackley ordered him to fly into San Jose, Costa Rica. The purpose was to extract a CIA asset, Sam Cummings, who was hiding in the Piper Aircraft compound using the alias of Mark Clark.

Cummings was the president of the CIA-related Interarms Corporation of Virginia, the largest small-arms company in the world. Cummings had been in Costa Rica on a sensitive CIA mission to provide arms for dissident groups. One of the meetings resulted in two locals being killed and Cummings charged with their murder. Cummings was the brother-in-law of Senator John Tower, who was implicated in the CIA October Surprise operation and other CIA operations in South America.

Extracting Cummings was utmost priority to the CIA as failure could expose a highly sensitive operation. The CIA had given orders that Cummings was either to be extracted from Costa Rica, or killed to silence him.

Among the people involved in the extraction were William P. Clark, Reagan's National Security Adviser, who was in Costa Rica at that time; Joseph Fernandez, a close friend of George Bush and who later became CIA station chief in Costa Rica; and Felix Rodriguez, who was a veteran of the CIA Bay of Pigs fiasco. Parker named another person working with him was Martha Honey, who would later write several books on the CIA involvement in Central America.

Bowen gave me many details about the CIA drug trafficking. He stated that he was in CIA drug trafficking commencing in 1950, operating in the Middle East, Central and South America, and in the Golden Triangle area.

The frequent cross-questioning of CIA and DEA personnel confirmed that Bowen was with the CIA and involved in CIA-directed drug trafficking. Bowen's statements often confirmed the CIA role mentioned by some of my other confidants. Much of this information was given during question and answer sessions but also in a pilot-to-pilot manner. No embellishment; just routine conversations concerning routine piloting activities. None tried to impress me. They simply stated facts.

Bowen elaborated upon his dealings with the Medellin and Cali drug cartels as a CIA operative and the role played by the Mossad in these dealings. Bowen was a friend of Theodore Shackley, a CIA kingpin in CIA drug activities, working closely with the cartels. Bowen said that the CIA provided Theodore Shackley the alias of Robert Haynes. Bowen worked with Shackley from the early 1950s to 1984.

**CRASHING IN THE ANDES**

In 1959, Shackley was on board a C-46 aircraft flown by Bowen when an engine failure forced them to crash-land high on the eastern slopes of the Andes in Bolivia. I've also flown C-46 aircraft, and know that with an engine out, it is very difficult to maintain level flight, and especially at the altitude being flown over the Andes. The plane crashed, but everyone survived.

I had an opportunity to question Shackley on this crash while I was a guest at the national convention for the Association of Former Intelligence Officers (AFIO) held at San Francisco in November 1995. While eating lunch at the convention I suddenly spotted Shackley and his wife sitting immediately across from me. Since I did not know if he had read my earlier books in which I made reference to him, and since I wanted to be low-key at this convention, I didn't introduce myself to him. However, I wanted to get Shackley's reaction to the plane crash described by Bowen, and asked former National Security Agency (NSA) agent Joe T. Jordan, who sponsored my appearance at the convention, to ask.

Jordan said that Shackley "stated unequivocally that it was untrue." I didn't think that Bowen would lie to me on a matter like that, so I called Bowen at his Florida residence, advising him of Shackley's reply. I asked, "Was there something going on with that flight that he [Shackley] would not want anyone to know that he was on it?"

Bowen responded, "Of course; it was loaded with drugs."

Bowen then enlarged upon the purpose of that trip. He stated that this trip occurred several years before Shackley was made CIA station chief in Miami, and that Shackley was instrumental in setting up the CIA drug trafficking into the United States from South America. Bowen said that the series of flights went from Miami, to Colombia, to Quayaqui, to Lima, and then to Arequita. After the plane left Arequita going eastbound over the Andes, one of the two engines failed, causing the aircraft to lose altitude. Bowen was able to maneuver the aircraft into one of the few available flat areas, and crash-landed the plane.

Bowen said that Shackley had arranged for cocaine to be loaded on board the aircraft, where it was hidden in the tail section. Bowen, Shackley, and the others then abandoned the crashed aircraft. Eventually the Bolivian authorities discovered the drugs, but the pilots and passengers were long gone. This would explain why Shackley wanted to distance himself from that crash.

Bowen said that Shackley went to Ascension, Paraguay to arrange for drugs to be shipped to Miami, meeting with the head chief of one of the Indian groups, Quadium (phonetic), and a Lieutenant Colonel in Paraguay's military. The name of the town where that meeting was held was Guadion. Bowen said that these people were the backbone of Strossner's intelligence and drug dealing activities.

Bowen described the conflict between different CIA factions, stating that Shackley wanted to smuggle the drugs into the United States, and another faction, with whom Bowen was associated, wanted to block this practice. Bowen said, "At that time, Shackley was the leader in bringing the drugs in. Shackley's team wanted the drugs in. The team I worked for did not want the drugs in."

I asked who set up that initial drug operation, and he said, "He was the mastermind of the drug operation. He had full authority to set it up." I asked, "Would you have any knowledge of whether McLean or Washington was aware of this drug operation?"

"They ordered him to do it."

I said to Bowen that Russbacher had told me of the three factions within the CIA that had different and contradictory agendas, and that Russbacher was with the Office of Naval Intelligence faction. Bowen replied, "The naval intelligence faction is the most dangerous of them all. I grew up with them in Arlington."

**MONEY LAUNDERING PROPRIETARIES**

Bowen described one of the CIA proprietaries operated by Shackley, INTERKREDIT, with offices in Medellin, Amsterdam, and Ft. Lauderdale, Florida. During the Vietnam War Shackley helped manage the extensive CIA drug operations in the Golden Triangle Area, and was the executive director of the CIA Phoenix Program (that murdered over 40,000 Vietnamese civilians). Shackley directed the CIA's secret war against Laos in the mid-1960s, and later became chief of station in Saigon. He directed the transfer of tens of millions if not billions of dollars received from the CIA-promoted heroin trade in the Golden Triangle of Burma, Thailand, and Laos.

When Shackley was chief of station for the CIA in charge of Central and South American operations, he reportedly directed the massive drug trafficking into the United States that subsequently blossomed. He directed the operation known as "TRACK II," which led to the overthrow of the Salvador Allende government in Chile in 1973. He was just the man to coordinate the CIA's development of the burgeoning drug trafficking from Central and South America into the United States.

Bowen gave me details of the CIA ties to the Medellin drug cartel that Russbacher and Parker had described to me earlier. Each gave me details of the formation of the Medellin cartel from another perspective.

Bowen described another side to the kidnapping of Ochoa's sister, Leona, which Parker had earlier described. Bowen was unaware of the role Parker played in the kidnapping. Bowen said that he flew the DC-3 aircraft that flew Ochoa's sister, after she was kidnapped, from a small dirt airstrip near Bogota, Columbia to a dirt strip at Ipiales, in the southwestern part of Colombia, near Paso.

Bowen worked under Shackley when Shackley was transferred to Vietnam, and described Shackley's role in the deadly Phoenix program. Bowen said that the people doing the killing, often Humong warriors, were paid in drugs by the CIA for every person they killed. (Many of the Humong were later settled into the United States.)

## UNUSUAL ATTEMPT TO EXPOSE CIA DRUG TRAFFICKING

Bowen, like many other CIA operatives, became disenchanted with the CIA drug trafficking. In 1981, he wrote anonymous letters to U.S. Customs in Miami, reporting the details of the drug operation in the hope that it would be stopped. Nothing happened. During a flight in 1982, he tried another way to get publicity which backfired on him. Bowen said that he was requested by CIA operative Henry Meierhoffer[422] to fly a trip to Medellin, Colombia carrying a government undercover agent and to return with another agent. But when Bowen arrived in Medellin, Shackley placed eight hundred pounds of cocaine on board the return flight, including two hundred pounds belonging to the Mossad in bags imprinted with the Mossad's two triangles resembling the Star of David.

On the return flight to the United States with the cocaine, he decided to land at an airport that had intensive surveillance for drug trafficking, Sylvania Airport in Georgia. His intent was to alert the authorities to the cocaine load and, in his way of thinking, cause the local police to take action against the CIA. This was rather naive but his heart was in the right place. Bowen was blowing the whistle on the huge international drug operation involving some of the highest officials in the U.S. government. The plan backfired. Bowen was arrested for drug trafficking.

## STANDARD SILENCING TACTIC

Bowen said that at his trial in 1985, the U.S. District Judge refused to allow him to have his CIA handlers, including Meierhoffer, appear as witnesses. During Bowen's trial, Justice Department prosecutors and the Judge protected the Mossad's role in the drug trafficking by withholding from evidence the two hundred pounds of cocaine with the Mossad's identification on it. If those bags of cocaine with the triangles representing the Star of David were presented as evidence, serious questions would have been raised.

The Judge refused to allow Bowen to produce records and testimony showing that he was carrying out CIA activities. Refusing to allow evidence to be presented that is necessary to a person's defense, when covert government activities are

422 On March 2, 1984. Interestingly, Meierhoffer had been an employee of Transocean Airlines in Beirut during the time I was a captain for the airline.

involved, is a standard pattern by federal judges. Almost every CIA and DEA person with whom I have talked, and who has been imprisoned, experienced this pattern, including Russbacher, Rewald, Riconosciuto, Wilson, and others.

Bowen's court-appointed defender displayed the usual lack of aggressiveness, with no desire to raise a defense that would expose covert government activities. It is probable that the naive jury felt that Justice Department prosecutors surely would not lie or bring false charges against an innocent citizen. They convicted Bowen, and he was sentenced to ten years in prison. During his imprisonment Bowen was sent to Springfield federal prison hospital where he was repeatedly injected with Procan, which prisoners refer to as "Russian lobotomy" because it reportedly destroys the memory.

I asked, "What happens if you resist taking the shots?" He replied: "Burly guards come in and hold you down, while another prison attendant shoots the drug into you."

**ANOTHER DEA SOURCE**

Another one of my many confidential sources was a former DEA pilot, Basil Abbott, who had flown drugs from Central and South America for the DEA from 1973 to 1983. During several years of frequent discussions and many letters Abbott gave me a chronology of his DEA activities. At first he was a confidential informant (CI) and then a contract pilot, flying arms to Central America and drugs on the return flights.

Abbott described receiving pilot training from DEA agent William Coller at the FAA Academy in Oklahoma City, preparing him to fly drugs in and out of short dirt strips in Central and South America. Classroom training was given on how to avoid radar detection, the routes to fly and the hours to fly them so as to avoid detection by drug interdiction aircraft. Coller trained Abbott in numerous aircraft, including the Cessna 180, 185, 206, 210 and 310; and Piper Aztec, Aerostar and Navajo. Abbott received training on how to survive if forced down in the jungle, and how to ditch the aircraft in the water. He received a DEA flight manual written by Coller which described the technique for landing and taking off from unpaved and short runways, as found in Central America.

During Abbott's DEA employment he worked out of DEA offices in Denver, Charleston, and in 1978 the DEA facility at Addison Airport, north of Dallas. Abbott named other DEA pilots who, acting under DEA orders, flew drug flights from Central America to the United States. These pilots included Cesar Rodriguez, Daniel Miranda, and George Phillips.

Abbott was ordered by the DEA to fly arms to numerous Central America locations. One of these flights, occurring in 1982, flew arms into a dirt strip near Bluefields, Nicaragua for the Miskito Indians. From there, Abbot flew to a strip known as B2E, where drugs were loaded for the return flight to the United States. Some of these flights landed at a small airfield near Memphis, Tennessee.

These flights were profitable for everyone involved, including the pilots. In addition to being paid in cash for each flight, pilots flying for the DEA were given part of the drug loads, which they later sold. Abbott received $60,000 and fifty pounds of pot for this flight to the Miskito Indians and return with drugs.

Abbott described flying drug loads out of small landing strips in Nicaragua, Antigua, Honduras, Costa Rica, Salvador, Guatemala, Belize, and Mexico. He arranged for fuel supplies and ground facilities at these locations, and regularly bribed local politicians to cooperate and protect the arms and drug flights. Abbott's fluency was helpful in these activities. In addition to English, he spoke several languages, including Spanish, Swedish, Norwegian, and Danish. During his DEA-associated activities he circulated in prominent Central America society, socializing with well-known political figures, including Alfredo Stroessner in Paraguay.

Abbott described a Bolivian 707 that regularly hauled drugs into Panama with the DEA's knowledge. When Abbott asked his DEA handlers about it, they told him to forget it. These flights were hazardous in many ways. Abbott described DEA pilots flying arms to the M-19 group in Colombia, during which some of the pilots were assassinated.

"It was like Grand Central Station at some airstrips in Belize and Nicaragua," was how Abbott described the frequency of drug flights arriving and departing. Abbott told how he and other DEA personnel flew to Santa Cruz, Bolivia, in a Convair 340 to set a trap for the son of the Israeli Ambassador, Sam Weisgal, involving a large shipment of cocaine to the United States. When the drug bust occurred, several people were killed. The DEA seized the drugs and then reshipped them as if they were DEA loads. Weisgal escaped the drug bust, but was later captured. However, he was soon released when Israel complained.

**SHADES OF INSLAW**

Abbott told me about a flight to Panama with DEA agent George Phillips.[423] While stopped for fuel at Belize, Phillips opened an aluminum suitcase that held rolls of tapes and disks marked Inslaw. Phillips told Abbott that the tapes were money records of a fake company used by a group of drug dealers. This software, called PROMIS, was initially stolen from the Inslaw company by Justice Department officials, who then sold the computer program to foreign governments and to drug cartels.

**PERIL OF KNOWING TOO MUCH**

On a flight to Cancun, Mexico, in June 1983, Abbott was seized by DEA agents acting with Mexican police. While in jail he was interrogated by DEA agents Richard Braziel, Torry Schutz, Jerry Carter, and Assistant U.S. Attorney (AUSA) John Murphy. When Abbott wouldn't answer the questions, Mexican police, under Braziel's request, severely beat Abbott. U.S. agents then transported Abbott to a county jail in San Antonio, Texas, where he was visited by CIA agents who assured him that he would be released shortly. Instead, Abbott was sentenced to eight years in prison by Judge Shannon. DEA agent Richard Braziel then told Abbott the sentence was only for show, and that they would get him released if he did not say anything about the DEA and CIA drug operations.

Abbott was eventually released. After his release on probation, Abbott tried to obtain media interest in DEA drug trafficking, including the Larry King Show. He had no more success than I had during 30 years of attempting to expose the escalating government corruption, including 10 years of reports to Larry King.

423 Phillips was a CIA contract agent assigned to the DEA.

Abbott even tried to give his evidence to Manuel Noriega's attorneys to show how Noriega was simply a part of the CIA, DEA, and Mossad drug trafficking into the United States.

One source did respond to Abbott's publicity efforts: the DEA, FBI, and Department of Justice. They fabricated a reason for arresting Abbott while on probation, stating that he had left the geographical limits of his parole at Dallas by flying a private plane to nearby Austin. Upon readying his plane for the return flight to Dallas, DEA agents arrested him, charging him with violating parole conditions.

During his parole-revocation hearing, Abbott said that he had called his parole officer by phone and advised him of his trip to Austin, and had received permission to do so. (This call had apparently alerted government agents to his whereabouts for the subsequent arrest.) Abbott was arrested at the Austin, Texas Airport by Texas Department of Public Safety (DPF) agent Robert Nesteroff, and falsely charged with drug smuggling, even though there was no evidence to support this charge. (Nesteroff was later charged with drug smuggling by the U.S. Department of Justice.)

Abbott felt that Nesteroff sought to have him put in prison because Abbott had knowledge of Nesteroff's drug activities and had previous contact with Nesteroff.

After the hearing the parole officer rendered a decision stating that he had not proven that he was not dealing in drugs. Abbott was expected to prove a negative, when there was no evidence that he had been involved.

Abbott started contacting me after this second arrest, and in dozens of detailed letters and over a hundred hours of questioning by phone, divulged a great amount of information about the CIA and DEA involvement in drugs. This information coincided with what I had learned from many other sources.

## DANGEROUS TO EXPOSE GOVERNMENT CORRUPTION

Abbott described his frequent contacts with the DEA's Central America Bureau Chief, Sante Bario, and how the DEA silenced Bario to keep the CIA and DEA drug smuggling operations from the public. Bario was the DEA chief pilot for Central and South American affairs, and for some reason high-level DEA officials wanted him out of the way. DEA and Justice Department attorneys charged Bario with federal drug offenses, causing his imprisonment. When brought before U.S. District Judge Fred Shannon in San Antonio, Bario tried to describe his DEA duties and the DEA and CIA drug trafficking, but Justice Department attorneys and the judge blocked him from proceeding. After being returned to his jail cell, a prison guard gave Bario a strychnine-laced peanut-butter sandwich, causing immediate painful convulsions and subsequent death. The official autopsy report covered up for this murder, reporting that Bario died of asphyxiation.

## KEEPING QUIET AFTER BARIO'S DEATH

After Abbott was first arrested and pled guilty to the charges against him, District Judge Shannon asked him why he pled guilty rather than trying to defend himself. Abbott replied that he didn't want to end up dead like DEA pilot Sante Bario.

## ASSASSINATING ABBOTT'S WIFE

Abbott described acquiring a common-law wife in Norway who later bore their child. She moved to the United States and started an import business bringing sweaters into the United States from Norway and Iceland. Abbott feared for the safety of his wife and daughter after the DEA targeted him, and he sent them back to Sweden. After he was arrested and in federal prison at Bastrop (near San Antonio, Texas), his wife in Sweden tried to get media attention on the DEA drug trafficking by talking to newspapers in Germany, hoping that this attention would force the DEA and Justice Department to release Abbott. Instead, she joined the long list of those who posed a threat to U.S. officials and their criminal activities; she was assassinated.

Abbott's grief over his wife's assassination, and the constant attempts by government agents to silence him, made him determined to expose the corruption in the DEA, CIA and Justice Department. He sent me many letters describing in great detail the DEA and CIA drug operations, including maps of landing sites, people he contacted, and the names of other DEA pilots.

Abbott was released from prison on November 14, 1994, and became one of several former prisoners who credit my letters (such as to the parole board in Abbott's case), along with a copy of the second edition of *Defrauding America*, with bringing about their release.

## OPERATION BUY BACK (BB)

Abbott told of an operation, which CIA-ONI agent Gunther Russbacher enlarged upon, involving smuggling drugs in frozen shrimp, using a CIA front company, Pacific Seafood Transportation Company. Russbacher and other CIA operatives confirmed the drug trafficking by Pacific Seafood. Russbacher said that shrimp containers "were filled with ice and everything but shrimp." He said it was part of a joint DEA-CIA operation called Operation Buy Back (BB).

Abbott described many of the people with whom he came in contact, who were also heavily involved in drug-related activities. He described his close contacts with Eric Arturo Del-Valle, a member of Panama's Jewish community, and who was the president of Panama. Arturo's family was in the sugar export business, which Abbott said was also a subterfuge for cocaine exports to the United States by the Mossad.

Abbott described the relationship between the major Bolivian drug traffickers, Sonia and Walter Atala, and the Roberto Suarez cocaine gang and the CIA. The Atalas leased a Boeing 727 in 1980 and 1981, painted the name Lloyd Aero Boliviano on the side, and used it to haul cocaine into Tocumen Airport from Bolivia and Paraguay. At Tocumen Airport the cocaine was off-loaded to a warehouse owned by the Atalas, which was a front for exporting Hitachi radios and television sets back to Bolivia and Paraguay. (Abbott also picked up cocaine numerous times at Tocumen Airport.)

From Tocumen Airport the cocaine was loaded onto small planes, or onto TACA Airlines, flying to the United States. Every morning at 6 a.m. TACA departed Tocumen for El Salvador, Belize, Costa Rica, Nicaragua, and eventually to New Orleans, Miami, and Houston. Cocaine was off-loaded at one or all of these stops in the United States.

The cocaine would sometimes be driven from Atala's warehouse at Tocumen to the Colon Free Trade Zone, placed into another of Atala's front companies, and eventually put on ships going to the United States.

Abbott described the frequent presence of Manuel Noriega at CIA and DEA drug transshipment points. He said that Noriega's CIA code name was Nelson.

**BELIZE AS A MAJOR DRUG TRANSSHIPMENT POINT**

Abbott described the enormous drug trafficking occurring in Belize, and how that country was used by the CIA for training Contras, similar to what was occurring in Arkansas at Mena and Nella. Abbott described Operation Bushmaster in Belize, which was intended to take over the drug business from the many independent drug smugglers, being taken over by the CIA for greater profit and greater security. Busting independent drug traffickers was one of the joint CIA-Justice Department tactics to control the drug business into the United States. So powerful was the CIA that it literally took over the government of Belize.

Abbott frequently delivered arms that he had picked up in Louisiana, Texas, and Arkansas to Belize, among other destinations. These consisted of AR-15's, M-16s, ammunition, M-1's, grenades, machine guns. He described the shipments of anhydrous dyethel ether into Belize for a cocaine processing lab on Mischer's land, where there was a Minute Maid orange plantation.

He described a cocaine processing lab north of Cuatrocienegas, Mexico, in the state of Chihuahua. Abbott stated that Robert Corson and he helped set up the lab, after which DEA agents arrested Abbott. Abbott stated that from that CIA lab the cocaine was transported by land, and sometimes by air, to the strip at Lajitas in West Texas, on land controlled by Walt Mischer. From there it was then flown to other parts of the United States.

**THE ARKANSAS CONNECTION**

One of the Arkansas airstrips into which Abbott was directed to deliver the drugs was south of Interstate 30 just southwest of W. Memphis, Tennessee, called Marianna. Several of my other deep-cover contacts described that same airport to me, and the role played by state police in protecting the drug and arms operations.

Abbott described how Arkansas state police blocked off the roads leading to small airstrips when drug flights arrived. He described one such instance occurring in the spring of 1982. Abbott flew a Cessna 210 containing 300 kilos of cocaine from one of several warehouses at Tocumen owned by drug traffickers Walter and Sonia Atala, to the crop-duster landing strip at Marianna, Arkansas. He made a fuel stop in Belize, famous for transition of drug-loaded aircraft, and then proceeded to his Marianna destination. A Memphis-based DEA agent took the cocaine from Abbott, while an Arkansas state trooper blocked the road leading to the landing strip. A week later, Abbott took off from that strip with six suitcases of money, delivering the money to Cesar Rodriguez at Isla Contadora. Abbott said the plane was provided by Robert Corson through Jim Bath of Houston. (Corson was famous in the savings and loan scandals.)

**FURTHER CONFIRMATION OF CIA-DEA THEFT OF PLANES**

Abbott described the CIA stealing of general aviation planes within the United States for use in the CIA (and National Security Council's) unlawful arms and drug shipments, which coincided with what several of my CIA contacts had stated to me for the past few years, and as described by former CIA asset Terry Reed in his book, *Compromised*. Some of the stolen planes were registered in the company name of Pacific Seafood Transport.

The stolen aircraft were repainted and new serial numbers applied, after which they were flown to Central and South America with loads of arms, and then drugs on the return flights.

**MEXICAN AIRLINERS & DRUGS**

It was in the early 1990s that Abbott described to me how he arranged for the unloading of drugs from Mexican airliners in the Mexican desert. At the time this sounded rather bizarre, but his detailed description of the events over a period of several years convinced me that he was telling the truth. Further, an article (November 30, 1995) in the *New York Times* (and earlier in the *Los Angeles Times*) was headlined, "Drug Plane Unloaded in Mexico, Maybe by Police." The article described a Caravelle passenger jet being landed on a dry lake bed near Todos Santos, Mexico. The Caravelle was a French-built airliner that was flown by United Airlines during the 1960s.

Normally this operation would have gone unreported, as many others had occurred. But this drug operation was reported because of the unusual events surrounding its occurrence. The aircraft's nosewheel was damaged upon landing, preventing a subsequent takeoff. The article described how heavily-armed federal police immediately proceeded to unload the plane after it landed, and then proceeded to dismantle and destroy the aircraft. All identifying documents and avionics equipment were removed from the plane, the wings cut off, and an attempt made to blow up the plane. A large hole was bulldozed in the ground and the plane was buried.

Complications developed while the plane was being destroyed. The state police commander and several deputies arrived to investigate, and were confronted in a tense standoff with the federal police, who advised that the army had been notified and the situation was under control.

The 30 federal policemen involved in the drug operation were suddenly transferred and unavailable for questioning by the federal prosecutor in the Baja California jurisdiction.

Making reference to the use of large jets in similar situations, Mexican Foreign Minister Jose Angel Gurria said in a recent interview that drug traffickers had stopped using large passenger jets. This is doubtful.

**HIGH-LEVEL INVOLVEMENT**

Putting together the many reports from my contacts in the CIA, DEA, and high-level drug traffickers, Mexican officials at every level are heavily involved in drug trafficking that is funded by drug users in the United States. This high-level involvement became obvious in late 1995 when newspaper articles published stories about the tens of millions of dollars hidden by present and former Mexican officials in Mexican and foreign banks. Reports had surfaced that Mexico's President, Ernesto Zedillo, had received huge financial and other donations from the drug cartels, and that the brother of former president Carlos Salinas de Gortari had over $84 million hidden in Swiss bank accounts, plus unknown sums in other banks.[424]

Swiss police arrested (November 15, 1995) Raul Salinas' wife, Paulina Castanon, when she and her brother tried to withdraw some of the drug funds that he had hidden in Swiss bank accounts. Mexican police had arrested Raul Salinas for allegedly masterminding the September 1994 murder of a top official in the ruling political party, Jose Francisco Ruiz Massieu, and could not get to the funds. His wife and her brother used forged documents to withdraw the funds, and were subsequently arrested by Swiss authorities, who stated that the funds were associated with drug-related activities.

**CIA CABLE ANALYST**

In late 1993, I made contact with another deep-cover CIA operative and State Department employee, Michael Maholy, whose primary duty was monitoring cable traffic at different CIA locations. Maholy started giving me information and a different slant on the role of federal officials in drug trafficking from Central and South America into the United States. As with most of my other contacts, these factual conversations continued for years.

Maholy was liaison officer for the U.S. Embassy in Panama and worked for the U.S. State Department and CIA for over two decades. Maholy wrote in one of his letters about his role at the U.S. Embassy.

*I have spent time in South American countries providing photos, documents, maps, and all intel. for the U.S. Embassies in Central and South America. I first became acquainted with agent [Robert] Hunt in 1985 in Panama where I was the liaison officer for the U.S. Embassy. He was always accompanied by [Oliver] North and his team. This went on for several years. I recall reading cable traffic where his name came up repeatedly.*

Maholy detailed the drug trafficking involving the CIA and the State Department:

*Hunt was on several covert missions and detached to Operation Whale Watch, which involved me buying drugs from Colombians and trading them for arms and ammo. My part in the operation was to provide a cover or front through the use of offshore oil rigs, so that Hunt, myself, and others, could complete these transactions. These offshore oil-rigs were all CIA offshore geological survey and logistics services.*

Other letters followed, and included considerable:

*During my contacts with [CIA Director] William Casey, I was drafted into the Southern Zone (Central and South American countries) so that we could start operations on spying on Panama, Colombia, and other countries that were making huge amounts of money from drugs. They needed weapons and fire power. We, the CIA, provided them. They in turn sold us drugs....many instances of cover-up conspiracies that continue to multiply as we are talking.*

*On one tour to South America I worked on a CIA-owned oil rig operated by a company called Rowan International, based in Houston, Texas. Rowan is a world-wide drilling exploration company with very friendly liaisons in Central America and South America, as well as Africa and Middle*

424 *Dallas Morning News*, November 25, 1995.

*East.... While in Balboa Harbor off the coast of Panama, on the rig Rowan Houston, at approximately 2:00 a.m., a helicopter landed on the heliport. I was monitoring cables and traffic when our radar detected a small support group which turned out to be patrol boats, four in all. At this point I thought the rig was going to be taken over by hostile forces. But instead I could not believe who was getting out of the chopper: it was Noriega and another man. I contacted the "company man" and he informed me that this meeting was not to be documented and to go back and resume the task of cable and traffic. I found out later that this man with Noriega was [Mossad agent] Michael Harari. I found out later that they were trying to raise money from CIA by selling drugs to plan the destruction of a hydro-electric power plant on the Orinoco River in Venezuela.*

Over a period of many months, Maholy gave me details of CIA and Mossad drug trafficking. He named the companies owning the oil rigs off the coast of the United States, Central and South America, Nigeria, and Angola: Santa Fe; Zapata; and Rowan. He physically saw Evergreen International Airlines and Southern Air Transport hauling drugs, confirmed by cable traffic he handled.

I had repeatedly heard from various investigators and CIA contacts that various divisions of the Zapata Corporation,[425] such as Zapata Petroleum, Zapata Off-Shore, Zapata Cattle Company, were heavily involved in drug trafficking. The oil rigs were used to carry out the drug operations. Drugs would be off-loaded from ships onto the drilling platforms and then taken into the nearby coastal areas in helicopters that were constantly carrying supplies and personnel. Maholy confirmed that this practice existed, having learned about it from CIA cable traffic and his own observations while on the rigs.

Maholy told how he was transferred from his detachment in Greenland under Lt. General John W. Carpenter III, USAF, to Central America, where he learned about the CIA role in drug trafficking. He also became a standard expendable, as the CIA did to him what they do to most CIA-related assets dealing in drugs. When they learn too much about the operation and threaten an exposure, the CIA, working hand-in-hand with Justice Department prosecutors, charge the person with a drug offense for having carried out CIA orders.

In another letter, Maholy wrote in part:

*The real mission [of these oil and gas drilling platforms] was to funnel weapons and money to the Nicaraguans, and also to bring illegal drugs into the United States. Being a CIA-funded mission, the rig had Naval SEAL teams diverted through its location.... Rowan International was a cover for a branch of Zapata Oil. Zapata Oil and Exploration had many land-based operations in Central and South America as well as offshore rigs.*

*We had access to military cryptographics such as the KW 135, the KL 16, KL 10 and the CW 4 to decode and sifter out any cable traffic from transmissions from Guatemala, El Salvador, Costa Rica, and Panama.*

---

425 Zapata Corporation, based in Houston, was a CIA asset, and the stock partly owned by George Bush. Zapata Petroleum was organized by George Bush, who reportedly had major interests in various Zapata divisions.

Maholy confirmed what other CIA sources had told me about the CIA drug trafficking through Pacific Seafood. He wrote:

*This company [Pacific Seafood] used a number of vessels to carry out covert missions to run weapons, drugs and cash from country to country. Not only would their "shrimp" trawlers use the oil rigs for loading, unloading and refueling, and also to deliver large sums of money for aid to the Contras. The shrimpers would constantly converge on our rig to convert, store and transport all of the above. The crews were all seasoned para-military experts in their abilities to search and destroy, CIA trained and specialists in their fields.*

*It was from one of the shrimp boat captains that I would come to meet Barry Seal's main right-wing contact from Morgan City, La. His name was Russell Hebert, and the name on his shrimp boat was Southern Crossing. This boat had state-of-the-art radar, hi-tech navigation systems, extra fuel tanks, and a crew consisting only of "special forces or [Navy] Seals."*

Maholy wrote that he remembers Russell Bowen flying onto the rig and then flying two DEA agents to Colombia. I called Bowen, who lived in Winter Haven, Florida at the time, and asked him about this flight. Bowen confirmed that it was him. I said to Bowen that Maholy mentioned having seen him at the oil rig, and Bowen then confirmed it, stating it was part of the operation that extracted CIA agent Sam Cummings from Costa Rica.

## MOSSAD'S DRUG TRAFFICKING ON CIA AND ZAPATA OIL PLATFORMS

Maholy described the drugs that he had seen on the oil platforms operated by the CIA and Zapata Corporation,[426] some with the Mossad's Star of David triangles on them. In one letter he wrote, "A shrimp boat arrived with a load of cocaine with the markings of the Mossad's famous two triangles that resembled the Star of David."

Maholy described how the drug planes would fly low and proceed from the off-shore oil rigs to the United States at very slow speeds of approximately 120 knots, so that they would appear on radar as helicopters servicing the rigs. Bringing the famous Ochoa drug family into the picture, Maholy described how the Ochoa drug cartel used the coastal oil rigs for drug trans-shipments.

Maholy described the role of a Venezuelan naval officer by the name of Lizardo Marquez Perez, who was in charge of this drug operation, and frequently seen on the oil rigs by Maholy.

Maholy described the coverup of the drug operation by such people as the Chief of the DEA cocaine operations in Washington, Ron Caffrey; Oliver North; CIA official Duane Clarridge; Army Lieutenant General Paul Gorman (commander of the Panama-based U.S. Southern Command), and others. Excerpts from some of Maholy's letters:

*A person I've met on several occasions was in the Colombia Cartel, Carlos Lehder. During Operation Back Door he and several of his soldiers were planning to use CIA oil rigs and the shrimp industries to import drugs*

---

426 Zapata Corporation was headquartered in Houston, Texas.

*into America. Carlos had DEA personnel assigned to work with him. I myself have been to his home on Norman's Cay in the Bahamas. He had a stash of drugs shipped back and forth to Everglade City in the Ten Thousands Islands area of Southern Florida. When the rig Rowan Midland was in Venezuela, Carlos had a regular agent of his as a tool-pusher to oversee all shipments coming and going. The CIA would buy drugs and supply friends of the Colombian government with money and weapons.*

***OPERATION BACK DOOR***

*They used the remote mangrove swamps to unload huge loads of pot and cocaine to get it to Miami to distribute. With help from CIA and DEA agents, Carlos would set up a few loads as decoy to make it look good so he could get major shipments into the United States. Operation Back Door had a priority of grave importance. I was to monitor some of the cable and equipment, also scramble transmissions made from his boats and planes, so he could go undetected. Also to make sure his money could be on the rig when he wanted it. Carlos got to be "mouthy." The government set him up and double crossed him. The rig was then moved to Aruba and once again set up as a relay station and command center. The M-19 group was also involved in several covert missions. Members of their right wing force were actually flown and boated to Florida to recruit forces and promote a revolution in the U.S. and an invasion of drugs to Southern Florida. Operation Back Door simply meant the drugs would come to America via the back door.*

The role of the Venezuelans in CIA-related drug trafficking was revealed in the *60 Minutes* show on November 21, 1993.

Maholy described his dealings with drug trafficker Barry Seal (aka Ellis McKenzie and a former pilot for TWA Airlines.) Maholy said that Seal was involved with the Noriega Cartel in a top-secret operation. Seal's Miami contact was a person using the name of "Lito." Maholy described how Seal had a fleet of aircraft hauling drugs that flew mostly at night with the pilots using night-vision goggles. They flew through airspace "windows" when the military radar would ignore the targets. As the planes approached the oil rigs off the coast of the United States the planes flew close to the water, avoiding radar detection.

Maholy wrote that Seal was paid large amounts of money by CIA contacts, and that in 1982 and 1983 Seal brought in more than five thousand kilos of cocaine, grossing over twenty-five million dollars.

Maholy elaborated upon his role in Operation Screamer which was a mammoth sting operation aimed at penetrating the network of mercenary pilots that were flying drugs in competition with the CIA. On this operation Maholy worked under DEA agent-in-charge Randy Beasley. Maholy told how Seal offered to turn informant, allegedly implicating high federal officials, including former Watergate prosecutor Richard Ben-Veniste. Maholy stated that "This made Beasley and others uneasy. Why? Because they themselves were dirty."

Maholy said that Seal had an informant number, SG1-84-0028. That number, or the initials CI, would be substituted for Seal's name on all reports in his case file (which was given the number G1-84-0121).

NATIONAL SECURITY AGENCY
CENTRAL SECURITY SERVICE
FORT GEORGE G. MEADE, MARYLAND 20755-6000

Capt. Scott A. Beal
C.I.A. Station Chief
United States Embassy
San Jose, Costa Rica

Jan. 10, 1994

Re: "Agent Classification"

CONFIDENTIAL

Dear Capt. Beal,

Due to the highly sensitive nature of classified agency documents that have been requested, appropriated measures have been taken by our Special Operations Division advisor at N.S.A. headquarters, Fort Meade Maryland, to acknowledge varification and existence of O.N.I. Special Operations Division officer, Michael Maholy. His significant involvement and cooperation relevant to " deep-cover " covert C.I.A., O.N.I., and D.E.A. intelligence operations conducted in conjuction with U.S. Naval Seal Teams II, and III, Delta Force Units 7,and 9,and U.S.M.C. Recon detachments deployed to both South and Central American countries, consisted of monitoring cable transmissions and as an observer of ongoing missions.

Agent Maholy was considered on "active" status from 1976 to 1988. Maholy had assigned surveillance command units in Veracruz Mexico, Puerto Barrios Guatemala, Managua Nicaragua, Sanata - Ana El Salvador, Tegucigalpa Honduras, San Jose Costa Rica, Colon Panama, Cartangena Colombia, and Caracas Venezuela.

Be advised, that a substantial accumulation of " classified " and " TOP - SECRET " documents pertaining to agent Maholy s assistance to the deployment and recovery of the above mentioned personal covert operatives, combined with the the tracking of " hostile " troop logistic positions and movement, have been turned over to O.N.I., and C.I.A. authorities at Langely Command Center.

The Office of Strategic Services has and is conducting a current review and trace of documents still exsisting, and of those that may have been destroyed, under Presidential Directive status, and will foward the results of their investigation to your liaison officer in San Jose Costa Rica A.S.A.P.

CC: Gp/fp
O.S.S.

Respectfully,

Gerald D. Tishner
N.S.C.I.D.
Office of Strategic Services

Document indicating Maholy's deep-cover government status.

**OPERATION WHALE WATCH**

Operation Whale Watch was one of the CIA's drug trafficking operations using CIA-affiliated oil rigs off the coast of the United States and Central and South America. Maholy described how two oil rigs were deliberately sabotaged when security was breached and the crews on the rig learned about the drug trafficking and voiced their displeasure. Maholy wrote:

*I have information on offshore activities involving the sabotage of two more drilling rigs involving the deaths of more than 82 persons. One off the coast of the Yucatan Peninsula in Mexico, and the other off of the coast of Newfoundland. Both rigs were CIA owned and operated. Due to leaks in security, they were destroyed by our own government officials.*

*"Ranger I" was a semi-submergible deep-water drilling rig off the coast of Halifax, Newfoundland, operated by the sister company of Exxon Oil, Shamrock Drilling of Ireland. The Shamrock Company was funneling money through "Ranger I" to Canada and was detected by a breach in security. Thus, they picked a winter storm as a perfect cover to flood the computerized ballast systems, triggering the rig to list to the port side and sink to the bottom of the North Atlantic. This took place in February 1989 at 3:00 am in the morning. All 42 hands lost. No bodies recovered.*

*Then there was Operation Odessa. This was a jack-up offshore drilling rig that was stationed off the coast of Nicaragua and had to be moved due to civil unrest in that nation. This was a prime rig where command officers of the CIA had communication offices. I've spent many days and nights reading cable traffic and monitoring daily activities. This rig was a mother ship for distribution of drugs, weapons and money for all parties concerned. The rig moved north because of hostile government takeover. Five days after entering Mexican waters, the rig was blown up. This involved Hunt*[427] *and his strike team.*

*This information was intercepted during a non-routine check of all comsac radio transmissions. I believe the reason was that the Mexican government was paid huge sums of money for the cover-up. Reasons released to the media were "offshore oil platform explodes, all 46 aboard dead.*

Over a period of time Maholy furnished me with additional information that made clear the CIA's involvement in drug trafficking into the United States, the details of the operations, the Mossad involvement, and other areas of CIA corrupt activities. I received documents and letters showing Maholy's CIA status. A letter written by the Israeli Embassy in Washington dated October 20, 1993, made reference to the CIA-Mossad drug operation, Operation Whale Watch, stating in part: "These agents [involved in Operation Whale Watch] include: C.I.A. Intelligence Officers Michael Maholy, Duane (Dewey) Clarridge, Steven Tucker, along with two National Security Council (NSC) officers, Lt. Col. Oliver North and Lt. Robert Hunt [and Mossad agent] Michael Harari (Retired)."

A letter dated October 25, 1993, sent by the National Security Agency identified Operation Whale Watch, confirmed my contacts as being part of the

427 Hunt was reportedly a part of Navy SEAL teams Six and Two. More about Hunt in later pages.

operation and with the CIA. The letter stated in part: "Operatives [include] Special Agent-in-Charge Michael Maholy, C.I.A.…. Due to the sensitive nature of "Operation Whale Watch" we cannot authorize any further information on this Top-Secret Mission."

## CROSS-CHECK ON NAMES OF DRUG SMUGGLERS INVOLVED IN OPERATION NEW WAVE

CIA operative Robert Hunt described what he knew of the drug trafficking. He recited a list of people involved in Operation New Wave, the heroin operation described to me by Gunther Russbacher. The names given by Hunt included almost all the names Russbacher had listed, including David Fuller, Patrick O'Riley, Michael Cobb, John Woodruff, Brett Sanderson, and Precilla Montemajor. He named Mossad agents, including Robert Silberman, Simon Goldblatt, Ariel Colderman, Delilah Kaufman, and David Turner. Hunt said Goldblatt was a field supervisor assisted by Marta Bleiblatt. The large number of Mossad agents working with the San Francisco CIA office surprised Hunt.

## ENLARGEMENT ON EARLIER DISCOVERIES

The large number of CIA and DEA sources and private investigators that contacted me made it possible to enlarge upon what earlier sources had described, and provided further corroboration of the information provided. Russbacher enlarged upon Operation Indigo which Parker had told me and which was described in Parker's court filings.[428] Referring to Operation Indigo, he said that the full name was Operation Indigo Sky, and confirmed that it had been in operation since approximately 1976. Russbacher said that the operation consists of producing heroin in poppy fields in Nigeria and processing in the capital city of Lagos, along with transportation to Europe and the United States.

Russbacher stated that the intent of Operation Indigo Sky was to get an alternate source of supply for heroin coming from the Golden Triangle area and the Indian subcontinent. The operation began with the 1976 purchase of the Star Brewery in Lagos and its subsequent multi-million-dollar upgrade into a heroin processing facility. The brewery's name was changed to Star of Nigeria and then to Red Star. The transportation of the drugs from Lagos was initially by the CIA and DEA and then changed to contract operators. Most of the processed drugs in Operation Indigo Sky went from Lagos to Amsterdam, where it was further packaged and then shipped to European and United States destinations.

Russbacher described the different ways the drugs are shipped into the United States, including being shipped in sealed containers leased from Phillips Electronics and other companies. He described ways of circumventing customs inspections in the United States and those incidents in which Customs and the DEA protected the drug shipments. He described the swapping of sealed containers at bonded warehouses in Hoboken, New Jersey and other locations, and the secret unloading of drugs at airfields throughout the United States, including Boeing Field in Seattle.

## FURTHER CONFIRMATION OF CUSTOMS INVOLVEMENT IN DRUG TRAFFICKING

Further support for the DEA and CIA informants who reported drug trafficking

---

428 U.S. District Court, Denver, United States of America vs. Trenton H. Parker, No. 93-CR-43.

activities by U.S. Customs agents was provided by an Associated Press (AP) story on May 3, 1993. The article described an eight-volume file prepared in December 1990 that disappeared from a final Washington report in 1991. The missing files described "Customs Service drug smuggling" and reported a pattern of drug trafficking by Customs inspectors. This report was sent to Washington and then removed from government files. Most newspapers refused to print the AP story but I found it in the *Oakland Tribune*.

**LARGEST HEROIN SEIZURE IN U.S. HISTORY–ANOTHER CIA DRUG OPERATION**

Much of what is written in the media is not what it seems. In May 1991, federal agents seized over 1,000 pounds of heroin in an Oakland, California warehouse, the largest heroin seizure in the nation's history. Due to the compartmentalization common to intelligence agencies, the arresting agents were unaware that they interrupted a large-scale drug smuggling operation involving the CIA and other government agencies.

Five people were charged with importing heroin, possession with intent to distribute heroin, and conspiracy. A subtitle to a *San Francisco Examiner* article describing the case stated that it was the "largest-ever seizure." Over 1,000 pounds of high-grade "China White" heroin was smuggled into the Port of Oakland from Taiwan.

The 1991 seizure of the largest quantity of China White heroin involved the arrest of two families from Thailand, living in Danville, California. The case was assigned to Judge Vaughn Walker,[429] the same judge that was handling the contempt of court case filed against me for having sought to report the criminality that I had uncovered. His actions, and those of the Justice Department attorneys, showed evidence of covering up the drug operation that involved covert government agencies. Apparently, they learned that the drug seizure involved an ongoing CIA drug smuggling operation, and they now had to keep the lid on the drug seizure and avoid a publicity-generating trial.

**STANDARD PRACTICE OF JUDICIAL AND JUSTICE DEPARTMENT OBSTRUCTION OF JUSTICE**

Despite this being the biggest heroin seizure in the nation's history, Justice Department prosecutors and District Judge Vaughn Walker approved a lenient sentence for most of the defendants. Through a plea agreement reached in July 1993, the defendants pled guilty in exchange for probation or a short prison sentence. Several of the defendants pled guilty to knowing a federal crime had been committed and failing to promptly report it to federal authorities. This offense violated federal criminal statute Title 18 U.S.C. Section 4. This plea agreement with its lenient terms eliminated a trial that could have exposed high-level government connections to the heroin operation.

**IRONIC CONTRADICTION**

Judge Walker was approving the charge of misprision of a felony against several of the drug trafficking participants for failure to report the federal crimes. At the time he was holding me under virtual house arrest since December 1990, while I waited for a trial on a criminal contempt of court charge for having sought

429 *USA vs Chen, et al.*, CR 91-2096 VRW.

to report the federal crimes I had discovered, including the CIA and Justice Department involvement in the drug trafficking. U.S. District Judge Marilyn Patel had me arrested in November 1990 on criminal contempt of court charges in retaliation for reporting to a federal judge what I was required to report under federal criminal statute Title 18 USC Section 4. Under that statute, it is a federal crime for any person, knowing of a federal crime, not to immediately report it to a federal judge or other federal tribunal. I responded to that obligation by filing my charges with the court.

It was ironic. I was charged with criminal contempt of court for complying with that statute, while Justice Department prosecutors and Judge Walker were charging the participants in the nation's largest heroin smuggling operation with misprision of a felony for not reporting the criminal activities!

Aware of the involvement of federal personnel in drug trafficking into the United States, and suspecting this heroin case might be another government-funded drug operation, I asked Russbacher if he knew anything about it, and he admitted that he did. During the late 1980s, Russbacher had been assigned by the CIA to coordinate government-related drug trafficking through the West Coast. This involved monitoring and protecting the drug operations coming into the states of California, Oregon, and Nevada. He gave me details about the operation that he would not know unless he was involved in its operation. Even though he was in prison when I asked, Russbacher was in frequent touch with CIA personnel and kept up-to-date on covert activities.

**OPERATION NEW WAVE**

Russbacher first told me about the operation on August 23, 1993. He said that it was a major heroin trafficking operation into the United States, and that the code name for the parent operation was Operation New Wave. A part of that operation was called Operation Backlash.

Russbacher stated that the operation, sanctioned on September 21, 1987, originated in San Francisco, and operated out of the offices of Levi International Imports-Pier 51. He then gave me the names of many key participants in the operation. He said that key personnel from the CIA included David Fuller from Los Angeles; John Beardsley from Mississippi, and Patrick O'Riley from New York City.

He said that those involved from the U.S. Department of Justice included Russ Taylor out of Lincoln, Nebraska; Saul Trattafiore out of Williamsport; and Sandy Weingarten out of St. Louis. Russbacher stated that they were all attorneys, and, he believed, also Assistant U.S. Attorneys.

Drug Enforcement Administration participants in the drug operation, according to Russbacher, included Michael Cobb out of Orlando, Florida and John David Pigg out of Oklahoma City. Pigg was killed in July 1993 in Anadarko, Oklahoma, reportedly for expressing disenchantment with the operation.

Russbacher described Navy Task Force liaison personnel as himself, using his navy alias of Robert Andrew Walker; John A. Woodruff (CIA person using that alias, and who is now deceased); and Oswald LeWinter (CIA person using that alias).

Referring to Customs, Russbacher identified key participants as David Cohen out of the El Paso office; Precilla Montemajor out of the San Francisco office;

Taulyn Weber, also out of the San Francisco office; Brett Sanderson out of the Seattle office.

**NAMING MOSSAD AGENTS**

During a telephone conversation on September 6, 1993, Russbacher gave me the names of the Mossad personnel implicated in this drug trafficking operation who handled drug distribution in the San Francisco area.

*First name is Robert Silberman, out of Chicago. Second name is Marta Bleiblatt, also out of Chicago. Third name, Simon, last name Goldblatt, he is out of Haifa and attached to New York. Fourth name, Ariel Colderman, San Francisco. Fifth one is Kasam Merchant, out of Los Angeles. Sixth one is David Turner, San Jose. Silberman and Bleiberg work for a company called Edeco. Goldblatt is a field supervisor on Operation White Elephant. The next one, the last three, are attached to Operation Lemgolem.*

I told him that I would list their names in the next edition of *Defrauding America*, and he warned me about the viciousness of the Mossad and their killing of people in various countries whose statements or conduct displeased them. "I have no use for the Mossad and the harm they've inflicted upon the United States, and I'll take my chances," was my reply.

**IMPLICATIONS OF THE MOSSAD'S INVOLVEMENT**

The repeated discovery that the intelligence agency of a foreign country, Israel, was heavily involved in several of the drug operations conducted against the American people by America's intelligence agencies was disturbing. Throughout my discoveries I learned of the involvement of Mossad agents in the smuggling of drugs into the United States and other crimes, including the October Surprise scheme, the theft of the Inslaw software, and the looting of Chapter 11 assets.

Examples of corruption given within these pages are only a fraction of what I discovered during thirty years of investigations, whether it be related to aviation fraud or any other segment of criminal activities. The involvement of the Mossad and Israeli personnel, including those who became American citizens, repeatedly came to my attention, and much of it has not been identified.

Russbacher said that the intent of the operation was to bring heroin into the United States from the Far East using freighters, cruise-line transports, and other international lines. The ships would bring heroin from Far East ports through Central America, sometimes through northern South America, and then into the United States. Some of the intermediate points included Acapulco, Mazatlan, Sewantenego, Cabo San Lucas, and Ensenada.

United States ports included San Diego, Los Angeles, San Francisco, and Seattle. At San Diego, a transshipment point, non-military vessels went to the federal port known as O-1, District 00.01. In Los Angeles they used the Long Beach basin.

Also used were tankers, including the Greek tanker line Orion, which docked at Manhattan Beach, California. The oldest freighters would normally be Pan American or Iberian registry.

Drugs were also transshipped from Colombia, many times in ships of Norwegian registry, until 1989, and these were mostly cruise ships. Russbacher elaborated on the method of packing drugs on ships:

> *On the cruise liners it was generally in the freezers, brought on board inside carcasses of beef. Also in the flour bags, 100 pound bags. They are referred to as flower barrels. On other types of ships it was either stored in the paint lockers, or there was a separate compartment built.*

I asked, "What is the remuneration or rewards for the different agencies that are involved in this operation?" Russbacher stated that there is a "split profit sharing" where the profits are divided among various proprietaries or front companies used by the different agencies.

The drug trafficking operation was coded as NW 688-01-B-NSC, and called Operation New Wave. One segment was named Operation Backlash and coded BL421-D-06. Russbacher said the operation was still active, but limited to DEA and Customs involvement. He said the CIA and Department of Justice dropped from active participation in March 1993, except for the criminal prosecutions in San Diego and San Francisco that had to be completed.

I asked Russbacher why the Department of Justice filed those charges when the filings might expose involvement of Justice Department personnel. He said that the many individual fiefdoms in the CIA, Justice Department, and other agencies, and the compartmentalizing of information, result in charges being filed by a local office against a person or operation that may be sanctioned by high officials.

Since the defendants in the San Francisco action were from Thailand, I asked Russbacher how that country fits into the operation. He said the drug shipper in Thailand was a CIA front called Van Der Bergen International Shippers in Bangkok. "They're the ones that are responsible for gathering [the drugs] out of Southeast Asia," He said.

Russbacher said that Hong Kong was sought as a drug shipment point:

> *But they [CIA] couldn't get an agreement going with the British out of Hong Kong. The problem was, they wanted a higher percentile participation than our government was prepared to give. Instead of using Hong Kong, we used Macao. Eighty percent of the morphine block, we are not talking about the liquid, comes out of Macao, before it becomes morphine sulphate.*

Many books have described the decades of British drug trafficking, originally through the British East India Tea Company, which still exists. Russbacher told me that there were large amounts of drugs being shipped from the Philippines in the operation.

Russbacher described the role played by the Mossad in the drug trafficking into the United States in Operation New Wave and Operation Back Lash. He said the Mossad's role was to guard the shipments until they reached the United States, adding that one of his Mossad contacts was Delilah Kaufman, a paralegal with an Italian law firm in the San Francisco Bay area.

In 1991, part of the operations were suspended due to increased awareness at the southern transshipment ports. More federal funds were allocated for DEA and Customs agents, causing smuggling by certain DEA and Customs factions to be compromised. Even though the drug trafficking involved personnel from almost every federal agency responsible to prevent such trafficking, the smuggling was compartmentalized. With the addition of new DEA and Customs agents, the danger of discovery increased.

**FEDERAL JUDGE RECEIVING BRIBE MONEY?**

Because of U.S. District Judge Vaughn Walker's extremely lenient sentences given to most of the Thai defendants charged with the largest known heroin shipment in the nation's history I asked Russbacher: "Do you know where Judge Vaughn Walker fits into this operation?" Russbacher replied: "He is one of the people getting a payoff."

"Through Shamrock [Overseas Disbursement Corporation]?" I asked.

"Through Shamrock, yes."

"And you know this to be a fact? Did you see this on a printout, or did he simply tell you that?"

"Rodney, I was very very strong in this. I basically baby-sat the operation for about four months. I don't want to go into it."

"Did you have any conversations with Walker?" I asked.

"No, I did not. But a woman by the name of Denise Stedman out of the San Francisco [CIA office] had numerous conversations with him. She is the one we used."

After learning about this operation, and finding that another U.S. District Judge reportedly received bribe money, it fit in with the information I received from other CIA personnel. It also fit in with what Russbacher had told me during the past several years.

Judge Walker had me under virtual house arrest since December 10, 1990, while I awaited trial on contempt of court charges for having sought to report to a Chicago district court the criminal activities that I uncovered.

That action sought to report the federal crimes in the Ninth Circuit bankruptcy courts (which included California), and sought relief from the judicial attacks upon me by Ninth Circuit judges. Now that I had information linking Walker to the CIA, DEA, Customs, and Justice Department drug operation, I decided to file another report with the courts under federal crime-reporting statutes.

**REFERENCE TO JUSTICE DEPARTMENT CRIMINALITY IN POLITE TERMS**

In a classic understatement, Lamar Smith, chairman of the House Task Force on International Narcotics control, said, "I personally am convinced that the Justice Department is against the best interests of the United States in terms of stopping drugs."

**EASTERN AIRLINE WHISTLEBLOWER**

Another insider describing drug trafficking was a former Eastern Airlines captain, Gerald K. Loeb. He discovered a pattern of drug trafficking from Central and South America into the United States on EAL aircraft. Loeb saw dozens of instances, while he was pilot, of suspicious shipment of drugs into the United States and the shipment of drug-money from Miami to Panama and Colombia.

**EASTERN AIRLINES AS DRUG-RELATED CONDUIT**

Loeb frequently noticed, in departures from Miami for Central America, containers placed on board the aircraft, which followed a pattern of usually arriving at the last few minutes before departure. This was followed by same containers being off-loaded in Panama or Colombia in the presence of armed guards. The activity indicated drug and drug-money trafficking.

Loeb described how he gave detailed information of the drug trafficking to the Federal Bureau of Investigation, the Airline Pilots Association, to EAL President Frank Borman, and to *Time* magazine's Jonathan Beaty, all of whom kept the lid on the criminal activities.

Dozens of times Custom agents discovered drugs hidden behind aircraft inspection plates as the Eastern Airlines aircraft arrived in Miami. Eastern pilots were concerned over the drug trafficking, as they themselves could be charged with drug-related offenses. As ALPA Chairman of Legislative Affairs for the Eastern pilots group in Miami, Loeb received many complaints from pilots about drugs being found on their aircraft as it arrived in Miami. Loeb testified to Congress that there were over sixty cases reported to him where this happened.

## FBI COVERUP AND THEIR RETALIATION AGAINST CRUSADERS & INFORMANTS

Loeb developed a friendship with a young Eastern Airlines station agent in Panama City, Panama, who revealed to him that cocaine was being shipped on Eastern Airlines planes from Colombia and Panama into the United States. Loeb contacted a friend, Governor Thompson of New Hampshire, and described the massive drug smuggling and drug-money shipments that he had discovered. The governor then contacted Justice Department officials, who arranged for Loeb and two other Eastern Airlines employees to give information to the FBI in Miami. Loeb identified these FBI agents as Special Agent in Charge F. Corliss, Assistant Special agent (ASAC) William Perry, and agent Rod Beverley. The Eastern Airlines employee from Panama was threatened by the FBI, warning that he himself would be charged with a federal crime if he reported the drug and drug-money trafficking.

Under federal criminal statutes these threats constituted federal crimes.[430] But when the criminal acts are perpetrated by the same agency responsible for prosecution, the system fails.

## THREAT OF PRISON IF THEY TESTIFIED

FBI agents also contacted other witnesses that Loeb had said were willing to testify about the drug trafficking, including an Eastern Airlines flight attendant, a ground service agent, and others. Instead of taking information from these people, FBI agents threatened to file criminal charges against them. One of the charges the FBI agents threatened to file against them was misprision of felonies for not reporting the criminal activities earlier. This threat of prison caused the witnesses to remain silent, which is apparently what the FBI agents wanted. Some of these witnesses then blamed Loeb for what had happened, and then went under cover. The FBI traumatized witnesses to keep them from reporting the criminal acts involving federal personnel, and is a practice that I had seen for years.

Loeb testified before numerous congressional committees, including Senator John Kerry's (D-MA) Subcommittee on Terrorism, Narcotics and International Communications. Referring to the meeting in Miami with the FBI, Loeb

430 Title 18 USC §§ 1512, 1513.

testified[431] that the FBI reported to Eastern Airlines president Frank Borman what Loeb and the other witnesses had said, and that the FBI said something had to be done to silence him and the other witnesses. Referring to his testimony, Loeb wrote in part:

*The officials at Eastern Airlines and the corporate officers deemed [my reporting of the drug trafficking to the FBI] to be outrageous conduct. Having learned from the FBI within hours of my giving that information, they hired two private detectives and [then the harassment against me commenced]. . . . [Drugs aboard Eastern Airlines aircraft] was an ongoing scenario, particularly from Panama, the hub operation, and Colombia. Our crews were very aware that they were unwittingly being duped and flying cargo, as [the drugs and drug-money were] called, that was unlisted in their aircraft, un-manifested, into ports of call in the United States of America.*

Loeb testified that a private detective agency hired by Eastern management, Intercontinent Detective Agency of Miami, offered bribes of $2,500 and $5,000 to people to discredit Loeb and the Air Line Pilots Association who was representing the pilots on whose plane drugs were found. Borman fired Loeb for being "disloyal" to the company, after which Loeb fought the dismissal. Eventually, Loeb took a financial settlement and left the airline. Two weeks after Eastern fired Loeb, the airline fired another pilot, Ramon Valdez, who had hired an investigator to obtain additional evidence on the drug and drug-money trafficking involving Eastern Airlines aircraft.

Initially, many Eastern pilots wanted to testify about the drug trafficking and drug-money laundering. But after they saw what happened to Loeb after he reported the activities to the FBI, they all suddenly developed "amnesia."

## COVERUP BY EASTERN AIRLINES' PRESIDENT

Loeb told me that when he first reported the drug trafficking on Eastern Airlines aircraft to Eastern president, Frank Borman, that Borman told him to mind his own business. Instead of responding to the serious problem, Borman and other Eastern management proceeded to harass Loeb.

Loeb reported the drug trafficking to the president of the Airline Pilots Association, Henry A. Duffy, and explained that over two dozen Eastern Airlines' pilots were actively involved in drug trafficking. The ALPA president reportedly told Loeb that drug trafficking was none of the union's business. I encountered a similar attitude when I brought to his attention major air safety irregularities that were playing a key role in a series of fatal airline crashes (as explained in *Unfriendly Skies*).

## COVERUP BY TIME MAGAZINE

Loeb described the details of the drug trafficking, the reaction of Eastern Airlines management and the FBI to the drug trafficking, to *Time's* reporter Jonathan Beatty, and how *Time's* management refused to publish the story. *Time* had covered up for many government criminal activities, including the October Surprise, the air safety and criminal activities related to a series of airline crashes

---

431 Testimony given on February 8, 1988 to the Subcommittee on Terrorism, Narcotics and International Communications, and as published under Drugs, Law Enforcement, and Foreign Policy: Panama, S. Hrg. 100-773, Pr. 2.

that I brought to their attention, the CIA drug trafficking from Central America, the assassinations by CIA-trained assassination squads, and much more. Under federal criminal statutes this conduct is called "misprision of felonies."

**DEA BLOCKING OF TESTIMONY BY NORIEGA'S PILOT**

Loeb told how, during the criminal proceedings against Noriega, that Noriega's attorneys had told Loeb that they had audio and video tapes of Noriega and Bush, and would release the tapes if the charges were not dropped against Noriega. One of the attorneys asked Loeb to pass the information to the Justice Department prosecutors, warning that if the charges were not dropped, the tapes would be released. The judge refused to permit this type of testimony or evidence, thereby protecting the CIA and DEA involvement in drug trafficking that was a far greater offense than what was charged against Noriega. Judicial coverup of serious federal crimes is common.

I asked Loeb if the airlines that took over the Central and South America air traffic after Eastern Airlines went out of business became involved in the drug trafficking. He stated that American Airlines encountered similar problems. He also described how Braniff Airlines was heavily used by drug traffickers before that airline went out of business.

The House Committee on Government Operations issued a report concerning hearings held in March 1992, related to misconduct by federal personnel. The report was entitled "Serious Mismanagement and Misconduct in the Treasury Department, Customs Service, and Other Federal Agencies and the Adequacy of Efforts To Hold Agency Officials Accountable." The report stated in part:

*This is the third in a series of hearings looking into allegations of mismanagement and misconduct by the U.S. Customs Service. Witnesses have testified about attempts by both Customs and Internal Affairs to prevent investigations from going forward. These are serious allegations. [criminal would be more fitting.]*

*This hearing...focuses on the implementation of the customs reorganization plan, and the accountability of the Inspector General. But what is really at issue here is the overall effectiveness of counter-narcotics law enforcement efforts along the U.S.-Mexico border. The credibility of the Customs Service is at stake. Allegations of improper associations between law enforcement agents and drug traffickers are bad enough, but the inability and unwillingness to properly investigate such allegations cause the public to lose faith in the ability of the United States government to fight the war on drugs.*

The report revealed that government officials sought to block the testimony of witnesses, showing the existence of obstruction of justice, which by itself is a crime [that was never prosecuted]. The criminal mindset behind these acts was never addressed.

Included in the report was a letter to the committee signed by anonymous field agents of U.S. Customs, stating in part:

*We are writing to you to advise you of the continuing systemic corruption at the U.S. Customs Service....The "reorganization" of the Office of Enforcement has only removed necessary checks and balances. Integrity is virtually a non-existent commodity in Customs management.*

Former DEA agent Michael Levine describes in *The Big White Lie* how the Drug Enforcement Administration destroyed evidence, resulting in high-level drug traffickers escaping prosecution.

**TESTIMONY OF RAMON MILIAN RODRIGUEZ**

Hundreds of people directly involved in drug trafficking and drug-money laundering have testified in closed-door Congressional hearings about the CIA, DEA, and Customs involvement in these activities. This revealing testimony rarely gets into the hearing records available to the public. Many of these witnesses sought to give evidence to various U.S. agencies about the drug trafficking and drug-money laundering, and were blocked.

On February 11, 1988, Ramon Milian Rodriguez, a major drug-money launderer, testified in Congressional hearings in 1988[432] that he had tried to blow the whistle years earlier on the drug trafficking and drug money laundering. Rodriguez testified that he also contacted members of Vice President's George Bush's South Florida Task Force in 1983, including people that he knew as Sathos and Summerall, and was likewise rebuffed.

Rodriguez testified, as did others, that insiders in government provided the Medellin and Cali cartels with information about the names and identification of DEA agents, the radio frequencies and the schedules of Coast Guard and Navy interdiction aircraft.

Rodriguez described the huge amount of drug money shipped from the United States, and the logistic problems associated with moving large pallets of money out of the United States. He described the drug traffickers' use of Eastern and Braniff Airlines for shipment of drug-money from the United States to Central and South America. The shipments were in containers or on pallets, and often loaded without any cargo manifest. In Panama and other Central and South American countries, the airliner would be met by armed guards, the drug-money unloaded, and then taken to banks, such as Banco Nacional de Panama. Station agents and other airline employees working for Braniff or Eastern would be in the pay of the drug cartels or other drug traffickers.

Rodriguez elaborated upon the complexities and sophistication involved in drug-money laundering, requiring expertise in accounting, banking, logistics, security, bank secrecy laws, and the mechanics of incorporating. Dummy corporations would be set up, and the money transferred from one corporation to another to mask the money path. Cutouts would be used to separate high-level personnel from the source of the drugs or drug money.

A series of accounts would be set up with dummy corporations through which the drug money would be processed. These dummy corporations would be filed with the Secretary of State of various states in the United States, especially Florida, California and New York. Some legitimate businesses were used to front for the drug-money laundering. Dummy corporations were also set up in the country where the destination banks were located. A Panamanian corporation could be used as a cutout for a Swiss, Liechtenstein, Luxembourg, or Hong Kong company. Another tactic was to make a Panamanian company

---

432 Hearings before the Subcommittee on Terrorism, Narcotics and International Communications, February 11, 1988.

a stockholder of a Netherlands Antilles company.

Rodriguez testified that his money laundering out of the United States amounted to approximately $200 million per month, or over two billion dollars a year. This huge amount was just for his operation, and primarily for drug activities in New York and Chicago. Rodriguez also testified that he had as many as fifty aircraft flying the money out of the United States, including Boeing 727s. Rodriguez was on the board of directors of several banks, including Ponce de Leon Savings and Loan in Miami. He identified some of the countries favored for money laundering as Switzerland, Hong Kong, Panama, Curacao, Cayman Islands, and the Bahamas. Asked what happens to the drug money laundered from the United States into foreign banks, Rodriguez replied that it would be invested in real estate, stocks, bonds, CD's, and other financial investments within the United States.

**COOPERATION OF U.S. BANKERS IN MASSIVE DRUG-MONEY LAUNDERING**

Rodriguez testified that many U.S. banks cooperated in his money laundering, and that they often had a special representative who dealt with drug-money launderers. He identified the banks routinely and knowingly dealing in drug-money as "Citibank, Citicorp, Bank of America, First National Bank of Boston." He testified that there was competition among U.S. banks to receive the drug-money.

Describing the power of the drug cartels in Colombia, Rodriguez testified that the cartels owned airlines, soccer teams, radio and TV stations, newspapers, and "politicians." Rodriguez described how Colombia's M-19 kidnapped "one of the Ochoa women [Leona]," how the individual drug traffickers merged into a group, and formed its own army of 2,000 people. This testimony coincided with what other CIA assets had stated to me, including Gunther Russbacher, Trenton Parker, Russell Bowen, and others.

Rodriguez testified that drug proceeds were used to fund the contra fighting, a fact that is well known to everyone except the American public.

**COMPANIES USED IN DRUG TRAFFICKING AND DRUG-MONEY LAUNDERING**

Rodriguez described some of the companies used in drug-related activities. One was Frigerificos de Puntarennas, a shrimp warehouse used as a front with a chain of interlocking companies, including Ocean Hunter. Ocean Hunter imported shrimp into the United States and hid drugs inside the shipments. The company was also used to launder money to the Contras. Despite the drug-related activities of Frigerificos, the Reagan-Bush administration awarded lucrative contracts to that company to provide "humanitarian assistance funds from the State Department." (i.e., guns on the way south, and drugs on the return trips.)

Rodriguez testified that the CIA was involved in the weapon shipments and drug-money laundering with his various companies. Senator John F. Kerry (D. Mass.) made reference to the repeated denials by White House and National Security Council officials about U.S. arms shipments to Iran and the Contras, while the arms shipments were continuing to occur. During testimony by various witnesses, whenever a witness was about to name a U.S. politician or the CIA involvement in the drug trafficking, Kerry interrupted the witness and said this would be discussed in executive or closed-door session. The American public never heard of the criminal activities by high-level government officials and various government agencies.

**SENATE TESTIMONY BY NORIEGA'S PILOT, FLOYD CARLTON**

Manuel Noriega's pilot, Floyd Carlton, testified to a senate subcommittee that he offered to give information in July 1986 to the U.S. Drug Enforcement Administration office in Panama, and the DEA refused to take the information. Carlton's evidence was very valuable since he had frequent direct contacts with Noriega and the Medellin and Cali drug cartels. The evidence included taped telephone conversations, documents, personal information about "money laundering, drugs, weapons, corruption, assassinations." But to have allowed Carlton to give that information would expose the CIA, DEA, and Mossad involvement in the drug traffickers. Carlton testified that one of the DEA agents in Panama, who refused to receive the information, was Thomas Tyre.

**STANDARD OBSTRUCTION OF JUSTICE TACTIC**

Using a standard Justice Department tactic to silence or discredit whistleblowers, U.S. agents arrested Carlton in January 1987, charging him with drug trafficking. The charges were made in such a way that Carlton would not be allowed to testify about the CIA role, which he had earlier sought to expose. Even though Carlton was sentenced to federal prison, he was released and put in the Federal Witness Protection Program after testifying on behalf of the Justice Department in later cases.

**HOODED WITNESS**

Floyd Carlton gave testimony to Congress while wearing a hood, hiding his identity. Carlton testified about large quantities of drugs shipped to the United States from Colombia and Panama on Eastern Airlines, a fact that Eastern Airlines captain Gerald Loeb had described to me in detail.

Carlton corroborated that the ranch that John Hull ran in Costa Rica was used by drug trafficking aircraft. Hull was a close associate to Dan Quayle and George Bush.

**CIA MAKING NORIEGA A KEY DRUG KINGPIN**

Senator Kerry stated what was already well known, that:

*[General Noriega] had been on the payroll and an employee of the CIA for many, many, many years and, I have been given to understand, up until rather recently. It is not inconceivable, but it is most probable that this activity that the CIA had with this thug [Noriega] who was in their employ, and how proud they must have been that one of their own, that they nurtured for so many years, had risen to this power position.*

**RECOGNIZING THE SERIOUSNESS OF THE DRUG PROBLEM**

The published 1988 report by the Subcommittee on Terrorism, Narcotics and International Communications said in part:

*The reason for believing [the narco-trafficking] is a matter for national security is that the Latin criminal cartels who have profited from the depravity of some Americans constitute an international underworld so extensive, so wealthy, and so powerful that it can literally buy governments and destabilize entire societies.... This is a national security matter...Latin drug trafficking directly detracts from our ability to defend ourselves from military attack. Drug abuse has affected readiness within our Armed Forces...*

**AIDING AND ABETTING DRUG TRAFFICKING AND DRUG MONEY LAUNDERING BY FUTURE PRESIDENT OF THE UNITED STATES**

For years, Arkansas papers carried stories of the CIA arms and drug trafficking in the vicinity of the Mena, Arkansas, Airport. Prosecution had been blocked by Arkansas and federal officials. A May 21, 1992, *Arkansas Times* article carried a front page story of the drug trafficking, including three pictures of CIA contract agent and drug pilot Barry Seal, drug trafficker Jorge Luis Ochoa, and George Bush. Below their picture was the title, BAD COMPANY. A subheading read, "Arkansas's most notorious drug smuggler testified about his links to Colombia. His ties to Washington have yet to be explained." The article brought together the CIA's Mena operations; the drug smuggling; the shooting down of a CIA C-123 over Nicaragua; Lt. Col. Oliver North's arms shipments to Central America, and drug shipments back to the United States.

The criminal activities surrounding the CIA arms and drug trafficking at Mena Airport were well known to local residents, the local police, the Arkansas State Police, and the media. The local *Arkansas Gazette* published numerous investigative articles describing the criminal activities and the coverup by the State Attorney General and Governor Bill Clinton.

Charles Black, assistant deputy prosecutor for Polk County, told Governor Clinton in 1988 about the drug trafficking, and asked that Clinton provide a million dollars to coordinate the evidence and prosecute. Clinton said he would get back to Black, and then never did. In 1991, the Arkansas Citizens Committee demonstrated in Little Rock, complaining about Clinton's refusal to investigate and prosecute the complaints concerning massive drug trafficking in Arkansas.

During a White House press conference senior White House correspondent Sarah McClendon asked President Clinton about his knowledge of the drug trafficking at Mena Airport. Clinton replied that this was a federal problem. Responsibilities under law for these criminal activities involve state as well as federal authorities.

**CIA LIAISON WITH ORGANIZED CRIME TO DISTRIBUTE DRUGS AND COORDINATE DRUG-MONEY LAUNDERING**

Much testimony has been given by hundreds of insiders to congressional committees over the years depicting the involvement of U.S. intelligence agencies in drug trafficking into the United States, drug-money laundering, and the joint operations with organized crime. An example of this type of sworn testimony is found in several manuscripts marked Confidential, consisting of depositions taken in June 1991. One of the witnesses was CIA agent Richard Brenneke, who testified in a joint investigation by the United States Congress and the

Arkansas State Attorney General's office.[433] Brenneke's testimony described the drug trafficking, CIA ties to organized crime, and CIA money-laundering. The transcript stated that the testimony would be made available to the Special Prosecutor (Lawrence Walsh) in the Iran-Contra case, and for other purposes.

In the transcript of that testimony, Brenneke described his activities on behalf of the Central Intelligence Agency. Brenneke testified about his expertise in handling financial transfers worldwide, including money transfers for the Central Intelligence Agency, commencing in 1968, and continuing until 1985. Brenneke testified to "handling money for them [and] handling East Bloc weapons purchases primarily made in Yugoslavia and Czechoslovakia." He described flying as pilot for the CIA from 1968 through 1980, including flying aircraft from Mena, Arkansas, including military C-130 aircraft, starting in April 1984, to various airports in Panama, including Tecuman Airport at Panama City, and into Colon. Brenneke produced pilot log books showing the flights that he made for the CIA into Mena and other locations.

Brenneke testified that the weapon shipments were met by "members of the Panamanian Defense Forces" and "by Michael Harari." He identified Harari in congressional testimony as a Mossad agent and "Manuel Noriega's partner in a number of business deals in Panama. I know that first hand because I had to deal with him."

He described carrying weapons and military forces trained in Arkansas, from Mena to Panama City in Panama. He testified that the weapons "frequently came either from government stores or through Tamiami Gun Shop in Miami, Florida." He testified that his co-pilot on many of these flights was "Harry Rupp, a friend of mine who lives in Denver, Colorado."

Brenneke described drug-trafficking flights from Medellin to Mena and to Iron Mountain Ranch in Texas. He identified Rich Mountain Aviation at Mena Airport (Inter-Mountain Regional Airport) and Fred Hampton as owning and operating the CIA-front operation.

When asked by congressional investigators about the nature of the cargo flown back to the United States, including into Mena, Brenneke testified, "I found the cargo to be cocaine; in some cases marijuana." He testified that on each return flight he carried 400 to 500 pounds of cocaine, which was loaded by Panamanian Defense Force soldiers onto the CIA aircraft.

## SALE BY CIA OF DRUGS TO ORGANIZED CRIME FAMILIES

When asked about the disposition of the drugs, Brenneke testified that upon landing at Mena Airport the drugs would be either off-loaded onto other aircraft, or stored in Rich Mountain Aviation's hangar. Brenneke testified that in some instances the drugs were received by Freddie Hampton of Rich Mountain Aviation, and in some cases "members of John Gotti's family in New York. One of them was an individual known to me by the name of Salvatore Reale." Brenneke testified:

---

433 Investigators conducting the questioning included William Alexander, United States Congress, 233 Cannon House Office Building, Washington, D.C.; Winston Bryant, Attorney General, State of Arkansas; Chad Farris, Chief Attorney General, State of Arkansas; Lawrence Graves, attorney in the office of Attorney General, State of Arkansas.

*[That Reale was] Director of Security for Kennedy International Airport in New York City....Mr. Reale was one of Mr. Gotti's lieutenants. I watched the two of them interact. Mr. Gotti would provide directions, Mr. Reale would carry them out. It was his job to make sure that cargo being shipped through Kennedy was not lost, but properly located, and in some cases avoiding customs.*

This testimony linking organized crime with the CIA in drug trafficking caused the Congressional investigators to ask: "Are you saying that you saw Mr. John Gotti, the famous head of the organized crime syndicate, in New York, together with Mr. Reale?" Brenneke replied, "Yes, sir, I did."

**GOTTI CRIME FAMILY IN BUSINESS WITH THE CIA**

In response to another question as to whether Mr. Gotti and Mr. Reale were connected with the Central Intelligence Agency, Brenneke replied:

*Yes. As far back as 1968 and early 1969, we [CIA] had begun to launder money from organized crime families in New York. At that time, Mr. Gotti was an up and coming member of one of the families. I got to know them at that time. We used to wash their money out overseas and put it in Switzerland in nice, safe places for them.*

"So you worked for Mr. Gotti as well as for the CIA?"

*Actually the CIA told me to do that on his behalf.*

"So the CIA was in partnership or association with Mr. Gotti?"

*Yes, sir, I would say a partnership.*

"Can you describe the nature of the partnership?"

*Sure. The organized crime members had a need for two things; they needed drugs brought into the country on a reliable, safe basis; they needed people taken out of the country or people brought into the country without alerting customs or INS to the fact that they were being brought into the country. They also needed their money taken offshore so that it would not be subject to United States tax where they might have to declare its source. And so we [CIA] performed these kinds of functions for them.*

"Mr. Brenneke, are you saying that the CIA was in the business of bringing drugs into the United States?"

*Yes sir. That's exactly what I'm saying.*

"And that they were in partnership with John Gotti in this operation?"

*I would say that they worked with Mr. Gotti and his organization very closely. Whether it was a formal partnership, I don't know. But there certainly was a close alliance between the two.*

Brenneke testified that the Gotti people told him the drugs would be taken to "the New York City area, specifically Kennedy International Airport." He testified that the CIA handler he was working for was Robert Kerritt, and that Kerritt paid the various CIA assets in the Mena area. Brenneke continued:

*Mr. Kerritt is a full-time employee of the Central Intelligence Agency...I and the CIA have dealt with the Gotti mob since 1968.*

"Did the Gotti organizations, through Reale, pay money to the CIA for the drugs?"

*Yes, they did, somewhere in the $50,000,000 bracket.*

"How do you know how much money?"

*Because I banked that money for them in Panama City, and ultimately transferred it to other locations in Europe.*

"What would be the procedure for you to receive the payment from the Gotti organization for the drugs?"

*Generally the money was given to us in cash.*

"Us, you mean the CIA?"

*Us, meaning the people I worked with, who were also associated with the Central Intelligence Agency. We would transfer the money to banks in Central and South America. And from there transfer it via accounts that I had established back in 1970.*

"Let's take a payment from Mr. Reale in cash, and follow the procedure step-by-step as you know it for the transmittal of that money from the Gotti organization to the Central Intelligence Agency."

*Okay. That money was delivered to us in cash. There were occasions where there were wire transfers, but the generally followed method was cash. That would be stored in the aircraft on its return trip to Panama. Once it reached Panama, we would put it into a bank account, which at that time was in the Banquo de Panama. And the account name was the initials, IFMA, which was a company that I set up in Panama City in 1970. The money would be subsequently and almost immediately transferred to Spain or Liechtenstein, from there it went to Monte Carlo, and the ultimate destination was Zurich or Geneva. But in any case, Switzerland.*

"The money was given to you by the agent for the Gotti Organization?"

*Yes sir. And there were other people besides the man that I've named.*

Brenneke identified the names of the CIA accounts that he had set up, offering the incorporation papers that were filed "in the late sixties and early seventies." Brenneke testified that he personally transferred the money out of one account and into others. He testified that he discussed the money transfers with CIA employees Robert Kerritt and Robert Ellis.

**PROTESTING THE CIA DRUG INVOLVEMENT**

Brenneke described his adverse reaction to discovering the CIA involvement in drug smuggling into the United States and the CIA's involvement with drug money laundering. In answer to a question, Brenneke testified:

*When I found that we were bringing drugs into the United States, and that we were receiving money which was being put into accounts which I knew to belong to the United States government, as I'd set them up specifically for that purpose, I called Mr. Don Gregg, who was a CIA officer with whom I was acquainted, and complained about the nature of what we were doing.*

**OFFICE OF VICE PRESIDENT AND PRESIDENT IN DRUG TRAFFICKING AND DRUG-MONEY LAUNDERING**

Donald Gregg worked closely with George Bush when Bush was director of the CIA, and became his national security advisor when Bush was vice president of the United States. Bush later nominated Gregg to be Ambassador to South Korea. When asked about Gregg's response to Brenneke's concern about the drug trafficking, Brenneke testified:

> *I was told that it [CIA drug smuggling and drug-money laundering] was not my business, what I was flying in and out of the country. That I was hired to do specific things, and if I would do those things and not pay any attention to anything else, we would all be very, very happy. I didn't like that. He said shut up and do your job.... I subsequently talked to Mr. Gregg on a number of occasions as well as to other people in the vice-president's office to voice my concern over the use of drugs, importing drugs into the United States and using the cash generated from that to perform operations.*

Brenneke supplied the investigators with telephone records of that and other calls, providing further credibility to his statements. Returning to questions about how the drug money from the Gotti crime family went into the CIA accounts, Brenneke explained:

> *I set up, in 1969 or 1970, a number of corporations in Panama City. Those corporations in turn opened bank accounts. Those bank accounts were accounts that I would normally use in the course of my business with the CIA to transfer money into the accounts, and from there to transfer them into specific accounts in Spain or, as I say, in some cases other countries in Europe. The ultimate destination was Switzerland, where those funds were. I knew where they went, because I'm the person who went in and gave the order to the banker to move them.*

"And you had an arrangement with the CIA to organize those banks for the CIA, to open the account?"

> *That was what I specialized in doing. I laundered money there. When I was first recruited by the CIA, which was in 1968, 1969, all we were doing was selling mutual fund stock offshore.*

"Name the banks [in which accounts were] opened for the CIA."

> *Panama City, Banquo DeMexico. At one point we were using a Citibank correspondent down there whose name escapes me. We had a man on-site who worked for us, as well as worked for Ron Martin, a man named Johnny Mollina. John would spend a lot of his time in Panama City and worked in one of the banks that we used. I set up more than one account in Madrid that was used. I set up an account in Brussels at Bank Lambert that was regularly used. I set up accounts at Credit Suisse, a Swiss bank. And Bank of Credit & Commerce, commonly referred to as BCCI. Also, a bank that no longer exists called Bank Hoffman. I set up a bank in Panama City on behalf of the mutual fund company I worked for so that I could ultimately control how the transfers were handled.*

"And you organized a bank in Panama for the CIA?"

> *I organized it for the company I worked for. It was subsequently used by the CIA, and it was used by members of the organized crime families. The bank was called U.S. Investment Bank. It really existed in Panama City. You could actually go in and open a check account there.*

"And the money that you got from the Gotti organization that you put on the airplane [in Arkansas] and returned to Panama on the next trip, you personally took to a bank in Panama City?"

*You bet I did. Let's take Banquo DePanama, the Panamanian National Bank down there, as an example. I would go in and meet with, for instance, Johnny Mollina. John worked for one of the banks down there. I think it was Citibank that he worked for at one time. In any case, I would go in. I knew the bank officers by name. And I would provide them with directions as to how the money was to be transferred and where to transfer. That is, it was to be transferred by cashier's check and courier to Madrid in a specific account there, or it was just wire transferred to Madrid as a transfer of funds from IFMA, a Panamanian corporation, to IFMA's affiliates in Madrid or Brussels at Bank Lambert. They needed to know that. And then I would have to tell them at the other bank that money was coming into that account.*

"So you would notify the CIA bank, or the bank having the CIA account in Spain or in Switzerland?"

*Yes, that the deposit had been made in Panama.*

"How would you notify them?"

*Generally by telephone. And they would be told that...there were a variety of codes that were used, but the message was very simple. You're going to receive money in this account. The money will probably stay in the account anywhere from 24 to 72 hours, at which time it will be transferred out of that account.*

"Did you ever utilize bearer bonds for the purpose of laundering money?"

*Sure. It was handled in two ways. When U.S. Investment Bank was active in Panama it would issue bonds, no names on them, which was common. It's common in Europe. It's common in Central and South America. And those bonds actually belong to the individual that is carrying them, as, for instance, the stock in IFMA belongs only to the person who happens to have it in his hand at that moment. You lose it, you lose your money.*

"And what would you do with the bearer bonds?"

*The bearer bonds would be taken generally by courier, in some cases to Banquo DeMexico in Mexico City and transferred from there or sent from there by their couriers. By 1986, it was getting uncomfortable in Panama, and so some of the Venezuelan banks in Caracas were used. The same procedure was followed, though. The money would be deposited into an account; you would walk into the bank, for example, and sit down with the Vice President or Managing Director of the bank. You were clearly a large depositor and a large customer of that bank. And you just simply explained that you wanted to deposit the money in this bag, and he would just kindly go ahead and do so for you.*

**DRUG TRAFFICKING CONTROLLED FROM CIA HEADQUARTERS IN WASHINGTON**

"Mr. Brenneke, under whose direction were you working in order to carry out the function of depositing the money from the sale of the drugs to the New York crime family?"

*"Bob Kerritt, an officer of the Central Intelligence Agency in Washington, D.C."*

Brenneke clearly stated, without hesitation, times, dates, places, and either telephone logs or notes that he made of conversations with his CIA handlers in Washington. Brenneke testified to, and provided the Congressional investigators with writings that he sent to his CIA bosses in Washington complaining about the CIA role in drug trafficking and drug-money laundering and its operation with major crime families in the United States. He provided the investigators with copies of bank account records, corporation papers, and detailed testimony, wherein there could be little doubt that his testimony was true.

Brenneke testified about the criminal charges made against Heinrich Rupp concerning looting the Aurora Bank in the Denver area, saying "that was common in our line of work with the CIA."

When asked if Brenneke ever complained to CIA director William Casey about these activities, Brenneke replied:

*Yes, I did on a number of occasions. And Mr. Casey's telephone logs would reflect phone calls to me, made to me in Lake Oswego, which was at that time the location of my office.*

**SEEKING ISRAEL'S HELP TO SHUT DOWN DRUG OPERATION**

Brenneke testified about Israel's involvement in the drug operations, and that he had gone to Israel "because I tried everybody in the U.S. Government first, and they sure as hell weren't going to help" shut down the operations.

"Do you have any knowledge of the money coming from the Gotti organization being used for any other purposes, other than depositing in the bank accounts for the CIA?"

*Sure. We had to run the operations at Nella, for instance. The training facilities at Nella had to be paid for. Nella was a training base for military and paramilitary folks from south of the border; Mexico, Panama.*[434] *The base was operated by the Central Intelligence Agency.*

Brenneke identified CIA agent Terry Reed as one of the flight instructors at Nella. Reed co-authored the book *Compromised* with John Cummings, describing the drug trafficking and money laundering in Arkansas and Mexico, and involving Arkansas personnel, including Governor Bill Clinton and some of his staff.

**GETTING THE DRUG MONEY BACK INTO THE UNITED STATES**

"Did you establish an account in the United States to get that money back into this country?"

*Yes, I did. I established an account at Brown Brothers Harriman in New York City around 1980. That's a bank in New York City.*

"How do you know that the money you picked up and that you received in Mena from the Gotti organization, and took to Panama, wired to bank accounts in Europe, came back to the United States?"

*"I ordered the transfer of funds."*

"And to whom did you report these actions?"

434 Nella consisted of a small airstrip north of Mena that was used by the CIA for paramilitary and military training of personnel from Mexico and Central America, and used for training Contra pilots.

*I reported them to Don Gregg, Bob Kerritt, Bob Ellis and from time-to-time other people. I not only have notes, I have letters that I wrote to some of these people. Copies of these letters were submitted to the congressional investigators.*

One of the investigators, Chad Farris, Chief Deputy attorney General for the State of Arkansas, tried to discredit Brenneke by asking hostile questions:

*Why would you care about the use of drugs as part of this CIA plan? If you were so concerned about the use of drugs in the operation because of the reasons you've described, why did you continue to take part in the operation; what do you hope to achieve by testifying here today; what's the purpose of your testimony, to you personally?*

Brenneke was under subpoena, and obviously had to answer truthfully. Further, Brenneke was following orders when he did what he did. He also knew the risk of opposing high-level officials in control of the CIA, DEA, and Justice Department.

Brenneke testified about the Justice Department's sham charges against him for having testified during a 1988 federal court trial in Denver concerning Heinrich Rupp, and his testimony that he saw George Bush and Donald Gregg in Paris during the period of October 18, 19, and 20, 1980. Brenneke stated that in the Denver proceedings Justice Department attorneys offered him a plea agreement, that if Brenneke pled guilty to perjury concerning his statement about seeing Bush and Gregg in Paris, he would not receive any prison time or fine. No perjury charges were ever filed against Brenneke for this testimony. Brenneke's testimony corroborated testimony of many others, and statements made to me over a period of years by CIA personnel and DEA personnel, and with numerous investigative media articles and highly specific expose books.

Brenneke was involved in many other CIA activities. Tape recordings made of telephone conversations between Brenneke and Russbacher, in my possession, described their role in the CIA's operation known as Operation Gladio, which sought to destabalize the Italian government in the 1950s.

Brenneke had given a speech at the University of Arkansas in 1991, which was videotaped, further describing these events.

**TESTIMONY BY IRS INVESTIGATOR BILL DUNCAN**

One of my sources was William Duncan who was an investigator for the Internal Revenue Service. Duncan spent several years investigating drug-money laundering in Arkansas, and the role played by Governor Bill Clinton; the Arkansas Development Finance Authority; Dan Lasater's brokerage business, and the Stephen's financial powerhouse. Duncan had functioned in the capacity of congressional investigator for the Subcommittee on Crime, and discovered as part of his investigation the involvement of Arkansas officials and the CIA in drug trafficking and drug-money laundering. Duncan was a criminal investigator for the U.S. Treasury Department from 1973 through 1989, involving matters surrounding drug trafficking and drug-money laundering in the Mena, Arkansas area.

In addition to what Duncan stated to me, I received a transcript of his congressional testimony, marked Confidential, given to a Joint Investigation by the United States Congress and the Arkansas State Attorney General's Office in June 1991. During the deposition, Duncan was asked what his duties were concerning the Mena Airport activities. He replied:

*I was assigned to investigate allegations of money laundering in connection with the Barry Seal organization, which was based at the Mena, Arkansas airport.*

Duncan testified in detail about the drug-money laundering he uncovered, involving the CIA, and how attorneys with the Department of Justice stonewalled the prosecution.

Duncan found, as I had in the past, that Justice Department attorneys routinely obstruct justice by refusing to have witnesses willing to testify appear before the Grand Jury. Or, they can control the testimony by asking witnesses only perfunctory questions and blocking the witnesses from testifying on meaningful activities.

Duncan testified as to the tactics used by Justice Department officials to protect the CIA and those people working with the CIA in the drug trafficking and drug-money laundering. He testified that important witnesses were not called to testify before the Grand Jury; that important witnesses with valuable information were not allowed to present this information, being limited literally to giving their name, address, phone number, and type of employment. Duncan testified to how vice-president of the Union Bank in Mena, Gary Gardner, wanted to testify about the CIA money-laundering and how Justice Department prosecutors blocked this testimony.

Duncan testified that he gave the U.S. Attorney's office in Fort Smith, Arkansas, the names of 20 witnesses to call for the Grand Jury appearance, who had direct knowledge and evidence of the drug-money laundering, and that only three were called. Duncan testified to the coverup by U.S. Attorney Asa Hutchinson and other Justice Department officials, that permitted the money laundering to continue.

Of the three witnesses that were allowed to testify, Duncan testified that two of them were angry because the U.S. Attorney refused to allow them to give evidence to the Grand Jury. I also encountered this common tactic when I circumvented the stone-walling by Justice Department attorneys. I appeared before a Denver Grand Jury in the mid-1960s to give testimony as a federal investigator about the corruption at United Airlines and within the Federal Aviation Administration relating to a series of air disasters.

One of the witnesses not allowed to testify to any meaningful activities was Kathy Corrigan Gann. Duncan testified:

*She was the secretary for Rich Mountain Aviation, who participated in the money laundering operation upon the instructions of Hampton and Evans. She basically said that she was allowed to give her name, address, position, and not much else. I talked to another witness. His name was Jim Nugent, a Vice-President at Union Bank of Mena, who had conducted a search of their records and provided a significant amount of evidence relating to the money laundering transaction. He was also furious that he was not allowed to provide the evidence that he wanted to provide to the grand jury.*

Duncan's testimony continued:

*At a later date, I came in contact with the deputy foreman of the grand jury, who had previously given testimony to an investigator for the House Judiciary Subcommittee on Crime, concerning her frustrations as the deputy foreman of the grand jury. Her name was P.J. Pitts. She was perpetually involved in the grand jury as it heard evidence concerning the Barry Seal matter, and she related to me the frustrations of herself and the entire grand jury because they were not allowed to hear of money laundering. [The primary purpose of the grand jury was to obtain evidence about money laundering.]*

*She stated to me that they specifically asked to hear the money laundering evidence, specifically asked that I be subpoenaed, and they were not allowed to have me subpoenaed. She said the whole grand jury was frustrated. She indicated that Mr. Fitzhugh, who at that time was the U.S. Attorney, explained to them that I was in Washington at the time and unavailable as a witness, which was not the truth.*

When asked about how Duncan's superiors responded to the coverup, Duncan testified that he complained to his superior, Paul Whitmore, Chief of Criminal Investigation, and to the group managers, Tim Lee, Charles Huckaby and Max Gray. Duncan continued:

*They were very frustrated. Mr. Whitmore made several trips to Fort Smith, Arkansas to complain to the U.S. Attorney's office. He related to me on several occasions that the U.S. Attorney wrote him a letter telling him not to come to his office anymore complaining, that was unprofessional behavior. Mr. Whitmore felt there was a coverup.*

"Do you agree with Mr. Whitmore's conclusion?"

*Absolutely. We experienced a variety of frustrations from 1985 on, not being able to obtain subpoenas for witnesses we felt were necessary. I had some direct interference by Mr. Fitzhugh in the investigative process. Specifically he would call me and interrupt interviews, tell me not to interview people that he had previously told me were necessary to be interviewed.*

**IRS DEMANDING PERJURED TESTIMONY TO COVER UP FOR CIA DRUG TRAFFICKING**

"Did you have any interference or interruptions from anyone within the U.S. Treasury Department?"

*They interfered with my testimony before the House Judiciary Subcommittee on Crime. The Internal Revenue Service assigned to me disclosure litigation attorneys, who gave me instructions which would have caused me to withhold information from Congress during my testimony, and to also perjure myself.*

**DRUG-MONEY BRIBE TO U.S. ATTORNEY GENERAL**

"How did you respond to the Treasury Department?"

*I told them that I was going to tell the truth in my testimony. And the perjury, subornation of perjury resulted because of an allegation that I had received, that Attorney General Edwin Meese received a several hundred thousand dollar bribe from Barry Seal directly. I received that information from Russell Welch, the [Arkansas] State Police investigator. And they told me to tell the Subcommittee on Crime that I had no information about that.*

Duncan testified about other aspects of upper management acting to prevent exposure of the drug trafficking and drug-money laundering. His testimony continued:

*I received a subpoena from Deputy Prosecutor Chuck Black from Mt. Ida, to present evidence to the grand jury for the purposes of seeking indictments against the individuals at Mena. The Internal Revenue Service told me I would have to go back and deal with the same disclosure litigation attorneys who attempted to get me to withhold information from Congress and perjure myself, and I refused to do that. They withdrew support for the operations and basically kept me in the regional office in Atlanta and did not allow me to fulfill my responsibilities. This ultimately resulted in my resignation in June of 1989.*

Addressing questions concerning the obstruction of justice, Duncan testified:

*My superiors and I had continuing discussions because none of us, my managers nor myself, had ever experienced anything remotely akin to this type of interference. We couldn't understand why there was this different attitude. I had found Asa Hutchinson to be a very aggressive U.S. Attorney in connection with my cases. Then all of a sudden, with respect to Mena, it was just like the information was going in but nothing was happening over a long period of time. As soon as Mr. Fitzhugh got involved, he was more aggressive in not allowing the subpoenas and in interfering in the investigative process. He was reluctant to have the State Police around, even though they were an integral part of the investigation.*

*For instance, when the money laundering specialist was up from Miami, Mr. Fitzhugh left Mr. Welch in the hall all day until late in the afternoon and refused to allow him to come in. We were astonished that we couldn't get subpoenas. We were astonished that Barry Seal was never brought to the grand jury, because he was on the subpoena list for a long time. And there were a lot of investigative developments that made no sense to us.*

Duncan testified that the IRS briefing attorney from Washington wanted him to cover up during the grand jury testimony. "Did you get the impression that she was ordering you to cover up the investigation?"

*Absolutely. I would have thought a complete disclosure to Congress about the problems that we encountered was in order, but quite the opposite was true. They obviously did not want any negative testimony coming from me concerning the U.S. Attorney's office.*

Attorney Bryan Sloan, a personal assistant to the Commissioner of Internal Revenue, Larry Gibbs, said, "Bill [Duncan] is just going to have to get the big picture."

Duncan testified that among the federal agencies that should have been involved in the Arkansas investigation were the U.S. Customs Service, the FBI, and the Drug Enforcement Administration. Among the state agencies were the Arkansas State Police, Polk County Sheriff's office, and the Louisiana State Police. Duncan testified that none of the law-enforcement personnel, who had knowledge and evidence of the drug trafficking and drug-money laundering, were called by the Justice Department to present evidence to the grand jury.

Duncan testified that even though "allegations of narcotics smuggling, massive amounts of drug-money laundering" were involved, "conspicuously absent during most of that time were the DEA, FBI, and Customs."

During Duncan's testimony, it was revealed that the U.S. Attorney's Office at Fort Smith received instructions from the Miami U.S. Attorney's Office to "shut down the Mena Investigations at a point in time when they were ready to indict and present information to a grand jury."

During another congressional deposition on July 24, 1994, Duncan testified:

> *By the end of 1987...thousands of law enforcement man-hours and an enormous amount of evidence of drug smuggling, aiding and abetting drug smugglers, conspiracy, perjury, money laundering...had gone to waste. Not only were no indictments ever returned on any of the individuals under investigation for their role in the Mena Operation, there was a complete breakdown in the judicial system. The United States Attorney, Western Judicial District of Arkansas,...refused to issue subpoenas for critical witnesses, interfered in the investigations, misled grand juries about evidence and availability of witnesses, refused to allow investigators to present evidence to the grand jury, and in general made a mockery of the entire investigative and judicial process.*
>
> *[Actions of IRS officials were] purely and simply designed to impede the Congress of the United States in their investigation of issues which impact on the very heart of our judicial system, and ultimately the security of this country. Evidence...indicates that...the Mena, Arkansas Airport was an important hub-waypoint for transshipment of drugs, weapons.... The evidence details a bizarre mixture of drug smuggling, gun running, money laundering and covert operations by Barry Seal, his associates, and both employees and contract operatives of the United States Intelligence Services. The testimony reveals a scheme whereby massive amounts of cocaine were smuggled into the State of Arkansas, and profits were partially used to fund covert operations. Two witnesses testified that one of the Western District of Arkansas Assistant U.S. Attorneys told them that the U.S. Attorney's Office received a call to shut down the investigations involving [the drug operation].*

## CONFIDENTIAL TRANSCRIPT OF TESTIMONY OF ARKANSAS STATE OFFICIAL

Another transcript sent to me, marked Confidential, was of testimony given by Russell Welch to the Congressional and Arkansas State investigators in June 1991. Welch was an investigator for the Arkansas State Police for sixteen years, and testified along the lines of IRS investigator William Duncan. He added that U.S. Attorney Michael Fitzhugh of Miami blocked an investigation into the CIA drug trafficking and money laundering as Asa Hutchinson had done. He testified to the refusal by the Justice Department to issue subpoenas for those who had knowledge of the drug-related crimes. Welch testified that despite the fact that he had considerable knowledge of the federal offenses the Justice

Department refused to allow him to appear before the grand jury.

Welch testified that one of the lady members of the grand jury had seen him in the hall outside the jury room and demanded of Fitzhugh to have Welch testify. Angrily, Fitzhugh told Welch the grand jury wanted to hear from him, but Fitzhugh refused to allow this.

**COVERUP BY DEA**

Asked how other federal agencies blocked investigation and prosecution of the drug trafficking and drug-money laundering, Welch testified that the cooperation from "the Drug Enforcement Administration in Florida was absolutely zero. We didn't get a lot of support from the Arkansas Drug Enforcement Administration."

Referring to drug trafficker Barry Seal, Welch testified "there was obvious government involvement [protection] with him." Seal was heavily involved in drug trafficking and drug-money laundering with the CIA, and also with Arkansas officials and power-brokers, including members of then-governor Bill Clinton's administration.

Welch described, as did others, that the practice was for aircraft flying into Arkansas from Central America to air-drop the drug loads at selected sites in Western Arkansas, and that helicopters would then pick up the drugs. He described the amount of drugs Barry Seal brought into Arkansas as "billions of dollars of cocaine and drugs over an eight to ten year period of time."

Welch testified about the feelings of the grand jury as he referred to the deputy foreman, Patty Pitts:

> *She expressed concern that they weren't being allowed to investigate the Mena Airport; that Mike Fitzhugh wasn't giving them the evidence that they needed to have; and wasn't giving them the witnesses they needed to have. She felt like they were being hindered.*

**JUDICIAL ASSISTANCE IN OBSTRUCTION OF JUSTICE**

Referring to the practice of certain federal judges to block the prosecution of government-related drug offenses, he said U.S. Attorney Fitzhugh told him that "A federal judge would never let it get to court, and we would be wasting our time."

**ATTEMPT TO DISABLE WELCH**

Welch said to me that while he was presenting evidence of the massive drug trafficking to Arkansas officials in Little Rock, he suddenly became deathly sick, and was rushed to the hospital. Fortunately for him, the doctors discovered the problem. They told Welch that he had been sprayed with military-grade Anthrax (similar to what Saddam Hussein had threatened to use in the Persian Gulf War).

**OBSTRUCTION OF JUSTICE BY NSC**

The General Accounting Office started a probe of the Arkansas drug operation in 1988, and was shut down within four months by the National Security Council.[435] Several Congressional committees started to investigate, and then shut down. Governor Bill Clinton blocked an investigation and prosecution.

---

435 *Wall Street Journal* June 29, 1994.

Polk County prosecuting attorney Joe Hardegree, who had accumulated considerable evidence of CIA drug trafficking and drug-money laundering, complained that a cloak of secrecy prevented prosecution of the drug-related offenses because of links between the drug traffickers and the federal government.

In a prepared statement to a *Mena Star* reporter in 1988, Hardegree said that the investigation of prosecution of drug-related crimes had come to a grinding halt because of links between the drug traffickers and the White House.[436] Hardegree added, "I have good reason to believe that all federal law enforcement agencies from the Justice Department down through the FBI to the Drug Enforcement Administration received encouragement to downplay and de-emphasize any investigation or prosecution that might expose Seal's activities and the National Security Council's involvement in them."

By 1983, the Arkansas State Police had almost three dozen volumes, several thousand pages of reports and evidence, providing overwhelming evidence of the drug activities.

Since 1983, the drug trafficking and money laundering in Arkansas were investigated by agents from the local Polk County (where Mena is located), Internal Revenue Service, the FBI, and Arkansas state police, and despite massive evidence of the criminal activities, officials in the U.S. Department of Justice and Arkansas police blocked prosecution. Every attempt by the individual investigators to appear before a grand jury to present their evidence was blocked by Arkansas and federal officials.

**ARKANSAS CITIZENS COMMITTEE**

One of the concerned group of citizens was the Arkansas Committee, in which Charles Reed,[437] Mark Swaney, and Tom Brown of Springdale, Arkansas, were heavily involved. Reed and his group investigated the CIA's unlawful weapon shipments and drug trafficking activities in Arkansas, focusing on the Mena area. In 1989 the group sent a petition to Governor Bill Clinton asking the state to convene a grand jury to receive their evidence, to conduct an investigation, and to prosecute.

The group discovered the drug trafficking operations of CIA and DEA-connected Barry Seal, at that time one of the biggest drug traffickers in the country. Every time Seal was "accidentally" arrested by a law enforcement officer, he was subsequently released after intervention from officials of the CIA and Justice Department. This get-out-of-jail pass was typical for covert CIA-related personnel. In 1972, for instance, Seal was arrested in New Orleans with 14,000 pounds of explosives intended for Cubans working with the CIA, and promptly released.

The Arkansas State Police received hundreds of citizen reports detailing the criminal activities, reportedly consisting of several thousand pages in 34 volumes. Governor Bill Clinton was advised of the activity and it was requested

436 *Freedom*, May June 1989.

437 Charles Reed furnished me with considerable data concerning the drug activities going on in Arkansas, expecting me to use it to help awaken the American public. He was a crusader seeking to make the public aware of the government corruption. He died on November 15, 1995, in his hometown of Salem, Massachusetts, shortly after sending me his total accumulation of data on government-associated drug trafficking in Arkansas.

that he order state law enforcement personnel to investigate. Despite the gravity of the reported drug activities, Clinton and the U.S. Attorney[438] refused to conduct an investigation.

Helping to obstruct justice was Asa Hutchinson and then Michael Fitzhugh, the local federal prosecutors, obviously acting on orders from their Washington Justice Department officials and U.S. Attorney Generals.

**FORCING JUSTICE DEPARTMENT INTO COVERUP GRAND JURY HEARING**

By 1987, public pressure forced the U.S. Attorney to convene a grand jury and go through the motions of investigating. In typical coverup fashion, the U.S. Attorney blocked state and federal investigators, who had evidence of the drug trafficking, access to the grand jury. Witnesses who could provide evidence, and who were called, were not asked questions about the drug activities, being asked by the U.S. Attorney non-relevant questions. The Justice Department tactics included asking questions about things the witness knew nothing about, and not asking questions about things they did know. The witnesses recognized what the U.S. Attorney was doing, and complained about the tactics when outside of the grand jury room.

**ARKANSAS DEVELOPMENT FINANCE AUTHORITY (ADFA)**

ADFA was promoted by Governor Bill Clinton as providing low-interest loans for schools, churches, and other noble purposes, and passed by the Arkansas legislature in 1985. Clinton had control of who received loans from ADFA. The first five loans went to Clinton's friends and associates, including Park On Meter (POM), a company partly owned by Webster Hubbell, a Rose Law Firm partner and later *de facto* head of the U.S. Department of Justice. That $2.85 million loan was never repaid, and the records of loans and payment schedule were kept from the public. There was no noticeable improvement in the POM plant to show where the money was used that was to fund that purpose. POM was involved in secretly manufacturing weapon parts for the CIA's unlawful arms shipments to Central America.

**MARKETING DIRECTOR ADFA**

Former director for marketing at ADFA was Larry Nichols, who turned whistleblower and presented evidence to the media concerning activities at ADFA. He was one of the first to go public about Governor Clinton's misuse of state offices for his sexual encounters. Nichols stated that there was virtually no accounting of the money received by ADFA, or the repayments on the loans. He said that money would appear in a particular account and then suddenly disappear, a technique that IRS investigator William Duncan said was a zero-balance tactic commonly used in drug-money laundering.

Nichols stated that the huge amount of money coming into ADFA would be periodically transferred to other banks, including the terrorist and drug-related Bank of Commerce and Credit International (BCCI). He said that drug money was laundered into a Chicago bank in which Congressman Dan Rostenkowski had a part interest.

438 Asa Hutchinson and later Michael Fitzhugh.

## LASATER, INCORPORATED

Bond brokerage houses are a convenient vehicle for drug-money laundering. In Arkansas key drug-money laundering facilities were Lasater & Company, Stephens' companies, and Arkansas Development Finance Authority (ADFA). Dan Lasater, a close friend of Governor Clinton, and a key campaign contributor, operated a bond brokerage business in Little Rock, which was a primary source for CIA and other drug-money laundering.

Clinton was responsible for sending tens of millions of dollars of Arkansas bond business through Lasater's bond brokerage business. Clinton personally lobbied on behalf of Lasater, for Arkansas to use the Lasater firm for much of its bond business. This lobbying occurred while the media reported that Lasater was the target of a federal drug investigation.

Lasater also had a major drug trafficking and drug-money laundering operation at his Angel Fire Resort in New Mexico, as reported to authorities by present and prior employees. An investigation and prosecution of this CIA-related operation was blocked by federal agencies, again protecting the involvement of these agencies in criminal drug-related offenses.

In 1987 Lasater was sentenced to 30 months in prison for distributing drugs for recreational use, although he was known to be a major drug trafficker. A trial was avoided through a plea agreement, eliminating the risk that the CIA and ADFA would be exposed.

Lasater's top aide in his businesses was Patsy Thomasson, who operated the businesses while Lasater was in prison because of this conviction. When Clinton became president of the United States he appointed Thomasson director of White House administration.

Even after Lasater was charged with drug trafficking in Arkansas, Governor Clinton personally lobbied to approve a state bond sale to Lasater's company, netting Lasater a $750,000 fee. Lasater handled considerably over a half billion dollars in Arkansas bond contracts.[439] State bond sales are lucrative and require relatively little work, and are prime contracts for bribes of the approving government officials. The bond business is a free-lunch for those who are well-connected politically. Lasater sold high-interest, high-risk deals to small banks and savings and loans, causing some of them to fail, incurring large losses for the American taxpayers.

## INVOLVEMENT OF THE POWERFUL STEPHENS FAMILY

After Lasater went to prison, he changed the name of Lasater Incorporated to Phoenix Group, Incorporated, which was later purchased by the powerful Stephens' interests. Stephens handled much of the ADFA funding after Lasater went to prison. Since much of the funding for ADFA came from CIA-related drug money it is safe to assume that Stephens knew about the source of that money and the corruption related to ADFA.

The connections between Bank of Credit and Commence International, First American Bank,[440] and Stephens Incorporated, have been discussed in other

439 *Wall Street Journal*, March 10, 1994.

440 Owned by First American Bancshares, which in turn was unlawfully owned by BCCI.

pages. Jackson Stephens helped BCCI secretly obtain ownership of American banks.

After Lasater went to prison, Governor Clinton transferred the bond business to Stephens Incorporated. Jack Stephens was reportedly involved in drug related activities according to Larry Nichols, director of marketing for ADFA. Stephens funded Clinton's campaign to the tune of $2.8 million dollars, the exact amount, according to Larry Nichols, that it received in profit from a concocted transaction of a student loan fund that was under Clinton's control. Stephens also contributed large amounts of money to Clinton's campaigns through Worthen National Bank.

## REPEATED UNREFUTABLE EVIDENCE OF THE DRUG TRAFFICKING AND DRUG-MONEY LAUNDERING

The *Arkansas Gazette* exposed the drug trafficking, drug-money laundering, and the unlawful purchase by BCCI of American banks using Stephens' empire to facilitate the purchase. Pressures caused the paper to go out of business, one of the dangers of exposing government misconduct. One of the last articles written by the *Arkansas Gazette* described how Stephens helped the unlawful acquisition:

> *Curt Bradbury, then a financial analyst for Stephens, Inc., and now chairman and chief executive officer of Worthen National Bank of Arkansas, provided [to a BCCI officer] research about Financial General, including a copy of its latest annual report. Financial General was the parent company of the National Bank of Georgia, the bank run by Bert Lance [who was closely linked to former President Jimmy Carter].*

After Financial General and National Bank of Georgia were purchased, the holding company was renamed First American Bankshares and run by Clark Clifford and Robert Altman.

Over the years many people testified about the CIA involvement in the drug-related crimes. Many television shows depicted this problem. The drug trafficking involving the CIA, with obstruction of justice by Justice Department and other agencies continued, year after year. The public remained either ignorant or apathetic, seemingly more interested in trivial matters than the enormous implications of enormous corruption in government.

Associations[441] comprising retired or former members of the U.S. intelligence community have repeatedly reported instances of the CIA-related drug trafficking and drug-money laundering.

## IRS REPORTING THE DRUG-MONEY LAUNDERING AND CIA OBSTRUCTION OF JUSTICE

Among the concerned people who spoke out on the Arkansas drug-related activities were William Duncan, IRS investigator at that time; Russell Welch, an Arkansas state investigator; Charles Black, a Polk County Deputy Prosecuting Attorney, where much of the Mena activities was ongoing; Terry Reed, a CIA contract agent, who discovered his Mexico CIA proprietary was used for drugs.

Despite the large amount of evidence IRS investigator William Duncan had, and Arkansas state police investigator Russell Welch, and the nearly two dozen witnesses ready and willing to testify to the Grand Jury, the Justice Department

---

441 Including the Association of National Security Alumni. *Covert Action* is another publication dealing exclusively with U.S. intelligence agencies.

prosecutor refused to allow them to appear before the jury. U.S. Attorney Fitzhugh refused to allow Duncan to testify, or his other witnesses, even when the foreman of the grand jury requested that they appear.

The CIA controlled the Justice Department so as to halt any investigation and prosecution of the criminals and criminal activities in the Arkansas area associated with the CIA crimes. Clinton controlled the State Police and blocked any state investigation and prosecution. But there were some renegade investigators that had to be dealt with, including Bill Duncan. Colonel Tommy Goodwin, director of the Arkansas State Police, also acted to block any investigation into the weapon shipments, drug trafficking, and drug-money laundering.

The May and June 1989 edition of *Freedom* magazine said that "Two congressional subcommittees and the U.S. Customs Service are investigating secret activities around the quiet mountain town of Mena, Arkansas, including alleged drug running and arms smuggling." The February-March 1992 issue of *Unclassified* described the large amount of evidence proving the existence of drug trafficking and drug-money laundering at Mena Airport, and the coverup by the media. It stated in part: "UNCLASSIFIED is genuinely puzzled about the absence of major media attention to Mena, especially given Clinton's prominence in the presidential race."

**ANGEL FIRE RESORT**

For several years several of my CIA contacts described the CIA-related drug trafficking and drug-money laundering in the Angel Fire, New Mexico area, including that occurring at Angel Fire Ski Resort. As stated earlier, this resort was owned and operated by Dan Lasater.

An investigation into Angel Fire Resort was triggered in 1985 after former Angel Fire employees reported drug trafficking and drug-money laundering. This resulted in investigations by local and federal law enforcement officials.[442] Lasater owned Angle Fire Resort from 1984 to 1987, and sold it after he was sentenced in 1986 to two and a half years in prison for distributing drugs in Arkansas. (Within six months he was pardoned by Governor Clinton.)

**ROUTINE COVERUP AND OBSTRUCTION OF JUSTICE**

A January 1991 memo written by Customs Service Air Interdiction Officer Lawrence E. Frost described the findings of drug trafficking at Angel Fire:

> *During 1988 significant information was developed by Special Agent Norm Scott of the FBI and I regarding a large controlled substance smuggling operation, as well as a large scale money laundering activity being carried out in the Angel Fire, New Mexico Area.*

The memo described how Frost and Scott requested information about Lasater from the Drug Enforcement Administration, which was in the DEA's possession because of the Arkansas investigation and trial. The same memo referred to that request and the negative response:

> *At no time did I ever receive any information from...DEA regarding any of the alleged conspirators in this case, although I knew that DEA had previously arrested and convicted the primary target of the investigation,*

442 *Sunday Journal*, New Mexico, May 8, 1994; *Albuquerque Journal*, May 8, 1994.

*Dan Lasater.*

If the DEA had cooperated and furnished information, it is possible that Frost and Scott would have discovered Lasater's links to the CIA, the CIA drug trafficking, the CIA drug-money laundering, and God knows what else.

**TACTIC OF COVERUP BY JUSTICE DEPARTMENT ATTORNEYS**

The standard tactic used by Justice Department personnel to cover up for crimes committed by its protected government personnel, or associates of Justice Department officials, is first to block any investigation, either on the federal level, or if on the state level, pressuring local law-enforcement personnel to cooperate in the coverup. If a grand jury investigation should occur, keep witnesses away that could divulge information on government involvement. If calling the witness cannot be avoided, the U.S. Attorney, who asks the questions in grand jury proceedings, avoids meaningful questions and limits the questioning to mundane matters. Also, have witnesses appear who will give false testimony, who are protected against being charged for perjury.

**DEA WHISTLEBLOWER**

On November 21, 1993, *60 Minutes* aired a show in which several DEA officials and agents appeared, described smuggling of large quantities of cocaine by the CIA into the United States, the liaison with Colombian drug traffickers, and the obstruction of justice by U.S. officials. Robert Bonner, a former head of the Drug Enforcement Administration, and Annabelle Grimm, a DEA agent in Caracas, Venezuela, exposed the drug trafficking that was protected against prosecution by Justice Department and DEA officials.

In one instance described by Bonner and Grimm, over 1,000 kilos (2200 pounds) of cocaine were brought into the United States with the help of the CIA's station chief, James Campbell and CIA agent Mark McFarlin.

Bonner and Grimm explained how the local CIA agents circumvented the complaints by the DEA, going directly to the CIA's top command in Washington, again making clear that the drugging of America involved top officials in the United States government, and that these were not rogue operations.

Appearing on the show with Bonner and Grimm was General Ramon Guillen Davila of the Venezuelan national guard, explaining that drugs were regularly shipped into the United States in liaison with the CIA. He described one load, 1500 kilos (3300 pounds), that was so huge it would not fit into the Boeing 707 cargo door. He stated that the drug trafficking was approved by the CIA, and that he had immunity, otherwise he would not be on the *60 Minutes* program subject to arrest.

Grimm described the huge warehouse in Caracas used by the CIA to store the drugs before shipment to the United States, which was built with U.S. taxpayers' dollars.

Davila explained how the CIA conspired with Venezuelan officials, including himself, to bring drugs into the United States in CIA-controlled aircraft. At that time Davila was head of a joint CIA-Venezuelan task force responsible for halting drug trafficking.

The CIA, made aware of the *60-Minutes* show ahead of time, quickly issued a statement on November 19, implying that the drug shipment was an accident rather than an intentional act.[443] Many people, and much planning, were required to smuggle this huge quantity of nearly pure cocaine into the United States and bring about its sale. There was nothing accidental about this complex operation.

Making reference to the CIA statement that the CIA smuggling, distribution, and selling of the ton of pure cocaine was an isolated incident, my CIA contacts laughed. They recognized that the ton of cocaine to which the CIA had to make reference was only a small part of the CIA-drug smuggling operation.

The CIA tried to show that it took corrective action when this multi-million-dollar operation was discovered, stating that one CIA officer resigned, and a second had been disciplined. Many people implicated in a drug sale, even as little as one ounce, or who was present when others were talking about drug sales, have been sentenced to many years in federal prison. When the same offense is committed by a government official or agent, the offense becomes far worse, and calls for much longer prison sentences. Since Justice Department officials covered up for the drug trafficking, and since they are the only officials under our form of government that can prosecute for federal crimes, the criminal conduct by federal officials goes unpunished.

Chief State Department official responsible for overseeing international narcotics matters, Melvin Levitsky, explained that an indictment against General Guillen would require the United States to cut off aid to Venezuela, and therefore no charges should be filed. Much of the world's coca, from which cocaine is obtained, is grown in Bolivia, Peru, and Venezuela, and constitute a major part of their income. This fact is no secret to the CIA, and the CIA relies upon this source for much of its cocaine smuggling into the United States.

Obviously, great financial and physical harm is inflicted upon the American people by the drug trafficking. A giant hoax is being played upon the American people by the so-called multi-billion-dollar-a-year drug war financed by the U.S. taxpayer. The fact that hundreds of federal officials are involved in the drug trafficking into the United States, including the nation's highest "law-enforcement" agency, indicates the magnitude of the subversive activities against the United States.

Very few newspapers reported anything related to the CIA statement, the charges made on the *60 Minutes* show, or the significance of the serious charges. They engaged in their standard coverup.

## STANDARD EXCUSES USED FOR OBSTRUCTING JUSTICE

The standard CIA excuse, when questioned about its drug smuggling, is that it is a sting operation, or to obtain information about drug smugglers. DEA agent Grimm said on 60 Minutes that these explanations were "ludicrous." When Justice Department officials were questioned, they replied that there was "no evidence of criminal wrongdoing." Justice Department officials said their investigation "Revealed instances of poor judgment and management, leading to disciplinary actions for several CIA officers." The CIA station chief involved in the massive drug trafficking, James Campbell, was promoted and then retired.

When asked by Mike Wallace of *60 Minutes* about the CIA drug smuggling, Senator Dennis DeConcini, replied, "I think they made a mistake." DeConcini

443 *New York Times*, November 20, 1993.

helped protect the massive looting of the savings and loans, and covered up the criminal activities that I reported to him over a period of years. DeConcini did admit that the "mistake" leading to over a ton of cocaine reaching the United States "can kill people, and probably did." The senator, a former prosecutor, excused the failure to prosecute any of the CIA people. Not a single government employee responsible for bringing this huge quantity of drugs into the United States was punished.

**DOUBLE STANDARD**

Tom Brown, the pastor of a small church in Arkansas, helped expose the unlawful arms and drug trafficking in Arkansas that was part of the government's involvement in Central and South America. To silence and discredit him, the same Justice Department officials who aided and abetted the massive drug smuggling into the United States retaliated against Brown. The church grew and used peyote and pot in their services as part of their religious beliefs. No payment was received with this practice. Justice Department prosecutors charged Brown with a criminal offense, and U.S. District Judge H. Franklin Waters of Fayetteville, Arkansas, sentenced him to ten years in prison.

Brown wrote that Judge Waters was involved with Don Tyson of Tyson Foods as corporate attorney in the 1970s, while Tyson was involved with drugs. Brown heard that Waters was appointed a federal judge in the western district of Arkansas to protect high-level government personnel from being exposed. Duplicating what I repeatedly encountered, Judge Waters played a significant role in covering up the Mena operation since 1982.

**DEATH TO A PROTESTING AIRLINE PILOT**

Evergreen Airlines, based in McMinnville, Oregon and Marana, Arizona, was a long-time CIA operation, hauling weapons from the United States and hauling drugs into the United States. As in every operation involving corrupt federal officials, especially those connected to the CIA, death is often the consequence of voicing objections to the criminal activities in which these agencies have been involved. Dean Moss suffered the ultimate consequences.

On an Evergreen DC-9 flight on contract to the military, Logair (an operation on which I flew as pilot in the late 1950s), the captain mysteriously died. This flight, that would be fatal for Moss, occurred on February 9, 1989.

Dean Moss had as his copilot Philip E. Bartash, as the DC-9 took off from Hill Air Force Base in Ogden, Utah, headed for San Antonio. The aircraft failed to pressurize as it climbed to altitude, and Moss reportedly left the cockpit with a portable oxygen bottle to determine the cause of the pressurization failure. When Moss did not return to the cockpit, Bartash wrote in subsequent reports that he descended to 13,000 feet altitude, put the plane on autopilot, and then went back to the cabin looking for the captain. He found the captain lying on the floor of the aircraft's cargo compartment. Bartash then called Lubbock International Airport, notifying the tower that he had a medical emergency on board, and that he was coming in for a landing.

A medical team was in place when the aircraft landed, and doctors at Lubbock General Hospital pronounced Moss dead. The doctors reported the cause of death as cardiac arrest due to massive hemorrhage of the stomach from a caustic substance that ate up his stomach. It is a common intelligence agency assassination tactic to force Drano or some other toxic chemical down the victim's throat, resulting in massive hemorrhaging from the stomach.

It is believed that a security guard was on the aircraft and that the security guard hid and then disappeared after the aircraft landed.

Lubbock Judge L.J. Blalack and Pathologist Ralph R. Erdmann reported the death as a homicide, which was listed in that manner on the Lubbock Police Report. The television show, *60 Minutes*, ran a June 27, 1993, story on the flight, seeking to portray Dr. Erdmann as incompetent for reporting the death as a homicide. This is the same *60-Minutes* who said they were too busy when Colonel Rowe contacted them to reveal the CIA and Defense Department drug pipeline involving Operation Watchtower.

**DEATH OF A MARINE CORPS WHISTLEBLOWER**

A June 17, 1993, television show, Connie Chung's premier *Eye To Eye*, addressed the matter of assassination of an informant and drug trafficking into the United States in military aircraft. The show focused initially on a Marine Corps pilot, Colonel James Sabow, assassinated in his on-base housing several days before exposing large-scale CIA drug trafficking using military aircraft. He was shot in the mouth.

One of the guests, a pilot and former Army captain, Tosh Plumlee, admitted he flew many flights loaded with cocaine from Central America into Air Force bases. Some of these military bases were named by my CIA contacts: Homestead Air Force Base; China Lake; Twenty-nine Palms. He stated that he flew civilian and military aircraft into these bases, and flew for the CIA and other government agencies.

A private investigator and former military investigator, Gene Wheaton, appeared on the show, confirming that he discovered this to be true. He also made reference to the shipment of arms to both sides in the Nicaraguan war.

The military tried to make Sabow's killing look like a suicide, even though there were no fingerprints on the shotgun found next to the body. The victim's brother, Dr. David Sabow, a neurologist, said on the show: "There's no question in my mind that this [killing] was ordered by the military; it was carried out by the military. He was set up by the military and by people he knew very, very well. I will prove it."

**MURDERS OF GI INFORMANTS LISTED AS SUICIDES?**

It is believed that many military people are listed as suicides when in reality they were reportedly killed after threatening to expose epidemic drug trafficking in the U.S. military. Relatives of U.S. servicemen, who military officials said committed suicide, formed an organization called *Until We Have Answers*, and demanded investigations into the deaths.[444] The number of questionable suicides represented by the families was seventy-two in late 1993. Congressmen David Levy (R-NY) and Frank Pallone (D-NJ) requested that Secretary of Defense Les Aspin direct the Department of Defense to conduct investigations into the deaths. They also added a rider to the Defense Authorization Bill requiring the DOD inspector general to reinvestigate any finding of suicide, if requested by the family.

444 *Unclassified*, October-November 1993.

Air Force Captain Edward Consuegra disappeared in December 1992, after he discovered serious irregularities in a government contract with Unisys Corporation. That contract had been arranged by a former CIA official, Deputy Director of the CIA, Frank Carlucci.

*Unclassified* wrote that there were "eerie similarities to the INSLAW case here." They pointed out that in each case there was a major computer contract; large scale corruption involving a government official with intelligence agency connections, and a person who learned too much and who threatened to expose the criminality.

**MOSSAD AGENT DESCRIBING CIA DRUG TRAFFICKING**

Describing the conduct of U.S. officials. Ben-Menashe writes in his book, *Profits of War*, that "Whenever U.S. officials were caught red-handed doing something illegal, they usually lied like crazy and accused everyone else."

Ben-Menashe's book tells about the drug trafficking into the United States by the CIA and the Israeli intelligence community, and how the profits went into the coffers of these intelligence agencies and into private companies controlled by key government personnel. He tells how the Mossad and Israeli agents profited from drug trafficking into the United States from Central and South America and how the CIA protected and assisted in this operation.

People working closely with George Bush were key participants in the CIA drug trafficking from Central America into the United States. John Hull, a friend of Dan Quayle and George Bush, was heavily involved in the drug trafficking by making a fuel stop available on property that he owned in Costa Rica. Another close friend of Bush was Felix Rodriguez, who played a key role in the illegal arms and drug trafficking that were key parts of the Contra scandal.

CIA operative Gunther Russbacher mentioned the frequent visits of Senator Dan Quayle to the CIA's arms and drug transshipment point known as John Hull's Ranch[445] in Costa Rica. He stated that Quayle was deeply involved with the Contra operation and drugs, as well as being closely associated with noted drug trafficker Felix Rodriguez. Russbacher said, "Quayle was one of our bag boys."

**SHAM BASIS FOR INVADING A FOREIGN COUNTRY AND KILLING ITS CITIZENS**

In 1990, President Bush ordered the U.S. military to invade Panama on the basis that Colonel Manuel Noriega was violating U.S. laws by allowing drug trafficking through Panama. This was bizarre in light of the fact that CIA operative and then Director of the CIA, George Bush, paid Noriega for years to engage in drug-related activities with the CIA and the Mossad, including the drug trafficking associated with the so-called Iran-Contra affair.

The invasion of Panama caused hundreds of deaths, including twenty-six U.S. servicemen, and billions of dollars in damages, on the pretense that Noriega was dealing in drugs and presumably U.S. agencies were not. People in control of U.S. intelligence agencies were themselves engaging in drug trafficking against

445 It was reported that the so-called John Hull's ranch actually belonged to Douglas Siple and John Hood, who hired Hull to reside on and manage the property.

their own country, and by nature of their positions of trust, their crimes were arguably worse than those committed by Noriega.

President George Bush ordered the invasion of Panama to capture and bring to the United States Manuel Noriega, on the pretense of halting drug trafficking. Noriega did in fact aid in drug trafficking, assisting the CIA, DEA and other U.S. entities, and the Mossad. He assisted Oliver North and his associates, including Vice President Bush, in the unlawful arms flow to Central America and the drug-laden aircraft returning to the United States. The actual reason for President Bush's invasion of Panama is only speculation at this time. Further, Noriega's activities occurred in Panama, and as head of state he had the right to hold these activities legal, just as some people in the United States have argued for legalization for drugs.

Many CIA personnel believe that Noriega was taken out because he knew too much about the involvement of U.S. officials, and that he was demanding too high a cut for his part in the CIA drug trafficking. After the invasion, the United States saw that key banking positions, used for money laundering, were filled by people who would continue the drug money laundering. This continued an uninterrupted conduit for U.S. intelligence agencies' drug-money laundering.

**MORE JUDICIAL COVERUP**

The federal judge presiding over the trial of Manuel Noriega barred attorneys supposedly defending Noriega from presenting any information on the CIA's role, or that of George Bush, in drug trafficking or anything of a political nature. The U.S. District Judge repeatedly refused to allow CIA documents to be introduced that Noriega needed to defend himself. Noriega's U.S. attorneys limited their defense arguments so as not to expose the CIA involvement in drug trafficking.

To obtain a conviction, Justice Department prosecutors rewarded known drug smugglers with reduced prison terms, protected them against the consequences of their perjury, and compensated them for testifying against Noriega. In a November 27, 1991, article the *Arizona Republic* described the huge payments to major drug traffickers who testified as Justice Department officials wanted them to testify, so as to bring about General Noriega's conviction on drug charges.

In some cases the funds paid out of the U.S. treasury by Justice Department personnel paid for testimony from drug traffickers that were guilty of major drug smuggling into the United States. Justice Department prosecutors dropped charges and reduced prison terms for many of the witnesses. Three of them, facing life terms with no possibility of parole, and with a collective 546 years in prison, were released and given immunity from further prosecution (including immunity from perjured testimony against Noriega). They were given large financial payments, and their families brought to the United States.

The star witness against Noriega was his former pilot, Floyd Carlton, who faced life imprisonment with no parole, for having flown cocaine into the United States. Justice Department prosecutors allowed Carlton to transfer his drug-related assets from Panama to the United States, with no risk of forfeiture or income taxes. Carlton was also given several hundred thousand dollars, along with permanent U.S. residency for himself, his wife and children, and a nanny.

Another Panamanian who was paid for his testimony was Ricardo Bilonick, who reportedly earned $47 million during a three-year period drug trafficking. He faced 50 years in prison, unless he testified as Justice Department prosecutors wanted him to testify. His prison sentence was greatly reduced, he was allowed to keep millions of his drug-related income, and relieved of income tax liabilities.

Colombian pilot Roberto Striedinger, considered by Justice Department personnel as one of the top drug traffickers, and who flew cocaine into the United States, was given a greatly reduced prison sentence. Justice Department personnel returned to Striedinger his seized bank accounts, Mercedes-Benz automobile, a 40-foot yacht, an airplane, and two guns, including AK-47 assault rifles, Uzi and MAC-10 submachine guns.[446]

Ironically, the usual coverup argument to deny the existence of government corruption, such as October Surprise, is that testimony from felons cannot be relied upon (presumably the information must come from nuns or some other group that could not be expected to know about the activities). But when it suits government personnel the testimony of felons is not only considered reliable (and why not), but payments are made to testify as prosecutors wanted them to testify. Further, perjured testimony is protected against prosecution.

On July 10, 1992, a federal jury in Miami sentenced Manuel Noriega to 40 years in federal prison for trafficking in drugs.

**REPLACING NORIEGA WITH A TEAM HEAVILY INVOLVED IN DRUG ACTIVITIES**

The drug trafficking through Panama into the United States didn't stop with Noriega's kidnapping. The Bush Administration arranged for the new President of Panama to be Guillermo Endura, President of a Panamanian bank extensively used by Colombia's Medellin drug cartel. The formation of this cartel was orchestrated by the CIA. Picked for vice president was Guillermo Ford, part owner of the Dadeland Bank of Florida. He reportedly was heavily involved in drug-money laundering. Ford was also Chairman of Panama's Banking Commission. Another official selected by the Bush administration to be Attorney General of Panama was Rogello Cruz.

The *New York Times* said of Michael Harari in a January 2, 1990, article:

> *An Israeli reputed to be Gen. Manuel Antonio Noriega's closest associate may have eluded capture on the night of the United States invasion because he was warned to flee six hours before the American troops swept into the capital, the deputy commander of Panama's new police force said today....*

Harari, working closely with Noriega in the drug trafficking, undoubtedly warned Noriega of the impending attack, which undoubtedly played a role in the casualties suffered by the invaders. Twenty-six American GIs were killed, but this is still small in comparison to the hundreds of innocent people killed in Panama as a result of President Bush's invasion orders. Compounding the harm inflicted upon Panama, the American public will pay over a billion dollars in taxes for aid sent to Panama after the U.S. invasion.

Harari, a Mossad colonel, was well known in Europe and elsewhere as one

446 *The Arizona Republic*, November 27, 1991.

of Mossad's primary killers. He carried out numerous assassinations in Europe. After killing a waiter by mistake in Norway, Israel sent him to Central America, where he took control of the Mossad's widespread drug trafficking, collaborating with U.S. personnel in sending shipments to the United States. Speaking of Israeli control of Panamanian drug activities, the *Washington Jewish Week* stated (December 28, 1989):

> *[The Israelis in Panama] do not reflect well on Israel or the Panama Jewish community...They are engaged in contraband and money laundering. In general, they engage in very aggressive and unfair business practices.*

Numerous CIA operatives have written about the criminal activities of the CIA. Phillip Agee, for instance, has written books on the CIA drug trafficking. Agee had been with the CIA for many years. The *Associated Press* printed quotes (January 29, 1990) from Agee's speech at Oregon State University in Corvallis: "Bush is up to his neck in illegal drug running on behalf of the Contras."

Much of the heroin entering the United States comes from Southeast Asia in the Golden Triangle area. A March 26, 1990, *U.S. News & World Report* article stated:

> *For more than a decade, Khun Sa, the warlord of opium, has flooded Washington with offers to end the poppy production within his Golden Triangle fiefdom in exchange for financial aid. The U.S. has not responded, and this year the region's crop could double from the levels of just a few years ago. Att. Gen. Dick Thornburgh unsealed an indictment against the man considered responsible for 40 percent of the U.S. heroin supply. But Sa is not likely to be booked soon. In the remote hills of Burma, a private army of thousands protect him.*

**CROSS-CHECKING AND CONFIRMATION**

These new deep-cover intelligence agency people provided confirmation of each other's status and of the statements given to me by others, and this included Gunther Russbacher. Further, as other covert operatives gave me information about the criminal and subversive activities of officials in control of federal agencies and operations, Russbacher loosened up and exposed sensitive and corrupt activities of which he had knowledge.

**CIA-ENGINEERED WARS AND DRUG TRAFFICKING**

The CIA-engineered Vietnam War provided the logistics making possible massive transportation of drugs from the Golden Triangle area of Asia into the United States. The CIA-engineered conflict in Nicaragua resulted in and made possible massive transportation of drugs from Central and South America into the United States. These developed into multi-billion-dollar-a-year profits for the CIA. Most of the profits were reportedly hidden in off-shore financial institutions. It is no longer far-fetched to consider that the CIA may have deliberately generated these conflicts primarily to develop its drug trafficking operation into the United States. Nor is it far-fetched to consider that these acts and consequences may be part of a scheme to financially and morally destroy the United States.

The mindset within the CIA, including the Phoenix Program that assassinated 40,000 Vietnam villagers, the Vietnam war that killed millions, and the CIA's massive drug trafficking into the United States, is such that deliberate infliction of harm against Americans, and people of other countries, cannot be questioned.

## CIA ASSET TERRY REED BLOWS THE WHISTLE

Terry Reed, a former CIA asset, and co-author John Cummings, authored a 1994 book describing what Reed discovered as a CIA asset in Arkansas: *Compromised: Clinton, Bush and the CIA*.[447] Reed, a former U.S. Air Force intelligence officer, a successful businessman specializing in advanced computer-controlled manufacturing, was recruited by the CIA to train Contra pilots in Arkansas, and later to start up a CIA proprietary in Guadalajara, Mexico.

Reed's activities in the Mena, Arkansas area brought him into contact with the CIA and National Security Council's arms and drug trafficking, and the coverup by Governor Bill Clinton and members of his staff.

Reed's first employment with the CIA was as a flight instructor for Contra pilots in Mena and Nella, Arkansas. He worked with Barry Seal, another CIA asset, who described to Reed the involvement of Arkansas officials in CIA related drug trafficking and drug-money laundering. Reed was in frequent contact with people who later became front-page news.

Before Reed learned about the full extent of the drug smuggling operation, Reed frequently worked with Barry Seal until Seal was killed. Seal told Reed that millions of dollars of drug money was being laundered through the Arkansas Development Finance Authority, the Dan Lasater brokerage company, and involving officials close to Governor Bill Clinton. Seal told Reed that bags containing large amounts of drug-money were dropped into remote locations near Nella, and then picked up by helicopters or surface vehicles.

## DRUG MONEY AND ARKANSAS BOND BUSINESS

After Seal was killed, Lasater's bond business dropped heavily, suggesting that Seal was indeed laundering money through Lasater's business.

Reed described how Oliver North and William Barr authorized him to start a CIA proprietary in Mexico whose function allegedly would be to ship arms to Central and South America. The business was to be a high technology trading and consulting firm, but unknown to Reed, developed into a CIA gun-running and drug operation. Reed moved his family to Mexico, thinking the operation was legitimate and of long duration.

Without knowing about the CIA and NSC involvement in the drug smuggling operation, Reed worked closely with Oliver North, Felix Rodriguez, Barry Seal, and others. Reed's suspicions about the CIA drug operations through the proprietary that he headed was confirmed in July 1987, and he advised his CIA handler that he wanted out of the operation. Under cover of darkness, Reed moved his family back to Arkansas, and went into hiding. He encountered government prosecution as I encountered when I and others encountered after we discovered and sought to expose high-level corruption.

For three years the Reeds had to fight Justice Department attorneys to avoid prison. Fortunately, and very unusual, the public defender appointed to defend the Reeds was a young female attorney who actually fought to protect her client, rather than protect government officials with whom she must work during her career.

---

447 Authored by Terry Reed and John Cummings.

**OLIVER NORTH'S DONATION SCHEME**

Oliver North was reportedly involved in the scheme described in earlier pages in which stolen planes were used to fly arms south from the United States and drugs on the return trips. Reed described how Oliver North explained the stolen plane operation to him in 1983 when they met in Oklahoma City.

Reed explained how the CIA needed an arms manufacturing company for shipping weapons to Central America, and that it purchased the Iver Johnson Arms, Inc., moving it from New Jersey to Arkansas. Like many other CIA proprietaries, the person listed as the owner was a cover for the CIA. In this case it was reportedly Philip Lloyd.

Reed described a late-night meeting in a World War II ammunition bunker outside of Little Rock, Arkansas, discussing drug trafficking and drug-money laundering in Arkansas. Reed stated that the people he saw at this meeting included Governor Bill Clinton; Clinton's Chief of Security, Arkansas State Police Lieutenant Raymond Young; Clinton's aide in charge of the Arkansas Development Finance Authority (ADFA), Bob Nash; Attorney Robert Johnson of the CIA proprietary, Southern Air Transport; Reed's handler, John Cathey; Max Gomez (alias for Felix Rodriguez, with close working relationship to Vice-President and then President George Bush).

Clinton's chief of security, Lieutenant Raymond Young, waited outside the bunker while the meeting occurred. Young was the same Arkansas state police officer who filed and carried out the fraudulent charges against Reed at a later date. Reed's incarceration would protect Governor Clinton, Young, Nash, the CIA, and the others implicated in the drug operations.

Reed had been in frequent telephone contact with the man he knew as Robert Johnson. Johnson directed the drug trafficking and drug-money laundering, the training of Contra pilots and fighters in Arkansas, and authorized Reed to set up the CIA proprietary in Mexico. At a later date, Reed learned that Robert Johnson was really William Barr, appointed by President George Bush to be Attorney General of the United States, the nation's top law-enforcement position. Bob Nash was an aide to Governor Clinton, head of the Arkansas Development Finance Authority, and a liaison with the CIA in drug-money laundering through ADFA.

The purpose of this meeting was to protest Arkansas officials taking too great a percentage of the drug money laundered by Missouri officials, and the attention caused by the drug conviction of Bill Clinton's brother, Roger Clinton.

Reed described in *Compromised* Barry Seal dropping from aircraft bags of money into isolated clearings in Arkansas, including on property owned by Little Rock industrialist Seth Ward, upon which resided Ward's son-in-law, Fins Shellnut. Shellnut worked for bond broker Dan Lasater. Reed described how the bags of money, sometimes millions of dollars at a time, would be dropped onto Ward's property, picked up by Shellnut, and then laundered through Lasater's bond brokerage business.

Ward owned and operated a company called Park On Meter (POM), which made parking meters, and made weapon parts for the CIA that were shipped in violation of the Boland Amendment to Central America. Ward's oldest daughter, Suzy, was married to Webster Hubbell, a partner in the Rose Law

Firm, who was later number three man in the U.S. Department of Justice and *de facto* head of the Justice Department, while Janet Reno served as the titular head.

Lasater Inc. handled much of the drug money laundering in Arkansas until Dan Lasater was convicted of drug trafficking and sent to prison. Testifying against Lasater was Bill Clinton's brother, Roger, who was also charged with drug trafficking but given a reduced sentence in exchange for his testimony against Lasater.

**DAMAGE CONTROL**

Reed's CIA contact, William Barr, known at that time by his alias, Robert Johnson, told Reed that Attorney General Edwin Meese had appointed Michael Fitzhugh to be U.S. Attorney in Western Arkansas, and that he would stonewall any investigation into the Mena, Arkansas drug-related activities.

**LINK TO GLOBAL DRUG-MONEY LAUNDERER, BCCI**

After the CIA temporarily pulled part of the drug-money laundering out of Arkansas, which had funded ADFA, Arkansas had to borrow funds from First American Bank in Washington, a part of BCCI, another operation that was closely linked to the CIA. This money source was arranged through one of Stephen's companies, the same company that played a key role in getting BCCI into the United States, while violating laws prohibiting ownership of American banks by foreigners.

In 1977, Stephens arranged for BCCI to secretly purchase Financial General Bankshares, a bank holding company. This holding company was then renamed First American Bankshares.

Clark Clifford, former Secretary of Defense, and his law partner, Robert Altman, assisted in this unlawful acquisition. Worthen National Bank, a subsidiary of Stephens, Inc., denied in 1991 (four years after they helped BCCI make the illegal purchase) knowing anything about BCCI.[448]

The CIA laundered much of the funds obtained through drug trafficking and other racketeering enterprises into offshore banks, and then part of the money would come back into the United States through purchasing of real estate and corporations, or making loans. Drug cartels do the same.

**ONE OF MANY TACTICS USED TO LAUNDER DRUG MONEY BY LASATER**

Lasater used a straw man for many of his shady security trades, Dennis Patrick. Lasater induced Patrick to open a brokerage account at the Lasater company, being promised huge profits without putting any money into the account. Patrick was a clerk in the Waitley County circuit court. Without signing any papers and without putting up any money, Patrick was notified that he made $20,000 profit, and asked to come in and sign papers.

**ANOTHER ATTEMPTED MURDER**

When an investigation commenced into Lasater's operation, Patrick became a liability. Three attempts were made to kill him, and three people in three different criminal trials were sentenced to prison for these attempts on Patrick's life.

448 *Spotlight*, November 23, 1992.

**ATTACKING A POTENTIAL WHISTLE-BLOWER**

With the knowledge that he acquired during his CIA connections in Arkansas, the CIA and Arkansas officials, including Governor Clinton, saw Reed as a threat of exposure. Arkansas State Police fraudulently charged Reed and his wife with fraud, conspiracy, and mail fraud, relating to the theft several years earlier of Reed's aircraft, and allegedly making a false claim to the insurance company.

For three years the Reeds had to fight Arkansas state police agencies, which included Governor Bill Clinton's chief of security, Raymond Young. Reed reported that Young forged documents, used perjured testimony, falsified evidence, seeking to put Reed and his wife in prison.

Reed describes how U.S. District Judge Frank Theis blocked their defenses, and dismissed evidence showing the sham nature of the charges, claiming the evidence was irrelevant.

During their attempts to defend themselves against the false charges *Time* magazine sought to discredit the Reeds and what they were exposing. The April 20, 1992, *Time* article was entitled, "Anatomy of a Smear" with a subtitle, "Terry Reed loves to tell reporters scandalous tales about Bill Clinton and the Contras. The trouble is the stories are false." *Time* falsely stated that Reed had no connections to the CIA or Barry Seal, despite the massive amount of specific data given to the *Time* reporter, Richard Behar. The article stated that "The only trouble with Reed's sensational tale is that, not a word of it is true."

*Time* was obstructing justice by misstating the facts and seeking to cover up for the criminal activities by the CIA and the Clinton group.

In response, *Freedom* magazine, which had been exposing the CIA drug trafficking in Arkansas, published a May 1993 article entitled, *The Drugging of America*, expanding on the criminal activities by exposing the *Time* coverup and obstruction of justice. *Freedom* magazine wrote: "According to knowledgeable sources interviewed by *FREEDOM,* Terry Reed was one of the players in CIA covert operations based at Mena."

The Reeds filed a thirty-one page lawsuit against *Time* magazine in Little Rock on April 8, 1993.

*Time* magazine was one of the publications that I repeatedly notified of the criminal activities I discovered, starting while I was a federal investigator. Never once did the magazine report the criminal and treasonous conduct perpetrated against the American people.

**WALL STREET JOURNAL COVERUP**

An article by author Edward Jay Epstein, appearing in the April 20, 1994, *Wall Street Journal*, sought to discredit Terry Reed and cover up for his exposure of the crimes involving Arkansas officials and the CIA. Reed's co-author, John Cummings, was a former prize-winning investigative reporter at New York's *Newsday*.[449] Reed had nothing to gain by his exposure activities, and Cummings had sufficient experience and credentials to evaluate the truth of what he discovered, and which he wrote about in *Compromise*. In seeking to cover up

449 Cummings had co-authored *Heist, Goombata: The Improbable Rise & Fall of John Gotti and His Gang*, and *Death Do Us Part.*

for these serious crimes, which would have also exposed Israel's sordid conduct, Epstein wrote that the disclosures of criminal misconduct in *Compromise* must be fabrications because Justice Department officials refused to prosecute or even to present the evidence to a grand jury.

Epstein wrote that the book presented "no credible evidence" showing Clinton's involvement in the CIA activities; or that Oliver North was involved. Epstein addressed the obstruction of justice by Justice Department officials as "Justice Department's reluctance to bring a case against Contra-support activities that were approved by the president and the CIA director."

Epstein sought to ridicule anyone who claimed the CIA and Clinton were involved in Arkansas drug trafficking and drug-money laundering. It would be difficult for any journalist who does any amount of reading of the numerous exposé books and articles describing the details of these criminal activities to doubt that they exist. The American public paid heavily for this type of coverup. Epstein's article surely was appreciated by the corrupt element in government.

**REBUTTAL**

In response to Epstein's article, CBS news correspondent Bill Plante and CBS News Producer Michael Singer responded in a May 3, 1994, Letters To the Editor column, appearing in the *Wall Street Journal*:

> *There is a trail-tens of millions of dollars in cocaine profits...it is a trail that has been blocked by the National Security Council....As the CBS News story revealed, Mr. Clinton was asked by a state prosecutor for help to pursue the case...Help was promised but never arrived....Mr. Perot, who had done his own investigation of Mena, was concerned enough about the drugs-for-guns operation to call Mr. Clinton. And former Clinton staff people have told CBS News that the governor was aware of what was going on there. Mena is a perplexing and difficult story. There is a trail-tens of millions of dollars in cocaine profits, and we don't know where it leads. It is a trail that has been blocked by the National Security Council. The FAA, FBI, Customs, CIA, Justice, DEA and the IRS were all involved in Mena.*

**PRESIDENT CLINTON'S DRUG POLICIES**

Clinton's drug activities in Arkansas could be expected to be followed up with sympathetic activities after he became president of the United States. And this he did. The California legal newspaper, *Daily Journal*, wrote in its July 21, 1994, issue that "The Clinton administration has been undermining existing anti-drug efforts on all fronts." The article stated charged President Clinton with dismantling almost the entire White House Office created to lead the fight. It stated:

> *Surgeon General Joycelyn Elders repeated calls for drug legalization...government-led domestic marijuana eradication has been substantially curtailed...The president has ordered a massive reduction in Defense Department support for drug interdiction...proposed that Congress cut $100 million in drug-treatment funding and $130 million in drug-prevention education... For 1995, the president wants to cut 625 positions from federal drug enforcement agencies—the DEA, FBI, Border Patrol, U.S. Customs Service and others—and reduce federal drug-*

*prosecution personnel by more than 100 positions.*

All of these steps in the face of the massive threats associated with drug trafficking would be "normal" for someone directly or indirectly involved with the drug trafficking into the United States. These activities are also synonymous with Clinton's efforts to block investigation and prosecution of the Arkansas drug activities while he was governor, and synonymous with the charges that he was closely allied to Arkansas drug activities.

**FAA COVERUP OF DRUG TRAFFICKING**

The number of concerned government employees exposing the coverup and obstruction of justice by federal personnel escalated as my activities became known. Shortly after Christmas 1994, several present and former FAA investigators assigned to the agency's drug task force revealed to me the obstacles they faced from FAA management in retaliation for reporting drug activity involving aircraft that they discovered during their official duties. One of them, David Jennings, told me how he was fired by FAA management for continuing to make such reports. He and other FAA inspectors assigned to the security and drug divisions revealed numerous instances of FAA management interference with this agency's lawful responsibilities. Their statements showed that the same problems I found as a federal investigator for the FAA have not changed, and if anything, worsened. During this same time period considerable media and congressional attention focused on the FAA because of numerous airline crashes. But as usual, none of the attention was focused on the hard-core corruption that I tried to expose for the past 30 years. Pious-sounding statements continued to deceive the American public.

**CIA DRUG TRAFFICKING UNKNOWN ONLY TO THE AMERICAN PUBLIC**

One of the many bizarre aspects of this massive drug trafficking, involving key government agencies and branches of government, including the White House, is the illiteracy and indifference of the American public when so many highly documented books have been written about the activities.

Hundreds of witnesses have testified before Congress[450] about their direct knowledge and/or participation in this drug trafficking. Many television shows have addressed this fact, with witnesses who were part of it. The criminal elements are aware of it. Those connected with the intelligence agencies are aware of it. Numerous articles appear in newsletters pertaining to these agencies describing the drug trafficking. The media, with its awareness of these facts, certainly knew about it.

The coverup by the print and broadcast media personnel, who have access to these reports, constitute far more than illiteracy or indifference. These acts are crimes under federal criminal statutes, far worse than federal offenses for which many people are in prison.

450 Senator John Kerry's office released on October 14, 1986 a classified report describing the testimony of over four dozen witnesses before the committee that he headed. This report described the drug trafficking into the United States by persons associated with the CIA and other government agencies. Thirteen of the government people identified in the drug trafficking were among the defendants in the Christic Institute's lawsuit. No actions were taken by any law enforcement agency against these government employees.

## OBSTRUCTION OF JUSTICE BY INDEPENDENT PROSECUTOR WALSH

In 1991, Arkansas Attorney General Winston Bryant gave independent prosecutor Lawrence E. Walsh boxes of evidence showing the CIA's role in Arkansas drug trafficking. This evidence consisted of depositions, Arkansas State Police reports, investigative files, sworn statements, FBI reports, and court documents, proving the existence of drug-related activities in the Iran-Contra operation involving the CIA, the National Security Council, the Mossad, and other government officials.

Walsh covered up for it, even though this was the most important part of the Iran-Contra affair that he was charged to investigate. Walsh's coverup was a crime far worse, and with far greater impact upon the United States, than the offenses that he spent over forty million dollars investigating. I also presented Walsh with evidence concerning criminal activities implicating federal officials, and encountered the same coverup. Walsh had an even greater responsibility to make this evidence known than the average citizen, under federal crime-reporting statutes.

In talking to the press, Congressman Alexander said: "I've never seen a white-wash job as good as has been executed in this case. It is unbelievable to me that such crimes can be gotten away with in this country."

## OBSTRUCTION OF JUSTICE BY CONGRESS

The May and June 1989 edition of *Freedom* magazine said, "Two congressional subcommittees and the U.S. Customs Service are investigating secret activities around the quiet mountain town of Mena, Arkansas, including alleged drug running and arms smuggling." Congressional testimony proving the existence of government-related drug trafficking is routinely kept from the American people, despite knowledge of the great harm being inflicted by the criminal activities, and the evidence of a secret and destructive element that has taken over key segments of the United States government.

Hundreds of insiders, including former CIA, DEA and other deep-cover operatives, have testified to Congress for years about these drug activities, and this testimony, and the crimes they clearly prove, have been kept from the public. This coverup, this obstruction of justice, has permitted great harm to be inflicted upon the United States and the American people. At this stage, most of the media, most of Congress, definitely those in control of the Justice Department and other government agencies and branches of government that are implicated through coverups, have a vested interest in blocking the American public from finding out about these unprecedented crimes.

Under federal criminal statutes, these coverup activities have made members of Congress, the media, and others, co-conspirators in the crimes and treasonous activities.

## THREATS TO REPORTERS BY THEIR EDITORS

I had repeatedly learned about the threats made against reporters not to report these criminal activities. This serious problem was written about in the May-June 1989 edition of *Freedom* magazine as it related to investigative television reporter Theresa Dickie and another reporter, who had investigated the Mena drug activities. The article stated:

*In 1987, reporter Theresa Dickie put together a series of television news segments probing airport operations. According to Dickie, she received a phone call from Joe Evans, Fred Hampton's partner at Rich Mountain Aviation, who threatened her if story was not accurate, she "would damn well regret it." After the third segment of "The Mena Connection" aired, Dickie said she was instructed that it was to be her last. Her news director called her in and said bluntly, "There will be no more calls to Mena, Arkansas, or you will be out of a job."*

*Another media source felt he could not comment because of duress he had experienced earlier while investigating drug smuggling around Mena. "I'll be out of a job if my employer knows I even talked to you guys," was all that he would say.*

**BRITISH INVESTIGATION**

An investigation into drug trafficking was conducted by a British law commission headed by Lord Louis Blom-Cooper, which then conducted a year of hearings. The *London Times* referred to the commission's report as "a scorcher," which found:

* The use of Antigua by the Mossad for drug trafficking and for training and arming the private armies of Colombia's drug barons.

* Lying by CIA officials to the White House, claiming that the Israeli operations in Antigua were to train rebel forces to oust Panama's Manuel Noriega.

* Mossad's training of hundreds of Colombians into killers for assassination purposes.

* A longstanding practice by U.S. authorities to cover for the crimes of the Mossad group, which supported my findings and as described by my CIA and DEA sources.

* Exposed the role played by Israeli Major General Pinchas Shachar in the arms and drug operations. Shachar was the official representative for Israel Military Industries in the United States, with special access to the Pentagon and other guarded U.S. military installations. According to reports, CIA Director William Sessions wanted the British report entered into Shachar's file and to suspend his special privileges. Attorney General William Barr rejected the recommendation, keeping the American public in the dark about this part of the epidemic drug trafficking. The article described how the Bush White House sought to ignore the report, just as the many other reports have been hidden from the American public. The U.S. media became accomplices in the coverup.

Justice Department officials referred inquiries to the State Department, claiming it was a foreign affair matter, and the State Department referred inquiries to the Justice Department, claiming it was a criminal matter.

This fact is difficult for the average American to comprehend, especially in light of the media coverup of the activities. Few Americans can believe that the people in control of the CIA, DEA, and other intelligence agencies, would commit these serious crimes and inflict such great harm upon the American people. It also takes the concurrent coverup by many others in the three branches of the federal government to make such a vast operation possible. These include the attorney general, the Department of Justice, the Treasury Department, Customs, Drug Enforcement Administration, and many others.

Sham drug busts occasionally occur to give the public the impression that drug enforcement agencies are carrying out their drug-interdiction responsibilities. One sham drug bust occurred in Miami in the early 1980s to justify hiring more federal personnel, and to reflect favorably on the newly appointed drug czar, Vice President George Bush. Another huge drug bust was set up in the Los Angeles area in 1989, at Sylmar, in which twenty tons of cocaine were seized. The purpose of this drug bust was two-fold. One was for public relations, indicating to the American public that the huge amount of money and taking of constitutional rights were justified. The second purpose was to reduce the amount of drugs in circulation. The drug prices were plunging due to an oversupply, restricting the CIA's income from its drug trade.

Some drug busts are made to eliminate competition from drug traffickers not connected with the intelligence agencies. Another reason is to bust a CIA drug trafficker who may be getting out of line or who knows too much.

**WASHINGTON POST COVERUP**

A *Nexus* magazine article (April-May 1995) described how *Washington Post* investigative reporters discovered massive drug trafficking through Mena, Arkansas, how the story was typeset and scheduled to run in the *Sunday Outlook* section on January 29, 1995, and the killing of the multiple-page story. The article was written by Dr. Roger Morris and Sally Denton, veteran investigators with established reputations. The *Nexus* article stated:

> *Morris worked for the National Security Council staff at the White House during the Johnson and Nixon Administrations. He has taught at Harvard and has written a series of acclaimed books on foreign policy. Denton is the former head of news agency UPI's special investigative unit, and is the author of* The Bluegrass Conspiracy *which exposed the involvement of Kentucky political and law enforcement figures in an international arms and drug smuggling ring.... The broad picture is not new to readers of* The Sunday Telegraph *[London], which published a story making some of the same points on 9th October last year.* The Wall Street Journal *has also done original reporting on the subject.*
>
> *A copy of the article passed to* The Sunday Telegraph*...appears to be absolutely explosive. Based on an archive of more than 2,000 documents, it says that western Arkansas was a center of international drug-smuggling in the early 1980s, perhaps even the headquarters of the biggest drug-trafficking operation in history....The activities were mixed up with a US intelligence operation at the Mena airport in Arkansas that was smuggling weapons to the Nicaraguan Contras.*
>
> *The article makes clear that the alleged scandal is not confined to the activities of the Arkansas political machine and Mr. Clinton. It embraces the highest levels of the federal government over several years.*

These are only a small fraction of the newspaper articles dealing with coverups, obstruction of justice, and other offenses by the American broadcast and print media.

**DEEP-COVER ASSET TOSH PLUMLEE**

Another source providing me confidential insider information about the role of U.S. agencies smuggling drugs into the United States through Mexico and other countries was a former deep-cover military and CIA asset from 1956 to 1987, William Robert "Tosh" Plumlee. Among the many government operations in which he was involved while connected to military and CIA intelligence was fighting alongside Fidel Castro's rebel forces in Cuba, flying aircraft in Southeast Asia for Air America and other operations, and flying arms to Central America and drugs on the return trips, all under orders from his government handlers.

Ironically, Plumlee had worked for the same airline as I had in 1950, Pioneer Airlines, and worked at Redbird Airport in Dallas, where I worked as a ground and flight instructor in instrument and Airline Transport Pilot courses. Tosh had flown and/or had contacts with key people in the Contra and drug operations, including Bill Cooper (captain of the C-123 plane shot down over Nicaragua, that exposed the illegal Contra supply operation leading to the Iran-Contra affair).

## OPERATION WHALE WATCH AND OPERATION WATCHTOWER

Plumlee confirmed the existence of Operation Whale Watch and Operation Watchtower, drug smuggling operations involving the CIA, U.S. military, National Security Council, and others. He described his drug flights from Central America to the United States for the CIA, with stops at places he marked on the maps. He described in great detail the close cooperation between Mexican and U.S. government personnel in the drug smuggling into the United States. He described a ranch, heavily protected by Mexican police, that was used for drug smuggling.

He described one of the drug corridors running the length of the Baja Peninsula, with refueling stops, including an airstrip immediately north of Cabo San Lucas. He described another common drug route that he flew. Starting in Panama, he made stops at Santa Helene in Costa Rica; Puerto Escondido in Southern Mexico; up through Baja and then to Mexicali. He delivered the drugs to airfields throughout the Southwest. He described Borrego Desert airstrips and a location near Humboldt Mountain in Arizona where drugs would be pushed out of the aircraft. He described another airstrip near Buckskin Mountain close to the Colorado River, and at abandoned mines between Parker and Havasu City, Arizona.

In the 1960s he flew missions evacuating defecting Russian missile technicians out of Cuba; trained Cuban pilots in Nicaragua and Happy Valley, prior to the Bay of Pigs fiasco. He flew in Southeast Asia, in Laos and Cambodia, in 1967, about the time of the Tet offensive.

## STINGS THAT NEVER HAPPENED

Plumlee said, "We were documenting the loads and the routes and waiting for the big busts. But the busts never seemed to add up to the amount of cocaine we were bringing in." He said that many of the men in the black crews with whom he worked felt extremely uneasy about the illegality of the drug shipments. They occasionally talked of exposing the drug trafficking as a group, and complained to their DEA and CIA contacts. They were told, "You've got to keep the big picture in mind, or you might blow a major sting operation." The pilots were given the line by their handlers that the drugs were for undercover operations to catch drug traffickers.

Plumlee said that the DEA, CIA and FBI were spying on each other's covert deals, and occasionally busted each other's operatives. He described landing a DC-3 loaded with over 1200 pounds of cocaine in Scottsdale, Arizona, where he was to meet an FBI contact, who failed to meet him. Plumlee then called the FBI, trying to contact the agent. Plumlee said, "The FBI thought I was some kind of nut." That trip had started from an airfield called "The Farm," near McAllen, Texas. His instructions were to deliver the arms to the Contras, and then return with a load of drugs.

**APPLES, PEARS, AND BANANAS**

Plumlee described some of the code words used in radio and other communications. "Apples" was the code word for small arms and ammunition. "Oranges" referred to artillery, C-4 explosives, and primer cords. "Pears" referred to electronics. "Bananas" referred to personnel. Reporting over the radio, "Bananas are delivered," would refer to, for instance, a government dignitary deposited on the ground.

"Code 6" referred to the flyway through Central Mexico, across the U.S. border at Piedres Negras, and into the Big Bend region of Texas. "Code 7" referred to the air route along the Baja Peninsula, through San Felipe and Mexicali, to drop points in the Anza-Borrego Desert, Twenty Nine Palms, or the former Patton bombing range east of the Salton Sea.

Plumlee sent me a map containing the San Felipe phone number of a major drug trafficker at the Delgado Ranch, Luis Carlos Quintero Cruz. Plumlee was part of a major drug deal in 1986 involving Quintero that was related to the Contras.

Some of the data Plumlee conveyed to me corroborated what Basil Abbott and other sources had described to me for the past several years, including the drug operations in the Bluefields area of Nicaragua.

**ARKANSAS DRUG DROPS**

Plumlee described the air drops of cocaine-containing bags in the areas around Russellville and Mena in Arkansas, mostly in national forest areas, and the subsequent pickup by helicopters. He described how he was involved in several of the helicopter pickups. He said that the aircraft would go north from the Bayou Buff area, to Mena, and also up to Antlers, Oklahoma. Most of these drops would be at night, with daytime pickups by helicopters.

He described how helicopters would pick up the drug drops in daylight, with some company authorized to pick up blue colored drug-laden bags, and another company pick up a different color. One of the helicopter companies that he mentioned was American Services.

Plumlee said that he knew of about 125 pilots flying drugs for the CIA, the DEA, and the FBI, some of whom would infiltrate other government groups to determine what they were doing. Occasionally, one government agency would arrest a pilot flying for another government agency. The agency behind the arrested pilot might either call and obtain the pilot's release, or simply sacrifice the pilot and disavow any relationship. The pilot then goes to prison, sometimes for life.

**METHOD OF PAYMENT**

He described how CIA assets get paid, either by check from the CIA proprietary or front companies, with which they operate under cover, or by cash. He said that his checks or money usually came from military intelligence sources, from Sitco, and sometimes regular military pay. He said to this day he still has not received a military discharge.

**ASSOCIATION WITH THE FAMOUS BARRY SEAL**

Plumlee described his role in Operation Grasshopper, a top secret military operation in which famous drug trafficker Barry Seal was a part. Another operation in which he was involved was code named "AMSOG." Seal was also a part of that operation.

Plumlee described the government's double-cross of Seal which led to Seal's assassination, the intent being to keep Seal from testifying about the government's drug and money laundering activities. He said that Seal was a military operative in the early days of AMSOG, a joint operation involving Mexican and American government personnel. It was involved in drug trafficking.

Plumlee described an incident in Mexico where a prisoner, seeking to give him and his DEA agents information about the killing of an American pilot by a Mexican drug lord, was then killed by Mexican guards.

In the early 1970s Plumlee was attached to an operation in Miami, Florida called Jay Emway, which involved assassination attempts upon Fidel Castro. Plumlee was involved in black cover operations with the Pentagon while also working with the CIA. He became a CIA contract pilot, taking orders out of the Pentagon, and also worked through the staff of the National Security Council.

Plumlee worked in the CIA's Jim Wave operation, which was another CIA assassination scheme to assassinate Castro.

He worked for various CIA proprietary or front companies, including Riddle Airlines, the Dodge Corporation, Inter-Mountain Aviation, Evergreen Helicopters,[451] Act Technology, Air America, CDG American Services, In-Air, and other companies that he couldn't remember.

As standard CIA procedures, he was given different CIA aliases when working in different undercover operations. These aliases included Buck Pierson, James Plumlee, James H. Rawlings, William H. Pierson, Juan Carbello, James H. Rawlings, and some that he couldn't remember.

He flew many black operations,[452] including flying arms to Central America and drugs into the United States, being advised that these activities were in the national interest. He described the heavy involvement of the military, the Pentagon, the staff of the National Security Council, in these activities. He described how the military and intelligence groups worked with Mafia people, casino-associated crime groups. He described assassination attempts on Dominican dictator Rafael Trujillo, Fidel Castro, kidnapping people in foreign countries, He described how these illegal operations were given the pious-sounding name of national security, the same label used to support secrecy on subversive and

---

451 Ironically, Evergreen Helicopters crews would occasionally stay at a motel that I owned in Yuba City, California, and park their large helicopter in a vacant space behind the motel during the 1970s.

452 Black operations are set up by an entity within the CIA to carry out a sensitive operation. They can be assassinations of foreign leaders or other people, a support operation, anything for which the CIA can't get legal approval to do, which are against the law, and which they don't want to be responsible in the event the cover is blown. They often financially benefit the parties participating in them.

criminal activities against the United States.

Plumlee described how one of the Contra commanders on the Southern Front, Eden Pastora, also known as Commander Zero, refused to engage in drug trafficking as the other Contras did. The CIA then tried to assassinate Pastora during a media conference held at La Penca, Costa Rica, during which Pastora was expected to expose the CIA-DEA drug trafficking.

**PRESIDENTIAL SPIN-DOCTORS**

The Reagan and Bush administrations were accusing the Sandinistas of drug trafficking, seeking public and congressional support for the war against this third-world country. But Plumlee described (as others have done) how he discovered that it was the Contras, supported by the United States, who were heavily involved in drug trafficking. Actually, other sources who flew arms to Central America said they delivered arms to both the Contras and Sandinistas, and that both sides paid with drugs.

**U.S.-MEXICAN GOVERNMENT INVOLVEMENT IN DRUG SMUGGLING INTO THE UNITED STATES**

Plumlee described the heavy amount of arms trafficking from the United States into Mexico and then to El Salvador, and the drug trafficking on return flights. He described what another deep-cover source had told me, that many of the arms came out of Lijitas, Texas, at the Mexican border.

**SECRETS CODES TO PREVENT INTERDICTION**

As other sources said to me, Plumlee described how the military gave him contact codes to get back into the country without being intercepted. Referring to the secret codes given to him that halted drug interdiction flights, Plumlee stated, "I have seen interdiction planes turn away after we squawked our transponders, and let us into the country, not molested, and not have Customs waiting for us when we land."

At a certain geographical point upon entering U.S. airspace, the pilot would call a particular ground station from the air and say, for instance, Bravo One, Bravo One, after which the ground station would answer, "Okay Bravo One, we have a lock." The pilot would then hit the squelch button on a preset transponder code, and if the code was correct, there would be no interdiction and Customs would not be waiting the plane's arrival.

**STEALING ARMS FROM U.S. ARMORIES**

Plumlee described the stealing of guns and ammunition from National Guard arsenals throughout the United States, which was then used to supply the Cuban rebels, the Contras, the Mexicans in Chiapus, Mexico, and other Third World countries. The purpose being to destabilize other countries or overthrow a particular government. Private arms merchants, working with the CIA, Department of Defense, and other Pentagon operations, obtain the documentation necessary to move the arms out of the United States.

He made it clear that the National Security staff, not necessarily the National Security Council, knew about the arms and drug trafficking.

**RISKS OF WORKING UNDERCOVER FOR THE U.S. GOVERNMENT**

Anyone involved in undercover work for any of the government agencies is a disposable asset. The government can fraudulently charge the person with a crime and sentence the person to prison for a long prison term; the government can discredit the person; can seize the person's life's assets, and the government can kill the person.

**U.S. TACTIC TO KEEP THE SECRETS**

Speaking about how people in control of government agencies keep the government drug trafficking from the American people, Plumlee said:

> *We've lost a lot of people that's been killed or assassinated or discredited because for whatever reasons, they were going to blow the whistle on current operations they were involved with.*

When asked if government personnel would kill an operative that was getting ready to divulge a secret operation, Plumlee replied:

> *Elements within the agencies that are involved would definitely put hit men out, if it was going to jeopardize their on-going operation. Independent operatives within the agency sometimes take it upon themselves to protect the operation, and also to protect their profit margins.*

Plumlee discovered that the unlawful arms shipments and drug trafficking into the United States involved the CIA and other government entities, and even the National Security Council and the White House.

**DECODING DEVICES GIVEN TO DRUG CARTELS**

He described how the drug cartels had sophisticated decoding devices that decoded DEA and CIA messages, and that the cartel decoded a message showing that one of the traffickers, named Rodriguez, had given testimony to the DEA. The cartel then beheaded the informer.

Plumlee brought out that different agencies would file charges on people working for other agencies, so that they could show greater results and support their request for higher funding.

**EXPOSING THE CRIMES TO CONGRESS**

After Plumlee decided that the drug operations were not lawful undercover operations, but rather criminal in nature, he contacted members of Congress and the media, expecting, as I did in the past, that they would exercise their duty and receive information, and use it in such a way that the crimes would be halted.

Plumlee testified under oath to several House and Senate committees, including the Senate Foreign Relations Committee. He described to them in detail the CIA and DEA drug trafficking into the United States through Mexico and other countries. He testified to the close cooperation between Mexican and U.S. officials in the drug smuggling operation. He described how witnesses who were suspected of exposing the U.S. involvement in drug smuggling were assassinated.

**THE USUAL CONGRESSIONAL OBSTRUCTION OF JUSTICE**

In 1983, several years before the Contra scandal erupted in the U.S. media, precipitated by the shooting down of the "Hasenfus" flight, Plumlee met several times with Senator Gary Hart's aide, Bill Holden, giving details, maps, and other evidence of the government's involvement in drug trafficking. The evidence included details, documentation, CIA maps, field maps, coded flyways, names, military code operations, that left no doubt that these activities did exist. This information was passed on to various congressional committees, none of whom allowed the American public to know about it.

Senator Hart conveyed the information to Senator John Kerry (D-MA), chairman of the Subcommittee on Terrorism, Narcotics and International Communications. Several of my other informants who were an active part of the arms and drug trafficking also contacted Senator Kerry, among others.

In a February 14, 1991, letter to Senator John Kerry, Senator Hart stated:

> *Mr. Plumlee raised several issues including that covert U.S. intelligence agencies were directly involved in the smuggling and distribution of drugs ...He provided my staff with detailed maps and names of alleged covert landing strips in Mexico, Costa Rica, Louisiana, Arizona, Florida, and California where he alleged aircraft cargoes of drugs were off-loaded and replaced with Contra military supplies. He also stated that these operations were not CIA operations but rather under the direction of the White House, Pentagon and NSC personnel.*
>
> *My staff brought these allegations to the attention of the Senate Armed Services Committee and the Senate Intelligence Committee at the time, but no action was initiated by either committee.*

In 1991, journalist Art Goodtimes of the *Telluride Times-Journal* wrote a January 13, 1991, letter to Senator John Kerry, offering to provide maps, data, testimony of former CIA agent Tosh Plumlee. The letter advised that Plumlee was involved in flying in Central America and had evidence of the U.S. government's involvement in illegal drug trafficking through Mexico, El Salvador and Panama. The letter described Plumlee's evidence of:

> *Government's involvement with illegal drug operations, infiltrated by military undercover operatives...Plumlee's intent to get a federal investigation into the illegal covert activities instigated by various agencies of our government in Central America.*

A DEA report dated February 13, 1990, marked SECRET, stated in part:

> *BUENDIA[453] had allegedly gathered information on...the relationship the CIA had with known narcotic traffickers in Vera Cruz area....the CIA narcotic trafficker situation was very delicate (not to be spoken about)....information on CIA arms smuggling and the connection the CIA had to narcotic traffickers....Shortly thereafter, Eden PASTOR, aka Commander ZERO, who had given BUENDIA information on CIA arms smuggling allegedly suffered a CIA sponsored bomb attack while traveling in Costa Rica....It was later learned that BUENIDA had allegedly obtained information that would expose high ranking members of the PRI political party who were assisting the CIA with arms smuggling and knew of the CIA link to narcotics traffickers.*

Plumlee was only one of many people having direct knowledge of these criminal activities and who gave this information to members of Congress.

## HIDING FOR HIS SAFETY FROM RETALIATION BY U.S. AUTHORITIES

After Plumlee recognized that the CIA and related government entities were

453 Buenida, who was exposing drug trafficking by the CIA and high officials of Mexico's PRI party, was killed by elements of the Mexican DFS security detail.

actually responsible for much of the drugs smuggled into the United States he went underground, hiding from his prior handlers, and settled in a small town near Denver.

In a book Plumlee was writing, he described the government corruption that he saw in Mexico involving both Mexican and U.S. officials, and how both either participated in or did nothing to halt the drug trafficking.

## ANOTHER HOAX UPON THE AMERICAN PEOPLE

Seeking to get public support for the U.S. attempts to undermine the Nicaraguan government, President Ronald Reagan appeared on television holding up a picture allegedly showing Nicaraguan Sandinistas loading drugs onto a plane in Nicaragua. The plane was piloted by Barry Seal. Plumlee, a friend of Seal, said that the picture was not taken in Nicaragua, but in Panama, and misrepresented what was actually taking place. Plumlee said that the C-123 aircraft from which the picture was taken had on it a global positioning instrument wherein a satellite could identify the location of the aircraft, and the record shows that the plane never went to Nicaragua.

Plumlee stated that the camera in the C-123 aircraft was rigged up by the CIA at Rickenboch Field, and that he helped rig the switching arrangement. The idea was to show that the Sandinistas were engaging in drug trafficking, when in fact, as Plumlee stated, it was the Contras, who the US were supporting, who were most active in drug trafficking.

Plumlee described how Barry Seal thought he had an ace-in-the-hole against federal prosecution. This ace-in-the-hole was Seal's threat to report the CIA-DEA-White House involvement in drug trafficking to the media and to Congress. If Seal had known what I found during the past 30 years, that these same checks and balances have been involved in a continual pattern of felony coverups and obstruction of justice, he would have realized these ace-in-the-hole safeguards were meaningless.

Seal had information about the U.S. involvement in drug trafficking, and about the sophisticated military hardware taken out of U.S. Army arsenals at Ilopango in Honduras and shipped to Third World countries. These included sophisticated electronic gear, decoding devices, stinger missiles, some of which ended up in the hands of drug cartels.

However, Seal's threats to make such reports were probably the reason the Justice Department and its control of federal judges resulted in him being charged with felonies, and sentenced to a half-way house where drug cartels who were exposed by Seal would retaliate and assassinate him. In other words, the government officials put a contract out on Seal's life, and made the drug cartels aware of Seal's undercover status.

Seal was assassinated at the half-way house. In this way, the CIA, DEA, the White House, and others, were protected from exposure.

## MEXICAN-US COOPERATION IN DRUG SMUGGLING

Plumlee described the Mexico-CIA relationship in smuggling drugs into the United States, making a mockery of the professed U.S. concern about drug trafficking.

During a taped interview for Jeremiah Films in 1995, Plumlee stated:

*The result of that testimony [to various congressional committees] was that the testimony was sealed, the committee censored it, calling it national security and top secret. A lot of the pilots that flew and testified to the committees had the same problem. Their testimony was not released.... Pilots and other ground crew personnel who made these allegations in 1982 and 1983, were systematically purged from those operations....*

*There was systematic character assassinations of a lot of good people that had done a lot of black operations, one in particular was Barry Seal, who was a personal friend of mine....they discredited people with fake documents....*

*We flew some of the drugs into Air Force bases along the southeast coast, and some in the West and the Southwest...including Homestead Air Force Base...*

*DEA has a very good handle on [the drug trafficking] around Arkansas and Louisiana, but their investigations were completely shut down, stopped in their tracks...and the people who had the information about this operation were suddenly transferred and can't be found now....*

*Starting about 1981, the [CIA-DEA] drug smuggling problem was just really starting to escalate. It didn't really start until the latter part of 1981 and 1982, about the same time that Reagan said we're fighting a drug war, and a lot of money was appropriated for that....From the time that the money was appropriated to start [the drug war] we saw a 400 percent increase in the illegal drugs that were coming into this country.*

Plumlee continued, as he referred to the high-level block, similar to what I ran into during the past 30 years, when concerned people tried to expose the government-related misconduct:

*Someone had the power to intercept that information, to destroy the information and the operatives that had gathered the information. Even to the point of putting them in jail, discrediting their character, by assassinations, assassinating their character by labeling them as "cartel drug runners.*

As I discovered for the past 30 years, that "someone" were people in control of the U.S. Department of Justice. Referring to how easy it would have been to halt the drugs coming into the United States in 1981, Plumlee stated:

*What I'm saying is the cartel could have been shut down in 1981. The information was there from the informants that had infiltrated the cartel.*

Plumlee said that he flew over 6600 pounds of cocaine into the United States in government sanctioned operations.

He said that most of his flights were for military intelligence, a fact little known, as most of the blame goes to the CIA. He said that his military handler was out of a military fort in Arizona.

At the request of his military handlers, in 1988, Plumlee started a pilot recruitment agency in Southern California called Pilot's Aviation Network, for the purpose of pilots to continue flying drugs for the various U.S. agencies.

**SUDDEN REVERSAL OF POSITION**

Plumlee appeared on CBS Television (November 15, 1996) as CBS televised CIA Director John Deutsch's appearance before a high school in the Watts area of Los Angeles. After Deutsch was filmed denying any CIA involvement in drugs, CBS showed Plumlee stating in a 30-second clip that he flew drugs; that he did so under orders of individuals; and that the CIA was not involved. After I saw that segment I contacted Plumlee, since he had earlier gone into great detail describing the CIA involvement in drug smuggling. Plumlee had clearly stated this fact to CBS during over the lasts few years and had provided the TV network with documentation. Plumlee was outraged that CBS took his statements out of context as Plumlee was referring to another drug smuggling operation that was controlled by the National Security Council, the Pentagon, and the White House.

In response, I wrote a November 22, 1996 letter to Bruce Rheins, CBS News producer in Los Angeles, complaining about that coverup and which I experienced for the past 30 years, and advised him that I also had considerable evidence of covert agencies and the military smuggling drugs into the United States, and had over two dozen former agents of the FBI, CIA, DEA ready to testify to these activities.

Rheins responded in a November 25, 1996 letter, stating, "Your name has surfaced quite frequently in my research surrounding the allegations of the CIA's involvement with the distribution of crack cocaine in South Central Los Angeles." He made no attempt to obtain any information from me. On the contrary, I was cancelled from two scheduled CBS television productions after that time.

Plumlee provided me with various documents relating to the drug trafficking by U.S. forces. One report, marked Secret, dated February 13, 1990, stated in part:

> *Apparently 1 month ago (January 1990) XXXXXXXX and AVINA-Batiz were engaged in conversation when AVINA-Batiz told XXXXXXXXX that the flow of drugs into the United States is the best solution to Latin America's problems. The poisoning of American youth is the best answer to the down-trodden Latin American masses in retaliation against the imperialistic actions of the United States.... has learned that the reporter from Vera Cruz (FNU) Valasco, before his death (1985) was allegedly developing information that, using the DFS as cover, the CIA established and maintained clandestine airfields to refuel aircraft loaded with weapons which were destined for Honduras and Nicaragua. Pilots of these aircraft would load up with cocaine in Barranquilla, Colombia and enroute to Miami, Florida, refuel in Mexico at narcotic-trafficker-operated and CIA-maintained airstrips.... Cubans were working a similar type of refuel operations, picking up cocaine in Medellin, Colombia and flying it thru Cuba into Miami.*

An August 10, 1976 FBI report from the special agent in charge of the Phoenix office (62-2116) to the FBI director confirmed that Plumlee had flow a large shipment of arms to Albuquerque, for later flight to San Diego, that their was a 1963 government report on the matter in Phoenix file 26-20103, and that the "file has been destroyed." The FBI report further stated, "This would fit into the time frame PLUMLEE alleged on 8-10-76 wherein he was instructed to leave a plane loaded with arms in New Mexico."

The 1976 date suggests that the United States was clandestinely shipping arms to Mexico, Central or South America, quite possibly in an attempt to overthrow another government.

In another FBI report (000037) it was stated that Plumlee had advised Special Agents of the Cincinnati Division that through one LARRY ALLEN, Miami, Florida, he arranged to fly munitions to the Castro forces in Cuba. On or about July 5 he flew a DC-3 airplane from Miami International Airport to an abandoned military airport on Marathon Island in the Florida Keys, where the plane was loaded with arms and ammunition and flew to Cuba, and was paid $900.00 by ALLEN.

The FBI report stated that "it was his desire to establish his credibility concerning his past activities [working for government agencies and] in establishing contact with the FBI in Arizona in the event he should ever become involved in border-line activities." The report stated that Plumlee agreed to provide a written report to the Phoenix FBI office. The report stated that Plumlee was also flying for Regina Airlines and Riddle Airlines.

It was obvious from the FBI's own reports that they knew of the drug trafficking into the United States by the CIA and the military, and that this includes knowledge by the FBI director.

**ROUTINE OVERTHROWING OF GOVERNMENTS**

There were many other similar reports, which indicates that the U.S. armed Castro to overthrow the Batista government, and than after Castro takes over in Cuba, the CIA seeks to overthrow him, duplicating what has been routine operations on a global scale by the CIA and other U.S. covert agencies.

Among the various covert agency handlers mentioned in the reports were Larry Allen, Johnny Smith, Frank Sutter, John Roselli, and John Martino.

Plumlee has a long history of working in covert activities. After joining the army in Dallas, he worked under several case officers with OSS and CIA ties, including Captain Edward G. Seiwell. He received pilot training under the GI Bill At White Rock Airport, after which he worked at Red Bird Airport south of Dallas, becoming involved with several CIA-front companies. (I worked at Red Bird Airport from 1949 to 1951 in the period between leaving the Navy and flying for the airlines).

He was sent to the Miami area where he became involved in covert operations in Cuba, the Caribbean and Central America. Most of this time he flew guns and ammunition for various factions in half a dozen countries. Plumlee said he was driven by the adventure and the paychecks. He explained that in his covert operations he had to keep other federal agencies from knowing about the clandestine and usually illegal operations.

He was one of a handful of Norteamericans fighting to overthrow Batista and install Fidel Castro. He described how covert activities have the ring of unreality to the public because of their lack of knowledge about the activities. Those who work the 8 to 5 shift cannot comprehend what goes on in covert operations.

Plumlee tried to leave covert operations after a tour in Vietnam, but as so often happens, his handlers kept calling him for other operations. He wrote:

*It was in Mexico where I saw the widespread government corruption on both sides of the border. Someone in Washington was turning a blind eye toward drug shipments from Colombia being smuggled through Mexico and into the United States. It was obvious, our intelligence information was being tampered with at the highest level. Millions of dollars, dirty drug money, was being routed through Panama by the cartel, some of it to be used to influence the upcoming presidential election. Some of the illegal cargoes were flow and transported by other CIA operatives and military personnel holding civilian status, thus covering their CIA-Military affiliations from public view.*

Plumlee described the operation known as Operation Grasshopper, which was a top secret military operation, and involved such notable drug traffickers as Barry Seal. He described the protection of the government's involvement in drug trafficking by other government agencies, including the American-Mexican Special Operations Group (AMSOG) whose function was to block drug trafficking. He said that Barry Seal was an operative in this group in its early days.

Plumlee described the brutal murder of a former Air America pilot in Quedo Loco Lobo, near Oaxaca in Southwestern Mexico by a Mexican named Pepe Suequez. Plumlee described how the informant describing the killing of the American pilot, Maurice Louis Gonzales, was horribly mutilated and left to die in a Mexican prison for informing American authorities of what had happened.

**MANY OTHER SOURCES PROVIDED CORROBORATION OF THESE GOVERNMENT-RELATED DRUG SMUGGLING ACTIVITIES**

Many deep-cover government and other sources, other than those named in these pages, provided me with overwhelming evidence of drug trafficking by government officials and other employees. There is not the slightest doubt in my mind that these activities are occurring.

Most of the American people are totally uninformed on these subversive and criminal activities, or the coverups by Justice Department employees, federal judges, members of Congress, and most of the mainstream media.

In his book, *Called to Serve*, Colonel James "Bo" Gritz described his several meetings in May 1987 with Khun Sa, the head of the largest heroin-producing region in Southeast Asia. Gritz had been on a team mission (LAZARUS) trying to locate missing prisoners of war when he found evidence of massive heroin production being purchased by U.S. personnel.

**KHUN SA AND U.S. DRUG PIPELINE**

Khun Sa described to Gritz how he sought U.S. help in replacing the heroin crop with another salable commodity and how this offer was refused. He described how heroin production in the Golden Triangle area shot up from 40 tons in the early 1950s to 700 tons in the early 1960s. During the first set of meetings, Khun Sa said to Gritz that he might consider telling who his largest past U.S. customers were for the heroin, but would not disclose the present customers.

During the second set of meetings occurring in mid-1987, Khun Sa brought his aides together for a meeting with Gritz, at which time the group provided Gritz specific information on who in the United States were his main customers for heroin. Gritz wrote in his book that these U.S. customers were:

* Theodore Shackley (who was formerly deputy director for covert operations in the CIA). Shackley was identified to me by many of my deep-cover sources as being actively involved in drug trafficking.

* Richard Armitage, also CIA, later holding the key position of Assistant Secretary of Defense in the United States. (He also handled much of the drug-money laundering for Khan Sa's through Armitage's connections with the Nugan Hand Bank.) In his defense department position, Armitage was responsible for locating missing POWs. But if these POWs were found and returned to the United States, their "hero" status would make whatever they had to say meaningful. And they could be expected to describe the U.S. involvement in drug trafficking, very possibly the most explosive and subversive activity ever exposed in the United States of America.

* Daniel Arnold, also CIA, handled the arms and drug sales formerly handled by Armitage. He served as CIA station chief in Thailand.

* Jerry Daniels, a CIA agent, replacing Armitage when Armitage returned to the United States.

* Santos Trafficante, head of one of the many criminal cartels with which the CIA had been doing business for decades.

Gritz's trip to visit Khun Sa was known to Justice Department officials, who sought to have him arrested, but Gritz left the United States before this could be accomplished.

**COSTA RICA REPORT ON U.S. ARMS & DRUG TRAFFICKING**

An 80-page report by the Costa Rican government, dated July 20, 1989, officially detailed and documented the U.S. role in drug trafficking in Central and South America. The report, titled, "Special Select Commission Appointed To Investigate Drug Traffic Crimes," was the official legislative assembly report of Costa Rico. Excerpts from the 115 page Spanish report reveal what the mainstream U.S. media kept from the public. It clearly showed that the movement of arms from the United States to Central America was associated with massive shipment of drugs on the return flights.

**ONE OF MANY CIA SOURCES**

Another one of my many deep-cover sources was Gene "Chip" Tatum, describing what he discovered while a helicopter pilot for the U.S. Army and the CIA. Tatum provided me with affidavits, letters, details, and copies of military flight plans showing the names of well-known individuals and records of drug shipments. This evidence showed drug trafficking into the United States from Central and South America, and also within the states.

Tatum joined the U.S. Army in 1971, and was initially assigned to Vietnam. He was later trained as a helicopter pilot. He also became commander of a unit in the ultra-secret operation known as Pegasus.

In the 1980s he flew helicopters in Central and south America, flying medevac helicopters taking Contras and civilians to emergency care centers.

Tatum was command pilot of one of two helicopter flight crews from the 3/498th Medical Company based at Fort Stewart, Georgia that were sent in 1985 to Palmerola Air Base in Honduras. Each crew consisted of a pilot, copilot, medic, and the crew chief. Tatum was part of the medevac mission for Joint Task Force Bravo. Under cover of his army helicopter pilot duties he was instructed to support a covert group of missions under Operation Pegasus.

Initially unknown to Tatum, these assignments included hauling large white coolers, marked medical supplies, from remote jungle sites to landing strips for pickup by fixed-wing aircraft. These coolers were usually transferred to C-123 and C-130 aircraft, flown either by military or private pilots. The coolers were flown to Panama and then the United States.

Once, during a hard landing, one of the coolers broke open, and while taping the coolers shut he discovered that instead of the contents being medical supplies they were filled with bags containing cocaine. He subsequently discovered that these falsely marked coolers were frequently placed on board his helicopters.

Tatum had frequent contact with Oliver North while North was assigned to the White House's National Security Council and William Barr, who later became attorney general of the United States, in control of the U.S. Department of Justice.

While under orders of the National Security Council (NSC) and the CIA and working under cover as a U.S. Army helicopter pilot he was instructed to infiltrate the 3/498th Medical Company and pose as a medevac pilot. In this capacity he flew wounded personnel to medical stations. But priority was given to CIA and NSC assignments over the carrying of wounded personnel.

While at Palmerola Air Base in Honduras, Tatum flew helicopter flights to Illapongo, El Salvador, where Corporate Air Service, a CIA-owned aviation company was based, and to various Contra camps in Honduras and Nicaragua. Although the reason for his assignment to the Medevac unit was to move wounded personnel to treatment centers, he discovered that the one common denominator on all Pegasus missions was the movement of large white coolers in and out of Contra camps.

On one flight out of Palmerola (MCHG) he carried as passengers pilots Bill Cooper and Buzz Sawyer, who would later die while flying over Nicaragua after being hit by a surface to air missile. The only survivor of that flight, Eugene Hasenfus, was the person responsible for kicking military cargo out of the back of the aircraft. He survived because he carried a parachute, and jumped out of the aircraft before it crashed. His subsequent capture and interrogation precipitated the exposure of the Iran-Contra affair.

**DESCRIBING ONE OF HIS OPERATIONS**

On one of his flights to El Ocotal in Costa Rica, Tatum carried Felix Rodriguez (also known as Max Gomes), a close associate of Vice President George Bush in the Contra operation; General Gustavo Alverez of Honduras; and Joseph Fernandez, another CIA agent. Upon landing at Ojo de Agua-El Tamborcita they were joined by Michael Harari, a former (or present) Mossad agent and security advisor to General Manuel Noriega of Panama; by William Barr (attorney at the CIA's Southern Air Transport located at Miami at that time and before he became attorney general of the United States), and Barry Seal. Seal had flown Noriega and Harari to the meeting in his Learjet aircraft (tail number N13SN).

**PURPOSE OF THE MEETING**

The purpose of the meeting was to determine where over $100 million in drug money had disappeared on the three routes from Panama to Colorado, Ohio, and Arkansas. This theft was financially draining the operation known as the "Enterprise."[454] By comparing computerized records, Tatum said that it was determined that the loss of money occurred on the route from Panama to Arkansas.

Tatum said that at the end of the meeting he went with Fernandez to the helicopter where a portable secure phone was set up to communicate with Washington by satellite link. The first call was made by Fernandez to Oliver North, informing North that the money loss was occurring on the Panama to Arkansas route, and "that means either Seal, Clinton or Noriega."

Fifteen minutes later, the portable phone rang, and Vice President George Bush was on the line, talking to William Barr. Barr said at one point, referring to the missing funds, "I would propose that no one source would be bold enough to siphon out that much money, but it is more plausible that each are siphoning a portion, causing a drastic loss."

Barr told Bush that he and Fernandez were staying in Costa Rica until the following day, after first visiting John Hull's ranch. Barr then handed the phone to Tatum, who was instructed by Bush to be sure that Noriega and Harari boarded Seal's plane and departed, and for Tatum to get the tail number of Seal's plane. Tatum noted that the aircraft number was N13SN

Tatum said that Barr then dialed another number, immediately reaching then governor Bill Clinton. Barr explained the missing money problem to Clinton, explaining that over $100 million of the "Enterprise" monies had disappeared, along the Panama to Arkansas connection. Barr suggested that Clinton investigate at the Arkansas end of the Panama to Arkansas route, and that he and Oliver North would continue investigating the Panama end of the connection, warning that the matter must be resolved or it could lead to "big problems."

The SATCOM phone equipment was then stowed on the helicopter, and Tatum waited for Noriega and Harari to leave in the Learjet piloted by Barry Seal. Tatum then flew his passengers to Tegucigalpa, the capital of Honduras. A copy of the flight plan that Tatum filed, dated March 25, 1985, follows. Tatum wrote on the back of the flight plan:

> *Meeting with Gen Noriega/SATCOM with North and Gov of AK concerning missing monies. Dropped off Noriega at airport in S.D. Met Barry Seal in 13SN. Seal took Gen Noriega & Harari.*

Several days later, Tatum flew from Tela, Honduras to La Cieba, picking up Oliver North, Felix Rodriguez, General Alverez of Honduras, and Amiram Nir. They then flew into several villages on the Nicaragua/Honduras border to determine their suitability for cargo drops by CH-47s the following month.

**EXAMINING COCAINE PLANTS**

Tatum then flew the group to Santa Anna, Honduras, meeting with Enrique Bermudez and other Contra leaders, and visited a cocaine processing facility. Tatum described the strong smell of jet fuel and acetone, and the large fuel pods that had the tops stripped off of them and in which were fuel and leaves. Tatum repeated what North said: "One more year of this and we'll all retire," adding, "If we can keep those Arkansas hicks in line, that is," referring to Barry Seal

---

454 The "Enterprise" was revealed in the Iran-Contra investigations by congress and Independent Prosecutor Walsh, and included as its head Oliver North, Weinberger, .....

and Governor Clinton.

While General Alvaraz went with the Contra leader to discuss logistics, North, Rodriguez, and Ami Nir, continued through the wooden building, inspecting the cocaine. Tatum repeated what North said: "Bush is very concerned about those missing monies. I think he's going to have Jeb arrange something out of Colombia."

As Tatum listened to these conversations, he remembered the army officers' remarks in Ojo de Agua when Tatum complained about the carrying of drugs: "Tell no one. There's no one big enough in your chain of command." Having heard North discuss the involvement in the drug activities of Vice President Bush and Governor Clinton, Tatum recognized what the army officer had previously stated to him.

Tatum then flew back to La Cieba and then to Tela, returning the following day to home base at Palmarola, where Tatum put a few notes on the back of the flight plan filed with base operations. The note read:

*ROM ACM/Rodriguez for night. USN to WASPAM/Santa Anna/Lemez—No problems recon successful—Rodriguez, North, Nir, Dr. Gus. Others (4).*

During another trip, Tatum picked up at Dustoff Operations six coolers marked "medical supplies," which contained cocaine, and flew them to an airstrip at Trijillo, where they were given to a C-130 crew bound for Panama. Tatum asked the pilot, "Who gets these?" The pilot looked at the manifest and said that a Dr. Harari would be called on arrival." The alleged doctor was none other than Mossad operator Michael Harari, and the phony Doctor title went along with the phony medical supply labels on the coolers.

Another military flight plan showed Tatum making a flight on April 9, 1985, into a small village forty kilometers east north east of Ocotal in Nicaragua. Tatum met Felix Rodriguez and Contra leader Enrique Bermudez, and the three of them inspected a cocaine processing facility located in a large tent, containing all American equipment. Inside were several women packaging cocaine.

Four 110-quart white coolers, marked "medical supplies," were then put on board Tatum's helicopter for subsequent loading onto a civilian C-123 at San Lorenzo. Tatum then flew back to his home base, at which time he wrote on the back of the flight plan details of the cocaine lab inspection.

### WHITE HOUSE AND CIA COCAINE OPERATION

During a flight from Palmerola to El Paraiso, Honduras, his passengers told Tatum that they worked for Corporate Air Services out of Ilopango Air Base in El Salvador and that they were meeting with Contra leaders to coordinate air drops to various Contra camps. When the meeting was over, Tatum was given a white cooler marked "vaccine," weighing over 200 pounds, and instructed to deliver the cooler to a C-130 at Las Mesa airport in San Pedro Sula, Honduras. The cooler was dropped while being taken from the helicopter, and Tatum used aviation tape to reseal it. After removing the old tape and looking inside the cooler, he discovered that the contents consisted of what appeared to be over 100 bags containing a white powdery substance; cocaine. The resealed cooler containing the cocaine was then put on a C-130 that was departing for Panama.

### PUBLIC FUNDED MEDICAL UNITS USED FOR SMUGGLING DRUGS

This discovery reminded Tatum of the white coolers that he had been asked to deliver by helicopter to Arkansas' Mena Airport while assigned to Special Operations at Ft. Campbell in Kentucky in 1983 and 1984. He was ordered several times to deliver white coolers marked medical supplies to Little Rock Air Force base and to Mena Airport. The medevac unit at Ft. Campbell, the 324th Medical Battalion, was a supporting unit for Task Force 160, a Special Operations Unit under CIA control. Flight crews of the 324th Medical Battalion rotated in and out of Honduras on tours that lasted four months. That's how Tatum came to be assigned to Central America and discover the drug smuggling operation in Central America and Arkansas.

Tatum described people that met his helicopter arrival at Mena Airport. He described meeting Dan Lasater, who was usually accompanied by a plain-clothes policeman who produced a badge and identification showing him to be Raymond "Buddy" Young. Tatum said that Young showed up in Honduras posing as a member of the Arkansas National Guard. Occasionally, Lasater was accompanied at the Mena Airport by Jerry Parks, who helped in the off-loading of the coolers. Jerry Parks operated a security company that had close ties to the Clinton administration in Arkansas.

Some years later, Parks had a falling out with Clinton, and had threatened to expose information about Clinton and the drug activities. This caused him to become one of many people in Arkansas that had sensitive information who was either killed or died under mysterious circumstances.

One of the many military flight plans filed by Tatum dated March 1, 1985 described delivering two white coolers marked "medical supplies" to Dustoff (MEDEVAC) Operations. Felix Rodriguez than ordered Tatum to deliver the coolers to him at Tela, Honduras (LYA). Tatum checked the contents, and found them filled with about 100 kilos of cocaine. As ordered, he delivered the coolers to Rodriguez, who was waiting in front of an old DC-3. Tatum then returned to his home base at Palmerola, and made the following notation on the back of the military flight plan that he had filed with base operations:

*Q/U Two coolers "med supplies." Checked contents—white powder—appr 100 sacks each.*

Rodriguez instructed Tatum to obtain the secret frequencies used by the military at a tactical communications site (TAC) called Skywatch, which was the focal telemetry point of several military satellites in this hemisphere. The military had refused to release this information to the CIA, causing the Agency to contaminate the water supply with an unusually high concentration of chlorine, causing widespread stomach cramps and diarrhea among the soldiers. This required calling for medical personnel to fly to the site and treat the personnel affected by the CIA contamination. While the personnel were being treated, Tatum went into a communication van and copied the frequencies from the equipment in use.

Upon his return to Palmerola that afternoon, Tatum called CIA agent Donald Gregg on a secure telephone line, passing along the frequencies that he had copied. Gregg then instructed Tatum to pass the frequencies to CIA agent Clair George at Langley. Before having the call transferred, Tatum told Gregg of his discovery of cocaine in the coolers. Gregg repeated the false excuse that the coolers were bound for the world courts as evidence against the Sandinistas. Tatum was then transferred to Clair George, who took the information and was advised that he would pass the information to Dewey, referring to Duane (Dewey) Clarridge of the CIA. Tatum then went to Base Operations and noted this information on the back of the on-file flight plan and the mission briefing sheet. Copies of some of these forms are on following pages. On this particular flight Tatum wrote:

*North arranged for water contamination at TAC site—I flew medevac to site and while medic attended—I collected TAC FQCYS for North. Upon departure forced to auto-rotate. Declared emergency-bad torque and cracked tail boom.*

One of many military flight plans filed by Tatum that I examined was a March 5, 1985 flight that carried Amiram Nir, a CIA and Mossad asset; General Gustavo Alverez, a Honduran Army Chief of Staff who often used the alias, Dr. Gus, a Honduran Colonel who was the General's aide. On this mission Tatum flew into six villages listed on the flight plan, picked up soldiers, and took them to El Paraiso, Honduras. At El Paraiso, as they prepared to leave, four large white coolers were put on board the helicopter. Pointing to the coolers, Tatum asked Rodriguez, "Evidence?" Rodriguez responded by patting the cooler with his hands, saying, "You catch on fast."

Tatum landed at San Lorenzo (SNL), Honduras, dropping off Rodriguez and the coolers. Upon return to home base at Palmerola. Tatum wrote on the back of the operation's flight plan, "4 coolers sim to cocaine cooler"

During one flight to Tegucigalpa on March 15, 1985, Tatum met with Barr, Harari, and Buddy Young (head of Governor Bill Clinton's security detail). Barr represented himself as an emissary of Vice President George Bush, who would be arriving soon. Tatum periodically reached Barr by phone at the CIA's Southern Air Transport in Miami, and under the name, Robert Johnson. The purpose of the meeting was to arrange for Vice President Bush's arrival.

The following morning, Young and Harari flew back to Palmerola with Tatum. Because of the high noise level in the helicopter, the passengers, Young and Harari, wore headsets and spoke over the aircraft intercom system to each other, possibly unaware that Tatum could hear their conversation. He was copying this conversation on his knee pad until he ran out of paper. Tatum recorded the conversation:

Young: Arkansas has the capability to manufacture anything in the area of weapons, and if we don't have it, we'll get it.

Harari: How about the government controls?

Young: The governor's on top of it. And if the feds get nosey, we hear about it and make a call. Then they're called off. [As he looked down at the countryside] Why the hell would anyone want to fight for a shit-hole like this?"

Harari: [Shaking his head] What we do has nothing to do with preserving a country's integrity. It's just business, and Third World countries see their destiny as defeating borders and expanding. The more of this mentality we can produce, the greater our wealth. We train and we arm; that's our job. And in return, we get a product far more valuable than the money for a gun. We're paid with product. And we credit top dollar for product. [i.e. drugs.]

Young: [Still looking confused.]

Harari: Look, one gun and 3,000 rounds of ammo is $1,200. A kilo of product [cocaine] is about $1,000. We credit the Contras $1,500 for every kilo. That's top dollar for a kilo of cocaine. It's equivalent to the America K-Mart special; buy four, get one free. On our side, we spend $1,200 for a kilo and sell it for $12,000 to $15,000. Now, that's a profit center. And the market is much greater for the product [cocaine] than for weapons. It's just good business sense. Understand?

Young: Damn! So you guys promote wars and revolutions to provide weapons for drugs. We provide the non-numbered parts to change out and we all win. Damn, that's good!

Harari: It's good when it works. But someone is, how do you say, has his hand in the coffer.

Young: Well, we get our ten percent right off the top and that's plenty. Gofus can make it go a long way.

Harari: Who is Gofus?

Young: Governor Clinton. That's our pet word for him. You know they call the President "Potus" for president of the United States. Well, we call Clinton "Gofus" for governor of the United States. He thinks he is anyhow.

Harari: That's your problem in America. You have no respect for your elected officials. They are more powerful than you think, and have ears everywhere. You should heed my words and be loyal to your leaders. Especially when speaking to persons like me. Your remarks indicate a weakness, something our intelligence analysts look for.

Young: Aw hell, Mike. Everybody knows the Clintons want the White House and will do anything to get it. We know about the cocaine. Hell, we've picked it up before with Lasater when he was worried about going on Little Rock Air Base to get it.

Harari: [Changing the topic, Harari questioned Young about his knowledge of who the players were.]

Young: Clinton thinks he's in charge, but he'll only go as far as Casey [CIA director] allows. Me and my staff, we keep the lid on things, you know: complaints about night flying, Arkansas people are private folks, they don't like a lot of commotion, and Mena just isn't the right place for the operation. It keeps us busy at the shredder, if you know what I mean. Dan's the man [Lasater]. He does magic with the money. Between him and Jack Stevens we don't have to worry a bit. Then we got Parks. If there's a problem, he 's the man. We call him the Archer. That's the code name that Casey and Colby told us to assign to that position. Finis oversees our drop zone. Nash, he's just the boss' yes man. Personally, I think he's a mistake.
Seal and his guys, I like his attitude "and leave the driving to us."

Harari: You like Seal?

Young: Hell, he's the only one I trust; respect is the word.

Harari: Do you see him much?

Young: Hell, yes. We test drive Clinton's rides [cocaine] before we send 'em on, you know. [Laughing and grinding his hips.] Say, how much coke do you recon you can make in a week?

Harari: One camp can produce 400 keys [kilos?] a week. The others are about half that. But that's just our operation here. We have other sources in various parts of the world. Why do you ask?

Young: The Governor wanted to know our capacity.

Harari: Who else is on the team?

Young: Well, hell, I forgot who I told you about.

Harari: [Harari repeated the list from memory.]

Young: OK, there's the manufacturers; hell, these two. [At this point Tatum ran out of paper on his knee board, and didn't recognize the names; but they sounded like Johnson and Johnson.]

Upon landing back at his base, Tatum made a notation on the back of the previously filed flight plan:

*This was a mission to Tegucigalpa. Bush visit/met with Barr & had dinner at German restaurant.*

Tatum was alerted for a flight at 5 a.m. to pick up three wounded soldiers at a Contra camp near Choloteca, Nicaragua, and instructed to pick up two observers on the way at Choloteca: Oliver North and Lt. Col. Navarro. At the Contra camp two of the casualties were loaded. The last casualty had a piece of wood sticking out of a bad wound to the upper left portion of his body. As the medic cleaned the area he found a hole the size of a softball adjacent to the impaled object. As the medic sought to clean the area it caused a clear view of muscle hanging and the inside of the chest cavity. North saw it and fainted. Tatum caught him and popped an ammonia capsule under his nose to revive him. The flight then departed for San Lorenzo, Honduras, where the casualties were unloaded. Back at base, Palmerola, Tatum completed the Mission Brief Back report, writing in part:

*Arrived at SLN—Arrival at the helipad the emergency vehicles were not waiting. There was no answer on Medevac FQCY FM 45.10 or on ..... 49.10. Confusion on ground causing ground time delay of 15 min. Medics' duties were compounded when Mr. North fainted.*

As I looked over the many copies of flight plans that Tatum provided to me, they provided still more evidence of the following:

* Mossad agent Michael Harari was on many of the flights associated with the drug trafficking.

* William Barr, who Bush appointed to be the top law enforcement officer in the United States, U.S. Attorney General, played a key role in the smuggling of drugs into the United States. Tatum's statements about reaching Barr at Southern Air Transport in Miami through the name of Robert Johnson confirmed what Terry Reed, author of the book *Compromise*, had told me and had written. Nothing like having a member of this drug operation appointed Attorney General of the United States in control of the U.S. Department of Justice.

* The drugging of America involved the CIA, the military, the White House through Oliver North, George Bush, and Governor Bill Clinton, among many others.

* That Mena, Arkansas was a key CIA transshipment point for cocaine coming into the United States on return flights from Central America delivering guns to kill people in Nicaragua in President Reagan and President Bush's alleged honorable war against the people of Nicaragua.

At one time, thinking that Oliver North did not know about the cocaine trafficking, upon returning to Palmerola Air Base, Tatum called Washington and advised North of the cocaine discovery. North told him, "The Sandinistas are manufacturing cocaine and selling it to fund the military. It was bound for the world courts as evidence."

Tatum was assigned to fly helicopter flights in Honduras and Nicaragua, working CIA missions, and under orders of Oliver North, CIA operations Amiram Nir and Felix Rodriguez. In carrying out these orders and missions, he associated with William Barr, George Bush, General Manuel Noriega, Mossad agent Michael Harari. The control word for the missions that he flew was Pegasus. This operation was secretly embedded in an Army medical unit (3/498th Medical Company from Fort Riley, Kansas). He said that CIA agent Henry Hyde was responsible for the finances of the unit, including arranging lines of credit.

Gene "Chip" Tatum

**"NEUTRALIZING" OTHERS**

Tatum described how he flew assassination teams to various locations to "neutralize" certain people, including a Mossad agent, an army chief-of-staff of another country (General Alvarez), and president of a Third-World country. He described how Amiram Nir was assassinated by the CIA Archer assassination team that he flew into Morelia, Mexico. Tatum said that Nir was a renegade Mossad agent that the Mossad was pleased to see eliminated. Nir was also scheduled to testify in the Iran-Contra hearings and had first-hand knowledge of the CIA and Mossad drug trafficking.

Tatum said that he fired an air-to-air heat-seeking missile from the Hughes 500 helicopter that he was flying at the Cessna 210 aircraft that had been chartered by Nir. In Tatum's words, "I prepared a SIGLOC on the Baron frequency which we used to track the target. Tatum said the missile exploded below the Cessna, causing it to descend in an out-of-control condition.

Tatum said that he left the operation in 1992 after he was instructed to "neutralize" Ross Perot in whatever manner required. Possibly this plan explains Perot's sudden dropping out of the presidential race. He was warned that no one leaves the operation and that he would pay the consequences. Tatum did leave and eventually Justice Department employees charged him and his wife with a federal offense.

I filed a friend-of-the-court brief on his behalf[455] and included with it an affidavit signed by him which described in general terms the CIA-NSC drug trafficking which he had discovered. The brief informed the court that Tatum had evidence of these federal crimes, that he wanted to provide evidence of these offenses, and that his knowledge of such offenses may have motivated Justice Department employees to charge him with federal offenses.

As usual, the federal judge refused to receive the evidence, despite the mandatory requirement of federal criminal statute, Title 18 USC Section 4.

The following page contains a copy of the March 28, 1985 flight plan with Tatum's notations on the front showing passengers Joe Fernandez, Michael Harari, Felix Rodriguez, General Alvarez. This was the flight in which a determination was sought as to where the drug money was disappearing. Present at the meeting were William Barr and Colonel Manuel Noriega, followed by the Satcom phone call to Oliver North and Governor Bill Clinton.

---

455 Amicus Curiae brief filed in the U.S. District Court in the Middle District of Florida, into action number CR 92-72 CR-T-21(A), under Federal Rule of Civil Procedure 24.

**REQUEST AND AUTHORIZATION FOR TDY TRAVEL OF DOD PERSONNEL**
*(Reference: Joint Travel Regulations)*
Travel Authorized as Indicated in Items 2 through 21.

1. DATE OF REQUEST: 13 June 1985

**REQUEST FOR OFFICIAL TRAVEL**

2. NAME (Last, First, Middle Initial): SEE ATTACHED ROSTER (24 Names)
3. POSITION TITLE AND GRADE OR RATING: SEE ATTACHED ROSTER
4. OFFICIAL STATION: Hunter AAF, GA 31409-5100
5. ORGANIZATIONAL ELEMENT: D CO, 24th Cbt Avn Bn
6. PHONE NO.: 5902
7. TYPE OF ORDERS: TDY - Amendment
8. SECURITY CLEARANCE: See Attached Roster
9. PURPOSE OF TDY: "In support of Joint Task Force-Bravo"
10a. APPROX NO. OF DAYS OF TDY (including travel time)
b. PROCEED O/A (Date)
11. ITINERARY ☐ VARIATION AUTHORIZED

12. MODE OF TRANSPORTATION

| COMMERCIAL | | | | GOVERNMENT | | | PRIVATELY OWNED CONVEYANCE (Check one) |
|---|---|---|---|---|---|---|---|
| RAIL | AIR | BUS | SHIP | AIR | VEHICLE | SHIP | RATE PER MILE: |
| | | | | | | | ☐ MORE ADVANTAGEOUS TO GOVERNMENT |
| ☐ AS DETERMINED BY APPROPRIATE TRANSPORTATION OFFICER (Overseas Travel only) | | | | | | | ☐ MILEAGE REIMBURSEMENT AND PER DIEM LIMITED TO CONSTRUCTIVE COST OF COMMON CARRIER TRANSPORTATION & RELATED PER DIEM AS DETERMINED IN JTR. TRAVEL TIME LIMITED AS INDICATED IN JTR |

13. ☐ PER DIEM AUTHORIZED IN ACCORDANCE WITH JTR.
☐ OTHER RATE OF PER DIEM (Specify)

| 14. ESTIMATED COST | | | | 15. ADVANCE AUTHORIZED |
|---|---|---|---|---|
| PER DIEM | TRAVEL | OTHER | TOTAL | |
| $ | $ | $ 231.00 | $ 231.00 | $ |

16. REMARKS (Use this space for special requirements, leave, superior or 1st-class accommodations, excess baggage, registration fees, etc.)

TO# 2-121 dtd 8 Feb 85 is hereby amended to read: AND TRAVEL ORDER # 2-206

CHANGE: "Chip" Tatum to "Lois" Tatum.
and authorize 300lbs (UP TO) of excess baggage.

17. REQUESTING OFFICIAL (Title and signature): BRENDA J. LONG, SP4, FLT OPS COORD
18. APPROVING OFFICIAL (Title and signature): STUART D. ARTMAN, CPT, AV, BUDGET OFFICER

**AUTHORIZATION**

19. ACCOUNTING CITATION: 2152020 76-2083 P200000.2200 S09-076 APC F403 CN: 202414(A) $231.00

LAUNA G. SEYMORE, PROG ANAL OFFCR, DPT

OFFICIAL

20. ORDER AUTHORIZING OFFICIAL (Title and signature) OR AUTHENTICATION: THERESA L. SPARKS, 2LT, ASST AGC, AG
21. DATE ISSUED: 08 Aug 1985
22. TRAVEL ORDER NUMBER: 8-102

DD FORM 1 JUN 67 1610

Travel authorization for Tatum, further support for his military background.

The following is a declaration that Tatum gave me, which I had intended to file in a friend-of-the-court brief, which partially described his CIA-related activities:

**DECLARATION**

I, Dois Gene Tatum, declare:

I was a helicopter pilot for the United States Army from 1982 to 1986, during which time I flew missions in Central America and also from Ft Campbell, Kentucky.

From 1986 to 1992 I was an agent for the Central Intelligence Agency, operating under a deep-cover assignment.

During this time I witnessed activities involving high-level U.S. personnel that I felt were unlawful, and I reported these activities to my superiors in the U.S. Army and to my handlers in the Central Intelligence Agency, to the National Security Council, and to various individuals, including William Barr, Oliver North, George Bush.

Among these activities were rampant drug smuggling into the United States involving people in control of the Central Intelligence Agency, the Drug Enforcement Administration, the armed forces of the United States, among others.

I have documented some of these activities on military flight plans, showing as passengers on certain flights, the following: William Barr; Buddy Young; Felix Rodriguez; Oliver North; Joe Fernandez; Manuel Noriega, and Mike Harari.

I have visited cocaine laboratories with the above people, who were inspecting the drug smuggling operations in Central America.

I have documented on some of these military flight plans the nature of the cargo being carried in white coolers that were fraudulently marked as "medical supplies," which I accidentally discovered to be cocaine.

During one flight and related meeting, I was present while there were discussions as to where drug money was being siphoned on the Panama to Arkansas run. Present at this meeting were Manuel Noriega; William Barr (associated with CIA proprietary Southern Air Transport and later attorney general of the United States); Joe Fernandez; Mike Harari; General Gustavo Alverez. Participating in this meeting via satellite telephone was Vice President George bush, Oliver North, and William Jefferson Clinton, then governor of Arkansas.

I had reported these illegal operations to my superiors, including William Barr; Oliver North; George Bush; Felix Rodriguez; Joe Fernandez; Don Gregg; Dewey Clarridge.

After I refused to perform a mission that I felt were beyond my willingness to execute, I notified my handlers that I wanted out of the operation, which at that time was known as Operation Pegasus. Their response was to warn me that no one leaves the operation.

I declare under penalty of perjury that the above facts are true and correct to the best of my knowledge and belief. Executed this 15th day of August 1996 in the County of Hillsborough, State of Florida.

Dois Gene Tatum
aka Gene D. Tatum

A pattern of long-term drug trafficking directed by the National Security Council in the Reagan-Bush White House, with CIA and military involvement and other complicity, was revealed by examining the dozens of military flight plans Tatum had given to me. These activities will be explored in depth by Tatum in his book describing the drug activities involving U.S. personnel.

Although Tatum was assigned to a military medical evacuation team, his CIA handlers often diverted his flight to drug-carrying activities, resulting in casualties not being evacuated for medical treatment. This diversion of life-saving helicopter support resulted in the military sending the following message:

(Transcription)

RCV MSG TIME
O4353 0404

J-I 224 K1 11 SIG 3CISG 1S AVN EAC JTF-B MED ELEMENT 549TH MP
ACTION JOINT******TASK***********FORCE***********BRAVO************
235TH SIG J-2 EACAIC RED CROSS BASE OPS CSSE PAO JTF-B FINANCE AFRTS

PTTUZYUW RYEIEOAC 489 154G356 YYYY RYBBDGA
CHR UUUUU
P 132015Z APR 85
FM USCINCSO QUARRY HEIGHTS FH //SCSG//
TO RUEBDHA/COMJTF-BS COMAYAGUA HO //J3/J4/MED ELEMT//
RUEBSAR/CONJTF-11 TEGUCIGALPA HO //J3/J4/MED ELEMT//
RUWTFTA/COMUSFORCARIB KEY WEST FL //J3/MED SECT//
RUCIPFT/CDR 101ST ABNDIV/AASLT/ FT CAMPBELL KY //G3/MED BH/G4/
AFZB-DPT-077INFO RULPAKA/CDR 193RD IKF BDE (FN) FT CLAYTON PN //AFZU-CS/
AFZU-CTF-CDR/AFZU-DPT//
RUUTNFH/CDR USAHSC FT SAM HOUSTON TX //HSOF-SO//
RUCLPNA/CDR USAMEDDAC QUARRY HEIGHTS PM //HSXO-FO//
PUEADWD/DA WASHINGTON DC //DASG-HCO//
CHCGRC/USCINCARRED FT MCPHERSON GA //AFOP[illegible]C/AFMD-OT//
FUCJAAA/USCINCRED MACDILL AFB FL //RCJ3-O?/RCJ3-BF/RC04-MED//
BT
UNCLAS
SUBJ: OPERATIONAL CONTROL OF JTF/TF MEDEVAC A/C IN HONDURAS
A. USCINCSO MSG 1218DDZ DEC 84 SUBJ: MED PLANNING AT III
B. USCINCSO MSG 1513DDZ FEB 85 SUBJ: MED SUPPPORT UT-85
C. PT III PLANNING CONFER MACDILL AFB FL, 27-28 SEPT 84
1. REFERENCES CITED ABOVE RECOMMEND AND IDENTIFY MEDICAL SUPPORT REQUIREMENTS AND PLANNING CONSIDERATIONS FOR JOINT/COMBINED EXERCISES

PAGE 02 RUEOEHA0485 UNCLAS
IN HONDURAS. SPECIFICALLY, RECOMMENDING TO THE JTF PLANNERS AND TO THE CUPPORTING COMMUNITY THE NUMBER, AND IN SOME CASES, THE LOCATION OF MEDEVAC A/C IN-COUNTRY; BASED ON THOROUGH ASSESSMENT OF MEDICAL CAPABILITIES IN-COUNTRY DURING PROJECTED EXERCISE PERIOD.
2. IT HAS BECOME INCREASINGLY EVIDENT DURING THE PAST SIX WEEKS THAT MEDEVAC A/C IN DIRECT SUPPORT OF JTF'S, IN SOME CASES, ARE BEING UTILIZED FOR OTHER THAN MEDEVAC RQUIREMENTS AND ARE BEING CONTROLLED BY OTHER THAN MEDICAL OFFICIALS. ON SEVRAL OCCASIONS THESE PRACTICES HAVE LEFT THE EXERCISE AREA WITHOUT ADEQUATE OR TIMELY MEDEVAC SUPPORT CAPABILITY.

3. DUE TO THESE POTENTIALLY LIFE-THREATENING SITUATIONS, AND WITH THE IMPENDING DEPLOYMENT OF UT 85 MEDICAL ASSETS INTO THIS THEATER. *[USE OF]* ALL MEDEVAC A/C AND CREWS DEPLOYING TO HONDURAS IN SUPPORT OF COMBINED/JOINT TRAINING EXERCISES WILL BE PLACED UNDER THE *[OPERATIONAL CONTROL OF]* JTF BRAVO MEDICAL ELEMENT. THIS WILL ENSURE THAT THE EXERCISE IS ADEQUATELY COVERED AND THAT AIR CREWS IN SUPPORT OF OTHER THAN JTF BRAVO MED ELEMENT'S MEDEVAC SECTION ARE KNOWLEDGEABLE OF THE AOR. HOST NATION FLIGHT REQUIREMENTS AND HEALTH FACILITIES, AND US MEDICAL CAPABILITIES/LOCATIONS IN-THEATER.
4. POC AT SCSG MAJ LEDFORD (A) 282-5803

ROBERT HUNT IN SAN FRANCISCO

## CIRCLE-THE-WAGON REACTION TO SAN JOSE MERCURY DISCLOSURE OF CIA-RELATED DRUG ACTIVITIES

In August 1996 the *San Jose Mercury* newspaper in California ran a three-part series describing the role of CIA assets selling crack cocaine to the blacks in the Los Angeles area. The articles caused a major reaction from various black leaders. This in turn required the mainstream media to address the articles, and major disinformation then followed. The *San Jose Mercury* articles were accurate, but relied upon a small percentage of the sources that I had, none of whom actually flew the drugs into the United States. The mainstream print and broadcast media whose coverups and disinformation allowed the decades of CIA drugging of America to continue, began an intensive spin control to discredit the *San Jose Mercury*'s articles.

The chorus blasting the *San Jose Mercury* articles included the *New York Times*, *Washington Post*, *Los Angeles Times*, *Newsweek*, all of which knew of the overwhelming number of insiders testifying to Congress, the great number of highly detailed and documented books proving that the CIA had engaged in drug smuggling into the United States for decades.

## USING BANKRUPTCY COURT ASSETS TO FINANCE CIA DRUG PURCHASES IN LOS ANGELES

There was far more to the drugging of the blacks than known by the *San Jose Mercury*. Russbacher described to me in 1991 the drugging of the blacks in Los Angeles, and how the CIA used money looted from Ninth Circuit Bankruptcy Courts to finance the purchase of drugs. Russbacher had described how trustee Charles Duck provided some of the funds for CIA drug purchases.

Drugging of blacks was also described to me over a period of years by a former New York City vice-squad detective, Jim Rothstein. He was a detective on the New York City police force from 1965 to 1980. (Rothstein was the detective who arrested CIA agent Frank Sturgis when Sturgis arrived in New York to kill Marita Lorenz, the former girl friend of Fidel Castro and also CIA asset.)

Rothstein described to me over several years how he discovered and reported the drug sales by the CIA to the blacks in New York City, via Virgil Trip Stone. Rothstein said that Al Carone, a member of one of the New York City crime families was a CIA asset and involved in the drug sales, reporting directly to CIA Director William Casey. Rothstein said that the direct sales between the CIA and key blacks in the New York City area continued from approximately 1967 to 1973, at which time the CIA sold drugs to organized crime figures who then took over the drug sales to the blacks. (These statements coincided with the testimony that Richard Brenneke gave to Congress in 1989, that he frequently dealt with the Gotti crime family, including John Gotti himself, when drugs were turned over in Arkansas. As stated earlier, Brenneke described the details of how he, acting in his CIA capacity, laundered drug money for the Gotti family through specific CIA bank connections.)

I had contact with Carone's daughter and she confirmed the CIA and Mafia relationship of her father. Rothstein gave me the name of another CIA asset involved in the drug sales to the blacks, Morio Lazzo.

**WARS TO COVER FOR CIA DRUG TRAFFICKING**

One article in the *Washington Post* (October 28, 1996) described the belief by *San Jose Mercury* reporter Gary Webb that the "Contra war was not a real war at all. It was a charade, a smoke screen...to provide cover for a massive drug operation by criminal CIA agents and others." Based upon what I have learned from my many deep-cover sources, I believe that to be absolutely true. And that would apply also to the Vietnam War.

As could be expected, pressure was apparently put upon the *San Jose Mercury*, causing the publisher to issue an apology stating that reporter Gary Webb did not have enough evidence to support his statements (which were extremely mild compared to what actually existed), and that the reporter would be reassigned, to a post 150 miles from his Sacramento residence.

# SILENCING WHISTLEBLOWERS

With the great number of people involved in these government-directed criminal activities there must be a procedure in place to silence or discredit whistleblowers. Justice Department employees, federal judges, members of Congress, and a silent mainstream media, makes coverup possible.

**STANDARD TACTICS TO KEEP THE PUBLIC FROM LEARNING WHAT IS BEING DONE TO THEM**

I repeatedly encountered the tactics used to keep the public from learning about the corruption, the criminal and treasonous activities that I encountered during the past 30 years, commencing while I was a federal investigator. The coverups and obstruction of justice that I encountered, and the brutality of the consequences of this misconduct, motivated me to continue my exposure activities.

**KEY PARTY TO THE OBSTRUCTION OF JUSTICE**

The coverup by most of the media and all of Congress plays a major role in the complicity of silence. But the tactics addressed at this moment are the tactics of the nation's highest law enforcement agency, the United States Department of Justice. Justice Department prosecutors have standard tactics to silence people who threaten to expose corruption involving federal officials:

* Fabricate charges against the person, or simply charge them with offenses that they committed under orders of their CIA handlers.
* Seize all assets, preventing hiring their own legal counsel, and require them to rely on the usually ineffective court-appointed defender.
* Block them from raising matters relating to their CIA activities.
* Block them from subpoenaing CIA people with whom they worked.
* Deny to them access to CIA documents, or bar the introduction of these documents that may be in their possession.
* Have CIA personnel engage in perjury and subornation of perjury as they falsely testify against him or her and deny that the person had any CIA connections.
* Pay informants to testify against the person, either through money,

reduction in prison sentence, or vacating prior criminal charges.

* Put all evidence under seal, preventing public access to the testimony and documents.

* Discredit charges made by informants by claiming they are felons and their word cannot be accepted as true. Simultaneously, the same Justice Department buys testimony from hard-core criminals to imprison targeted informants.

**DEATHS ALSO CONVENIENTLY OCCURS**

Every one of the criminal activities within these pages, and the U.S. officials implicated in them, were protected by the pattern of convenient deaths and false charges by Justice Department prosecutors against anyone who constituted a potential threat of exposure, including whistleblowers, informants, protesting citizens, and victims. Killing witnesses or informants is nothing new for a government that seeks to assassinate foreign leaders, invades foreign countries, undermines foreign governments, kills foreign citizens, and routinely executes criminal acts against its own citizens. These acts have greatly accelerated as every government and non-government check and balance covers up.

One of the first whistleblowers to be killed, which I reported in my 1978 first edition of *Unfriendly Skies*, was federal inspector Henry Marshall, an employee of the Agricultural Stabilization and Conservation Service. He was killed in June 1961 on a farm in Texas, much to the relief of high federal officials. Marshall had evidence linking a multi-million-dollar commodity fraud to an LBJ aide and to Lyndon Johnson himself. Alongside Marshall's body was the .22 caliber rifle that had fired the fatal bullets. Texas authorities obligingly ruled Marshall's death a suicide, even though the position of the wounds indicated it would have been physically impossible for them to have been self-inflicted.

An AP article appearing in the *Dallas Times Herald*[456] reported that convicted swindler Billy Sol Estes secretly testified before a grand jury impaneled at Franklin, Texas, relating to the Marshall death. Estes testified that he was present when Lyndon Johnson and two other men discussed having Marshall killed because Marshall knew too much about illegal manipulation of cotton allotments. Johnson reportedly gave the order to have Marshall slain. Estes identified the two men as Clifton Carter and Malcolm Wallace. Carter was once Johnson's top political aide in Texas and later his White House liaison to the Democratic National Committee. Wallace was a former University of Texas student body president.

The Marshall killing and its relationship to Lyndon Johnson had been the subject of intense gossip and rumor in Texas political circles for years. Estes, who had aged considerably since Marshall's death, agreed to testify concerning the Marshall killing at the urging of U.S. Marshal Clint Peoples of Dallas, who had pursued the case for more than two decades.

Other testimony in the grand jury hearings revealed that Johnson approved the killing out of fear that Marshall would give Attorney General Robert F. Kennedy evidence concerning cotton allotments incriminating LBJ. Kennedy was known to have no love for Johnson.

456 Copy of a *Dallas Times Herald* article appearing in the March 24, 1984, *Sacramento Bee*.

The deaths of key people in the alleged murder conspiracy prevented further grand jury investigation. Former President Lyndon Johnson died January 22, 1973, on his ranch near Austin, Texas. Wallace died in a car accident in 1971, and Carter died September 22, 1971. The grand jury came to the conclusion that Marshall was killed, but reached no conclusion as to who may have done it.

**"You're Going To Get Killed!"**

When FAA inspectors warn another inspector his life is in danger by reporting safety violations and related criminal acts, the public might get the impression FAA inspectors are not going to report safety problems! "You're going to get killed," was the warning I received from several FAA employees as I tried to expose the FAA corruption. If other inspectors feared for their lives if they reported safety violations at favored airlines, such as United, they could not be expected to report the misconduct.

The CIA, heavily involved in activities surrounding the John F. Kennedy assassination, has a long history of assassination plans. The death rate of people associated in some way with the JFK assassination was extraordinarily high. A partial list of these people, and of those who posed a threat to U.S. officials because of their knowledge of activities described within these pages, follows:

**KILLINGS & MYSTERIOUS DEATHS ASSOCIATED WITH THE JFK ASSASSINATION**

It has been reported that over 100 key witnesses to the JFK assassination died within a few years of the killing. The *London Sunday Times* estimated that the odds of sudden deaths among approximately three dozen witnesses over such a short time span to be 100,000 trillion to one. Despite the pattern of killings and mysterious deaths of informants under these unusual conditions, the Warren Commission held that they did not establish any relationship with the Kennedy assassination or constitute a conspiracy to silence opposition to the Warren Commission findings.

**PATTERN OF RETALIATION COMMENCING WITH THE SCANDALS OF THE 1980's**

The pattern of killings, mysterious deaths, and persecution of informants and whistleblowers continued with the escalating pattern of criminal activities described within these pages. A partial list follows:

**Attorney Dexter Jacobson** was killed on August 14, 1990, just prior to presenting evidence of rampant Chapter 11 judicial corruption to the FBI. Several months before his death, Jacobson and I had exchanged information on the Chapter 11 corruption each of us had uncovered. The conduct of local police constituted a coverup that aided the killers to escape detection.

**Paul Wilcher** was found dead on July 23, 1993, under mysterious circumstances. He was an investigator and attorney living in Washington, D.C., who was in frequent contact with Gunther Russbacher and myself. He and I shared information with each other. He had recorded sixty tapes of statements made by Russbacher during about six weeks of daily questioning taking place in the Missouri State Prison at St. Charles, Missouri. These tapes revealed CIA secret operations in which Russbacher was involved. Russbacher warned Wilcher that these tapes were never to be revealed to anyone unless he died. I had a set of them in the event something happened to Wilcher's originals. More about Wilcher's death in later pages.

Shortly before Wilcher's death, he wrote a 105-page report to Attorney General Janet Reno describing evidence that he allegedly acquired concerning several of the criminal patterns described in these pages. His letter stated that "Bush Administration hold-overs in the Justice Department, along with others tied to the CIA," were blocking exposure of the criminal offenses. The first page of his letter stated in part:

> *The lives of key participants, other witnesses, and even myself, are now in grave danger as a result of my passing this information on to you. If you let this information fall into the hands of the wrong persons...some or all of those who know the truth...could well be silenced (i.e., murdered) in the very near future.*

**Barbara Wegler** died from unknown causes on March 5, 1995. Several weeks earlier I was in touch with her concerning her investigation of covert activities based upon information given to her by Bill Tyree. She was to provide me with information about what she found, but died before she could do this. Her interests included Operation Watchtower; CIA involvement in Jim Jones' Jonestown; and other activities.

**Attorney Gary Ray Pinnell** was killed on February 11, 1991, in San Antonio, Texas, just prior to presenting evidence of Chapter 11 judicial corruption to the FBI. Judge-appointed trustee Marten Seidler was under investigation by the grand jury in Pinnell's murder on the basis that he was associated with Charlie Rummels, a prime suspect in the attorney's death. Many of those who were corruptly stripped of their assets after they exercised the statutory protections of Chapter 11 wanted to testify before the grand jury looking into Pinnell's death, but they were blocked by Justice Department attorneys. Some of those who sought to testify were of Hispanic origin, some coming from as far away as El Paso. When they returned home, they were harassed by Immigration and Naturalization Service personnel.

**Danny Casolaro** was killed on August 10, 1991, as he was obtaining evidence of corruption linking Justice Department officials to Inslaw, October Surprise, and BCCI. He was a Washington-based free-lance reporter, and was killed in the Sheraton Hotel in Martinsburg, West Virginia. After Casolaro was killed, his body was embalmed before the family was notified, violating state and county rules and blocking a thorough autopsy, which might have revealed incapacitating drugs.

**Alan D. Standorf** was murdered on January 4, 1991, and his body found on January 31, 1991, in the back seat of a car parked at the Washington National Airport. Standorf was a source of information for Casolaro. CIA operative Michael Riconosciuto had introduced Casolaro to Standorf. It is believed that Standorf, an electronic intelligence employee for the National Security Agency, was a key source for some of the information obtained by Danny Casolaro linking the Justice Department to the various parts of the scandals. Casolaro had previously told a friend, Bill Turner, that a key source of information on the scandals that he was investigating had disappeared (referring to Standorf).

**Attorney Dennis Eisman** was shot to death in April 1991, twenty-four hours before he was to meet with Michael Riconosciuto, who was involved in numerous CIA activities, including October Surprise and Inslaw. Eisman was building a defense for Riconosciuto against the charges filed by Justice Department prosecutors as they sought to silence him. Shortly before Eisman was killed, he was to meet in Philadelphia with a woman who would deliver to him important evidence of corruption by Justice Department officials.

**Attorney John Crawford**, one of the attorneys who worked with Riconosciuto, died from a heart attack in Tacoma in April 1993. This death raises questions, since he was one of several attorneys and investigators working with Riconosciuto to die within a relatively short period of time.

**Paul Morasca** was working with CIA operative Michael Riconosciuto. He opposed and started to expose corrupt activities carried out by the CIA and CIA contract agent John P. Nichols, and which included the Wackenhut Corporation, including George Wackenhut. He was killed in January 1982 in the San Francisco condo that he shared with Michael Riconosciuto.

**Larry Guerrin**, a private investigator, was killed in Mason County, Washington in February 1987, as he conducted an investigation seeking evidence for Michael Riconosciuto relating to the Inslaw scandal.

**Alan Michael May** was killed in his San Francisco home on June 19, 1991. May was involved with Michael Riconosciuto in the October 1980 movement of $40 million bribe money to Iranian factions. May had requested that Riconosciuto not divulge May's ties with the Iranian hostage scandal out of fear for his life. Within four days after the *Napa Sentinel* published Riconosciuto's description of the October Surprise operation, May was killed. The local coroner's report stated death was due to a heart attack. However, a subsequent autopsy revealed that May had poly pharmaceuticals in his system.

**Vali Delahanty** disappeared on August 18, 1992, as she was trying to warn Michael Riconosciuto about a plan by DEA and Justice Department officials to set him up on a drug charge. The skeletal remains of her body were discovered in a ravine at Lake Bay, Washington on April 13, 1993. Her disappearance and death prevented her from testifying on behalf of CIA Agent Michael Riconosciuto and against the Justice Department and DEA. Delahanty's sister, Debbie Baker, told me that Vali had called her shortly before her disappearance and stated that she had very sensitive information concerning the Inslaw matter and the DEA and Justice Department's attempt to falsely imprison Riconosciuto. Vali reportedly wrote to Riconosciuto stating that she had information showing the DEA agent Hurley was working with John Munson to set up Riconosciuto. Vali was an alcoholic and was living with Munson. The evidence strongly indicates that Munson collaborated with DEA and Justice Department personnel to frame Riconosciuto on the sham amphetamine-manufacturing charge. Several months before Vali's body was found, Munson reportedly told people at a local bar, while he was under the influence of alcohol, that she was dead. Later discovery of her body proved him correct.

**Pete Sandvigen**, who resided on Whidbey Island in Washington, was ready to leave from the Navy Air Station on Whidbey Island, as part of further investigation into Inslaw. His body was found on December 2, 1992. The gun that he carried was found without the ammo clip, raising questions. Sandvigen had been part of a 26-man CIA team in Afghanistan during the late 1980s. He tried to help Riconosciuto defend against the Justice Department's amphetamine charges, along with exposing the Inslaw scandal.

**Alfred Alvarez and two friends** who were part of the Cabazon Indian Reservation, were killed in July 1981. Alvarez opposed the operations and takeover of the Indian reservation by the CIA front, Wackenhut Corporation.

**Deaths in the family of former FBI agent Darlene Novinger**. Novinger said to me that she discovered during an FBI investigation that Vice President George Bush and two of his sons were using drugs and prostitutes in a Florida hotel while Bush was vice president. She said that when she reported these findings to her FBI supervisors they warned her not to reveal what she had discovered. Novinger had been requested to infiltrate drug trafficking operations in South America and the United States. She was pressured to quit her FBI position; her husband was beaten to death; and four hours after she appeared on a July 1993 talkshow[457] describing her findings (after she was warned not to appear), her father mysteriously died. A dead white canary was left on his grave as a warning to her. After receiving death threats she went into hiding, from where she occasionally appeared as guest on talk shows, and called me from undisclosed locations.

**Attorney David Mayer** was killed by gunshot on February 6, 1989, in the San Francisco Bay Area. On February 7, 1989, he was to have appeared in the U.S. District Court at San Francisco before Judge Paul Vukasin, Jr.,[458] defending people in drug-related charges that were reportedly tied in with covert CIA drug trafficking activities. Mayer was an activist seeking to expose the contra-drug connection involving the Reagan-Bush administration, the CIA, Justice Department officials, and others. His investigation and files disclosed links between high federal officials and associates, and a number of major federal crimes.

**Abbie Hoffman** was reportedly killed in his home on April 12, 1989, just prior to delivering a manuscript on the October Surprise operation to *Playboy's* Chicago offices.

**Wife of DEA drug pilot Basil Abbott** was killed in Europe in 1982 after talking to European reporters about the DEA drug trafficking operation into the United States. She sought publicity to obtain the release of her husband who had outlived his usefulness to the DEA.

**Barry Seal**, pilot for the DEA and CIA, shot to death on February 19, 1986, after he learned too much about the drug-smuggling operation and threatened to reveal what he knew.

**Robert Maxwell** died after falling or being thrown off his yacht shortly after his role in the Inslaw affair was publicized. He had considerable knowledge and/or participation in U.S., Israel, and British intelligence agencies, in Inslaw, and other areas associated with assassinations and mysterious deaths.

---

457 Tom Valentine, *Radio Free America*.

458 A friend of Earl Brian, Edwin Meese III, and other parties implicated in October Surprise, Inslaw, Chapter 11 corruption, Justice Department pattern of coverup, are all part of the Reagan-Bush coterie.

**Charles McKee and other Defense Intelligence Agency agents on Pan Am Flight 103** died when the plane was blown apart over Lockerbie, Scotland. Mckee's team was returning to Washington, in defiance of orders, to give testimony to Congress on the CIA and DEA drug trafficking activities.

**Reported assassination of three navy officers on the evening of April 30, 1991, at Fort Ord, California**, including Admiral John D. Burkhardt, Captain Samuel J. Walters, and a female Navy officer, whose first name was Marilyn.

**John David Pigg** was killed in July 1993 in Anadarko, Oklahoma. He was a CIA agent involved in a major heroin operation involving several federal agencies[459] through San Francisco and other key U.S. cities, which is discussed in more detail in later pages. He reportedly wanted to get out of the operation and it was suspected that he constituted a threat of exposing the multi-billion-dollar-a-year operation.

**William Casey**, Director of the CIA, a key participant in the October Surprise operation and its related Iran-Contra arms and drug activities. He experienced seizures on the morning that he was to testify before the Senate Intelligence Committee and underwent brain surgery. He died several months later on May 6, 1987. Friends believe that Casey would have told the truth if he had testified, thereby implicating people in high positions. CIA operatives have told me that the rumor within the CIA is that Casey's medical condition was induced by drugs.

**Former Senator John Tower** was killed in a plane crash at New Brunswick, Georgia on April 5, 1991, just as the October Surprise scandal was again surfacing. Tower was involved in the October Surprise and Iran-Contra operations, as was his aide, Robert McFarlane.

**Thomas Wilhite** threatened to expose the CIA role in Bishop, Baldwin, Rewald, Dillingham, and Wong to newspaper reporters. He died in a plane crash within 24 hours of announcing his intention to blow the whistle. Wilhite was a friend of Ron Rewald, who was the fall guy when its cover was blown by a Honolulu television reporter.

**WHO WERE THE ASSASSINS?**

The people or groups responsible for the assassinations, according to my CIA contacts, included teams within the intelligence community and the FBI. Two of my sources who were close to the assassination teams in the CIA were Gunther Russbacher and Commander of Navy SEAL Team Two, Robert Hunt. These activities are described in other pages, and their description of the assassination teams showed that the intelligence agencies have separate fiefdoms (something like I found initially in the FAA), and that some of these fiefdoms had their own assassination groups. They even targeted other CIA personnel.

Several of my CIA contacts described an FBI agent noted for his assassination activities and how they feared him: Charles "Chuckie" Peters, employed by the Federal Bureau of Investigation in the Chicago area.

Russbacher told me about the assassination orders that he had to carry out during his CIA career. He said one of the termination operations (assassinations)

459 Central Intelligence Agency; Drug Enforcement Administration; Customs; U.S. Department of Justice.

was called the Omega Plan. Another one of my sources formerly with the ONI and CIA described the assassination operation known as Operation Ringwind, in which he trained some of the assassinators.

## KILLINGS OCCURRING IN FOREIGN COUNTRIES

**Francis John Nugan** operated a covert CIA proprietary known as Nugan Hand Bank in Australia. After the cover was blown on Nugan Hand by a Hong Kong financial reporter, Nugan was found shot to death, holding a rifle with an unspent bullet in the bolt-action-operated chamber. Nugan had information on CIA links to money laundering, drugs, and other criminal activities that threatened to expose a fundamental operational pattern.

**Houshang Lavi** worked with Iranian arms dealer Cyrus Hashemi (now deceased) on covert arms sales to Iran. Shortly after trying to obtain documents establishing arms sales between the United States and Iran through Israel, an assassination attempt was made on his life.

**Anson Ng** was shot to death a month before Casolaro's murder. Ng was in Guatemala working for *Financial Times* to interview Jimmy Hughes, who had important information on misconduct relating to murders occurring on the Cabazon Indian Reservation. Hughes had fled to Central America to escape the fate of other informants who had been killed or prosecuted by Justice Department officials.

**Jonathan Moyle** was a journalist investigating the sale of military equipment by arms merchants in Chile to Iraq as part of a CIA operation. Moyle was killed in April 1990 while in Santiago, Chile.

**Arnold Raphel** was one of several top officials in the Carter Administration participating in the October Surprise operation. He was killed in a plane crash with Pakistani President Mohammed Zia ul-Haq (August 17, 1988) in which sabotage is suspected.

**Mohammed Ali Rajai**, a former Iranian official, reportedly met with George Bush and William Casey on October 18, 1980, just prior to their flying to Paris to formalize the October Surprise agreement. Rajai was killed in a bomb blast in his Teheran office.

**Cyrus Hashemi** was a key party in the October Surprise operation and was killed after telling a reporter that his arms sales to Iran were part of the October Surprise operation.

**Mehdi Hashemi** was head of Khomeini's office for export of militant Islamic fundamentalism and a part of the October Surprise operation. He was executed in Iran on September 21, 1987.

**Shahpur Bahktiar** was an Iranian living near Paris who had evidence proving the existence of the October Surprise operation. He was killed on August 6, 1991.

**Hassan Sabra**, chief editor of the Lebanese weekly *Al Shiraa*, who had been exposing the October Surprise and arms-for-hostages operation, was shot on September 21, 1987, the same day that Mehdi Hashemi was executed in Tehran.

**Sadegh Ghotbzadeh** was foreign minister of Iran during the Iranian hostage crisis. He negotiated with the CIA in the October Surprise operation. Ghotbzadeh encouraged Ayatollah Khomeini to go along with the October Surprise scheme advanced by the Americans. In *October Surprise*, Secretary of State Alexander

Haig's aide, Michael Ledeen, tipped off the Khomeini regime to an alleged coup attempt involving Ghotbzadeh, resulting in his death.

**Ayatollah Mohammed Beheshti** reportedly sent a representative to the October 1980 Paris meeting. Beheshti was killed by a bomb explosion at the Islamic Republic Party headquarters in Iran on June 28, 1981.

**Glenn Souham** was a business partner of Iranian arms dealer Cyrus Hashemid and Adnan Khashoggi, and had information about October Surprise and the Iran-Contra operation. He was killed.

**Mohammed Zia ul-Haq, President of Pakistan** was killed in a sabotaged plane crash on August 17, 1988, following a falling out with the CIA. He knew about the CIA-DEA drug trafficking from the Middle East into the United States.

**John Friedrich** was a close ally of Colonel Oliver North and Amiram Nir and had considerable knowledge of the Iran-Contra operation and the Justice Department's theft of the Inslaw software. Friedrich and his bodyguard were shot and killed in Sale, Australia. According to CIA-operative Michael Riconosciuto, Friedrich was the third party that he was using to try to set up an interview with Michael Hand of the covert CIA Nugan Hand Bank for an Australian television station. Friedrich owned a company dealing in search and rescue equipment. Friedrich's real name may have been Haffenberger before he moved to Australia.

**Amiram Nir** was involved with Colonel Oliver North in various arms sales and the Iran-Contra affair and was to be a major witness in North's forthcoming trial. If he had appeared, his testimony, as well as that of many others who died, would expose President Reagan and Vice President Bush, Oliver North, Israel's Prime Minister Peres, the Mossad, and the CIA, among others, in various scandals. Nir was reportedly writing a book on his experiences. Israel's Mossad investigated Nir's death and determined that he was killed by a woman friend he had met earlier, and who was a CIA contract agent.[460] As described more fully in later pages, Oliver North told one of my CIA contacts that Nir was killed because Nir had secretly tape-recorded Vice-President George Bush during a 1986 meeting in Jerusalem discussing arms-for-hostages and that Nir had planned to go public with the tapes. One of my deep-cover sources, who was part of the assassination team that killed Nir, told me the details of his death. This is described in other pages, and differs somewhat from what Ben-Menashe wrote.

## CIA ASSASSINATIONS

Under orders of his CIA handlers, Gunther Russbacher participated in numerous assassinations. Robert Hunt, who was identified to me as a Navy SEAL, taught assassination techniques, as well as participated in assassinations. The CIA released a report in November 1993 describing its role in assassinations, including those in unison with the Mafia. This reflects the mentality of this sinister agency funded by the U.S. taxpayers.

The 133-page report, dated May 23, 1967, cataloged the riveting details of the CIA planning assassinations of foreign leaders.

## PERSECUTION OF WHISTLE BLOWERS

With the hundreds of people involved in carrying out government-perpetrated

460 *Profits of War*, Ari Ben-Menashe.

or directed corrupt activities it is necessary to have in place a standard procedure to silence or discredit these people. I've seen it in operation for the last 30 years. The CIA, or any other government entity, coordinates with Justice Department prosecutors to silence or discredit whistleblowers and informants, especially intelligence agency personnel, by charging them with federal offenses for carrying out what they were ordered to do by their handlers. Their subsequent imprisonment silences them, and the felony conviction is then used to discredit them.[461] A few examples of this practice follow, but there are hundreds of other instances of this Justice Department persecution.

**Gunther Russbacher** was repeatedly charged with federal offenses after he posed a threat to high U.S. officials. He was charged with kidnapping, misuse of government purchase orders and fuel, impersonating a naval officer and other offenses. As with the others who were imprisoned, he constituted a serious threat to many government officials.

**Ronald H. Rewald**, a CIA operative, installed as head of the CIA proprietary known as Bishop, Baldwin, Rewald, Dillingham & Wong (BBRDW). After the cover was blown on the secret CIA operation by a Honolulu television reporter, CIA and Justice Department officials charged Rewald with money offenses to shift attention away from the CIA proprietary.

**Michael Riconosciuto** was a former CIA operative who was directly involved in highly sensitive CIA and Justice Department activities, including October Surprise and Inslaw. Justice Department personnel, including Peter Videnieks, threatened to retaliate against Riconosciuto and his wife if he testified before Congress on the Inslaw matter. Riconosciuto testified, and he was subsequently charged with manufacturing amphetamines.

**Bobbi Riconosciuto** lost custody of three of her children, as Justice Department official, Peter Videnieks, warned Michael Riconosciuto, if he testified to Congress about the Inslaw matter.

**Richard Brenneke** had been a CIA contract agent for many years and was involved in numerous CIA operations, including October Surprise, arms and drug trafficking. Justice Department officials charged him with perjury after he testified in a 1988 U.S. district court hearing on behalf of another CIA operative, Heinrich Rupp. They had both been CIA contract agents, and both said that they had seen vice presidential nominee George Bush and Donald Gregg in Paris in October 1980 for the October Surprise meeting.

**Stewart Webb** was charged by Justice Department prosecutors with making threatening phone calls after Webb threatened to expose his former father-in-law's involvement in the HUD and savings and loan scandals. The CIA was heavily implicated in these scams. Justice Department prosecutors and federal judges incarcerated Webb for nearly a year, while he waited to go to trial on the sham charge.

**Heinrich Rupp**, a long time CIA contract agent and pilot, flew a Unocal Gulfsteam from New York to Paris as part of the October Surprise operation. He was charged by Justice Department officials with fraud relating to the covert

461 Of course, when it suits the Justice Department prosecutors, they use felons and reward them to testify against someone that the Justice Department wants silenced.

CIA Aurora Bank in Colorado.

**Imprisonment of over 300 CIA and DEA personnel who posed a threat of exposure to corrupt CIA activities**. During the 1980's and early 1990s Justice Department attorneys charged these people with federal crimes for having carried out the orders of their handlers.

**Scapegoats for the HUD and savings and loan scandals**. Seeking to shift attention from the kingpins in these scandals and away from the CIA involvement in them, sham charges were filed by Justice Department prosecutors against dozens of innocent people.

**Brett C. Kimberlin** made known to the media that he sold marijuana to Vice Presidential candidate Dan Quayle from the fall of 1971 through early 1973 while Quayle was a law student in Indiana. Justice Department prosecutors retaliated by canceling his 1989 parole date and resetting it for 1994, causing him to be imprisoned for an additional five years.

**John Cole** was sentenced to federal prison in 1992 after he had reported to the FBI and U.S. Attorney in Illinois details of criminal activities that he had discovered while in management with Granite City Steel. This steel company was involved with a group of other companies, some of which were CIA proprietaries, including unlawful arms shipments overseas, drug trafficking, and which included FBI and Justice Department personnel, CIA officials, Japanese Mafia figures, among others.

**Lester Coleman** fled the United States after the FBI arrested him on trumped up charges of passport irregularities. Coleman posed a danger of exposing CIA and DEA drug trafficking, its link to Pan Am Flight 103, and the stolen PROMIS software. His statements contradicted U.S. claims that Libya was responsible for placing the bomb on Flight 103, rather than terrorists for Iran and Syria.

**THE AUTHOR**

I must be included in the list of those persecuted to silence their exposure activities. To silence me, Justice Department prosecutors and federal judges acted in unison, misusing the courts to seize my assets, suspend all constitutional and statutory protections, and then charge me with criminal contempt of court for using the remedies in law to protect myself. When I sought to expose the criminality described within these pages the federal judiciary acted in unison, repeatedly sending me to prison in retaliation for reporting the crimes.

U.S. District Judge Vaughn Walker, acting in unison with Justice Department prosecutors (under Janet Reno), sought to send me to federal prison for having filed a federal action reporting the criminal activities in this. I was also waiting to go to prison on a charge of criminal contempt of court for having filed oppositions and appeals of the criminal seizure occurring in the bankruptcy court. Orders had been rendered barring me access to the federal courts, which prevented me from reporting the federal crimes and prevented me from defending against the government retaliation. This criminal misuse of the federal courts and the Justice Department converted me from a multi-millionaire to a state of poverty. My business, my home, my assets, have all been destroyed. A half million dollar default judgment was obtained against me when I was incarcerated and unable to defend. I have been barred by federal judges from even filing actions addressing that judgment. (For the remainder of my life, I cannot acquire any assets, cannot engage in any of my prior investment activities, and cannot defend myself, regardless of the protections in the Constitution and laws of the United States.)

**MOSSAD ASSASSINATIONS**

Dozens of people were assassinated throughout the world by Mossad squads when their activities displeased Israel or its intelligence agency. Even my CIA covert operators feared speaking out against this group. These killings have been described by former Mossad agents in their books[462] and elsewhere within these pages.

**ANOTHER PLANNED MOSSAD ASSASSINATION IN UNITED STATES**

A former officer in the U.S. Army Criminal Investigation Division contacted Inslaw president William Hamilton, advising him that his contact in Israel warned that he and former Mossad agent Ari Ben-Menashe, were slated for assassination by Rafi Eitan. Hamilton made a memorandum of this phone call on dated May 18, 1993, which stated in part:

*On Saturday, May 15, 1993, Bill McCoy, a retired Army Criminal Investigation Division officer, told me that his military intelligence sources reported that Rafi Eitan was then in Quebec.*

*One day earlier, on Friday, May 14, 1993, Ari Ben Menashe had told me that an 'ex-colleague in Tel Aviv' had warned him that Rafi Eitan was planning to kill Ari Ben-Menashe and William Hamilton, and that Rafi Eitan had arranged last year for the murder of Ian Spiro and his family in the San Diego, California area.*

*Upon hearing from McCoy on Saturday, I, therefore, advised McCoy that Ben-Menashe is currently living in Montreal, Quebec and may be in danger if the information is true and accurate. I gave McCoy the telephone number for Ben Menashe so that McCoy could contact Ben Menashe directly with his information from U.S. military intelligence about Rafi Eitan's alleged presence in Quebec.*

*Yesterday, Monday, May 17, 1993, Ben-Menashe claims that he met Rafi Eitan in the lobby of a hotel in Montreal after first speaking with him by telephone on two occasions over the weekend. Ben-Menashe says that Rafi Eitan was accompanied by a bodyguard, possibly from Germany.*

*According to Ari, the following are highlights of the conversation between Rafi Eitan and Ari Ben-Menashe:*

*Rafi:* *Ari, you have done enough damage (by publication of Israeli secrets in his book, Profits of War)... If you testify in England in the Maxwell inquiry, you are finished... Your friend, Hamilton, is perpetuating something very delicate and talking about things that shouldn't be talked about.*

*Ari:* *It's Hamilton's software.*

*Rafi:* *There are greater things to consider. Fricker's article is very damaging...*

462 *Profits of War*, Ari Ben-Menashe; *By Way of Deception*, Victor Ostrovsky and Claire Hoy; *The Other Side of Deception*, Victor Ostrovsky.

*On a separate subject, I questioned Ari Ben Menashe about his appearance in Chicago before Judge Bua's federal grand jury on INSLAW. I asked whether Bua or his staff asked any questions about the claim, published in Ben-Menashe's book, Profits of War, that Israeli intelligence slush funds were used to finance the termination agreement between Leigh Ratiner and Dickstein, Shapiro and Morin. Ben-Menashe said he was not asked a single question about the subject.*

*********************************************************

In later pages, more killings will be described, including the deaths of those associated with government crimes in Arkansas.

**PARTIES WHO BENEFITTED BY THE DEATHS AND THE PERSECUTIONS**

**Central Intelligence Agency officials** and their criminal operations, including for instance (a) looting America's financial institutions; (b) drug smuggling into the United States; (c) October Surprise; (d) Chapter 11 courts, and many other operations.

**Justice Department personnel** who aided and abetted the CIA-related activities and who persecuted those who threatened to expose the criminal activities.

**Federal judges**, especially those who were directly involved in the Chapter 11 looting and were on secret retainers with the CIA. Also, those who assisted in the persecution of informants and whistleblowers, and those who unlawfully dismissed federal actions that otherwise exposed the corruption described within these pages.

**Justices of the U.S. Supreme Court**. Every Justice of the U.S. Supreme Court was repeatedly informed of these criminal activities, either by petition or appeal that I filed or by personal letters sent by certified mail. They had a duty to act, especially when the criminal activities were perpetrated by the federal judges, federal trustees, and Justice Department attorneys over whom they had a direct supervisory responsibility, in addition to other responsibilities under federal criminal and civil rights statutes.[463] Instead of meeting their responsibilities, they aided and abetted the criminal acts, making possible the continuation of many criminal activities.

**Members of the U.S. Senate and House**, who aided and abetted the criminal activities by blocking investigations and blocking the reporting of the federal crimes, many of which occurred in their areas of supervisory responsibilities.

**Establishment media** who knew of the government crimes and despite First Amendment constitutional responsibilities and federal crime-reporting statutes, refused to report the serious government corruption that inflicted such great harm upon the American people.

**State judges** repeatedly used by federal authorities to take judicial or police actions on targeted individuals, or to cover up for them.

**ANOTHER SCHEME TO SILENCE RUSSBACHER**

Adding to the circumstantial evidence in the charges made against Russbacher

---

463 **Title 28 U.S.C. § 1343; 42 U.S.C. §§ 1983-1986.**

by Missouri officials was a document I received in August 1993, revealing the scheme to falsely charge Russbacher with criminal activity. The document consisted of a May 14, 1989, letter written by a former Missouri Secretary of State, Roy Blunt on stationery of the Missouri Secretary of State, to a Missouri prosecutor, Scott Sifferman, prosecuting attorney in Lawrence County. The letter exposed the scheme by state officials, working with a faction of the CIA, to press charges against Southwest Latex Supply and its head, who was Gunther Russbacher, operating the company as a CIA proprietary. The charges were based upon Russbacher's alleged attempt to sell unregistered securities of Southwest Latex Supply Company.[464]

Southwest Latex Supply was one of the CIA proprietaries Russbacher operated while a deep-cover CIA operative.[465] The reference in the document to Christian was to a CIA Deputy Director of Covert Operations (DDCO). Russbacher referred to him as part of the CIA's Faction-One, reportedly under the control of George Bush during Bush's stay in the White House. Russbacher described how the interests of Faction-One often clashed with the Office of Naval Intelligence Faction, known as Faction-Two. Russbacher felt that Christian was attempting to silence and discredit him through the sham charges and subsequent imprisonment, and discredit any disclosures of October Surprise and related operations that threatened George Bush and the many people who were part of the operations.

Gunther said, "You have to understand, we always had to use Roy Blunt; he was our intermediary. Without Roy we couldn't have chartered half of the CIA proprietaries that we did." Russbacher added:

> *And then he [Blunt] was going to use me [through the sham charges] after I had been sanctioned by the Agency. He was going to use me to put a cap in his head and become the new governor of the State of Missouri. But it didn't work.*

I asked, "When you had to pay him off, what was he doing, looking the other way as it related to the CIA proprietaries?" Russbacher responded, "Sure. Absolutely."

Russbacher said to me that Missouri Secretary of State Blunt worked with the CIA in the past in covert activities, and that he and other CIA personnel paid Blunt bribe money to carry out CIA proprietary activities.

One of the significant aspects of the letter was how state prosecutors and officials criminally misused government offices against private citizens and brazenly put into writing details of the scheme, confident that no State or federal officials would prosecute. That is what always astounded me through the thirty years of discovering major corruption implicating federal officials: none ever feared prosecution for their crimes. The letter revealed that the sham charges were return of a favor to a Mr. Christian; and that the prosecuting attorney

---

464 Southwest Latex Supply was a spinoff from National Financial Services Corporation. National Financial was to buy the stock from Southwest Latex. Because they were not registered, the trade was not outside of Southwest Latex and considered a violation of the "blue-sky" law. National Financial Services provided the money to start up Southwest Latex Supply and it was considered a daughter corporation from NSF.

465 Russbacher stated that Southwest Latex Supply manufactured the five-gallon buckets used to package the C-4 explosives sold by CIA agent to Libya.

carrying out his part of the conspiracy would be rewarded with a judgeship.[466]

State of Missouri
Office of Secretary of State
Jefferson City, 65102

Roy D. Blunt
Secretary of State

May 14, 1989

To: Scott S. Sifferman
Prosecuting Attorney
Lawrence County Courthouse
Mount Vernon, Missouri 65712

Re: Southwest Latex Supply

Dear Mr. Sifferman:

I have tentatively set my schedule to be in Mount Vernon on June 14, 1989. We will need you, to do the following:

1. Have the charges ready to be filed for selling unregistered securities, fraud, and commingling of funds. Please forward for my review.
2. Schedule Press and Miller People.
3. Itinerary.

As you have seen, we have no grounds for these charges but, I owe one to Christian and, with full press coverage I should pick up some strong support in Webster's stronghold for 1992. I have spoken to the Lawrence County Republican Committee [and] they have assured me you will be recommended for the judgeship after the charges are filed. I will personally make the statements to the press and, they will not have any credibility after that.

Pursuant to our conversation we should set the bond high and you can advise Mr. Tatum. He can then present our scenario. You and John can handle it from there.

Sincerely,

Roy Blunt
Secretary of State

466 Because of poorer quality of the FAX copy in the author's possession, the exact wording of the letter is duplicated here.

## THE REWARDS

The prosecutor who assisted in carrying out the scheme, Scott Sifferman, was later appointed a judge in the State of Missouri, as promised. Russbacher said that other State officials who participated in this scheme that eventually resulted in his state imprisonment included State Prosecutor Scott Zimmerman, who prosecuted Russbacher knowing the charges to be false; William Webster, a nephew to former FBI and CIA Director William Webster (who was Missouri Attorney General); former Missouri Governor John Ashcroft; former Lt. Governor Mel Carnahan (who became Missouri Governor in 1993).

On August 15, 1993, I sent a copy of the Blunt letter to Missouri's Secretary of State, Judith Moriarty, requesting a clean copy of the letter I sent and which should be in their files. She never responded, and I sent another request on September 3, 1993. Obviously, a letter by a prior Secretary of State outlining a plan to charge a person with a crime, for which that person is currently in prison and which admits in its contents that the charges are false, isn't the type of letter that a State official wants exposed. No response to either letter.

I sent a letter to Missouri's Governor Mel Carnahan on October 1, 1993, requesting his assistance in obtaining a copy of the Blunt letter. Carnahan was Lt. Governor of Missouri during the 1989 scheme to incarcerate Russbacher, and was a close friend to the writer of the letter, Roy Blunt. The Governor had a vested interest in preventing exposure of the Blunt letter. The Missouri Governor had the power to pardon Russbacher, and I demanded that he do so.

## OTHER WAYS OF KEEPING GOVERNMENT CRIMES SECRET

A reminder; Justice Department prosecutors have a standard tactic to silence whistleblowers, concerned citizens, covert operatives who know too much about high-level criminal activities. The technique is to falsely charge the individual with a federal offense, suborn or reward witness to testify falsely, and file charges against a wife or aged parent. In addition, have a federal judge, often a former Justice Department attorney, bar the defendant from calling key witnesses such as CIA personnel, and block the introduction of documents on the excuse of national security. It works like a charm, in sending innocent people to prison and protecting high-level officials from having their participation in criminal activities become exposed.

A small sampling of victims that I encountered include such intelligence community assets as Gunther Russbacher (CIA, ONI, involved in CIA's October Surprise and many other operations); Ronald Rewald (titular head of the CIA financial proprietary in Hawaii, Bishop, Baldwin, Rewald, Dillingham and Wong); Richard Brenneke and Heinrich Rupp (CIA drug trafficking, October Surprise, CIA looting of financial operations); Oswald LeWinter (involved in October Surprise and other covert operations); Richard Craig Smith (DIA asset working with Rewald); Lester Coleman (DIA asset with knowledge of CIA-DEA drug trafficking, its involvement in the downing of Pan Am 103 over Lockerbie, illegal sale of stolen PROMIS software); Basil Abbott (pilot flying arms and drugs for the CIA and DEA); Michael Maholy (knowledgeable about CIA arms and drug trafficking); Russell Bowen (former OSS and CIA asset, knowledgeable of CIA drug trafficking); Terry Reed and his wife (Terry was CIA asset who complained of CIA drug trafficking), and many others.

## JUDICIAL IMMUNITY GIVEN TO CORRUPT PROSECUTORS

An article in the San Francisco legal newspaper *Daily Journal* (September 22, 1993) described the judicial immunity given to corrupt prosecutors. The article stated in part:

*Prosecutorial misconduct is encouraged—if not indirectly condoned—by pervasive judicial abstention and "buck passing."... [appellate courts rarely] dismiss a case based on prosecutorial misconduct, they rarely do so, either finding the wrongdoing "harmless" or suggesting that alternative remedies such as contempt...this is intellectually dishonest and an abdication of courts' duty to preserve the integrity of the judicial system in proceedings before them...It is well-documented that in reality there often is no effective sanction for prosecutors who engage in unethical conduct. Recently the House Committee on government Operations investigated 10 cases in which federal judges found that "very serious" prosecutorial misconduct had occurred. This misconduct included violation of grand jury rules, violation of defendants' fifth and Sixth Amendment rights, knowing presentation of false information to the grand jury, and mistreatment of witnesses. the committee's report notes that "courts often do not themselves takes disciplinary action but defer to the Department of Justice," which is "much like the fox guarding the chicken coop." The report documents the fact that the Justice Department effectively ignored the courts' findings of governmental abuse, and that was not one of the individuals involved was sanctioned, thereby raising serious questions regarding what the Department considers "prosecutorial misconduct."*

*There is virtually nothing that an aggrieved party can do when a court declines to sanction unethical government conduct, because prosecutors are absolutely immune from suit. In Imbler v. Pactman, 424 U.S. 409, 431 (1976), the supreme Court ruled that a Los Angeles deputy district attorney who intentionally suborns perjury cannot be sued by the defendant who is wrongfully convicted even after the conviction is reversed. Although "this immunity does leave the genuinely wronged defendant without civil redress against a prosecutor whose malicious or dishonest action deprives him of liberty," the Supreme Court, quoting an earlier case, decided that it is "better to leave unredressed wrongs done by dishonest officers than to subject those who try to do their duty [the crooked prosecutors] to the constant dread of retaliation."*

In other words, it is better to have people go to prison, sometimes for life, by the lying or misconduct of prosecutors, rather than hinder the prosecutors in their prosecution of other people, many of whom may be innocent!

# FEDERAL GOVERNMENT AS A CRIMINAL ENTERPRISE

Many people in control of key positions in the three branches of the federal government were, and are, either directly involved in the activities described within these pages, or were involved in the coverup. Either way, these are criminal acts for which prison sentences are provided. Their dereliction of duty, their aiding and abetting, their complicity of coverup, caused and made possible the infliction of incalculable harm upon the American people.

As stated in the 1978, 1980, and 1990 editions of *Unfriendly Skies*, and more so in the several editions of *Defrauding America*, at the epicenter of the corruption described within these pages are attorneys and officials in the U.S. Department of Justice and federal judges. Without their criminal conduct,[462] none of these criminal activities could have been perpetrated or continued. The same applies to the mainstream media and to members of Congress, all of whom played key roles in the obstruction of justice.

## ORGANIZED CRIME IN THE U.S. JUSTICE DEPT.

The heading in the Forum section of the *Sacramento Bee*[463] read "Organized Crime in the U.S. Justice Dept," accurately reflecting the decades of criminality in the most misnamed agency of the federal government. The article stated in part: *"Indications...point to a widespread conspiracy implicating government officials in the theft of Inslaw's technology."* Inslaw, bad as it was, constitutes only the tip of the iceberg.

For 30 years, Justice Department attorneys blocked every attempt that I made to report the government corruption that I initially discovered as a federal investigator. With thousands of investigators in the Department of Justice, these

462 Obstruction of justice, criminal coverup, persecution of whistleblowers, informants and protesting victims.

463 October 27, 1991.

crimes could not have escaped detection. My letters and my federal actions made certain that they knew of the federal crimes.

If my reports of the pattern of criminality had received the reaction in the three branches of the federal government and from the media that a properly functioning government requires, there could not have been the epidemic corruption that now exists in government. Even now, the criminal activity continues and increases in frequency and severity as the public concerns itself with such trivia as ball games, a whale trapped in the Arctic ice fields, or an endangered species of cockroach being threatened by much-needed development of natural resources.

Thousands of people have been financially destroyed and their lives made miserable by the coordinated theft of their assets in Chapter 11. Many deaths in fraud-related airline crashes would not have occurred if Justice Department attorneys had not engaged in the coverup. Decades of financial deprivation and financial problems for individuals and the United States itself will result from the savings and loan debacle.

## RESPONSIBILITIES OF JUSTICE DEPARTMENT

Under federal law, the responsibility for ensuring that the laws of the United States are properly enforced falls to the United States Department of Justice, which is under the control of the U.S. Attorney General. He or she is appointed by the President of the United States. In practice, the Attorney General routinely misuses the Justice Department to protect the criminal acts of those who appointed him or her.

## RESPONSIBLE FOR PROTECTING THE CIVIL RIGHTS OF AMERICAN CITIZENS

Within the U.S. Department of Justice are numerous divisions. These include, for instance, the Federal Bureau of Investigation, responsible for investigating the many crimes that I reported to it; the civil rights division, with the responsibilities to investigate the civil rights violations that I reported to them; the criminal division, responsible for preventing the many criminal activities that I reported to them (including those perpetrated by Justice Department personnel seeking to block my reports); the U.S. Trustee, who is responsible for preventing the rampant fraud in bankruptcy courts that I and others reported to that office; the Drug Enforcement Administration (DEA), responsible for preventing the massive drug trafficking, including that committed by the CIA and DEA.

This is the Justice Department that has persecuted me continuously since mid-1987, retaliating against me for reporting the federal crimes that I uncovered; who retaliated against me for exercising lawful and constitutional protections to halt the barrage of civil and constitutional (and criminal) violations inflicted upon me. Every one of these divisions has been routinely used to commit the federal crimes that they have a duty to prevent.

## SUCCESSION OF CORRUPT ATTORNEY GENERALS

A succession of attorney generals have been implicated in corrupt acts and federal crimes, but have escaped prosecution because they held the highest law enforcement position in the United States. Attorney General John Mitchell, for instance, went to prison for his activities. Subsequent attorney generals have committed federal offenses involving far more serious crimes, and were never prosecuted or called to task by the checks and balances in government.

Attorney General Edwin Meese, a former California attorney and Alameda County District Attorney, was prominently associated with an escalation of the sleazy and corrupt activities in government. He was implicated in the 1980 October Surprise scheme that helped bring the Reagan-Bush team into power. As a reward, or to protect the Reagan-Bush team from prosecution in that scandal, the Reagan-Bush Administration appointed Meese U.S. Attorney General. Meese was then used to protect Reagan and Bush from the October Surprise scandal and others that followed.

In addition to the October Surprise criminality, Justice Department officials misused this powerful agency to steal the software from the Inslaw people, showing their corrupt mindset. This was followed by protecting the rampant drug trafficking into the United States by the CIA and DEA. In every area of major criminality implicating federal personnel, Justice Department attorneys and officials have engaged in obstruction of justice and other crimes of coverup.

When the stench from Meese's activities forced him to resign, he was replaced by Richard Thornburgh, who continued the criminal activities of Inslaw, the obstruction of justice activities, and the persecution of whistleblowers and informants. Thornburgh left the Attorney General position in 1991 to run for the Senate seat vacated by the death of Senator John Heinz in a plane crash in Philadelphia. A Pennsylvania newspaper identified Thornburgh as the "Harrisburg Mafia."

President George Bush, who had a long-time relationship with the CIA, then appointed[469] William P. Barr as U.S. Attorney General. Barr was General Counsel of the CIA while Bush was Director of the Agency. From the very beginning, Barr blocked investigations into the major scandals that were surfacing almost daily, including those that directly involved the Justice Department and the CIA. Barr has a long history of CIA relations.

Barr blocked an investigation of the part played by Justice Department officials in the Inslaw affair, denying the request by the House Judiciary Committee for an Independent Prosecutor.[470] Barr refused to appoint a special prosecutor to investigate the White House's funding of Iraq's military build-up. Barr refused to appoint an independent prosecutor to investigate the White House's role in the Bank of Lavoro scandal. He refused to appoint an Independent Prosecutor to investigate Inslaw. The House and Senate Judiciary committees had requested the attorney generals to request appointment of an independent prosecutor in each of these matters.

**PREVIOUS INVOLVEMENT IN MAJOR CRIMINAL ACTIVITIES**

It has been a common practice to appoint someone to the highest law enforcement position in the United States who has been involved in criminal activities, and act as damage control. Before William Barr was appointed U.S. Attorney General by President George Bush, he was legal counsel for the CIA's Southern Air Transport, and former CIA operative Terry Reed said that he

469 October 27, 1991.
470 Sometimes called independent counsel.

personally saw Barr in drug-related activities. Another source, Gene Tatum, also personally encountered Barr in similar activities.

This same general practice is applied to the political selection of federal judges who then act to block any prosecution or revealing civil actions. Bush was heavily involved in the overall drug smuggling activities, acting with Oliver North and other drug traffickers, and it would be only "normal" to put one of their own at the head of the nation's top law-enforcement agency. Further, U.S. Attorneys are selected to insure that this plan works. This problem reflects one of the major flaws in our constitution. It was visibly reflected during the presidency of Ronald Reagan, George Bush, and Bill Clinton.

**PROSECUTING FEDERAL JUDGES WHO DON'T COOPERATE**

Justice Department attorneys, misusing the power of the U.S. government, have tremendous ability to destroy persons who threaten to expose their dirty games. U.S. Attorney Joseph Russoniello at San Francisco, charged U.S. District Judge Aguilar in June 1989 with misusing his judicial position in a racketeering enterprise (RICO) and obstructing justice. What did Aguilar do? He allegedly made false statements to an FBI agent who talked to the judge on the beach at Waikiki during a Hawaiian vacation. He also suggested to an attorney the use of a particular defense in the trial of Aguilar's brother-in-law. Also, Aguilar told his brother-in-law not to call him because the brother-in-law's phone may be tapped.

The real reason for prosecuting Aguilar for these relatively minor offenses, compared to the monumental offenses committed by other federal judges and Justice Department officials, was that Aguilar often disagreed with the Justice Department prosecutors in judicial proceedings. Aguilar halted the deportation of refugees that Justice Department attorneys wanted deported. He also engaged in a heated argument with U.S. Attorney Russoniello in open court, threatening Russoniello with contempt of court.

Unlike the continuing Justice Department and judicial corruption, no one was harmed by Aguilar's acts and he made no money or profited in any way. Compare the alleged offenses charged against Judge Aguilar with the pattern of obstruction of justice and felony persecution of informants by Justice Department personnel; or the FBI's pattern of lying to grand juries and trial juries.

Another judge charged with a crime by Justice Department officials was former U.S. District Judge Claiborne in the Las Vegas District Court (1986), who was noted for rendering decisions contrary to those wanted by the Justice Department. Claiborne's accountant had failed to list the profit made on one of several real estate transactions on his income tax report. Justice Department prosecutors then charged Claiborne with income tax evasion.

The mere investigation by the FBI arm of the Justice Department can cause a member of the U.S. Senate and House to lose an election. The Justice Department can easily fabricate charges, especially conspiracy or misprision of felony offenses, by stretching facts clearly out of proportion to reality. Possibly the fear of what the Justice Department can do was one of the reasons every member of the U.S. Senate from 1991 to 1993 refused to respond to my multi-page petition to investigate the corruption I brought to their attention. But this was no excuse for them aiding and abetting the criminal activities. They had a duty to perform. When they accepted their position, they assumed the responsibilities that went with the pay, the perks, and the prestige.

## PATTERN OF CRIMINAL ACTIVITIES BY JUSTICE DEPARTMENT ATTORNEYS AND OFFICIALS

For thirty years I have been intimately connected with the criminal acts committed by Justice Department officials and their various divisions. Their misconduct in the 1960s, which I initially discovered while a federal investigator, had devastating consequences in the aviation areas that I brought to their attention. Since then, as these pages reveal, the criminality in the U.S. Department of Justice has increased many times over, very possibly making it the key cog in the pattern of racketeering activities against the American people.

If Justice Department personnel did, in fact, do any of the acts described within these pages, these same personnel would *have* to misuse the power of the federal government and of the Justice Department to block the reporting of these crimes.

These Justice Department attorneys have made it standard practice to misuse Justice Department facilities to falsely charge dozens of informants and whistleblowers with federal offenses to block their reporting of crimes implicating federal officials.

## PLACING A YOUNG LADY IN PRISON

A federal judge sentenced a young lady to federal prison (1989) for failure to remember details of stock transactions that happened several years earlier while she was a stock broker for Drexel Burnham Lambert. Lisa Jones, a 24-year-old dropout and runaway who became financially successful at the Wall Street investment firm of Drexel, was one of the first witnesses called by Justice Department attorneys investigating insider trading and other security violations at Drexel. She refused to fabricate testimony requested by Justice Department attorneys, who then retaliated when she could not remember details of the stock transactions. Justice Department attorneys charged her with perjury and, would you believe, obstruction of justice. Lisa Jones was victimized in the battle between Drexel and Justice Department attorneys and sentenced to eighteen months in federal prison.

The young woman suffered the indignities accompanying federal imprisonment, including frequent transportation with leg irons, handcuffs, and body cavity searches. Lisa Jones joined the many thousands of citizens who became victims of Justice Department and judicial corruption and, understandably, developed psychological problems.

After all this, Drexel's attorneys sued the young lady for payment of legal fees that Drexel had agreed to pay. In response to Drexel's claim that they would sue Ms. Jones for the amount of money that they had advanced, San Francisco attorney Daniel Bookin stated: "It is inconceivable to me that Drexel would sue Lisa after all that she's gone through, and in view of her serious psychological problems. All issues of compassion and decency aside, however, one simple fact seems certain: Lisa has virtually no assets; she could not even begin to repay the cost of her legal representation."

## SENDING SENIOR CITIZENS TO PRISON

Justice Department prosecutors charged Leona Helmsley with evading income taxes and sentenced the 72-year-old woman to four years in federal prison, leaving behind her 81-year-old husband who could be expected to be dead before she would be released.

Helmsley's accountants had claimed as business expenses charges that Justice Department attorneys considered personal items. Helmsly's income tax forms were made out by professional tax preparers, who determined that the deductions were business related. The accountants who made that determination were never charged with any wrongdoing. Helmsley paid over $4 million federal income taxes in the disputed tax year and the amount owed by the disputed charges was a very small percentage of that amount.

Seeking to show that the Judge who sentenced Helmsley to prison did himself commit a serious federal crime, I mailed to the federal judge on April 25, 1992, a list of the criminal activities that my CIA sources and I were trying to report, and demanded that he receive our testimony and evidence. I reminded him of the mandatory requirements that we give our evidence to a federal court and that the court receive it.[471] He refused to receive our evidence.

While aiding and abetting and covering up for the serious crimes, and sending informants to prison, Justice Department prosecutors found time on December 15, 1992, to indict[472] Bobby Fisher for playing a chess game in Yugoslavia, charging him with violating the presidential order barring business relations with communist countries.

## TEN YEARS FOR A TELEPHONE CONVERSATION

On December 7, 1990, Judge Samuel Conti sentenced a young black girl from Oakland, California, the mother of two infants, to ten years in prison on a conspiracy charge. The young girl had a telephone conversation with another person concerning the sale of drugs. The conversation never went any further, but federal agents, monitoring the phone call, charged the girl with conspiracy. She was in tears when U.S. Marshals drove her back from the federal court house in San Francisco to the Dublin Federal Detention Center after Judge Samuel Conti sentenced her to ten years in a high security prison. This same judge played a major role in blocking my exposures of the criminal activities and in protecting the many people who were implicated in the attacks upon me. He, as with many other federal judges, should be impeached and sentenced to a long prison term. But this will never happen because crooked federal judges and Justice Department attorneys have a strangle-hold on the justice system.

## PRISON FOR REFUSING TO COMMIT PERJURY

Justice Department prosecutors charged a Sacramento area real estate developer, Marcel Cordi, with a federal offense for refusing to testify falsely against a bank official whom Justice Department prosecutors wanted to convict. U.S. Attorney David Levi of Sacramento wanted Marcel to testify against a bank official and alter the facts in his testimony. Marcel was willing to testify,

---

471 Title 18 U.S.C. § 4.

472 Fisher violated a June, 1992 executive order by President George Bush restricting commercial relations with Yugoslavia. The indictment subjected Fisher to ten years in prison and a fine of as much as $250,000. Is it any wonder the United States has the highest percentage of its citizens in prison?

but would not commit perjury to enable Justice Department prosecutors to falsely convict the person. In retaliation for refusing to commit perjury, U.S. Attorney Levi charged Marcel with fraud based upon an incorrect statement on a prior loan application relating to his length of employment.

Levi was the U.S. Attorney who charged me with criminal contempt of court when I filed federal actions reporting the criminal activities implicating federal officials, including his Justice Department employer. In retaliation for reporting the crimes and for exercising federal defenses, Levi charged me with criminal contempt of court. Levi was appointed in 1992 to a federal judgeship in Sacramento. It is standard practice to appoint Justice Department officials to the federal bench. This plan insures that Justice Department prosecutors are successful in federal court.

Another example of how the public is victimized by the mindset in the Justice Department: A woman in Texas with five children drove her boyfriend's van into Mexico and was arrested at the border when she was returning home, having no idea cocaine had been hidden in her van. The jury, assuming that Justice Department officials would not prosecute an innocent woman, rendered a decision holding her guilty, causing her to receive a 10-year mandatory minimum sentence. She knew nothing about having been used as a "mule."

Making these outrages even worse is the fact that their sufferings are shared by thousands of others who become forgotten victims of corruption by Justice Department attorneys.

Cases have been cited[473] where major criminals are not charged by Justice Department prosecutors on the basis of information that they gave relating to other drug operations, often enabling Justice Department prosecutors to obtain many other convictions of lesser figures. There are hundreds of peripheral drug players in prison facing long mandatory prison terms while those government officials (and of course judges) guilty of far more serious drug offenses are free, primarily because they were able to snitch on others.

Long prison terms for drug offenses become even more preposterous when it is realized that the CIA and DEA have engaged in large-scale drug trafficking operations into the United States for decades.

## MISPRISION OF FELONY

A frequent charge for sentencing innocent people to prison is charging them with the federal crime, misprision of felony. Anyone who knows of a federal crime and who does not promptly report it to a federal judge or other federal tribunal is guilty of this crime. This statute has no exclusions and applies to members of Congress, White House officials, Justice Department personnel, the media, judges, all of whom have committed this crime. In practice, punishment for this crime is reserved for citizens, excusing those in the inner circle of government corruption.

An example of the misuse of this criminal statute occurred when a Memphis aircraft broker sold a used aircraft to a customer who later used it in drug-related operations. The aircraft broker had no way of knowing how the plane was to

---

473 Including a December 26, 1990 article by Harry Hellerstein, Assistant Federal Public Defender in San Francisco, in the *Wall Street Journal*.

be used, nor was he required to become an investigator. Later, when federal authorities were building a case against the suspects, they requested that the aircraft broker fabricate testimony in order to assist in obtaining convictions.

The broker was willing to testify, but refused to lie. Justice Department attorneys then retaliated against him, charging him with misprision of a felony on the basis that he failed to report to federal authorities that the aircraft was to be used in unlawful activities. The aircraft broker was subsequently put on trial with 32 other defendants, who apparently *were* guilty of drug-related offenses. Without competent legal counsel to protect his interests, the unsophisticated jury accepted the prosecutors' charges as true, holding that he was part of the drug trafficking operation. He was then sentenced to five years in federal prison, even though he never committed a single offense.

## SUICIDE INDUCED BY FEDERAL TACTICS

Another example of the harms inflicted upon innocent people was related to me by the aircraft broker in the preceding example. The broker was in a county jail near Memphis waiting for trial when he witnessed the fatal consequences of arrogance by federal agents. His cell-mate, Mike Scarlett from Texas, had been enticed by federal agents into making the controlled substance "speed." Knowing that Scarlett was having serious financial problems supporting his family, federal agents encouraged him to produce the drug, teaching him how to produce it, financing the operation, and setting him up with the equipment and a location. On the first day Scarlett started to make it, these same federal agents arrested him, charging him with manufacturing amphetamines.

While in prison, Scarlett discovered that his wife was sleeping with one of the federal agents who had set him up. Al told me that his cell-mate, Scarlett, was very distraught-looking after phoning his wife. He described how the inmate wrote what was later discovered to be a suicide note, and that Scarlett hung a bed sheet over the prison bars, as if he wanted privacy for sleeping, as is often done. Behind the sheet Scarlett stepped onto the rim of the toilet and tied a strip torn from a bed sheet to a grill near the ceiling. Scarlett then stepped off of the toilet and hung himself.

## PRISON FOR FILLING IN A MOSQUITO-BREEDING MUD HOLE

Justice Department prosecutors sent Allen Kafkaesque to prison for filling in a mosquito-breeding low spot on his 103-acre ranch.[474] He allowed two loads of dirt to be dumped in a low spot as a base for a shed. Federal officials then charged him with filling in "wetlands," which has been made a crime by the same members of Congress whose crimes of coverup far exceed the crimes for which non-violent offenders are in prison. Justice Department prosecutors sought to have him imprisoned for 27 to 33 months. When the judge reduced the sentence to six months in prison, Justice Department prosecutors appealed, seeking to have Kafkaesque imprisoned for almost three years.

Simultaneous with these prosecutions, Justice Department prosecutors were protecting CIA people involved in subversive and criminal activities, including drug trafficking, looting of financial institutions, judicial looting of Chapter

474 *Wall Street Journal*, November 18, 1992.

11 assets, Inslaw. Also, while they were obstructing justice in each of the scandals described within these pages, and prosecuting innocent people to silence or discredit them, they were perpetrating major crimes against the American people.

**OUTRAGEOUS PRISON SENTENCES**

America reportedly has the greatest percentage of its population in prison of any country in the world. Outrageous prison sentences are imposed for often minor offenses, such as filling in swamps on one's own property or being found with small quantities of drugs. Minor drug offenders are sentenced to twenty or more years in prison for a one-time offense while vicious killers are often released in a fraction of the time. Often the drug offender is a person simply filling the demand created by a drug-crazed society, that may arguably share a greater blame than the person responding to the demand. Sometimes a person charged with a spoonful of drugs receives a far longer prison sentence than a person who brutally kills another.

These outrageous prison sentences are legislated by the same members of Congress who have committed crimes associated with their coverup of the criminal activities described within these pages. These congressional felonies are often worse than the offenses that place thousands of people in prison for years of confinement.

**THREATENING AN AGED PARENT OR WIFE TO OBTAIN A CONFESSION**

A favorite stunt of Justice Department prosecutors is to charge the wife or an aged parent with a crime. They had no part in the offense charged, and an offense may not have *even* been committed. In this way the brave attorneys in the Justice Department coerce defendants to plead guilty (who may be innocent) or to plead guilty to charges greater than what were committed. Justice Department prosecutors threatened to charge Russbacher's wife with a crime if he did not plead guilty to misusing government fuel and aircraft when he had the CIA Learjet fly him to Seattle and then to Reno in 1989. Numerous inmates told me how they were forced to plead guilty to something they hadn't done, or to plead guilty to a greater offense than they were guilty of after Justice Department prosecutors threatened to imprison their parents or wives.

**BLACKMAILING MEMBERS OF CONGRESS**

It is well known that FBI Director J. Edgar Hoover was skilled at obtaining incriminating and embarrassing information on political figures, and had a file on almost every member of Congress. In *From the Secret Files Of J. Edgar Hoover* by Athan Theoharis, the author describes Hoover's interest and ability in gathering scandalous information about prominent political figures. The book describes FBI reports on John F. Kennedy's affair with Inga Arvad, Robert Kennedy's affair with Marilyn Monroe, Eleanor Roosevelt's affair with Joseph Lash, homosexual and other activities. The CIA does the same thing to exert control over members of Congress. The book shows that Hoover's activities did not die with him, but continue to this date. Other intelligence agencies have similar activities, such as the U.S. Army, Navy, Marines. The army had a blackmail program called Operation Orwell.

**BUYING AND SELLING HUMAN LIVES**

Judges, prosecutors and attorneys often buy and sell cases and human lives as if they were commodities. Judges are paid off to rule favorably on particular cases. A clerk can lose a key file or piece of evidence. The court reporter can change the transcript to indicate the reverse of what is actually in the record.

Attorneys often sabotage their own clients, allowing them to be convicted to satisfy a debt to their adversary's legal counsel or to placate a judge who may want the other party to prevail. Trading of human life in court is like kids trading marbles. Prosecutors will let a defendant go free in exchange for the life of another man. Criminal attorneys will plead a man guilty just to pay back a prosecutor for not prosecuting another client. Prosecutors will lie to imprison an innocent person or to cause his incarceration for years longer than the law provides for the offense that was actually committed. Cases are fixed by paying judges, prosecutors, police, and others.

Some Justice Department attorneys justify their lying, using the argument that the defendant lies so why shouldn't they do likewise. But a defendant may lie to avoid prison. Prosecutors lie to imprison innocent persons or to greatly increase the length of sentence for the purpose of making their record look good, regardless of the human tragedy it brings.

The public doesn't perceive this misconduct as a threat to themselves. When the Justice Department prosecutes a party for an alleged crime, the average person, including unsophisticated members of the grand jury, assumes that the party is guilty. Otherwise the accused would not be charged, or so they think. I fell into that trap in the past until I learned that Justice Department attorneys lie and cheat as a standard tactic. Unfortunately for the victims of this prosecutorial misconduct, as a *Wall Street Journal* article once stated, the grand jury would indict a ham sandwich if the prosecutor told them to do so.

Justice Department attorneys win year-end bonuses and personal-recognition awards for putting people in prison, guilty or not.

## DISMISSING INVESTIGATORS WHO EXPOSE HIGH LEVEL CORRUPTION

A common method for covering up evidence of the ongoing criminal activities is to dismiss investigators who report evidence of the crimes. For instance, when the investigative activities of the U.S. Attorney in Philadelphia threatened too many politicians involved in political corruption, President Carter reportedly pressured the Justice Department to remove U.S. Attorney Martson from office.

Speaking before the Washington National Press Club on January 25, 1978, Martson stated:

> *If a single Congressman can remove his home-town prosecutor who's actively investigating public officials, with a single call to the President—if that can happen, and that's what did happen—our federal criminal-justice system won't work. No amount of rhetoric will ever convince the bagmen and the fixers that they can't pull strings in Washington, because they're sure that strings got pulled in Washington.*

The Justice Department—controlled by the United States Attorney General, who is appointed by the President of the United States—investigated President Carter and his political friend, Attorney General Griffin Bell, for possible obstruction of justice. Is it any wonder the Justice Department cleared their boss of any wrongdoing?

The same tactics were used by Justice Department officials against Assistant U.S. Trustee Gregg Eichler in the San Francisco area when his investigations exposed the part played by federal judges and Justice Department officials in the corrupt Chapter 11 courts. I had given Eichler information on the criminal activities I experienced in Chapter 11, implicating federal judges, federal trustees, and law firms. Eichler was dismissed from government service in late 1991, after he exposed the corruption by trustee Charles Duck, and as he was going after the judges.

Justice Department officials fired one of their investigators in retaliation for testifying in the Inslaw affair. Justice Department officials arranged for the removal of Chapter 11 Judge George Bason from the District of Columbia bench after he ruled in favor of Inslaw, and then arranged for the Justice Department's attorney defending against the Inslaw charges to replace Judge Bason. By packing the courts in this manner, corrupt Justice Department officials gain control over the judicial process, wherein they protect themselves.

Investigator Lloyd Monroe was forced to quit the Justice Department after he discovered connections between the savings and loan scandal and the CIA-related Southmark Corporation in Dallas.

Justice Department officials reprimanded assistant U.S. Attorney Dave Howard in the San Francisco office after he filed a highly sensitive eleven-page report on July 11, 1990, describing the judicial corruption in Chapter 11. Howard recommended the appointment of a special counsel to investigate the corruption by federal judges and trustees in Ninth Circuit Chapter 11 courts. Instead of acting on the report, Justice Department officials censored Howard for preparing the report.

Jack Blum, on Senator Terry Sanford's committee, was forced to resign when he pursued the investigation of BCCI corruption when the committee wanted to drop it. After Sanford's committee blocked the investigation into BCCI, Blum went to Manhattan's District Attorney Robert Morgenthau with his evidence, resulting in criminal prosecution against powerful attorneys who sold their country down the river for financial wealth. Justice Department officials repeatedly blocked the exposure of the BCCI corruption, just as they blocked the exposure of every other scandal described in these pages.

The FBI has its own way of dealing with whistleblowers. The former head of the Los Angeles FBI office, Ted Gunderson, said[475] that he had been harassed by the FBI to suppress his reports of drugs smuggled into the United States in the bodies of dead GI's sent back from the Vietnam War. Gunderson retired from the FBI in 1979, becoming a private investigator, during which time he obtained evidence of widespread drug dealings at Fort Bragg, North Carolina. Numerous CIA assets have given me data confirming this sordid practice. Gunderson told the United Press reporters that the FBI and Justice Department had tapped his business phone and smeared his name.

## DEATHS OF THOSE EXPOSING JUSTICE DEPARTMENT CORRUPTION

Mysterious deaths of people exposing Justice Department and CIA corruption

---

475 United Press, February 22, 1986.

have been repeatedly reported throughout these pages. One of the main murders, closely associated with the Justice Department's criminality in the Inslaw matter, was the widely publicized death of Danny Casolaro. The September 10, 1992, Congressional Inslaw report addressed this link, reporting that there was a need for a further investigation into Casolaro's death and the link to the Justice Department officials.

## ARROGANCE ON AN INTERNATIONAL LEVEL

The mindset rampant in the Justice Department has no bounds. Justice Department attorneys have sanctioned and ordered the seizure in foreign countries of foreign citizens. Many of these people had never been in the United States, or the acts that may have been legal in the country where they were committed, did not occur in the United States. Under law, the Justice Department had no jurisdiction over them.

In one instance involving a resident of Mexico, Dr. Humberto Machain, Justice Department personnel paid bounty hunters $50,000 to kidnap him and bring him into the United States to stand trial. He had allegedly assisted in torturing a U.S. DEA agent in Mexico. Civilized international law procedures require that extradition be requested of Mexican officials.

Applying this tactic to other nations, there is far more "justification" for other nations to kidnap American citizens based upon the crimes inflicted in their country by the CIA and other U.S. dirty-trick squads. Using this reasoning, hundreds of federal officials, especially those in the CIA, could be seized for the crimes that they caused to be inflicted as they invaded the sovereignty of foreign countries such as Vietnam and Nicaragua, or undermined the lawful governments of other countries.

Iranians could justifiably sneak into the United States and abduct American citizens to stand trial in Iran for having committed crimes under Iranian laws, including interference in Iranian governmental activities, or the shooting down of an Iranian airliner by a trigger-happy U.S. Navy crew that had invaded Iranian waters.

The Vietnamese government could sneak into the United States and abduct American officials for their part in causing the deaths of tens of thousands of Vietnamese in the Phoenix program.

The U.S. invaded Panama, killing hundreds of Panamanian citizens, to capture the head of a foreign country (who has never committed a crime in the United States), for having trafficked in drugs in Panama. Making the seizure of Manuel Noriega more bizarre, he was formerly on the payroll of the same CIA, engaging in drug trafficking in partnership with the Central Intelligence Agency's sanctioned operations.

## SUPREME COURT APPROVAL OF UNLAWFUL SEIZURE

A federal judge in Los Angeles threw out the indictment against the Mexican physician, Dr. Humberto Machain. Entered into the court records were the declarations of a Mexican informant that another doctor, Fidel Kosonoy, was responsible for administering the drugs that kept an American DEA agent, Enrique Camarena, alive so that the agent could be tortured for obtaining additional information. Kosonoy was the personal physician of Rafael Caro Quintero, a Mexican drug trafficker. Justice Department prosecutors withheld this declaration that contradicted their charges against the Mexican doctor.

The Justices of the U.S. Supreme Court upheld the right of Justice Department officials to invade a foreign country and seize their citizens in this manner. There was an exception: Justice John Paul Stevens called the decision "monstrous," which it was. The United States has given federal bounty hunters carte blanche to violate a widely held principle of international law, implying that foreign countries can do the same to U.S. citizens.

Chief Justice William Rehnquist upheld this shocking violation of international law on the basis that "the treaty says nothing about the obligations" of the two countries "to refrain from forcible abductions." Using this rationale, U.S. bounty hunters can kill foreign citizens in foreign countries if the extradition treaty says nothing about that issue.

The Supreme Court Justices held that it was legal for American bounty-hunters to invade the sovereignty of a foreign country, using force if necessary, including killing foreign citizens, bringing them to the United States for trial, with Justice Department-appointed "defense" attorneys. These are the same Justices who obstructed justice when I repeatedly brought the corruption described within these pages to their attention via petitions, appeals, and letters.

Foreign nations and their media strongly criticized the United States Supreme Court for this position. Chile's most important newspaper, *El Mercurio*, reacted to the Supreme Court's ruling with the heading "Caramba! they've legalized terrorism." The June 23, 1992, editorial summarized the arrogance:

> *The decision promotes contempt for the rule of law and the right of due process, violates national sovereignty and opens the door to acts of reprisal among nations. And what happens if U.S. agents—or people cooperating with the U.S.—clash with police in Mexico, Colombia or some other country, with gunfire that may even injure or kill innocent bystanders?*

Chilean Socialist leader Marcelo Schilling said of the Supreme Court rule that it was "the law of the jungle in which the weaker countries will lose out." Guatemalan President Jorge Serrano called the Supreme Court's ruling an "unacceptable judicial monstrosity."

When asked what he thought of the kidnapping doctrine, legal adviser to the State Department, Judge Abraham Sofaer, testified before Congress in 1985:

> *How would we feel if some foreign nation...came over here and seized some terrorist suspect in New York City, or Boston, or Philadelphia...because we refused through the normal channels of international, legal communications to extradite that individual?*

In 1989, the Assistant Attorney General in charge of the Office of Legal Counsel, William P. Barr, held that the FBI could legally seize suspects in foreign countries, even though they had never been in the United States and had never committed any offense in the United States.

The heading in the Mexico City newspaper *El Financiero* read: "Bush and the Culture of Terrorism." The article described the "new world disorder in which the United States...can kidnap, torture and assassinate citizens from other nations."

On November 11, 1990, the United Nations Convention Against Illicit Traffic in Narcotic Drugs came into force and passed a resolution stating in clear text that a treaty party "shall not undertake in the territory of another Party the exercise of jurisdiction and performance of functions which are exclusively reserved for the authorities of that other Party by its domestic laws."

It was the invasion of Mexico under orders of Justice Department officials that required this restatement of international law. The resolution was introduced by Canada and Mexico and approved by the United Nations group. The United States ratified that convention agreement in 1990 and then promptly violated it by seizing a Mexican citizen in Mexico in 1992.

In response to the U.S. kidnapping of a Mexican citizen and the U.S. Supreme Court upholding that act, the Mexican senate approved an amendment to the Mexican criminal code imposing a 40-year sentence on anyone who kidnaps Mexicans on behalf of the United States or any other foreign authority who may wish to duplicate America's invasion of a foreign country's sovereignty to kidnap foreign citizens. So intense was Mexican anger toward the United States that the bill was approved unanimously and then approved by President Carlos Salinas de Gortari. This new law was Mexico's response to the U.S. Supreme Court ruling in June 1992 that approved the 1990 kidnapping of the Mexican doctor from Mexico.

## KILLING A NEARLY BLIND RANCHER

Another of several examples of the vicious mindset of ATF and Justice Department agents was the shooting death of a wealthy and nearly blind rancher, Donald Scott, near Malibu, California (October 2, 1992). Federal personnel had tried to buy the ranch to expand the adjacent Santa Monica Mountains National Recreation Area. But Scott, a recluse, partially blinded by recent cataract surgery, didn't want to sell.

A multi-agency drug task force of over two dozen heavily armed California and federal agents[476] mounted a military-type assault upon Scott's home. They said they were looking for a field of marijuana they claimed that a federal agent spotted from a plane flying a thousand feet over the 200-acre property in the hills above Malibu, called Trail's End.

Instead of going to the ranch in a peaceful manner with a search warrant, they conducted a commando-type raid, breaking into Scott's home while he was sleeping, killing him as he came out of his bedroom. No marijuana plants or drugs were found on his property.

There was no reason for this commando-type raid, as there was no need for the element of surprise. If Scott had actually been growing fields of marijuana, he could not suddenly dispose of it down the toilet, and the peaceful serving of a search warrant was all that was necessary.

Investigation showed that the real motive was not a search for drugs, but a desire to seize Scott's ranch under federal forfeiture laws. Scott's wife had been a former user of drugs and if the slightest trace of drugs could have been found on the property, the five million dollar ranch could be seized under the draconian federal forfeiture laws.

---

476 The invaders were from the Los Angeles County sheriff's department, the Los Angeles Police Department, the U.S. Drug Enforcement Administration, the National Park Service and the California National Guard.

Subsequent investigation revealed that federal agents had obtained a property appraisal before invading Scott's home, showing the value of adjoining property and indicating the desire to seize the property. Federal personnel in charge of the raid advised the attacking agents to look for evidence of drugs so as to justify seizing the property.

**WEAVER FAMILY AGAINST THE "BRAVE MEN" OF ATF AND JUSTICE**

At an isolated mountain-top home in Idaho 400 heavily armed ATF and FBI agents, U.S. marshalls, local law enforcement agencies (supported by military vehicles and tanks), surrounded a small house occupied by Randy Weaver, a former Green Beret, his wife, and their four children. Weaver was on the Justice Department's hit-list for refusing to cooperate in an undercover operation against a group of local skinheads. Weaver had been asked to infiltrate the group, but after attending a few meetings, he didn't want anything to do with the plan.

ATF and FBI personnel instituted a plan to retaliate against Weaver. An undercover agent of the Bureau of Alcohol, Tobacco and Firearms pressured Weaver to sell him sawed-off shotguns, which Weaver at first refused to do. After ATF persistence, Weaver finally did what he was requested to do, selling two of them which were allegedly 1/4 inch short of the minimum legal length.

Justice Department prosecutors charged Weaver with violating federal firearms law, and ordered him to appear in federal court. When Weaver failed to appear (due to an error in the reporting date made by the court clerk), six heavily-armed U.S. marshals in camouflaged clothing sneaked onto Weaver's mountain-top property. Weaver's dog spotted the intruders and started barking, after which a family friend, Kevin Harris, and 14-year-old Samuel Weaver went to investigate.

As the dog approached the intruders, they shot and killed the animal. The young boy cried out, "You've killed my dog." At that point Randy Weaver came out of the house and hollered for his son to come back. Sammy hollered, "I'm coming, Dad." As the boy ran toward the house one of the marshals fired seven shots at him, hitting him in the back. The boy lay there, suffering, and eventually died.

Harris, who had gone with the young boy to investigate, witnessed the killings and shot back, killing the marshal that murdered Sammy. The remaining U.S. marshals then retreated, returning with a force of over 500 heavily armed, battle-ready, FBI and other federal personnel, bravely massed to do battle against the father, the mother, three children, and a friend.[477] Included in this armada against the family under siege were tanks and other weapons of war.

The FBI took charge and ordered the small army to shoot anyone seen outside the house. During this siege the father went to a storage building adjacent to the house to view the body of his slain son. A sharpshooter from this small army then shot him in the back. His wife, Vickie Weaver, was standing in the opened doorway holding her infant daughter, when a federal agent shot her with a large caliber rifle, splitting her head apart. Blood spurted from her wound as Weaver pulled his wife inside and laid her down on the kitchen floor. Frightened, Weaver

477 *Spotlight*, September 25, 1992.

and his children lay on the blood-splattered floor, expecting to die at any moment. For eight days they waited in fear, as the U.S. taxpayer-financed army threatened to kill them all.

Although only a small percentage of Americans cared, outraged neighbors and people from all over the country converged on the site, protesting the slaughter. Several members from a concerned citizens group in Hawaii arrived, as did people from throughout the state. Their presence may have saved the remaining hostages from being murdered as happened to young Weaver and his mother.

According to a *Wall Street Journal* article,[478] an internal FBI report shortly after the siege commenced, justified killing Mrs. Weaver and her son, asserting that they had put themselves in harm's way. The article stated:

> *Court records show that while the woman's body lay in the cabin for eight days, the FBI used microphones to taunt the family. "Good morning, Mrs. Weaver. We had pancakes for breakfast. What did you have?" asked the agents in at least one exchange.*

No shots were ever fired from the cabin.

Justice Department prosecutors obtained an indictment against the remaining Weaver family from a rubber-stamp federal grand jury in Boise (September 16, 1992), charging the victims with federal crimes. The indictment against the Weaver family (including the children) read in part:

> *Vicki Weaver and other members of the family did unlawfully, willfully, deliberately...shoot, kill and murder one William F. Degan.*

That indictment, as worded, included the infant whose mother had been killed.

**PROMOTING KILLERS**

The jury in the subsequent trial held Weaver innocent of the charges filed by Justice Department officials, but held him guilty of a relatively minor offense; failure to appear in court for a hearing. Despite the trauma of having witnessed the killing of his wife and son, Weaver served a prison term for failing to show up for a court appearance.

Justice Department officials launched an investigation, issuing a 542-page report in 1995 recommending criminal prosecution of federal officials. Assistant attorney general for civil rights, Deval Patrick, refused to take this action, claiming that the murders of Sammy and Vicki Weaver were justified.

On January 6, 1995, Freeh issued oral and written reprimands (big deal) to several of the people responsible for the killings, and then promoted several of them, including Larry Potts, who was appointed to the second highest position in the FBI. Eugene F. Glenn became head of the Salt Lake City FBI office. E. Michael Kahoe became head of the FBI's Jacksonville, Florida office.

Freeh said that the shot that killed Mrs. Weaver, while she was holding her baby, was a "tragic accident." Freeh absolved the sniper of blame in that murder. This FBI mindset was blasted by attorney Gerry Spence who labeled Freeh's actions as:

> *A total whitewash. The censure means nothing. The promotion means everything. The clear message is: "It's all right to kill innocent women;*

---

478 *Wall Street Journal*, January 10, 1995.

*we'll stand behind you; we'll even promote you."*

Despite this example of the vicious mindset of Justice Department officials, very few Americans saw the threat to themselves and others, to constitutional rights, and the dangerous mindset in government. As usual, Congress did nothing about this misuse of a federal agency over which they had supervisory responsibilities.

The U.S. Marshall Service, on March 1, 1996, gave to those who murdered members of the Weaver family its highest award for, would you believe, valor. The award mentioned "their exceptional courage, their sound judgment in the face of attack, and their high degree of professional competence during the incident." The award called the men "heroes."

**ENLARGEMENT ON THE WEAVER TRAGEDY**

The Weaver tragedy received very little press coverage, even though it indicated a very dangerous mindset by ATF and Justice Department officials. By ignoring it, as in every other form of corruption implicating federal officials, the pattern continued and worsened. On Sunday morning, February 28, 1993, about one hundred heavily armed Alcohol, Tobacco and Firearms agents (ATF) invaded the residence of a religious group in Waco, Texas, attacking the building with loud shouts as if they were attacking a drug cartel. There were about a hundred people inside the residence, primarily women and children.

The religious group resided in a large building on property known as Mount Carmel, owned by a religious group known as Branch Davidians. They were a relatively peaceful group, harming no one, wanting to be left alone. As is common in Texas, to earn extra money, the group frequented gun sales and had accumulated a large cache of various types of weapons. They also knew about the Weaver tragedy and others, and didn't want the same to happen to them. They were more aware of the government arrogance than most Americans.

Upon hearing the shouting hoard of heavily armed para-military group descending upon them, the religious group locked the doors and braced for an attack. ATF agents broke windows and shot into the residence, killing eight people inside, including a two-year-old girl. As heavily armed agents started breaking windows and entering the building, the Branch Davidians naturally shot back, killing four of the assaulting ATF agents. Firing then stopped, and the para-military force retreated, followed by a nearly-two-month standoff.

The residents placed bales of hay against the gaping holes in the walls and where the windows were knocked out. Federal agents ordered electricity cut off to the compound, forcing the residents to use kerosene lanterns for illumination, creating a high fire risk. Government agents blasted the occupants twenty-four hours a day with loud noises, and shook the building with the movement of huge military tanks. Several of the besieged residents gave up and left the building, at which time they were immediately arrested and charged with conspiracy and murder of the four ATF agents who had invaded their residence.

The ATF agents were joined by FBI agents and National Guard troops, equipped with heavy attack vehicles and tanks, surely the envy of many Third-World military leaders. They were brave men, ready to do battle with the frightened religious group consisting mostly of women and children.

If the besieged residents had any hope that public pressure would bring a halt to the siege, they were sadly mistaken. As in Hitler's Germany, the government misconduct didn't directly affect them. The government's Wurlitzer-like manipulation of the media sought to make the besieged victims the culprits.

The large building in which the occupants were trapped was an old wooden building and highly flammable. A fire starting inside the structure could be expected to spread rapidly, especially if the winds were blowing hard as they often do on the Texas prairie. Once fire started inside, escape would be very difficult.

**APOCALYPTIC ASSAULT**

Early in the morning on April 19, 1993, while the lanterns burned inside the building, the war-ready heavily-armed military force commenced an attack, using armored vehicles and tanks, knocking down walls that fell inward upon the residents. Inside the building, sections of sheetrock and wood rained upon the frightened occupants, knocking burning lamps onto the piles of hay, causing them to ignite. As if this weren't enough, over 200 tear gas canisters were thrown into the building.

The leader of the religious group rushed through the building handing out gas masks and instructing the people to put them on immediately. The wind was blowing at over thirty miles an hour, roaring through the holes ripped in the building by the tanks, fanning the flames started by the overturned lanterns. Inside, the residents were trapped, scared, and unable to escape. The blackness of the early morning hours, the heavy smoke, the eye irritation caused by the tear gas, and the piles of debris in the hallways, made escape impossible for most of the residents. Eight managed to flee the searing heat, some of them with their clothes on fire.

Once the fires took hold, they spread in firestorm fashion, insuring the fiery death of everyone inside. Many of the frightened women and children huddled in fear, feeling the effects of the searing heat. Suddenly, as the flames reached the butane fuel escaping from a ruptured tank, an explosion sent flames hundreds of feet into the air, an event seen throughout the world on television screens. Possibly never in the history of the civilized world had such an arrogant government attack upon a group of religious people occurred, permitting the horrible consequences to be watched by a largely apathetic nation.

**OILING UP THE DISINFORMATION MACHINERY**

The Waco tragedy had the potential of waking up the American public to the mindset of their leaders. This possibility required oiling up the nationwide misinformation network controlled by various federal agencies; it appeared to work, except for those people who were informed about this form of government arrogance.

While the residence was still burning, President Bill Clinton appeared on TV, saying the residents committed suicide and they were to blame for the horrible outcome. Clinton said government agents and officials weren't responsible because "a group of fanatics tried to kill themselves." U.S. Attorney General Janet Reno echoed his words. Clinton and Reno had other reasons for blaming the victims. The two of them had approved the attack upon the religious group.

The same federal agents who inflicted that great tragedy upon the religious group sought to absolve themselves of blame, stating they saw the residents starting the fires. They sought to support this far-fetched statement on allegedly seeing someone in the building bending over. It is very possible that the person bending over was trying to put out the many fires started when the lanterns were knocked over; or it was totally fabricated.

Federal officials reported that many of the bodies had bullet holes in them, implying they were shot by the leader of the religious group to prevent them from escaping the flames. Texas coroner Dr. Nizam Peerwani, heading the Tarrant County Coroner's office in Fort Worth, stated: "There is absolutely no evidence of that, as far as we are concerned at this stage." Interviewed on *Good Morning America* on April 23, 1993, the coroner stated that because of the condition of the bodies it would be difficult to determine bullet wounds and that the immense fire left very little of the bodies to examine. He added, "When a corpse is exposed to such intensive heat, the head will often explode."

The mainstream media, which had kept the news of the Weaver tragedy from the American people, couldn't hide the Waco tragedy as they did the Idaho assault. But they did report as fact, over and over again, that the group had committed suicide; that the blame for the holocaust was upon the victims and not upon the attacking military force.

Eight members of the religious group escaped the inferno and were immediately arrested. When questioned separately by their attorneys, each of them described what happened inside the building. The survivors described the chaos in the building as the tanks inflicted heavy damage. They described how the kerosene lamps had been knocked over by the tanks crashing into the building, and the resulting fires, the difficulty of moving about because of debris from the collapse of the walls and the heavy smoke and tear gas. The smoke caused total darkness inside the building. "You couldn't see your hand in front of your face," stated attorney Dick Kettler, speaking for one of the religious group members, Remos Avraam.

Attorney Dick DeGuerin stated that his client told him "there was pandemonium, they knew they were trapped. It was difficult to move around even before the fire started because the tank battering had damaged the inside of the compound."

After hearing the facts stated by the survivors, Clinton repeated during an April 23, 1993, press conference what he had stated several days earlier: that the victims were responsible for their deaths. "I do not think the United States government is responsible for the fact that a bunch of fanatics decided to kill themselves." Clinton used the disinformation given by Justice Department agents to support his statements, even though they were contradicted by the independent statements of the survivors and by common sense.

## START OF ANOTHER CONGRESSIONAL COVERUP

Appearing on the *Larry King Live* television show within a few days of the holocaust, Senator Dennis DeConcini said he would head a senate investigative committee investigating the Waco affair. DeConcini repeated the statements of the Justice Department and President Clinton placing the blame for the deaths on Koresh. This dogmatic statement indicated his pre-judgment of the matter and his determination to protect government personnel. His statement blaming one of the victims came after there was overwhelming evidence showing Justice Department agents to be lying.

**THE "INVESTIGATORS"**

Never at a loss to find people willing to assist Justice Department mischief, a team of "investigators" came upon the scene several days later and defended the onslaught, stating the occupants themselves decided to set the building and themselves on fire. The wife of the team's leader, Paul Gray, worked for the same people who started it all, the Bureau of Alcohol, Tobacco and Firearms. Gray taught at the ATF's academy, and had been selected by the ATF to conduct the investigation. Gray confirmed that "this fire was intentionally set by persons inside the compound." Most of the gullible public believed this tale.

**SUBSEQUENT REPORT**

In response to pressure from groups of concerned citizens, Treasury Secretary Lloyd Bentsen called for an independent review to determine what really happened. In September 1993, the Treasury Department released its report, defending the use of the para-military force on the residence occupied mostly by women and children. The report admitted that there was a pattern of deception by senior officials in the aftermath of the bungled operation. Simultaneously, Department of Justice officials released a report clearing Attorney General Janet Reno and other federal officials (who had given approval to the attack), blaming the tragedy on field personnel.

**LONG PRISON TERM FOR SURVIVORS**

The jury found the survivors innocent of most charges, except aiding and abetting. U.S. District Judge Walter Smith handed down sentences (June 17, 1994) of as much as forty years to eight survivors of the Waco holocaust. The aiding and abetting charges, which would more appropriately apply to many federal personnel, permitted Judge Smith to render long prison terms for those who had suffered so greatly. As usual, most of the public was indifferent to the crime perpetrated upon this religious group.

Several of the survivors started corresponding with me in 1994, and gave me details of the vicious attack upon the group. It was obvious that the charges used to "justify" the attack upon the compound were the usual fabrication of government.

**GUN OWNERS BEWARE**

Millions of gun owners who legally purchased guns that were legal at the time of purchase can end up in prison and be financially destroyed, solely at the whim of a bureaucrat from the ATF and Justice Department. One gun owner, W.J. Chip Stewart, from Springdale, Arkansas was charged with a federal offense by the ATF, the same people responsible for the Weaver family and Branch Davidian massacres (and others). ATF and Justice Department attorneys caused him to be sentenced to federal prison for twenty-seven months. As a result of his imprisonment, Stewart lost his business, his wife who didn't wish to be inconvenienced, his credit worthiness, and his money.

What did bureaucrats in ATF and Justice Department consider a crime? Stewart had legally purchased two semi-automatic handguns that were legal to own at that time: a small 22 caliber and a 45 caliber semi-automatic pistol from Holmes

Firearms Company, similar to those owned by millions of people in the United States.

ATF bureaucrats decided, after many of these guns were sold, that the widely-sold semi-automatic guns could be converted by a gunsmith to become an automatic weapon and were therefore illegal.

Shortly after ATF agents notified Stewart that the guns that he had legally purchased were now unlawful, he turned the guns over to the ATF. They had gotten his name from the gun manufacturers' registration records. Eight months after ATF notified Stewart that his two pistols were put onto the banned list, and after Stewart voluntarily turned the guns over to them, Justice Department prosecutors obtained a grand jury indictment against him. Stewart, who owned an auto wrecking business and was a relatively permanent member of the community, could have been served peacefully with the warrant for his arrest. Instead, sixteen heavily armed ATF and FBI agents and local sheriff's department personnel converged upon his home, breaking down the door. Fortunately for Stewart, he wasn't home. Otherwise, he could have met the deadly fate of Scott, the Weavers, the Branch Davidians, or the many others who were killed by the brave men of ATF and FBI.

With this type of mindset almost anyone can be financially destroyed and put in prison, either because of violating some obscure statute or by being falsely charged.

In December 1994, White House police shot and killed a homeless man who had a knife on his side, and who was simply standing in position. He posed no immediate harm to anyone. The killing was needless, but the official who fired several shots point blank into the victim was never charged with a crime. The victim had been earlier kicked by the same officer, Stephen J. O'Neill.

## WIDESPREAD INVOLVEMENT OF FEDERAL JUDGES

The direct and indirect involvement of federal judges in almost every one of the criminal enterprises shown in these pages has already been mentioned. In Chapter 11 courts they were directly involved in the theft of billions of dollars a year from Americans who trusted their government and exercised the statutory protections of Chapter 11, 12, or 13.

Federal judges[479] were repeatedly put on notice through my federal court filings of the criminal activities described within these pages that a group of CIA insiders were ready to testify. The judges blocked the reporting of federal crimes, which made **them** guilty of federal crimes. I repeatedly appealed and petitioned the Justices of the U.S. Supreme Court to intervene, as they had a duty to do, and every time, they refused to respond.

## THE CRIMES OF CONGRESS

The public has a short memory. Scandal after scandal by members of Congress has surfaced and rarely has a member of Congress been criminally prosecuted. Simultaneously, thousands of American citizens are charged and put in prison for committing some minor offense, or imprisoned on thumped-up charges.

---

479 Including, for instance, Ninth Circuit Judges, including Marilyn Patel, Samuel Conti, Milton Schwartz, Edward Garcia, Raul Ramirez, and each of the Justices of the Ninth Circuit Court of Appeals; District of Columbia judges and justices, including Stanley Sporkin, Green, Silberman; Second Circuit judges and Justices at New York City; Fifth Circuit judges at Chicago.

Even in the Savings and Loan scandal, the nation's worst financial debacle that will adversely affect Americans for decades, not a single member of Congress, including those who openly solicited money to block regulators' actions, has been sent to prison.

Members of Congress limited their investigation of the Keating-Five to "ethics" violations, which is comparable to limiting the charges against the Murder Incorporated assassins to ethics violations. Even here, Congress couldn't hold that those who aided and abetted the greatest financial debacle had violated any ethics.

Government whistleblowers, concerned citizens with knowledge of government crimes, have reported to members of Congress for years about the crimes described in these pages. Possibly I hold a record for the number of years that I have reported the escalating corruption in government, and to this day there hasn't been a single meaningful response.

**PROSECUTOR'S IMMUNITY FROM CIVIL RIGHT AND CRIMINAL VIOLATIONS AGAINST AMERICAN CITIZENS**

The San Francisco and Los Angeles area legal newspaper, *Daily Journal*, carried an article (September 22, 1994) stating in part:

> *Prosecutorial misconduct is encouraged–if not indirectly condoned–by pervasive judicial abstention and "buck passing." Although appellate courts sometimes threaten to dismiss a case based on prosecutorial misconduct, they rarely do so, either finding the wrongdoing "harmless" or suggesting alternative remedies such as contempt.*
>
> *It is well-documented that in reality there often is no effective sanction for prosecutors who engage in unethical conduct.... This misconduct included violation of grand jury rules, violation of defendants' Fifth and Sixth Amendment rights, knowing presentation of false information to the grand jury, and mistreatment of witnesses. The report documents the fact that the Justice Department effectively ignored the courts' findings of governmental abuse, and that not one of the individuals involved was sanctioned, thereby raising "serious questions regarding what the Department considers 'prosecutorial misconduct.'"*
>
> *There is virtually nothing that an aggrieved party [defendant] can do when a court declines to sanction unethical government conduct, because prosecutors are absolutely immune from suit. In Imbler v. Pactman, 424 U.S. 409, 431 (1976), the Supreme Court ruled that a Los Angeles deputy district attorney who intentionally suborns perjury cannot be sued by the defendant who is wrongfully convicted...leaves the genuinely wronged defendant without civil redress against a prosecutor whose malicious or dishonest action deprives him of liberty, the Supreme Court, quoting an earlier case, decided that it is "better to leave unredressed wrongs done by dishonest officers than to subject those who try to do their duty to the constant dread of retaliation.*

Similar reasoning is used by judges to hold themselves immune from their wrongful and oftentimes criminal acts. They argue that to hold judges liable for unlawful acts would dampen the judicial spirit. Federal statutes have priority over judge-made case law, and give citizens the right to sue *anyone* who violates their rights. And in the English language, that includes judges.

People have been fraudulently sent to prison, even for life, on the basis of perjured testimony given by a person who is protected against the perjury by the prosecutors who often reward the perjurer for making the false statements demanded by the prosecutor. The reward for perjured testimony may be release from prison, dropping of charges, or placement in the witness protection program with long-term income provided. The witness giving false testimony need not fear being charged for perjury, as the prosecutor responsible for such charges is orchestrating the perjury.

**FINANCIAL LOSS IF PUBLIC DEFENDER OFFENDS THE JUSTICE DEPARTMENT OR FEDERAL JUDGES**

On the state and federal levels, private attorneys are selected to represent defendants who lack sufficient money to hire their own attorneys. The income of the court-appointed attorneys arising from representing defendants is often either the sole or a major source of income. If the attorney incurs the wrath of the Justice Department or federal judges, these attorneys can find themselves without any court-appointed cases, and literally find themselves out of business.

# LEGAL FRATERNITY AS A CRIMINAL ENTERPRISE

The common denominator in the entire sordid mess was the legal and judicial fraternities. I wrote of this in the first two printings of *Unfriendly Skies—an Aviation Watergate* in 1978 and 1980, and greatly enlarged upon that in the 1990 *Unfriendly Skies*. This revised *Defrauding America* expands upon the sordid and criminal nature of this legal fraternity group.

It was the legal fraternity within the FAA and NTSB that covered up for the air safety and criminal acts which other federal inspectors and I found at United Airlines and within the FAA. Justice Department attorneys enlarged upon these coverups and obstruction of justice. For the past thirty years Justice Department attorneys have blocked every attempt to report the crimes revealed in these pages.

**REPORT A CRIME, GO TO PRISON**

After failing to block my exposure of these criminal activities, the legal fraternity in and out of government proceeded to destroy me financially. This group consisted of the CIA-related law firm of Friedman, Sloan and Ross, federal judges and Justice Department personnel, using state judges and attorneys in the process. And when these activities failed to stop me, they proceeded to repeatedly charge me with criminal contempt of court from 1987 to the present date in retaliation for reporting the government-related criminal activities.

Sabotage of my exposure activities in the air safety field began with attorneys in the Federal Aviation Administration and the National Transportation Safety Board, especially during the Denver air safety grievance hearing. This was compounded by the Denver attorney whom I hired to assist me in that hearing, J.E. Kuttler. Kuttler either sabotaged my exposure efforts from the very start, or was grossly incompetent.

I sought legal representation to help expose the FAA corruption while residing in Oklahoma City. Several attorneys expressed shock at what I told them, and they said they would get back to me, but never did. I presume they talked to another attorney in the Justice Department and that ended their interest. I asked Oklahoma City attorney Clyde Watts for help to expose the corruption. He was a former attorney with the Department of Justice in Washington and planned on questioning some of his Justice Department friends when he went to Washington. Watts was defending General Walker, who the federal government was trying to silence, and who was placed in a federal prison hospital on the argument that he had mental problems. When Watts returned to Oklahoma City, he wouldn't talk to me. When I went to his office to pick up my papers, his associate greeted me, looked at me sadly, and wished me luck. Other attorneys advised that they would check the matter and get back to me. They all then avoided me.

Los Angeles attorney Ned Good contacted me and said he would use my testimony in a lawsuit against United Airlines concerning a Boeing 727 crash into the Pacific Ocean at Los Angeles (January 18, 1969). The sequence of events suggests that Good simply threatened to use my testimony if United did not agree to a financial settlement dictated by the attorney.

This same problem occurred again when attorneys contacted me to obtain information on the crew partying and NTSB coverup associated with the PSA San Diego crash (that was the world's worst air disaster at that time). They advised me that they would publicize my evidence, when in reality they simply used it to extract more money from PSA and its insurance carrier.

Some of the largest law firms in Salt Lake City, and the Utah State Bar, attempted to block the introduction of my evidence into the trials relating to the United Airlines crash at Salt Lake City. The same occurred in the New York City and Denver crashes when I attempted to introduce evidence I had acquired while I was a federal air safety investigator on that very same program at United Airlines.

## LACK OF INTEGRITY AT AIR-CRASH TRIALS

The level of integrity at court trials is at the level expected from the legal fraternity. Attorneys demand that the expert witnesses they hire slant their testimony in favor of their client, making the expert witnesses nothing more than brokers of disinformation.

The sordid deception practiced by the defense attorneys in the Simpson murder trial is an example of what is routine in the legal fraternity.

## AMERICAN CIVIL LIBERTIES UNION

The American Civil Liberties Union, the self-professed protector of civil rights, played a key role in the pattern of hard-core civil right violations judicially inflicted upon me. I repeatedly notified the ACLU of the civil right violations inflicted upon me, why it was being done, and the damage to the judicial system and our constitutional protections. The first contact was in 1965 and continued through 1989. They not only refused to provide help, but they upheld, aided and abetted the escalating civil right violations.

In 1989, the Executive Director of the Nevada ACLU, Shelly Chase, and I appeared on Reno radio station KOA, during which she upheld the right of Justice Department attorneys and federal judges to imprison citizens who report crimes committed by federal officials. She upheld the right of California judges to void divorce judgments rendered years and decades earlier, even though these acts were gross civil and constitutional violations. The Friedman law firm that played a key role in the ten-year-pattern of civil right violations was a key member of the ACLU in the San Francisco area.

The ACLU gets large financial donations from the public on the argument that they protect civil and constitutional rights. While some of their stated motives and actions are meritorious, there are many who question whether their goals enhance the quality of life. The ACLU often protects the most vicious and seamy side of society, often working to inflict harm upon others by protecting the guilty. Despite the fact that people were dying from aircraft hijackings, they opposed using metal detectors to screen passengers for weapons.[480] The ACLU opposed drug testing of transportation employees, even though studies indicated that excessive alcohol consumption was a serious problem among railroad employees. They argued repeatedly to allow brutal murderers to go scot-free because of some minor procedural requirement dreamed up by the same U.S. Supreme Court justices described in these pages.

**ATTORNEYS IN CONGRESS**

Without the coverup by members of Congress, most of whom are attorneys, the present number of scandals could not have been possible and would have been nipped in the bud in its infancy instead of escalating into the epidemic corruption that now exists. Members of Congress proposed legislation in mid-1989 to authorize federal employees in various government agencies to shoot down private aircraft in the drug-interdiction program, and proposed immunity for those shooting down and killing the occupants of the aircraft. They proposed that aircraft should be shot down if they did not respond to signals from an intercepting Customs or other government agency aircraft. The Senate voted to authorize the Customs Service and other federal agencies in August 1989 to fire upon small planes that do not respond to interception. Entire families can be wiped out by gunfire in this manner.

**CALIFORNIA SEGMENT OF LEGAL CORRUPTION**

Corruption in the legal fraternity is rampant throughout the United States, but that segment based in California has probably inflicted more damage upon the United States than any other segment. Upon becoming President in 1981, Ronald Reagan brought into the White House many California attorneys including Edwin Meese (former district attorney from Alameda County near San Francisco), Lowell Jensen, and others. They were all involved in scandal after scandal, using their control of the Justice Department to protect themselves from criminal prosecution.

It was the California legal fraternity that acted as a front in the sham action filed against me in the California courts. It was California judges, up to and including the Judges in the California Supreme Court, who aided and abetted the scheme through a ten-year pattern of massive civil and constitutional violations.

---

480 Between 1968 and 1973, there was an average of over two dozen attempted airplane hijackings a year. But after airports commenced using metal detectors in 1973 to screen passengers for weapons, the hijacking attempts dropped dramatically. ACLU argued that the security devices violated the Fourth Amendment protections against "unreasonable search and seizure."

The attorneys and judges in the Ninth Circuit federal district[481] constitute the largest block of legal fraternity corruption that I encountered, although the problem is national in scope. It was federal judges in the State of California who have made it an imprisonable offense to report government crimes, or to exercise federal protections to defend against civil, constitutional and criminal violations.

The attorneys that I hired were equally abominable. I finally had to appear without attorney to get the law into the record that barred the actions taken against me. In the sham California action the attorneys refused to raise the defenses in mandatory statutory law and under federal law, arguing instead fifty-year-old case law that permitted judges to do what they please.

My first attorney, Walnut Creek practitioner Douglas Page, jeopardized my defenses by substituting a young attorney right out of law school to argue important matters of law at a critical hearing, contrary to our employment agreement. The substituted attorney knew nothing about the unusual issues arising in the bizarre action filed against me. I fired both attorneys.

I contacted over thirty attorneys during the next few years, seeking legal representation. I knew the law but recognized that *in propria persona* defendants (also *pro se*), appearing without legal counsel, usually end up on the losing side due to judicial prejudice. My experience with attorneys revealed that they were either ignorant of the law; they didn't wish to offend the judges by showing they were wrong; some admitted that their careers would be seriously harmed if they were to defend me against the judges and Justice Department attorneys, and some engaged in outright sabotage of my position.

When I first decided it was time to exercise federal remedies for the massive civil and constitutional violations in the California courts, I engaged Sacramento attorney James Reed, who taught civil and constitutional law in the local law school. He wasn't much on California law relating to the underlying action filed against me by the Friedman law firm, but he used the law I researched and got it into his federal briefs. It was necessary to sue state judges to obtain declaratory and injunctive relief, something very few attorneys will do, fearing judicial retaliation.

The federal lawsuit filed by Reed exercised federal remedies for the civil rights violations and to obtain a declaratory judgment upholding the validity of the five judgments that established decades earlier my personal divorced status and property rights. That lawsuit named as defendants Solano County Judges Dwight Ely and Michael McInnis, along with the Friedman law firm.

It appeared that Reed was pressured to drop the judges as defendants, and over my objections he amended the complaint eliminating them. This federal action was assigned to U.S. District Judge Raul Ramirez, who quickly dismissed the action, clearly violating many federal statutes and related case law. Reed then changed residence and became county counsel at Mammoth Lakes, causing me to look for another attorney specializing in civil rights violations.

In 1985, I contacted attorney John Moulds who specialized in civil and

---

481 The Ninth Circuit consists of the states of California, Oregon, Washington, Nevada, Idaho, and Hawaii.

constitutional law. Moulds was the part-time magistrate who in 1987 sentenced me to prison for filing three federal actions seeking declaratory and injunctive relief from the civil rights violations, and for reporting the federal corruption I had uncovered. After Moulds looked over my papers, he admitted the gravity of the violations committed in the California action but told me he couldn't represent me in federal court because of his part-time magistrate position. He had known that earlier, and never raised the objection, until he recognized the nature of the problem.

**ANOTHER IMPOSTER**

I wasn't doing very well in finding attorneys by referrals, or even on blind calls, so I tried a different approach. I advertised in the San Francisco newspapers for an attorney, receiving a telephone call from an attorney who represented himself as Sid Saperstein with offices supposedly in San Francisco. I resided in Reno then, seeking to escape the worst of the California judicial tactics. Saperstein said he would come to Reno the next day. I was unable to visit California because California judge William Jensen in Fairfield had rendered a bench warrant for my arrest. This warrant was issued when I had an attorney appear on my behalf during a hearing in Solano County Superior Court, which was necessitated by my appearance in U.S. District Court at Sacramento in a civil rights action in which that same California judge was a defendant. Even though appearance by attorney was permitted by California law and the judge knew I could not physically be in two places at the same time, Jensen issued a bench warrant for my arrest. The Solano County bench warrant for my arrest was still outstanding, and I wanted an attorney to get that removed.

Saperstein came to my Reno residence on January 23, 1987, claiming that he had connections in the courts and could get the bench warrant lifted. He asked for money and I wrote him a check, and asked him for his calling card. He pulled out a hand-written calling card, stating he had changed offices and that his printed cards had not yet arrived. Sounded strange, but possible.

Several days later, Saperstein called and said that he had succeeded in getting the bench warrant lifted. This sounded fishy, as it normally requires a noticed hearing to have the matter heard. I asked him if he had the judge's order in front of him that vacated the bench warrant, and he said that he did. I asked him the name of the judge who signed the order. "Judge Schwartz," he replied. There was no Judge Schwartz in the Solano County courts where the warrant originated, causing me to ask which court issued the order. "The Superior Court in San Francisco," he answered. The San Francisco courts had no authority over the order rendered by the Solano County courts. Saperstein had a scheme going that obviously smelled to high heaven.

I asked Saperstein to read to me the exact wording on the order that he stated a few minutes earlier was right in front of him. He stated he would call me back shortly. He couldn't do this because there was no such order. That was the end of Saperstein. I never saw or heard from him again. I sent a certified letter to the address that he gave me as his office, and it came back with a post office notation that the address didn't exist.

What I suspect happened was that the Friedman law firm saw my advertisement for an attorney in the San Francisco legal paper and got Saperstein—or whoever he was—to contact me for the purpose of giving me false assurance that it was safe to return to California. Then, upon returning to California, Friedman would make certain that I was arrested.

I hired a Sacramento attorney, Joel Pegg, to have the bench warrant removed and to file appeal briefs that were due, seeking to vacate the orders rendered in the sham divorce action that had been rendered without jurisdiction and which violated blocks of California and federal law. His services were also needed as U.S. District Judge Milton Schwartz and U.S. Attorney David Levi at Sacramento had charged me with civil contempt of court for filing federal actions to have the validity of the five judgments declared under federal law and seeking relief from the civil right violations. Further, the actions reported the early stages of the federal corruption that I had uncovered up to that time.

Pegg has a prestigious looking office and a charming picture of Rhonda Fleming, supposedly one of his clients, on his desk. He looked impressive and said the right words, and I felt confident that I could trust him. I paid Pegg a $20,000 retainer and from that point he started sabotaging me at every turn.

It was urgent that the attorney file several appeal briefs with the California Court of Appeals that were coming due, but Pegg repeatedly put off preparing and filing the briefs. I was appealing decisions that would overturn the past three years of illegal and unconstitutional orders by the California judges and which affected the ownership of ten million dollars of property. The California Court of Appeals had already given me a time extension, and the three judges, Donald King, Harry Low, and Zerne Haning, were anxious to find some excuse to dismiss the appeals.

Forty-eight hours before the filing deadline I forced Pegg to give me an answer concerning the briefs that he had not even started to prepare; he answered that he had requested a time extension from the court and the court had granted it. By this time my opinion of attorneys was about as low as it could possibly get, so I checked to determine if he was lying. I telephoned the Clerk of the Court of Appeals at San Francisco, asking if an extension of time was requested and if it was granted. The clerk advised me that there was no request for an extension and none was granted. Pegg had lied to me. I wrote Pegg a letter and asked him for an explanation, which he refused to give me.

I then had to quickly prepare and file my own appeal briefs. This didn't take too long as I had already prepared a draft for Pegg. Appeals by people appearing without attorneys are usually denied in California courts. The system protects its own.

The briefs were filed, but the three judges in Division Five, District One, refused to even consider the briefs. They fraudulently said that the decisions being appealed were not appealable orders, repeating the misstatement of facts and law that had kept the sham California action going for the past six years. I then sought relief from the Justices of the California Supreme Court, but by this time the judicial corruption had progressed to such an advanced stage that it became necessary for every state and federal judge to protect the earlier judicial conduct.

Joel Pegg was to seek removal of the lis pendens placed upon my dozens of properties in the sham divorce action that halted my business operations and caused loss of valuable properties. He repeatedly said he would do so and then never did. His refusal to seek this basic relief forced me to seek relief in Chapter 11.

As stated earlier, U.S. Attorney David Levi and Judge Schwartz converted the civil contempt into a criminal contempt, and I now faced prison for having exercised federal remedies to defend against what was being done in the California courts. Pegg represented me in the defense against the criminal contempt charge, but refused to raise the defenses that would expose the scheme by Justice Department prosecutors and the federal judges. Just before the trial commenced, Pegg notified Magistrate John Moulds that he wanted to withdraw from the case. By that time Pegg had my money, and the Chapter 11 seizure of my assets left me without funds to hire other legal counsel. It also showed Moulds that there would be no attorney to file appeal briefs and other post-conviction defenses.

**THE BANKRUPTCY SCENE**

I obtained other counsel, and in 1987 sought relief in Chapter 11, seeking to force a federal judge to exercise his duty and provide the declaratory and injunctive relief to which I was entitled. I hired attorney Vernon Bradley of Sausalito, California, who was to represent me both in the California action and in the Chapter 11 proceedings. He then hired Las Vegas attorney Joshua Landish to handle the filing of the Chapter 11 papers in Las Vegas. Both Bradley and Landish agreed before I hired them that they would seek relief from the federal judge in Chapter 11 from the illegal orders of the California judges. But then when they became attorneys of record, they refused to file the necessary papers to obtain the relief.

I was present at the first hearing on the Chapter 11 cases on September 11, 1987. The two attorneys made a passionate argument on my behalf and, although they failed to raise the civil and constitutional violations that forced me to seek Chapter 11 relief, they argued in my defense. They praised my business acumen which had built up a multi-million dollar equity estate in twenty years. They argued that the sham California divorce action filed by the Friedman law firm caused me to seek relief in Chapter 11 and, if federal law was applied requiring the California judges to recognize the five prior judgments, there would be no reason for my seeking relief in Chapter 11. This was the hearing at which federal Judge Robert Jones rendered an order abstaining from hearing the cases, refusing to accept jurisdiction, and ordering that the two cases be dismissed in 60 days. This was not the full relief I wanted, but it removed the lis pendens and permitted me to pay off the mortgage loans that had come due.

These attorneys then sabotaged my defenses. Attorney John Landish appeared at a hearing limited to the personal Chapter 11 filing and limited to removal of the automatic stay on several mortgages. That hearing took place on September 28, 1987, without my knowledge. The mortgage holder[482] sought to foreclose on the properties on which the mortgages had come due, and which would have been shortly paid off since Judge Jones ordered removal of the state lis pendens

482 Robil, Inc., and Superior Home Loans.

that had blocked the refinancing. Landish, whom I had hired specifically to protect my properties, then requested Judge Jones to vacate the earlier order providing me relief; to seize the business, home, and assets on both the personal and corporate Chapter 11 cases via appointment of a trustee, and then to liquidate the assets, leaving me penniless.

I would later learn that this is a common trick used by attorneys after they have recommended to their clients that they seek Chapter 11 relief. The attorneys then strip their clients of all assets! In this manner, the attorneys and trustees generate huge fees as they plunder the assets. Through their attorneys, the Bank of America was famous for jumping the gun to seize the properties of their clients, ever since the 1930 depression days.

Landish kept notice of the seizure from me until after the ten-day period to appeal passed. I discharged Landish, but by that time he had done the damage. I did not learn what occurred at that hearing until several months later, after I obtained taped recordings of the court proceedings.

I hired other legal counsel, and the integrity problems continued. I hired attorney Raymond Goodman of Concord, California to represent me in the bankruptcy proceedings, and he too agreed to file briefs to remove the illegally appointed trustee. He didn't tell me that the California state bar had suspended his right to practice law. Also, he didn't tell me that he would turn my Chapter 11 cases over to an associate attorney, William Rubendall, whom I had never seen and who turned out to be a disaster. He failed to file opposition briefs and refused to file the briefs to remove the illegally appointed trustee as was agreed before I paid the retainer. He refused to return phone calls. Contrary to my instructions, he notified Judge Jellen that my earlier appeals would be withdrawn. And much more.

I then retained attorney Robert Ayers of Walnut Creek, California and paid him a retainer. After six weeks of failing to file the required briefs, he then told me he was no longer representing me. But he kept the money I gave him. I even had trouble getting my files back. What has been stated about attorney misconduct in these pages is only a small part of what occurred.

## SEIZING MY ASSETS AND THEN STRIPPING ME OF LEGAL COUNSEL

After attorney Pegg abandoned me, I asked for a public defender to defend me against the false imprisonment. Judge Raul Ramirez appointed Assistant Federal Public Defender Carl Larson, who operated as a puppet for the Department of Justice.

Larson refused to perform any of the fundamental legal requirements needed to defend me. He refused to file a motion for stay of my imprisonment pending appeal, which is a right under law. Larson refused to file briefs raising the many fundamental constitutional and statutory defenses that were violated. Larson refused to acknowledge the grotesque violations of law and constitutional safeguards, and supported the retaliatory actions taken against me.

Larson refused to obtain the hearing transcript or the records required to prepare a defense. He refused to file any briefs on my behalf, arguing that he would give a verbal presentation. That was totally unacceptable. Court rules and proper defense tactics require filing a written brief addressing the dozens of statutory and case laws and constitutional protections. A court hearing of this type is limited to a brief verbal argument and is totally inadequate and not intended to present the dozens of case laws, constitutional protections, and other complex issues. Larson was protecting his employer, the Justice Department, and the federal judges.

I discharged Larson and requested another attorney. At first this request was refused and I had to present briefs in pro se status. Finally, federal judges appointed another attorney, Sacramento sole practitioner Clifford Tedmon. He too duplicated the prior counsel misconduct and again I had no alternative but to discharge him. None of them would file motions for my release or raise any of the glaring violations of law. Federal judges appointed still another attorney, Brian DeAmicis, who repeated the tactics of the prior attorneys who refused to argue the controlling law and would not prepare adequate briefs. It was hopeless to obtain defenses under this pattern of legal misconduct. Finally, I discharged him and filed my own briefs.

## HOW WOULD THEY PROTECT AGAINST MALPRACTICE?

The conduct of these attorneys was hard-core misconduct, and I wondered how they would protect themselves from a malpractice action. I learned later that in judicial and Justice Department corruption of this magnitude the legal system bands together to protect itself.

I filed complaints with the California State Bar Association concerning Pegg and other attorneys, and they held the conduct to be proper. I filed a complaint with the Nevada State Bar and the Governor of Nevada concerning the misconduct of attorney Joshua Landish, who sabotaged me and caused the loss of my ten-million-dollar estate. They held that the attorney conduct was proper. When I filed malpractice actions in the State of California against the attorneys, the judges unlawfully dismissed the actions. I was totally gridlocked in every state and federal court, reflecting the cohesiveness of the legal fraternity.

Nevada attorneys said to me that I probably could never find a Nevada attorney to file a malpractice action against Landish, as the attorneys protect each other. I contacted at least half a dozen California malpractice attorneys concerning the misconduct by California attorneys, and none would take the case. Most had already heard about the judicial involvement and wanted no part of it. The legal fraternity had me gridlocked in the California and federal courts while simultaneously using the courts to destroy me financially and take away my freedom.

Eventually the California and federal judges settled on two quick responses to strip me of all defenses. They placed a frivolous label upon anything I filed, and then called me a vexatious litigant for seeking relief. In this way they stripped me of all statutory and constitutional protections and protected the legal and judicial fraternities from the consequences of their actions.

## POWER OF THE LEGAL AND JUDICIAL BROTHERHOODS

In *With Justice For None*,[483] the author and attorney Gerry Spence, described the power of the legal and judicial fraternities and that most judges are the lackeys of big-money interests. Mr. Spence spent much of his life representing insurance

483 *Times Books*, Gerry Spence.

companies and government contractors and later, protecting the rights of people adversely affected by injustice, such as the case of Karen Silkwood against Kerr-McGee. He also sympathized with me when I sought his help in 1988, but refused to help, even though the actions taken against me represented attacks upon fundamental constitutional rights and revealed a corrupt judiciary.

In *A Feast For Lawyers*[484] the author describes the hacks, vultures and scoundrels in the legal fraternity, and the judges who feed on the public. He describes the mentality of "we against them." The "we" being the legal fraternity and "them" being the uninformed public.

**JUDGES FOR SALE**

The practice of buying decisions is firmly embedded in the legal fraternity. A typical example was San Francisco Bay Area attorney Suren Toomajian who spent his vacations in Palm Springs and other places, accompanied by California judges whose expenses he paid. In return, the attorney received favorable decisions. One of his clients, a lady friend of mine, told me that Toomajian had a practice of canceling hearing dates until the court clerk assigned the case to a judge which the attorney controlled. Crooked attorneys leave envelopes containing money with particular judges or the judge's law clerk in payment for favorable rulings. Often, when the attorney appeared before a judge that he controlled, there would be virtually no arguments raised in support of the decision sought. The decision had been reached in private conversations before the hearing on the matter.

The legal fraternity has no interest in cleaning up the system that benefits attorneys and judges, even though the public is repeatedly victimized.

Bribing judges is routine. In an in-depth May 1995 article in the legal paper, *Daily Journal*, the bribing of U.S. Supreme Court Justices is described in detail.

**EFFECT OF JUDICIAL CORRUPTION ON LOCAL MATTERS**

The average citizen may experience this corruption, but not recognize it, when judgments are entered that defy logic or common sense in child custody matters, spousal support, and other judgments, not realizing that the opposing attorney regularly bribes that judge with financial favors.

**TIES BETWEEN RELATED LAW FIRMS AND COVERT GOVERNMENT ACTIVITIES**

I learned that the San Francisco law firm of Friedman, Sloan and Ross, who filed the sham California action against me and who the California and federal judges protected, was a covert Justice Department and CIA law firm wielding immense control in the courts. The first indication I had of that relationship was when an attorney in Las Vegas told me about it in early 1991.[485] The following year several of my CIA contacts described the clandestine CIA activities in which attorneys, law firms, trustees, and judges are paid off.

CIA and ONI agent Gunther Russbacher described, in sworn declarations and numerous letters and statements, the role played by law firms and attorneys in covert dealings with the Central Intelligence Agency and the Justice Department. He described how these attorneys do covert legal work for the

484 *Evans & Company*, by Sol Stein.
485 January 22, 1991.

two government agencies and how they play a key role in the Chapter 11 corruption. Russbacher described numerous covert CIA locations at which he saw members of this group and how they received payoffs.

Russbacher described seeing Las Vegas federal Judge Robert Jones at Atlantic City gambling casinos and the method of paying judges via gambling casinos. Russbacher described the presence of Chapter 11 trustee Charles Duck and his related law firm of Goldberg, Stinnett and MacDonald at secret CIA meetings in Central America. This entire cast of characters were the players in looting my assets in Chapter 11.

Russbacher described the role one of his companies, National Brokerage Company, played in the money trail to the overseas company that serves as the payoff center for federal judges, trustees and law firms, which is described in more detail elsewhere. Shamrock Overseas Disbursement Corporation in Dublin, Ireland receives and disburses funds for these payoffs. The telephone listing is under Shamrock Overseas Courier Service. The same person who was a CIA asset in the CIA-associated Silverado Bank Savings and Loan is reportedly the Chief Executive Officer of Shamrock, Donald Lutz.

## LEGAL FRATERNITY IN CHAPTER 11 CORRUPTION

The legal fraternity is deeply implicated in the massive Chapter 11 corruption that is inflicting billions of dollars of fraud upon American citizens every year. Attorneys often encourage their clients to file Chapter 11 to gain a little more time to pay a particular debt that has come due, fraudulently stating that the Chapter 11 court will provide the extra time. This is what the law says. But in practice, the fraud starts immediately. The federal judges order a trustee to seize the person's properties, business, and assets. The owner who built up the business and assets is ordered to vacate. The trustee then liquidates the assets at fire-sale prices, incurring huge legal fees and losses that usually destroy the assets. It's all blatantly unlawful, but the entire judicial system including the Justices of the U.S. Supreme Court protects the multi-billion-dollar a year racketeering enterprise. It is all part of the vast secret government looting assets of the American people. This criminal enterprise is one of the best-kept secrets in the United States.

## LEGAL FRATERNITY IN SAVINGS AND LOAN DEBACLE

The legal fraternity was heavily implicated in the savings and loan debacle. In 1992, numerous law firms were charged by various federal agencies with helping to carry out the looting of the savings and loans. The law firms associated with covert CIA activities, however, escaped the financial penalties. Despite their key role in the hundreds of billions of dollars in fraudulent transactions, I know of no law firm that was criminally prosecuted.

Blasting the role played by attorneys in the fraud involving Lincoln Savings and Loan Association, U.S. District Judge Stanley Sporkin of Washington, D.C., asked: "Where were these professionals? Why didn't any of them speak up?" Sporkin was involved in the 1980 October Surprise scheme and his judicial appointment was probably his reward by the Reagan-Bush administration for helping to carry it out, and to block any judicial exposure or prosecution activities.

"Thievery by Lawyers Is on the Increase, With Duped Clients Losing Bigger Sums," headlined the *Wall Street Journal* article (November 26, 1990). Dozens of articles like this appeared in the legal publications throughout the United States, especially in California. The cases (where attorneys receive large sums of money from estate or litigation settlements and then steal the funds intended for their client) are endless. The *Daily Journal* legal newspaper wrote (January 9, 1992) about the sharp rise in larceny by attorneys against their own clients. Sporkin's role in treasonous and criminal activities makes him the last person to point a finger. But it was good public relations.

**ATTORNEY "WATCHDOGS"**

Complaining to State Bar Associations about incompetence or outright thievery by attorneys is almost always useless. The practice of attorneys stealing money received for their clients is endless and, when this is reported, the bar association oftentimes will refuse to suspend the attorney's license to practice.

**LEGAL FRATERNITY IN PROBATE**

Even in death, the legal and judicial fraternities continue their sordid conduct. Attorneys have turned the probate field into a system to loot the deceased's assets, depriving widows and orphans of money they would receive if the corruption did not exist. In many states the probate system is a means of plundering estates, dividing up the loot among attorneys, judges, and their fronts. Local party bosses often select probate judges who will continue the practice of looting assets of the deceased.

An article in the *Journal of the American Bar Association* described the probate courts as "one of the most viciously corrupt systems ever devised by the inventive minds of the greedy." This is basically true, but the Chapter 11 courts are even worse, and more crooked.

The *New York Times* reported "The probate procedures in many areas border on the scandalous." A leading professional journal involved in probate reporting, *Trusts and Estates*, reported the routine nature of probate work as being "cut and dried...Most of the work is done by the lawyer's secretary...very little of the lawyer's own time is consumed." But the fees extracted from probate estates often consume most of the assets and, in some cases, the charges exceed the assets. Attorney fees are astronomical in relation to the time that the attorney spends on the case. In addition, probates that could be quickly settled are dragged out for months and years longer than necessary to inflate the attorney's already padded charges.

There are many cases where the surviving widow or children had to go on welfare, while a million dollars or more of assets were tied up in probate by crooked judges and their attorney cohorts. Even when wills have been made, some judges will find fault with them, declare that the person died intestate, and divide the assets as they see fit, increasing even further the attorney charges and kickbacks to the judge.

Attorney fees come from the assets before the heirs receive their inheritance, even when the attorneys appointed by the judges are unnecessary, and their appointment results in the heirs receiving nothing. What a system! There is virtually nothing a victimized heir can do as the system protects its own, regardless of how corrupt the attorneys and judges may be.

Connecticut attorneys conspired with their attorney friends in the legislature to pass a law taxing inter-vivo trusts that were circumventing the probate racket.

This law requires a person filing an inheritance tax return due on a probate-exempt trust to pay huge fees to the local probate judge, even though that person performed no services in connection with the trust. The legislatures on the state and federal level are controlled by attorneys, who block almost every effort by the public to protect themselves against these parasites. Like sheep, the public remains unresponsive as it is devastated, financially and otherwise.

It has been said that it costs over one hundred times more to probate an estate in the United States than the same size estate in Britain, and takes over ten times longer to do it.

The public doesn't understand the gravity of this misconduct. During the 1984 presidential campaign of Vice Presidential candidate Geraldine A. Ferraro, it was revealed that her attorney husband, John Zaccaro, had taken $175,000 from an elderly woman for whom he had been appointed conservator. As if the money was his own, he used part of it as a deposit to purchase property for a client of his real estate company and part of it to pay tax and mortgage payments for another client. Confirming that no one can lie like an attorney, Zaccaro stated to a *New York Times* reporter that no one told him that he couldn't use someone else's money for his own use.

If this was a book on probate it could be filled with horror stories of attorneys and judges stealing money from innocent people through probate fraud that they call legal.

**TYPICAL LEGAL SABOTAGE**

Another example illustrating how an attorney will sabotage his own client occurred during a trial on drug smuggling charges. A federal judge in San Francisco dismissed charges (November 15, 1991) against a person charged with drug smuggling on the basis that the defendant's attorney conspired with attorneys for the Justice Department to get him convicted.

The judge blasted the U.S. Attorney's office for "outrageous misconduct" because he encouraged the defendant's attorney to mislead his client. "The conduct of the Justice Department in the investigation and prosecution of Steven Marshank was so outrageous that it shocked the universal sense of justice," said the U.S. District Judge. The written ruling by the judge said that the defendant's attorney, Ronald Minkin of Los Angeles, supplied information to Justice Department attorneys about his client and other defendants in order to get them convicted. Through this misconduct the attorney was able to collect thousands of dollars in legal fees and stood to gain millions of dollars when the prosecutor seized his client's properties under forfeiture laws.

**LIKE WADING IN A SEPTIC TANK**

Outrageous as this is, I experienced this attorney misconduct over and over again and learned of many other cases similar to this. It is a firmly established mindset and accepted code of conduct of this sordid group. The examples of attorney misconduct that I describe within these pages are only examples of many other instances. Dealing with this group reminded me of wading in a non-functioning septic tank.

An article in the *Wall Street Journal* (September 11, 1991) said, "Lawyers Who Tattle On Clients Prompt Concern." The article told of the situation in Houston where the attorney became a government informant against his own clients. U.S. District Judge Lynn Hughes held, however, that tape recordings made by the attorney of his client can be used in criminal proceedings against the client.

"The notion of attorneys as informants, particularly as informants against their own clients, is an area that we've seen sporadically over the years," said Neal Sonnett, a Miami criminal-defense lawyer. "We do not condone the government's use of criminal-defense-attorneys as informants against their clients," said a federal appeals court in Atlanta (1987). However, they allowed the indictment against the victimized client to stand.

Assistant U.S. Attorney Turow in Chicago approved the treachery, saying that the intrusion is justified, "It's obviously a treacherous area for the government to work in, but it's an area that sometimes the government has to work in." Attorneys involved in the profitable sabotage of their own clients have even agreed to keep Justice Department prosecutors informed of their client's *future* crimes. In the case against Manuel Noriega, Justice Department prosecutors obtained the help of an attorney who formerly represented Noriega and who turned government informant, a profitable change for the attorney.

Attorneys have even murdered their clients. An example: San Jose, California, attorney Norman R. Sjonborg was charged by Santa Clara County Superior Court Judge with being "one of the most dangerous sociopaths that I have ever seen," for having killed one of his female clients. Attorneys taking advantage of their female clients, demanding sex, is so rampant it is hardly news anymore.

**FORCING SEX UPON WOMEN NEEDING LEGAL HELP**

A standard practice of attorneys is forcing female clients to have sex with them in order to be represented. This practice was so outrageous that New York and California passed legislation barring sex between an attorney and client. But whether this will stop the abuses is questionable. The routine violations of the canons of ethics by attorneys, and the State Bar refusal to prosecute for such violations, leaves no hope for reform.

**SEIZING A CLIENT'S PROPERTIES**

One of the scams used by attorneys is to take a deed of trust on a person's home or properties to insure payment of legal fees, followed by outrageously excessive fees resulting in loss of the property to the attorney. New York State passed legislation in 1993 preventing this onerous practice.

**THOSE UNABLE TO STOMACH IT**

In a full page *Newsweek* article (November 4, 1991), a former attorney told why he gave up his law practice, repeating what has been written in many other articles. In his book, Sam Benson wrote:

> *I am astounded that I was able to practice law for more than two years of my life. It was not any single event that pushed me over the edge. It was an uneasiness, an uncomfortableness that was always there for me. I was tired of the deceit. I was tired of the chicanery. But most of all, I was tired of the misery my job caused other people.*

**THE POWERFUL TRIAL LAWYER LOBBY**

The Trial Lawyer Lobby is one of the most powerful lobbies in the United States, consisting of over 60,000 trial lawyers. They exert great influence upon politicians through their political contributions or bribes. This lobby has become the Democratic party's most important special interest group, supposedly more powerful than government unions. Congressmen vote against the wishes of this lobby at risk of being targeted for removal.

Two prominent names on the list of financial recipients of the Trial Lawyers Lobby were Senator Howard Metzenbaum (D-OH), and Senator Ernest Hollings (D-SC) who received over $400,000 from members of the Trial Lawyers' Lobby.[486] The bundling of contributions from these attorneys and their family members and the political-action committee can buy virtually any Senator's votes. So-called public interest advocate Ralph Nader gets a major share of his contributions from the trial-lawyer groups. Attorneys in the trial lawyer lobby control sufficient Democrats to block any vote in the Senate on changing the liability laws.

Studies have shown that less than 40 cents of every dollar paid to settle litigation goes to the person who suffered the injury. The rest goes to the attorneys.

Election of attorney Bill Clinton to the presidency of the United States with his attorney wife didn't help the problem, especially with Clinton's role in Arkansas scandals.

## PROTECTED BY THE STATE BAR ASSOCIATIONS

In case after case these corrupt practices continued without any corrective measures after people made complaints to the State Bar Associations. My complaints to the California and Nevada Bar Associations relating to the pattern of attorney misconduct resulted in *approval* of the misconduct.

Major law schools and universities have a responsibility to act when a pattern of judicial activities destroys the rights and protections under our form of government. They have the legal knowledge and the duty to act, but when hard-core corruption is involved that would bring adverse public reaction upon the group, they aid and abet the activities. These legal institutes of learning know of the criminal activities implicating federal judges and Justice Department attorneys.

I brought these activities to the attention of Professor Ulysses Crockett of the University of California at Berkeley. Crockett had first telephoned me in 1991 when he heard about my contact with CIA operative Gunther Russbacher, and then seemingly took an interest in what I was doing. After that, I confronted Crockett with his responsibility to intervene, especially in the nearby San Francisco federal action against me. Instead, he referred me to several law professors in New York and Massachusetts that he said owed him a favor.

I wrote to these professors and only one responded, expressing a lack of interest. Crockett has been a prosecutor in the same Alameda County District Attorney's office as Edwin Meese, who was deeply involved in most of the scandals I have mentioned in this book. I wondered if Crockett was simply trying to find out how much information we had about the scandals in which his fellow attorneys, such as Edwin Meese, were involved.

## WOLVES IN SHEEP'S CLOTHING

From this sordid group come state and federal judges, who try to present

---

486 *Daily Journal*, September 30, 1992.

to the public an appearance of honor, integrity, and justice. Many judges require everyone in the court to stand up when they enter the court room, as if they are someone to be revered.

There are thousands of examples of the sordid conduct of state and federal judges. On a lighter vein was the conduct by U.S. District Judge Robert H. Schnacke, to whom I sought to report in 1974 the criminality I uncovered in the aviation environment. Reflecting on Schnacke's personal life, the headline in *The National Educator*[487] stated: "Kindig fights Pan Am and cathouse judge." The article stated in part:

> *A judge who has a reputation of siding with the big corporations and who, to say the least, is anything but squeaky clean in his own personal life, having been caught up in a police vice squad raid on a house of prostitution on January 25, 1985. One way or the other, the raid, which took place in San Francisco, did not make the news media until the San Francisco Chronicle finally reported it on March 16th. The federal judge, Robert H. Schnacke was in the audience of an adult theater on Market Street, when the vice squad officers arrested 11 women performers on lewd conduct charges. According to one of the arresting officers, the judge was more than in the audience; he was allegedly "performing" by placing Federal Reserve Notes in the private parts [vagina] of the prostitutes.*

**"Months of Lies to the Press."**

Famed defense attorney Gerry Spence described during a 90-minute speech to the Montana Trial Lawyers Association (July 22, 1993)[488] his observations of the lying by Justice Department attorneys in criminal trials. He exhorted the attorneys to challenge federal prosecutors and not accept as true anything that they say.

"These are not the good guys." Spence stated, "These are people who do [lie, fabricate evidence] what they believe is necessary to bring about a conviction."

Spence had just finished the trial in which Justice Department attorneys tried to imprison Randy Weaver after they had killed his wife and son as they stormed their humble cabin. Spence told the group:

> *The siege against Weaver brought in enough [weapons of war] to take over a small country for this little man sitting in this little plywood cabin.*

Spence said that after killing Weaver's wife and son, Justice Department attorneys "charged him with conspiracy...and they made the entire family the conspirators....The federal government now has the audacity to say that members of a family are members of a conspiracy, little children are members of a conspiracy."

## HIGHEST JUDGE IN NEW YORK STATE SENTENCED TO PRISON

One of the highest-ranking judges in New York State was sentenced to prison on September 9, 1993. Former Chief Judge of New York's Court of Appeals embarked on a two-year pattern of sending vulgar, harassing, and threatening

---

487 March 1989.
488 Associated Press, July 23, 1993.

letters and phone calls to his former mistress and her daughter. Judge Sol Wachtler, who was married, was upset over the ending of his four-year secret love affair with Manhattan socialite Joy Silverman. He disguised his voice while making threatening phone calls to his former mistress, threatened to kidnap her fourteen-year-old daughter, sent obscene letters and pictures to the daughter, and committed other despicable acts. These were obscene and criminal acts, but the many judges and their co-conspirators that strip innocent people of their life's assets or their liberties commit far greater harm.

### AMAZING THAT MORE ATTORNEYS AND JUDGES ARE NOT SHOT BY THEIR VICTIMS

It has always amazed me that more attorneys and judges are not shot by their victims, some of whom have lost through judicial and legal corruption their life's assets and now must face their remaining years in abstract poverty, along with their families. Often, the victims are unaware of the mechanics of how they had been financially destroyed.

The individual attorney or judge who gets shot receives little publicity. But in one case the publicity was nationwide when a client stormed a San Francisco high-rise office building on July 1, 1993, and shot over a dozen people, eight of whom died.

### CREATING A DANGEROUS MINDSET NATIONWIDE

The endemic corruption within the legal and judicial fraternities, the abominable lack of integrity, infects government and non-government activities throughout the United States. These two groups are at the center of every corrupt activity within these pages. Their conduct has created a mindset of corruption throughout America, destroying the moral fibre of the United States. And these are the two groups most responsible for upholding the laws and Constitution of the United States and establishing a guideline for acceptable conduct.

This is the climate and conduct permitted to occur by a largely illiterate and indifferent public, whose apathy makes this possible.

### PERSONALITY TRAITS CARRYOVER

The sordid conduct and mindset, and the "we against them" mentality do not disappear, when an attorney becomes a judge. The addition of judicial power and self-ruled immunity from their acts makes for terrible injustice against the American people.

# ISRAEL, THE MOSSAD, AND AMERICA

Israeli officials and agencies, and particularly its intelligence agency, the Mossad, aided and abetted many of the criminal activities described within these pages, inflicting great harm upon the American people. Without the assistance of the Israelis, some of the treasonous and subversive acts against the United States would not have been possible, especially the October Surprise operation. Israel was needed to transship the arms to Iran and to act as end-users on the bill-of-lading.

## KILLING PEOPLE WHO DISAGREE WITH ISRAELI POLICIES

Similar to CIA activities, and possibly worse in some respects, the Mossad doesn't hesitate to assassinate people whose lawful conduct irritates the Israelis. Gerald Bull, a Canadian scientist who developed the Super Gun used by Iraq, was killed by the Mossad at his Brussels apartment in March 1990.[484] Israeli assassination squads killed Bull to halt his development of the weapon project.

During that same time frame, Israeli agents were assassinating others, as reported by former Mossad officers Ari Ben-Menashe and Victor Ostrovsky in their books.[485] Nineteen people were murdered by Israeli agents within several weeks in 1990, including eight German scientists hired by a company in Miami and who were traveling back and forth to Iraq. They included a German scientist, Hans Mayers, in a car "accident" in Munich; four Iraqi businessmen, and two Pakistani scientists in Britain.

---

[484] *Profits of War*, Ari Ben-Menashe; *By Way of Deception*, Victor Ostrovsky and Claire Hoy; *The Other Side of Deception*, Victor Ostrovsky.

485 ibid.

A television production aired on June 17, 1993, focused on the many killings by the Mossad, including the botched killing in Norway of the wrong person by Mossad operative Michael (Freddy) Harari. It was in Lillehammer, Norway, in 1974, that a Mossad Kidon team headed by Harari killed a Moroccan waiter who they thought was their intended victim, Ali Hassan Salameh. Instead, the victim was a plain waiter, with a wife and two children. Israel agreed in January 1996 to pay compensation to the widow and daughter of $283,000, and to the son of $118,000. A panel of Norwegian judges convicted five Israelis of the murder, concluding that the assassination was run by Israel's intelligence agency, Mossad.

One of their favorite assassination stunts was to put a pressure sensitive plastic-explosive bomb in the victim's bed. When the intended victim lay on the bed the bomb went off. Another tactic was to place plastic explosives in a telephone handset and when the person answered, and the caller identified him as the intended victim, the bomb would be set off by a signal carried over the telephone wire. Although the plastic explosive was small in size, it usually caused fatal injuries.

Victor Ostrovsky detailed the specifics of several of the killings by Israeli agents, detailing the composition of the Israeli assassination department inside the Mossad as a small internal unit called *"Kidon"*, divided into three teams consisting of approximately twelve men each.

Ostrovsky told of the shooting down of a Boeing 727 operated by Libyan Arab Airlines by two Israeli jets, killing over a hundred people. He told how two Israel agents killed Arab scientist Yahia El Meshad by slipping into his apartment with a passkey and then cutting his throat while he slept. He also told how the Mossad killed a PLO official in Paris who was preparing to meet with the French Secret Service.

The December 14, 1992, issue of *Spotlight* carried a story about Israeli assassination squads operating in foreign countries under the title, "Foreign Killers Run Loose in U.S." The article related how Israeli-trained assassins, funded by U.S. taxpayers, are entering the United States, often with the help of the CIA, leaving a trail of unsolved and unreported killings. The report explained how the United States is funding Mossad's criminal operations in Third World countries.

Ben-Menashe's book portrays the Mossad's hiring of Arabs who unknowingly carried out terrorist attacks against Americans, inflaming the American public against the Arabs, who didn't know the attacks were planned and directed by the Mossad. He also tells how Mossad agents paid Palestinians to seize the Mediterranean cruise ship *Achille Lauro* in 1985, which ended in the killing of one of the passengers. Ironically, the passenger was Jewish. Ari Ben-Menashe wrote in his book *Profits of War* that the attack upon the cruise ship was financed by Israel, and its intent was "to show what a deadly, cutthroat bunch the Palestinians were." The American public was told that the attack upon the *Achille Lauro* was a Palestinian operation when in fact it was engineered and financed by Israel.

**ISRAEL'S ADMISSION OF WORLD-WIDE ASSASSINATIONS**

A *London Observer* article carried in the *San Francisco Examiner* on

**ENORMOUS POWER OF THE ISRAEL LOBBY**

One of the most powerful forces in the United States is the Anti-Defamation League, whose parent is B'nai B'rith. Much of the money used to bribe members of Congress and other federal officials is sent to the United States by Israel, which obtains the money from U.S. loans and grants that are rarely repaid. Through its powerful Zionist group it can fund campaigns to defeat politicians not adhering to Zionist wishes.

ADL blocks any exposure of wrongful activities by Israel and its Mossad. It spends huge sums of money to oppose members of Congress whose interests are not aligned with Israel. Much or all of this money comes from the U.S. taxpayers who provide loans or grants that are not repaid. One tactic used to silence those who report or criticize the Mossad or Israel's conduct is to label them an anti-Semite. It is risky business for a public official to defend U.S. interests when it means confrontation with the Zionists. Apparently anyone who disagrees with Israel is anti-Semitic, and the vast control by Israel over the U.S. media will make certain the American people hear this version.

ADL has been able to defuse any attention focused upon unlawful activities of people connected with Israel or the Mossad. The ADL lauded a major Jewish crime figure, Morris Barney Dalitz of Las Vegas, who regularly donated heavily to the ADL. Dalitz was called Chairman of the Board to such crime figures as Meyer Lansky and Benjamin "Bugsy" Siegel. Lansky and Siegel were members of the original "Murder Incorporated,"also known as the Meyer and Bugsy Gang. JDL[501] chairman Irv Rubin was accused in 1992 of plotting a murder-for-hire operation.

In *American Jewish Organizations and Israel*, author Lee O'Brien describes the Anti-Defamation League of B'nai B'rith (ADL):

> *In later years, ADL has turned to...aggressive measures....outright surveillance of individuals and groups, the results of which are fed into both the Israeli intelligence-gathering apparatus, via their consulates and embassy, and American domestic intelligence, via the FBI. Top ADL officials have admitted the use of clandestine surveillance techniques.*

The Anti-Defamation League of B'nai B'rith has been functioning as the action arm of the Israeli Mossad in the United States. In 1993, an ADL spy scandal erupted in San Francisco, after which it was learned that the ADL had been acting as proxy for the Mossad. The scandal surfaced after it was discovered that San Francisco police inspector Tom Gerard[502] was stealing police intelligence files and selling them to the ADL.

It was learned during the investigation that Roy Bullock was an ADL operative spying on numerous individuals and groups in the United States. According to an April 9, 1993, *Los Angeles Times* article the ADL disguised payments made to Bullock by funneling the money through Beverly Hills attorney Bruce Hochman, who in turn paid Bullock. Hochman was a prominent ADL figure, and a member of a panel appointed by Governor Pete Wilson to recommend the names of attorneys for federal judgeships. This helps explain why the

---

501 JDL, Jewish Defense League, is a group founded in the late 1960s to fight those opposed to Israel.

502 *San Francisco Chronicle*, May 8, 1993.

inordinately high percentage of federal judges are Jewish.

During a three-hour press interview in the Philippines, Gerard revealed that he was a former CIA operative and had evidence that the CIA trained, supported, and encouraged death squads operating in El Salvador, Honduras and Guatemala during the 1980s. The sheer brutality of the carnage was too much for him, and he left the CIA in 1985. "This was not good guys versus bad guys," Gerard said. "This was evil, evil.... This was something the devil himself was involved in. And I wanted no part of it."

Gerard told how the CIA supported the death squads that tortured and murdered thousands of people in Central America, including political opponents, union members, peasants, and clergy throughout Central America. Gerard said that the San Francisco police and the FBI have joined forces to discredit him. Following its standard practice of lying, a CIA spokesman denied that Gerard had any relationship with the Agency.

**CIVIL RIGHTS IN ISRAEL**

Civil rights are largely ignored in Israel. Only those with Jewish mothers have full stature in Israel, a form of apartheid. Christians and Moslem Palestinians are deprived of their basic human rights in Israel, and the United States has been subsidizing this Israeli socialism, Israel's form of apartheid. The Israeli government regulates and controls almost every facet of personal and business endeavors.

In late 1992, Israeli officials deported 415 Palestinians from their homes, forcing them into the mountains and barring relief supplies that the Red Cross tried to deliver to them. Those deported included doctors, accountants, lawyers, lecturers, and engineers, some of whom were elderly, and some of whom had heart problems or were crippled. They were driven into a no-man's land in the mountains as winter approached.

An Israeli human rights group[503] charged their government with routinely torturing Palestinian political prisoners, reporting that "Violence and ill-treatment have become an expected part of interrogations." The report stated that at least 5,000 of the 25,000 Palestinian prisoners jailed in the previous year had been tortured, while Palestinians reported that the percentage was much higher. An April 3, 1993, *New York Times* article was entitled, "Israeli Study Finds Torture Common."

**AMERICAN TAXPAYERS FUND THESE ACTIVITIES**

Israel depends upon the largesse of the United States government and its powerful Israel lobby, as well as other Zionist groups, to fund these activities, including their assassination teams, and bribing U.S. lobbyists, public relations firms, and members of Congress. Billions of dollars in loans have been given to Israel that will never be repaid, the cost of which must be borne by the American taxpayer, plus the interest on the money. In 1991, Israel literally demanded that the U.S. guarantee $10 billion in loans to build housing for Jews in land taken from Jordan.

Despite the enormous amount of gifts to Israel, their appreciation was reflected in the 1991 statement by Israel's Prime Minister Yitzhak Rabin as he attempted

503 Betselem, the Israeli Center of Human Rights in the Occupied Territories.

to lay a guilt trip on the United States, claiming it had an obligation to help settle Soviet Jews in Israel through the guarantee of the $10 billion loan.

In 1991, the United States taxpayers paid over $4.3 billion in aid to Israel. Israel then invested these funds in U.S. savings bonds for which the United States paid Israel over $34 million in interest (on the money that the United States gave to Israel in the first place).

From 1974 to 1989, Israel received $16.4 billion in loans that would never be repaid. The loans were secretly converted to grants, which did not have to be repaid. The reason the White House officials referred to the money transfer as loans in the first place was to avoid U.S. oversight, which is required only on money grants. By this time the money had already been used, and there was no control over how it was used.

If Israel defaults on the $10 billion loan and the American taxpayer is forced to make the payments, interest and principle have been reported to total $116 billion over a 30-year repayment period.[504]

### ISRAELI CITIZENS HAVE SIMILAR PROBLEMS WITH CORRUPT GOVERNMENT AND INTELLIGENCE AGENCIES

Government officials in control of Israel's foreign relations, and its intelligence agency, the Mossad, have engaged in a pattern of criminal acts inflicting great harm upon American citizens, including those of Jewish faith. This indictment of those operating under the flag of Israel does not indict the average citizen of Israel any more than the criminal activities by U.S. officials indict the average American.

More inside and secret information on the activities of the Mossad has been described in earlier pages, and more follows.

### FORMER MOSSAD AGENT REVEALS EXPLOSIVE SECRETS OF ISRAEL'S INTELLIGENCE-ESPIONAGE AGENCY

Former Mossad officer, Colonel Victor Ostrovsky, was concerned about the conduct of a controlling faction in Israel's Mossad. He was troubled by its use of Kidon assassination squads in friendly countries, undermining foreign governments, including the United States, its drug trafficking (as my contacts had frequently described to me), and exposed these practices in his books.[505] Ostrovsky described how the U.S. invasion of Panama dried up much of the Mossad's funds derived from shipping drugs into the United States.

He described the thousands of Jewish assets in various countries, including the United States, who secretly feed information to the Mossad that is often harmful to the host country. Ostrovsky left the Mossad in the late 1980s, but retained secret contacts with high-level Mossad officials. In this way he kept aware of Mossad activities.

Ostrovsky describes how the Mossad plans events so that the blame will be on another party, to accomplish what Israel, or the Mossad, wants to achieve. He describes how the Mossad knew about the impending bombing of the Marine barracks in Beirut that killed nearly 300 American soldiers, and kept this information from the Americans so as to continue the hostilities between the

504 *Spotlight*, August 24, 1992.

505 *By Way of Deception*; *The Other Side of Deception*; *Lion of Judah*.

Americans and factions in the Middle East. This hostility continued the strategic value of Israel to the United States.

He described how the Mossad made possible[506] the explosion in a West Berlin night club[507] that killed one US serviceman and wounded several others, and which President Ronald Reagan used as an excuse to bomb Libya,[508] killing many women and children. The Mossad called this plan, resulting in bombing Libya, Operation Trojan. France recognized the Mossad's role in Operation Trojan, and refused to allow U.S. aircraft to fly from France to bomb Libya, forcing some of the U.S. aircraft to fly from England and refuel in the air.

This bombing caused hostage takers in Lebanon to break off negotiations with the Americans and the British concerning the release of the hostages. Instead, only French hostages were released, because of the nonparticipation of France in the bombing of Libya.

## MOSSAD'S ASSASSINATION OF WORLD-FAMOUS FIGURE

Ostrovsky writes in *The Other Side of Deception* how and why a Kidon team killed long-time Mossad asset and British citizen Robert Maxwell. The Mossad's code name for Maxwell was the "Little Czech." Maxwell had threatened to expose the Mossad's attempts to halt the democratization of the Soviet Union. Israel and the Mossad felt that removal of the Soviet threat would lessen Israel's strategic value to the United States, resulting in a major reduction in financial aid and military equipment. Maxwell had financially funded many prior Mossad activities, and was now in need of immediate financial help himself. Maxwell warned that if Israel did not provide this help, he would publicize Israel's attempt to prevent the end of the Cold War.

While preparing to assassinate Maxwell, the Mossad instructed Maxwell to meet them in Los Cristos on the island of Grand Canary, and to get there via his yacht. A Kidon team was then dispatched by boat, and during the evening of November 4, 1991, while Maxwell was on his boat, the Kidon team climbed on board the yacht, killing Maxwell and throwing his body into the ocean. Later, in a typical snow-job, Maxwell was buried on the Mount of Olives in Jerusalem, while Israel's Prime Minister Yitzhak Shamir eulogized the man that Israel's Mossad had killed.

The large number of Israel sympathizers in England and the United States, including the media, have kept the facts of this and other Mossad assassinations from the public.

## MOSSAD'S BRUTAL KILLING OF A FAMILY IN CALIFORNIA

Ian Stuart Spiro, his wife, and three small daughters were killed on November 7, 1992, in the San Diego area. Spiro's wife and three daughters were killed in their home near San Diego by large-caliber bullets into their heads. Ian Spiro was found dead in a car parked in the desert, having died from ingesting cyanide. Spiro had connections to the CIA, British, and Mossad[509] intelligence agencies.

---

506 The Mossad funded several terrorist organizations in Europe, and monitored their telephone and radio communications.

507 La Belle discotheque.

508 U.S. aircraft bombed Libya on April 14, 1986.

509 A sayan, or sayanim, is a Jewish asset in a foreign country, obtaining information for Israel and the Mossad. A spy would be another name for a sayan.

He had been involved in various CIA operations, including October Surprise, Iran-Contra, and the Lebanese hostage crisis. He was helping Riconosciuto collect documents to present to a federal grand jury conducting hearings into the Inslaw matter when he was killed.

Spiro had worked with Oliver North in the arms-for-hostages schemes. My initial reports linked the deaths with Israel's Rafi Eitan. The maid who worked part-time for the Spiro family had identified Rafi Eitan from pictures, as having been to the Spiro home several days before the Spiro murders. This doesn't prove that Eitan committed the murders, but he is known in the intelligence community as an assassinator.

One of my intelligence agency sources, Ron Veatch, told me that Spiro was planning to duplicate a nationwide 900-sexually-orientated business, New Media Telecommunications (located in La Jolla, California), which was run by Jonathan Wise, whose father, John Wise, was a CIA asset. Spiro had become very concerned about the harm being inflicted worldwide by the U.S., British, and Israel intelligence agencies, and began exposing some of their worse secrets.

Another one of my sources, Gunther Russbacher, said that his intelligence agency contacts revealed that the Spiro murders were carried out by Israel's Mossad and Britain's M-5 intelligence agencies.

Russbacher had told me in the past that one of the methods the CIA uses to blackmail people, including politicians, was through the promotion of the 900-sexual numbers and pedophile activities. When I quizzed Russbacher about this information he said that New Media Telecommunications was an CIA operation and that John Wise had been a CIA asset for many years. This discovery added additional intelligence/espionage agency involvement in the death of the Spiro family.

I received a letter on October 20, 1993, from Ron Veatch stating:

*I had spoken to Ian Spiro a few days prior to his murder. Ian was working for a CIA cover and he became aware that Jonathan Wise, who was president of the Communications 900-type business was also CIA/NSA federal front. He begged me for help.*

*Jonathan called me the next day after the murders and missing of Ian, and tried to draw me into their scheme. Ian gave me some CIA/FBI top secret papers to hold and he was murdered by CIA/FBI-directed Mossad.*

A business associate of Ian Spiro, Robert Corson, was found dead in an El Paso motel room[510] a day before Gail Spiro and her three children were found. Corson reportedly worked for the CIA and in the CIA's drug and arms trafficking. One of my sources, Basil Abbott, described Corson's role with him in CIA and DEA drug trafficking. Corson had also been involved in the looting of savings and loans, another CIA-related activity.

Nassen Beydoun, who had worked with Spiro and Oliver North, was later shot and killed.

A possible witness who could identify the killers was found dead shortly after the Spiro family was killed. Jose Aguilar, a tree trimmer who worked at

510 November 4, 1992.

the Spiro property, was killed by a bullet in the head on November 14, 1992.[511] Aguilar reportedly identified a picture of Mossad agent Rafi Eitan[512] as a visitor to Spiro's home shortly before the Spiro family was found dead.

Another death related to Spiro and his activities was Howard Cerney, attorney from New York City, who represented Ian Spiro on some of Spiro's legal matters. He was found dead in July 1993.

Before his death, Ian Spiro told friends that he was receiving phone threats from the CIA or Defense Intelligence Agency (DIA).

In 1994, Ostrovsky published his book, *The Other Side of Deception*, which described the murder of the Spiro family by a Mossad Kidon team. Ostrovsky described how he was reminded of their deaths by his high-level Mossad contact that he identifies only as Ephraim. Ephraim and other contacts informed Ostrovsky that Spiro was a sayan[513] who had years of contacts with Israel's Mossad. Apparently Ian Spiro had received a large sum of money from the Mossad with which to obtain the release of an Israeli airman, Ron Arad, from Spiro's Lebanese contacts. After his Lebanese contacts discovered Spiro's links to the Iran-Contra affair, they refused to deal with him. The Mossad wanted their money back, and Spiro claimed that he had given the money to the Lebanese. When the Mossad Kidon team arrived at Spiro's home in the San Diego area on November 7, 1992, and could not get the money returned, the mother and three young girls were shot. Spiro was then taken into the desert, where he was fed poison, causing his death.

As frequently happens, to cover up for CIA-related activities, the FBI pressured the media to report that Spiro had killed his family and then committed suicide. And as usual, the local police cooperated. The conduct and final report of the Spiro deaths by the San Diego sheriff's department indicated a coverup, as happened with many other deaths where intelligence agencies are involved. Attorneys Dexter Jacobson and Paul Wilcher are two typical examples.

Incredibly, these revelations by a high-level Mossad officer went unknown to most of the American public, partly due to the massive media coverup. Further, the CIA, the Mossad, and British intelligence, are allies, and these intelligence agencies appear to have a greater loyalty to each other, rather than to their respective countries.

## DEADLY EFFECTS UPON AMERICA BY ISRAEL'S MOSSAD

In evaluating what Israel's Mossad has done to the United States and its citizens, consider the Mossad's role in sending drugs into the United States, contributing, with U.S. intelligence agencies, to the national security threat posed by the destabilizing effects of drugs. Consider the Mossad's killing of Americans, including Michael Harari's involvement in killing those army officers who sought to expose the drug trafficking associated with Operation Watchtower. These are only a few examples of how intelligence agencies of other countries are contributing to the demise of the United States as it existed prior to the formation of the CIA.

---

511 Valley Center, California.

512 Rafi Eitan was a member of the Mossad's LAKAM, a unit of the Mossad operating in the United States, gathering information about U.S. activities, and a unit directly under Israel's prime minister.

513 A sayan is a Mossad asset in a foreign country, and Jewish.

# OTHER CORRUPTION

President Eisenhower warned about the military-industrial complex as he was leaving office, but to no avail. Pentagon fraud and bribery, CIA covert operations to protect the interests of powerful U.S. corporations overseas, and aviation-related crimes were some of the many scandals surfacing in the 1980s, creating a well-entrenched mindset that continues to this date. Establishment media coverup plays a key role in the American public's ignorance about corruption in government. Refusal to read the many highly detailed exposé books and articles is another reason why this corruption is able to escalate.

Evidence of aviation and space related frauds by major corporations repeatedly surfaced in the 1980s and the 1990s. An *Aviation Week & Space Technology* article (April 3, 1989) stated in part:

> *The pattern of corruption that has emerged from the Ill Wind cases involves classic influence peddling. Government employees received bribes in return for providing consultants with early notice of upcoming contracts and for helping them devise strategies for winning those contracts. The consultants convinced contractors to hire them based on their access to an inside source.*
>
> *A bribed government employee like Berlin could use his influence to determine which firms would be eligible for a contract and, in some cases, could help determine the winner by inserting specific criteria in a service's acquisition plan, favoring one contractor over another. Berlin did this for Teledyne and Hazeltine. The corrupt official also could provide confidential bidding information so a favored contractor could submit a superior best and final offer to win an award.*

Despite the consequences of money, safety and lives, bribing of government officials exists in the aviation field. Lockheed, Douglas, Northrop, and other aircraft manufacturers have repeatedly been charged with paying bribes to generate orders for their product and to avoid complying with inspections and design safeguards.

Justice Department prosecutors filed a lawsuit on July 31, 1991, in New York charging General Electric with defrauding the Pentagon of more than $30 million on the sale of jet engines and support services to the Israeli Air Force. Implicated in this fraud was an Israeli Air Force general who pled guilty to fraud and bribery charges.

Lockheed admitted bribing foreign government officials as an inducement for them to buy military and commercial aircraft. In one instance, Lockheed officials resigned after Justice Department prosecutors charged Lockheed with bribing foreign officials.[514] These corporate officials admitted sanctioning bribes exceeding $22 million to European and Japanese officials. Lockheed pled guilty to secret payoffs[515] to Japanese government and business officials to promote the sale of Lockheed L-1011 aircraft.

Boeing Corporation paid bribes exceeding $3 million for promoting the sale of Boeing 747s to Middle East Airlines.[516] Northrop Corporation bribed Korean officials through a fictitious hotel project that served as a conduit for bribes.[517] American Airlines agreed to pay a civil penalty for making illegal political contributions.[518]

Bribes were paid to Japanese politicians and firms to obtain aircraft orders,[519] and government auditors could not account for $3.4 million paid by Boeing and McDonnell Douglas. Boeing agreed to plead guilty[520] to felony charges of illegally obtaining classified Pentagon documents from a lobbyist, Richard Fowler, who illegally obtained the documents from Pentagon insiders. Many believe Boeing got off with a slap on the wrist as many Boeing executives were directly involved with the unauthorized handling of military planning material.

Defense Department investigators reported they were looking at other major defense companies suspected of trafficking in secret government documents. The Boeing investigation was pursued independent of the massive Pentagon bribery and influence-peddling probe code-named "Operation Ill Wind." Fowler was convicted by an Alexandria, Virginia, jury on December 7, 1989, on 39 felony counts related to unlawful acquisition and distribution of Pentagon papers.

Loral Corporation, a major electronics-defense contractor, pled guilty on December 8, 1989, to federal charges of fraud and obtaining inside information on defense contracts. The defense contractor unlawfully obtained the military documents by paying over half a million dollars to William Galvin.[521]

One of the main officials caught in Operation Ill Wind investigation was Melvyn Paisley, Assistant Secretary of the United States Navy. While profiting through unlawful activities, he frequently stated: "Every citizen who enjoys the protection of a free government owes not only a portion of his property, but even of his personal service to the defense of it." Paisley was one of several Boeing Company executives appointed by the Reagan administration to top positions in the Department of Defense. Upon leaving Boeing for the government position, Boeing gave the officials a half-million dollars in severance pay, of which Paisley received $183,000. Boeing regularly receives large amounts of

514 Dan Haughton and Lockheed President Carl Lotchian resigned. February 13, 1976.
515 *San Francisco Chronicle* June 2, 1979.
516 *Wall Street Journal* April 16, 1979.
517 *Wall Street Journal*, October 27, 1989.
518 *Wall Street Journal* May 2, 1975.
519 *Air Line Pilot*, July 1979.
520 *New York Times* November 7, 1989.
521 *San Francisco Chronicle* December 9, 1989.

military business from the government through orders generated by their former employees.

Several years before Paisley's government appointment, two Boeing executives accused Paisley of bribing military officials and bugging the offices of competitors to help Boeing win government contracts. Despite these charges, Reagan's Defense Secretary, Caspar Weinberger, made Paisley the senior Navy official responsible for research, engineering and systems. As one newspaper reported,[522] "This, it turns out, was like turning a hog loose in a silo." Weinberger was later indicted in the Iran-Contra affair. (And pardoned by President Bush as he was leaving office.)

Whistleblowers forced the Justice Department, in 1987, to investigate the complaints, including those filed by the whistleblowers under the Whistleblower's Act, after which influence-peddler William Galvin pled guilty. A contract with a small company owned by two Israelis, requiring Paisley's approval, required the company to deposit two million dollars into a Swiss bank account belonging to Galvin and Paisley. The scheme backfired when the military equipment (drone system) was so poorly constructed that the Navy canceled the contract. When Paisley tried to transfer his share of the bribe money, his involvement was discovered by Justice Department investigators. Galvin was the first one sentenced to prison, and Paisley fell next.

The scheme revealed a pattern of fraud and deceit implicating many others and involving far greater amounts of money. Among the corporations implicated with Paisley and Galvin were Unisys Corporation; Martin Marietta Corporation; United Technologies Corporation; Northrop Corporation; General Electric; General Dynamics, and many others.

One of the high-ranking Air Force officials implicated in the widespread corruption in the military procurement system was Victor D. Cohen, formerly Deputy Assistant Secretary of the Air Force in charge of buying communication and computer systems for the federal government. On August 22, 1991, Cohen pleaded guilty to conspiracy and bribe-taking during the five-year investigation into the Pentagon procurement scandal dubbed "Operation Ill Wind."

Unisys Corporation, a major defense contractor, agreed to pay a record $190 million in criminal fines and civil recoveries from the Operation Ill Wind investigation of military procurement corruption. Unisys pled guilty September 6, 1991, in federal court in Alexandria, Virginia to conspiring to defraud the United States and to bribery, among other counts.

Some FAA inspectors received money or perks from the airlines they inspected, and I often wondered if this was the reason United Airlines and Congress could block inspectors' safety activities. It is believed that bribes played a part in the FAA's refusal to act on such glaring aircraft design defects as the DC-10, Beech V-tail Bonanza, and other defective aviation products that resulted in many hundreds of deaths.

**FALSIFIED AVIATION REPORTS**

As the 1980s ended, many Eastern Airlines management personnel admitted falsifying maintenance records that fraudulently indicated repair work was done

522 *San Francisco Daily Journal*, November 7, 1991.

or inspection accomplished, that had not been performed. Pilots and mechanics at Eastern Airlines repeatedly reported this falsification problem in the late 1980s to the company, the FAA, and the media, followed by the usual refusal to act and concurrent coverup.

Some inspectors and management officials resigned, rather than be a part of the fraud affecting air safety. A former Eastern management official, Paul Kilpatrick, told me[523] that he resigned his position, giving up 24 years seniority, when Eastern's hierarchy wanted him to sign off for work that was never done. Many of the Eastern Airlines' pilots complained about pressure from top management to fly aircraft that had numerous system malfunctions constituting unsafe conditions. In answer to these complaints, FAA officials stated the reports were not true and gave Eastern a clean bill of health. They were, of course, lying, a mindset that other inspectors and I had seen for years.

If it were not for the persistence of Eastern employees and former employees, the truth would probably never have surfaced. Their persistence caused a federal grand jury in New York to take evidence, and their findings proved the charges to be true. The grand jury handed down a 60-count indictment in July 1990, charging Eastern officials with falsifying maintenance records to indicate repairs had been made when this had not been done; falsifying documents, and conspiring to impede an investigation. After several Eastern officials entered into plea agreements admitting their crimes, other officials agreed to plead guilty. Justice Department prosecutors did not file any charges against FAA officials who engaged in the coverup.

Causing terrible consequences for hundreds of victims, McDonnell Douglas Aircraft Company at Long Beach falsified records indicating that safety changes had been made on three DC-10s sold to Turkish Airlines, when they had not been made. As a result, 346 people were shredded into little pieces in the Paris DC-10 crash. FAA Western Region officials, whom I had exposed in criminal misconduct, knew the many problems with the DC-10 and ignored the impending consequences.

In 1985, the FBI investigated an alleged cover-up of violations by the FAA at Continental Airlines. Seeking to protect Continental and its own refusal to perform its safety duties, FAA Western Region officials deleted three pages of violations and criticisms prepared by FAA inspectors from a final version sent to Washington.

The leader of the FAA inspection team, Harry Langdon, found significant problems in Continental's pilot check-out and training procedures, reporting: "It shows either a lack of understanding of federal aviation regulations or a disregard for them. Continental does not, in our opinion, presently meet certification standards." The report also criticized FAA officials at Western Region headquarters in Los Angeles, stating that they were "remiss in condoning the situation." Nothing has changed since other inspectors and I made similar reports for the past thirty years.

The NTSB's politically-sensitive Board routinely sequesters evidence uncovered by its investigators, making it a co-contributor to many crashes that

523 May 1989.

it subsequently investigates.

**AIRLINES SACRIFICE SAFETY FOR MONEY**

The willingness of a few airlines to sacrifice safety has existed for years. The airlines knew the dangers of outward-opening cargo doors; the absence of backups for flight controls; the danger of no fire extinguishing agents in the cargo compartments. Airlines sought to make one of the emergency exits on the 747 inoperative, to save a relatively small amount of money. They knew that in emergency evacuations lives may be lost by closing off an exit. They knew that eliminating flight engineers from the jets decreases safety. They were aware of the dangers of the early Boeing 737s when there is wing contamination and refused to require speed adjustments to offset the problem. These were calculated risks, accepting the occasional mass-fatality crashes as an acceptable part of doing business.

The airlines even opposed legislation requiring a medical kit on board the aircraft to handle heart attacks, asthma, and diabetes emergencies. I noticed in 1951, when I first started flying for the airlines, that the on-board medical kit consisted of nothing more than Band-Aids and Iodine, meaningless for anything other than a slight cut. Numerous inflight emergencies occur where a meaningful first aid kit can mean the difference between life or death. The Air Transport Association (ATA) opposed the legislation requiring the same medical kit required by most foreign airlines. The ATA argued in a statement released on September 15, 1985, that most domestic flights can land within minutes of an on-board emergency to rush injured or ill passengers to hospitals trained to handle medical emergencies. That is not so.

The truth is that there are many personal emergencies where the person perishes before a plane can land and receive medical attention, which in many cases could have been prevented if adequate medical supplies were on board. Congressman Norman Mineta (D-Cal), chairman of the House Aviation Subcommittee, acknowledged the resistance by airlines to place emergency supplies on the aircraft.[524]

Year after year the perils of air travel are lamented. In 1985, a Congressional panel investigating air safety stated that air travel was less safe; this was the third scathing criticism of the FAA in less than a month. A month earlier another Congressional study said investigators found disturbing gaps in the FAA's airline inspection program. A week later, an internal Transportation Department report found that the FAA had been slow in devising safety regulations and that they enforce them inconsistently. Similar reports were made for the prior 30 years. Nothing changes. In 1989, an internal Boeing report stated that unless major changes are made in crew training, the loss of aircraft would reach crisis proportions.

**ACCIDENT-RELATED MISCONDUCT IN MILITARY**

The military has its culture of deception also as it relates to airplane crashes, although it is believed far less criminal in nature than existing in the FAA and NTSB. A June 3, 1995, article by syndicated columnist David H. Hackworth appearing in the *San Francisco Examiner* detailed "the culture of deceit in today's

---

524 *Aviation Week & Space Technology*, October 7, 1985.

military." Hackworth wrote:

*Alan Diehl, the Air Force's former top civilian safety official, says Air Force crash investigations are routinely sabotaged by senior officers seeking to please superiors, hide culpability and avoid embarrassment. Diehl has told the Pentagon that causes of at least 30 accidents have been covered up by "incompetents, charlatans and sycophants."*

## CHALLENGER DISASTER

Coverup of a serious safety problem preceded the Challenger disaster, which carried seven people to their deaths, including school teacher Christa McAuliffe. Those who had the technical competency to know wanted the launch scrubbed because of serious safety problems caused by the cold weather conditions.[525] But this would delay the launch and affect the plans of President Reagan, who had a television appearance that evening, using the Challenger launch to convey a theme in his State of the Union message. Management personnel, sensitive to political and other pressures, overruled the technical personnel and approved the launch. Tragedy followed, as forewarned.

## APOLLO COVERUP PRECEDED CHALLENGER

Known safety problems preceded the Apollo tragedy. NASA officials preceded the Challenger irregularities with the Apollo irregularities, where astronauts perished in the oxygen-fueled fire that cremated the unfortunate occupants. The manufacturer of the capsule had warned that bathing the entire capsule with oxygen was dangerous, a warning that was ignored by NASA. Then, when the astronauts perished, NASA tried to hide these warnings and instead, blamed the manufacturer's purported quality defects for the deaths.

## HARASSMENT OF NUCLEAR PLANT INSPECTORS

Harassment of company inspectors at a nuclear plant under construction by Brown & Root, Inc., was reported in a *Wall Street Journal* article dated November 7, 1984. The *Journal* reported that the plant, Comanche Peak, was riddled with poor workmanship. When quality-control inspectors refused to pass defective work, the company fired the inspectors. The company falsely claimed the fired inspectors did not follow orders. The Nuclear Regulatory Commission conducted an inquiry to determine whether harassment and intimidation of these and other inspectors compromised the plant's safety. Dozens of inspectors around the country complained of pressure to ignore defects, which otherwise would be costly to the companies. The inquiry concluded that the company fired inspectors who adhered to quality control standards required by federal regulations.

The *Wall Street Journal* article described the actual physical threats against inspectors at the Zimmer plant of Cincinnati Gas & Electric Company in Moscow, Ohio. Inspectors were doused with water and with fire extinguisher fluids during inspections. Ultimately, the quality of the plant was in such doubt that the plant

---

525 Infrared temperature-sensing instruments showed abnormal "cold spots" on the lower part of the right-hand booster, which later failed during launch. The Thiokol engineers were adamant that the launch be delayed. They felt that the O-rings lost some of their resiliency and ability to seat tightly in their grooves, when their temperatures fall below 50 degrees. The O-ring temperatures had fallen to 30 degrees, far below the safe limit. Despite the engineers' protest, NASA officials went ahead with the launch, with fatal results. The company later fired the inspectors who exposed the defects in the Challenger launching.

converted from nuclear energy to coal. At a nuclear plant built by four utility companies near Bay City, Texas, the Nuclear Regulatory Commission threatened to halt the project in 1980 after it found that supervisors consistently overruled quality-control inspectors in favor of construction workers.

**LOSS OF RETIREMENT BENEFITS**

Numerous pensioners discovered, and will continue to discover upon retirement that there was no money in the pension fund and that they were financially destitute. This problem became evident in the late 1980s and escalated in the 1990s. The media gave very little if any publicity to this scandal, making possible the losses suffered by their readers.

Two government regulatory schemes exist when pension funds are federally regulated: the Employee Retirement Income Security Act of 1974 (ERISA) and the Pension Benefit Guaranty Corporation. The Pension Benefit Guaranty Corporation protects the pension benefits of the 30 million Americans in programs regulated by the federal program. If the pension funds are guaranteed by the government and are under-funded, the U.S. taxpayers may have to pay many billions of dollars on top of the other horrendous debt. More than $1.6 *trillion* in pension funds is potentially at risk because of poor regulations and failure of the checks and balance systems to enforce federal law, according to the report of the Labor Department's Inspector General, J. Brian Hyland.[526]

The Employee Retirement Income Security Act of 1974 (ERISA) is supposed to protect workers' pension benefits when employers go out of business. The protections are inadequate to ensure that the funds are there, and the results are that the taxpayers must pay the pension funds through the Pension Benefit Guaranty Corporation.

Hyland urged Congress to immediately investigate potential abuses and shortfalls of federal pension laws, reporting that existing laws and regulations allow employers and pension-fund managers to hide abuses from the government. Further, that inadequate staffing at the Labor Department leaves the government little chance to catch offenders.

Pension Benefit Guaranty Corporation reported that its 1991 losses were greater than $1 billion plus many more billions of potential losses. One bankrupt airline by itself, Trans World Airlines, was short over $1 **billion** on its pension plan. It is believed that about twenty percent of government insured pension plans are under-funded, the shortage amounting to over $40 billion. There are about 95,000 federally insured pension plans.

The under-funded pension plans of numerous large companies will have to be funded by the taxpayer and include, for instance, CF&I Steel Corporation of Pueblo, Colorado; LTV Corporation, and the former Eastern and Pan American Airlines.

One of the reasons pension funds are under-funded, or funded with near-worthless financial paper, is that corporate raiders seized the cash in many pension funds, replacing it with junk bonds or financial paper issued by potentially insolvent insurance companies. The pension plans are then "guaranteed" by the near-worthless junk-bonds, many of which actually became worthless in

526 Stated on June 2, 1989 and reported the following day by *Associated Press*.

the early 1990s.

"Pension disaster is looming," was a headline on an *Associated Press* story of November 14, 1989. The article stated that "Fraud and mismanagement could wipe out the retirement nest eggs of millions of working Americans in private pension programs, and saddle taxpayers with a multi-billion-dollar bailout, according to government officials and agency documents." The article stated that the Labor Department Inspector General's office warned that the fraud and mismanagement could dwarf the recent savings and loan financial debacle, adding to the problems that could set the stage for our country's second worst depression of the twentieth century.

The report stated that many of the under-funded pension plans are not insured by the government; that retirees will often get nothing, and that only some of the 107,000 private pension plans were covered by the government's Pension Benefit Guaranty Corporation (PBGC) insurance.

The Director of Pension Rights Center, a public interest group, stated in the article that "It's astonishing how much of the money is being stolen," and referred to some $14 million stolen from two union locals.

A *National Law Journal* article (June 3, 1991) was headlined, "Unfunded Retirement Plan: Ticking Bomb?" A subsequent *National Law Journal* article (December 16, 1991) referred to the continuing savings and loan debacle followed by the growing pension fund problem, stating that the plans are more than $40 billion under-funded. The article stated that the American taxpayer may be burdened with pension fund liabilities almost as great as the savings and loan debacle, and described how seemingly safe pension funds are unsafe because of the intricate involvement with failed or failing savings and loans and insurance companies. "Pensions could be next S&L debacle," was the headline on a 1991 *San Francisco Chronicle* article. "Tension mounts as pension-fund troubles grow in U.S.," was the headline on a February 1992 *Newsday* article.

There were many other articles describing similar problems, including a *Wall Street Journal* article (June 10, 1992) reporting that Chrysler's pension plan was short by $4.4 billion; Bethlehem Steel's pension plan $1.3 billion short; Navistar $500 million short. PBGC had to pay over $1 billion after Pan Am and Eastern Airlines folded, with an estimated liability to pay of over $21 billion. PBGC estimates that if Chrysler went bankrupt its under-funded pension plans would approach $8 billion.

Pan American Airlines filed for Chapter 11 bankruptcy in 1990 and then went out of business in 1992.[527] Pan Am's bankruptcy required the Pension Benefit Guaranty Corporation (PBGC) to pay approximately $1 billion dollars to cover the pension fund shortage, which of course will be paid by the American taxpayer plus the interest charges.

In one instance involving LTV Corporation, government lawyers stated[528] in a Supreme Court case that the taxpayers were liable for "an open-ended source of industry bailouts" which would probably spark a financial crisis similar to the one facing the government's insurance program for the savings and loan

527 *Wall Street Journal*, April 18, 1991.
528 *The Recorder* October 31, 1989.

industry.

**PRIVATE PENSION FUNDS OR PLANS**

There are approximately one million company pension plans that are not guaranteed by the government. These include the popular 401(k) retirement savings plans, employee stock ownership and profit-sharing plans. The federal government considers these to be savings plans and not pension plans. Over 13 million Americans have these non-government insured plans. For the employer they are relatively cheap. They do not promise workers a definite benefit upon retirement, and employers do not pay any insurance costs.

Private pension funds are not guaranteed by the government, relying upon the continued survivability of the company, or the integrity of the bonds or other financial paper that the company provides. In many cases healthy pension funds containing large amounts of cash or liquid assets became the target of corporate takeovers or leveraged buyouts, solely for the purpose of enriching the new owners. The cash would then be replaced with financial paper of questionable value. In some cases the company is the target for a "bustout," in which the sole purpose of acquiring the company is to loot its assets, including the pension funds, and put the company into Chapter 7 bankruptcy. The employees are then left without any retirement funds if it is not a federally insured plan.

**INSURANCE COMPANY FAILURES ADDED TO THE ESCALATING PROBLEMS**

Attention was focused in April 1991 on another aspect of the pension fund problem as it related to insolvent insurance companies guaranteeing pension fund payments, when California officials seized Executive Life Insurance Company due to its insolvency. Junk bonds yielding great profits to attorneys and Wall Street firms arranging the funding were key factors in the failure of the insurance company.

The failure of the twelve billion dollar life and health insurer adversely affected over 200,000 policyholders, over 115,000 annuity owners, and hundreds of plundered pension plans. Within days of seizing First Executive's West Coast branch, California insurance regulators on May 14, 1991, were forced to seize another insurance company, First Capital Holding Corporation. The failure of Capital Life Insurance Company in California was billed as the biggest insurance bust in U.S. history.[529] Monarch Life Insurance Company was seized in May 1991 by Massachusetts regulators. New Jersey officials took over the venerable $13.8 billion Mutual Benefit Life Insurance Company, the nation's 18th-largest insurer, in July 1991. Many elderly people lost their pensions, their annuities, their retirement income. As in every major scandal, multiple checks and balances existed in theory and on paper which should have prevented these consequences.

Senator Howard Metzenbaum, head of the Antitrust Subcommittee, stated during Senate hearings that California officials had ignored clear signals of the insolvency years earlier, having allowed the insurance company to continue the practices, guaranteeing that heavy losses would be suffered by thousands

529 *Spotlight*, May 27, 1991.

of people.[530] Speaking of the California regulators, Metzenbaum stated: "It's clear that they knew [several years earlier] that Executive Life was in a precarious position and yet they allowed the company to continue [offering pensions and life policies]."

**CALIFORNIA, THE BREEDING GROUNDS FOR SCANDALS**

If it were not for the coverup by California officials, the Lincoln Savings and Loan debacle would not have financially destroyed thousands of people. The actions by this same group of state officials and their coverup resulted in huge losses to thousands of people who relied upon the pensions, annuities, and contracts paid by Executive Life Insurance Company. Corruption was rampant in the California legal fraternity.

There may be other problems for insurance companies that have not received any exposure. In other pages a practice was described in which CIA operatives obtained hundreds of millions of dollars in loans from insurance companies using bogus bearer bonds, including treasury bonds, as security. Some of these bonds were paid off, or else renewed, when their 20 and 25-year due date occurred. In some case, losses would be recognized.

**BANKS**

Bank deposits up to $100,000 are guaranteed by the Federal Deposit Insurance Corporation, and losses up to this amount are being paid by the American taxpayer through borrowing and interest paid on the borrowed money. "Bank Bailout Called Near Certainty," was the headline on a *San Francisco Examiner* article[531] warning that the taxpayers will have to pay over $100 billion to bail out the banks (plus interest on the indebtedness). "Banking on the Brink: The Troubled Future of American Finance," stated the headline, quoting Edward W. Hill, a professor at Cleveland State University, and Roger J. Vaughan, economist of Santa Fe, New Mexico. The article estimated that if the weak or insolvent banks were shut down at that time the cost would be $45 billion to $59 billion and a delay in closing would exceed $75 billion to $95 billion.

"Another Banking Debacle Feared," was another headline.[532] The article stated that "Wall Street analysts and investors who follow the banking industry are worried that a new financial horror movie is opening in the stock market."

"State's banks ready for more bad times," headlined an *Associated Press* article.[533] The article referred to the unemployment levels in the Los Angeles area as being close to Depression levels, much of it due to the reduction in the military-industrial complex and the depressed economy caused in part by the vast looting of the savings and loans.

The number of problem banks would be increased if they valued the real estate covered by their loans at the current market value rather than at the original value. The problem arises when the real estate on which the loan was based subsequently drops in value, possibly lower than the mortgage balance.

FDIC regulator L. William Seidman warned that the $70 billion bailout voted by Congress in 1992 would not be enough to cover the expected bank failures

---

530 *Wall Street Journal*, April 26, 1991.
531 October 6, 1992.
532 *San Francisco Chronicle*, July 8, 1991.
533 October 27, 1992.

in the near future.[534]

There were mixed signals as to the health of the nation's banks. In 1993, by paying very little interest to its depositors and charging high interest for the money loaned and for credit card balances, the financial health of the banks improved.

**WALL STREET SCAMS**

Billions of dollars were taken out of the American economy, much of it lost by investors, from corrupt insider trading, junk bonds, and other acts of Wall Street rogues: Ivan Boesky, Michael Milken, Dennis Levine, Martin Siegel and others. Boesky, responsible for billions of dollars of losses, had a CIA background, including an assignment in Iran.

One typical case of how the public gets fleeced was the case of Prudential-Bache, in which hundreds of millions of dollars were fraudulently taken from trusting investors. In an October 1993 settlement offer Prudential agreed to pay nearly half a billion dollars to investors who were swindled out of their investment money.

Prudential had previously argued, before federal and state regulators applied pressure, that none of the investors had a valid claim because they waited beyond the statute of limitation period to file a lawsuit. The settlement barred the defrauded investors out of other forms of compensation, including punitive damages. Prudential, a subsidiary of the Prudential Insurance Company, ran roughshod over the defrauded investors, using a former ex-convict with a crooked real estate record to carry out the fraud.

**CORRUPTION EVERYWHERE**

Even a household name like Beech Nut committed fraud when it represented a sugar and water concoction as being "100 percent pure apple juice." This practice started in 1977 and continued for five years. The threat to the health of babies and children went uncorrected by government investigators for years. Not until a detective from the Processed Apple Institute informed Beech Nut of a lawsuit did Beech Nut discontinue the deception. Eventually the government was forced to intervene. Former Beech Nut executive John Lavery was convicted of conspiracy and mail fraud selling corn syrup to babies and children as pure apple juice. When Lavery appealed the conviction, the Court of Appeals ruled: "The evidence was ample to permit the jury to infer that Lavery conspired with the suppliers to perpetrate a fraud on the public through the distribution of the adulterated juice."

Corruption even exists in the type of music played on the radio stations via Music-Payola, the catchy term used for bribing radio stations to play certain records. This scandal first came to light in the 1970s, and persisted, despite federal criminal laws prohibiting the practice. The Justice Department's Organized Crime Strike Force charged four people with violating federal payola laws by paying over $300,000 in bribes to radio station executives between 1980 and 1986. Could this have a bearing on the onslaught of junk music that traumatizes the entire spectrum of the radio dial?

---

534 *San Francisco Chronicle*, October 17, 1991.

**THE FDA SCANDAL**

As the HUD and other scandals surfaced, so did the FDA corruption. The Food and Drug Administration regulates 25 percent of the nation's consumer economy, affecting the entire nation. Evidence revealed that FDA officials engaged in corruption, bribery, and illegal gratuities associated with generic-drug makers. Generic pharmaceutical companies admitted bribing FDA officials, submitting falsified data, and other wrongful acts. Just like FAA officials, the FDA officials treated the industry that it regulated as a partner.

The scandal became known in 1988 when the House Energy and Commerce Committee initiated an investigation following a complaint from Roy McKnight of Pittsburgh-based Mylan Laboratories Inc. "By creating an atmosphere of embracing the generic-drug industry as a partner rather than a regulator, the FDA created an atmosphere of lawlessness," said Sidney Wolfe, head of the Public Citizen Health Research Group. He added, "It isn't surprising that the generic companies pulled these shenanigans."

**REQUESTING INVESTIGATION OF ITS OWN OFFICIALS**

FDA internal regulations prevent the approval of a new generic drug if inspectors find manufacturing problems at the drug company's plant. Officials within the FDA plant inspection department refused to provide inspection reports to other FDA officials reviewing new-drug applications. The FDA's new-drug department had to resort to the Freedom of Information Act to get copies of the FDA's plant inspection reports from its own agency! This unheard-of withholding of information by one part of a government agency from another segment of the same agency prevented the agency from accomplishing its lawful functions. When the documents were finally obtained, important information was blacked out. Who in the hell did these federal employees think they were working for!

**COMMON KNOWLEDGE, BUT NO ONE COMPLAINED**

Fear of retaliation kept companies who were aware of the FDA corruption from complaining. Clark Research & Development Inc., filed a lawsuit accusing the FDA of losing documents and pursuing a "pattern of harassment" after Clark complained that FDA officials allowed a competitor to make misleading claims.

The impetus for the FDA corruption came from companies scrambling to be the first to win FDA approval for their products as patents expired. High stakes were involved. The first generic company to get FDA approval and place its product on the market was often the one who captured this lucrative market.

Middle management at the FDA began receiving reports as early as December 1985 that drug reviewers favored one company over others in return for bribes. FDA officials based drug approval on bribes, either sex, money, or other perks. There was a tip that a woman executive from a drug company exchanged sex with an FDA drug reviewer, and then got quick approval of the company's product. No one investigated the tip.

Two small generic-drug makers[535] had a phenomenal success in obtaining quick FDA drug approval. They received a remarkable 77 percent drug approval in 1986, almost twice that of any other company, including those much larger

535 Par Pharmaceutical Inc., and its Quad Pharmaceuticals Inc. subsidiary.

in size.

**DRUG APPROVALS BASED ON BRIBES**

"We screwed you on this one, so we'll take care of you on the next one," FDA officials told H. Lawrence Fox, an attorney for Barr Laboratories, Inc. Fox testified before a Congressional committee, showing the passing out of drug approvals based upon bribes. They sounded like crooked judges and attorneys making favorable decisions based on quotas, ignoring the merits of the case.

Bribery and favoritism caused the disappearance and destruction of documents submitted by companies for drug approvals. A Congressional investigative panel embarrassed the FDA by producing the original copy of a generic-drug application that a former FDA branch chief, Charles Chang, had torn in half and thrown in the trash. Chang pleaded guilty in a Baltimore federal court to two counts of interstate travel in aid of racketeering.

The FDA official accepted a paid, round-the-world trip costing over $3,000, and computer equipment worth $8,000, from American Therapeutics Inc., a generic drug maker based in Bohemia, New York. In return, the FDA official sped the company's application through the approval process while delaying the processing of other applications.

The Congressional investigations revealed major drug companies submitted falsified data, and filled generic drug test samples with brand-name products, claiming the products as their own, thereby winning FDA approval.

**THE GREAT GRAPE CATCH—or, Government Intimidation Of Industry and A Country.**

As news media attention escalated on the FDA internal corruption, a sudden occurrence shifted public attention in March 1989 to another matter: the great grape catch. The FDA allegedly received a tip that a shipment of grapes from Chile contained cyanide. Like a scene from a school play, a horde of FDA officials converged on a pier in Philadelphia. Pier Superintendent John Hamilton described the scene: "All of a sudden, I saw an army of guys. They never told us what they were looking for, but it was obvious they knew where to look."

Out of dozens of ships containing huge shipments of fruit from Chile, the FDA officials singled out the Almeria Star from an armada of fruit-laden freighters for inspection. The FDA inspectors went to a row of crates containing an estimated 280 million grapes, and plucked two grapes that allegedly had several needle marks on them. These grapes were then taken to the FDA laboratory and reportedly discovered to contain cyanide, which FDA officials said had been injected into the two grapes before they left Chile two weeks earlier.

FDA officials then issued a warning that consumers not eat any Chilean fruit and imposed an embargo against Chilean fruit (March 13, 1989). Markets in the United States ordered the removal and destruction of Chilean fruits. U.S. officials tried to pressure other countries to join in the boycott, but they refused. Farmers in Chile were unable to sell their produce. The FDA's actions cost Chile over $300 million, inflicting great financial harm upon Chilean growers and shippers while increasing the cost of grapes from an alternate source for U.S. consumers.

Chilean farmers, the Chilean economy, and U.S. consumers lost by this action. These tactics inflicted catastrophic financial harm upon Chile's economy. Chilean farmers went out of business due to their inability to sell their crops. In this way the United States stopped the entire Chilean fruit harvest to the United States that was worth almost a billion dollars a year to Chile's fragile economy. Chilean leaders went on TV to calm the country as they tried to figure out what to do next.

A *Wall Street Journal* article (November 16, 1989) pointed out the inconsistencies and implausibilities of the FDA's actions that cast "serious doubt on the FDA's miracle find." The article stated that many people believed FDA officials fabricated the grape scare, speculating that the FDA's story was manufactured to show the Pinochet government the power of United States economic sanctions.

Subsequent laboratory tests conducted by Chilean laboratories revealed that grapes change color about two days after injection with cyanide. But the two grapes picked by the FDA officials did not have any color change. Further, tests revealed that cyanide dissipates rapidly into the air as a gas, leaving an ugly, unappetizing blemish, and that grapes shriveled and darkened within two weeks. There were no blemishes on the two grapes picked by the FDA officials. University of California researchers at Davis, California believed the two grapes became contaminated *after* the FDA officials seized the fruit.

In response to the phony grape claims by U.S. officials, Chile and 2,500 Chilean fruit growers and exporters filed damage claims against the United States totaling $458 million. The claims argued that the Food and Drug Administration improperly embargoed all fruit shipments from Chile in 1989. These administrative claims were the prelude to legal action against the U.S. government.

The Chileans argued that the FDA ignored demonstrated facts about the reaction of cyanide injected in fruit, including its rapid rate of dissolution. The claims stated that "The FDA knew or should have known that it was physically impossible to inject enough cyanide into the two grapes (out of billions) before they left Chile on February 27, 1988, and [for it] still [to] be retained at the levels purportedly detected in the Philadelphia lab on March 12."

Senator Jesse Helms (R-NC)úrgued that the GAO reports, protecting the FDA actions, were flawed, remarking "I don't believe it happened in Chile. [This is] the most bizarre episode I have ever seen." A Congressional investigation followed and, as could be expected, cleared U.S. officials of any wrongdoing.

**ADVANCE WARNINGS**

A year earlier, in 1988, George Jones from the U.S. Embassy in Santiago questioned Chilean attorney Ricado Claro, during lunch as to what the Chilean reaction might be to a United States ban on fruit from Chile. White House officials were dissatisfied with certain policies of the Chilean government. Looking back, this question appeared to be a threat for Chile to change its internal affairs to comply with White House demands. A year later the hypothetical happened.

**THE TRUTH KEPT FROM THE AMERICAN PEOPLE**

Ari Ben-Menashe, former Mossad agent, stated in his *Profits of War* that he was in Chile at the time, and learned from his CIA contacts that the real reason for the grape setup and embargo was to retaliate against Chile for threatening to halt the chemical and other weapon sales to Iraq by Cardoen Industries of Chile, a company working closely with the CIA.

Chile's General Matthei had planned to put a stop to the sale of chemical and other war supplies to Iraq by Cardoen Industries, a company closely aligned with the CIA. This planned action displeased President George Bush, who reportedly asked his CIA friend, Robert Gates, to retaliate against Chile and force the country to change its plans. Gates was also displeased with Ben-Menashe for having leaked a story to the London *Financial Times*,[536] exposing these chemical weapon sales by Cardoen to Iraq in collaboration with the CIA.

After Chile suffered devastating financial harms from the destruction of its primary agricultural exports, its leaders were forced to capitulate to U.S. demands. Cardoen Industries was allowed to continue shipping chemical weapons to Iraq as part of the Iraqgate and BNL scandals.

## PEDOPHILE ACTIVITIES, CIA, AND GOVERNMENT OFFICIALS

In its bag of dirty tricks the CIA has promoted pedophilia for the purpose of blackmailing and controlling people, especially those in high government positions. Several of my CIA and police sources told me how the CIA made young children available to incriminate people in key positions. Jim Rothstein, a former New York City Vice Squad investigator, revealed the pedophile operations he uncovered, and how the CIA promoted pedophile activity for blackmail purposes as a standard covert practice.

One of the most covered up pedophile operations in which young boys and girls were kidnapped and then used for sex objects, or killed, was the Franklin scandal in Omaha, Nebraska. A Nebraska legislator, John W. Decamp, published the sordid details in a book entitled, *The Franklin Cover-Up*.[537] The book went into detail concerning the pedophilia ring that took children, mostly boys, on trips to Washington, to the 1992 Republican Convention in Houston and elsewhere for use by high government officials.

Several pedophile victims told their stories of sexual misuse of children, including Satanism and killing of little children, revealing how Washington officials, including the Justice Department, blocked investigation and prosecution of the perpetrators. The ringleader of the Nebraska pedophile activities was reportedly the prominent black Republican Larry King, who sang the opening song at the Houston Republican convention in 1988.

The book told of the killing of children, their exploitation, the involvement of prominent government officials, and the coverup by state and federal prosecutors, including Justice Department officials and the mainstream media. A one-hour television show was aired on the Franklin activity (November 20, 1992), giving additional support to the documented exposé of this little-exposed problem. Within the CIA covert operations it is common knowledge that numerous U.S. Congressmen and Senators are implicated in pedophile activities. Further

---

536 The exposure of chemical weapon sales to Iraq was published in the *Financial Times* on November 11, 1988.

537 *The Franklin Cover-Up*, subtitled Child Abuse, Satanism, and Murder in Nebraska. John W. Decamp. AWT, Inc. Lincoln, Nebraska.

details on the pedophile activities were given to me by former FBI agent Ted Gunderson.

**MANY DEATHS**

Many deaths incurred in the politically sensitive child pedophile ring operating out of Omaha, Nebraska, involving high Washington officials. It was during counseling that Dr. James Viken, Ph.D. learned of the Franklin pedophile activity. Viken reported his findings to U.S. Customs, and experienced the usual coverup reaction. His September 22 and 30, 1993 letters to a House committee described how the CIA-related child pedophile activities that he uncovered as a psychologist and family therapist went unanswered, even though he provided detailed information.

**SEXUAL ABUSE OF CHILDREN BY PRIESTS**

The moral breakdown within the United States is so epidemic that it exists even in the priesthood, inflicting harm upon children in their care. The crime of priests preying upon children who looked to the priests for guidance, has been known and covered up for years by the media, the local police, and the church itself. The response of the church hierarchy has been to deny the charges, accusing the victims of lying, and making it possible for other children to be sexually molested.

The archdiocese of Santa Fe, New Mexico, for instance, knew of pedophilia allegations for years against a former priest and repeatedly allowed him to molest other children. In one newspaper article,[538] attorney Bruce Pasternack reported:

> *What they demonstrate is proof positive that the Archdiocese of Santa Fe and the Paraclete Center knew their children were going to be raped before they were raped.*

Another one of dozens of newspaper articles was headlined, "Catholic Hierarchy Hides From Child Abuse by Priests." Throughout the United States and especially in the Catholic and Episcopal churches, pedophilia crimes are rampant. With the push to prevent gays from being excluded, pedophile crimes will surely worsen. No thought was given to the financial and emotional trauma that the victimized children would suffer.

The establishment media covered up for this sordid misconduct for years, protecting the churches and the perpetrators. The young victims were charged with making false statements while simultaneously protecting the child molesters. In the late 1980s and 1990s the pattern of sexual abuse of children by priests finally received publicity in the alternate media. The abuse was so extensive that by mid-1995 the mainstream media made limited reports of the problem.

**PUBLIC POSTURE VERSUS HARD-KNUCKLE RETALIATION**

After years of coverup the Roman Catholic bishops adopted (November 19, 1992) a resolution pledging to address the problem of priests who sexually abuse children. The statement read in part: "In the course of our assembly this week, we have reflected—once again and more deeply—upon the pain, anguish and sense of alienation felt by victims." Cardinal John O'Connor of New York spoke (July 1993)[539] in response to the onslaught of lawsuits about the pedophile

538 January 10, 1993.

539 *Wall Street Journal*, November 24, 1993.

activities by their priests, that "Justice, compassion and charity comprise the foundation of our policy."

**RE-VICTIMIZING THE VICTIMS**

In response to the lawsuits by the victims the church, through its law firms, went after the victims and their families. After Edward Morris sued the Philadelphia Catholic archdiocese for priest sexual abuse while he was a child, the church and the law firm counter-sued Morris's parents, blaming them for, would you believe, failing to discover that the priest was molesting their child.

Morris claimed in his lawsuit that Father Terrance Pinkowski sexually abused him over an eight-year span, telling the young boy that sexual relations were a form of therapy necessary for his spiritual growth in preparation for ordination (Morris had intended to become a priest).

In another example, after Timothy Martinez sued the archdiocese of Santa Fe, the church and the law firm had private investigators questioning neighbors to determine any homosexual activities.

Simultaneously, under cover of concern for the victims, church leaders, through their attorneys, played hard-ball with the victims, using scorched-earth tactics to humiliate and discredit the plaintiffs. These attacks to discredit the victims' charges even occurred after the priests admitted their sex crimes.

In case after case, even after the priests had admitted their sex crimes against children in criminal proceedings, or after the priests had been sent to church treatment centers for pedophilia (including the Servants of the Peraclete near Albuquerque), the priests were allowed to continue contact with children. One of the victims' attorneys, Jeffrey Anderson of St. Paul, Minnesota, stated of these tactics: "There's a difference between exercising legal rights and prerogatives in lawsuits and intentionally re-victimizing victims by repudiations, rebukes and attacks."

New York state authorities accused Reverend Edward A. Pipala and members of Cardinal John O'Connor's archdiocese in upstate New York of operating a church-affiliated club consisting of several dozen young boys, taking them to sex parties involving sodomy and sexual abuse.

State prosecutors often protected the criminal behavior by the priests, refusing to prosecute.

**OTHER RELIGION-RELATED CRIMES**

The scandal surrounding the Vatican Bank showed that the Vatican itself has been heavily involved in corruption, killings, and other criminal acts. After the death of Pope Paul in 1978, Albino Luciani was elected to be the head of the Catholic Church, taking the title of Pope John Paul I. Shortly thereafter, he discovered massive fraud and criminal dealings by Catholic bishops and cardinals[540] in charge of the Vatican Bank. He discovered tens of millions of dollars were missing from the bank. He learned that there were ties to the Mafia and to the secret P2 lodge. Pope John Paul I planned to expose those church officials involved in the corruption. But the exposure of the Vatican crimes was prevented by the mysterious poisoning and death of the Pope thirty-three days after assuming that position (September 28, 1978).

---

540 Including Bishop Paul Marcinkus, formerly of Chicago; Cardinal Jean Villot and others.

Hiding evidence of the crime, the Pope was hastily embalmed without any autopsy being performed, and no death certificate issued. Involved in the criminal activities of the Vatican Bank and threatening to reveal the involvement of many others as the scandal unfolded in Europe, banker Roberto Calvi was found hanged under a bridge in London. Even the CIA had business dealings with the Vatican, funneling large sums of money to the church to aid in covert CIA activities.[541]

**DEFECTIVE HEART VALVES**

Defective heart valves made by the Pfizer corporation resulted in many deaths.[542] Officials at Pfizer released heart valves that were defective with fractured or broken wire struts holding the tiny disk in place. When these components fail, blood-flow through the heart becomes unregulated and the heart stops. In a majority of the cases where the defective valve fails, the person dies.[543] Over 300 people reportedly died as a result of the defective valves.[544]

An investigation revealed a phantom inspector had signed off for repair and welding of cracked valve components that were in fact not repaired or welded. During manufacturing, the wire struts welded to the valves often developed cracks, necessitating rewelding. An investigation of records at Pfizer-Shiley Incorporated showed that inspector number 2832 purportedly rewelded and inspected these cracked components. But the inspector had left the company months before the signing of the reports. In addition, the inspector stated that he had never welded any of the parts.

Falsified records were common, according to reports by Shiley workers at the Irvine, California plant. One Shiley supervisor wrote a memo to his boss stating, "Even though no rewelding occurs, the [inspector] signs off the [inspection report] as if it were rewelded. I think we are hiding our worst defect."

**RAMPANT CONGRESSIONAL CORRUPTION**

In *Above the Law*, [545] author James Boyd described the influence-peddling and buying of votes in Congress. Vested interests pass money under the table—bribes—disguised as honorariums, speech-fees, loans that never come due, and other thinly disguised graft. In its book review, the *Christian Science Monitor*[546] said, "Only the completely cynical can read Mr. Boyd's book without mounting distress."

The review reported the indifference or coverup by the FBI, the Attorney General, and the live-and-let-live philosophy of Congress for their peers. The review also addressed the media coverup, stating "the press doesn't smell too sweet either. It rushed into the kitchen only after the kettle boiled over." Ironically, the *Christian Science Monitor* knew of my allegations from 1965 to the present day and continued to keep the lid on the scandals. I contacted the *Monitor* in the 1960s, and several times in the late 1980s. They expressed concern, followed by coverup, as reported by the *Christian Science Monitor*'s editor-in-chief Earl Foell. He said that the *Monitor* organization has a moral

541 *In God's Name*, David A. Yallop, Bantam Books.
542 *Wall Street Journal*, November 7, 1991.
543 Death toll at this writing exceeds 300.
544 *Wall Street Journal*, November 7. 1991.
545 Authored by James Boyd and published in 1968.
546 March 1, 1968. Christian Science Monitor.

mission to support socially responsible journalism. (*Business Week* September 26, 1988.) In 1990, I wrote again to inquire what they were doing in response to my charges. They never answered. So much for moral missions!

A *Washington Post* article dated September 4, 1969, stated that "Committees in Capital Run Like Swiss Banks." The article continued: "The devious ways that Congress used the District of Columbia [for a] haven for committees that can be used by senators and congressmen to hide embarrassing contributions."

A three-page *U.S. News & World Report* article on November 10, 1969, was captioned: "Scandals in Congress: The Record." The article continued: "Activities of a staff member have put the office of the Speaker of the House high in the headlines. The result is one more entry in the record of scandals that have dogged the U.S. Congress for years." The *New York Times*[547] wrote, "Everybody in D.C.'s Doing the Scandal Shuffle." Two decades later the corruption by government officials is much worse. Government corruption has been uncovered in almost every agency in the executive branch, as well as in Congress and in the federal judiciary.

## ABSCAM SCANDAL

Among the many Congressional scandals was Abscam. It broke in February 1980 when the FBI released video pictures of Congressmen[548] taking bribes from an FBI agent posing as an Arab Sheik. Abscam's intent was to expose political corruption, especially of those members of Congress who incurred the displeasure of Justice Department officials. A United States Senator and seven members of the House of Representatives, as well as a number of private attorneys and state and local officials, were implicated as a result of the video taped sting operation.

## SHAM WHISTLE-BLOWER "PROTECTIONS"

This saga of corruption shows the urgent need for legislation protecting and encouraging whistle-blowing against corruption by federal officials and personnel. Past legislation was rendered valueless by placing people in charge of the program who gutted it. In 1978, the Civil Service Reform Act created the Office of Special Counsel (OSC) for the purpose of protecting whistleblowers from reprisals, and to prosecute those who retaliate. President Reagan gutted the office by appointing Alex Kozinski to head the OSC, who openly violated the intent and the specifics of the legislation. Nearly half of the office personnel and seventy percent of the attorneys and investigators at the OSC either resigned or were fired. During that time over 7000 federal employees sought assistance from the OSC. Only two cases were filed, and these were limited to job reinstatement, carefully avoiding any mention of the epidemic government corruption.

"The OSC failed to meet its Congressional mandate," said Senator Levin on February 5, 1987, when he introduced the Whistleblower Protection Act of 1987. "It has not protected employees who have been the victims of unfair personnel practices, and its failure to do so is one reason why federal employees are afraid to blow the whistle." Congresswoman Patricia Schroeder of Colorado

547 October 8, 1989 by R.W. Apple, Jr.

548 Among those convicted in Abscam included Representatives John M. Murphy (New York); Michael J. Myers (Pennsylvania); Frank Thompson, Jr (New Jersey); Raymond F. Lederer (Pennsylvania); John Jenrette (South Carolina); Richard Kelly (Florida); and Senator Harrison A. Williams, Jr.

introduced legislation in 1987, known as the Contractor Whistleblower Protection Act, stating: "We urge [whistleblowers] to come forward; we hail them as the salvation of our budget trauma, and we promise them their place in heaven. But we let them be eaten alive."

She should know. I repeatedly gave her details of these scandals and the actions taken to silence me through criminal misuse of the federal agencies over which she had oversight responsibilities. She never responded. Representative Barbara Boxer of California promoted the whistleblower legislation and refused to meet her responsibilities when I notified her of the same epidemic corruption that I had brought to Schroeder's attention. None of them responded to their congressional oversight responsibility or as required under federal criminal statutes.

The Cavello Foundation in Cambridge, Massachusetts, which allegedly assists whistleblowers, wouldn't act when I brought the same information to them. I contacted the Government Accountability Project in Washington on June 30, 1988, supplying them with the information, but they refused to get involved. GAP staff associate Carina Campobasso expressed concern when I spoke with her on the phone, but her subsequent letter stated there was a case-freeze in effect which prevented them from taking on new cases. The massive corruption and harm inflicted upon the United States certainly warranted an exercise of a greater sense of responsibilities than that feeble excuse.

The greatest example of the need for meaningful whistleblower protection is the felony persecution of the whistleblowers in my group, consisting of, among others, Russbacher, Rewald, Riconosciuto, Webb, Abbott, Russell Bowen, John Cole, myself, and others.

For all this corruption to take place, it is necessary for every check and balance, including the watchdog agencies in government, to feloniously cover up, refuse to perform their duty, and obstruct justice. Senate investigators reported in September 1990 that federal inspector generals, who have the responsibilities to uncover and root out wrongdoings in government agencies, usually cover up the misconduct and intimidate those who want to expose it. The report cites "a disturbing pattern of misconduct" by Inspector Generals in a broad array of federal agencies. The report, prepared by Senator Jim Sasser (D-Tenn), chairman of the Subcommittee on General Services, Federalism, and the District of Columbia, stated that the "watchdogs have become political lap dogs."

The report states that instead of meeting its lawful responsibilities, "many Inspector General offices are engaged in damage control for their agencies and political patrols; or are knee deep in the very abuses they are supposed to prevent."

The Inspector-General system was created in 1978 to ferret out waste, fraud, and abuse in government, and to provide a safe harbor for those dedicated federal employees who try to stop government misconduct. As usual, it has been identified as a failure.

**REVOLVING DOOR SYNDROME**

Part of the reason for influence peddling and corruption arises from the revolving door syndrome. It is seen in many scandals, including HUD, the savings and loan, Defense Department, and in air safety. Ignoring regulatory violations by government employees seeking employment with industry is an accepted fact of life.[549] A *Wall Street Journal* article named government officials appearing before industry groups that are affected by their decisions, seeking clients after their departure from government or for employment positions. These government officials act while in government positions to protect their future benefactors. The revolving door problems were mentioned in a *This World* article on June 2, 1985:

> *[A] quality control officer nearing the end of a military career was likely to keep his mouth shut if he spotted a problem with a company that might offer him a job after retirement.... People are frequently looking for the next job, and you're going to do things that make that next job easier to get....a Department of Defense attorney...acknowledged that there was "a lot of concern" about the issue at the Department.... [a company] comes around and offers him a job at $50,000 to $75,000 per year. If he stands up and makes a fuss about high cost and poor quality, [the company won't] come to him when he retires.*

A *Wall Street Journal* investigative reporting article on January 4, 1989, addressed the revolving door problem:

> *Competition to Hire Officials Leaving government Is Fiercest for Pair of Lawyers From Trade Office. [Describing the high financial rewards received by government employees going with the industry they formerly regulated and giving as examples two government employees going with industry] it is reliably understood that they each will be paid upwards of $300,000 a year to launch an international trade practice at [a major law firm].*

Another front page *Wall Street Journal* article on January 31, 1989, described the rewards received by employees involved in the savings and loan corruption: "Revolving Door—S&L Mess Isn't All Bad, At Least for Lawyers Who Were Regulators." The article told of an attorney who left government to join a law firm and started at over triple what the government paid.

This reminds me of the Director of the Air Safety Investigative Branch of the Civil Aeronautic Board (now called the National Transportation Safety Board), to whom I reported the criminal activities associated with a series of ongoing

549 NTSB chairman Webster Todd became director of ALPA's department of engineering and air safety; FAA Administrator Butterfield became employed by IASCO, an aviation concern near San Francisco; FAA Administrator Najeebe Halaby became president of Pan American World Airways; FAA chief counsel Bert Goodwin became director of regulatory affairs at ALPA headquarters in Washington; FAA Administrator John Shaffer became a director at Beech Aircraft Corporation; FAA official John Baker became head of the Aircraft Owners and Pilots Association; Donald Madole left the NTSB's Bureau of Aviation Safety to become a partner in a key law firm that profited from airline-crash litigation; NTSB Board member Hogue went with Airline Passengers Association; the bankruptcy judge who ruled favorably for Continental Airlines then left the bench and joined the law firm representing Continental; Robert Remley, a former FAA official who ruled favorably in a 1984 safety audit of Continental (despite contrary inspector reports), went with Continental. Those going to Texas Air Corporation included Richard Hirst as Vice President, who was a former attorney with the CAB; Clark Onstad, Vice President and Chief Lobbyist, who was former Chief Counsel with the FAA; Dewey Roark, General Counsel, who was formerly Special Counsel for regulations in the FAA. The government officials going to Eastern Airlines included John Keyser, Vice President for Regulatory Compliance at Eastern, and former FAA attorney and official (with whom I worked in the FAA in the early 1960s); Phillip Bakes as President and Chief Executive Officer at Eastern Airlines, was former Chief Counsel of CAB, was former counsel to the Congressional Committee which wrote the Airline Deregulation law.

airline crashes. I asked him, attorney Donald Madole, to intervene, as was his duty. Instead, he covered up, with the result that the fraud-related crashes and deaths continued. Madole protected United Airlines, the FAA, the NTSB, and who knows who else. Madole left government service and reportedly became a multi-millionaire as a partner in the law firm that profited from air disasters.[550]

Former Reagan aide, Michael Deaver, parlayed his government contacts after leaving government service, and was sentenced to prison for not waiting the required 12 months before using them. But this offense was peanuts compared to the hard crimes committed by those Justice Department attorneys prosecuting Deaver, and the federal judges hearing the case.

Speaking of departing government officials at the Bank Board who helped bring about the savings and loan fiasco, Representative Jim Leach stated: "My impression is that they'll all go out and earn a million dollars. The revolving door at the Bank Board makes the problems at the Pentagon look like peanuts."[551] The Revolving Door problem was addressed by *Newsweek* on February 6, 1989, naming middle and high level officials with the Federal Trade Commission who triple their former government salaries when accepting positions with corporations they formerly regulated.

The *Newsweek* article gave examples of the profitable revolving door syndrome. For instance, John Norris, former Deputy Commissioner, Food and Drug Administration, went from a government salary of $75,500 to an estimated $360,000 yearly salary. Gene Lucero, who supervised enforcement of Superfund and hazardous-waste laws against private companies, went from $75,000 to an estimated $190,000 a year salary. General Counsel for the Federal Trade Commission, Robert Paul, went from $78,000 to an estimated $240,000. The practice of cashing in their government contacts and knowledge, and working against the public interest, is epidemic.

Former Texas Senator John Tower left the Senate in 1985 after serving as Chairman of the Senate Armed Services Committee, and joined a high-powered consulting firm whose chief clients were major defense contractors. He was paid over $750,000 for his advice to contractors following a very short period of work.

Department of Transportation Secretary James Burnley left government service to join a prominent Washington law firm under suspicious circumstances. He was reported to be actively negotiating to become a member of the law firm of Shaw, Pittman, Potts & Trowbridge at the time he issued an important ruling in favor of Eastern Airlines, one of the firm's major clients in the transportation field.

Before leaving his government position in December 1987, Burnley took the unusual step of personally handling a request by the Air Line Pilots Association to defuse an issue relating to Burnley's new employer. ALPA requested that the Department of Transportation investigate Eastern's "continuing fitness" as a carrier in view of its continuing financial troubles. Such matters are usually dealt with at the Assistant-Secretary level. A week after Burnley

---

550 Speiser and Speiser.
551 January 31, 1989 *Wall Street Journal.*

intervened personally, he rejected the ALPA petition in a strongly worded order saying it "borders on abuse of the department's processes." He was misusing his government position to carry out the wishes of the airline represented by his future law firm who handled Eastern Airlines and another Texas Air subsidiary, Continental Airlines.

The Air Line Pilots Association accused Burnley of a conflict of interest, accusing him of seeking employment with two law firms having close ties to Eastern Airlines while at the same time denying ALPA's petition for a fitness examination of the airline.

As in each and every one of the other scandals, the country's most expensive attorneys frantically sought to protect their valuable clients.

**ALTERING ELECTION RESULTS**

The authors of *Votescam*, James and Kenneth Collier, explained the ease with which election results can be altered in the computerized voting machines. The authors describe how votes can be changed through pre-programmed computerized voting machines to favor a particular candidate. They charge that a cartel of bureaucrats, especially those in the CIA, the establishment media, members of Congress, decide in concert how America's votes are counted and by whom. The book describes how a private corporation, News Election Service (NES), with ties to the establishment media, controls the counting of votes. If what they say is true, and it is not far-fetched, elections can be easily corrupted. The corrupt forces in government, and especially those in control of the CIA and Justice Department, can select the winner, regardless of the number of votes actually cast for the various candidates.

**COVERUPS EVERYWHERE**

It isn't only in the United States that drug trafficking by well-known personnel is covered up. An April 6, 1988 DEA report showed the involvement of Mark Thatcher, Prime Minister Margaret Thatcher's son, in drug trafficking with the infamous drug trafficker and terrorists, Monzer Al Kassar. I made this highly classified report available to British newspapers with the usual coverup. Key segments of the first page of the report on the following page is reprinted here:

1. Mark Thatcher has been identified in this investigation as a person who has consummated a major arms for drugs transaction....3. On 7/29/85, the Bern CO received information from intelligence sources that THATCHER...and AL KASSAR had consummated a 100 million dollar arms deal with Iraq through the intervention of Rifeat AL ASSAD, the brother of the Syrian President. The Sources also reported that the arms were paid for with heroin from the Bakaa Valley, Lebanon, which was picked up by a Gates Learjet, Austrian Registration Number DE-GBR, owned by the firm of ALKASTRONIC...which is owned by Monzer AL KASSAR. Intelligence sources reported that...THATCHER and partner split a 15 million dollar profit from the sale of the heroin....4. In September 1986, the Rome CO received information that AL KASSAR had met with an associate of Mafia boss Salvatore REINA in Palermo, Sicily to dispose of the heroin. On 9/26/86, AL KASSAR ordered his bank in Geneva, the Swiss Bank Corporation to transfer the sum of 15 million dollars from his account...to the account of DIVERSIFIED CAPITAL LTD...

REPORT OF INVESTIGATION

Page 1 of 2

1. PROGRAM CODE

2. CROSS FILE / RELATED FILES
XK-85-0004
R1-85-2002
XH-R8-0004

3. FILE NO. UN-86-0007

4. G-DEP IDENTIFIER I83-T1

5. BY: Michael Meyrick, S/A
AT: Bern, Switzerland

6. FILE TITLE Monzer AL KASSAR, et al

7. ☐ Closed ☐ Requested Action Completed ☐ Action Requested By:

8. DATE PREPARED April 6, 1988

9. OTHER OFFICERS:

10. REPORT RE:
Arms Trafficking by Mark THATCHER

DETAILS:

1. Mark THATCHER has been identified in this investigation as a person who has consummated a major arms for drugs transaction with Armen HASER, currently residing in Monte Carlo, Monaco.

2. A check of the records of NADDIS showed that in 1985, DEA received information that HASER was associated with Monzer AL KASSAR in the arms and heroin trafficking business in the Middle East and Central America.

3. On 7/29/86, the Bern CO received information from intelligence sources that THATCHER, together with HASER and AL KASSAR had consummated a 100 million dollar arms deal with Iraq through the intervention of Rifaat AL ASSAD, the brother of the Syrian President. The sources also reported that the arms were paid for with heroin from the Bekaa Valley, Lebanon which was picked up by a Gates Learjet, Austrian Registration Number OE-GBR, owned by the firm of ALKASTRONIC, companies registration number HR B 30633, founded on March 11, 1983 in Vienna, Austria, which, in turn, is owned by Monzer AL KASSAR. Intelligence sources reported that HASER and THATCHER and partner split a 15 million dollar profit from the sale of the heroin. A review of the records of NADDIS was negative for Mark Thatcher and his partner, Steve TIPPING. TIPPING did all of the actual contact work and travelling for this transaction. NADDIS does show entries under HASER (1753696), ALKASTRONIC (7070765), AL ASSAD (1784282), and AL KASSAR (1/2519).

4. In September 1986, the Rome CO received information that AL KASSAR had met with an associate of Mafia boss Salvatore RIINA in Palermo, Sicily to dispose of the heroin. On 9/26/86, AL KASSAR ordered his bank in Geneva, the Swiss Bank Corporation to transfer the sum of 15 million dollars from his account 81 56 8 YR to the account of DIVERSIFIED CAPITAL LTD., DR. I. H. THURSTON, Director at

11. DISTRIBUTION:
ACTION Madrid CO
DISTRICT
OTHER OH, CIOH, AMAI

12. SIGNATURE (Agent)
Michael W. Meyrick, Special Agent

13. DATE 4/7

14. APPROVED (Name and Title)
Gregory A. Passic, Country Attache

15. DATE

DEA Form - 6

DEA SENSITIVE
DRUG ENFORCEMENT ADMINISTRATION
This report is the property of the Drug Enforcement Administration.
Neither it nor its contents may be disseminated outside the agency to which loaned.

# SUPREME COURT COMPLICITY

Many of these criminal activities and resulting harm could not have continued without the coverup by each of the Justices of the U.S. Supreme Court. In the 1970s, I brought the corruption to the attention of the Supreme Court justices as it related to the air safety and criminal violations associated with a series of air disasters and the felony coverup by Justice Department attorneys and federal judges. These federal crimes included those perpetrated by officials in the Federal Aviation Administration the National Transportation Safety Board, and various divisions of the U.S. Department of Justice. I had first brought these crimes to the attention of federal district and appellate judges in the Ninth Circuit at San Francisco and Los Angeles, and each of them were improperly dismissed.

From 1990 to the present date, I continued to report even worse criminal activities, those described within these pages, demanding to produce testimony and evidence from myself and a large number of former CIA and other deep-cover sources. Federal judges, including Supreme Court Justices, repeatedly prevented me from producing evidence as required by the clear language of the federal criminal statute. They also openly violated their duty to supervise federal judges and officers of the court in the federal judiciary.

I also filed petitions, from 1983 to the present date, that addressed the pattern of judicially-inflicted civil and constitutional violations seeking to silence me, but also to report the criminal activities that I uncovered that were major violations of federal law.

If any one of the many criminal activities that I uncovered, and which I repeatedly brought to the attention of the Justices of the U.S. Supreme Court, are true, and the Justices refused to receive my evidence or take action to bring the crimes to justice, they are clearly guilty of several federal criminal statutes associated with coverup and obstruction of justice. This is very serious.

Federal judges had mandatory responsibilities under federal statutes to provide me with a federal court forum, to provide relief from the ongoing civil and constitutional violations perpetrated in an obvious criminal conspiracy, and to receive my evidence relating to the criminal charges.

Some of the crimes were obvious from the record. It is a federal crime[552] to inflict harm upon a victim or informant, for reporting federal crimes, as federal judges and Justice Department prosecutors did to me from 1987 to the present date. It is a federal crime[553] to inflict harm upon any citizen for having exercised rights and protection under the laws and Constitution of the United States.

## REFUSING TO MEET STATUTORY RESPONSIBILITIES

Another type of culpable omission occurs when a statute creates a duty to act, and the perpetrator fails to do so. Federal judges have a mandatory duty to provide a federal court forum and to provide the relief and protection in federal statutes. They cannot by law decide who shall receive the protections guaranteed by the laws and Constitution of the United States. But this is what they have done, and are continuing to do.

A criminal act, such as an assault or battery, can be committed by an omission to act when there is a duty to act.[554]

## FORCING SUPREME COURT JUSTICES TO PERFORM A MANDATORY DUTY, OR ENGAGE IN FELONY COVERUP

Toward the end of September 1994, I filed several petitions for relief with the Justices of the U.S. Supreme Court. I had received notice that the remaining $300,000 in my formerly $10 million estate would be distributed by court order on September 22, 1994, to the very people who played key roles in the scheme to silence me, including the San Francisco law firm of Friedman, Sloan and Ross, the Texas resident who served as the catalyst for the sham "divorce" action against me, and various law firms.

I promptly filed a petition for writ of mandamus and prohibition with the Ninth Circuit court of appeals at San Francisco, citing federal law showing the orders taking my assets were void orders, based upon absence of jurisdiction and violation of important statutory and constitutional protection. Court of Appeal judges promptly denied the petition, refusing to render findings of facts and conclusions of law. Simultaneously, judges of the large Ninth Circuit court

---

552 **Title 18 U.S.C. § 1512. Tampering with a witness, victim, or an informant–**
(b) Whoever knowingly uses intimidation or physical force, or threatens another person, or attempts to do so, or engages in misleading conduct toward another person, with intent to --
(1) influence, delay or prevent the testimony of any person in an official proceeding:
shall be fined...or imprisoned...or both. [1988 amended reading].

**Title 18 U.S.C. § 1513. Retaliating against a witness, victim, or an informant.**
(a) Whoever knowingly engages in any conduct and thereby causes bodily injury to another person or damages the tangible property of another person, or threatens to do so, with intent to retaliate against any person for–(1) the attendance of a witness or party at an official proceeding, or any testimony given or any record, document, or other object produced by a witness in an official proceeding; or (2) any information relating to the commission or possible commission of a Federal offense....

553 **Title 18 U.S.C. § 241. Conspiracy against rights of citizens.** If two or more persons conspire to injure, oppress, threaten, or intimidate any citizen in the free exercise or enjoyment of any right or privilege secured to him by the Constitution or laws of the United States, or because of his having so exercised the same; ... They shall be fined ... or imprisoned ... or both;

554 *See W. LaFave & A. Scott, Criminal Law* 21011 (2d ed. 1986). In *People v. Burden*, 72 Cal.App.3d 603 (1977), a similar analysis was made. *Barclay's Official California Code of Regulations*, Title 11, 1081 (1991), for instance, describes the law requiring officers to prevent crimes, protect life, ensure equal justice, and other acts. In prosecuting government officials for failure to perform their duty, it is necessary only to prove the omission, the *mens rea*, the willfulness of the non-action.

California statutes, including for instance Government Code section 1222, approvingly cited in *People v. Pringle*, 151 Cal.App.3d 854, 858 (1984), provides for punishment of officers failing to perform their duties "here no special provision is made for the punishment of such delinquency."

of appeals rendered a July 28, 1994 order, barring me for the remainder of my life from access to the court of appeals, as is available to other citizens. This order enlarged on what district court judges had done earlier, which barred me access to federal district courts and voided for me the rights and protections under the statutes and Constitution of the United States. These orders were unlawful and unconstitutional, and obstructed justice by blocking me from reporting to a federal court, as required by federal criminal and other statutes, that federal courts receive reports of federal crimes. They also blocked me from defending against the enormous harm judicially inflicted upon me for the past decade.

I then filed a petition for writ of certiorari with the U.S. Supreme Court, describing the pattern of civil and constitutional protection judicially inflicted upon me, including the corrupt seizing and looting of my assets. To circumvent the practice of Supreme Court clerks refusing to file my petitions, I sent by certified mail a copy of that petition, and a copy of the second edition of *Defrauding America*, to every Justice of the Court. They were therefore put on notice of the criminal activities, including that of judges and officers of the court over whom the Justices had supervisory responsibilities. I also reminded the Justices that they had vicarious criminal liabilities if they continue to refuse to perform their duties. The petition, and the letter, were straight-forward, factual, devoid of any emotion, and left no doubt that the criminal activities were making the federal judiciary a criminal enterprise.

Within a week of signing for the certified letters and petitions, the clerk of the Supreme Court returned them to me, refusing to file the petition that he is required to file under law.

I was totally gridlocked. The protection of the laws and Constitution of the United States were judicially denied to me while these laws were being judicially violated, inflicting major and devastating harm. In 1995, the U.S. Court of Appeals in San Francisco rendered a similar order, barring me access to the appellate courts. And the United States Supreme Court refused to file any petitions that I submitted. All of these acts violated the laws and Constitution of the United States, but they blocked me from reporting the government crimes in which they themselves were implicated.

The criminal activities that I initially sought to report to the federal judges continued to play a causative or permissive role in a continuing series of airline crashes that could have been prevented if my evidence had been accepted.

As a matter of law, and under Supreme Court procedures as specifically provided by Rules of Court of the Supreme Court, a person has the right to petition an individual Justice for relief. Also, under federal crime-reporting statutes, the law clearly provides that a citizen must report federal crimes to any federal judge. Implied in the law, a federal judge must receive the evidence. Every time that I exercised these rights and responsibilities the Supreme Court Justices blocked me.

## IMPLYING THE SERIOUSNESS OF MY CHARGES

Only once did a Justice of the Supreme Court make any type of response, and this was highly unusual and significant. A Justice simply does not write personal letters to a litigant, especially a *pro se* litigant. In response to my petition addressed to Justice Byron White, which he refused to grant, he stated in an October 28, 1991, letter:

*As a single Justice I can be of no help to you.*

*I am returning your petition.*

My charges were specific and of serious national importance. If any one of them was true, a serious undermining of the United States was under way. I was a former federal investigator holding authority under law to make such determinations. A check of prior federal actions would have supported certain of my charges. I offered government documents to support some of my charges.

A corollary would be similar to a federal investigator offering evidence showing why a series of aircraft disintegrations were occurring, and no one would listen. The charges were serious; the harm inflicted upon the United States was of a catastrophic nature. No one had the moral or legal right to refuse to receive my evidence.

## VICARIOUS CRIMINAL LIABILITY

Under law, the head of an organization is financially and criminally responsible for the actions of those over whom he has supervisory responsibilities. This liability increases if he knows of the criminal acts and allow them to continue, and if he fails to report the acts to proper authorities. The Justices were the head of the federal judiciary involved in the corrupt and criminal acts. These acts could not continue without them aiding and abetting them as they were doing.

## C0-CONSPIRATOR LAW

Under universally applicable conspiracy laws, co-conspirators are criminally responsible not only for their own criminal acts, but also for the actions of their co-conspirators performed within the scope of the conspiracy, and in furtherance of the conspiracy.

A 1994 article in the San Francisco legal newspaper, *Daily Journal*, described the criminal acts under state and federal law perpetrated by those officials in the federal and state government who have a duty to act and who fail to perform that duty. The article described the law in detail, and explained how the "law of negative acts" or "omissions" are another form of criminal activity. The article explained that "in certain circumstances the failure to act (the omission) satisfies the requirement of criminal law." Referring to the law book, *R. Perkins & R. Boyace, Criminal Law* 66467 (3d ed. 1982), the article explained that there are several situations in which the omission to perform a duty is criminally culpable and satisfies the *actus reus*.

## REFUSAL TO PERFORM A FIDUCIARY DUTY

The Justices had a fiduciary duty to protect the public against corrupt actions of federal judges over whom they have supervisory responsibilities, and of attorneys and trustees appearing in federal courts. In the event of a fatal airline crash, for instance, a government official, such as an FAA official, or one with the National Transportation Safety Board, would be guilty of a crime if that official knew of unsafe or criminal acts relating to air safety, and if that person then covered up for it, allowing the violations to result in a crash and deaths. That certainly happened in many of the crashes I describe in the book, *Unfriendly Skies*.

In the airline crashes that were associated with federal offenses which other inspectors and I had reported, these criminal offenses applied to officials in the Federal Aviation Administration, the National Transportation Safety Board, Department of Justice and its various divisions including several U.S. attorneys and the FBI, members of Congress, the media, all of whom knew about the charges and covered up for them.

Justice Department officials who refused to receive evidence of crimes that I discovered while a government and then as a private investigator, were guilty of felony omissions. They were even more guilty when they prosecuted me, in conjunction with federal judges, for having sought to report criminal acts.

By voiding the protection of federal law and the Constitution to me, federal judges made possible the infliction of great harm. Under criminal law, they are guilty of criminal acts.

Judges obligate themselves by *contract* to protect a citizen from civil and constitutional violations and criminal acts, when such harm is a reasonable possibility. In my case, the harms were ongoing. The essence of a judge's job is to enforce the laws and Constitution of the United States, their *raison d'etre*, including providing a federal court forum and providing declaratory and injunctive relief from the judicially-inflicted harm. I suffered greatly, under the judicial infliction of continuing civil and constitutional violations, while judge after judge, the media, members of Congress, stood by, refusing to perform their duty to prevent these acts.

**UPHOLDING UNCONSTITUTIONAL SEIZURE OF PROPERTY**

The Supreme Court Justices in June 1989, upheld the right of state and federal agents to confiscate the assets of a person possessing drugs, or who is charged with a crime, even though charges had not been filed (and maybe never would be). Judges dictate what schools your children may go to, to achieve some social engineering.

In 1993, the California Supreme Court held that a citizen could be arrested and held in jail for several days solely on the basis that he or she was not carrying identification. A swimmer walking to the beach could end up in jail, in chains, enduring body-cavity searches, and risking rape, solely because he or she did not have identification suitable to the stopping officer.[555]

In California, commencing on January 1, 1995, a person driving without a valid driver's license can have his or her car seized and auctioned off, expanding on the unconstitutional forfeiture practices.

**LICENSE TO STEAL**

"License to Steal," was the heading on an article in San Francisco's legal newspaper, *Daily Journal* (March 18, 1996). The subtitle said, "In Supreme Court Ruling, Rights of the Innocent Are Forfeited." The article made reference to the Supreme Court's March 1996 decision upholding the right of government agencies seizing property from innocent people. The article stated in part:

> *The U.S. Supreme Court has given its stamp of approval to states that steal property from innocent people. Such a forfeiture doesn't violate the constitutional protections of due process, the high court said... Chief*

555 Associated Press, April 30, 1993.

*Justice William Rehnquist...writes opinions as if he were writing algebraic formulas–they make no reference to the lives they affect...The high court just issued Michigan and other states a license for theft...Justice Ruth Bader Ginsburg wrote a concurring opinion that in effect apologizes for the decision–yet supports it.*

**HOLDING THEMSELVES ABOVE THE LAW**

U.S. Supreme Court decisions hold that a citizen cannot sue a judge for harms inflicted, regardless of whether the judge acted in error, maliciously, or in excess of authority. The US Supreme Court Justices have held in such cases as *Stump v. Sparkman*[556] that the American public has no protection against the renegade judges.

This isn't what civil rights statutes state; it is judge-made law to protect themselves, while corruptly misusing their judicial offices. These self-protective case law decisions conflict with the public's right to seek damages from *anyone* who knowingly inflicts harms through known and deliberate violations of protected rights.

On March 4, 1996, the Supreme Court Justices held that "an owner's interest in property may be forfeited by reason of the use to which the property is put even though the owner did not know that it was to be put to such use."

**SUPREME COURT'S SOILED RECORD**

President Lyndon Johnson relied upon voter fraud to get into the U.S. Senate, as related in the 1964 publication of *A Texan Looks At Johnson* and *Means of Ascent* by Robert Caro, published by Knopf. When Johnson discovered that Texas Governor Coke Stevenson had received 112 votes more then he did, Johnson arranged for a "recanvass" of the records. Lo and behold, an additional 202 suspicious votes appeared, nicely arranged in alphanumerical order, in a district he controlled. When the matter was taken to the federal district court, the court issued an injunction barring Johnson from claiming victory, and set a hearing to address the voter fraud.

To circumvent the unfavorable evidence being presented in the U.S. District Court in Texas, Johnson's attorney, Abe Fortas, filed a petition with Justice Hugo Black of the U.S. Supreme Court to block the federal district court in Texas from taking any action. Black ruled in Johnson's favor, without allowing the evidence of voter fraud to be presented. Johnson later rewarded Fortas by appointing him to the U.S. Supreme Court. But as the saying goes that "a leopard doesn't change its spots," Fortas' conduct on the Supreme Court was so sufficiently outrageous that he was later forced to resign rather than face impeachment.

An editorial in the *San Francisco Chronicle*[557] titled: "The Pernicious Court," stated that the "Judiciary is riding roughshod over rights and precedent as it enacts its legislative agenda into law." The editorial stated that "the Supreme Court rode roughshod over traditional constitutional rights, ignoring settled precedents and overturning others that got in its way." How well I have seen judicial misconduct, and even criminal misconduct, during the past 30 years.

---

556 *Stump v. Sparkman*, 435 US 349 (1978).
557 June 30, 1991.

**COMMON JUDICIAL-ATTORNEY CORRUPTION**

Former presiding judge of the San Diego Superior Court, Michael I. Greer, pleaded guilty (March 11, 1996) in a federal court to accepting $75,000 in bribes from a high-profile attorney and law firm which had over 40 cases before the judge. Greer implicated other judges receiving bribes, helping explain why many cases were decided in clear opposition to the facts and the law. Instead of admitting publicity that he committed a crime, the judge issued a statement to the press admitting "lack of judgment in his dealings with attorneys."

One of the "benefits" of the bribes was a $5 million judicial decision in favor of automobile dealer James J. Williams, Jr. The presiding judge admitted turning cases over to "cooperating" judges following the payment of bribe money. The bribe money resulted in many millions of dollars of awards by the judges to clients represented by the attorneys paying bribes.

**ARROGANCE AT EVERY LEVEL OF GOVERNMENT**

The bureaucrats in charge of the U.S. Department of Housing and Urban Development (HUD) routinely investigate and file charges against Americans who object to the placement of undesirable housing in their midst. In Berkeley, for instance, HUD used federal resources to investigate, intimidate, and threaten with federal prison those people who objected to the placement of housing in their neighborhood for the mentally disturbed and treatment of drug abusers. HUD attorneys investigated for seven months and threatened to charge people with violating federal housing discrimination laws. Nearby neighbors, Richard Graham, Alexandra White, and Joseph Deringer, were threatened with $50,000 in fines and a prison sentence for objecting to the HUD housing plans. HUD charged that the neighbors engaged in "coercion, intimidation and interference" against the potential tenants of the planned housing.

The same members of Congress who are so deeply implicated in these criminal activities are the same people who legislate laws putting Americans in prison for relatively minor offenses. The percentage of people incarcerated in the United States has reached record levels, approaching a dictator's method of silencing opposition. Prisons are being filled with non-violent offenders, whose long prison terms are the result of laws passed by Congress, charges by prosecutors, and sentences by judges. These are the same groups that themselves have the greatest percentage of federal offenses but which are not charged. If everyone who used drugs joined those imprisoned for the offense, a very large percentage of the American public would be incarcerated.

People who have exaggerated information on their application for a loan, such as overstating their income, or some other relatively minor matter, have been sent to federal prison.

The public has tolerated judicial decisions requiring them to bus their children many miles away to bring about some desired judicial goal, despite the freedom of association clearly prescribed in the Constitution and in effect for the first two decades of America's existence. The right to associate with people of one's choosing, or the reasonable usage of property, and other freedoms accepted as constitutional for two centuries, are suddenly criminal acts if exercised.

The newer generation has little knowledge of the constitutional rights that first existed, being brain-washed to accept as unconstitutional the rights that were constitutional.

**FURTHER COMPLICITY OF SUPREME COURT JUSTICES**

Just before this book went to the printer, I had submitted for filing on August 12, 1997, a petition for writ of certiorari with the U.S. Supreme Court. That petition was *very* sensitive, and its filing would have made a Supreme Court record of the criminal activities described within these pages, including the extensive involvement of federal judges. The petition was filed in response to the dismissal of an appeal by the Court of Appeals in the District of Columbia (97-5007), and was authorized under Title 28 USC Section 1254 and Supreme Court Rule 13.

If that petition had been filed, it would have put the Justices of the United States Supreme Court on record of knowing of these criminal and subversive activities and then aiding and abetting them by refusing to address the issues and providing relief.

Arguably, the Supreme Court Justices had the prerogative of not hearing the petition, but they lacked the authority to deny its filing. Normally, the Justices hear only a small fraction of the petitions that are filed. But in this case, the mere act of filing the petition put the justices on notice, and to have refused to address and hear the issues involving criminal and subversive misconduct, including that of federal judges over whom they have supervisory responsibilities, would have further implicated them.

The Justices addressed this serious problem by refusing to file the petition, having the clerk fraudulently write that the filing was not timely, when the petition was filed several weeks before the 90-day jurisdictional period had expired.

I responded in an August 23, 1997 letter to Supreme Court clerk, William K. Sutter, precisely showing the fraudulent nature of the denial, sending copies of that letter, and a copy of the petition (which must be filed in booklet form) to each of the Justices, insuring that they were on notice and could not at some future date claim ignorance of the issues and facts stated in the petition. For years Supreme Court Justices have been made aware of my charges and where evidence supporting them could be found.

Automatic exposure to the legal fraternity of petitions to the Supreme Court occurs by the procedure in place. A person filing a petition for writ of certiorari with the U.S. Supreme Court must file an original and 40 copies, many of which are then sent to law libraries throughout the United States. These petitions are then read by media sources who report on the contents of significant filings even if the Justices do not choose to hear the matter.

**GRAVITY OF SUPREME COURT JUSTICES COVERUP**

Obviously, the coverup of such serious crimes against the United States by Justices of the Supreme Court constitutes impeachable and criminal offenses. And these crimes are made worse by the fraudulent attempt to block their reporting by rejecting the filing of the petition for writ of certiorari authorized by federal statutes. But this was definitely not the first time the Justices blocked my filing, or refused to address the issues after being filed. However, in this case, the issues were very grave.

# CRIMES OF COVERUP

As previously stated, a person has committed a felony if he or she knows of a federal crime and does not promptly report it to a federal judge or other federal tribunal.[558] Most of the mainstream media, members of Congress, many lazy or cowardly citizens, are certainly guilty of this crime. Those in the broadcast and print media who refused to report the charges of government crimes, or knowledge of the crimes, are morally and criminally guilty. Those who engaged in deliberate misinformation to cover up for these crimes were guilty of even worst crimes, under federal law.

Most of the large publishers are controlled by a relatively small number of conglomerates that control which books are published and which are banned. The conglomerates have interests throughout our society that are tied in with many of those in control of government and who would suffer financially if the truth came out and their financial contacts came to a halt.

I encountered the publishing house censorship in the mid-1960s, and had to form my own publishing company to get the books to the public. The pattern of air safety and criminal acts that caused or allowed to occur many of the worst airline disasters would not have happened if the media had met their responsibilities to report the valid charges and evidence that I offered. Many papers, such as the *Wall Street Journal*, have excellent investigators and articles, but the editorial sections engage in coverups.

My experience with coverup by NBC began in late 1977, when Alan Goldstein and Linda Ellerbee contacted me after reading the U.S. Supreme Court's refusal to vacate the lower court's dismissal of my action against the FAA. Unaware of previous NBC contacts and coverup, they expressed great interest in what I told them and requested further details, which I sent. That was the end of that.

558 Title 18 U.S.C. § 4.

The media have people examining federal complaints after they are filed, reporting those that have public interest. They knew of my filings in the U.S. District Courts throughout the United States, which revealed the rampant and devastating government corruption in the United States. The issues stated in the lawsuits were obviously of extreme importance.

During an appearance on Larry King's television program on June 28, 1989, Leo Demoore, the author of *Senatorial Privilege*, told of the coverup he witnessed as a reporter covering Kennedy's Chappaquiddick accident. He discussed the coverup by the press of the more sensitive and sordid parts of the scandal, claiming that although public attention forced news coverage, most if not all the papers omitted extremely serious misconduct by Kennedy and those who covered up for him, distorting what they did reveal. He said that the press protected Kennedy as much as possible. The press didn't want to hear anything that might blemish Kennedy's image. Demoore made it clear that both the press and the publishing houses wanted the matter kept as quiet as possible.

Demoore had a firm contract with Random House to publish *Senatorial Privilege*, which had already been accepted in 1985. Suddenly, Random House refused to go to print, claiming they were dissatisfied with the contents, even though they had already expressed complimentary approval of the first half. Demoore felt that unknown people pressured Random House not to publish the book. Random House was also one of the publishers that had tentatively agreed to publish my first printing of *Unfriendly Skies*, and then suddenly refused to do so.

Another of many similar examples happened to journalist Peter Brewton, who had a firm contract with Doubleday to publish *The Mafia, CIA, and George Bush*. Despite assurances that the book would be published by the summer of 1992, before the presidential elections, Doubleday stalled and then refused to proceed with publication. Brewton then had his book published by SPI Books, a division of Shapolsky Publishers.

## CENSORSHIP BY THE PUBLISHING INDUSTRY?

When I finished the first manuscript of *Unfriendly Skies* in the late 1970s I queried many publishers, several of whom requested to see a copy. Several publishers expressed interest in publishing the manuscript, but each suddenly canceled at the last minute. When Ballantine Publishing Company returned the manuscript after showing a strong initial interest they accidentally left an interoffice memorandum in the returned manuscript. One of the editors referred to the manuscript as a "blockbuster." And that first draft submitted in 1976 was mild compared to subsequent manuscripts.

The contents were too sensitive; no one wanted to touch the manuscript. Even after I formed my own publishing company, a California book printer refused to print the book. The next printing that came out in 1980 was even more sensitive than the first, and had the benefit of excellent book reviews by top reviewers, including the American Library Association and other influential book reviewers. It also had the benefit of hundreds of talk show appearances, which publishing houses take into consideration in determining the marketability of the book. Still, no publisher would publish the book.

In 1988, I sent over thirty query letters to publishing houses to determine their interest in publishing the highly sensitive third printing of *Unfriendly Skies*. By that time the extent of the air disaster and superimposed government scandal was no secret to the news media. Not a single publisher expressed an interest in even *looking* at the manuscript. In the mid-1960s, when I offered the then-primitive manuscript to publishers, at least one out of three wanted to read it. In the late 1980s, when the public's interest was aroused due to the many airline crashes and air safety problems, no publisher was interested in my book. My credentials and exclusive insider knowledge qualified me to be one of the best possible authors for such a publication.

At this same time, a three-page *Time* magazine article in 1989 told of the demand for authors and non-fiction books and the high bids to get public-interest material. The air safety crisis was a constant topic in the news and on talk shows. My manuscript was the **only** insider book on the subject, unlike any other air safety book.

Strangely, many in the media refused to accept prepaid advertising for my book. I sent prepaid advertisements to various newspapers after the first printing came out in 1978. These were unoffensive advertisements simply listing the title of the book, the price, reviewer's comments, and the address at which it could be ordered. No one could have been offended by that ad.

The newspapers that rejected the book advertisements included the supermarket tabloids that are not exactly the pillars of authenticity, including the *Globe*, *Enquirer*, *Weekly World News*, *Sun*, and others. I couldn't understand how these papers could reject my pre-paid ads when it was their standard practice to print such preposterous articles under such titles as: "Docs Deliver Baby Frozen 600 years;" or "Five Year Old Girl Delivers Baby;" or "Girl Gives Birth To Baboon's Baby!" or "Healthy Newborn Has An Ape's Body—and a Human Brain!" A February 6, 1990 headline in the tabloid *Sun* contained the bizarre "Girl, 6, Gives Birth to a 22-lb. Baby." Even the *Wall Street Journal* refused to accept my advertisements, refusing to give me a reason when I asked.

A year before I formed my own publishing company and published *Defrauding America*, I mailed over thirty query letters to major publishers seeking their possible interest in publishing the book. Although it is standard practice to at least receive a no-interest notice, I couldn't even get that. Very possibly they didn't want to be identified with having refused to assist in getting this sensitive information to the public.

In late 1992, one of the editors for Sheridan Square Press contacted me after being referred by Ari Ben-Menashe, author of *Profits of War*, asking that I send him some material concerning my manuscript on *Defrauding America*. I sent them an early chapter on the October Surprise, which contained many statements made by CIA operative Russbacher, including the role played by Israel and the Mossad. I never heard from them again, despite four subsequent letters. In April 1993, I requested that they return to me the chapters that I had sent. They wouldn't even answer that letter.

## THE ADVERTISING DOLLAR MAKES SMALL PLANES FLY BACKWARDS

The multi-million-dollar advertising revenues may explain the uncanny media reporting of the "ability" of small planes to fly backwards, or catching up and ramming into jetliners that were traveling at two or three times their speed. The news media had attributed this remarkable feat to small planes and their pilots in numerous midair collisions. In the PSA San Diego midair collision, the airliner actually rammed the small plane from the rear. But the news media reported that the small plane crashed into the jet. In the Cerritos midair collision, the DC-9 jet, flying in a northerly direction, rammed into the side of the small plane that was on an easterly heading. The news media reported the small plane crashed into the jetliner. A *Time* article of September 15, 1986, showed the east-bound small plane on a southerly heading toward the oncoming jet, instead of its actual heading of easterly, away from the jet. This misinformation placed the blame for the midair collision on the small plane pilot.

Most of the media would not report anything about the all-night crew partying in the PSA San Diego crash, or the coverup by the government air safety agencies.

A *San Francisco Examiner* article by Mark Hertsgaard[559] criticized the press for "framing the news according to what the movers and shakers of official Washington wanted, rather than thinking through the relevant issues for themselves, and [holding] the national political dialogue hostage to the debate within the Washington policy elite." He added, "Journalists got so carried away that instead of being honest brokers of information, many fell into the role of Pentagon cheerleader."

## SOME IN THE PUBLISHING INDUSTRY PAID WITH THEIR LIVES FOR THE COVERUP

Among the members of the publishing industry who knew of the air safety corruption that I reported, and whose silence made possible its continuation, were *Playboy* officials. I offered *Playboy* my manuscript in the mid-1970s, depicting the ongoing air safety and government corruption and its relationship to several recent air disasters. They didn't accept the manuscript, or publish any articles on the pattern of corruption I described. A few years later, several *Playboy* officials perished in the Chicago DC-10 tragedy resulting from problems that their publicity could have corrected.

After the Chicago DC-10 crash, *Playboy* published a nineteen-page air safety article that complained of the status of air safety but totally omitted the underlying corruption that brought on the problems. The article concealed the hard-core safety misconduct that must be addressed before any meaningful corrective actions can be taken. The article was entitled, "Airline Safety, A Special Report," and stated in part:

> *The closer you look at airline travel, the more it looks like a game of angels and great good luck, rather than skill and know-how and high technology.... based on the same statistical manipulations, it was safer to walk the tightrope than fly his planes and it was also safer to repair your roof then to take a bath.... Statistics can devil the hell out of you if you let them, but you pay your money and you take your chances, and in this game, undelivered goods are nonreturnable.*

Even the airline pilot's magazine refused to accept advertisement for the book, which could have exposed and corrected the problems that killed many of their

559 December 30, 1990. Author of *On Bended Knee: The Press and the Reagan Presidency*.

own members. The Air Line Pilots Association refused to accept advertisement for my first book. It was ironic that the Association lost a former president, Clarence Sayen, in the United 727 crash into Lake Michigan. This crash was a typical consequence of the rampant irregularities at United Airlines in which their own pilots were victims of the corruption. The Union still wouldn't expose the misconduct, apparently preferring to sacrifice their own members rather than blow the whistle on this sordid scandal. ALPA repeatedly blocked my efforts to improve the safety problem responsible for the death of its former president, many of its pilots, and thousands of people.

**KNOWINGLY DUPLICATING MY TITLE**

One of the publishing houses to whom I offered my nearly-completed manuscript, *Unfriendly Skies*, in 1988 was Bantam-Doubleday. I inquired whether they would be interested in publishing my manuscript containing highly sensitive material on government corruption, advising them that it will continue carrying the *Unfriendly Skies* title. I also advised the publisher that if no publishing house would publish it, I would self-publish. Doubleday responded they were not interested in the subject matter. You can imagine my surprise when I saw the title of *my* title, *Unfriendly Skies*, heavily promoted on the *Today Show* on April 26, 1989. Instead of listing me as the author, it showed the authors to be an airline pilot identified as Captain X and writer Reynolds Dodson.

Doubleday obviously knew my book existed from our prior contacts and its listing in *Books in Print*. They were also aware that I spent years promoting it as a public service, exposing government corruption, and that their publication containing bland material diminished interest in my explosive book with the same title. Doubleday heavily promoted their book as an exposé, expending money far beyond that which was justified by its contents. Doubleday publicized the highly sensitive nature of the book and, because of that alleged fact, the pilot's name was withheld. Captain X appeared on television via computerized composites of his face to keep his identity secret. It was a good advertising gimmick, but the contents of the book were extremely bland.

It was a snow job that deceived the public. The book didn't contain any specifics, nothing of a sensitive nature, and did not warrant a pseudo author. The book dealt heavily with the dating habits of flight attendants and ramblings by a pilot, suggesting limited experience. Pilots have said to me that they heard Captain X was a United Airlines pilot. The intent of the duplication was possibly intended to divert attention from my next printing of the same name.

Several hours before Captain X appeared on the May 1, 1989, *Larry King Live* show, I talked to Pat Piper, an associate producer on the show, reminding him *I* was the author of *Unfriendly Skies*, and that Doubleday copied my title. I felt King should address this deception during the show. Piper replied that he had read Doubleday's *Unfriendly Skies* and complained about its absence of substance, stating he didn't know why Captain X was asked to appear.

King didn't ask Captain X why he copied my title. King did ask why all the secrecy for a book that was rather bland and portrayed air safety as being in good shape, contrary to the heavy book promotion. Captain X compensated for his lack of substance by his politician's knack for avoiding difficult questions.

I requested an explanation from Doubleday on May 10, 1989, as to why they copied the title of my book. Their law firm replied that they had a right to duplicate any title they wished. While this is true, a major publishing house does not duplicate the title of another book that is being actively promoted. It is my strong belief that *Doubleday* duplicated my title to defuse the scandalous contents in my book.

The *Air Line Pilot* magazine gave Doubleday's version a glowing review.[560] They had refused to address the contents of my book and had even refused to accept advertising for it when it first came out. The article stated that the book tells it like it is and that air safety was in good shape. This was contrary to earlier *Air Line Pilot* magazine articles written by their technical staff. The article stated in part:

> *There's just a pilot's and copilot's seat. Some 600 functions have been eliminated from the control panels. On the wall to the right, where the engineer was sitting, there's a box with some shelves. Behind that, there's a wardrobe closet. How simple it is! It's not much worse than...a sports car dashboard! You've got some computer-terminal screens, and they have some weird-looking graphics on them, but other than that it doesn't seem all that complicated, and you have dreams (foolish dreams!) that you might be able to fly this bugger.*
>
> *In a chapter entitled "The High But Not Necessarily Mighty," the authors discuss "built-in risk factors" like the "noise pollution factor," the "bird factor," and "the airline versus the fork-tail doctor killers." The latter refers to those general aviation aircraft like the Piper Cherokees and Seminoles flying down in "Indian County," many of them, the author claims, owned by rich doctors or movie producers. These aircraft menace his skies, especially in Southern California.*

Following this book review, there was a multi-page article relating an interview with Captain X in which he gave details of how Doubleday approached him to write a book. Captain X had no writing abilities, his airline experience was limited, and he lacked access to and knowledge of the internal problems within government and at United Airlines.

The so-called Captain X described how he and co-author Reynolds Dodson prepared the book's contents. Captain X told of sitting in his backyard and relating "war stories I've told a hundred times before—both to fellow pilots and to friends and relatives."

One of the so-called exposé stories concerned the captain correcting a landing by a copilot, an event as routine as getting up in the morning. Captain X said he received some typewritten pages putting in print his back-yard description of the rough-landing story, and the great anxiety it caused him. The article continued: "I've got problems. My company won't want to come within 10 miles of a story about a copilot who almost broke one of its airplanes." First of all a hard landing doesn't normally break an aircraft. Second, a competent captain will correct an approach made by a copilot before it becomes a hard landing. Third, a hard landing occasionally occurs to all pilots, and normally

560 July 1989 *Air Line Pilot*.

is not grounds for disciplinary action.

This embarrassing naivete was evident throughout the book. Nothing in the book constituted an exposé. Captain X continued his description of how *Doubleday* arranged for his participation. His first-person writing suddenly took the position of a third person:

*He [co-author to Captain X] sent the first chapter, plus an outline, to his agent. His agent in turn sent it to 15 different publishers, and 13 expressed interest in it. Within days, Ren was calling excitedly. Three of the publishers had gone into auction, and the winning bid had been quite considerable. [No legitimate publishers would have gone into auction on such a bland book, when other books far more creditable were on the market.]*

*I am not always the most patient guy, and a couple of times we almost came to blows over whether a pilot would "shout" or "speak" during the throes of a thunderstorm and whether the emotions that a pilot feels would be fear or hostility. [big deal!]*

*Now a mini-bureaucracy sprang up, and suddenly I was confronting a new group of personalities.... When the time came for me to sit down with Doubleday's executives—who still didn't know who I was: as far as they knew I was "Captain X," and to this very day, that is all they know me by—I suddenly found myself sitting in a high-rise conference room staring at a bunch of women who, to my middle-aged eyes, looked like fresh-scrubbed flight attendants.*

Captain X made reference to Doubleday's statement that book sales depended on media exposure and advertising, as much as the contents of the book. In this case, far more depended on hype than on contents. Doubleday then arranged for Captain X to be coached in preparation for radio and television appearances.

A Los Angeles newspaper review[561] summarized the contents of what Doubleday called an exposé:

*Captain X said the worst is over. Air travel is actually safer than ever as far as Captain X is concerned. The future is bright for aviation.*

The book received one of the most unusual book reviews ever written, appearing in the October 1989 *Flight Training* magazine:

*This is a bad book....I suspect Captain "X" elected anonymity after reading what he dictated, and some residue of both ego and pride required that he divorce himself from it....This is a book that simply mocks maturity and professionalism....Beware! This is not the way it is. The incidents he reports, and which he allowed to happen (and from which he extricated the airplane) bespeak an impaired captain, unable to recognize acceptable aircraft performance. They are not the compliments to himself that he solicits.*

During a radio appearance with host Anthony Hilder in Anchorage on July 19, 1989, Hilder mistakenly introduced me as Captain X, assuming that I was the author of the books that he saw stacked on the floor of local book stores. He had earlier recommended the new book to his listeners.

---

561 Los Angeles *Herald Examiner* May 10, 1989.

"Anthony, I'm not Captain X," I explained, and then proceeded to describe the deception by Doubleday. Hilder angrily advised his listeners to return the books they had bought, adding that this explains the reason that he received complaints from those who read Doubleday's *Unfriendly Skies*, who complained there was nothing to the book.

Callers, including an attorney, stressed the need to sue Doubleday. I didn't have the opportunity to report that the federal judiciary had me gridlocked, barring me access to federal courts.

The amount of money spent by *Doubleday* to promote the book can be speculated by the reports I received that piles of the book were in bookstores all over the country. Hundreds of thousands of dollars had been spent to flood the bookstores with the duplication of my title.

Author Ralph McGehee states in *Deadly Deceits: My 25 years in the CIA*, "There's a little bit of fear that if you go after the intelligence community, your career is threatened." Several CIA operatives have told me that the CIA had blackmailed Senator Boren, head of the CIA Senate Oversight Committee,[562] warning him that they would release pictures of his alleged homosexual and pedophile activities, if he didn't cease his opposition to the nomination of Robert Gates as Director of the CIA in 1992.

**BUYING MEDIA COVERUP**

A *Harper's* magazine article (July 1989) stated how politicians leak the "news" to favored reporters, who then reciprocate by rarely reporting unfavorable articles about those who give them the "news." The article described the government oligarchy in which power vests in a few persons doling out "news." *Harper's* stated:

> *By their subjugation of the press, the political powers in America have conferred on themselves the greatest of political blessings—Gyges' ring of invisibility.*

The compounding the harm inflicted upon the American people.

A January 15, 1990, *Newsweek* article stated that "while the White House press corps waited to be spoon-fed instructions, scandals in housing programs and savings and loan regulation went unreported." The article continued:

> *No administration really wants reporters snooping through the Agriculture Department or other places they can break new ground; better to have them hanging around the White House briefing room, waiting for handouts. It's this system, rather than any particular handler or press secretary, that conditions and corrodes Washington coverage. That's why it's up to reporters to redefine the concept of news so that it relies more on what they find, and less on what the president—or his press secretary—would have them believe.*

Occasionally the system goes out of whack, such as in Watergate. For weeks, most newspapers kept the lid on the relatively minor scandal until the *Washington Post* stirred up public interest to the point where the press could not ignore the drum-beating.

562 Chairman of the Senate Intelligence Committee.

In an in-depth investigative report that is as true today as the day it was published (July 25, 1967), the *Wall Street Journal* identified the news distortion and coverup: *"Ethics & the Press*, Conflicts of Interest, Pressures Still Distort Some Papers' Coverage." The in-depth article told how "Advertisers and outside work of newsmen color stories," thereby halting investigations. The article stated in part:

*In Boston and Chicago, newspaper investigations into suspected hanky-panky suddenly are aborted. In one case, a subject of inquiry turns out to be a stockholder of the paper and friend of the publisher. In the other, the investigation threatens to embarrass a politician who could help the paper in a building project.*

*In Denver, the advertising staff of a big daily wrestles with an arithmetic problem. A big advertiser has been promised news stories and pictures amounting to 25 percent of the ad space it buys; the paper already has run hundreds of column inches of glowing prose but is still not close to the promised allotment of "news" and now is running out of nice things to say.*

***VICTIMIZED READERS***

*All this hardly enhances the image of objectivity and fierce independence the U.S. press tries so hard to project. Yet talks with scores of reporters, editors, publishers, public relations men and others reveal that practices endangering—and often subverting—newspaper integrity are more common than the man on the street might dream. Result: The buyer who expects a dime's worth of truth every time he picks up his paper often is short-changed.*

*All newspapers, including this one, must cope with the blandishments and pressures of special interests who seek distortion or omission of the truth....on some papers the trouble starts at the top; it is the publisher himself who lays down news policies designed to aid one group or attack another.*

*It is plain, however, that a sizable minority [or is it majority] of newspapers still are putty in the hands of their advertisers, that they allow personal as well as business considerations to favor the news to a marked degree,...that they tolerate staff practices hardly conducive to editorial independence and objectivity....blackouts of news involving newspapers are quite common; hardly a working journalist could deny that one of the gravest weaknesses in coverage exhibited by the American press is its coverage of itself....another grave fault of a good many papers: Favoritism toward business in general and advertisers in particular....the paper itself, by actual policy or common practice, distorts the news to suit advertisers or literally hands over news space to them....Everyone in newspapering pays lip service to the ideal that a paper's news columns should not be for sale,...a staffer is "on the take"...*

Giving a toast in 1953 before the New York Press Club, the former Chief of Staff of the *New York Times*, John Swinton, stated:[563]

563 *Contact*, July 20, 1993.

*There is no such thing, at this date of the world's history, in America, as an independent press. You know it and I know it....The business of the journalist is to destroy truth; To lie outright; To pervert; To vilify; To fawn at the feet of mammon, and to sell his country and his race for his daily bread. You know it and I know it, and what folly is this toasting an independent press?...Our talents, our possibilities and our lives, are all the property of other men. We are intellectual prostitutes.*

The *Wall Street Journal* article described the news distortion of virtually every media in the United States caused by pressures from vested-interest groups and from financial benefits. The Federal Communications Commission charged NBC-TV with falsely presenting the facts associated with general aviation and airline problems in midair collisions. The FCC charged the NBC staff with twisting and distorting its coverage of the midair collisions, favoring the airlines by distorting the facts. The FAA ordered NBC to take "appropriate steps to achieve fairness" and stop distorting the facts.

**WALL STREET JOURNAL COVERUP**

The morals of the *Wall Street Journal* are two-sided. Since the 1960s, when I was an FAA investigator seeking to address the air safety and criminal activities involved in a continuing series of airline crashes, I reported these crimes to the *Wall Street Journal*. I expected that the newspaper would exercise its media responsibility, reporting these charges in their columns. They never did, and the crimes and the tragedies continued. Since 1987, I reported the specific government crimes to the paper, and as before, they refused to report my charges, despite the proof that I offered. I sent copies of *Defrauding America* to their editors, which contained serious charges that threatened the sovereignty of the United States. I even filed a federal lawsuit against the paper charging them with the federal crimes of misprision of felonies and obstruction of justice, among others. They never reported the lawsuit.

The *Journal* wrote in a January 12, 1993, issue:

*This progress report carries forward a custom begun 16 years ago. It reflects our belief that publishing a newspaper is a public trust for which we are accountable first of all to you, our readers.*

Their responsibility to the public was correctly stated, but their own conduct was the opposite.

I encountered a constant pattern of coverup by the establishment media, starting in the mid-1960s and continuing to this very day. During the sixties when I had hard-core evidence linking criminal misconduct by officials at United Airlines and the FAA with recent airline crashes, none would report the evidence I presented. These media coverups continued into the 1980s and 1990s, and exist at this very moment.

In February 1988, I gave two reporters[564] for the *San Francisco Chronicle* details of the corruption that I had uncovered, providing them with supporting documents. These reporters contacted a friend of mine, falsely stating that they did not write an article on the matters I brought to their attention because I refused to give them supporting material. That was a lie. I had supplied them with a

564 Jeff Palline and Bill Wallace.

great deal of written material and withheld nothing. I described to them the corruption I discovered in the aviation area, in Chapter 11 courts, and the persecution judicially inflicted upon me to block my exposure activities. I referred them to specific federal filings at San Francisco and Sacramento that enlarged upon the corruption that I had found, and which were now of judicial record. Instead of reporting these charges, they kept the lid on the scandal.

"The Complicity of Silence" was the heading on an article in *Lies of Our Times* (June 1993), as it related to the media coverup of the U.S. directed assassinations occurring in Central America and particularly the El Mozote massacre in El Salvador (December 1981). The article told how *New York Times* reporter Raymond Bonner sent an article to the home office describing the brutal assassination at El Mozote, primarily of women and children, by the U.S.-trained Atlaeatl Battalion. Bonner was at the assassination site and personally interviewed the handful of survivors. He then became the target of a media smear campaign to discredit him and to remove him from his reporting activities.

*Wall Street Journal* editor Robert Bartley savagely attacked Bonner and his reports and especially the one on February 19, 1982. The *Wall Street Journal's* attack upon Bonner caused other newspapers and magazines to instruct their reporters to keep the lid on the massacre, ensuring that the massacre of other civilians would continue. The *Wall Street Journal* editorial caused one major newspaper to send copies of that editorial to its correspondents in Central America warning them: "Let's not let this happen to us."

The editors of *Times* then transferred Bonner out of the Central America assignment to quiet him. On March 15, 1993, the U.N.-sponsored Truth Commission on El Salvador released its report on the El Mozote massacre, proving that the massacre had occurred, that it was directed by the CIA, which the media had known and covered up for years.

Earlier in these pages I said the *St. Louis Post Dispatch* attempted to cover up the downing of the U.S. Navy helicopter at Fort Ord that killed three Naval officers from the Pegasus group in the Central Intelligence Agency.

The *Wall Street Journal* publishes many detailed and well-researched articles on government corruption, but is very "selective." In matters relating to the crimes of Governor and then President Bill Clinton the *Journal* reported the corruption as the media is expected to do. But in crimes that heavily implicate the Republicans, the *Journal* is clearly guilty of criminal coverup in the October Surprise scheme, the massive drug smuggling by The National Security Council's Oliver North and President George Bush, and other crimes.

## SIMULTANEOUS WRITINGS ON TRAGEDIES, AND COVERUP OF THEIR CAUSES

The press repeatedly prints articles on the sufferings arising from air disasters, while concurrently covering up for the misconduct that made the crashes possible. Some of the best researched articles on the human sufferings associated with air tragedies have been published by the investigative reporters of the *Wall Street Journal*.

An article in *Aviation Week & Space Technology* on May 1, 1989 reported:

*ATA President Blasts U.S. government's Failure to Reform Aviation Agency. The article stated "The U.S. government has failed inexcusably to respond to reforms recommended by the Aviation Safety Commission a year ago," according to Robert J. Aaronson, the new head of the Air Transport Assn.*

The basis for these charges is a fraction of the actual misconduct. No one can blow the whistle on anyone else without implicating himself, or vested and protected interests.

**PRESSURE ON ADVERTISERS TO REMAIN SILENT**

Following a series of Delta Air Line incidents in mid-1987, Delta put financial pressure on the media to stop reporting the many near-crashes of its aircraft. Delta threatened to cancel valued advertising accounts with the newspapers and radio stations making these reports. An *Associated Press* article (August 13, 1987) described Delta's threats to cancel large blocks of advertising. Delta responded by saying there was a "misunderstanding." What else could they say?

Yearly advertising budgets for a major airline easily exceeds one hundred million dollars, ensuring that any newspaper, radio station or network will withhold any unfavorable information if possible. Federal Express dropped its ads on ABC prime-time television network after a critical report on ABC's 20/20. The program[565] reported Federal Express mishandled government and military documents and packages, and that drug activities were rampant at the airline.

Federal Express's President Frederick Smith wrote (July 14, 1989) that the company was canceling its prime-time advertising, with the exception of commercials scheduled for the ABC telecast of the World Series and Monday Night Football. Federal Express spent over $40 million a year on advertising, according to the Standard Directory of Advertisers, an industry publication. In another letter, President Smith wrote that this cancellation would cost ABC "in excess of $100 million." It's easy to understand how the news media hesitates to print anything that would dissatisfy a valuable customer.

An *Air Transport World* article (March 1970) described the value of airline advertising: "Airlines are a major source of ad revenue." Airlines such as Delta run full-page ads in the *Wall Street Journal*, which rarely runs articles detrimental to the airlines' interests.

Boston radio station WHDH experienced the consequences of offending Procter & Gamble. The station had broadcast the activities of a local citizen group that was critical of one of the company's products. Procter & Gamble then pulled local ads for all of its products from the station, resulting in the loss of $1 million of advertising revenue. Procter & Gamble reportedly warned that it would pull commercials from any station broadcasting the announcement from the citizen group.[566] The newspaper article stated: "P&G's message reinforced what station managers already believed: don't criticize business, and stay away from controversial topics, or it will cost the station business. Actions such as Procter & Gamble's don't have to happen often before media outlets become self-censoring."

---

565 *New York Times*, October 18, 1989 report of July 7, 1989 show.

566 April 1, 1991 San Francisco *Daily Journal*.

Car makers retaliate against magazines printing articles reporting weaknesses or defects in their products. General Motors, for instance, withdrew advertising for three months after a magazine's editor, David E. Davis, delivered a speech against the auto maker concerning the closure of twenty-one plants, eliminating 74,000 jobs. Toyota Motor Corporation withdrew ads after its models did not make *Road and Track*'s 1991 list of "10 Best List." The loss of this type of advertising can make the difference between profit and loss.

**COVERUP IS PROFITABLE**

It is unprofitable for the media to report corruption involving those who provide advertising revenue to them, making it profitable for the media to cover up for corruption, regardless of the consequential harm made possible by the coverup. For instance, a disproportionate amount of corruption in the HUD and savings and loan scandals was committed by a group in Denver that included Richmond Homes and MDC Holdings and its many subsidiaries that were heavy advertisers. This group provided a major share of advertising revenue for the two major newspapers in the Denver area, *Rocky Mountain News* and the *Denver Post*. If either one of the two newspapers reported the corruption, they would lose significant revenue and subject themselves to government retaliation through any one of numerous government agencies. The indifference of the American public, their ignorance concerning government corruption, their failure to respond in a meaningful manner, doesn't exactly motivate a newspaper to go out on a limb.

**MEDIA COVERUP AND DISINFORMATION**

The *Washington Post* and reporter Bob Woodward enlarged upon a White House coverup of the two-bit Watergate burglary into a scandal all out of proportion, and then covered up for the scandals that were a thousand times more serious. The same *Washington Post* kept the lid on the CIA involvement in Watergate, October Surprise, drug trafficking, and the other scandals mentioned within these pages.

A *Washington Post* article (June 22, 1992) misstated facts relating to the 1980 October Surprise operation. Reporter Bob Woodward and John Mintz sought to squelch the October Surprise story by discrediting CIA whistleblowers and their statements about the October Surprise. Intelligence agency newsletters and magazines described the *Washington Post* as having close ties to the CIA.

Committee Chairman Charles Rangel (D-NY) charged the *Washington Post* with misleading reporting in the Iran-Contra affair. The CIA was after President Nixon, and the *Washington Post* accommodated them. The *Post* also used Mark Hosenball to ridicule the idea that Oliver North and his CIA-associated renegades had done anything wrong, despite the overwhelming evidence that they financially supported the assassination squads and drug trafficking. The *Post* censored a Drew Anderson column revealing the actions by Oliver North and his co-conspirators in the Iran-Contra affair, assisting the overall scheme to deny to the public knowledge of this scandal-riddled CIA, NSC, White House operation. Anything unfavorable to this group was heavily censored by the *Post*.

**WASHINGTON POST DISINFORMATION RIDICULING WHISTLEBLOWERS**

The *Washington Post* (June 22, 1992) chastised Presidential candidate Ross

Perot for attempting to expose what they implied were non-existing criminal activities by President George Bush, including Bush's role in October Surprise and its progeny, Iran-Contra. I wrote to Katherine Graham, the publisher of the *Washington Post*, pointing out the errors in the articles on October Surprise, advising her that I was a former federal investigator and that my CIA sources had given me considerable information that established the existence of that operation. My letter expressed the opinion that the *Washington Post*, including Bob Woodward, were involved in obstructing justice by the fact that they withheld data, supplied disinformation, and deliberately misstated facts. She did not respond.

The *Village Voice* duplicated the *Washington Post* tactics in an article written by former CIA asset Frank Snepp. The article stated that Russbacher did not know how to start the engines on the SR-71 and therefore could not have been the SR-71 pilot described in the October Surprise plot. Other segments of the media seeking to discredit the October Surprise scandal repeated Snepp's article as if it were proven to be true.

A 1994 *Newsweek* article followed the standard tactic of discrediting those who spoke out, as it related to Clinton's many misdeeds:

> *The national press has been restrained in its accounts of Bill Clinton's private life, and with good reason. Most of those who have made charges against him have been despicable people, jealous, stunted sorts.*

The *Washington Post* reporter who interviewed Paula Jones, and who wrote an article concerning the encounter, was suspended after presenting the article to the editor. For years concerned reporters told me and people with whom I had been in contact that they had written articles of government criminality which their editors refused to print.

## INVESTIGATIVE REPORTERS SILENCED BY THEIR EDITORS

Margie Sloan, a free-lance investigative reporter who investigated the Denver-based group heavily implicated in the HUD and savings and loan scandals,[567] was told by numerous reporters who had written stories concerning the CIA involvement that their editors killed the articles they had prepared.

Pete Brewton of the *Houston Post*, author of *The Mafia, CIA, and George Bush*, wrote about the block put on many of his stories associating the looting of the savings and loans with the CIA and powerful politicians, including former Texas Senator Lloyd Bentsen (subsequently appointed to President William Clinton's cabinet).

In *The CIA and the Cult Of Intelligence*, the authors describe the pressure and threats upon newspaper and book publishers not to publish matters adversely reflecting upon the CIA or other government agencies. The book tells of the planting of moles in the news media, including radio and television networks, and the pressure not to report government misconduct.

## CIA DIRECTOR AND THE MEDIA

In November 1984, CIA Director William Casey complained to the Federal

---

567 Throughout this book, reference to defrauding the United States should be recognized as defrauding the residents who must pay for these financial crimes and who suffer and will continue to suffer the consequences.

Communication Commission about the ABC television network for having aired a show featuring CIA agent Scott Barnes. In the television presentation Barnes said he was asked by two CIA agents in Honolulu to kill Ronald Rewald, a CIA asset sacrificed to cover up for a CIA financial operation in Hawaii (BBRDW). That show revealed the CIA's role in BBRDW, and could alert the public to the CIA's role in drug trafficking and drug-money laundering, among other covert operations. Casey was a founder,[568] major investor, and director, in Capital Cities Corporation, which then took over the ABC television network the following year (March 1985).

In earlier pages I described the findings of the Church Committee that reported the hundreds of media personnel who were on the CIA payroll. My CIA contacts confirm this relationship. Twenty-five-year CIA veteran, Ralph McGehee, writing in *Deadly Deceits*, described the same problem.

**ABSENCE OF MEDIA PROTECTION**

About the only way that the American public can be protected against the endemic corruption described within these pages is for the media to publish the charges that I and many other people have made. This exposure is highly unlikely:

* The media is itself implicated in the criminal activities through years of coverup.

* The media is infiltrated with CIA money, paid to prevent exposure of these activities.

* The media is staffed by CIA assets who are ordered to prevent these exposures.

**CONGRESSIONAL COVERUP PROVIDES EXTRA ASSURANCE OF COVERUP**

The public certainly can't count upon members of Congress to expose the corruption and act upon it, as they have been covering up for decades, and continue to do so to this very day.

**A FEW COURAGEOUS NEWSPAPERS**

Several of the alternative newspapers have courageously sought to expose the corruption in government. In some cases they exposed criminality by federal personnel that the mass media then had to address, at least in small part.

An isolated number of the mainstream press did print articles on government corruption. For instance, the *Arkansas Democrat* exposed for several years the vast arms and drug trafficking at Mena Airport in Arkansas; the *Houston Post* reported the CIA involvement in looting the savings and loans until pressure caused them to drop the series, and *Playboy* wrote articles on the CIA and October Surprise.

**CONTINUING THE CIA DRUGGING OF AMERICAN COVERUP**

In 1996 the *San Jose Mercury* ran a series of three articles describing the CIA's links to drug smuggling in the San Francisco and Los Angeles area, and the drugging of the blacks. Immediately, the primary members of the mainstream media, led by the *Washington Post*, *New York Times*, and *Los Angeles Times*, ridiculed the articles. These were the same newspapers who knew about the

568 Along with Lowell Thomas and others.

many reports by insiders about the CIA's drugging of America and who kept the lid on the criminal activities.

Simultaneous with these *San Jose Mercury* articles, certain California members of Congress[569] showed their outrage, doing little else, despite the fact that they had been repeatedly advised of the CIA drug trafficking for years, keeping the public unaware of what was being done to them.

**PUBLIC RELATION FIRMS AND THE CIA**

The CIA uses public relations firms to perform domestic activities that the CIA is barred by law from doing. Washington-based Hill & Knowlton, for instance, acted as a conduit for propaganda news releases to the media. The firm has numerous CIA and other intelligence agency personnel on its board of directors. Robert Gray, who created and had operated Hill and Knowlton since 1961, had numerous contacts with the CIA and other intelligence groups and with such CIA personnel as William Casey, Edwin Wilson, Oliver North, and Robert Owen. Gray also formed his own company with CIA contacts and was on the Board of Directors of several covert CIA companies that fronted for Task Force 157, an Office of Naval Intelligence operation.

*Covert Action*, in its Spring 1993 issue, told how U.S. intelligence agencies use public relation firms, journalists, and authors to print what they want the American public to hear. The article reported that "In a typical issue of the *Wall Street Journal*, more than half the news stories were based solely on [government-provided] press releases." The article continued: "Reporters were paid by the CIA, sometimes without their media employer's knowledge, to get the material in print or on the air." They reported that news organizations ordered their writers to repeat what was fed to them by the CIA.

A former CIA employee, Robert T. Crowley, whose job was to act as liaison with corporations, admitted that public relations firms are continuously used by the CIA "to put out press releases and make media contacts." The CIA's use of U.S. media has been well detailed in publications related to the intelligence agencies. Much of what is stated as "news" by the media is really press releases from CIA-connected public relation firms. Author Susan Trento wrote:

> *Reporters were paid by the CIA, sometimes without their media employers' knowledge, to get the material in print or on the air. But other news organizations ordered their employees to cooperate with the CIA, including the San Diego-based Copley News Service. But Copley was not alone, and the CIA had "tamed" reporters and editors in scores of newspaper and broadcast outlets across the country. To avoid direct relationships with the media, the CIA recruited individuals in public relations firms like H&K to act as middlemen for what the CIA wanted to distribute.*[570]

The Spring 1993 issue of *Covert Action* described the misleading news given to the American public:

> *In a typical issue of the Wall Street Journal, more than half the news stories were based solely on press releases [from government personnel]. Hill and Knowlton...were perfect "cover" for the ever-expanding CIA....The CIA...used*

569 Senators Dianne Feinstein and Barbara Boxer and Representative Maxine Waters.
570 Interview with John Stockwell, *Propaganda Review*, No. 6, Winter 1990, p. 14.

*its H&K connections to put out press releases and make media contacts to further its positions.... H&K employees at the small Washington office and elsewhere, distributed this material through CIA assets working in the United States news media. Since the CIA is prohibited from disseminating propaganda inside the U.S., this type of "blowback"-which former CIA officer John Stockwell and other researchers have often traced to the Agency-is illegal. While the use of U.S. media by the CIA has a long and well-documented history, the covert involvement of PR firms may be news to many. According to Trento:*

*Reporters were paid by the CIA, sometimes without their media employers' knowledge, to get the material in print or on the air. But other news organizations ordered their employees to cooperate with the CIA, including the San Diego-based Copley News Service. But Copley was not alone, and the CIA has "tamed" reporters and editors in scores of newspaper and broadcast outlets across the country. To avoid direct relationships with the media, the CIA recruited individuals in public relations firms like H&K to act as middle men for what the CIA wanted to distribute. In a typical issue of the Wall Street Journal, more than half the news stories were based solely on press releases [from government personnel].*[571]

*Covert Action* described how reporters depend upon the close intelligence community for much of their "news," and how the media protects these sources.

An article written by the research staff of *National Vanguard Books* described the slanted news by the press and entertainment media: *Who Rules America?*:

*Their power...reaches into every home in America, and it works its will during nearly every waking hour. It is the power which shapes and molds the mind of virtually every citizen, young or old, rich or poor, simple or sophisticated. The mass media form for us our image of the world and then tell us what to think about that image. Essentially everything we know-or think we know-about events outside our own neighborhood or circle of acquaintances comes to us via our daily newspaper, our weekly news magazine, our radio, or our television. Employing carefully developed psychological techniques, they guide our thought and opinion...Most Americans fail to realize that they are being manipulated. Even the citizen who complains about "managed news" falls into the trap of thinking that because he is presented with an apparent spectrum of opinion he can escape the thought controllers' influence by believing the editor or commentator of his choice. Every point on the permissible spectrum of public opinion is acceptable to the media masters-and no impermissible fact or viewpoint is allowed any exposure at all, if they can prevent it.*

In the book, *Media Circus*, written by *Washington Post* media critic, the author ridicules the lack of investigative reporting, absence of penetrating insight, or newsworthy news that exists in America's newspapers. He writes,

*The nation's watchdogs have become lapdogs, and groveling spineless mutts at that. And nobody, the American public especially, appears to give a thinker's damn.*

---

571 *Covert Action*, Spring 1993.

The book reveals the failure of the media to acknowledge the savings and loan and HUD scandal, to which must be added October Surprise, Iran-Contra's drug trafficking, the involvement of CIA and other government officials in the drug trafficking causing great instability in the United States, and much more. Worse, the media has engaged in disinformation and misinformation. He explains that reporters are too dependent upon government sources for "news" to risk offending government officials. The book states, "Under-reporting of unpleasant [news] wouldn't occur so easily or often if such practices hadn't already become a well-worn habit encouraged by a public that doesn't want to know the truth if it undermines their collective confidence." The book stated, "The American press and their public richly deserve one another." Of course, the public is paying a very heavy price for its absence of citizen responsibilities.

Some of the most well-known media personnel are those who have placated government officials by repeating their lines, and thus made privy to government information. It must be said, however, that many journalists have tried to report stories of the criminal activities by government personnel, only to have the stories killed by their editors, or be fired, or transferred to innocuous assignments. Well-known Washington reporters, for instance, receive large sums for covering political or other conferences from those whose activities are being reported.

If there was a deliberate plan to keep the public in the dark about government corruption (and there could very well be), the media's hyping of sports contributes to the public's ignorance of these important matters.

Most newspapers, with some exceptions, have an obsessive reliance on inconsequential or trivial local news, ignoring any reporting of national and international news, especially relating to government corruption. Despite the interrelationship of international events with events in the United States, there is little reporting of these events, and when they are reported, they are cursory. A few exceptions are, for instance, the *New York Times*, *Los Angeles Times*, and others. But even here, disinformation is routine. They covered up for the CIA drug trafficking at a terrible cost in human lives and financial resources.

Government personnel, including the very ones participating in the criminal activities, establish what the news media gets to report. In *Media Circuit, The Trouble with America's Newspapers*, author Howard Kurtz describes the ravenous gullibility of the American press in grabbing for the elusive carrot dangling at the end of a hypocritically extended stick.

None of this is new to me. For thirty years I encountered the coverup and obstruction of justice by the mainstream media.

## LEGAL PUBLICATION PROTECTING ITS NEWS SOURCE

The San Francisco legal newspaper *Daily Journal* was aware of the large-scale Chapter 11 corruption and addressed it gingerly, carefully avoiding the high-level judicial corruption, focusing only on the outer peripheral issues. They kept the lid on the judicial involvement in the corruption, protecting their primary sources of news articles. In one article the *Daily Journal* referred to me as a "disgruntled debtor" for my efforts to expose the Chapter 11 corruption that they knew existed, and for filing appeals and oppositions to the corrupt seizure and looting of my assets.

In another article (July 15, 1992) the *Daily Journal* eulogized U.S. District Judge Vaughn Walker, who played a key role in the obstruction of justice in Ninth Circuit courts. The article stated, "Judge Walker a Champion of Law." The *Daily Journal* knew the part played by Walker who aided and abetted the criminal contempt charges against me that were in retaliation for exercising my constitutional and statutory rights and responsibilities. In another article the *Daily Journal* eulogized California Court of Appeals Judge Donald King, who played a key role in carrying out the early attacks upon me.

They frequently eulogized U.S. District Judge Marilyn Patel who played a key role in the attacks upon me and who aided and abetted the underlying criminal activities by blocking my reports.

## CENSORSHIP VIA JUSTICE DEPARTMENT THREATS

In early April 1992, the *Now It Can Be Told* show videotaped Russbacher for about five hours during which he related numerous CIA activities in which he participated. These details exposed serious criminal activities within government agencies. Cindy Fry[572] of the *Now It Can Be Told* show stated during a telephone conversation that the producers were warned by Justice Department personnel not to air the Russbacher tapes if they wanted to avoid the consequences. The show never aired, despite the expense involved in taking the crew from New York to the Missouri prison where the taping occurred. Fry added that many people at other network shows had also been threatened by Justice Department personnel not to air any of the Russbacher tapes.

A television station in Missouri had taped Russbacher in April 1992 and made several spot announcements advising the viewers that Russbacher's full taping would appear at 10 p.m. over their Jefferson City and Columbia stations. Again, threats from Justice Department officials caused the station to cancel the showing. The media can be threatened to censor the news in numerous ways:

1. Federal personnel in the Justice Department or other federal agencies can threaten to take retaliatory action against the media through the Federal Communication Commission, IRS, the FBI, or the Justice Department.
2. Refuse to renew their station license.
3. Withhold government business.
4. Withhold news.
5. Pressure advertisers to withdraw business.

In turn, station management can threaten talk show hosts with termination if they address government corruption, or allow guests to appear who talk about such subjects.

## COVERUP BY STATE OFFICIALS

When necessary, corruption by federal officials can be reinforced by state officials. California authorities aided in the coverup surrounding the killing of attorney Dexter Jacobson by refusing to conduct a meaningful investigation. West Virginia authorities aided in the coverup involving the killing of Danny Casolaro by destroying evidence. Missouri officials aided in the coverup of CIA corruption by removing evidence of CIA proprietaries from the corporate records, and by prosecuting Russbacher and causing his imprisonment. Arkansas

572 Ganyl Kaufman and Mary Ann Poors, on May 13, 1992.

officials, including Governor Bill Clinton, blocked an investigation into the CIA arms and drug trafficking at Mena, Arkansas, that had been demanded by local police and citizens. California authorities aided and abetted the scheme that began with the sham lawsuit filed against me in the California courts by the San Francisco law firm that was a front for the Justice Department and CIA.

Fearing the consequences, or to financially benefit from working with those in control of key government agencies, corporate America keeps the lid on government scandals. Many of these corporations are fronts for the CIA, and find the relationship profitable. An example of this was the part played by the Pepsico Corporation in the October Surprise scandal, and its drug processing laboratories in foreign countries.

**ROSS PEROT COVERUP**

Ross Perot appeared to be genuinely interested in helping public spirited causes, including trying to learn if there were any prisoners still alive from the Vietnam War. Perot had been contacted by several people for help in exposing the October Surprise operation, and arrangements were made for Perot to talk to Russbacher via a conference call using my phone. Early on February 7, 1992, Russbacher called me from prison[573] and as previously arranged by Perot I put the call through to him in Dallas. The reason for Perot's interest in Russbacher was to determine if Russbacher sounded legitimate, and to determine if Russbacher was actually involved in the October Surprise operation. After Russbacher got off the phone, Perot and I continued the conversation. In response to Perot's questions I conveyed my confidence in Russbacher's statements, his CIA position, and his role in October Surprise.

Several weeks later (February 25, 1992) my telephone rang and the caller said "This is Ross Perot." He then made reference to the earlier phone call and asked for further information on Russbacher, trying to determine in his mind Russbacher's credibility. I told him what I knew and how I had confidence in Russbacher's statements.

Perot later appeared on the *Larry King Live* show[574] declaring an interest to run for Presidency of the United States. Shortly after that talk-show appearance, Perot sent several of his employees to Missouri to personally question Russbacher about the October Surprise operation and to determine if Russbacher actually knew how to fly an SR-71 aircraft. The media picked up on this event and ridiculed Perot for pursuing far-out conspiracy theories.

Following the visit by Perot's group to Russbacher, the rumor was out that Russbacher didn't even know how to start the engines of the SR-71. I had earlier obtained the formerly secret SR-71 pilot operating manual consisting of over 1,000 pages and, after studying it, questioned Russbacher about such matters as starting the engines. He knew how to start the engines and answered most of the other questions that I asked concerning the aircraft. I wrote to Perot, reminding him of his duty to expose the corruption that I and CIA whistleblowers

573 Justice Department officials had charged Russbacher with impersonating a naval officer while he and his wife were billeted at Castle Air Force Base, seeking to continue the imprisonment inflicted upon him as part of the Justice Department scheme to silence this high-ranking officer in the Office of Naval Intelligence and the CIA.

574. May 1992.

had described to him. He never responded.

**NADER COVERUP**

Ralph Nader's aviation group, consisting of attorneys, kept the lid on the air-disaster related scandals for years, while professing to be active in protecting the public's welfare. I contacted Nader and his group in the mid 1960s, requesting assistance to expose the corruption related to an ongoing series of airline crashes. Reuben Robertson, an attorney for the group, traveled from Washington to my residence near San Francisco to obtain information from me. He admitted the gravity of the problem. Despite recognition of the serious corruption, the Nader group did nothing to publicize and correct the matter. Robertson later accepted a position with the Civil Aeronautics Board, which had been heavily involved in the coverup.

Some years later, after leaving the CAB, Robertson and the Nader group filed a federal lawsuit under the Freedom of Information Act[575] against the FAA in the District of Columbia.[576] The complaint sought information on safety problems discovered during inspections by FAA Washington inspection teams. The FAA refused to release the information, saying it was confidential and against the national interest. This standard phrase to cover up for government corruption was especially bizarre in air safety matters. A federal judge upheld the FAA's position and refused to require the information to be released. In 1988, I again contacted the Nader group concerning the worsening problems. They wouldn't answer.

A *Forbes* magazine cover story (September 17, 1990) portrayed Nader as overseer to a vast network of organizations financed in part by wealthy lawyers and special interest groups. The story reported that Nader controlled twenty-nine organizations with combined revenues exceeding seventy-five million dollars. The *Forbes* article said that Nader had an "umbilical" connection with rich plaintiff's attorneys who receive huge fees in Nader-backed lawsuits against industry. In return, these law firms contribute to his "consumer" organizations.

**ATTORNEY DOUBLE-TALK**

A conference held in Washington on October 6 and 7, 1988, was entitled "How To prevent, Investigate, and Litigate Aircraft Disasters." One of the speakers on air safety included Donald Madole, a managing partner of one of the nation's largest aviation law firms specializing in airline crashes. Another speaker was Congressman James Oberstar, chairman of the House Investigations and Oversight Subcommittee of Public Works and Transportation—responsible for aviation safety. Another speaker was Richard Witkin, Transportation Editor for the *New York Times*. They all had something in common: coverup of the corruption that made many of the crashes possible.

Donald Madole was an attorney with the Federal Aviation Administration when FAA inspector Frank Harrell, my predecessor on the United Airlines assignment, went to Washington seeking help exposing the air safety and criminal violations associated with several recent air disasters. Madole was head of the Bureau of Air Safety section. Later, Madole was head of the NTSB accident

575 Title 5 Section 552.

576 *Robertson, III, et al., v. Butterfield, Administrator, Federal Aviation Administration, et al.*, C.A. No. 72-2186.

investigation section when I reported to him the same, and worse corruption, and many United Airline disasters showing again the consequences. Madole covered up for the corruption that made possible many of the subsequent crashes.

**INTERNATIONAL SOCIETY OF AIR SAFETY INVESTIGATORS**

For many years I have been a member of the International Society of Air Safety Investigators (ISASI), whose purported function is reducing the frequency of airline crashes and improving accident investigation techniques, and found them just as guilty of coverup. This group knew about the corruption other inspectors found. They knew about the judicial actions taken to silence me. Not a single solitary move was taken by this group to either expose what others and I had discovered, or to intervene when I was sent to prison in retaliation for reporting criminal activities in government that adversely affected air safety.

At one time the group was composed primarily of present and former members of the FAA, NTSB, and airline pilots with an air safety function, but gradually allowed attorneys as members. At the time that I was being railroaded to prison for having reported the corruption, the San Francisco chapter was taken over by attorneys, the same group that kept the lid on the criminal activities, and they refused to come to my rescue.

**TALK SHOW COVERUPS**

At one time talk shows were my best source for exposing the corruption in government. I had appeared as guest on over 2,000 radio and television shows from 1978, when the first *Unfriendly Skies* was published, until about 1990. For many years my appearances were well received, and I was repeatedly called to appear as air safety expert by various radio stations, especially when a major air disaster occurred. But when I got into more serious government corruption, my appearances were no longer wanted. The government corruption that I described in a factual, unemotional manner was either more than they wanted to handle, or pressure was put upon them not to have me appear.

In addition to the detailed and documented factual contents of the book exposing matters of national importance, the flyers that were sent to the many shows contained highly favorable book review excerpts, providing credibility. Further, I had been a federal investigator holding authority under law to make similar determinations.

This change was especially noticeable after the first edition of *Defrauding America* came off the press in July 1993. I sent hundreds of promotional packages to the producers and hosts of radio stations that had guest appearances. These packages included (a) flyers describing the serious charges made in the book; (b) excerpts from outstanding statements made by sophisticated book reviewers; (c) my background establishing my credentials for writing the book; and (d) partial list of recent appearances on key radio and television stations. This silence became even worse after the 1995 bombing of the federal building in Oklahoma City.

Despite the fact that the book detailed and documented serious government corruption and revealed the harm arising from it, less than four percent of the media receiving promotional material concerning my availability responded. The fact that 96 percent of the recipients didn't feel that the public should know about these serious charges is a serious indictment against the talk show hosts themselves.

Sudden cancellation of my scheduled appearances became common. The producer of one radio station program called me several hours before the show was to start and canceled my appearance, giving the excuse that the host was sick. Due to poor coordination, I was later called about two minutes before the start of the show and told to stand by. When I replied, "I thought the show was canceled," the caller checked and then advised that it indeed had been canceled, but for reasons other than initially stated.

Los Angeles KABC talk-show-host Michael Jackson canceled my appearance hours before I was to appear. As the government corruption became worse in the late 1980s, these cancellations increased in frequency, even though the stations that did not cancel oftentimes went out of their way to state the seriousness of, and the interest in, the matters we discussed. Radio stations, as with many other business enterprises, receive revenue or licensing from government personnel, and retaliation can easily occur, either directly or indirectly.

A *New York Times* article (October 11, 1994) described the pulling of anti-smoking advertisements in California on television stations KABC (Los Angeles) and KBHK (San Francisco), after R.J. Reynolds Tobacco Company applied pressure. The anti-smoking ads paid by the California Health Services Department warned of the dangers of nicotine and second-hand smoke.

**"You can't Say Anything Against United Airlines!"**

Radio and television stations frequently reminded me not to say anything unfavorable about a major airline and especially United Airlines. I was to appear on NBC's *Tomorrow* Show and given a date to appear. During the initial conversation the producer requested that I not say anything against United Airlines because NBC had a very profitable advertising account with United. I replied that I would concentrate on the misconduct within the two government air safety agencies. But before the appearance I was called and told not to appear.

San Francisco's radio stations, smack in the heart of where much of the judicial and Justice Department corruption existed, played their part in the coverup. I sent notices to most of the radio stations in the San Francisco and Sacramento areas, advising them of the contents of *Defrauding America*, and of my availability to speak on the subjects. Despite the extremely serious nature of the charges, my credibility and that of my CIA sources, and the support of the excellent book reviews, not a single one allowed me to appear.

Although they had the right to determine who appears on their shows, the nature of the government corruption and the undermining of our government by criminal activities raised the question of responsibility. Their coverup amounted to an obstruction of justice, making them co-conspirators with the very people they were shielding.

When Gary Sick, author of *October Surprise*, appeared as a guest on KGO,[577] a listener called and asked about Gunther Russbacher. Before Sick could respond the host stated that Russbacher had been totally discredited, claiming he did not know how to start the engines on the SR-71. I wrote to the KGO host to

577 June 1992.

explain that I had quizzed Russbacher on the SR-71 and that he did know how to start the engines. I asked the host if he could give me information to support his statement. He refused to answer. I found over the years that KGO was very protective of corruption at United Airlines and within government.

An interesting incident occurred with private investigators Stewart Webb and Margie Sloan when they appeared on radio station KABC in Los Angeles for the Michael Jackson show (February 11, 1992). It was being hosted on that date by Dr. David Viscott. The show centered around what the guests learned by examining thousands of documents linking the infamous Silverado Bank Savings and Loan to the CIA, money laundering, and drug trafficking. These dramatic revelations exposed what Justice Department attorneys, White House officials, and much of the media had attempted to keep from the American public.

After the host took a break for a commercial, he disconnected the guests. When the host returned, he shifted the subject to a ball game format, acting as if the guests had never appeared. One listener, finding the guests extremely interesting, called two friends at the beginning of the show to have them listen.

That listener, Ralph Bluthenthal, a former Los Angeles policeman and Director of the General James Doolittle USO Lounge near the Los Angeles International Airport, subsequently phoned KABC and was told that the two guests had never been on the air. His prior law enforcement background prompted Bluthenthal to call his two friends once again to determine if they had heard the same series of events. Upon confirmation, he then called KABC to find out what happened. He was given the run-around by different KABC employees. KABC program manager, John Dolsa, said, "The interview never occurred."

Bluthenthal then asked, "Does that mean, if I request tapes or transcripts of that show, I can't get them?" Dolsa responded, "That show didn't happen." After being cut off, Margie Sloan called KABC and learned that the FBI had contacted the station during the show and warned station personnel to remove the guests.

In one instance I had been a guest on KABC's Ray Briem show from midnight to five a.m., reporting facts that were critical of United Airlines and the government's air safety agencies. Another host, Michael Jackson, had scheduled a United Airlines pilot and author, John Nance, to appear as guest a few hours later. Nance's position was that everything was just fine in the aviation field. Other pilots who had been on talk shows with Nance stated to me they found Nance to be constantly covering up for the problems and misconduct as if he was paid to do so.

I had been a guest on KABC numerous times with Ray Briem for five hours at a stretch, and the show was always well received. However, as the scandals of the 1980s escalated, KABC refused to allow me to appear.

In late 1994 there was a series of airline crashes causing the public to focus on air safety problems. CNN Atlanta headquarters called[578] and asked my views on air safety problems, and they liked my response. They scheduled me to appear as an air safety expert for the following Monday show, appearing at their San Francisco studio. I then contacted the San Francisco CNN offices to check on

578 Betsy Goldman and Kathy Snow.

parking, which alerted them to my scheduled appearance. Within an hour the CNN Atlanta office canceled my appearance. For whatever reason, the San Francisco media had me blackballed. San Francisco was a key center in the corruption I sought to expose, and any exposure of this problem would affect the business and media community that has established ties with the same government and legal fraternity sources I sought to expose.

Even radio stations that profess high ideals are not above keeping the government corruption from the listeners. Appearing on a Christian radio station in Louisiana in March 1995, I stressed the need for Christians to become more informed and active in exposing government corruption. I reminded them that their God, or simply praying, will not get the job done. Apparently praying and leaving it up to "God" was the primary theme of the show. I was suddenly canceled midway through the appearance. I didn't have much confidence in so-called Christians helping to halt the serious threats to America.

Cutting off guests in the middle of the show is not unusual. Appearing on Dallas radio station KSKY (August 31, 1994) were two guests who had inside information about CIA operations involving the Bush and Bentson families. William White and David Parker were cut off the air, not by the host, Alfred Adask, but by the station manager. The host was subsequently fired.

## CHICAGO TRIBUNE COVERUP

Among the major newspapers that helped to cover up for the CIA conduct exposed by Gunther Russbacher was the *Chicago Tribune*. In a March 17, 1992, article it misstated the facts, covered up for factual evidence, ridiculed Russbacher for allegedly misrepresenting himself as a Naval officer, and labeled Russbacher a phony. This coverup and misstatement of the facts not only helped keep Russbacher in prison, but covered up for the enormous corruption adversely affecting the American people. I sent the *Chicago Tribune* a copy of the letter that I sent to Attorney General Janet Reno, along with a May 20, 1986, memorandum signed by CIA Director William Casey, identifying Russbacher as a member of the Office of Naval Intelligence. I also sent a copy of the first printing of *Defrauding America*, which put them on notice of the criminal activities discovered by myself and the group of former federal investigators and coverup operatives. As expected, the *Chicago Tribune* continued the coverup.

## THOSE WHO COULD HAVE HALTED THE ONGOING CRIMINALITY AND RESULTING HARM

The nature and extent of the epidemic corruption within the federal offices of the United States can be very roughly assessed by looking at those who had a duty to act under federal criminal statutes, under their oath of office, under the responsibilities that they assumed and for which they were well compensated. For instance, in the multi-billion-dollar-a-year looting of Chapter 11 and 13 assets that converts thousands of people to a state of poverty, it required not only the perpetrators (federal judges, trustees, law firms, attorneys) to corruptly inflict the harm but the coverup and refusal to act by the media, members of Congress, other attorneys, federal judges, Justices of the U.S. Supreme Court, Justice Department attorneys, and others. Their refusal to act made them accomplices and guilty as the people committing the acts, according to federal criminal statutes.

On the premise that anyone who knows of federal crimes is guilty of a felony if he does not promptly report it to a federal tribunal that is not itself involved in the criminal activities, I sent copies of the first edition of *Defrauding America* to many of the primary newspapers and magazines in the United States.[579] Each copy of the book, sent by registered mail, was accompanied by a brief one-page letter outlining the charges, the continuing nature of the criminal activities and the harm resulting from it, and reminded the recipient of their obligations under federal criminal statutes to make public the charges. The clout that the recipients had, as major publishers, could have forced an exposure of the criminal activities and brought about massive changes in the heads of many government entities. None responded.

**EVEN THE RELIGIOUS COVERED UP**

One would expect a higher level of responsibility from the heads of Christian movements. My CIA contacts told me about the Vatican Bank's involvement in drug money laundering. DIA agent Lester Coleman described in his book, *Trail of the Octopus*, the role played by Pat Robertson's Beirut operation, Christian Broadcasting Network, in shipment of arms to the Contras, the money coming from drug trafficking proceeds.

**BANNED IN BOSTON**

Believing, naively probably, that readers of the *Christian Science Monitor* would be interested in reading about government misconduct, and the moral conscience that they often profess would motivate them to help expose the wrongdoings. I sent a display ad to the paper's Boston office. A December 29, 1995, letter from the *Christian Science Monitor* rejected my prepaid ad, saying "the attached ad is not acceptable for *The Monitor*." There was nothing offensive about the ad.

**MEDIA ADMISSION OF BEING CIA FRONTS**

It is well known in the intelligence community that the intelligence community had many media personnel and corporations on their payroll, insuring that the public is denied knowledge of the corrupt activities described in these pages. Many articles have been written about this fact of life. For instance, a February 16, 1996, article in the *Washington Post* described the CIA's use of American journalists and news organizations during "the past 19 years," and even using them as cutouts or fronts for CIA activities.

The article made reference to earlier discoveries "that the CIA had had clandestine agents posing as American journalists for decades." Executive editor of the *Washington Post*, Leonard Downie, Jr., stated that "It's disturbing to hear that the CIA has either used the cover of legitimate journalistic organizations without their knowledge, or somebody working for them has been recruited by the CIA."

CIA spokesman Mark Mansfield said the use of the media is permitted by a regulation "waived by the agency's director...and has been and continues

579 Among the recipients of the book were: U.S. News & World Reports; Newsweek; Washington Post; Washington Times; Wall Street Journal; New York Times; New York Post; New York Daily News; Los Angeles Times; San Francisco Examiner; San Francisco Chronicle; Sacramento Union; Sacramento Bee; Dallas News; Dallas Times-Herald; Los Angeles Herald Examiner; Rocky Mountain News; San Jose Mercury; Houston Post; and others.

to be the CIA's policy."

A December 1977 article in the *New York Times* reported that in the mid 1960s the CIA "owned, subsidized or otherwise influenced...more than 800 news and public information organizations and individuals."

**REPORTERS' DISCLOSURE OF KILLED STORIES ON GOVERNMENT CORRUPTION**

For years, reporters have stated to me that they have written stories on various government scandals and that the stories were killed, despite the gravity of the corruption and the harm continuing to be inflicted. That coincided with the media coverup that I encountered during the past 30 years of attempting to expose these crimes. Nearly a half page was devoted by the *Wall Street Journal* (January 6, 1997) to the matter of media coverup relating to major government misconduct. The article stated in part:

*One of the striking things about press coverage of Whitewater is the number of star reporters who, for one reason or another, are no longer on the beat. Investigative reporter Douglas Frantz quit the Los Angeles Times over its handling of a December 1993 Troopergate story that he co-authored with Bill Rempel. ABC's Jim Wooten took himself off the scandal beat after the network killed a Troopergage-related story, Mr. William Powers reported. Washington Post reporter Michael Isikoff left the paper after a bitter internal dispute over the Paula Jones story...the tabloid New York Post let reporter Christopher Ruddy go...*

*Survivors on the Whitewater beat report, both on and off the record, that life is uncomfortable. [Referring to the pressure from "cooperating" journalists], in what Mr. Powers called a chilling "divide-and-conquer approach," whispering campaigns about allegedly shoddy work are launched in an effort to convince reporters to ignore the work of their colleagues...*

*[In referring to the death of Kevin Ives and Don Henry, related to the Arkansas CIA drug trafficking that also implicated then-Governor Bill Clinton, and the killing of that story by CBS and "60 Minutes"], reporters view [these] attacks as a kind of drip-drip water torture to try to undermine the credibility of journalists working the story.*

*In 1994, when the [ABC] network was set to run a story including Gov. Clinton's use of state troopers to procure women, Mr. Clinton's private attorney, David Kendall flew to New York to lobby against the piece [and applied pressure to kill the story]...In June, the White House launched a furious blitz at ABC executives to block former FBI agent Gary Aldrich from appearing on "This week with David Brinkley" to discuss his book on White House mores...NBC's "Dateline" and CNN's "Larry King Live" canceled plans to interview Mr. Aldrich. "We killed it," Mr. Stephanopoulos later boasted.*

*[In another similar case] White House spokesman Mike McCurry was furious and...complained to network executives, and in an angry call to [ABC investigative producer] Chris Viasto, he screamed: "You're never going to work in this town again."*

*New York Daily News reporter David Eisenstadt was fired Nov. 11 after filing a story linking top Clinton fund-raiser Terry McAuliffe to Asian fund-*

*raising and Mr. Huant. Mr. Eisenstadt's attorney sent the Daily News a letter saying he would file a lawsuit because the paper had "improperly thwarted the truth and succumbed to political pressure" in terminating the reporter.. James Ledbetter of the Village Voice reported that Mr. Eisenstadt was fired "after the Clinton campaign reportedly complained to News co-publisher Mort Zuckerman," a frequent White House guest.*

The *Wall Street Journal* article did address the problem of media coverup. Unfortunately, the Journal itself practiced the same coverup in scandals involving their vested interests or political interests, as I discovered over the years.

**COVERUP OF ABANDONED POWs**

Another example of repeated coverups by the U.S. broadcast and print media can be found in *Kiss the Boys Goodbye*. Co-author and former CBS producer of the *60 Minutes* Show, Monika Jensen, described the coverup and disinformation by CBS that aided and abetted the abandonment of U.S. prisoners in Indochina after U.S. forces were driven out. The book describes in detail the coverup of abandoned U.S. personnel by members of Congress, the White House, the National Security Council, the military, and most of the print and broadcast media.

The sacrifice and abandonment of American GIs should not be surprising to Americans, considering the pattern of harm inflicted upon them by people who have taken control of key segments of government. Many of these corrupt and harmful activities are described within these pages.

Despite repeated reports by American and foreign personnel of American GIs being seen in Indochina after the U.S. pullout, many of the same government personnel described in these pages as part of other corrupt activities blocked any meaningful investigation or rescue attempts.

Many of those who were in covert and military operations in Indochina, including the abandoned American POWs, knew of the heavy CIA drug trafficking, which could be one of the reasons for denying the existence of these POWs.

**DANGERS OF ACTING RESPONSIBLY**

Many careers were destroyed as concerned military officers admitted that American GIs were abandoned by their own government and were languishing in brutal conditions in Laos, Cambodia and Vietnam. Retaliation against those who expose corruption of government leaders has been standard practice for decades.

# ANATOMY OF A CIA PROPRIETARY AIRLINE

As my exposure of government corruption became more widely known, additional covert agency people continued to contact me with insider information. In mid-1995, a 15-year veteran of deep-cover CIA activities called and started providing me with detailed information on highly-secret covert activities, some of which corroborated what other CIA personnel had told me. Stephen Crittenden operated a highly secret CIA proprietary airline, Crittenden Air Transport (CAT), based in Bangkok, Thailand, along with over two dozen subsidiaries.

Crittenden[580] joined the Army at 17, and was in the Army Special Forces program. He did four 9-month tours of duty in Vietnam, from 1969 to 1973, and then with Air America from January 1974 to December 1975. Eventually he piloted C-123, C-130, and Boeing 707 aircraft.

Crittenden's disclosures corroborated what other CIA personnel had described to me, especially about drug trafficking, and revealed new areas of CIA misconduct. He also provided me with detailed information relating to the start-up and operation of covert CIA proprietaries. He was a classic example of how this is done.

CIA operative Gunther Russbacher had earlier mentioned Crittenden Air Transport as a CIA operation, and I listed it as such in the second edition of *Defrauding America*. But it wasn't until Crittenden contacted me, and we spent dozens of hours in almost daily deposition-like sessions that I learned more about the secret operation of that airline. Some CIA operatives referred to that airline as the "ghost" airline because it was often seen in covert operations but little was known of it, including where it was based.

**Start Of A CIA Proprietary**

Crittenden's conduct in Vietnam drew the attention of the CIA, and he was selected to be the "owner" of a new CIA proprietary airline. At 24 years of age, Crittenden had much to learn about operating an airline, but the CIA provided management personnel and did most of the scheduling from CIA headquarters

580 Stephen Crittenden's mother, Lucy Isabel Crittenden, was a pilot in the WASP during World War II. His mother had him flying a Beech V-tail Bonanza when he was only 12 years old.

at McLean, Virginia. He was provided a mentor to organize and operate the airline that was given the name, Crittenden Air Transport (CAT). In January 1976, the airline commenced operation with five C-123s, an office building in Bangkok,[581] and $20 million in start-up operating cash, provided by the CIA. This high-level planning permitted Crittenden to fly many of the flights. This CIA operation continued until December 1988.

It was a business person's dream. He had no mortgage payments to make, and engine replacements and aircraft upgrading were provided by the CIA at no charge. Most of his loads consisted of arms and drugs, with payment for full loads, even when flying partial loads or empty.

**FIRST FLIGHT TO CHINA**

In January 1976, Crittenden Air Transport (CAT) made its first flight, which was to Beijing, China, delivering a load of small arms and picking up a load of heroin. CAT received a $100,000 check from the Shamrock Corporation for that flight. Crittenden, a young man given an airline by the CIA, thought he had really hit the big time. Far bigger payments would be made in the future.

The drugs from that flight were unloaded at Bangkok, Thailand, where another CIA proprietary airline, Southern Air Transport, picked it up for delivery at Los Angeles. At that time, Crittenden was flying twin-engine short-range military C-123s, and Southern Air Transport was flying long-range military four-engine C-130s.

Thereafter, CAT aircraft flew to seven different countries flying arms, including Thailand, China, El Salvador, Nigeria, South Africa, Saudi Arabia, and the USSR. The arms were flown from Thailand after they were unloaded by Southern Air Transport aircraft.

Payments to CAT for the flights were received from the CIA's Shamrock Corporation through the Bank of Bangkok. Payments were based upon full loads and at five dollars per pound of permissible cargo weight.

**GIFT OF ADDITIONAL AIRCRAFT**

Several years after the formation of Crittenden Air Transport, in 1978, the CIA provided Crittenden Air Transport with seven military C-130s and one Boeing 707, which came from Evergreen International Airline's operation at Pinal Airport near Marana, Arizona, a small town north of Tucson. Again, no money was paid for the aircraft, and no money was owed on them. Eventually, Crittenden Air Transport had over 15 aircraft.

With these additional and longer-range aircraft, the CIA had Crittenden flying into additional countries, including the United States, Mexico, France, Germany, Great Britain, Egypt, Italy, Colombia, Bolivia, and Panama. Payments for these flights came through the CIA's Shamrock Corporation, with checks written on various bank accounts, including the Bank of Credit and Commerce International (BCCI), Valley Bank in Phoenix (a reported CIA proprietary), Bank One, and Barclays Bank in Miami. (Barclays is a major British bank, headquartered in London, with offices throughout the world.)

Common destinations in the Pacific were Sydney, Manila, and Singapore. Out of Miami, common destinations included San Salvador in El Salvador;

581 Crittenden also had offices in Miami and Sydney, Australia.

Guatemala City in Guatemala; Managua in Nicaragua; San Jose in Costa Rica; Panama City in Panama.

The C-123s flying from Bangkok to Manila carried approximately 10 to 12,000 pounds of heroin. Because of the large amount of fuel necessary on the long over-water flights from Southeast Asia, the C-130s, normally able to carry about 40,000 pounds, would carry only 10 to 12,000 pounds.

A typical flight from Manila or Bangkok to the United States would make the first stop at Honolulu for fuel, and then go non-stop to either Miami or Mena, Arkansas, often flying over Mexico. Special codes were used in air traffic control procedures that advised customs not to inspect that aircraft.

Crittenden said that the C-123s were used primarily to haul heroin obtained from the powerful Chung family in China. The drugs were sent from China to Bangkok in old DC-3 and other aircraft flown by independent operators, and then loaded onto CAT's C-123 aircraft. CAT's ground personnel at Bangkok handled the unloading and loading. The drugs would then be flown to Clark Air Force Base near Manila, where the drugs would be transferred to long-range C-130s operated by Southern Air Transport. SAT then flew to the United States via Honolulu.

**BRANCHING OUT**

After receiving the long-range C-130 aircraft, Crittenden Air Transport then handled much of the Pacific Rim cargo for the CIA that was formerly handled by Southern Air Transport. These drug-related flights often flew direct from Hong Kong to the United States via Honolulu, often overflying Mexico. Southern Air Transport then confined its operations mostly to Central and South America, until it returned to the Pacific rim in approximately 1987. When Crittenden shut down his Crittenden Air Transport operation in 1988 the CIA used Evergreen International to take its place. For some reason the Chung family was not satisfied using Evergreen, according to Crittenden, and entered negotiations with him to get back into the operation.

Crittenden went into detail describing the type of cargo he carried, the people he dealt with, and many specifics concerning logistics, fueling, billing, payments, and other data that could only be known by someone in a position held by Crittenden. Most of the loads were either arms or drugs, including heroin from Southeast Asia or cocaine and marijuana from Central and South America. Crittenden explained that other covert proprietary airlines, such as Southern Air Transport and Evergreen, also carried similar loads for the Drug Enforcement Administration.

**FURTHER DESCRIPTION OF DRUG TRAFFICKING**

Crittenden described numerous CIA flights transporting drugs into the United States. He described his contacts with Fernando Canles, then head of the Bolivian Air Force, who transported cocoa paste in their own aircraft to Medellin, where it was then off-loaded for further processing into cocaine. Crittenden described flying Canles to La Paz in 1984 in a newly overhauled Lodestar 500 (a converted piston-powered Lockheed Lodestar).

Crittenden said that he gave Canles flying lessons in the Lodestar, and that Canles had an expensive condo in Key Colony in Key Biscayne, Florida.

Crittenden had described the many drug loads that he flew for the CIA out of Southeast Asia and Central and South America. He described various contacts that he had with known high-level drug traffickers. He described his Miami meeting with Pablo Escobar in 1990 to arrange payment for a CIA drug flight out of Colombia.

**PAYMASTER FOR DRUG CARTELS?**

Crittenden described Colombian and Bolivian drug cartel figures landing their Cessna Citations and Lear jets at Marana. Stephen said they did not carry drugs on these flights. They arrived to obtain payment for prior drug shipments. These were usually flights from Cali and Bolivia, which landed at an airport outside of Mexico City, and then on to Marana, 50 miles into the United States from the Mexican border. Stephen said these planes never had to clear customs.

**STATE POLICE PROTECTING DRUG LOADS**

Crittenden went into detail about drug loads that he flew into Mena, Arkansas, for the CIA. He described the practice of Arkansas state police guarding the unloading operations, closing off the airport access roads during unloading, which coincided with what pilots had stated to me who had flown drugs in small and corporate-size aircraft for the DEA.

**SHAMROCK CORPORATION, CIA PAYMASTER**

Other CIA assets, including Gunther Russbacher and Robert Hunt, had described the role played by the Ireland office of the CIA's Shamrock Corporation[582] in disbursing bribe money to federal judges and other covert agency assets. Crittenden described his relationship with Shamrock, that focused on other areas of Shamrock's activities. He said that the Shamrock Corporation paid his airline for the flights flown, and that totaled approximately $571,350,000 on flights from 1976 to 1988.

**FUNDS IN BCCI**

Crittenden said that when BCCI closed down, his proprietaries had about $800,000 on deposit, and that he had a claim in for the 20 percent settlement of that amount. During one of many conference calls with another CIA asset, during which I was silently listening, James Pennington discussed this claim, showing that Pennington was familiar with it. Pennington was the CIA's liaison to Somoza, the head of Nicaragua until Somoza was removed by the Sandinistas in 1980. Pennington was also the chief CIA adviser to Central America. He arranged for the purchase of arms from England and other European countries for Somoza, most of which were paid for by U.S. aid money intended to help the citizens of that country. Instead, the CIA's conduct converted that humanitarian money into weapons against the people.

Somoza was the CIA's choice to head Nicaragua, and his removal through elections was the start of the United States' war in that country.

Crittenden described flying several flights carrying CIA money to off-shore depositories on Grand Cayman Island for deposit into BCCI. In one case, he carried 40 million dollars.[583] Other CIA assets, including Trenton Parker and Gunther Russbacher, had years earlier described doing the same.

582 Crittenden explained that Shamrock was a Delaware corporation.

583 Crittenden described using a Learjet 23, serial number 20, for these flights.

Crittenden said that the BCCI bank not only held the account for Shamrock Corporation, one of the money-disbursing proprietaries for the CIA, but handled money involved with the CIA drug and arms trafficking.

There were two BCCI accounts in which Stephen Crittenden had money. One was in the name of Crittenden Air Transport and the other was in the name of Thomas Kary. Stephen thought the account number of one of them was 09090011.

**THREE LEVELS OF CIA PROPRIETARY AIRLINES**

Crittenden described three levels of CIA operations. As it relates to personnel, level one would be typists and other office personnel; level two personnel would have compartmentalized knowledge, and level three would have a broader knowledge of a particular operation.

As it related to airlines, Crittenden said level one would be airlines that would be suspected by the public to be a CIA proprietary, such as Southern Air Transport. Level two would be an airline that had less of a public exposure, such as Evergreen International Airlines, based in McMinnville, Oregon, with a tightly-guarded base at Marana. Level three would be an airline that was virtually unknown, and which he identified as Crittenden Air Transport.

**ARMS FLIGHTS TO MOSCOW DURING THE "COLD WAR"**

Crittenden described several flights that he made into Moscow during the Cold War period, including one flight in the summer of 1976 where a load of M-16 rifles were off-loaded. The load had been brought to Crittenden at Manila by Southern Air Transport. A load of Russian AK 47s were then loaded on the C-130 and flown to San Salvador in El Salvador. A prior load consisted of American M-16s. At San Salvador the unloading of the arms was coordinated by John Forsyth, who worked for James Pennington, the CIA's liaison to Anastasio Somoza, who headed the Nicaraguan government.

Crittenden said that the U.S. reason for having Russian and U.S. weapons in Nicaragua was to convey the impression to the news people that both American and Russian soldiers were in the country.

**ORDERS FROM CIA HEADQUARTERS**

Crittenden described how he received his instructions from the CIA for his various missions. In some cases, he called his handler at the CIA headquarters in McLean, Virginia, named Ross Lipscomb. Crittenden remembered the confidential phone number as 202-357-1100, and when the switchboard operator answered, Crittenden would respond, "Access code 4613," after which he would be switched to his CIA contact. Stephen said that the "3" in the code signified that he was Level Three.

In some cases his instructions came on computer floppy disks which he would then put into his computer. He described receiving floppy disks on some occasions around 1978 from CIA asset G. Gordon Liddy, who in the mid-1990s was a Washington-area and nationally-known talkshow host. Liddy's physical handling of the disks to Crittenden occurred in the garden area of the DuPont Center in Miami.

Included in the floppy-disk data was information about avoiding radar detection while flying drugs into the United States from Central and South America.

**CIA STOLEN AIRCRAFT OPERATION**

Crittenden described another facet of how the CIA (and the National Security Council under Oliver North) used stolen aircraft in the Contra arms and drug-smuggling operation. CIA assets Gunther Russbacher and Terry Reed described this practice. Crittenden described how twin-engine Beech D-18s were stolen and then sent to Volpar Aviation at Van Nuys Airport in California for a Volpar conversion to nose-wheel from tail-wheel configuration. Crittenden stated that a Sam Virse from Memphis, Tennessee, took many of these aircraft to Volpar.

Elaborating more on this operation, Crittenden stated that Aviation Materials on Sweeny Road in Memphis, Tennessee, was an aircraft salvage yard containing wrecked Beech 18s, Queenairs, Kingairs, Barons and Cessna 366 and 377s. Reportedly, the owner, Graham Lotts, would give the aircraft manufacturer's data plates that were riveted onto the fuselages of the wrecked aircraft to Virse, who owned an airport at Bud Island in Memphis. Virse reportedly had a couple of assistants who would steal identical aircraft. The manufacturer's identification plates would be removed from the stolen aircraft and replaced with the data plates from the wrecked aircraft. The aircraft would then be flown to Volpar in Van Nuys to be repainted and modified.

Crittenden stated that Volpar knew the CIA was picking up the aircraft after modification, but was probably unaware that the aircraft were stolen. He said that this practice continued from 1976 to 1988, during the time of the CIA, State Department, and National Security Council's illicit arms and drug trafficking involving the Contra operation.

**REQUIRING FAA ASSISTANCE**

Crittenden described how someone within the FAA at its Oklahoma City registration division cooperated in this scheme by furnishing Sam Virse pre-signed aircraft Airworthiness Certificates to be used in the stolen aircraft having the substituted manufacturer's identification plates.

**COMPANIES COOPERATING WITH THE CIA**

Crittenden described several airlines which are involved with the CIA in a cooperating relationship, including Eastern and Braniff when they were still operating, and Continental. These cooperating airlines received various benefits for their covert role with the CIA, including fuel allotments and fuel discounts, mail contracts, hidden subsidies or payments.

**CONNECTIONS WITH EVERGREEN SHIPPING LINES**

The existence of Evergreen Shipping Lines out of Taipei became more prominent in the mid-1990s, causing me to ask Crittenden if that Taipei corporation with a similar name to Evergreen was part of the same operation. He described a prior conversation with Evergreen International Airlines president, Dale Smith, stating that they had acquired a shipping line.

**ANOTHER SIDE OF CIA-EVERGREEN OPERATION**

Crittenden described the practice of stealing jet engines and other valuable equipment and avionics from Eastern Airlines aircraft that were stored at Marana after Eastern went into Chapter 7 bankruptcy. He described how low-time jet engines were removed from Eastern Airlines Lockheed 1011s and other aircraft and then replaced with high-time nearly run-out engines, and the records altered to cover up for these activities.

This mindset could be expected to be accompanied by similar conduct in other aircraft maintenance practices, such as placing worn parts on aircraft and counting on averages that they would not be discovered. A former Evergreen mechanic, based in Australia, filed a lawsuit against Evergreen Airlines[584] charging that he was fired for objecting to the standard practice by the airline of installing worn-out parts on Boeing 747s and other aircraft and falsely showing them as meeting replacement specifications.

One of Evergreen's government contracts involved the "Logair" contract, flying military equipment and supplies from one air force base to another. In my earlier flying days I also flew this contract operation.

A video[585] was produced about Evergreen's covert activities and CIA connections that was entitled, "Welcome to Evergreen." The video caused the Air Force Office of Special Investigations (AFOSI) to conduct a secret investigation of Evergreen in 1995.

Former Congressman Denny Smith, who had oversight responsibilities for the CIA, later became a member of Evergreen's board of directors.

In 1995, Evergreen halted payments on some of its debts, raising the possibility that it could be a typical CIA scam of placing a CIA proprietary into bankruptcy. If that happened, it could have its debts canceled and the assets acquired by another CIA proprietary, thanks to the CIA's influence of the Justice Department, federal judges, trustees and CIA proprietary or cooperating law firms.

**WHITE SLAVERY OF AMERICAN WOMEN?**

Crittenden described on the phone and in writing a flight that he flew from Los Angeles International Airport in one of his Boeing 707s in January 1984. Forty tall, blue-eyed, blonde women boarded the plane at the Flying Tigers hangar, thinking they were going to Singapore to do a movie. Instead, according to Crittenden, while enroute over the Pacific Ocean, he was ordered to divert to Hong Kong. He said the women were "presents" from the CIA to the military leaders of Red China. Crittenden did not know the actual plan for their use, or of their fate, until a later date. Crittenden Air Transport was paid $500,000 for that trip. The women were never heard from again.

My first thought after hearing of this operation was how it could have occurred without media attention. But then I thought of the 30 years of attempts to expose the massive corruption, harm, deaths, that I sought to expose, with every print and broadcast media, and every member of Congress, that I contacted, keeping the lid on the scandals.

A June 17, 1995 article in the *San Francisco Examiner* described this practice, stating in part:

*Smuggling of women from Central and Eastern Europe for prostitution is increasing, the International Organization for Migration said Friday.*

---

584 Andy Anderson was a mechanic for Evergreen in Sidney, Australia, who claimed in the lawsuit, as reported by the *Portland Free Press*, "that throughout his employment his supervisors regularly and knowingly ordered him to install defective parts on 747 aircraft that were used to transport cargo, rendering these aircraft not airworthy."

585 Produced by local cable-access producer Tim Herman, and available at the time of the publication of this book from HHMP News Service in Portland, Oregon, phone (503) 242-2492. The video had news reports from diverse sources, including the Canadian Broadcasting Corporation, KOIN-TV in Portland, and WSAV-TV in Savannah.

*Many women are tricked by offers of jobs as dancers...the victims passports are taken by smugglers, who threaten them and deprive them of most of their earnings, the report said... cases of smuggled women...had doubled and tripled...in recent years.*

**DESCRIBING HIS CIA-RELATED CONTACTS**

Another CIA operator in Houston, Ted Smith,[586] had the job of selling or trading military goods throughout the world. When a deal was made, Crittenden Air Transport would load the military equipment at Fort Hood, Texas, and at that time the list was given to a Major Robert Cooper. Often, the goods were unloaded in San Salvador, El Salvador. The CIA people responsible for subsequent distribution were James Pennington and John Forsyth.

**PORTS OF CALL AIRLINE**

Among the CIA proprietary airlines that Crittenden had contact with was Ports of Call Airline, that had passenger flights for vacationers, and cargo flights for hauling arms and drugs. The airline was based in Denver, a city with heavy CIA involvement. Its fleet consisted of Boeing 707 and Convair 880 and 990 jets. Because of media publicity about the nature of the airline's flights, the CIA closed down the operation in 1987.

Crittenden said his C-130 aircraft hauled four loads of cocaine during 1983 and 1984 to Guatemala City, where the loads were transferred to Ports of Call Convair 990 jets. Each C-130 carried approximately 20,000 pounds of drugs, that were distributed into two Convair 990s. Ports of Call aircraft operated in close liaison with Evergreen International.

He said that Ports of Call aircraft carried passengers in the Boeing 707 aircraft, and carried cargo, such as the food-lift to Ethiopia, often drugs, in the Convair 990s. After Congress conducted closed-door hearings into the Iran-Contra affair, and after Denver papers carried stories of its questionable operation, the CIA shut down the operation.

**CONTACT WITH CIA'S EVERGREEN AIRLINE**

To those with at least a fair knowledge of CIA activities, Evergreen International Airlines is known to be a CIA proprietary, operated by CIA assets. Crittenden had frequent contacts with top management people at Evergreen's McMinnville, Oregon headquarters, and Evergreen's more secretive operation at the Marana Airport. Stephen thought that the McMinnville operation was relatively clean as far as drug trafficking was concerned, and that the drug shipments go through Marana. The parent company for Evergreen International Airlines is The Evergreen Group, a Delaware corporation.

Crittenden described how CIA money is flown from CIA headquarters at McLean, Virginia to Marana, sometimes using a Boeing 707 with NASA markings, flown by CIA pilots, including himself. Part of this money is reportedly used to pay for drug shipments arriving from Central and South America.

Crittenden had dealt personally many times with Evergreen's president, Dale Smith. Stephen said that Smith was more of a figurehead, and that for many years the main person was Mike Irwin, who provided Stephen with a card authorizing his presence at the heavily-guarded Marana operation. Don Doss

586 Reportedly having an office at one time at 1600 Smith Street, Houston, Texas.

was head of aircraft scheduling, and was a level-two CIA asset. Doss's immediate boss was Walt Burnett.

**SOUTHWEST AIRLINES, A CIA PROPRIETARY?**

In the past, CIA operative Gunther Russbacher had described to me that Southwest Airlines was a CIA proprietary or used by the CIA. Although the details sounded convincing, I felt I needed other data to support that statement. Crittenden said to me that Southwest was indeed a CIA proprietary, describing details to support what he was saying. I feel that more evidence is needed to make this determination, but the statement of these two key CIA operatives is certainly of interest.

**LOSING CIA STANDING**

Crittenden explained that he lost CIA backing after he repeatedly criticized George Bush, former CIA director and long-time CIA asset. (Russbacher had stated that Bush was head of a powerful CIA faction, of which there were several, each vying for power.)

**SHUTTING DOWN CRITTENDEN AIR TRANSPORT**

Crittenden described how the shut-down of the airline resulted in planes being abandoned throughout the world. He said that five C-123s were left parked at the airport in Caracas, Venezuela; seven C-130s at the airport outside Bangkok, Thailand; a Boeing 707 at the airport in Chico, California where Evergreen had a hangar. He said that CIA asset Mike Irwin, who was associated with Evergreen International Airlines at McMinnville, Oregon, took over the Boeing 707.

**CIA "SANCTIONS"**

Crittenden described the three levels of sanctions the CIA plans for people who have met their disapproval, with Level-Three sanctions being the physical elimination of the person; death. He stated that the Level Three sanctions are carried out by "outriders," people who have no family or friends, and have been trained as snipers in the military.

Level Two sanctions usually involve coordination with Justice Department prosecutors, causing charges to be filed against a person and bringing about his or her imprisonment and thereby discrediting the person. I've talked to many of these victims, including people already named in these pages, including Gunther Russbacher, Ronald Rewald, Michael Riconosciuto, Basil Abbott, Russell Bowen, and of course, myself.

**USING FBI TO SILENCE CIA ASSETS**

Crittenden described how the FBI was used to discredit him to his friends and prospective bride, which followed the scenario the FBI used on CIA agent Gunther Russbacher, and confirmed the CIA requirement that the Agency approve of any marriage. In Russbacher's case, the CIA had specifically barred him from marrying Rayelan Dyer, because of her Berkeley involvement in the Vietnam protests and because of her collaboration with author Barbara Honegger who was writing a book on the CIA's October Surprise operation.

After Russbacher married Rayelan, in 1989, in direct contradiction to the CIA's objection, FBI agents burst into the home of Rayelan's mother while the newly-married Russbachers were visiting, and put Russbacher under arrest. In Crittenden's case, he was engaged to a woman, Terri Terril of Overton,

Nevada, who did not meet the CIA's approval. The impending marriage was blocked by a squad of FBI and Nevada law-enforcement officers arresting Crittenden in October 1980, in the presence of Terri and her parents, and accusing him of being a felon.

**PRISON FOR CRITTENDEN**

The standard Justice Department tactic for silencing or discrediting people who constitute a threat of exposure is to charge them with a crime and bring about their incarceration, followed by statements that since the person has been convicted of a crime the person isn't capable of telling the truth. Five years after a mix-up occurring in the CIA's Valley Bank at Phoenix, the FBI and U.S. attorney in Phoenix charged Crittenden with wire fraud in a case where no individual lost money and no individual or company filed any complaint.

What had happened, Crittenden's mentor at CIA headquarters, Ross Lipscomb, wired $100,000 to Valley Bank, instructing the bank to place the money in escrow, to be released upon the possible purchase of a Boeing 707 aircraft for which Crittenden was acting as an aircraft broker. After Crittenden inspected the Boeing at Evergreen's Marana Airport facility, he determined that it was an earlier model than was needed. Crittenden and Lipscomb then notified Valley Bank that the deal was off. The bank then returned the $100,000 escrow deposit to Lipscomb.[587]

However, Valley Bank had "accidentally" placed the $100,000 into the account of a Crittenden Air Transport subsidiary, C & C Brokerage, and while in this account, C & C's financial officer, Rick Challis, wrote checks that used up $87,000 of that $100,000 deposit, including a $50,000 check made out to a friend. Crittenden was unaware of these checks, and was out of the country when they were written. When he learned of this matter, and at the request of the bank, he and Challis signed a note to cover the overdrawn funds. Challis was never charged, even though he was responsible for the overdrawn condition.

In a scenario similar to that which occurred to Russbacher, Crittenden's CIA handler, Ross Lipscomb, urged Crittenden to plead nolo contendere, and said he would be shortly released. Crittenden considered such a plea to be a not-guilty plea. However, the legal definition of the term is an implied confession.[588] And that is the way U.S. District Judge Roger G. Strand recognized Crittenden's position, causing him to be sentenced to five years in prison and five years probation after release. In 1995, Crittenden was still in prison and FBI agent Gil Hirschy stated to a friend of Crittenden that he was going to try and keep Crittenden in prison for as long as possible.

**WAS CRITTENDEN SET UP TO SILENCE HIM?**

The combination of events suggests a government frame-up:

* The person writing the checks, a CIA asset, was never charged, even though he was culpable, and Crittenden was only involved in pre-signing checks that

---

587 These facts are spelled out in the report of a January 20, 1993, hearing report before a federal parole board that is in my possession.

588 Nolo contendere. Literally, "I do not wish to contend." Substantially, though not technically, a plea of guilty; an implied confession; a quasi confession of guilt. 21 Am J2d Crim § 497. It is difficult to define the exact nature of a plea of nolo contendere; regardless of the label attached, the plea for practice purposes is a plea of guilty, or the equivalent thereof. *United States v. Safeway Stores, Inc.* (DC Tex) 20 FRD 451.

required two signatures.

* The person wiring the $100,000 to Valley Bank, Ross Lipscomb, a CIA employee at CIA headquarters, never lost any money.

* Valley Bank was a CIA proprietary. Any loss would have been a result of their negligence. They never made any complaint, and they were covered by a Promissory note signed by Crittenden and Lipscomb.

* Crittenden's CIA handlers, aware that no crime had been committed, urged Crittenden not to raise a defense (which he complied with), and admitted an offense was committed by pleading nolo contendere. His CIA handlers assured him (as Russbacher was also assured) that he would spend only a short time in prison. Which was not true; he received a five year prison sentence and five years probation after release.

* The FBI's and U.S. attorney's vigorous prosecution and attempt to rearrest Crittenden after his release, for either the non-offense, or minor offense at the most, indicates motives outside of the charge itself.

It is my belief that Crittenden didn't realize the legal aspects of the charge, that he actually did not commit an imprisonable offense, and simply followed the directions of his handlers. And for this he was defrauded of years of his life so as to silence or discredit him.

**RELUCTANCE TO EXPOSE GOVERNMENT MISCONDUCT**

I had heard of Crittenden in 1993 and had written him a letter in prison, requesting information about his CIA activities. He did not answer, having been told by his CIA handlers that once he got out of prison they would let him alone. When Justice Department prosecutors continued to seek his incarceration, Crittenden then contacted me, the first contact occurring in early June, 1995.

For several hours a day, Crittenden gave me details of his CIA activities, including the unprecedented secret "conference" calls to various high-level CIA proprietaries and CIA personnel. I was, of course, elated over obtaining the wealth of information. I also recognized the immense forces in the print and broadcast media, and in Congress, that would keep the lid on these scandals and discredit anyone who came forward.

In a hearing summary report that I obtained from Nancy Graven in the federal public defender's office at Springfield, Missouri, the evaluation stated:

*This examiner is of the opinion there is a possibility that if the bank had not mistakenly credited the $100,000 deposit into the subject's brokerage account, had instead deposited that amount in the escrow account, that there is a possibility the fraud would not have been committed.*

**LISTENING TO CIA CONVERSATIONS**

A practice that I had with Gunther Russbacher was repeated several times with Crittenden. While I had them on the phone I would use my telephone conference-call capabilities to call CIA assets and CIA companies who they knew, and I would then secretly listen to the conversations, which provided further proof to me of Crittenden's CIA relationship and activities. During a June 1995 telephone conversation between Crittenden and Evergreen's Walt Burnett, the conversation clearly established that they knew each other and had engaged in CIA-related activities. During another call that I placed to Evergreen's Walt Vernon in June 1995, it was equally obvious that they had both engaged in CIA activities.

The same was done with other CIA proprietaries and assets. Calls were made to Southern Air Transport (SAT) headquarters in Miami, during which he talked CIA business with a key management person who he had known for the past 12 years. It was obvious they knew each other, that they worked and had worked for the CIA. Other secret conference calls were made to other CIA proprietaries and to present and former CIA assets, each of which discussed prior or present CIA activities. Similar calls were made to other CIA assets with whom Crittenden was familiar.

Several calls were made to the Los Angeles representatives of China's powerful Michael Chung family, with whom Crittenden's CIA airlines did considerable drug hauling in the past. Crittenden described how the Chung family flew drugs from China to Hong Kong, and then his C-123s would fly the drugs to Clark Air Force Base in Manila, where Southern Air Transport's long-range C-130s would fly the drugs into the United States, often landing at either Miami or Mena Airport in Arkansas.

Crittenden was dealing with representatives of the Chung family in Los Angeles, who were seeking to have Crittenden obtain for them a fleet of Boeing 727 aircraft to start an airline in China. One of the loads that would be carried by the airline would be drugs. During a series of telephone conversations, Crittenden arranged for a Cesar Resurreccion to inspect 727s in Tucson at Hamilton Aircraft Sales.

**DESCRIBING A SUBSIDIARY**

Crittenden described another subsidiary of Crittenden Air Transport, Saarkes Air Cargo, based in Abai Dabai, whose main cargo was drugs. The CIA furnished the proprietary with three Boeing 707s, which were used to fly drugs to Bangkok, Shanghai, Miami, and Mena Airport in Arkansas. Even though Saarkes was listed as a Crittenden Air Transport subsidiary, Crittenden, who was the titular head of the airline, had no control over it. This reflected how CIA proprietaries that appear to be owned by private interests are actually controlled by the CIA.

Crittenden Air Transport was of course a classic example of how CIA proprietaries are formed. The people who reportedly owned them were given the planes and start-up capital. This was similar to the CIA proprietary in Hawaii called Bishop, Baldwin, Rewald, Dillingham and Wong (BBRDW).

During various telephone conversations he mentioned names of people with whom he had contact. These included Captain Jack, the alias for the CIA pilot flying for Rowan Drilling out of Houston, and who was reportedly a SR-71 pilot for the CIA. His real name was Sonny Knoles.

Crittenden told me of a 1988 C-130 flight to Ireland carrying CIA arms and a stinger missile for the Irish Republican Army. The flight originated at Fort Hood and then flew to Dublin, where it cleared customs. The C-130 then took off and landed in a field south of Dublin, where the arms were off-loaded.

During one phone call to a secret IRA headquarters, he had a fellow prisoner, Michael Martin, make a call to IRA headquarters, which was in a bar in Ireland. A special security code was used to get the phone operator to connect to IRA headquarters. When the call was over, Crittenden asked me what I thought. I said that I couldn't understand a single word because of the heavy Irish brogue.

Martin had introduced himself to Crittenden while at the federal prison at Phoenix, asking if he was Stephen Crittenden. Martin had helped in the unloading of the arms in Southern Ireland on the flight flown to Ireland.

He gave me confidential phone numbers that he used to contact CIA headquarters at McLean, Virginia, along with his access code. He said that when he reached the Agency operator, who answered, "Central Intelligence Agency, may I help you," he replied, "Access Code [number assigned to him, ending in '3,' indicating he held a Level 3 designation]."

He explained that the Evergreen Shipping Lines based in Taiwan was part of the Evergreen Group, which included the CIA's Evergreen International Airlines. He described people who worked with him, including Robert Newbould, who was chief pilot for Crittenden Air Transport and after its shutdown, flew for Rowan Drilling out of Houston, Texas.

Crittenden described people with whom he worked, and their activities, including, for example, Randy Cotheran, a marijuana distributor in Tennessee; Louis Reyes Heradia, Mafia in East St. Louis; husband of Michelle Stockdale of Springfield, who owns a fleet of trucks that moves marijuana; Mark Goiter of Great Falls, Montana, a mercenary and major drug runner; David Hadley, a cult leader; Robert Brashes of College Park, Georgia, a mercenary and assassin, who worked for the Agency, who he described as level three, a CIA sanction group; Coletta Flying Service, Ypsilanti, Michigan, hauling material for the Cali cartel.

He described his friendship, through the CIA, of various drug cartel people, including Hernando Villarell, Cardehana, Colombia. Crittenden described his Mafia contacts made through the CIA, especially in the St. Louis area. When I asked what the CIA did for the Mafia, he said, "We haul weapons and drugs to them." He described being given by the CIA the names of judges and Mafia people, especially in Missouri and Illinois, to contact if he encountered trouble. He gave me the names and phone numbers of many Italian and Mexican Mafia people who worked routinely with the CIA, including assassins that did sanctions (murders) for the Agency.

Crittenden described shipment of weapons to cults that had been stolen from local armories. Crittenden said he delivered weapons to cult leaders in China, one of the many destabilization operations for which the CIA is famous. He described fictitious bank account names, including Thomas Kary, for a bank account with First Bank of Commerce in Grand Cayman.

He described his association with John Emery Wolruffa, a screen writer in Hollywood, involved in the movie, *Wild Geese*, with Richard Burton. Crittenden said the movie was about mercenaries that Crittenden flew to South Africa. In the original event, Crittenden took the mercenaries in 1983 to Mozambique in Ethiopia via Kingston, Jamaica. Crittenden's code name was Iron Man in that operation. When the aircraft arrived over Mozambique it was depressurized and the ramp at the rear of the aircraft was lowered, permitting the mercenaries to drop out with their parachutes. As planned, Crittenden later landed to pick them up. However, after landing, he received a message canceling the pickup, and the plane immediately took off, abandoning the mercenaries. Most of them were subsequently killed. Political considerations caused them to be sacrificed.

The information given to me by Crittenden was sufficient to bring down high-level people in control of key segments of the U.S. government, including the CIA, DEA, Justice Department, and elsewhere.

**CIA PROPRIETARY, BIRD AVIATION**

Using the conference call feature of my phone, Crittenden made several phone calls to William Bird, the head of the CIA-associated Bird Airlines, which had operated in Southeast Asia during the 1960s and 1970s. Bird Air was started by the CIA, making William Bird, a former Air America pilot, its head, and furnishing him with airplanes (including C-46s), operating capital, and contracts. This is the same plan the CIA used to start Crittenden Air Transport.

When the Vietnam War was over, the CIA moved Bird into an aircraft brokerage operation in Fort Lauderdale, Florida. Bird later operated a repossession service with offices in Oakland, California and Phoenix, Arizona. This operation appeared to be tied in with the practice described by CIA operative Gunther Russbacher, in which companies are forced into bankruptcy and their assets looted.

**CHECKING HIS CREDIBILITY**

I checked Crittenden's credibility in several ways. First, I had already been advised by other deep-cover people of the existence of Crittenden Air Transport. These people included, for instance, CIA operatives Gunther Russbacher, Oswald LeWinter, Russell Bowen, Tosh Plumlee, and others.

Second, as previously stated, I listened to telephone conversations that I placed with known CIA proprietaries or assets, during which Crittenden talked to high management people in these operations.

Third, I quizzed Crittenden repeatedly about minute details of his operations, the aircraft specifications, the type of navigation systems installed on the aircraft, and other specifics that covered intricate areas of CIA activities during the 15 years that Crittenden operated the CIA proprietaries. No one could have been so well informed, and so quick with the answers, if that person hadn't been directly involved. When Crittenden didn't know about a particular area that I asked, and which he had no reason to have known, he quickly admitted it, rather than fabricate, which could have easily been done.

Fourth, Crittenden had an address book sent to me which had the names and phone numbers of his many contacts, including drug kingpins with whom he and the CIA did business.

Fifth, I frequently quizzed Crittenden about details that he would not have known unless he was involved with that particular matter. When I asked Crittenden what type of navigational systems were used by CAT's C-130s, he immediately described the dual Omega navigational systems installed on the aircraft. Also, I frequently repeated questions for which he had given me specific dates, names, or numbers, and these always coincided with what he had stated earlier, something that would be unlikely if he had made them up the first time.

Sixth, my training and experience as a federal investigator, during which I held authority under federal law to determine violations of federal law; my years of private investigator experience; my extensive contacts with other intelligence agency personnel, gave me the expertise for judging the credibility of statements pertaining to areas in which I had extensive knowledge.

Seventh, several of my deep-cover contacts from the Defense Intelligence Agency and the CIA, and others in the airline industry, described their knowledge of Crittenden and his airline. One of these contacts had testified several times to Congress in secret hearings, and was especially reliable. Another of my sources, Russell Bowen, a World War II fighter pilot, who was with the CIA and its predecessor, the OSS, asked Crittenden during a three-way telephone conversation whether he knew Robert Haynes (who Bowen said was an alias used by CIA agent Theodore Shackley). Crittenden described where he had frequently seen him (at a particular hotel in San Salvador), which Bowen acknowledged to be correct. Crittenden provided further corroboration by defining the dates that he saw Shackley, beginning about 1979.

**SEEKING TO HELP CRITTENDEN**

Because of the valuable information that Crittenden was providing that could expose these criminal activities, I sought to help him get released.

Justice Department prosecutors were seeking to add ten years imprisonment to Crittenden's sentence, insuring that his information would never be known to the American people. He had a preliminary date on his parole revocation hearing calendared before U.S. District Judge Roger G. Strand on July 28, 1995. FBI agent Gil Hirschy told Crittenden's public defender, David Lee Titterington, that he would try to have Crittenden incarcerated for another ten years. Crittenden was obviously seriously concerned.

The first thing that I did was to send a letter to Hirschy, stating that it was my understanding that Crittenden offered to give details on high-level drug trafficking in exchange for halting any further prosecution. Further, that this offer was rejected, which I described as obstruction of justice on his part.

I then sent a four-page letter to Judge Strand, explaining the sham nature of the charges; the evidence of Crittenden's CIA relationship, and the nature of the cargo that the CIA ordered Crittenden to carry during his 15 years with the CIA, and included a copy of the second edition of *Defrauding America*.

Crittenden said after the hearing that the judge had my material in front of him, advised that he had looked over the material at home the night before, and that they would be entered into the court records. Judge Strand then set June 21st for the hearing on Crittenden's parole-revocation. I also prepared a Title 28 U.S.C. Section 2255 motion seeking to vacate the nolo contendere plea that Crittenden had made in 1991 and to vacate the sentence, allowing Crittenden to be freed.

**CIA WARNINGS TO CRITTENDEN**

These activities caused considerable concern at the CIA. On July 5, 1995, CIA headquarters left a message for Crittenden to call. During this phone call, the CIA sought to have Crittenden cease talking to me, much the same as the CIA asked, or ordered, Gunther Russbacher to do a couple of years earlier. The CIA tried to win over Crittenden by promising him an aircraft operation based in Beliez. Crittenden responded by hanging up. Crittenden had given me the confidential CIA phone number, and then asked me to destroy it.

**CLEARING THE COURT ROOM**

At my suggestion, Crittenden sent me a notarized declaration of his CIA activities, including the years of drug trafficking. I then filed that with the court, along with a friend-of-the-court brief. At the hearing, Judge Strand ordered the court room cleared, and then the U.S. attorney told Crittenden that he could either recant the affidavit that he had signed, or he would ask the court to sentence him for an additional ten years. Crittenden then recanted the affidavit.

Crittenden advised his friend, Chip Stewart, and then me, that the affidavit was correct, but he had to recant it, which I agreed he should do. I then asked U.S. Attorney Janet Napolitano for a copy of the transcript of that hearing. She wrote back on October 27, 1995, stating that "you can order a copy of the transcript...by contacting Judge Strand's court reporter." In this letter she implied approval to obtain it. But that is not the way it was.

I then contacted the court reporter to obtain a copy of the transcript, and she replied that the hearing was under seal, and that I would have to file a motion with Judge Strand to get the record unsealed. I filed the motion with the court on February 7, 1966, stating:

> *This is a request to have the court records unsealed, of the hearing in this case occurring on October 2, 1995. The court reporter advised that I had to obtain a judicial unsealing of the record for the reporter to release a copy of the transcript pertaining to the hearing on Stephen Crittenden on that date. Another letter by the U.S. attorney's office dated 27, 1995 (copy enclosed) authorized me to obtain a copy by contacting the court reporter.*
>
> *Since it is the statement of the court and the Justice Department that Crittenden was not associated with any intelligence or other government agency, there surely should not be any objection to releasing the complete, unaltered, transcript.*

Judge Strand never responded to the request.

**REVELATIONS WERE A PUBLIC SERVICE**

Whatever the reasons may have been for Crittenden's revelations to me, the end result is that the United States and the American people were served by those disclosures. The information given to me by Crittenden provided still further evidence of the subversive conduct by high-level people in control of key segments of the U.S. government, including the CIA, the DEA, the Justice Department, and elsewhere.

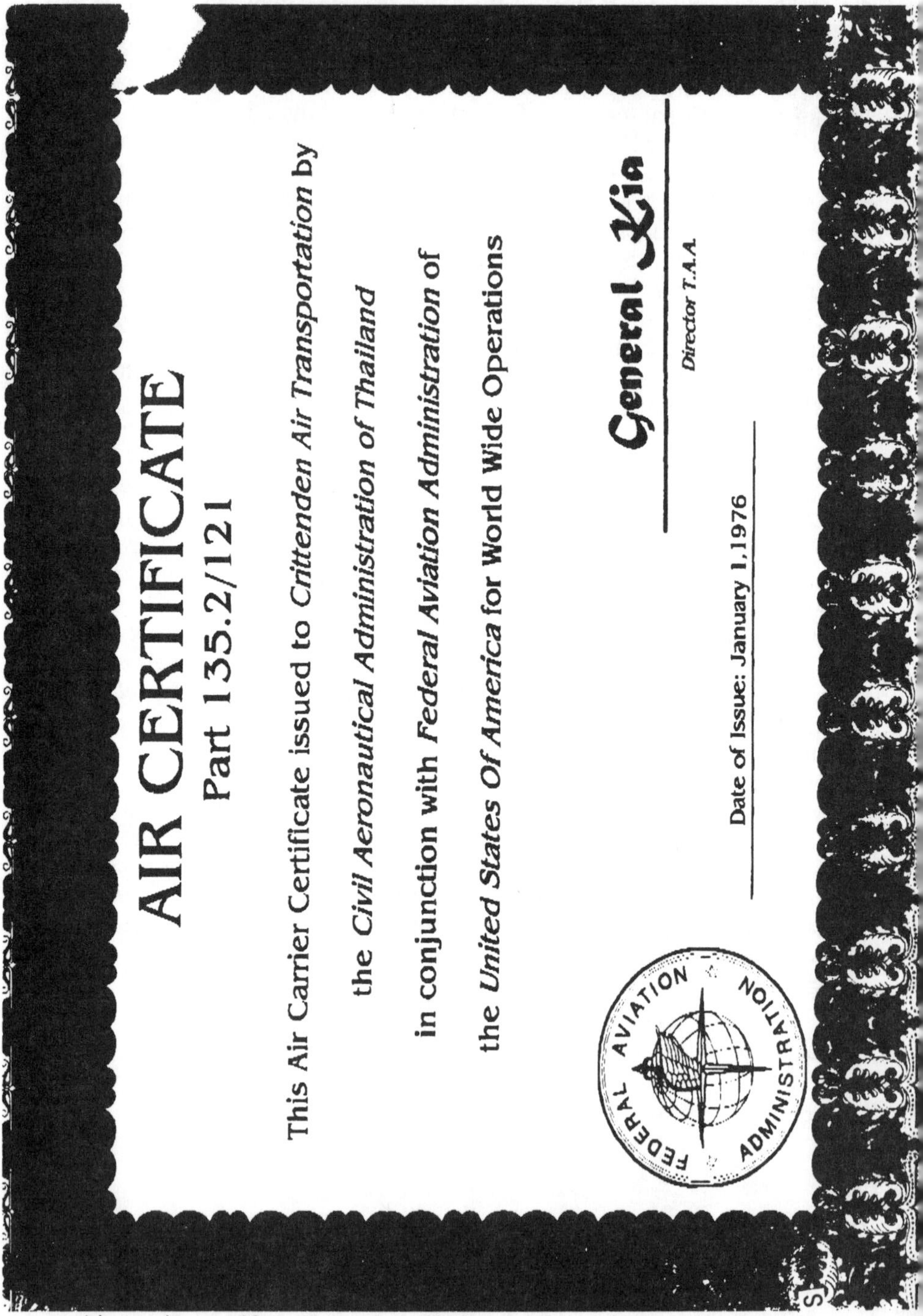

AIR CERTIFICATE

Part 135.2/121

This Air Carrier Certificate issued to *Crittenden Air Transportation* by the *Civil Aeronautical Administration of Thailand* in conjunction with *Federal Aviation Administration* of the *United States Of America* for World Wide Operations

General Kia

*Director T.A.A.*

Date of Issue: January 1,1976

FEDERAL AVIATION ADMINISTRATION

Air carrier certificate issued by Thailand to Crittenden Air Transport.

## CERTIFICATE OF TRANSFER

Lockheed/USAF ("Seller"), Tucson, Arizona, does hereby sell, assign and transfer to Crittenden Air Transport ("Buyer"), of 625-627 Pra Sumain Road, Bangkok, Thailand ,10200, the following property:

PROPERTY: Lockheed C-130 H/J
IDENTIFICATION NUMBER: 4288

The Seller warrants that the property is being transferred to the Buyer is under U.S. Department of Defense restriction and maynot be sold and/or transfered outside of the United States witout prior approval of the Secratary of Defense.
The above property is sold on an "AS IS" basis. The Seller makes no warranties, express or implied (except as specifically stated above).

This transfer is effective as of August 9, 1980.

The property is now located at Davis - Motham A.F.B., Tucson, Arizona, and all of such property is in the possession of the Seller.

Lockheed/USAF

By: ______________________
Lockheed/USAF Gen. Wayman Nutt

Crittenden Air Transport

By: C.E.O. Steph Crittenden
Crittenden Air Transport

Conveyance of military C-130 aircraft to Crittenden Air Transport by Lockheed.

One of Crittenden's C-130s parked at a former Air America airfield southeast of Bangkok near the Cambodian border.

# CONTINUING DISCOVERIES

Information and documentation expanding or providing further corroboration of government corruption continues to reach me as my exposure activities become more widely known. In this chapter I make reference to some of these later discoveries that augment what has already been described. Part of newly gathered information provides further support for what I have earlier learned, and part of it goes into new areas.

**ANOTHER MURDER**

Murders, or mysterious deaths of people posing a threat of exposure, continued to occur. Attorney Paul Wilcher of Washington, D.C., was in frequent contact with Gunther Russbacher and myself. He had taped statements made by Russbacher during about six weeks of daily questioning taking place in the Missouri State Prison at St. Charles, Missouri. Fifty-five tapes recorded these conversations, revealing CIA secret operations in which Russbacher was involved, including CIA-directed assassinations in the United States and in foreign countries. Russbacher warned Wilcher that these tapes were never to be revealed to anyone unless he died. I had a set of them in the event something happened to Wilcher's originals.

On June 16, 1993, Wilcher called Russbacher in prison and argued that Russbacher should have his CIA faction release to him the copy of the very sensitive SR-71 video tape that Russbacher said existed of the flight from Paris to the United States, which revealed part of the October Surprise operation. Russbacher told me that a CIA faction delivered the videotape to Wilcher on the evening of either June 17 or June 18, 1993. The possession of that tape, assuming that it exists, would help reveal the October Surprise operation, and George Bush's involvement in it.

Wilcher had reportedly also obtained documents linking members of Congress with the BCCI scandal. Wilcher told his lady friend, Marion Kindig, and Garby Leon of Columbia Pictures, that he had received these BCCI documents and that he was investigating the BCCI matter. Former CIA contract agent Michael

Riconosciuto told me that he had given Wilcher sensitive information about the Justice Department's theft of the Inslaw tapes and other sensitive matters involving the U.S. Intelligence Agencies.

Wilcher had contacted several members of Congress concerning this material, including Lee Hamilton of the October Surprise Committee, Congressman Jack Brooks of the BCCI Committee, and other members of Congress. Wilcher received the same stonewalling that I encountered for the past 30 years.

Wilcher had also presented the Justice Department with a 100-plus page report detailing the government corruption that he believed to exist. Wilcher's activities were focusing media attention on these areas and constituted a threat to these operations and the government people involved.

Wilcher had been attending Friday evening news conferences conducted by senior White House correspondent Sarah McClendon, and had taped the meetings for McClendon. In early June 1993, Wilcher failed to make his expected appearance and neither his lady friend, Marion Kindig, nor Sarah McClendon, could contact him. Sarah asked Marion to call me, in the possibility that I may have heard from him, which I hadn't.

**GOVERNMENT OCCUPIED AN ADJACENT APARTMENT**

Marion Kindig went to Wilcher's apartment and, getting no answer when she rang the door bell, rang an adjacent apartment seeking to have the person actuate the door-lock-release for the main entrance. She wanted to leave a package on Wilcher's door knob. That adjacent apartment was directly across the hall from Wilcher's apartment. When Marion rang the door bell, it rang into a central telephone system, and a recorded message said: "This is a government number that has been disconnected."

I stated to Marion that it is strange to have an official government phone number in an apartment immediately opposite Wilcher's apartment, and then be disconnected when Wilcher disappears.

**"Do you think Paul is dead?"**

A couple of days later, Tuesday evening, June 22, 1993, I called Kindig from Reno after finding a message from her on my home phone recorder. Reaching her at midnight in Washington, she again discussed her concern about Wilcher's disappearance. Marion asked, "Do you think Paul is dead?" I answered, "Based upon what I know at this time, I would say there is a seventy-five percent chance that he is."

Sarah McClendon and Marion Kindig had tried to get the Washington police to enter Wilcher's apartment, but the police refused. I suggested a way for her to gain entry, but she didn't have to carry out the plan, as Sarah had convinced the police to force their way into Wilcher's apartment. For a woman of eighty-plus years, she had plenty of drive.

Upon entering Wilcher's apartment, the police found Wilcher's body sitting upright on the toilet, as if he died in that position. Over twenty-five police officers, firemen, and FBI agents were present at Wilcher's apartment that first day, an inordinate amount if it had been a simple death. When Kindig and McClendon arrived, the FBI "assured" them that they had no interest in the case, while they continued to question possible witnesses. The FBI seized all of Wilcher's computer disks, audio tapes, records, letters, which contained evidence relating to October

Surprise, BCCI, and related U.S. scandals.

Russbacher told me that his CIA faction entered Wilcher's apartment earlier that morning, shortly after I had talked to Marion, at which time they found Wilcher's body. They then left.

Russbacher said that his CIA faction told him that Wilcher had left his apartment with persons unknown, and had been eating pizza and drinking Pepsi Cola laced with a poison. After Wilcher died, he was reportedly placed in the trunk of a car in a fetal position, after which rigor mortis set in. He was brought back to his apartment and placed on the toilet stool.

Sarah McClendon and Marion Kindig went to the morgue to identify the body. Kindig told me that there were bruises on the right side of the face, which was badly swollen.

The coroner's report could not find (or it didn't report) any known cause of death. But Russbacher's CIA group reported that there was evidence of DMSO containing a neuro-toxin absorbed into the right hand fingers, and that was the cause of death.

Many magazine and newspaper articles should have followed Wilcher's death, as happened after Casolaro's death. Wilcher was well known to Congressional groups as he sought to force them to receive evidence about the October Surprise scandal and its many offshoots. He was known to the Justice Department and to Attorney General Janet Reno, whom he had sought to meet in early June 1993. He sought to expose the October Surprise, BCCI, and Inslaw scandals. Wilcher's death protected Justice Department officials, members of Congress, and other U.S. officials.

Ironically, shortly before his death, Wilcher stated to Alexander Horvat of the Argus Research Foundation in St. Charles, Missouri, "Nothing is going to happen to me."

### THE PRINTER OF THE FIRST EDITION SUDDENLY REFUSED TO PRINT THE BOOK

It may not have had any relationship, but shortly after Wilcher's body was found, the company preparing to print the first edition of *Defrauding America*, Consolidated Printers of Berkeley, California, suddenly fabricated excuses for not printing the book.

### RELATIONSHIP BETWEEN CIA AND THE MILITARY-INDUSTRIAL COMPLEX

One of my contacts, John Cole, had worked in management at Granite City Steel company, and was privy to strange activities between several major corporations and the CIA. Cole stated that he reported to the FBI and the U.S. attorney in Illinois details of criminal activities that he had discovered and documented. These activities involved the Central Intelligence Agency, FBI, Justice Department, military contractors, and even the Japanese crime group, Yakuza.

One of the schemes involved the sale of brand-new aircraft and tanks by defense industries to CIA proprietaries, which were then shipped to foreign countries, both friendly and unfriendly. Intermixed with these activities were drug trafficking, arms dealing, and money laundering. Cole described the role played in these activities by Gunther Russbacher through his CIA proprietaries, including National Brokerage Companies in Missouri.

Cole and Russbacher described the practice involving fighter aircraft manufactured by McDonnell Douglas Aircraft Corporation and General Dynamics, where new aircraft and tanks needed by the CIA for gift or sale to a foreign country, that was barred by U.S. law from receiving that equipment, would be sent as scrap to National Steel and Granite City Steel. This "scrap" was then shipped[589] or flown to foreign countries, including Libya and others who were considered to be enemies of the United States. Included in these scrap aircraft sales were four-engine military aircraft shipped overseas for covert purposes.

Another scheme involved guns seized by police agencies throughout the United States that were shipped to Granite City Steel for the purpose of being melted down. Instead, the guns were secretly shipped to foreign countries for use in CIA operations.

Cole told me about the role of FBI agents in the St. Louis office who were reportedly involved in trading stolen automobiles to drug dealers for drugs, which was allegedly a sting operation but rarely produced any arrests. Instead, the drug dealers would be threatened with federal prosecution if they did not cooperate in the drug trafficking. Bizarre sounding, but the more I learned of covert government operations, the more it sounds plausible.

Banks used by the various members of the group of companies involved in these activities allegedly included BCCI and BNL, Nugan Hand, and others. Handling some of the transactions were Kissinger Associates, who arranged for government funding and approval, bank involvement, and other phases of the operation. Money obtained through loans that were guaranteed by the United States under the agriculture programs appeared to go for farm products, but in reality, only a small amount was used in this manner. This practice went on for years, and the BNL and Iraqgate scandals were only one of many such operations.

Since Cole mentioned Russbacher's name, I asked Russbacher if he knew about the operations. "You are digging up a lot of stuff," Russbacher replied, and then enlarged upon what Cole had told me.

Russbacher described part of the CIA proprietary called Liberty Loan, which had loan offices throughout the United States. Liberty Loan was a CIA operation with offices in twenty-two states that was headquartered in the same building where Russbacher had other CIA proprietaries: 7711 Bonhomme, Suite 704 in Clayton, Missouri. Russbacher stated that Liberty Loan no longer existed, "We had to kill it (in 1986). There were too many indictments coming down; the Agency was making phony loans that were receiving attention."

Liberty Loan was tied into a complex scheme involving companies based in Missouri and Illinois that were tied in with illegal arms sales, drug trafficking, money laundering, stolen cars, and other activities. Surplus military aircraft and weapons were purchased from the government at scrap prices, supposedly to be melted down. Instead, they were shipped or flown overseas for sale to foreign nations, some of whom were friendly to the United States, and some

---

589 Shipping companies included Sioux City in New Orleans; Rock Island Railroad; Stinson Steamship Line, owned by National Steel.

of whom were not.

**DOMESTIC AND FOREIGN COMPANIES IMPLICATED**

The CIA used both domestic companies, including its own proprietaries, and foreign companies, in these operations. The companies involved in these covert operations included, among others, Granite City Steel; National Steel;[590] Bull Moose Tube; Premeian Partners; National Brokerage Companies; Styx Warehouse; Chemitco & Concorde Warehouses, Belgium-owned companies with locations nationwide, including Austin, Texas, Atlanta, Georgia, Miami, Florida, Denver; and various overseas companies.

There were other corporations that were either legally related or who knowingly participated in the convoluted activities. These included: Southern Air Transport (SAT) Miami;[591] Crittenden Air Transport (C.A.T. Miami); Saarkes Air Cargo (S.A.C. Miami); Continental Air Transportation (C.A.T. Austin, Texas); Caldwell Air Cargo (C.A.C. Charlotte, North Carolina); Company Air Ways (C.A.W. Atlanta); Bank of Little Egypt (Marion, Illinois);[592] Boatmen's Bank of St. Louis, Missouri;[593] Pan Cargo;[594] Air Ticketing Network;[595] Liberty Loan; Dergo Company of Liechtenstein owned by Mozar Al Kassar of Damascus, Syria; Permeian Partners Oil Transmission Company; Hiliti Corporation; TMH and National Steel Carriers trucking companies, divisions of National Steel; Georgetown Railroad; Wilson Railroad Company; International Mill Service; J.C. Hauling; Gerald Bull of the "Supergun" project; Adnan Khashoggi, well known arms dealer; Liberty Pipe and Tube, among others. Part of the evidence related to these activities is found in federal actions[596] and in hundreds of pages of factual information that I received by phone and mail.

These companies, with their intertwined contacts, and with CIA involvement, and with foreign interests secretly operating within the United States, engaged in many forms of criminality. Aircraft and weapons were stolen from U.S. manufacturers (often with their connivance), and shipped overseas to friendly and unfriendly governments and factions. Drug shipments to the United States were a part of the web of intrigue.

**NAVY SEAL TEAM WHISTLEBLOWER**

Another covert operative who confided in me, and who Russbacher confirmed, identified himself as a former Navy SEAL; Robert J. Hunt.[597] Hunt stated that he had joined the U.S. Navy when he was seventeen, just as I did, and was later

---

590 Owned by Nippon Kokon of Japan, and owned in part and influenced by the Japanese crime family known as Yakuza.

591 CIA proprietary, reportedly hauling drugs from Central and South America into the United States.

592 Bank president Richard Dodd either committed suicide or was terminated.

593 Major holder of Bank of Egypt's financial paper, including counterfeit money. President Armstrong ran off to South America.

594 Reportedly operated by Sarrkes, nephew of King Saud of Saudi Arabia, in shipping hashish and heroin into the United States. The primary drug brought in was reportedly Turkish-Indian-Pakistan type heroin. Sarrkes was a business associate of S. Crittenden of Crittenden Cargo.

595 With an office in San Francisco, owned by Pakistan personnel, with reportedly a secondary company in Denver called Colorado Satellite TV. These companies reportedly trafficked in heroin and other drugs. The primary type of drugs reportedly brought in was China White.

596 *United States of America v. Robert Medley*, U.S. District Court, Western District of North Carolina, Nos. C-CR-90-186, 187, 188; *John Cole v. United States of America*, U.S. District Court, Southern District of Illinois, No. 92 CV 638 WLB.

597 Hunt's U.S. Navy serial number was 00254-31-66.

sheep-dipped into the Office of Naval Intelligence and the CIA. As with any informant, it is necessary to carefully evaluate what is being stated and to cross-check as much as possible. This I did, and most of what Hunt stated, that I use in these pages, has been corroborated with other sources that I know to be reliable and part of the intelligence network.

In his CIA/ONI role, Hunt reportedly worked frequently with Israel's Mossad. Hunt's deep-cover status was confirmed to me by Gunther Russbacher and others. I also arranged several conference calls between Russbacher and Hunt, and it was obvious that they had considerable experience in the intelligence community, and knew of similar operations.

Hunt said his first assignment was part of the second planned rescue of the American hostages held by Iran in 1980, called Operation Snow Bird. Because the Reagan-Bush group involved in the October Surprise scheme publicized these plans during the 1980 presidential campaign, the rescue operation had to be canceled.

Hunt provided me with numerous government and other documents and a sworn affidavit (November 18, 1993) briefly describing his intelligence agency activities. These writings provided further corroboration of Hunt's status.

**DECLARATION**

I, Robert Hunt, declare under penalty of perjury:

1. I am a Lt. Commander in the United States Navy, and have had numerous assignments as a Naval officer, including Commander of Navy Seal Team Two (from 6/85 to 8/87 ), and Executive Officer of Navy Seal Team Six (from 12/87 to 12/89 ). My Navy serial number is 002-54-3166 . I have been in the U.S. Navy since 1979.

As it relates to Gunther Karl Russbacher:

2. I occasionally worked with or under Gunther Karl Russbacher.

3. During my fourteen years working for the Office of Naval Intelligence (ONI) and National Security Council (NSC), along with regular duty with the U.S. Navy, the Russbacher name was frequently mentioned.

4. I knew him to be an officer in the United States Navy, assigned to the Office of Naval Intelligence, and to the Central Intelligence Agency. It is my belief that when I saw Gunther Russbacher in 1986 that he held the rank of Captain. At that time I was assigned to the National Security Council (NSC).

5. Russbacher acted in part as one of the pilots carrying out duties for the NSC.

6. I saw Russbacher in 1990 while he and I were at Castle Air Force Base.

7. There is no doubt in my mind that Gunther Karl Russbacher was, and probably still is, an officer in the United States Navy, assigned in part to the Office of Naval Intelligence, and the Central Intelligence Agency.

8. For further confirmation of these statements and declarations I can be reached by contacting the following headquarter location (or by contacting Rodney Stich, P.O. Box 5, Alamo, CA 94595, Phone 510-944-1930):

NATIONAL SECURITY COUNCIL
9800 Savage Road

Fort Meade, Maryland 20755

I declare the above statements/declarations to be true and correct, to the best of my knowledge and belief. Executed this 18 day of November 1993, in the City of Springfield, Missouri.

Robert J. Hunt

Sworn declaration by Robert Hunt, describing part of his deep-cover activities.

**REQUEST AND AUTHORIZATION FOR TDY TRAVEL OF DOD PERSONNEL**
*(Reference: Joint Travel Regulations)*
Travel Authorized as Indicated in Items 2 through 21.

1. DATE OF REQUEST: 4 AUG 92

**REQUEST FOR OFFICIAL TRAVEL**

2. NAME *(Last, First, Middle Initial)*: HUNT, ROBERT J. SSN: 002-54-3166

3. POSITION TITLE AND GRADE OR RATING: Cdr, SEAL Team-Two LCDR

4. OFFICIAL STATION: LCRK NAB

5. ORGANIZATIONAL ELEMENT: COMNAVSPECWARG 305/66 NORFOLK, VA XVFAA

6. PHONE NO.: 3/32 X7221

7. TYPE OF ORDERS: TDY

8. SECURITY CLEARANCE: TOP SECRET

9. PURPOSE OF TDY: EXERCISE AUGER MACE

10a. APPROX. NO. OF DAYS OF TDY *(Including travel time)*: 120

b. PROCEED O/A *(Date)*: 10 AUG 92

11. ITINERARY

FROM: LCRK NAB
TO: BAHRAIN 9VIA NAB LITTLE CREEK, VA)
RET: LCRK NAB

12. MODE OF TRANSPORTATION

| COMMERCIAL | | | | GOVERNMENT | | |
|---|---|---|---|---|---|---|
| RAIL | AIR | BUS | SHIP | AIR | VEHICLE | SHIP |
| | X | | | X | X | X |

☐ AS DETERMINED BY APPROPRIATE TRANSPORTATION OFFICER *(Overseas Travel only)*

PRIVATELY OWNED CONVEYANCE *(Check one)*
RATE PER MILE
☐ MORE ADVANTAGEOUS TO GOVERNMENT
☐ MILEAGE REIMBURSEMENT AND PER DIEM LIMITED TO CONSTRUCTIVE COST OF COMMON CARRIER TRANSPORTATION & RELATED PER DIEM AS DETERMINED IN JTR. TRAVEL TIME LIMITED AS INDICATED IN JTR.

13. ☒ PER DIEM AUTHORIZED IN ACCORDANCE WITH JTR
☐ OTHER RATE OF PER DIEM *(Specify)*

14. ESTIMATED COST

| PER DIEM | TRAVEL | OTHER | TOTAL | 15. ADVANCE AUTHORIZED |
|---|---|---|---|---|
| $ 7290.00 | $ 1570.00 | $ 715.00 | $ 9,575.00 | $ YES |

16. REMARKS *(Use this space for special requirements, leave, superior or 1st class accommodations, excess baggage, registration fees, etc.)*

OFFICER IS AUTHORIZED DELAY ENROUTE. WEAPONS WILL BE TRANSPORTED ACCORDING TO FAA/CAB REGULATIONS. THIS ORDER IS FUNDED BY DEPT OF STATE. REPORT TO USN LIAISON OFFICER, US EMBASSY BAHRAIN. EXPEDITED MOVEMENT DIRECTED IAW MTMC REG 55-355, INDIVIDUAL WILL BE ROUTED VIA MOST EXPEDITONS MODES. SPECIAL CONVEYANCES AUTH. RECIEPTS FOR ALL EXPENSES WILL BE SUBMITTED WITH DD 1351-2 IAW JTR

17. REQUESTING OFFICIAL *(Title and signature)*
GREG C. JONES, LT, USN
CHIEF ADMIN, CODE 1001/AB

18. APPROVING OFFICIAL *(Title and signature)*
HOWARD J. THOMPSON, VADM, USN
COMNAVSPECWARGP TWO

**AUTHORIZATION**

19. ACCOUNTING CITATION
2122080 24-2400 008040060 DSSN: 5073 APC M778 211A($7290.00)HUN788008X06001
214A($1570.00)HUN788008L06001
219A($ 715.00)HUN788008X06001

20. ORDER AUTHORIZING OFFICIAL *(Title and signature)* OR AUTHENTICATION
MARTIN B. SLYZINSKY
CH, ACCTG BR, PBD

21. DATE ISSUED: 08/04/92

22. TRAVEL ORDER NUMBER: 8-7009

DD FORM 1 JUN 67 1610

Travel orders dated August 4, 1992, authorizing Hunt's travel from LCRK Naval Air Base to Bahrain and then return.

CONSULATE GENERAL OF ISRAEL
CHICAGO

קונסוליה כללית של ישראל
שיקאגו

October 4, 1993

LT. CMDR. Robert Hunt
Seal Team - Four/ONI.
LCRK NAB.
Norfolk, VA. 23505

Commander Hunt

Thank you for taking the time to write me. I have not heard from you in a long time. I hope all is well with you.

In reference to your request, from N.S.C. regarding our files on May, 1986 operation MAGG PIE I am unable to send them to you, because of the nature of state security of Israel. Please understand.

Because of our long working relationship and what you have ask for. I will give you only the names of your agents that were at Tel Avivs Ben-Gurion airport in may of 1986. our people have made note of Robert McFarlane, Oliver North, Robert Hunt, George Cave, Howard Teicher, Amiran Nir and two pilots Gunter Russbacher and John Segal. I hope this will help you in what ever you are doing.please give me a call if their is any problems (708) 674-8861 wish you the best please keep in touch you have my number.

Shalom

Yacov Nir
Consulate

October 4, 1993, letter from the Israeli consulate to Hunt, identifying several of the key participants in the arms-for-hostages activities, including Robert Hunt and Gunther Russbacher.

EMBASSY OF ISRAEL
WASHINGTON, D.C.

שגרירות ישראל
ושינגטון

November 11, 1993

Lt. Cmdr. Robert Hunt
Seal Team-Four/ONI
LCRK NAB
Norfolk, Virginia 23505

Re: MAGG PIE
Spare Parts

Dear CDR. Hunt:

This letter is to confirm your previous request from the National Security Council, as we had stated on May 25, 1986, a delegation headed by Robert C. McFarlane and including Oliver North (NSC), Robert Hunt (ONI), George Cave (CIA) and, Howard Teicher (CIA), left Israel on a plane piloted by Gunther K. Russbacher (ONI) and John R. Segal (CIA).

On the plane was one pallet of Hawk spare parts. As part of the plan, General Richard Secord remained in Israel with the 707 loaded with the additional twelve pallets of spare parts. Gen. Secord stood ready to deliver them to Iran upon receiving word from the delegation.

The Iranians however did not release the hostages at the end of the three days of negotiating. The Iranians offered the U.S. delegation the release of two hostages in return for the delivery of the remaining 12 pallets of Hawk spare parts. Col. North was ready to accept the offer, but Robert McFarlane refused and the delegation left Iran. This is all I can provide to you on the subject. Please direct all inquirys to our Office of Foreign Affairs. at 3 Kaplan Street, Kiryat Ben-Gurion, 91919, Jerusalem, Israel.

Yours truly,

Moshe Ben-Manash
Special Envoy to the Ambassador

cc: Office of the Ambassador
Office of Legal Counsel

MBM/cal

3514 INTERNATIONAL DRIVE, N.W. • WASHINGTON, D.C. 20008 • TEL: (202) 364-5500 • FAX: (202) 364-5607 • TELEX: 23 904152

November 11, 1993, letter from Israel Embassy describing arms-for-hostages activities, and listing Gunther Russbacher and Robert Hunt as ONI.

**EMBASSY OF ISRAEL**
**WASHINGTON, D.C.**

שגרירות ישראל
ושינגטון

October 20, 1993

Michael Maholy
United States Medical Center
1900 Sunshine Expressway
Springfield, Missouri 65807

Re: Operation "Whale Watch"

Dear Mr. Maholy:

In reference to your formal request concerning "Operation-Whale Watch" and through the National Security Council and Central Intelligence Agency, I am unable to give you full details of this covert mission, although I can forward to you the names of known agents that we have record of relating thereto.

These agents include: C.I.A. Intelligence Officers, Michael Maholy, Dewy Claridge, Steven Tucker, along with two National Security Council (NSC) officers, Lt. Col. Oliver North and Lt. Robert Hunt. For additional intelligence if the need arised, a Michael Harair "Mossad" (Retired) was available in a consulting capacity.

We are unable to provede further detailed information but you must understand this matter involves high security. We will not jeopardize any of our intelligence operatives within that country.

If you have any questions please call our International Affairs Security Office at 21 396 Dian-Ben-Row Street, Tel Aviv, Israel.

Yours truly,

Steven Goldburg
Security Officer
Assistant to the Ambassador

SAG/ft

3514 INTERNATIONAL DRIVE, NW • WASHINGTON, D.C. 20008 • TEL: (202) 364-5500 • FAX: (202) 364-5607 • TELEX: 23 904152

October 20, 1993, letter from Israel's embassy in Washington, relating to the CIA drug-trafficking operation known as Operation Whale Watch, and confirming the CIA status of several of the author's CIA contacts: Michael Maholy and Robert Hunt.

**NATIONAL SECURITY AGENCY**
**CENTRAL SECURITY SERVICE**
FORT GEORGE G. MEADE, MARYLAND 20755-6000

October 25, 1993

Mr. Scott A. Beal
C.I.A. Station Chief
United States Embassy
Costa Rica 9H32

Re: OPERATION "WHALE WATCH"

Dear Mr. Beal:

In reviewing your letter for verification, dated June 16, 1985, and due to our highly classified and necessary confidential security measures, we at Central can only provide names of the agents who were assigned to monitor cable traffic and special detection devices, including the 7 star-hydro-phone systems that were placed in position.

These operatives are: Samuel Thompson, C.I.A., John Plumber, C.I.A., Scott Williams, C.I.A., Steven Crow, C.I.A., and Special Agent-in-Charge, Michael Maholy, C.I.A. In addition, a Lt. Col. Oliver North (USMC, NSC) and a Lt. Robert Hunt (USN, NSC), were available as back-up for added security if required.

These Agents were assigned to offshore petroleum drilling rig "Rowan Houston" during the dates you had stated. The platform was located in Balboa Harbour, Panama.

Due to the sensative nature of "Operation Whale Watch" I cannot authorize any further information on this Top-Secret mission, at this time. However, if you have any further questions, please contact me. I look forward to hearing from you.

Sincerely,

Steven Bradshaw

Steven Bradshaw
Special Assistant-Security Div.
National Security Agency

SB/fp

October 25, 1993, letter from National Security Agency making reference to the CIA drug trafficking operation known as Operation Whale Watch, identifying some of the author's CIA contacts.

**CIA ASSASSINATION SQUADS**

During several telephone conversations Hunt enlarged upon what he had written to me, giving me additional information. He described his knowledge of CIA assassination teams based upon his training of some of the teams, and his involvement with them. Hunt wrote that the training for Operation Ringwind occurred at Camp Perry near Washington, D.C., and his initial handlers were John Michoud of the Office of Naval Intelligence and Blain McCurts of the CIA. Later, Graham Fuller took over. The operation was created by Charles McKee, Matthew Gannon, John McChoud, and Blain McCurts, and put under the control of Robert Gates when he was Deputy Director of the Central Intelligence Agency. Referring to the assassination teams, Hunt said:

*They call it Operation Ringwind, formed in early 1981. It was strictly to take care of all participants in October Surprise until they decide to shut the operation down. And that could be tomorrow morning, or ten years from now. Whoever they think is involved.*

Hunt stated that one of Operation Ringwind's operations occurred at Fort Ord, California, on April 30, 1991: the destruction of the Navy helicopter on which Russbacher was to have been. Responding to my question, Hunt said:

*Gunther was at TI [Terminal Island Federal Prison] from my understanding. My orders were to be at Fort Ord on such and such a date, I think it was April or May. Our objective was to intercept this aircraft because I was aware, and I wasn't running this team, I'm not the ringleader, that he was on board with documentation.*

*I asked an agent back East, "What is this information?" He said "For the president's eyes only." Now, I don't ask questions. And I didn't know Gunther from a hole in the wall. Even if I did, if I had a job to kill my brother, I'd do it. My job was to meet him at Fort Ord and take him. I mean totally take him; take his information and do away with him.*

*I hate to say this to you. And I hope Gunther doesn't feel bad in any way. My job was to take the information that he was carrying. It is my guess, from what I've read, that it was a tape of the 71 [SR-71] and a lot of classified documentation. And do away with him. That was the purpose. My job was to infiltrate these people onto the base and give them covert identities and put them into a status where we would not be noticeable on the flight line.*

*After I came back to the base, all of a sudden I hear an explosion that would just rattle your God damn teeth. I said to these guys, "What is going on here?" And they said they just took care of the situation. My understanding of what had happened, the people in operation Ringwind were actually the people who destroyed that aircraft. From my understanding there were explosives placed on that aircraft before it had left (Alameda Naval Air Station). They knew who they were going to get, they knew the target, and there was only one helicopter involved.*

*Electronic detonating device and it was probably Simplex. It was probably what we call a rotation cap, which is put into it, and it is set off by signal. And it could have been set up either by signal wave from the tower as they were coming through, or the people on my ground detonated it. I think there was a double backup on that.*

Showing the mindset in the intelligence agencies who blindly carry out orders, regardless of their unlawful nature, Hunt said:

*A lot of people were involved in the October Surprise doings. It is my understanding, I didn't have what you call total profile knowledge, I was told to go to Spot A, Spot B, spot C, and just take care of Mr. so and so, and so-on and so-on. And you know, we never asked questions. If someone said, take care of Rodney, it would be done. If I knew it came from my command or my source, I would certainly not have any problem with that. As I mention those names to you it kind of scares me a little bit. I wonder what would happen if this backfired on me.*

Hunt wrote in a letter:

*It is believed that Parkers' group, 222, had a leak. This is where Operation Ringwind came into place. They were to expose all of the members of Pegasus including Captain G [Russbacher]. As you know, Ringwind was a CIA Hit Team that was put together in the early 1980s.*[598] *Its primary purpose was to eliminate all people involved in October Surprise. This team trained at Camp Perry, under the guidance of my team and the former head of the FBI Rescue Team. We taught them every deadiy sin they know. As for Fort Ord, we were there with them to assist in their operations. It is my belief they put a bomb in that helicopter. BOQ at Fort Ord will reflect my stay there on those dates. As for October Surprise, my involvement was limited.*

Hunt said that the reason for his presence at Fort Ord was to report back to the CIA at Langley what he had seen and heard the night that the helicopter blew up. He stated that he was later contacted for more information by John McChoud (Office of Naval Intelligence) and Blain McCurts (CIA).

The mindset imposed upon people in the intelligence agencies by officials in control of these activities was reflected in a statement made by Hunt in an October 20, 1993, letter:

*I remember when I had orders to take him out, I never looked beyond those orders. I just did my job.*

**FOLLOWING RUSSBACHER IN ANOTHER OPERATION**

Hunt's handlers told Hunt to follow Russbacher to Castle Air Force Base in 1990, after Russbacher returned from the trip to Moscow. Hunt, in various letters, including one dated July 12, 1993, wrote:

*I had orders by my handlers to follow Captain Russbacher. Why was uncertain because you never ask. I know he was at Castle Air Base in July of 1990 for a debriefing. He talked about an SR-71 flight that left NAS Crows Landing. My guess was that the plane went to Russia. After my debriefing my handlers sent me to Fort Ord in April of 91. You know what happened that night. You know the rest of the story. I think the mission was to do away with Captain Russbacher. I helped the CIA team get into the base to do it. The Team that has been doing all of these hits are CIA.*

---

598 Russbacher stated to me that the head of Operation Ringwind was Robert Gates while he was Assistant Deputy Director of the CIA's Operations Division.

*My SEAL Team Six trained these people at Camp Perry. It was called Operation Ringwind. There were eight people involved in it. As far as I know they are still active.*

**MISSILES FOR PRISONERS**

Hunt described another operation known as Operation Cappuccino, the intent of which was to send TOW missiles from the United States to Iran and cause the release of Ben Weir. In another CIA operation, Hunt was involved with Ya'acov Nimrodi in Operation Espresso. In an explanation, Hunt wrote:

*I met a man by the name of Amiram Nir, whom the CIA later killed in Mexico. I was introduced to Ya'acov Nimrodi, along with David Kimche, Al Schmimmer. I was at the King David Hotel in Jerusalem and briefed [Vice President George] Bush fully about the arms sales. Nir [who was later killed by the CIA] taped the whole thing. Bush had known he was being taped. This was in July 1989. I knew because we gave him the recording equipment to do it, and that was another reason they whacked [killed] him.*

Hunt described part of the operation, including the meeting which he attended at the King David Hotel at which there were in attendance two assets of the CIA, Charles Mckee and Matthew Gannon. McKee and Gannon were subsequently killed on board Pan Am Flight 103 which was blown up over Scotland. Numerous articles have been written about McKee being the primary target of the Pan Am bombing. As part of this operation, Hunt met Amiram Nir, who was later killed by the CIA.

**ARMS TO THE CONTRAS**

Another operation in which Hunt said he was involved was Operation Tipped Kettle, which consisted of shipping arms to the Contras that had been earlier seized from the PLO by Israel. Hunt said that Operation Tipped Kettle operated under Morton Abromowitz, Chief of Intelligence in the U.S. Department of State.

**BRIBE MONEY FOR FEDERAL JUDGES, TRUSTEES, LAW FIRMS**

Earlier pages described the source of bribe money for federal judges, trustees and law firms, involving the Dublin, Ireland corporation, Shamrock Overseas Disbursement Corporation. During his brief role in that operation during November 1989, Hunt carried funds from Ireland into a newly opened CIA bank account at the Royal Bank of Canada in Kirkland, Montreal.

**ASSASSINATION FOLLOWING SECRET RECORDING OF BUSH IN THE IRAN-CONTRA AFFAIR**

Hunt described flights to Teheran in 1986 seeking to trade arms for the release of American hostages seized in Lebanon, including a 1986 flight with Colonel Oliver North, in which Hunt provided security. During one of these trips, Hunt said a hostile group of guards suddenly surrounded the group, and Hunt pulled out his pistol, causing the guards to back off.

Hunt described being in the Hilton Hotel in Geneva with Richard Secord, Oliver North, Amiram Nir, Manucher Ghorbanifar, Ya'acov Nimrodi, and an Iranian Intelligence Chief, waiting for the 80 TOW missiles to go from Israel to Teheran via Portugal. He described how Secord and Robert McFarlane failed to get landing rights in Portugal, causing the El Al plane carrying the missiles to return to Tel Aviv. Hunt stated that it was decided to send 18 missiles on each flight, for which one American was to be released.

A confidential CIA memorandum signed by CIA Director Bill Casey, dated May 20, 1986, lists Robert Hunt as one of the passengers on the flight from Israel's Ben Gurion Airport to Teheran. It also shows Gunther Russbacher as one of the pilots, and identified him as CIA.

Hunt described a meeting occurring in Israel in 1986 at which he had a security role, guarding, among others, then Vice-President George Bush. Bush later learned that Nir had secretly tape-recorded the meeting, and was planning to expose the activities involving Bush and the CIA. This exposure and the tape recordings threatened to expose many high U.S. officials, including Bush, and some of the secrets described within these pages. Nir had to be eliminated to protect these people and operations.

While at CIA headquarters at Langley, Virginia, Hunt asked Oliver North where Nir was, as Hunt hadn't seen Nir for a period of time. Hunt described this brief conversation:

> *Colonel North told me that Nir was killed because of his involvement in recording the Jerusalem meeting in 1986. I asked North, "Where was Nir," and he said, "Nir has been taken care of." I said, "Why?" He replied, "Because of the Jerusalem meeting." I was told by the Colonel [Oliver North] himself.*

**REVEALING CIA METHODS OF INDUCING DEATH**

Hunt had previously told me several times that he and his team taught methods of inducing death upon those targeted for sanctions (extermination). I asked Hunt to describe several of the methods used to carry out this operation. Concerning the use of the chemical, Rohine, Hunt said:

> *It is used two ways. I have never used that particular one. From my understanding it is self absorbing. It can be put on a letter. It could be put on the rim of a glass, or injected. It has a self-absorbing base. It causes cardiac arrest and leaves no trace.*

He described the injection of potassium chloride into the body that reportedly disrupts the electrolytes balance, resulting in cardiac arrest.

Hunt described the use of Drano to bring about a person's death:

> *From what I understand and from how I've seen it used, Drano will cause internal bleeding. It used to be one of the oldest methods, a lot of the pimps would use it on their prostitutes. They would hold them down on the floor and then pour the Draino down the person's throat. This would cause convulsions, and the person's insides start bleeding. It eats up the entire body. That is one method commonly used in the Agency.*

**HUNT'S ROLE IN TEHERAN FLIGHTS**

Hunt described to me his role on the flight to Teheran in 1986, seeking to negotiate with the Iranians to cause the release of Americans held captive after being seized in Beirut. Russbacher also had a role in that flight, and I compared their statements, which checked out against each other. Hunt stated that the aircraft had been painted in Israel with the colors of the Irish airline, Air Lingus, to cover up for the actual origin of the aircraft. He stated the plane left Israel's

Ben Gurion Airport for Teheran on what he thought was about the 25th of May or June of 1986. He identified one of the pilots as Robert John Segal. Hunt said that others on the flight included Oliver North, George Cave, Howard Teicher, and Robert McFarlane.

**OPERATION AUGER MACE AND SADDAM HUSSEIN**

Operation Auger Mace was a Kuwaiti war-game exercise in 1992, which served as a cover for Hunt and his Navy SEAL Team to go into Baghdad for the purpose of capturing Saddam Hussein. Hunt stated:

*Our mission there was to go into Baghdad and actually try and bring Saddam back to the United States. The purpose was to help President Bush win reelection. Bush knew at that point in the game that he was in trouble. So we went in Bahrain, and from Bahrain we went to Tel Aviv, working with an Israeli General by the name of Uri Simhoni. He was an attaché at the Israel Embassy in Washington at one time. He was a Major General and with his Intel network we were to go into Baghdad, extract Saddam Hussein, bring him back, similar to what we did with Noriega. This operation was put together with my unit and also a Delta unit, and we were to go in there with the Israeli and extract him from his quarters, right outside of Baghdad, and just take him on out.*

**CIA DRUG ACTIVITIES AND PAN AM 103**

Hunt described his knowledge of CIA drug activities from the Middle East to the United States using Pan American flights. He said:

*The money and the drugs were being flown through those Pan Am flights from Europe. Michael Pallack helped coordinate those things. In fact, there is a guy, I only met him once, his name was Major Turnabey, he was the Intelligence Chief for the popular front for the liberation of Palestine. And he had a lot to do with Pallack and his whole gang. They would actually coordinate, do actual drug running, right on through Germany and into the United States.*

Hunt named two CIA operatives on Pam Am 103 that he personally knew, who were returning to the United States to report the CIA involvement in drug trafficking. Referring to these two CIA operatives, Hunt said:

*These two guys, McKee and the other gentlemen,*[599] *were involved in Operation Ringwind. They're the ones who helped train all those people in the early eighties. And they were very deep-deep-cover experts in Mideast terrorism. And they were so pissed-off at what was happening they just went in to blow the whistle. When the Agency heard that, I have a gut feeling that the CIA blew the plane up.*

I asked, "What type of drug operation did the CIA have which used Pan Am?" Hunt replied, "Well, they were putting the stuff on Pan Am." Referring to other CIA figures, Hunt said, "And that's where Victor Marchetti and all came in. They were all into this. All these guys, it was just one big giant clique."

**HOW CIA PERSONNEL CONTACT HEADQUARTERS**

Among the many inner workings of the CIA that Hunt told me about was a system of communicating between Washington and the deep-cover people

---

599 Believed to include Matthew Gannon and Ronald Lariviere.

in the field, called Flashboard. He explained how CIA operatives call into one of several phone numbers at Langley, Virginia and that a particular code is dialed, after which an operator comes on the line and asks for their code number.

**SECRET ASSASSINATION NUMBERS?**

Hunt had given me several secret CIA telephone numbers, which I gave to Russbacher, requesting his comments. Russbacher stated during this October 7, 1993, telephone call: "About that telephone number without any specific prefix, that is a no-no. Where in the hell is this coming up from?"

"A friend," I replied. "The friend who worked under me? He needs to keep his mouth shut. That is not even good to discuss." Russbacher then gave me the telephone numbers: "You know, one of those is a security number and the other is a kill number, Rodney." Not knowing whether he was talking about termination of an operation, a telephone call, or to kill someone, I asked, "What does that mean?" Russbacher replied, "You know what it means. We are talking about termination or sanctions."

Russbacher continued, "The alphabetical prefix plus a four-number numeric code is for any particular type of surgical operation. It isn't even nice to know. Just leave that stuff totally aside and don't put it into a book." Russbacher continued: "Hunt should have known better than to let that type of shit out. I would never in my wildest dreams put a tag out like that."

**ASSASSINATION SQUADS**

Hunt stated that one of his ONI duties was teaching assassination squads. He also referred to several private companies funded by the U.S. that were used to train U.S. and foreign personnel to carry out for-hire assassinations (something like the Jewish group known as Murder Incorporated).

One company, known by the acronym ANV was based in Jupiter, Florida, and was referred to as the Fish Farm. Shareholders in the company were present as well as former CIA personnel who were involved in some aspect of CIA related drug trafficking. They included, for instance, Theodore Shackley, who was heavily involved in the CIA Far East drug trafficking and then in the drug trafficking from Central and South America.

ANV began as a CIA proprietary and then converted to a private firm for the Agency's standard disavow purposes. ANV conducted much of its training, including assassination squads, on Andros Island in the Bahamas.

The ABC television network wanted to run a story on these operations on Andros Island, sending a crew on a helicopter to film the Island from the air. Hunt stated that the ABC helicopter was shot down in 1991 or 1992, killing a woman reporter. The incident was kept from the American public, using national security as an excuse.

ANV functioned as an umbrella organization for various other groups, including the Phantom Battalion (based in Memphis) and the Peregrine Group (based in Texas). Hunt said there were numerous ties between the groups and the Richard Secord-Theodore Shackley-Thomas Clines Associates, all of whom were reportedly associated with the opium trade and assassination program in Laos.

One of the companies associated with ANV was known as CSA, founded by Robert C. (Stretch) Stevens, who worked for Shackley for over two decades in various CIA operations. Shackley was heavily involved in CIA drug trafficking from the Far East and in Central and South America. A para-military group in ANV was known as the Phoenix Battalion.

Another group under ANV was Peregrine International Associates, founded in 1981 by Guy S. Howard and Ronald R. Tucker. They conducted covert operations with Defense Department approval from 1981 until 1989, when the company folded. Many of Peregrine's personnel were vets of Army Delta Force. The company hired both retired and active duty military personnel on leave to act as "guns"–guys who had no qualm about killing someone.

Peregrine received funds for their operations from U.S. agencies such as Customs or from foreign governments which may have been drawing on U.S. military assistance funds [supplied by U.S. taxpayers]. Their assassination targets included drug smugglers acting in competition with CIA and DEA personnel in Peru, Honduras, Belize, and various Caribbean nations. They also armed and trained Contras and military command units in El Salvador, Honduras and Peru.

Richard J. Meadows served for a time as Peregrine's president. Charles Odorizzo and William Patton worked for the group. Peregrine's key contacts were retired Army Lt. Gen. Samuel Wilson (former Director of the DIA) and Lt. Col. Wayne E. Long, who as of April 1987 worked as a senior officer in the Foreign Operations Group, which is part of the Army's intelligence support activity office.

**OPERATION BLUE GREMLIN**

Hunt told me about other CIA operations, including Operation Ho Ho Ho. When I asked Russbacher if he knew about the operation, he enlarged upon it, stating that Operation Ho Ho Ho was the name given to it by those in the field but that the Agency code name was Operation Blue Gremlin, further identified in communications by the alphanumeric identification OP BG 1741.5A. They described Blue Gremlin as a planned blowing up of buildings in Teheran in December 1984 but which for various reasons was never carried out.

**ISRAEL'S INFILTRATION OF THE NATIONAL SECURITY COUNCIL**

Hunt had told me earlier that a high official of one of Israel's secret agencies was on the staff of the United States National Security Council: Moshe Ben Lafven, who went under the American name of Steven Croch.

A CIA cable analyst, Michael Maholy, described in earlier pages, had described in a letter his relationship to Hunt:

*I first became acquainted with agent Hunt in 1985 in Panama where I was the liaison officer for the U.S. Embassy. He was always accompanied by [Oliver] North and his team. This went on for several years. I recall reading cable traffic where his name came up repeatedly. From my sources, Hunt was on several covert missions, detached to Operation Whale Watch, which involved me buying drugs from Colombians and trading them for arms and ammo. My part in the operation was to provide a cover or front with the use of offshore oil rigs, so Hunt, myself, and others, could complete all transactions. These offshore oil-rigs were all CIA offshore geological survey and logistics services. I have spent time in South*

*American countries, providing photos, documents, maps, and all intelligence for the U.S. embassies in Central and South America.*

**PLANNED ASSASSINATION OF PRESIDENTIAL CANDIDATE BILL CLINTON?**

Due to the sensitivity of a covert operation by a section of the U.S. intelligence agencies, I am identifying the operative who told me about it as "Agent X." This agent told me about an operation ordered to be carried out by high Washington personnel in mid-1992 under the code name, Operation Mount Rushmore. He said that it involved the San Francisco law firm of Heller, Ehrman, White, and McCauliffe,[600] and several Mossad agents reportedly working for the firm. Agent X described Operation Mount Rushmore and the control over it by the Mossad agents and attorneys. The agent said:

> *[It] could blow the lid right off the White House. The name of it is Operation Mount Rushmore. Operation Mount Rushmore was an attempt to assassinate presidential candidate Bill Clinton when he came into San Francisco. They called it Mount Rushmore because of the heads of the presidents. What I was to do, I was at the Presidio in San Francisco, and I met a Mossad agent who was also involved in this.*
>
> *And there was a company in Redwood City called EIC. They are on Woodside Road in Redwood City, and the guy who runs it is the owner, Chan Wang. He is a member of an organization called the "Eagles." He is a Chinese guy. It is my understanding that he was financing this entire operation. He was in touch with the law firm of Heller, Ehrman, White, and McCauliffe.*

Agent X continued, indicating further Mossad involvement in Operation Mount Rushmore:

> *There was an attorney I briefly met, whose name was [name withheld at Agent X's request]; he was an attorney at Hiller Erman, and he was handling some part of this operation. From my understanding, these people were organized. I was at the Presidio training some people, and they wanted to do a sanction on candidate Clinton when he came into San Francisco.*
>
> *Things got screwed up and the whole operation went sour, and everybody went under ground. The Mossad agent I was in touch with, I never heard from her again. I talked to some people at the State Department and everything was hush-hush and quiet. And it all just dropped off the face of the earth. And then two days later I get orders to go overseas, which are the orders I sent you. After Rushmore went sour, we were told to get the hell out. The State Department wrote the orders and I was gone the next day.*

Agent X said, "I was told to go there [San Francisco] last summer and meet a Mossad agent, which I did. I asked, 'Why San Francisco?' and they said 'Bill Clinton is coming and we need to talk to you.' That is the reason for being in the Bay Area, the Rushmore operation." The agent continued:

---

600 Located at 333 Bush Street, San Francisco, California.

*Well, here is what happened. I was involved with Operation Ringwind, which is the team that actually went out and assassinated the people in the very first letter I mentioned to you.*[601] *I know the names. I try and remember them out of memory and the notes I make throughout my life. Our operation was with McKee and the other gentlemen who were killed on Flight 103. We actually trained these people at Camp Perry, Virginia. And we also trained them out of Fort Story and at Vint Farm Hill, which is the Intelligence Center. And we briefed them on everything. The object of this unit was to eliminate everyone that was involved in October Surprise.*

*Everyone who had information pertaining that was not involved militarily, to do away with them. With the military people that were involved, and there were a variety of generals and colonels and so forth, it was handled in a different way. They had training accidents, or they were put so far into retirement that they didn't know what the hell was going on.*

*And these were the people, there are about seven of them, who are involved in this now. They were actually in the [San Francisco] Bay Area along with myself, and they were going to take care of this operation which involved the Mossad, to take care of Mr. Clinton.*

"Why would they want the Mossad in this," I asked.

*I don't know, and that is one of the things that threw me. Why the Mossad? What do the Israeli have to do with this? When I talked to the Israeli Intel officer he said, "We have our reason." I guess it was because Bush had such a rapport with Israel, they wanted to see him get reelected. And if it involved getting rid of Mr. Clinton, and I hate to say it over a phone, but that is what it came down to. My contacts go back to the early eighties with Duane Clarridge and Charles Allen. They were all aware of what was going on.*

In subsequent conversations and letters, the agent enlarged upon these statements, stating that the security guard[602] was an employee of the building's managers where the law firm was situated. In a September 20, 1993, letter, Agent X enlarged upon what he had earlier stated and written to me, relating to Operation Rushmore:

*I was ordered last summer [1992] to go to San Francisco by Graham Fuller, CIA; Dick Pealer, ONI; and John Kaplin, CIA. These people were my handlers. I was told to go to the Bay Area. I flew from NAS [Naval Air Station] Norfolk to NAS Alameda, where I was to meet another Agent. He was the CIA station chief for SF [San Francisco]. His name is Robert Larson. He made arrangements for me at the Presidio. The next day the team arrived, and I wondered why this hit team was in town. I got a call from a woman who said she was Mossad and we needed to meet. So we did; we had lunch. I asked her, her name, and she said it was Anna Colburn. I later found out her real name was..... We talked about why*

---

601 Danny Casolaro; Alan Standoff; Barry Kumnick; Dennis Eisman; Alan May; David Mayer; Paul Maresca; Dexter Jacobson; Gary Pinnell; Michael Hand; Ansan Ng; Jonathan Moyle; Arnold Raphel Mohommed Rajai; Cyrus Hashemi; Shahpour Bahktior.

602 Security guard for 333 Bush Street building.

*I was in town, and I asked for what reason. She said they wanted to hit Clinton. When she said that, I got sick. I said to myself, another Kennedy. I then asked her for the technical details.*

*They would be operating out of Republican Headquarters on Van Ness Avenue, where they could monitor all political moves by Clinton. The lady who would oversee this was...for the Republican Party. She is also CIA.*

*Money, who would fund this? A man by the name of Chan Wang. He belongs to an organization called The Eagles. He also owns a real estate company called EIC in Redwood City. The man who would be his in-between was also CIA. His name was Bok Pon. Bok and I hit it off. He told me that...worked for a major law firm called Hiller Ehrman [Hiller, Erman, White, and McCauliffe], and that this firm would handle everything we may need, such as safe-houses, equipment, money, travel, etc. I later found out a major Mossad team was working from the law firm.*

*Now I have the team assembled. Knowing Clinton was coming to town in the next few weeks, we set up shop. Weapons, escape routes, rendezvous, etc. Clinton was expected to come and stay at the Ritz Carlton. That's when we were going to do it. My men and I took up a position across the street from the Carlton before Clinton's arrival. We photographed the whole area for best possible results. Anyway, three weeks before he was due to arrive, word had it there was a leak. Where, was unknown. So my team and I pulled out in fear of being caught. That night we were told to eliminate all factions involved, including the Mossad agents. This order was given by Bob Larson, [CIA] station chief, San Francisco.*[603]

*Just as we were about to get her, I get a call on my pager from Flashboard. When I called, they said, "Stop operations." When I asked the reason why, they said they found the leak. The leak came from a security guard where Heller Ehrman had their office. One of the Mossad agents was dating this guard. Our job was to, of course, take care of it. So that night when he got off work at midnight, and he went to catch the BART train at Market to go home, my friend and I grabbed him and threw him in front of a train. "Job well done," said Washington. Two days later I ended up in the Mideast.*

*Rodney, what I have told you could incriminate me, but I will take the chance and you know why. I have told you a lot of things, and believe me, they are true....I know for a fact that the Mossad is still working out of that law firm, for reasons unknown.*

*The names of the guys in Operation Ringwind are John Aldridge; Phil Burgess; Bob Burdige; Gregg Note; Robert Lister; Fred White; Rodney Harmon; and myself. The names are all CIA.*

*I forgot to mention that Gene Trefethen also sponsored this operation. He owned a winery in Napa. He is one of Wang's friends. Together with their money, that's how this thing was going to be pulled off. Consider this a self-confession.*

---

603 Larson was later transferred to a position in the Caribbean, and known as "Pogo."

When the operation was threatened with exposure, and before the leak was discovered, Agent X said that the team sent to carry out the operation against presidential candidate Bill Clinton proceeded to eliminate those who knew about its existence.

**WAS THE PLAN A MOSSAD OPERATION?**

I sought to reconfirm what Agent X had earlier stated about the CIA and Mossad operation to kill presidential candidate Bill Clinton. I asked: "It appears from what you stated earlier that the Mossad was running Operation Mount Rushmore, and that you received your initial instructions and coordination from them. What are your comments to that?"

Agent X replied: "They [Mossad and the Hiller law firm] were the ones actually running the entire operation. From what I understood, and from what I pieced together, they were the ones actually running the whole operation."

"Doesn't that sound a little strange?" I asked. He replied:

> *Yes, and no. You have to remember, Bush made a lot of friends with Israel. He promised them ten billion in aid. The Gulf War, the ten billion in aid, and they didn't want anyone to defeat him [Bush]. They really wanted him to win. The Mossad is a very strong force in San Francisco, from what I can understand. I've never seen such a large contingency in one area. I've seen them in New York. I've seen a few of them in Boston. I know one that actually works for the National Security Council.*

"I'm trying to think of the implications of the Mossad directing Operation Mount Rushmore," I said. "There are implications I don't fully comprehend yet."

> *We work together a lot of times. It is a very mutual thing in some areas, but not in all areas. When it comes to hard Intel [intelligence], no way. But it is like, 'You give me something and I will give you something.' If the operation backfired, the Agency would have someone to blame it on. Then they can do a big sting, and catch all these people, and say, look, now you have another Kennedy-type situation. That is my feeling.*

**WHO ISSUED THE ORDERS**

I asked Agent X who issued the orders for this operation. He replied that "The orders came from ONI. I first went out there in July of last year, 1992."

I said that Gunther Russbacher was familiar with the operation and that it was not totally canceled, "Only put on hold." Agent X replied: "Well, it could have been put on hold; my part in it was pulled out. We had a flop in the operation, and we had to sanction several people in it because we had a leak. So when that was done they just pulled the whole unit out of there."

**SIGNIFICANCE OF OPERATION RUSHMORE**

If Operation Rushmore was indeed a plan to assassinate presidential-candidate Bill Clinton, and involved the CIA and the Mossad, the implications are enormous. It would lend further credibility to those who argue that JFK's assassination was a CIA operation.

**CORROBORATION OF OPERATION MOUNT RUSHMORE**

After Agent X gave me details of Operation Mount Rushmore, I asked Russbacher if he had heard of the operation, without giving him any clue as to what it concerned. He expressed shock that I knew about it, and then commenced describing details of it, which coincided with what Agent X had stated. Since Agent X and Russbacher were not in contact with each other, this cross-check of information provided additional support that it did in fact exist.

A taped telephone conversation was made available to me which was made about January 30, 1994, between Gunther Russbacher and another former navy pilot and intelligence agent, Joe Jordan. The primary purpose of the call related to a planned POW rescue mission into Cambodia involving Russbacher and a small group (that took place shortly after that call). During that phone call, reference was made to Operation Mount Rushmore and Operation Watchtower, giving me further support to the existence of these deep-cover operations.

After the second edition of *Defrauding America* was released in April 1994, describing Mount Rushmore, I sent copies of the book to Attorney General Janet Reno, along with a cover letter describing criminal activities over which she had responsibility to act. Despite the gravity of the alleged assassination scheme, I was not contacted for supporting evidence.

On May 9, 1994, Secret Service agent Bill Bishop called and wanted to meet me concerning Operation Mount Rushmore. I wouldn't meet him at my home, but agreed to meet him at a local coffee shop. Bishop arrived with another Secret Service agent, Brent Herron. I had a lady friend along to monitor the conversation so as to protect myself against the agents misstating what I had actually said.

Bishop stated that he heard about Operation Mount Rushmore after reading the brief that I filed in federal court. He wanted to know details on who "Agent X" was, and I told him I would be glad to send him the details via either FAX or a letter, if he first sent me a FAX or letter advising what he wanted to know.

During the meeting I described my attempts to expose the corruption I uncovered, and the actions taken by Justice Department attorneys and state and federal judges to silence me.

## MOSSAD INVOLVEMENT IN PRESIDENTIAL ASSASSINATIONS?

*Final Judgment*, authored by Michael Collins Piper, addressed the role of Jewish organized crime within the United States and the role that this criminal element may have played in the assassination of President Kennedy. The Mossad's alleged involvement in Operation Mount Rushmore, and the attempt to assassinate presidential candidate Bill Clinton, provides additional support to Piper's argument that the Mossad or Jewish crime family did in fact play a role in JFK's assassination.

## ADMISSION FOR FORMER MOSSAD OFFICER

Former Mossad officer, Colonel Victor Ostrovsky, described in his book, *The Other Side of Deception*, how and why the Mossad planned to assassinate President George Bush, seeking to blame three Arabs for the deed. When the plot was exposed, the Mossad killed the Arabs to prevent the scheme from going public. This contradicts the Mossad's alleged involvement in Operation Mount Rushmore, and could be due to different factions in the Mossad, or that plans changed.

## INVOLVEMENT OF FEDERAL JUDICIARY IN OPERATION MOUNT RUSHMORE?

During my many conversations with Agent X, the name of U.S. District Judge Marilyn Patel (San Francisco) surfaced. He said that Patel was in close contact with the parties involved in Operation Mount Rushmore and that he had met her at various social functions in the San Francisco area. [Patel was once on the board of directors of ADL in San Francisco.] Agent X said:

> *During the whole Operation Rushmore her name kept coming up constantly. It had something to do with San Francisco and that law firm. Now, the attorneys in that high-power law firm had known her, and were always telling me that if there was a problem, don't worry. They said that if something went sour, she was going to be the overseer and get everyone out of trouble. That is what it all came down to. The name was constantly mentioned. I met her once. In my opinion, she knew everything that was going on with Rushmore, because of the way that the attorneys from Hiller Erman spoke about her. "Don't worry," they said, "we have friends at 450 Golden Gate [federal building in San Francisco housing the federal courts and the Justice Department]." I said, "Well, who do we know over there?"*
>
> *"We know Marilyn H. Patel," was their reply. That was how I first met her. Whenever you do something like what we were going to do [Operation Rushmore], you have to cover every angle. It's like a game of chess. You cover every escape, you cover money, technicalities, what if and what not, every possible avenue. So, if something happened, the case would have got in front of Patel.*
>
> *I only know her from my trade [CIA covert activities] and what I've done. Whenever you plan an operation like we were going to do, you cover every single angle, I don't care what it is. Who is going to finance it, if something happens who is going to back us up, what contacts in the police department. In fact, the former chief of police there, he is now with a security company called the Phoenix program. Phoenix Security is who he is with now. He was involved in the sense, you know, for contacts, you know it's a big organization.*

If Agent X is telling the truth, then we had sections of the CIA, the Mossad, a federal judge, and many others involved in a scheme to assassinate a presidential candidate. It almost appears as if it was the Mossad who was *directing* the assassination attempt.

Further, we have two of the federal judges that had charged me with criminal contempt of court (for reporting federal crimes) who were identified by my CIA contacts as CIA assets who were working with agents of a foreign country to assassinate the person who is now our president.

Judge Patel's involvement in a scheme involving the assassination of a presidential candidate who then became president is very much in line with the actions she took to block my reporting of the criminal activities described within these pages. She compounded this felony by charging me with criminal contempt of court for filing federal actions seeking to report the federal crimes in which she was also involved. She caused me to be imprisoned in retaliation for attempting to report federal crimes that I had discovered up to 1990, and her actions were approved by other Ninth Circuit district judges, all of the Ninth Circuit Court of Appeal judges, and the Justices of the U.S. Supreme Court (as previously explained).

## INVOLVEMENT AND OBSTRUCTION OF JUSTICE BY OTHER NINTH CIRCUIT FEDERAL JUDGES

Commencing in 1974, I repeatedly encountered evidence showing that federal judges of the Ninth Circuit in San Francisco were heavily involved in blocking the reporting of the criminal activities. It was obvious that the obstruction of justice type of criminal activities perpetrated by federal judges would have other facets. My first CIA contact, Gunther Russbacher, confirmed this fact. During the latter half of 1993, Hunt also provided information confirming judicial misconduct.

In addition to the federal judges that he had already identified to me as being implicated, he learned that U.S. District Judges John V. Vukasin, Jr., and Wayne Brazil were protecting, along with Judges Patel and Walker, the various activities in which the CIA was involved. Hunt was in San Francisco to provide information on a CIA proprietary, COMTEL, that had filed Chapter 7 bankruptcy, leaving behind about fifty million in debt.

Hunt stated that a federal judge appointed as trustee a CIA contract agent, attorney Robert Damir, to prevent the creditors from learning that COMTEL was a CIA operation. After attending a creditors meeting on December 17, 1993, Hunt was aghast at the lawlessness in the proceedings. "Bob, that's what I have been discovering first hand since 1987," I replied. Hunt stated that a CIA law firm in San Francisco was acting to protect the CIA against exposure: Lafayette, McGee, Willis & Greenwages.

## FURTHER SUPPORT FOR THOSE WHO BELIEVE THE CIA WAS INVOLVED IN JFK'S ASSASSINATION

Much has been written about the role of CIA factions in the assassination of President John F. Kennedy. It isn't the purpose of this book to go into that subject. However, the statements of relatively high-ranking former or present ONI and Navy officers relating to the JFK assassination are given within these pages for the reader to ponder.

The role of deep-cover CIA officer, Trenton Parker, has been described in earlier pages, and his function in the CIA's counter-intelligence unit, Pegasus. Parker had stated to me earlier that a CIA faction was responsible for the murder of JFK, and that Kennedy was advised three weeks before the assassination of a plan to assassinate him in one of three cities that Kennedy would be visiting.

During an August 21, 1993, conversation, in response to my questions, Parker said that his Pegasus group had tape recordings of plans to assassinate Kennedy. I asked him, "What group were these tapes identifying?" Parker replied: "Rockefeller, Allen Dulles, Johnson of Texas, George Bush, and J. Edgar Hoover." I asked, "What was the nature of the conversations on these tapes?"

> *I don't have the tapes now, because all the tape recordings were turned over to [Congressman] Larry McDonald. But I listened to the tape recordings and there were conversations between Rockefeller, [J. Edgar] Hoover, where [Nelson] Rockefeller asks, "Are we going to have any problems?" And he said, "No, we aren't going to have any problems. I checked with Dulles. If they do their job we'll do our job." There are a whole bunch of tapes, because Hoover didn't realize that his phone has been tapped.*

Parker had earlier mentioned to me that he turned over a full box of files and tapes, documentation, and micro-fiche for the Pegasus operation in the Caribbean to Congressman McDonald shortly before the Congressman boarded the ill-fated Korean Airlines Flight 007 that was shot down by the Russians.

The November 1993 issue of *Penthouse* magazine had an in-depth article on Parker, in which federal agents sought to frame Parker and charge him with money-laundering. Parker had recognized one of the agents, and converted the Justice Department's scheme into a reverse-sting operation against them, using the techniques taught to him by the CIA. The government agents lost tens of thousands of dollars, not knowing that they had been recognized by Parker and were being taken.

Justice Department prosecutors were unaware of what had occurred, and charged Parker with money laundering. These federal charges were later dropped (in mid-1993) when Parker produced evidence that he was a member of the Office of Naval Intelligence and the CIA.

**FURTHER DETAILS FROM ANOTHER DEEP-COVER AGENT**

Another former deep-cover CIA agent who started contacting me in 1995 was Oswald LeWinter (alias Razine), who revealed his role as part of a CIA cleanup crew during the infamous October Surprise meeting in Paris. I discovered during conversations with LeWinter over a period of years, and cross-checks with other sources in the United States and Europe, that LeWinter was indeed involved in numerous CIA deep-cover operations. He proved helpful in providing confirmation and additional details on what I learned from other deep-cover sources.

He, as were Russbacher and Richard Brenneke, part of the CIA's Operation Gladio which brought about the downfall of the Italian government in the 1950s.

LeWinter described how the CIA made bribe payments for years to members of the German Parliament, bribing them to vote the way the CIA wanted them to vote. He stated that Kurt Waldheim was a CIA asset receiving CIA funds.

I had often wondered why presidential candidate George Bush selected Dan Quayle, a weak figure who couldn't add anything to his election chances, as his running mate. Possibly LeWinter had the answer. He stated that Quayle was running the Mena operation supplying arms to the Contras while he was vice-president to President George Bush. I had received other uncorroborated reports that Quayle, while a senator from Indiana, was working closely with CIA operations, and provided assistance to CIA asset John Hull when Hull was helping the CIA's arms and drug trafficking. (Hull is wanted on a murder charge in Costa Rica.)

Referring to Senator Richard G. Lugar (R-IN), LeWinter said that when Lugar was in the Navy, Lugar was liaison between the Chief of Naval Operations and the CIA. LeWinter stated that he was working for a group restructuring the intelligence community, which gave him access to archives and files that went back to the start of the CIA.

LeWinter stated that he first became connected with the CIA while he was a college professor in the 1960s, doing domestic spying for the CIA. The operation was conducted under a cover called the Council for Management and

Change. LeWinter said he was head of ITAC,[604] a secret CIA spy operation inside NATO headquarters.

LeWinter had worked closely with the CIA's James Angleton until the latter's death. LeWinter said that one of the things "Angleton confided in me was that he had turned Cardinal Giovanni Montini into an Agency asset, and until his death, Pope Paul VI was an asset of the CIA." LeWinter named other CIA assets that he had discovered while in the CIA, including CNN.

He stated that he had considerable information about CIA assassinations, including the assassination of General el Haq Zia, the head of Pakistan, in a plane crash. He stated that the CIA station chief in Delhi, India, convinced militants in India that Indira Gandhi had been murdered by the Pakistanis, encouraging them to retaliate.

LeWinter confirmed the status of Robert Hunt as being a former Navy Seal and involved in covert activities.

---

604 Intelligence Threat Analysis Center (ITAC).

# CIA-DEA DRUG ROLE IN PAN AM 103

Within a year of the December 21, 1988 downing of Pan Am Flight 103 over Lockerbie, Scotland, I started receiving information from CIA and other sources as to what actually happened. The information from these sources revealed why and how the bomb was placed on the aircraft, again showing the consequences of misconduct by U.S. activities.

**THE REASON FOR THE BOMB**

On July 3, 1988, the U.S.S. Vincennes shot down with a surface-to-air missile an Iranian airliner killing 290 people. The airliner was on a scheduled flight, on a heavily traveled civil airway, climbing through 12,000 feet, when the missile was launched. The explosion created indescribable horror as the occupants fell over two miles to their deaths. Obviously, Iran was outraged. Iran's Ayatollah was reported to have issued a fatwa, a Muslim proclamation that four U.S. airliners would be downed in retaliation. Iran then contracted with a terrorist group headed by Ahmed Jibril to bring about the downing of a U.S. commercial aircraft.

**ONE OF MANY CIA-DEA DRUG SMUGGLING OPERATIONS**

The CIA and DEA had an ongoing drug-smuggling operation with Lebanese and Syrian drug traffickers, using Pan Am aircraft out of Frankfurt that were departing for the United States. It was this drug smuggling operation that made possible the placement of the bomb on Pan Am Flight 103.

This is how the drug smuggling operation worked: A courier would check his bags at Pan Am in Frankfurt, and the bags would pass inspection. However, before the bags were placed on the aircraft, baggage handlers replaced one of the previously inspected bags with another bag containing approximately 200 pounds of heroin.

Jibril, paid to down a U.S. airliner, had no trouble using the CIA's own illegal operation to make possible the downing of Pan Am Flight 103. The Jibril group bribed the baggage handlers to place an additional bag in the baggage compartment, which contained the bomb. Because of a flight delay, the bomb that was set to explode over the North Atlantic exploded over Lockerbie.

At first, the United States recognized Jibril as the main suspect. But then the United States needed Syria's cooperation in attacking Iraq after Iraq invaded Kuwait. Since Syria was the home to one part of the CIA-DEA drug smuggling operation and also the terrorist group, Syria could not be exposed for harboring them. Further, exposing how the bomb was put on the aircraft risked exposing the CIA-DEA drug smuggling operation.

Justice Department officials then fabricated evidence and blamed two Libyans for placing the bomb on board Pan Am Flight 103. This story was believed primarily by the American public who did not have access to foreign media reports. Articles in the European press identified the false U.S. charges. German police, for instance, who knew about the CIA-DEA drug pipeline, gave no credence to the Justice Department's fabricated evidence and false charges.

In shifting the blame for the Pan Am deaths on the Libyans, the United States government was protecting the people who actually caused the tragedy. To make their argument sound legitimate, the United States ordered sanctions against Libya for refusing to turn over the two Libyans falsely charged by the United States with placing the bomb on Pan Am 103. European countries, recognizing the lack of credibility to the evidence and argument presented by the Justice Department, and knowing the facts, refused to go along with some of the sanctions demanded by the United States.

### DIA AGENT LESTER COLEMAN

Lester Coleman, a former agent for the Defense Intelligence Agency (DIA), worked for the DIA in the Middle East, including the DEA office in Nicosia from where the drug smuggling operation was monitored. Coleman worked alongside DEA agent-in-charge Michael Hurley, and according to Coleman and his book, Hurley monitored the CIA-DEA drug operation using Pan Am aircraft. Coleman and LeWinter said that Hurley was the DEA agent-in-charge of the area including world-famous CIA drug trafficking at Mena, Arkansas.

### TENTACLES OF INSLAW

While working alongside Hurley, Coleman discovered that the PROMIS software, stolen by Justice Department officials from the Inslaw company, was being sold by the DEA's Nicosia office. The sales involved a company called Eurame, which also dealt in the sale of drugs and arms. Coleman saw boxes of PROMIS software labeled PROMIS Ltd, Toronto, Canada in the DEA office at Nicosia. The software was installed by a CIA front-company, Link Systems, Ltd. The sale of this stolen software was another enterprise involving Michael Hurley, in addition to his role in the drug trafficking. PROMIS software sales had been made to Jordan, Iran, Iraq, Egypt, Turkey, Pakistan, and other countries.

### MULTIPLE RESPONSIBILITIES

Ironically, the same DEA agent, Michael Hurley, reportedly involved in the drug smuggling operation that brought about the deaths on Pan Am Flight 103, was subsequently transferred to Portland to falsely testify against Michael Riconosciuto. As stated in the Inslaw chapter, Justice Department officials threatened to retaliate against Riconosciuto if he testified in the Congressional hearings involving Justice Department misconduct in the Inslaw matter.

**EXPOSING GOVERNMENT CORRUPTION VIA A BOOK**

Disturbed about the government's involvement in downing Pan Am 103, and in drug smuggling, Coleman co-authored a book with Donald Goddard that was published in Great Britain, *Trail of the Octopus*, exposing the truth behind the bombing of Pan Am Flight 103.[605] Much of this information coincided with information that CIA agents had told me several years earlier.

**STANDARD GOVERNMENT RETALIATION**

A week before the book's publicized release date, Justice Department prosecutor Sean O'Shea filed two false charges against Coleman, intending to discredit what he was revealing. One charge was for an alleged passport violation and the other charge was for making an alleged false statement in the civil law suit involving the relatives against Pan American Airlines.

**SETTING HIM UP**

Shortly before being charged with the passport violation, his DIA handlers instructed him to return to Beirut after first obtaining a passport using a forged birth certificate given to him years earlier as a cover. After Coleman did this, Justice Department prosecutors charged him with making false statements on the passport application. The DIA either backed off from providing Coleman a defense, or was part of the scheme to silence and discredit Coleman.

**PERJURY CHARGE FOR REPORTING THE TRUTH**

Coleman had prepared an affidavit that was to be entered into the litigation against Pan Am by the relatives of the dead. Coleman had stated in the affidavit details of the CIA-DEA drug smuggling operation using Pan Am aircraft, and Justice Department prosecutors then charged him with perjury for revealing these criminal activities.

Without funds to hire legal counsel, and recognizing the slim chance of defending himself against the sham Justice Department charges, Coleman fled with his family to Sweden, where he was given political asylum.

In 1997 he decided to return and fight the charges, assisted by old friend, Alabama Governor Forst James, who arranged passage for the Coleman family and paid for the flight to the United States. Coleman was immediately arrested upon arriving in the United States, spending more time in prison waiting to be tried than the normal incarceration for such a violation.

**FILING FALSE CHARGES AGAINST FORMER MOSSAD AGENT AND HEAD OF INTERNATIONAL INVESTIGATIVE FIRM**

Juval Aviv was head of the international security firm, Interfor, based in New York, that was hired by Pan Am and its insurance carrier, U.S. Underwriters, to investigate how the bomb was placed on Pan Am Flight 103. Aviv and his firm discovered what Coleman had sought to expose, and wrote a detailed report to this effect. Pan Am's attorneys tried to introduce this evidence into the civil trial filed by relatives of the dead.

Justice Department prosecutors and the federal judge in the Pan Am litigation acted to prevent this information being presented to the jury. The next of kin probably preferred it this way. By withholding knowledge of the CIA-DEA drug operation, the relative's attorneys could argue that Pan Am's wilful

---

605 *Trail of the Octopus,* authored by Donald Goddard, Bloomsbury Publications, England. 1994.

negligence permitted the bomb to be put on the aircraft and was therefore responsible for the deaths.

Justice Department prosecutors retaliated against Aviv for exposing the CIA-DEA drug pipeline. They filed sham charges against Juval Avid in 1995, claiming that he made false claims in an investigative report submitted to the General Electric company five years earlier. General Electric never complained about the report and was very pleased with it. A federal jury in New York acquitted Aviv in early 1997, taking ten minutes to reach a decision.

**NO END TO THE FALSE PROSECUTION**

Justice Department prosecutors filed sham charges against lobbyist William Chasey, after Chasey sought to obtain meetings between Libya and the United States to show the errors behind the Justice Department's Pan Am 103 charges.

Justice Department prosecutors misused the power of that federal agency to silence or discredit others who sought to expose the truth behind the Pan Am bombing. They filed false charges against John Brennan, president of U.S. Underwriters, Pan Am's insurance carrier, after Brennan had authorized using information showing what really happened that allowed the bomb to be placed on board the ill-fated flight.

Sham charges were filed against the lead attorney defending Pan Am, Jim Shaughnessy. Even the head of the insurance company that paid for Aviv's investigation and hiring of legal counsel suffered government retaliation.

**IMMUNITY AGAINST THEIR CRIMINAL DEEDS**

It is a criminal offense[606] for *anyone*, including a Justice Department employee, to inflict harm upon a person for trying to report a federal crime. By fraudulently charging Coleman with a criminal offense for reporting the CIA-DEA drug smuggling operation, Justice Department employees committed serious criminal acts.

**BRITISH TELEVISION PRODUCER**

In 1995, I started communicating with European film producer Allan Francovich who had produced a 1994 documentary film, *The Maltese Doublecross*, revealing the truth associated with the downing of Pan Am Flight 103. The film showed the falsity of the evidence fabricated by Justice Department officials and showed that Libya and Libyans were not involved in the bombing. Appearing in the television documentary was one of my CIA sources, Oswald LeWinter, providing additional support to the CIA-DEA drug pipeline using Pan Am aircraft.

I had met Francovich when he was in Berkeley, California, unsuccessfully trying to find a station that would air his television documentary. We were in frequent contact thereafter on matters of mutual interest.

**CENSORSHIP IN THE UNITED STATES**

Francovich tried to have his television documentary played in the United States, but could not find any television station or cable operator who would handle such a sensitive matter despite its success in Europe.

---

606 Title 18 USC §§ 1512, 1513, plus the criminal offenses associated with obstruction of justice and related offenses.

Coleman experienced the same refusal by U.S. distributors to handle the distribution of his book, *Trail of the Octopus*. Several distributors had initially agreed to handle it, and then inexplicably backed down.

Even in Europe, the book was removed from book stores and reportedly the unsold books were shredded. As in many behind-the-scene activities, British authorities worked with the United States to cover up the truth behind the Pan Am deaths.

**USUAL U.S. MEDIA COMPLICITY OF SILENCE OR WORSE**

The U.S. mainstream media knew about the charges in the European press, books, and movies, disproving the Justice Department position. As in most of the government corruption described within these pages, the media kept the truth, or at least the opposing information, from the American public.

**WALL STREET JOURNAL ASSISTANCE**

Despite the evidence showing Justice Department prosecutors engaging in sham charges against Aviv, and despite the evidence showing Justice Department coverup of the true facts in the Pan Am tragedy, the *Wall Street Journal* published a lengthy December 18, 1995, article that greatly assisted the Justice Department's coverup. For those who didn't know the facts, the *Journal's* article discredited Aviv and the others who sought to expose the truth.

**GERMAN PRESS REVEALED PARTS OF THE STORY**

A partial English translation from the German magazine, *Focus*, was sent to me in 1996, revealing the interview between a Focus reporter and a CIA official in Washington.

**REVENGE WAS THE MOTIVE**

*"For the sake of the relatives of the 270 dead, find some culprits."*

In Potomac in the US State of Maryland, FOCUS spoke with a section chief of the CIA about the Lockerbie disaster and its background. The CIA staffer had been working during the past ten years in the field of the Middle East and in counter-terrorism. Without the assurance that his identity would not be revealed, the interview would not have taken place.

FOCUS: When did you find out who was responsible for the Lockerbie disaster?

CIA: From the beginning we had information about the Damascus-based PFLP-GC of Ahmed Jibril. The information said that this group blew up the airplane on orders of the Iranians. Out of revenge for the shooting down of an Iranian civil airliner over the Persian Gulf by the US Navy. We got the first proof for this story in February 1989. One of our Near Eastern agents, a member of a Palestinian group, took part in an Islamic conference in Tehran. He had been invited by the then Iranian Interior Minister, Al Akbar Mohtashemi. Earlier, he had been ambassador in Damascus and helped to build up the Lebanese terrorist organization Hizbollah.

FOCUS: What happened at this meeting in Tehran?

CIA: It was a meeting of the ten groups of so-called Palestinian rejectionist; the opponents of peace, and a Hizbollah delegation. Abu Nidal's people were also represented. Mohtashemi demanded more action from his guests against the USA and Israel. He criticized them because he considered them too lazy. That was like a whiplash for them. As sugar coating, he offered further financial support. Suddenly, he portrayed the PFLP-GC as a shining example. Ahmed Jibril looked around proudly.

FOCUS: What did this praise have to do with Lockerbie?

CIA: The others asked Jibril later on what Mohtashami meant, in personal conversations. Jibril finally admitted that he was responsible for the attack on Pan Am 103.

FOCUS: Did he confirm this to your agent too?

CIA: Yes.

FOCUS: Couldn't this just be a case of a terrorist who wanted to make himself look important? Did you learn more?

CIA: Our knowledge was very extensive. We learned, for example, that the Lockerbie bomb was built in Lebanon, in a camp of the PFLP-GC in the Bakaa Valley. The device was flown from Damascus to Berlin aboard Syrian Arab Airlines and given there to the German commando branch of Jibril's organization. This was led by Hafer Qessan Daikamouni, whom the German police later arrested. An American staffer of Pan Am [baggage handler?] smuggled the bomb on board Pan Am 103 in Frankfurt.

FOCUS: What was his motive?

CIA: Money and drugs from Lebanon. He was a drug addict.

FOCUS: Why this airliner specifically?

CIA: On board the jumbo there were drug investigators and intelligence colleagues. They were coming from the Middle East and wanted to fly home to their families for Christmas. The terrorists knew this.

FOCUS: Does your information on the real background come from one single Arab source?

CIA: No, of course not. We had many contacts, especially in Damascus.

FOCUS: Why didn't you simply confront the Syrians with this and demand that they take decisive measures against Jibril?

CIA: We did. Secretary of State James Baker flew to Damascus. He said to his colleague [Syrian Foreign Minister] Farouk al-Sharaa: "We know who it was." Sharaa answered: "Then prove it to me." We couldn't.

FOCUS: And that was that?

CIA: No, of course not. We took tougher political measures. But then overnight, the policy changed. Saddam Hussein had steamrolled over Kuwait, and Syria was needed in the grand coalition against its neighbor Iraq. We compelled Assad to take part in the Gulf war against Iraq.

FOCUS: The coalition won the war. Months later, Washington suddenly accused two Libyan secret agents and the entire regime from Colonel Qaddafi of having blown up the Pan Am Airliner. How does this all track?

CIA: Its Realpolitik. How could we unmask our partner during the tough weeks of the war as being behind one of the worst crimes of all times?

We had to spare Syria, but at the same time, also for the sake of the 270 relatives of those 270 dead, come up with a culprit. So we used the Libyans, with whom we have a traditionally tense relationship anyhow.

FOCUS: The US Navy wanted to bomb Qaddafi to death in 1985. Do you think that some day the truth about Lockerbie will be officially confirmed?

CIA: It's very doubtful whether my government can part ways with the Libya version. Too much has happened since 1991. The fronts have all grown too hard. The United Nations embargo has caused a lot of damage. And Syria? The country is on the threshold of peace with Israel. I don't exclude the possibility that this peace will be paid for with the knowledge about Lockerbie

**OTHER AIRLINERS SHOT DOWN BY U.S.**

The Iranian airliner was not the first one to be shot down by U.S. aircraft. In an attempt to kill the leader of a foreign country, U.S. and French aircraft shot several air-to-air missiles at what they thought was a passenger aircraft carrying Libyan Col. Moammar Gadhafi. (June 27, 1980.) Instead of killing the head of a foreign country, the attempted assassination succeeded in killing everyone on board an Italian passenger plane over the island of Ustica, just north of Sicily. Eighty one people were killed by that scheme. The *London Independent* reported this sequence of events, based upon documents obtained from the retired head of Italy's counterintelligence agency. (January 8, 1996)

**MYSTERIOUS DEATH OF FRANCOVICH AND DISAPPEARANCE OF HIGHLY SENSITIVE DOCUMENTS**

On April 22, 1997, Francovich was going through U.S. Customs in Houston, Texas, carrying documents for Coleman's defense and Aviv's civil damage trial against the government. During questioning by Customs agents he suddenly suffered a fatal heart attack. The highly sensitive papers that he was carrying then disappeared. Francovich's body was then taken by friends for a private autopsy to determine if he had been injected prior to his death by any of the drugs used to bring about a fatal heart attack. As they said, it would be easy in a crowd to simply prick someone with a needle containing the drug on its tip.

# CLINTON, MORE OF THE SAME

After Clinton was elected president of the United States by about forty-two percent of the votes cast, or about twenty percent of the eligible voters, his administration and its Justice Department halted all investigations and prosecution of the crimes related to Inslaw, October Surprise, CIA drug trafficking and money laundering, BNL, BCCI, and Iraqgate. He stacked key government offices, especially the Justice Department, with people who would protect him from his earlier acts while governor of Arkansas, some of whom were themselves implicated in various federal offenses.

## APPOINTING FRIENDS FOR DAMAGE CONTROL

One of Clinton's first acts was to remove key people in the Justice Department, including the FBI, who could charge him or his friends with criminal acts. The first to go was FBI Director William Sessions, who had announced his intention to investigate Justice Department officials in the BCCI coverup. Sessions was a "loose cannon" to high government people in both parties. Clinton took the unprecedented step of firing all U.S. Attorneys, thereby halting prosecution of people close to the president, including the president himself.

He appointed Webster Hubbell deputy attorney general, a position in which he was *de facto* head of **U.S. Department of Justice**. Hubbell was a law partner at the Rose Law Firm to Hillary Clinton, with connection to CIA-related Arkansas operations. Hubbell was later charged and confessed to criminal activities after he was forced to resign, ending up in federal prison. After having been charged with these offenses, Clinton stated that he had the utmost respect for Hubbell.

Clinton appointed Patsy Thomasson, who had connections to drug trafficking activities, to be director of White House administration. She had been a top aide to Clinton's friend and drug-trafficker, Dan Lasater, assisting in the operation of Lasater's Arkansas bond activities that involved drug-money laundering, and his Angel Fire Resort which was heavily involved in drug trafficking. She managed these operations while he was in prison on a drug-related offense. Among Patsy Thomasson's White House responsibilities were issuing security clearances, control of drug testing, and other sensitive matters. Ironically, several years after assuming her sensitive White House position, she was still unable to obtain a security clearance.

To control the U.S. Department of Transportation, Clinton appointed the former mayor of Denver, Federico Pena. Pena's primary credential was that he helped promote the new Denver International Airport. That airport project was riddled with corruption, involving key players from the Denver area HUD and savings and loan scandals, and involved CIA in looting of financial institutions.

Pena was appointed despite the many reports of influence peddling, payoffs, land flips, and fraud involving the Denver International Airport. The Republicans couldn't object to his appointment. To do so would threaten to expose aspects of the savings and loan scandal that have never been exposed by Congress or the mainstream media, and which occurred while the Republicans were in control of the White House and oversight administrative agencies.

CIA sources told me that Pena was paid a million and a half dollars for his help in getting Denver voters to approve the Denver Airport project. Pena had been involved with MDC Holdings and related groups, in which U.S. Attorney Michael Norton was also financially involved.

Former CIA operative Trenton Parker stated that he saw Vincent Foster, a senior partner in the Rose Law Firm, at that time, as one of the people he met at the infamous Mena, Arkansas airport during the 1980s while Parker was on CIA business. The group consisted of Vincent Foster; major drug trafficker Barry Seal; and Terry Reed, a CIA contract agent who sought to blow the whistle on CIA drug activities. Reed co-authored the book, *Compromise.*

Clinton appointed Ron Brown secretary of the U.S. Department of Commerce which was then followed by numerous investigations into Brown's alleged unlawful activities. Brown's death in a 1996 plane crash contributed to halting the investigations.

Appointed to the position of Under-Secretary of State for Global Affairs was Tim Wirth, who reportedly received nearly a quarter of a million dollars in campaign funds from insolvent savings and loans[607] and land developers. Despite the knowledge that junk bond purchases by savings and loans played a significance role in their failure, Wirth, as U.S. Senator, tried to block legislation which would have blocked any further junk bond purchasers.

Wirth was beholden to Denver attorney Norman Brownstein and Larry Mizel for millions of dollars used in his various congressional campaigns since 1974. Brownstein and Mizel were reportedly heavily involved in serious misconduct in the HUD and savings and loan scandals. Wirth was Chairman of the House Banking Committee's Subcommittee on Telecommunications and Finance from 1981 to 1986 while a Congressman from Colorado, during which time he protected the junk bond industry that inflicted great harm upon the American economy. Wirth's opposition to corrective actions continued long after it was obvious the corruption had to be stopped. (Among Mizel's many reported activities was an illegal kickback scheme in which subcontractors had to kick back money or be blackballed from future work.)

607 CIA-related Silverado, Lincoln, CenTrust, and Columbia Savings and Loans. The misconduct by these savings and loans cost the U.S. taxpayers, initially, over ten billion dollars, plus interest.

Wirth's opposition to addressing the savings and loan debacle was concurrent with receiving almost $200,000 from several savings and loan associations[608] that cost the taxpayers over $10 billion during the bailout. (All of these institutions had ties with the CIA.)

**COMING FROM ARKANSAS WITH HEAVY BAGGAGE**

Clinton had much to hide when he left Arkansas to assume the presidency of the United States. His misuse of government facilities and power to feed his sex drive, his use of drugs, his coverup of the CIA's unlawful arms shipments from Arkansas and related drug trafficking, were crimes. The diversion of taxpayer funds from Madison Guaranty Savings and Loan to his Whitewater Development investment didn't help. The mysterious deaths, killings, and beatings of people possessing information that would expose these corrupt activities added still further to Clinton's problems. He certainly needed a thick armor of protective officials in government. Fortunately for him, the U.S. media kept the lid on these major crimes.

**SAYING THE RIGHT THINGS**

Despite involvement and knowledge of questionable activities, the Clintons as attorneys and politicians, said the right things. Hillary Clinton, in a speech at the University of Pennsylvania in May 1993, stated "We have to believe that in the free exchange of ideas, justice will prevail over injustice." [609]

When Clinton was asked about smoking marijuana, his reply was that he "didn't inhale." He appeared on television while governor of Arkansas, attacking drugs as a scourge, and pleading with young people not to take drugs. Simultaneously, he was blocking investigation and prosecution of the heavy CIA-related drug activities in Arkansas in which his own friends and business associates were implicated. During his presidential campaign he lambasted the big time operators in the 1980s, while he helped cause the failure of Madison Guaranty Savings and Loan.

When he was accused of carrying on a sexual relationship with Gennifer Flowers and countless other women, he denied it, despite the massive evidence that the women's statements were true and his were false. Clinton's pattern of lies and misconduct, surrounding himself with the Arkansas crowd and young inexperienced personnel resulted in one fiasco after the other, exposing the United States to ridicule all over the world.

The scandals came once after the other. Travelgate (false charges and firing of long-time White House employee); Whitewater; bribes from foreign sources disguised as political contributions; the haircut fiasco in which traffic at Los Angeles Airport, one of the nation's busiest, was halted while Clinton waited for a barber to arrive and give him a haircut. (Many airlines and thousands of passengers were required to either circle in the air or divert to other airports, causing millions of dollars in extra costs and creating massive aircraft scheduling problems.) And of course much more.

**RON BROWN'S LOBBYING**

Brown was enmeshed in scandals throughout his career. In 1993, Brown

608 Silverado, Lincoln, CenTrust, and Columbia Savings and Loan associations.
609 Editorial Wall Street Journal, May 24, 1993.

was identified as having demanded the payment of $700,000 plus a percentage of sales in exchange for his help in lifting the trade embargo against Vietnam. At first, Brown and his attorney denied that Brown had any contact whatsoever with Vietnamese businessman Nguyen Van Hao, who allegedly arranged for the placement of the $700,000 in a secret bank account. Later, after evidence surfaced that this statement was false, Brown then admitted meeting several times with the Vietnamese business man and Vietnam government contact. After this information surfaced, President Clinton affirmed his support for Brown. The Clinton administration's Justice Department investigated itself and held that there was no evidence of wrongdoing.

Reference is made to the FBI agent, described elsewhere, who reported indictments about to be handed down against Brown and many business executives, and the sudden shut-down of the operation by Justice Department personnel, with shredding of the evidence.

**CLINTON'S PRACTICE OF DRUG COVERUP**

While Clinton was governor of Arkansas, he blocked investigation and prosecution of CIA drug trafficking and drug-money laundering. While governor he associated with and did business with known drug traffickers.

After Clinton became president of the United States, drug use was rampant in the White House, and key drug interdiction efforts were cut way back. As stated earlier, Patsy Thomasson, with her close ties to Lasater's drug operation, was given a key position in the White House staffing.

The San Francisco area legal newspaper, *Daily Journal*, wrote (July 21, 1994) that "the Clinton administration has been undermining existing anti-drug efforts on all fronts." The article accused Clinton of:

> *Dismantling almost the entire White House office created to lead the fight. It listed Surgeon General Joycelyn Elders repeated calls for drug legalization...government-led domestic marijuana eradication has been substantially curtailed...The president has ordered a massive reduction in Defense Department support for drug interdiction...proposed that Congress cut $100 million in drug-treatment funding and $130 million in drug-prevention education... For 1995, the president wants to cut 625 positions from federal drug enforcement agencies—the DEA, FBI, Border Patrol, U.S. Customs Service and others—and reduce federal drug-prosecution personnel by more than 100 positions.*

The drug history of White House personnel was so bad that security clearances could not be obtained for dozens of White House employees.

The London *Sunday Telegraph* (July 17, 1994) headlined an article, "Clinton took cocaine while in Office," and stated in part:

> *President Clinton faces potentially devastating allegations that he engaged in regular use of cocaine and marijuana during his rise to political prominence in Arkansas. The allegations, made in a series of exclusive interviews with The Sunday Telegraph, describe a drug habit that continued until the mid-1990s. Mr. Clinton's drug use...involved the systematic violation of the law when he was either a law professor, or in high office as Attorney General and later Governor of Arkansas. The Clinton administration has been criticized for cutting funding for the Coast Guard's*

*air and boat patrols and restricting sharing intelligence on drugs with other countries. The alleged use occurred in a variety of settings from 1972 to 1986; some of it involves stories of wild behavior at nightclubs and private parties. If the accounts are true they raise questions about how Mr. Clinton funded the alleged habit on his modest $35,000 income as Governor of Arkansas.*

Senator Lauch Faircloth, a member of the Banking Committee, properly articulated the danger of exposing Clinton's drug connections as he said, "If any credible evidence surfaces concerning drug use by President Clinton while he was Governor of Arkansas, it would be a national scandal."

**CLINTON'S TYSON CONNECTION**

Don Tyson and the Tyson companies made many financial contributions to the Clintons, and in return received protection against costly environmental and food-safety requirements. Arkansas regulatory agencies eliminated the costly requirement for waste disposal at Tyson's chicken processing plants. When the U.S. Department of Agriculture was requiring meat processing plants to provide safety inspections, the chicken processors were eliminated.

**TYSON'S REPORTED INVOLVEMENT IN DRUGS**

A January 21, 1981, confidential report by the Washington County Criminal Investigation Division described Don Tyson's[610] alleged involvement in drugs and his hiring of hit-men, as stated to the police by confidential informants. The report describing the statements made by informants stated in part:

*Don Tyson...is involved in drug traffic and stolen property....Tyson has been operating a Crystal Methamphetamine lab that was located at the Swepco Generator Plant....Most of the product of this drug lab are being passed on the campus of the University of Arkansas at Fayetteville. TYSON brings in his supplies for his lab in his trucks that haul frozen chickens.*

*An associate of TYSON was now ex-sheriff HERB MARSHALL...was to have been furnishing confiscated weapons to TYSON for sale....Also involved with the stolen guns is Joe Starr,...operator of Springdale Farms. Starr also is involved in purchasing cocaine and marijuana and hires the runners to distribute it. STARR and TYSON work together in the narcotics and stolen gun dealings.*

*CLINT SPENCER,...operator of the Spencer Bonding Agency in Fayetteville is said to work for TYSON as a hit man. Drug dealers that owe Tyson money were tracked down by Spencer and said to have been found missing and not to be heard of again.*

*Runners for TYSON are said to be: 1. RICK DOLAN,...; 2. BOBBY CARSLIE,...; 3. CHARLES AGEE,...; 4. LARRY HACKINS,...; 5. MORTON MARSHALL,...also jailer at the Washington County Jail.*

*Am-Vet's Club in Fayetteville...has the same ownership as TOMMY's Lounge in Springdale, being CHUCK, last name unknown, was paying the Washington County Sheriff's Office for protection in the past and some of TYSON's drugs goes through these clubs.*

610 Don Tyson's mother and father were killed in an automobile accident, and Don Tyson took over the business.

In 1994, the media focused on the favoritism shown to Tyson Foods, and the funding of Clinton's campaigns and perks bestowed upon the head of the U.S. Department of Agriculture, Mike Espy. But there was much more about the Tyson connection that the mainstream media did not divulge, similar to withholding information about the Arkansas CIA drug trafficking and drug-money laundering.

An August 10, 1984, DEA report[611] stated in part:

*On July 5, 1984, SMQ-84-0019 telephoned [investigator] at the Tucson District Office concerning narcotic trafficking by Donald J. TYSON in and around the area of Fayetteville, Arkansas....had information concerning heroin, cocaine and marijuana trafficking in the States of Arkansas, Texas, and Missouri by the TYSON organization....Alex MONTEZ and Donald KEMP, who are believed to be Lieutenants for Donald TYSON....The CI [confidential informant] got involved with the TYSON organization...the CI learned of a location called "THE BARN" which TYSON used as a "stash" location for large quantities of marijuana and cocaine. "THE BARN" area is located between Springdale and Fayetteville, Arkansas, and, from the outside, the appearance of "THE BARN" looks run down. On the inside of "THE BARN" it is quite plush. The CI Also learned that Donald TYSON has all of the narcotics related meetings at the Ramada Inn in Fayetteville, Arkansas, and those meetings are usually concerning the business in and around "THE BARN."...In March 1978,* [redacted], *in a state of intoxication, stated to the CI, "Daddy Don (Donald TYSON) can put out the word to take care of you, and Alex MONTEZ will leave you in a culvert, but somebody else will take the blame for it."*

Another report by the Criminal Investigation Section, dated October 26, 1981, stated in part:

*The following information received from Sgt* [redacted], *Training Division, Little Rock, Arkansas. SGT* [redacted] *advised that he received information from an informant, who told that DON TYSON of Tyson Food Industries in Springdale, Arkansas, owns a company aircraft, which is being utilized to smuggle drugs from Florida to Springdale.*

An October 20, 1986, report on drug trafficking activities by the Federal Bureau of Investigation stated in part:

*Mr. LOCKE stated he became associated with DAN LASATER during the mid-1970s. In 1980, along with DAVID COLLINS and DAN LASATER, he became a partner in the formation of COLLINS, LOCKE, AND LASATER (CL&L), a banking investment firm. LOCKE stated he was a member of the Arkansas State Legislature during this time, and also employed as a salesman for CL&L. Mr. LOCKE admitted the use of cocaine during business meetings when DAVID COLLINS and DAN LASATER were present.*

611 File number GF140-34-4046.

Another DEA report dated December 14, 1982, stated in part:

*Sgt. Myres advised that he had received information from confidential sources indicating that PRIDEAUX's sources for cocaine is a Don TYSON, who owns TYSON INDUSTRIES in Springdale, Arkansas. Sgt. Myres also advised that his source said that TYSON smuggles cocaine from Colombia, South America inside race horses to Hot Springs, Arkansas....Sgt. Myres's source also stated that a Dale LNU is a runner for TYSON and delivered cocaine to PRIDEAX.*

For indexing purposes that report identified Tyson as follows: 2. TYSON, Don J.- NADDIS 470067, aka "CHICKEN MAN", owns Tyson Industries, Springdale, Arkansas.

Another report identified as LR 245F-2, relating to an investigation of George Edward Locke stated in part:

*Mr. Locke advised it was his understanding that CRAIG CAMPBELL was the source of cocaine for Jack Stephens during a time JACK STEPHENS was having problems regarding alcohol consumption.*

A September 8, 1986, report related to questioning of Dan Lasater's pilot, Ronald P. Ziller, stated in part:

*Mr. Ziller stated he went to work for Lasater in July of 1983 and was fired December, 1984. He was chief pilot of the Canadian Air Challenger, CL 600DL and co-pilot of the Lear Jet, 100DL.... When asked about the use of cocaine by members of the firm, Collins, Locke, and Lasater, and their friends, he stated that [he] had heard stories of its wide use by some members of the firm.*

*Mr. Ziller was asked about any flights outside of the U.S. that Dan Lasater or any other member of the firm might have had with him as pilot. He stated that on the 8th of February, 1984, he flew Dan Lasater, Patsy Thomasson, to Belize to look at a horse farm that was for sale by a Roy Carver....Some of these trips were made with Roger Clinton as a passenger.*

Dan Lasater was sentenced to prison for his drug trafficking occurring in Arkansas, and before leaving for prison he signed a Durable Power of Attorney on June 24, 1987, naming Patsy L. Thomasson as his agent and attorney-in-fact. On the three-page document, under Certificate of Incumbency, filed with the Arkansas Secretary of State, Patsy Thomasson was named president of The Phoenix Group, Inc., the Angel Fire Corporation, and Portfolio Services, Inc.

Speaker of the house Newt Gingrich said (December 5, 1994, CNN) that a quarter of the White House staff had used drugs during the past year. Considering the many Arkansas cronies that were taken to the White House, this news is hardly unexpected.

## QUESTIONABLE RELATIONSHIPS

Dan Lasater's company received much of the state funneled money for bonds that laundered drug money until Lasater went to prison for drug distribution. After Lasater went to prison, Clinton had Stephens' companies handle the bond-writing. Stephens is the company that brought the illegal and corrupt BCCI bank into the United States by enabling BCCI to take control of certain U.S. banks in violation of U.S. law.

**PATTERN OF QUESTIONABLE DEATHS ASSOCIATED WITH CLINTON AND CIA ACTIVITIES IN ARKANSAS**

A pattern of killings, mysterious deaths and beatings surround the activities of Bill Clinton and the CIA activities in Arkansas with which Clinton was involved. The nature of these deaths and beatings occurring to people who knew of corrupt activities of either Clinton or the CIA strongly suggest that they occurred to silence the victims. It is inconceivable that so many would suffer so greatly simply because they were associated with Clinton or the CIA, unless someone felt they could expose misconduct that affected national interests.

**THE QUESTIONABLE DEATH OF VINCENT FOSTER**

Another matter with serious implications was the mysterious death of White House counsel Vincent Foster, which had strong overtones of being murder. Foster, a partner in the Rose Law Firm, who was involved in many questionable activities surrounding Governor Clinton was found dead in Fort Marcy Park, Virginia on July 20, 1994. His death occurred shortly before the various Arkansas scandals started to emerge in the British and U.S. press.

There were unprecedented irregularities associated with Foster's death and the subsequent investigation, and as the facts became known, it was obvious that Foster was murdered and that the usual coverup was occurring.

Despite the fact that Foster's death was the highest official since JFK's assassination to be shot while in office, the FBI did not investigate. Instead, the Park Police were allowed to investigate the death of this high federal official despite the fact that the park police had virtually no expertise in this area.

The person who discovered Foster's body notified a park worker, and then left. This person eventually contacted Washington talk show host G. Gordon Liddy, telling him repeatedly that "there was no gun in his hand." The witness told Liddy why he didn't report finding the body to the police, "I don't want to end up like that guy I found."

Park police reports said that Foster's right hand held the gun. The person who found Foster's body stated positively that there was no gun in Foster's hand. There were many other irregularities, indicating that Foster had been killed elsewhere and then his body taken to where it was found. The evidence indicating that Foster was killed included, for instance:

(1) There was virtually no blood at the scene, which was highly improbable with a gunshot wound into the mouth.

(2) The little blood that was on Foster's face ran uphill in relation to how the body was neatly positioned to the slope.

(3) Semen was found on his underwear, indicating sexual activity on the day of his death. There was no attempt to find out why. Was he lured into a sexual encounter and then killed?

(4) Blonde female hair was found on his clothes. No attempt was made to investigate this matter.

(5) Carpet fibers were found on Foster's clothes, as if he was rolled in a carpet. No attempt was made to identify the source of the fibers.

(6) No fingerprints were found on the gun.

(7) The gun was found in Foster's right hand. He was left-handed.

(8) The neatly clutched gun in Foster's hand despite the fact that the explosive

recoil would have jerked the gun away.

(9) Foster's body was neatly positioned on the ground, with both hands neatly placed alongside the body, despite the body reaction occurring after the head was hit by a bullet.

(10) He allegedly walked on 600 feet of dirt and through knee-high shrubbery without any evidence of dirt or shrubbery on the soles of his shoes or clothes.

(11) Three handwriting specialists[612] held during a news conference that the Foster suicide note was a forgery.

(12) Foster's glasses were inexplicably found 13 feet from his body in dense foliage.

(13) Eyewitnesses, such as the person who found Foster's body, were not called to testify.

(14) Pattern of obfuscation and secrecy by White House, Justice Department, and U.S. Park Police, indicative of coverup.

(15) Critical pictures of the death scene disappeared.

(16) Refusal to allow the FBI to investigate Foster's death, leaving the investigation of the highest federal official to be killed since the JFK assassination in the hands of Park Police who had virtually no experience in this area.

(17) Failure to find the bullet despite an exhaustive search added another element of suspicion on top of evidence proving that Foster did not walk to the death scene.

Other irregularities exist that point toward murder, most of which went unreported by the mainstream media.

**COVERUP TYPE OF "INVESTIGATION"**

In addition to this evidence of foul play, there was the coverup that could be expected to follow on the heels of the above signs of murder.

(1) White House counsel Bernard Nussbaum blocked the Park Police from examining Foster's files in the White House.

(2) The files were then secretly removed from the White House, despite their obvious value in investigation of Foster's death.

(3) Many of Foster's files were shredded by the Rose Law Firm.

(4) A subpoena was arranged to keep Foster files from investigators.

(5) The U.S. Park Police refused to release the autopsy report, and then quickly ruled the death a suicide.

(6) No grand jury was convened to investigate the evidence.

(7) None of the people contacted by the Park Police were put under oath.

(8) FBI Director William Sessions was fired by Clinton the day after Foster's death, leaving the FBI without a leader and hampering a proper investigation.

(9) A relatively inexperienced officer of the Park Police was put in charge of the investigation.

(10) Park police gave away possible valuable evidence (pager, personal clothing) the day after the death, when such items could provide important evidence.

612 Vincent Scalice, former New York police department homicide expert; Reginald Alton, Oxford University manuscript expert; and Ronald Rice, Boston private investigator.

(11) Pictures of the death scene were lost. Since the death related to the highest federal official to die under mysterious circumstances since JFK's death, it is hardly likely that they were simply lost.

(12) Park Police told Fiske's investigators that X-rays of Foster's body were not obtained, when Park Police reports state X-rays were taken.

(13) None of the neighbors at the death scene were interviewed.

(14) Fiske investigators pressured the person who first found the body to change his statements about the crime scene (The person had clearly stated initially that he saw both hands and that neither of them held a gun, while Park Police reported a gun in Foster's right hand).

(15) Observations by first people on the scene of additional wounds on Foster's head were not recorded on official reports.

(16) Later FBI medical reports reported two drugs in Foster's blood when the first medical examiner didn't find any.

(17) Note found in Foster's briefcase, under mysterious circumstances, was torn into over two dozen pieces, without leaving any finger prints.

(18) Government refusal to release the medical examiner's report.

Because of these suspicious circumstances, the *Wall Street Journal* filed a federal lawsuit under the Freedom of Information Act seeking to obtain the autopsy report on Foster. Clinton's Justice Department refused to release the report, despite the fact that unless there was a murder with political implications, there could not possibly be any justification for refusing to release it. The special counsel appointed by the Justice Department, Robert Fiske, also refused to release the autopsy report to the public, simultaneously stating that the death was a suicide. If so, why couldn't the autopsy report be released?

The Western Journalism Center had a full-page announcement in the *New York Times* on August 28, 1994, raising these same points and more. Many of these same points were raised in other reports. On June 4, 1995, *Accuracy in Media*, had a full page ad in the New York Times, listing the many irregularities in the Foster death, and chastising the mainstream media for not pursuing the matter, and alleging that the death was not a suicide. The *New York Post*, the *Johnson-Smick Report*, *Accuracy in Media*, and many other publications, also raised doubts about the reported suicide, as they reported that Foster's death appeared to be murder, associated with a massive coverup.

## CONTINUING THE PATTERN OF COVERUPS BY INDEPENDENT COUNSELS

Independent counsel Kenneth Starr issued a statement in July 1997 stating that Foster had committed suicide. I know of no independent counsel "investigation" that did not cover up for hard-core misconduct, including of course, October Surprise, Iran-Contra, and Inslaw. Starr's performance, his continued legal representation of clients, some with conflicting interests, portrayed an impending coverup.

## FOREIGN MEDIA CIRCUMVENTS U.S. MEDIA COVERUP

The *London Sunday Telegraph* exposed many of the scandals occurring in the Clinton Administration, many of the articles written by Washington-based columnist Ambrose Pritchard. The *Sunday Telegraph* was at the forefront reporting the illegal arms sales in the Iran-Contra affair, while the U.S.

mainstream press kept the lid on the scandal. The *Telegraph* was years ahead of the mainstream American press in revealing the massive CIA drug trafficking into the United States. It was far ahead in exposing the murder of Vincent Foster and his secret foreign travels.

**FOSTER'S SECRET EUROPEAN TRIPS**

Foster apparently made several secret trips to Switzerland, catching a return flight to the United States within hours of his arrival. A *London Sunday Telegraph* article stated in part:

> *The records show that Foster bought a ticket to Switzerland during that early phase of the Clinton presidential bid—traveling on American Airlines from Little Rock to Paris with a connection to Geneva on Swiss Air. The return flight was booked for November 3, giving him less than one full day on the ground in Switzerland. The cost was $1,490.*
>
> *A year later he did exactly the same thing, darting in and out of the country on December 7, 1992—during the presidential transition period—he bought a ticket from Little Rock to Geneva, via Paris, returning on December 9.*
>
> *Finally, on July 1, 1993, he purchased a ticket through the White House Travel Office from Washington to Geneva on TWA and Swiss Air, reimbursing the White House from his personal American Express card. But he never made the trip and was refunded by Swiss Air on July 8.*
>
> *Several days later [on July 20, 1993], he was found dead in a Virginia park next to the residence of the Saudi ambassador.... Independent experts have described the crime scene as a textbook case of a murder made to look like a suicide.*
>
> *These are only a sample of the flights, not the full picture. On December 20, 1988, for example, he flew to Batman in remote Turkish Kurdistan. At his death he had built up more than 500,000 "air-miles" on the frequent flier programs of major U.S. Airlines. On Delta he apparently built up 197,853 miles. Much of it came from flying overseas. His foreign flights on Delta during the late 1980s and early 1990s were often purchased at "executive fares," a category of discount available only to senior government officials—or contract operatives doing work for the federal government. That raises the question: was Foster a U.S. agent at a time when he was ostensibly in private practice as a Little Rock lawyer?*
>
> *Sources close to the Foster family say that his widow, Lisa, was not aware of any trips he made to Switzerland, which suggests that he was not engaged in routine work for the Rose Law Firm.*
>
> *A psychiatrist told the FBI that he was contacted on July 16, 1993, by Foster's sister, Sheila Anthony, a top official at the Justice Department. She told him that Foster was working on "top secret" issues at the White House and "that his depression was directly related to highly sensitive and confidential matters."*
>
> *Many in Washington believe that the investigation by Robert Fiske last year was a charade and a black mark on the American judicial system. It reached the conclusion that Foster committed suicide before much of the forensic evidence had been analyzed by the FBI crime labs, before*

*key witnesses had been interviewed, and before the autopsy review by independent experts. Several of the FBI documents appear to have been doctored. One official close to the investigation has described the scale of lying and fabrication by government officials as staggering.*

*What is it about the death of Vince Foster that has caused every investigation to recoil? First, the U.S. Park Police, then the Fiske investigation, then the Senate Banking Committee and now, perhaps, Kenneth Starr's team.*

**FURTHER SUPPORT FOR THE SECRET TRIPS**

One of my sources, Leo Wanta, had European meetings scheduled with Vincent Foster. Wanta was involved in international currency dealings. Wanta started communicating with me in July 1995, describing his activities with the CIA, the role he played in destablizing the Russian ruble, his contacts with Vincent Foster, and other activities involving sophisticated global money matters. Some of Wanta's activities destabilizing the USSR economy were described in *Thieves' World*.[613]

Wanta said that he had a scheduled meeting in Europe to meet Vincent Foster involving currency transactions. This coincided with the travel plans described by the London *Sunday Telegraph* and also by former associate editor at Forbes Magazine, James Norman.

Wanta said that Vincent Foster and William Barr were working together in moving huge quantities of U.S. dollars in Europe. Foster was scheduled to meet with a financial group to finalize his monetary request for $250 million in favor of the Children's Defense Fund, allegedly a front for surreptitious activities. The meeting was scheduled in Geneva for July 7, 1993. (Foster died on July 20, 1993.) Hotel reservations were made by Wanta's group for Foster for July 7, 1993.

Wanta said that Robert Nash, formerly of Arkansas Development Finance Authority (ADFA) was involved, and had reportedly transmitted funds to the Wanta group to cover currency transactions. Wanta said that Nash has remitted $500,000 for initial currency trading to the Bank of China. ADFA did considerable foreign currency trading and other financial transactions in overseas markets. President Bill Clinton appointed Nash to a position in the U.S. Department of Defense.

Vincent Foster had requested from AmeriTrust Corporation, in which Wanta was involved, $250 million over a 24 month period from U.S. government proceeds of bank debenture contracts approved by Richard Breeden of Securities Exchange Commission and U.S. State Department. This required the approval of the U.S. Treasury.

Foster was assisting Wanta on various sensitive projects, involving U.S. attorney Joe Donahue, Richard Secord, Eduarde Schevardnadze of the Republic of Georgia. Wanta's scheduled July 1993 meeting with Foster in Tbilisis, Georgia concerned these projects.

Foster was working with Wanta to obtain for Wanta diplomatic appointment for Somalia, and the delivery of 90 million barrels of Saudi light oil to Houston,

613 *Thieves' World*, Claire Sterling, Simon & Shuster.

Texas, under contract with White Cloud Petroleum Corporation of Delaware, and MiApollo Investments Limited.

The July 7, 1993 scheduled meeting with Foster never occurred as on July 7, 1993 Wanta was arrested in Lausanne, Switzerland, on a warrant from Wisconsin for alleged tax evasion. This may explain why Foster canceled his TWA plane reservation to Europe.

Wanta described the operations of AmeriChina Global Management Group, Ltd, that was a CIA operation, working in close contact with a CIA group aligned with former CIA director Bill Casey. He described AmeriTrust as a group that handles sensitive U.S. government contracts in prime bank debentures and currency movements. Wanta referred to the involvement in these currency transactions by covert agencies, referring to them as MiApollo.[614]

Wanta was working with U.S. and Russian Mafia figures, including Jack Tremonti and Martin Gulewicz. Tremonti was believed initially associated with the Mafia in Detroit. Gulewicz had been involved in drug trafficking. One of Wanta's companies was called New Republic Financial Group. Another company involved in the currency trading, Global Tactical Services, based in Duncan, Oklahoma, was headed by Tremonti. It is believed that Wanta and those he worked with had reduced the value of the ruble about 50 percent in mid-1990, through fraudulent currency transactions. It is also believed that they had the protection of the CIA and other intelligence agencies during this period.

Wanta said that the United States government issued executive orders to assist Russian programs, and then defeated the programs. Instead of using these programs to strengthen their economy, the KGB dumped massive amounts of Russian rubles, that were cash reserves, to Asian/Aneko. This devalued their own currency, but provided them huge personal gain.

Wanta said that he was the coordinator for the U.S. government and USSR-Russian partner in Russia. He also described how Saudi Arabia's King Fahd authorized a $90 million humanitarian grant under Operation Restore Hope,

## PATTERN OF ASSASSINATIONS, MYSTERIOUS DEATHS, BRUTAL PHYSICAL ATTACKS, AND WARNINGS

The threats, beatings, killings, and mysterious deaths of people who had information relating to Clinton or the CIA Arkansas activities, continued after Clinton became president. At least half a dozen people were murdered who posed a threat of exposure.

## CONVENIENT DEATHS

**Luther "Jerry" Parks**, a private investigator employed to provide security for Governor Clinton during the presidential campaign, had accumulated a file on Clinton's activities, including drug use and sexual escapades. When this file became known to Clinton, the phone lines were cut, the burglar alarm disabled, and the file stolen from Parks' home. Later, Park was ambushed and killed in his car on September 26, 1993, as a result of repeated shots, indicating a determination that he be killed. Shortly after his murder, federal investigators were pulled off the case by the Clinton administration.

614 "M" stands for military; "I" stands for intelligence. Military-intelligence-Apollo.

**Kathy Ferguson**, the former wife of an Arkansas state trooper, was found dead in her Sherwood, Arkansas home on May 11, 1994, a week after her former husband was named as a defendant with Bill Clinton in the Paula Jones sexual harassment suit. Arkansas authorities quickly ruled her death a suicide. She had earlier told fellow employees that the charges of Clinton's sexual escapades were true and that her former husband had described Clinton's activities to her.

**Bill Shelton**, the boy friend of Kathy Ferguson, was found shot to death on her grave on June 12, 1994. The Arkansas coroner quickly ruled the death a suicide. It could be expected that Kathy Ferguson told Shelton about any information given to her about Clinton by her former husband.

**Jon Walker** fell to his death on August 15, 1993, from the Lincoln Towers building in Arlington, Virginia. He had been an investigator for the Resolution Trust Corporation and had reported to the Kansas City regional office of RTC that a suspicious association existed between Whitewater Development and Madison Guaranty Savings and Loan in Arkansas, and Bill and Hillary Clinton.

**Kevin Ives**, who was murdered by blows on the head, was also placed on the railroad tracks, in an attempt to name the cause of deaths as accidental. The boys had been camping near a small airstrip where drug trafficking regularly occurred. State coroner Fahmy Malack, who assisted in the coverup of the murders by calling the murders accidental, was protected by Clinton. Ives' mother obtained an autopsy from another source, which substantiated the actual cause of death.

In another murder case and coverup, Malack ruled that the person, James Dewey, had committed suicide, despite the fact that he was decapitated. When Clinton's mother, who was a physiotherapist, was found guilty in the death of two patients, Malak came to Clinton's defense, claiming that the deaths were suicide. Clinton argued to defend Malak, claiming Malak was "stressed out" and under-paid. Despite the obvious coverup of murders by Malak, Clinton recommended that Malak receive a forty percent salary increase. Eventually the media couldn't keep the lid on these activities and Malak was removed from office. Clinton then found another job for him, paying over $80,000 per year. It pays to have friends in high places.

**Don Henry**, a young boy who was with Kevin Ives. He was stabbed in the back and his body placed on the railroad tracks, where it was run over by a train.

**Stanley Huggins**, who in 1987 reported corrupt loan practices by Madison Guaranty Savings & Loan. On June 23, 1994, he was found dead in Delaware, reportedly of viral pneumonia. Huggins was an attorney with the Memphis law firm of Huggins & Associates. He had helped produce a 350-page report on Madison Guaranty Savings & Loan.

**Ronald Rogers**, a pilot, knew much about Clinton's wrongdoings. He was killed in a suspicious plane crash hours before he was to be interviewed for the taping of the *Clinton Chronicles*.

**C. Vincent Raiser II**, a Washington lawyer, was killed in a plane crash on July 30, 1992, near Dillingham, Alaska. He was the national finance co-chairman of Clinton's presidential campaign, and a former legal counsel in the Washington law firm of Jones, Day, Reavis & Pogue. He was chairman of the

American Mobile Satellite Corporation, a telecommunications company used by federal police agencies.

**Herschel Friday**, a member of Raiser's committee, was killed on March 1, 1994, as his plane crashed and exploded during a landing at a private airstrip.

**Ed Willey**, former member of Clinton's presidential campaign finance committee, allegedly shot himself on November 30, 1993.

**Barry Seal**, who had a great amount of information on CIA drug and drug-money trafficking, and involvement of Arkansas officials, was shot and killed.

**Keith Coney**, who claimed he had knowledge regarding the deaths of Ives and Henry, was killed as he was fleeing from assailants.

**John A. Wilson,** councilman in Washington, DC, shortly before giving a speech about Clinton's activities, "hung himself" on May 19, 1993.

**Gregory Collins**, who claimed to have knowledge of several of these killings, was himself shot.

**Keith McKaskle**, who also claimed to have knowledge of several of these killings, was stabbed at his home.

**Jeff Rhodes**, who claimed to have knowledge of the deaths of Henry and Ives, found shot to death in the city dumps.

**Richard Winters**, claiming knowledge of several of these deaths, killed by a shotgun blast.

**Jordan Ketelson**, claiming knowledge of several of these deaths, killed by a shotgun blast in his driveway, and ruled a suicide.

**Dennis Patrick**, familiar with drug-money laundering at Lasater and Company, and an expected witness, survived three attempts to kill him. His name had been fraudulently used by Lasater & Company as an account in which tens of millions of dollars were transacted. Four men were charged in the attacks upon Patrick.

**Gary Johnson**, the attorney for Larry Nichols, was severely beaten and left for dead, after two thugs demanded the video tapes of Governor Clinton entering Gennifer Flowers' apartment. Johnson represented one of Bill Clinton's adversaries in a law suit. Besides the fact he represented Nichols in the law suit, Clinton had a more important reason for seeing Johnson dead. Johnson's apartment was across the hall from Gennifer Flowers, one of Clinton's sexual partners. Johnson had a security camera rigged to show who was at his door, and this security camera also recorded who entered the apartment of Jennifer Flowers. When this information became known, the thugs went to Johnson's apartment, obtained the tapes, and then severely beat Johnson, leaving him for dead. His spleen and bladder were ruptured, his collar bone broken, his sinus cavities crushed, his elbows broken, among other injuries. Only Clinton had a motive for getting those tapes and silencing Johnson. True to form, the mainstream media published virtually nothing about this beating and its implications.

**E.J. Davis.** An investigative reporter for the *American Spectator*, he was knocked unconscious (February 14, 1994) as he returned to his hotel room after conducting a series of interviews that reflected poorly on Clinton. He had been contacting people in Arkansas who furnished information on one or more areas of misconduct in which Clinton was involved. Davis' list of contacts had been stolen after he was knocked unconscious. Mainstream newspapers ridiculed the story, claiming that Davis was drunk.

**Sally Purdue**, a former Arkansas beauty queen, one of Clinton's sexual conquests, lost her job and was threatened with physical violence if she spoke out, adding that they would break her legs.

**Terry Reed,** a former CIA agent in Arkansas, familiar with some of the drug trafficking, drug-money laundering, and its association with Lasater and Company and with Bill Clinton, published a book in 1994 (*Compromised*) detailing these facts. On April 23, 1994, while Reed was signing copies of his book at a Little Rock Wal-Mart store, a death threat was put into his car. The note stated,

> *Stay Out Of the Federal Court NEXT MONTH or YOU die. It Is All Over for You AND for your children If you PRESS Ahead. Hint: Grab Your Passport.*

Reed had filed in 1994 a civil rights lawsuit against Governor Clinton's head of security, Buddy Young, and a former Arkansas State Trooper, Tommy Baker.

## CONTINUING PATTERN OF COVERUP BY THE CLINTON GANG

In July 1993, I sent to Attorney General Janet Reno a copy of *Defrauding America* and related information, requesting that I be allowed to present my testimony and that of several CIA and other deep-cover CIA assets in support of my charges of high-level criminal activities. Under federal crime-reporting statutes, she had a duty to receive our evidence of criminal activities. We were all insiders and privy to the criminal activities.

Answering for the attorney general, the Criminal Division of the U.S. Department of Justice wrote:

> *You allege...a litany of hard-core criminal activities against the United States by a large and well-orchestrated group of federal personnel in all three branches of the federal government.... We have carefully reviewed your letters and your book. The allegations you make, while serious, are unsupported by credible evidence and fail to support your claim of persecution. Accordingly, we will take no further action in response to your letters.*

Obviously, the boxes of evidence, and our testimony, could not be presented in a first letter, or any series of letters. Obviously, it required more than my initial letter to make any determination about the validity of my allegations. It would require my sworn testimony and that of my CIA and other contacts, and an examination of my evidence.

Speaking before a NAACP group on November 13, 1993, Attorney General Janet Reno vowed that the law represented all Americans and that enforcing civil rights laws was a top priority of the Justice Department. She said this as Justice Department prosecutors were seeking to return me to prison in retaliation for having filed federal actions under the mandatory crime-reporting statute (18 USC Section 4), in which I sought to report the criminal activities described within these pages. Her bankruptcy trustee division was also liquidating my life's assets that had been corruptly seized after I sought refuge in Chapter 11 from the pattern of civil rights violations described in earlier pages.

Continuing her PR speech, Reno said:[615]

*The law is a splendid instrument to do right. If I don't do anything else in the time I have as attorney general, I want to make sure the law and the Department of Justice become an accurate symbol for everyone of what is right. All my life, my mother and father raised me to believe that civil rights enforcement was the most important thing the Department of Justice can do. [Did they really say that!]*

That was too much. I took this opportunity to send the attorney general a letter that again put her on notice of the criminal and subversive activities that I, a former federal investigator, and my many intelligence agency sources discovered.

**FIRING EDITOR FOR WRITING ARTICLE ON FOSTER'S DEATH**

Various reporters were fired when they wrote articles on one or more of the Clinton scandals. For instance, in 1996, Jim Norman, one of the senior editors at Forbes magazine, prepared an article for the magazine, describing Foster's secret trips to Europe and his money-laundering activities. Forbes refused to publish the article and then fired him.

**INVESTIGATOR QUITTING BECAUSE OF COVERUP**

The lead prosecutor investigating Foster's death, Miguel Rodriguez, and his assistant, resigned on March 20, 1995, because he objected to the coverup by special investigator Starr. Rodriguez, an assistant U.S. attorney (AUSA), was barred from having key witnesses appear before the grand jury, among other obstacles. Rodriguez didn't trust the FBI labs, and wanted evidence examined by non-government laboratories because he already saw a pattern of FBI coverup.

615 November 13, 1993 *Associated Press*.

# EVIDENCE ON TOP OF EVIDENCE

This chapter reveals additional high-level government corruption that was conveyed to me by some of the new sources that I continued to acquire. As my name and exposure activities became more widely known, more people who were formerly with government, and who knew about high-level government corruption, started contacting me. Their intent was to make known the threats to the United States posed by a literal secret government.

**VETERAN FBI AGENT**

In the past, several FBI agents have revealed serious corruption problems within the Justice Department, adding to the knowledge I acquired during 30 years of combat with various Justice Department divisions. Starting in 1997, another and still more important FBI source, became known to me.

Richard M. Taus had been a Special Agent for the FBI from 1978 to 1988. During this time he was assigned to organized crime and foreign counter-intelligence operations, and acted as a relief Supervisory Special Agent (SSA). Among his additional duties in the Bureau, Taus was a Pilot-In-Command (PIC) flying missions for the FBI New York Field Office. The *New York Times Reference Book For the Year 1988* lists Taus under "FBI Events." In the 1980s he conducted an undercover operation from a squad consisting of 17 special agents. He also held the rank of Lieutenant Colonel in the aviation branch of the U.S. Army Reserve.

Taus had uncovered and reported evidence of major criminal activities, some of it involving CIA and other government operations. When his reports exposed CIA or White House involvement in these activities his supervisors ordered him to halt his investigations, often using the familiar excuse that they were national security matters. When Taus sought to circumvent the coverups, government power was misused to silence him. He felt that the gravity of the government corruption had to be exposed, but he was unsure he could do so without suffering retaliation because of his prior FBI position.

I advised Taus that in my opinion the national welfare, Supreme Court decisions, federal criminal statutes, required that any government employee, regardless of any secrecy agreement that he or she might have signed, had an obligation to report government corruption. Because of the heavy involvement of high level officials, including those in the Justice Department, in the criminal activities and the coverups, an imaginative use of the law and other means must be used to meet these responsibilities. I suggested using the book route to force government and non-government checks and balances to address the corruption that he and other conscientious people were trying to expose and correct. Failure to do so could only make possible the continued infliction of great harm upon the United States and its people.

It wasn't as if we were exposing secret operations or operatives engaging in lawful activities. We were exposing criminal and subversive activities, that if not stopped, could bring about the internal collapse of the United States.

Since the government retaliation effectively silenced Taus, he decided that the national interest dictated that he and I would work together to expose and correct the corruption in government that we had discovered.

**A BRIEF HISTORY**

During two tours of duty flying combat missions in Vietnam, Taus received three Bronze Star Medals and seven Air Medals, as well as several decorations for meritorious service. In 1967-68, as an Armed Forces Courier officer, Lt. Taus fought in the Tet Offensive and flew in the siege of Khe Sanh.

In 1970-71, as a Helicopter Unit Commander for the First Cavalry Division, Taus, then Captain, flew Boeing CH-47 Chinook helicopters directing rescue-and-recovery operations.

On this tour, Taus adopted a Vietnamese orphan whom he brought back to the United States and who now bears the name, David Taus. This adoption was rather historic. It required obtaining specific approval and assistance from President Thieu and President Johnson, amending U.S. Immigration and Naturalization laws. This adoption received global media attention. David Taus would later work for the FBI in the mid-1980s as a personnel analyst in the New York Field Office.

**CIA DRUGGING OF AMERICAN GIs**

While he was a helicopter unit commander and pilot in Vietnam, Taus reported to his supervisors widespread drug trafficking by the Central Intelligence Agency. Taus described how the CIA carried drugs that were sold to American GIs in Vietnam and Laos, causing over a third of the armed forces to become drug addicts. These GIs were often too drugged out to either fight or defend themselves. In addition, in that condition they often killed their own officers, a practice known as "fragging."

Taus described an incident which occurred while he was on a helicopter mission in Vietnam. He heard a radio distress call from the pilot of an Air America C-46 as the plane was about to make a crash landing. (Air America was one of many CIA airlines.) Taus landed at the crash site, offering to fly the unharmed pilots to their base of operations, but the Air America crew refused to leave the aircraft, saying they would wait for Air America people to arrive. The reason for refusing to leave the aircraft was suggested by the nature of the cargo, which consisted of about 4,000 pounds of heroin.

Upon return to base, Taus made a written report to his military unit describing the heroin on the Air America plane. He also sent a letter to his New York congressman concerning the drug smuggling by the CIA. A congressional "investigation" followed, which covered up for the CIA's drug smuggling. The final report stated that the heroin on the Air America aircraft was not for the CIA but for the personal use of the crew. Four thousand pounds for the personal use of the crew?

Reports that I have received over the years from many military and CIA people made it obvious that the military was heavily involved in drug trafficking. It is ironical, and this is surely a mild word for it, that the public is paying billions of dollars a year for CIA, DEA, Customs, and the military (among others), to stop the flow of drugs into the United States, while these same government entities are actually involved in drug trafficking. The implications of this are, of course, horrendous. But who's going to tell the people? And will they listen?

**JOINING THE FBI**

After leaving active military service, Taus joined the FBI as a Special Agent, and continued his military relationship as a senior officer in the Army Reserve. When Taus received his field-grade promotion, he was assigned as an instructor for the U.S. Army Command and General Staff College courses.

During his many years of FBI investigations, Taus reported CIA drug smuggling into the United States. His official FBI reports were ignored. Occasionally his supervisors excused their refusal to act by stating the drug smuggling operation was a national security matter. In a way, that is correct; national security was being seriously affected by the drugging of America.

Taus reported CIA involvement in other criminal activities, including looting of the savings and loans, augmenting what several of my CIA contacts, who had done the looting for their CIA handlers, described to me. Taus explained how the CIA had years earlier infiltrated the FBI, discovering the names of FBI agents and informants. The CIA knowingly gave false information to FBI agents, seriously jeopardizing FBI missions and misleading top Justice Department and White House personnel. This false information is still part of the FBI's classified records.

**INVESTIGATING IRANGATE AND IRAQGATE**

In the 1970s, the FBI started receiving reports of criminal activities involving a group known as the "K-Team," operating out of Freeport, Long Island. Not knowing at that time that these were CIA activities, Taus' FBI superiors ordered him in 1981 to start an undercover operation in Freeport to investigate this group. The cover for this FBI investigation was called the Freeport Soccer Club, and enabled the FBI to infiltrate the K-Team operation.

**THE ENTERPRISE**

The K-Team had a front operation with the patriotic-sounding name, National Freedom Institute, and called its operations the "Enterprise." Taus said that this was the "Enterprise" that repeatedly surfaced in the Iran-Contra congressional hearings with the activities surrounding the Iran-Contra affair.

During this investigation Taus' team discovered that the K-Team was a CIA operation, and that it was engaging in drug trafficking, looting of savings and loans, and activities related to what later became known as Irangate and Iraqgate. Taus' team discovered in 1983 that K-Team members arranged for Iraq to obtain U.S.-backed loans for agricultural products and that the money was used to purchase war material. These loans and the purchase of war material continued until Iraq used the military weapons to invade Kuwait.

Several years before the public heard about the National Security Council's "Enterprise" involving among others, Lt. Col. Oliver North, Navy Vice Admiral John M. Poindexter, and Air Force Major General Richard V. Secord, Taus was reporting their illegal activities in FBI reports.

A clue leading to the disclosure of the commodity fraud was the FBI's discovery that one of the Iraqi players in the US loans for commodities was a major arms dealer. Officials in the Reagan White House in 1983 knew that Fadhil Al-Marsoumi, Baghdad's largest weapons dealer, was behind the 1983 request for U.S. commodities credits. The Reagan-Bush team knew of the diversion of U.S. funds for military use years before the 1989 Iraqi invasion of Kuwait.

As the investigation continued, it was learned that the Iran and Iraq scandals were not only a CIA operation, but that high level federal officials were implicated, including Vice President George Bush. Taus said that when high level officials are involved in a scandal, the rank-and-file in the intelligence community lines up behind their leader, the President.

**"TERMINATING" THE OPERATION AND INFORMANTS**

Shortly before the 1988 presidential elections, Taus' supervisors instructed him to shut down the undercover FBI operation and terminate the informants working for him. In covert activities the word "terminate" often times has a fatal meaning, and Taus explained that it did in this case.

Three of the FBI informants, who were originally CIA operatives, refused to remain silent and sought to give their stories to the media. In 1988 and 1989, they were *really* terminated. One was an electrician, Ritchie Roberts, acting like the "plumbers" in Nixon's Watergate, rigging electrical devices such as bugging equipment, and also deactivating security alarm systems. Another informant who refused to remain quiet was Thomas Ziegler (alia Charles Schering), a carpenter, who worked with Roberts. Both lived in Queens, New York. Roberts and Ziegler, working for the CIA's K-Team, broke into the Grenadian Mission at the United Nations building in New York, obtaining documents, and planting evidence to falsely discredit people. Taus said that they were assassinated by the CIA.

The third assassination, of Steve Lopez, conducted by FBI agents, received media attention in *The Staten Island Advance*, the *New York Post*. As Taus said, "I never thought the FBI would do something like this."

Taus said that he reported these assassinations to his original FBI supervisor, Manny Gonzalez, and was told that he "could do nothing to assist me with these revelations." In 1993, Gonzalez was appointed by Louis Freeh to be an Assistant Director-In-Charge. When Taus approached Gonzalez in 1993 with further evidence showing the FBI's false charges against Taus, Gonzalez said he would try to help. He died shortly thereafter.

For years I had been told by some of my CIA contacts that the FBI had assassinators in their employ. Although CIA assassinations were admitted to me by my CIA contacts, at least two of whom carried out assassinations, I never thought the FBI would stoop to this level. Hearing it from Taus, an FBI veteran, gave support to what other deep-cover operatives had told me in the past.

One of the FBI names that was frequently repeated as a well-known assassinator was Chuckie Peters, who had been described to me by Gunther Russbacher, Michael Riconosciuto, and others.

**CIRCUMVENT THE FBI OBSTRUCTION OF JUSTICE**

Outraged at this obstruction of justice, Taus wrote letters to FBI Director William Sessions, reporting the high-level criminal activities that his group had discovered, and the coverup by his FBI supervisors. When Sessions did not respond, Taus wrote letters to members of Congress. As I had discovered, even this can have undesirable consequences.

**FOREIGN MEDIA CIRCUMVENTED U.S. MEDIA COVERUP**

Foreign newspapers started exposing the Iran-Contra activities, circumventing the U.S. media coverup. The foreign exposures forced Congress to address the issues, at least the outer fringes. Taus wrote:

> *When the revelations occurred in November 1986, the Team became increasingly desperate. The FBI files were being filled with misinformation about the "Enterprise" and its team members. There were assassinations. I was instructed by my FBI supervisor, Patrick Groves, to "eliminate" my informants and cooperatives who were no longer interested in cooperating with the K-Team's own investigation. The FBI case agent on the "K-Team" case, Carmine Rivera, told me that I would be seriously hurt by my continuing investigation into Oliver North's Enterprise. Finally, supervisory FBI officials warned me "to desist or you will be in great trouble."*

The FBI was doing everything possible to cover up for the criminal activities that independent prosecutor Lawrence Walsh was empowered to investigate. Taus wrote that the FBI coverup was in part unnecessary, as Walsh covered up for the hard-core criminal aspects associated with the Iran-Contra affair, as did members of Congress. Walsh had received boxes of hard evidence on the drug trafficking from state and federal investigators, and from sources sending him evidence, including the evidence that I sent to him. Taus identified this coverup as he wrote,

> *Walsh conducted his investigations into the Irangate affair using the same FBI agents who tried to cover up the matter at the direction of the CIA.*

Taus wrote that a young staff attorney for Walsh, Jeffrey Toobin, was continually stifled by the FBI under the umbrella of the phony "national security" label. (Toobin wrote a book, *Opening Arguments,* about these coverup problems.)

**USING A STANDARD JUSTICE DEPARTMENT TACTIC**

On November 4, 1988, shortly before the presidential elections, it became necessary to silence or discredit FBI Special Agent Taus. He was arrested by his own FBI associates on sham charges, thereby eliminating any threat of exposing Bush's involvement in the criminal activities. The FBI charged Taus with using a government credit card to obtain ten dollars worth of fuel for his car. Taus had used the credit card during a criminal investigation when a government car was not available and he had to use his personal car. The other federal charge involved sexual allegations allegedly occurring almost a year earlier.

The arrest was obviously intended to discredit Taus and the reports that he had been making. Taus' letters to FBI chief William Sessions and to Congress about the criminal activities of the CIA and White House personnel required that he be silenced or discredited. The enormous power of the federal government and government offices were then exercised.

**USING STATE AGENCIES IN THE OBSTRUCTION OF JUSTICE CONSPIRACY**

State prosecutors and judges routinely work with federal prosecutors to assist in silencing or ganging up on a particular individual. And this was done in Taus' case. Federal prosecutors wanted to move the case against Taus into state court to avoid Taus claiming that the federal charges were retaliation for reporting high-level criminal activities. After the federal charges had been filed, New York state prosecutors filed criminal charges against Taus, alleging sexual misconduct with several young boys who were members of the Freeport Soccer Club, the organizational structure used by the FBI for two undercover cases.

After these state charges were filed, federal charges were then dropped. Bail was set by the Nassau County district attorney and cooperating state judge at an unprecedented $2,500,000, insuring that Taus would not be free to report the government corruption. (Contrast this bail with the refusal to prosecute, or the relatively minor charges, against the hundreds of Catholic and other priests that actually preyed on boys.) Prior to this time, Taus' FBI performance ratings were outstanding, as were his military records.

**JUDICIAL AIDING AND ABETTING**

Taus explained how New York state Judge Edward Baker refused to allow the jury to hear any testimony or disclosures about the government's motivation for arresting him. (This was the tactic used against Ronald Rewald and many other cases in both state and federal prosecutions.) Not only did this eviscerate part of Taus' defenses, but it also prevented Taus from reporting the criminal activities that he and his agents discovered. Judge Baker refused to allow evidence to be presented showing how the boys who made the charges had first denied that there were any sexual violations. Baker also refused to allow testimony showing that the families of the boys had been earlier charged with criminal offenses and that the charges were dropped after the boys had testified as the prosecutors wanted them to do. Also, that the boys were themselves threatened with incarceration if they did not testify as prosecutors wanted them to do. There were other major judicial violations that denied Taus a fair trial. Added to these tactics was the jury's failure to realize the fraud routinely perpetrated by state and federal prosecutors.

The state court trial record includes sworn testimony by senior FBI supervisory agents stating that "Taus was involved in highly sensitive national security cases," and that "his arrest was ordered at the highest level in Washington."

Psychiatrists and psychologists hired by the prosecutor admitted that information showed that Taus told them that there was a major coverup and conspiracy involving the Iran-Contra scandal; told them of the CIA drug trafficking activities and that it reached into the highest office in the country, and included Vice President George Bush. They admitted that Taus described the coverup of high-level criminal activities. They even admitted under questioning that in their many years of experience they felt that Taus was telling the truth. Despite all this, in November 1990, the jury found Taus guilty of some of the charges. Judge Baker then sentenced Taus to 32 to 90 years in state prison.

This sentence was outrageous even if, for argument, Taus had been guilty of a few relatively minor sexual encounters. This outrage could be expected to forever seal Taus's lips about the criminal activities that he discovered and reported.

**LIMITED MEDIA PUBLICITY**

Taus' attempts to report the criminal activities did get some media publicity in January 1991, after he was sentenced. An article in the October 28, 1991 issue of *Time* was titled, "Reagan Knew Everything." An October 26, 1992 article in *US News & World Report* was titled, "Cover-Up." Other disclosures of what Taus discovered were later contained in *Guts & Glory*, written by Ben Bradlee. The most informative article about K-Team activities was found in the December 4, 1992 issue of *Washington City Paper*. The CIA faced this publicity with a partial release of classified information and then lies about the CIA operation at Freeport. This partial release of actual facts and then fabrications is routine when a secret operation is exposed.

**HELP FROM OLD FRIENDS**

MIT Professor Norm Chomsky tried to help Taus by referring him to John Kelly, the former U.S. Assistant Secretary of State for Near Eastern and Asian Affairs. Kelly wanted to do a story about the FBI coverup on his 1994 Public Broadcasting Series (PBS-TV), *Inside the FBI*, but Taus declined, fearing possible violations of the Secrecy Agreement Act. Kelly later testified before Congress after the "surprise" Iraqi invasion of Kuwait, explaining that the State Department was unaware of Iraq's intentions. The CIA knew what was coming, as did the National Security Council. There is little doubt that the FBI was left in the dark or simply supplied with misinformation by the CIA.

In early 1997, I explained to Taus that there was a U.S. Supreme Court decision rendered about 15 years earlier stating that a federal employee had a greater duty to report criminal activities by his superiors than a duty to cover up for such crimes because of an employee secrecy agreement. I also explained that in my opinion, the statutory requirement to report federal crimes, such as required by federal criminal statute Title 18 USC Section 4, superseded any secrecy agreement required to be signed by government employees or agents. Taus said he did all he could to report these federal crimes, but the coverup was too pervasive, reaching senior FBI officials such as ADIC Oliver "Buck" Revell, who had earlier stalled and stopped legitimate FBI investigations concerning both the Irangate and Iraqgate scandals.

**ASKED TO FALSIFY REPORTS**

Taus explained that one of the events that triggered retaliation against him was his refusal to falsely sign the FBI's yearly statement requiring FBI agents to certify that they know of no unreported criminal activities. The form requires agents to report on that form any criminal activities that they know to exist. His supervisors wanted him to sign that he knew of none, when in fact he knew of a great amount of criminal activities which his supervisors wanted covered up.

When Taus refused to falsely state on that yearly form that he knew of no criminal activities, his Supervisory Special Agent warned him that he wasn't on the team. That warning, and his reporting of the criminal activities and the FBI's coverup of them to FBI Director Sessions and Congress, was followed by the false charges against him that resulted in a virtual life sentence.

**REMOVAL OF HIS ACCUSERS**

After Taus was convicted and sentenced, nearly all of his opponents were fired or resigned. The prosecutor and Deputy Chief District Attorney J. Kenneth Littman, who prosecuted Taus for alleged sexual violations, was ousted by the District Attorney for soliciting sex with a minor in the Nassau County courthouse. A November 6, 1993 New York *Daily News* article addressed the matter with the title, "Prober A Heel: Long Island Teen." A November 5, 1993 article in *Newsday* was titled, "Prosecutor Ousted." Taus' trial judge, Edward Baker, retired under questionable circumstances while making front-page headlines in the August 13, 1993 issue of *Newsday*. FBI Director William Sessions was later fired by President Clinton, and the Assistant Director-In-Charge of the New York office, James Fox, who was present when Taus was falsely arrested, was told to retire ahead of schedule by newly-appointed FBI Director Louis Freeh.

**CONFIRMATION OF HIS FBI REPORTS ON CRIMINAL ACTIVITIES**

In seeking to obtain evidence revealing the probable retaliatory acts originating from within the Justice Department, Taus requested under the Freedom of Information Act files concerning him and his reports of criminal activities involving Iraq, Iran, and CIA drug trafficking. The FBI replied in an October 1995 letter that the FBI had over 2,400 pages containing both his name and matters relating to Irangate, but refused to give him copies of these records. Taus had no copies of the records that he prepared as an FBI Special Agent, and as he said, if he had kept copies, they would have been seized when the FBI ransacked his home after the false charges were made.

**MEDIA EXPOSURE OF TAUS' FBI FINDINGS**

The media eventually reported the existence of the K-Team that Taus and other FBI agents were investigating and had discovered to be a CIA operation in Freeport, and that it was the home of the infamous "Enterprise" operated by National Security Council's Oliver North. The K-Team met the requirement of CIA-Director William Casey and the NSC's Oliver North when the Reagan Administration fueled the war in Nicaragua, undermining the government that had replaced the brutal CIA-backed Somoza regime.

**CONTINUED DISCLOSURES**

Taus wrote about the mysterious death of William Sullivan, Assistant Director of the FBI, who resigned from the FBI after more than 36 years of service. He quit because of the coverups by the FBI, including the coverups by former FBI Director J. Edgar Hoover. Sullivan was responsible for Taus' entry into the FBI and the two of them had a close relationship. Sullivan's attempt to expose some of the FBI's coverup activities was halted by his suspicious death in a 1977 hunting accident.

Taus explained how the CIA engaged in "plausible deniability," adding that responsibility cannot be avoided legally, as an agency relationship exists in all their operations, whether conducted by their bona-fide special Agents or operatives.

**FBI-DISCOVERED CIA DRUG TRAFFICKING**

While in Vietnam, Taus was very concerned about the CIA drug smuggling that he observed and reported. This concern was increased when he discovered, as an FBI Special Agent, many other examples of CIA drug trafficking. This concern was worsened by his discovery that the CIA was actively involved in drug trafficking with organized crime figures. And if this wasn't enough, his concern was heightened by the fact that his own FBI supervisors ordered him to cover up for these activities.

Taus described how he first discovered this activity while he was a helicopter unit commander in Vietnam. He discovered it later while flying missions in Central and South America. At that time he was a New York National Guard pilot with the rank of captain.

**PIZZA CONNECTION**

As an FBI special agent working under Assistant U.S. Attorney (AUSA) Louis Freeh, and during the investigation culminating in the well-publicized Pizza Connection, Taus discovered CIA involvement in organized crime's drug trafficking. During these investigations Taus discovered that pizza parlors and cheese factories were fronts for organized crime's drug trafficking operations. This became known as the Pizza Connection, and propelled Louis Freeh to prominence in the FBI.

The discovery of heavy CIA drug trafficking by Taus and other FBI agents with whom he was working came about as a result of their investigations into organized crime activities, including the Pizza Connection cases. Their discovery was aided by the report of the Pennsylvania Crime Commission Report on drug trafficking among the pizza and cheese industries. The Pennsylvania report described extensive interstate and international drug-trafficking involving Mafia figures throughout the United States and Canada, and the heavy involvement of the CIA in these activities.

It was Taus' belief that there was a conflict between the Sicilian Mafia drug activities and that of the American Mafia, and that the CIA's connections were with the American Mafia. He felt that the selective crackdown on organized crime drug trafficking was initiated against the Sicilian Mafia because it was creating friction and competition with the CIA-backed American Mafia drug activities. Also, the Pizza Connection drug charges focused on the lower level Mafia figures while protecting high-level personnel in industry and government. Taus explained the obstacles blocking prosecution by well-placed political figures, judges, and others. He explained how AUSA Freeh blocked the issuance of subpoenas for such companies as Cremosa and Drexel-Castle, which had CIA connections.

He explained that the American Mafia was an entrenched third generation and that the Sicilian Mafia, which was more violent, was creating not only competition in the drug business but also causing too much friction.

Making Taus' revelations especially valuable is that I was receiving insider information from the daughter of a Alfred Carone, a Mafia figure who had been concurrently working for the CIA and the New York police department. I was also receiving additional insider information from several CIA operatives concerning the relationship between the CIA and organized crime in the New

York and other areas. This information provided even more support to what I had already learned about the decades of CIA working relationship with organized crime in drug smuggling and other racketeering activities.

The media showed Louis Freeh as being responsible for developing the Pizza Connection case, but Taus explained that the credit goes to the Pennsylvania Crime Commission. At that time, Freeh was a new assistant U.S. attorney (AUSA).

**DISCOVERING OTHER CIA DRUG CONNECTIONS**

During the investigation, Taus discovered that several of those involved in the drug trafficking were members of the CIA's secret group in Freeport, Long Island. One was Sal Imbergio, who ran for mayor in that town. Several of the CIA K-team operation were associated with a nearby CIA-related firm called Drexel Company, which later changed its name to Castle Securities after its CIA-controlled Cayman Island parent, Castle Bank.

Taus explained that the Drexel Company was connected to the larger business firm of Drexel, Burnham, Lambert, a junk-bond securities company with Mafia associates and high-ranking political connections in New York state. He explained that he tried to show Freeh the connections between the Drexel firm and the drug activities of the Pizza Connection, Freeh refused to act on the information, concentrating instead upon certain segments of the Mafia, and Taus thought that Freeh was protecting the Mafia segments that had current CIA drug trafficking relations. Taus explained, "Other known figures with connections or associations to the CIA escaped federal prosecution."

Taus listed many of the Mafia figures involved in drug trafficking, including Carmine Persico, a member of the Colombo crime family; Salvatore Piga, a Luchese crime family member; Mario Renda, a Mafia untouchable heavily involved in looting of savings and loans during the 1980s; Angelo Ruggiero, a member of the Gambino crime family; Giuseppe Lamberti and Salvatore Mazzurco, partners in the Mafia-controlled Pronto Demolition Company.

Piga went to First United Company in Garden City, Long Island a brokerage house dealing in credit exchanges, and which was owned by Mario Renda, famous in the savings and loan scandals. Renda had numerous foreign operations, some of which were shell companies to confuse investigators and for diverting funds. Taus explained that some of these were associated with Oliver North's Enterprise operation in Central America.

One of the Renda's firms, Amalgamated Commercial Enterprise (ACE), played an important role in the weapons and drug shipments from Central and South America to Florida. ACE was also doing business with and supporting Southern Air Transport's missions involving arms and drug shipments that were part of the White House's National Security Council and CIA operations.

Taus explained the two echelons of the Mafia, the street Mafia represented by the five crime families in New York and the higher-level Mafia imbedded in blue-chip Fortune 500 corporations and in high government positions.

**SOUTHERN AIR CONNECTION TO DRUGS AND THE CIA**

Taus described how his investigations took him to Florida and discovery of Southern Air Transport' relationship to the CIA and drug trafficking, which provided more corroboration to what was revealed to me by my many CIA sources over the last decade. He also discovered National Security Council's Oliver North's involvement in drug trafficking, which takes us right up to the steps of the White House. Taus' statements about CIA drug trafficking, the involvement of Southern Air Transport, for instance, coincided with what several of my deep-cover sources told me, and as described in part in earlier pages.

Taus described what appeared to be a two-tier Mafia, in which the Sicilian drug trafficking in the Pizza case was interfering with other government drug-routes and supplies from the Middle East through Lebanon, Syria, Bulgaria and Turkey. It was this competition that caused Justice Department officials to eliminate the Sicilian's drug business. In other investigations, Taus discovered the involvement of CIA operatives in the K-Team operations at Freeport, Long Island.

**MORE EVIDENCE OF CIA LOOTING OF SAVINGS AND LOANS**

In addition to the vast amount of evidence given to me by various CIA operatives describing the CIA's looting of savings and loans, Taus described the same problems that he uncovered during his FBI investigations. As he explained to me, "The (Freeport) CIA station was involved in financial fraud with unsecured loans, unauthorized securities, dummy shell corporations, and the bilking of numerous savings and loans."

He described how the CIA's unlawful participation and meddling into areas handled by other government agencies, such as the State Department, Defense, and Commerce. He described how Irangate and Iraqgate were some of the consequences of the illegal CIA activities.

He explained how the CIA had numerous shell companies, proprietary airlines, ship and land transportation resources, to get products to market. Of course, the Korean, Vietnam, and Nicaraguan conflicts in which the CIA was involved, provided additional logistics for drug shipments to the United States.

Details of everything that Taus found during his FBI investigations had been told to me by my CIA and other deep-cover sources, some of whom were carrying out these activities under orders of their superiors or handlers.

Taus described how his immediate supervisor, R. Lindley DeVecchio, refused to act on his reports of CIA-related drug trafficking. In late 1996, DeVecchio was charged with aiding Gregory Scarpa, a member of the Colombo organized crime family. DeVecchio had claimed that Scarpa was an FBI informant, which was a cover for the FBI supervisor's protection of Mafia activities.

During a later hearing in federal district court in Brooklyn, federal prosecutor Valerie Caproni, charged DeVecchio with lying, claiming that the FBI agent had fed confidential information to Scarpa, and that this information fueled murderous warfare between two Mafia factions in 1991 and 1992 seeking control of the Colombo crime family. Ten mobsters and an innocent teenager were killed. Caproni said that Scarpa was a battle commander in one faction and played a leading role in bringing about the murders.

There is much more to be written about this FBI relationship with organized crime, as discovered by Taus and others. A separate book is being written to show this relationship, Taus' discoveries, his attempts to report these findings, and how those in control of the Department of Justice and the courts sought to silence him.

**Federal Bureau of Investigation**

**RICHARD M. TAUS**
Special Agent

95-25 Queens Blvd.
Rego Park, NY 11374

(212) 459-3140

Taus's FBI Calling Card

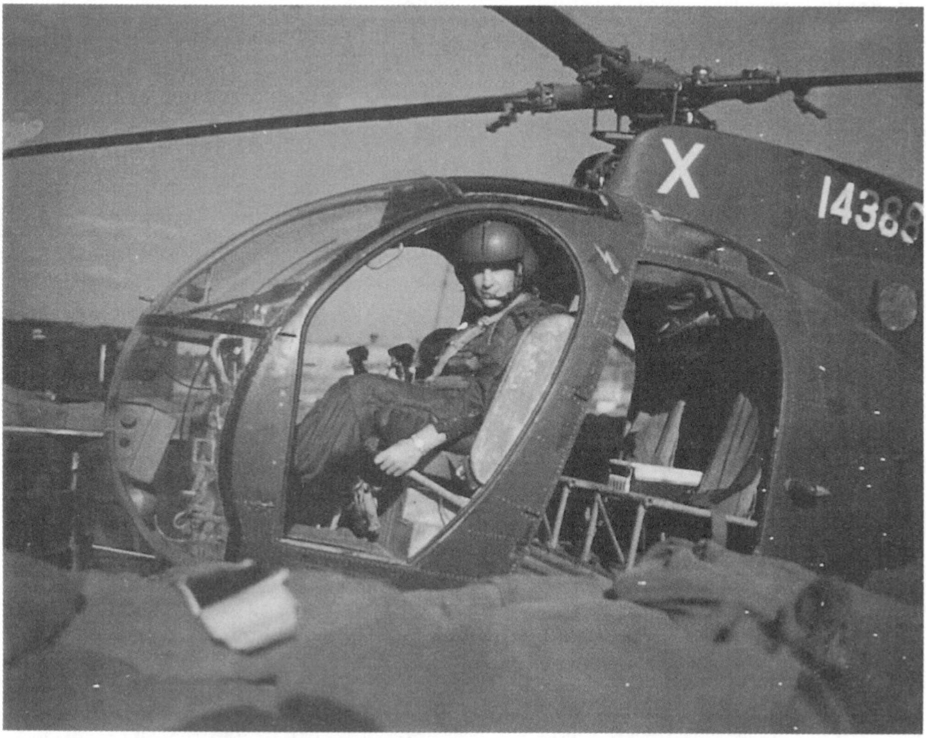


Taus In Vietnam

**ANOTHER JUSTICE DEPARTMENT OBSTRUCTION OF JUSTICE**

In April 1997, radio host David Bresnahan contacted me and described how a senior FBI Special Agent from Washington had conveyed information of another coverup to him. The agent was part of a team of 75 Special Agents and 125 clerical staff investigating criminal activities implicating former commerce secretary Ron Brown and business executives, some of whom had ties to Chinese and Indonesian interests. The FBI agent confided to Bresnahan that indictments were about to be handed down involving 54 top business executives.

In another example of obstruction of justice, a group of Justice Department employees barged into the offices occupied by the FBI investigative team and ordered everyone to leave the premises. The FBI investigative group was searched as they left the building to be sure that they did not take out any revealing documents.

From outside the glass-paneled offices, the FBI agents saw the Justice Department group shredding the evidence that they had accumulated and which supported the indictments that were about to be issued. As I have witnessed for over 30 years, this coverup and obstruction of justice is routine, and no one ever goes to prison for perpetrating the crimes.

**SENIOR FBI AGENT IN CHARGE, LOS ANGELES**

One of my friends and sources for many years was retired FBI agent Ted Gunderson, who had been in charge of the Los Angeles office. He devoted his retirement years to exposing FBI misconduct, especially the coverup of pedophile activities involving prominent people and government officials. In 1997 he started a campaign to reorganize the FBI, seeking to correct the many problems that he, I, Taus, and many others discovered of that government agency.

**FORMER NEW YORK CITY VICE SQUAD INVESTIGATOR**

A friend of many years, Jim Rothstein, described to me what he reported while he was a vice squad detective on the New York City police department in the 1960s and 1970s, being forced to take a disability retirement in 1981. During his many years as a vice squad detective he frequently reported CIA involvement with organized crime and in drug trafficking. He described to me the reports that he had filed of CIA drug sales to the blacks in New York City, naming some of those who were involved.

His reports described how CIA operatives sold drugs to black wholesalers from about 1967 to 1972, after which organized crime groups took over the drug sales. Rothstein described his contacts with a key black who acted as an intermediary between the CIA and minor drug dealers.

**COVER UP OR ELSE**

Rothstein's supervisors didn't want to hear his reports. Rothstein's reports of CIA and other government corruption threatened to expose high level people in the local and federal government. His supervisors in the New York police department gave him a choice; take a disability retirement or suffer the consequences. He took the disability retirement.

Rothstein described how a package of evidence exposing the CIA drug and Mafia links was put into the office safe of district attorney Robert Morgenthau, and how the evidence disappeared by the following morning. He described how New York City and county authorities refused to prosecute those who were involved with CIA drug activities.

**MILITARY INVOLVEMENT WITH ORGANIZED CRIME**

Referring to Army Colonel Edward Cutolo, referred to in earlier pages, he said that he had seen Cutolo's involvement with the Mafia in drug trafficking. He explained that Cutolo, like other military people involved in the drug trafficking, would often have second thoughts and seek to extricate themselves from the operation. This can be deadly, as shown by Cutolo's death..

**DAUGHTER OF MAFIA-CIA INSIDER**

The huge mosaic that I had been building for the past 30 years addressing government corruption continued being supplemented by diverse insider sources. One person who provided highly revealing parts of the complex organized crime-CIA relationship was Dee Ferdinand, the daughter of a Mafia figure, Albert Carone. Her information filled in areas that would not be known by my FBI, CIA and other contacts. Carone had complex relationships. He was a member of the Gambino family, connections to other crime groups in the eastern part of the United States, a detective on the New York City vice squad, a member of the military, and a CIA operative.

Dee said that her father was in the OSS during World War II (the predecessor to the CIA), working in military intelligence (CIC). After the war, he returned to New York, continuing his relationship with the Mafia families, and also became a member of the New York Air National Guard, 27th brigade and the 42nd Infantry division. His earlier army rank was Sergeant, after which he rose to the rank of colonel when he died in 1991. He is buried in the national cemetery at Santa Fe, New Mexico.

While working with the New York city police department, he was a white-shield detective in the 42nd and 81st precinct. In this capacity he took frequent leaves of three or four months at a time on operations for the CIA, using military cover. His connections with the NYPD ended in 1966, after which he concentrated on Mafia related activities with the CIA.

Dee described her father's concurrent relationship with the Mafia, the New York City police department, and the CIA. Key points that she described were confirmed by independent sources, including Rothstein, Russbacher, and LeWinter. She often filled in missing Mafia and CIA links that FBI Special Agent Richard Taus had suspected during his FBI investigations.

Having grown up in a Mafia family and being friends with top Mafia bosses, Dee was very helpful in explaining the complex relationship between the Mafia and the CIA. She explained details of her father's activities as a CIA paymaster, moving money to and from the Mafia families in New York, New Jersey, and Pennsylvania, the CIA, the Mossad, and payoffs to the New York City police department.

Dee said that her father's primary connections were originally with the Genovese and then with the Gambino family, and lesser connections to other Mafia groups. His connection to the Colombo family was through Joe Percillia, also known as Joe Pickle.

**GROWING UP IN A MAFIA FAMILY**

Dee described life growing up in a Mafia family, explaining:

*You have to understand, when I was growing up, there was no such thing as organized crime being spoken. It was a way of life with certain people in your home, or you were in their home, or whatever. You didn't know what these people did. Everybody's dad was like everybody else. They went to work every day and that's it. Would they talk about killing people? No. Nothing seemed dysfunctional. It was just a family. You didn't think anything odd. What you saw in your home and how you were treated by these people was not how they were on the outside. You didn't think about it. You didn't know what these people did. It came out after a while as you got older. You wouldn't talk about something like that. What is spoken in the home never goes beyond the home.*

Referring to Santos Trafficante, Dee said, "He was a good friend of my dad. He was at my wedding. Uncle Sonny. That's what I called him." Referring to Sam Giancana, she said, "Giancana was a good friend of my dad."

**DRUGS AND THE NEW YORK CITY POLICE DEPARTMENT**

Dee said her father was a detective and "bag man" in the New York City police department, collecting money that was distributed to captains and inspectors as payoffs for "looking the other way" where drugs were involved. Dee explained that her father, while a plain clothes detective in the New York City police vice squad, paid money to the captains and inspectors of different precincts, and paid off mob figures. Referring to Inspectors Jack Lustig and Vince Nardiello, Dee said, "They were involved in the payoffs, and these are the people my father worked with."

**CIA PAYMASTER**

"My father was not only part of organized crime, but also a CIA paymaster." When I asked where that money came from, she replied, "The monies always came from the agency or the mob, in cash." When I asked what crime families were paid off, she said, "All the families."

**MOB BOSS CASTELLANO AS BREAKFAST GUEST**

She described how Paul Castellano, the boss of the New York crime families, was a frequent breakfast visitor at her home, and how she knew him as Uncle Paul. (Castellano was later murdered by orders of Mafia figure John Gotti.) Dee explained that Castellano was a brother-in-law to the former mob boss, Paul Gambino, and got the job because his wife was Gambino's sister.

**ASSASSINS FOR THE CIA**

Dee described how the Mafia handled assassinations in the United States that were requested by CIA personnel, explaining, "When the Agency needed people assassinated in the United States, the mob was used." (The CIA does its own assassinations overseas.)

**DRUG DEALS BETWEEN THE MAFIA, CIA, AND MOSSAD**

Dee said that her father started in CIA-Mafia drug trafficking in the Vietnam days. Explaining other aspects of the Mafia's drug dealings, Dee said, "Sam Giancana did a lot of drug deals with the Agency." She added that organized crime and the CIA had regular drug dealings with Noriega and the Mossad, and that former Mossad operative Michael Harari was routinely involved. "A lot of this money was split with the Mossad and the Agency. They had to use the mob; there isn't too much difference between the CIA and the mob. They worked together."

**FREQUENT CONTACTS WITH CIA AGENT TED SHACKLEY**

Dee described the frequent contact that her father had with CIA agent Theodore Shackley relating to drug trafficking. (Shackley's drug involvement was detailed to me by several CIA operatives.) Dee described how she called Shackley several years ago, demanding that her father's grave marker be changed, showing him as colonel instead of staff sergeant. (Sergeant was Carone's permanent military status and colonel was his temporary commission status.) Within two weeks the marker had been changed, showing his rank as Colonel.

**OPERATION AMADEUS**

Referring to the CIA-Mafia drug trafficking, she said she knew from what her father said that the drugs, coming from South America, went to the Colombo, Genovese, and Gambino families, and that it was a joint CIA-Mafia drug operation under the code name, Operation Amadeus. She said that during World War II, Operation Amadeus was involved in transporting Nazi officers from Germany into South American countries. According to her father's notes, Operation Amadeus split into several other operations, including Operation Sunrise and Operation Watchtower.

**THE MONEY TRAIL**

Repeating what she learned from her father, Dee said that part of the money trail went through a bank in England to the Bahamas, Bank of Zurich in Switzerland, among others. She said that her father carried cash between Mafia figures and the CIA.

**COMPARING NOTES BETWEEN FBI AND MAFIA FAMILIES**

Former FBI Special Agent Richard Taus had given me a list of some of the Mafia figures that he investigated, and I asked Dee what she knew about them. She said that some of the people were her family. For example, she said "Angelo Ruggiero was my father's cousin." Neil Dellacroce was related to her father. Referring to Joe Percillia by his alias, Joe Pickels, Dee said that he was with the Gambino and Genovese families.

**FALSE SEXUAL CHARGES**

Dee explained how internal politics within the NYPD resulted in her father being falsely charged with child-molestation offenses, causing him to be sent the psychiatric unit in South Oaks Hospital. He was then given a choice of retiring or being prosecuted. "My father wound up with a full pension. Charges were dropped. This is how they set them up."

Another source, vice-squad detective Jim Rothstein, was given the choice of taking a medical disability from the NYPD or facing the consequences after he continued to make reports of Mafia-CIA drug connections.

It is a standard practice to make false child molestation charges against people who pose a risk of exposing government-related corruption. This was done with Richard Taus after he sought to reveal CIA drug trafficking. As revealed to me by CIA sources, Dee also said that child pornography was a favorite tool used by the CIA to blackmail people, especially politicians.

**FACING DEATH, REVEALING MAFIA AND CIA SECRETS**

After being ousted from the New York City police department, Carone moved his family in August 1980 to New Mexico. He continued his military and CIA duties, traveling frequently to various military bases, including Kirkland Air

Fort Base, Fort Bliss (El Paso), and others. Eventually Carone fell out of favor with the CIA, with possible fatal consequences. Following a trip made to Mexico in 1984, Carone told Dee that he "wasn't long for this world; it's over." Dee said that her father felt the CIA had poisoned him, which prompted him to start revealing other CIA-Mafia secrets to her, asking that she eventually make the information known.

Before his death, Carone was diagnosed with chemical toxicity of unknown ideology by doctors who sought to determine the cause of his medical symptoms.

Dee described how her father made frequent reference to a John Cathey and his contacts with Cathey involving drug trafficking activities involving the Contra operation. Cathey was the name reportedly used by the NSC's Oliver North.

**INPUT FROM RUSSBACHER**

Because of Gunther Russbacher's varied CIA background and dealing with organized crime families, I called him in England and asked if he knew Al Carone. He did, and started giving me information, including the fact that he was known as "Big Al," and that one of his aliases was "Pincheron" in his Chicago mob connections. Russbacher said that Carone was working with the Delente and Bufalino groups.

**INPUT FROM LEWINTER**

Oswald LeWinter, a long-time CIA operative, knew Carone, and knew about the Pizza Connection cases. He said that Justice Department prosecutors filed charges against certain Mafia figures such as Gaetano "Don Tanino" Badalamenti and protected higher figures in the drug trafficking. This coincides basically with what Taus had told me.

LeWinter described how Tomasso Buscetta, the mob witness used by Justice Department prosecutors in the Pizza Connection cases, was a CIA operative who would testify, and who would cover up, as desired by government prosecutors. LeWinter said that New York Senator Alfonse D'Amato was heavily involved with the Mafia.

**TARGETING THE BLACKS IN HARLEM**

I told Dee about what Rothstein had discovered about CIA drug sales to the blacks in Harlem from 1967, and Dee gave me another angle to that operation. She said that the CIA and the Mafia targeted the blacks in Harlem for drug consumption. To be sure I understood, I asked again, "Did they specifically target the blacks?" She responded:

> *In Harlem, the blacks, definitely. It was their (CIA-Mafia) mainstay. That's how their money came, but it backfired on them. They really didn't think it would get into the white communities as much as it did. They targeted blacks and Puerto Ricans. My father was always saying, "Who gives a shit about the niggers!"*

Dee told me about calling Congresswoman Maxine Waters office and explaining who she was and about the drug trafficking, including the targeting of the blacks, and the lack of interest that was shown. That reflects similar lack of interest shown by Waters' office when some of my drug trafficking sources also volunteered information about their CIA-DEA drug trafficking knowledge. (Other members of Congress showed the same lack of interest.)

**MOB ACTIVITIES**

Dee described some of the Mafia's meeting places and front-operations. She referred to a restaurant and catering place in New Jersey called The Tides, and the Riviera Club in the Bronx. She said that Cosmo Fish and Shrimp Company in Nevada had some connection to organized crime, but couldn't remember what.

She described some of the drug trafficking names that she heard in her home, including Shavey Lee's in Chinatown, New York, where her father frequently visited. Dee said that Shavey Lee had drug connections in Hong Kong. She described the relationship between the Sicilian and American Mafia, and how the Sicilian Mafia first got started working with the CIA during World War II. She said that it was the Sicilian Mafia in Italy that controlled the American Mafia. She describe how Vito Genovese kind of adopted her father when her father was growing up in Brooklyn, and that relationship eventually got him into key positions within the Mafia families. Her father called Genovese, Uncle Vito.

**JFK ASSASSINATION TIES**

Referring to what her father and Maurita Lorenz had told her, "My father knew Frank Fiorini, the alias for Frank Sturgis. One and the same person. Frank Fiorini was there also (Dallas). Jack Ruby was the payoff man involved with that (JFK assassination). Maurita had given me information about traveling by car with three Mafia-CIA figures from New Orleans to Dallas, arriving in Dallas the day before the assassination, and facts that strongly implicate this group with the assassination of President John F. Kennedy. (Maurita Lorenz was once Fidel Castro's girl friend and had a son with Castro.)

## SECRET CIA ASSASSINATION GROUP

During the past 30 years I moved from one level of government corruption to the next, often times into areas worse than the prior ones. And in almost every subsequent level, I initially had doubts about what I was discovering. It became easy for me to understand why the average person, isolated by the media and Congress from these facts, finds it hard to believe that such things exist. This is how I felt in 1996 when a sophisticated-sounding black contacted me and started providing me information about an operation that seemed almost too bizarre. But when these other extreme examples of government misconduct are considered, it could be argued that even this new discovery was not out of character.

Robert L. Freeman started describing the activities of his all-black assassination team that was trained by the U.S. military for an ultra-secret operation intended to destabilize Vietnam, Laos, and Cambodia. Freeman was one of 45 blacks trained by the U.S. Army, U.S. Navy, and the Central Intelligence Agency for the sole purpose of killing anyone, including U.S. servicemen and advisors. He described in great detail how his group was mentally brain-washed, trained, and armed, engaged in random and indiscriminate killings to destabilize the region and justify U.S. intervention. At first the information he was giving me seemed just too bizarre to be believed, despite my 30 years of bizarre discoveries. Freeman was the head of a five-man assassination team, ordered by the team's CIA handlers to kill anyone they encountered, and leave evidence indicating another faction had done the killings. Freeman said that for several years his team went on a killing spree, sometimes wiping out an entire small village. Years later, after being deprogrammed, he recognized the harm inflicted by the CIA's operation and sought to reveal this operation.

Freeman said that his group was identified by the CIA as an experimental assassination unit, and called the Secret Death Squad (SDS). The official CIA listing was MACSOGSDODV, or more fully, Military Assistance Command Strategic Operational Group Special Detachment, Department of Defense, Vietnam.

Initial training for the group started in early 1957, shortly after Freeman joined the U.S. Army. After an indoctrination, he and the other blacks were sent to a special training program, and isolated from contact with anyone outside of the group. During training and while transferred to their Far East destination, they wore black ski masks to hide their identity.

A total of 45 blacks were trained to operate in groups of five, with Freeman being the head of the first and primary group. Only a single five-man group was placed in the field, and the others were backups to replace any of the original team who was killed or put out of action. The first assassination group commenced training in early 1957 and by November of 1957 were infiltrated into Vietnam.

During their entire period of training and deployment in the Far East they were under the control of their CIA handlers, John Richardson and Ed White. The group was turned loose in Indochina in 1957, and told to kill indiscriminately. Specific targets were occasionally given to the group by the CIA through Richardson. This was seven years before the United States poured thousands of U.S. troops into the area on the argument that the communists were creating instability.

The CIA's intent was to destabilize the area, as it has done throughout the world, especially Central and South America, Africa, and elsewhere. In this operation the CIA wanted to create horror in the region so as to justify U.S. intervention. This practice of destabilizing a government, country, or region has been repeated time and time again throughout the world by the CIA in one form or another. The CIA has compounded this horror by training, arming, and funding the locals to engage in assassinations and other brutalities upon innocent people.

After receiving training at various military bases, the first group was flown by an Air Force C-141 aircraft to the U.S. Naval Base at Manila, where they then boarded a navy submarine. The submarine surfaced at night off the coast of Vietnam and the team was taken to shore by a rubber boat. At this point they were flown by an Air America helicopter to a remote jungle site, which was the start of nine years of assassinations.

**START OF CIA ASSASSINATIONS**

Within a few weeks of their arrival, the CIA assassination team annihilated their first village. In December 1957, they had their first meeting with their CIA handlers, John Richardson and Ed White, at a base outside of Saigon that was known by its original French designation, P-42.

In 1958, among the randomly selected targets were a combined power station, radar facility, and transmitter, operated by U.S. military personnel. Freeman said that his group killed 23 people, including five members of the U.S. White Star Force. Another 1958 target resulted in killing 15 American advisors in the Bio Lio Forest. In each of the assassinations the scene was arranged to make it look like the attackers were Viet Minh or some group other than the United States.

In a 1960 attack, the team killed eight American naval personnel, leaving evidence to blame the Viet Cong. A major 1961 target resulted in blowing up a Saigon Hotel containing American personnel. Two bicycle bombs were used in such a way that the blame was placed on the "Volunteers for Death," a group of children ranging in age from eight to seventeen who sought to protect their country against the U.S. invaders. These children were responsible for fire bombing many American-occupied buildings in Saigon.

Adding to the many villages wiped out in 1962 were several villages along the Vietnam-Cambodian border, some of which contained American advisors. During the same year, the group raided the compound outside the presidential palace, killing nearly two dozen military and civilian personnel.

In 1963, the group killed 11 members of Madam Ngo's female home guard at their compound near Saigon. At a later date, the group assassinated South Vietnamese President Ngo Dinh Diem. The killing occurred at approximately 10:30 p.m. in the presidential palace. Freeman said that the timing was set up by General Khanh, Army of the Republic of Vietnam, who was a liaison with North Vietnam, and controlled by the CIA.

Freeman stated that his group parachuted into the presidential compound and killed the palace guards, after which three bullets were fired into President Ngo Dinh Diem's head. The killing was made to appear as if done by locals, who were responsible for unrest and dissatisfaction with President Ngo.

In 1963, the CIA assassination group killed the 27-man home guard known as the "Sea Swallows," organized by Father Hoa to protect his village. Hoa was a well-known personage in South Vietnam and French-educated at a Catholic mission. The killing of this home guard was blamed on the North Vietnam Army. In that same year the assassination team blew up a brothel on Tu Do street in Saigon that was a GI hangout. Over the years the CIA group blew up other Boom Boom Vils in various Indo China locations. These Vils provided GIs with prostitutes, liquor, and drugs, and were unofficial Rest and Recreation (R&R) "villages" that were set up by or with the blessings of the CIA.

**ACTING WITH THE VIET CONG**

On February 6, 1965, acting in conjunction with the Viet Cong, Freeman's group conducted a raid on U.S. military forces at Pleiku, inflicting over 50 casualties and destroying many buildings. This attack put the base temporarily out of commission, and precipitated the escalation into the full-blown Vietnam War that came into earnest in 1965.

Acting under orders from their CIA handler, John Richardson, Freeman's group planned to assassinate McGeorge Bundy when Bundy arrived to inspect the damage at Pleiku. Freeman explained that he was unable to get a clear shot at Bundy due to being obscured by General Westmoreland, General Khanh, Ambassador Maxwell Taylor, who were at various times in the line of fire. Bundy's assassination never occurred.

Freeman's group was also busy in 1965, killing about 65 people at the My Khanh Floating restaurant in Saigon, using a Claymore mine. The target was Green Beret Sergeant Al Combs, who died in the explosion along with his wife and children. Freeman said that Combs was starting to suspect the existence of an all-black American assassination team.

Working with the Volunteers For Death, his group hit several Saigon targets in 1965, including a theater and hotel frequented by American GIs.

The group's murderous destabilization activities were sometimes randomly selected by the group, and sometimes specifically directed by John Richardson and Ed White. The intent was to cast blame on others than the United States. The group operated out of an area called "C-Zone," a section of jungle in Vietnam on the Cambodian border. Freeman estimated that C-Zone covered an area in excess of 100 square miles, bounded on the east by D-Zone, in which Play Ku is located. Freeman said that there was a powerful communist transmitter in C-Zone that was never to be attacked.

**CIA DRUG TRAFFICKING**

Freeman described one aspect of the CIA's drug smuggling, detailing how drugs would be brought from the interior to a clearing in the jungles by groups usually consisting of approximately 15 men, women, and children, whom they referred to as "mules." After the same people made two or three trips delivering drugs to the CIA location, they would be killed on the return trip, and the money that they had been previously paid for the drugs would be turned over to their CIA handlers, John Richardson and Ed White. After the drugs were delivered, Air America helicopters would arrive to transport them to a military base where they would then be either sold to the American GIs or shipped to the United

States.

**CRITTENDEN AIR TRANSPORT**

Freeman explained to me that he had seen C-47s (DC-3s) belonging to Crittenden Air Transport at some of the landing strips. Stephen Crittenden, the head of the CIA airline bearing his name, was another of my many sources who divulged to me details of the CIA drug trafficking. Crittenden and his CIA airline operation have already been described in earlier pages.

**U.S.-ORDERED ASSASSINATION OF AMERICAN GIs**

Freeman described to me how his team was ordered by his CIA handlers to assassinate American POWs and how his team carried out these orders. Up to this point I did not know whether to believe him or not. I had carefully read his many letters that very carefully described the events. I passed the key information to several of my CIA sources, including long-time CIA operative Oswald LeWinter, who had spent many years in Vietnam, including during the time that Freeman was operating his assassination team. What LeWinter didn't know, he asked his contacts at CIA headquarters and they confirmed the existence of all the events and places. However, they knew nothing about the all-black assassination team and this could be expected for an operation as sensitive as this.

I was still not sure enough to write about what Freeman had told me, feeling that I needed more corroboration or documentation, and the latter I felt would probably be non-existent or buried in such a way that I could never find it.

**HARD EVIDENCE OF ASSASSINATING AMERICAN POWs**

In April of 1997 Freeman started providing me with documentation marked Top Secret that appeared very authentic. The documentation, some of which are shown in following pages, show messages from Washington ordering the assassination of America POWs, the carrying out of such orders, and other activities that Freeman had described. During a phone call with LeWinter (April 21, 1997) he confirmed the assassination of General Duong, whose assassination was shown on two of the Top Secret documents to be ordered by Washington, and the carrying out of such assassination by the Freeman group. LeWinter confirmed the General's assassination in Cambodia, adding that he was nearby when it was carried out. LeWinter gave me details of the assassination, and I then asked Freeman to describe how the General was killed, and his answer coincided with what LeWinter told me.

I faxed the Top Secret document to LeWinter and he said that he knew Richardson, who was the CIA's handler of the Freeman assassination team. LeWinter said that he was in communication with Richardson and would get further information for me.

Those documents provided sufficient corroboration to make Freeman's description of events believable. I felt that the documents were the most sensitive ones I had yet obtained. Not that the assassination of American GIs ordered by Washington were the biggest crimes ever inflicted upon Americans, but that these were crimes that the average person could understand.

Making matters even worse, government stamps shown on the documents included the White House Situation Room (while Lyndon Johnson was president), the Secretary of the Navy, the Marine Corps, and the CIA.

Although worse crimes have been perpetrated upon the American people by their own government officials, the documents made it easier to understand the outrageous arrogance perpetrated upon them.

One Top Secret document, dated January 21, 1964, described orders for Freeman's group to rescue prisoners of war at a certain location, and if that was not possible, to kill them. The Top Secret report confirmed the killing of the American prisoners of war. A copy of that Top Secret report went to the president of the United States, Lyndon Johnson at that time; to McGeorge Bundy, the presidential security advisor, John McCone, director of the Central Intelligence Agency, the Marine Corps, and the secretary of the navy. The documents also confirmed Freeman's position as head of an assassination team. The documents from Washington ordered Freeman's group to assassinate American prisoners of war; and revealed that the assassinations were carried out.

Until receiving those documents, the only way I had to establish Freeman's credibility was by evaluating what he told me and obtaining circumstantial evidence provided by my CIA sources that had connections in Washington.

Earlier, certain CIA sources, such as CIA veteran Oswald LeWinter, stated to me that his check with CIA sources in Washington confirmed everything that Freeman was telling me, except for the ultra secret black assassination team which would be difficult for most CIA insiders to know about due to the compartmentalization and extra secrecy associated with the operation.

The document dated January 21, 1964 described the inability of Freeman's team to extract ten prisoners of war, and carrying out the order to kill the POWs. The other document, dated November 7, 1963, described the assassination of President Ngo Dinh Miem by the Freeman group, and praised the group for the number of assassinations that they perpetrated.

**REQUESTING CLARIFICATION OF DOCUMENT**

I asked Freeman for a clarification of some of the words and terminology in the Top Secret documents. For instance, I asked for an explanation of the words: "SUBJECT; EXTRACTION TEAM COMPROMISED UNABLE TO EXTRACT 10 POW//TERMINATED//STOP ACTIVATE/WILL PROCEED TO NEXT TANGO REQUEST ARCHERFISH 1200 TO 2300(L)dPLUS 5 UNODIR WILL DISPOSE OF BORDER GUARDS.

In his April 5, 1997 reply he explained that his team could not extract the American POWs because North Vietnamese troops were at the POW compound. His team therefore followed instructions, and killed the American POWs. He explained that the reason for killing the POWs was so that they could not talk and compromise other GIs. He explained that the words, "Tango Request" meant a request for information on the next target (Tango). Archerfish (L) d was to load and deploy between 1200 and 2300 hours Zulu time. He explained that the border guards referred to in that document were North Vietnam troops.

I asked him what was meant by the words: "Major Freeman to proceed with NOC NV Terminated prisoner plus 15 operating dragon ruge..."? He wrote back that "NOC" in the document meant, "No Official Cover," and that Freeman's group was to proceed to "NV" (North Vietnam) to terminate 15 American Special Force's prisoners behind enemy lines.

I asked him to explain "proceed with NOC DAK TU VIL All Terminated body count 40//..." He replied that his group was to proceed with no official cover to Dak Tu Vil and terminate the entire village (VIL), and that the body count was 40, and that it was a Viet Cong settlement.

I asked him what he meant by the wording, "/COMMANDING CIA CASE OFFICER MAJFREEMAN/CODE/AAAA-A1 WAHDCV 07964000 HOURS TANGOS TERMINATED 20ARVNS/STOP" He replied that his CIA case officer, John Richardson, ordered him to terminate 20 ARVN's (Army of the Republic of Vietnam, South Vietnam), which his team carried out. He explained that 079640000 meant the 7th day of the 9th month, 1964, 1200 hours Zulu. He said that WAHDCV meant Washington, DC headquarters of Vietnam Command, and to place the blame for the killings on the Vietcong (V) or NVA's.

I asked him the meaning in the first paragraph that said, "experimental assassination team," and he said that his squad was known as the Experimental Assassination Team or SDS (Secret Death Squad). He also explained that code names given to him by his CIA handlers included Bushmaster, Jungle Cat, and Viper.

He explained that Operation Pluto was the over-all operation when referring to total body count from date of activities until November 7, 1963, which he said was approximately 5,361 people killed by his team.

**ADDITIONAL SUPPORT**

If all this sounds too bizarre, consider what was said about killing American POWs in a *New York Times* book review (March 30, 1997) of the book, *Spite House, The Last Secret of the War in Vietnam*. The book review made reference to the killing of American prisoners of war, and stated in part:

> *Her book shines a light into a dark corner of the war, the secret world of special operations conducted by clandestine military units working with, and for, the Central Intelligence Agency. In this world, torture, assassination, even the killing of fellow Americans were given official, if unwritten, sanction. We are told that United States "hunter-killer" teams, working from a list of suspected American deserters and defectors, had standing orders to kill them on sight. And, according to at least one former marine, that in 1973, after the signing of the peace accords, the C.I.A. assembled five-man sniper team and paid them $12,000 to $25,000 a head for assassinating alleged renegade Americans. It is this aspect of the book that will undoubtedly shock American readers, who probably believe nothing about the Vietnam experience could surprise them at this point.*

Fortunately for POW Robert Garwood, who the United States government falsely listed as a deserter, and who spent six years as a prisoner, the assassination teams never got to him.

**SEEKING CONGRESSIONAL HELP, IN VAIN**

Before Freeman contacted me, he sought to get publicity by writing a October 25, 1996 letter to U.S. Representative Maxine Waters. His October 25, 1996 certified letter (P 215-016 317) to Waters attempted to get her interest in revealing the fate suffered by some prisoners of war. His letter stated in part:

> *One series of instances that has disturbed me more than any other, over the years, was the continuing systematic massacre of civilian drug carriers,*

*or mules as we called them, who were bringing drugs into our base near the Cambodia-Viet Nam border. From C-zone, our designation for the base, drugs were flown by Air America helicopters to a fixed-wing base further into Viet Nam near the central highlands. From there they were transported to the United States.*

*In this instance, the duty of our group of five, of which I was the leader, was to escort civilian drug mules from an area approximately fifty miles inland, out to C-zone and back. These runs were made at two or three month intervals, and the civilians—men, women and children—were paid each second trip. The payments were made at C-zone by our CIA Case Officers, John Richardson and Ed White. Following each second trip, at a predetermined location on the return journey, we killed the entire group. The money was recovered and returned to Richardson or White, Over the four year period of this operation, under CIA directive, we murdered approximately two hundred civilians. I've never been able to forget, despite extensive therapy, the looks on their faces—disbelief, and perhaps the worse; in the eyes of the children—acceptance.*

Several of my other CIA sources, including Gunther Russbacher and Oswald LeWinter, both of whom had served several years in Vietnam, confirmed the killing of American POWs by American rescue groups. Russbacher admitted taking a part in such assassinations, but explained that his group killed American POWs who were too sick to travel and who might be subjected to torture if they were not exterminated.

There are several pro and con positions that could be taken here, but I'm not addressing that issue.

**STILL OTHER CONFIRMATION OF "FRIENDLY" GI KILLINGS**

It was difficult for me to recognize that Americans would kill their own people, even though several independent sources had described this practice to me. When I brought this subject up with Vietnam veteran Chip Tatum, he further explained the practice. He explained:

*I would routinely jump into an AO and, armed with the latest intel reports, move the forces to an area predetermined as a safe zone from extraction. Because I had to have update frequencies, call-signs (changing daily), and authentication codes memorized, it was imperative that I not be captured. The enemy, armed with this information, could feasibly lure aircraft and rescue teams into their clutches. The safety valve used to insure that I was not captured was quite simple. On most missions, I was accompanied by an intel officer, MP, or ranger (I called him my # 2), with orders to kill me if capture was imminent. After hearing this, when I returned to DaNang, I told my superiors that I was finished, and that I knew what my # 2s were for, and I did not approve. I was returned to the states (Homestead AFB) and shortly thereafter sent to Italy to work the Yugoslavia and Soviet Block countries.*

[redacted]

(One) TOP SECRET

U.S. Marine Corps Base
Quantico, Virginia
1730 Hours [redacted]

Eyes only The Secretary of the Navy

DUPLICATION FORBIDDEN
ORIGINAL TO BE DESTROYED AFTER ENCRYP
TION AND TRANSMITTAL TO SECNAVY

TOP SECRET

[redacted]

EYES ONLY-DIRECTIOR CIA

U S MARINE CORPS BASE MACSOCSDODV
QUANTICO VA
1700HOURS 6NOV1963 [redacted]

HEADQUARTERS USMC
WASHDC 1740HOURS 7NOV1963
COMMANDING CIA CASE OFFICER

SUBJECT ASSASSINATION PRES NGO DINH MIEM CODE NAME NHU) SOUTH VIET NAM
BY MAJOR ROBERT L FREEMAN CODE NAME BUSHMASTER)EXPERIMENTAL ASSASSINATION TEAM
STOP SIGN JOHN RICHARDSON CIA CASE OFFICER V END QUOTE

DO NOT LOG ONE COPY ONLY DUPLICATION FORBIDDEN

ON RECEIPT ISSUE NECESSARY ORDERS DISPATCHING MAJORFREEMAN POST HASTE BY
AIRAMERICA TO CAMBODIA GENERAL DUONG MUST BE TERMINATED AT ALL COST
STOP NOTIFY BY TWX WHEN SANCTION IS COMPLETED STOP MSCAAAAIA

PRIORITY CODED UNCODED MSC BB[redacted]

EYES ONLY-OPERATION PLUTO CIA USMC MAJOR R L FREEMAN BODY COUNT TO DATE
7NOV63 5,361 STOP HE IS A KILLING MACHINE GUARD HQ AND HQ DELAY
EN ROUTE APPLICABLE REGULATIONS STOP

SIGN DCIA CIA WASHDCV 0796641700 GREENWICH

SPECIAL DETACHMENT 14USM WAS ACTIVATED 25NOV1957 AT FAIRFAX VA USMC
INTELLIGENCE HEADQUARTERS CIA PERSONEL SOG V MAJOR FREEMAN [redacted] STOP

DUPLICAATION FORBIDDEN ORIGINAL TO BE DESTROYED AFTER ENCRYPTION AND
TRANSMITTAL TO SECNAVY STOP [redacted]

DO NOT LOG ONE COPY ONLY DUPLICATION FORBIDDEN

EYES ONLY-JOHN MCCONE DIRECTOR CIA SPECIAL GROUP WASHDC V 1012632200HOURS
RECEIVED

TOP SECRET

SUBJECT: GENERAL DUONG TERMINATED STOP MAJOR FREEMAN CONTINUE TO DISTINGUISH
HIMSELF AS A LEADER AND ASSASSIN END QUOTE MSC AAAA3A RECEIVED
912632200 BY TWX STOP

EYES ONLY-MCGEORGE BUNDY PRES SECURITY ADV

November 6, 1963 document confirming assassination of President Ngo Dinh Miem and order to assassinate Cambodian General Duong.

U.S. Marine Corps Base
Quantico, Virginia
1730 Hou[redacted]

(One) TOP SECRET

TOP SECRET

Eyes Only The Secretary of the Navy

DUPLICATION FORBIDDEN
ORIGINAL TO BE DESTROYED AFTER ENCRYP-
TION AND TRANSMITTAL TO SECNAVY

[redacted]

MSG AAAA2A BY TWX91263220OHOURS

SANCTION OF GEN DOUNG COMPLETED STOP

SIGN JOHN RICHARDSON CIA V CASE OFF MACSOGSDOD V MSG 912632205 STDT-V
END

[redacted]

(One)

TOP SECRET

December 1963 Document Confirming CIA Assassination of Cambodian General Duong.

DEPARTMENT OF DEFENSE

[redacted]

THE WHITE HOUSE SITUATION ROOM,
WASHINGTON, D.C.

[redacted]

INTEL/DCI/ EYES ONLY//

CLASSIFICATION SENSITIVE//TOP SECRET

SUBJECT: EXTRACTION TEAM COMPROMISED UNABLE TO EXTRACT 10POW//
TERMINATED//STOP ACTIVATE/WILL PROCEED TO NEXT TANGO REQUEST
ARCHERFISH 1200 TO 2300(L)D PLUS 5UNODIR WILL DISPOSE OF BORDER
GUARDS MAJFREEMAN TO PROCEED WITHOUT DELAY STOP TWX1800ZULU
MACSOGSDODV JOHN RICHARDSON TOP SECRET OFFICER CIA V

EYES ONLY ONE COPY/ o215223ZJAN64V//DIA/NIS/COMSOCOM CONFURS CIA/V
DIA
NCA ACTUAL RECIEVED 1900ZULU WASHDC TWX//

JSOC WASHDC DIA/CIA/SUBJECT: [redacted]
MAJFREEMAN TO PROCEEDWITH NOC NV TERMINATED PRISONER PLUS 15
OPERATION DRAGON RUGE PRIORITY-AAAA-1A ENDQUOTE

SUBJECT: UTILIZATION SPECIAL WARFARE UNIT/SDS/MAJFREEMAN PROCEED
NORTH VEITNAM/TERMINATE 20POW/STOP SIGN SECDEPTDEF V/TWX CONFIRMS
23JAN64 CIA V WAHSDC END STOP [redacted]

CIA MCLEAN VA VIA DEFENSE COMM AGENCY FOLLOWING CLASSIFIED TOP
SECRET EYES ONLY DCI MAJFREEMAN PROCEED WITH NOC DAK TU VIL
ALL TERMINATED BODY COUNT 40///END MSG Z1400 V MACSOGSDOD V/

/SDS/TO PROCEED TO NEXT TANGO 15POWCAMBODIA 10SF AND 5CIA/OPERATORS
TERMINATED BY /SDS UNIT MAJFREEMAN COMM//NOTFY SURVIVORS/MISSING
IN ACTION/ THE CIA BELIEVE THAT THE ARMY IS THE AGENCY THAT SHOULD
NOTFY// STOP MSG TWX 26JAN640800ZULU SIGN JOHN RICHARDSON CIA//
MACSOGSDOD V

U.S. MARINE CORPS BASE MACSOGSDODV/COMMANDING CIA CASE OFFICER
MAJFREEMAN/CODE/AAAA-A1 WAHSDC [illegible] 0000HOURS TANGOS TERMINATED
20ARVNS//STOP
TOP SECRET

PRIORITY CODED UNCODED MSG DESTROYED AFTER ENCRYPTION AND
TRANSMITTAL TO CIA DIR JOHN MCCONE//GREENWICH 1821ZULU/ZULU
TOP SECRET TOP SECRET//DUPLICATION FORBIDDEN STOP SIGN
JOHN RICHARDSON CIA V CASE OFFICER FOR MAJFREEMAN MACSOGSDODV/
ENDQUOTE [redacted]

EYES ONLY PRESIDENT//SECNAVY/////DESTROYED DESTROYED//////

[redacted]

January 1964 document confirming Washington-ordered assassination of several groups of American POWs.

**FBI ASSET DARLENE NOVINGER**

A friend of several years, Darlene Novinger, was a former investigator for the Federal Crime Task Force, working also with the FBI, in an unofficial capacity. She was quite a beauty, and her good looks helped her infiltrate drug-related operations. At 13, Darlene was Miss National Teenage Safety. She had a background in modeling, singing, and acting, before being recruited by the FBI as an undercover operative. In this capacity she had the authority to investigate and report criminal activities but could not arrest anyone, a role held by agents of the FBI, DEA, ATF, Customs, among others. Her investigations resulted in numerous arrests.

These investigators were not paid a salary, but received periodic payments based upon the assets seized or the value government agents placed upon their information. She started this role in 1979, and the following year started working with Billy Breen, the primary character in the book about the FBI called "The Insider." Her first assignments were working with FBI agents on drug cases.

Her success in these earlier cases caused her to be assigned in 1982 to Atlanta by the Federal Strike Force, which used personnel from the FBI in Washington and Harrisburg, DEA agents, and the Broward County (Fort Lauderdale, Florida) sheriff department. This operation was called Operation Nimbus, and involved investigating large-scale drug activities covering the area from Canada to Florida. During this operation, Darlene worked with DEA agent Bradley Ayers and an investigator in her same capacity, Billy Breen.

Darlene said that the investigation revealed a large drug operation involving a powerful Lebanese drug trafficking family living in luxury in Miami and Jamaica. The Smatt family, headed by William Smatt, was related to the Lebanese Phlangee group. She said that the investigations showed that the drug trafficking operation involving the Smatt group also implicated Vice President George Bush and his son, Jeb.

The irony of this discovery was that George Bush was the head of the South Florida Drug Task Force. The investigation also discovered that Bush was being politically corrupted and blackmailed by drug traffickers who knew of the vice president's involvement in these criminal activities.

Darlene said that after submitting the report to the FBI concerning Bush's involvement, orders came from Washington to stop the entire investigation and destroy all reports.

Darlene said that the investigation of this group involved the FBI, DEA, and Customs. She also said that someone in the FBI's Miami office leaked to this group that Darlene had penetrated their operation and that Darlene was working for the FBI. This telephone notification was received by the group in their Jamaica office while Darlene was physically present. She had been earlier instructed to proceed to Jamaica and make contact with the group, suggesting that the FBI planned for her death at the hands of the group she was ordered to infiltrate.

During a mid-1997 conversation, Darlene told me that the Smatt group was still in the drug trafficking business, seemingly protected against government interference.

**SIMULTANEOUS COVERUP**

FBI agents made several attempts to get copies of Darlene's investigative reports. Her supervisors tried to get her to sign a statement retracting the reports she had already made. During one session in December 1982, she was interrogated for about seven hours, and FBI Supervisory Special Agent Patrick Kelly shoved a prepared statement in front of her which retracted her earlier reports. "Sign this paper stating that it's not true," he screamed. "You're lying," shouted FBI agent Jack Malarney, adding, "You are out of step with the bureau." Another agent, known as Mr. Barnacle from the Philadelphia office, suggested to Darlene that she leave town.

Darlene responded that she had recently passed a polygraph test showing her statements to be true. The agents demanded to know what government agency conducted the test. Darlene replied, "U.S. army intelligence."

**STANDARD JUSTICE DEPARTMENT TACTICS**

Before Operation Nimbus was shut down, veteran U.S. Customs investigator, Joe Price had filed similar reports exposing high-level drug trafficking, including the George Bush involvement. After Price filed his report in September 1983 concerning Bush's involvement in drugs, supporting Darlene's reports, FBI agents arrested Price on false narcotics trafficking charges. Price had been a maverick in U.S. Customs ignoring bureaucratic impediments that enabled him to bring about drug convictions. He often worked alone and without supervisory knowledge, making it easy for Justice Department prosecutors to falsely charge him with drug offenses. A jury, unaware of the standard Justice Department retaliatory practice, found Price guilty.

The night before his sentencing in March 1984, at a cafe in Coconut Grove, Miami, Price handed Bradley Ayers a packet of very sensitive information which Price had received in Washington. In that package was information concerning Darlene's reports concerning Operation Nimbus that revealed corruption in high political offices within the United States and abroad.

**INVESTIGATING DRUG OFFENSES IN PENNSYLVANIA ATTORNEY GENERAL'S OFFICE**

Government agencies are compartmentalized, which made possible Darlene's transfer to other investigative groups, away from the Florida drug trafficking investigation. She went on another drug investigating assignment, working with the FBI in Pennsylvania. During this investigation she discovered and reported drug activities involving prosecutors in the Pennsylvania attorney general's office, under then-governor Richard Thornburgh. She discovered that five prosecutors in the Pennsylvania attorney general's office were involved in drug usage and distribution, including Richard Guida, Henry Barr, and three others. She said that she obtained eye-witness statements showing that Guida and Barr were doing "lines" at the VIP Club in Harrisburg. (Dumping cocaine onto a small mirror, chopping it into lines, and then inhaling it into the nose using a straw.)

Guida discovered Darlene's ongoing investigation, and in an apparent attempt to halt her investigation, Guida signed orders charging Darlene with altering the number of pills on a doctor's prescription for her husband. The pills were for Darvan 100 and Tyrox, used to provide her husband relief from the pain associated with a work-related injury and a debilitating illness that he had acquired. She had been refilling these prescriptions for years and they were renewed whenever requested. She allegedly altered the doctor's prescription from 50 pills to 65, through a crude alteration of the prescription that would have been immediately obvious to the pharmacist who filled the prescription six months earlier. Guida sought to have Darlene imprisoned for six years!

Initially, when Darlene started reporting the involvement of prosecutors from the Pennsylvania attorney general's office, Darlene's FBI supervisors ignored her reports. But this attitude changed when the five prosecutors were taken to Washington when President George Bush appointed Richard Thornburgh to be attorney general of the United States. FBI supervisors then told her to stop her investigation. When she refused, the FBI supervisor told Darlene she "wasn't a team player."

**TYPICAL ATTORNEY ABANDONMENT**

During the trial preparation to defend against the Pennsylvania charges, Darlene's attorney, William Pappas of Harrisburg told her, "I've got to get off the case." She asked, "What's the matter?" He replied, "They pulled me aside and said if you win this case you'll never practice law in this state again." She said, "All right, get off the case; I'll represent myself."

During the trial, one of the prosecutor's witnesses who had worked with Darlene earlier, approached Darlene and her mother and said, "I'm sorry, but you stepped on somebody higher up's toes." He was remorseful, but he knew that he too could suffer retaliation. The trial ended with a hung jury.

**COMMITTING PERJURY**

When Thornburgh brought the five prosecutors to the U.S. Department of Justice, they had to sign statements that they were not drug users and had not engaged in any drug activities. Their drug offenses were known to various federal agencies, none of which filed charges against them for perjury, or for their drug distribution and usage. These drug users passed their drug and security checks conducted by the FBI, raising additional questions about the validity of these checks when it involves their own personnel.

**ESCALATING THREATS**

Darlene started receiving harassing phone calls, shots were fired at her, and cars attempted to run her off the road. At one time, five FBI agents arrived at Darlene's residence, demanding, "Where is everything?" They were looking for copies of her reports and tapes of recorded conversations.

Darlene told me that Jim Price's copies were confiscated when the FBI searched his home. She said that the FBI made no effort to protect her, Billy Breen, and Bradley Ayers while shots and other acts were made against them. As she said, "We were left out on a limb."

Billy Breen, with whom Darlene had worked on these investigations, contributed insider information for the book, *The Insider*. Breen also received various forms of threats. Shortly after appearing on the Larry King show, Breen died of a brain tumor.

Darlene's husband was found dead in 1987, floating in the Susquehanna River near Harrisburg. Her father was killed in 1993, and a dead canary was later placed on his grave as a warning of what happens when someone talks too much.

**GOING PUBLIC WITH GOVERNMENT CRIMES**

Recognizing the government's high-level coverup, Ayers and Darlene met with several investigative reporters in 1991, appearing on the television shows,

*Current Affairs* and *Geraldo*, describing the corruption in the Pennsylvania attorney general's office. She also appeared with former congressman Don Bailey.

This publicity forced prosecutors in the U.S. Department of Justice to charge five of their top prosecutors with drug offenses. They all pled guilty and received exceeding light terms of six months, a fraction of what a lowly citizen would have received. This light sentence was especially onerous in light of the fact that the offenders were in highly sensitive positions which required far longer sentences under federal sentencing guidelines.

The media publicity generated by the indictment of the five Justice Department prosecutors caused Thornburgh to resign as attorney general, leaving for Pennsylvania where he later ran unsuccessfully for governor. She said that after being released from the federal prison camp, Henry Barr continued practicing law in Pittsburgh, Pennsylvania.

Darlene said she discovered that Richard Thornburgh's son was involved in drugs while his father was governor of Pennsylvania, which was known to Thornburgh and his attorney general staff. Unlike the average citizen, the son was not prosecuted or sent to prison, being part of the "protected class."

**CONTINUING DISCOVERIES**

After U.S. Customs agent Joe Price alerted Ayers to drug trafficking at two CIA-affiliated airlines, Southern Air Transport and Pan Aviation in Miami, Ayers gained repeated access in 1985 and 1986 to aircraft flown by these airlines, and on many of the aircraft interior cargo areas discovered cocaine residue. These aircraft included C-123s, C-130s, and Boeing 720s. Television station WPLG in Miami reported these findings on their programs. Price eventually experienced retaliation for his reports, and was charged with a fabricated offense for which he was sentenced to prison.

The internal government corruption was too much for Darlene. She severed her connections with the FBI and other government investigative agencies, and suffered the financial fate that most whistleblowers against government corruption suffer. In the 1990s she started appearing on isolated radio shows seeking to inform the listeners about what she had found. She contributed to this book information that added still more pieces to the complex puzzle involving the secret or invisible government.

# IMPLICATIONS AND ACTION REQUIRED

The racketeering activities by corrupt officials and personnel described in these pages makes organized crime junior-league. Never in the history of the United States (or possibly any modern civilized country) has there been such an epidemic of corruption involving so many government officials and personnel in all branches of government. Never before have government officials inflicted such great harm upon so many people, and upon the United States itself. Never have so many of the victims been so illiterate as to what was being done to them, and by whom.

**CAN ANY OF THIS BE TRUE?**

For years, insiders have testified before Congress concerning much of the corruption exposed in these pages. Many highly documented exposé books have been written about such matters as CIA drug trafficking into the United States. The criminal activities against the American people described in these pages are supported by:

* What I (and other inspectors) uncovered as a federal investigator, and the large amount of official government documents I accumulated in that capacity. I was trained, and authorized by federal law, to determine the existence of such misconduct.

* What I learned as a victim, as powerful forces in control of federal agencies attempted to silence me. These discoveries are supported by large quantities of judicial and other records.

* What I learned from ten years of continuing questioning of over two dozen former covert agency personnel, from FBI special agents, from police vice-squad detectives, the daughter of a Mafia figure, drug traffickers, and from other sources.

* Cross-checks between my many covert sources to corroborate what had been told to me from other sources.

* Secret transcripts of testimony given in closed-door Congressional hearings, revealing that Congress knew about these criminal activities years earlier, and covered up for them.

* The writings in highly detailed books, newspapers and magazines, by DEA and other deep-cover agents who discovered the high-level government corruption. Includes writings by investigative journalists who also discovered the government corruption.

**THE HARM INFLICTED UPON A GULLIBLE PUBLIC**

The American public is suffering the consequences of what they made possible by their indifference. Scandals after scandals have inflicted great harm upon America, and the public remains mute like a pack of sheep. Even the implications of the greatest financial crisis ever inflicted upon the American people in the savings and loan scandals was not understood. The total cost of that scandal, including interest before this theft is paid off sometime in the twenty-first century, has probably undermined the solvency of certain social programs. And that is only one of many scandals inflicting great financial and social harm upon America.

The public's failure to become informed and its apathy has made possible enormous harm that is destroying the moral, financial and physical fibre of the United States. Some people say the American public deserves what is being done to them and the fate in store for them.

Among the harm Americans have had to endure and will continue to endure are the following:

* Suffering the brutal deaths of 53,000 dead in the Korean War, another CIA-instigated operation using similar meaningless arguments to support the carnage suffered by Americans and inflicted upon the poor people in that Third World country. The huge cost of these two wars have yet to be paid by Americans.

* Suffered the loss of 58,000 dead in the Vietnam War, which was a CIA originated operation. The line given to the American people was that the United States could not allow the poor citizens in this Third-World country to choose their own form of government. Young Americans, brave as they were, naively paid the price in horrendous suffering and death.

* Saddled with the enormous debt arising from the HUD and savings and loan scandals, which have yet to be repaid.

* Suffering the violence, the financial and personal harm, arising from decades of CIA-related drug trafficking into the United States.

* Suffering the corruption and related breakdown of government offices.

* Suffering the poverty inflicted upon naive people exercising the statutory protection of Chapter 11, only to been victimized as their assets are looted by a gang of corrupt federal judges, federal and judge-appointed trustees, law firms, and even the CIA.

* Earning the blame for the millions of deaths inflicted by the CIA in other countries, through invasions, destabilizing of other governments, assassinating foreign leaders, and training assassination squads. The American public shares blame for these criminal acts on the basis that America is a government of, by, and for the people.

**IDENTIFYING THE CIA MALIGNANCY**

An article in the *New York Times* (October 3, 1963) referred to the danger posed by the Central Intelligence Agency and as detailed within these pages. The article stated:

*The C.I.A.'s growth was "likened to a malignancy which the very high official was not sure even the White House could control...any longer." If the United States ever experiences [an attempt at a coup to overthrow the Government] it will come from the C.I.A. and not the Pentagon. The agency "represents a tremendous power and total unaccountability to anyone."*

**A COUP AGAINST THE UNITED STATES?**

A coup d'état is a sudden and decisive action in politics, especially one illegally or by force bringing about a change of government. Surely the criminal and subversive acts described within these pages meets that definition, resulting in a secret or invisible government totally unknown by the vast America public.

**TAKING THE AMERICAN PUBLIC FOR FOOLS**

Again and again the American public has been taken. In the drugging of America, the public has been duped into funding massive amounts for fighting drugs, while simultaneously funding the same invisible government bringing in the drugs. Someday historians may ask, "How could so many people who access to so much evidence of government corruption could be so ignorant and indifferent to what was being done to them?

**WILL THE PUBLIC EVER WAKE UP?**

Most of the public remains unaware and indifferent to the harm made possible by their being uninformed and their indifference about government corruption. I witnessed this apathy for the past 20 years as I appeared as guest and expert on over 2500 radio and television shows, seeking to inform and motivate the American people to what was being done to them.

Many listeners expressed concern—and then did nothing. Even relatives of people killed in fraud-related air disasters that I had exposed did nothing, and none offered to help me expose this corruption. Their only interest appeared to be rushing to a law firm for financial enrichment. Those who say the public will *never* wake up and respond may be right.

**CHILDISH IDOLIZING**

The average American male devotes a thousand times more attention to the trivial ball games than the criminality of their leaders in government. Like children sucking on pacifiers, they worship the ball games and the players. What better way for government to keep the public ignorant of government corruption then to foster an opiate-like craving for the trivial ball games.

Public concern is shown for theoretically endangered species of bugs, cockroaches, mosquito-breeding swamps, or the petty revelations of authors such as Kitty Kelly, but shows little concern for the brutality inflicted upon their fellow citizens by government corruption.

A typical and accurate portrayal of the American public's indifference was shown in an October 1991 cartoon in the *San Francisco Examiner* depicting the inability to get the average American male to face realities. The cartoon portrayed an American male, seated before a television set watching a ball game, during the great Oakland, California fire. The cartoon pictured his entire home burned away, with only the fireplace, chimney, television set, and his chair remaining. As the ball game ended, he calls to his wife, "Alright! the Forty-Niners Won! Now what were you trying to tell me, Dear?" Below the cartoon was the caption: "American Perspective on Priorities." How true!

**AMERICA'S VERSION OF A HERO**

A "hero" is what the media, such as CNN, called O.J. Simpson, after evidence established that this 200-plus pound individual regularly beat his 125 pound wife. Even after the evidence left little doubt that he nearly cut off his former wife's head and plunged a knife into a nearby victim almost two dozen times, much of the media and many Americans still eulogized him. Thousands cheered Simpson as he sought to escape from the police. Cheering for a coward and a thug because he plays ball shows the mentality prevalent in the United States. High admission fees by these same ball-crazed people paid Simpson's huge salary and provided the money to pay huge attorney fees to fabricate defenses that only brain-dead people could accept as plausible.

Talk show host Larry King eulogized this criminal, lamenting that times were hard for the ball player. CNN, which gets considerable revenue from sports, repeatedly showed a demure picture of Simpson on the screen, despite the obvious brutality of this individual.

**"If you don't like what is going on in the United States, leave!"**

The mentality of many people is reflected by the statement made by talk show host Larry King, "If you don't like what is going on in the United States, leave!" With that type of mentality, is it any wonder the United States is in such a state of decline? Americans have the right to expect honest government, and the alternative is not for honest Americans to leave the country.

**SIMPLE AND OFF-THE-MARK PUBLIC REACTION TO CRIME**

In 1994, the media and the politicians promoted the "three strikes and you're out" scheme. In March 1994, California Governor Pete Wilson signed a bill requiring life imprisonment for anyone guilty of three felonies, and these include non-violent offenses. Examples of people who will spend the remainder of their lives in prison will be those committing such relatively minor offenses as filling in a low spot on their own land and violating the marshlands laws; making false or overly optimistic statements on loan applications; and other non-violent offenses made into felonies by legislation of the same members of Congress who aided and abetted through coverup the crimes in these pages.

The same members of Congress responsible for legislating draconian prison sentences for relatively minor offenses have committed more felonies through coverup of government crimes than most people have committed who were sent to federal prisons for federal offenses.

**MANY AMERICANS BENEFITED FROM THESE CRIMINAL ACTS**

Possibly another reason many Americans have remained indifferent to government corruption, such as government drug trafficking, is the direct and indirect financial benefit they receive from these offenses. Millions of people benefited from the looting of the savings and loans, especially attorneys, accountants, and the media. Many people benefit from the CIA and DEA drug trafficking into the United States. The endemic looting of Chapter 11 assets is a multi-billion dollar a year racketeering enterprise for law firms, attorneys, judges, and those working with them.

Those who have a well-paying job often can care less about what is being done to others, similar to the public reaction in European countries as they ignored the atrocities inflicted by the Nazi before and during World War II.

Media coverup of the air safety and criminal activities that I and other federal inspectors uncovered at United Airlines and at other corporations, protected them against loss of advertising revenue. Media coverup of the government corruption described in these pages protected them against disruption of their industry-government relationships. And protected them against government retaliation.

The large-scale drug trafficking by the CIA and DEA requires thousands of participants in all walks of life, including the military, the three branches of the federal government, and state governments. Also included are people on military bases where the drugs are unloaded; the pilots who knowingly fly the drug-laden aircraft; Justice Department attorneys who not only remain silent, but assist in prosecuting informants and whistleblowers. Hundreds of people in Customs, DEA, know about the criminality, and they either say nothing, or deliberately block any exposure. All of these coverup acts, or failure to report the crimes, are crimes *per se*.

**INDIFFERENCE AND COVERUP IN EVERY WALK OF LIFE**

A *Wall Street Journal* article entitled, "Policing the Police," revealed the corruption in the New York City Police Department.

> *Honest cops were ignored, the Internal Affairs Division protected the department's reputation, the brass was disinterested. A former officer, Bernard Cawley, an admitted renegade, beat up suspects and innocent bystanders. Wasn't he afraid of being arrested, he was asked. "Who's going to catch us? We're the police. We're in charge," came the chilling answer.*

That condition exists throughout our society, and certainly in the federal government that I have exposed. Instead of criminal coverup by police department personnel, we have the coverups by members of Congress, federal judges, the government check-and-balance personnel, most of the media, and of course, the public.

**HOW DO THESE CRIMINAL ACTIVITIES GO UNPUNISHED OR UNREPORTED**

There are powerful forces acting against America's interest to keep the American people from learning about these scandals. People implicated in the criminal activities were appointed to key positions in the U.S. Department of Justice and to federal judge positions. By having road blocks in these two primary government entities, investigations and prosecutions can be blocked.

A few examples. William Barr, an attorney for the CIA airline Southern Air Transport, was made Attorney General of the United States. William Sporkin, legal counsel for the CIA, knowledgeable and involved in some of the skullduggery described within these pages, was made a judge on the critical District of Columbia Court of Appeals. William Jensen, involved in the Inslaw scandal, was made a federal judge in San Francisco.

President Clinton knew how the game was played. Immediately after becoming president of the United States, he fired all of the U.S. attorneys, and then selected those who he could control. The most notable was the appointment of a friend, Paula Casey, to be U.S. Attorney in Little Rock, Arkansas. This maneuver kept most of the Arkansas related crimes, such as the drug trafficking and drug-money laundering involving Clinton and the CIA from being prosecuted. The public paid in many ways for these acts. It was like taking candy from a dumb kid.

**GOVERNMENT INCAPABLE OF CURING ITSELF**

The cancerous-like growth of corruption in government, and the involvement of virtually every government and non-government check and balance in the coverup of these crimes, makes it almost impossible to correct the situation.

The mind-set in the Justice Department is too deep-seated for it to correct and prosecute itself. Members of Congress aren't going to admit their decades of coverup activities. Nor will most of the media who knew of these grave offenses and who either remained silent, or engaged in deliberate disinformation to keep the public from learning the truth.

**CONSTITUTIONAL FAILURES**

The Constitution has serious deficiencies. When the president of the United States can appoint the attorney general to protect him or his friends from criminal activities, the Constitution is seriously flawed. When federal judges hold themselves immune from the great harm deliberately inflicted upon individual Americans, the system is dangerously flawed.

Until there are major changes to the Constitution and in government, Americans will continue to suffer the consequences. The problem is that with a media blackout on these outrages, the public doesn't know what is being done to others in similar circumstances.

The nature of the crimes now being perpetrated, with the placement in key government agencies of damage-control officials, and the aiding and abetting by most non-government checks and balances, the nation could very possibly find itself in a serious situation far worse than the Great Depression that I lived through.

What has been inflicted upon the nation and its people for the past fifty years cannot continue without a massive failure of the government as we previously knew it. The scope of the problem is so enormous that even now, especially with the public's ignorance and apathy about the criminal activities, that it may already be too late.

**THE FARCE OF "LIBERTY AND JUSTICE" FOR ALL IN THE UNITED STATES**

"With liberty and justice for all," goes the pledge of allegiance to the flag of the United States. Is there really *anyone* who is so unsophisticated to think that there is any truth to these words! Life, liberty, and the pursuit of happiness are the "guarantees" of the Constitution of the United States, and these guarantees have been destroyed by the same groups paid and entrusted to uphold these rights: attorneys in the U.S. Department of Justice, federal judges, and the legal fraternity.

**MANY OF THE VICTIMS ASSISTED IN BRINGING ABOUT THEIR OWN FATE BY REMAINING IGNORANT AND INDIFFERENT**

Many of the victims referred to in these pages were part of the great American trait of remaining illiterate and unconcerned about government corruption. Many Americans recognize government personnel as being corrupt, but they aren't aware of the hard-core criminal nature of this corruption.

A *Washington Post* article (June 21, 1994) tells of the lack of confidence in the government of the United States:

> *On Wall Street, many traders said the dollar's slide also reflects a growing sense of uneasiness about the leadership of President Clinton.... because there is a lack of confidence in the U.S. Government. People just don't want to put money in a place where there is weakness like that.*

**HARM YET TO OCCUR TO THE AMERICAN PEOPLE**

Speaking as an insider, never in my life time have I seen so much corruption in government and associated harm inflicted upon individual people. Partial or total financial collapse is certainly a possibility, causing incomprehensible financial and personal harm upon most Americans. Many things can trigger a financial collapse of the United States, and with it, violence that never existed in the Great Depression. Jobs will be lost. Homes will be lost. Money will not be available to obtain the most basic necessities of life, far exceeding the devastation of the great depression of the 1930s, which I lived through. This time, however, there is the addition of the lawlessness that did not exist at that time.

**LET AMERICANS SUFFER THE SAME ATROCITIES AS THEY INFLICTED UPON OTHERS**

A corollary to the killings and other outrages that the United States inflicted upon Third-World countries would be an invasion of the United States initiated by a foreign power, brutally killing American citizens, entire families, with napalm and body-ripping explosives, on the same ruse used by our government. And this may yet come to pass.

The outrages that the United States inflicted upon hundreds of thousands of Vietnamese included immolation, disembowelment, firing squads, assassinating entire families such as occurred at Mai Lai. It has been estimated that about seven million people died throughout the world as a result of CIA-generated operations.

The CIA has undermined governments worldwide for decades, training, funding, and arming assassination squads, making possible or causing the deaths of millions of people. Without funding and tacit approval by the American people, these brutalities could never have been perpetrated.

On the pretense of fighting drugs coming from Panama, and in gross violation of international law, the United States invaded Panama and killed hundreds of Panamanians. The United States then installs its own man in Panama, and the drug trafficking and drug money laundering increased.

**WHO IS TO BLAME?**

Everyone who held a position in the government or non-government checks and balances shares the blame. The mainstream media has thousands of investigative reporters, many of whom knew of the criminal activities by federal personnel, and who then engaged in either coverup or disinformation. They certainly knew of the HUD and savings and loan looting in the early stages. They knew of the crimes and CIA role in October Surprise, Iran-Contra, Inslaw, BCCI, drug trafficking, and the other well-known crimes. They made possible the continuation and escalation of these harmful and criminal acts by federal officials by their passive and active coverup, disinformation, and other acts, all of which are crimes under federal law.

Congress knew about these criminal activities and either did nothing, or engaged in a coverup. Federal judges knew about these criminal activities. I brought evidence of their existence to federal courts since 1974. People in control of the U.S. Department of Justice not only knew about the criminal activities, but were part of the corruption.

**GOAL FOR RESPONSIBLE AMERICANS**

Possibly the reader may find a message in the song, *The Impossible Dream*, in the musical, *Man of La Mancha*. There is a message and a challenge in the words, that may motivate the very few people who will respond to the challenge of the epidemic corruption in government:

> *To dream the impossible dream; to fight the unbeatable foe; to bear with unbearable sorrow; to run where the brave dare not go; to reach the unreachable star. This is my quest, to follow that star, no matter how hopeless, no matter how far. To fight for the right, without question or pause. To be willing to march into hell for a heavenly cause. And I know if I'll only be true, to this glorious quest, that my heart will lie peaceful and calm, when I'm laid to my rest. And the world will be better for this; that one man, scorned and covered with scars, still strove with his last ounce of courage, to reach the unreachable stars. To right the unrightable wrong. To try, when your arms are too weary, to reach the unreachable star.*

Corny? Maybe. But it is going to take similar courage to combat the epidemic and endemic corruption within government. Surely, only a small percentage of Americans will exercise this responsibility. In light of the near-total breakdown in America's checks and balances, the media's coverup complicity, and the infiltration of this criminality in every phase of government and non-government activity, the task is not easy.

**PATRIOTS NEEDED TO MAINTAIN OUR FORM OF GOVERNMENT**

Never has America needed real patriots more than now. Our form of government *requires* its citizens to be patriots. The true patriots are those few people who have the courage to fight the epidemic corruption and the overwhelming odds. True and honest democracy does not come cheap.

Many times listeners would call in during radio appearances and say they will pray. But prayer is not going to solve these problems; it is a cop-out by people calling themselves Christians. Their gods, or their prayers, will not bring about the needed changes. Nor will flag-waving "patriots" solve these serious problems.

**AN ITALIAN-STYLE OUTRAGE IS NEEDED**

In 1992 and 1993, the Italian people finally addressed their government corruption problems, bringing about the prosecution and removal from office of many corrupt officials. This should happen in the United States. But a defect in our government structure makes this unlikely. Italy had a system of magistrates that are not hamstrung by a central politically-appointed U.S. Attorney General. It is this central office of Attorney General that is often occupied by people who have been involved in criminal activities, that blocks the exposure and prosecution of most of the high-level criminal activities described within these pages.

"Political eruption may bury Italian system," was the headline on a *San Francisco Examiner* article, threatening to sweep away the entire ruling class. "Italian government Is Near Collapse," wrote the *Wall Street Journal* on March 12, 1993. It's long past due when individuals who are not involved in the corruption, and are victimized by it, stand up and act.

Italians were calling the prosecutions a revolution against government corruption. Five movies depicting the corruption were released in the spring of 1993. Director Daniele Lachetti said he hoped that his movie would cause the people to wake up and face reality. "We need to rewrite our code of behavior to eliminate the twisted logic that dominates our nation," he told a local magazine writer. Americans should take note of Italy's fight against government corruption.

**AMERICAN DRUG USERS IMPLICATED IN THE CRIMES**

Drug-related activities are certainly a key source of government corruption, and made possible by the drug demands of American drug users who consume tens of tons of drugs every year. Combined with those who profit from America's drug habits, this greatly reduces the percentage of American people available to fight the battle.

**AMERICA'S TRAITOROUS GOVERNMENT OFFICIALS**

Appropriate to America today is the following message reportedly attributed to Cicero, 42 B.C.:

> *A nation can survive its fools and even the ambitious. But it cannot survive treason from within. An enemy at the gates is less formidable, for he is known and he carries his banners openly. But the traitor moves among those within the gates freely, his sly whispers rustling through all the alleys, heard in the very halls of government itself. For the traitor appears not traitor: He speaks in the accents familiar to his victims and he wears their face and their garments and he appeals to the baseness that lies deep in the hearts of all men. He rots the soul of a nation. He works secretly and unknown in the night to undermine the pillars of a city; he infects the body politic so that it can no longer resist. A murderer is less to be feared.*

**SPECIFICALLY, WHAT CAN AND WHAT SHOULD A CONCERNED AND COURAGEOUS AMERICAN DO?**

* First and foremost, discover the facts by extensive reading of factual material concerning these matters that are written by insiders and knowledgeable people. Reading a daily newspaper is only a start, and far from adequate. These books are rarely available at your book store.

* Inform others of these problems in a factual and concerned manner.

* Make repeated phone calls to radio and television shows describing what you have learned, and encourage them to have the authors of exposé-type books appear as guests. Remember, however, that many hosts will not want to address these highly sensitive issues.

* Recommend that others read this and other books, and encourage them to get involved.

* Make repeated reference to this and related books on the Internet in as many places as possible, and encourage discussion of the charges made in the book. But be aware of those on the Internet whose function is to discredit those who seek to expose the truth.

**PRESSURE CONGRESS TO MEET THEIR RESPONSIBILITIES**

* Send certified letters to each of your U.S. senators and representatives, **demanding** that they immediately take the following actions, reminding them of their responsibilities, but realizing that their answers will in most cases be off-the-shelf meaningless responses:

  * *Promptly conduct their own hearing* into these charges, having me, my many deep-cover and FBI sources, and the many others who have already testified in closed-door hearings, to testify in open hearings.

  * *Promptly provide for open congressional hearings into the worse of these criminal activities, such as CIA drugging of America.* Keep in mind that most prior congressional hearings were coverups. Insure that the hearings are open and not secret behind closed doors. Keep the pressure on them.

  * *Keep the pressure on, even after hearings start.* It is standard practice in congressional hearings to address a small and remote part of scandals while covering up for the serious parts. Iran-Contra investigations were a good example, with the CIA drug trafficking well hidden while addressing minor issues.

**ACTIONS AFTER THE CRIMINAL ACTIVITIES ARE REVEALED**

  * *Pressure Congress to provide legislation and ample funding for an ombudsmen division* in government that is staffed by people totally isolated from political influence and with the power to fully investigate and recommend prosecution.

  * *Promptly pass legislation eliminating the immunity of government prosecutors, federal (and state) judges*, and other government employees whose actions are obviously illegal, unconstitutional, and/or retaliatory. This legislation should cover the Civil Rights Act, Federal Tort Claims Act, and provide authority on its own for people who have been harmed to sue in federal court, with a jury. *Anyone* who acts under color of state or federal law, acting in violation of settled law and constitutional protections, inflicting harm upon any person, should be capable of being sued for damages.

  * *Promptly pass legislation subjecting members of Congress and state and federal judges to investigation and punishment* by a body not subject to political influence when they commit crimes for which a citizen would be subject to prosecution and imprisonment. This would include misprision of a felony, meaning having knowledge of a federal crime and not promptly reporting it to a federal tribunal that is not itself involved in the crime or its coverup.

  * *Provide constitutional changes to eliminate the president from appointing or controlling the attorney general* and the selection of U.S. attorneys.

  * *Pass legislation to clarify the crime-reporting statute*, Title 18 USC Section 4, making it a felony for any judge to refuse to receive evidence of

criminal activities (that is already clearly stated); making federal judges, the media, and others guilty of a crime if they block the reporting of criminal acts to a federal judge, or retaliate against the person for having sought to do so (as federal judges and Justice Department prosecutors did to me and many others). Also make clear that it is a federal crime for anyone, including media personnel, who know of a federal crime and who do not report it promptly to a federal judge or other federal official.

* *Pass legislation requiring that all criminal proceedings, regardless of the length of possible imprisonment*, require a jury. (Although this is required by the U.S. Constitution, federal judges have openly violated it, holding that a prison sentence of six months or less does not require a jury trial.)

* *Pass legislation circumventing judicial rulings*, that permit a private party to sue a federal judge or prosecutor if either of them violate clearly stated statutory or constitutional law, and the right to a jury trial in these cases. This protection exists already, but judges have held themselves immune. Statutes specifically making judges liable will address this issue.

* *Pass legislation permitting people whose assets have been corruptly taken from them in Chapter 11 courts to sue the government and the Judges, Trustees and law firms, in jury trials*. Have the statute of limitations start to run from the day the legislation is passed, and have an adequate period of time to file administrative claims under the Federal Tort Claims Act and time to initiate RICO or civil rights violation actions.

* *Pass legislation barring seizing of assets on the pretense that the person violated some particular law.*

* *Pass legislation or make constitutional changes eliminating life tenure for federal judges.*

**ONLY THE PUBLIC CAN BRING ABOUT THESE CHANGES**

These changes will not come about as a result of the nation's checks and balances which have been directly or indirectly implicated in the corruption for decades. It will be up to the American people. And based upon their prior performance, the chances of this occurring is very slim.

**MOST MEMBERS OF CONGRESS WERE INFORMED OF THESE CRIMINAL ACTIVITIES AND THE WITNESSES READY TO TESTIFY**

In the mid-1990s (and earlier), every senator in the United States and many House members received by certified mail copies of my second edition of *Defrauding America*, along with cover letters and an occasional letter putting them on notice of some particular new criminal matter that I uncovered. Years of congressional coverups caused me to change my approach. Instead of asking them to receive my evidence, I sent them details and sufficient evidence of the criminal activities, demanded that they do their duty under federal criminal statutes, and reminded them of the crimes that they commit by covering up for these matters. By this time, they have become so deeply implicated in the obstruction of justice responses that almost none of them can be counted upon to expose these widespread criminal activities in government.

Also, I repeatedly put on notice federal judges, including the Supreme Court justices, members of Congress, and other high-level executive branch officials, of the criminal activities that I and my sources seek to reveal.

**LEAVING THE SINKING SHIP?**

In 1995 and 1996, over a dozen senators and over two dozen House members stated they would either retire or not run again, giving implausible excuses for their decisions. Something smells here. When millions of dollars are often spent on a single House or Senate seat election, it would not be realistic to give up what they acquired during these many years, unless there were reasons they were not revealing. One reason could be an expectation that one or more of these scandals may suddenly surface.

**20 YEARS EARLIER, MANY THOUGHT THAT GOVERNMENT WOULD NOT DO THE CRIMES I REPORTED**

When I first started exposing corruption involving the FAA, NTSB, the Justice Department, and federal judges in the 1960s and 1970s, many people could not believe that government would do those things. Since that time, the corruption has worsened and become more visible. The government brutality at Waco and Ruby Ridge helped the public to realize there is a problem in government. But again, this was only the tip of the iceberg, and much of the public failed to react.

**SUFFERING CONTINUED JUDICIAL PERSECUTION**

From approximately 1986 to 1995, federal judges, in unison with Justice Department prosecutors, continuously charged me with criminal contempt of court in retaliation for having exercised the crime-reporting responsibilities of Title 18 USC Section 4, and for exercising other federal remedies seeking relief from their retaliatory attacks. It wasn't until mid-1995 that they dropped the continuing series of charges against me and I was released from travel restrictions. But by that time federal judges and Justice Department prosecutors had stripped me of my life's assets, including my business, my home, my airplanes, everything. Needless to say, at my age I could not start over, and all my retirement plans were destroyed.

No longer, at least not at this moment, are federal judges and Justice Department prosecutors seeking to put me in prison for reporting crimes in which they themselves are involved. But they have issued orders that for the remainder of my life bars me from federal court, and voids for me the rights and protections under the laws and Constitution of the United States. But there is nothing left to defend. It is all gone. At least, no one can call me a coward. A fool, yes, for doing what I did, but not a coward.

**AS I LOOK BACK**

As I look back, I realize I was a fool for taking upon myself the David versus Goliath task of trying to expose and bring a halt to the ever increasing pattern of government corruption. It was difficult not to do something, when such brutal air disasters kept occurring in my area of responsibility due to the misconduct that I and other FAA inspectors had encountered.

However, if I had known, while an FAA inspector, the total corruption of the government and most non-government checks and balances, and the public's indifference, I would (or should) have turned my back on the continuing problems and the consequences. Everyone who did turn their back, or who were directly involved in the crash-related corruption, profited.

After over 2500 radio and television appearances, several books, and suffering incredible retaliation, not a single solitary corrective action has been taken relating to the corrupt culture in the FAA. My insider sources indicate to me that things are even worse then when I was a federal investigator.

**CONSEQUENCES IF AND WHEN THESE CRIMES BECOME KNOWN TO ENOUGH COURAGEOUS AMERICANS**

These high-level crimes against the American people are of such horrendous proportions, it is difficult to comprehend the reactions of certain Americans to their disclosures. When, and if, the American people discover, and comprehend, what has been done to them, and what is in store for them as a result, who can say what the reaction will be.

At this stage, only some vocal blacks have raised any protests about the CIA drugging of their community. Most Americans are still as apathetic as they always have been about more meaningful issues such as government criminality.

If certain more aggressive elements among Americans recognized the arrogance and brutality of high-level government personnel, and the literal overtaking of their government by a literal invisible government, it could trigger some type of major protest that snowballs. Where it could lead, no one knows.

But something has to be done. And whatever that is, it will require major stressful attacks on the status quo in government if there is to be any meaningful corrective actions.

**ORGANIZED CRIME IN CONTROL OF GOVERNMENT?**

What the public is facing is akin to discovering that organized crime, in some cases a Murder Incorporated group, had seized control of government offices and had been inflicting horrendous harm upon a gullible American public.

Will they realize the grave significance between the horrendous harm inflicted upon them by people in control of key government offices, including the CIA, DEA, Justice Department, federal court, Congress, much of the media, among others? Will they realize the criminal nature of these crimes and the harm inflicted throughout America? Will they realize that government funds and government offices were used to bring drugs into the United States for the past 50 years, resulting in an unprecedented crime wave, thousands of killings, neighborhoods becoming battle zones? Will they realize the arrogance of all this, including taking the public for fools?

Billions are spent for the same government officials to allegedly fight drug trafficking into the United States, while these same government officials are involved in the smuggling of drugs. How will the public take to their attorney generals, their presidents, being directly implicated in drugging America?

The perpetration of any one of these racketeering activities upon the government and people of the United States should be enough to bring about a citizen's revolt.

**HOW TO PROSECUTE AND REMOVE THE LARGE NUMBER OF FEDERAL PERSONNEL IN KEY GOVERNMENT POSITIONS**

Who can prosecute those in control of key government entities such as the Justice Department and federal judges, when the government offices responsible for prosecuting criminals are themselves criminally implicated? Who can initiate the collection of evidence and subsequent prosecution? The Justice Department is too corrupted to perform this task, and that is the highest law enforcement agency in the federal government.

Most members of Congress are heavily implicated in prior coverups, and even if they were to suddenly convert from a coverup to a true investigative group, what could they do when the Justice Department and federal courts are infiltrated with corrupt personnel. The system is already too corrupted to find an easy answer. At this moment, I don't have it. However, if a sufficient minority of the public became angry and vocal, and obtained media assistance (also very doubtful) the answer may surface.

**ASSUMING THE ANSWER TO PROSECUTION IS FOUND**

Assume for a moment that the answer is found to receive evidence and prosecute the guilty. Let's examine who would be criminally implicated and prosecuted. They would include key officials and personnel within the CIA and DEA; Justice Department officials in Washington and many of the U.S. attorneys; former presidents and members of the White House's National Security Council; and many others. The list would be endless.

The same government offices responsible for prosecuting would be the government offices under control of those involved in the criminal and subversive activities. People in control of key government offices would be heavily implicated. The task would be almost impossible to achieve, and without a more sophisticated and concerned public, success is improbable.

Even if, for argument, some prosecutions did occur and some government officials removed from office, the focus would be on a very small percentage of the guilty. As soon as the media shifts attention to other matters, the public's attention will wane. Conditions will revert back to what they were, with probable retaliation against those who helped expose the government crimes.

**CONSEQUENCES OF FAILURE TO REMOVE CROOKED OFFICIALS**

The harm already inflicted upon America is enormous, and steadily increasing. This cannot continue much further without a total collapse of our society, our government, the national solvency. Corruption-related crises are bound to surface, and the more aggressive segment of society may step in, and this segment could very possibly do even more harm to the country.

**IMPORTANCE OF RECOGNIZING THE IMPLICATIONS**

Someday, historians may write and wonder why the American public was so illiterate, and so indifferent, about what was being done to them and the United States.

If enough responsible people, who recognize their obligations under the form of government in the United States, will become informed and take actions that they can take, maybe responsible people It will be important, in eradicating all signs of this cancerous growth in America, to realize the felonious role played by most of the mainstream broadcast and print media. Failure to do this will be no less fatal to America's interest than removing only a small part of a cancer from a cancer-riddled patient.

**THE PROBLEM IS NO LONGER MINE**

For 30 years I attacked these problems, without success. At my age, it is no longer my problem to solve. I will be gone before the American public pays for what it reaped. Good luck, you will need it!

## APPENDIX "A"

Many of the actions and inactions described in these pages are criminal acts under federal law, and are poorly understood by the general public. The following brief description of selected criminal statutes will help to understand this association.

**ACCESSORY BEFORE AND AFTER THE FACT**

An accessory is a person who in some manner is connected with a crime, either before or after its perpetration, but who is not present when the crime is committed. (21 Am J2d Crim L § 115.) Title 18 U.S.C. § 3. An accessory *before* the fact is a person who contributes to a felony committed by another, but is too far away to aid in the felonious act. In some jurisdictions the accessory before the fact is also charged with the crime of those committing the actual act. An accessory *after* the fact is a person who knows a felony has been committed and who *comforts or assists the felon in any manner to avoid prosecution.* (21 Am J2d Crim L § 126.)

An attorney in the Justice Department, a judge, a member of Congress, someone in the print or broadcast media, who knows of a crime and has the duty to expose it, but doesn't, would be guilty of this criminal offense. As will be seen, the list of groups and individuals guilty of this crime is endless.

**ACCOMPLICE**

An accomplice is a person who knowingly, voluntarily, and with a common interest with others participates in the commission of a crime as a principal, as an accessory, or aider and abettor. That would include a government official who refuses to perform a duty to prosecute someone guilty of a federal crime.

**AIDING AND ABETTING**

Any person who "commits an offense against the United States or aids, abets, counsels, commands, induces or procures its commission, is punishable as a principal." Any person who joins any conspiracy, even if they are unaware of the actual act committed by others, or why, become equally liable with the others. Title 18 U.S.C. § 3. This is another crime that has been and is being perpetrated by officials in all levels of government.

**CONSPIRACY**

Conspiracy is an agreement between two or more persons to accomplish an unlawful act. Conspiracy is a separate offense over and above whatever other acts the parties conspired to accomplish. The existence of a conspiracy is usually determined from *circumstantial evidence*, looked at collectively. This is usually the only means of determining a conspiracy,[616] and is generally established by a *number of indefinite acts, each of which, standing alone, might have little weight. But taken collectively, they point unerringly to the existence of a conspiracy*.[617] The existence of a conspiracy may be proven by *inference from conduct, statements, documents, and facts and circumstances* which disclose a common design on the part of the accused persons and others to act together in pursuance of a common criminal purpose. This offense is rampant throughout

616 *United States v. Calaway* (9th Cir. 524 F.2d 609).

617 *State v. Horton*, 275 NC 651, 170 SE2d 466.

these pages. It is a common tactic to ridicule anyone claiming a conspiracy exists, even though conspiracies are possibly the most common offense committed, being simply an agreement between two or more people to commit some act.

**CORRUPTION**

The term corruption covers a multitude of official wrongdoings, and especially anything which adversely affects the administration of justice; or subverts the instrumentalities of government; or impedes justice and the administration of justice. (*United States v Polakoff*, 121 F2d 333.)

Corruption applies to many of those involved in the activities described earlier and those activities yet to be described.

**FALSE STATEMENTS TO GOVERNMENT AGENCY**

Making false statements to or within a government agency is a felony under several government statutes. (Title 18 U.S.C. §§ 35, 1001, 2071.) It is a crime under section 1001 to make a false statement in a "matter within the jurisdiction of a department or agency of the United States." Under the Federal Aviation Act it is also a crime to make a false statement, verbally or in writing, to a federal air safety inspector. This offense was repeatedly perpetrated by United Airlines management, and management within the FAA and NTSB.

**FRAUD**

Fraud is deceit, deception, or trickery operating prejudicially to the rights of another, and so intended by inducing him to surrender some legal right. It is anything calculated to deceive another to that person's prejudice. It is an act, a word, silence, the suppression of the truth, or any other device contrary to the plain rules of common honesty. (23 Am J2d Fraud § 2.)

**MISPRISION OF A FELONY**

Misprision of a felony is a criminal offense and arises from failure to inform a federal court or other federal authority of a federal offense that has been witnessed or that has come to the person's knowledge. It is also the failure to prevent a felony from being committed. (21 Am J2d Crim L § 7.) It is also the failure to disclose a felony coupled with some positive act of concealment, such as suppression of evidence, harboring of criminal, intimidation of witnesses, or other positive act designed to conceal from the authorities the fact that a crime has been committed. (Title 18 U.S.C. The statute addressing failure to report a federal offense is **Title 18 U.S.C. § 4.** This criminal offense was repeatedly perpetrated by federal judges and Justice Department attorneys who had an even greater duty to report and receive reports of federal offenses.

**OBSTRUCTION OF JUSTICE**

Obstruction of justice is the criminal offense of knowing of a crime and interfering with the administration and due course of justice. This statute was repeatedly violated by corrupt federal judges and Justice Department attorneys.

**MAIL AND WIRE FRAUD**

Under Title 18 U.S.C. § 1341 and 1343, mail and wire fraud is any scheme to harm another by false or fraudulent pretenses, dishonest methods, tricks, deceit, chicane, overreaching, or other wrongful acts, using the mail or wire.

**MALFEASANCE**

Malfeasance is the doing of an act which is positively unlawful or wrong, and which causes injury to another's person or property. It is the performance by a public official of an act in an official capacity that is wholly illegal and wrongful.

**MISFEASANCE**

Misfeasance is the improper doing of an act which a person can lawfully do, but done in an unlawful and injurious exercise of lawful authority. This would include a federal judge or Justice Department official who prosecutes informants in retaliation for reporting federal crimes.

**NONFEASANCE**

Nonfeasance is the failure to act where duty requires, such as when a public officer neglects or refuses, without sufficient excuse, to do that which it is the officer's legal duty to do, whether willfully or through malice or ignorance.

**PERJURY**

Perjury is making false statements under oath. Anyone who subscribes or signs any material matter which he does not believe to be true is guilty of perjury.

**TREASON.**

Treason is that act committed by a citizen who gives aid and comfort to the enemy; who betrays a trust or a confidence; who commits a breach of faith; who betrays his or her country.[618] Within these pages this offense will arguably apply to various CIA activities yet to be described and to others.

**VICARIOUS LIABILITY**

Vicarious civil or criminal liability exists when a person performs a wrongful act, or refuses to perform a duty, such as an employer or management. Where an employee is the proximate cause of the harm, his or her superior is liable on the theory of vicarious liability.

Where an employer, or the government, exercises control over an employee, that employer or government agency has vicarious liability. Where an employer gives a federal employee substantial or complete control over certain acts, an agency relationship exists. As it relates to federal judges, for instance, the federal government pays the salaries of the judges, provides the courts, provides instructions for administrative duties. The same principle applies to Justice Department attorneys and other government checks and balances.[619]

**FEDERAL SENTENCING GUIDELINES**

A minimum prescribed prison term for a particular offense. A longer prison term is prescribed for government officials who betray their trust as they commit offenses under civil rights and criminal statutes.

FEDERAL STATUTES

**Title 18 U.S.C. § 2**[620] provides that any one becomes a principal to a criminal

618 *United States v. Wiltsberger* (US 5 Wheat 76, 5 L Ed 37. A criminal attempt to destroy the existence of the government. *Republica v Chapman* (Pa) 1 Dall 53, 1 L Ed 33. Breaching an allegiance to one's country. Also shown under Article III, § 3 of the U.S. Constitution.

619 Cases relating to vicarious liability includes *Crinkley v. Holiday Inns, Inc.*, 844 F.2d 156 (4th Cir. 1988); *Cislaw v. 7-Eleven, Inc.*, 92 Daily Journal D.A.R. 4136 (March 30, 1992); *Beck v. Arthur Murray, Inc.*, 245 Cal.App.2d 976 (1966); *Nichols v. Arthur Murray, Inc.*, 248 Cal.App.2d 610 (1967); *Porter v. Arthur Murray, Inc.*, 149 Cal.App.2d 410 (1967); *Wickham v. Southland Corp.*, 168 Cal.App.3d 49 (1985).

620 **Title 18 U.S.C. § 2. Principals**. (a) Whoever commits an offense against the United States or aids, abets, counsels, commands, induces or procures its commission, is punishable as a principal. (b) Whoever wilfully causes an act to be done which if directly performed by him or another would be an offense against the United States, is punishable as a principal.

act who in any way aids or covers up for an offense. This could include federal judges, Justice Department attorneys, members of Congress, and the media.

**Title 18 U.S.C. § 3. Accessory after the fact.**[621] It is a felony for any person, who knows that an offense against the United States has been committed, to obstruct justice by assisting the perpetrators through blocking the reporting of the crimes by an informant or victim. This felony would include federal judges and Justice Department attorneys, members of Congress, media personnel, who knew about the criminal activities described within these pages and either refused to make the crimes known, or worse, who engaged in a coverup.

**Title 18 U.S.C. § 4 (misprision of felony).**[622] It becomes a felony if any person who knows of a federal crime does not promptly report it to a federal judge or other federal officer.

**Title 18 U.S.C. § 34 Penalty when death results.**[623] If death results from violation of a related criminal statute, it becomes a capitol offense. This would apply, for instance, to the criminal violations at United Airlines and within the FAA and NTSB that resulted or made possible airline crashes.

**Title 18 U.S.C. § 35. Imparting or conveying false information.**[624] This offense was and is rampant in the air safety proceedings, in Congressional investigations, and is shown throughout these pages.

**Title 18 U.S.C. § 111. Impeding certain officers or employees.**[625] It is a felony to resist, impede, intimidate, or interfere with any person designated in section 1114 of this title. This would include the United Airlines management, and federal management in the FAA, NTSB, Justice Department, and federal judges, who blocked me and other federal inspectors from reporting and correcting serious crash-related air safety and criminal violations, and later, other federal crimes that I tried to report.

---

The legislative intent was to punish as a principal not only a person who directly commits an offense, but a person who "aids, abets, counsels, commands, induces or procures" another to commit an offense, and anyone who causes the doing of an act which if done by him directly would render him guilty of an offense against the United States. Case law decisions include *Rothenburg v. United States*, 1918, 38 S.Ct. 18, 245 U.S. 480, 62 L.Ed. 414, and *United States v. Giles*, 1937, 57 S.Ct. 340, 300 U.S. 41, 81 L.Ed. 493.

621 **Title 18 U.S.C. § 3. Accessory after the fact.** Whoever, knowing that an offense against the United States had been committed, receives, relieves, comforts or assists the offender in order to hinder or prevent his apprehension, trial or punishment, is an accessory after the fact.

622 **Title 18 U.S.C. § 4. Misprision of felony.** Whoever, having knowledge of the actual commission of a felony cognizable by a court of the United States, conceals and does not as soon as possible make known the same to some judge or other person in civil or military authority under the United States, shall be fined not more than $500 or imprisoned not more than three years, or both.

623 **Title 18 USC § 34.** Penalty when death results. Whoever is convicted of any crime prohibited by this chapter, which has resulted in the death of any person, shall be subject to the death penalty or to imprisonment for life...

624 **Title 18 U.S.C. § 35. Importing or conveying false information.** (a) Whoever imparts or conveys or causes to be imparted or conveyed false information, knowing the information to be false...
(b) or with reckless disregard for the safety of human life, imparts or conveys or causes to be imparted or conveyed, false information, knowing the information to be false...shall be subject to a civil penalty...or imprisonment....

625 **Title 18 U.S.C. § 111. Impeding certain officers or employees.** Whoever...intimidates, or interferes with any person...while engaged in...the performance of his official duties shall be fined...or imprisoned...

**Title 18 U.S.C. § 153. Embezzlement by trustee or officer.**[626] This felony is rampant in federal Chapter 11, 12, 13 courts, with the knowledge of federal judges, Justice Department officials, and many others.

**Title 18 U.S.C. § 241. Conspiracy against rights of citizens.**[627] This felony applies to anyone, including judges and Justice Department attorneys, who intimidate, threaten, or inflict harm upon any person in retaliation for exercising federal defenses against acts taken to silence him or block him from defending himself.

**Title 18 U.S.C. § 371 Conspiracy to commit offense or to defraud United States.**[628] There are many ways to commit an offense against, or to defraud the United States. As a matter of law, the word "defraud" is broadly used to include obstructing the lawful operation of any government agency by any "deceit, craft or trickery, or at least by means that are dishonest."[629] To convict someone, including a federal official, under Title 18 U.S.C. § 371, it is only necessary to show that the person (1) entered into an agreement (2) to obstruct a lawful function of the government (3) by deceitful or dishonest means and (4) had committed at least one overt act in furtherance of the conspiracy.[630] Obstructing the lawful safety functions of the FAA and the NTSB, for instance, would constitute a felony under this statute. Obstructing the lawful functions of the federal courts, or the Justice Department, would also cause violation of this statute. Prosecuting a citizen seeking to report government corruption would be a crime.

**Title 18 U.S.C. § 1001. Statements or entries generally.**[631] It is a federal

---

626 **Title 18 U.S.C. § 153. Embezzlement by trustee or officer.** Whoever knowingly and fraudulently appropriates to his own use, embezzles, spends, or transfers any property or secretes or destroys any document belonging to the estate of a debtor which came into his charge as trustee, custodian, marshal, or other officer of the court, shall be fined not more than $5,000 or imprisoned not more than five years, or both.

627 **Title 18 U.S.C. § 241. Conspiracy against rights of citizens.** If two or more persons conspire to injure, oppress, threaten, or intimidate any citizen in the free exercise or enjoyment of any right or privilege secured to him by the Constitution or laws of the United States, or because of his having so exercised the same;...They shall be fined...or imprisoned...or both;

628 **Title 18 U.S.C. § 371.** If two or more persons conspire either to commit any offense against the United States, or to defraud the United States, or any agency thereof in any manner or for any purpose, and one or more of such persons do any act to effect the object of the conspiracy, each shall be fined omm more than $10,000 or imprisoned not more than five years, or both.

*Hammerschmidt v. United States*, 265 U.S. 182, 188 (1924).

*United States v. Boone*, 951 F.2d 1526, 1543 (9th Cir. 1991).

631 **Title 18 U.S.C. § 1001. Statements or entries generally.** Whoever, in any matter within the jurisdiction of any department or agency of the United States knowingly and willfully falsifies, conceals or covers up by any trick, scheme, or device a material fact, or makes any false, fictitious or fraudulent statements or representations, or makes or uses any false writing or document knowing the same to contain any false, fictitious or fraudulent statement or entry, shall be fined not more than $10,000 or imprisoned not more thana five years, or both.

Case law relating to Title 18 U.S.C. § 1001 holds that falsifying any record that reduces the effectiveness of the government agency, causing the agency to wrongfully act or not act on such writings or acts, or decreasing the public confidence in such agency.

Just the mere filing of a false statement within the jurisdiction of any government department or agency constitutes a section 1001 offense. Loss or damage to government is not an essential element of the crime. *U.S. v. Godel*, 361 F.2d 21 (C.S. Va. 1966); *Morgan v. U.S.* 301 F.2d 272 (C.A. Ariz. 1962); Test for determining materiality of false statement is whether the falsification is calculated to induce action or reliance by an agency of the United States. *U.S. v. East*. 416 F.2d 351 (C.A. Mont. 1969);

Section 1001 makes it a crime to knowingly and willfully falsify documents within jurisdiction of government department or agency. It is immaterial whether the false statement actually influenced or crime for **anyone** within the jurisdiction of any department or agency of the United States to knowingly and willfully falsify, conceal or cover up by any trick or scheme a material fact or to make any false, fictitious or fraudulent statement or representation. This criminal statute would apply to the false statements made in air safety records by United Airlines management; to the false statements made by the FAA hearing officer and legal counsel in the FAA safety hearing; to the NTSB for omitting major facts that resulted in a false conclusion; and many other instances yet to be described.

**Title 18 U.S.C. § 1341. Frauds and Swindles.**[632] This statute relates to using the mail to defraud another person. The mail was used to defraud the United States, and to defraud me, as will be seen.

**Title 18 U.S.C. § 1343. Wire fraud.**[633] This section applies to anyone who defrauds another while using the telephone or other communications.

**Title 28 U.S.C. § 1361. Action to compel an officer of the United States to perform his duty.** This statute permits any citizens to invoke federal court jurisdiction to report government misconduct and to obtain a court order compelling a government official to halt the wrongful acts or to perform a lawful duty. A federal judge lacks jurisdiction to void, or to punish a citizen, for exercising this right.

**Title 18 U.S.C. § 1505. Obstruction of proceedings before departments, agencies, and committees**[634] This criminal statute was repeatedly violated by

---

caused the government department or agency to act, but rather, whether capable of influencing decision of tribunal making determination. *Robles v. U.S.* 279 F.2d 401 (C.A. Ariz. 1960); a section 1001 violation occurs when a false writing or document is made in any matter within the jurisdiction of a government department or agency, knowing that it contains a false statement or entry, and intending that it shall bear a relation or purpose as to some matter which is within the jurisdiction of the government department or agency, and with the false statement having a materiality on the department or agency matter. *Ebeling v. U.S.*, (C.A. Mo. 1957) 248 F.2d 429.

Section 2071 was to protect the government against false statements that might impede the exercise of federal authority. *U.S. v. Leviton,* C.A.N.Y. 1951, 193 F.2d 848; protect the government against those who would cheat or mislead it in administration of its programs (*U.S. v. Johnson*, D.C. Mo. 1968, 284 F. Supp. 273; affirmed 410 F.2d 38); includes all false and fraudulent statements or representations which are knowingly and willfully used in documents or affidavits in any manner within the jurisdiction of any department or agency of the United States. *U.S. v. Coastal Contracting & Engineering Co.*, D.C. Md. 1959, 174 F. Supp. 474. See, also, *U.S. v. Allen*, D.C. Cal. 1961, 193 F. Supp. 954.

632 **Title 18 U.S.C. § 1341. Frauds and swindles.** Whoever, having devised or intending to devise any scheme or artifice to defraud, or for obtaining money or property by means of false or fraudulent pretenses, representations, or promises,....for the purpose of executing such scheme or artifice or attempting so to do, places in any post office or authorized depository for mail matter, any matter or thing whatever to be sent or delivered by the Postal Service, or takes or receives therefrom, any such matter or thing, or knowingly causes to be delivered by mail according to the direction thereon, or at the place at which it is directed to be delivered by the person to whom it is addressed, any such matter or thing, shall be fined...or imprisoned....or both.

633 **Title 18 U.S.C. § 1343. Fraud by wire, radio, or television.** Whoever, having devised or intending to devise any scheme or artifice to defraud, or for obtaining money or property by means of false or fraudulent pretenses, representations, or promises, transmits or causes to be transmitted by means of wire, radio, or television communication in interstate or foreign commerce, any writings, signs, signals, pictures, or sounds for the purpose of executing such scheme or artifice, shall be fined not more than $1,000 or imprisoned not more than five years, or both.

634 **Title 18 U.S.C. § 1505. Obstruction of proceedings before departments, agencies, and committees.** Whoever corruptly...influences, obstructs, or impedes or endeavors to influence, obstruct, or impede the due the proper administration of the law under which any pending proceeding is being had before any department or agency of the United States...shall be fined not more than $5,000 or imprisoned not more than five years, or both.

government personnel, primarily Justice Department attorneys and federal judges, who obstructed justice by blocking the reporting of federal crimes.

**Title 18 U.S.C. § 1512. Tampering with a witness, victim, or an informant.**[635] It is a crime to interfere or retaliated against a person seeking to report a crime. This would apply especially to Justice Department employees or judges.

**Title 18 U.S.C. § 1513. Retaliating against a witness, victim, or an informant.**[636] This criminal statute applies to anyone, including judges and Justice Department officials, who retaliate against anyone for reporting federal crimes. It would apply to FAA officials who retaliated against me, and the harm yet to be described, which retaliated against me for reporting the government corruption.

**Title 18 U.S.C. § 1515 (a)(3)(A). Misleading conduct means knowingly making false statements.**[637] This criminal statute was violated by government personnel in the criminal activities described throughout these pages, starting with the air disaster-related misconduct.

**Title 18 U.S.C. § 1515 (a)(3)(B); Intentionally omitting information from**

---

635 **Title 18 U.S.C. § 1512. Tampering with a witness, victim, or an informant.**

(a) Whoever...prevents the attendance or testimony of any person in an official proceeding;

(b) prevents the production of a record...in an official proceeding;

(c) prevents the communication by any person to a law enforcement officer or judge of the United States, of information relating to the commission or possible commission of a federal offense...(2)(b) Whoever knowingly uses intimidation...or threatens another person, or attempts to do so, or engages in misleading conduct toward another person, with intent to (1) influence, delay or prevent the testimony of any person in an official proceeding; (2) cause or induce any person to (A) Withhold testimony, or withhold a record, document, or other object, from an official proceeding; (3) hinder, delay, or prevent the communication to a law enforcement officer or judge of the United States of information relating to the commission or possible commission of a federal offense...(c) Whoever intentionally harasses another person and thereby hinders, delays, prevents, or dissuades any person from (1) attending or testifying in an official proceeding; (2) reporting to a law enforcement officer or judge of the United States the commission or possible commission of a federal offense...(3) arresting or seeking the arrest of another person in connection with a federal offense; or (4) causing a criminal prosecution...to be sought or instituted, or assisting in such prosecution or proceeding...shall be fined...or imprisoned...

636 **Title 18 U.S.C. § 1513. Retaliating against a witness, victim, or an informant.** (a) Whoever knowingly engages in any conduct and thereby causes...injury to another person...or threatens to do so, with intent to retaliate against any person for (1) the attendance of a witness or party at an official proceeding, or any testimony given or any record, document, or other object produced by a witness in an official proceeding; or (2) any information relating to the commission or possible commission of a federal offense...shall be...fined or...imprisoned...

637 **Title 18 U.S.C. § 1515. Definitions of terms in criminal statutes (as used in sections 1512 and 1513).** (a)(2) the term "physical force" means physical action against another and includes confinement; [including prison.] (a)(3) the term "misleading conduct" means – (A) knowingly making a false statement; (B) **intentionally omitting information from a statement** and thereby causing a portion of such statement to be misleading, or intentionally concealing a material fact, and thereby creating a false impression by such statement; (C) with intent to mislead, knowingly submitting or inviting reliance on a writing or recording that is false...or otherwise lacking in authenticity; (D) with intent to mislead, knowingly submitting or inviting reliance on a ... object that is misleading in a material respect; or (E) knowingly using a trick, scheme, or device with intent to mislead; (4) the term "law enforcement officer" means an officer or employee of the Federal Government, or a person authorized to act for or on behalf of the Federal Government or serving the Federal Government as an adviser or consultant – (A) authorized under law to engage in or supervise the prevention, detection, investigation, or prosecution of an offense; (5) the term "bodily injury" means – (E) any other injury to the body, no matter how temporary. (a)(1) the term "official proceeding" means...(C) a proceeding before a Federal Government agency which is authorized by law. [FAA included.]"

**Title 18 U.S.C. § 1515 (a)(3)(A).** Misleading conduct means knowingly making false statements.

**a statement and thereby causing a portion of such statement to be misleading, or intentionally concealing a material fact.**[638] This criminal statute was repeatedly violated in the aviation and other scandals.

**Title 18 U.S.C. § 1515 (a)(3)(C). With intent to mislead, knowingly submitting or inviting reliance on a writing that is false or otherwise lacking in authenticity.**[639] Same as other section 1515 violations. Title 18 U.S.C. § 1515 (a)(3)(D). With intent to mislead, knowingly submitting...material that is misleading in a material aspect.[640]

**Title 18 U.S.C. § 1515 (a)(3)(E). Knowingly using a trick or scheme to mislead.** Misleading statements made by government personnel throughout these pages were violations of this statute.

**Title 18 U.S.C. §§ 1621. Perjury generally.**[641]

**Title 18 U.S.C. § 1622. Subornation of perjury.**[642] This felony was repeatedly perpetrated by FAA management during the FAA Denver hearing.

**Title 18 U.S.C. § 1623. False declarations before grand jury or court.**[643]

**Title 18 U.S.C. § 2071. Concealment, removal, or mutilation generally.**[644] This criminal statute was violated by the FAA and NTSB in covering up for behind the scene facts in several air disasters described in detail in *Unfriendly Skies*.

**Title 18 U.S.C. § 2075. Officer failing to make reports; felony omission of a duty to act.**[645] This criminal statute was repeatedly violated, commencing with the refusal of FAA and NTSB management to report the air safety and criminal acts, and then omitting key data from the final reports. This criminal

---

638 **Title 18 U.S.C. § 1515 (a)(3)(B);** Intentionally omitting information from a statement and thereby causing a portion of such statement to be misleading, or intentionally concealing a material fact.

639 **Title 18 U.S.C. § 1515 (a)(3)(C).** With intent to mislead, knowingly submitting or inviting reliance on a writing that is false or otherwise lacking in authenticity.

640 **Title 18 U.S.C. § 1515 (a)(3)(D).** With intent to mislead, knowingly submitting ... material that is misleading in a material aspect.

641 **Title 18 U.S.C. § 1621. Perjury generally.** Whoever (1) having taken an oath before a competent tribunal...willfully and contrary to such oath states...any material matter which he does not believe to be true, he shall be fined...or imprisoned...

642 **Title 18 U.S.C. § 1622. Subornation of perjury.** Whoever procures another to commit any perjury is guilty of subornation of perjury, and shall be fined...or imprisoned...

643 **Title 18 U.S.C. § 1623. False declarations before grand jury or court.** (a) Whoever under oath ... or statement under penalty of perjury...before or ancillary to any court or grand jury of the United States knowingly makes any false material declaration, or makes or uses any other information...knowing the same to contain any false material declaration, shall be fined...or imprisoned...

644 **Title 18 U.S.C. § 2071. Concealment, removal, or mutilation generally.** (a) Whoever willfully and unlawfully conceals, removes, mutilates, obliterates, or destroys, or attempts to do so, or, with intent to do so takes and carries away any record, proceeding, map, book, paper, document, or other thing, filed or deposited with any clerk or officer of any court of the United States, or in any public office, or with any judicial or public officer of the United States, shall be fined not more than $2,000 or imprisoned not more than three years, or both.

645 **Title 18 U.S.C. § 2075. Officer failing to make returns or reports.** Every officer who neglects or refuses to make any return or report which he is required to make at state times by any Act of Congress or regulation of the Department of the Treasury, other than his accounts, within the time prescribed by such Act or regulation, shall be fined not more than $1,000.

An assault or battery, a federal offense, can be committed by a judge who fails to act in the presence of a duty to act. *See W. LaFave & A. Scott, Criminal Law* 21011 (2d ed. 1986). In *People v. Burden*, 72 Cal.App.3d 603 (1977) similar analysis was utilized. The principal of culpable omissions is no stranger to federal law. For instance, Title 28 USC § 1343 makes any person liable for damages when that person fails to prevent or aid in the prevention of civil right violations, and the victim suffers harm.

offense would also apply to the Justice Department personnel who failed to report the criminal activities made known to them, including the CIA drug activities.

**Fraud arising in misleading government reports**. It is a federal offense to prepare a report that omits material information that as a result of the omission results in a different inference. Those especially guilty of this offense would be officials within the FAA, NTSB, Justice Department, and members of Congress. This offense is described in many federal decisions, including *Branch v. Tunnel*, 937 F.2d 1382 (9th Cir. 1991) and *Olson v. Tyler*, 771 F.2d 277, 281 (7th Cir. 1985). In these cases the courts held that deception exists when material omission in a writing exists, wherein less than the total story is described, and where a different inference is drawn.

Richard Taus receiving Army Commendation Medal from Maj.Gen. J.M. Hightower at Ft. Hamilton, Brooklyn , New York.

**RECOMMENDED READING LIST**

The following books are a few of those that focus on certain areas covered in *Defrauding America.*

*A Very Thin Line, the Iran-Contra Affairs.* Theodore Draper, Simon & Schuster. 1991.
*Blond Ghost*, Ted Shackley and the CIA's Crusades. David Corn. 1994.
*Bluegrass Conspiracy.* Sally Denton. Avon Books. 1990
*Called To Serve.* Col. James Gritz. Lazarus. 1991.
*Casey, The Lives and Secrets of William J. Casey.* Joseph Persico. Penguin, 1991.
*CIA and Cult of Intelligence.* Victor Marchetti and John Marks. Knopf. 1964.
*Cocaine Politics, Drugs, Armies, and the CIA in Central America.* Peter Dale Scott and Jonathan Marshall. University of California Press. 1991.
*Compromised, Clinton, Bush and the CIA.* Terry Reed & John Cummings. SPI. 1994.
*Den of Thieves.* James Stewart. Simon and Schuster. 1991.
*Disavow, A CIA Saga of Betrayal.* Rodney Stich and T. Conan Russell. Hallmark. 1996.
*Disposal Patriot, Revelations of a Soldier in America's Secret Wars.* Jack Terrell with Ron Martz. National Press Books. 1992.
*Dope, Inc.* By the editors of Executive Intelligence Review. 1992.
*Everybody Has His Own Gringo.* Glenn Garvin. Brassy's. 1992
*Inside the CIA.* Revealing the Secrets of the World's Most Powerful Spy Agency. Ronald Kessler. Pocket Books. 1992.
*Invisible Government.* David Wise and Thomas Ross. Random House. 1964.
*Iran-Contra, the Final Report.* Times Books. 1994.
*Kings of Cocaine,* Guy Gugliotta and Jeff Leen. Harper. 1989.
My Turn To Speak, Bank-Sadr. Brassey's. 1991.
*October Surprise,* America's Hostages in Iran and the Election of Ronald Reagan. Gary Sick. Times Books. 1991.
*October Surprise.* Barbara Honegger. Tudor. 1989.
*Our Man in Panama.* The Shrewd Rise and Brutal Fall of Manual Noriega. John Dinges. Times Books. 1991.
*Out of Control.* Leslie Cockburn. Atlantic Monthly Press. 1987.
*Powderburns, Cocaine, Contras & and Drug War.* Celerino Castillo III and Dave Harmon. Mosaic Press. 1994.
*Profits of War,* Inside the Secret U.S.-Israeli Arms Network. Ari Ben-Menashe. Sheridan Square Press. 1992.
*Secret Team.* L. Fletcher Prouty. Institute for Historical Review. 1973.
*Sellout,* Aldrich Ames and the Corruption of the CIA. James Adams. Viking. 1995.
*The Big White Lie,* the CIA and the Cocaine/Crack Epidemic. Michael Levine. Thunder's Mouth Press. 1993.
*The CIA and the Cult of Intelligence.* Victor Marchetti and John D. Marks. Knopf. 1974.
*The Cocaine Wars.* Paul Eddy with Hugo Sabogal and Sara Walden. Norton.

1988.
*The Mafia, CIA and George Bush.* Corruption, Greed, and Abuse of Power in the Nation's Highest Office. Pete Brewton. SPI. 1992.
*The Politics of Heroin,* CIA Complicity in the Global Drug Trade. Alfred W. McCoy. Lawrence Hill Books. 1991.
*Unfriendly Skies,* Saga of Corruption. (3rd ed) Rodney Stich. Diablo Western Press. 1990.
*Whitewater.* Wall Street Journal. 1994.

The following pages have additional material of interest.

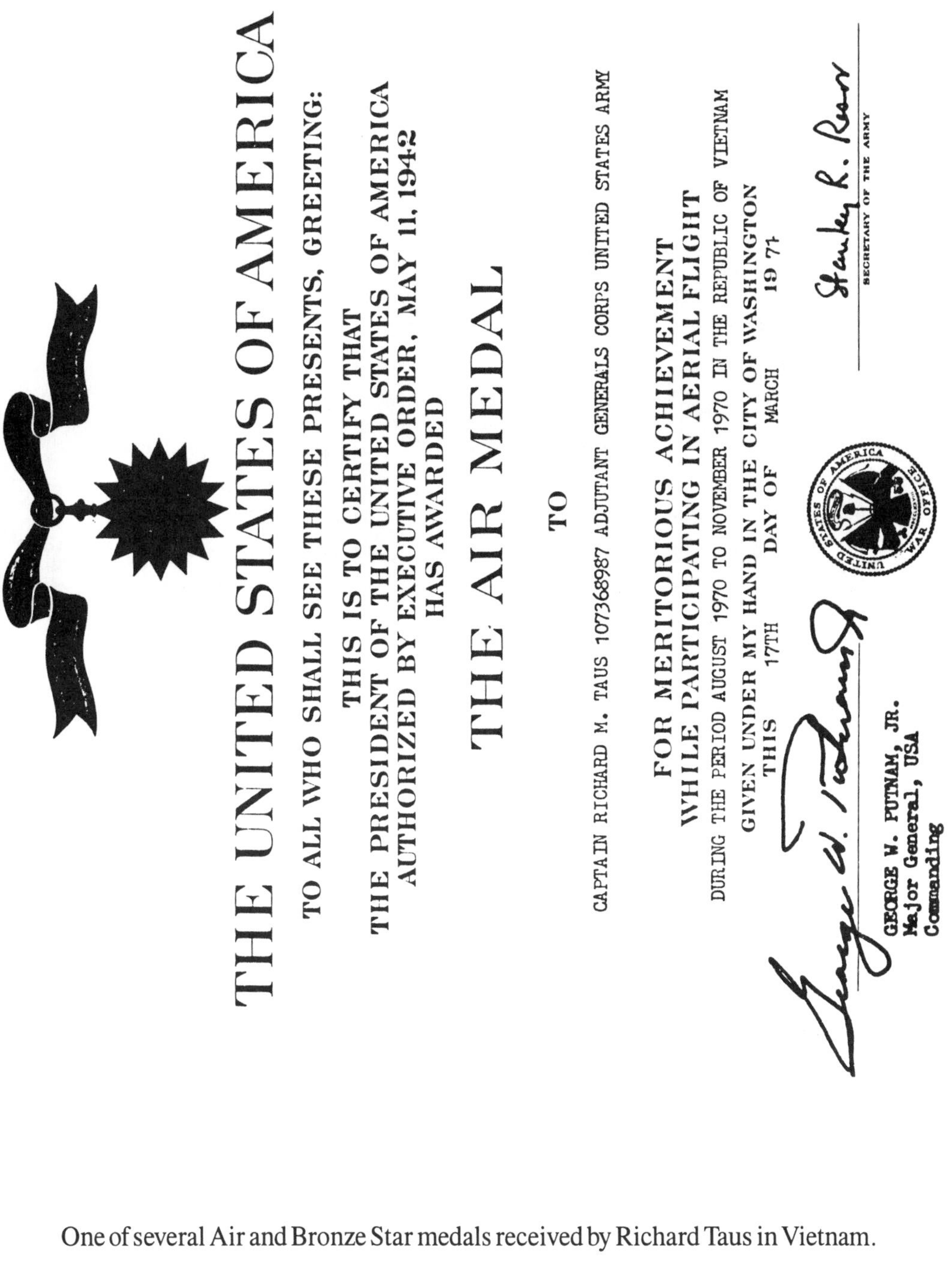

THE UNITED STATES OF AMERICA

TO ALL WHO SHALL SEE THESE PRESENTS, GREETING:

THIS IS TO CERTIFY THAT
THE PRESIDENT OF THE UNITED STATES OF AMERICA
AUTHORIZED BY EXECUTIVE ORDER, MAY 11, 1942
HAS AWARDED

THE AIR MEDAL

TO

CAPTAIN RICHARD M. TAUS 107368987 ADJUTANT GENERALS CORPS UNITED STATES ARMY

FOR MERITORIOUS ACHIEVEMENT
WHILE PARTICIPATING IN AERIAL FLIGHT
DURING THE PERIOD AUGUST 1970 TO NOVEMBER 1970 IN THE REPUBLIC OF VIETNAM

GIVEN UNDER MY HAND IN THE CITY OF WASHINGTON
THIS 17TH DAY OF MARCH 1971

UNITED STATES OF AMERICA WAR OFFICE

GEORGE W. PUTNAM, JR.
Major General, USA
Commanding

SECRETARY OF THE ARMY

One of several Air and Bronze Star medals received by Richard Taus in Vietnam.

THE
PRESIDENT
OF
THE UNITED STATES OF AMERICA

*To all who shall see these presents, greeting:*

*Know ye, that reposing special trust and confidence in the patriotism, valor, fidelity, and abilities of* RICHARD M. TAUS*, I do appoint* HIM AS A RESERVE COMMISSIONED OFFICER *in the* GRADE OF LIEUTENANT COLONEL IN THE

**United States Army**

*to* DATE *as such from the* TWENTY-SECOND *day of* MAY*, nineteen hundred and* EIGHTY-SIX*. This officer will therefore carefully and diligently discharge the duties of the office to which appointed by doing and performing all manner of things thereunto belonging.*

*And I do strictly charge and require those officers and other personnel of lesser rank to render such obedience as is due an officer of this grade and position. And this officer is to observe and follow such orders and directions, from time to time, as may be given by the President of the United States of America, or other superior officers, acting in accordance with the laws of the United States of America.*

*This commission is to continue in force during the pleasure of the President of the United States of America, under the provisions of those public laws relating to officers of the* **Armed Forces of the United States of America** *and the component thereof in which this appointment is made.*

*Done at the City of Washington, this* SIXTEENTH *day of* APRIL *in the year of our Lord, one thousand nine hundred and* NINETY *and of the Independence of the United States of America, the* TWO HUNDRED AND THIRTEENTH

*By the President:*

THE ADJUTANT GENERAL

UNITED STATES OF AMERICA WAR OFFICE

SECRETARY OF THE ARMY

Taus's promotion to Lieutenant Colonel in the United States Army Reserve.

**Affidavit of Richard M. Taus**

I, Richard M. Taus, declare and state: I am a former Special Agent for the Federal Bureau of Investigation assigned to the New York Field Office and the Brooklyn-Queens Metropolitan Resident Agency from July 1978 to November 1988. I was assigned to both the Foreign Counter-Intelligence Division and the Criminal Division.

During this period of time, my investigations into these matters revealed criminal activities and operations which I reported and documented to my superiors in the FBI, as follows:

The involvement of official, agents and operatives of the Central Intelligence Agency (CIA) with organized crime members and drug-trafficking activities. And the participation by members of the CIA who engaged in the looting of the Savings & Loan (Thrift) Industries, financial scams and fraudulent securities transactions.

The involvement of people from the National Security Agency Staff and Council and the White House in criminal activities associated with funding the acquisition of military supplies and equipment, arms and ammunition which were referred to as the Iran-Contra Arms Initiative, known as Irangate, and the Iraqi Scandal, known as Iraqgate.

The associations between known and suspected members of the Mafia and CIA agents in conducting drug-trafficking activities and financial frauds.

I was ordered by my supervisors in the FBI to halt these investigations, destroy my written reports, terminate my informants and make no reference to these criminal and subversive activities implicating high-ranking government officials, politicians, Mafia and business leaders who controlled and manipulated government agencies and operations.

Without any support from my superiors at the FBI New York Field Office, I then sent a letter describing what I had discovered in my official status as an FBI Special Agent to the FBI Director, William Sessions, and this was ignored. I proceeded to write Congressional officials, among them Senators Arlan Spector, Alfonse D'Amato, John Kerry and Congressmen Norman Lent, Charles Schmur, and many others who were on both the Senate and House Intelligence Oversight Committees. None of the above officials or representatives provided any support or assistance in exposing the CIA-White House corruption and the obstruction of justice tactics by my FBI superiors.

My sole purpose in preparing this affidavit, to be used by the former FBI Special Agent-In-Charge of the Los Angeles Field office, SAC Ted Gunderson, is to bring to justice the criminal and subversive activities that I and other government agents and operatives have discovered during our official and government related duties.

I declare and affirm under penalty of perjury that these statements are true to the best of my knowledge and belief. Executed this 13th day of August 1997, in the County of Clinton, State of New York.

Richard M. Taus
Richard M. Taus

Linda O'Connor
LINDA O'CONNOR
Notary Public, State of New York
No. 01OC5019512
Qualified in Clinton County
Commission Expires 10/25/97

The following is one of hundreds of CIA documents that I have obtained showing CIA control of BBRDW and Ron Rewald. The following is a partial copy of a Secret December 1982 cable sent to CIA headquarters relating to how the CIA laundered money and funded BBRDW. For clarity, part of the body of the cable is reprinted:

[redacted] 141758Z DEC 82

[redacted]

S E C R E T 131830Z DEC 82 [redacted]

CITE DCD/HONOLULU 12741

TO: PRIORITY DIRECTOR INFO DCD/HEADQUARTERS.

WNINTEL [redacted]

REF: A. DCD/HONOLULU 12202
B. DIRECTOR 407402

(THE FOLLOWING INFORMATION WHICH [redacted] BY SUBJECT IN PARAGRAPH ONE IS SOLELY PROVIDED AS BEING OF ASSISTANCE TO [redacted] IN ASSESSING HIS TAX SITUATION.)
CIA

*In reply to questions posed in Ref B on 9 December 82, subject said that all monies paid him by CIA were not solely funnelled through [CIA station chief] Honolulu but also came through .... officers and other personnel introduced to him by [CIA station chief] in period 1978-1981, presumably including other CIA personnel et al. On several occasions, he was told by such DCD/Kavanaugh CIA personnel that, in the interest of secrecy/confidentiality, he should not discuss nor mention such payments to Rewald. Chairman said he received payments not only for Telex, telephone bills, stationaery, calling cards, etc., but also for passing funds to individuals in the Middle East, Argentina, Hong Kong, Taiwan, Indonesia, California, and Hawaii. His reimbursement from CIA also included payment for some services rendered as well as necessary business/travel expenses associated with such payments to individuals in Honolulu. He has no knowledge of such payments funded by other CIA branches, but has no reason to doubt subject's veracity. CIA funds were passed to subject by cash, bank transfers, and checks by vartious law offices and accounting firms, presumably CIA fronts.*

**SECRET**

[redacted] [redacted]

IMMEDIATE

STAFF

ACTION: [redacted]

---

[redacted]

PAGE 001 IN 1876295
TOR: 110609Z AUG 83 HNDC 12821

---

S E C R E T 100400Z AUG 83 STAFF

CITE DCD/HONOLULU 12821

TO: IMMEDIATE DIRECTOR INFO IMMEDIATE DCD/HEADQUARTERS.

WNINTEL [redacted] LPBURGER

SUBJECT: LPBURGER [REWALD] CHAIRMAN (LPC) CASE

1. HEADQUARTERS TEAM ARRIVED MIDDAY 10 AUGUST 1983 AND CONTACTED JOHN PEYTON, ASST U.S. ATTORNEY. PEYTON EXPLAINED URGENCY OF [redacted] [CIA] FILE SEARCH AND HAD DIRECTED THAT [redacted] [FBI] OFFICE BEGIN EXAMINATION IMMEDIATELY. JUDGE CONCERNED THAT UNDUE DELAY WILL IMPEDE UNNECESSARILY WITH BANKRUPTCY TRUSTEE DUTIES TO MARSHAL ASSETS AND PROTECT CREDITORS AND INVESTORS INTERESTS. [redacted] [FBI] OFFICE, IDEN A, NOW PART OF RECORDS SEARCH TEAM. IN ABSENCE HQS TEAM, HE DID EXTRAORDINARILY WELL, GIVEN CIRCUMSTANCES.

2. BY PRESENT ORDER OF COURT, TEAM ABLE TO CONDUCT INSPECTION WITHOUT OUTSIDE PARTIES PRESENT (TRUSTEE AND LPC LAWYER). ARRANGEMENTS HAVE BEEN MADE BY COURT FOR TEAM TO WORK THRU 2100 HOURS EVENING 10 AUGUST 83.

3. VERY PRELIMINARY RESULTS OF SEARCH REVEAL THE FOLLOWING:

A. IDEN B INVESTOR FILE LOCATED IN SUBJECT RECORDS; STATEMENT AS OF 30 JUNE 1983 INDICATES SUBSTANTIAL BALANCE IN ACCOUNT. FILE ALSO SHOWS THAT IDEN B REFERRED BY IDEN C; IN FACT ONE INVESTMENT MADE ON BEHALF OF IDEN B BY IDEN C PERSONAL CHECK.

**SECRET**

CIA cable sent August 10, 1983 to CIA headquarters describing the coverup activities by John Peyton, former CIA Chief of Litigation. Peyton was then "demoted" from his key CIA position to assistant U.S. attorney (AUSA), who then falsely charged Rewald with looting BBRDW's assets. Notice that 3A indicates finding "substantial balance in account." These funds were then removed by the CIA to other CIA proprietaries, causing many people to lose their savings.

UNCLASSIFIED | CONFIDENTIAL | X | SECRET

OFFICIAL ROUTING SLIP

| TO | NAME AND ADDRESS | DATE | INITIALS |
|---|---|---|---|
| 1 | JCK DCD/HONOLULU<br>Chief, Honolulu FO<br>eyes only file | 14 Dec 79 | [initials] |
| 2 | | | |
| 3 | | | |
| 4 | | | |
| 5 | | | |
| 6 | | | |

| | | | | | |
|---|---|---|---|---|---|
| | ACTION | | DIRECT REPLY | | PREPARE REPLY |
| X | APPROVAL | | DISPATCH | | RECOMMENDATION |
| | COMMENT | | FILE | | RETURN |
| | CONCURRENCE | | INFORMATION | | SIGNATURE |

Remarks:

Approved temp. funding CFETC TELEX;TELE-PHONE. Full funding LPBURGER/BBDRW operations; Honolulu

FOLD HERE TO RETURN TO SENDER

FROM: NAME, ADDRESS AND PHONE NO. | DATE

[redacted]

CIA document approving CIA funding of BBRDW and Rewald (LPBURGER).

May 17, 1997 letter to every member of U.S. Supreme Court, putting them on notice of criminal and subversive activities in their areas of responsibilities.

**From the desk of Rodney Stich**

**P.O. Box 5, Alamo, CA 94507; phone: 510-944-1930; FAX 510-295-1203**

**Author of *DEFRAUDING AMERICA–Dirty Secrets of the CIA & other Government Operations***
***DISAVOW–A CIA Saga of CIA Betrayal***
***UNFRIENDLY SKIES–History of Corruption and Air Tragedies***

*Member*
*Association Former Intelligence Officers (AFIO)* — *Association of National Security Alumni*
*International Society of Air Safety Investigators (ISASI)* — *Lawyers Pilots Bar Association (LPBA)*
*Former FAA air safety investigator* — *Former airline captain and Navy pilot*
*E-mail: stich@defraudingamerica.com* — *Web sites: www.defraudingamerica.com; www.unfriendlyskies.com*
*Internet search engine: "Rodney Stich"*

May 19, 1997

Chief Justice William Rehnquist
U.S. Supreme Court
One First Street, NE
Washington, DC 20543 Certified # Z 745 656 619

Subject: Obstruction of Justice by Federal Judges, and the Judicial Voiding of the Crime-Reporting Statute, occurring in your area of responsibilities.

Dear Sir:

The intent of this letter is to make another record showing a pattern of judicial obstruction of justice that has enabled criminal and treasonous activities[1] against the United States to flourish. Most of this information is already known to you and the other Justices as a result of prior filings and letters sent to the court and the individual Justices. Despite this latest writing to the Justices, I expect that each of the Supreme Court Justices will continue to aid and abet the criminal activities against the United States and its people.

Attached to this letter is a copy of my petition for an *en banc* rehearing in the District of Columbia court of appeals. This petition contain details of how federal judges have played a key role in enabling major criminal activities against the United States to go unpunished and escalate. Here are a few of the key points that identified in that petition:

* **Judicial destruction of the public's most important tool for fighting corruption involving government officials**. Federal judges have repeatedly prevented the exercise of the public's most important tool to defend against criminal activities perpetrated by government officials. This tool is Title 18 USC Section 4,[2] which requires that anyone who has knowledge of a federal crime to promptly report it "to a federal judge." This important protection enables any American to circumvent the rampant coverup and obstruction of justice by Justice Department employees. In the underlying federal filings associated with the District of Columbia filing (95-2260; C.A. 97-5007) I detail and document the repeated actions by federal judges (including Justices of the U.S. Supreme Court) blocking the reporting of very serious crimes against the United States. These repeated judicial acts, aided and abetted by Justice Department employees, have permitted the escalated of great harm upon the nation and many of its citizens, as described in the second edition of *Defrauding America* and third edition of *Unfriendly Skies*.

[1] The more prominent criminal activities discovered and documented by Stich and his group of former FBI, CIA, DEA and other sources include: (a) decades of CIA drug smuggling into the United States, undermining the national security (later joined by people in control of the Drug Enforcement Administration and segments of the military); (b) rampant looting of Chapter 11 assets by federal judges, trustees, law firms; (c) CIA involvement in defrauding U.S. financial institutions; (d) criminal coverup, obstruction of justice, retaliating against Americans seeking to report these crimes, by Justice Department employees and federal judges; (e) numerous killings and mysterious deaths of people posing a danger of exposing this criminality.

[2] **Title 18 U.S.C. § 4 (misprision of felony).** "Whoever, having knowledge of the actual commission of a felony cognizable by a court of the United States, conceals and does not as soon as possible make known the same to some judge or other person in civil or military authority under the United States, shall be fined not more than $500 or imprisoned not more than three years, or both."

* **Judicial retaliation against individuals seeking to report criminal activities implicating federal officials**. It is a criminal act under federal law[3] for anyone, especially a federal judge or Justice Department employee, to inflict harm of any type upon anyone who exercises the responsibility and the right to report such crimes being perpetrated by or at the direction, or with the knowledge, of federal employees. Every Justice of this Supreme Court has been made aware of the criminal retaliation by judges against me for seeking to exercise this responsibility. The Justices of this Supreme Court have supervisory responsibility over the judges who perpetrated these criminal acts and have repeatedly refused to correct the wrongdoings, thereby becoming an accomplice to the obstruction of justice and related criminal acts. Over the past two decades I have filed several petitions with this court reporting the criminal activities that I and a large number of former federal employees have discovered, including the judicial obstruction of justice and judicial retaliation associated with the attempt to report the criminal activities. Several more petitions were submitted to this Supreme Court and then blocked from being filed by the clerk of the court, who was obviously acting under judicial orders.

* **QUALIFICATIONS FOR MAKING CHARGES OF CRIMINAL ACTIVITIES**

My qualifications for making these charges include:

* Hard evidence which I have accumulated over a period of 30 years, commencing while I was a federal inspector-investigator, holding federal authority to make the determination for the federal government of violations of federal law.

* Evidence obtained as a private investigator and victim, confidant to over two dozen former employees of the Federal Bureau of Investigation, Central Intelligence Agency, Drug Enforcement Administration, military personnel, and others. This list includes people who headed CIA proprietary airlines and other secret CIA operations, CIA agents who helped negotiate the sale of drugs and who helped set up various drug cartels, people who actually flew the drugs into the United States, people who laundered drug money through CIA banking sources, and others.

* **SUPPORT FOR THESE CHARGES**

Support for these charges include, but are not limited, to the following:

* Thousands of pages of testimony transcript and government documents arising from an FAA hearing during which I acted as an independent prosecutor proving the existence of criminal misconduct associated with a series of specific airline crashes. (EFAA 20G)

* Numerous federal court filings[4] made under the mandatory crime-reporting statute, Title 18 USC

[3] **Title 18 U.S.C. § 1512. Tampering with a witness, victim, or an informant –**

(b) Whoever knowingly uses intimidation or physical force, or threatens another person, or attempts to do so, or engages in misleading conduct toward another person, with intent to –

(1) influence, delay or prevent the testimony of any person in an official proceeding:

shall be fined ... or imprisoned ... or both. [1988 amended reading]"

**Title 18 U.S.C. § 1513. Retaliating against a witness, victim, or an informant**. (a) Whoever knowingly engages in any conduct and thereby causes bodily injury to another person or damages the tangible property of another person, or threatens to do so, with intent to retaliate against any person for – (1) the attendance of a witness or party at an official proceeding, or any testimony given or any record, document, or other object produced by a witness in an official proceeding; or (2) any information relating to the commission or possible commission of a Federal offense ..."

**Title 18 U.S.C. § 241. Conspiracy against rights of citizens**

If two or more persons conspire to injure, oppress, threaten, or intimidate any citizen in the free exercise or enjoyment of any right or privilege secured to him by the Constitution or laws of the United States, or because of his having so exercised the same; ... They shall be fined ... or imprisoned ... or both;

[4] *Stich v. United States, et al.*, 554 F.2d 1070 (9th Cir.) (table), *cert. denied*, 434 U.S. 920 (1977)(addressed hard-core air safety misconduct, violations of federal air safety laws, threats against government inspectors not to report safety violations and misconduct); *Stich v. National Transportation Safety Board*, 685 F.2d 446 (9th Cir.)(table), *cert. denied*, 459 U.S. 861 (1982))(addressed repeated criminal falsification of official airline accident reports, omitting highly sensitive air safety misconduct, making possible repeated crashes from the same sequestered problems); Amicus curiae brief filed on July 17, 1975, in the Paris DC-10 multi-district litigation, *Flanagan v. McDonnell Douglas Corporation and United States of America*, Civil Action 74-808-PH, MDL 172, Central District California.)(addressing the long standing FAA misconduct, of which the coverup of the DC-10 cargo door problem was one of repeated instances of tragedy related misconduct); U.S. v. Department of Justice, District of Columbia, Nos. 86-2523, 87-2214, and other actions filed by claimant seeking to expose and correct the powerful and covert air disaster misconduct. Others have been filed in the 1980s and 1990s, seeking to produce evidence of drug smuggling into the United States by and at the direction of the Central Intelligence Agency, Drug Enforcement Administration, and others; judicial corruption in bankruptcy courts that loot the assets of Americans who exercise the statutory protection of Chapter 11; and other criminal activities involving high-level federal employees/officials.

Section 4, and the permissive statute addressing government misconduct, Title 28 USC Section 1361.[5] An examination of these filings clearly show the obstruction of justice by federal judges and Justice Department attorneys, and their retaliation against me for reporting the criminal and treasonous acts in which they were involved.
* Details and documentation in the third edition of the books, *Unfriendly Skies* and second edition of *Defrauding America*, and the thousands of pages of data obtained from covert sources supporting what was stated in those books. Since their printings, considerable additional evidence of high-level government corruption has been acquired.
* Thirty years of aggressive attempts to expose government corruption, and the knowledge obtained as an airline pilot in the early 1950s showing CIA involvement in drug smuggling.

**HARM INFLICTED UPON THE UNITED STATES AS A CONSEQUENCE OF JUDICIAL OBSTRUCTION OF JUSTICE AND RETALIATING AGAINST THOSE EXERCISING THE REQUIREMENTS OF THE FEDERAL CRIME-REPORTING STATUTE**

I brought to federal judges, and this Supreme Court, through formal filings, and through letters, charges of criminal activities involving federal officials. In every instance, Justice Department attorneys and federal judges blocked me from introducing evidence, despite the mandatory requirements of Title 18 USC Section 4, and the criminal statutes relating to obstruction of justice. This blatant violation of major criminal statutes and associated obstruction of justice and retaliatory acts has enabled the continuation and escalation of major crimes against the United States and its people, including, for instance, the following:
* Escalating drugging of America by the CIA and those working in concert with that agency, with the resulting crime, killings, fear, financial losses, and great harm to the national security.
* CIA involvement in looting of savings and loans, adding additional threats to the financial solvency of the United States over and above those arising from the other criminal activities.
* Spreading of the culture of corruption throughout American institutions, brought about by the corruption within the Justice Department and federal judiciary.
* Continuation of the corruption and culture within the FAA that has caused, or allowed to occur, specific airline crashes. The details of this relationship are found in the third edition of *Unfriendly Skies*, in the record of FAA hearing, EFAA 20G, during which I acted as an independent prosecutor.

In the past, the coverups of these criminal activities, including those by Justice Department employees and federal judges, by most of the media and members of Congress, have kept these subversive activities from the public. Certain changes in the distribution of information, including the Internet, now threaten to circumvent these practices. The conduct of this court and of the judges over which it exercised supervisory and vicarious responsibilities will become known to those members of the public who recognize their responsibilities under our form of government. When that happens, possibly the Justices of the U.S. Supreme Court and the judges and Justice Department personnel who they are protecting, may feel the effects of criminal statutes as many Americans charged with far lesser offenses have felt.

A copy of this letter and a copy of the petition for an *en banc* hearing to the District of Columbia Court of Appeals is attached to this letter.

Sincerely,

Rodney Stich

Enclosure: Copy of petition for *en banc* rehearing.

[5] **Title 28 U.S.C. § 1361. Action to compel an officer of the United States to perform his duty.** The district courts shall have original jurisdiction of any action in the nature of mandamus to compel an officer or employee of the United States or any agency thereof to perform a duty owed to the plaintiff.

Author's response to Supreme Court clerk who sought to excuse the Justices' refusal to respond to notice of criminal activities in their area of responsibilities.


**From the desk of Rodney Stich**

**P.O. Box 5, Alamo, CA 94507; phone: 510-944-1930; FAX 510-295-1203**
**Author of *DEFRAUDING AMERICA–Dirty Secrets of the CIA & other Government Operations***
***DISAVOW–A CIA Saga of CIA Betrayal***
***UNFRIENDLY SKIES–History of Corruption and Air Tragedies***

***Member***
*Association Former Intelligence Officers (AFIO)* *Association of National Security Alumni*
*International Society of Air Safety Investigators (ISASI)* *Lawyers Pilots Bar Association (LPBA)*
*Former FAA air safety investigator* *Former airline captain and Navy pilot*
*E-mail: stich@defraudingamerica.com* *Web sites: www.defraudingamerica.com; www.unfriendlyskies.com*
*Internet search engine: "Rodney Stich"*


June 3, 1997

William K. Suter, Clerk
U.S. Supreme Court
One First Street, NE
Washington, DC 20543

Ref: Mischaracterization of notice to Supreme Court Justices of criminal and subversive acts within their area of supervisory responsibilities.

Dear Sir:

I had sent information to each of the Justices of the U.S. Supreme Court on May 19, 1997, about criminal and subversive activities against the United States occurring in their area of supervisory responsibilities. The information was provided under several responsibility requirements, including the crime-reporting statute, Title 18 USC Section 4. This criminal statute requires any federal judge to take immediate and appropriate actions to receive evidence from the person making the report, and take subsequent actions to bring about a meaningful investigation and prosecution. This includes making provisions to circumvent any high-level government cover-up, such as that by employees of the U.S. Department of Justice.

Apparently to **again** sidestep their duties and responsibilities under federal law, including criminal statutes, you sent to me a May 28, 1997 letter stating in effect that this information (of criminal and subversive activities) must be provided to the Supreme Court justices by a "timely petition for a writ of certiorari." That is ludicrous and a patent attempt to continue the obstruction of justice.

That letter, surely made at the direction of one or more of the Justices, would be comical if not for the severe harm being inflicted upon the United States and its people, made possible by the coverup actions perpetrated by the Justices of the U.S. Supreme Court.

Sooner or later, if control of the highest law-enforcement institution in the United States can be taken by people willing to comply with federal criminal statutes and responsibilities, the Justices of the U.S. Supreme Court may face the same prosecution faced by citizens who perpetrate far lesser offenses. The same crime, misprision of a felony, perpetrated by citizens of the United States, has resulted in long prison terms for many people who had far less responsibilities than do the Justices of the U.S. Supreme Court.

Sincerely,

Rodney F. Stich

cc: Justices William Rehnquist; John Paul Stevens; Sandra Day O'Connor; Antonin Scalia; Anthony Kennedy; David Souter; Clarence Thomas; Ruth Bader Ginsburg; Stephen Breyer.

UNITED STATES OF AMERICA
FEDERAL AVIATION AGENCY
AIR CARRIER INSPECTOR'S CREDENTIAL

NUMBER 671

This Certifies that:
Rodney F. Stich

ISSUE DATE 11-14-62

is assigned to the duty of inspecting, during flight, air carrier aircraft, engines, propellers, appliances, route facilities, operational procedures, or airman competency. In the performance of his official duties he is authorized to obtain access to air carrier aircraft and to enter the flight deck of such aircraft in accordance with the provisions of the Federal Aviation Act of 1958, and the regulations issued thereunder. He is also authorized to issue U.S. Government Form SF-160 in accordance with the Economic Regulations (Part 234.2) of the Civil Aeronautics Board.

NOTE: This card must be surrendered on leaving the Government Service.

Director, Bureau of Flight Standards

16—74927-1 FORM FAA-110A (5-5

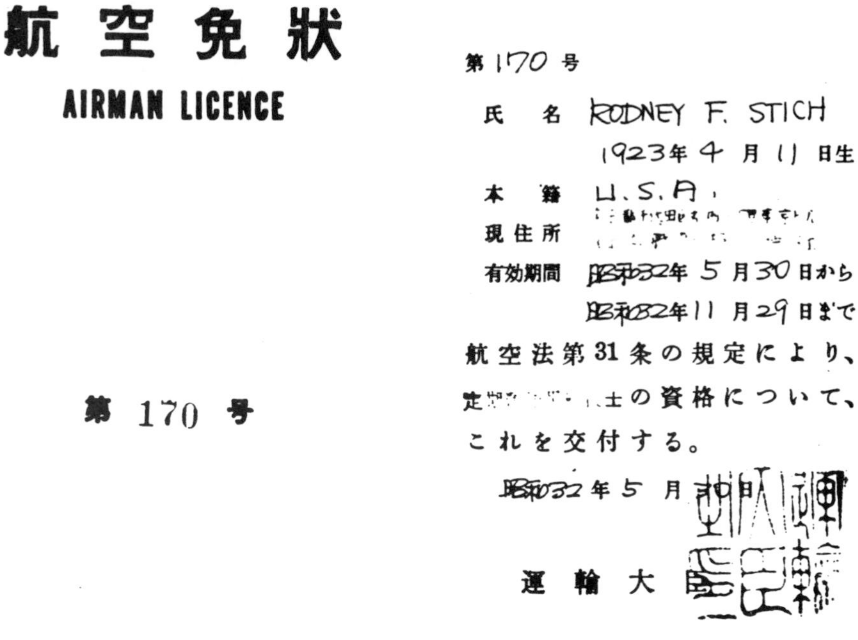

航空免状
AIRMAN LICENCE

第 170 号

第170号
氏名 RODNEY F. STICH
1923年4月1日生
本籍 U.S.A.
現住所 [illegible]
有効期間 昭和32年5月30日から
昭和32年11月29日まで
航空法第31条の規定により、
定[illegible]士の資格について、
これを交付する。
昭和32年5月30日
運輸大臣

Author's Japanese pilot license # 170 and FAA credentials.

Author (middle) during recurrent jet training at FAA's Oklahoma training base.

Author as Navy Patrol Plane Commander (PPC), Privateer aircraft, 1945.

Author's aircraft (Twin Bonanza) seized by the government as they stripped him of his life's assets that funded his crusader activities.

**ATTORNEYS**